The Return of Glory

1969 Lectures

NEVILLE

Order this book online at www.trafford.com
or email orders@trafford.com

Most Trafford titles are also available at major online book retailers.

© Copyright 2022 Neville.
All rights reserved. No part of this publication may be reproduced, stored in a retrieval system, or transmitted, in any form or by any means, electronic, mechanical, photocopying, recording, or otherwise, without the written prior permission of the author.

(1969 lectures transcribed from tapes recorded in live audiences in Los Angeles. Transcriptions and books compiled by Natalie).

Print information available on the last page.

ISBN: 978-1-6987-0489-0 (sc)
ISBN: 978-1-6987-0491-3 (hc)
ISBN: 978-1-6987-0490-6 (e)

Library of Congress Control Number: 2021917388

Because of the dynamic nature of the Internet, any web addresses or links contained in this book may have changed since publication and may no longer be valid. The views expressed in this work are solely those of the author and do not necessarily reflect the views of the publisher, and the publisher hereby disclaims any responsibility for them.

Any people depicted in stock imagery provided by Getty Images are models, and such images are being used for illustrative purposes only.
Certain stock imagery © Getty Images.

Scripture quotations marked KJV are from the Holy Bible, King James Version (Authorized Version). First published in 1611. Quoted from the KJV Classic Reference Bible, Copyright © 1983 by The Zondervan Corporation.

Scripture quotations marked RSV are taken from the Revised Standard Version of the Bible, copyright © 1946, 1952, 1971 by the Division of Christian Education of the National Council of the Churches of Christ in the USA. Used by permission.

Trafford rev. 03/09/2022

 www.trafford.com

North America & international
toll-free: 844-688-6899 (USA & Canada)
fax: 812 355 4082

OTHER WORKS BY NEVILLE

Your Faith Is Your Fortune
The Search
Awakened Imagination
He Breaks the Shell
The Neville Reader (reissue of Neville or Resurrection containing):

> *Out of This World*
> *Freedom for All*
> *Feeling is the Secret*
> *Prayer—the Art of Believing*
> *Seedtime and Harvest*
> *The Law and the Promise*
> *Resurrection*

The Awakening: 1963 Lectures
Imagining and the Transformation of Man: 1964 Lectures
The Wonder Working Power of Imagination: 1965 Lectures
I AM is The Way: 1966 Lectures
Imagining Creates Reality: 1967 Lectures
The Fall and Restoration: 1968 Lectures
The Return of Glory: 1969 Lectures

CONTENTS

Note From Author xi
Foreword xiii
Acknowledgments xv

The Mystery of Imagination 1
The Mystery of Grace 14
The Mystery of Forgiveness 25
Foreknowledge 35
The Mystery of Eschatology 49
The Mystery of Election 64
The Mystery of Inspiration 76
The Real Baptism 91
The Wonder Working Power of Attachment 103
The Maker and The Maker of Things 117
When the Spirit of Truth Comes 130
We Are the Gods Who Came Down 145
The Rock 156
As He is So Are We 172
Christ Bore our Sins 183
Can You Believe in Jesus, a Pattern 195
The Goal of Life 208
The Game of Life 222
The Only God is I AM 236
The Mystery of the Bible 251
Simon Lifts the Cross 262
God's Plan of Redemption 276
Word Became Flesh, Dwelt in Us 289
The Two Sides of This Teaching 301

Our Religion of Easter	313
Crucifixion: I AM the True Vine	329
Outer World Responds to Imaginal Acts	344
Creating One New Man Instead of the Two	357
Man is Soul and Body is Emanation	371
Forgiveness and the Immortal Eyes	385
The Law and the Plan of Redemption	398
Persons Represent States in Scripture	410
A Riddle	424
One Being Fell Containing All	435
The Wisdom, Power, Glory Buried in Us	447
Holding to Our Faith?	460
All Things Possible to Him Who Believes	472
The Lord's Anointed	484
God is The Great Artist	498
Revelation of the Word within Us	512
The True Battle of Armageddon	523
The Law of Liberty	538
Love: God Bestows Himself	553
The Nature of God is Revealed in Us	566
Pursue Truth with Ceaseless Questioning	581
God's Mystery of Christ	598
The I in Me is God Himself	612
Personifications, Not Persons	628
Forming of Christ in Us	641
We Find the Father In Us	656
Imagination's Power	668
The Dreamer	683
Who is Paul?	700
All are Men in Eternity	715
Judas Betrays Messianic Secret	725
J, E, and P Manuscripts	737
Believe It In	752
No Other Foundation	766
The State of Paul: The Free Man	779
Scripture Must Be Fulfilled In Me	794
Sorrow Produces Glorious End	806
We Are God Himself	819
The Invisible God Behind The Made	833
Fundamental Revelation: Jesus Christ in Us	847
The Riddle	860

Thou Art Our Father, Our Potter 871
Kingdom of God: The One Body 883
Experience the Mystery of Christ 895
Thy Words Were Found... 908
God Only Acts and Is 924
All Dreams Proceed from God...937
The Christian Mystery Experienced... 947
The Season of Advent 961
The Secret of Causation 973
Christmas: Gospel Proclaims Event 986
The Mystery of Christmas 999

Glossary 1011
Production Notes 1015

NOTE FROM AUTHOR

(This is Neville's last piece of writing, given to me by Mrs. Goddard after his death in 1972. Neville felt "that the chapter Resurrection needed something to lead into it.") Natalie

Introduction to *Resurrection*

If I tell you what I know and how I came to know about it, I may give hope to those who would gladly believe the Bible but who do not understand it or who may have thought that the ancient scriptures are but a record of extravagant claims. Therefore, the reason for this report from me, rather than from another whose scholarly knowledge of the scriptures is more erudite, is that I am speaking from experience. I am not speculating about the Bible, trusting that my guesses about its meaning are not too wide of the mark. I will tell you what I have experienced that I should convey more of God's plan than the opinions of those who may know the Bible so intimately that they could recite it from end to end, although they have not experienced it. He who knows something out of his own experience knows something that makes the finest and wisest opinion look shadowy. True knowledge is experience. I bear witness to what I have experienced. Looking back, I do not know of anything that I heard or read to call forth this knowledge. I did not receive it from man, nor was I taught it, but it came through a series of supernatural experiences in which God revealed himself in action for my salvation.

He unveiled me. And I am he. We mature only as we become our own Father.

I do not honestly expect the world to believe it, and I know all the varieties of explanation I myself should give for such a belief had I not experienced it. But I cannot unknow that which I have experienced. When it occurred it was the most amazing thing that every happened to me. I could not explain it with my intelligence. But God's plan of redemption unfolded within me with such undeniable insistence that finally it became both a mystery and a burden laid upon me. I literally did not know what to do with what I knew. I tried to explain it to friends, and I know that with all good will they could only think, "Poor Neville, he has evidently had a very bad time."

From the first experience, I felt commissioned. I could not unknow it, and I am burdened with that knowledge. The warnings of my friends could make no difference to the truth I had experienced. That truth remained. Whether I could be a living instrument of it or not, I could not say at all. But until I put it into words so that others could read it, I did not feel that I had accomplished the work I was sent to do.

Now that I have written it, I feel that I have finished what I came to do. And that is to reveal the true identity of Jesus Christ. Jesus is the I AM of everyone. He is the Lord, the one God and Father of us all, who is above all and through and in all. Therefore, if the words *Lord, God, Jesus* convey the sense of an existent someone outside of man, he has a false God. Christ is the Son of God. The Son of God is David, the sweet psalmist of Israel.

It's the Father's purpose to give himself to all of us, to each of us. And it is his Son, David, calling us Father, who reveals the Father's gift to us. The Father's gift of himself to us is not discovered until the very end. And all discovery implies suffering to be endured in the process of discovery. The Father became as we are that we may be as he is. He is never so far off as even to be near, for nearness implies separation. He suffers as us, but we know it not. God as Father is made known only through his Son, David. The core and essence of David's work is his revelation of the Father. Can one come to an identity of oneself with the Father without the Son's revelation of him? Personally, I feel quite sure the answer is no, one cannot. "No one knows the Son except the Father, and no one knows the Father except the Son and anyone to whom the Son chooses to reveal him."

If two different witnesses agree in testimony, it is conclusive. I now present my two witnesses: the internal witness of the Spirit, my experience, and the external witness of scripture, the written Word of God.

Neville
September 1972

FOREWORD

(to 1969 book)

Welcome to the world of practical imagining, of visionary and mystical experiences, of a deeper appreciation of the meaning of life, the inward journey, and the eternal ancient wisdom revisited.

We are led to the truth when we are ready for it. I was led to Neville when answers had to be found, where changes in thinking had to take place in order to expand spiritual awareness. The first most compelling concept encountered was that a change in attitude begets a change in the outer world, stated by Neville as "imagining creates reality." It followed that one's world is a reflection of one's inner thinking plus the attendant emotions; and that to dwell on anything you desire, feeling the possession of it in the present moment, remaining faithful to that feeling of having it now, believing it wholeheartedly, produces that result.

I tried it and it worked. To my joy, a three-and-a-half-month trip to Europe, all expenses paid, came in within about a month after doing an imaginal act of feeling myself flying in a jet over the ocean and then seeing through the window well-known landmarks of Europe below. I did not lift a finger to make it so, told no one about it, and it came out of the blue. This is the pragmatic and provable law that everyone can test endlessly to their satisfaction. It's truly the way to everything in the world; and it's being done by every person every moment of time, either wittingly or unwittingly. It's a magical overcoming of limitation when done deliberately. And it is, you learn, God the I AM, your "I am," in action.

Neville taught from his own visions, mystical experiences, discernment (not speculation) and Bible study, not only that imagining creates reality but that every soul is destined to spiritually awaken eventually as God, yet retaining one's individual identity. He never claimed to be more than the messenger of this eternal story that all will one day experience…a gift which can't be conjured or earned. This book of 1968 talks (the sixth in a series) chronicles a continuing growth in understanding of his six major visions that began in 1959 with the last one occurring after three-and-a-half years. Through extensive study and insight, he found these visions paralleled those in the Bible, the story of Christ; and they proved to be the keys to explaining the hidden mysteries of the prophetic Old Testament and their fulfillment in the New Testament. Perhaps an appropriate analogy would be the Rosetta stone and what it did for the Egyptian hieroglyphics. Once understood and accepted, the larger picture emerges. The questions "Who am I? What am I doing here? Where did I come from? What is the purpose of life?" are all answered in this new at the same time ancient revelation. A sense of power is returned to the individual, plus a great sense of peace comes knowing life really does have a glorious meaning…in spite of the seeming chaos and horrors of the world.

As Browning said in his *Paracelsus,* "Truth is within ourselves; it takes no rise in outward things…There is an inmost center in us all where truth abides in fullness…and to know rather consists in opening out a way whence the imprisoned splendor may escape, than in effecting entry for a light supposed to be without." Neville's teaching gives us the way to that center and how to help open out the way so that the imprisoned splendor may escape. So the story needs time to be understood, to be heard repeatedly, and to be internalized by the seeker. And that is why the eleven years of his lectures are so precious and unique, gradually leading one through the process that culminates in an awakened individual.

Study of this higher level of being helps stir the sleeping giant in all who have been made by their Inner Being into the good soil, that is, made ready to awaken. To awaken is to personally experience those same six visions. These are the signs that the transformation has been completed, and that our divine heritage has been returned. (As encouragement to all, this writer can also bear witness to experiencing the last of the six visions.) Then we can go back to eternity expanded and triumphant having overcome death and the illusion of this world.

Natalie 3/15/22

ACKNOWLEDGMENTS

Deepest thanks to Neville for being the source of these wonderful insights. The inspiration they will forever engender in readers of his work is undeniable and it is that which is the incentive to preserve his lectures for posterity.

In memory and thanks to William Machgan for his love of Neville's teachings which led him to lend support to this project.

To all who will find help in these volumes, grateful thanks for your interest and for helping spread the good news.

N

THE MYSTERY OF IMAGINATION

1/6/69

Tonight's subject is "The Mystery of Imagination." I could have titled it "The Mystery of God, the Mystery of Man, the Mystery of Christ." It would have been the same thing. But I took for tonight the use of the word Imagination—it would not offend. But these three are interchangeable words.

So here, I imagine as do you. We cannot imagine differently. All the differences lie in content. And so, we ask the little question "Who am I?" and our response to that question determines content…and there we differ. The whole vast world differs based upon their response to that enormous question, which we find in scripture. Who am I? I could tell you that you are God. You wouldn't believe it. You can read it in scripture: "Be still and know that I am God." You'll read it in the 46th Psalm, but you won't believe it. If I told you that you are Christ, you might be offended; you may have some external concept of a being and you call him Christ. When I say that you *do* imagine, that wouldn't offend you because you know we do imagine. And you may not believe for one moment that this power of imagining is the power of God, but, nevertheless, you do imagine. That wouldn't offend anybody.

So tonight we'll take…first of all, we'll start with Blake's *Jerusalem*. Now Blake claimed this entire poem was dictated by the Spirit of Prophesy or the Savior of the world. He said, "Morning after morning, when I return I've found the spirit of the Savior spreading his beams of love over me and dictating the words of this mild song." And in this he said, "Babel mocks, saying there is no God nor Son of God, that thou, O Human Imagination, O Divine Body, art all a delusion; but I know thee, O Lord, when thou arisest upon my weary eyes, even in this dungeon and this iron mill…for thou also sufferest with me." And then the Divine Voice replied: "Fear not! Lo, I am with thee always, only believe in me, that I have power to raise from death thy Brother who sleepeth in Albion" (Plate 60). Now could you honestly believe to that point that you would say, "But I know thee, O Lord" meaning your own wonderful human Imagination, no other being, your Imagination, the eternal you. Could you say with him that "Man is all Imagination and God is man and he in us and we in him. The Eternal Body of man is the Imagination and that is God himself" (*Laocoon/Annot. to Berkeley*). Could you believe it?

Well now, let us show you. We're told in scripture that all things were made through Christ and without him was not anything made that was made, but all things, good, bad and indifferent (Jn. 1:2). Now who made this? The year is 1951—my brother-in-law because he is married to my wife's sister—called and asked if I would see him that evening…it was very important. He knew that we were sailing for Barbados in about two weeks and he wanted to see me before we sailed. So he came home and this was his problem. First, I'll give you his background. He graduated from Harvard and then remained on and took the business course at Harvard, Harvard Business School's graduate course. Came out of college and went straight into the bank, the Bank of New York. Well, as you know banks have different departments and some departments do not advance rapidly. He was in the Trust Dept. That is almost a service; that is not a money making section of the bank. So he was in the Trust Dept. and after eighteen years he concluded that traveling as he's traveling now at the bank he couldn't see how he could possibly put his two children through college. He went through college and his wife went through Smith, and he couldn't see how he could possibly put these two children through college. They were bright, desired to go to college but with that fixed salary he couldn't see how he could do it. So he went to the president and the manager of the bank and explained the facts of life. They in turn reminded him that that department did not allow any further increases in salary, that eventually someone would resign or someone would retire, someone would leave the bank, or they may die. In that event, he would be promoted, but without this, he had to remain and move forward just as they all do in banks. They made it very, very clear to him that if he didn't like it he could quit.

Now he said, "That's my problem." I said, "All right." First of all, I'll tell you he was at that time and still is the head usher of a very prominent 5th Avenue church, the Church of the Ascension. He was on the financial board because he was a banker and could advise them on how to invest their funds and to raise funds. But he couldn't find any comfort in an interview with his minister. The minister didn't know what to say to him,

The Return of Glory

how to solve this problem. I said to Sam, "You know Sam that I'm leaving in a couple of weeks and we'll be gone for about three months. Will you do this? I assure you it will work. It will not fail you *if* you do it. You are the operant power, it doesn't operate itself. I can tell you from now to the ends of time, but if you don't operate it by becoming the operant power, it won't work. But if you actually do what I'm going to ask you to do, I tell you that it will work." Well, he said, "Tell me." I said, "When you go to bed tonight—I don't mean tomorrow night or the next night—I mean tonight and every night thereafter, you feel as though you had the most heavenly day in business, that you invested fantastic funds." By the by, I must tell you that I asked him, what would you like to do? Well, he said, "I'm trained to invest funds. I know the money market. I would like to handle the funds of a great foundation like Harvard, Yale, Princeton, Columbia, the Rockefellers or the Fords. That's the kind of a thing I would like." I said, alright, as you sleep tonight you feel this is the most heavenly day, the most wonderful day! What a portfolio and what I did with it, this enormous sum of money that you invested, and feel that you've never known such a wonderful day in your business. He started that night.

We sailed to Barbados and returned three months later. As is our custom, that very first day they always came home for dinner. So the wife came first and we had a round of drinks and she said, "Let's wait for Sam. I want Sam to be here before we have any drinks." I said, "All right, we'll wait for Sam." So Sam came in straight from the bank and when he came in I made a round of Martinis, and Sam rose and said, "Dear, did you tell them?" She said, "No, it's your story. I want you to tell them." Well, this is the story. Being a member of the financial board of the church this meeting was held two weeks after we sailed. At the end of the meeting when they came to the sidewalk this man who handles all the funds of the Rockefeller brothers, not the Rockefeller Foundation, it's something entirely different, the five brothers and their sisters and then their wives and children. The fund runs well in excess of a billion dollars…it's just their private funds. The man said, "Sam, I've been thinking of this for the last couple of weeks." Right on the heels of Sam beginning to put this into practice he entertains the thought and said to Sam, "Would you consider quitting the bank? I know you have to lose all the seniority, lose all that you've built up in the bank, I can't give you that. I'll start you at a much, much bigger salary and guarantee you an increase in salary every year. But what an opportunity! Here you have a portfolio well in excess of a billion dollars, and I'm asking you to quit the bank and join me and help me with the Rockefeller money." He said, "I can't say yes to it now, but I'll go home and discuss it with my wife."

Well, they agreed that it was quite a challenge…and so they would do it. The bank was thrilled beyond measure that the Rockefellers would see in one of their men that they trained one with that ability, and they were just all smiles, all love. When one broke forth they almost offered him to quit. Now they're thrilled beyond measure because he could throw some business in their direction, handling one portfolio one day, $394 million. At the same time, a $4,000 investment…some grandchild just got an A or B or something in school, and he was given $4,000. He had to take that $4,000 and be just as careful with that investment as the $394 million that he was one day switching in a certain portfolio.

Well, that was Sam. I wrote a book a year later 1952 in which I told this story. I did it without Sam's consent or knowledge. Knowing the story I wrote the story myself and simply signed his initials. As is my custom, I bring out a new book and I always give Sam a copy. Sam took the book and he saw his story. Now he's entranced, mind you, in this. He still is a powerhouse in his church. He knows exactly what he did and he knows how it works…but that book was hidden. When I called on Sam the next time there was no discussion of this theory and the book was not available. All my other books were put away. You couldn't find one of my books in Sam's house today, because to him this is irrational. Some friend of his in the social world may come to his apartment and see a book, and ___(??) by the title, or take it from the library, see Sam's story in the book, and that would embarrass him. He's very prominent in his own minds eye in the social world and in the banking world and these worlds.

So he denied I introduced him to Christ. He goes to church every Sunday morning, is the head usher…doesn't know Christ. I introduced him to Christ and proved to him the existence of Christ *in* him. For all things are made by Christ and without him is not anything made that is made. And who made it? *He* dared to imagine himself returning from a job where everything was perfect, just as he wanted it. In two weeks the offer came out of the blue. The man began to entertain the thought of suggesting it to Sam soon after Sam began to go to bed night after night imagining that he had such a job. Now he buries the evidence: The old, old story, "he denies the ladder by which he did ascend." Oh no, that's not…so I introduced him to Christ, he met Christ and did not recognize him, and did what you're told in scripture, he denied him. He rejected Christ although he goes every Sunday and ushers them down the aisle. There he is in his cutaway, leading in that manner.

Now, I'll tell you the story in scripture that is related to it. "He who is not with me is against me" (Luke 11:23). There is no room for neutrality, none whatsoever, in this conflict. You are either with me or against me.

Now, he makes that bold statement and then it seems irrelevant what follows. And this is what he states in the Book of Luke, the 11th chapter:

"When an evil spirit, an unclean spirit goes out of a man, it wanders through waterless places seeking rest; and finding none it says, 'I'll return to the house from which I came.' When he comes to the house he finds it swept and put in order (verse 24). He goes and gets seven other spirits more evil than itself; and they come and they enter and dwell in that house; and the last state of that man is worse than the first" (verse 26). "Now a woman in the crowd raised her voice and said, 'Blessed is the womb that bore you and blessed the breasts you sucked.' He replied, 'Blessed rather are those who hear the word of God and keep it!'"

Here is a man brought into the very presence of the only creative power in the world, his own wonderful human Imagination, his eternal being, who is Christ Jesus in him. He tests him and proves his creative power to the full satisfaction. He tests him and Christ proved himself in performance, and then he buries the evidence. He wants no part of it, none whatsoever; it isn't socially prominent. It will do nothing for him in the social world to have that story heard concerning him. So, having turned his back upon Christ, he'll be confronted tomorrow, next year…I use the word loosely… and he will forget what he did to get the job with the Rockefellers. He held it for eight years and then his boss quit, and as is the custom when the new boss came in he brought his own personnel so Sam was out. But because of eight years service in that capacity, he was offered all kinds of jobs and he took a junior partnership in a brokerage house. So now he's a partner in a brokerage house doing remarkably well…a man my age, in fact, the same month in the same year. We never discuss this principle at all. He wants his own archaic concept of a man he calls Jesus Christ. He doesn't want a living Christ within himself that is his own wonderful human Imagination. He doesn't want that, no, he wants something that is historical, something that happened 2,000 years ago, and that to him is Christ.

I introduce you to Christ. I can't make that ____(?). It is customary that you reject him. I can tell you it's not the easiest thing in the world having once been trained in an orthodox manner to believe in an eternal Christ to suddenly find that he's your own wonderful human Imagination; that this is the eternal you, the immortal you, the one that cannot die, and the one that you can put to the test every moment of time. So when Blake said, "Thou also sufferest with me although I do not behold thee" you never behold him as another. He will one day through a series of events reveal himself *as you.* Because these events are only related to Christ Jesus and only as these events are experienced by you and you are cast in the central role will you know who you are. So you never see him as another as told us in scripture: "It does not yet appear what we shall be, but we know that when he appears we shall know him because we shall be like him" (1 Jn. 3:2). So when he appears, I am he. So you'll know by a series of events which you will experience who you really are. Until then, you will know him, but you will not behold him because you don't behold him. He is God the Father and you can only behold him in the face of his Son. You beholding the Son, knowing the Son is *your* son, then you know who you are…that you are God the Father.

But long before you know and behold yourself as God the Father, you can know him. So I can bring you this night as I have…I've brought you this night and introduced you to Jesus Christ. You can call him Jesus Christ, I do. You can call him, as Blake in *Jerusalem* calls him, the Lord: "But I know thee, O Lord, when thou arisest upon my weary eyes." Here yesterday morning, Sunday morning, I returned after a full night of instruction to ethnic groups. When I was addressing Negroes, I was a Negro, as black as the ace of spades, and I'm talking to Negroes. When I addressed the Oriental, I was an Oriental. When I addressed the Caucasian, I was a Caucasian. And yet I am not white, yellow or black; I am Spirit. But to be seen, I had to wear the form of man and wear a pigment acceptable to those I addressed, so here I am, black as the ace of spades speaking to Negroes, and then I am a blond speaking to Caucasians, and again I am the Oriental speaking to Orientals. I came back as gently upon the eyelids as Blake in that 60th Plate tells us: "I know thee, O Lord, when thou arisest upon my weary eyes." I could actually feel the contact upon this dungeon, this iron mill. And then I spent maybe five minutes just reveling in all that I knew I brought back and what I had done, and then I got up and went about my chores for the day.

So these words are not idle words with Blake. One day you'll experience them. One day you'll awaken from the dream of life, and you'll know that you are God the Father. You will know it by a set series of events. You can't alter them, don't try to change them, they will actually unfold in you. They will erupt like a flower erupting on the bush, and the whole thing will reveal you as the being that you've been seeking throughout the ages, the being called Jesus Christ or God the Father. But it does not offend man when you speak of the human Imagination, because all admit they do imagine. They may never be that courageous to identify their own wonderful human Imagination with God, but I tell you the day will come when you'll be forced to identify him and actually interchange a term…that God and your own wonderful human Imagination are one and the same, they're not two.

You put it to the test. Well, all right, you put it to the test. You know what you want? Well, dare this night to assume that you have it, and sleep in the assumption that you have it, and that assumption will slowly harden into fact. That will harden into fact just as Sam's hardened into fact. For God is emerging in the direct line of descent from us. When we read the genealogy of Christ that is a direct line of descent from us. Slowly, painfully but surely he is weaving himself on us. And who is he? Your wonderful human Imagination, my wonderful human Imagination, that's the immortal you that comes out, comes right out of this strange, wonderful line of descent. When it comes out, it's not anything that you see here; it's an immortal being, a body that is altogether different.

You are then Spirit, "For flesh and blood cannot inherit the kingdom of God" (1 Cor. 15:50). So that which comes out can inherit the kingdom of God, but this cannot, for this is a corruptible body, this is a body that is excrementitious. I certainly don't want a body of this nature forever of bondage and slavery. For here is a body that no matter how much I have in this world, I could have all the wealth in the world, and I cannot command any slave of mine to perform the normal functions of this body for me, I've got to do them all by myself. No money in the world can buy that service. The man who wears such a body has to perform the normal natural functions of that body all by himself or simply give it up. If he ceases to perform them, well then, it means his exit from this world, for he can't command anyone to perform them for him.

So these bodies are certainly not bodies that you think of that you'd want to have throughout eternity. For the body you'll have, the immortal body is your own wonderful human Imagination. And you can't describe it. It is Spirit. It's a protean being and by that I mean it can assume any shape as I did all through Saturday night. I woke on Sunday morning knowing that I'd played the part of the Caucasian, the Oriental and the Negro teaching the word of God. I was just that body; that was the mask that I wore, and was received by these ethnic groups as their teacher clothed in a garment just like theirs. But the being that was masked by the body, no one saw him, for that one was Spirit, pure Spirit.

Now, a friend of mine wrote me this letter. He says, "I came back from a vast, vast section of space and time, and for one short interval I encountered a fish, and the fish was standing erect on its tail. In what you would call a hand, its flipper, its right flipper or the right fin, it held a fishing rod, and it looked at me so intently. It conveyed the thought to me, 'I never lose a man that I go after...I catch everyone that I see.' Then I had a flash that it was all past history, as though through the ages he had been fishing for me and I had been ___(??) the hound of heaven. I had been running, running, running away, but he was infinitely patient, and he the great fish would one day catch him." Well, this being who wrote the letter, I must tell him that the fish has always been the symbol of Jesus Christ. To this day, you will

7

find it on the crown of the pope, the sign of Pisces, always on the crown of the pope. The "great fish" he is called. So a protean being…it was he clothed as the fish speaking to himself; for he really is in search of *self*, not in search of another. Everyone is in search of self and that self is God the Father. That being that appeared before him clothed as the fish symbolized what he is searching for. But he got the impression no matter how he tries to escape he will never escape this one, he will always get him. So in the end you get him. And I would say from this vision he isn't far from being caught.

Now a lady wrote, she said, "You were supposed to close on Friday the 30th," and she sent this lovely Christmas card from both she and her husband, she said, "On Thursday morning on the 19th I heard your voice distinctly and you were calling to everyone who comes to your meetings on Mondays and Fridays telling them not to come on Friday the 20th for you would not be there. You kept on calling to all the regulars and I was so impressed I went to the telephone and picked up that receiver to call. 'You know,' I said, 'this is stupid. Neville will think me insane' and I put down the receiver. I still heard the voice, I could not shut it out, and you were eager to call the regulars. Again I went to the telephone and again I restrained the impulse, thinking you might think me stupid. So again I didn't do it. Just imagine my chagrin when I came on Friday and was told you would not be there, that you were unwell, that you had the flu. And so you didn't come the closing night and I knew all day Thursday that you would not be there because I heard your voice calling all the regulars not to come." If you could only test and trust, completely trust this Inner Being. One day you will. One day you will trust it…you will need no phone. You will be so intuitive your every thought that radiates from a seeming other…for in the end you will know that "All that you behold, though it *appears* without it is within, in your Imagination of which this world of mortality is but a shadow" (Blake, *Jerusalem*, Plt.71).

So here, this mystery of imagining as Fawcett said, "It is the greatest of all problems to the solution of which the mystic aspires; for supreme power, supreme wisdom, supreme delight lie in the far off solution of this mystery." Now notice he uses three definitions, power, wisdom and delight and these are the three defined in scripture that define Christ. Paul speaks of Christ as the power of God and the wisdom of God (1 Cor. 1:24). In the 8th chapter of Proverbs they speak of Christ as the delight of God: "He was with him constantly, delighting before him always, delighting in the affairs of men" (verse 30). "He who finds me finds life; he who misses me injures himself; all who hate me love death" (verse 35). So this that you heard this night if it is denied by you or ignored, it's because you're in love with the world of death. Everything here dies…but everything in the world begins and ends, it all dies, but Christ lives forever! Those who hate him it's because they're in love with death and they'll build up enormous fortunes, bigger and bigger, and have to leave it behind them. They haven't found a way yet of taking it. They'll leave their little garment and leave their funds no matter what size it is, but *this* you can't leave behind. If you find him here, you've found him, and death means nothing to you then for you are one with what the world speaks of as Christ.

One day you will know him, you will have all the experiences recorded in scripture concerning Jesus Christ. You'll be cast in the central role and then you will know beyond all doubt who you really are. You will have found him not as another; you will have found him as *yourself*. So some find him because they seek him; others find him because they're brought to him by one who found him. And so, some here this night you didn't seek him but you've been exposed to him. You may not accept it. You may go out and think that's blasphemy what that man said tonight, because it's in conflict with your concept of what you think it ought to be. But I tell you from experience. I am not speculating, I am not theorizing, for I'm telling you I know what I know from experience. I have experienced the entire drama as recorded in scripture concerning Jesus Christ, from the resurrection, through the birth, up to the very descent of the dove, the grand baptism.

So everything recorded and all the outstanding events of his life I have experienced while walking in this little mortal frame. The frame is not exempt from all the bugs of the world. So a hundred million Americans got it, I was one of them. And so they burned and so did I...five days of intense fever where you melt...so you take off twelve pounds and you do it certainly the hard way. You can consume all the liquids of the world, weight still isn't going to remain on you...off it goes. At the end of your little episode you're weak, physically weak, and someone will say, "Well, if you are really the one that you claim and you've had all these experiences, then why?" They do not realize that "I do not consider the sufferings of the present time worth comparing with the glory that is to be revealed in me" (Rom.8:18). I am not exempt from anything that man is heir to, and man is heir to all the nonsense of the world. It's all within us, I know.

So here this night, the mystery of Imagination is simply the mystery of your own being. It's the mystery of God. The more you discover the workings of your own Imagination, the more you discover the secret of God. So don't put it aside. When you go home tonight be perfectly honest with yourself. Do you know what you want either for yourself or for another, do you really know? Well then, do what Sam did, persuade yourself that things are as you desire them to be. To the degree that you're self-persuaded that they are so, to that degree they will become so and they will externalize themselves in your world. For these assumptions though at the moment that I make them are denied by my senses if persisted in will harden into fact. So, before you say no to it, test it! When you prove it in performance, you have found Christ. Now, do not do what my brother-in-law did; he buried the book, and forgot it.

The same family...a friend of mine, who is now gone from this world, said to me, "Neville, wouldn't you like me to put Vicki in the social register in New York City?" I said, "Certainly not." Well, she said, "It's the most marvelous thing for her." I said, "Let Vicki make that decision. She's a child now and so she can't possibly make that decision and I might be doing her a great injustice." So I said, "No, Helen, thank you very much. I presume you're in it." She said, "Well, when I was born I was registered in it and all my children, three of them, and my husband. My second husband, he came over, and I got him into it. So we're all in the social register...my entire background. So it's easy for me to get Vicki in the social register." So I declined. Well, casually I said it to Cynthia, Sam's wife, I think a month later, and she said, "You think she would sponsor me?" I said, "Why not? I'll ask her." So I called Helen and said, "Helen, my sister-in-law, Bill's sister, would like to be in the social register." She said, "Certainly, Neville, I'll get her in." That book is so prominently displayed in her living room that you can't miss it. They leave it ___(??). It's all over the living room and quite casually open at the page. She loves that sort of life. Naturally, she's not going to take the story which is the true story. For that thing in the social register isn't true at all. Yes that she graduated from Smith, that her husband graduated from Harvard these are true. But I mean the phoniness surrounding the whole thing. But the story I told concerning his use of Christ, that's the true story, and you'll find it if the book is not out of print called *The Power of Awareness*. That's where I tell this story.

So when you go to bed tonight, instead of just sleeping as you do normally, dare to assume things are as you desire them to be and try to catch the mood that would be your mood were it so. Try to catch the feeling of the wish fulfilled...and then sleep. Tomorrow night do the same thing. The next night do the same. And while you are sleeping, this immortal you will be pulling every wire in the world that is necessary to bring to birth your assumption.

Now let us go into the Silence.

* * *

Q: In Luke regarding the unclean spirit that comes out of a man, I don't understand it.

A: When the unclean spirit has been caste out of a man? This is a disembodied *idea*. For a demon is not some disembodied spirit; it's a prejudice, a superstition, a false pride. All these bedevil man. And so you entertain one and you're going to get two, you get seven, and they never stop there. You start with one superstition and all of a sudden you have a thousand of them, but they have to have a man as the agent to express themselves. They can't express themselves without a man. Man is the agent that expresses all the unlovely things in the world…these unclean spirits. So in my brother-in-law's case it was a false pride, and so he entertained this false pride that he went to Harvard. All right, so what! And then he was a banker…alright, wonderful…and now he's in the social register. He won't tell you that I got him there at the same time I declined for my daughter. She's never expressed any opinion since that she wanted it. I told her afterwards that I said no to it, that you, when you get old enough to know what's what in this world, you may decide you want it and it's always there for you if you want it.

So the water displaces it, it passes through and it must go back to a man. So the idea goes back to Sam. He got the job, he knows exactly how he did it, and now he puts it behind him and denies the ladder by which he did ascend. So the demons returned…all the false pride. He will think he's doing a wonderful job for God on Sunday morning and there he is every Sunday morning, regardless of weather, as the head usher ushering all the ladies and gentlemen down to their pews, and he thinks he's doing God a service. He knows nothing of God. They'll sing all the hymns, get on their knees, and pray to what? Certainly not to any God, for the *only* one that you could ever know is the God that you know in the first-person, present tense. You'll know him within yourself and his name is I AM. That's his eternal, immortal being. So you'll know him.

When you go outside and turn to a false god, you'll never find him. When you start with one idol, you multiply it. So these are the demons spoken of in scripture. You have a superstition, you can't stop at one. Were you ever in the theater? There you find them by the millions. Can't whistle in your own room, you can't put your shoe above where your head would be, can't open an umbrella in the place, and multiply them. Talk about the superstitions, go into the theater, and I'm not fooling. They make you go outside and do all kinds of nonsense if you absent mindedly whistle in your own dressing room or do any of these silly little things. But they really believe it brings bad luck and to the degree that they are self-convinced that it does, it does.

So these are the demons that possess the mind of man. And certainly false pride is a frightful demon: I must be seen with what I call the proper people, and I can't be seen in certain areas, certain restaurants, and certain this, that and the other, because it isn't the thing to do. Well, that's false pride.

Q: Like Jean Dixon? You know who she is?

A: Yes, I've heard of her.

Q: Ok. She prophesizes...like she gets these messages. Don't you think it's her Imagination that when she thinks something dire is going to happen and says it that that's why it happens...because she has imagined it? Is that the way it works?

A: First of all, she's not a woman of vision. She's not a woman who actually has the vision of scripture, but she can become self-persuaded using any little technique. She can use cards, use the stars, use monkey bones, and to the degree that she is self-persuaded that these things mean what she thinks they do, well, to that degree they'll come to pass. But you never hear them tell you of their mistakes. For instance, we had two candidates running for the presidency. All right, you can tell them both secretly that you're going to be president. One has to be, so you're fifty percent right. Well, that's such a major thing, but you're also fifty percent wrong. But you don't talk about that...only talk about that which has been publicized ___(??).

Q: ___(??) how to shorten the time period?

A: I would call it *intensity* of *feeling*. If you can feel the mood and become possessed by that mood. If I could only catch the mood...what would the feeling be like if it were true? Just what would it be like? Well, dwell upon just what it would be like...and suddenly you're bathed in that mood. Now sleep in it. Your own wonderful human Imagination is doing it, and one day when you least expect it that same being is doing it. That same being that you exercised without beholding him will be beheld because you won't see him as another. You will see the events related only to him, and this time they are related to you. And then you will know who you are.

Q: (Inaudible)

A: When you find him, you are not in this dimension at all. It is not in this world at all. One day you'll discover that the story of scripture is true, that in the end there is only one man, and all are gathered into one man and *you* are that one man. God is not a ___(??); God is a person...one man as told us in Ephesians: "There's only one body, one Spirit, one hope, one Lord, one faith, one baptism, one God and Father of all" (4:4). So in the end there is really only one. Here is a universally-diffused individuality gradually being gathered together one by one by one into one body, one Spirit, one Lord. So you will not be some little thing; you will be the actual body after the journey. And it's a terrible journey. No one denies the journey in this world is a horrible journey. No matter how luscious a life may be, there must come in the lives of all those moments when you are sad. You must say goodbye to your mother, your father, your husband or wife or child through the gate of death and you are left behind to mourn. Well, if you don't have a heart then you can take it. When you love someone dearly it's difficult to say goodbye, because clothed as you are in these garments of flesh and blood you miss the physical contact, you miss the voice, you miss the touch, you miss everything about the one you loved dearly. And you're kidding yourself if you say ___(??) that. You don't do it that way…not if you have a heart.

Q: (Inaudible)

A: I have *Your Faith is Your Fortune* coming out in about two weeks. That's been out of print for years. Now I have one with five books in it called *Resurrection* and they are out of print, four of them, for years. Well, my friend brought it back and I added one chapter…rather long…I call it a book, a small book, and it bears the title of that new one, called *Resurrection*. So there are four that are out of print plus the one that's new. And now *Your Faith is Your Fortune* will be in, I think the publication is the 16th, and DeVorss tells me that it will be ready by the 16th of this month.

No, it is not revised. They couldn't use the old plates because they're worn out. That book has gone way beyond what I thought. I always thought that it went 70,000. It's well over a hundred thousand that it sold and they use the same plates. But the plates are so completely worn he had to set it from the beginning to the very end, so he has placed it differently and it's not such a crowded page. It has wider spaces so it's a much bigger book in appearance but the identical content.

Well, until the next time. We will be here Monday and Friday nights. Thank you. Good night.

THE MYSTERY OF GRACE

1/10/69

Tonight is "The Mystery of Grace." Grace is so unlike what man is taught to believe. Grace is God's gift to man, a gift that is unmerited, unearned. It is not man's due, it is not conferred as a reward, it's a free gift by God to man. We are saved by grace. We are told that God chose us in him before the foundation of the world. Before the physical creation he chose us, chose all that you see in this world, that we should be holy and blameless before him. He destined us in love to be his sons through Christ Jesus, according to the purpose of his will. Therefore, no one in eternity can stop that purpose from coming to its fullness. God himself is present in the historical struggle directing the course of human history toward *his* own end.

Now we are given different gifts, all varied endowments that you and I bring. And we are able to bring it because we received it as a gift to the corporate life of the body of the risen Lord. They are called gifts of grace. The greatest of these gifts—far outstripping more spectacular gifts such as tongues—is love. Just imagine you face an audience of a thousand, no two speak the same tongue, they cannot communicate…and you address an audience of a thousand who cannot communicate and each hears you in their own tongue wherein they were born, as told us in the 2nd chapter of Acts. Each present of the thousand hears you in their own tongue wherein they were born. That's a spectacular gift. But the gift of love is God's gift of himself, for God is love; for all the other gifts are attributes of God and they are essential to the corporate life of the risen Lord. But when God gives you love, he gives you himself…for God is love. Power, wisdom, all these are attributes of God. The gift of prophecy, even that of the apostle, all these are attributes of God and all these, wonderful as they are and essential to the body of the risen Lord, are attributes. But when God gives you love, he has actually given you himself.

Now let me share with you the experience I had in 1929. I certainly did not expect it, and to this moment I feel unworthy of the gift. I felt then as I feel now not equipped to express that gift. Nevertheless, I was taken in spirit into the divine council, the assembly of the gods. I was taken first to the recording angel and there she checked off my name written in the book of life. Then I was taken before the risen Lord and he asked a simple question, asked me to name the greatest thing in the world. I quoted from the works of Paul, the 13th chapter of 1st Corinthians, "Faith, hope and love, these three, but the greatest of these is love." With that the risen Lord embraced me, we became one body, we became one Spirit. It was not the Lord and the speaker; I became the one body of the Lord, the one Spirit of the Lord, I became the Lord. Then I was commanded, ill-equipped as I was and still am, to tell the story. I came out and my room was filled with light. There was no reason for it. There was no light lit in my room, no moonlight, just radiant light. It did not subside for the longest while. It seemed to have no source…it was simply light in the wee hours of the morning.

So here, I stood in the presence of the risen Lord and he gave me himself; for he was infinite love when he embraced me. As he embraced me, I felt an ecstasy that I've never known before or since. For that return awaits me after I take off this little garment and return to that. For I have it only at rare intervals when I do my work at night in the region beyond dreams. So that was a gift—unearned, unwarranted, unmerited. It remains the Father's secret why he gave me *that* gift. There are other gifts, the gift of the miracle worker, a spectacular gift; the gift of the apostle, it's a glorious gift. It ranks so high in all the gifts it comes first in the list as Paul makes out the list. And it is a glorious gift because as you're sent, the sender and the one sent are one. But the gift of love is God's gift of his very self to the one that he embraces when he is wearing the human form divine which is all love. I cannot tell anyone why, I do not know. I only know that was the gift that he gave me. All the other gifts are attributes of God and they are essential to the corporate life of the body of the risen Lord.

So when the *whole* that he chose before the world was—and he chose it in him and destined it in love according to the purpose of his will; no one can stop it—that body will rise completely, each endowed with that special gift of grace. God treats us as if we were innocent, as if we were righteous, as if we were without guilt. In spite of what all the churches will tell you concerning condemnation…*not* to God. There is no one in this world that is guilty in the eyes of God. We are all innocent in the eyes of God and I don't care what the individual has ever done. That is God's love for man. He chose us in him before the world was and this whole vast universe is only a theater for God to manifest his power and his love, making of us sons. All sons but each endowed with different gifts to serve God and radiate his glory in the life of that corporate body when we all play our part within it. So no matter if you got the smallest gift, it is still beyond the wildest dream of mortal man, for that gift has to be exercised in the body of the risen Lord.

Now, while we are here we are called upon to do something. Not that we are going to earn it; the gift was ours and it was before the world was. But we are in the world of Caesar called upon to watch our thoughts, to watch our words, whether they are expressed audibly or simply entertained. I have stressed this through the years that I have been telling you. I received a letter yesterday from a friend of mine (she's here). She said, "Now this goes back…the dream only took place a few days ago…but the dream takes me back to when I was married, that is before I met you, because my husband has departed this world and he departed before I met you…yet as I go back in my experience I was married. All the friends I knew were of that era, and I said to a friend something that was an idle, oh, uncalled for remark. It was idle, it might have been mischievous, but I said it innocently. Then the room that was dark suddenly the corner lit, and there were two that she to whom I spoke told it. They in turn told it to four, and four to eight, eight to sixteen, sixteen to thirty-two, and finally the room seems crowded. I would estimate it to be 300. They were all aware of what they had heard and how they heard it, and here we had 300 in the room filled with a malice and an anger and violence all directed towards me based upon my idle remark. I realized then what we do unwittingly when we entertain a thought or express a thought. We think, oh, what does it matter? And here I saw the room crowded with animosity directed towards me that I myself had set in motion."

Well, the Book of James speaks of it. But in *Jerusalem* Blake makes the statement, "Oh, what have I said, what have I done, O all powerful human words." So I think I can stifle it. I entertain the thought and it's an unlovely thought of someone…maybe someone I do not even know. You read it in the paper and you react, and you've told it, and a corner of your room is lit and two are hearing it. The two repeat it…all directed now towards you. And you wonder why certain things happen in your world. This animosity *you* yourself created because "All that you behold, though it appears without, it is within, in your Imagination of which this world of mortality is but a shadow." So I start it in my Imagination, an idle, thoughtless word, and I said it to a friend and the friend repeated it to two, two to four, four to eight, and so on.

So here in our world we must be careful what thoughts we entertain, and I tell you, because imagining creates reality. You could entertain any lovely thought in this world that has no support on the outside—your reason denies it, your senses deny it, but you can entertain it as though it were true. And that is just as true as the most factual thing in this world. Something that is now in your world unlovely and it's factual you can now in your mind's eye entertain a contrary thought concerning it and persuade yourself of the reality of what you are now entertaining. Two will hear it, and four will hear it, and eight and they will look at you differently because of this change of attitude in you.

But here, after years the same God in us is the God in her and revealed to her the truth of scripture, for it is beautifully told in the Book of James. It's beautifully told in Galatians, it's told in the gospels, concerning the word that man entertains. So if I don't take hold of what I am thinking, well then, the world will reflect it and they will show me by their animosity what I actually have been doing. And it's all within me; it's not on the outside at all.

So here, after years these gifts of grace…we are saved by grace. So let no one frighten you, you *are* saved, for you were chosen in God before the physical creation was brought into being. It's not an afterthought. This is not some emergency thinking on the part of God. You were chosen in God before the foundation of the world, and he never saw you in any other light than the innocent one. It is God and God himself who puts you through the paces as we are told in the 11th chapter of the Book of Romans, "He has consigned all men to disobedience, that he may have mercy upon all" (verse 32) so that none may boast, that none may brag. So you have a billion, don't brag. You have nothing, don't be remorseful. So you think you are perfect in the eyes of the world, don't boast. You've not a thing to boast about. If there is anything to boast about, boast that you were chosen; and you *were* chosen before the foundation of the world, and you were chosen to play a specific part in the corporate life of the body of the risen Lord.

The first great act of grace, the supreme act, was incarnation. For you and I were helpless. "And when you were helpless," said Paul—I think it's the 5th chapter of Romans—"Christ died for the ungodly" (verse 6). He hadn't yet become us…God became man at a certain point in time that man may become God. So here we are the scattered. We were chosen and then we are scattered. And this universally diffused individuality is diffused in us. Paul, who uses the word "grace" more than all the other books of the Bible put together made this statement and I think it's the clearest definition of the meaning of the word as Paul expressed it. You'll find it in his 2nd letter to the Corinthians, the 8th chapter, the 9th verse: "You know the grace of our Lord Jesus Christ, who though he was rich, yet for your sake he became poor that by his poverty you might become rich." Now he drives this thought home in another letter to the Philippians and in this he makes the statement: "Jesus

Christ, who was in the form of God, emptied himself and took upon himself the form of a slave and was born in the likeness of man…and being formed in human form he became obedient unto death, even death upon the cross" (Phil.2:5-8). The cross and the *only* cross on which he is crucified is man. This is the cross. This is the supreme act of grace when he actually became me that I may become as he is.

So, all are destined to become sons of God through Jesus Christ. Jesus Christ is the *pattern man*, the perfect pattern, and the *only* way to the Father. There is no other way. He is the pattern man and were that pattern not in you, you'd never find the Father. Even though you're endowed with a different gift, nevertheless, you will be taken to the Father and you will know the Father. If you do not know him as yourself, you will still know the Father. If you have the gift of tongues, the gift of the miracle worker, the gift of the teacher, the healer, the prophet, all these are glorious gifts, you will still by this pattern in you be led to the Father. "For I am the way, the truth and the life; no one comes unto the Father, except by me" (Jn. 14:6). You follow this pattern and the pattern will unfold within you and take you to the Father.

Now, I received a letter today from a lady who is here tonight. She said, "My husband gets up and he's on the go and at four in the morning he's off to work. So on the morning of the 8th of this month I said goodbye to him and then went back to sleep. I addressed the brothers, I said, 'Oh brothers, please, please take me to the Father. I'm so tired of being here, take me to the Father.' And then I heard female voices, all laughing in a friendly lovely manner and they seemed to tuck me in. Then I saw three of them, although I knew my physical eyes were shut, I saw three of them. One came over, embraced me and kissed me and tucked me in. I said again, 'Please take me to the Father.' Again this one said yes and she kissed me and I began to float. I found myself in this marvelous golden mansion, and I knew it was my Father's house. Then I saw the human form, golden form, seated on this golden, well, it could have been a throne…but he was seated and his body was golden. I could only get to the shoulder, and then with a supreme effort I raised my eyes…they were spiritual eyes, for I knew my lids were shut… and I saw your face. I knew that you were the Father. I said, 'It's Neville. But of course, he is one with the Father.'" May I tell you, the Father is a hero wearing billions of faces…that's the Father. You follow that pattern, which is the pattern laid down in scripture as the life of Jesus Christ, and when it unfolds within you, you are he. And he who sees me has seen the Father, for I and my Father are one. So when that pattern erupts and unfolds within you, you are the Father, whether mortal man believes it or not.

But there are those who still walk the earth who will have the experience of this lady and who will know beyond all doubt from her own wonderful mystical experience that what I tell you is true. The Father became us that we may become the Father. The one to whom he gave himself by the embrace of love is destined to be the Father. The body he wears is the same body that embraced him, the body of love. For love is the human form divine. She saw the symbolism of the golden mansion. It need not be a golden mansion; that's what she saw. But she did see a being that she knows and respects in this world, a being that's quite limited, limited as Paul was limited. Paul cried out three times…he appealed to have the thorn removed from him. Well, the thorn need not be something physical as many have speculated it could be his feeling of inadequacy, that's his thorn, the feeling of being not properly equipped for the job at hand. And the voice replied, "My grace is sufficient for thee; my power is made perfect in weakness" (2Cor.12:9).

So you are weak, you're inadequate in the eyes of yourself and therefore, naturally, the world. Well, "my power is sufficient for your weakness" and so he did not remove the thorn, the thorn being Paul's feeling of being inadequate. How often I've felt the lack of a formal education. How often I've been asked, "Well, what is your college background?" and I've never once made any claim other than the truth. I never went to college and I never graduated from high school. In a group of men and women who treasure degrees out of the world of Caesar it was quite a confession and a feeling of inadequacy in their presence. Yet I knew I had experienced in the world of Caesar that which if I told them they would not understand. They would turn aside and smile as one a little bit demented, a little bit off.

Yet I knew I stood in the presence of the risen Lord who embraced me, that there is such a thing as a book called *The Book of Life* where names are recorded as told us in the 12th chapter of the Book of Daniel. When the seventy returned and they were so proud that by their power they had cast out all the devils, he said, "It would be far better if you rejoiced because your names are written in heaven; not to rejoice that you cast out demons but that your names are written in heaven." For, there *is* such a ledger, where in the book…it's the *Book of Life*. Well, the Father has life in himself and the one written in it will have life in himself. So the moment he embraces you and you become one with him he transfers to you all that is his. So he has life in himself and you the son become one with life in yourself—no longer an automaton, an animated being moved from without—but now a life-giving Spirit. One that is truly wearing the garment of love which is not seen by mortal eye in this world, but you know it and you feel it constantly. When you sleep at night you know what you are about to wear the moment the eyes shut in what the world calls sleep.

So grace is God's gift to man. Not one child born of woman will be exempt of grace, for by grace we are saved. We are incapable of saving ourselves, no man is wise enough, strong enough...we are helpless beings in the world of Caesar. While you are yet helpless, Christ died for the ungodly. His death was the incarnation; his incarnation is your breath. It was not always so, but since the moment of the incarnation, the universally diffused individuality that is the Cosmic Christ, and now he shares his gifts with all as he had predetermined before that the world was. It will not be an afterthought when you receive the gift. There are those here this night who have received gifts...one the incurrent witness where the eyes are "open inwardly into the world of thought, into eternity, ever expanding on the bosom of God, the human Imagination" (Blake, *Jerusalem*, Ch.1, Plt.5). That's a glorious gift, that's a gift of prophecy, for it sees as present what is still future. That is the gift of the prophet. It comes second in the list of gifts as described in Paul's letters to the Corinthians: the apostle first, the prophet second (12:28). So, the incurrent eye witness is the gift of the prophet. She sits here this night and she has that gift. It's a fantastic gift.

Others will have the gift of the teacher, the gift of the healer, the gift of the helper, the gift of the administrator, for that's essential, the gift of tongues, the gift of faith, the gift of hope. I have no power to decide any gift for anyone...that rests entirely with the risen Lord. So to whom he will give the gift of love that is his secret. I only know when I was called in '29 then I felt unworthy and today I still feel unworthy in the world of Caesar to have received the greatest of all gifts, for there is no greater gift than the gift of God himself. For all other gifts are attributes of God and therefore eternal, but love is God himself. God is love.

So I tell you what I have this night from my own personal experience: No one will be lost. No one will be unredeemed. No one has ever been other than holy and blameless in the eyes of God. He has never seen anyone other than the innocent, other than the guiltless...I don't care what they have done. Man sees them guilty, man judges, man condemns, but not God. He sees nothing to condemn, for *he* committed us and consigned us to disobedience. If you ever thought other than that...you could keep all the commandments externally and break every one internally. When he comes into the world he interprets the Commandments *psychologically* and no man can ever tell me he has kept the Commandments psychologically. "'Thou shalt not commit adultery' you have heard it said'...said he, "...but I say to you any man who looks on a woman lustfully has already committed the act of adultery with her" (Mat. 5:27). Let the man rise who has not; let him cast the stone if he has not. Who has not coveted, who has not in his mind's eye stolen? If he didn't have the courage to steal outwardly, who did not entertain the thought but restrained the impulse because he didn't have the courage thinking of consequences? So every Commandment has been broken by man, and God made it so that he may have mercy upon all.

So everyone in the end is justified. Paul equates justification with grace. So in his letter to the Romans, the 8th chapter, "And those whom he foreknew…" Well, if he chose me in him before the foundation of the world, then he knew me to have chosen me as he knew you to have chosen you. So he starts, "Those whom he foreknew he predestined to the conformed to the image of his son. And those whom he predestined he also called; and those whom he called he also justified; and those whom he justified he also glorified" (verse 29). Well, justification is divine acquittal. So everyone is destined to be completely acquitted of anything and everything that he has ever done in this world. There will be no suffering for him. In spite of what others may wish for him, God does not, for he played the part.

Now, to go back into the Old Testament into Genesis for it…when all the brothers begged forgiveness and got on their knees and bowed before Joseph, he made them rise. He said, "You meant evil against me, but God meant it for good (Gen. 50:20). Therefore, it was not you who sold me into slavery but God. It wasn't any person other than God. He sold me into slavery using you as the medium through whom he could carry me into slavery, that I with my gift of prophesy, my gift to interpret vision, would interpret Pharaoh's vision and save civilization from starvation. So I interpreted his vision and began to save the wheat and save the corn and save everything that could be saved and built barns…knowing in seven years after this abundance there would be seven years of nothing. You'll even forget there ever was abundance. So you sold me into slavery that I with my gift of grace, the gift to see and understand what I see mentally—for he was called the dreamer who could interpret dreams, interpret visions." He interpreted the vision of Pharaoh and then told Pharaoh exactly what it meant. Pharaoh gave him the order to start building the barns and taking x-number of percentages of all things grown and building for the future that would have nothing. It came to pass just as he interpreted it.

So in spite of the brothers feeling that they were guilty, God didn't see them guilty at all. God used them, knowing the weaknesses of the heart, of the flesh, he could use them through envy to dispose of a brother that they envied. So God didn't see them as guilty… that they were justified. And after justification comes glorification. So in the 17th chapter of John, when the work is done, when he has brought to climax the *sacred* history of Israel, he brought it to climax and complete fulfillment, he said, "I have finished the work thou gavest me to do. Now Father return unto me the glory that was mine, the glory that I had with thee before that the world was" (verse 5). He was one with the Father and emptied himself of his glory, of his divine form, and took upon himself the form of man, a slave, and then became obedient unto death (Phil. 2:7) as we all are obedient unto death. Then came the sacred history of Israel erupting within him. And so he brought that sacred history of Israel to climax and fulfillment within himself and the work was completed. Now he asks only to return to the glory that was his that he gave up to come into the world of slaves to lift them all to his level.

So may I tell you, you are saved! And I wouldn't care what the world will tell you, I don't care what you have done, what you may still have to do; you have been saved by grace...not by any effort on your own part. But you have been saved. The gift will appear and you will know the part you will play in the corporate life of the body of the risen Lord, for every gift is essential to that living body. So do not envy anyone who has a different kind of a gift. But if one has the gift of love, which is God himself, he will be seen by those who really are seeking the Father. If they know him, they'll see his face on the body of love. They'll see it and interpret it in their own way...a golden body, a radiant body. The body that I saw was a glorious, radiant body of love. You can't describe it, it was simply all love. There's no way to describe that risen form other than love. There's not one word that you entertain in the presence of the risen Lord but love. So when asked to name the greatest thing, it was automatic. You could name faith and hope, but you knew you're looking at the greatest thing in the world, it is right before you and it's love. Then he embraces you and you fuse. I can't quite describe how two people become one, but we became one without loss of identity. I was still aware that I am who I am, and yet I wore the garment of love, and I became one with the Spirit of the Lord, one with God the Father. Then I was commissioned and sent out of that assembly, and told "Time to act!" No more preparation is necessary, time to act. Inadequate as you are, unprepared as you are, unequipped as you are: "My grace is sufficient for you, for my power is made perfect in your weakness. So you go, be ashamed of nothing. I have chosen you to be my messenger and I've sent you."

So here, another gift he gave me was that of the apostle. He gave me himself, but having sent me...the word apostle means "one who is sent." So the command as he sent me was, "You are now my apostle to tell my story to everyone who will hear it. And those who I call to you will come and no one will stop them. No one can come unless my Father calls them." And the ones who my Father called in no way can I cast off...and *only* those that he calls. It's a most selective thing in the world, for he is restoring his fallen body, but lifting it up to a higher and higher level of being. This fall of God was deliberate for a creative purpose. So then the fallen form, scattered as it is, is restored and everyone is brought back into the one body, the one Spirit, the one Lord, the one God and Father of all. All are raised by means of the fall, therefore, all are justified and all are glorified.

So this glorious thing called grace, which today we cheapen so much, the Greek word that is translated grace is "charis" and we use it now that he has charisma. Some firm brought out a perfume and called the perfume Charisma. This is such a sacred word in scripture; c-h-a-r-i-s, that is the root of the word. In fact, that is the word that is translated "grace." Hasn't a thing to do with perfume, hasn't a thing to do with some individual's out-going personality. So, certainly he has a lovely personality and so he's out-going and they say he has charisma. But that one doesn't have charisma. They go around judging each other. Hasn't a thing to do with God's grace. God's gifts differ from these little things that men see and all these gifts are true gifts. One day you will be in the one body where all these gifts are exercised. Which one you individually will receive I do not now. I only know I received the gift of love, and therefore with the gift of love which is God himself I would automatically have all his attributes. So all the others below the level of God himself which are attributes I would have to have. If they're not exercised now—there's no reason for the exercise of them here, but when I shed this for the last time I will be exercising all the gifts, for I received the gift of love.

Now let us go into the Silence.

*   *   *

Q: (inaudible)

A: Yes, God is a protean being. By a protean being, he plays all the parts. Proteus in mythology was this mythological figure who served Neptune, the god Neptune; and he could assume the form of a fish or that of a man as it served his purpose as he went about serving his lord who was Neptune. Well, God is a protean being and can appear in any form that is his choice if that is the form best suited for the work at hand. So when I address the Orientals, it was better that I was an Oriental that they would receive me and hear the Word of God. When I addressed the Negro, I was the Negro. When I addressed the Caucasians, I was a very blond person that they would see me with blond hair and blue eyes. Well, you can't conceive that I have blond hair or blue eyes, yet that's what I was to those who saw me, for I can assume any mask when I am in the region beyond the region of dream where I'm instructing. Others will see me in different forms, depending upon what I'm doing. But God is Spirit and he wears masks…these are all masks, very much so. They're called persona. Persona is the mask, that of the actor, the actor's mask. "God only acts and is in existing beings or men." Like the ancient actor, he put on a mask, and God is the supreme actor who plays all the parts. So there isn't an Oriental in the world that is not being played by God, there isn't a Negro in the world who is not being played by God. But man doesn't know that and so while the masks are on, they hate each other's masks. The being playing it is God, nothing but God.

The 82nd said by our scholars to be the most difficult of all the psalms…there are 150…and Thomas Cheney—who was the editor-in-chief of the *Encyclopedia Biblica*, the most scholarly of all the higher criticisms of scripture—said that the ideas in this psalm might be perennial, but their meanings have long ceased to exist. We do not know. Well, it's a beautiful psalm and the psalm is this: "And God has taken his place in the divine council; in the midst of the gods he holds judgment" (verse 1). Now he addresses the gods, and same word translated singular, which is God, is now translated in the plural, same Elohim, and he addresses the gods now. He said, "I say ye are gods, sons of the Most High, all of you; nevertheless, you shall die like men, and fall as one man, O ye princes" (verse 6). So he gathered all within himself and one man fell taking all within himself, and they were gods before they fell. For this is for the purpose of lifting up the one being containing all to a higher level. And so ___(??) to be given back, "Return unto me the glory that *was* mine before that the world was" (Jn. 17:5). One day when the whole drama is over the glory will be returned that was yours before the world was, only it will be far more radiant because of the experience in the world of death.

Until the next time. Thank you.

THE MYSTERY OF FORGIVENESS

1/13/69

Tonight's title is "The Mystery of Forgiveness." The glory of Christianity is to conquer by forgiveness. We are so apt to attribute our ills and our troubles to outward causes, to our environment, to the conditions that surround us, to things—desirable things lacking, or undesirable things that are present—while all the time the real cause is sin. Now, sin is simply "missing the mark." You have an objective and you haven't realized it, and after a while you're frustrated...that is sin. The gospel teaches that all ills, all troubles can be traced to sin.

Now let us take the story as told us in the Book of Mark: "After John was arrested, Jesus came into Galilee, preaching the gospel of God, and saying, 'The time is fulfilled, and the kingdom of God is at hand; repent, and believe in the gospel'" (Mk. 1:14). Now this drama takes place *in* the individual. This is not something on the outside; it's all on the inside, after John was arrested. So we read the story of John, this is John the Baptist, who wore camel's hair and a leather girdle and did violence to his appetite, living on locusts and wild honey, believing that he could acquire merit by this violence to his body, to himself. As millions today really believe...if I can restrain these impulses and I do this, that and the other, well then, I'm acquiring merit and this will get me into the kingdom of heaven after this state of mind in us is arrested. Having tried it, having gone on, say, an extreme vegetable diet—no meat, no fish, no fowl, no not even eggs, no liquor, no tobacco—and I think by these restraints that some being on the outside is seeing my goodness, and will simply chalk it up in my favor...and here, I'm doing violence to my being. Then a man goes through that and discovers that's *not* the way and arrests that state of mind, arrests it within himself. He doesn't criticize others for indulging in it or for practicing it...

leave them alone. But you the individual who has gone through it, you realize that's not the way.

So, "After John was arrested" then comes the new man, one that is waiting in man to be awakened, to be born. Then he makes the proclamation that the kingdom of heaven is at hand. But he puts a condition now, "repent and believe in the gospel." He is the gospel; this is the *pattern* man. He has experienced scripture, experienced it in detail, and he knows that he is the central figure of scripture. So Jesus now interprets the Old Testament with himself as the very center of it. Now, to the rabbi that is not merely shocking that's blasphemy! For he said, "In the volume of the book it is written about me" (Heb. 10:7). "Everything said, all the things prophesied were all about me." Now he calls himself the "Son of man." You will never find this title on the lips of anyone outside of Jesus, and you'll find it scores of times in the gospels.

Now, they bring him a paralytic. Well now, a paralytic need not be a physical being that is incapacitated; you could have a paralysis of business where the merchandise is not flowing. If it does not flow and become alive, there will be bankruptcy, and therefore you're dead as far as your business is concerned. You could have a paralysis in your social world where you're now ostracized, you're not invited as you were, and then all of a sudden that can continue and then you are not the being that you were, there's a paralysis. You can have a paralysis in the art world where a man loses inspiration. The painting isn't coming, the poetry isn't coming, the writing isn't coming, the architecture isn't coming. If it is not coming, there is a paralysis there. Now this being represents this paralysis in our world.

So all the miracles are parables, and a parable is a story told as if it were true leaving the one who hears it to discover the fictitious character of that parable and then learn its meaning and apply it. So they bring him a paralytic and he said to the paralytic, "Your sins are forgiven" (Mat. 9:2). Well, the scribes and the Pharisees who heard this statement said, "Why does he speak thus, its blasphemy. Who can forgive sins but God alone?" And he discerning their hearts said to them, "Which is easier, to say 'Your sins are forgiven,' or to say 'Rise, take up your pallet and walk'? But that you may know that the Son of man has authority on earth to forgive sins—I now say, 'Rise, take up your pallet and go home'" (verses 3-7). The man rose and went out, and they had never seen anything comparable to it.

Now, how do I put that into practice as an individual? What am I called upon to do? He started off by saying, "Repent and believe in the gospel." Repentance and faith are the conditions of forgiveness. I can't forgive without repentance. Repent means "a radical change of attitude, a change of mind, a reversal of my thinking, or a revision of my thinking, or a reformation of my thinking. I need not go down to the root, I can change a portion of it, but I must change my attitude. A change of attitude will then be repentance.

If I can actually change my attitude towards anyone in this world, I can forgive them. So someone stands before me and he is unemployed. He is a family man…he has not only himself to support, but he has a wife and he has a family and he's unemployed. I represent that man to myself as one who is gainfully employed, and I persuade myself that he *is* gainfully employed. To the degree that I am self-persuaded he becomes employed. Now I need not the man's consent or the man's permission or his knowledge that I am doing what I'm doing. I see the need and seeing the need, and moved by this authority within me, I simply act as the Son of man is called upon to act. Well, if I do it and I get the result that I desired then I have found who the Son of man is.

Now, the Son of man is Christ and Christ is God. Well, I didn't pray to any outside God, I didn't go to any individual and ask them for help, I simply tried it. I did what I believe should work. Having interpreted scripture correctly, I tried it and it worked. I tried it again and it worked. Then I kept on trying it and it kept on working like a charm. Well, if it works, then I know who the Son of man is. So are we not told, "Do you not realize that Jesus Christ is in you? Test yourselves and see." We're called upon to make a test…to test ourselves and see. I trust that you will realize that we have not failed to meet the test. Now this is Paul's letter to us, the 13th chapter of 2nd Corinthians, and he's calling upon man to test himself. For *in him* is the Son of man, and the Son of man is the title most often used by Jesus of himself. Yes he confessed that he was the Christ. He confessed that he was the Son of the Blessed; he confessed that he was the Son of God. He also confessed that he was God, that "He who sees me sees the Father. How can you say, 'Show us the Father'?" (Jn. 12:45). So he said, "I am the Father" and so the Son and the Father are one. He confessed these, but the title most often on his lips and only on *his* lips is that of the Son of man.

So the Son of man has authority to forgive sins. Well now, you can forgive sin. And sin is simply a man missing the mark. You don't ask the man's permission, you don't ask his consent, he doesn't know what you're doing, but you are moved by some emotion. Instead of sympathizing with him and keeping him in that state, you empathize with him. You do it in your own Imagination. Having done it in your Imagination, you've found out who Christ is…and Christ is your own wonderful human Imagination. There never was another Christ and never will be another. So, the cry on the cross, "Father, forgive them, for they know not what they do." Here is one asking forgiveness for what they are doing to him. Well, you are doing it to your own wonderful human Imagination every time you misuse it. So I misuse my Imagination by indulging in some unlovely thing concerning myself or another, that is a misuse of Christ. So I am saying, forgive them, they don't know what they're doing or they would not do it. So I'm crying out to my own self to forgive every man for his misuse of the being that I am; for I am in you just as you are in me. We are one and our Imagination is this one universal Christ.

So, "Father, forgive them!" the cry on the cross. Well, this body is the cross. There is no other cross that he bears. He became man that man may become God. So while he's here, I've proven where he is; I have proven that he is my Imagination. For what did I do but represent the individual to myself as I would like to see him in the world and I persuaded myself that this representation was true, that it was real, and in time it became real. Well, he doesn't know that I did this so there is no praise, no thank you. I don't expect any thanks for it. My thanks is to see the law work. Well then, if I see it work I know who I am, that I am he.

So this is the paralysis, the paralytic being that was brought into his presence. Anyone who is missing the mark is paralyzed, he's frustrated. But he invariably blames outside causes and he points to his environment, he points to conditions round about him, he points to things…always things. These things may be, as I said earlier, desirable things that are not now present, they are lacking, or undesirable things that are now present in my world. But still they are things. But that is not the *cause* of man's ills, not the cause of his troubles; the real cause is man's sinning…he is missing the mark. After a while he's frustrated and frustration is sin, because frustration is simply missing the mark.

So the glory of Christianity is to conquer by forgiveness. If I can practice it morning, noon and night, I'm putting into practice what the whole story of Christianity is all about. While I am here on this earth I have an authority, my authority is to forgive sin while waiting for that moment in time when I will fulfill in myself the sacred history of Israel, and bring it to climax and bring it to fulfillment in myself. When I do, I will know that the Bible is all about me; it was not written about any other, just about me. But who is this me, Neville? No my own wonderful human Imagination. It was all written about Christ and Christ is my Imagination; Christ is the Son of man that is my own wonderful human Imagination. There is no other Christ.

So this is forgiveness and throughout the scripture it is all about forgiveness. Peter said to him, "Lord, how often must I forgive my brother, as many times as seven times?" He said, "I do not say seven times, but seventy times seven" (Mat. 18:21)…in other words until it happens. It is an endless number. You are self-persuaded that the thing is done. If you are self-persuaded, forget it; you will see the evidence in your world. But until you are self-persuaded of what you're doing you haven't yet succeeded in forgiving.

Now, to forgive is also to forget. Man cannot forgive and not forget. So as Blake said, "In heaven the only art of living is forgetting and forgiving." There is no other art. In hell everything is self-justification; there is no forgiving and no forgetting. So when our priesthoods of the world forgive you and meet you on the street an hour later and still remember your confession, they haven't forgiven at all. They have not represented you to themselves as the woman or as the man that you would like to be; they see you as the one who confessed. Well, that's not forgiving, because it's not forgetting; and where there's no forgetting there is no forgiving. So when I see someone who is gainfully employed, you forget he was ever unemployed. You represent him to yourself just as you want him to be. Well, how often, Lord?—seventy times seven. Doesn't really matter how often he sins and becomes frustrated…practice the art of forgiveness and go through life simply forgiving every being in this world, for they're not really to be condemned. They are in states and the state is the thing, not the man.

So a man falls into a state and that state is undesirable. He didn't know he's falling into it. He could be persuaded to move into it by what he reads in the paper and he reacts to things that he shouldn't. Nevertheless, he falls into a state. Well, the state is the thing. You lift him out of the state by representing him to yourself as being in another state, and you persuade yourself of the reality of this other state in which your friend is placed. So you'll see, if you do it this way, there's no condemnation. A man has to be in the state of violence to commit violence. He has to be in the state of anything to express that state. So if the state expressed is undesirable, it's the state, not the one who is in it. He who is in it is the agent expressing the state. Well, if you know this, you will not condemn anyone. If he is in an undesirable state, you represent him to yourself as being in a desirable state. And to the degree that you can persuade yourself that he is—forget all the past, how long he's been in that horrible past state—he will come out of it and find himself expressing the state that you represented to yourself that he is now occupying.

So the story…all these miracles are parables and they're simply conveying a certain story. Well, the story of Jesus Christ himself is an *acted parable*. It is an acted parable, the whole story from the beginning to the end, dramatizing God's plan of redemption. Well, if you see the story and know that now that is an acted parable, well then, one day you are going to experience that parable. But when you experience it then you know the reality of it. The whole thing will erupt within you, like a flower erupting upon a vine and you will *know* the truth of the gospel. For he took the entire Old Testament (there was no other story) and having read the entire Old Testament, he then interpreted the Old Testament with himself as the central figure.

Well, that simply shocked every rabbi in the world who heard it, for that's not what they were looking for…that's not the Messiah. They were expecting something entirely different from a normal man moving on the streets of the world, not educated, not anyone to hail, not anything. But all of a sudden, it happened in him, and being familiar with the Old Testament, which was the only scripture, he realized "Well, this is what is taking place in me." And then he begins to tell it. Those who followed him were also the uneducated as told us in the Book of Acts…that John and Peter began to do fantastic things in the name of Jesus. The Sanhedrin, the great leaders of the day, stopped them and with their great political power threatened them and told them never again to teach in the name of Jesus and not to mention anything concerning Jesus. Then they said to those who would stop them, "Whether it is right in the eyes of God to listen to you rather than to God, you must judge; for we cannot but speak of anything other than what we have heard" (Acts 4:19). So, we have heard it, we've experienced it, what else can we talk about?

If the whole vast world rose tonight and told me that what I am saying is misleading and that I must no longer talk about it, well, how could I ignore what has happened? I could no more deny what has happened to me than I could the simplest evidence of my senses, I couldn't. I know what I had for dinner tonight, but that is not as graphic in my mind's eye as the unfolding of scripture within me. That happened back in 1929, but here in 1959 the dramatic scenes began to unfold. In the short interval of 1,260 days they all unfolded. They are more indelibly impressed upon my mind than yesterday's meal. I couldn't tell you what I had yesterday…it doesn't interest me. I ate, I know I ate, and I know that I read, and know that I studied, I know that I lived a normal life, but I couldn't tell you the details of yesterday. But I can give you the details of these dramatic scenes as they unfolded within me, all from scripture. So how could I now deny them? I can't deny that anymore than the simplest little evidence of my senses.

So Peter and John said, "If it is right in the eyes of God, you be the judge. I cannot do other than speak of what we have heard and seen" and so they went through life forgiving. Forgiving was simply putting into practice repentance and faith, for repentance and faith are the conditions of forgiveness. I repent by simply changing my attitude, reforming the being before me. You are unemployed? Well now, not in my mind's eye. You are gainfully employed. You're missing your mark in life? You haven't found your goal? Not in my mind's eye, you've found the goal. Now, to the degree that I'm self-persuaded you should conform, for I have a new form for you, a new state. You should come into that state if I am faithful to that state and faith is simply remaining loyal to unseen reality. The world hasn't seen it as yet, but I've seen it. So this unseen reality I am loyal to it. I will not violate this pledge: I pledge myself to remain loyal to a state relative to you or to myself. And to *that* degree you should conform to this state if I am loyal to it. But repentance came first, because it meant changing or reforming what I saw with my senses. In my mind's eye I changed it.

Well, if it works—and I have all the evidence in the world that it does work if we the operant power will operate it—well, if it does work, I have found Christ. And there is no other Christ because "By him all things are made, and without him was not made anything that is made" (Jn. 1:3). Well, if this thing is made and made without effort, made without appealing to anyone in the world, it just happens, yes, they can reflect and say, well, it happened in this way, that way and the other way, and give all credit to the means because the *cause* remains hidden. The cause was in the mind of someone, in one's Imagination, so that was the hidden side, the *real* cause. Now when it begins to unfold they will look at the means that was used in order to unfold it and objectify it, but that was *not* the cause. The cause remains hidden because Christ is hidden. Who sees your Imagination? So, he is the unseen being in the midst of us. "You know him not. There is one in the midst of you, one within you whom you do not know, whose very buckles you are not worthy to untie" (Jn. 1:26).

Here is the one who will one day actually baptize you with the Holy Spirit. He'll be so satisfied with what he's accomplished in you that he'll actually come down in fullness and possess you and wear you as a garment. Then you and he are one. But we are invited in the earliest gospel, which is Mark, to start practicing repentance. This comes after the outer man is arrested, when I no longer think I can get into the kingdom of heaven by doing violence to my appetites. Someone will say, you can't smoke and get in. I've heard these arguments, "Can you imagine Jesus smoking?" Well, I see him smoking all day long…everyone who does…who else do you think is doing it? Can you imagine Jesus eating meat? Well, everyone who eats meat, that's Jesus. There is nothing but Jesus; there is nothing but God in this world. Can you imagine him doing this, that and the other? Well, any man who does anything, that's what Jesus is doing, so "Forgive them, Father, they know not what they do." They're doing violence to me because they don't know who I am. But forgive them for whatever they do to me. Eventually,

I will not give up, I'll persist to the very end, and I will awaken in them. When I awaken in them we are one, we aren't two.

So this is forgiveness and if you'll practice it you start with repentance and it's simply a lovely change of attitude. Change it towards anything that is undesirable, and then represent to yourself what you would like in the place of what you see. Now, can you believe in the reality of what you have done in your Imagination? So you have the two conditions and you've met them: One is repentance and the other is faith. To believe in this rearrangement of your mind and to really believe in it, that's faith, in the rearrangement which is repentance. Now these two conditions will result in forgiveness and it's always the forgiveness of sin, it's nothing else. The cause of every ill in the world, of every distress, of all the problems in the world is nothing more than sin. It has no outer cause; the cause is sin. And you'll find it all through the Bible: "Your sins are forgiven. Your sins are forgiven. Your sins are forgiven." Well, they're all different requests. One came paralyzed, one came talking adultery, one came and it was dead, and no matter what it was, he said, "Your sins are forgiven." He represents them to himself as they would like to be seen by themselves, and persuaded himself that this representation was true, and they became exactly what he in his mind's eye believed them to be.

Well, having found the Son of man and knowing that the Son of man is Christ Jesus, then one should expect that all that is said of him in scripture one should realize, one should experience. For if you can prove by this drama that you can actually change the life of one person in this world, without his consent, without his knowledge, and change it into the ideal state that you know he would like, or she would like to be, you only need one. If you do it once, you've proven who Jesus Christ is, who the Son of man is. Now everything said of the Son of man who is Jesus must be experienced by you. When it's experienced by you, well then, who are you but God the Father? So he said, "Who sees me sees the Father." Oh yes, in the world of men I am the Son of God, I'm the creative power of God, the wisdom of God. But "I came out from the Father and I came into the world; again, I am leaving the world and I am going to the Father" (Jn. 16:28). I return to myself having come into the world, with all the limitations imposed upon me, and proven who I really am, with all the limitations, and then I take off the limitations and return to the being that I am.

So the glory of Christianity is to conquer by forgiveness…that's the glory. Hasn't a thing to do with your giving fortunes to the world. Foundations will give two million, ten million, fifty million…wonderful! Let them all give it, perfectly alright. But that doesn't do a thing for the individual in his giving of that. Let him take an individual and change the individual in his mind's eye and see that change take place in his world. Then he should know who he is. But if I have all the millions in the world and I give it to charity and give it impersonally, that's not it. God is a person and we are treated as persons by God. Let no one tell you that God is not a person. I tell you God is a person. You stand in the presence of the risen Lord and it's man: "Thou art a man, God is no more, thine own humanity learn to adore" (Blake). So I say, you will one day actually stand in the presence of the risen Lord and it's man. Infinite love yes, but man. So don't think of God as some over-soul, some impersonal force; think of God as man. He actually is man and that's why you are man: he became you. Now he's raising you to his glory, to his love, to his power, to his wisdom, to all the things that he is.

So you practice forgiveness. That's the first thing in the earliest gospel, the Book of Mark, that man is called upon to do. These are the first words of Jesus. And after the outer man is arrested...well, I know in my own case I was seven years a strict vegetarian, teetotaler, a celibate, and all when I was in my twenties. Here, when the sap of life is running rampantly in my body for expression, and because of my own frustration in my first marriage, which was like a living hell, I then assumed the vows of celibacy. For seven years that was my vow. No meat, no fish, no fowl, no liquor, no smoking. I thought I was acquiring merit. One day I discovered I wasn't acquiring any merit so I arrested John. I arrested that attitude of mine within me and then did everything I had not done in seven years without any self-condemnation, without any self-blame. Then here came this marvelous unfolding of the entire story of Christ within me. So when I speak to you I speak not from theory, I speak from experience. I tell you what I know that I have experienced. I have experienced the entire story as recorded in the gospel of Jesus Christ. It's the most dramatic thing that one could ever imagine, and it happened so suddenly, so unexpectedly.

So tonight, when you go out you practice forgiveness. And you start with a simple change of attitude, that's repentance. Believe in the reality of that change...that's faith. Remain loyal to that unseen reality. That's your real trust, your real faith. Walk in that state as though it were true, and in a way you do not know, you could not devise, it becomes true. Let no one then call you up to say "when?" It's not your concern as to when...you've done it. I imagine it so to be, I am still imagining it so to be, I will continue to imagine it so to be until what I have imagined is externalized in my world. And so I'm not concerned. Don't ask me any questions, I've done it! If I've done it, well then, let it come into being in its own fullness of time. It's not for me to do it.

Today a lovely little booklet came to my wife to comfort her in her present distress and the back page was…one of the little thoughts recorded in it was from Thoreau. If one would advance confidently in the direction of his dreams—just advancing confidently in the direction of his dreams—what he imagines will come to pass. "If one would advance confidently in the direction of his dreams, endeavoring to live the life which he has imagined, he will meet with the success unexpected in common hours." Just imagine that was Henry Thoreau. I have a dream and then I advance confidently in the direction of my dream, endeavoring to live the life that I have imagined, dwelling in it, though reason denies it and my senses deny it, I will then meet with the success beyond that of common hours. So here was this glorious concept that Henry David Thoreau gave to the world. And this lady and her husband sent it off today as a little comforting thought to Bill. But it was quite an impressive thing…in fact, the entire booklet…but this last one was by Thoreau.

So, if in heaven the only art of living is forgetting and forgiving, we might just as well start practicing that now on earth. So we go forward simply putting it into practice. It costs nothing and only takes a moment of one's time, but it actually costs you nothing to do it. Because you *don't* sit down and burst a blood vessel trying to do it, you simply imagine that all things are possible to one's Imagination and you imagine it done, knowing that Imagination is God, that is Jesus Christ. Well, if that is Jesus Christ and I've imagined it and believed in the reality of what I've imagined, it should come to pass; because all things are possible to God and my Imagination is God, the *only* God. So if I imagine it and I do not swerve from what I've imagined, it should come to pass.

Well now, in your letters not only your mystical experiences which are the most glorious things ever but things concerning forgiveness share that with me…how you took someone who was in great need. That need could be anything. It need not be financial need, it could be a physical condition, it could be a marital condition, a family condition, whatever it is, and then you resolved it. When you resolve it without their knowledge or consent and you get results then write me about it. Write me that I may share it with those who are present and encourage all by our mutual trust.

Now let us go into the Silence.

FOREKNOWLEDGE

1/17/69

Tonight's subject is "Foreknowledge." We're told in scripture that "Thus said the Lord of hosts, 'As I have planned, so shall it be; as I have purposed, so shall it stand. And the Lord will not turn back until he has executed and accomplished the intents of his mind'" (Is. 14:24; Jer. 23:20). Now the structure of God's plan is given us in the Book of Romans. Here we have it in five terms: "Those whom he foreknew he also predestined to be conformed to the image of his son. And those whom he predestined he also called; and those whom he called he also justified; and those whom he justified he also glorified" (8:29).

Now here, in these five terms we have a very strong case for *predestination*, and there is no way that you can interpret these terms and avoid that conclusion. But does it rob us on this level of our freedom?—no. "He who began a good work in us will bring it to completion at the day of Jesus Christ" (Phil. 1:6). He will bring it to completion. But on the surface of his being, where we are, while that work is taking place in us we are not robbed of our freedom. On the contrary, the certainty that our salvation is in the hand of God frees us from worldly anxieties; and then we can say with Paul, "In all these things we are more than conquerors through him who loved us" (Rom. 8:37). For, never would you have made anything if you had not loved it. Well, he so loved you that he is molding himself within you, and when he completes his job *that* is Jesus Christ. So when Christ is formed in us, then we are born from above in the same manner that when this physical garment was formed in our mothers it was born from below. So when the image of God is formed within us from above, we are born from above; and that image radiates the glory of God and is the express image of his person. So anyone seeing a being who is born from above would see God.

It's the express image of his person, and they would have no other feeling on meeting that being who is born from above other than that they are now in the presence of God; for he radiates the glory of God and is the express image of his person.

But, although that is taking place in us unknown to the surface mind, that predestined will of God that he will not turn back until he has executed and accomplished the intents of his mind, in the latter days you will know it clearly. But in the meanwhile, on the surface we are as free as anyone could ever wish to be to exercise a power, which is God, whether we do it wisely or unwisely. I state over and over that imagining creates reality... your wonderful Imagination is God. He's enslaved himself on the surface of our being, allowing us to misuse him for any purpose in the world. But in everything God works for good, so he takes the most horrible thing in the world and still can convert it to good. But God which is our Imagination will not respond to compulsion. You can't compel him. "God only acts and is in existing beings or men," but he acts only if *we* have *imagined* the wish fulfilled. He will not act under any other circumstances. *Persuasion* is the sugar that best sweetens his medicine...you persuade.

Well, how would I persuade? Well, what would the feeling be like if it were true? What would it be like were it true, and I toy with that thought until I get the mood, the feeling that would be mine if what I desire in this world were true. When I can actually feel that, well then, I can expect the results projected upon the screen of space, and I will encounter confirmation of this act. Listen to the words as given us in the 11th chapter of the Book of Mark, "Whoever believes that what he says will come to pass, it will be done for him. Therefore I tell you, whatever you ask in prayer, believe that you have received it, and you will" (verse 23-24). Now there is no limitation placed upon man, whether you be a good man or a bad man, whether what you ask is considered good in the world or evil in the world. There is no restriction other than the one condition: Can you believe it? Can you imagine that it really is done? If you can, the promise is there: it will be done. You don't have to think of the ways and means by which it will be done, it will be done. "Whoever believes that what he says will come to pass, it will be done for him." It didn't say you had to think out the means by which it will be done; it will be done *for* you.

Over a hundred years ago, a Frenchman by the name of Jules Verne wrote a book and called it *From Earth to Moon*. The book was published in 1865. He actually conceived the drama that you and I have just witnessed and rejoiced that it happened here: The capsule that took three, launched from America, and took them around the moon and brought them back safely. He said in his book that this capsule is launched in Florida and he had it not where we have Cape Canaveral (now we call it Cape Kennedy) but Tampa, which is about a hundred miles away. He had three men and he said it would travel approximately 25,000 miles an hour. Well, that's exactly what it did. He gave the dimensions. If you remove the Saturn booster and just take the capsule, the dimensions of the capsule are exactly what he wrote a hundred and three years ago. He said it would be launched in December and ours was launched in December; and it would splash down in the Pacific, well, ours was splashed down in the Pacific. He made it a very successful voyage that the Yankee engineers would have the knowhow to do it. Well, they did it to the rejoicing of the whole vast world, save the few who are envious of the accomplishment of those in our land who can imagine, who can dream. For we are a nation of dreamers…that's what we did with the world.

Here, someone said, in fact, it was Webster, Daniel Webster, that he would not vote one penny of our treasury to bring any part west of the Mississippi into the Union. It was a wild, wild land, wild people, deserts, and mountains that towered into the heavens, and you never saw them because they were always filled and covered with snow. He would not vote one penny of our treasury to bring anything west of the Mississippi an inch nearer to Massachusetts. To him that was the heart. But he couldn't stop us dreaming. He couldn't stop us dreaming of extending the borders right straight to the Pacific, because someone had to entertain the dream in spite of him. He was an able man, a very able man.

So for everyone who would stop us, we go beyond it and simply bring our dreams to pass in this world. If you can dream and not just wish but assume the feeling of the wish fulfilled, then I can prophesy for you. If you can honestly tell me what you have imagined and convince yourself of it, I'll prophesy, because no power in the world can stop it. There is no power in the world that can stop your dream that you have imagined fulfilled from coming to pass. You don't need any technique, you don't need any wise concepts of how to bring it to pass—it will be done for you. Here Jules Verne departed this world, but his dream in 1865 came to pass in the very land where he said it would come to pass. It came to pass just as he had predicted a hundred and three years ago.

Now you may say, "But I want to see my dreams." You'll see them. Don't think that man ends where he vanishes from this world. This world does not terminate at the point where my senses cease to register it. Don't think that Jules Verne is not aware of his prophecy fulfilled…not for one moment. So don't think for one moment that because you depart the world and the world will say, well, she left unsatisfied or he left unsatisfied…don't for a moment. Your dreams will all be realized. Just in *this* case it took a hundred years, 103 years, to bring it to pass. But just imagine, he predicted this before we had an airplane. Airplanes were not invented in the year 1865. He told of going around the moon; and told of the land where it would be launched, and the area where it would come down, and how many men would be aboard it, and everything about it. He told it in detail…even to the speed that it would take, even to the dimensions of the capsule. That book I presume is still available, *From the Earth to the Moon*, published in 1865.

So God cannot be compelled. God is your own wonderful human Imagination and he can be persuaded. Then you master the art of persuasion—what would the feeling be like if it were true?—and you toy with the idea until that mood possesses you. Then you wear the mood as you would a coat, put it on as you would a garment, and then as you wear that garment it *will* project itself on the screen of space. When?—I do not know. How?—that is not my concern, I do not know. I can only tell you if I could get into the Imagination of any man and know what he believes, I don't care how he comes to believe it, if he believes it I can predict for him. If you took an astrology chart and used that to persuade yourself. If you are actually self-persuaded…it isn't there, but your self-persuasion is the cause of what's going to happen. To the degree you are self-persuaded it will happen. Now you may give all credit to the chart…it wasn't there at all. Anymore than it was in teacup leaves or coffee grounds or anything on the outside, but you could use these things to persuade yourself.

I would say, why use anything? Take nothing on the outside and become self-persuaded. For, "God only acts and is in existing beings or men" and this being who acts is your own wonderful human Imagination. But you can't compel him. He will do little that we wish until we have imagined the wish fulfilled. So, on the surface of our being we are free, free to exercise our talent. In the depth of our being, that being that we speak of as God the Father is molding us, shaping us. It's the shaping of the unbegotten, for that is Isaac. Isaac is simply the molding of the unbegotten, and when he's completely formed and reflecting the invisible God, well then, he's born. When he's born, he radiates the glory of that God and is the express image of his person.

So anyone seeing one who is born from above automatically knows he's in the presence of God, for he is the express image of God and he's radiating the glory of God. So what is taking place in the depths should assure us. Leave it alone. We should not then be concerned if I know that my end is already predetermined: he foreknew me, and he predestined me, and he called me, and he justified me, and he glorified me (Rom. 8:29). If I know that that is the pattern on which God is working, well then, I'm completely free of all worldly anxieties. Why should I be concerned of what is taking place?

So not a thing in this world has happened or ever will happen but what some man or woman imagined it. What is now proved was once only imagined. So foreknowledge is nothing more than what men and women are imagining. If I could only get into the minds of men and see what they are imagining, I can tell you what's going to happen. If I could take the sum of this room, if I could only get a true confession—not what you would like me to believe of you but what you really are imagining. Because when we're called upon to make a confession, we don't really confess, we can't stand it. We simply tell what we would like to tell, but we don't really tell what we have imagined. So in the depth of our soul we are imagining all kinds of things, unlovely things, lovely things, all kinds of things, but they all operate if we have imagined it with conviction.

So there isn't a thing…my father, who certainly was no prophet, he had his ten children, and one day I can hear him vividly, the year was 1919. The boys from Barbados who went overseas during the First World War were returning in 1919. The war came to an end in November 1918, but they couldn't get them back because of a lack of ships until quite late in 1919. In the meanwhile, he entertained, being a ship chandler, he entertained the captains, stewards and the officers for business reasons, and they all told the same old story: there will be another war in twenty years. Germany will still be the main enemy, but this time she will have Japan and she will have Italy. Now that's what they said. Well, he didn't know. He was a wonderful man, but you wouldn't call him an intellectual giant…just a perfectly wonderful father and husband. I can hear him now at table and he said to my mother, "There will be another war in twenty years." Mother said to him, "Oh, Joseph, why do you say that? Look, we have all our boys. They all will be of age in twenty years from now." He said, "There'll be a war in twenty years!" That was 1919. Well, add it up. War broke September the first, 1939. That's when England declared war on Germany when Germany moved into Poland, twenty years. But he was no prophet, he was simply repeating with conviction what he heard from the men of the ships, the captains and the stewards and the officers as he drank with them and did business with them. So they were convinced of this. Well, the very ones who formed the triumvirate—Italy, Germany, Japan—were the ones he named back in 1919.

He's done it in business. When looking out to sea and looking over our land, he said, "This is a perfect spot for a hotel." Then in his mind's eye he saw the hotel, saw everything about it and then turned to the little ladies who owned it and said, "If you ever want to sell, think of me." Well, two died years later and then the third one thought it was too much to keep up—thirty-five acres, the gardeners and the servants and all these things—so she would move into a hotel and spend the last days living in a hotel where everything was done for her, and she wouldn't have the problem of taking care of people. Well, he bought it. Years and years before when he made this statement, he had no money, but when the sale took place he could raise the money and buy the thirty-five acres. A hotel does stand on it plus many other things, because thirty-five acres would be too many acres for a hotel. But a lovely hotel, a very successful hotel stands on the premises plus dozens of homes, beautiful homes. He saw the entire thing in his mind's eye, believed it and voiced it.

So whoever will believe what he says will come to pass, it will be done for him. For when that sale was made, there was one man who had all the cash in the world but at that moment he was in Brazil. When he realized that the thing is about to be sold and when he cabled his lawyer to bid, it was twenty-four hours too late. The sale was over by twenty-four hours. So it will be done for you. He firmly believed it and it worked.

So I say to every one of you here, don't be ashamed or afraid of noble dreams. I don't care how big the dream is...I don't care how big it is! If you can actually believe it and say to yourself, "It will come to pass," to the degree you are persuaded that it will come to pass it will be done for you. You don't have to know what are called the "right" people or have the necessary means at this moment, but whatever it will take, you will find will happen in your world, but everything!

So, you should always dwell upon that glorious thing that is taking place within you. Just imagine that God himself entered death's door, your own wonderful skull, with you when you entered, and he laid down in the grave with you in visions of eternity 'til you awake. When you awake you see Jesus and the linen cloths that the females had woven for you (Jn. 20:5). Well, this body, not this suit, the body is the linen cloth of scripture and my mother wove it for me...it came from below. Now he said, "And you will see Jesus"...but you're told in 1st John, "It does not yet appear what we shall be, but we know that when he appears," meaning Jesus. "we shall be like him, and see him as he is" (3:2). So when he appears, he appears *as you*. You don't see someone that you resemble; he appears because he awakes within you. The Lord himself entered death's door with you when you entered this skull, and he laid down in the grave with you. You didn't realize that you were in that grave and it was properly sealed. And there you remain in visions of eternity, all these are visions of eternity, until you awake and see Jesus. When you "see" Jesus, the word "to see" and "to know" in Greek are the same. So you will awake and know who Jesus really is, and when you do, you are he.

Then you find the gate of your Father's house and come out of it…that's when you are born from above. You see the linen cloths, the garment out of which you emerged. When you come out, you are the one who entered with you. But in that interval while he was forming you, he was actually forming you into himself…so you are he. Then you come out and from then on you radiate the glory of God the Father and you are the express image of his person. So from then on, who sees you sees God (Jn. 14:9). "Show you the Father, Philip? He who has seen me has seen the Father. How can you say, 'Show me the Father?' Have I been so long with you and you do not know the Father?" So anyone whose eye is open after one is born from above if they encounter that being, they see God. It's the only God; there aren't multiple gods. Unnumbered faces he will wear, but if you meet him he wears the body of God and he reflects and radiates the glory of God.

So when we are told by Paul, "He has made known unto us, in all wisdom and insight the mystery of his will"—made known to us the mystery of his will—"which he set forth as a plan in Christ for the fullness of time, to unite all things in him, things in heaven and on earth" (Eph. 1:9). Well, here is the most marvelous, exciting passage. Here it is, he sets it forth to unite all things in him, but he has made known his plan. Well, if he made known the plan, that's foreknowledge. That's not something that's taking place as he moves forward. Here is a plan and the plan is contained in what is called the image, Jesus Christ, waiting for the fullness of time to unite all things in him.

Now this is the most exciting thing! The Greek word which we translate into the phrase "to unite all things" that's the Revised Standard Version. The King James Version is "to gather together in one all things." But regardless of which phrase you prefer, that phrase, the Greek word that is used to translate that phrase if translated literally means "head. That's all that it means—"to head up or to sum up." But "head"…that's the word, same word. Well, strangely enough the whole thing takes place in your head. You enter the head and there you sleep in visions of eternity. How long you are asleep I do not know. Mystics have said 6,000 years, 8,000 years; no one seems to make it less than 6,000 years. And you didn't realize you were in a head, sealed, completely sealed, and dreaming these visions of eternity until one day you awoke.

When you woke, you woke in your head and when you came out, you came out of the head. But strangely enough, in all the major events that followed it, all lead to the head. When the head exploded, you discovered the fatherhood of God: here comes the Son standing before you, but it all was in your head. When you were split from top to bottom, it was your head to the base of the spine. When you ascended, it was back into the head.

When the heavens opened and became translucent without circumference, it was the head. So here, to unite *all* things in him, things in heaven and thing on earth, but it's all united in the head. So here, it's like this one grand brain and we but brain cells in the mind of the dreamer; and each cell is awakening in the head, for that's where the brain is. And finally, it is only being the head. He will head up everything, sum it up so each in turn will become the one that radiates the glory of God and bears the express image of his person.

So foreknowledge…don't go to any person who calls himself a fortune teller, they do not know. But do tell in confidence tell yourself, what am I really imagining? What have I imagined today? Have I been persuaded by the press, by radio, by TV, is that what I've imagined? Or have I this day imagined what I really want to imagine? I have a family, I have children, I have rent to pay, food to buy, clothes to buy. There is everything in my world…I have obligations to life, well, have I imagined something that would take care of all these things? For if I could imagine all of these things done, as we are told, "Whoever can believe that what he says will come to pass, it will be done for him." Well, can I really now imagine that they're done, that whatever income I need, double it, treble it, make it bigger and bigger and bigger in your own mind's eye. Don't ask how! Your present job may not be the one that can do it. You may be fired. You may be fired tomorrow if you imagine tonight your income three times what it is. Maybe the present job cannot pay it, and you will do something that will simply displease the one above you and he'll fire you. You will find it was the great turning point in your fortunes.

I was fired from J. C. Penney, making twenty-two dollars a week and I wondered, what am I going to use for money? He said to me, "That's not my problem. When we have a recession, we let people out." "I have been working there for a year, doing everything you asked me to do. I've never once been late; I haven't missed one day, and here I'm fired." Well, he said, "That's not our problem." But he realized that I was a greenhorn and a kid eighteen years old, so he gave me a letter to his friend at Macy's saying "He doesn't understand our system in America. If you have an opening, give him a job." So they gave me an opening, a reduction of four dollars a week, down to eighteen, working just as hard doing the same stupid things. One day I figured, now he isn't going to fire me, I'm going to quit. So I quit…had no money, but I quit and started for myself. I wasn't a dancer and I persuaded myself that I could dance. Oh, I did social dancing, but I persuaded myself I can dance as well as anyone can. Well, in no time flat I was making five-hundred dollars a week dancing. They sent me off to England. What dancer! I was not a trained dancer, but I was *self-persuaded* that I could do it! Well, I did it. Then I came back and I had six Broadway shows. I was no actor, but I played the parts, played second-leads in many a show…because I was self-persuaded. You call that arrogance, well, call it what you want, but I did it. From then on I started just working for myself. Oh, I worked for producers, but I never called it that they employed me. I was giving them a talent that they needed, and so it was simply a mutual exchange. They were not doing what Macy's did to me or J. C. Penney did. I was through with that.

Well, I say to everyone, dream nobly, I don't care what it is. And you can start as I did behind the eight-ball, completely behind the eight-ball. Then go as far as you can dream. You have no limit outside of your own ability to dream and occupy the dream…and that is foreknowledge. If I know exactly what I'm dwelling in, I can foretell. If I don't realize what I'm imagining, I can't foretell. There is no astrology, no teacup leaves, nothing on the outside that can tell me. Oh, they will confirm it if I am persuaded. Because I read unnumbered charts and to the degree that I was absolutely convinced of the truth of what I said, it came to pass. Yet it wasn't there; it was my own conviction. So I say to everyone, dream nobly, imagine the wish fulfilled, for he will do little if anything that we wish *until* we have imagined the wish fulfilled. And after we have done it, no power in the world can stop it from coming to pass.

Now, you may say, I don't want to be like Jules Verne and wait a hundred years for my dream. Alright, dream nobly anyway, even if such dreams take a hundred years or a thousand years. For tonight I'm telling you that you are destined to be God! Well now, what could stop you tonight from losing all worldly anxiety in the knowledge that he is doing it and that in the immediate present he'll finish it? When he finishes it I will know by the series of events which he will unfold within me—beginning with waking me in the tomb of my skull and bringing me out. I will have that intuitive knowledge how to get out: I will know the gate of my Father at the base of that skull and I will come out. Then in a little interval I will know the next and the next and the next, and whenever that happens I will know exactly what to do.

So, I'll be gathering all things both in heaven and on earth all within me in my head. How interesting it is when you think the word "beginning" means "head"; the same word in the Book of John, "In the beginning was the Logos," the word "beginning" is "head." So "In the head is the Logos, and the Logos was with God, and the Logos *was* God" (1:1). "In the head God created the heavens and the earth." It's all in the head. It will begin there and end there, for "I am the beginning and the end" (Rev. 21:6). You'll find the whole head then becoming translucent, and you'll discover the meaning that Blake meant to convey when he said "All that you behold, though it appears without, it is within, in your Imagination, of which this world of mortality is but a shadow" (*Jer.*, Plt.71)...and that "within" is ever expanding in the bosom of God.

So, seek no one on the outside to tell you your fortune. But do look into your own wonderful Imagination and ask yourself, "What am I imagining? For myself, for my husband, for my wife, for my friends, what am I imagining? Am I taking them at face value and seeing them in want? Well, that's their future. Or will I now reform them in my own mind's eye and see them as I would like them to be so that when we get together there's no down-in-the-mouth conversation? They come home to dinner and it's a lovely, wonderful atmosphere...it's all marvelous. Well, I want that for my friends. Now, am I seeing that in my friend? If I'm seeing that in my friend, well then, he has to conform to it, for if I can say something and believe it, it will be done for him. I don't have to give him some advice, no good advice, just good news. The word gospel is "good news" it's not advice. You don't give any advice, it's simply, it will be done for you if you are self-persuaded that it is *already* done. So when you meet him and he doesn't confirm it, perfectly alright—you know it's done and you are faithful to what you have done, and that will then project itself in the world.

So foreknowledge is not to tell anyone that you are now destined because of your birth to be this, that and the other. You're not...no matter what the world will tell you. You are destined to fulfill what you have imagined. So whatever you have imagined and accepted as factual, as fact, you are going to encounter. So, there is no fiction in this world, none whatsoever. Today's fact was yesterday's fiction. Just as in Jules Verne, he was a fiction writer, science fiction. How in that day before an airplane was conceived, or rather, before it was built (we had no airplanes in 1865) he could write a novel and call it *From the Earth to the Moon* and put in detail what Apollo the 8th has already accomplished. Same month it launched, same month it came down. Launched from this land and came down in the Pacific, just as he foresaw, and he had three men aboard. Now, being a Frenchman, he wanted a Frenchman aboard, too, and so one of the men he called Andon. Well, one of our men was Anders. In his day the French would be mostly Catholic. But that one was called Andon while our man was Anders. He got so much within that fictional picture.

So when I tell you there is no fiction, I mean it! You and I sit down together and you tell me your dreams and all of a sudden you get excited about the dream, and I'm moving you into the feeling that it's done. When you get up, you walk as though it's done. Well, I can prophesy for you: it's done! At that moment it's done. But when will be the birth? Well, there's always an interval in pregnancy, between that conception and birth...always an interval. No two animals in the world have the same interval: One bird twenty-one days; another bird longer, into the months; a sheep five months; the horse twelve; man nine. All have different intervals between the moment of conception and the moment of birth. So you conceive it. Alright, know that you conceived it and say within yourself, "I've imagined it so to be, I'm still imagining it so to be, and I will continue to imagine it so to be until what I have imagined is perfectly expressed." Then you will know what foreknowledge is.

You don't have to be concerned with divine foreknowledge, for that is fixed, and "He will not turn back until he has executed and accomplished the intents of his mind" (Jer. 23:20). Now, that sentence begins on a peculiar phrase, "The anger of the Lord will not turn back", but the word "anger" means literally "to breathe heavily." Well, the word "breath" in Hebrew and in Greek means "Spirit," so a better translation would have been "the Spirit of the Lord will not turn back." But whoever said, "the anger," alright, so they have the anger; for it was a forceful breathing, a heavy, heavy breathing, which meant a kind of passion. But that doesn't mean passion as man would interpret it if I used the word passion…and it certainly doesn't mean anger as we today use the word anger. It simply means the Spirit, but the Spirit with passion, it's determined, "it has purpose, and it will not turn back until it has executed and accomplished the intents of its mind. In the latter days you will understand it clearly." And so, that which I have planned will be, and what I have purposed will stand, and no one is going to change it. All the plots and plans of man on the surface let them be; it will all be used for good.

But what he planned, which is what? To mold you into his image and endow you with himself, with all the power that is his so that you can radiate the glory of God. Not only radiate it, but when you are met, you *are* the express image of his being, of his person. And so that no one with the eye open, on meeting you, will not know you as God; for there's only God in the end, nothing but God. So all are being awakened towards *that* end and that's predetermined, that's foreknowledge. But here in the world of Caesar let no one tell you that you're fated. You aren't fated one bit save what you yourself do. You aren't fated, so you can forget karma, forget all these things in the world. You're here and you will play your part, so what are you imagining? Tell it to yourself, persuade yourself that it's noble and lovely, and to the degree that you are self-persuaded, you will encounter that in the world and you are it.

Now let us go into the Silence.

*   *   *

Q: (inaudible)

A: Well, I can only say that I acquaint you with the principle and leave you to your choice and its risk. But to tell you that you must follow along a certain line, I'm setting myself up as the criterion of what is good and what is wrong. So I can't do that if I'm teaching principle. So I will give you a principle by which you can be the man that you want to be, and leave you…we all have a certain ethical code, I mean, in our cradle we were conditioned to believe in certain things. I know that I was…that I was spanked for doing certain things that Mother didn't think right, I was criticized for doing other things, and finally you build within yourself a certain ethical code by which you live. If you violate the code, well now, it's your choice. But I give you a principle and I tell you in the end everyone is exonerated, everyone is forgiven, because everything is used by God for good. He will use the horrors of a Hitler and the horrors of a Stalin and turn it into good.

It is: love is the answer…love is the end. If you're ever in doubt, do the loving thing and you have done the right thing. If you're ever in doubt, would I like it done to me? It's the eternal story called the Golden Rule: do unto others as you would have them do unto you. So I imagine you to be and I name it…because the same thing I imagined for you I wouldn't mind if I had it myself. To me that's the only way to give a gift. When I go to give a person a gift, I always think "Would I like it? Would I wear it? Would I like to have it and keep it?" Well, buy it as though you were buying it for yourself and then give it. I mean, to me that's giving in this world. Not to get rid of something you really don't want yourself. That's how most people give in this world. Well, I mean, would I like it? If I would like it, well, that's the one thing I want to give. So I ask myself, "Would I like it?" Then, I give it to you in the sense in my Imagination. I clothe you with what I myself would like to have… good fortune, health, this, that and the other.

But I am free to choose unlovely things, and most people, unfortunately, choose unlovely things and imagine horrible things for individuals, for communities, for nations. But I cannot avoid that risk. I can't hold back the principle as I've discovered it. I can talk about the principle and try my best to explain it, but leave you who hear it to your choice and its risks. It's like showing a child how to light a stove. Well, he may blow himself up, but I've got to teach him how to light that stove; got to teach him how to light, how to draw a match, because eventually he has to know how to do it. He may behind my back go and set fire to the barn, but I've got to in some way teach him how to use power. Well, a match is fire…that's power. Now *this* is the greatest power in the world, one's own wonderful human Imagination, and you can't start too early teaching a child how to use the Imagination.

Q: (inaudible)

A: Right, David, absolutely right. I know the one day I went off to my tailor in New York City…he's been my tailor now for thirty-five years…and I ordered a few suits, and when I brought them home after they were completed, my wife naturally would look at the suits, and when she saw one she said, "What on earth possessed you when you ordered this suit?" Well, I put myself into the suit, looked at myself before the mirror and I agreed with her…never wore it once. My son was about my size at the time (he's much bigger now) I said, "Can you use this suit?" "Oh, lovely!"…he wanted a new suit. Well, he took the suit and he just loved it. But when I saw it at home! And I ordered the suit, my tailor didn't persuade me. I thought, "Well now, I like that suit." I saw it just in the piece, these are all individual pieces, and when I got it home I didn't want any part of it. So I never wore it once. So then I had the pleasure of giving it to one who seemed to have enjoyed it. Well, whatever possessed me? Maybe he was treading in the winepress for a suit and I was the means through which he got a suit. It could happen that way. He wanted a suit, he assumed that he had a suit, his father goes and buys one he wouldn't wear to a dog fight, and then he wants that suit. So he got it. You never can tell how these things work.

I could give you a story…and I think I've told it before. This lady in New York City and she was a lady of the evening, and so I could discuss all kinds of things with her. She met me at the corner of Broadway and 72nd Street one night, and she said to me, "Neville, you said that whatever I desire I can have. Well, I would like a new hat." I said, "Alright, imagine that you have the hat." About ten days later or two weeks later, I ran into Ann again and she said, "Now, Neville, I have the hat…see I'm wearing it…but why didn't God give me the money to buy the hat?" Then she told me the story. She said, "I walked up the street and I saw this hat in the window and I closed my eyes and assumed I was wearing it. Then I walked further up. On my way back I would not look into the window to become disillusioned that the hat was in the window as I thought I had it on my head. So I went home wearing this hat, all in my Imagination. When I got home, I wouldn't even look into the mirror. I took off the hat, wouldn't look at it, and put it up as my hat. The next day the old hat is still there, so I put on the old hat.

"Several days later a friend of mine called me, said she would like to see me if I had the time, so I went up and saw her. She said, "Ann, I have something for you. I know it's going to look lovely on you. I bought it and I wondered why I bought it. I can't wear it." She brought out not *a* hat but *the* hat. Ann put the hat on and she loved it. But Ann's problem was this, "Why didn't God give me the money to buy the hat instead of giving it to me this way?" So knowing her profession and the uncertainty of the profession, I said, "Ann, tell me, do you owe any rent? Bet you owe two weeks rent." She said, "I do, exactly two weeks." I said, "Maybe you pay $17.50 a week?" "That's exactly what I pay," she said. "Well, you owe $35.00 rent. Now what price hats do you usually buy?" "Oh," she said, "$3.00, 3.50." I said, "What did this hat cost?" She said, "$18." I said, "Have you ever bought an $18 hat?" She said, "Never." I said, "Now tell me, how much money would you really have to have to buy an $18 hat? You owe $35 in rent. If you found a hundred dollar bill while you're looking at the hat, you wouldn't have bought it. Know what you would have done? You'd have gone in and paid your two weeks rent and possibly put down another week in advance or two weeks in advance to feel a little secure, and you would not with the remaining money come out and buy that hat." She said, "You're right…but you're too nosey." So how could God give her the hat by giving her money? She never would have bought the hat…she wasn't in the habit.

I'll tell you, in New York City I'll go to Tiffany's to buy a present, say for a wedding or an engagement or an anniversary. I get a far better present, beautifully wrapped than I would at Macy's and at Macy's it would cost more. But people will pass by Tiffany because it has the reputation of being at the very top in quality, and they wouldn't dream of going in…they feel embarrassed. They wouldn't go in and look at this beautiful display of merchandise, they feel embarrassed. But they feel at home in Macy's or in Gimbel's and go into Gimbel's and spend more than you would at Tiffany, and when it comes it's a Macy's package and not a Tiffany package. But I've gone to Tiffany time and again and bought eight glasses, beautiful glasses, different kinds of glasses (it's a good present) and bought them at a modest price. A similar glass would be twice the price at Macy's, but people feel at home going to Macy's and they feel ill at ease going to Tiffany. So if you never bought an $18 hat and you always bought $3 hats, I'd have to give you $2,000 to buy an $18 hat. God knew exactly what she needed. She wanted a hat and so he got someone to buy the hat who didn't want the hat and then gave it to her. And that's how it worked.

* * *

THE MYSTERY OF ESCHATOLOGY

1/20/69

Tonight's subject is eschatology. Eschatology is the doctrine of the last things. It is the dramatic end of history and the beginning of the eternal salvation of the individual who arrives at that point in time. The end of history and the appearance of the Son of man who is God come together after the tribulation of human experience. And of that day and hour only the Father knows.

So you will say, you speak of the Father as another and yet you say we are destined to awaken *as* the Father. Well, I do not deny that. God the Father is other, but *not* other than ourselves. Other yes, but not really and wholly other than ourselves: his Spirit is *in* us. Were that not so, he could not commune with us. So we are told, "Bring my sons from afar and my daughters from the ends of the earth; bring them all who are called by my name, whom I created for my glory, whom I formed and made" (Is. 43:6-7). Created for *his* glory because his glory cannot be given to another; therefore, if I'm created for his glory, I have to be the very one who created me (Is. 42:8).

Well now, that is eschatology—when we come to the very end of human tribulation. No one will avoid it, not one person in the world will avoid playing *all* the parts. So envy no one! You either have played it or you will play it. You may pity yes, we pity others, but you've played that part or you will play it. And you will not come to this dramatic end until you've played all the parts. In that day...and no one knows it but the Father within you knows the day. Now all the events were predicted and are fulfilled. Their full meaning is now understood in the light of the new things. What new things? We read in Isaiah—and bear in mind, all the stories are visions—the Book of Isaiah begins "This is the vision of Isaiah, the son of Amos." He tells you it's a vision and the sixty-six chapters do not deny it or modify it or in any way contradict it as a vision. We speak of the vision of Obadiah, Jeremiah ("And the word of the Lord came to Jeremiah"), the vision of Ezekiel, and they're all visions. This is *not* secular history.

So here, in the Book of Isaiah, the 42nd chapter, "Behold, the former things have come to pass and new things I now declare to you; before they spring forth I tell you of them" (verse 9). A literal rendering of the first part of that verse would be, "The former things, behold they have come." But man will not believe the individual to whom they come; it's not what the world was looking for. The world was looking for something entirely different than that which happened in the first one, and he told them exactly what happened in him: the entire vision of all the prophets unfolded in him. He knew this was "the end," the end of history, the end of the tribulation of human experience, and his entry into what he called the kingdom of God. It's entirely different from what the world expected. The world expects some physical being coming from without to save. And so today it came to Israel, for the entire eschatology of the Old Testament is the coming of Jehovah. He came, but they would not believe it. They thought of him in terms of something entirely different from the way in which he comes. He comes only to fulfill what he had predicted. He predicted it through his prophets and said that something *new* would happen.

"These former things, behold, they have come and now they're here." What are they? Well, the experiences of the one who fulfilled scripture. Everything in scripture is fulfilled in man in the last day. So he is the fulfillment of the prophecy of himself, for he prophesied what he would do. He would enter into the limitation of man and take upon himself the restriction of man. Become man by emptying himself of all that was his and take upon himself the form of a slave, and was born in the likeness of man; and became obedient unto death, even death upon the cross of man (Phil. 2:7). This is what God became, having foretold through the prophets what he would experience as man—but not on the outside. And when the one in whom it began to unfold told the story, they did not believe it.

So today, we still have that fundamental rock, Israel, carrying on by its calendar year—it's now approaching the 6,000th year because to them he has not come. When it comes to the individual, then his B.C. turns into A.D. We cannot claim although we write letters and say this is now the year 1969, and we will write it out because it's part of the world of Caesar. And so will the Jew write out 1969, but in his faith he keeps alive the long passage of time because he feels Jehovah did not come. He counts in an entirely different way, and everything said through his prophets that he inspired, the individual experiences personally.

Now here, if the whole thing is a vision, what must I do to experience it in vision? I must actually re-enact the entire drama within myself. Aside from the resurrection which takes place within us; aside from the birth as foretold to Abraham which takes place within us; aside from the three who appear unexpectedly…they were not seen approaching, they just simply suddenly appeared to bear witness to the birth foretold; aside from the story of the serpent in the wilderness when man himself becomes the serpent and ascends into heaven; aside from all the things told, man himself experiences them. Now here, who would have thought for one moment, I know I didn't, that I would re-enact the story of the 22nd of Isaiah and the 53rd of Isaiah in one night? For remember, these things are all written out and they're not paragraphed, they're not in chapter form, in fact they're not even punctuated so that there are commas between them. In fact, one word goes into the other. It is only man who has taken this manuscript and tried to give verses, paragraphs and chapters to it.

But here, the 22nd and 53rd of Isaiah one night without expecting it or dreaming about it, it suddenly unfolded within me. As we are told in the 53rd, "Who has believed our report? And to whom has the arm of the Lord been revealed?" (Verse 1). Well, here I find myself in the presence of twelve men in a room like this, just like this, not as big, and I'm seated on the floor facing my twelve and simply explaining the Word of God. One of the twelve rose quickly and departed, and I knew intuitively that he was going to tell the authorities what he had just heard. I knew he was going to tell them. He had no sooner departed than a tall, handsome, wonderful looking man, I would say about 6'4" or 6'6", a tall, good looking lad, well-dressed in costly robes, entered. He walked through, as straight as an arrow, walked to the end of the room, turned at right angles, walked to the end, turned at right angles, came down the center. But the minute he entered the room he was so important that all of us rose…the eleven who were left and myself. So we all rose and stood at attention while he came down, turned, and then down, turned, and came in front of me. As he came in front of me he took a mallet and a wooden peg and hammered it into my shoulder. I felt every blow, but it was not painful. I felt the impact of this wooden peg into my shoulder. Then he took a sharp instrument and with one quick circular motion severed my sleeve and pulled it off and discarded it. Then he stretched his arms out and he formed the cross. Then he embraced me and he kissed me on the right side of my neck, and I in turn kissed him on the right side of his neck. As the vision faded, I could see that lovely shade of baby-blue, a light, light blue that was the severed robe. His robe was costly, but this seemed to be a priceless robe that he severed from my arm. So, "Who would believe our report? And to whom has the arm of the Lord been revealed?"

In the 22nd, he puts a peg into the shoulder of the one that he has chosen and on that peg he hangs all the burdens of Israel. Then after he has worn it for awhile, the peg is broken and all these utensils of the temple fall from the peg: he has played his part. It was the most dramatic night. Here was part of the eschatology, part of the end, when the whole drama which was not understood and could not be understood if you're looking for someone to come from without to play it. It's only understood when the individual experiences it. Then he tells it to those who would not believe it, but he tells it anyway…whether one believes it or not.

So it is not the end of the world as people interpret these things year after year. This past year we had a huge crowd leave California. They went off to Georgia, because we were going to have an earthquake that would completely inundate us. So they went off to the east, others went to other parts of the east, and the first time in recorded history they had an earthquake in the east that shook twelve states. So they went off to get away from what they called the earthquake that was going to inundate California. What does it matter…there is no death. The individual who seems to die is restored to life. He will find himself young, not a baby but young, about twenty years of age, and he will be in an environment best suited for the work that is still to be done in him. He will be cast in a role that he has not yet played, but he'll play every role in the book. Only when he has played all the tribulations of human experience will he arrive at that hour, that day called the Day of the Lord. And only the Father knows it and the Father in one, in man, knows it.

So here, everyone is going to play it…I don't care who you are. It is God's purpose and he is able to fulfill his purpose: to give himself to you. He created you for his glory that you may radiate the glory of God and that you may actually be the express image of his person. No one can stop it. But you will not arrive at that moment called the moment of eschatology until you have played all the parts and gone through all the tribulations of human experience.

So I say, envy no one. Doesn't matter what they've done, what they're doing, don't envy them. You either have played it or you will. You pity someone…you've played it or you will. So that all the parts in the world that can be conceived…for the Bible has every conceivable evil in the world described openly. There isn't one thing today that you can conceive of that man could do to man but what that is in the Bible, and it's described openly. Well, you've played them all.

So, the last days, the last things, are simply the events of scripture unfolding in you in the most dramatic form imaginable. You can't conceive of the drama when it really begins to happen within you…when it *actually* happens. I'm not speaking of an adumbration, I'm not speaking of a foreshadowing; I'm speaking of the actual event when it happens. It's the most dramatic thing in the world when it possesses you and here you are the center of the entire Bible: *you* are the Lord Jesus Christ! Well, these things happen, as scripture reveals it, to the Lord Jesus Christ and they happen to you. Then you know who you are. You are the Lord Jesus Christ…you are the Lord Jehovah. So you tell it. They say, "You, a little non-entity who suffers, who has nothing in the world that you can brag about, and you dare to make this bold assertion? Why that's blasphemy!" Well, that's what he's accused of being. He blasphemed by claiming that "I and the Father are one…that when you see me, you've seen the Father" (Jn. 10:30; 14:9). But no one had eyes to see him. He said, "Had you known me you would have known my Father also, but you know neither me nor my Father" (Jn. 8:19). So you will do these things because you do not know me, and therefore you do not know my Father, for I and my Father are one. So the Father in you is playing the part.

Now, the 42nd Psalm…the night that I fulfilled that, I certainly went to bed not expecting anything comparable to that. Here I found myself leading an enormous crowd in this gay procession to the house of God, and then a voice rings out, and the voice said "God walks with them." A woman at my side asks the voice, "If God walks with us, where is he?" and the voice answered, "At your side." She turned to her left and looked into my face and became hysterical it struck her so funnily, and she said, "What? Neville is God?" The voice replied, "Yes in the act of waking." Then the voice spoke only to me—others did not hear the voice—and the voice spoke in the depth of my soul and said to me, "I laid myself down within you to sleep and as I slept I dreamed a dream. I dreamed…" and I knew exactly how he's going to finish that sentence.

I became so excited that I was actually nailed upon this body in the same manner that we are told by tradition that he was nailed upon the cross. But it was not painful. There were vortices…a vortex held me here, a vortex held me here, a vortex in my hand, one in my side and two vortices each foot; and here I am with six nails but each nail was a vortex. And it was ecstatic, it was a joyful thing! It wasn't anything that was sad or painful. And I knew the story of the crucifixion: that "no man takes away my life, I lay it down myself. I have the power to lay it down and the power to take it up again" (Jn.10:18) and I deliberately took upon myself this limitation. Well, who did it?—the Father. For I heard the voice that night, "I laid myself down within you to sleep, and as I slept I dreamed a dream" and I knew what he was going to say, that he was dreaming that he was I, and when the dream is over and he awakes, I am he...that I can then radiate his glory and bear the express image of his person.

Well, that is not for me alone; that's for us. Now listen to the words, "The glory that thou gavest me I have given to them, that they may be one even as we are one"—the very glory thou gavest me by allowing me, your own creation, to radiate your glory and become the very image of your being. I have told them how it happened. I've told them how it's going to happen, so I've given them the glory that thou gavest me, that they may be one even as we are one. For now we're one. "I in them and thou in me that they may be made perfectly one. I have made known unto them thy name, and I will make it known, that the love by which thou lovest me may be in them" (Jn.17:26). The same love, not less than that which thou gavest me. So the whole then becomes one. But I say, in the end everyone in a very short interval of time will experience the whole Bible. You will tell it as I am telling it. You will find a few who will believe you and you will find a majority who will not believe you. But it's perfectly alright. They have to go through all the tribulations of human experience, every one. Not one person in the world will skip it.

You may play the part of what is called today the beautiful people. By that they mean they have money, inherited wealth, so they're called beautiful. Then they love at the end of the year to be named among the ten-best-dressed, so they can spend at the end of a year maybe a quarter of a million dollars on clothes for the one year, and will not be seen wearing the same thing a second time. That's sent off to charity or to someone else. I knew someone in New York City who used to go to these fabulous homes and buy their dresses, and then she had a shop and she would sell them. Notified her clientele that she had, say, Jackie's wardrobe of last year and they would all come flocking down to buy what Jackie wore the year before, because she wouldn't be seen in the same thing a second time. Well, she's playing her part and playing it beautifully, but maybe tomorrow she will have to play, if she hasn't played it, she'll have to play the part of the scrub woman. She will play it! Let no one tell you that you do not play *all* the parts. You will not arrive at eschatology until you have played every part as written in scripture, and there isn't one evil thing that man can do to man that is not described in the Bible openly. And you've played it.

So in the end I could see a man betraying me. I've played the part of the betrayer. It's all now coming back into my world. I was betrayed and I betrayed or I could not fulfill scripture. So everyone has played it all. Don't try to single out this part or that part. You'll be cast in it. You'll go through the gate, like leaving the set on a stage, and you go from view. You're not seen by the audience for awhile, but you aren't dead. You'll re-enter, maybe coming back playing a different part. But in the great theater you depart this world and people call you dead, burn the little body and turn it into dust, but you are not dead. You are restored to life instantly and finding yourself in an environment best suited for the work that is still to be done in you. For you must play all the tribulations of human existence.

So, eschatology is not the ending of the world where the earth collapses and the moon ceases to be and the stars fall. No it is the end of history, human history, and the beginning of the time of eternal salvation: that abrupt cleavage between this world and the transcendental world of God where now you're in an entirely different world, radiating his glory created by your very being. For now you've become the Father. And the Father created you to radiate his glory and to bear the express image of his person. So do not look when these fellows begin to talk about the world coming to an end, meaning that the earth is going to dissolve or we're going to have some frightful, catastrophic thing in the world. Forget it! So, it's simply a dramatic ending of your world of history as human history, and the beginning of an eternal history where it's entirely different. You can't describe it, because there aren't any images on earth that one can use to describe what happens. You can't describe it. Slight little things you may bring in, but you can't possibly describe the new life. It's something entirely different: you're equipped to do it all and you are God. You are not some little pygmy; you are actually God himself.

So you see someone and you condemn him…the chances are you're going to play it tomorrow. So don't condemn, for you're simply moving towards the fulfillment of what you condemn. And let no one be the judge. Don't you be the judge…you know too much now. All you can do is hope you have played them all so far and that tonight may come your eschatology. That tonight may come the end of history as the world understands it. For sacred history has been brought to its climax and fulfillment in Jesus Christ. But Jesus Christ *in you* is the one that brings it to climax and fulfillment. He said, "I in them and thou in me." Well, as he addresses the Father, he says, "Oh righteous Father." Well now, if the Father is in me and I am in you, is not the Father in you? So the Father is in you and Christ is in you, and Christ is the pattern man that must fulfill scripture. So as it erupts in Christ—for in him the plan was made—and so the whole thing erupts *in you* and everything in scripture unfolds.

So you are the one spoken of as Abraham. The promise was made to Abraham that you will have a child. Well now, you have the child, therefore, what part are you playing? Suddenly he looked up and three men stood before him and they were messengers of the Lord, and he didn't realize it was the Lord himself. But he did entertain them and then prepared a feast for them. They come so suddenly you don't see them approaching just as told you in scripture. They're not approaching; they suddenly are there. You're diverted for one second, say, three, four seconds, you're diverted from the thing out of which you've emerged by the wind, the unearthly wind, which is Spirit, which is God. As you're diverted and look back, suddenly those that you did not see approaching are sitting where what was a body and the body is gone. They removed the Lord…where have they put his body? The body is gone, because he only wore it for awhile, and while he wore it something happened in him.

Now a lady wrote me this past week and she said, "I had a dream. I was digging in the earth, digging and digging, and I was using a shovel. The earth seemed loose, yet I was digging and digging and I knew as I was digging in the earth I was digging my own brain." It's a lovely vision! It's a true vision: that's where everything takes place. She was digging in her own brain, for it takes place in the earth, and man is made of the dust of the earth. So she was actually digging in her own brain. That vision came perfectly for her. Well, she is "on the verge," but I could not tell her the day as no one knows the day or the hour. But many of you are "on the verge" of eschatology…coming to the end of the journey. Let no one tell you that he knows when it will be, for only the Father knows. The Father knows the day and the hour. You sleep and suddenly out of the nowhere this thing happens.

Now a strange thing…here, if you read the Book of John…and it differs somewhat from the synoptics…John pinpoints the very day of the week on which it will happen. He pinpointed, if you know scripture, that it will happen between six PM on Sunday and six PM on Monday when the birth will take place. Well, the birth is followed (really preceded) by the resurrection. They take place the same night. Well, it happened that way with me. It was the wee hours, four in the morning on Monday. I went to bed on Sunday night about eleven and here in the wee hours of the morning—which is Sunday night but really Monday morning—that's when it happened. So it seems that you follow the same pattern. And you can talk about it and tell it and they'll point their finger at you and say, "What on earth is he trying to say? Is he trying to tell me that he has experienced the story of Jesus Christ? That's blasphemy!" Well, they have to say it. They repeat the same thing over and over— whenever he comes he blasphemes. Whenever he comes he is denied by those who hear him. It's the *eternal* story.

But everyone comes into the world from B.C. Then suddenly when it happens his world turns into the year of the Lord, A.D., and from that moment on he is in the world of A.D. No one until it happens is actually in A.D. They are still living before the coming of Jehovah. So, the Old

Testament is simply crowded with eschatology and it is the coming of Jehovah. But he came and was not recognized. It was not what they were expecting; they were expecting something entirely different from what happened. All that is going to happen, I'm going to tell you, in your world you're going to fulfill scripture. You're going to feel so wonderful within you that you are the central character of the Bible…that everything written in the Bible was all about you! Even though it happened to others it was all about you, because in the end there is no other. We're all one. And so, I dwell in them and thou dwellest in me that we may be one, perfectly one. So in the end all are gathered together into one body and they're one Spirit, they're one Lord, one God and Father of all (Eph. 4:4).

You will not have a different Son from the speaker; it will be the same Son. I tell that to priests and to rabbis and to ministers of the Protestant church, why they throw their hands up in holy horror. They say, "Well, you've taken all of my religion from me. If that is true, all that I have been taught as a minister is now false." I said, no, it isn't false but I'm telling you what I know from experience. I have actually experienced scripture. This is true; it is not what you have been taught. Jesus Christ is God the Father, and Jesus Christ is *in* you. One day you will find out that you *are* God the Father; and because you are God the Father, there must be a Son to bear witness, for no one knows the Father except the Son (Mat. 11:27). The Son must come into your world and then you will see who the Son really is. You will know him; you don't have to ask anyone. The minute you look at him, you know exactly the character that he is, and he knows who he is and he knows who you are. This relationship reveals you as God the Father.

Yet here you are in this little garment that suffers as all garments do. You are in the world of Caesar until the very end. You are not going to be restored to life at the end; you're finished with it. This dramatic end has come, the end of history. But until you've finished telling the story as told us in the Book of Acts he remained, and it doesn't say how he ended. The story of Paul, he was at home talking from morning to night about the Word of God and the kingdom of heaven. It does not give us any way how Paul ended…in spite of tradition where they claimed he was a martyr, meaning that he was murdered. He wasn't murdered. The word martyr means "witness." Yes, he was a martyr in that sense: he was a witness to the truth of God's Word. But all these so-called martyrs were not martyrs as we speak of a martyr; they were witnesses to the truth of the Word of God. For, the word is true and someone has to witness it. So he was a witness to the very end, but it does not tell us when he departed or how he departed. In spite of what the churches claim, it is not found in scripture.

So when it happens to you, you will tell it. You may not tell it as I tell it, publicly from a platform, but you will tell it. You can't restrain the impulse to tell it. As we are told in Jeremiah: "If I say, 'I will not mention it or speak anymore in his name,' then there is in my heart as it were a burning fire, and I am tired of holding it in, and I cannot" (Jer. 20:9). It is simply something within you and you cannot stop it. So someone will ask you to please not mention it anymore, because you disturb those around about you. They don't want to hear it. They're quite satisfied with their church, quite satisfied with their concept of who Jesus Christ is—he was someone who was born 2,000 years ago back in time and space and he is my Lord to whom I pray, so forget it, that's the one I want. So don't you come with any stupidness that Christ is *in* you, and that the same Christ that is written up in scripture is the Christ in you, and that the same thing must happen to you. That it must be said of you, and you will know it's true: "In the volume of the book it's all about me" (Ps. 40:7; Heb. 10:7)).

So when David calls me Father, it's all about me. So he said to David… and David called him "my lord." Well, "my Lord" is simply the expression of a son of a father. He always referred to his father as "my lord." But no one seems to have seen it because they haven't had the vision. So you talk to a rabbi, talk to a minister, you talk to a priest, "Oh, no, couldn't be" and yet he said he's a father. If he's a father, he has to have a son. So he said, "When you see me you see the Father." Well, if I'm a father, then where is the child? If there is no child to bear witness to my fatherhood, I am not a father. Therefore, if he is not a father then he's not God, for God is Father. "I have made known unto them thy name and I will make it known that the love by which thou hast loved me may be in them" (Jn. 17), same love. Well, the name he made real was the name "Father." I made thy name real to them—I told them your name. What was the name?—the name was Father, and I and my Father are one (Jn. 10:30). Well, if I and my Father are one, then where is the one to bear witness that I'm a father? For, "No one knows the Son except the Father, and no one knows who the Father is except the Son, and anyone to whom the Son chooses to reveal him" (Mat. 11:27). So here comes the Son.

Well, it isn't Jesus Christ standing before himself calling himself Father. It is his Son David who calls him Father. When he calls you Father, you have to be Jesus Christ, because David called him Father. So if he calls you Father, you are the same Jesus Christ. So I can say to every one of you, you're going to have this experience and you'll know that you are Jesus Christ. There are not a number of little Jesus Christs running around, there is only God the Father…only one Father. So if I'm the Father of God's only begotten Son, as told me in the 2nd Psalm (verse 7), and then you have the same experience, then you and I are one, the same Father. And then if the whole vast world will have that experience then are we not one? So his prayer is that we be one, that they all become one as we are one. He speaks of the glory…just as Isaiah did…"I created them for my glory." He said, "Now, the glory thou gavest me I have given unto them." Didn't take a little bit for myself and then share something else with them, the *same* glory, because there can't be another. So in the end there is only one God, only one Lord, only one Father, and, may I tell you, only one Son. You will be the Father of that one Son, as I from my own experience know I'm the Father of that one and only Son.

So this is eschatology—when we arrive at the end, the very end and that dramatic sundering of the two, the end of history because I've experienced all the tribulations of human experience. I can't bring it back to mind now, but I do know I've had to have played every part in this world to arrive at the fulfillment of scripture—the blind man, the deaf man, the poor man, the rich man, the beggar, the thief, the murderer, the betrayer, the betrayed, you name it, and scripture has mentioned every one of them. You can't name one state in this world that is vile or evil that is not described in the Bible openly. So I've played them all. I think you have or you will. But I think you who come here have played them all. You would not be this constant had you not played them all. You'd find something far more interesting tonight, raining as it is, to be elsewhere. But no, you've played them or you would not be here, I'm telling you. So in the not distant future you will be fulfilling scripture and everything in it you will play.

But I can't tell anyone the thrill when any one scene in scripture unfolds within you…it's so dramatic. It's so unlike anything. Now we today saw this great event in Washington, a new president, and it was colorful and perfectly marvelous, no question about it. It pales into insignificance compared to the dramatic quality that possesses you when scripture unfolds within you. Can you imagine yourself actually in the presence of the child bearing witness? "Unto us a child is born." The child is there and you know exactly what happened to you and how you came out like one from a womb, but it was your skull. Then, five months later, "A son is given." They're two different events. So this 9th of Isaiah (verse 6), "Unto us a child is born, unto us a son is given" are two entirely different. The son is given to bear witness to my fatherhood; the child is there to bear witness to my birth. I am the one born and a child is simply the symbol of birth. It's an infant wrapped in swaddling clothes. So my birth from above was symbolized in that of a child; but when the son is given it's your fatherhood because he calls you Father. They are two entirely different events though they come together seemingly as one: "To us a child is born, to us a son is given." And you think, well, the child and the son are the same, but they are not. They signify two dramatic events within you.

When they'll happen I can't tell anyone. I am quite sure that our new president today could feel the thrill when the crowd walked by and when he was actually sworn in by our chief justice…and it was a thrill. Undoubtedly he felt a tremendous thrill of accomplishment. But not like these. These thrills are so fantastic you can't describe them. You know they will be experienced and only when they are experienced can one understand. It's beyond anything you can describe! It belongs to the transcendental world of God…it's not this world of history. A dramatic state when you like a serpent, a fiery serpent at that, ascend into heaven. And it reverberates, as you're told, they all take it by storm. For, it's simply like thunder when you enter or re-enter, I should say, heaven, having been sent out. You've played the part of the degenerate, you've played the part of one in generation; you've played all those parts, and now comes *regeneration*. All that you ever did is forgiven…I don't care what it is. Everything man has ever done is forgiven when he begins to unfold scripture.

So eschatology is simply the doctrine of the last things. I've shared with you as you've shared with me your visions. I've shared with you the last things. I've told you exactly what happened to me, how these events unfolded within me. They came unexpectedly, suddenly. I certainly did not expect them and they came so suddenly upon me. Well, that's how they come. They come like a thief in the night. You can't watch for them, they happen suddenly. I certainly did not expect them and they came so suddenly upon me. Well, that's how they come, like a thief in the night. But they will not happen until after you have experienced all the tribulations of human experience. So don't try to go back…God in his infinite mercy has hidden from you the memory of the past. For if you could remember some of the horrible things that you have done as you've played the part, you couldn't live with yourself. That you may not have that memory, it's been taken from you for a purpose, because in the end it's all washed out anyway. "Though your sins were as scarlet, they shall be as white as snow." So it doesn't matter.

So condemn no one, for you have played it or you will play it. But I say in your part you have played it. And you will know it because you are compassionate. You meet anyone and you have no condemnation, none whatsoever. Someone called me up and said, "My brother shot a man, killed him." I didn't ask why. He loved his brother as he loved his mother, who was weeping and weeping and carrying on. I said, I will hear the good news for you. It went on and on for about nine months and the verdict came in, freed, acquitted. He killed him and he knew he killed him, shot him. Why he shot him I never once asked the brother. It's not my concern. He asked me to help. Well, all I could do was simply do what if I were the father of such a boy, I would want him set free. I can't bring the one he killed back, but I would certainly want my son set free if I were the father of such a person. I do not believe in an eye for an eye, a tooth for a tooth. So I simply assumed that I heard his voice and it was ecstatic as he told me that his brother was set free. Well, his brother *was* set free.

So I say to everyone, in the end having played all the parts, you will have compassion for every being in this world, and you will see nothing to condemn, nothing. What a play! It's a horrible play! But in the end you will fully understand the meaning behind all the events and you will see that the one who conceived it in the beginning knew only through this play could he create beings to whom he could give himself. But *really* give himself in the full sense of the word. So it was God's purpose to give himself to what he created so that the thing created became God. Whatever God was prior to that, that individual created, formed and made by God, *had* to be that as though he was never anything but. Here, something is formed in time and enters eternity, so it has no beginning, none. Can you conceive of something formed in time and receiving the gift of eternity so it has no beginning? Well, that's what you are.

Now let us go into the Silence.

*   *   *

Now are there any questions, please?

Q: (inaudible)

A: You don't understand? That's a very good question, my dear. You could not be a father unless there's a child to bear witness to the fact that you are a father, could you? If you say I'm a mother, well, the child might have died, but you would have proof that you did bear a child. So you can't be a parent unless there is a child, can there be? In the 2nd Psalm we read, "I will tell of the decree of the Lord, he said unto me, 'Thou art my son, today I have begotten thee'" (verse 7). Now bear in mind the Bible from beginning to end is all vision; it is not secular history. We speak of David as an actual physical being of flesh and blood—that is *not* the David of scripture. The David of scripture is an eternal state and that state is the being that you are playing now. You will play it perfectly. Everything that you play, you're going to play it perfectly whether it be the thief or the honest one, the betrayer or the betrayed. You're going to play that part perfectly.

So he said of David, "I have found in David, the son of Jesse"—now Jesse means "I am"—and that is God's name forever and forever (Exod. 3:14). So, "I have found in David, the son of Jesse, a man after my own heart who will do all my will" (Acts 13:22). So, the part that you play will do all your will. At the very end having played *all* you come to eschatology and then the summary of it all is David, the very essence, the summary of all the parts you've ever played. For in the Hebrew mind, history is made up of all the generations of men and their experiences, fused into a single whole, and this concentrated time into which all the generations and from which they spring is called eternity, called Olam. The word is Olam. Well, you can translate that eternity "the world," but Olam which is called in another translation "the age." We speak of an age...this age or that age. There are two ages. Now, if I took all of the parts I've ever played and bring them all into one and personify it, it would be David. That then is my son. I am so pleased with him because he didn't falter. He obeyed my will when I said, now, you'll be a thief in this part...you'll be an honest man in this part.

David, may I tell you, if you read the story of David, you'll wonder why anyone ever looked upon him as a noble, honorable king. He fell in love with a woman, Bathsheba. She was married to a man who only had one and David had many wives. He could afford many wives and he had them. This one, Uriah, only had one and it was Bathsheba. But he saw her and fell in love with her and wanted her lustfully, so he takes her husband and puts him in the front rank of the army knowing he would be killed so that then he could get Bathsheba. He violated every commandment. He danced nude before the ark when he was king, he played the part of the mad person to avoid being arrested, he did everything imaginable and yet that was David. So all the parts you have ever played put them all together and fuse them into one and it's David, the eternal youth. The word Olam means "eternity," so, "He's put eternity into the mind of man, yet so that man cannot find out what God has done from the beginning to the end" (Ecc. 3:11).

And that was in man, so he plays all the parts...every one is already inwoven in man. You betrayed a love...you played the part where you swore that you would love one person and found yourself giving yourself to others. You also played the part of the one betrayed who kept the vows, and you played the one who did not keep the vows. So you played all the parts.

Q: (inaudible)
A: Both. You've played the male and female. You've also played the homo. You play everything in this world. One tells you, "Well, I've never played

that!" Forget it. I had my dancing partner's father and he had a peculiar fetish against homosexuals. I used to call him Pop—he was like a father to me—I said, "Pop, what possesses you?" because in my act I had this flamboyant homosexual. He was a terrific dancer and he was just simply carried away. So Pop condemned and condemned and I wouldn't fire him. I said, "No, I like him...like the boy immensely. He does exactly what I want him to do in my act." Well, this night Pop Johnson, who thought himself very much a man, had a dream and he had the most orgasmic experience with his brother. He was so...the next day he felt so unclean he couldn't live with himself for over a month, because his own brother was the one who played the part in his dream. I said, "It serves you right!" Howard was in my act and Howard was a wonderful dancer. Why should I fire Howard to please him? Howard went to what they call the Mummers' Ball back east. It's the Mummers' Ball where they all dress up and just carry on and have a most marvelous parade. It started in Philadelphia. Well, we had them in New York City. So this next day Howard didn't come to the show. I had to rearrange the entire act, because Howard came on twice which allowed me to change my costume. So Howard was not only late, he didn't come. So when he came in, I said "Well, Howard, what on earth has happened to you?" "Oh," he said, "Neville, last night I went to the Mummers' Ball." I said, "You did?" He said, "Yes and I won the prize." He said, "I was escorted on my right by three from West Point and on my left three from Annapolis, and here they walked me down the aisle, and I got first prize. I not only got the first prize, but I also won one of the judges!"

Good night.

THE MYSTERY OF ELECTION

1/24/69

Now tonight is "Election." Election is an act of God not based on any inherent superiority of those elected, but grounded in the love and grace of God and his promises. His promises were made to us before the foundation of the world, for we're the ones spoken of in that 82nd Psalm: "I say you are gods, sons of the Most High, all of you; nevertheless, you will die like men and fall as one man, O you princes" (Ps. 82:1,6). So, one man contained all. And we deliberately, purposely forgot all that we were, to experience the world of death, knowing that we had the power in the end. And we trusted the one, for we all made up the one. The word "elohim" is plural, it's "gods." The word "the Lord" which is I AM, that's singular, but it's made up of all, all of us. So we are the sons, as elohim, of the Most High. To be a son of God and no longer a slave is the theme of the New Testament.

So here, election…let no one tell you that someone who is called—for the word "election" also is translated "called or favored or chosen"—so one who is called does not in any way transcend one who has not yet been called—for all will in time be called, every one in his own order. So, "to be in Christ" as the scripture speaks of being "in Christ" a new universal humanity comes into existence, something entirely different from what we were prior to our descent. And, may I tell you in my own words and my own experience exactly how it happens. Not that the one who is called or the one who is elected is in any way better than the other who is not yet called, but it is all a plan and all in order. We are called and grafted into the body of the risen Lord. Everyone is called eventually and grafted into the body of the risen Lord. So in the end there is only one being containing all that were chosen in the beginning before the so-called "fall." The fall was not a fault and it was not anything that we did that was wrong; it was simply a deliberate plan to expand our own creative power. So the promise was that although we would go into the world of death, we would be redeemed. All would be redeemed in the same one body that contained all when it fell, a deliberate, fall into death.

Now, back in 1929 suddenly—unexpectedly, certainly unprepared for it—I was called. I was elected. It was simply that moment in time when I, having borne the fardel for the allotted time, was simply now released from my burden and my long lost rank restored. For when I was taken in Spirit into the divine assembly and here my name was already written in the Book of Life—as yours is written in the Book of Life—and it's simply the formality of being checked off; and then to stand in the presence of the risen Lord, and to be embraced. It's like the impression of a seal upon wax, upon clay, so now when you are sent you are God himself sent out…it's God sent out into the world. For in the end there is only God. God is made up of all of his sons, and it's an ever-expanding wisdom and power of God through his sons. So when I stood in his presence and answered what he asked, the embrace, which was a fusion as far as I'm concerned, was at the same time the impression made by a seal upon wax. For I was simply liquefied and made ready to receive the imprint of God, so that when I would come out now I would bear the express image of his person and radiate his glory covered by a garment of flesh and blood that no one here can see it. It can only be seen when the eyes are open in Spirit…but certainly not here.

So election is simply that moment in time when having borne the burden that was allotted in the beginning…for we are told, "You are sons of God, all of you, sons of the Most High; nevertheless, you will die like men and fall as one man, O princes." If then you are princes, well then, your father is the king. He is the King of Kings or the Most High Lord. So in the end, all are gathered together; but we're gathered in a certain order, and no one on earth can tell you that order or how you actually come back into now a far greater state than we were prior to the fall. For he who never experienced the world of death, the unmanifested, the eternal, comes into time expressing death, overcomes it, and returns glorified beyond what it was, having overcome the experience of death. So everyone in the world will be redeemed, will be elected, will be called, I don't care who they are. For, everyone is playing a part that was written for him. I have played all the parts. Having played all the parts I was qualified to take off that burden, and then came the split where the imprisoned splendor or that Spirit that was trapped is set free. It was set free and then my rank, long lost rank, was restored, but augmented beyond what it was before the fall of the one man.

So let no one tell you that when one is elected that he's better than you are. Not for one moment! For we all were chosen before the foundation of the world, and chosen in him who was God. So everyone in the world will be elected and returned to the body that is God but beyond the wildest dream of what he represented prior to the descent. That I know from my own personal experience, I'm not speculating. I'm not asking others to tell me. I am like Paul, so when Paul said in his first letter that he wrote to the Galatians: "Paul, an apostle, not from men nor through man, but through Jesus Christ and God the Father, who raised him from the dead" (1:1). The only one in us is Jesus Christ. We are Jesus Christ, and he only raises Jesus Christ. Jesus Christ is his power and his wisdom. His power and his wisdom took on the wildest temptation in the world, death, and experienced death and over came it. For he rose; but he hasn't risen in all. So, "Though Christ a thousand times in Bethlehem be born, if he is not born in thee, thy soul is still forlorn." Christ rose not from the dead…Christ still is in the grave if you for whom he died still are asleep in that grave.

So when you wake in the grave, which is your own skull, Christ awoke, for you are he. When one speaks of Christ, they think of the third-person; when they address him in prayer, they think of a second-person. Christ is not a third or a second-person; he must be thought of in the first-person. Only when you experience him in the first-person…for I know, in my own case, I awoke. It wasn't another that I saw, I awoke. I was raised. I, myself, was resurrected in a tomb—the same tomb in which Christ was buried, this universal diffused being in all the tombs of the world, our skulls. When I emerged from it, *I* emerged, it wasn't another. And so, the entire thing reinterpreted itself in me, the entire story as told and recorded in scripture. The whole thing having unfolded in me I couldn't find a second person, I couldn't find a third person of whom I could speak after the experience. Although the world will think you insane and arrogant and that you're blaspheming, I can't deny the experience. I know exactly what happened to me, so I know exactly what has happened to those to whom it happened, and what must happen to everyone who will experience it. And everyone will!

For the story is the story of God and there's nothing but God. God chose us in him before the foundation of the world and told us that we would—though gods, sons of the Most High, all of us, not one less than the other—that we would die like men. Well, I know I've said goodbye to my father, my mother, my brother, my nephew, my friends, and hundreds I have said goodbye to that I knew here and could touch and talk to. So I saw them go and I know that I must go and others see me go…they must. But in my own case, having been elected, having been called—not because of any superiority—but the time was up. I bore the burden for the allotted span, and after that span I was told I would be redeemed. Well, I have been. So he called me, he elected me, and brought me into his being once more, and impressed me with himself, like the seal upon wax, and sent me. Well, having sent me and I'm his very image it is simply God who goes forth into the world. There is no other way he's sent. For, there's only God in the end and all of his sons reflect it. It takes all of the sons to actually make God the Father.

So here, all these were told, it is said in scripture to the fathers. The promises were made to the fathers. *We* are the fathers. "When your days are fulfilled and you lie down with your fathers, I will raise up your son after you, who will come forth from your body. I will be his father and he shall be my son" (2Sam. 7:12)…that is said to David. Well, David is the very end—for all the parts you are playing, when you summarize all the parts, the quintessence of all the parts is David. So at the very end and you lie down with your fathers, then is when something comes out of you, that which played you, and played all the parts that you represented. For, the root of the word which is "to elect" means "to try." You try this on approval and you try it and try it. Then all of a sudden you come to a certain point where now the play is perfect and I know he will do all my will, but *all* my will, and then I start. I play every part in the world. There isn't a part that ever was played on earth that I have not played or I could not reach the point of having the time strike to relieve me of the burden.

So when he strikes that note, all of a sudden you hear it within you and it's simply what is known in scripture as "the trumpet." But the trumpet is a reverberation, and it reverberates like thunder, and you hear it in your head. You can't stop it, you can't in any way divert it; you are helpless while it is blowing. It's a peculiar unearthly wind. You begin to awaken and you awaken and didn't realize that you have been so sound asleep in your own skull, which is a tomb, for so many years. Then you awake and then you emerge from that grave, and you leave that grave empty. You come out and all the things are round about you as recorded in scripture. So that moment you hear the vibration, and you can't stop it, and the vibration awakens you. As Blake said: "And the dead heard the sound of the child and began to awake from sleep." Well, in my own case, I knew the area was a place of death, but I personally felt myself waking. I had no feeling of being dead, but when I found myself sealed in a tomb, I knew that only the dead were placed in a tomb. So he equates…both Blake does and scripture, "Wake you sleeper and rise from the dead." So if I am a sleeper and I must rise from the dead, he equates sleep, this kind of a sleep, with death.

And that moment when you hear that peculiar vibration you wake. That's when you are elected. Not because of anything that you have done… you have done everything that is condemned in this world and everything that is praised in this world. But you have borne the fardel for the allotted span and you can't go beyond that. There was a promise that after 400 years you will be brought out into an imperishable inheritance, something that is beyond the wildest dream of any person in the world...*after* you have borne it for 400 years. Well, 400 is a symbolic number of this body that I wear. I will wear this body of flesh and blood for the unnumbered centuries whether it be 6,000 or whatever it is, until the very end. And I will not for one moment fail. I will drink that cup to the very last and drain it. And then I've been promised that after I have borne the burden for the allotted span he will then call me, he will elect me, and then graft me into his body. Well, I was. So I know from experience there is a risen Lord. You're grafted into that body and *you are* the Lord. And there are all things you have ever done and you've done everything, I don't care what the world will say, you have done everything...or you will still have to do it, because not one in the end will reach the point where he cannot say, "Forgive them. They know not what they do!" So that every being in the world is completely forgiven for all that he has ever done because all have done it.

Now, this is election. So let no one tell you that one who is elected is something better than another. There is no historical continuity of any biological descent concerning this election as some will try to tell you. No social, no political, no religious institution is relevant as a criterion to this election. They cannot in any way explain it based upon any institution in the world. So when you read in the papers and magazines, as I do, that a certain order, certain religious order, dares to claim that they are the sole custodian of a great mystery of life based upon an unbroken chain back to Peter, what absolute rubbish! What nonsense! He calls us from every walk of life; in my own case, from no walk at all. For in 1929 the unemployed...the Crash came, and what would you do with a dancer? Well, you couldn't eat. All the theaters in New York City closed. There were only four legitimate theaters running, and running at a loss just to keep something going. Four, mind you, out of fifty legitimate theaters. All of the vaudeville houses closed. Well, I was simply a dancer, therefore unemployed. And while unemployed I was called...with no background whatsoever. I was called into the presence of the risen Lord. So you're told in Daniel, he will give it to the lowliest of men after man realizes that the Most High rules the kingdom of men and gives it to whom he will...even to the lowliest of men (4:7).

Well, I was as low as one could get. And so he gives it not based upon any background whatsoever, for he will take the foolish to confound the wise and the weak to confound the mighty. So if you took that standard, I certainly fitted it...but I had played the parts. I have memories, occasional flashes of fabulous wealth, and in such peculiar fabulous wealth. I've actually gone into the very homes and the full complement of servants and actually

The Return of Glory

relived what I did live at some moment in time. I realize that I once on one occasion I gave it up voluntarily. I did not return. What I did to move from the world, I do not know, but I gave it up voluntarily because to me it was decadent. I was getting nowhere with all this enormous possession and there I left it behind me. So I know from my own visions that I have played them. I know that you've played them, but you may not have brought back the visions. But you have played all these parts so that in the end you will condemn no part in this world, and that at the end you are called. To be called is to be elected and to be elected is to be grafted into the body of the risen Lord. From then on, for a little while, you are sent and because you are now one with God, to be sent is to be simply God sent out. That's all…it's simply God sent out.

So, election is not some strange, peculiar thing that the churches talk about that *they* are the elect and this one is chosen and that one is so and so. I tell you, in the end everyone will be elected, everyone will be redeemed, as the promise was given in the beginning: you will experience death, my sons, you're sons of the Most High; nevertheless, though you experience all of this and you will fall as one man, I will raise you up at the last day. After you have borne the burden, then I will split that which encased you, and the Spirit that was trapped will be set free. You'll be set free and once more return to the one body, the one God, the one Lord, the Father of all…and you will be he.

So this is really the story of election. No secret to it. And every child born of woman will be elected, will be redeemed, but not until he has borne the burden for the full span of time. No one knows how near you are to that final hour, no one knows. I assure you from my own experience I didn't know. If anyone the night before it happened to me had told me or asked me if I had any hope, I think I would have said no. In the world of Caesar where would I turn to earn a dollar when I only knew how to dance? What would I do? And yet seventeen million unemployed and only 125 million of us in the country, do you know the percentage? Seventeen million workers unemployed, so what would you do with a dancer? And he wasn't trained to do anything else. So ask me then what I thought my future would be, well, it would be a huge big zero. Yet it was that moment in time that I had borne the burden right through to the very end. And in his infinite mercy he hides from me the horrors that I have done, so that in the end I can say to everyone, "Forgive him, I don't care what he has done. I played that part too." For all parts we've played and if we haven't, we will. But I am convinced that those who are here have played them. Oh, you've played them, but he is infinitely merciful and he hides from you the parts that you may not be drowned by them. So, in the end you will simply proclaim the entire thing.

A lady wrote me this day, she said, "I had the strangest experience this past week. I saw stairways leading to the right, to the left and forward. All the people…so many moving…and they all were in dark modern clothes, all dark clothes. I was dressed in white flowing Grecian robes and I had on golden slippers. But they didn't recognize me, not one of them knew me or recognized me. Then I saw in the distance coming from the right side a man clothed as I was clothed in white robes, Grecian in style and golden slippers. As he approached, it was you, Neville, but you had golden hair. Your hair was gold. You greeted me because you recognized me. Still, they didn't see you; I saw you. And after the greeting I wondered to myself, 'Why does Neville have golden hair?' Then I said within myself without voicing it, 'Well, I know this is a vision and time will prove to me that this has a significance, and therefore I will extract the meaning, in time. Why he has golden hair now, I do not know.' And then that was it."

Then, another perfectly lovely experience given to me this past week, this lady said, "I heard this wonderful chorus of male voices and they were singing our wonderful battle hymn, *Mine Eyes Have Seen the Glory of the Coming of the Lord,* and I within myself repeated it, just the first little section of it. Then I found myself standing on the rim of a very large wheel and all around the rim on the wheel were strong, strapping, muscular men, and they wee singing at the top of their lungs. Glorious voices! And they were like laborers, muscular. I could see the one to my left with a bare chest and all the muscles on his chest and his arms. What lovely voices! I was the only woman present. In the center on the hub of the wheel was a small wiry man with hair that was mussed, and he was simply waving his hands with a baton. He kept on looking, and there were all these voices singing, and then he turned and looked at me. At that moment we were singing the most glorious hymn—I can't repeat the words, I haven't memorized them—but it was to the effect that we are one. We are one in hope, one in honor, one in charity. Even though we seem by the spokes to be divided, and they're all around the wheel, we are really one. That was the essence of the song. Then he turned to me and came forward and gave me the baton. And then I woke."

Then she said, "In the same interval, soon after that, you made the statement that you would give only what you yourself would like to receive. It gives you a thrill to give what you would like to receive. I thought that was a lovely thing. So when I went to bed that night I thought of my friend Jan and I wondered, now what will I give her? Something that she has never *really* had…and I thought, well I'll give her love. I actually felt I was giving her love when I became like the ocean, a fabulous ocean, and Jan appeared walking on the ocean. She was all gold...the whole body was gold. Even when she opened her mouth to smile, it was gold...everything was gold. Then she seemed to disappear, yet she left that golden reflection that I could see reflected in the ocean. And I felt so satisfied that I had picked up love to give it to her and endowed her with a gift. Well, I know she must receive it in some tangible form in this world of Caesar." That was a gift. You do not have to have one penny in your pocket to give; you can give as this lady gave. She gave her that wonderful feeling of love, that she was encompassed by love and everything was love. Then she saw her appear walking on the water. Well, water is psychological, therefore, this was a psychological gift...but it will harden into the rock. It will harden into fact in the world of Caesar.

So here, I promise you. I hope—but I cannot say it would happen tonight—I hope it comes in the not distant future that you, too, are called; because I can't tell you the thrill that is in store when you are elected. When you stand in the presence of the risen Lord and know he is risen, that he's alive and that he is love, infinite love and nothing but love. That everything is forgiven in his presence. Whatever I did is completely wiped out, the fault forgiven, and the monster tamed. For may I tell you when you take upon yourself these bodies of flesh and blood you take on an animal. And you speak of the world of the animals? Well, they are tame compared to this animal. The whole vast world of animals, may I tell you, would never hurt you if you didn't first hurt them. There isn't an animal in the world that really would hurt you if man had not gone out to murder and destroy them, they wouldn't. I saw it one night so clearly where I was at the very top of a ladder and down below were all the animals of the forest, the lion, the tiger, the panther, every wild beast. For a moment I was apprehensive, and I looked and they roared and carried on in the most violent manner. While standing at the top of the ladder with nothing between us but simply the steps of the ladder, I realized that they were only an expression of me. At that moment I arrested in me the activity that caused them to move, and they all froze and became as though they were made of clay. I descended the ladder and went down, and they were just like dead, dead things. Then when I lost all fear of them, I released the activity within me and they were like domesticated cats, playful and wonderful, altogether lovely.

I know from my own experience if we were not what we are...and we are a violent being. We came down into the world and took the heart of violence and the mind of violence and gave up the being that we were to experience this. Then in the end the monster is tamed. Because the night that I had the experience suddenly I saw two beings: one below me, a horrible monster all full of hair, the Esau of the world; but it was an animal like a gorilla, hair from head to feet, a strong monstrous beast; and above me, this glorious angel, just an angel, beauty beyond description, radiant. This monster called her "mother." I pummeled it and as I beat it, it gloated. It loved blows, it loved violence. Then as I realized what was happening: every time I beat it, it grew stronger, and I was vying with it, and the thing grew stronger; and this one above me, this glowing, beautiful creature.

I realized here is the embodiment, the personification of every violent act that I have ever done. I can't describe to anyone my compassion for it…I felt so compassionate. I've never felt it before or since for anything or anyone in this world. As I looked at it, I swore to myself—I had no one to swear by and I swore inwardly—if it took me eternity I would redeem this monstrous thing, because it had no right to existence. It came into being through my misused power; it was not brought in in some deliberate act of love. It only personified my misuse of power. As I made that pledge to myself, this enormous monstrous being melted, actually melted. As it melted before my eyes, becoming smaller and smaller, all of its energy came back to me, and I felt as strong as he who said, "I am God Almighty." I felt like El Shaddai when the energy misused and personified and held in that state dissolved and returned to me out of whom it came. As it did so, this angelic being glowed like the sun. And then I returned to this world of Caesar. So I redeemed him. I redeemed that which had followed me all through the centuries. I unknowingly created him, but he was unseen by me, invisible to my eyes until the last days. For the last day is this world now in which I am. It began in 1905 and this is my last day.

Only a few years ago when I went back to Barbados, my brother Victor—he had never told me this before and what brought it up I don't know—but he said to me, "You know, when I was a boy of eight and therefore you were six, the prophet Jordan"—we had a man in Barbados who was known as "the prophet" and his name was Jordan—"the prophet Jordan said to me, 'Vic, what do you want to be when you become a man?' I said, 'I want to be a businessman.' He said, 'You're going to be the most successful businessman in the island,'" which he is today. "Then he said, 'Now the third brother' (didn't mention the first at all), 'what does he want to be?'" Well, strangely enough, my brother Lawrence from the time he was a little child of three or four wanted to be a doctor, and Jordan said to my brother Victor, "He is going to be a very, very successful doctor" which he was when he died a few years ago. He left the most modern clinic in the island that could take care of thirty patients; that is, he had thirty rooms, fully staffed, and all the other doctors to assist in all that was needed plus his own diagnostic lab. He had everything, which he left to his two sons who were doctors.

Then he said "Now the fourth one...don't touch him! He belongs to God. He was sent this time into the world to do the work of God, so don't try to persuade him." In spite of that prophecy by the prophet Jordan—and Victor became exactly what he said, my brother Lawrence became what he said—they all have tried throughout the years to persuade me to give up what I'm doing and come back to Barbados and become a businessman and enter the businesses with my family. When I was only six, the prophet Jordan said, "Don't touch him, he's the fourth one, and he belongs to God. God sent him in for a purpose at this time, and you can't change him, Vic. He'll do exactly what he has to do, because he's under compulsion by God."

I didn't know that story until a few years ago when around, I presume, the tea hour or cocktail hour Vic told me the story. He never told me before because he didn't want to influence me. So here, in spite of his not telling me, I was moved by that unknown force— which my mother felt when I came into the world. But she interpreted it to mean that I would be a minister, because she had felt that something in her when she was carrying me, and said, "Now this one is going to be a minister." Well, a minister but not in the orthodox sense of the word.

So I'm telling you all of these things from experience that everyone will be elected, everyone will be redeemed, because you were the son of God before your descent. You didn't begin in the mother's womb and you didn't begin 6,000 years ago; you were in eternity the son of God. You are the son spoken of in the 82nd Psalm. So what can happen to us after the burden but restoration of our long lost rank? But the restoration will be now glorified, enhanced beyond what it was because we came into death and overcame it as he who decided the whole thing said we would. But *he* is made up of *us*— there would be no Lord without the gods: the Lord is made up of his sons. We are his creative power and wisdom...we are, all of us. We are the Christ spoken of in scripture.

So tonight when you go out, you dwell upon it. Don't just let it remain here for the evening, dwell upon it. So when you go to bed tonight you dwell upon the glory that is yours, that you really are the son of God. If as yet it hasn't been revealed to you, take my word for it, it *will be* revealed to you. So that no one can persuade you otherwise, it's going to happen *in* you. You'll know that you are the Christ; that you don't see one rising, *you* rise. You rise in the same place where he was buried. Well, who was buried there? You were buried there; you were that power, that wisdom that was buried in Golgotha. You're the one who will come out of Golgotha to find yourself surrounded by the symbolism of scripture now bearing witness to your birth into a higher echelon and all of these things will unfold within you. You will be elected.

So if I said, as I quoted earlier the great mystic of the 17th Century Scheffler: "Christ," said he in his third stanza, "Christ rose not from the dead. Christ is still in the grave if you for whom he died art still asleep in the grave." But it won't be long when you awake in that grave and *you* will awake. All that follows will convince you that *you* are the Christ of scripture. It is you who died. It is you who entered that state, convinced that the power which is yours was enough; that after you had borne the burden for the allotted time you could rise, having experienced death numberless times and having played everything, and in the end forgiven everything.

Now, let us go into the Silence.

* * *

Q: (inaudible)

A: No, I wouldn't say that. I wouldn't say that a deep desire for something means you haven't experienced it. No I wouldn't say that. When you find yourself…as Paul said, "In whatever state I find myself to be, in that state I am satisfied" because he knows he has to play the states. But you, knowing this law, can get out of certain states that are unpleasant, for if you play it only for a day, you've played it. So you've played all the parts, but every part in this world. If you condemn a thing, you're moving towards it; you're always moving towards that which you really condemn. You might have visions of it in a dream, where you experience the condition that you condemn in dream…but you're moving towards it. But not a thing is going to be left behind. You will play it all and bear the burden. Having borne it fully, then you'll be set free and once more return to the body of the risen Lord. And all of us will recognize each other and know ourselves more intimately than we know here, because we were the gods before we came here. We knew each other intimately and we will know each other intimately there. But here we are wearing masks…all of us are wearing masks. We do impress upon that mask a certain thing, but we're wearing masks.

Q: (inaudible)

A: I would not question that for one moment. I do know, in my own case, that if I play a certain part here, at the same time I am elsewhere playing all other kinds of parts. I know that much. But when you depart this world, you don't cease to be, waiting to return, because the world into which you go is part of this world. You are restored to life and you find yourself very much alive in a world just like this, so there is no end because others cannot see you or touch you. You still survive and you are restored and you carry on, but you may be playing a different part.

But here, I know when people see me in different parts at night, playing different parts, I am a scattered being. You are a scattered being and you are playing many, many parts. You're a fabulous being because you're the son of God, and the son of God and God are one. He and his power are inseparable. We seem helpless in this world, but we did it purposely… emptied ourselves and took upon ourselves the form of a slave, and were found in the form of man.

I do not know if that satisfies you, Jack, but you are playing all the parts now, as you said, simultaneously. But even in this world many a person plays many parts simultaneously. He plays the part of the devoted husband and a bigamist at the same time. He plays the part of a devout religious person and a thief at the same time, and they find him out and he is the most holy of all people in his neighborhood. We don't have to go very far in our lifetime…we see them all over if one reads the papers. We have a Sol Estes who taught Sunday school, and he still in his own mind's eye, having stolen millions from the government, which means from the taxpayers, he can't see where he did wrong. He knows…well, the opportunity was there. And we have a Bobby Baker…we have all these characters in government…but they are only a few. There are millions not yet unearthed. No reason to unearth them because everyone has stolen…if not physically, he's stolen mentally. He may not have had the courage to do it physically. Everyone has committed adultery by worshipping a false god. But even in the world of Caesar he has committed adultery, because he's committed it in his mind's eye. And we're told the drama is psychological, so if I look at anyone lustfully, though I haven't performed the act physically, I've done it. So who is free of that sin…if it's a sin?

Until the next time…thank you. Good night.

THE MYSTERY OF INSPIRATION

1/27/69

Tonight's subject is "The Mystery of Inspiration." We are told that all scripture is inspired by God...that is, "God breathes." It is defined as, well, how will I put it...a divine action upon the lives of certain people that qualified them to receive and communicate sacred revelations—the prophets, the apostles, the incurrent eyewitnesses. Many of them like the prophets do not know what they are receiving. As we are told, "The prophets who prophesy of the grace that was to be yours searched and inquired concerning this salvation; they inquired what person or time was indicated by the Spirit of Christ within them when they predicted the sufferings of Christ and the subsequent glory. It was revealed to them that they were serving not themselves but you" (1Pet. 1:10-12). Their vision was foreshortened, so they saw as present what was really future.

Now, the apostles are sent to point out the fulfillment of scripture. When they come into the world, sent by the risen Lord, they simply have the same experience, and they point out all parts of the Old Testament to show the fulfillment of scripture. It's so difficult to get over to man, to an individual that he is God. They rebel at the very thought. They've been conditioned to believe that God is someplace in space, something outside of man. And they can't believe that all that they behold, though it appears without, it is within, in their own wonderful human Imagination. It's so difficult...they think it's blasphemy when you speak to man and try to imply that he is God. He rebels against it.

Listen to these words. You'll find them in the 10th chapter of Matthew, "He who receives you receives me." Now listen to it carefully, "He who receives you receives me, and he who receives me receives him who sent me" (10:40). Now we go to the 8th chapter of Romans and here we are told,

"If Christ is in you, though the body is dead, he who raised Christ Jesus from the dead will raise you also through his Spirit who is in you" (8:10, 11). Now, the very first that we quoted from the 10th chapter of Matthew should tell you that God is *in you*. Whatever you think of Jesus Christ, the Bible identifies the Lord God Jehovah with Jesus Christ. The writers of the New Testament identified the Christ that governed their lives with Jehovah, who influenced and inspired the prophets…one being. So here in this 8th of Romans the inspired writer known to us as Paul tells us that "If Christ is in you, though your body is dead"—and I can tell you from experience it *is* dead. I have stopped it. I have time and again moved into a certain society, arrested within me—not in you, in me—the activity that caused the animation that I am observing; and as I arrested it, everything stood still and it was just as dead as anything in a museum. If you walked into a museum and saw all the wonderful things round about you, they are dead, they are made of clay or marble. Well, I have seen people just like this, and then suddenly I desired it, and felt the motion within me, this possession as it were, that inspired state, I arrested it. As I arrested it, it all stood still. I walked among them and they were just as dead as dead could be.

So he makes the statement, "If Christ is in you, though the body is dead"—and he states it quite clearly—"he who raised Christ from the dead *will raise* you also through his Spirit that dwells in you." How to convince man that the Lord God Jehovah is *in* man, he is dreaming man, and in the end he will awaken *as* man? How to convince man that the prophets, whose vision was foreshortened and they always saw as present what really was future, and they told it in mysterious images and types? They say that Christ is the Rock…the Rock is Christ (1 Cor. 10:4). "And of the Rock that begot you, you are unmindful, and you've forgotten the God that gave you birth" (Deut. 32:18). They equate the Rock with God, the Lord God Jehovah.

Then you sit in the Silence, thinking of nothing in particular and suddenly a rock appears before your vision, it's a quartz. You look at it… it's just simply a quartz, nothing much about it…and suddenly it becomes fragmented into numberless pieces. You look at this fragmented rock and then it molds itself into a human form seated in the lotus posture in deep, profound meditation. As you look at it, you recognize it to be yourself… you're looking at yourself. Here is a rock, shapeless, a quartz, fragmented, gathered together and formed into the human form. It's now a meditative figure and you're looking at it and you see yourself. Then it begins to glow and it glows and glows and glows and when it reaches the limit of translucency it explodes. Then you realize the truth of the vision that one saw, that a *Rock* begot me.

Out of the state of death comes life. You are the God spoken of in scripture. You came down into this world and took upon yourself the limit of contraction, the limit of opacity, which is man. And man is dead. Here, three and a half billion of us walking the earth, fighting and carrying on; and we're fighting and carrying on because the being within us who makes us alive is dreaming and he hasn't awakened. When he awakes, he puts an end to all the conflict. But until he awakens he thinks all of the animation is taking place independent of his perception of it and he doesn't realize *he* is animating everything in his world; and his dreams are projected on the screen of space, and he's fighting with his own visions, his own dreams. One day he awakens, and he awakens within the dead body; it's a grave where he deliberately and purposely entered and began his dream. The whole vast world is his projected dream. One day he suddenly awakens within himself. When he awakens, the symmetry and the poetry of scripture and all the imagery of scripture surrounds him, everything surrounds him. He realizes then for the first time that he really is the central figure of the Bible; that it is written about him and it's not written about anyone else. There is no one else, because God is one and his name is one...and his name is I AM. He awakens and he knows I am now awake, and he didn't even realize that he was asleep.

He was asleep in a body that really was dead, but he being life itself animated it...because he and the breath are one. In Hebrew and Greek the word "breath" is the same word. So he enters death, the body; his entrance is the breath entering. God breathed once and the body became animated. And this animated body with the dreamer within it is dreaming the world. One day he awakens from the dream of life, and then all the confusion comes to an end within him. Then at the very end after he tells his story— not everyone will believe it— having told his story or recorded his story, he takes off the garment of death and returns, but enhanced, to the being that he was before he entered the garment of death. For now there's no limit to expansion, no limit to translucency; there was a limit set to contraction, to opacity, and that limit was the body of death which is man.

Well, who would have thought that the imagery of the prophet was true when in the 32nd chapter of Deuteronomy he speaks of this Rock: "Of the Rock that begot you you are unmindful, and you have forgotten the God that gave you birth." He equates the Rock with God. Then someone seated in the Silence, not thinking of anything in particular suddenly sees a huge quartz, a rock...not anything to write home about...just a rock. Then it fragments itself, and you realize that this one being, this universal being is defused in all. Here is a universally diffused individuality that is...and the Rock's name is I AM forever and forever. Well, you say "I am," and I say "I am," we all say "I am." Well, everybody born of woman says "I am." It's a completely universally diffused individuality that is the fragmented Rock. You realize in the end that not a being on the outside exists independently of your perception of it. It's all really *within* and you project it on the whole vast world. Everything is contained within you I don't care what it is. So you desire this, that or the other, it is all contained within you.

Now, this inspiration comes...not the whole Bible is inspired. There are certain passages in Paul's letters he confesses are not inspired. When he passes his own personal opinion, it's just as erroneous as mine...if it's an opinion. If I tell you what I know from inspiration, what happened to me that's true, can I find passages in the Old Testament that bear witness? I must have two witnesses: I must have a passage in the Word of God and I must have it actually parallel my own experience. If it parallels my experience, I have two witnesses. When two different persons agree in testimony it is conclusive. So I bring the Bible, the Word of God, and I bring my own experience and there they parallel. Here is the Rock that begot me. Well, I saw myself begotten out of a rock. I looked at this rock, the whole thing is fragmented, it gathers itself together, and here is a person seated in this wonderful lotus posture. I'm looking, and all of a sudden, why, I'm looking at myself. But not myself as I see when I shave in the morning, I am seeing the most glorious, the most beautiful being that I could ever imagine. Well, I'm certainly not that to myself when I shave in the morning or at any other time of the day for that matter. But this is myself raised to the nth degree of perfection. He's in meditation and he's meditating me. And I must be as perfect as he is perfect. When in his own eye, he who's meditating me, I am as perfect as he is he awakes within me and I am he. But that being is eternal life and it came into a body that is dead, and started the dream of life. Well, that is true of everyone in the world...this completely diffused being. Everyone knows that he is, and everyone because he knows he is, is saying "I am," and that is God's name forever and forever (Exod. 3:15).

So there are passages in Paul when he begins to talk about marriage that are *not* inspired. He said...he confesses he's not married, and he wishes that everyone was as he is. Well, if everyone was as he is, there would be no offspring. But he said that it's far better to marry than to burn. In other words, it is far better to have union in what he calls the marriage state than to long for such satisfaction and burn rather than marry. Well, that is his opinion; that is not inspiration. When he condemns the homosexual in his letter to the Romans that's his opinion, because he forgot scripture. Scripture is the Old Testament, and in the Old Testament God made *everything* and then he said it was good and very good (Gen. 1:31). So he forgot that God made everything and pronounced it good when he begins to insert his own opinion. So not every word in scripture is inspired, but you will know the passages that are inspired; because as you awake you begin to unfold scripture. So he expounded to his disciples in all the scriptures the things concerning himself. Not everything concerning, but the things concerning, himself. Beginning with Moses and all the prophets and the psalms, he interpreted to them in all the scriptures those things that concerned him (Luke 24:27).

Now, the only scripture that he had was the Old Testament; there was no other scripture. The New Testament came afterwards to point to passages in the Old Testament that he had pointed out. So when you read the New Testament, any passage quoted by the risen Lord from the Old (he only quotes from the Old Testament), you pay strict attention to it. In the 10th of John when he said, "So you condemn me for saying that I am the son of God," (Jn. 10:34-38), he makes the statement, "I and my Father are one" (Jn. 10:30). He said, "Why do you condemn me for saying I am the son of God? Is it not written in your law"—and now he quotes the 110th Psalm—is it not written, "And the Lord said unto my Lord: 'Sit at my right hand'"? And then he quotes the 82nd Psalm, (verse 6), Is it not written that "I say, 'Ye are gods'"? "If it is said that you are gods and scripture cannot be broken, do you condemn me whom God consecrated and sent into the world?" So he's quoting only scripture. Every passage he quotes or any passage quoted of him is quoting of the same Christ in you, but he is the risen Christ who is fulfilling scripture. The minute you awake within yourself you are the *risen* Christ. There aren't a bunch of little Christs running around, only one; and one is being gathered together into one being.

Eventually everyone will be sent. I can't conceive…although we have different talents and we're all called upon and given different talents as told in scripture…I still cannot believe that one is left out of the embrace, which is the insufflation of God; and therefore the minute that you stand in his presence you are qualified as an apostle. For the one outstanding requirement is to have seen the risen Lord. And so if I see him, I am qualified for apostleship, which means "qualified to be sent." Well, if I am sent, then I go to experience scripture. Then I must tell it to everyone and point out the passages of scripture, meaning the Old Testament, to show the parallel between what has happened to me and what the Word of God said through his inspired prophets. So when the prophets inquired, it was said to them that you are serving not yourselves or your time, but you are serving our time. So it was not yet fulfilled for them to do it. And so *now* the time is here. Since the first one began and the first one awoke, from that moment on all are awaking. We are in the act of awakening *as God* who actually became man, and man being a dead being, he took upon himself death to prove his own power of overcoming death.

So the inspired one…you can't stop it. When it comes upon you, it comes unexpectedly, it comes suddenly, and no one knows. I know in my own case, whenever it happened to me it would happen when I'm sitting in my chair in the living room awake, or it would happen at night on the bed. But I can't stop it. Whenever it happens I am possessed, and possessed as though something is wearing me. Then all of a sudden the vision appears and the ears are opened and everything. Then you know you are now seeing things that kings and prophets longed to see and did not, and you are hearing what they longed to hear and did not. You know the time had not fully come; but *now* it has come to *you* and suddenly you are seeing and hearing what they longed to see and hear, but they did not. Then the entire scripture is unfolding within you passage after passage.

So you will know the inspired passages from what is taking place in you. Not everything is inspired; there were times when they wrote certain laws, dietary laws, based upon what they called the need of the time. But that is not inspired scripture. The *inspired* scripture you must fulfill, for that is the Word of God. So just as we have in the New Testament passages that are certainly not inspired, we have in the Old Testament passages that are not inspired and they enslave the minds of men. So he said, "You will deny the Word of God for the traditions of your fathers" and these traditions are man-made. If you're going to accept the man-made traditions, you will never know the Word of God. But the Word of God being inspired whenever you awaken *that's* what you're going to fulfill. Everything that is inspired in scripture you fulfill.

So the inspired Word of God comes to certain individuals…eventually to everyone. But as it unfolds, it comes to certain ones, for he is re-building his temple. The temple was purposely shattered. And now instead of having dead stones, we become living stones in the temple of God, and that is the body of God. The body of God is not any church, as the churches talk about. They speak of the church as the body of God; hasn't a thing to do with the church. For the temple of God is not made with human hands; it is made of the redeemed. Everyone who has awakened becomes a living stone in the body of God, and it's one body and one God, one Lord, one Spirit… and *you* are that one Lord. So listen to it carefully, "If the Spirit of Christ is in you, though the body is dead, he who raised Christ from the dead will raise you also through his Spirit that dwells in you." Well, if he isn't dwelling in me, he couldn't raise me. And I know from my own experience when I awoke I didn't see anyone else; there was no one lifting me up. But the wind was there, the breath was there, so the invisible God was present and present in me. But I saw no one other than myself.

So I awoke within myself. The body was dead, and when I came out of it...if you've ever gone into a recovery room in a hospital...in my own case, in 1952 I had my gall bladder removed, and by then they had recovery rooms. This was in New York City. So they wheeled this body of mine into the recovery room. Instead of taking you back to your room on, maybe, ten or twenty floors below the operating room, if something went wrong, they'd have to simply wheel you back upstairs. So to avoid that, they wheel you out of the operating room into an adjoining room, so that if something goes wrong you can quickly be sent back into the operating room and they can correct it, repair it, whatever it is. When I came to after about four hours, I looked around and thought everyone...this is the morgue. I thought everyone I saw was dead; they all looked dead. But I knew that I at least was aware, so being aware I knew in some strange way I may be dead to the world but still I'm aware. Everyone I saw...I looked over...everything that I saw was simply like on a slab, a dead, dead body.

Well, these *are* dead. It's the presence of God and you are God within these bodies that animates them. Therefore, I tell you, you cannot die. You cannot go to eternal death in that which cannot die, for God is the God of life. So nothing can die, I don't care what it is, it just can't die. But the body it wears returns to the dust out of which it was made. But *you* can't die, for you are *God* himself. God actually became man and man was dead. In the body of man, because of his presence, man became a living being. His presence is called his "breath" for his breath and Spirit are one. So when he breathed into man he entered man and man became a living being. So when you're told that he breathed upon his disciples and said, "Receive the Holy Spirit" he is the risen Lord now. He is disappearing from the visible world, but he enters within. That's the story, that's the mystery. That's inspired history, inspired scripture. And so, he enters by the breath. Well, what breath?—he himself is the breath. So one who tells you the story having experienced it, when he disappears where do you think he's going to go? Where else could he go but within? And yet he contains all within himself. But he has to go within; doesn't go without because he's left the outer world.

So this mystery of inspiration is simply, if he has possessed you, you know it. There is no doubt in your mind when you are possessed, none whatsoever, because you can't stop it. And you aren't determining the visions consciously...they are happening. All of a sudden you are cast in the central role. You are not an actor on the outside, you're the star, and you're playing the central role in that particular drama. When suddenly it is all over, you search the scriptures and there is the inspired Word of God that you have just fulfilled. All of the inspired passages of scripture you will fulfill and then you tell it. Not everyone's going to believe you, because they've been conditioned to believe in some little external Jesus Christ. It annoys them to hear you speak that way, because they don't want you to refer to Christ, the false Christ as "some little thing on the outside." The whole vast world worships a false Christ. It is Christ *in* you that is the hope of glory (Col. 1:27), and it is that Christ in you that fulfills scripture. "Scripture must be fulfilled in me. And so beginning with Moses and the prophets and the psalms, he interpreted to them in all the scriptures the things concerning himself," nothing else. "For everything was written about me," he said.

So don't be embarrassed when I tell you that you are God. Dwell upon it! When you leave here tonight, go out believing yourself to be that important. If you want someone in your world to be important, you must start treating him as though he is important. He will never react to you as an important person until you treat him as though he is. If in your mind's eye he's a little person, well, that's what he's going to be to you. Well, the same thing is true of yourself. You don't have to become arrogant. Oh no, there's no arrogance about it, but you've got to assume that this thing is true. And you dwell upon it and then the visions will come to confirm it. Everything in scripture is all about Christ, and *you* are Christ, and Christ is Jehovah. So, "When you've seen me, you've seen the Father. Why do you say, 'Show me the Father?' Whoever has seen me has seen the Father. There is no other Father."

So here, in the 89th Psalm, these three words are used, "I have found David and he has cried unto me, 'Thou art my Father" (verses 20, 26). That I know from experience. But he also called me "God,'" called me "My Lord." And I also know that I am his Rock that begot him, for all these fragmented parts I played, and put them all together it is my son David. When I take all the things I've ever done in this world, and I've played all the parts, good parts, bad parts, horrible parts, but every conceivable part I've played. Now you take it altogether and fuse it into one grand whole, and the whole personified is eternity, and that eternal state is a youth called David. So he calls me Father, he calls me his God, he calls me the Rock of his salvation, and then you know who the Rock is that we have forgotten. You know who the Lord is and you know who the Father is. And you tell it and if he is still asleep in those that hear you, they think you're mad…because all inspired men appear mad to those who hear them. It's always so. They'll judge you as a mad person. They call him mad: "Why listen to him? This man is mad and he has a spirit." So in the 10th chapter (verse 20) of John he is called insane and said to have a demon, he has a spirit, so why listen to him? Then he points to scripture.

83

But no one expects that one coming into this world today is coming to fulfill scripture. They think scripture is a prophecy, and it's going to be fulfilled in a secular manner. It's not going to be fulfilled in any secular manner. While I walk in garments of death I will fulfill it. I will animate these garments as long as I occupy them. And I'm telling you, if you've never had this experience it's the most exciting thing imaginable. When you are possessed by the Spirit and taken into a room like this and you know intuitively who you are. You know the power that you're feeling you can arrest it, stop it. But you also know that if you stop it, everything in the world that you had perceived is dead…if you stop it. You arrest that activity and everything stands still, perfectly still, and it's dead. You go over and examine it…it's all dead. Then you release it and as you release it—not there but here in your own Imagination—everything once more becomes not only animated but it continues its purpose. If the bird was in flight when you arrested it, it continues to fulfill its purpose to go to the branch. If someone was waiting on a table and they were arrested while they were carrying the food, you can keep them there as long as you want to. After a while you release it. They continue and they fulfill their purpose and serve the table.

Now, if you can imagine that taking place all over the world. Well, I'm telling you it's true. But it's difficult for man so identified with the body of death and believing himself to be it. He shaves it every morning and he bathes it and cleans it and dresses it…and he thinks he is it. He doesn't realize he is *in it*. "Christ *in* you is the hope of glory." So this body that I take so much care to keep it well and to do all things for it is dead; and I who entered it, I am the living being who experiences scripture while I am in it. So I came down into the world and took upon myself the body of a slave and was born in the likeness of man; and being found in the form of man, made myself obedient unto death, even death upon the cross which is man (Phil. 2:7). While in this state of death, I experience my own Word that I inspired the prophets to write. For who else inspired them but God and you are God! So you foretold what you're going to do, and it was the most incredible thing in the world: that you would actually die, become dead and overcome it. The last enemy to overcome is death and you are victorious, so you overcome death.

You awaken within the grave, and then unassisted you come out and find yourself the being that you *were,* but now enhanced. Those who still thought of you only in terms of the outer form, they come to the grave and they see the things that were foretold, but him they did not see. How could you see him with mortal eyes? You can't see him. So he said, "You have eyes and you see not, you have ears and hear not"; and now he gives them eyes that they may see and bores ears for them that they may hear. Now you see and you hear what kings and prophets longed to see and hear but did not. Then the whole thing unfolds within you.

So let no one tell you and believe it. They can tell you, but don't you believe it, about going to some retreat so that you can in some way cultivate inspiration. It comes out of the blue and it comes when you least expect it. So when teachers come telling you take a five-month course with me or a six-month and then we will develop this capacity to be inspired, forget it! They sit for hours over a period of months and years to raise the kundalini fire. Well, they can sit until the end of time and they'll raise nothing. It doesn't come that way. When that fire rises within you, it first comes down like some bolt of lightning and splits you in two, and then you, as that fiery serpent, you rise. It happens so suddenly and so unexpectedly, you can't sit in any way and lift it up…it hasn't yet come down. Only *he* ascends into heaven who first descended. And it's actually a bolt of lightening that splits you in two, which is called in scripture, "the curtain of the temple" which is the flesh. Takes that dead body and splits it, and then the Spirit trapped is set free and up you go, back into the heavenly state from which you came. You are the God spoken of in scripture: "I say ye are gods, sons of the Most High, all of you; nevertheless, you will die like men and fall as one man, O princes" (Ps. 82:1, 6). How else could you tell it? Could you tell it clearer?

So, if you can take it, from tonight on, when you think of yourself, don't think of any physical descent. People tonight are so proud that they came out of certain physical lines. If they really knew the background of that one, they'd be ashamed of it. Many a person has paid a fortune after having made a fortune to trace his line, and then paid another fortune to forget it. When he finds what the physical descent was he wants to forget it completely. Here I was reading recently that Frederick Myers—and this is the attitude of the whole religious world—he was the head of the Society for Psychical Research in London. Well, he's gone from this world now. He thought he would ask the priests and the ministers and all those associated with religion a very simple question. The question was this, "What do you think is going to happen to you when you die?" This minister answered, "I suppose I will enter into the joy of the Lord. But why bring up such an unpleasant subject?" Now here is a man teaching…now this is an actual fact…it is given as actual fact by Mr. Myers himself that he asked this minister and he's going to enter into the joy of the Lord. For you're told, "Well done, my good servant. Enter into the joy of the Lord." Well, he takes that literally and he thinks because he serves with a certain suit of clothes and a turned back collar that he is something set apart, that he is one of the chosen, so he will enter joy of the Lord. But he's scared to death to enter into the joy of the Lord…why bring up such an unpleasant subject. Well, that is true of the whole vast world over.

I tell you, you are immortal, you cannot die. You come into death—this world is a world of death—and the bodies will return because they're dead anyway and they'll return to dust. But you, the occupant of that body cannot die. You still remain asleep and you'll find yourself clothed in another body of death, but you being alive, you animate it. You will animate a young body, a lovely young body, say, twenty years old, and you'll animate a world just like this. It's terrestrial, it's alive, it's real, and you'll find yourself doing similar things in an environment which you in the depth of your being find best suited for what you still want to do. You'll continue doing it until one day you awaken in that garment and fulfill scripture. Everyone *must* fulfill scripture; that is the goal. At the end, you take it off and then you return to the glory that was yours before that the world was. We will all meet in that state, and we knew each other intimately before we came down. We will know each other just as intimately when we ascend and all the masks are taken off. No one in this world could ever know anyone as intimately as we know each other in eternity, for in eternity we form *one*; we are many and yet one. "Hear, O Israel: The Lord our God, the Lord is one" (Deut. 6:4). And in that day there shall be only one Lord, one king, one God and Father of all...and all form the One...so not one will be missing. I don't care what frightful dream the individual has had, it will still in the end be but the dream. You take it off, and when he returns we will love him as dearly as we did before the descent; for we're all one and not one can be lost.

So inspiration in a sense is a gift of God. You cannot acquire it, it just happens suddenly, and it happens by the God in you. For that is the God of whom I am speaking tonight...the one being right *in* man. If you read scripture carefully, it is not inspired from without, it is from within. So when he asks the question, "If Christ is in you...", if it is, well, I say yes he is in all of us: that is the power of God and the wisdom of God personified as you. Well now, "If the body is dead, he who raised Christ from the dead will raise you also," for he only raises up Christ. Christ is risen, so Christ in you is the one who will be risen and you are he. "Through his Spirit who dwells in you" and his Spirit is breath. The God breathed his inspiration and you hear the wind and you feel it, but it is all you. So he is now the image of the invisible breath who radiates the glory of that God-breath. So it's *in you* and that's why you can awaken...and everyone will awaken.

Now let us go into the Silence.

*   *   *

Q: (inaudible)
A: No, I say the Bible is inspired, all scripture is inspired by God and profitable for instruction as we are told in the 2nd letter of Paul to Timothy. But not every passage is inspired, because he has certain passages that are only opinions, and he tells you they are opinions. So, his opinion doesn't differ from my opinion. If I pass an opinion, it's subject to all the errors of the world. But if I tell you of any inspired event in my life, like the fulfillment of the Word of God, that is *not* an opinion, that is an eternal truth. Whether one believes it or not, that is unalterable. But if I pass an opinion…you ask, "What do you think of Nixon?"…well, I can pass an opinion and I'd be so far amiss…history may disprove me and make me completely false. So my opinions are just as subject to error as any man's opinion in the world. But when it comes to inspiration which is "God breathes"…literally the word means "God breathes."

Q: (inaudible)
A: O, my dear, you feel it. You can't read that book and not feel it. When it begins to become alive within you, you know what is inspired and what is not. If you take the story of the diets, that's not inspired; that was based upon a need, a necessity at the time that it was written…because if he made everything and called it good (Gen. 1:31). And then we find in the Book of Acts when Peter said he could not eat the unclean thing, Peter fell into a trance, and a sheet came down from heaven and on it all manner of food. The voice said to him, "Peter, slay and eat, for that which I have cleansed I have cleansed" (10:13). Then when Paul writes in the 14th chapter of Romans, he said, "I know and I am persuaded by the Spirit of Christ that there is nothing unclean in itself; but any man who sees anything to be unclean, to him it is unclean" (14:14). That goes not only for food but for any act of man. So through the eyes of the inspired man, "God made everything and called it good and very good." But man sets himself up as the criterion of what is good and what is evil, because he ate of the tree of good and evil. One day he's going to eat of the Tree of Life, and leave behind him this concept of good and evil. It's a play for a divine purpose: to expand the being that we are beyond what we were before we took upon ourselves this challenge.

Q: (inaudible)
A: That's an opinion…all the traditions. We are told, "You deny the Word of God for the traditions of your fathers." So we have traditions, and so when someone comes up and gives this pontifical statement as though he's in communion with God, it's like Putnam on TV…same thing. He's always in communion with God and he speaks in the same manner. He

is speaking this way and all opinions in the world. Well now, that's not scripture…scripture hasn't a thing to do with that. Scripture is inspired, true scripture is inspired.

When I start passing opinions, setting myself up as the criterion of what is right and what is wrong, that could be as false as all outdoors. There are certain isms in this world…I think of one, she's blonde, or was blonde, and someone told her she looked lovely in lavender, so lavender became the perfect color and all of her followers had to wear lavender. Then onions and garlic disagreed with her, so that was simply the fruit of the devil. And red was awful on her, so red was taboo. They built up this ism on her own little superstitions, and then she called it something from God. Well, you find these false prophets all over the world. Prophecy is over. Predictions and fortune telling as always has been. That's not prophecy.

Prophecy is over and you'll find it in the Old Testament, that's prophecy. The New Testament is the fulfillment of prophecy. So Man comes into the world to fulfill the Word of God, but when he fulfills it, he re-interprets the Old in light of his own experience. And man having these traditions of the fathers will not accept his re-interpretation of the Old; because to them Abraham lived and that's all there is to it. He lived thousands of years ago. He was promised a child, that child was called Isaac, and that happened thousands of years ago. He will not believe the whole thing is prophecy and that Isaac *is* born…the little child that was born not according to the flesh but according to the Promise, as we're told in Galatians…and that little child is the Christ child bearing witness of the birth of God. So when it happens in him, he simply takes the Old Testament and shows the passage where he has fulfilled it. And his name isn't Abraham, his name could be anything. But he knows that Abraham was a state that he entered to receive the Promise and fulfill it. But man…if you take this story as secular history then you'll never see the scripture…never see it.

My old friend, Abdullah, who was born and raised in the Jewish faith, said, "Not only was I raised in the most orthodox environment in Judaism, but for forty years I was a strict vegetarian. I had never tasted pork in my life, no part of the animal. The voice said to me, 'If you will not eat what they give you, how do you expect them to take what you give them? So you are feasting them and you expect them to accept what you teach and yet you will not eat what they offer you.'" And he said, "I broke my fast after the vision, and what do you think was served me, and it had never happened before? I was the guest of honor and I went to this lovely party, and they brought in a little roasted pig. The whole animal, right at the top of the table, and I am the guest of honor. I broke not only my fast from not having had meat in forty years, but never in my life had I ever had a piece of pork...and here I am breaking my fast on pork." So, you won't take what I'm offering, well, have I taken what you offered? So, *all* things are clean if you see them clean. As we are told, "Food will not commend you to God; you're no worse off if you do not eat it and no better if you do,' as told us in Paul's letters, no worse off if you don't, no better if you do.

But there are people who believe they're going to get into heaven by not smoking, not drinking, and not doing this and not doing that. I was one of those and when I met old Abdullah, having observed me for a while, said "You know, Neville, you're so good you're good for nothing." He told me that "Because you thought you could acquire merit by not doing things." After a while you see everything in this world and allow it...you just allow it. You don't want to duplicate it. I have no desire to take from you anything in your purse...like someone left a coat here last night, 250 in this party, and this lady came in with the coat over her hand and she went into the kitchen...had no right to be there. These were all men, 250 men, the motorcycle club, and here she had the coat. Well, Mr. Harrison who is supervisor here saw this woman with the coat, and just said to her, "What are you doing with the coat?" She said, "My brother left it here." He said, "Your brother left it here? Well, what does he do?" "He works for Lockheed." Well, he said, "The man who left that here doesn't work for Lockheed, he works for Blue Chip Stamps and he's a red-headed man, about thirty-five," and then he took the coat from her. She gave it up quite innocently, quite freely. She's just one of those people who walk around and pick up anything...saw the coat hanging there, so she picked up the coat. She must have heard from someone or she didn't have to hear...she walks in and picks up the coat. But Mr. Harrison redeemed it. And maybe it is not Larry's, but she gave it up so quickly that he knew that she was fully aware of the fact it wasn't her coat. She saw the coat and she's going to take it. Well now, forgive her as that's part of her life, just part of her life.

In little Barbados where I come from we've always been in business and some of the richest families on the island and their wives...they couldn't help it, they were simply conditioned that way...kleptomaniacs. They'll pick up everything and then pay for nothing. Well, the clerk saw them do it, would tell my brothers that she has so and so, and she has so and so. Well, they never said one word to her. The husband knew she had this peculiar habit and they'd make a little note, and he never complained. The bill was sent to him and he paid it. So she went home thinking she got something for nothing. They were the richest families. These are not people who are hungry. They were rich, I mean *really* wealthy. Come in and pick up silly little things like apples. Put six little apples in quickly…and she could have bought the store. Well, what can you do? When you invited her to dinner, you nailed things down; but in her social capacity you had to have her to dinner. I recall her vividly…I can see her now before my mind's eye…a sweet, lovely, cultured lady. But don't you leave anything, because off it would go. It's not an economic set-up; it's part of the mind.

You know who made her?—God. And so, that's it. When you know that God made everything in this world, you forgive everything in this world. God wrote the part for her and God played the part and is playing the part. And so, he will go through all the sufferings, because he has to stand the embarrassment of the part he wrote when he's arrested. Well, who is arrested? Well, the body is dead and the occupant of the body is God, and he has to stand the embarrassment for the part he wrote. You go to a play and people will hiss the actor. You want to hiss someone call the author on the stage…he did it. The actor's only expressing what the author wrote.

I recall vividly…I played in a show on Broadway for about, I think it was about twenty-five to thirty weeks of being hissed eight times a week, six shows and two matinees. Yet the author is unseen as God is unseen. Then you'll know the meaning of the cry on the cross: "Father, forgive them; they know not what they do (Luke 23:34).

Good night.

THE REAL BAPTISM

1/31/69

____(??) on this level it's only a symbolic representation of the dying, being buried, and being raised with Christ. The action itself, although it represents all of this, is not really important. In the mystical sense it's all important, for it comes just before the realization of being God the Father. As Paul describes it in his letter to the Ephesians, and he puts it sixth in the great unit, and he said, "There's but one body, one Spirit, one hope, one Lord, one faith, one baptism, one God and Father of us all" (Eph. 4:4). So he puts it just before the realization of being God the Father.

Now, he tells in his letter to the Romans that "We were buried with Christ by a baptism into death, so as Christ was raised from the dead by the glory of the Father, we too may walk in newness of life" (6:4). Baptism implies complete immersion. As we are told, "As Jesus rose up out of the water, immediately he saw the heavens opened and the Spirit descending upon him like a dove" (Mark 1:10). He rose up out of the water…did it ever occur to you that the bodies that we wear are almost 100 percent water? In these bodies we are buried: this is the great water in which we are buried and remain buried until that moment in time when we rise up out of the water and see the Spirit—not only the heavens completely transparent—but then we see the Spirit in bodily form as the dove descending upon us. This descent upon us is the gift of a new form; that is to say, a new manner of existence, a new unification, so that each while conserving his individuality actually becomes God the Father.

So Paul places it as sixth in the great unit. He mentions seven, but the last would have to be the source of it all, God the Father who is above all, who is in all, and who is through all. But he places baptism as the sixth. So he starts off with the body…there is in the end only one body. This is unification, one body. One Spirit he places second, then the one hope, the one Lord, one faith. Now he comes to baptism, the sixth, one baptism, one God and Father of us all. So just before we become aware of being God the Father of all—not just God the Father but of all—this baptism takes place.

Now, the clarity spoken of in scripture...the heavens were rent and then he saw not only this complete translucency but he heard a voice and then he saw the Spirit in bodily form as a dove. All of these took place in the soul of the individual who experienced them. They were not seen or heard by the crowd. Jesus is the personification of *redeemed* humanity, so I can use the word Jesus representing all who have had the experience. So all that is said concerning this story took place in the soul of Jesus, that is, the individual who has had the experience. It was not shared by another, not on this level.

So he said, "I have a baptism to be baptized with; and how I am constrained until it is accomplished!" (Luke 12:50). Well, all scholars interpret this to mean the crucifixion; but it is not, for the crucifixion began the whole thing; that was the death...buried in these bodies of mortals. It reminds us of that 2nd verse of Genesis, the 1st chapter, "And the Spirit of God hovered upon the water." It's a creative act. The word means "incubate, to hatch out." It's all buried there, for "We were all united with Christ in a death like his and we will certainly be united with him in a resurrection like his" (Rom. 6:5). So we're all hatched out after incubation, one by one, from these bodies of water. We come out of this; this is the great flood in which all of us are inundated in a world of illusion. Then the Spirit is hovering, incubating, and then one day we are lifted up out of this body.

So we are told, "And when Jesus came up out of the water, immediately the heavens opened and then he saw the Spirit just like a dove descending upon him" (Jn. 1:32-34). Well, that was not seen. If you read the Book of Mark and the Book of Matthew it wasn't seen by anyone but Jesus. So bear in mind Jesus only represents redeemed humanity. It's the one body into which every being who has that experience is incorporated...incorporated into that one body, that one Spirit. It's the only hope of man, the one hope; it's the only Lord, not a bunch of little lords running around; the only faith by which we should live, faith in this; and it's the one baptism culminating in the one God and Father of all. You become the God and Father of all. So here, this is baptism in the true sense of the word.

I know in 1926 when my mother came to see me in New York City she hadn't seen my son, who was then two years old. One of the first questions she asked, "Is he baptized?" I said no he's not. "Oh, how could you do this? Suppose he dies tonight?" I said, "What would that matter? I would lose a lovely boy, but what would it matter?" Well, she said, "He wouldn't go to heaven. If he isn't baptized he couldn't go to heaven." I said, "For your sake,

Mother, next Sunday we will have him baptized." So I arranged with this minister in the Episcopal Church to take him in and name him and he'd baptize him by sprinkling a little water on him in the name of the Father and of the Son and Holy Spirit. She was satisfied that should something happen to him and he died right then or right after, he is saved in the sense that he could get into heaven.

We are told in scripture, "Unless you are born of water and the Spirit, you cannot enter the kingdom of heaven" (Jn. 3:5). This is the water; you actually come out of this body. Your whole head opens up and it's transparent. You've never seen such translucency. You don't realize that you're still inundated until you see the dove. The dove is not moving its wings, it's not in any way making any effort. It's floating. If it's floating, then it's on water. And you're coming up towards that which is above you, which is floating. It simply is the fulfillment of the story of Genesis, for man is the ark of God; he's not a phantom of the earth and the water. He is the true ark containing everything within him. There isn't a thing good or evil that is not contained within him. So he is the ark and the dove is the symbol of the Holy Spirit.

We're told that Noah stretched forth his hand and received the dove and brought her in unto himself. There she remained within the ark. So on his hand the dove descended. I know in my own case when the whole thing became completely translucent, I only knew that I am inundated by reason of the hovering of the dove…it was simply floating. Well, a dove doesn't float. It was simply floating, seemed to be floating, and then I ascended and came out of the body of water. So when he came up out of the water, then the heavens opened, and there he saw the Spirit like a dove descending upon him and smothering him with love.

Well, I know in my own case, when this voice of God personified as a woman spoke and said, "He loves you" when it was so obvious this bird did love me, it's smothering me with love. But she added, "They avoid man because man gives off such an offensive odor. And so, because of the offense, they avoid man, but his love was so great for you that he penetrated the ring of offense to demonstrate his love for you." Well, I was reading recently a work called *The Dialogues of Buddha*. Now these are the alleged works, for how would anyone know what Buddha said? These are called *The Dialogues of The Buddha*, not just *a* Buddha, translated from the Sanskrit by Rhys Davids. Now, these words—and I've never seen them before, they came long after my own experience—he said, "In the eyes of the gods, human beings are stinking, disgusting, revolting, and are counted as such." Well, I know in my own case, this voice of God spoke similar words, but not in that manner. She did say that "Man gives off the most offensive odor, but his love was so great he came through and penetrated the ring of offense to demonstrate his love for you."

Well, I mean, on this level you wouldn't think that Buddha was wrong or that she was wrong if you think of TV and all the others and the deodorants. We must really be stinking, because one of the biggest things is simply deodorants…that everyone in this world must have a guard, this guard against this, this guard against that. We really must be in the eyes of someone the most offensive. But he wasn't speaking ___(??). We are in a world of death. We are actually put into a world of death, and came down deliberately, not because of anything we did that was wrong. For, when the whole drama is over and the incubation is over and we once more rise from the world of death, we are infinitely greater than we were prior to the descent into death. It was for a deliberate purpose. If you can call it a fault to overcome any limitations ___(??) prior to the descent, for we're ever expanding, forever and forever. There is no limit to expansion; there is a limit to contraction, a limit to this opacity that is this water-body called man.

So here, we are all in these bodies. Have you ever seen the result after cremation of one who weighed 200, 300 pounds?—just a little bit of ash. You could put it in a small, little can, no bigger than a little Campbell Soup can. Well, where did those 300 pounds go? It was all water, all water. So here we are inundated, not in some general flood, but general humanity. And individually we are put into these garments of water. So as Paul said quite wisely in the 6th chapter of Romans, that "We have actually been buried with Christ by a baptism into death, and just as he rose by the glory of the Father, we too in newness of life" (verse 4). When this happens in a man's world, no one here sees the results, because they didn't even see the events that he encountered. No one saw the dove descend upon him; no one saw the transparency that he saw; no one heard the voice that he heard of the love and affection of the one who descended upon him. It was all something transpiring in the soul of the one who had the experiences. You tell it; some believe it and some do not. The majority do not believe it, for they have been conditioned to believe in Jesus as a little individual unit who lived and died 2,000 years ago. They can't see Jesus as the personification of humanity, the *redeemed* humanity. They can't see Christ as a cosmic presence buried in all; they see him only as some tiny little thing. And that is not the story at all.

So, if I cannot enter into the kingdom of God unless I am born of the water and the Spirit, well, this is the birth of the water: you finally emerge. Having been immersed in the water, your exit from that state is *your birth*. And then the descent of the Spirit upon you is your birth in Spirit. This then qualifies you for the new form, the new manner of existence, the new unification with Christ on an entirely different level. For God is now raised to an entirely different level by his descent into this world. So it started out one person at a time, and then the second, the third…but all form into "one body, one Spirit, one hope, one Lord, one faith, one baptism," and then comes the final, "one God and Father of us all, who is above all, through all and in all" (Eph. 4:4).

So whether you were baptized or not hasn't a thing to do with it. That is only a symbolic representation of this great mystery, and it *is* the final mystery, and it's the last in the great series. So when one experiences the baptism as I'm trying to explain it tonight, at that moment you are an entirely different being. No one sees it unless they have incurrent eyes. But no one in the outer world looking at you can see it. You are one with God the Father. You *are* God the Father, without loss of identity. That is the great mystery. There is no absorption into that—yes, one body, one Spirit, one God—but no loss of that individuality. That is the great mystery. That was the purpose of it all. We were individualized before. We aren't going to lose that individualization; by coming down we simply increase it. We tend forever and forever toward greater and greater individualization…that is the descent into this world of death.

But the bodies were bodies of water. And he hovers for that interval of time over the water, because something precious is buried there. It is himself that is buried there, and he simply hovers over it, he incubates it until it hatches. When it hatches, it breaks the water. It comes up out of the water, and immediately the heavens open and the Spirit, in bodily form of a dove, descends upon him. Then the voice of God, Bath qol, the woman who speaks, or she speaks the words of God, and then you hear of the tremendous love that God holds for you in bringing you out…to raise you up by his glory. Therefore, you now receive the glory that is God and become one with God the Father, remaining in the world for a short interval to tell it to those who are on the verge. But tell it to all in the written form, because what you leave behind you and they may, tomorrow or tomorrow or tomorrow, pick it up and read it. It might spark something because everyone eventually must be seeking God more than anything else in this world. On a certain level they seek money, they seek security, they seek love and affection in the world of Caesar. Well, that's all right, but there will come a day when he will seek God more than anything else in this world. Nothing will satisfy him but an experience of God.

So this is the baptism of which I speak. If you have not been baptized, take my advice, don't become ___(??). I did it for my mother's sake. But if you are not baptized in the Christian faith, it doesn't make any difference whatsoever. That is only a symbolic representation of this great dying, being buried, and being raised again with Christ. But you don't have to go through the shadow world in order to actually fulfill the story. Hope one hope, that you may fulfill the *real* baptism tonight or tomorrow, whenever it is. For this is what I speak of when it comes to the mysteries of scripture.

So here, if you know of anyone who is not baptized and they are desirous…like a friend of mine one day came to me and said, "You spoke of baptizing your son…well, I have five children and I haven't baptized them, and I would like to baptize them, and would you be the godfather? Would you arrange the baptismal for me?" Well, I arranged it and he and his wife came over with their five children and they were all baptized. It was the most dried and cut thing ever, but he wanted it, he felt it should be done. Well, it satisfied him and I was the godfather, the proxy. Now he has his five and they're all baptized. Well, it's all right. I was, without my consent, at the age of three or four. Mother had me baptized, and we're all baptized, but certainly I had no knowledge of what was taking place.

But the *real* baptism, you are the sole actor; there's no one but you. The crowds do announce it. Now, Luke implies in his story that others saw it, and if you read Luke carefully and take the first four verses, you will see that Luke is not telling anyone that he is going to be exact either chronologically or in any other way. He starts off in the most marvelous way: "That in as much as many have undertaken to compile a narrative of the things that have been accomplished among us, just as they were delivered to us by those who from the beginning were eyewitnesses and ministers of the Word" (Luke 1:1-4). Now that phrase "from the beginning" is a translation of the Greek word Anothin. Anothin means "from above." We find it in his argument with the great Sanhedrin, Nicodemus, when he said to him, "Unless you are born from above you cannot enter the kingdom of heaven" (Jn. 3:3). Well, that word Anothin is translated here "from the beginning." He tells us that there were eyewitnesses and ministers of the Word.

Now he goes on to say, "Well, it seemed good to me also, having followed all things accurately for sometime past"—that phrase "for sometime past" is a translation of the same word Anothin. In other words, he's telling you that he too has had the experience, for he's not listening to people. He has had it, for here "from above" he knows exactly what he's doing. But he does not claim that the story that he's going to write is going to be an exact chronological story. He rearranges it…because he ends with the crucifixion, and he knows from his own experience it comes first. But, he's going to tell a story. As Tennyson said, "Truth told," or "embodied, in a tale shall enter in at lowly doors," so you tell it on a certain level where people can accept it. So, truth embodied in a tale shall enter in at lowly doors. You tell it as though it took place here in the outer world for the whole world to observe. And the story is not true...it's not true on *this* level. But the whole vast world has accepted it on that level...which has kept the story alive.

So Luke cannot be condemned for telling it the way that he did, because he addresses now the one for whom he wrote it, "That you, O excellent Theophilus"—that means "one who loves God" as you do—"that you may know the truth concerning the things of which you have been informed." Alright, so you have been told these stories and you've been informed that you may know the truth. Well, he knows in his heart that the truth one day will come to the surface, but he will keep it alive by some eternal form, and you will hear it as though it took place on the outside and you will worship an exterior Christ. You will worship some outside God and live by it and go to church and do all the things that the church demands of you until one day it erupts within you and you know the truth of the story. So there is no judgment concerning what the Evangelist did.

But Mark doesn't do it that way. When Mark tells the story he just tells it. You cannot read that first chapter of Mark and find anyone present who saw the descent of the dove, who saw the clarity of the heavens other than the one who is having the experience. The same thing is true of Matthew. But Luke, for reasons which undoubtedly are very good, told it as though the crowd watched and so did John. At least John the Baptist witnessed it... he had at least one outside. But, there is no one who *witnesses* this story. And that's why when you tell it, because you still are in the eyes of those that you address the little one that they know, and you don't make an impression. They know all your weaknesses, all your limitations, all you frustrations, everything..."And so how can you tell me that the story written of our dear Lord has unfolded in you?" because they are looking for something entirely different. They don't know that re-enactment is constantly coming. So when he said, "I have a baptism to be baptized with; and now, just now, I simply wait for its fulfillment. Now I am simply constrained until it is accomplished."

Well, you take the one body waiting for all to come...that is the constraint. The one Spirit waiting for everyone to awaken...that is the constraint. The one being waiting for all to that hope—"Set your hope fully upon this grace that is coming to you at the unveiling of Jesus Christ" (1Pet.1:13)...to have that one faith. Well, he is constrained until everyone was once more brought into the one body, the one Spirit, the one God and Father of all. So, baptism comes at the very end, just prior to the taking off of the garment for the last time, when at that moment you are one with actually God the Father, who is above all, through all and in all. And so where would you go after the last? You're in all, actually in all, and once more hovering, waiting for those that you're incubating to rise from the dead, for they are all buried in these garments of water.

So, then you read it carefully...and don't be misled by what you've been conditioned to believe. For I know in my own case I was trained as my mother was trained concerning baptism. Yet because of my divorce... not my divorce, I was separated...and it was one of those peculiar feelings between my first wife and myself. She had the little boy for a while, then I got him for a while, then she got him for a while. He went back and forth like a swinging door. So when my mother came, naturally, she was concerned was he baptized? When I said no then she went through the ritual and we baptized him. She was so concerned for his Christian future that she persuaded my wife to allow her to take him to Barbados. So off she went, thrilled, and she took him down for a couple of years. Then my wife, unannounced, uninvited, appeared and demanded him. So she brought him back...again swinging doors, back and forth, until finally when the divorce was granted he was given to me. At the age of twelve, I got him outright. And that was his background. But her concern was for his Christian future, because that was how she was trained and that's how she trained us.

So, whether you were baptized on this level or not, it doesn't really matter. Set your hope fully on the real baptism: when suddenly the heavens open and you're coming up out of the water and hovering above you is the Spirit of God, looking at you with the most loving expression...but floating and you are coming out. As you come out you do exactly what Noah did, for you're only fulfilling scripture, and Noah put forth his hand and the dove lit upon him, then he brought the dove in to himself. And then the dove, from my own experience, smothers you with love, smothers you with affection; and the voice of God will speak and it does need a person as its agent. It doesn't come in some strange way, it comes as a person. And so the voice comes as a person. Here is the woman who tells you of his great love for you...that's why he penetrated the ring of offense. Then, you never thought yourself offensive prior to that, you never thought anyone offensive, but it is to those who contemplate the world of death a horrible disgusting place. But nevertheless, whether you were horrible to those or not, it happens this way, and this is the great mystery of baptism.

Everyone will have *this* baptism even though they did not have the other baptism. For the other is only a symbolic representation of this great mystery of the death of God, the burial of God, and the rising of God. He was buried in a body of water as told us in that 6th of Romans (verse 4)—also in the 12th chapter of 1st Corinthians. You'll find it all through the letters of Paul, so much is said of his baptism. Well, one thing this baptism does for us, we lose completely all human divisions as told us in the 3rd chapter of Galatians (verse 27). After the baptism we are "in Christ," and when we are also "in Christ," there is neither Greek nor Jew, neither bond nor free, neither male nor female. In other words, there is no division whether that division be of race, whether it be of class, or of sex, because in this resurrection of which I speak we are beyond the organization of class, of race or of sex. For, we are one with the risen Lord who is all.

He is everything in the world. So if it's black, he's black; if it's pink, he's pink; if it's white, he's white; if it's male, he's male; if it's female, he's female. No matter what it is! So he's above all divisions in this world. It's put an end to all human divisions and you don't see people as you formerly saw them. You do not in your dreams meet them as you formerly did…everything changes. And the only thing that hasn't is your little body which is still limited with all the frailties, all the weaknesses of man, until that moment in time that you are relieved of it. The moment will come to depart this world, but it will come after this. For after this, you have finished the race and you've fought the good fight and you've kept the faith, and now there's laid up for you the crown of righteousness (2Tim.4:7). The crown is the laurel leaf…not some little ___(??) in your head…it's the laurel, the leaf of the victor who really ran the race and came out. He fought the battle, because this certainly is a battle, a horrible battle, when all day long man fights in this world. He doesn't know the law of God, so he doesn't know how to apply it. He wars against the shadows of his own creation.

But here, set your hope tonight upon this: it's the final of the seven unities. We start with the great unity in the confession of Israel, "Hear, O Israel: The Lord, our God, the Lord is one" (Deut.6:4). Now in the language of the Christian, this great creed, this great shema of Israel, is that which we find in the 4th chapter of Ephesians, "the one body, the one Spirit, the one Lord." And here it is emphasized right through, so it parallels this. But the sixth is this wonderful one concerning baptism. I can't tell anyone the thrill when it happened to me on the first day of January 1963. It was the 1,260th day from the first to the last. The last day was the first of January 1963, that's when the whole thing was fulfilled, the whole thing was done. Well then, now here it is six years later and I am still, like Paul, telling the story. He spends his day from morning 'til night telling the story of the fulfillment of God's promises to the fathers. Many believed, many did not…but he kept on telling it. And no one knows how he departed this world, for not a thing is said in the Book of Acts—which is the story from the 9th chapter on to the end—how he left the world. The churches tell you he was martyred; not a thing in scripture tells you that at all. The word martyr means "witness"— he witnessed to the truth of the Word of God. And they call it a martyr. I call nothing in my life a martyrdom. Even if I was shot this very moment,

I wouldn't call it a martyrdom. My martyrdom is witnessing to the truth of the Word of God. Man has completely misunderstood the word martyr and they call it someone who is violently destroyed from this world. It isn't that at all. Are you a witness to the Word of God? Everyone must be in the end.

And the very end is the baptism. That's when you're incorporated into the body of the risen Lord *as* the risen Lord, without loss of identity. So you're given a new form, a new manner of existence, a new unification. Because you are unified with Christ in death, now you're unified with Christ in the resurrection, a complete new unification. In this unification there is no loss of identity, none whatsoever, and yet *you are* the risen Lord. You are God the Father, Father of all. And I will know you more intimately than I could ever know you in this world. No one in this world could ever know another as he will know that other after the resurrection. Because he knew him before the descent, he will know him after the ascent. There will be no loss of individuality, just simply a greater and greater individuality; and all back into the one body, the one Lord, the one God and Father of all.

So you set your hope this night fully upon this grace that is coming to you. And may it come now! On the other hand, I must confess from my own experience that it does take 1,260 days from the first to the baptism of which I speak. But what is that to wait? It's only three and a half years from the first. So may the first take place tonight, because no one knows when it happens. Do not for one moment dwell upon what you have done in this world as any restraining power, because no one can tell me that he is innocent of unnumbered things of which he is ashamed. In my own case, I have a perfect example of one who could never have judged myself so kindly. I could never in eternity judge Neville that I know as kindly, as gently, as compassionately, as mercifully as I was judged to be what I became. So how on earth could I say to anyone that you aren't qualified! I didn't come to judge. I do not know what you did and, may I tell you, I don't care. But don't you put up a barrier because you did certain things of which you may be ashamed...that that is a delaying motion in your world. Forget it! Because when he shines his mercy upon you then all the past is wiped out. "Though your sins be as scarlet, they shall be white as snow" (Is. 1:18).

So it doesn't really matter. I'm not encouraging you to go out and violate your codes, no. But I'll tell you, you have a burden that you're carrying, that you shouldn't carry it. You're carrying a burden of things you have done or things you should have done that you did not do. And that burden...in your own mind's eye you think "I've got to unload it first, overcome it first, before I'm qualified." Not a thing could be further from the truth because you cannot *earn* the kingdom of heaven. You cannot acquire any merit towards it. So if you're carrying such a burden, just forget it if you can, and hope...

set your hope *fully* upon this regardless of what you've done. The Father, maybe this night, hovering over you…and you don't see him because you're immersed in water and don't see him, but he is incubating you and warming you into this that could actually break through the surface of the water. And so one day…and I hope it is in the immediate present…that he will come.

Now let us go into the Silence.

*   *   *

Q: (inaudible)

A: The ad will be in tomorrow's *Times*…a small little ad. It always comes out on Saturday on the religious page, and so to get within the ad, I cut the title down to *Wonder Working Power*, but I really mean *The Wonder Working Power of Attachment*. And it works miracles in this world. Everyone in the world who has succeeded, they have used it either knowingly or unknowingly. So I have the two titles. I couldn't now tell you the second one; I'll have to read it tomorrow morning. But I do know on Monday it's *The Wonder Working Power*.

No questions? Was it that clear? I hope so! Because I couldn't tell you anything lovelier than the story that comes just before the end… and this is the one that comes on the very last day of the 1,260 days that are allotted in scripture. On that day, you come up out of the water, and then the heavens really are rent, a translucency that has no circumference; and then you see him floating, looking at you so lovingly, in the form of a dove. Then you do exactly what you're told in Genesis that Noah did, you stick your hand out and he lights upon you. And then comes that affection and love that is indescribable, and the voice of God speaks.

Little did I know that in *The Dialogues of Buddha*, which I only recently read, that centuries before our story was told, he said that in the eyes of the gods human beings are stinking, disgusting, revolting, and are counted as such. Well, that is exactly what in her own wonderful way the voice of God spoke to me, but it was the most pleasant way to describe it. She said, "Men give off such an offense, a frightful offense that they avoid them, but he so loved you he penetrated the ring of offense." Well, the word offense would encompass all the terms used in *The Dialogues of Buddha*, but they are not as offensive as that one word…because it leaves you to use your own Imagination as to what are we that we offend. But Buddha said "stinking"…and this is the world of death. But one can get accustomed to anything. If you work in the stockyards in Chicago, I dare say that you could get accustomed to it and it would not be to you offensive when you went to work in the morning. You can go to any place and after a while of adjusting the thing doesn't offend. So we are adjusted to the world of death and it doesn't offend us. But those who are not, who are living in eternity and who contemplate the world of death, it *is* offensive.

Q: Traditionally, Neville, at least in my experience, water as been equated with Spirit. But your experience seems to indicate that water is synonymous with body, of this physical world.

A: I would say that Spirit to me, I equate Spirit with wind as I do in both Hebrew and Greek. You hear the wind and you can't deny it's a peculiar, unearthly wind. That is the current of air that you hear and you don't think of any other element but wind. Wind and Spirit are the same word in both Hebrew and Greek. But in water…I know in my own case when I experienced it, I came up out of the water. The reason I knew it…in spite of the transparency which would not allow me to see water, I knew it by reason of the floating of the Spirit, for he hovered over me. He actually hovered. But he's not a water bird; it's a dove. There it was on top of the water. So in rising, I came up out of the water.

So I know that Jesus is the personification of the redeemed. But man has taken Jesus to be a single little being when he really is the corporate body…he is God himself. As the word implies, Jesus is God, it's Jehovah, same root, Yod He Vau. But water to me is not Spirit. Water to me is simply just what is said here…the bodies are water. I am not a chemist, but I am told that almost 100 percent of the body is water. What actual percentage I do not know. But I do know I've seen an urn retuned to me after cremation when I cremated my dear friend Bob ___(??). Well, there was just a little handful of ash. He was a small man, but even if he weighed 300 pounds it would be no bigger. For all the others ___(??), it's simply water. So they may put it in a big urn for you, but when you open the top you're going to see just…like a few little ashes of cigar if you went right down to the end. It would be practically nothing left from the body after cremation. So out of the dust ___(??) and then comes the water ___(??) that second verse, "The Spirit of God hovers upon the water," and then everything begins to come up out of the water. So he's bringing up out of these the being that was buried with himself, as you're told in that wonderful 6th chapter of Romans. It's a marvelous…of course, the whole of Romans is written so orderly, the whole thing. From beginning to end it's the most orderly of the entire works as though this, if he never wrote anything else, this is it. But then he does elaborate on it in all the other letters… (Tape ends before Neville finishes.)

THE WONDER WORKING POWER OF ATTACHMENT

2/3/69

I hope you will find this subject tonight practical, very practical. It is "The Wonder Working Power of Attachment." To understand it let us go first to the greatest book in the world, the Bible. We are told in the Book of Joshua that "Wherever the sole of your foot shall tread upon I have given to you" (Josh.5:3).

Now you must understand who Joshua is if you would apply this principle. The word Joshua is the Hebrew form of the word Jesus, and Jesus is Jehovah…same root, Yod He Vau. The word means "Jehovah is salvation" or "Jehovah will save" or "Jehovah saves." So really, it is all to himself; it's not one being promising another, it's one being promising *himself*. God needs the dance of life and his dancers are also himself. We are the dancers but we are also God. God's name and himself are one: his eternal name is I AM. Could you be any place in this world and not know that you are? Before you know who you are or what you are or where you are, you do know that you are. So without voicing it you're saying "I am." That's God. Is there any place where God is not? There is no place where he is not and there is nothing that he is not. If there is something, then it would have to be God.

Now, "All things by a law divine in one another's being mingle." If you will accept this interpenetration seriously—and I'm speaking from experience—there are possibilities that are fabulous. You penetrate my brain, not only you but everything in the world. My apartment in this city seems, well, miles away, New York City 3,000 miles away, where I was born 5,000 miles away. I'm not denying that they are not here, but if I accept interpenetration then they're also in my brain. So if I desire to go tonight to where I was born, I may not have the means, I may not have the time, unnumbered things may stand between me and my desire. But if I accept interpenetration, I could while standing here be in my island home of Barbados. I could "enter into this image in my Imagination, approaching it on the fiery chariot of my contemplative thought." I've done it. I do not do it lightly any more, because I know from experience if I do it, having done it, I may now lose the desire, but I will be compelled to make the journey. Conditions will so arrange themselves I will be compelled to make that journey...so I do not treat it lightly.

Now, this is not just a journey in space. But anything in this world that you desire, I don't care what it is it now penetrates your brain and it's right here where you are wherever you are. I am not denying that Barbados is in what is called the outer world. But I know from my own experience that I really am, the being that I really am, is all Imagination. I also know that "God is man and exists in us and we in him...that the eternal body of man is the Imagination, and that is God himself" (Blake, *Annot. Berkeley, Laocoon*). If I, in Imagination will enter into any image in this world that I desire, if I will actually enter into it, there is no power in the world that can stop it from becoming an objective fact in my world, no power.

Now, what is the secret that makes it so? Reality is controlled by *feeling*. You find this in the greatest book in the world, in the 27th chapter of the Book of Genesis. All of these are states spoken of as individuals in scripture, but they are states of consciousness, all contained within you. The central character here is Isaac; and here he has two sons, one called Esau, clothed in the outer world. This room is Esau and everything in my objective world is Esau. He has a second son, his name is Jacob. All subjective states, my longings, my wishes, my desires, that's Jacob. Now, he turns to Jacob, who has clothed himself to disguise himself as an objective fact, and comes to his father, and the drama unfolds within me. The father said to him, "Come near that I may *feel* you, my son, whether you are really Esau or not." Then he said to him, "Are you really Esau?" and Jacob answered, "I am."

Put yourself into a state that is subjective, completely subjective, and then gather the mood that would be yours if it were objective fact. What would the *feeling* be like if it were really objective? How would you feel? And while clothed in that state, giving it all the sensory vividness you can possibly muster, all the tones of reality, making it as *real* as you possibly can, you feel it, and deceive yourself into the belief that the image into which you entered is really objective. Well, when he opened up his eyes (the man was blind)...and we are told that all of a sudden the objective world came back—Esau came back from the hunt and Jacob was blessed. He discovered he was *self*-deceived, but he could not take back the blessing that he gave to the subjective state. He was self-deceived, he did it purposely, and then he opened his eyes upon the objective world and it denied the reality of what he had done. But he still could not bring it back…it's on its way. It's going to supplant. The word Jacob means "supplant." It's going to supplant the objective fact that denies its existence. Then it becomes in turn Esau. And we go through life playing the part of you being Isaac with your two sons, an objective fact and a subjective feeling, un-reality. But you enter into the image of the subjective state.

Now this is how I do it. I've done it unnumbered times. I've told it in my books how I do it and told how others did it. I could stand here and shut out the world, and the easiest thing to do is to close my eyes so that I don't see. Because, if I keep the eyes open, well then, you remind me that I really am in this room and you are present and you are fact. But I don't want this, so I simply begin with the story of Isaac…he is blind. Well, to be blind is simply to shut the eyes so you don't see the outer world. And so Isaac is blind. Then while in this state, he imagines himself to be in the state that he desires to be in, and he feels himself into that state until *that* state becomes real to him… it seems real, he's in it. And then with the *inner* eye he sees the world as he would see it if it were true. How would I see the world if it were true? Well, he begins to visualize his world and senses it to be real, and the dream takes on its tones of reality. When to him he reaches a point of what I call *relief*— for of all the pleasures of the world, relief is the most keenly felt. When I feel it's done, I open my eyes and instantly Esau, the outer world, returns and tries to persuade me that what I did is unreal. But having done it time and time again, it may see unreal at the moment, but it is moving towards objective fulfillment…and no power in the world can stop it.

So this is what I mean by this wonderful wonder working power. It's all within your own wonderful human Imagination, for that is God. This promise to Joshua is God's promise to himself. There is no one to play the part but God. He conceived a poem, a beautiful poem and no one to play it—they existed only for him, not for themselves—and so God, the director, the author of the poem simply became the dancers himself. And his name is I Am. That's God's name: "That is my name forever and forever…and for all generations I will be known only as I AM" (Exod. 3:13-15). Before I say I am John or Neville or Peter or a man or a woman, I simply am. Now I clothe myself with what I would like to be. Rich, poor, known, unknown, anything in this world, simply clothe yourself in it and feel as you would feel if it were true, and then drop it. Open your eyes upon an objective world that denies the reality of what you have done, it doesn't matter. As you're told in scripture, "I have blessed you and I cannot take back my blessing." I felt that which was subjective to be objective, and it seemed to me to be real, and so I gave him a blessing…now I cannot take it back. So Esau went out disappointed, the outer world that is now is going to be supplanted. He's disappointed that it will be supplanted by something other than itself. His brother, the subjective state, will clothe itself in objectivity, and take the place. If you're poor and you've clothed yourself in the feeling of being secure, what feels secure to me it comes into your world and removes the objective insecurity. Well, the insecurity vanishes, disappointed that it didn't get the blessing to remain alive forever and forever. All these are states within you, all states of consciousness. Everything in this world is God made visible…there's nothing but God. There's no room for anything but God.

So, all things by this law divine in one another's being mingle. Go to the moon, as we have just circled it, is remote in space and yet it penetrates my brain and therefore it is there in my brain. Now I can't take you with me and show you the earth from the moon, but you can do it to yourself. You can be in any point in space that you can conceive and imagine yourself to be there and view the world as you would see it from that point in space. When I was actually denied freedom in the Army, I did not appeal. I couldn't appeal because the laws of Caesar denied my right to appeal beyond my commanding officer, and so I couldn't appeal it. But I could by this principle! So he said, "Disapproved" and that was final in the world of Caesar. But it wasn't final in the world of God and I simply assumed that very day that I was honorably discharged and in my apartment in New York City. That's 2,000 miles away from Camp Polk, Louisiana. So I gave it feeling. I, first of all, slept on this little cot in the barracks, but I assumed that I was on my own wonderful comfortable bed and I was *not* then on furlough. I made that very, very clear to my mind's eye that I was honorably discharged and now once more a civilian. Then I felt the little cot I felt it to be my bed. My wife is on the other bed in my Imagination. My little girl is in her bed. Then I got off the bed and I went to the window and looked out upon a familiar scene that could only be seen from my bedroom window, and that was the Holly Apartments across the way on Washington Square. I imagined I looked to 6th Avenue. I imagined I looked to Washington Square and then I walked through my familiar scenery, my living room, my dining room, kitchen, everything. Then I retired, went back to bed, got back in bed, and slept in my bed in New York City as though it were fact.

Now, a mystical experience happened that morning, but it need not happen. The chances are it will happen that you will not bring it back to consciousness but in my case it happened. I saw a sheet of paper and I saw a hand from here down and it held a pen. It scratched out the word "Disapproved" from this sheet of paper that resembled the application that I had made that day. Then it wrote in, in a very bold way, "Approved." Then the voice spoke to me, it was my own voice, and the voice said, "That which I have done I have done. Do nothing!" Then I woke in this world and it's four in the morning. So I did nothing, but nine days later the same one who disapproved my application called me in and I was that day honorably discharged from the Army and I did nothing. I knew exactly what I *had* done and it was moving towards its objective confirmation, and no power in the world could have stopped it. The same man who disapproved it was the man who approved it nine days later, without further application on my part. I was called into his presence and that was it. I can multiply these beyond number...not only in my own case but those who believed it as I told the story.

So I tell you, everything is possible to the individual if he knows who he is. You are the Joshua of that 5th book in the Bible, and Joshua is the Jesus of the New Testament, and Jesus of the New Testament is the Jehovah of the Old Testament, and that Jehovah, who is Joshua, who is Jesus, is your own wonderful human Imagination. When you say "I am," that is he. But as long as you see him as something other than yourself outside to whom you turn and pray, well then, you will not apply this principle. You simply give up all foreign gods, all idols, and come down to the one and only God, and his name is I AM. But if you say Jesus—trained as I was, born and raised in a Christian faith, and I still call myself Christian, I am a Christian—well, if I think of Jesus as I was trained, he's on the outside. I had to have this revelation and then to put it to the test and *prove* it to know who Jesus really is; and there never was another Jesus. There never was another Joshua, there never was another Jehovah. There's no place in this world for one other than God. He is actually the director of the great dance of life and all the dancers are himself...whether you play the part of a bum, that's God dancing the part of the bum...but you need not play the part of a bum. If you play the part of a billionaire that's God dancing to the tune of billions. If you play the part of anything, that's God...and there's nothing but God.

Now, nothing can act but where it is, only where it is. But where is it? If I am God, and I know that we are God, where would you go that God is not? If you make your bed in hell, God is there; if you make it in heaven, God is there, so where could I go that God is not? Everything penetrates me, but everything, therefore I don't have to go any place, it's all here. I simply adjust...adjust within myself and move from one state to another state. I don't have to travel to go to Barbados. I will go to Barbados if I make the adjustment here, that I do know.

It was a very cold September night in New York City and I had brought out my book *Your Faith is Your Fortune*, and the usual crowd...usually in excess of a thousand. I gave three lectures a week on Wednesdays, Fridays and Sundays, Sunday nights. There was no charge just a voluntary offering, so naturally there was no place big enough. I rented a church just off Time Square that sat about 1,100 and it was always crowded. But this night because of the snow, twelve or fourteen inches of snow, people couldn't get through and that night we had not more than a 150 or 200 and it was my first book, in the true sense of the word, *Your Faith is Your Fortune*. Well that night, maybe fifty copies were sold. I ran the presses on five thousand. That night because of the cold and the snow I said, "Oh, to be in Barbados...just to be with all the palm trees and the warmth and odors of the tropics." I went to bed in my place in New York City and felt myself in my mother's home in Barbados, even to the hearing of the moving of the leaves, that tropical atmosphere. I could smell it and I could see it...went sound asleep in that atmosphere.

Then came a cable from my family saying that they knew I couldn't come because of the lack of transportation; for no planes in those days were flying, war was on, and mother was dying and if I could possibly make it, if any ship was coming, this would be the only time to see her. My wife and I sailed within twenty-four hours on the one ship that was moving out, the old Argentina. I had put myself in Barbados and I had to fulfill it, and cancel all my other plans, for my wife and I had sent off a check to Maine to reserve accommodations for the summer. In fact, the year would be '41, not '42, and we had to cancel that because this was under compulsion and I had to make the trip. So I don't treat it lightly. When I say you adjust yourself to a certain state and make that state real, you feel it...for reality really is controlled by *feeling*. The day will come that all we now think to be laws of nature and laws of science and laws of this, they will discover they aren't so at all. Feeling will modify or even void them, and they aren't so at all.

So this wonder-working power is all within you if you know who you are. If you're going to get down on your knees and pray to an external God, you don't know the power. If you ___(??) you are, whether you be in church or in a bar, doesn't make any difference, wherever you are, God is there, and wherever God is it's holy. Take off your shoes for the place on which you stand is holy ground, no matter where you are. Let no one tell you because you're in church you are in a more holy place than if you were actually now in what is called a brothel. For if *you* are there and you know who you are, then you know the holy place. And while standing there or sitting there you can make an adjustment all within yourself and then give it the tones of reality, give it all the sensory vividness that you can possibly muster. You *feel* it. If you can feel it and make it real, when you open your eyes upon the objective world and it denies the reality of what you just did subjectively, it doesn't matter: it's moving toward its fulfillment!

The Return of Glory

Everything in this world works in this strange and wonderful way. Most of us who are doing it are totally unaware of what we are doing. As Blake said, "I will never be certain that it was not some woman treading in the winepress who started the subtle change in men's minds, or that the passion because of which so many countries have been given to the sword did not begin in the mind of some shepherd boy, lighting up his eye for a moment before it ran upon its way." Someone in a dungeon feeling themselves, well, abused by society, and while they're there they simply imagine and imagine, and carry on within themselves what they would like to happen to those who placed them there. The ones who placed them there think that now we are safe because he is in the dungeon, and they do not realize that that one in the dungeon is going to actually *cause* the convulsion of the world. Who knows who tonight is actually carrying on in their Imagination…you can't stop them…who in the world can stop them? Well, in their Imaginations they are simply conjuring numberless things that may be unlovely. But if I know there is only God, who in this world would I want to hurt? No man could ever in eternity shoot another. He could only shoot himself who is God. There is no other. So I think I'll rub him out with a bullet, so I shoot him and I think that's the end of it. It is only myself that I did it to.

There is nothing but God; he is the one and only reality. This is the great shema, the great confession of faith of Israel: "Hear, O Israel! The Lord our God the Lord is one" (Deut.6:4). If you keep that in mind and never wander from it, you can't go wrong. If God is one then I can't be another. I *can't* be another. It's the one body fragmented, because all use the same name: I say "I am." So the whole vast world is God fragmented. And now the poem will become alive and he gathers himself, not another—but this time they are *living* stones, not dead stones—all back into the same destroyed temple, for the body of God is the great temple. That one body deliberately shattered itself and all became simply one body. Now as I gather it one by one back into the same body, the body becomes more luminous, more transparent, more creative, for God is ever-expanding. People speak of an absolute, an absolute what? This is an ever-expanding creative being that is God.

So this wonder-working power is in your own wonderful human Imagination, that is God. "Man is all Imagination and God is man, and exists in us and we in him. The eternal body of man is the Imagination, and that is God himself" (Blake, *Annot. to Berkeley/The Laocoon*). If you are a Christian, you call it Jesus; if you are a Jew, you call it Jehovah. Well, these names are beautiful, only tradition has it that they are *other* than yourself, and you bow before them and speak to them as idols. But if I could only supplant this and call it I AM, my own wonderful human

109

Imagination, that's God. I can't get away from it. Where can I go that I am not imagining? Where in this world could I go and still not be one who is aware that I am? A little child comes into the world...it doesn't know who it is, where it is, or what it is, but it knows that it is. Well, that's what I mean by God, this wonderful Awareness, this wonderful Imagination.

Now, if you take it seriously, and I do hope you will, this interpenetration, that I don't have to move from wherever I am to be where I want to be, because all things penetrate me. Everything in this world penetrates my brain. I can't see the sun if the sun didn't penetrate me. I cannot be aware of anything good, bad or indifferent if it didn't penetrate my brain. Therefore, at once it is within and still seemingly in the outer world. But I don't have to make the journey in the outer world to get it; I simply adjust myself within myself. For no matter what I behold "Though it appears without, it is within, in my Imagination of which this world of mortality is but a shadow" (Blake, *Jerusalem*, Plt. 71). So I simply adjust within myself. When I do it with *feeling* to the point of *relief*, where I can feel relief, it's a committed act and it's done. Then in a way that no one knows I'll be led across some bridge of incidence, some series of events that will lead me from where I was up to the fulfillment of what I did within myself. I don't have to consciously build the bridge; it simply unfolds in my world. I will meet a seeming stranger, I will meet others, and all will add up towards the fulfillment of that which I did within myself. On reflection, I may even give them the credit...maybe they want to feel that they had much to do with my success, all right, give them the credit. But I must always bear in mind they are only playing the part they had to play because all things by a law divine in one another's being mingle. So they penetrated me, I penetrate them, and we are one. If they can play the part necessary for that rung in the ladder that I must walk, well then, they'll play the part without their knowledge, without their consent. I don't think of them as individuals, I just think of what I want as an *end*.

So if I would really steer my thoughts wisely in this world, I must be aware of my imaginal activity, or at any rate, the "end" which I am shaping. For without a purpose, without an end, there is no vital life. Vital life would be an impossibility, as impossible as to expect a light bulb to give off light when it is not attached to the power line: the power line is I AM. Well, what am I? Well now, that is the light...as I name it that is the bulb. Is it attached to the power line? Then it will become luminous, it will become objective in my world.

So here this night, dream nobly. I don't care what the dream is, but make it a noble dream, because everyone in your world is yourself pushed out. Just take some noble concept of life that you would like to experience and without asking anyone whether it's possible, without asking anyone to aid you in the fulfillment of it, adjust yourself within yourself and you don't have to do anything. This very night, just simply move within yourself and feel it. Then give it reality—feel what it would be like if it were true. Look at your world from this point. And then open your eyes upon the objective world that denies it, doesn't matter. Read the story carefully when you read in the 27th chapter of the Book of Genesis…but bear in mind who the characters are: all the characters of scripture are *personifications* of eternal *states*, not persons as we are. They are states, eternal states, and learn to discriminate between the state and the occupant of the state. So Isaac is a state and his sons are states; and you always have the two sons—your present objective world and your present longing which is subjective.

Now the story is to put the subjective, if you really desire it, into the place of the objective by clothing yourself with the subjective and giving it tones of objective reality. Then it supplants! It's done! And you go from there to another state and another state, and one day you'll reach the state called Jesus. You will have the story that is described in the books of the gospels, the four gospels, that entire story from beginning to end will recreate itself within you, and then you'll know who you are. Everything said of him will be recreated within you, casting you in the central role. Not an observer, no spectator—you are the star in the drama from beginning to end. Then you will know who you are. The story is truer than those who talk about it and teach it dream it is. Our priesthoods of the world haven't the slightest concept of the depth of this story and what it really is. One day, everyone is going to recreate within himself the story of Jesus, and then he will know who he is. And Jesus and Jehovah are one…and only this saves man from this world of Caesar. You are redeemed from within yourself by recreation at a certain moment in your life of the story of Christ Jesus.

Now let us go into the Silence.

*   *   *

I know it's not the easiest thing in the world if you've never heard anything like it before…to suddenly accept this premise, but I tell you I'm speaking from experience. I am not theorizing and I am not speculating.

Q: That woman in the dungeon you were speaking of imagining all these horrible things, suppose there were someone on the outside knowing she was imagining these terrible things, could the other person conquer? There might be a clash…

A: Well, no I would not think that there is such a person, but I'm not denying that there are such people in the world who feel resentful if any good happens to another. For instance, I can sympathize; it's so easy to sympathize. How many of us can *empathize*? You go into a bar and someone has lost a friend or just notified that their son was killed in Vietnam, and the whole neighborhood comes to commiserate. They will simply show all their sympathy. The same family, now, let it be known that they just won a sweepstake ticket for a half-million dollars and you find enmity. You don't find empathy, where they all want to run over and rejoice with her. But you say, "Why didn't it happen to me? Why should she get it? She smokes, she drinks, she carouses...I know things about her." All these things happen and no one empathizes with her, but they're willing to sympathize with her. So we haven't actually exercised within us that quality of empathy.

So I wouldn't think of someone who may be doing it. Let me think only in terms of myself, because it's one anyway. I cannot deny the fact that this shattered being, fragmented as God is into unnumbered centers of awareness that there are centers though God, not knowing who he is or she is, exercise it unknowingly and in an unlovely manner. Well, let me be concerned with what I am doing rather than what I think the other may be doing.

Q: (inaudible) To that degree could you not...?

A: Well, you simply would modify, but you can't stop someone from actually exercising their unlovely ideas. The other person would say, "I only imagined it, therefore that isn't real" and they don't believe they are the cause of convulsions. I can't conceive that a drop of rain, that a vibration, that a patch of color is not a miracle produced by an imaginal activity. *Everything* is the result of an imaginal activity. God is all Imagination and so is man, because they are one. Look into the world and see if there is something that wasn't first imagined. The room is real, but before we call it reality it was first imagined, the dress you wear, your hair, everything about you, was first *only* imagined and then it became what we call reality, a proven fact. But it's preceded by a cause and the cause was an imaginal act.

Q: (inaudible) (concerning Esau and Jacob)

A: The story is that they both were in the same womb together...that Rebecca felt a conflict within herself. Well, I am Rebecca, and I'm also Isaac, I am Jacob, and all the characters of the Bible. Well, there is a conflict in everyone who has a desire that is not realized. So what is now realized is his Esau...it's the objective world that's clothed in hair. He was covered in hair all over. Well, there's nothing more external to man than hair. You may not see it, but you put it under a magnifying glass his whole body is a forest. Sometimes it becomes very obvious and if he didn't have a human face, they'd think he was a monkey because he's covered all over with hair. They said that Esau came out and he was covered all over with hair. It's showing you that the external state is Esau. It comes first in a man's world; then Jacob came after him holding onto the heel of his brother. When Jacob came out he was called Jacob because he was a supplanter; he supplanted his brother in the affections of God. God preferred Jacob to Esau…in fact, he said "I hate Esau, but Jacob I have loved" as told us in the last book of the Old Testament.

So here, the conflict is taking place within me. Two souls are locked within my breast—one to heaven doth aspire and one to earth doth cling. The eternal story, whether you are taking the story of Faust or you're taking the story of the Bible…but I prefer the story of the Bible. And Rebecca wonders, "Why does this thing take place within me?" And then before they came out, judgment was passed upon them, that one who was not yet born I hate, and the other one who was not yet born I love. Well now, that…I go through the world with that. And remember Isaac is blind. It's a very strange thing, but you'll find the same story repeating itself all the way through.

So, I have a desire but the desire isn't realized. What is in its place I would like to rub it out. A person tonight desires to be happily married and they're not happily married…that's Esau. They'd like to be *happily* married. Well, *if* they were happily married, that other state would have to vanish, so they put themselves into a state of being blissfully happy, proud of the new name that they bear, and live in that state as though it were true. Well, they open their eyes upon the world and what they see denies the reality of what they've just done. But let them be faithful to this subjective fact, which is not now an objective one, and tomorrow it will become the objective fact supplanting the present objective state of singleness or barrenness, or call it what you wish. This is the law, this is the principle.

So, all these are eternal states. I know that the entire Bible as I've seen it in vision is eternal states. And yet when you see the state it's a person…but you know in vision that it's a state. But you as you see it, you are the power and you animate it. And you don't have to ask, "Who are you?" The name is automatic—Abraham is Abraham whether you see him or I see him, and yet it's a state. Moses is a state. All these are states of consciousness that man has been taught to believe that they are secular history. It's not secular history. The Bible is simply supernatural from beginning to end; it is speaking of an entirely different world.

But man has been taught to believe that all these things are part of the world of Caesar and they're not. You and I were expelled from a garden of bliss purposely. In a state of innocence we came out into the world of experience and we go back *awakened* Imagination. Well now, the expulsion is to see ourselves in an external world where everything that is real is external to ourselves. And that had to be reversed so that eventually there's a complete reversal that takes place in the Bible: "The first shall be last, the last first." So the first son is denied and the second son takes his place. And so, something takes place within me when I'm born from above and I see the reality is within and not without at all. I was ___(??) I am producing the reality without. So the whole thing is a complete reversal within me *after* I am born from above.

So I am pushed out. Well, this is the "pushed out" state, where everything seems to be completely independent of my perception of it and external to myself; when eventually the whole thing is turned around and "All that I behold, though it appears without, it is within, in my Imagination of which this world of mortality is but a shadow." So here, we are actually living scripture, but scripture is not what the world tells you that it is. And here, if this world isn't horrible enough when you think of all the nonsense that people imagine, and our priests who are supposed to be our teachers had to go and invent hell. It isn't bad enough, so they invent hell.

Q: When is the Sabbath? In our imaginal activity when do we rest?

A: When do we rest? Having done it, you are not concerned. You know it must come to pass. Having done it, you simply drop it. If I plant in confidence a seed in my garden today, I don't pick it up tomorrow morning to see how it's coming. I leave it in confidence that it contains within itself a pattern of itself and therefore it must come out, bearing witness of the nature of the seed I planted. So I don't dig it up. I walk in confidence that that's done, and I'm too busy planting other things.

Q: In your own experience have you found a reaction within yourself that tells you when you have done the imaging process sufficiently to bring into reality that which you have done?

A: Well, I tell you that …did you hear the question? When you've done it, is there something within you that tells you, you really have done it and therefore it will come to pass? In my own case it's a sense of relief. It's a creative act and this is a sense of relief. But beyond that moment of relief you can't continue in the act…it's something within you. In fact, I would suggest to anyone, try it and fall asleep in the act. Just put yourself into it, and then if it's only a little nap of, say, one minute, a few seconds, so you could drop it. It's the dropping of it. If you hold onto it still thinking, "Well, did I do it?" then you didn't do it. So you get into a state and all of sudden you fall asleep. You may find yourself waking with a huge big snore. Others will think, "Well, what's wrong?" Now at that moment you simply drop it. It's something you practice...you just practice it. But it works! I'm telling you it just will not fail you.

Q: You get sort of bored with it if you don't fall asleep. Well, you can't do it any more.

A: Well, I don't use the word boredom with it. Can you put yourself into a mood, a receptive mood, where instead of being a petition, as people think it is, it's communion with self. As you are told in the Psalms, "Commune with our own heart upon your bed and be still" (Ps. 4:04). So I'm communing with self, because I can't turn to another asking the other to help me. You get to the point that you just can't do it...that you cannot ask another. You cannot turn to any being, whether it be your ideal of Jesus or your ideal of this state or your ideal of something else, you can't. It's all communion with self. You're told that in the 4th Psalm, "Be still," all right, "then commune with your own heart upon your bed." Well now, what would the feeling be like...just what would it be like? Catch the *mood* and then try to sleep.

Q: When you do it over again, haven't you had the experience of boredom?

A: Boredom? I presume I've been bored...certainly, I've been bored.

Q: The first time around it was exhilarating. You get such a feeling, and then you go over it the next night or day and that for some reason...

A: No, well, I don't do it beyond the first. I don't plant the seed over and over. No, I just do it once. When I do it, I do it. And then I *know* I've done it. I have a memory so I know I did it. So if I did it, the thing is done! Now, some seeds will come up overnight; other seeds will take a year, other seeds a different length of time. We know in our animal life, a little child comes into the world at the end of nine months after pregnancy. Well, a horse takes twelve months, the sheep takes five months, a chicken takes twenty-one days. So there are different intervals. As you plant something you always have a time interval for it to mature in the world.

Q: Your books are confusing because you said night after night you went to sleep thinking of something lovely...

A: If I am telling the story that someone else told me, I must tell it in their language without altering it to fit a certain pattern. So in *The Law and The Promise* I told forty case histories and not one was my own. I told my own in other books. Therefore, if someone writes me a letter, I can't modify or change that letter because I told them I would not change it, but that I would conceal their identity by using only the initials. So the forty letters that I received, in fact, I've received hundreds, and from the hundreds I picked out forty, using only the initials of those who wrote them; and I didn't add one word or change anything from the letter that I received, because that's the way it came to me. If I tell the story as I should have told it…I think I did say this is how this one did it. If I add a little poem to it just to lift it somewhat—not in the body of the letter but either preceding or following the letter—but I told the letter just as I received it. I did not in any way change it in *The Law and The Promise*.

Q: Are the limits to imagining self-imposed? For example, in a move one might make to a different locale. You know very little about the locale and it's difficult to imagine much about it in terms of what you know of Barbados and your return there. When you start imagining this scene in the locale where you will be when you feel you are limited, are these self-imposed?

A: The Bible places no limit on the power of Imagination. Listen to the words carefully, "Whatever you desire, when you pray believe that you have received it, and you will," the 11th chapter, the 24th verse of the Book of Mark. There is no limit placed upon that promise, none whatsoever. If you can *believe* it, well then, it's done…it promises it will be done. Man places the limit because "I know no one to whom I could turn to feel that I have a hundred thousand dollars. I have no power to leave it to you. I have no friend that I think wealthy enough to put me in his will who had that sort of money, and how could I ever get a hundred thousand dollars?" So, in other words, he says no to what he wants. But there is no limit placed upon principle. Man places the limit. Yet everyone in the world that has reached any point, almost everyone at birth had nothing, and no one would have put a dime on a bet that he would ever become something. So here, we have it before us every day, but we didn't know about that. We know now. But look how many ___ (??). We always try to find something to justify our own limitations, but the limit is placed by us.

Q: How can you imagine on something that is completely unknown to you?

A: If it's unknown then you wouldn't think of it.

Q: Say a move to Chicago and you've never been there and know nothing about it, where do you go from here?

A: Well, if Chicago is 2,000 miles from here and it's east of us, if I stood here now and adjust myself to an area that I would say is Chicago, I would think of a city I know well, Los Angeles, and see it 2,000 miles to the west of me. If Los Angeles is 2,000 miles to the southwest of where I'm standing then I must be in Chicago.

Good night.

THE MAKER AND THE MAKER OF THINGS

2/7/69

___(??) the very platform right on this level of Caesar. The subject is concerning the making of things in this world. There is a Maker and we are called upon to test this Maker. That which appears as made points to an activity that does not appear. As we are told, "What we see was made out of things which do not appear" (Heb. 11:3).

Now, I am asked to test this principle. So in Paul's letter to the Corinthians he said, "Test yourselves"...first of all, "Examine yourselves, to see whether you are holding to your faith. Test yourselves. Do you not realize that Jesus Christ is in you?—unless indeed you fail to meet the test" (2 Cor. 13:5). So tonight we want to test this principle, for he tells us that "By him all things were made and without him was not anything made that was made" (Jn. 1:3). And this presence that makes everything is *within us*. Now I must find him and put him to the test, for I'm called upon to test him. It didn't say he makes only the good but everything—good, bad or indifferent.

So I must now really test him, this presence. I tell you I have tested him and I know who he is. He is my own wonderful human Imagination. That is Jesus Christ...there never was another Christ. There never will be another... my own wonderful human Imagination. When I say "my" I'm speaking of all of us. As Blake said, "I know of no other Christianity and of no other gospel than the liberty of both body and mind to exercise the divine art of Imagination. Imagination the eternal world into which we shall all go after these vegetable mortal bodies are no more." And then he adds, "The apostles knew of no other gospel than this wonderful human Imagination that creates everything in this world."

Now how does he create? John Stuart Mill defined causation in this manner: "Causation," said he "is the assemblage of phenomena which occurring some outer phenomena commences and begins to appear in this world." To put it in our language, I would say, causation is the assemblage of imaginal states implying the fulfillment of what we desire. If now we can set it in motion, activating it, it will produce that which the assemblage implies. Its potency is in its *implication*. Now, you and I are confronted every moment in time with a new problem. As H. G. Wells said, "All life throughout all the ages is nothing more than a continuing solution to a continuous synthetic problem." You and I think if I only had x-number of dollars I could live for the rest of my earthly days comfortably. So I map the whole thing out. I think that's going to do it…but it won't do it. I have it all set, then comes something penetrating my wonderful setup, like inflation or the unforeseen, and it disturbs my wonderful ___(??) and makes me now conceive an imaginal solution to this continuous problem. I will not in eternity find a set state, not in this world. So I think if I had so much money I could live beautifully and then all of a sudden it doesn't work, it doesn't fit, because something penetrates it, inflation or this, that or the other, and all of sudden the whole thing is disturbed forcing me now to use my Imagination, my creative power, to construct some imaginal solution to this new problem.

This synthetic problem is defined in the dictionary as "the compiling of separate elements which produces a new form." So something penetrates my form, and then it forces me with this new form to conceive a new solution to that form. Now this is how we do it. I'm confronted with any problem I don't care what it is. I look at the problem, I don't duck it I see it. Now, what is the solution to that problem? Suppose I were in jail, well, the solution would be to be out of jail and not ___(??), to have someone simply discharge me for reasons I need not know, but I am out of jail. I'm sleeping at home and I'm not listening to anyone knocking at the door to re-arrest me. If I were not in jail and I were free, where would I sleep? I would sleep at home. Well then, while in jail sleeping, I assume I am at home sleeping. I construct a scene implying the fulfillment of my desire.

You say, "Well, will it work?" I know it works. In San Francisco a few years ago this lady rose in the audience and she said, "My brother has been sentenced to six months hard labor in the Army. I don't know what he did, but something he did and he is sentenced. He tells me he is innocent." I said, "I'm not asking you whether he is innocent or not, what do you want?" She said, "I want him set free." I said, "Were I you…would he come to your place if he were free?" "Oh yes he would. That's exactly where he would come." Well, she went home and she simply imagined she heard the doorbell ringing downstairs and she imagined that it was her brother. She rushed down the stairs, flung open the door, and here is her brother standing a free man. She did that until it took on all the tones of reality it seemed so natural to her. One week later while seated upstairs the doorbell rang and she rushed downstairs, threw the door open and there's her brother. I asked no question as to how, but he was discharged. Who brought this action or who discharged him I don't know, but he was not running away from that prison. If they simply heard the case over again and found that they had faulted, I do not know. I only know she rose the following Sunday in my audience in San Francisco and told that story. In one week he was out and just as she had imagined. Now if she didn't know this principle, she would have remained at home and stewed and stewed for six months until he'd done the time and then he was out.

I tell you, everyone, use your Imagination, for that is Jesus Christ and by him all things are made and without him there was not anything made that was made (Jn. 1:3). You name one thing that wasn't first imagined, just name it. Tell me something in this world. You might point to the mountains or to the earth, to the stars, but is Imagination limited to this level? Can't you conceive of levels…and levels of Imagination? Your dream proves that and your visions certainly prove that. You go into divine imagining, same as human imagining only on higher levels. This whole vast world is sustained by divine imagining, and our imagining and divine imagining aren't two but one. We are keyed low. So we are called upon to exercise this talent of ours, this power.

Now, faith is not complete until through experiment it becomes experience. That is, on this level you can experiment with the great promises of God, and God is your own wonderful human Imagination. You can on this level experiment with all that he tells you: "Whatever you desire, believe that you have it and you will." You can experiment with that. So, faith is not complete until through experiment it becomes experience, and then you are on sure ground and you can walk safely. If you know an unseen objective, something that's seen differently, and then you constructed a certain scene, an assemblage of mental states which would imply the fulfillment of it; then you activated it…you entered into the very center of it and you imagined the whole thing is taking place, and you felt all the tones of reality concerning this, and then you close the book on it. Then it happens in a way you did not devise…it seemed to come into your world across a bridge of incidence that you did not rationalize. You didn't construct the bridge. You simply had to walk across this bridge to the fulfillment of what you had done. After you've done it, repeat it, and then try it again, and it worked, well, then you are on sure ground. You know exactly what to do whenever you are confronted with any problem. You see the problem, you don't duck, you look at it, and then you construct some imaginal scene which would imply the solution, the fulfillment. Having activated it, you simply drop it and let it come into this world. And it does! If you are so sure of that then you can tell it and share it with others.

But many of us, I speak now of the Christian faith, and it's so fatally easy to make the acceptance of Christianity a substitute for living by it. So, I say I'm a Christian. All right, you say you're a Christian. Tonight, in New York City alone there are one million on relief and I dare say that ninety percent of them will tell you if you ask them that they are Christians. So they accept the very word "I'm a Christian" but they do not know the beginning of Christianity. For, I am told that Christ is not on the outside: "Do you not know that Jesus Christ is *in you*?" that's what Paul challenges us with in that 13th chapter of 2nd Corinthians. If I say yes to that then I can't look for any Christ on the outside. I can't go seeking anything, for I'm told in the Book of John that when he appears I am like him (1 Jn. 3:2). Can I go looking for someone who really looks like me? When he appears I am like him. Well, I better start looking for him now and Paul tells us where to look for him: "Do you not realize that Jesus Christ is in you?" Well, if he's in me and he makes me and he makes all things, I've got to find what in me makes all things. Then I discover, why, it's my Imagination. That I imagined this… that when I was a boy I dreamt of leaving little Barbados, unschooled, with no background, and coming to America. Didn't want to go to England, I didn't want to go to any part of the world, I just wanted America. So when I was seventeen, I became so restless that my parents put me on the boat and put $600 in my pocket and sent me off to America, knowing, so they thought, I would come back after I spent the money. That would take me no time they thought, spend the 600 and come on back. Well, that's forty-odd years ago…the year was 1922. Oh, I've gone back many a time on vacation, but certainly not to live. I've gone back time and again just to see the family and to have a nice vacation.

But this I felt as a boy…I wanted it, so I began to dream I would live in America. When they came home I wanted to hear every American voice. Englishmen came, Frenchmen came, all kinds of people came, because it's a little island with ships coming and going. But it was simply the Americans that fascinated me. And so, eventually through my fascination I had to come to America. Can you become enamored over something I don't care what it is? So you say, "Well, I would like to be" and you name it. Now, if you would become that then how would you see the world if it were true? Then in your Imagination begin to see the world as you would see it if it *were* true. If you do it in this manner, no power in the world can stop you from becoming it, but no power! Well, if it becomes true, haven't you found Christ? Or the words of scripture are false: "By him all things were made and without him there was not anything made that was made." Well, if that is true and

I have found a Maker in me that produced a certain thing—I have done it numberless times; I've taught it to others and they have done it numberless times—haven't we found him? Haven't we found who Jesus Christ really is?

Now listen to the words, "Unless you believe that I am he, you will die in your sins" (Jn. 8:24). This is not a man on the outside talking to you. This is something taking place *in you*: unless I believe that I am he I die in my sins. Oh, I know in the world of Caesar when one wears the garment of flesh even though they have completely experienced the entire drama of Christ, when they tell it, the world just simply puts their hands over their ears to shut out this blasphemy. Because they firmly believe that he is coming from without if he ever comes and that he came from without and died 2,000 years ago and that is an historical fact. They can't believe in the true Jesus Christ, that when he comes to any individual he comes *within* that individual, unfolding the entire story as recorded in scripture. When the individual has the entire story recorded in him, or re-experiences in him, he knows who he is. There's only *one* story and only *one* being plays the part and that is God. "God alone acts and is in all existing beings or men" (Blake, *A Memorable Fancy*). Only God plays that part and that story is told in the gospel, which is the fulfillment of the Old Testament. So if the individual has the entire story unfolding within him and finds himself cast in the central role—that he is not a spectator observing the drama, he *is* the central actor, and God alone acts—then he knows who he is.

Then he goes out and he tells it. But while he wears the garment of flesh they will not listen and they will say to him "You have a devil. You must have a devil because you're blaspheming the name of God." He said, "My Father is he whom you call God and I know my Father and you know not your God." He knew his origin and his destiny, and no one would believe him because he wore a garment of flesh. But he knew the entire story unfolding within him and the whole thing awakened within him. Those who heard it were not expecting that kind of revelation, so they simply would shut him out as one who blasphemed the name of God. But here, within me I hear it: Unless I believe that I am he I will continue missing my mark in life, which means "sinning." For "to sin" means "to miss the mark," miss the goal. So I have a goal...if I don't believe I am really the Maker, the Creator of all things, and I pray to another, I am missing the mark. So the words are, "Unless you believe that I am he, you die in your sins."

So anyone who will not believe...you go to bed tonight...you must assume that you are *already* what you want to be. That assumption though at the moment is denied by you reason, denied by your senses and is false, if persisted in will harden into fact. This is how we create. I create and make something out of things that do not appear. So I assume that I am...and to prove that I am it in my mind's eye I bring a circle of friends to congratulate me and allow them to congratulate me on my good fortune. Then I sleep having received the congratulations of those who would empathize with me were it true. So they actually believe because they now congratulate me they have witnessed my good fortune. Then I sleep in that assumption. I wake tomorrow morning, I'm in the same environment, but I've set things in motion and now some bridge of incidence, some series of events will appear in my world which will compel me to move across that bridge up to the fulfillment of that which I have assumed.

Well, if it happens and I repeat it, and share it with another, the other tries it and it works, then what does it matter what the world thinks? I have found him and I have found the one the world worships as someone on the outside. They make pictures of him and it doesn't resemble the Maker. You make a picture of Jesus Christ, hang it on the wall, bow before it, and it's so unlike the artist who painted it or who wrote it, and it's not that at all. "When he appears, we will be like him" (1Jn.3:2). That's what we are told in the first epistle of John: whenever he appears then I am just like him. So I know from my own experience when he appears the drama as told in scripture unfolds within me. You are the one playing the central part and only God acts. God alone acts and is in all existing beings and men, so he simply puts himself into the central part and unfolds the eternal drama in you; then you know that you are God.

Last year in San Francisco just before the first meeting (I gave ten lectures) and this lady came to me and she said, "You know, Dr. ___(??) died suddenly. He was sitting quietly and all of a sudden he dropped over and he was gone. I always thought that you and Dr. ___(??) were the greatest in the world teaching." I said nothing. I didn't know Dr. ___(??). I saw him in book stores when I went into bookstores in New York City. I met him just casually, but I never once heard him speak. She sat in the audience and I started on the concept that man is God and God is man. "Man is all Imagination, and God is man, he exists in us and we in him; that the eternal body of man is the Imagination, and that is God himself" (Blake, *Annot. to Berkeley; Laocoon*). Then I told the story of a lady who is now departed this world, how she had this experience where she was in this enormous room with these huge pillars, alone, one chair in which she sat. Then she noticed a carriage, not drawn by a horse, self-propelled, and it came up. Then the door opened and I stepped out with a briefcase, wearing a cape. I came through this door into this enormous area and I began to proclaim the power of God, sheer power. And she said to herself, "Why that's Neville and yet it is God. It's Neville and it's God… Neville and it's God." And then when I got through, without recognizing her I turned and then as though by appointment the carriage came back into sight and I stepped in and it vanished.

Well, it so impressed her that she wrote me the letter and told me. I simply told her that everyone is destined to discover that he is God, everyone in the world. There's nothing but God. God conceived it. There was no one to play it and he played the whole thing himself like conceiving a glorious poem that exists only for the one who conceived it, the poet…it doesn't exist for itself. But he so loved it he wants all the characters to exist for themselves and finding no one to play it he buries himself…he dies to all that he really is and takes on the limitations of the characters. Then he goes through all the tribulations and then slowly awakens in all the characters. Now he's individualized but he is God. He is still Neville, the character in the play, but he is now God. He is still John, he is still Jim, he is still everyone, but he is God in the very end. This is the story.

Well, she wouldn't come back after the meeting to greet me and never came back the other nine. She was so shocked, yet a few minutes before she is telling me I am the greatest in teaching the Truth. She hoped I would conform to her little concept of what Jesus is and what God is, and I didn't. I came right out and boldly proclaimed that we were all God, but all are not yet aware of it, and that we become aware of it when the story as told in the gospels concerning Jesus Christ, who is buried in everyone, suddenly awakens in the individual. When he awakens, the story unfolds in that individual and that individual then knows that he is Jesus Christ. For if Christ is in me, where is he? "Do you not realize," said Paul, "that Jesus Christ is *in you*?—unless, indeed, you fail to meet the test" (2 Cor. 13:5).

So I take a test and prove him on this level. I want to go some place and I can't afford the money, I can't afford the time, and conditions around me deny that I can do it. So I put myself there any way, just as though I had made the trip, and I sleep in the assumption that I am where I would be if I made the trip. Then everything changes and compels the trip, the money comes, the time is allowed, everything comes and I make the trip. Then where is Jesus Christ? Was he not my Imagination? Well, that's what scripture teaches. But man has taken this wonderful story, personified it into one little being, and then has made of him a little icon so that all men bow before a little man-made god when the true God is your own wonderful human Imagination…that's God.

Now, if all things are made by him, and you can this night imagine something that is not now a fact, and persist in that imaginal act, and tomorrow it becomes fact, haven't you found him? Well now, having found him don't give him up. As you are told in the end of the drama, "Now that you have found me, let these men go, but don't let me go." At the very end of the drama they're looking for him and no one knows him. One knows him and he betrays him. Well, to betray someone you must first know that one's secret. I can't betray you if I don't know your secret. So the one who knows the secret betrays him and that one is himself. It's self-revealed; he reveals himself. Unless God reveals himself, how would you know him? So he turns to all the others who did not know him and said, "Now that you have found me don't let me go, but let all these go." Let everything on the outside go, but don't let me go. The drama is within oneself. If I find him in myself, then don't, no matter what argument the wise men of the world give me don't listen if it is in conflict with what I have found. I have found Christ and Christ is my own wonderful human Imagination.

I may tomorrow forget it and be penetrated by the rumors of the world. Then suddenly the body collapses and I suffer the penetration because I am penetrated by something that disturbs the mold. I must then instantly re-establish my harmony by imagining what I would feel like if things were as I desired them to be to get back into that state. I can't stop the penetration. I'm living in this wonderful, fabulous world. As we brought out in the last lecture that to perceive you, you must first penetrate my brain; therefore, at once you are within me and at the same time without and independent of my perception. But you are within me. That's enough for me. If you are within me, I don't have to go searching for you. Everything penetrates me, like cities and mountains and rivers, everything, or I would not be aware of them. It must penetrate my brain for me to become aware of them. So at the moment of penetration it's within you even though it still maintains a certain independence of my perception of it and it is without.

Now, if I will treat this inter-penetration seriously, oh what possibilities! I don't need to go any place other than where I stand now to adjust myself to be elsewhere. For if I am all Imagination I must be wherever I am in Imagination. So someone penetrates me and I want to contact him, all right, I simply in my mind's eye adjust myself to this communion that they're here, not there. I make there here and then now, and then adjust myself within myself to everything that has ever penetrated me. For if God is within me, is there any place where God is not? There's no place where he's not. Then where would I go to be where I want to be? And so, if everything penetrates me, well then, I will simply single out that which has penetrated me and adjust myself to it.

Like tonight, if I want to be elsewhere in this world, I will adjust myself to that and put myself there through the feeling that I am that. How would I know I'm there? I view the world from there and I will see it as I would have to see it if I were there. How do I know I have moved? Motion can be detected only by a change of position relative to another object. So I'm standing here and as far as the world goes I haven't moved, but in my mind's eye I have moved because I now observe the world differently, and I see it as

I would see it were I there…yet physically I'm still here. Everything is here because everything has penetrated me. So I simply by a mental adjustment, I adjust myself to being the man that I want to be.

Well, how will I know that I've made that motion? Have my friends look at me, and if they see me as they formerly saw me, I didn't move. Try it again. If they now see me and I see it on their faces the expression which implies they see in me the man that I'm assuming that I am, I've moved. I have moved from whatever I was to where I'm now assuming that I am. So let them look at me 'til I see on their faces that which would imply to me that they see in me that which I'm assuming that I am. Now, there's no other way to tell that you've moved, for motion cannot be detected save by a change of position relative to another object. The motion of a single object is stupid. They couldn't tell unless there is a frame of reference against which it moved. Well, I have a frame of reference. I have my friends in this world and they will know if anything happens to me. If tonight I drop dead, there will be a little motion, and one friend will call another friend, another friend, and finally dozens will know Neville died. So they will know. If on the other hand something good happens to me, they'll know it in the same way, that little chain reaction. One will call another and say, "You know what happened to Neville? He did so and so or so and so happened." They'll all know it. Now, let me bring into my mind's eye a small circle of those who know me. I'm assuming now that I am what I want to be and then I assume that they're looking at me, and they're congratulating me, and they're empathizing with me. Well then, at that moment having felt the reality of all that I'm doing I drop it.

Now, if it comes to pass just as I have imagined it, haven't I found Jesus Christ? If he does all things and not a thing in this world ever was made that he didn't make and I made that, well, haven't I found him? Who is he then? Is he not my Imagination? So I tell you that my Imagination, your Imagination, is Jesus Christ. God became man that man may become God. And God is all Imagination, and becoming man, he's man's Imagination. So "Man is all Imagination and God is man, and exists in us and we in him. The eternal body of man is the Imagination that is God himself." God alone acts; he's the only actor in the entire world. So I can act the part of a fool, the perfect fool. I can act the part of a very poor man and play it beautifully. I can act the part of a rich man and play it. It all depends on what I want to be in this world. Not everyone wants to be rich…you may think they do, but no they don't really. They want enough to live on and to live well, but not everyone is really moved to be rich. If they are moved to be rich and they don't know this principle, they remain poor, because they're looking to a God on the outside and trying to coerce him into doing something for them by acquiring merit. You can acquire all the merit in the world, you can be so good that the whole vast world will think you're the best person in the world, and yet remain the being that you don't want to be. You've got to know who you really are. And no man really knows himself who does not know the revealer, and the revealer unveils himself within you as your very being.

In my experiences, I never saw another one do it. I was not a spectator of another; I was the actor playing the part, the very part that is written up in the gospels as played by Jesus Christ. So you tell the story while you wear this little garment that decays…and they are simply shocked beyond measure. You seem to be so blasphemous when you make these bold, bold claims, and yet you can't deny what happened to you. I could no more deny this than I could the simplest evidence of my senses. I know what I ate tonight and yet it is not as vivid in my Imagination as the experiences of playing the story in the gospels. If I now relive tonight's dinner, why, it fades in color, in everything, compared to these dramatic events that took place in me many years ago. These are as though they're taking place now they are so vivid and so real.

So I say to everyone, the one who makes everything in your world is your own wonderful human Imagination. It may seem a cruel thing to say to one who is now experiencing something that he does not want that he made it, but I have to be honest with myself. I have suffered, I have gone through all kinds of physical pains, but I could not deny…even though I could point to something and say, "Well, I caught the flu." So I caught the flu. Caught it where?—all within me. Read the paper that forty to fifty percent of the country, well that would run in to tens of millions of people, so I got it just like fifty million or maybe eighty million, I don't know, and went through all the pains and all the fevers and all the heat, and dropped off twelve pounds (which I haven't regained). But I learned a lesson: I can't deny that I am subject to everything that man is subject to, even though I have experienced the drama of Christ Jesus. The entire story unfolded within me, placing myself in the central character. Yet, in spite of that I have to go through everything, because I cannot point to any other cause other than my own Imagination, I can't. The cause cannot come from without I don't care what it is. If I'm in pain tonight, the cause has to be traced back to me. As we're told in Galatians (6:7), "Be not deceived; God is not mocked"—and God is my own Imagination, so he isn't mocked—"as a man sows so shall he reap." "You see yonder hills, the sesamum was sesamum, the corn was corn, the silence and the darkness knew, and so is a man's fate born" (*Light of Asia*). So I can't pass the buck. Anyone who comes to me, they tell me a story, I've got to go right back to the imaginal act in that being and try in some way to resolve it.

So I tell you here, to go back to quote once more John Stuart Mill, "Causation is the assemblage..." and now I'll quote it in our words, "the assemblage of mental states, which occurring produces that which the assemblage *implies*." So you create some assemblage of mental states implying you are what you want to be. Now you enter that state and you believe it... you become one with it. Perform all these inner acts just as though they were outer acts, and then watch it come to pass in this world. The whole thing will come to pass. And don't think you'll ever find a stopping place in this world. If you live to be a thousand, you'll never find that you have built one little mold that will endure unmoved, undisturbed forever, because you're being penetrated morning, noon and night by everything in this world. So I think I now need to be perfectly harmonious for the rest of my days and tomorrow it is disturbed, forcing me to use my talent to construct an imaginal solution. Then having constructed an imaginal solution ___(??) it and then it's resolved. But do not expect you're going to find any permanent state between now and the end when you depart this world.

May I tell you, you aren't departing it. You depart it relative to those who cannot follow you, but you haven't departed it. You've entered another section of the same world and will continue to do so until that story as told in the gospel repeats itself in you. Because of his indwelling in you, it will be repeated, for that is the story of God being born in man and coming awake in man. Were he not in man, it could not be repeated; but he is in man as man's own wonderful human imagination. So when you depart this world before you experience this story, don't think that you are dead...dead only relative to those who can't follow you. To yourself you are very much alive and once more made young—not a baby but young, about twenty—in a world best suited for the work yet to be done within you, until this thing erupts and unfolds within you. After that, the next time you depart a section of time you leave *this age* altogether and enter an entirely *new* age, that age spoken of in scripture as "the kingdom of God." Don't try to visualize what it is because images of earth will not enter to help you at all. It's something entirely different, a new life, a new being, a new body.

Now here, treat it seriously tonight, because it's right down on this level, and you can prove it. Before we meet again you can prove it if you really believe it. We live by our beliefs...giving it lip service is not enough. Just as the whole vast world of Christians give lip service to Christianity and make that a substitute for living by it. It is not...it must become something alive within us. Do I really believe in Christ? Yes I do. Well, do I know who he is? Yes I do. Who is he?—my own wonderful human Imagination. Does he make everything in your world? Yes. Well then, test him and see. I will. Now, instead of saying I will and forget it, will I keep that always in mind so that when confronted with any problem I will simply construct an imaginal solution which would be the true solution of that problem, and then enter into that image and abide in it as though it were true? Well, I will…I'll try to, try to always remember who the Maker is, for he makes things out of things that do not appear and he himself does not appear. He's like quicksilver. You can catch him best in a daydream. As Fawcett said, "Divine Imagining, which is God, is like pure imagining in ourselves. He lives in the very depths of our souls, underlying all of our faculties, including perception, but he streams into our surface mind least disguised in the form of productive fancy." So in that form of creative fancy and suddenly I'm daydreaming I could catch him…that is God. For he who is dreaming that's God. God is the dreamer. All dreams proceed from God, whether it be a day dream or a night dream and everything in this world was preceded by a dream, or call it an imaginal act. So you take it seriously and test it, you are invited to test it. You who have a Bible (I hope you all have Bibles) it's the 13th chapter of 2nd Corinthians, and you'll find what I told you in the 5th verse. It's a very short chapter, you can't miss it: "Examine yourselves to see whether you are holding to your faith. Test yourselves. Do you not realize that Jesus Christ is *in* you?" And it's stated all through his letters that "Christ in you is the hope of glory" (Col.1.27)…not Christ in history. Well now, if he makes all things, then put him this night to the test.

Now, let us go into the Silence.

*   *   *

Q: What version of the Bible do you use?
A: I use both the *King James* and the *Revised Standard Version*. I have them both at home in what is known as *The Interpreter's Bible* and they are paralleled, the King James on one side, the Revised Standard Version on the other, so I can compare them. Then comes the *Exegesis;* then come the commentaries—there are twelve very large volumes; and four large volumes of the dictionaries. These sixteen are my daily, I would say, fare, my joy. I get up in the morning around 4:30 with a cup of tea. I start reading the Bible until the paper comes. Some passages in the *King James* I prefer to that in the *Revised Standard*, but I will compare them and I'll take my choice. Then read the *Exegesis* to give me the original meaning of the words when it was written, so that the scholar does not try to force you to accept certain things. He will tell you what it was written in that day, because words change their meaning.
Q: How do you really distinguish between wishful thinking and visualizing what you want to obtain?

A: Well, all these begin with a wish. I mean, you wish and so that's a wishful thought. But instead of leaving it that way, you enter into the feeling of the wish *fulfilled*. What would the feeling be like if it were true? Now it goes beyond just a wish…leaving it as a wish. As Shakespeare brings out so beautifully, "We have been taught from the primal state that that which is was wished until it were." So it begins with a wish. There isn't a man in this world who is doing anything—be it something that he is proud of or not—but he finds he goes back…it was a wish. I wished to come to this country and in those days in 1922, as I presumed they had certain restrictions more so than today…but I came. I had no training to get any job. No matter where I'd go they would say "You aren't trained." Well, I knew I wasn't trained. I tried to get a job climbing the poles of electricity for the telephone company and they said that you aren't trained, you're not educated. I said, "What?—to climb a pole? Show me what to do and I'll do it." I tried to get a job as a lumberjack in Canada. I went up, they said, "You aren't trained." "Trained for what? I'm strong!" I was at the age of seventeen, eighteen, a very strong boy… unusually strong for my age and for my size. But strength didn't mean a thing for them or to any of them.

But I do know the whole thing is within us. In spite of my limitations, my social background, financial background, educational background, I kept on dreaming of transcending the limitations that were placed upon me but that I did not overcome when given the opportunity. In school…I went to school but when I heard the ball against the bat in cricket or a foot against the soccer ball that was something far more interesting to me than reading the book. And so, all these things so fascinated me that I wasn't interested in school. I dare say I came out as I came in, untouched. Then I realized when I came here that something else had to happen, and I wasn't aroused until I went to England. In 1925 I met an old Scotchman who was interested in certain mystical subjects and he read the *Bhagavad-Gita* and *The Light of Asia* and these lovely things to me, and then he gave them to me. Well, he inflamed…he touched a little wick within me so when I came back to America four months later, I was so moved by all that I had heard and read in the interval that I went wild. Every penny that I had that I could afford outside of my rent I bought books on related subjects. When I traveled I carried enormous amounts of books. While others were playing cards in the dressing rooms, I was reading my books. So I was not really aroused until I was twenty years old in 1925…completely untouched…a virgin until then.

Good night.

WHEN THE SPIRIT OF TRUTH COMES

2/10/69

In the Book of John we are told, "I have many things to tell you, but you cannot bear them now. When the Spirit of truth comes, he will lead you into all things" (Jn. 16:13). Here, the incomplete form of the incarnate revelation will be continued by the Spirit of truth until there can be seen all the truth. When he comes you will know it. I will show you tonight how he comes into this world.

We think we are completely free to receive everything in the world that is true, but are we? I read recently a work called *Vanished Pomps of Yesterday* by Lord Frederick Hamilton, and in it he tells this story that Catherine the Great finding the first violet of spring ordered a sentry to be placed over it to protect it from being plucked. She forgot to rescind the order and so eventually it became a tradition, and day and night, summer and winter, a sentry stood where a violet a hundred and fifty years ago once grew. Now, these are researched stories that Lord Hamilton gave us in his works…150 years later a sentry was standing where a violet once grew. The generation that came didn't know why he was there and he didn't know. Well, make sure that some sentry is not standing now on the lawn keeping you from the Word of God. As we are told, just as this was the tradition in the Book of Mark and in the Book of Matthew that here you make the traditions of your fathers to void the Word of God and then you hand it on. You void the Word of God through your traditions and hand it on.

Now tonight, let me share with you (and the lady is here). When I got home on Friday night and read it, I was thrilled beyond measure, for the Spirit of truth has come to her. She said, "I found myself on a movie lot, I seemed to be in the company of two others. In the center of the lot sat a man and I walked up to him and he seemed to take on the appearance of John Wayne. He greeted me, he said, 'Hello, Peggy'" Well now, that's her name. "I in turn said, 'Hello, John' and I was thrilled and amazed that he knew me. Then he said something to me which I didn't hear and I asked him to repeat it. He did, but he did in a softer tone and I didn't hear it. I was embarrassed to ask him again. So when I woke I knew it was the most important thing that was said to me…and then I remembered what he said. This is what he said, 'It is *not* "Before Abraham was, I am"; it is "Before Abraham, was I am" (Jn. 8:58). You dwell upon it. It will make all the difference in the world to your concept of this statement. In all translations the comma is after "was." Now bear in mind that the original manuscripts from which all of our translations are made had *no* punctuation marks. These are all man made. There were no verses, there were no paragraphs, there were no chapters. We did not have punctuation and verses and paragraphs and chapters until almost the 16th Century.

So man thought, well certainly, it is "Before Abraham was, I am" and a man is speaking. No. Here is the incarnate revelation trying to reveal the source of all the phenomena of life, and that source is I AM. When you read it with the punctuation after "was," you think a man is telling you that he as a man preceded Abraham. But if you read it as it was revealed to my friend—I should say *our* friend for she now shares with us her revelation—read it "Before Abraham (comma), was I am." He is not making any claim that would now separate him from us; for he said, "Go unto my Father and my brothers and say unto my brothers, I am ascending unto my Father and your Father, unto my God and your God" (Jn. 20:17). Now there's no separation from this revelation of the incarnate Word…not putting himself apart as something different that you and I should worship…just revealing to us what the I AM is unfolding *within* us. So I can't thank her enough for this revelation. So when the Spirit of truth comes, he will lead us into all things as we are prepared to receive it.

Now tonight, can we really receive that revelation? Can we turn only to this one presence, I AM, and know it to be the source of everything in this world whether it is good, bad or indifferent? Now, we may think that God certainly could not produce wars and all the conflicts. There is no other God, there is no other source and there is no other Creator but God. What to us may seem the most horrible thing in the world…I would rather liken it unto a tapestry: one side it's ugly, it's horrible, but come on the right side and see the beauty of the tapestry. We cannot here playing the parts that we play know why we do what we do. I know certain very able imaginists who would like to see that all the things of the world are collected and they're all preserved. But they cannot become eternally so. In other words, they can't forever follow the eternal events. How it could be changed they confess they do not know. I would say to them *revision* would do it...but I would rather not. They say, "Let us look upon it and regard the entire history of man as so much material for the artistry of God." Well, that's beautifully said and it's marvelous and you could be right, but I rather think that this event is coming up out of all the horrors that you and I experience. That everything that we do is simply in some strange, wonderful, magical way being transformed under that wonderful event that was the concept in the beginning.

As we are told in Genesis, "You meant it for evil but God meant it for good." So you played what you thought to be the evil part in selling me into slavery and yet by selling me into slavery I by my visions and my ability to interpret the visions of Pharaoh, I can now save enough of the harvest over a period of seven years to save civilization from death. For no one would have put away twenty percent of the yield of the field. But I know what the vision meant, and therefore interpreted it just as I knew that it ought to be and I saved twenty percent over seven years and saved civilization from starvation (Gen. 50:20). So I rather believe that whatever we are doing is being instantly transformed into the beauty of this great event.

But if you dwell upon this lady's revelation, it could only come to her through the Spirit of truth. First she saw John...well, John means "Jehovah favored"...that's what the word means. But bear in mind that the dreamer in her is also manufacturing the being who is sitting on the chair and that here she comes to a director. Now, John Wayne in her mind and in my mind always plays the leading role. He is never cast in a secondary role. Well, God is the chief actor who plays all the parts in the world. He has always played the chief parts. You don't see him playing the supporting role, he's always the star in the picture. Here he is in the director's chair, for that's the typical director's position. Here he's not only directing, but he's the chief actor. "God only acts and is in all existing beings or men." So his name forever is I AM and so when you say "I am" that's God. He actually became us that we may become God. So here she talks to him and she calls him John (Jehovah's favored one) and he knows her by name. Well, we are told in scripture that he numbered all the stars and called all by name. And then, do you think he would have made you and not know you by name? And you're *far* more precious than the stars...you are far more precious than all the stars and all the sands of the sea. Though we seem to be unnumbered, we are numbered in the mind of the Father and known by name, so when she comes forward he calls her "Hello, Peggy" and she in turn calls him, "Hello, John." Then he tells her something she couldn't hear. She asked him to repeat it, he does but softly and she couldn't hear it and she was embarrassed. Thrilled that she was known by this one who undoubtedly was most important and what he said was most important. But when she was waking she remembered what he said.

So let me repeat it if you haven't a recorder. It is *not* "Before Abraham was, I am"; it is "Before Abraham, was I am." Nothing came before him. So he's not making a claim—this quotation, by the way, comes from the 8th chapter of the gospel of John, at the very end—for here is the complete argument through the entire chapter concerning who is Father. "Did you know my father Abraham?" Well, they called Abraham father. And he said, "My Father is he whom you call God, but I know my Father and ye know not your God" (Jn. 8:54). He is trying to get them back beyond a physical state to something that is far ___(??). It is the source of all that is God, which he calls Father.

Now, I tell you tonight that you can test it. There is no other source. You can now assume that "I am" and you name it. You name exactly what you want to be and wear it as you would a suit of clothes until it seems natural. When you first put it on it seems unnatural. As a man I know from experience I buy a new hat and walk down the streets of New York City, no one knew me but I thought everyone knew I had a new hat. I was embarrassed with my new hat until I wore it long enough so that I could throw it in the corner and pick it up, put it on, and then it's an old hat. When it became an old hat then I could walk normally. Put on a new pair of shoes and you think everyone knows you have new shoes. You may deny this but if you are honest with yourself, when you put on a new dress, a new suit, a new...you think everyone knows it, and nobody knows you. They don't know you and they don't care as you walk by. But you are in something new. Well, the same thing is true of an assumption. So you have an assumption and you assume that I am what reason denies, what your senses deny; therefore, it is new and you haven't broken it in yet. All of a sudden wear it until it seems natural. At the moment it becomes natural, you walk in it and it externalizes itself in the world, and the whole vast world then reflects the truth of what you are assuming.

So the source of it all is I AM. There's only one God and Father of all and his name forever and forever is I AM. But if I think in terms of "the Lord," well, "the Lord" is something on the outside. He said, "The Lord will make himself known in a vision and will speak with man in a dream" (Num. 12:6). Well, the minute I say "the Lord" I think another, but the word translated "the Lord" is Yod He Vau He, which is actually translated "I am." So if I say "the I AM," then man is not quite ready for it. So when man is ready to receive the Spirit of truth then it comes. So she was ready and it came to her. She sat down and hastily wrote me last Friday night in script, for she had no time to type it our or write it in some other form, just hastily and gave it to me. I can say to her, The Spirit of truth comes to you and he will lead you into all things, for you're prepared to receive it. But to be prepared to receive that you had to overcome an awful lot, for trained as we all were in the belief of an external God—some source outside of self who brought us to wherever we are and will lead us to where he's going to lead us—is something on the outside. There is *nothing* on the outside! The being within you is the immortal, infinite being called God the Father. And you say "I am," that's God, that's God the Father. When one day you discover it, you will know that you and he are one.

So when the world rejects this revelation, it's because they do not know the Father. They *think* they know the Father and they call him by some other name and worship him as something external to themselves. Well, I tell you from my own revelation, from my own experience, the day will come—now this is revelation—that you will find scripture unfolding within you. One thing that is the most exciting thing ever is when that 2nd chapter of Psalms unfolds within you…when he stands before you and he calls you Father. You were taught to believe up until that moment that Jesus Christ was the Son of God, and you did not realize until that moment that Jesus Christ is simply God revealing himself, he is God himself; and the Son that reveals him as Father is David. So, "I will tell of the decree of the Lord: he said unto me, 'Thou art my son, today I have begotten thee'" (verse 7). These are the words of David. In the 89th Psalm, these are now the words of the Lord, of the I AM, "I have found David and he has cried unto me, 'Thou art my Father, my God and the Rock of my salvation" (verse 26). So when you tell people who have been conditioned to believe that Jesus Christ is the Son of God, and God is something other, something where?—no one knows—that conditioned mind must in some strange way be dissolved. And when truth comes, it will gradually seep through and then that individual will realize that *he* is God himself, for the Son of God calls him Father. Well now, if he calls me Father, which he has, and he calls you Father, which he will if he hasn't, are we not one?

There is only one Son and one Father, only one God and Father of all. If everyone has the identical son call him Father, then are we not one? Have we not proven that wonderful 4th chapter of Ephesians, "There is but one body, one Spirit, one hope, one Lord, one faith, one baptism, one God and Father of us all?" Well now, he became me, but if he became me, what was his purpose?—to give himself to me that I may actually become God. Then how will I ever know? He's a father. Well, you can call me Lord, but I would not believe it. You can call me by any name and I wouldn't believe it. But if the

Son calls me Father and he is supposed to have lived 3,000 years ago, well, here I am in the 20h Century, and here is one who by scripture preceded this age by 3,000 years. He stands before me and calls me Father, and I *know* I am his Father and he *knows* he is my Son. He isn't trying to prove it. It is as though I always knew it but I'd forgotten, like amnesia. I suffered from total amnesia and then he comes into my world and the memory returns. Now it's not memory any more, it now becomes actual fact. Because to God, God doesn't have a memory as we use the word memory…everything is actuality. So here comes the actual Son…I don't remember having him. He stands before me, it's actualized. So it's not memory, it's simply a returned memory which now ceases to be memory and it is now actual fact. He stands before me and here he is a youth as described in scripture, this beautiful…and you can't describe the beauty of David.

I have no sense that he ever had a mother. He is begotten and the verb "to beget" is always attached to the male; "to bear" would be attached to the female. So we speak in scripture of two forms of birth: there is one that is attached to the female, and this body was born of a woman, formed within her. But there is another birth, a birth from above, where the verb is "to beget," and that is always associated with the father. Here is "begotten," that "Today I have begotten you," said he to David. So in the 3rd chapter of John when the conversation between Nicodemus and himself takes place, he said, "You must be born from above." The word "anothin" is translated "from above." It is sometimes translated "anew" or "again" but, "Unless you are born from above (or again), you cannot enter the kingdom of God" (verse 3). Well, that is a must. No matter what man has achieved in the world, having been born first from below, from the womb of woman, he still then must be born from above. That birth from above is of the Father. Who is born?—it is the Father himself. As *you* are born from above then all that the Father is you will experience. He's a father, therefore if he is a father, "Where is my son?" Well, as you're asked in the last book of the Old Testament, "If I am a father, where is my son?" Now, here comes the son and the son stands before you.

That's one of the most difficult things for me as a teacher to get over to the mind that has been conditioned to believe…and it has that sentry standing over that little violet that grew 150 years ago. But in this case unnumbered centuries ago it was planted in the minds of man that Jesus Christ is the Son of God, God is other than man, Jesus Christ is other than man, and man is a little worm ___(??) here and he's sinful. I tell you, God actually became man—that's a fact of life—that man may become God. He is buried in man, he is crucified on man and this [body] is the only cross that he ever wore. The birth will take place from the skull of man, for that's where he's buried. When he awakes within man and comes out emerging from man, soon thereafter here comes confirmation of his fatherhood. Then you *know* it and you tell it to the world in hope that they will receive it. But now, whether they receive it or not, the Spirit of truth is coming and I can't tell you my joy because he has come to you. Whenever I depart this world he is still with you because he has come, he's appeared. You'll take whatever I told you plus what he is going to tell you from within all from within yourself, and then you will actually live in this vision that has been misunderstood through the centuries.

So I have come to reinterpret the story as it really *ought* to be: Jesus Christ is God the Father. He said, "He who sees me sees the Father: How can you say, 'Show me the Father' Philip?' Have I been so long with you and you do not know the Father?' He who has seen me has seen the Father" (Jn. 14:9). And so, in the end everyone will be the Father. And because there is only one Father and only one Son, this unity will be once more gathered together. It's now fragmented, it's now scattered, but eventually you and I will be so intimate, without loss of identity. I will know you more intimately than anyone in this world, no matter who knows you, could ever know you. The mother that you sucked, the father that loved you, the wife who bore you children, all these will be as nothing compared to the intimacy that we will have when all are raised and once more reunited into one body, the one Spirit, the one Lord, the one God and Father of all.

So you dwell upon this revelation that came from Peggy. It is not "Before Abraham was, I am"; it is, "Before Abraham, was I am." That is the foundation and that is that fountainhead of everything in this world. When you read of the horrors of the world as told to us morning, noon and night and all the things that would deny a divine event, bear in mind the story of the tapestry: one side isn't lovely at all and this side is called in scripture "below," the other side is called "above." So he is made to say, "You are from below," those who are having the experience here, and "I am from above; you are of this world, I am not of this world. But you shall be of my world" (Jn. 8:23). That's what he said. In this world you're playing your part and you'll play it perfectly and in the end you'll be lifted up. For he said, "I am lifted up" and that proves that all will be lifted up because we are one.

But I can't tell you the thrill in store for you when it happens. I can paint word pictures and could I draw I could paint that, but when it happens the thrill is beyond measure. You cannot describe the thrill that comes to the individual who has scripture unfold within him. For the purpose of life is to experience scripture. There is nothing but scripture to really fulfill in this world. Oh, I could become rich, I could become known, I could become anything if I so desire it and do not lose confidence in I AM; for if I put anything upon it, it will grow. You want to be rich? You can be rich.

The Return of Glory

You want to be known? You can be known. Anything at all! You simply assume it and wear it as though it were true and that assumption though at the moment you assumed it was denied by your senses if you persist in that assumption, it will harden into fact. It will objectify itself and become a reality. But that is not the purpose of life.

The purpose of life is to fulfill scripture. "Scripture must be fulfilled in me" (Luke 22:37). So when it is fulfilled in the individual he tells it, and that's not what the world believes it ought to be anyway. He doesn't look like the man that I thought would come. They're looking for something other than themselves and it's not another who comes. For when you say "I am," you never turn elsewhere. You can't divide it, it's one. It didn't say "we are"…that's not the revelation…the revelation is "I am." So when you go to Israel and they say, "What is his name?" just say "I am has sent me. I AM sent me." I can't think of another, for I'm not saying I AM meaning another whose name is I AM. But in translating it we call the I AM, the Lord. If I say, "The Lord sent me," you'd think of another right away…if I said I AM. When they said to Blake…one day they said, "What do you think of Jesus?" He said, "Jesus? Why, he is the only God," and then he hastily added, "But so am I and so are you." Then they went in to dinner and unfortunately the conversation stopped, and he only elaborated this for us. That's all we have from the conversation that he had with his friend that he had invited to dinner, or he invited him. "What do you think of Jesus?" "Jesus?" said he, "He is he only God, but so am I and so are you." Of course, Crabbe Robinson thought at that moment, "Well, this man is really touched…he's going off."

Nothing could be truer than what he said, because there is only God. You are God, actually God. But you deliberately came here to play these parts. You're weaving the most glorious event! When you and I all awaken and re-unite into the one body, oh! what we have done by this seeming horrible adventure. For I can't deny it's not the most pleasant thing in the world. The morning's paper delights in giving some headlines that are going to frighten you. You rarely find a headline that is pleasant. In fact, they go out of their way…if they can't find something that happened in our city that is horrible, they jump across the ocean to find something in some part of the world. We don't care what is happening in India, but they bring it back: this is what happened in India and three people died. They only have 500 million Three people died in an accident and they print it, some little accident, because they couldn't find something similar in our city. Well, the whole vast world is built that way; yet it is moving toward the most glorious divine event.

So when he said, "I have things to tell you that you cannot bear," he's not speaking to those to whom the Spirit of truth has come; he's speaking to those who are still so hidebound in their concepts of a personal God external to themselves to whom they pray, and that mind cannot accept a God within themselves who makes himself known in vision.

So I would say to someone...the lady who ran the bookstore in New York City from whom I bought so many books and knowing my passion for a book—if I wanted it I never thought of price—she always marked it up. If she knew my interest, I could see the figure that was there before and she'd rub it out. If it was $8.50, now it's $12.50...leave the .50, put in the twelve, and rub out the eight. She did it time and time again. I paid her as high as $100 for three books...she'd rub it out and put them all in. She always said to me, "You know, Neville, you have the most vivid dreams, don't you?" "Not dreams at all. These are *visions* where I commune with myself, but the self is God, and yet it is myself." "Oh, Neville!" she would say.

Two years ago when I went back to New York City I inquired about her..."Oh, she was killed just a month ago. She went out at night, no identification marks on her, she stepped off on a dark street and a huge truck nearby couldn't stop and she was instantly killed. Her husband couldn't locate her for four days, but finally found her in the morgue where they kept the body waiting for someone to come and identify her. There was Mary. So she still hasn't awakened. She went over believing all she believed and she's carrying all these beliefs with her. There's no transforming power in what the world calls death. You are placed in an environment best suited for the work yet to be done *in* you. So you are prejudiced here, you're prejudiced there, and you're this here, you're that there, whatever it is. You have to go through all these things until finally you're *willing* to have it all awaken within you. When he awakens, he's not coming from without, he comes from within. When we read in scripture, "And God said to Moses..." it seems as though he spoke from without; no, he whispers from within. It is from within that the whole thing came and Moses then spoke with him face to face...no longer in dream as we are told in the 12th chapter of Numbers... he became one with him.

So I say to you tonight, you can test it. Test what I'm telling you. Your own wonderful human Imagination...so when you say "I am" that's God. Would you like to be, and you name it. Don't let me tell you what you ought to be, you name it. Well then, what would it be like if it were true? How would it feel if it were true? And you dare to assume that it is true. How would I know that my assumption is in any way real? Well now, think of the people who know me. Now let them see you after you've assumed it. Do they see you as they formerly saw you? Then you haven't assumed it, so try again. Now, see the same people, do they see you as they formerly saw you? "Well, not quite...I'm trying to make them see me." You don't *make* them see you; you *let* them see you. And God, "Let there be light." You don't make it, you assume it; and then the world is simply a sounding box, sounding and reflecting what you've assumed. Well, you assume it. Now you think of those that would know if it were true. Let them see you as they would *have* to see you if it were true. Now, do they see you, do they congratulate you, do they discuss you in the new you? All right, it's done. Now, you don't take it off. You wear it as you wear now your present body...you wear it. When tomorrow morning you get up, you still wear the state. You wear this state and in no time it's going to harden into fact, the whole thing is going to objectify itself in your world and you'll confront it as a fact.

Then you'll know who the source, the cause of phenomena is, and there's only one source and the world calls that source God. It's a lovely name, never tire of it, but don't forget who God is. God is the translation of the word I AM—Yod He Vau He. In fact, no one can really sound it. It's a peculiar word...if you try to sound it as it ought to be sounded, it sounds like a belch. You cannot sound Yod He Vau He. The best they could do is simply put another name to it, so they called it "The Lord." Sometimes it's translated "God." But it is simply like a belch...it comes from the depths. You can't sound it. How're you going to sound Yod He Vau He? The best we can do is call it Jehovah (Anglicized) and Jah Adonay if you're going to speak it in Hebrew. But Jah Adonay does not express Yod He Vau He. But the letters do, these four letters are the sacred letters. In Hebrew, if you've attended some Hebrew service, when they come to the sacred word they cover it so that they may not see even the printed word of God. Well, this is covered by your body. Who sees I AM? They'll see what I tell them that I am. So I walk the earth and I'm a man...they'll see that all right...they know I'm a man. So I'm wearing a grey suit, they'll see that. They inquire where I live, so they know where I live. They'll ask a thousand questions and get answers to all these things, but all of these only cover the being that I am.

So they never actually *see* I AM, but they see my metamorphosis. Just as Peggy saw a metamorphosis that she herself created, for here seated is John and to her he seems to be John Wayne. The being in man is a protean being and can assume not only one but all metamorphoses at one and the same time. So here, she comes upon her own creation, and he speaks seemingly from without, and he whispers so softly she can't hear him because he's really whispering from within. In scripture we are told—not in these words but this will give meaning to it—whenever vision breaks forth into speech, the presence of deity is affirmed.

So whether it comes from a burning bush and speech comes from it, or the 6th chapter of the Book of Isaiah, speech comes from it: "Who will I send? Send me, O Lord." So the minute speech breaks forth in vision deity is affirmed. In this case, she was actually looking upon the form that I AM within her had instantly created. And she by association, John Wayne is a star, he is an important one, he's the actor of actors now, never supporting, always the star and he sits in the chair of the director. He directs and he acts. He whispers a great secret and on waking she remembers. The story is, "It is not 'Before Abraham was, I am'—every translation gives it that way—what it really is, is 'Before Abraham, was I am.'" You get it? It makes all the difference in the world.

So I can't thank Peggy enough for this revelation. How many will take it to heart and change the punctuation in future translations, I do not know. Because these punctuations are man made—we have none prior to that moment in Geneva when it was done either in the 15th or 16th century. But in the original manuscript there's no punctuation, no verses, no paragraphs, no chapters. So the little comma there, as it is in that cry on the cross, if you change the comma what a difference that makes. "Behold, I say unto you, today thou shalt be with me in paradise." Change the comma, "Behold, I say unto you today,"—I don't time it now—"thou shalt be with me in paradise" (Luke 23:42). All the difference in the world and what confusion that has made among those who read it. Because, he said forty days later, "Touch me not. I have not yet ascended" and yet he promised that *today* you'll be with me in paradise. Change the comma (man put it there) and you will see that *everyone* is saved and no one can be lost. How could God lose himself? He became man. Is there a man in whom God dwells who could be lost? How could it be? He has to redeem himself.

So, I'm *not* encouraging people to be violent and to go against their ethical code, no, far from it. When you discover this you hurt no one. You go out to help every being in the world. You can't hurt anyone because you know everyone is yourself pushed out, but everyone, I don't care who he is. So in this world of Caesar you mean what seems to be another; and they are in a sense because we're individualized and we do not lose our individuality for we are called by name. You'll be called by name…in heaven you'll be called by name, so there's no loss of individuality and yet there's a unity. There's an intermingling of beings and yet it's one. The one body is your body; the one Lord you are he; the one God and Father of all you are he, yet without loss of identity.

Now let us go into the Silence.

* * *

Q: Did you read a book put out by the St. Germaine Express, *The Unveiled Mysteries* and *The I AM Aberrations*, and so forth? And if you have, what do you think of them?

A: I haven't read them, but I've heard them discussed. I have had many people who come home and discuss these things with me. So I'm not qualified to pass judgment because I haven't read them. I've never attended one of their lectures, so I really don't know. But if they put I AM as something on the outside to worship, well then, that is not it. But again, I do not know what they do. But those who came home, if they are examples of what is taught, then I could not endorse it. I had someone who came home one day and she needed a little help and she asked me if I would close the door. I said yes, and she said close the window. It's New York City and I'm on the 16th floor, but still ___(??). She asked me to close all things in the room, and then she wondered if I would betray her.

What is all this nonsense about? She was a stranger to me and she came seeking help…and we had to be fair to her. So, all of a sudden she stood perfectly still and she began, "I am, I am so-and-so, I am this." It was such a contradiction. There was not one mood that she felt, just words, words, words, as though that would produce something. You don't have to declare anything, what would it be like if it were true? Well who is asking the question?—I am. Well, answer it yourself. You know the feeling that would be yours if it were true. Well then, you don't declare, you simply assume. "Commune with your own heart upon your bed and be still." So you do not get up in a crowd of a thousand and start shouting "I am"! They should all start running. So if she was any example of what they teach, I could not endorse it. But again, I am not qualified, I haven't read one of their books, I've never attended one of their meetings, so I do not know.

Q: Would you say some more about fulfilling life by fulfilling scripture.

A: Well, to me the purpose of life is to fulfill the Word of God. He said, "My word that went forth from my mouth shall not return unto me empty, but it shall accomplish that which I purposed, and prosper in the thing for which I sent it" (Is. 55:11). Well, the Bible is the Word of God. The Old Testament contains his promises to his servants the prophets; the New Testament is the fulfillment of the Old. Those who saw it or heard it could not believe that was what was intended. But the one in whom it unfolded re-interpreted the story in the light of his own experience. Well, they could not accept that…that's not the Messiah for whom they were looking. They were looking for something entirely different. He is telling them that he, a man, is not the Messiah, but this is how God redeems himself, for there is only God in the world and it happens in this manner. There is first a resurrection and he tells them it happens in Golgotha. Well, Golgotha means "skull." If you call it Calvary, that means "skull." Call it by any name as used in scripture. Luke calls it "skull" without any other name—"And they brought him to the place called the skull and there they crucified him and he was buried in a place close to where they crucified him" (Mat. 27:33). So it's the skull. It was there then that you have to rise. If I'm buried in the skull, when I resurrect it would have to be from the skull, and so you resurrect in the skull. Therefore, if I'm in the skull and I must leave it, the emergence from the skull is *birth*: I come out of that state.

Then I'm surrounded by the symbolism and the imagery of scripture, the child and the witnesses to *my birth*. They don't see me because now I'm Spirit and God is Spirit and "those who worship me worship me in Spirit and in truth." So they can only see the symbol of my birth, but him you are told they did not see. So you do not see the one who is born as God, but you see the symbolism proving that he is borne. For you're told, "Go into the city and this is a *sign* for you, you shall find a child wrapped in swaddling clothes and lying in a manger" (Luke 2:12). But you're told it's a *sign* and people who read it seem to be blind, for they don't see the word "sign." They see only the child. "Go and see the child wrapped in swaddling clothes." But the story is, go into the city and this shall be a sign for you. Here, if I want to know this night if the President is in the White House, I don't have to ask any guard. If I go to the city tomorrow, is the President's flag flying? That insignia should be there if he is in residence. If he is not in residence then the Presidential flag is not flying.

Well now, this is like an insignia. Here, God is born. Well, if he's born what's the sign to prove that God is born?—a child wrapped in swaddling clothes. So they go and they find him. That's exactly what you find when you come out of the skull. And others witness it. In fact, they find it, you don't find it, because it is not said that the one who bore it found it. It is said the one who came, the shepherd came and found him. And so the words of the angel were born out and proved true. So all the symbolism happens in you after you awake within your skull and you're born from above.

Now, it doesn't make you any different from anyone in the world, because all are going to be. But if you precede them, it doesn't really matter. So the body is being rebuilt out of the fragmented body, and so you go back into the body, this time a living stone rather than a dead stone. Now you have life in yourself and you're no longer an animated body or a living soul. You are a life-giving Spirit, for now you are God. You are born. You tell it and those who hear it accept it or not, but you can only tell it and you can't persuade them beyond telling it. You use no violence, you simply tell it. How many obstacles the one who hears it must overcome before they can accept it, you do not know; because some sentry may be standing over that little violet in their brain, and no one ever rescinded the order.

Q: To get these revelations, do you read the Bible?
A: My dear, as far as I'm concerned I've always loved the Bible. I've been in love with it, but I do not attribute my revelations to my love of the Bible. I've always loved it. It's just to me one of those things, I can always love scripture.
Q: Well, if one does not read the Bible, then one will not get revelation?
A: Oh no, don't for one moment believe that, not for one second! Who knows who this very night will be called? It is said, I was reading today, because Lincoln's birthday is this coming week, on Wednesday, that he was not a member of any church but he was a very deeply religious man...but he attended no church. Washington, whose birthday is this month also attended the Episcopalian Church. But Lincoln did not... and no one who ever sat in that White House was more deeply religious than Lincoln, but he didn't have to go to church. Undoubtedly he read the Bible. May I tell you, if for no other reason than to improve one's vocabulary...you can't conceive of any book...that and Shakespeare. You can go to all the schools in the world, go to all the great professors, and if you take the Bible and read just a passage every day, and take Shakespeare, any of the great poets...but I'll take Shakespeare as the outstanding one. Just read a passage and it will improve your vocabulary beyond measure, it increases and increases, and *all* is within you.

There is nothing more beautiful than passages of scripture. Take the 13th chapter of 1st Corinthians, which is a hymn in praise of love and oh what beauty: "Though I speak with the tongues of men and of angels, and have not love, I am a tinkling cymbal, sounding brass" (verse 1). No matter what it is, if I haven't love...and the whole chapter is devoted to love. The 11th chapter of Hebrews is a hymn in praise of faith. What beauty of words! If one reads it every day, just a passage, read one chapter. The longest chapter is not too long to read—that's the 119th Psalm—that's not too long. They're all short. But just the sheer beauty of words...and then the truth will seep in.

But you don't have to, my dear. God became you. You know why?—because he loved you. Never would he have made anything if he hadn't loved it. So nothing is lost, not one in all my holy mountain.

So when they speak of one who is damned forever, that's a little human tradition and has nothing to do with scripture. Damned forever, of all the nonsense in the world! So let them do what they want. They are not going to change God's Word and God so loved you he not only made you he became you. Can you say "I am"? That's he, my dear.

Good night.

WE ARE THE GODS WHO CAME DOWN

2/14/69

We are told that God became man that man may become God. And you may think that you are the man and God is the other that became you. Tonight I would have you reverse that: *you* are the God that became man that man may become you.

If I understand scripture correctly and if my visions which parallel scripture are accurate, and I know they are, I tell you that what I just told you is true. Then we are told in the 82nd Psalm that we shall die like men: "I say that you are gods, sons of the Most High, all of you; nevertheless, you will die like men, and fall as one man, O princes" (verses 1, 6). So we were the gods who became men that men may become as we are. So here we find ourselves today in the world of men. Now we are told, the day will come that we will tell posterity…posterity will serve us and tell of the Lord who wrought it…who actually brought about the deliverance of man. So you and I actually became humanity that humanity may become as we are. This I do know from my own personal mystical experience. So reverse it, don't think that you are some little worm and then God became as you are that you may be as he is. You *were* God and therefore you *are* God. *You* became man that man may become you, and that you *is* God. So you take the whole thing and reverse it and then you'll have an entirely different feeling about it.

I know from my own experience…I can't bring out the details, but I do know that my visions are true…they parallel scripture. There are certain passages you wonder what on earth does it mean? I know in the end the whole thing will be revealed, for I made everything because I loved it. When I say "I," I mean *we*. We made everything because we loved it…and then we became everything to raise everything to our level, to glorify everything in this world. I know in the 22nd Psalm when we are told that he wrought it (at the very end of the Psalm) yet it begins with a cry of despair: "My God, my God, why hast thou forsaken me?" That I am crying unto myself. For I came down and completely forgot who I am and assumed my creation to raise it to the level of what I am. But in the very end I cry out "I have wrought it!" and the whole thing is done. I will tell posterity will serve me. Men will tell of the Lord to the coming generations, to those that are yet unborn. It doesn't mean another generation; it means to the gods who came down, who are not yet born [from above] to discover that they did come down and assume human nature, and then raised it, and then they wrought it. They accomplished exactly what they set out to do.

The drama begins not with the birth; the drama begins with the crucifixion. That's how the entire drama begins. Told in the gospels, it begins with the birth and ends with the crucifixion, but that is *not* the story. It begins with the crucifixion, which is the union of God with man, and it ends with the resurrection, where he raises man to the level of himself. Everyone will be raised to that level, because we the gods came down. And so, in the divine society, "I say ye are gods, sons of he Most High, all of you; nevertheless, you will die like men"—just as everything dies in this world— "and fall as one man, O princes." Then having become man, we will actually assume the entire nature of man, the horror that is man, and then raise him to the level of *love*. In the end there is nothing but love. So I take upon myself the nature of man with all that is man. Well then, you look around and see what man has done, is doing, and is capable of doing. That's what we took upon ourselves, that nature. Not some little particular man called Jesus Christ did it, but the nature of man we the gods took on. And then we raise him to the level of ourselves which is God who is *infinite love*.

Now in the 42nd Psalm, many years ago…so I can't tell you other than to say that the beginning is the crucifixion and it did not begin in the year one A. D. I cannot pinpoint it, not now, but it was the beginning when this union took place between us the gods. For the word Elohim, the very first word that we find in the Bible: "In the beginning *God,*" that word is Elohim. It's a compound unity, it's a plural word. We are the gods that make up God. So, "In the beginning God created the heavens and the earth." So in that beginning the gods did it.

On this night many years ago in the 42nd Psalm, I relived it. When you relive scripture it is not a memory; memory becomes actuality. It's something that you re-enact. It's not something that you remember you simply all of a sudden play it. But as it's told in the 42nd Psalm it's told as a memory: "These things I remember…how I went with the throng to the house of God" (verse 4). But when I went with the throng, I wasn't remembering it, I was re-enacting it. Well, if you take the 42nd Psalm, it would be a thousand years B.C. if you took it chronologically. And that night *I* became man. For then I heard the voice from the depths of my own soul that "I am God in the act of waking" and that I re-enacted the union with man and *I* was the crucifix. I was the one who actually whirled in space and time, my hands vortices, my feet vortices, my side a vortex, my head a vortex and *I* was *life* itself who was sucked into man. I was not man waiting for it, I was that which came into man and took upon myself the *cross* that is man and bore it so that I will then lift man up to my level.

Then in this picture, who would have thought that in the unfolding of the drama and everything that is ever made is *love*. No matter what it is, it is love. The most horrible thing in the world was made in love. And so here, when this night that I broke the shell…and then 139 days later when it was revealed to me by the only one who could ever reveal it that I am the Father, I didn't become the Father at that moment. I was *always* the Father, but came down and took upon myself the cross that is man to raise it to that level. And here in the 22nd Psalm, "Deliver me, deliver my soul"—he asks why?—"Deliver my soul from the power of the dog." He asks to deliver "my darling" and the word is translated "my darling" in the King James Version and "my life" in the Revised Standard Version. But if you take the word, it appears twelve times in scripture. The first time it appears it's in Genesis and you read it in the 22nd chapter of Genesis, in the second and sixteenth verses, and here is the translation: "your only *son*." That's what the word means in Hebrew. Instead of saying "my darling" which completely hides it, or "my life," which completely hides it, "Deliver my only son from the power of the dog."

Now that night when I exploded and kept my promise that I would not leave my Son in hell…as you're told in the 16th Psalm, "Thou wouldst not leave my soul in hell" (verse 10). And the word translated "hell" means "uncovered, to disclose, to reveal, to take off the cover." You would not leave me uncovered, but you will reveal to me—then I in turn will reveal you, for the Father will never be known save the Son reveals him. So the *Father* does it all. And it takes the Son…if he is uncovered he will reveal the Father to himself. For, "No one knows who the Son is except the Father, and no one knows who the Father is except the Son and any one to whom the Son chooses to reveal him" (Mat. 11:27). But the Son cannot reveal the Father unless he is uncovered. So this moment was a complete explosion of the *uncovering* of my Son, who in turn revealed to me who actually died as I became man.

I became man, and then in a moment of time I uncovered my Son who would reveal me as God the Father. So I didn't *become* God the Father, I was always God the Father. And purposely clothed my Son within myself, and then played the part perfectly of man, and then unveiled my Son that he would reveal me as God the Father.

So he makes the statement, "Deliver my darling"...in other words, deliver your only Son from the power of the dog. Now this night in question when it first happened, I could hardly believe that this could be so altogether spiritual. But I know I made everything for its purpose and everything was made in love. These two men stood by my side, handsome men, about forty years of age, and my Son [David] a lad of about twelve or thirteen. They looked at him with such concupiscence, there was a lust beyond measure because he was so beautiful, and they wanted him more than they wanted anything in the world. I reminded them of his victories over Goliath...and here before me was the head [of Goliath]...the same imagery of scripture. I told them what he had done to the giant Goliath. David kept on looking at me and he was actually leaning on his left side against the open door looking out on a pastoral scene. If he looked leaning to the left side, then I was to his right (Col. 3:1). He said, "Thou art to my right" so I should always be saved for the Lord sitteth on my right. And I was seated and he was standing, leaning against the open door looking out on a pastoral scene...and I was to his right.

So the imagery is perfect. *We* are the Lord that came and assumed human form and play all these parts. Then in time we lift the part that we are playing up to ourselves, individualized. But before we actually descended into this world we were gods, we were the Elohim. It took all of us to form the Lord. And then we deliberately planned the play...to come down into our own creation and redeem it, and redeem man. So we are *not* man being redeemed, we are the Lord redeeming man. You dwell upon it. It may seem arrogant. And when I tell it to a large crowd not conditioned to hear it, they say "What madness! What sheer madness he's talking about!" Yet I mean what I am telling you. I know what I'm talking about. We are the gods of that 82nd Psalm of which Thomas Cheney said, "The meaning has long disappeared. It might have had some perennial meaning to those who heard it and who wrote it, but it has long, long ceased to have meaning for the world." And here was a man who was the editor of the most scholarly of the higher criticisms of the Bible, Thomas Cheney, for he was the editor of the *Encyclopedia Biblica*. He said, "Of all the Psalms this is the one that is the most confusing, for how could it be that God has taken his place in the divine assembly and in the midst of the gods he holds judgment?" (Ps.82:1,6). And then comes the agreement of the gods: we agreed to descend

The Return of Glory

and dream in concert. Then the One, made up of the many proclaims, "I say you are gods, sons of the Most High, all of you; nevertheless, you will die like men and fall as one man, O princes."

So we are the princes, the gods who make up *the* God who came down into mortal form to raise these forms to the level of ourselves. And man has completely reversed it. Today you read a prophetic book and it's all about mechanisms. More and better mechanics, so instead of plowing the field with a hoe, we now do it with a tractor. Instead of moving across with a little wheel barrow, we take a missile now and we go to the moon, around the moon, going all over the place with greater and greater and more wonderful mechanisms. But no one is telling of a lordlier humanity: of that which came down into man, and could not return until he was born from above, and then tell of this being that he's going to raise with him out of the skull of this mortal man. But no one writes about it, no one tells of this spiritual birth from the skull of mortal man; they only tell of greater and greater mechanisms. And yet, the story is the eternal story: that God became us in the most literal sense. But this man...*I am* the God that became this...and now the union is so complete that I feel that I am this, and I will lift it with me right up into the level, completely individualized.

We are the gods coming down. What we will do tomorrow, who knows? Will we again come down into another element called the animal world? For, we are animal too. Will we again come down into the plant world? Will we again come down into the mineral world and redeem everything that we have created? For, we are the gods who actually came down into man and took upon ourselves the cross that is man and now raises man to the level of God. But we can't leave the unredeemed. So when Tennyson said in his poem called *The Play*, "Be patient, our playwrite will show in some fifth act what this wild drama means." So I will not be satisfied just to take one section of Creation and redeem it but the whole of Creation. And so, this has been quite the challenge, but I have wrought it. And so you're told in the end of this wonderful story, "It will be told, posterity will serve him and men will tell of the Lord to coming generations, and proclaim that he has wrought it" (Ps. 22:30). Proclaim it to the yet unborn—meaning not the little children coming in, but to those who are not yet awake within this world—but the same God not yet awake within the skull where he emerges from it.

So I tell you, you are infinitely greater than you think you are. You and I were together in eternity. Now, eternity is not the domain of the timeless as some would indicate, like in today's paper they said it was a timeless "timeless state." No, it is the domain not of the timeless but of the everlastingly, the enduring, that which is forever and forever...*that* is eternity. What cannot forever endure ceases to be. We cease to imagine it and it vanishes. But you and I are eternal beings who came down into time. And as Blake said, "These things of time build mansions in eternity." "The ruins of time," he called them. So everything dies here, but everything dies, and yet they all build mansions in eternity. So not one thing has ever happened that was out of kilter, not a thing. It was all in order.

This morning's paper, you must have read it, where the pope said, "A man should not go against his conscience, but his conscience must be educated to conform to the doctrines of this church." Of all the nonsense of the world! Mustn't go against his conscience, but it must be educated to conform to the doctrines of the church, and he sets himself up as the doctrine, the one who is the criteria of all that is right and wrong. Let us get back to scripture and stop all this nonsense about the outside world. Hasn't a thing to do with these little things that are passing away. Go back to scripture.

Now, who would have thought for one moment in reading that passage if you just took it as I have quoted it "Deliver my darling from the power of the dog," who would have thought that it meant anything. It doesn't mean a thing…and yet when you it happens to you, you know exactly what it's all about and you wonder what is it all about? I made—and you and I together made—the bull, we made the mule, we made the harlot, we made the homosexual, we made the lesbian; we made everything in this world. You know why?—because we *loved* it. We would have made nothing that we did not love. And so why this…in the very end of the drama should stand to my right these two men? And look with such lust upon my only begotten Son… in the fulfillment of the 22nd Psalm, "Deliver your only Son from the power of the dog." The word "dog" means "a male temple harlot." That's what it means. So deliver…and they were looking with such concupiscence…and I simply loved them but warned them of his victory over the giant. Here was the giant's head before me completely severed from the body. And here he leaned against the open door looking out on a pastoral scene.

So everything is in order. They had to be there at that moment when I broke the tomb and did not leave my only Son in the grave. "Thou wilt not leave thy only Son in the grave" as we are told in the 16th Psalm. He makes the statement, "You will not leave me in the grave" (verse 10). The word translated means "in this world of death." Well, this is this world. I will not leave it in this world…I'll take him with me, for he's played the part perfectly. For "I have found in David"—the Son of myself called Jesse, which is I AM—"a man after my own heart who will do all my will" (Acts 13:22). Well, he did all my will. He played every part that I played, because I wore the part of man. And the sum total of all the parts that I played is David. And he is so beautiful because he is made up of everything I've done.

It took *everything* to form David. If one little part was left out, I couldn't have David. And so I've played every conceivable part in the world, for it takes everything to produce David. "Thou wouldst not leave thy loved one, thy Holy One, in the grave," in this world of death. No I will not. So in that moment when I broke the grave and he stood before me, resurrected, redeemed and I take him now into my heavenly state with me, that glorious being.

So we take everyone, we take ourselves, but we take with us our only begotten Son into this heavenly state where without speech we share in eternal wisdom. And no one writes of that; they write only of the more and more wonderful mechanisms of the world. So condemn no one in this world, no matter what he's ever done. You have played that part or you are going to play it or you are playing it. And every part in the world God created. By God I mean *we* created, for we are the gods who came down. We are actually God who came down and assumed human nature…not any particular little thing but human nature, and this union was real, and that was crucifixion.

So the night when I led them in procession to the house of God, I can feel it even now. I can't tell you the ecstasy of the vortices. There were six, like the Mogen David, the great cross or the great Star of David. Not five but six: the side was one plus the hands, the feet and the head. And this complete suction into man, but *I* was the being coming in. So I came in unto man and took upon myself the cross of man, for I was the cross. So you'll find in the story, especially in the works of Paul, everything was the cross. "I have preached nothing but the cross. I have preached Christ and him crucified." Well, *you* are Christ. He is now *in* you because he has already been unified with the body that you wear. But if you have the memory and you will when God remembers, he doesn't remember as man on this level remembers. It's all actuality; it's a re-enactment of the drama. So this night in question it was a complete re-enactment of the drama when the voice said within me, "In the act of waking." At that moment "in the act of waking" I felt the re-enactment of the *first* act which was the crucifixion. So, far from the crucifixion coming at the end of the drama, the crucifixion comes at the beginning and the resurrection comes at the end.

Now you dwell upon it. You may think tonight not practical, but, may I tell you, it's far more practical than anything I could tell you. Oh, I could tell you how to become better if you want to be better, how to become richer if you want to be richer, how to become this…that's simple. But this if you dwell upon it, you transcend all these things that all die. All these things disappear. You'll read in tomorrow morning's paper someone and we invariably say if a man dies who was a normal person who leaves no estate, they don't mention him in the paper, unless you pay for the little announcement or some mortuary pays for it. But if you die and you leave money, oh, it's always mentioned. If you leave a home and it's a normal house, no one...but if you leave a house that is a quarter of a million, they tell you of the house and the value of the house. Everything seems to have a tag on it in this world. You read the morning's paper and you will see everything that has any so-called ballooned figure is always mentioned. Now if you really want to be mentioned in some obituary, make a billion. You'll always be mentioned as one who had a billon who died...but you still die. You die as men whether you have a billion or you have nothing. But if you really want an obituary then leave a fortune or do something violent.

But if you really want to awaken, listen to what I have told you this night. I am not flattering you. You and I are the gods who came down, *literally* came down. We are not less than we were before; we are greater for having come down and we have redeemed this section of creation which is man. For man forms an eternal part of the structure of creation. And now we came down, became man and redeemed man. But we can't leave the other parts unredeemed. So we will redeem everything in our world, so that in the end there is nothing but God...but one thing at a time. So now we have proven we can come into the world of death and overcome death. Everything in the world, I don't care what it is, *we* created and *we* will redeem. So God, something other than yourself, didn't become you.

You are God that became your own creation that is man and then you raise man to the level of yourself who is God.

You dwell upon it. I am not making this up; I'm telling you what I know. And everything in the world, whether you be the thief or the one who is robbed, whether you be the bull of the world or the harlot of the world, whatever you are, we made it, and loved it when we made it. And we have played all the parts and the end, the quintessence of all the parts, is that eternal beloved being called David. He is the essence of everything that we have ever played. We take him with us for he is our only begotten Son and we take back the Son, because the Son revealed us to ourselves. Without the Son we would never know we were the Father. So we were the Father before we came down; we are the Father as we return, and we are conscious of being the Father only because our Son David that we brought forth as a result of what we did reveals us to ourselves. So David died and was buried, but we would not leave him in the pit. "Thou wouldst not leave me" said he "in hell"—in the world of death, in the grave.

So we don't. And may I tell you, when it happens, it's a terrific explosion, as though you actually exploded the whole skull, and then he stands before you because he was buried there. Then, as you look at him and the relationship he is the quintessence of all you've ever done. And then in time you take him back into the heavenly sphere, which means "eternal, the everlasting, enduring state." Certainly not a timelessness, as the world would think. An absence of time would be stupid. It's a living, living world!

Now let us go into the Silence.

*   *   *

Now are there any questions, please? No questions?

Q: (inaudible)

A: I could not answer that from experience, but I would presume it would be. But I could not answer it from experience and I try to confine myself to what I know from experience, what I've had in vision, what I've had in my supernatural experiences. But I tell you, that I know what I've told you tonight, that you are not a little man, that God became one with you in order to save you. You are the God who came down to redeem your own creation that is man. The fusion is so complete you had to actually forget you were God to play the part of man. Whatever part you are playing, that's the part. But I have played all the parts...you name one, I've played it...or I could not have encountered David. I can only now because of this I can't leave a part of my created world unredeemed for in the end there must be only God, and all things must be put under his foot. We are that God; we are the compound unity called the Elohim that make up the Lord. We all, when these masks are off know each other more intimately than we could ever know each other here behind the mask. No one here could ever know you more intimately no matter what you are to them—father, mother, uncle, brother, any one of these. Then you and I will know each other when the masks are off, for in that sphere all things intermingle and we are one.

Q: (inaudible)

A: Ina, my dear, there would be no consciousness, there would be no life were it not that God came down, for God is life, in him is life. He animates the world...that is, *we* animate the world. I know that from experience. Life is an activity of my Imagination... that I have experienced. And when I arrest that activity, things stand still. So I do know that I am that life. God is life. So that everything that seems alive and independent of my perception of it, it is only because that I am alive and am aware of it. I give it life. But I've got to redeem it. I came down into man and I am now identifying myself with man and this union is real. It's not something on the outside. I'm not pretending I am man, I actually became man, and played all the parts that man is heir to.

Having run the race and having fought the good fight and having kept the faith, and having done the whole, well then, I found "the end." And "the end" is the one who revealed me to myself that I purposely forgot. I had to forget that I am God to become man. So I became man, you became man, rather than think some being on the outside as taught by the world. The churches teach us that we are little worms and we did some horrible thing in the beginning and because of this, God in his infinite mercy is going to make a great sacrifice of his one and only son. One little man died and therefore you're going to be saved. Hasn't a thing to do with it. God, and you are God, became man to redeem your own creation. God didn't become you...you God became Ina. And that being that became Ina is I AM and that is God. A complete reversal... scripture teaches a reversal, but man doesn't quite see it. It was not Esau but Jacob; it wasn't Ishmael but Isaac; it wasn't John the Baptist but Jesus. You find this complete reversal: "And the first shall be last." So they're teaching all of this on the outside and the priesthoods of this world teach it that way.

I saw in this morning's paper they've just discovered that Peter's chair was not a chair that Peter ever sat in. They turned it over to the scientists to discover whether it really is as old as they thought it was. For centuries people went and saw this little chair, all broken down, and they worshipped it. It's all behind glass and it's a little shrine, the holy chair in which Peter sat. Now they discover it's not so old at all. Peter would have had to live another thousand years to have sat in it. Yet for all these years people worshipped this stupid little thing as the chair in which Peter sat.

Now priests can't get married. Yet in the 4th chapter of Luke, Peter's mother-in-law...if he had a mother-in-law he had a wife and was healed by Jesus. If he's the first pope and he was married, what's wrong with the pope now about not being married? Just analyze it...Peter's mother-in-law was healed is in the 4th chapter of Luke. So if he was the foundation of it all and called the first pope (which he was not) all of this is a man-made affair, for this whole drama takes place *in man*. When they all sat before me and listened to my unfolding of the Word of God, who was Peter? This drama is a perfect drama, but the way that established churches of the world have organized it, that's not religion. The head of the Jesuit Society said that if the church tells you that black is white you must accept it, no question to it. Well, that is part of the foundation of the church and you don't question the traditions of the church. You're told in scripture, you've made void the Word of God by your traditions which you hand on (Mat. 15:6).

The Return of Glory

You take all your traditions and you hand them on, and by so doing you make void the Word of God.

Now, some may think you're anti this. I'm not anti-anything. I just know my visions are true and they do not conform to these traditions of the church. You are the gods who came down! Now today you'll say, "How could I be God and I'm in need?" I don't care if you're in need or not, you're playing that part. You need not continue in that part because you're God and all things are possible to God. You can assume now that you are affluent. If you dare to believe that you really are God and all things are possible to God, then affluence will be yours...*if* you dare to persist in that assumption. But if you believe you're some little worm as the churches teach and you must pray to an external God and ask him to help you...and they tell you that if he doesn't help you it's because you're very wicked...and they're always passing the buck. But we are the gods!..though our scholars say that they can't understand that wonderful 82nd Psalm. We are the gods spoken of in that Psalm, but it's stated quite clearly, "Although you are gods, all sons of the Most High, all of you; nevertheless, you will die like men." We came down into a world that was dead and we had to take upon ourselves the death of the world, and then prove that we are God by making it alive and redeeming it, and then returning to our state, but enhanced by reason of the fact that we overcame this wonderful venture and we were victorious in a battle with death. For we all die. Who doesn't die, what doesn't die in this world? Show me a monument that does not die. Everything gradually decays, therefore it ceases to be; and yet there is something in this world—and we are that something—that cannot die. Well, we go through the experiences of death and then in the end we are all *self-redeemed*, and we redeem that one section of our creation that is man.

Good night.

THE ROCK

2/17/69

We are told in the Book of Deuteronomy that "The Rock, his work is perfect" (32:4). And then we are asked, "Is he not your father, who created you?" Then he goes on to tell us that "He fixed the bounds of the people according to the number of the sons of God" (verse 8). Today we are thinking in terms of curtailing the population and we have no chance really. It's all written here that not one child should be born were it not for the Son of God. Now, he speaks of the *sons* of God and he calls it "the Rock."

I will share with you tonight...and I have had those who were here in the past...my own personal experience of this claim of scripture. You're told in the Psalms "I will behold thy face in righteousness; and I shall be satisfied when I awake with thy likeness" (Ps. 17:15). Now you read these words and you'll say, "Well, certainly the Rock could not be God. It says, 'Our God is the Lord.'" Who else could be the Rock but our God? "And the Rock was Christ. And other foundations no one can lay than that which is laid, which is Jesus Christ" (1Cor. 10:4). And that is the Rock.

Now in scripture truth is literal; the words to express it may be figurative. Nevertheless, when you experience it, it is literal. First of all, the Rock becomes a person: "And the Rock, *his* work is perfect...and be ye perfect as your Father in heaven is perfect." So when the question is asked, "Is he not your Father who created you?" And then he sets fixed bounds to the people according to the number of the sons of God. Now the word translated God in scripture is a *compound* unity, one made up of others. There is a fixed number to the sons of God, a fixed number, and that unity knows each by name. I am telling you that you really are *now*, as told you in the first epistle of John, the son of God. You may not believe me, but "Beloved, now are we the sons of God, and it does not yet appear what we shall be; but we know that when he appears we shall be like him, and we shall see him as he is" (1 Jn. 3:2). So you look into the mirror and you see your face, and you know with anyone in this world there's always room for improvement. No matter how handsome, how beautiful they may be to others or maybe even to themselves, if they are honest they know there is really room for improvement; therefore, they're not perfect in their own eyes. But we are told, "You *must* be perfect as your Father in heaven is perfect" (Mat.5:48)...and Christ is called the Father, and Christ is the Rock.

Well, in 1934 I think it was, sitting in the Silence, not contemplating anything in particular, with my eyes shut as in sleep but certainly not asleep, contemplating the golden pulsing light that came out of my head. For if I sit in the Silence just for a minute or less than a minute, then if I look, here is this pulsing, golden, liquid light that is alive. All I was looking at was simply this light, when suddenly before my vision appeared this quartz...about that size...this solid, solid rock, but it's a quartz. And then before you could think, it fragments, broken into numberless little pieces, and then just as quickly, it re-assembles itself but not into the form of a rock. It reassembles itself into that of a human being seated in lotus posture. But it's not stone; it's flesh, it's a breathing, living being. As I look at it, I'm looking at myself, but with this difference: *it* is perfect. You can't describe the majesty, you can't describe the beauty, the dignity, the strength of character in that face. It would seem it would take more than eternity to turn this face into that... and yet I'm looking at myself. I have no doubt in my mind who I am looking at, I am looking at myself, but I am looking at myself raised to the nth degree of perfection. As I look at him, all of a sudden he begins to glow and he increases in luminosity. When it seems that he reaches the nth degree of luminosity, it explodes. And then I open my eyes and I am back in my room in New York City.

The Rock is Christ. The Rock is the limit of contraction. So here, the sons of God left the Father's glory and clothed themselves in mortal flesh. He is within me, that same being that I saw is housed within me and he's perfect. He's molding me into his likeness and when it's completed we aren't two, we are one. In the interval, I am his emanation yet his wife 'til the sleep of death is past. When *I* awake I'll be like him, as the psalmist says. "I shall be satisfied that when I awake I will have his likeness." I will not only have his likeness, I am *he* when the work is completed. So, "He who began a good work in me will bring it to completion at the day of Jesus Christ" (Phil. 1:6). So when the work is completed, *he* awakes, and when he awakes *I* awake and we are one, completely one, and that is God.

So we are limited in this world to the number of the sons of God, but who knows the number of the sons of God? So we are trying to stop the explosion in this world, because we say we can't afford to feed them, we can't clothe them. Well, I go back into the thirties and I heard George Washington Carver at a forum in New York City at the Waldorf Astoria. Every year in those days when the *Herald Tribune* was a New York paper (now it's gone), they held every year a forum that lasted about three weeks, seven days a week. All of the prominent men from all over the world, men and women, were invited—religious leaders, politicians, scientists, artists. There were always about a thousand of them who gathered and it would go on for hours. They had a luncheon and then the speeches. George Washington Carver—I'm quite sure you know who I'm talking about—one of the greatest Americans that ever walked the face of this earth who gave us all the by-products of the peanut and the Southern Pine. Over 300 by-products of the peanut, the ___(??). As he stood before that audience he said, "The clothes that I wear came out of the peanut; not only my tie but the color of my tie. All these pigments came out of the peanut. I asked God why he made the peanut and he said, 'I gave you a brain. Go into yourself and you'll find out why I made the peanut. Everything in the world is contained in the peanut, but everything! And it's contained in everything. So I brought out 300 by-products." He called it the "synthetic kingdom."

Now, he said, "From the southern states of America..." meaning that which is south of the Mason-Dixon line, not going into South America, just the United States. He said, "We can grow enough in the Southern states to feed and clothe the entire world." We don't need the Northern states, and we don't need any part of the outer world. So the problem is not curtailing the explosion that we're talking about, it's economics...how to distribute what we are capable of producing. Today we are paying billions every year *not* to grow what we could grow. You pay a man who has x-number of acres not to grow a certain number. And after he grows more than he really, well, when he produces more than they want him to produce, then he has to store it. So he spends millions storing it and all this money paying out for the interest on the storage bill. We haven't yet found out how to change our economic system to actually take care of what man is capable of producing. Communism is not the answer...that's failed. Socialism is not the answer... that has failed. And our present set-up is not the answer. But I have not the answer, I do not know. I am not an economist. But the problem is certainly not to curtail children in the world. First of all we can't do it, for he has given a fixed limit to the peoples of the world and it is according to the number of the sons of God.

Now what is that number? He said, "There are more than the stars of the heavens and more than the sands of the sea." Well, try to number it! And it takes all, and each is known by name, and it takes all together to form the Lord. For the word Elohim is that compound unity, one made up of others. We are the gods. I saw it clearly. Here is this rock and then the rock breaks into many parts, gathers itself together, and then it forms itself into the perfect human form seated in a lotus position. I'm looking at myself, but I am seeing myself that as a man I could not believe that it would not take eternity to actually mold me into its likeness. Yet the promise is, "Let us make man in our image" (Gen. 1:26). So here he is within me. That's where the Rock was and that's where the figure was and that's where that figure *is*. So "Rouse thyself, O Lord, why sleepest thou? Awake!" as we're told in the 44th Psalm. So in everyone is the son of God, known by name, known in eternity, and that has to awake, but it cannot awake until it completes its work. Its work is to make its emanation, which is this form it wears, as perfect as it is. When it is as perfect as it is, it awakes and naturally the emanation has to awake too; and they cease to be two, they become one (Eph.2:14). So he leaves everything and cleaves to his emanation, which is his wife, until they become one flesh, one being, one Lord. So in the end everyone will awake. But how to persuade man that he really is the son of God?

So I tell you, you *are* the son of God. And the day will come that you'll have the same experience that I've had…everyone will have it. You will see the Rock and you'll know why they said, "Of the Rock that begot you, you are unmindful, and you've forgotten the *God* who gave you birth" (Deut. 32:18). So here, a rock—you can't conceive of anything more dead than a rock, a quartz. So he died, in what sense?—he took upon himself the limit of contraction which is the symbol of the rock. The rock symbolizes that very *ultimate* of contraction, which is death. Then it forms itself. It leaves the Father's glory and then clothes itself with mortal flesh. And here *I'm* clothed in mortal flesh, but I know I'm awakening. I know that the whole thing is over as far as I'm concerned. I can only now remain just long enough to tell it. Whatever time is between now and the inevitable departure, it doesn't really matter; the whole thing is over in my case. I'm telling you this thing is true, true from beginning to end. We are the gods, we are the sons of God, and collectively we form *the* God, the only God. There is no other God.

Now, there is no other foundation stone. "I have laid the foundation," said he, "and no other foundation can any one lay than that which is laid, which is Jesus Christ" (1 Cor. 3:11).

That foundation is the Rock, and the Rock, I'm telling you, has formed itself into this beautiful you. So no matter what you look like today when you look into the mirror, there is that something that is breathing in you that is why you breathe. It's that in you that is your dreamer…that's the one. Every dream you've ever had it inspired, even the most horrible dream.

Every vision it inspired and all of your actions. It is the cause of everything in your world. When you are completed in *its* eyes, so that you actually can be superimposed upon him, and you aren't two you're one and it has to fit perfectly, then he awakes and the work is over. You awake and you are he. So we aren't making more gods. It's simply God in this venture, clothing himself in mortal flesh. By this experience he becomes more luminous, more expansive. Then we all go back because of the adventure greater than we were when we descended, having agreed to dream in concert. And this is our world in which we live.

Now here tonight…my friend just came through the door…and he called me today to tell me this story. He told me before and I asked him to write it out, but he's been frightfully busy. A little while ago, it might have been say two or three years ago, a friend of his read my book *Out of This World* and he said to himself…at the time he read it he was about to give up the theater because it was too difficult as he thought. He's a black man and yes a few big ones have broken through—the Belafontes yes, and the Poitiers yes, and the Eartha Kitts—but so few. He thought it would be simply an impossible task to continue in the theater being a black man. But he read *Out of This World* and he said, "In this book it said, 'An assumption, though false, if persisted in will harden into fact.' When you meet your friend Neville the next time, ask him for me if it doesn't work then what?" So Benny came to me and told me that this is what he said. The man's name, by the way, is David Moses. Benny gave me a book to autograph for him and he said, write something in it. Well, I only wrote one little thought from William Blake: "If the fool would persist in his folly, he will become wise." When he got it, it did something to him…"persisting in my folly, for certainly it is folly to assume that I am what the evidence of my senses deny, reason denies it. So I must persist in my folly?" Yes, and if you do, you'll prove it and you'll become wise.

Well, in the meanwhile, soon after that, in a matter of weeks, he got the commercial for Greyhound and undoubtedly you've seen his face in that commercial unnumbered times. If you know anything about the theatre, he was not only paid well for the commercial but there are residuals and they keep rolling in. From that he gets pictures, he gets TV spots. Tomorrow night he's on Diahann Carroll's show in the second spot. She is the star and he is second in tomorrow night's show. He has just done a pilot for Danny Thomas and Thomas tells him that he has every reason to believe, saying it is a ninety percent chance, that it will be accepted by the network to start in the spring. Well, if it starts in the spring…not the spring, September, pardon me…starts this coming September it will be either twenty-six or thirty-nine segments. And here is one who was about to give up his profession that he loved because he felt it was too much of a problem...and that one little thought conveyed to him.

Well, the dreamer in him is God. There is no other God, as you're told in that same 32nd of Deuteronomy: "See now that I, even I, am he, and there is no God beside me. I kill and I make alive; I wound and I heal; I do all these, and none can deliver out of my hand" (verse 39). So he's putting you through the paces because he is shaping you into his own image; and when he completes it there aren't two of you, just one; you are he. You are putting *yourself* through the paces. You clothed yourself in this mortal flesh for a purpose and you've gone through hell, for the world here is hell... there is no other hell. This is the hell spoken of in scripture and he will not leave himself here because God would lose something. If one of us were left behind, then God would cease to be that being that he is. We would have to leave the ninety and nine and go in search of the one.

So everyone *has* to awaken, but when he awakes he is the same being only enhanced in his beauty, enhanced in his luminosity, enhanced in everything that he was before. But I tell you from my own experience having seen that breathing, living figure...and I knew I'm looking at myself...well, I could not believe that I could ever in eternity be that handsome, not only handsome in face but I mean of character. There was a strength of character, there was a majesty, there was everything...put the superlative to every characteristic that you would love in this world, put it on it, the superlative, and that's what your face really is, not going to be, that's what it is *now*. But the clothes, the mortal form that it now wears, will conform to it, and when it conforms to it in *his* eye, not in the eye of the world, then he wakes. For he only sees the *heart;* he doesn't see the outer form at all (1 Sam. 16:7).

So I tell you, when you see Jesus Christ he looks just like you. So "Beloved, now are we the sons of God. And it does not yet appear what we shall be, but we know that when he *does* appear we shall be like him, and see him as he is" (1 Jn. 3:2). So when he appeared to me, I'm looking into my own face. Here I am looking right into my own face, but it's not a rock now, it is a living, pulsing, breathing man in deep, deep meditation, and he is meditating me. When he is complete, that the work is done, I awake. So we are told in that 17th Psalm, "I shall be satisfied when I awake with his likeness" (verse 15). Everyone will be satisfied when they awake with the likeness of perfection, "For be ye perfect as your Father in haven is perfect." And not one can fail, I don't care what man has ever done. Hitler can't fail for the son of God is in Hitler and the son of God is in Stalin. Not another one like Hitler; he looks just like Hitler raised to the nth degree of perfection...the nth degree of a Stalin...if you can imagine that. We on this level think, "How could it be?" But I tell you that's exactly what's going to happen and then we will all go back. We knew each other before we came down. We are the sons of God who as one man fell, as told us in the 82nd Psalm: "I say ye are sons of God, sons of the Most High, all of you; nevertheless, you will die like men and fall as one man, O princes" (verses 1, 6). So, we are the princes, the sons of God, and collectively we form the king that is the Lord.

So within you is the being. I'm telling you I know it from experience; I am not speculating. So then we are told he speaks with authority and not like the scribes. You can only speak with authority when you speak from experience. I am not speculating, I'm not theorizing, I am telling you exactly what happened to me. And I know I'm only the pattern man...that everyone will follow the same pattern. You're going to see that rock. The rock will form itself into a breathing, pulsing, living being, and when you look you're looking right into your own face. But a face that you could not believe you could ever in eternity see and yet you're going to be, because that's your face anyway. "So let us make man in our image after our likeness." And the word translated "perfect" in "And the Rock, his work is perfect" means "to set out for a goal, an end." And the goal of God is to make man in his own image after his own likeness. That is the end! It's not to make a country called America or Russia or any other thing in the world, not to make a man rich, but to make the *image* of God. That is the purpose and that is the *end* of God. This whole vast world came into being just for that purpose. Not to make one person more important than the other in this world, but to make you right into the image of the one and only God in you.

So you will never lose your identity, not in eternity. I cannot lose my identity. I am unlike every being in this world...and so are you. The being who is just the God forming me into his likeness is so completely unlike every being in the world, and he's known in eternity, known by name. But there are more sons of God than there are sands of the sea, and yet we all know each other. That's our wisdom. When we all go back, we know each other intimately—"all things by this law divine in one another's being mingle"—and we will have access to the wisdom of all and this fantastic experience in this world coming down into this mortal flesh.

So, just as Benny's friend...I haven't met him personally, I've only corresponded. He hasn't come to see me. He read the books and got the results, and so he feels, well now, all right, he knows, perfectly all right. I wish that some night Benny would bring him home and that we could chat. But at the moment he's a success, and quite often when people become a success they then turn their back upon the ladder by which they did ascend and completely forget it. But it was the little book *Out of This World* that fired that Imagination which is God. And the God in him is the eternal

The Return of Glory

God, perfect, absolutely perfect. No one gets off the wheel of recurrence until they are perfect as he who started the work in them judges perfection, and they must fit, superimposed, and no raw edges, just one.

A friend who came to see me tonight told me how he first came to hear me. He said, "It was early '67, I was over in the Glendale library, and I went to get a book. As I pulled the book off the shelf, a book fell to the floor. I picked it up and it was by Neville and I read the title, *Your Faith is Your Fortune,* and I stuck it back in, that wasn't the book I came to get. So a week later when I brought my book back, I went to the same area and pulled another book out, and that little book fell down again. Picked it up, it's *Your Faith is Your Fortune* by Neville, and I pushed it back into the area. The third week I pulled a book off and *it* fell again. Well, after three times falling to the floor, the same book, I took it over to the table and read about twelve pages. Having read it, it appealed to me so I checked it out, and before I brought it back I read if from cover to cover twice. Then a few weeks later I saw an ad in the paper where you were speaking and I haven't missed a Monday night since."

So he and his wife will come every Monday to these meetings because the little book fell three times. Well, that wasn't by accident either. That whole thing was done because in the same letter he encloses a vision. He said, "I'm driving my car at night"—this is all in vision—"and suddenly I feel that I'm going to have a baby. Well, my wife is going to have the baby…I couldn't have the baby. But I couldn't see her face." Evidently it wasn't his wife; nevertheless, it had to be a wife and she's going to have a baby. Well, all the streets are dark, only one house had lights in it, so he pulled over to the curb in his vision and then he saw behind these open windows where the lights were what seemed to be a night school. There was an instructor or at least a lecturer and students. He rushed on in saying, "Call a doctor, quick, quick, quick because I'm going to have a baby!" Then the instructor and the students ran out towards the car, he opened the door, and here on the seat is a baby. There is no wife, just a baby. He picked up the baby and he said, "I'm a father" and repeated it three times. "I am a father. I am a father."

Well, here is the most beautiful adumbration, a foreshadowing of the event. I tell you, this is the most marvelous foreshadowing of the event. Everyone is going to have it. We never leave this until the Father in us knows his job is done. And his only one work in this world is to make us conform to his own perfection. He was perfect when he came down; he'll be perfect when he ascends. When he ascends, by reason of this enhanced expansion he will still be the same perfection—you can't improve upon perfection—but you can be more expansive, more luminous, the same perfect being. So, all the sons of God are perfect, forming one body. As Paul in his analogy uses the body...there is a heart, lungs, kidneys, liver, all the vital organs and they have different functions, but they all form one body. So everything in my body still makes one body. We, together, form the one body, and each is known and loved by each other as brothers. So he said, "Go unto my brothers and say unto them I am ascending unto my Father and to your Father, unto my God and to your God." There can't be two Fathers, there can't be two Gods. So I'm ascending...so we are brothers, really brothers in the most intimate sense of the word, and collectively we form the Father.

So here, the Rock...I'm telling you it's literally true, and throughout scripture you will read about this Rock. "The Rock in the desert, they struck it and out came the living water" (Num. 20:11). In the psalms, they struck it and out came the honey...out came everything from this Rock. But the Rock is God and there's no source of anything in this world but God. So everything comes out of God and he's called the Rock. So the wise man builds his home upon the Rock. Let anything come now, the rains may come, all these come, and it cannot be washed away if you build upon the only foundation in the world.

And the Christ spoken of in scripture is in you—say "I am," *that's* he, your own wonderful human Imagination *that's* Christ. Don't entertain anything outside of what you want to see in your world. Don't imagine anything outside of exactly what you want in your world. If you do, you're going to get it, because all things come out of him. So take the most noble concepts in the world and entertain them as though they were true. Why shouldn't you be everything that you want to be? You should be, because all things are possible to him and he's inviting us all to simply *believe* it.

But I tell you, if you go through certain difficulties, certain sadness, all theses things, it's because he is weaving you, grinding you on the stone of life as it were into his image. But when I say grinding you, you're grinding yourself because you are that son of God, and you're taking this form that you wear, this mortal flesh, and grinding it. So when Blake said in his vision to Max Beckman—this is a work on art, *Looking at Modern Painting*—and Beckman when he came back from the vision said, "I saw this noble genius, Blake, and he waved to me, he said, 'Have confidence in objects... everything is ordered and correct and must fulfill its destiny in order to attain perfection. Follow this path, and you will receive from your own ego a deeper perception of the eternal beauty of creation; you will also receive an ever increasing release from that which seems so sad and terrible." He will show you why this event that is so sad and so hard to bear took place...and the whole thing is ordered and correct.

And in the end, then you awake and you are one with the infinite beauty that is your own being. And all the majesty in the world...you could

The Return of Glory

not conceive of such beauty, such character in the face that I saw. Until you see it, you can only speculate. Because I know that when I saw it I could hardly believe I am looking at the being I knew as Neville. I am looking at the most glorious being that one could ever see, and yet I'm looking at Neville. He's breathing, he's pulsing, eyes closed in deep, deep meditation, and I knew he's meditating me. When he's finished with his work, which is to make me conform to him, I must be just as perfect as he is perfect, then he's going to awake. And when he awakes I will awake. When both are awake, we are one, not two. That was the work he set out to do in the beginning when this whole vast world came into being.

So the Rock is not something out in space and a rock, it's a true statement: "And the Rock was Christ and the Rock is God, and "Who is the God but the Lord," said the psalmist. "And who is the Rock but our God, and who is our Redeemer but the Rock." So I am redeemed by what is called the Rock. I can see it now before my eyes…you couldn't get something more concentrated. It was completely down to the limit of a quartz, not sand, just a quartz. It could be one solid diamond, but it was dull in color, as though you just took it out, but dull, just one solid, solid quartz, about that big. Then as I looked at it, it broke. And then all these things quickly gathered themselves together, and here is this perfect being sitting in the lotus posture. I'm looking at him, I'm becoming so excited as I'm looking, and then he begins to glow like the sun. When he reaches the limit of luminosity it explodes, and I wake in my room, just simply awed and bewildered by what I had just seen. Then you start searching his Word, called the scripture, and you find in scripture confirmation of your own experience, exactly what happened to you…there it is.

So when our wise men today are speculating about curtailing the population explosion and doing all these things, they have not one chance of a snowball in the equator, none whatsoever. So maybe we'll have it here… some wise man may persuade our country to adopt a certain method. But it won't work. The Chinese will still be growing hundreds of millions and so will India. We will find ourselves in this land just simply out numbered. And we will think, well now, that's perfect. It is not a problem of biology, it's not a problem of children; it is a problem that is economic. Because when a man who knows what he is talking about can tell a gathering as intelligent as that gathering of a thousand people—here are the leaders in science, in government, in religion, all are present—and then Mr. Carver got up and addressed them and stood before them, as I stand before you, and "everything on my body came out of the peanut…the cloth, the color on my tie, 300 by-products." Then he said, "We can clothe and feed the entire world, not America, the whole world out of what we can produce in this synthetic kingdom from the Southern states of America."

Well, isn't the problem economic? But I do not have the solution, I am not an economist. I can't balance my own checkbook. There isn't a month I'm not told by the bank that I owe more, I mean, I have less than I thought I had. If it's only forty cents…it's always something less. Once, I think I got a credit for $100. We could hardly believe it…read it over and over and over again. And this is not a big checkbook, may I tell you, it's a very small little amount in that balance. Here, in spite of it we can't balance it…and my wife majored in mathematics at Smith. She took it in high school, she went to Smith, and that was her major subject. She can't balance the book.

So, I'm telling you that it is an economic problem. But what is the solution I do not know. I'm always amused when I hear all these wise men expounding, like the Toynbee's and all people who can speak maybe twenty languages more perfectly than we speak the one which is English, and they can speak all of these. I stand aghast at their nonsense, sheer utter nonsense. They seem not to know the Word of God at all. You read it carefully in the 32nd chapter of Deuteronomy: "He has fixed the bounds of the people according to the number of the sons of God…and the sons of God are more numerous than the stars of the heavens, more numerous than the sands of the sea." So here are the sons. Not one little child could come into this world were he not brought into the world as the mortal clothing of the son of God who is within him…and that's why he can breathe. God became man that man may become God. If that son of God who is perfect—he isn't becoming perfect he *is* perfect—was not actually resident in that little child, the child couldn't breathe, it couldn't be born alive. So every child that comes into the world is brought in by the son of God. And he had sons, unnumbered sons, and yet there's a limit to the number. This is not an infinite number; it's a fabulous number known only to the collective one that is God. But he knows each by name…you are known and loved as an individual. You aren't loved just as a collective being, no, you are loved as an individual and you are known by name, so that all gathered together that one speaks to you individually and loves you beyond measure.

So that so-called infinite number isn't infinite if you mean without boundaries…it is a limited number of sons. Now, sons are clothing themselves in mortal flesh, therefore, who is going to stop it? You can take all the things in the world. We go out to stop this and then nature seems to take over and rubs it out. So we think we are immune to a certain thing and all of a sudden nature fights it, something within us, and puts it to naught as though it were not. Because these sons are going to come in, these children are going to come in because the son of God meditating you can't stop it from coming in. I'm one of ten. There were twelve, but two at birth did not survive. But they're still the results of God's sons meditating, and they will still come in for the experiment. No one's going to stop it.

Every one of us here, if you could only dwell upon the fact that you really are the perfect son of God and you can't improve upon it. One day you're going to see your face and I can't tell you your thrill. You get an awful shock when you look into the mirror the next morning after having seen what you really are…and to see what is reflected in the mirror as against what you *know* it is. So, gradually it is woven into the likeness of the Father in you—for that is the Father that is Jesus Christ.

Now all things are possible to him. Don't turn to anyone on the outside, turn to him. He is your own wonderful human Imagination. You put yourself in the place tonight of David Moses. We cannot duck it any longer, here there is a barrier—for unnumbered years, it goes now into quite a few hundred years—where there was a limit as to what profession they could enter, where they could go. He heard the true story concerning Jesus Christ. Prior to that he was talking to and praying to something on the outside. Now he dares to assume that he is successful in the theater in spite of the limitation imposed upon that pigment of skin. Now all of a sudden he becomes a success. I only hope my friend Benny will remind him and constantly remind him that it is not an accident, and don't now go off because he is a success and forget the principle by which he became successful, because that's always possible. We become successful and all of a sudden we forget it and think it would have happened anyway, that it isn't because of what I read in the book or what that man wrote in the front page of the book about the fool persisting in his folly. "No, all of a sudden I got the 'breaks,'" he will say. He didn't get any breaks. All things move from a certain source and you can't plant one thing and reap something other than what you planted. You're told, "Be not deceived; God is not mocked, for as a man sows, so shall he reap" (Gal. 6:7). And so we put something in and we reap it.

So you having heard this story, you dare to assume the most noble thing in the world. I'll tell you one thing you could not achieve anything in this world of Caesar comparable to that which you really are: you are *already* perfect. But, you've taken this challenge! It was in the beginning: "Let us make man in our image after our likeness." That was the challenge and that's the only end you have in sight. While you're moving towards that end you play the part of the poor man, the rich man, the beggar man, the thief, the gunman, everything, you play them all. But all things were ordered and correct, so forget it. No matter what you've done, don't dwell upon it and feel remorseful. No…you did it and there was a purpose behind it all. Now, start towards dwelling upon this one being within you and his perfection. And then dream nobly…noble, noble dreams and have no other foundation. There is no other God: "See now that I, even I, am he and there is no God beside me; I kill, I make alive; I wound, I heal, and *none* can deliver out of my hand. I raise my hand to heaven, and cry, I live forever." Read it in the 32nd of Deuteronomy (verse 39). This is the being in you that is speaking to you if he could only get your ear. But I have been sent to get your ear for him that you may listen to him in you. And every noble thing that you desire in this world, he is telling you it's possible, you can get it because all things are possible to him. All *you* have to do is to dare to assume the feeling of the wish fulfilled and walk as though it were true. If you dare to walk as though it is true *now*, in spite of all lack of evidence it will become true. How? No one knows. He knows, because he has all the means. His ways and his means are past finding out, so don't try to find out the ways and don't try to find out the means. You dare to walk as though you were…and you name it. You actually assume it and walk, and it will become a fact.

Now let us go into the Silence.

* * *

Now, are there any questions, please?

Q: (inaudible)
A: I know it. We agreed to dream in concert, because all things by a law divine in one another's being mingle. We are one in the most intimate sense of the word and yet individualized. The word translated from the Hebrew is "Elohim" and it's plural. "In the beginning God" that word God is Elohim. It could be "in the head," for some translations use the word which we call "beginning," "head." In fact, some of the best and oldest translations will have "In the head, God created the heavens and the earth." I know from my own experience that you and I are one, but yet we are brothers. We are individualized and tend forever towards greater and greater individualization. "Go unto my brothers and say to them, I am ascending unto my Father and your Father, unto my God and your God." That's the 20th chapter of the Book of John (20:17). So here I am ascending to my Father and he is your Father, but he calls us brothers. The world does not seem to rest upon that; they still put him on the outside, and not a brother.

Now he said after the resurrection he knows that we are all one: "So go to my brothers and tell them I'm ascending to my Father and to your Father, to my God and to your God." But man still refuses to accept him as a brother. He tells you he is not only ascending to the Father, he *is* the Father: "I came out from the Father and came into the world; again, I am leaving the world and returning to the Father. And he who sees me has seen the Father" (Jn. 6:28; Jn. 14:9). He has discovered the Fatherhood of God and he is the Father. So *collectively* we are the Father, and yet individually we are brothers. We're all brothers, all individualized, and yet collectively we are the Father. Does that satisfy you?

Well, that is from the Book of Ecclesiastes, "Is there a thing of which it is said, See this is new? It has been already in ages past but there's no remembrance of former things, nor shall there be any remembrance of things to come later among those who will come after" (1:9). That's the most difficult thing for man to accept, because we say today we are living in an entirely different world and it has never happened in the history of man before. But we have such short memories. We say it couldn't happen in an intelligent community like Germany who gave so much to the arts, gave so much to science. Possibly the most cultured of all nations in the world at the time that a Hitler arose and they could follow a monster like that! Who could have believed it could happen? So we read scripture and it's all recorded in scripture, but they called those then Pharaoh and the Egyptians. We call them by other names. Genocide is in scripture. There isn't one evil act in the world that man is capable of doing that is not recorded in scripture openly. You name it, it's in scripture. And there's a *recurrence*, but man will not believe it. You could see the shadow coming, but "It couldn't happen *now*! That happened when man was barbarous." What was more barbaric than the Hitler regime and the Stalin regime? You can't conceive…and yet scripture records it. Well, we thought, "Oh, that's in the old days when they plowed with a hoe, but not today, when we have missiles and all these things." They've only increased the capacity to destroy more quickly, but the same tendency is to destroy.

But you can't destroy the being that you really are. For I saw him and he's perfect. He isn't becoming perfect, he *is* perfect. If you could look right into that being's face—and you're going to see your own face—and you will not see anything more majestic, you'll never see any greater measure of character, nothing more handsome, I assure you. I don't think, and you're a man, you will take it from me that you will enter a beauty contest tonight with expectancy of winning, and yet the being that you really are would put anything on earth to shame. You're not becoming that; that being *is* that. He is forming this mortal flesh into his likeness, and when they are formed they are one.

That's the story of Adam and Eve. She came out of him; then he leaves everyone and cleaves to her and they become one. But the most intimate relationship in the world between man and wife they still aren't one. They go to their sleep at night in their separate worlds of dreams. They have their day dreams and some of them may coalesce, but they have separate dreams too. She may be dreaming of something of which she would be ashamed to tell him and he the same way…so they aren't one. But the day will come you will be one. Their emanation is this [body] and yet it is your wife 'til the sleep of death is past. When it's past, we're one. That's when we wake and both awake. So in the 44th Psalm, "Rouse thyself, why sleepest thou, O Lord? Awake!" If he wakes, well then, what he meditates will wake. But he won't wake until he's finished his meditation, which is to make that thing meditated as perfect as he is. "So be ye perfect as your Father in heaven is perfect."

Q: (inaudible)

A: I can't tell you, Judith my dear. I know my mother was twenty, my father, my brother…I only know that death does not end this world at all. It's like going through a door on a huge stage where there are many stages at the same time. You go through but you do not cease to be at that moment in time when those who are on the stage cannot see you or touch you or hear you. You are suddenly…and what is the miracle behind it I don't know…save the being within you can do anything and he restores his image at the age twenty, approximately twenty, in an environment best suited for the work he is doing. He is doing that work. Now, you may not…if you drop tonight and the year is '69, it doesn't mean that 1969 is where you pick it up. You may find yourself in the year 4000 or the year 1000 or the year one.

As Richard Feynman said, our great physicist, and he is a theoretical physicist who just won the Nobel Prize, he said, "The time relationship is irrelevant"—he's speaking of the little positron—"It starts from where it hasn't been and it speeds to where it was an instant ago; arriving there it is bounced so hard it's time sense is reversed and then it returns to where it hasn't been." Now this is Feynman…for that he got a Nobel Prize. Now, it goes back to where it hasn't been. Then he ends his paper on this note "The time is irrelevant, whether it goes forward or backward is irrelevant. The whole thing is *closed*." Then he said what scripture teaches only he put it in a modern tongue. Ecclesiastes tells us there is nothing new under the sun and everything is ordered, a time to be born, a time to die, time to laugh, time to cry, and all these things are fixed like a play.

The Return of Glory

Now, he tells us that the Hamiltonian concept of the world was that the future is developing slowly out of the past. He said, "Not what we now know concerning the positron. We must now think of the space-time universe as *already* laid out, fixed, and we only become aware of increasing portions of it successively. What portion we become aware of, whether it's past relative to this moment or future relative to this moment is irrelevant." So if I drop now and my work isn't done, I may find myself in the world 3000, not 1969, and he in me who knows all, he'll make it perfectly normal to me in that age. It will seem familiar because it is to him. He was shown the entire play before he set out, as told us in the 3rd chapter of Galatians: "And scripture, foreseeing that God would justify the heathen by faith, preached the gospel *beforehand* to Abraham" (3:8). Abraham simply means "the father of the multitudes." That is another name for God. So here, he preached it to Abraham, so he saw the whole thing...and then he slept. There's not a thing in scripture that tells us that he's awakened—he will awake as Christ, but not a thing in scripture. And "A deep sleep fell upon Abraham and he slept" (Gen. 15:12). You read it carefully and all these things happened, but not a thing is said...it implies by the way it's written that he must have awakened, but it doesn't say so

In the Book of Job, no one reading the Book of Job...he heard these things, but he hadn't seen the face of God. He didn't know him. But in the end of Job, the very last chapter, the 42nd, you're told that all these things came upon Job by the Lord and all Job's friends came and comforted him through all the horrors and the evils that the Lord God had wrought upon him. So in the end, Job was innocent. He was in the beginning innocent...read the very first verse, "an innocent man." He was an innocent man and then these things happened. And in the end he got back not only what was taken from him but a hundred-fold more. That's what's going to happen to *every one* of us. We gave up the glory of the Father and clothed ourselves in mortal flesh, and as we clothed ourselves we had to give up the glory. But then, we return not only to the glory, but the experience will enhance that glory.

Good night.

AS HE IS SO ARE WE

2/21/69

We are told in the 45th of Isaiah that "I am the Lord, and there is no other. I form the light and create darkness, I make weal and create woe, I am the Lord, who does all these things" (45:5,7), and John tells us, "As he is so are we in this world" (1 Jn. 4:17). Man isn't taught that but scripture teaches it. Teachers do not teach it, they speak of another, something outside of man that is other than himself that creates the weal and the woe. Yet we are taught in scripture, "As he is so are we in this world."

Now all the stories told of Jesus Christ are acted parables. The story itself is an acted parable, the miracles are acted parables. Tonight, let us take just a couple. In the 2nd chapter of Luke, we are told that his parents went up to Jerusalem at the Passover, and when Jesus was twelve years of age they went up as was their custom. When the feast came to an end, they returned home and thinking that he was in the caravan they did not seek him out until a day had passed. Not finding him they searched among their kinfolk and acquaintances, and did not find him. So they returned to Jerusalem and after *three* days they found him in the temple. They said to him, "Son, how could you have done this to us? Your father and I have been seeking you anxiously." He said to them, "How is it that you sought me? Did you not know that I must be in my Father's house?" (Luke 2:48). And they did not understand the saying that he spoke to them.

So Luke records his first words claiming that God was his Father. Here his parents stand before him and he claims that God is my Father, and they did not understand him. Well, if you are seeking the cause of creation, the cause of the phenomena of your life among your kinfolk, among your acquaintances, among anything in this world outside of the temple, you'll never find him. For do you not know that you are God's temple and the

Spirit of God dwells in you? You will never find the cause of the phenomena of life outside of your own wonderful human Imagination that is God that is Jesus Christ. So you either find him in the temple or you'll never find him. You'll find him *in yourself*...that's the only place you will ever find him.

Now the whole story is a parable. His whole life is a *pattern*. He is the pattern man that the individual, in finding himself as the cause of the phenomena of his own life, will find Jesus Christ. You'll never find him in any other way. Now, as he is so are we in this world? Well, on the surface, believing him to be something on the outside, something that is different, something that overcame, something that is now living elsewhere, and yet we are as he is? Because the being spoken of is the Christ *in you* that is the hope of glory; so, as he is so are you.

Let us turn, in the same book, the 8th chapter now to see how it works. We are told, one day he entered a boat with his disciples and as they sailed he fell asleep. Then a great strong wind descended upon the lake and here in the storm the boat is filling. So they went to him and *woke* him saying "Master, master, we are perishing!" and he woke. As he woke, he rebuked the wind and the raging waves and they became quiet and there was a great calm. The one who caused the storm is the same one who quelled the storm. There is no other. He fell asleep. Well, when a man is in a sleep he dreams all kinds of things. Man may not believe it but here in this world Christ is asleep, and the wars and the confusion and the depressions and all the horrors of the world, all the blows, are because he's asleep. You only bring about the weal, the happiness, the wealth, the joy of the world when he awakes. If man is not aware of his own imaginal activities, well then, he's asleep, asleep relative to that activity. It could be that he's dreaming noble dreams and lovely dreams, or it could be that he's dreaming ignoble dreams, horrible dreams the woes of the world. But whatever he dreams he's going to externalize.

Well, in this case, it was a storm. He fell asleep the minute he got into the boat. What boat? You think of some little boast where man sails in the boat? *Man* is the ark of God containing within himself everything in the world. All the creative power in the world is contained in man. I am the ark of God; I am not a phantom of the sea and earth. I am the boat, the ark of God. And in this ark Christ is either asleep and the storm rages, or he is awake and then there is calm and there is weal. It's one or the other. So the story is telling us what we are in this world: that my own wonderful human Imagination is Jesus Christ and that is God. And so, as he is in me so am I... the outer projection of himself in this world. I am surrounded by woes or by weal based upon what he in my very being is dreaming. But he and I are one. For if he is my Imagination, he can never be so far off as even to be near, for nearness implies separation. So he can't even be near. They will speak,

"How near is God?" He can't be near. I can't go any place where I am not imagining. I can't imagine anything unless I am actually ___(??). So here, where could I go that I am not imagining? There's no place in the world I can go where I am not imagining; therefore, God is *never* so far off as *even* to be near. Can't be, for if I say he's near me, then we are two. And we aren't two, we are one. God is our own wonderful human Imagination, that's God.

Now, let me tell you a story that was given to me this past week. It was mailed I think late on the fifteenth, but I didn't get it until Tuesday. This friend who is here tonight he said that "In my vision I noticed around my feet clusters of little tiny seeds, like magnetic seeds, and they were miniatures of the world that I am observing. The entire terrain, the buildings, everything in the world on the outside were around my feet in clusters in little magnetic seeds. If I swept them off, as I did, they instantly reformed themselves, grew back instantly, maintaining the outer world in harmony with themselves. The outer world was big and magnified, but they were little tiny magnetic seeds. If perchance there was any change in the re-growth, there was an automatic change in the outer world to conform to the little magnetic seed around my foot, here on my foot, around my ankles."

Well, if you know scripture, the foot often is a symbol of a foot as you would use the foot, but there are passages that are fantastic. I would suggest to him above all, and to you who are here, to read the 40th chapter of Psalms. This is the second verse…how he lifts me up, meaning it becomes a symbol of the person himself. He lifts me up from the pit and out of the miry bog and places my feet upon a Rock (Ps.40:2). For the Rock of scripture is God: "Of the Rock that begot you, you are unmindful, and you have forgotten the God who gave you birth" (Deut.32:18). And the Rock was Christ. So he places my foot, which is myself, upon the only foundation worthy to be placed, which is the Rock, and that Rock is Christ, and Christ is my own wonderful human Imagination. (1Cor.10:4).

So I can say to him that vision is the most *glorious* thing. You are becoming more and more aware of causation and the *cause is you*, not on the outside, for the foot is the symbol of your own wonderful being, and now it's placed upon the Rock. For in this 40th chapter of the Book of Psalms, "In the volume of the book it is written about *me*." I thought it was about another person as everyone who gets the Bible thinks they are reading secular history that goes back in time thousands of years ago, and it's all about the one who is reading it, but he doesn't realize it. Now here is my friend who has come to the point by vision where he knows it's all about himself. That everything on the outside that he saw magnified he saw in miniature, a magnetic seed around his foot. And the foot is the symbol of himself as told you in that 2nd verse of the 40th Psalm.

So the whole vast world is a man pushed out. That, "All that I behold, though it *appears* without, it is within, in my Imagination of which this world of mortality is but a shadow." It's a shadow world that seems so big and overpowering. And causation is the being observing it, and within him are all the seeds, everything in the world. He is the ark of God and everything is contained within him. But if he is asleep, well, there could be a storm and the chances are it *will* be a storm. When he awakes he quiets the stormy seas. And no one quite understands that it's the difference between being awake to one's imaginal activities and being asleep to them. So when I'm asleep to what I'm imagining, well then, I may create frightful, frightful storms and think it is caused by something external to myself. I will try to trace causation and if I am asleep I will find something on the outside. I will say, "You know, the low pressure tonight." If you want a good laugh listen every night to the weather. In fact, it's become really a joke. His name is Gordon Wale, it's Channel Four and he comes on a little before six. It's gotten to the point now that the announcers when they announce "our great weather expert" they start laughing. You can hear the voices in the background laughing—the boom man, the sound man, the light man, the camera man... they're all laughing. He comes on with a straight face and some times he can't hold it, because the night before he told us about the lovely weather and then came the rain. But he has to justify it—the high pressure, the low pressure, the this pressure, and then suddenly it didn't happen but something else happened.

Causation is always on the outside to the whole vast world and it isn't on the outside at all. Causation is within the one observing everything in this world. He is the symbolized foot in that 2nd verse of the 40th Psalm. You also will read it in the 69th Psalm, you'll read it in Romans, you'll read it all through. In the end, when man actually overcomes it's victory, he puts all things under his foot. Do you recall the words? Everything then is right under the foot. So he sees the clusters of seeds, magnetic seeds around the ankle of his foot, and he's scraping them off and they reappear. As Blake said, "And the oak falls or is cut down by the axe, and the lamb is slain by the knife, but their forms eternal remain forever, returning by the seed of contemplative thought." So I contemplate the thing that *seems* to have vanished. It can't vanish, for the seed is in me, and then it all of a sudden reappears in the world. The whole thing reappears because the seed is within me, and as I contemplate it, it returns by the seed of contemplative thought.

So here, the storm spoken of in that 8th chapter of Luke is our world. If we enter the boat, which is this boat, and we are asleep the chances are we're going to have a storm. When we are awakened by our disciplined mind—for that's what the disciples are, aspects of the mind brought under control of the one who has disciples, so I have disciplined my mind—and as the mind becomes disciplined they awake the dreamer. He's no longer dreaming, he's awake and he quells the storm. As he quells the storm the whole thing is over, but now when he's awake he knows who he is. So, "Why did you seek me among your kinfolk? Why did you seek me among your acquaintances?" You will find in tomorrow's paper or the next day's paper that they are always finding some new guru, some new teacher, some new something and let us all go and hear him, because he or she is so marvelous, so wonderful. Always something on the outside and there is nothing on the outside. You will never find Christ as another; you can only find Christ as yourself, and when you find him he is God.

You will find him and then there's a series of events that unfolds within you bearing witness to your own fatherhood and you are the Father. But until it happens when his Son appears, you will never know, really know, that you are God the Father. You will believe me to a certain degree, but you cannot be convinced to that extent until he stands before you and you see him as Father. Then there is no more trinity that we speak of in this world. I have often thought should it not have been the doctrine of the unity of being, the oneness of being, rather than the doctrine of the trinity? For the trinity is difficult for man to grasp. It can be grasped, but it's easier if you speak of the doctrine, the great dogma of *revealed* Christianity as a unity. I tell you that you and I are one...that I do know. But you will not know it to the point of actual conviction and knowing it until my son David appears in your world and calls you Father. When he calls you Father, as he has called me Father and I know I am his Father, well then, you will know that you and I are one. In that day, you will actually know that you and I are one and you'll also know that everyone in the world must have the same experience, and therefore everyone is the same one. This is the great doctrine of the unity.

My old friend Ab whenever he entered the meeting always remained in the back, and when he came out he came out always intoning, "Praise be unto that unity that is our unity." That was his opening address to all of us as he came through the door. "Praise be unto that unity that is our unity." I wonder what percentage of the few who were present really understood what Ab was trying to tell: a unity of being, a diversity of faces all completely individualized and tending forever towards ever greater and greater individualization...and yet one. The same Father in unnumbered faces; but the same Father having only one Son, and that Son is the son of each in the world proving the unity of being.

So here in these stories every miracle is an acted parable. He enters the boat which is man, man being the ark of God. As he sets sail—and to set sail is to start the journey of life, that's when he sets sail—he falls asleep and then arises the storm. That storm could be a financial storm, a marital storm, a marshal storm, well, you name it, and it could be that kind of storm, all in the process. For a little while you could dream of something lovely and then that is the weal, the wealth, the happiness, the joy that comes with that kind of dreaming. But if you don't know who you really are and that the cause of the weal is your own imaginal activity, and you think it is caused by that relative who left you a fortune; or that this job that pays you well now and you get older and older and the job fades, there comes that day when you can't fit this bill any more, or maybe you have to retire because you reach a certain age, and then all things change because you don't know who your are. So if you don't know the imaginal activity that is the cause of the phenomena of your life, then once more you fall into the storm and the storm rages; and will continue raging until you are awakened, 'til the disciplined mind (called disciples) rouses you and all of a sudden you remember who you are and then become completely aware, morning, noon and night, even in the so-called dream of the night, of what you are imagining. You carry it right into the dream and you're imagining, and you do not falter. Because if you really want to build a certain world, then you've got to know what you're imagining, because that is the cause of the world that you're building.

So, do not seek him among things, seek him only in the temple. After three days they found him. Well, three is associated with *resurrection*. "And the third day the earth rose up out of the deep." Three and eight are the two numbers of resurrection in scripture. So here, after three days they found him, where?—in the temple. And then they asked him...well, he was teaching and instructing the wise men of the temple. He was asking questions and then answering questions and instructing. Now, twelve doesn't mean he was twelve years old; he had arrived at the point of adolescence and therefore he was creative. For when a boy reaches or a girl reaches the moment of adolescence, they can reproduce their kind, they can create. So he was at the point of creativity...that's what it's saying in scripture. After three days when he had reached that point where he can create then they found him. He said, "Why and how did you seek me? Did you not know where to seek me that I must be in my Father's house?" And now he identifies God as his Father and then goes on to claim "I and my Father are one" (Jn.10:30). There is no other Father and we are one. They did not understand the saying which he spoke to them.

The whole vast world does not understand it. You talk about it and your most intimate friend, your most intimate love, and you take them apart and tell them. Well, at the moment they can't quite get it...can't quite get it. You mean my own Imagination that I am capable of imagining all the unlovely things in the world…and *that* is the cause of the phenomena of my life? Can't be! It just can't be. I can imagine a lovely picture and execute it, a lovely poem and bring it forth, but don't tell me it's the cause of everything in my world. You mean when I have a toothache, when I have a pain? Yes when I have anything in this world I can only trace it back to one cause, for there's only one cause in the world: "I am the Lord and there is no other." Read it in the 45th chapter of Isaiah: "I am the Lord, and there is no other, I know not any, there is no God besides me. I form the light and I create the darkness, I make weal and create woe, I am the Lord who does all these things" (45:5,7).

So I could blame my wife, my husband, for my misfortunes. I could blame a friend for betraying my trust and it *seems* to be that they were the cause of my misfortunes…and they are not. My *dream* prompted me to act towards the friend that betrayed me as I did act, or to act towards my husband or my wife as I did act. And it isn't there at all…the causation cannot be on the outside; it has to be on the inside. When man begins to awake, he discovers there is no other God, none in the world; his own wonderful human Imagination that's the only God in the world. And just as my friend saw the little tiny—and he uses the word "tiny" advisedly—tiny magnetic seeds, that's the seed—but when it appears in the world it seems so magnified and the whole outer world seems so big compared to these little tiny causations. The whole thing is in man and it's so tiny that he ignored it, he scraped it off. It reforms itself instantly to maintain the outer world. If it didn't reform itself, the outer world would vanish and leave not a little trace behind. But they all reform themselves because they're all *in* man.

Now, he can rearrange the seed into a different pattern. As you rearrange it, the outer world instantly conforms to the rearrangement. Now you can rearrange it only by a change of attitude. I change my attitude toward the world, and as I change it and fix it, I have scraped off and rearranged the little tiny magnetic seed; and the world will conform to this rearrangement. That is the world in which we live. Now it puts us on our own feet…we can't stand on the foot of another. We're now on our own feet when we hear this, so we can't praise or blame the other. We can play the normal part of thanking another for the part they played in our drama, certainly, and being gracious and being civil in the world and so we give thanks for something received. But everything in the world that is coming into my world, good, bad or indifferent, I am drawing it by my attitude towards life. These are all animated and rearranged within me; so, as he is so are we in this world.

The Return of Glory

Well, you tell that to a good Christian and he will simply go through the ceiling, and yet you will read it in the 1st epistle, the 4th chapter of John: "As he is so are we in this world" (4:17). It just follows on the heel of the definition of God as love. He makes the statement, "God is love" and then he goes right into this statement, "As he is so are we in this world." So what a marvelous statement, because he is love, he isn't going to change the imaginal act. I imagine the most horrible thing in the world and love allows me to externalize it in the world. If he corrects me and rearranges it, well then, there are two of us, there isn't one, it's just two now. He is not going to rearrange it. He is within me playing the part and he will suffer this strange dream of mine that the world is taking advantage of me.

Well, within me he is dreaming. And when I awake, and may I tell you, I use the word advisedly, because when you awake, you awake within your own skull. You actually find yourself waking and you wake in your own skull...that's the resurrection and that's when the *real* drama begins. Then you come out of that skull of yours and all the imagery of scripture surrounds you, the child, the witnesses, everything—but you are unseen. For, they went to the tomb and this [skull] is the tomb, and they saw the witnesses there, but him they did not see. They do not see you. They *speak* of you and speak of the child, which they do see, and they speak of the child as your child, but him they did not see. Because you are Spirit you are invisible to mortal eye. Then comes the complete unfoldment of the great drama, all within you, but seen as it takes place, to be external; for everything is unfolding in the most beautiful manner externally, yet it's all taking place *within* you. For man contains eternity within himself; everything in eternity is *now* contained in man.

So the storm if it's raging now, remember it's only because you're not aware of your imaginal activity. If your disciplined mind will bring you to the point where it can rouse you from that deep sleep where you're unaware of what you are imagining, to make you aware of what you *want* to imagine in spite of what you have and still are imagining, well then, the world will change to conform to the change within you. And then the storm will subside and there will be a wonderful calm. But you cannot find him and don't seek for him in any place outside of the temple. Remember, it's in that 1st Corinthians, the 3rd chapter, the 16th verse: "Do you not know that you are God's temple and that the Spirit of God dwells in you?" The average person in the world if they are brutally honest with themselves, if asked that question they would say no, I do not know; for I thought if I went to the synagogue or I went to the cathedral or I went to some other church *that* would be God's temple. He does not dwell in houses made with hands. That's what you're told in scripture, "*You* are the temple of the living God and the Spirit of God dwells in you." Well, where is he then? Say "I am"... that's he.

Now begin to imagine...that's God in action...begin to imagine. But can you believe in the reality of what you have imagined? If you can believe in the reality of that, you will take those little clusters around the ankle and fix them. These little magnetic seeds will be fixed and the outer world will find itself conforming to this fixation around the foot, which is only the symbol of yourself...that you are this whole vast world pushed out. The world you see as something external to yourself is yourself pushed out. And the day will come we will all awake from this marvelous fantastic dream and return to our estate, but enhanced by the experience of falling asleep and having experienced the mystery of death. For, we are *immortal* beings, and we would have to forget completely our immortality in order to experience death. So we experience death by giving up the glory of our Father and clothing ourselves in mortal flesh, which experience is death.

Now, I ask you to take this challenge. You need not completely accept it. Because I know that I've had experiences where people have said to me, "You know, I so enjoy hating someone, I don't want to change it." It's a certain joy they get out of hating something; and they don't realize that they are only hating themselves. But until they awake they will continue to have that little vicarious pleasure. I know that from experience. In the 2nd World War in New York City, this man—he was an only child, had modest means, his parents had modest means, and for reasons not explained to me he despised Roosevelt, just hated him. Every morning when he shaved he would talk to himself in the mirror, but imagine that it was Roosevelt and tell him everything under the sun that he disliked about him. I told him, you come here to my meetings and you hear all that I'm talking about and you still do it? He said, "Yes Neville. I go to a show on Broadway and pay ten dollars. No show on Broadway can give me the joy that that ten minutes before the mirror in the morning gives me for nothing. I just have the most marvelous show telling him what I think of him."

Well, it paid off in the end to him...not to Roosevelt. So it all came back to him, that same venom that he simply spilled out on this imaginary face, all returned to him. They lost their home in Brooklyn...went down to Florida and the whole thing simply dissolved. That was the storm. And I'm trying to tell him to awake. You are sleeping when you dream that he is the cause of anything in this world. Well, he came from a Germanic background, his parents were German. Well, why should he take it out on Roosevelt because we went to war with Germany? That whole thing was a mad dream anyway. The war was a mad dream...but he simply took it out... he couldn't get over the fact that we were at war with Germany. And if I told him that Germany declared war on us and that we had no alternative if we are at war today because they declared war on us...couldn't see that. I said, "Forget it, the war is a bad dream anyway and you're only confusing it and making the storm a raging horrible storm." He said, "No, I get pleasure seven days a week."

So it's entirely up to us. If I want to hate someone and augment it with my intensified hate, all right, do it. But I tell you the only God that you will ever know you will find him in your own wonderful human Imagination, and your Imagination is God. You'll find him no place but in the temple, and *you* are the temple of the living God. Don't seek him out there. For "parents" only mean tradition, so tradition teaches us to look outside. And so, he said to the parents, "How is it that you sought me? Do you not know I must be in my Father's house?" and they did not understand. Tradition will not understand. If I say to all the priesthoods of the world today—and I have said it to rabbis, to Catholic priests, to ministers of the different denominations of the Protestant world—that I encountered David of biblical fame and they start laughing. When I go to the part that he called me Father and when I take the 89th Psalm and show them where the Lord said, "I have found David and he has cried unto me, 'Thou art my Father, my God and the Rock of my salvation' (verse 26), they stand a little bit silent, but they can't relate to it. They have not made the Bible *their* biography: the Bible is something that is talking about something other than themselves and it is not their biography. Until you make it your biography, you will never understand the Bible. The whole book from beginning to end is all about you individually.

So, you are the one who will find David and it is you he will call Father. It is you that he will call "My God and the Rock of my salvation," I mean literally. He will stand before you as just coming into adolescence, he's about twelve or thirteen. He's just arrived at the point where you will find him in the temple, for "He was twelve years old when they went to Jerusalem as was their custom." Then, on their return at the end of the feast they thought he was among them in the caravan. Not seeing him at the end of the day they sought him among their kinsfolk and acquaintances, and not finding him, they returned to Jerusalem. There after three days they found him. Where?—in the temple. "After three days" is resurrection and he's now resurrected. For, he would not be left in the pit. He cries out in the Psalm, "You would not leave me in the pit, in the miry bog" (Ps. 40:2). And so you will awaken me and then find me. So he finds him after three days in the temple.

So I tell everyone who will ever listen to me, you are immortal beings and the story is all about you. If you want your real biography, don't get some ghost writer to write it for you, you get the Bible. That is your *real auto*-biography. You inspired the writers of the Old; you came in and you fulfilled it in the New. But the same one who fulfilled it is fulfilling it, for there's only one Christ. Christ is the universally diffused individuality. No child could be born of woman who is not Christ, for Christ is the being *in* that child, meditating him into being, bringing him into the world.

So tonight you take seriously what I've told you. Also take the story of my friend…it's all within him, for the foot is the symbol of the person himself. Although it seems to be in miniature magnetic seeds in clusters and the world bearing witness of the arrangement on his foot, the foot is the symbol of himself; and any rearrangement of self produces a corresponding rearrangement in the outer world

Now let us go into the Silence.

* * *

Now are there any questions, well, if there aren't any questions, we will be here every Monday and Friday until we close in June. Until Monday… Good night.

CHRIST BORE OUR SINS

2/24/69

We are told in scripture that Christ bore our sins in his body on the cross. Sin is "missing the mark" whether it be a state of health (I'm in frightful pain) or I am sorry for some other reason, and *he* is doing the suffering for me. So you say to someone, "How do you feel?" and he tells you, "Well, I don't feel well…really I'm in great pain." If you told him that Christ is doing the suffering, he would think you're insane, because the average person has a concept of Christ as someone other than himself. That's what man believes: Christ is something on the outside, certainly not himself. Until man discovers who Christ *really* is the Bible makes no sense whatsoever, none.

Here we are told, "In the beginning was the Word and the Word was with God and the Word was God" (Jn. 1:1, 1:14). Now that is God dwelling in us, because if the Word is God and the Word dwells in us then God is dwelling in us. We are told that God is doing all the suffering. Now who is he? You said when I asked you "How do you feel," you said, "I am in pain." Well, that's he. "What do you mean that's God?" That's his name…and his name and himself are one. You said, "*I am* in pain," but you're telling me that God is in pain, for that is God. There is no other God. So you say, "I am in pain," well, is he not bearing all the sufferings? But you did not know that it was God.

Now, you may think that everyone in this world would like to awaken to that knowledge, you would think so. If I told you that it is a joy beyond measure to awaken to the knowledge of who God really is, and who you are because *you* are God, you would think the whole vast world would say yes to that; but may I tell you no, only an nth part would say yes to it, only an nth part. A friend of mine (who is here tonight) wrote me a letter saying,

"Six months ago, my husband, who was a carpenter working for the Los Angeles schools and he was let out. He said, 'Oh, they'll call me, they'll call me back.' And that was it. Well, here recently they did call him back. When he came in, she told him that the school had called, and then reminded him that that was exactly what he said six months ago. She said he was mad as anything, so mad! She was reminding him of the seed he had planted and he didn't want to recognize his own harvest, he didn't want it. Then she said, "What he said to me in his madness, in his anger, I cannot tell you, I don't remember it, but it was a contact of souls between us and I distinctly heard him say to me, 'I am asleep and don't you *dare* wake me!'" He doesn't want to be awakened. He's not alone, may I tell you, ninety-nine percent of the people of the world do not wish to be awakened. They feel if they awaken to this higher level, they will lose the pleasures of the flesh.

A friend of mine who was a very successful playwright in the old days of vaudeville and then radio…all the big ones were his clients. All of them that today you see on TV were his clients. He got ten percent of their gross. In those days if you made a thousand a week, that was a lot of money. He said that today people are making, well, he can't tell what enormous sums they're making, but something different. But in those days a cup of coffee was a nickel, it wasn't twenty-five cents, and he was getting ten percent out of Benny, out of all of these people. He used to love me to talk to him and just tell him about my visions and my interpretations of scripture; but he said, "Now that's enough, no more." He didn't want to go beyond the point to become interested, because he would lose his physical contact with life, and he was thinking only of sex. He had money, he had everything in the world that money could buy, lived beautifully, and he played the field. He was once married and he had two sons, then he was divorced, and then he became the bachelor for many, many years and he played the field in the theatrical world. Didn't want any part of it. So when I came west He had moved out here, and at his age, he was I would say about ten years my senior, he was still of the same opinion. He saw me on TV, called me up right away and invited me out. We had him home to dinner and he was the same wonderful man, but afraid to just touch it that he may awaken to the desire to want it. Well, then a few years ago, watching TV early in the morning right after breakfast he got up from the chair and fell flat on his face and he was gone. So now he's restored to a body just like the one before, only young, full of vigor, to continue his search and his sexual life.

But you'll say now why? Well, "I will send a famine upon the world; it will not be a hunger for food nor a thirst for water, but for the hearing of the words of God" (Amos 8:11). That's the famine. Until it possesses you, it makes no difference, you can talk from now to the ends of time and it doesn't interest anyone. You can talk from now 'til the very ends of time and tell people what I have experienced that parallels scripture and it wouldn't interest them at all unless that famine is upon them. When that *hunger* is upon them for the Word of God they'll listen and want to have the experience, and they'll have it. So when her husband could say to her...and he meant it and he was angry...I can't remember the words of anger, said she, but suddenly I heard him speak from within me and our souls seemed to be in communication, and we were one. He was saying to me "I am asleep. Don't you dare wake me up!" Now, that's that picture.

"He sent his Word into the world..." Well, if he is the Word then he sends himself, can't send another; therefore, "He who sees me sees him who sent me." There is no "other," there's only God. So whoever sees me sees him who sent me, for I am the Word, and "My word shall not return unto me void; it must accomplish that which I purpose and prosper in the thing for which I sent it" (Is. 55:11). Now what is the mission? I have sent him on a mission, sent myself on a mission. What is the mission?—to fulfill my Word. Well, I am the Word and to fulfill the Word?—yes. There is an external Word and that comes first...outer man comes first as recorded in scripture: "I send you now to fulfill my Word." So man comes into the world with that hunger, and when the hunger is upon him, then he fulfills scripture... everything said in scripture concerning God's plan of *self*-redemption. He isn't redeeming someone else...there is no one else. We are the gods that came down (Ps. 82: 1, 6). God can only redeem himself, because there is no one else. At that moment in time when the hunger is upon us, well then, we begin to erupt within us and we unfold and scripture unfolds within us. Everything said of the Christ of scripture the individual here must experience. So you will experience scripture.

Now here, I've just told you one wonderful story and two others that will fit perfectly into this picture. This lady writes that she had this experience, this dream she calls it. To me it's a vision, but call it a dream. "I am one of an enormous crowd and the crowd is yelling at a certain man and screaming at this man. I walk in quickly and I go to the very head of the crowd. I am not yelling, but the crowd is yelling and they're saying, 'He's mad! He's crazy!' Well, I knew he was not mad, that he was not crazy, so I got forward and then turned around, faced the man, and the enormous crowd in the background still yelling, and I feel that I must tell him how much I love him, and I am telling him that I love you, I love you, and repeating it over and over. This man has been really taken over by the crowd...he was pummeled, ill-treated...matted hair and everything that is undesirable. I am still persuading him or trying to that I love him. He puts his hands on my neck and his thumbs pressed into my throat and for a moment I lost my breath. I thought, well, he's going to kill me, but it doesn't matter, I still love him. Even if he kills me I still love him. And then at the end, he released that pressure and the breath returned, and I continued telling him how much I loved him. Then the crowds continue to declare that he was mad. Then he raised his hands and I said to myself that now he really is going to kill me, but it doesn't really matter because I love him, I *so* love him. Then the crowds vanished, he vanished, and the hands became two snow white wings, and they caressed me. All I can describe that feeling is to say that it was beyond any words to describe this love. It was a love beyond anything that one could describe when the wings came down upon me."

I can say to you, my dear, you have fulfilled scripture. If you want the chapters, read the 40th, the 48th, the 51st, 52nd, 53rd of Isaiah and you will know what you have fulfilled. So I can say to you without any doubt in my heart that you are very *near* to salvation and it is hurrying speedily to you, for you have fulfilled it. The man was yourself pushed out, the crowd was yourself, everything in that wonderful vision of yours was self-pushed out, made visible. You were the one that went through hell. Now you say "I love you." Well, can you love yourself? That wonderful thought of Blake's in *The Little Boy Lost*: "Nought loves another as itself, nor can it reverence another more. Nor can thought a greater than itself know" (*Songs of Experience*). It can't! How can thought know one greater than itself?

That may shock the world which thinks you can love someone more than yourself. But nought can love another more than self, nor reverence another so, nor is it possible to thought a greater than itself to know. So she was in love with the being that played all the parts…that one being with the matted hair, abused by the crowd. Well, she was the crowd over the centuries, for every time that I've entertained any feeling of distress, I was abusing Christ. Because, who was distressed?—I am, that's his name. So I felt little, I felt abased, I felt debased, I felt everything that was wrong. Well, who was feeling it?—I am. That's Christ, that's his name. For "Unless you believe that I am is he, you die in your sins" (Jn. 8:24). Just as my friend in that vision of hers said, "Before Abraham, was I am." When the vision revealed to her to change the comma: not "Before Abraham was, I am" but "Before Abraham, was I am" (Jn. 8:58). So in this, "Unless you believe that I am he" is recorded "Unless you believe that I am *is* he"—the one that you worship on the outside—"you die in your sins."

So here, he does bear all of my afflictions, all of my sorrows, all of my diseases. Because there's no record in scripture where a man looked at another who was in a terminal state of some disease and then took upon himself the disease, and set the man free while he went to his death with it. That's what it would imply if you take it on the surface. For he bears our sicknesses, he bears all of our weaknesses…takes them upon himself and sets man free. But there is no record and scholars have argued over this point over the centuries. They feel this must be some vicarious set of events and it can't be actual. It isn't! Christ is not something external to the one who is reading about him. The universal Christ is a universal diffusion of an individuality. You say "I am," but I say "I am"…it's the same "I am"…and this is Christ and Christ is God and God is Jehovah. There's only God in the world; there's nothing but God.

So here, we are told in the 8th chapter of Matthew and told in that 1st chapter of the 1st epistle of Peter, that he bears all of my afflictions, all of my weaknesses, all of my sins, and all of my diseases, but everything is mentioned. Now who is it who is bearing it? It is Christ. And then the mind thinks, you mean another outside of myself? No it's yourself who is bearing it and *that* is Christ. It's one of the most difficult things to get over to man.

In San Francisco several years ago this lady and her son came to my meetings. He was a lawyer and they took nineteen. I gave fifteen lectures and four Sunday mornings, so they attended the nineteen. At the end of the nineteen, she said to her son, "Do you believe him?" He said, "I was raised in a profession where one has to be practical. It's a rational profession, I'm a lawyer, but there's something about him, he sounds sincere. He may be sincerely wrong, but I will say he does sound sincere, and so I'll give it a go." So every night —he was not then married…since that time he's been married, I think, five or six times, but then he wasn't married and he lived in the mother's house. She would remind him every night as he went to his room to put into practice what he heard when he attended my lectures; then he would remind her to do the same thing.

Well, the next time I went back to San Francisco he had formed some organization and they were in the process of building the biggest, and it still is the biggest, and most modern co-op in San Francisco. It's called The Comstock. The rents are outrageous. First of all, you must buy your unit, and even maintenance is beyond what anyone would think of paying for rent. But this is not only rent, you have an equity in the building…you put that thing first. Then he began to build down the peninsula, then he began to build in Hawaii, and he made his millions. He never heard the Promise. She said to me one day, "I don't quite understand what you mean that Christ suffers for me. When I have a toothache, *I* have the toothache." And I could not persuade her, although she could apply this principle towards physical ends and the son toward this enormous co-op and they did remarkably well and still are. She departed this world, but he is still floating high, wide and handsome in the financial world.

But he could not grasp that he himself, his own wonderful human Imagination, is the cause of that wonderful co-op and is the cause of everything that happens in the world, whether he knows it or not. He can't quite believe that another other than himself is suffering…it's not another, there is no other. *You* are suffering, well, that's Christ. Who is suffering?—I am. Well, that's Christ and there never was another Christ. There is no other Christ. God is called the Word and the Word actually became flesh and dwells *within* us (Jn. 1:14). If he dwells within us, why turn on the outside for a Christ? There is no other Christ. He still couldn't get it, in spite of all that he accomplished in the world of Caesar, because the hunger is not upon him. He would not want this night to give up his fleshpots. He has all these things in the world. You turn to anyone who has enormous holding in the world and ask them—they don't have to give it up—but ask them if they would like to have the experience that would result in *regeneration*, where you don't kill it out, you don't go to some doctor and have yourself emasculated, you don't castrate yourself: there is no desire. The whole thing simply ceases to be. Ninety-nine percent of the people of the world would say, "What? No desire? Keep it! No desire? You just hold it! You mean I couldn't want a lovely big steak smothered with mushrooms?" I'm not saying you wouldn't want it, I'm not saying that at all. But I give you a pleasure transcending everything in this world…that when you go to bed at night, your night is not what it formerly was. You transcend the world of dream. You are in an entirely different world, a world of reality, a world of creativity, where those who have transcended this world are now once more part of the united body of the risen Lord and you are one with them. There's a communion that you cannot express here. There's not a thing here that would interest you when you are there. Well, until *that* famine comes upon you they cannot really accept it.

Now the third one…this lady is here tonight. She said, "In my vision you died and yet you returned. You died and not only I knew that you had died, everybody knew that you had died, and everyone knew that you had returned and that you were lecturing and teaching as you do. Well, we had to go a very long, long way to hear you. You were so far away, but you still returned after you died. I saw on your face my own earthly father's face, but I knew the bone structure that wore that face was *your* bone structure. I knew it was you and everyone knew it was Neville. They didn't know my earthly father so they didn't see him, they saw you. But I saw my earthly father on the bone structure of your face. I couldn't share it with anyone else because they didn't know my father. Then at the very end I awoke. I knew if I touched the face I would feel two: I would feel my father on the surface and I would feel *the* Father, because everyone referred to you as *the* Father."

See, there is only one Father and one God and Father of us all. It can wear every mask in the world. So here, in this wonderful picture that she had, this experience, she was seeing her earthly father upon the frame of *the* Father. Because *the* Father is a protean being and can assume every face in the world at will, instantly. To convey to her the story of Fatherhood she saw the one as foundation who told her the story of having realized Fatherhood through the Son calling him Father. So she saw the foundation, that bone structure that she knew was the man who told that story, but on it was the face of her earthly father.

So I tell you, the day is coming, and no one is going to stop it. But it can't be forced. You are here because you are hungry and that's why you are having the visions. That's why you are having these experiences. That's why you will all awaken in the not distant future. At the same time, that is why those who know of it and show a certain interest do not attend, because they don't want to awake. I am asleep, said he, and don't you dare wake me up! Then she said "Everything seemed all right after that. I realized then why he lost his temper, why he was angry, because in the depth of his soul he didn't want to give up the fleshpots." Man feels insecure if he gives up things in the world of Caesar.

So then we are told that he took upon himself the sins of the world and he was despised and rejected by men, a man of sorrows, that he was not comely that you should want to look at him, and he was not a man of beauty that you desired him. So there's no description of the man in whom he awoke, because it's not a man that is majestic outwardly, not a man that you want to turn around and look at, not a man that is comely and beautiful that you want to say, "Well now, isn't he a marvelous person." No…a perfectly normal person as she saw it in her vision…matted hair and he had really been put through the mill by the crowd. The crowd was herself when she denied the existence of Christ within her, and that whole crowd was herself shouting that he's mad.

Well now, she told me in her letter that she is very fond of the Book of John. That during the Depression she and her father would read the Book of John and it seemed to her a more loving book than any other book in the Bible. Well, I would not deny that, I would go along with that. She felt that in some strange way the answer to this experience would come to her from John. The 5th chapter, the 39th verse of John was her father's favorite. That is, if you do not know it: "You search the scriptures because you think in them you have eternal life; and it's all about me. All they have written, it's all about me." Well, I'll tell you, in the 10th chapter of John, he is called mad. He said, "The man is mad and he has a devil; why do you listen to him?" (10:20). So you came to that 10th chapter, you are the central character, and the crowd screaming that you are mad is not others; it's yourself because there is no other...there is only God.

Now, you can put this to the test and try it and see if it doesn't work. It will prove itself in performance. If it proves itself in the testing, then you know who he is...because "By him all things were made and without him was not one thing made that was made" (Jn.1:3). So now you can take something that to you is a desirable state. If in the world of Caesar you still want the *joy* of marriage, the joy of a love affair, the joy of a romance, whatever it is...well then, you have no one, you know no one, assume that you had it...just assume that you had it. I tell you, in the not distant future the experience will be yours. How it will happen, you don't know, no one knows. It will happen if you persist in the assumption that it *has* happened.

My wife told me this morning that when she got up on the early side, too early to really get up, and so she returned to bed. She said to herself, "What do I want *most* in this world? I want my husband and my daughter to be blissfully happy. Then I started thinking what would make them happy. I said, oh, no. I can't visualize what would make *them* happy. It's something that they and they alone would know. I mustn't tell them what would make them the happiest in the world. And so I began then to dwell only on their happiness, and I fell into a sleep. In my dream here are the three of us... you are on a couch and you're saying to me, 'I don't feel comfortable here.' I said, well, you know you don't like to sleep on the first floor, you like to be elevated and sleep above, so that's why you aren't comfortable on the couch. Then I ignored that section of it and then there was a puzzle and Vicky and I were putting all these pieces together. It was very, very amusing how these things would fall into their little places. I can't tell you what little thing I picked up or she picked up, but suddenly she began to laugh, and it was the most delightful laugh that I've ever heard coming from her. I looked at her after this thing fell into its place and it was perfect. I've never seen Vicky so pretty, so happy and so *blissfully* happy. And then I woke."

So in the immediate present it was answered in the depths of her being. It must now come to the surface. She figured why waste the time...it's too early to get up...let me be constructive and apply this principle now. So she wondered, "What do I want most in this world?" Forgetting herself and thinking of the two she loves most, she thought, well now, if they were the happiest people in the world, and that's what she wanted, it would make her happy if we were. I was on the couch and I couldn't find any rest in that first floor. So she ignored this part of it and she turned to Vicky and they found this puzzle. There she is putting all the pieces together and then this little chuckle that she never heard coming from her before. Then an expression and a feeling and a mood that transcended anything she had ever seen in Vicky before. Then she knew she did find that happiness that she had asked for.

So may I tell you, Jesus Christ is your own wonderful human Imagination. It can't be repeated too often, because when you read the story and you're told that *he*—for they use the pronoun, the third person—he is doing all the suffering for us and you know that *you* are suffering, well, he isn't taking it all because I'm suffering, and that's he. For "Unless you believe that *I am is* he"—you will continue to miss the mark—"you will continue in your sins," for that's what you're told in scripture. But, if I *really* believe that I am—when I say "I am" and I know I am is the *he* of scripture that is defined as Christ Jesus and Christ Jesus is defined as God the Father—well then, I know who I am.

So I came into the world for one purpose: to fulfill the Word. "My Word cannot return unto me empty' it must accomplish that which I purposed and prosper in the thing for which I sent it." So I sent *myself* into the world. I sent it to fulfill what I had dictated through the prophets. I inspired the prophets to tell a story: that I came not only to fulfill it, but in my fulfilling of that story to interpret it for the world. For on the surface, until you actually experience it you can't interpret it. It defies interpretation. But when one actually *fulfills* it, he interprets the prophecy. For the Old Testament is only a prophetic blueprint of what you and I must one day realize, and we realize it in ourselves as the central character of scripture. We are the Jehovah of the Bible; we are the Jesus Christ of the Bible. If it shocks anyone, let them be shocked, but don't retract for one moment. I tell you it's true. Don't take it back for one second and say, "Well, I'll modify it for you." Don't modify it! They either accept it or they don't accept it.

But I'm telling you it's true and there is no other Christ. The Christ of scripture is not a single little man; it's that universally diffused individuality, it's the *cosmic* Christ, and it's all one. So in one it awakes, in two it awakes, in the third it awakes, and eventually the whole will awake. And the one body that was fragmented is reunited into that one glorious body and we are once more reunited, after having gone into the world of death and overcome it. For this was our challenge: to be victorious over death. So everyone dies here, but everyone. The universe, they tell us, is actually melting. It may take unnumbered billions, but it melts and therefore it will one day come to its end…so they say. I'm not going to question these men. I only know in our own case, we came into the world of death for the purpose of overcoming death. Nothing dies in this world but nothing, because we are the immortal being clothed in these garments of flesh and only the garments of flesh die, they all die.

But I can't force anyone to want it [the Promise]. I go to Barbados to my family and they are not interested, not for one moment. I could not hold the interest of any member of my family for two minutes in telling them what I'm telling you tonight. They're not interested. They all live in comfort, live in clover, and they know that I don't earn what they earn. So their standard by which they judge success is what you have in the world of Caesar. They all have homes and cars and a lovely income and big salaries and perquisites beyond measure. Each gets a new car every year out of the business, all repairs on their homes, they pay no taxes; the business pays all taxes, all repairs. They have set it up so that they really live in clover. But I don't live there and I have to pay my own way here and they think me insane. Got a call yesterday that I'm coming back to Barbados in the summer. I said that I haven't the slightest plan to come to Barbados. Well, they are planning it anyway. Regardless of what I'm doing, they're planning it...that I must come and live there. They're determined on that score, because they can't see any reason for a man at my age persisting in doing what I'm doing when clover is there for me.

So, I can't persuade my family because the hunger is not upon them... it just isn't upon them. "I will send a famine upon the world and it will not be a hunger for bread or a thirst for water but for the hearing of the Word of God." Until that hunger possesses you, I don't care what the world will tell you, it doesn't make any difference. You will not truly...you may become a pope, but it doesn't mean because you become the pope that you had a hunger for the Word of God. You could have had a hunger for the power that rests in the office of the pope, a hunger for being president, an enormous power, and that could be the hunger. But the hunger—not to be recognized, not to be hailed—to experience the Word of God...for you know you were sent, you are a Word, and you sent yourself. Well, "He who sees me sees him who sent me" and you came in to fulfill the Word. Because there must be two witnesses: the external witness of scripture and the internal witness of the Spirit; because no one but you who has the experience could witness to it. So you know you parallel all the scriptures and you know in the depths of your own being stands the Father watching to see does it really fit? Is this the image of my declared purpose? For I have prophesied that this must take place and now *he* has fulfilled it...now he is the image of the invisible God and radiates the glory of God and is the express image of his person.

So he can be used as the bone structure on which every face can be placed to reveal to the one who has the experience the meaning of being God the Father. So, in her vision, she said, everyone, including herself, "referred to you as *the* Father," definitive, not *a* Father, but *the* Father. Her father was *a* father; I was *the* Father on which a father's face was placed. She knew that I had died and she knew that I had returned. Though I had died and everyone knew I had died, everyone knew I had returned to continue the telling of the only story worth while telling in the world: the story of God's plan of salvation to redeem not another, there is no other, to redeem himself. There is no other. It's all *self*-redemption, so no one can be lost, but no one; but each in its own order.

So, thank you for your three letters and please keep them up. No matter what they seem to you…as the lady wrote saying, "I don't quite understand this, but I'm going to write it anyway and this is what happened. That man I saw time and again in my dreams, I've seen him so often in my dreams, now he was really taken over. He was battered and beaten…matted hair." Read the 53rd chapter of the Book of Isaiah and you'll see what they do to the Christ in man. But the "they" is yourself pushed out, and not knowing *who* you are, you do it to yourself. So you represented all the people in the world or they represented you, and they were beating you, and you bore the stripes. As told in that chapter, like a lamb before his slaughter or slaughters he's dumb and opens not his mouth, so he, the servant of the Lord, opens not his mouth. So you read him when you go home, because you've fulfilled Isaiah, my dear, and you're right on the verge of salvation. May I tell you, with that I would say that it's hurrying towards you.

Now are there any questions? Before we go into the Silence are there any questions?

Q: (inaudible)

A: It means the words are not in the print and they've added those words to give meaning. So when you read it in the King James, all the little words put in italics, that's not in the print, that is not in the script, but to give meaning to the one who reads it in English, they added these words. They tell you it's not in the script…they put it that way.

Q: (inaudible)

A: No…the Revised Standard Version will give you footnotes concerning what the true meaning of the Hebrew or the Greek is. But all the little italics that means that the word isn't there, just isn't there. It's the most amazing thing when you sit down to read it to see what the scholars have done, because, if they haven't the vision, they must give meaning to the script, and so they add. I read today for instance in that 18th verse of the 1st chapter of John that "No one has ever seen God. The Son, who is in the bosom of the Father, he has made him known." Well, that word Son supplanted the word God in the 4th Century. We have no early manuscript before the 4th Century that uses the word Son…it is God.

It doesn't state that, but it does state that in the *Exegesis* that no earlier than the 4th Century. You'll find our earliest manuscripts are fantastic when you compare them to what man has done to give sense to the script. Yet to say that no one has ever seen God, that's a contradiction in the Sermon on the Mount; for you are told that a certain person or persons will see God. *All* will see God because they're going to find *themselves*. But here we are told, "Blessed are the pure in heart, for they shall see God," well, that certainly contradicts that statement. And it's not the Son called Jesus Christ. Jesus Christ is God the Father; the Son that reveals him is David. I will this very night put my head right here and not recant one little comma to that statement: it is David who reveals man as God the Father! I haven't met one priest, one rabbi, one minister, who will accept this, because they've been conditioned and they have a pre-fabricated misconception of scripture. We are the gods and collectively we form *the* God. We form God the Father.

Any other questions, please? Then let us go into the Silence.

* * *

I will ask this lady tonight when she goes home…in that 53rd chapter of Isaiah when it begins, "Who has believed our report? And to whom has the arm of the Lord been revealed?"…that "arm of the Lord" in Hebrew when it's translated literally it is "the arm of Jehovah upon whom has it been revealed?" The world thinks it's just might, sheer might, and this lady discovered that it was infinite mercy. The arms that she thought would kill her…and she didn't care because she loved him…turned into a love and a compassion that she found herself inadequate to describe. She couldn't describe the love, the feeling when these wings possessed her. So that instead of being hands that would squeeze her—a moment before they squeezed the wind out of her body—and now the same hands disappeared and turned into wings. You read the story of the wings in scripture. These are the wings of compassion, the wings of mercy. So his hands turned into the hands of mercy.

Good night.

CAN YOU BELIEVE IN JESUS, A PATTERN

2/28/69

Those whom a vision has changed must walk by faith through the mire of doubt. People will say, "Don't you believe that Jesus existed and that he rose from the dead and, therefore, that he exists?" And you answer yes. Well, it seems to satisfy them that he existed. It's like my wife saying to me "Do you believe in me?" and I answer yes, I believe that you exist. Is that what she intended that I believe that she exists, or that I trust her, that I believe in her to the point where I trust her? For that is what we are called upon in scripture to do, to believe in Jesus, to believe in the one who is sent.

So we are told, "What must we do, to be doing the works of God? And he answered, this is the work of God, that you believe in him whom he has sent" (Jn. 6:29). That's all that you have to do...salvation to everyone who believes in him. There is no aristocracy of privilege, none whatsoever. And to believe that he existed and that he exists means nothing. Can I believe in him? Well, how do I go about believing in him? If I trust him, I will trust the story that he tells, for he tells us he was *sent*. Everyone who is sent is Jesus and Jesus is the sender. We are called from this world here where the world is dead. We do not volunteer and we do not in any way choose the task. We are *selected* and we are called; and when we are called we are incorporated into the Lord, the risen Lord, and then we are sent. But if we are sent we are the one who sent us: for "He who sees me sees him who sent me." I am one with the being who called me after I am incorporated into his being. Then you come and you tell...what story did you tell? That you have a large family of brothers and sisters? No. Do you tell of any home that you built? No. For it is said of him when he entered the synagogue and began to teach, they wondered how can he have such learning? For is he not the carpenter, the son of Mary, the brother of James and Jose and Simon and Judas and his sisters (its plural) and are they not with us this day? Here is a large family... and he has no learning, so how does he do it? Now he tells them he was *sent* to do a work. What work did he come to do? There's no record that he built a home or repaired a house. He is called a carpenter in the 6th chapter of Mark, and here all the brothers are named, at least four of them are named, and the sisters, at least it's plural...so how many...at least two. So here is a large family.

Well, what did he come to do? He said, "I have come to fulfill scripture. And then, beginning with Moses and the law, and all the prophets and the Psalms, he interpreted to them in all the scriptures the things concerning himself." He didn't realize until then that the whole thing was about himself. He had first to be called...a man just like us, a man in a large family, a normal man, who had a trade, they called him a carpenter. He is called and incorporated into the man, the risen man, and then sent. And he tells you, I am one with the one who sent me. I can't divorce myself from that man who incorporated me into his being, and if you see me you see him who sent me. Now what did he send me to tell you? To tell you what I will now experience; and if you believe what I tell you, then all that I do you will do... if you believe me. But if you do not believe me, you will not do the things that I am telling you about.

So here, he who believes me will do all the works that I do and if he does not believe me he will not do them, and there is no other way to salvation. Unless these things unfold in him he will never depart from the world of death into the world of life. In Adam all die; in this man of which I speak all are made alive. So he made me alive in him and then sent me. The need was great to send me to tell you exactly what I experience and to tell you that if you believe my experiences that *you* will have them. If you have them then you are saved; you leave the world of death and enter the world of life. It doesn't make sense, but it is the incredible story that man is called upon to believe. Now he tells us, in spite of the fact that you know my parents... you say I am the son of Joseph, son of Mary, and you name my brothers, you mention sisters, mention my trade...and yet I tell you from now on I am not of this world. You are of this world; I am not of this world. I am from above; you are from below. But if you'll believe me, you too will be born from above and then you will not be of this world. You will actually be an entirely different being living in an entirely different world. But you cannot unless you hear my story and believe it.

Well, some believed him and the majority rejected him. He argued from scripture to point out what had happened to him, to show in scripture that he was the fulfillment of scripture. We read the story in the 16th of Acts. It's the story of one called Paul. First, there was a slave girl and she had the spirit of divination, and being a slave she was making a lot of money for her owners as a soothsayer. As Paul came by with his associates, she being a diviner said, "These men are proclaiming the way of salvation," and she followed them for days proclaiming that these know the way of salvation. Then came the keeper of the jail, the guard, and he said to these men, "What must I do to be saved?" They answered, "Believe in the Lord Jesus and you'll be saved." Believe in a man...as I would say to my wife, yes, I believe that you exist, is that believing? The Lord Jesus is only a *pattern*. It's *the* pattern. Well, the pattern gets encrusted with barnacles over the years and he calls one and sends that one into the world, having incorporated that one into himself, to scrape off the barnacles by telling exactly the path of salvation...how it happened to him.

So he goes and he tells it. You might think, after all, what does it matter, three billion people in the world and he tells it to what, a few dozen, a few hundred? Well, that's all you need to start it. You tell it to the few dozen or the few hundred or a few thousand, and a percentage, a *remnant* will believe it. That's all that you need. Others will reject it plus the billions who didn't hear it when you walked among them. So, as they hear it, they believe it, and then it happens in them, and it spreads once more until once more it's organized. As it becomes organized, it grows its barnacles, because those without vision will organize it and make a business out of it. Once more it becomes a *tradition* without the Spirit.

So he called me in 1929. I didn't volunteer. Standing in the presence of the risen Lord who is nothing but love, infinite love, he incorporated me into his body and then sent me. Sending me out of his body he sent himself, because I am one with the body. There's only one body, there's only one Spirit, there's only one Lord (Eph.4:4). But I had to be clothed in a garment that is fragile to talk to those who are equally fragile. They, knowing my biological background, knowing my large family, the limitations of that family; the limitations of my background in every sense of the word questioned against their background which is traditional and it doesn't fit; and so they reject it. A few will go outside of what they have heard and they will accept it; and to that *remnant* it happens...those who will believe in him. So, what must I do to be doing the work of God? Believe in him whom he has sent. I tell you, he has sent me. You may or may not believe it, that's your privilege. But I who have the vision, who had the experience and it so changed me that I must now walk by faith in this vision and keep this divine vision in spite of all the troubles of the world; and walk through the mire of doubt...even if the doubt comes from the most intimate circle, which is perfectly all right.

So, one is sent. He's first called, incorporated, and then sent. And that goes on eternally until *all* are redeemed, not one will be lost, not one. So, "As in Adam all die, so also by Christ shall all be made alive" (1Cor.1:22). But this Christ is a *pattern* of the eternal purpose of God. And there's only one way to escape from this world. There aren't two ways; there's one way: you must be born from above. That is essential. You must discover the fatherhood of God and that you are he. Your body must be torn from top to bottom and you must ascend into heaven and reverberate it. You must have the symbol of the Holy Spirit descend upon you and smother you with love. And you tell *that* story. It's in scripture. And they will say, "But it happened and I know I believe in the one who *existed*." You say, it's not that at all...that is only a pattern. I have come to renew the pattern. Your belief that Jesus Christ *existed* is not your belief in him. He is only a pattern of salvation, that's all that he is.

So he calls another after the barnacles have again encrusted the ship. Then he comes and he tries to scrape them off by retelling the story, the same story, as something that he himself has experienced. Beginning with your most intimate circle, your family, they say, "But Neville, you mean you don't believe in Jesus Christ?" I said, I do believe in Jesus Christ...far more than you do. "You couldn't because you don't talk that way. Don't you believe he existed?" I said, what does that matter? So he existed and he rose, therefore he exists, but that is not believing in Jesus Christ. To believe *in* Jesus Christ you believe in the *pattern*. He is the *pattern man*. So if you believe in *a* man...so you believe in Neville...what does it matter if you believe in Neville? Neville means nothing. If Neville was called and incorporated into the living being, who is a *pattern* of salvation, and then sent, he comes bearing the pattern and the pattern is within him. Then in an interval of time—in my case thirty years—then it erupted, the whole thing erupted within me, and it's then that you tell the story.

So he began his ministry when he was about thirty years of age. It doesn't mean thirty years physically; he's not speaking of the biological man. From that moment after he was incorporated, thirty years later he is then qualified by the eruption to tell what is happening in him. Then he actually uses scripture and so all of his arguments are based upon scripture. And some believed based upon it, they can see it; and others cannot see it because they've been so conditioned that they can't quite relate his experiences to that of scripture. You mean to tell me that when it is said in Zechariah that the Mount of Olives was split from top to bottom, and then one moved north and the other side moved south, leaving a huge, big valley, that that is related to your body when you were split from top to bottom and one side moved one way and one side moved the other, leaving an interval of about six inches...and that is related to the Mount of Olives? And you say yes...it is told in this symbolic manner, all this is metaphor...but *you* are the reality. And so they use the Mt. of Olives...but *you* are the Mt. of Olives. You are *everything* in scripture...that splitting was yourself. You mean to tell me that one who lived unnumbered years before you—at least a thousand years before you, if I take it in a secular manner as history—that all of a sudden he who lived 1000 years before you called you Father? And you say yes he did, he called me Father. Therefore is it not said in scripture that he just called me in *Spirit*, the Lord? And I point out the passage of scripture where I met him, I found him, and he told me who I was by calling me by my true name.

Some will believe it; the majority will deny it and think it's a huge strange fantasy. But you still through the mire of doubt walk and you tell the story. You mean that you born of your mother...we know your mother and we know your father, his name was Joseph and your mother's name was Wilhelmina, and you have so many brothers and one sister. We know your whole background that you had nothing, but nothing, no educational background, no financial background, nothing. And you dare to tell me these things happened in you when he could have easily called a financial giant or intellectual giant or some other giant judged by human standards... and he called you? I said, But he called me in the Spirit, he didn't call me in the flesh. I was not initiated in the flesh. I was sound asleep on my bed when I was taken in Spirit. So I was called in Spirit and I met him in Spirit and in truth. So I was called in Spirit. Then having been incorporated into his body which seemed to me solidly real...but it must have been Spirit. So when I came back into the garment I left on the bed, it was in that that I came back and in that I unfolded all that he incorporated into me...for that was his plan of salvation.

So I tell you now that this is the *only* way that man ever departs from the world of death, and he departs by simply believing the story. You don't believe that Neville existed, you don't believe in Neville as a man. He's frail, subject to all the weaknesses of the flesh, and everything in the world that man is heir to he is heir to it. But believe what he *experienced*. Do you believe it? So he takes scripture and he simply unfolds it before you and shows you where the experience that he has had is paralleled here. It was all *foretold*. And then you either believe it or you don't believe it. He repeats it over and over in the hope that those who hear him will believe it.

So in the story it ties the gospel to the reality. We find that in the Book of Acts. It was once part of the Book of Luke, but then it's detached and put into the chronological picture as the fifth book, when really it is part of the

Book of Luke. But it's divided for a purpose. Then you find that the story of Jesus (which is the pattern man) is now emptied into that of the apostles. The apostle is one who is sent, and that's the story of the ones who are sent to tell exactly how it happened.

Now, I do not know in any part of scripture where it is told as graphically as I have told you. I can go back and take the related passages in the Old Testament. "Is it possible," he said, "Can a man bear a child? Why then do I see every man with his hands pulling himself out of himself just like a woman in labor? Why has every face turned pale?" (Jer. 30:6). Well, I form within myself a child if I'm a woman. Well, is it not part of my body? So then I in labor then pull out of my body…for that's what primitive women did. There were no hospitals where you put them into a twilight sleep and then brought about the delivery. In the field while they were working they stopped for a moment and brought about the delivery by pulling out of themselves what they had formed within themselves. So, it seemed that a man is pulling out of himself his own being: "Why do I see every man pulling himself out of himself?" Well, you do, you pull yourself right out of yourself. And there you are fulfilling scripture.

Then comes, he has given us a child: "To us a child is born, to us a son is given" (Is. 9:6). And then this follows this picture at the same moment, the very same night. You go back and you point out to everyone who will listen to you this passage of scripture foreshadowing this event. Some believe it; the majority will deny it and they will not believe it. Then you go on to the next, the 89th Psalm, and then you find that you are fulfilling scripture. He called me Father. Who called me Father? The one who stands before me and he's David. But he preceded you by a thousand years and today in the 20th Century by 2,400 years. But he *did* call me Father. Then at that moment I knew he was telling me the truth because I *knew* it, and there was no uncertainty when it came to this relationship.

So here, I am telling you what scripture foretold and I have experienced scripture. Must that actually take place for man to depart this world? Yes it must take place. Well then, what must I do to bring it about?—only *believe* it. You don't do anything in this world outside of believing it. I don't care what you are…tonight if you are in this world a thief, if that is your profession; if tonight in this world you are an actor playing all kinds of parts on the outside; if you are anything in this world, I don't care what it is, that is not important. You heard the story and did you believe it? If you believed it and really believed it and set your hope fully upon having these experiences, then your salvation is assured. Eventually everyone is going to believe it; but by denying it and rejecting it they are delaying it. They delay the birth; the birth comes only after acceptance of the story of the one who was sent.

The one who was sent did not choose to be sent. He was called and he had no, well, what can I say, the night I fell asleep I would be the last person in the world that would have chosen myself as one worthy to be sent, one worthy to be called…that I would be called into the presence of the risen Lord. For are we not told that the pure in heart will see God? Well, I certainly did not feel myself pure in heart. I could not in the wildest stretch of the Imagination judge myself as one worthy to stand in the presence of God if to stand in his presence means that I am pure in heart. For here, I was having conflicts in my life with a wife from whom I was separated and my little boy moving back and forth between us and the conflicts that go with all these silly little things. I could never have judged myself worthy if to be pure in heart meant what the world thinks it is. Well, it isn't that at all. God sees the heart, he sees motives; he doesn't see the outer picture; he sees motive behind the act. Was it done in love or was it done to get even with another? Did you do it to hurt or did you really do it because you love? He sees that…he doesn't see the outer picture at all.

So, in '29 when I was called, judging superficially I could never have put myself up as one worthy of being called. But I was called. Then for thirty years you go through the picture and you're teaching only a law because you do not know the Promise. It's there in scripture but you don't know it. Then suddenly one day thirty years later the Promise erupts within you. You can do nothing but think about it and talk about it and tell it. Now you are the one sent. They know your background, your genealogy; you're biological set up—your father, your mother, your brothers, your sister—everything about you, your lack of education. And here, it's all recorded in scripture. But it's just about that that he calls…and then you tell it. Beginning with your own family they reject it, reject it 100 percent.

The one who came closest to it was my own father. In my discussion at home one day with a minister and the minister could not answer my question and could not for one moment throw any light on what I'm talking about, my father said to me, "Why son, you must be an apostle." Well, mother felt it in her womb when I was coming into this world, but she had no assurance of it because I became a dancer. Well, that was not what she thought. She thought I would be a minister in the Anglican Church… but certainly not in the theater. That would be so in conflict with what she believed I was sent to do…if I was sent to do anything. So, all these conflicts, and the closest to what I am doing about belief was my father… and it only lasted for a moment, just that moment of discussion with the minister.

But I'll tell you this night this is the only way of salvation. You don't believe in Neville...forget Neville. I'll go out with you any night and keep pace with you drink for drink and thoroughly enjoy it, every one. Eat with anyone and no food is distasteful to me love it all, no matter what it is, I take anything. I find nothing to condemn. And so because I can't condemn any being in this world for what part they're playing, well then, that is not discriminating enough. Well, in spite of all that, and I admit to all these weaknesses of the human flesh, he called me, sent me, and I didn't know for what purpose. But I realize now it was *after* his message erupted within me; then to tell it because you refresh the atmosphere. You simply clean it up after all the centuries of misunderstanding of the Christian mystery. For Christianity is only the fulfillment of Judaism. It's been fulfilled. And we are gathered one by one into that one man. We *are* that man when we are incorporated into that man...that is being "one in Christ"...Christ being the resurrected. Jesus is the pattern.

So, everyone who is sent is Jesus. I don't care what name you bear on earth, you are *then* Jesus, and you'll play the part. You tell it just as it happened to you. Don't elaborate, don't embellish it, tell it just as it is. Tell them this much that unless they believe it they will not depart. If they do not believe that it's going to happen to them and they believe only that he existed, well then, let them believe he existed. Just like saying to my wife, "Yes Bill, I believe you exist." What an insult! Do I trust her? Will I trust her with everything that I have in this world? Will I trust her completely? I do...well then, I believe *in* her. Now, a man tells you a story and he tells you the story of salvation as he has experienced it, do you believe in him? Forget the man...tomorrow you may read in the paper where he's guilty of something else that is in conflict with what he has told you, but do you believe his story? If you believe his story, then you believe in him, believe in him implicitly. All right then forget all that you hear about the man.

Someone said to me, "When I told the story about your experiences, I don't know why I said it but I said you know he is divorced and remarried." Then the book was closed instantly. The book became a closed book. She couldn't hear anything good about me because I'm divorced, so that closed everything. So she could not accept the story that I was called, incorporated into the body of God, and sent to tell what's going to happen within me when it happened. And then it took thirty years for maturity, and then it erupted, and then I began to tell it. She heard the telling of it, but when she heard I was divorced, she saw the outer man who could not adjust himself to married life with a certain person and they got a divorce. And that was the end in her world of anything to believe in me. She'll go right around the corner and believe that if you eat corn only you'll be satisfied and you'll be saved, because he isn't divorced...or she who told the story of eating corn is not divorced. So they'll eat corn from now 'til the ends of days and they will not depart from this world of death.

You can do anything in this world as the part calls for it, but believe the story. If you believe the story I don't care what you have done and what you're doing, if you believe the story and set your hope fully upon that grace that is coming to you, it will erupt within you. He will call you because he sees your belief, he sees your heart, and you are capable of believing the incredible story; for there's nothing in this world more incredible than the story of Christ, nothing. You mean that I born of this flesh and blood... and yet, you ask the man who will bring me out of this mother's womb to explain how the bones grew in my mother's womb, and he can't tell you how they were covered with flesh. Oh, he will give you 1,001 reasons on how these things happen, but he doesn't know a thing about how the bones grow in the womb of woman. As you're told in the Books of Ecclesiastes and Proverbs "Who knows how the bones grow in the womb of woman?" Ask them how a piece of bone, which is considered an inanimate and a dead object, how it grows. How does it grow and how does it cover itself with flesh and all the things that make it alive in the world? They do not know.

Now, you can tell them in spite of that miracle, and it *is* a miracle, there's another birth...something far, far greater than that. That something comes out of you that no one sees and yet it is so real. It is *God* coming out of you. He is born out of this thing that is a thing of death. They can't grasp that so they can't grasp the other. But I tell you only to believe it; you don't have to understand it. It doesn't call for any understanding on your part how it happens. All it calls for is to believe it. "So what must I do to be doing the works of God? Believe in him whom he has sent" (Jn.6:28). "Now what must I do to be saved? Believe in the Lord Jesus and you'll be saved." In other words, believe in the *pattern*, believe in the story that he has told you. If you believe in the story that he has told you, go about your business and try to live fully in this world. I don't care what it is, live fully. Enjoy life! Enjoy everything!

I saw a lady today who went to Barbados just for a short trip. She so loved it she got off the boat, flew back into Barbados to spend an extra week just to see the place that I told her about when I first spoke to her in Detroit many years ago. She came to Minneapolis to attend my classes. I told the story of my brother Victor visualizing a building that was not ours as though it were, and how in time we owned the building, and then from then on we became a very important business operation in Barbados. So she got off the boat as it went south of Barbados and flew back to Barbados and spent a week to meet the family, to see the building, and to ask all these questions.

She met Victor and met my family. So she came today to call on me and said "I'll tell you now I saw the building." It's gone now. We sold it to a bank, the Bank of Nova Scotia. They demolished the building and built a modern building in its place. So she saw where it was and met the family...and knows the truth of what I said. Then she said, "You know, when I heard you in Detroit and followed you to Minneapolis and took your classes, we had nothing"—speaking of her husband and herself—"but I believed you and so I began to put it into practice."

Well, it was a very sad story concerning her husband. He departed this world. He took his own life after spending many years in different mental hospitals. He always threatened that he would do it, and finally after nineteen years he did, going from one place to the other...thirteen of these hospitals. And she was blaming herself, wondering if she had failed and where did she fail? But the point of this...her brother who was a great business man, very thrifty, frugal, denying himself and living frugally, he died. Three weeks later his wife died and the only surviving relative was this sister. So now she has all that it takes to live lusciously, which was her dream. She assumed that she had it, not knowing where it would come from. She hadn't the slightest idea where one nickel ever would come from. It wouldn't come from her husband since he was always in a mental hospital, thirteen different ones. She didn't have it. She became distraught; she despaired because all the money which they didn't have was going out to take care of a mental case. Finally, about a year ago, he took care of that by departing this world through his own effort. Meanwhile, the brother dies and his wife three weeks later dies, and then the entire estate after all of his thrift goes to the sister. Now she can take these trips around the world and keep on going all the time. It makes no difference because the money is there.

So I tell you, this doesn't fail you on this level, this world of Caesar, and it will not fail you in the world of God *if* you believe the story. But you must believe *both* stories. If I tell you an assumption though false if persisted in will harden into fact that will prove itself in the world of Caesar as it did in her case. But now I tell you an incredible story that in you one day you're going to awaken in your skull to find the whole thing was really a grave, a sepulcher. Then all of a sudden you awake within it and then you come out. Then the birth as described in scripture is right before you and *you* are the one spoken of. I tell you the entire story and can you believe *that* as you believe an assumption though false will harden into fact? If you believe one, try after it proves itself in performance to believe the other. For unless you believe both you can't prove both. If you believe one in the world of Caesar, oh, you'll have the money...she has the money tonight, all that it takes...but she has to believe the other to depart from the world of Caesar.

Well, she doesn't need the money for the simple reason the earth is hers and all within it. When you depart from this world, you're God, and being God everything is yours. As he said, "If I were hungry, I wouldn't tell you, for the cattle on a thousand hills are mine. And were I hungry I would slay and eat" (Ps.50:10, 12). Why would I ask permission of anyone to eat that which is mine? So the world is yours when you are incorporated into the body of God. And having told the story, you depart this world to return unto the Father which is yourself…the body of the risen Lord where everything is yours. But in this world where you don't know it's all yours then apply the law, which is the law of assumption: I will assume the feeling of the wish fulfilled. All right, will it work?

This lady came today…I did not remember her. I don't see people at home. I gave it up when I came from New York because it was tiring as I told her. But she said, I have a message from your family in Barbados. Well, naturally that's going to trigger something. She wants to bring a message from my brother Victor and my brother Joe, so I said all right, I'll see you at 2:00. And to show you how tiring these things are she came at two, a little bit before two, and we discussed until quarter of three. Then I said, "May I call you a cab?" I called a cab and at 4:30 there's no cab. They said the cab will be there any minute now, but it's raining so no cab came. She felt embarrassed knowing that she had taken up all this time and she said, "I think I'll walk to the corner." I said, 'Well you're living at the Beverly Wilshire? Walk to the corner, go into the restaurant, the Cock and Bull, and because it's a very prominent restaurant the cabs will come there. If one is called at that place, they will come." So she walked up at 4:30 and she came at two. So you see why I don't like these private interviews. It's a very tiring thing, not only in time but in concentration when you concentrate on their problem and try to analyze it and to bring forth an answer for it.

But I tell you, just as on this level it works, it works on the other. You have to believe it on this level and apply it; you have to believe it on the higher level. So what must I do to be saved?—believe in the Lord Jesus. Well, how do I believe in him, that he existed? No. You can believe as millions of Christians believe that he existed, and they will go to bat to prove that he existed. No. That's not believing in Jesus: believe his message, the incredible message that he though born of flesh and blood and having four brothers (and they name the four brothers) and having sisters and having a family (they named the father and the mother), a normal person. He was a carpenter as named in the 6th chapter of Mark (verse 3). Then he tells you he wasn't this at all. He had a *second* birth and he is the man of the second birth, he is the *new* man. That he is not the man that you know, he is an entirely different being. "And this is what happened to me," said he, "and

205

now do you believe it?" Well, if you believe it then that's how you are saved. If you don't believe it, keep going, just keep going in the world with all the blows round about you.

So the hundreds of millions of those who call themselves Christians believe in the *existence* of Jesus, but they don't believe *in* Jesus. If they believed in him, they'd believe his story. And we are told, "Unless you be born from above you cannot enter the kingdom of heaven" (Jn.3:3). Now, I've told you in the most graphic form how it happens. I've recorded it in the book *Resurrection* exactly how it happens. Just as you're told in scripture it takes 1260 days (Rev.11:3); that's exactly the length of time that it took me from the first to the end. So the story is true. I have come to bear witness to it. So he who incorporated me sent me, and he who sent me is with me. So whoever sees me sees him who sent me. But you don't see him, the one who sent me by seeing the outer man. It's only the inner man that is the likeness and the very being of the one who sent me, for he *is* the inner being.

Now let us go into the Silence.

* * *

Q: What is the spiritual meaning of the term "carpenter"?
A: You know, Jack, I do not really know other than the carpenter is a builder. But I do not actually as I've never looked it up in the Concordance. Joseph was a carpenter. It is said in scripture, "Is he not the carpenter's son?" Well, in those days a man followed his father's trade, and so in the Book of Mark, "Is he not the carpenter, the son of Mary?" But it is said in other passages in scripture, "Is he not the carpenter's son?" So Joseph was called the carpenter and his son was called the carpenter. Well, he's a builder, an architect. But not a thing is mentioned in scripture concerning the appearance of Jesus, his physical appearance, or any physical accomplishment...like the building or repairing of a home. That was simply called a trade. But regardless of what trade one has in this world it would be the carpenter. I'm building...if I only bring home a dollar...I'm building something. So we are the carpenters of scripture in that sense.

But I do not know, Jack. Honestly I've never looked up the word "carpenter" in the Concordance for its definition. So I would just have to speculate. He is called the carpenter and his father is called the carpenter. But his brothers are named—James, Jose, Simon and Judas, and the sister is in the plural, "his sisters are with us today." There were at least seven in the family, a normal family, and they knew this man had no educational background..."How does he have his learning?"

Then he begins to explain scripture because he is having the experiences of scripture and no matter what tradition has to tell them he is telling them the truth of scripture, rather than what tradition has. A man without the experience is leading us to believe all kinds of things on the outside, which are not so at all.

Like our churches taking a piece of cloth and calling it the cloth that he wore on the cross…and there was no cross. If you take this one simple statement in the Book of Romans: "If we have been united with him in a death like his, surely we shall be united with him in a resurrection like his" (6:5). So all of us were in that act of crucifixion and where was the crucifixion? This is the only crucified state in the world: when I entered this body. And they dare to tell me that a piece of cloth was the cloth that he wore when he was on the cross? There was no cross outside of this. The pieces of wood where this was the cross, pieces of cloth, this was the robe that they fought over, and this isn't so at all. To this day there are hundreds of millions of people who believe it when they look at a piece of cloth. They've just discovered that the chair on which Peter sat wasn't so at all, unless Peter lived at least 1,400 years because it isn't older than that. Yet for centuries they've shown this stupid thing saying this is Peter's chair where he sat. Now that we have a way of discovering the age of a thing, we know it isn't so at all. But people go blindly on, forget it, and still accept the stupid traditional concept that is completely wrong.

But I will look up the word carpenter. I have my concordances at home, but I've never really looked it up. I should take every word as I read it and look it up. But I didn't look up carpenter.

Are there any other questions, please? Well, if there aren't any… Good night.

THE GOAL OF LIFE

3/3/69

Tonight's subject is "The Goal of Life." The goal of life is to find the Father, the cause of the phenomena of life. The Father has been built in from all eternity within us, for the kingdom of God is *within* you. You will never find him on the outside; and this God within us is our own wonderful human Imagination. So the true and full awakening of Imagination is what every man and woman aches for. It is a spiritual event that crowns and redeems experience. It doesn't matter what you have experienced. In the end, when you awaken from the dream of life to discover *yourself* as the Father, then it doesn't really matter. You can forgive all for anything they ever did to you, for *you* were the *cause* of all that they did to you and all that you did in this world.

Now we are told: "He has made known unto us the mystery of his will, according to his good pleasure, which he set forth in Christ as a *plan* for the fullness of time, to unite all things in him, in heaven and on earth" (Eph. 1:9). Here you and I are members of a body which shared in this glorious purposed end of everything in the universe—the end of the tree, the end of the mineral kingdom, the end of the animal kingdom, the end of man—that purposed end gathered together in one body...and you and I are members of that one body.

Now if this plan is contained in Christ, we have to find out who Christ is. And we are told, "Christ *in you* is the hope of glory" (Col.1:27). Not any Christ of history on the outside but Christ in you; for it contains the plan: here is the pattern man. Well, I read his story and see what it tells me. He said, "I came out from the Father and I came into the world; again, I am leaving the world and going to the Father" (Jn.16:28). Here in four short phrases we have pre-existence, we have incarnation, we have death, and we have ascension. "I came out from the Father." The Father sent me and "He who sees me sees him who sent me" (Jn.12:45)..."for I and my Father are one" (Jn.10:30). So I sent myself into expression and here I am clothed in a garment of flesh and blood; yet I am Spirit clothed in this limited state called man, flesh and blood, the limit of contraction. Then I have the experience now of being—that's God incarnated. Then I reach the end of my experiences and I have death. Then I return to the being who sent me, and the being who sent me and I the one sent are one; for when you see me you see him who sent me.

But in my journey, the purpose is to find and know that really I sent *myself* and to know that I truly am the Father who sent me. Well, how on earth will I know that? I search the scriptures to find in what way it could be done, for there's only one God and Father of all. "There's only one body, one Spirit, one hope, one Lord, one faith, one baptism, one God and Father of all" (Eph.4:4). Yet, I see billions in the world...I'm told there's only one Father. Now I want to find out how on earth if I be that Father and I look at billions in the world—they tell me there are three and a half billion today, and there were hundreds of millions prior, they're getting more and more—and yet only one Father. If I find I am that Father and I look on unnumbered billions in the world and each will find that they are the Father, how can we be one? Now, this is how we discover it. It doesn't make sense, but I tell you I'm speaking to you from experience; I am not theorizing, I am not speculating. I have experienced it, and so I tell you from my own personal experience how this is brought about.

We search the scriptures and we search the Old Testament, for that was the only scripture before the fatherhood revealed himself. It was foreshadowed and the whole book is simply a forecast, an adumbration in a not altogether inclusive manner. You have to search it and when you experience it, you go back and you search it again, and then you see what it really meant. But until it's experienced, reason cannot extract it...and there it is in the Old Testament. He said, "If I am a father, where is my son?" The verse is, "A son honors his father. If I then be a father, where is my honor?" (Mal.1:6). In other words, where is my son? So I search the scriptures to find out what is this son, who is his son? Born and raised in the Christian faith I was told it was Jesus Christ. My experience does not confirm that. So I started searching the scripture again, went all over the whole book, to find that Jesus Christ is God the Father: "He who sees me has seen the Father. How then can you say, 'Show us the Father?' (Jn.14:8). "I am the way"—to what? "No one comes to the Father but by me" and when you come to the Father you're going to find me...I am the Father. So, "Philip, I have been so long with you and yet you do not know me? He who has seen me has seen the Father." Well, if he is a father, then he has a son, because the son is the honor of the father. Well, no one talks about Jesus Christ having a son. We are taught in our churches, the Christian churches that he was the Son of God...yet he claims he is the Father. If he is a father, then he has a son.

Well now, who is his son? We read scripture, "What think ye of the Christ? Whose son is he? And they said, 'The son of David.' He said, 'Why then did David in the Spirit call him my Lord? If David thus calls him Lord, how can he be David's son?" (Mat.22:42). A son always referred to his father as 'my Lord.' David in the Spirit is calling him "my Father." He claims, "I have come only to fulfill scripture. Scripture must be fulfilled in me." Well, what portion of the Old Testament does that fulfill, when David in the Spirit calls him "my Father"? The 89th Psalm: "And the Lord said, I have found David and David has cried unto me, Thou art my Father, my God, and the Rock of my salvation" (verse 26). I go back now to find in the 2nd Psalm, "And I will tell of the decree of the Lord: The Lord said to me, 'Thou art my son, today I have begotten thee'" (2:7). The Psalm is attributed to David.

From my own experience I know it is true: to have this wonderful experience where your head explodes and then when it all subsides, you find yourself looking into the face of this heavenly youth. You know without any doubt, there is no uncertainty, you are looking right into the face of your son and he's David of biblical fame. There is no doubt whatsoever as to who he is and the relationship between the two: he is your son and he knows you are his father. It is *only* then that you know who you are: you have found the Father and found him in yourself. *You are* the Father. "No one knows who the son is except the Father and no one knows who the Father is except the son and anyone to whom the son chooses to reveal him" (Mat.11:27). For the son comes to reveal him. Without a son, no one would ever know he is the Father. So we search the scriptures to find the Son of God, and find him in David: "I have found in David, the son of Jesse, a man after my own heart who will do all my will" (Acts13:22). Well, Jesse means "I AM." It is any form of the verb "to be." What is God's name?—I AM. "When I come to the people of Israel and tell them that the God of your fathers sent me, the God of Abraham, the God of Isaac, and the God of Jacob, and they should say to me, 'What is his name?' what must I say?" "Say to them I AM has sent me. That is my name forever and forever" (Exod. 3:13-15). Well, Jesse is I AM...the Father of David. But you have to search it and even when you search it and reason confirms it, it doesn't make any sense until it actually happens to you.

Now, when you have this experience that I have had, you are the Father; and there's only one Father, therefore you and I must be one. We seem to be two. In my own case I did not lose my identity, I did not lose my individuality, yet I know I am the Father. The father of one, if tradition is to be taken in this secular world, well, he lived 1,000 B. C., and I was born in this century. But you're told in scripture that in the *Spirit* he called me Father. I make no claim of any reincarnation. I do not claim that I lived 1,000 B. C. and that I was Jesse, the father of a man called David...no. This whole thing is *supernatural*. The drama is completely supernatural from beginning to the end; it has not a thing to do with secular history.

So everyone is going to take this eternal story and unfold it within himself. As he unfolds it within himself, he knows he is God the Father; but he can't deny that *everyone* is God the Father not yet revealed. When it's revealed, we all return to the one God the Father, and we, the brothers, form the Lord. It takes all of us to form the one God and Father of all. We are the Elohim, it's a plural word...we are the brothers. So you'll be able to say, as you are told in scripture: "The works that I have done you'll do and greater than these you'll do, because I go to the Father" (Jn.4:12). You'll continue to fulfill scripture, and everyone is going to have the identical experience, so you'll be able to say, "Go to my brothers and say to them I am ascending unto my Father and to your Father, and to my God and to your God" (Jn.20:17). We are brothers regardless of sex, because in the resurrection there is no sex, there is no Greek, no Jew, no bond, no free, no male, no female, and we are above the organization of sex (Jn.3:28). We are brothers, not creating on a divided image as we do here in this world, but once more returned to the Fatherhood that we are. We are God the Father.

In this world, we seem to be sinners, horrible beings, the wars, the stealing, the horrors of the world. Well, I tell you in the end *all* is forgiven. These are only parts that we, the actor, play. And we are the actor: "God only acts and is in all existing beings or men" (Blake, *Memorable Fancy*). We are the actor, so a true actor can play the part of a bum and the part of the glorious one, the part of the pauper and the part of the fabulously wealthy, if he's a good actor. So God is the actor and his name is I AM. You meet someone on the street who's begging you for a quarter, there is God. Here is one you read in the paper he's a billionaire, that's God, same God. He's not rich because he has a billion and not poor because he only has a quarter... it is God the creator of it all. The whole vast world was created by God the Father and he became man to have the experience of death and to prove to himself that he could overcome death. So, "I say, 'Ye are gods, all of you, sons of the Most High; nevertheless, you will die like men and fall as one man, O ye princes" (Ps.82:1,6). So one man fell and became fragmented into all the brothers. These are the brothers...whether you're a lady or a gentleman, we're all brothers...and in the end we're all God the Father. You return: "I came out from the Father and I came into the world; again I am leaving the world and I'm going to the Father" (Jn.16:28).

Now we are told, "I no longer speak to you in figures" (Jn.16:25)—that is, in parable, in allegory, enigmatic statements, like saying 'I am the door, I am the true vine'—"but I will tell you truly and plainly of the Father." "I am the Father," that's what he said, "He who sees me sees the Father." And now knowing that we are brothers makes the statement, "And now may...I've told them your name that you gave me. And now the love by which you loved me may it be in them and I in them, and may we be one as you and I are one." He's praying for the oneness. For, what oneness? We are already one, but he's praying for the recognition of that unity...that all will have the experience of being God the Father. There's no way in eternity that I could persuade you that you're God the Father. The only way you'll ever know it is when the experience I have had you have, which is when David stands before you and you know he is your son. Then you see the Word of God cannot be broken. It cannot be broken! David says, "I will tell of the decree of the Lord: He said unto me, 'Thou art my son, today I have begotten thee" (Ps.2:7). As a Christian I was taught to believe that these words were addressed to Jesus Christ. I know today these words were *inspired* by Jesus Christ, *not* addressed to him. He inspired them and then came in to fulfill them: "I have come to fulfill scripture. Scripture must be fulfilled *in* me" (Luke22:37). So he comes in and takes upon himself the limitations of the flesh and blood, and is born of woman, and becomes obedient unto death, even death upon the cross... and this [body] is the cross. This is the only cross.

A friend of mine asked a question here last Friday and I did not have the true answer. I confess I had not yet looked up that word in the Concordance to give it its original meaning. The question he asked was what is the word "carpenter"? For, we are told in scripture, "Is this not the carpenter? Is he not the son of Mary, the brother of James, the brother of Simon and Jose and Judas and his sisters? Are they not with us today? How does he know these things?" Well, at the question period he asked the question concerning "carpenter." My concordance, which is *James Strong's Concordance*, defines the word in Greek as "to produce from seed, as a woman; a tree; the earth; to be born; to bring forth; to be delivered; to be in travail." So here is one who comes to fulfill the promise. For, the word "Moses" is also defined as the old perfective of the Egyptian verb "to be born"...not yet born. It's something *to be* born, and here comes one who actually unfolds the entire drama within himself. So here, something is to be born. Well, the carpenter is that which is to be delivered, to be born.

Now you and I reading it superficially will think of the man's trade, one who builds a house or repairs a house. Yet the actual meaning of the word as originally used was simply "to produce from seed." Well the seed was in the Old Testament…that is the foundation, that's the seed plot of the entire book. Now he comes to fulfill it, and he only fulfills scripture. He doesn't change anything in the world. He doesn't say we should not have a Caesar who rules it: "Render unto Caesar the things that are Caesar's." We have no description of the man in scripture, whether he was blond or dark, tall or short, no personal description. Here is a *pattern man*, a *plan* contained in every man, and every man contains Christ: for "Christ in you is the hope of glory" (Col.1:27).

So the goal of man is to find the Father and it comes in the most dramatic manner. You are first awakened within yourself; you find yourself completely awake in your skull. Your skull is where you were buried; that is the Golgotha in which Christ is buried. God actually enters the human skull and lies down in the grave and dreams himself *you*. At the end of what span of time I do not know—people speculate as to 6,000 years, 8,000 years—but I have no experience concerning the time so I cannot tell you from experience. I only know that one moment you begin to awaken. An unusual vibration possesses your head and then you can't stop it, you can't arrest it, and suddenly you find yourself waking. But it's unlike any awakening you've ever experienced before: you awake within your skull. You're fully awake and yet you're completely sealed in, there is no outlet. You intuitively know, it's an innate knowledge that if you push the base of the skull you can get out. You push the base of skull and there's an opening; you squeeze yourself out head first and then you come out inch by inch…like someone being born from a woman, only you're born from the skull. You look back and here is that out of which you came, your body, this little garment that your physical mother wove for you—that is the "linen cloth" of scripture—as you look back and see it lying there. And then, the entire drama as told in the Books of Matthew and Luke surround you. You are invisible to those who you see, but here is the infant that is presented and it's yours. They know it's yours and they call you by name, your earthly name, and tell that it's your child. They don't see you because now you are Spirit. So it's God that is born. And you came out of the garment that you wore.

That comes to an end, and then 139 days later is when you discover the fatherhood of God…and discover that *you* are the Father. A similar vibration starts in your head and when it reaches the limit of intensity you explode… your head *seems* to explode. Then standing before you leaning against the side of an open door is your son David of biblical fame looking out on a pastoral scene. You see him so clearly and, well, you can't describe the beauty of David…it's beyond description. The relationship is so established there's no doubt whatsoever: he is your son and you know it. Then that comes to an end.

And then 123 days later comes the third grand event and you are split from your head to the base of your spine and your body is actually in two parts. From top to bottom you're split and one side moves this way and one side moves this way. Again in fulfillment of scripture: "And he stood upon the Mount of Olives; and the Mount was split from east to west. One side moved northward and the other side moved southward" (Zech. 14:4). You think it is a mountain in the Near East? No, *you* are the entire scripture. It's your body, for we are told in scripture the curtain of the temple was his own flesh. You see your entire body split right down, and then at the base of your spine is this pool of golden liquid light. You contemplate it and strangely enough although it's a pool of living light, you know it is yourself. As you look at it, you fuse with it; and then like a serpent up you go into your skull, and it reverberates like thunder. As told in scripture, "As Moses lifted up the serpent in the wilderness, so must the Son of man be lifted up" (Jn.3:14). You go right up, right back into the same area that the Father is built in you...he's built within us. Right into this area as though you're only a brain...only this fantastic head that is yours.

Then 998 days later, your skull becomes luminous, translucent, there is no circumference, infinite transparency; and hovering above you, about maybe twenty feet, is a dove. The dove looks lovingly at you and you automatically raise your hand as you are told in the story of Noah. He stuck his hand out and the dove lit upon the hand and he drew her in unto himself (Gen.8:9). Well, the dove descends as though it's floating, descends upon your hand, and then as you draw it to your face it smothers you with affection, kissing your face, your neck, your head. While it is absolutely smothering you with love, a woman at your side will tell you that he loves you, and it is so obvious that he does. Then she will tell you "in a strange way that they avoid man because man gives off such an offensive odor, but to prove his love for you he penetrated the ring of offense and came down to demonstrate his love for you." While he is demonstrating his love in the form of a dove, the whole thing comes to an end.

Then you add all these little numbers up, from the very first one when you awoke in your skull to the end. The first, from the first day to the second experience, 139 days; from that day to the third experience, 123 days; and from that third to the fourth one, 998 days. They come to 1,260 days, the number given in Daniel (7:25) and Revelation (11:3). The child was born and then 1,260 days elapsed...and the entire drama is coming to an end.

Then all you can do is tell it. Some will believe it and others will disbelieve it, but all you can do is tell it; because eventually even those who disbelieve will have the experience. Not one can be lost, not one in eternity. The most horrible creature that walks the face of the earth will eventually have the experience. Though he stands today and claims that he is an atheist or agnostic, it really doesn't matter. Let him claim it and let him have fun. In the end we will all know from experience that there is God. Only the fool will say in his heart there is no God. So the wisest of men who today claim there is no God, they are wise in their own conceit, but in the eyes of those who know they're fools. They may have all the degrees in the world behind their name...oh, very wise...and make a nice big impression on those who are equally stupid. But, you know, there's an awful lot of learned ignorance in the world. So it doesn't really matter what they claim or what they do.

I'm telling you what I *know* from experience; I am not theorizing, I am not speculating. There is God the Father, and don't look for him outside of yourself. You'll not in eternity find him in any place other than yourself. When you find him, you are God the Father. And yet you are weak as all outdoors in the world of men. I stand before you just as weak as any man in the world, with little of the world's goods, and yet I know what I'm talking about. I have to continue in this weakness while I wear this garment of flesh; and when I take it off, I return to the being that I was before I sent myself out. Returning, I am one with the risen Lord. There's only one body. How can one body contain all? Well, how can your one brain contain billions of cells? So our brain, finite, yes, it's finite. They could be numbered if one is capable of doing it, but still finite...if it can be numbered. But it would run into unnumbered billions. And we are told in scripture, "He has put a limit to the peoples of the world according to the number of the sons of God." So there'll be no more in the world than there are sons ___(??) themselves in people. So every child born of woman is God incarnate. I don't care what the child is, any pigment of skin, any race, any nationality, that is God incarnate. There can be no more bodies in the world than there are sons of God to wear them; and sons of God wear all the garments in the world. And so we are simply fighting each other, fighting our own brothers.

Madam Schumman-Heink, maybe you don't know her, a grand old lady of the opera, a great singer of the Germanic world. She had six sons, three fought in the First World War on the German side, and three with the British Army. She traveled around the world and had her sons in different parts of the world. Here the poor soul was distraught. She was caught here when the war broke and she knew three sons were fighting with the Germans and three with the British. The Countess of ___(??)—I knew her well, she came to all of my lectures in New York City—she had a similar experience. She had sons, too, divided. They were born in different parts of the world and when war broke, the Second World War, the Germans called up her sons who were born on German soil and the British called up her sons who were born on British soil. Who knows if one was killed that it was not his own brother who killed him? Yet whoever was killed it was his own brother anyway. If the German was killed by a British, even though he had no one of a physical descent, he still shot his own brother; and shooting his brother he shot himself, because eventually we're all the same Father. All the Father of the one and only son, and that one and only son is David. There is no other son. And one day you'll find him.

How to persuade people who have been conditioned to think otherwise? I know it's difficult, because raised and trained in the Christian faith as I was, and I called myself a Christian, it would have been difficult to persuade me using only your visions to persuade me. I was so completely trained in the belief that Jesus Christ was a unit that was different and he was the Son of God. I went to my school, I studied scripture—we had it every Sunday in Sunday school—but where I was born and raised we also had it in our schools. We had to study scripture. I couldn't find in scripture that David was the Son until I had the experience. And it's the most difficult thing to persuade anyone to modify their concepts and come forward and hear one who has had the experience. So after, he tells you that "No one knows the Son but the Father, and no one knows the Father but the Son and anyone to whom the Son chooses to reveal him" (Mat.11:27). Then he goes on to say, "Take my yoke upon you and learn from me." Well, the yoke is simply a word for "teaching"—we speak of the yoke of the law, the yoke of adoption. Now, he is speaking from experience and he's asking those to exchange yokes. You've been taught this, that and the other, but I'm telling you I've experienced scripture, so take my yoke upon you and learn from me, because eventually you're going to have this experience.

Everyone's going to find that they are God the Father, and you'll never know you are God the Father unless the Son of God stands before you and calls you Father. And you know it, it's no longer the play; this is now the reality, and you know you are the Father because here comes David. He's a youth about twelve or thirteen, handsome beyond the wildest dream of man. You can't describe the *beauty* of David, because he is the quintessence of all the experiences that you, the Father, had in this world. "I have found in David the son of Jesse a man after my own heart who will do all my will" (Acts13:22). So the part you're playing does all your will and in the very end this eternal youth, which is the quintessence of your experience in the world of death, stands before you and reveals you are God the Father who is the cause of the phenomena of life. So the goal of life is to find the Father. We are led astray...we think it's to make a billion dollars or to become popular, to become famous. Well, these are things on the outside. I'm not denying that they're interesting; but that is not the goal. The goal of life is to find the Father and the Father is built in from all eternity *within* the individual born of woman. One day he's going to find the Father.

To the ladies, let me tell you, you will not be surprised when you know you are the Father. For in the resurrection you are above the organization of sex and you will not be surprised to know that you are the Father and he is your Son, and he has no mother…that he is begotten of you as a result of the experiences in this world of death. All of this is a *result*; he is the result, the end result, and he is as perfect as you are perfect. He is beautiful beyond measure and so are you. *That* day, you awaken to remember the being that you *really* are; but you had to forget it, empty yourself and become obedient unto death, even death upon this cross (Phil.2:7).

You dwell upon it. This may not seem to you tonight a practical lesson, but I've always felt that what is most profoundly spiritual is in reality most directly practical. Your Father which is yourself knows what you need. You dwell upon this and things will be good in your world. You don't have to seek the individual thing like a better job, this, that and the other. If you want to, you may, but you pursue this and he the being that you really are knows your need and you'll get it.

But in the end…in my own case this is my last round. Whenever the day comes, if it's tonight, when this is taken off, I will not be restored to life, as all must be restored who have not had the experience of the discovery of the Fatherhood. No more restoration to the garments of flesh; I ascend to the being that I really am, and that being is God the Father. Everyone who has the experience that I have had when they reach the point called death, no more restoration to garments of flesh. They ascend to the being that we are and that one body is made up of all the redeemed, all who are resurrected. As told us in scripture, "They die no more"—why?—"because they're sons of the resurrection, sons of God, and can die no more"—read it in scripture (Luke 20:35)—implying that if they haven't had the experience they must continue to die. But there is no death, not for the immortal God. For death here is simply going through the door to find yourself restored and clothed once more in a similar garment. But young, not a baby, about twenty years of age, same being that you are now, in a world terrestrial just like this, where you're afraid of death as you are here, where you marry, where you struggle, where you do everything just as you do here…until you find the Father. When you find the Father there are no more restorations in garments of flesh and blood, but ascent to the being that you really are: God the Father.

Now let us go into the Silence.

*   *   *

Now are there any questions, please?

Q: (inaudible)

A: You'll find that both in Matthew and in Luke...try the 20th chapter of Luke. The question is asked by those who do not believe in the resurrection, and they said, "Master, Moses in the law said that if a man marries and dies leaving no offspring, and he has a brother, the brother should marry the widow and raise up issue for him" (the brother who died). "There were seven brothers and one died leaving no offspring, and the second one married her. Then he died, leaving no offspring, and the third took her. Eventually all married her and they died leaving no offspring, and eventually she died." So they asked the question, "Whose wife will she be in the resurrection?" (20:28). Not believing in the resurrection, they did this to trip him. And he said, "You know not the scripture" and then he explained what happens to men who die. He said, "In this age men marry and are given in marriage; but those who are accounted worthy to attain to *that age*, unto the resurrection, they neither marry nor are they given in marriage, for they cannot die any more, because they are sons of God, being sons of the resurrection" (Luke20:34). So we marry and we are given in marriage in this age. So he speaks of the two ages: one in this world where we create on a divided image, and then in that world where we are unified into the one being which is God the Father. But it comes only after the resurrection. You cannot enter that age by doing things on the outside in this world; it can only be done by being awakened while in this world. You are awakened in the grave and the grave is your own skull. You are actually buried in your skull, which is called Golgotha and which means "skull." That's the Calvary.

Luke doesn't even use the word Golgotha: "And when they came to the place called The Skull, there they crucified him" (23:33). And then he was buried near to the place of crucifixion, the skull. Man thinks he's going to find the grave in the Near East. Well, he'll dig forever and he'll never find it. He never was buried there; he's buried in the skull of every little child that is born of woman. That's the universal Christ, the universal diffused individuality. And eventually all are gathered into the one being, the same being that came down.

Q: I don't understand coming from the skull and the number of days from one experience to another...coming into this world or going out?
A: No, my dear, no. The days that I mentioned are 1,260 days as told us in the 12th chapter of Daniel, and he said, "I heard it but I did not understand it." And they said, "Close the book, Daniel, until the end" (12:9). He could not understand what he heard, but the man spoke telling him of a time, times and half a time. Well, a "time" is a year; "times" would be twice that amount (that's now three years) and then "half a time" would be three and a half years, or forty-two months. The ancients divided a year into twelve equal parts of thirty days. Now you count them up and you come into the Book of Revelation and it spells it out as 1,260 days (Rev.11:2,3).

So from that moment you are awakened within your skull and you come out like one being born, and the babe wrapped in swaddling clothes confronts you and that unearthly wind possess you, then men come to bear witness to the event, and they surround the garment out of which you emerged. Now that vanishes and they remain and they find the infant on the floor. One announces calling you by name that it's your baby, and brings it over and places it on the bed where the body was (the body's no longer there). You pick the infant up in your hands and you speak in the most endearing terms to this infant wrapped in swaddling clothes. While you are completely entranced with this beauty, this little child, it breaks into a smile, the whole face becomes one wonderful radiant smile. You are told, "I will give you a son and his name is Isaac" (Gen.17:15,19). The word Isaac means "he laughs"...that's what the word means. I give you that which laughs and it's only a *sign*, a sign of *your* own birth out of the world of death into life eternal. Now count 139 days and the event of the Fatherhood of God comes upon you. Then comes 123 days and the splitting of your body from top to bottom comes upon you. Count 998 days, the dove descends upon you and smothers you with love. Put them all together and they come to 1,260 days. You simply fulfill scripture.

Q: Was that actually your experience?
A: My experience began on the 20th day of July, 1959, and then on Jan. 1, 1963 was the day of the descent of the dove. So July 20th of this year it will have been ten years since I've had the experience. So I'm talking from my own experience, I'm not speculating. It's only in the scriptures...but I did not know the scriptures until I had the experience. I thought I knew the Bible and I've been teaching since 1938, the second day of February, 1938, but I did not know anything but the law. I didn't know the Promise and this is the Promise *fulfilled*. But the law, I

thought I knew it. I know I know it and I can teach it. Next Friday will be the law, the game of life, and how to play it in the world of Caesar, that's Friday. But this is the *goal* of life, and you can't play it...only faith. The Promise is made and you walk by faith. You set your hope fully upon the *grace* that is coming to you at the revelation, at the unveiling of Christ within you; and Christ within you is God the Father. If he is a father, then he has a son to bear witness to his fatherhood. Therefore, who is his son? Well, *David* in the Spirit called him Father.

But people don't see it. I have talked with rabbis, with priests, with ministers of all denominations of the Protestant faith. Not one would even give an ear to it. They're as blind as blind can be. They are blind leaders of the blind and both fall into the ditch. They don't know it and they are unwilling to listen to one who has had the experience. Yet they go back to their books which they're always carrying in their hands for show. You see them on the subways in New York City, each of them has a book and he's not opening the book. If he does, he's not reading it at all. At their age they need glasses and they aren't wearing glasses, so they open the book just for show. I'm not speaking of that. I've gone on radio with them in all-night sessions, six hours, three ministers, a rabbi, a psychiatrist all these so-called learned men. Well, they completely closed the mind when it comes to my revelation. Yet I'm telling you what happened to me and it's all in scripture. But the mind conditioned is a strange thing to recondition. Try to recondition the mind.

A man comes to this country and he seeks the freedom that he feels he will find here. He finds it here, but he was born in some other area of the world and his heart hasn't left it. Let something come up between this country and that country where he was born, and he finds his little mind going back to protect that little land. Something tells him that this country may be right in the ultimate, but no, he's going to go right back and pick up the argument as the little country now presents it. It's so difficult to overcome and recondition the mind.

So you go to school...I was beaten once in my life in school, an unmerciful beating, where you brought blood from my buttocks down to my knees. For in those days they were allowed to beat the children, corporal punishment was in order. He had a cane...you could bend it around this way. He asked me a question and I quoted the Bible, "Take up thy bed and walk." He said, "Bring me your book." I didn't have my Bible with me. There were nine boys and a girl and you aren't going to have ten Bibles in the house. So I told him that my brother had it that day. That might have been a lie...but I said my brother had it. So I couldn't produce the Bible. He goes back into the room and brings out the long cane, taps it this way on the bench. I had to kneel on the bench, and he starts to beat me unmercifully. So he was a sadist; he blew his brains out a year later. He was simply taking it out on the boys. The boys would come to school padded from their buttocks down with all kinds of funny leather, books, and everything else, because they knew that someone had to be beaten that day. He took something out on the boys to give himself…it could have been an orgasm, I don't know…but he had to beat in order to get his own emotional thrill. And I was the one that day. That night when I undressed and my father discovered it through my brother Victor; Victor said, "Daddy, come and see what they've done to Neville." My father came back and said, "Take off your pants" because at dinner I didn't sit up as I should, and my mother said, "Come on, sit up, Neville." Well, I had to sit up…my mother told me to…but the pain and all the blood. When he saw what the man had done, he started to dress and Wilsey knew exactly what he was going to do. My mother's name was Wilhelmina and he called her Wilsey. She said, "Joseph, don't!" He said, "I'm going to kill hm. I'm going to kill him tonight" and do you know he would have if he was not restrained. So I never went back to that school. I was taken out of school that night and sent to another school. It was the one time I was severely beaten and that was for quoting the Bible accurately. But his translation said "couch" and mine said "bed": "Take up your bed and walk" and his said "Take up your couch and walk." That was the excuse to get someone beaten…just a sadist. Well, I'm not a masochist. So maybe it was a good thing that I was beaten for the Bible. And so, in the end he is. If it drove me to a greater search for the Truth then that is in order.

Until Friday…

THE GAME OF LIFE

3/7/69

Tonight's subject is "The Game of Life." The first thing we do in the playing of a game we must learn the rules and then we play the game within the frame of rules. Any violation of the rules carries a penalty. Now, this is the game of life and you and I play it from the cradle to the grave and beyond because the grave does not end our game of life. So while you're in *this* age, you can really learn how to play it.

Now first of all, we are told "Even in your thought, do not curse the king, nor in your bedchamber curse the rich; for a bird will carry your voice, or some winged creature will tell the matter." That you will find in Ecclesiastes in the 10th chapter (verse 29). Now we turn to the positive side, "Whatever you desire, believe that you have received it, and you will" (Mark11:24). Here we are taught to start at the end; the end is where we begin. When I know my goal that's where I start, for in my end is my beginning. I *feel* myself into that end, and I'm promised if I do and if I'm persistent, it will come to pass.

Now we are told, "Cast your bread upon the waters, for you shall find it after many days" (Eccles.11:1). Don't be concerned just cast your bread upon the waters. I know that many people have interpreted that as "to do good"…to go out trying to do good to build up a certain merit in the world, a certain credit in the book of God. Hasn't a thing to do with it. My friend the other night, when he asked me concerning the word carpenter, and I told you in the last meeting but he wasn't here, and for his benefit we'll tell him what the concordance, the biblical concordance tells us about it. The word means "to produce from seed, as a mother, a tree, the earth, to bring forth, to be born, to be delivered." So the seed of the Old Testament, which is the Promise, has to be born. So the carpenter called Christ Jesus brought it to birth, for in him all the promises found their fulfillment. He didn't come to *abolish* the law and the prophets but to *fulfill* them (Mat.5:17). He was the carpenter who produced from seed, the seed being the promises, as made through the prophets, and he simply fulfilled them.

Well now, this cast your bread upon the waters...and people go out to do good and give to charity. All these are lovely things and I wouldn't stop anyone from giving anything in this world that they really wanted to give, but that is not casting your bread upon the waters. The word bread means in the biblical concordance "to devour, to consume" and waters is a euphemism for "semen," that living water that carries the seed, the sperm of man. It's a *psychological* creative act; it's not a physical act. But it's the same *intensity* raised to an nth degree. You speak of a man who is consumed with hate or he could be on fire with love, but this is the *passion* of which it speaks; and that is casting your bread upon the waters. An intense imaginal act will draw to itself its own kin, its own affinity.

Now here we have one who has departed this world at the very peak of success. You all know him...this age could not forget him. He had so many failures and then he made a discovery which he put into print, and his words are these, "The mood decides the fortunes of people rather than the fortunes decide the mood" (Churchill). It is to those who continually compare what is within with what is without who have this certainty. Those who do not change in mood, who are consumed all day in anger, see not change and recognize no law. If there are changes of mood, there will be changes of circumstances. And then because of a change in circumstances related to the change of mood you recognize a law behind it, behind all these changes. But if all day long you are depressed...and there are people who from the cradle to the grave are depressed. I know of many. I go back to New York City where I was closer to people because the thing is smaller... this is a vast area in Los Angeles and I don't drive...but in New York City I would walk miles every day and encounter many friends. Well, I could spot a couple of dozen who when you met them you wanted to cross the street (if they hadn't seen you) because you're going to get the most depressing story. They'll tell you all about their wife or their husband or their children and it was always depressing. Over years the same thing...you never heard any change in mood. So they saw no change in their world; and therefore recognizing no change they saw no change in their world. And therefore, recognizing no change they recognized no law between the inner world that they maintained and the outer world that came in response to it.

But if I know this law I could predict that by the uprising of new moods within me that I would soon meet people of a certain character...and I met them. Even inanimate objects are under the sway of these affinities.

I have gone with a mood to my library and taken from the library a book that I have not touched in years, and opened it casually to find the answer confirming that mood, something beautifully stated, a book of poetry that I haven't touched. But something...you see a table differently for the first time based upon the mood, yet the table was there all along. And you see everything in the world reflecting the mood. For here we are told, the *mood* decides the fortunes and it's not the fortunes decide the mood. You can think, "If only I had a million dollars, oh, would I feel great!" Not knowing if they feel as though they had it, they would actually attract that state in their world, because we contain within ourselves "the lamp of the world."

We are told in the Book of Proverbs "The spirit of man is the lamp of the Lord" (20:27). The lamp of the Lord would be the light of the world. We are told we contain it, we actually contain it within ourselves. And nature, the genii, is slave of that lamp and must fashion life about us as we fashion it within ourselves. *It* has no choice. And when I say "nature," I'm not speaking only of the plants; I speak of humanity, I speak of the animal world, I speak of the plant world, I speak of the mineral world. I speak of everything that is seemingly on the outside that is slave of the lamp that is on the inside. But I must first fashion it on the inside and then this slave of the lamp will fashion it in harmony with that which I have done within. And no power in the world can stop it. If I am aware, I will recognize a law between my mood and circumstances which surround me. I don't have to go in search of it. I don't have to seek it. I could predict without search that I will meet certain characters, certain things in harmony with the mood...and I invariably do... whether that character is a living being or a book or something else. It's something that must bear witness.

So here, the game of life is to find out the rules. And the rule in the positive way to play it beautifully is to have a goal: you *must* know what you want. You can't just complain because you don't like what you have; you must know what you want in place of what you have. When you know what you want, you must assume the feeling of the wish fulfilled and although at the moment reason would deny it and your senses deny it, you must *persist* in that assumption, and if you persist in that assumption, that assumption will harden into fact. It will objectify itself upon the screen of space.

Now, I ask you to play it along that way. If you say, "Well, it doesn't work," you haven't tried it. You may say it's stupid. All right, maybe it's stupid. But the man who made his departure from this world a few years ago at the very top—no one achieved such greatness—and here he tells it in his own wonderful English that the mood decides the fortunes of people, and it 's not the reverse, that the fortunes decide the mood. Well, you either believe him or you don't believe him, but he certainly proved it in his own life. Although he was born to greatness he failed in Parliament. He was a washed up man in the Second World War. When Chamberlain was put aside after the conflict started, they called upon Churchill, and then Churchill was the one who galvanized the Western world by his words. He was putting into practice exactly what he told us, that the *mood* does it. And in spite of all the bombing of London and all the horrors, he sustained the mood, the mood of victory. Not for one moment did he waver even in the darkest days. He sustained it when his opponent didn't know the law and put his trust in armaments and numbers, all these things, and Churchill put his trust in the mood. He knew that the mood would fashion life around him, and it would externalize itself upon the world. He went to his grave leaving behind this wonderful statement. How many saw it, I don't know. I read it in the *New York Times* when he spoke to the Guild Hall in London and the *New York Times* printed his entire speech. That thing simply jumped off the page when I came to it. So I made a record of it and recorded it as I do all these things that hit me…for I am in search of principle. If I find the law, if I find the principle and abide by it, it should prove itself in performance. Well, it has proved itself in my case in performance by simply catching the mood and then I teach others how to catch it: what would the *feeling* be like if it were true? Well, you toy with that idea, you play with it for awhile and then all of a sudden the mood comes upon you. Well, keep that mood…just stay in that mood.

I can tell you of many who by playing on the mood are being secure… starting with nothing, not one penny in the world. And, here is a lady in her middle sixties, she confessed to that (I'm inclined to believe she is even older than that) but she had nothing and all of a sudden she began to put this into practice. "Something wonderful is happening to me now! Something wonderful!" and she kept playing upon it and playing upon it. Within that very week she received her first great return. A friend who had known her, and they were intimate for twenty-odd or maybe thirty-odd years, he often said to her that he'd never give her a nickel, not one nickel; that they had fun together and they saw every show that came to Broadway, all the operas, all the concerts, and they dined high, wide and handsome every night in some fabulous restaurant. He felt that was enough for her company of thirty years.

But he had a change of heart within that first few days after playing this part. She actually felt in the morning before she went to her job that paid her seventy-five dollars a week gross, that is before taxes, and she a single girl, living in a hotel room, and you know what you could take home…practically nothing. Luckily he did pick up all the checks when it came to food, but that is not what any woman wants in this world. Well, he settled on her a $100,000 trust fund. The trust is hers and she can will it away to anything in the world. She can give it to a dog kennel; he didn't so set it up that at her death it returned to his estate. It was detached from his estate and she receives the investment. He didn't give *her* the $100,000 because he thought she might go out and spend it, so he set it up in a trust to pay her the interest from that trust for the rest of her days.

Again she began to apply it beyond that. He set up another $100,000... and the same lady. Now she has $200,000 and she can't spend the income. I know where she lives; I know what she pays in rent. It's a lovely place, a modern apartment, and I know her rent is $165 a month and utilities...what would they be...I mean all the utilities in the place? It would be practically nil. I know how she lives...well, she can't spend the income. Then, of course, at her age she has a certain check from the government. All of that together, she must have, maybe, $1,500 a month, and she was making seventy-five dollars a week before taxes. She still isn't satisfied. Now, she knows the law. I tell her I don't give a darn what you want, I'm telling you only a principle and I leave you to your choice and its risk. So you simply apply the law and apply it wisely.

Now the old gentleman has a little hardening of the brain...and they've parted company. Because he refuses to see her—with advice of his nephews and nieces and all the others—she now curses him as we are warned *not* to do. "Even in your thought, do not curse the king, and even in your bedchamber, do not curse the rich; for a bird of the air will carry your voice, or some winged creature tells the matter." So she calls me every week from New York City to tell me she is overcoming the cursing of him, but has she? It will not take from her the trust fund—that is something established—but other things can come into her world that will hurt her beyond anything such as money. But unnumbered things if she continues to curse him, the rich man, because he didn't now put another million on her back as it were.

So, I'm just warning you of the law, the positive side of it and the negative side of it, and leave you to practice. It takes practice, for if you are in the habit of thinking negatively morning, noon and night you are not going to start tonight to go through the door and think that you are all that you want to be and sustain it. You can hold it for maybe a few seconds and then because it hasn't proved itself in performance in a matter of a minute, you may forget it and completely turn away to some other state. But the game of life is to first know the rules and when I know the rules I must then apply the rules. But I must see both sides of it, for in every game there are rules that are laid down and violation of the rules will cause a penalty. Now, "Be not deceived," we are told, "God is not mocked, for as a man soweth, so shall he also reap" (Gal.6:7). So in the world I can play a certain game and I may get away with a violation that the referee didn't see and I may do it several times, but *this* referee sees everything; for he is the lamp within us, for the "Spirit of the man is the lamp of the Lord." I cannot get away from that observer within me, for he and I are one. Do I know it? Then he knows it because I and my Father are one (Jn.10:30). So do not be deceived...I can't mock him. So whatever I do that's a violation of this, like feeling sad for myself and feeling very sorry for myself it is going to be recorded and as it's recorded there is no excuse that I can make, it's going to mold itself in harmony with my world.

Now here, a letter came today (and this gentleman is here tonight). He said, "A friend of mine last Monday night after your lecture asked me for help...the help being an imaginal help...that I would imagine the good for him that he wants to hear. So when I went home I spent a half an hour on him. I imagined exactly what I think I would hear if his desire had been realized. I heard it distinctly and then I retired. Just before I woke in the morning I saw in my dream his wife and the wife is thanking me profusely over and over for the help, the great help that I gave to her husband. It was such a vivid, vivid dream. When I awoke I knew she had no knowledge of what I had done and the help could only be my response to his request; so I began to think in some strange way she knows of the request because she certainly doesn't know of the help. Then during the day I thought maybe it has already been realized, could be, and in the deeper level of my being in dream she has thanked me for it.

Well, that night, which is Tuesday night of this week, while listening to music in my living room, suddenly he appears in my reverie and he uses the identical words that I used the previous night to hear him confirm the fulfillment of his desire. He spoke with such authority, such power, with such joy. But he used the identical words that I had formulated purposely to hear him tell me. I do hope that in the immediate present he will get confirmation from this man of the fulfillment of that imaginal act which he put in play for that man. But he heard it from both man and wife on two separate occasions, one in the dream and one in reverie. She came in the dream in the wee hours of Tuesday morning, and while he was listening to music on Tuesday evening then he came and spoke using the same words that he had used to hear.

Now, I can tell him from another part of his letter that this other one is a perfectly marvelous one. I won't go into all the details. In a dream he had to go to a certain city and when he registered he said to the man, "I want to be called at seven in the morning." The man said, "Yes sir," and made out a card and put seven. He looked at it and saw a big bold seven over his name. Then the man showed him what he did. He takes these cards and puts them in certain slots so when the operator comes on he will take ___(??) different times and those at this time he calls the different rooms to notify them that the time is up. So he was assured that he would be called at seven. And then he woke.

It's a marvelous vision. Seven is the numerical value of *spiritual perfection*. It also has much to do with gestation, incubation in all the worlds; in the insect world, in the animal world. Well, we are part animal, so in the animal world of man I am told that 280 days is the time between actual conception and birth. Well, that is a multiple of seven. We know the hen egg takes, if properly incubated, twenty-one days, a multiple of seven. So we find all these are multiples of seven and it has much to do with incubation. But in this case it is incubation of spiritual perfection. So I can say to him from this experience he's right on the verge. He sleeps one night and then the morning comes and he's called, for it is the Spirit within him. It is the Father calling him, and that cannot be far away for an actual conscious knowledge of the experience. So I say the conscious knowledge of the experience cannot be far away.

Another lady (she is here tonight) said, "I saw myself lying in state, ghastly pale like one that is dead, and then suddenly out of my body rises a giant of a man. I can see his feet now standing out of me. And that was it, this man." Well, let me tell a story of a mystic, a very able wonderful artist who was a great mystic. You know him best as A.E, the initials A. E. His name was George Russell and George Russell said, "I will tell this vision, but where it happened I will not say. It was a hall, vaster than any cathedral and its columns were made of living opal, as though you took the colors of dawn and eve and blended them into something alive...the columns were like that. In between the columns were thrones on which sat fire-crested kings. One wore the crest of the dragon, the others like plumes of fire. And in the middle of this place was a body, a dark, dark body stretched out on the floor as though in a trance, a deep trance. At the far end, on a throne higher than the others a being undoubtedly raised above the others, and behind him like the sun glowing. Then two of these crested kings came and passed their hands over this dark body on the floor. Where their hands passed over the body out came sparkles of light; and then rising out of this dark body was a figure as tall, as majestic as these fire-crested kings on the thrones. He looked around and recognized his kin and raised his hand in salutation. Then they all jumped from their thrones in the same wonderful greeting, and like brothers they altogether walked toward the end and disappeared into the sun" (*Candle of Vision*, The Many Colored Land).

Both were visions of what will take place; for he perceived it as coming from another; she saw it as coming from her own being as it was placed in space. It was an adumbration, a wonderful forecast, a foreshadowing of what's going to take place, for housed in man is that crested king, the Son of God. Whether you be woman as she is or whether it be man, the dark man as he saw the dark man, no matter what pigment of the skin, no matter what sex, within each is the Son of God. And that is the great lamp of the Lord, for these radiate his glory and they bear the express image of his person. So in each will rise one day these majestic beings that will come out of every being in the world. But while we are here, encased in these garments, let us learn the game of life. Learn the rules and play it.

Now here is a simple, simple statement of causation: it is the assemblage of mental states which occurring creates that which the assemblage implies. Simple…you simply assemble in your mind's eye a scene, as my friend did for the gentleman who asked him for help. Then he mentally heard only what he would hear if the man had received the desire fulfilled. So it's the assemblage of mental states which occurring creates that which the assemblage implies. So after you have done it, you don't have to repeat it. That intense moment, having done it, is casting your bread upon the waters.

May I tell you, when you do these things, although you do not have a physical expression in a sexual manner, there is a *relief* that is comparable, and of all the pleasures of the world relief is the most keenly felt. You are intense…someone is late…it could be someone you love dearly. You expect them at six and here it is seven and they aren't here and no telephone call to tell you what has happened. You are waiting anxiously. Then when the doorbell rings and it's their voice, the relief that comes when the one you so love suddenly appears. Well now, that of all the pleasures of the world, that is the most keenly felt. When you've done something of this nature, you feel a sense of relief and you don't have to do it a second time. This business of treating and treating and treating every day, you aren't casting your bread upon the waters. You may do it, but you only are going to *impregnate* once. Do what you want, but an impregnation is an impregnation. And if you reach the point of relief, well then, you've done it and you've cast your bread upon the waters and it shall return after many days (Ecc.11:1). Well, many days need not be days as we measure it, it could be in the matter of an hour. I have had the phone ring…having done it and the phone rang I would say within minutes to thank me for something that just happened when it was only a matter of moments before that I actually did it. That's when they got confirmation of it. I've done it when it took a day, took a week, took a month and sometimes it takes months. But I will not go over a thing…I did it! Having done it, what more can I do?

So this game of life is something that is serious, because you're playing it anyway. But you may never practice enough to really learn to master it, and you'll be complaining to the very ends of time. I'm quite sure tonight the million who are on relief in New York City—for over one million, just imagine, are on relief—and they're complaining as though the government owes them. There is no government; *we* are the government. So we aren't paying enough in taxes for them to get more, that's what they're saying. Because the government has no money, the government's money that they are putting out must first be taken from our pockets. And the million on relief are complaining they aren't getting enough out of our pockets. They think it's really due them, that it's theirs. The mood persists all through their day and they never change it. Changing nothing they see no change and recognize no law between the mood that they are sustaining and their outer world that they dislike so heartily. They dislike everything about it. If I told them that they are the cause of the phenomena of life, they would resent it and dislike me. No one wants to feel that he is solely responsible for the conditions of his life. And yet there is no other cause outside of God, and God is in man as man's own wonderful human Imagination.

So here, when I say human Imagination, I'm speaking of God. That's the God in man. And there are two sides to Imagination, imagining and contents. Contents are about what imagining is about. So there are only two sides…an imagining and imagining something. Well, the thing that I'm imagining I'm creating. God imagining creates. Well, don't think of something outside of yourself. When I say God imagining creates, man imagining is creating what he is imagining. Same God! Keyed low yes, I haven't the same *intensity* when I'm clothed in a garment of flesh and blood, but it's the same God.

So tonight I do hope that this is clear, that there are rules, the positive side of it and the negative side of it. Don't curse anyone. They use the word king and they use the word rich, because there are more poor people in the world than there are rich, and you'll find the poor man is inclined to curse the rich. He is envious of the rich. You need not be a millionaire to have someone envy you; you could be simply a little bit better off than he is. You could live, possibly, in a better neighborhood. You pay more rent because you can afford it. And maybe you can go into a better restaurant because you can afford it; and maybe you can buy a better suit because you can afford it. Even though you're not rich in the eyes of the world, there are those who are not as well off as you are and they will envy you the things that you can do. So you are warned even in your thoughts do not curse the king nor in your bedchamber curse the rich. Don't think for one second you are going to conceal it, for all things by a law divine in one another's being mingle. We are completely one. Though you seem to be completely scattered on the outside, but I don't have to ask you to aid the change of my world if I change it on the inside. If you are necessary to bring about the change, you will be used whether you consent to it or not. You'll be doing it unwittingly, but you'll be doing it if you can be used. I don't have to single out the individual as to who will play the part in bringing about the change in my world. You will play the part if you can be used, because we're all intermingled.

All I have to do is know that I start at the end: "That place to which I would travel, I myself must there become." I know it from experience. If I would travel on a boat and they say you can't get on that boat, not for at least seven months, and I want the next trip—I don't want it today, I want the next trip—I'll get on that boat. Well, if I would go on that boat, then I on that boat must become. ___(??) on that boat. I may view the place where I'm departing from the boat. When that boat comes, in a way I do not know and I couldn't devise it I'll be on that boat...that I speak from experience. If I would go any place in this world and they wouldn't give me permission to go and I *sleep there*, I'll go there. They may even try to get me to go there, those who now deny it. That I know from my own experience of getting out of the Army honorably discharged. I didn't have to run away and then have to face a court martial as one who ran away, and be dishonorably discharged possibly with a few years in jail at hard labor. I got out in a very short space of time honorably discharged by simply putting myself where I would be if I were there.

Well, anyone can do it. This is not something that takes a really fantastically disciplined mind. You can take in your mind's eye this much. Do you know some object where you would be that you desire to be? Could be a piano, it could be a lamp, it could be, well, anything. Do you know one object in that room? Well then mentally hold it, just hold it, and feel it until it takes on *sensory vividness*; but not *any* lamp *that* lamp; not *any* table *that* table, just hold it. That chair, just sit in it and feel it all around you and feel *that* chair, not just a chair. Now view the world from that chair. Well, if you see it as you would see it were you there, you're there; for man is all Imagination and he must be wherever he is in Imagination. So you're there. You *do* nothing...you cast your bread upon the water. And then this genii, which is nature, that is the slave of this lamp which is your own wonderful human Imagination will now without the consent of anyone build a bridge of incidence, and take you wherever you are and lead you across that bridge to sit in that chair, or to hold that lamp, or do whatever you did to anchor yourself there.

As you are told in Genesis: "Come close, my son, that I may *feel* you. Your voice sounds like my son Esau...but come close that I may feel you" (27:21). Well, he came close and he felt him and he felt the hair which Jacob didn't have, so that must be Esau. And it had all the qualities of objective reality, for Esau simply means "the objective world." So he gave to this imaginary state, which is purely subjective, the objective tones, the objective reality.

Now, you can prove it right now. Sit here and see the difference between a simple little object like a ball. Take for instance a tennis ball, take a billiard ball, take a baseball, take a football, and you can discriminate between all these different balls. Well, you can't discriminate between *nothing*. If they're all nothing because they're not objective to your senses now, you couldn't discriminate. But if you can discriminate in texture and you can feel the difference between a tennis ball and a billiard ball, and between these two and another ball, a baseball or a football, if you can discriminate between these different so-called un-realities, well then, they are not unreal. They are real, but not yet made objective to your senses. But now you make it real in your own mind's eye and then it *becomes* real.

You can try it just for fun…but don't do it to hurt another. Never hurt the other! You can take it with a flower. It gets to the point where you don't do it any more, because although the one who sent you the flowers took pleasure in sending it, you are almost embarrassed because it cost money. You figure, oh well, why do I do it? So you stop doing it because the flowers come…the impulse is there to send you lovely flowers and it was just a thing that you had envisioned and saw and gave thanks for. You didn't thank the individual; you thank the being within you for presenting you with the flowers. Then the one on the outside even without an occasion sends flowers. And you have flowers, because you simply could get the odor or the looks or the feel and you simply did it. After a while you just don't do it…at least not as often.

So here, in this game of life…it's a game. Paul calls it a race, he said, "I've finished the race, I've fought the good fight, and I've kept the faith" (2Tim.4:7). But you can call it a race or you can call it a game. Both are competitive, but the competition is with self, not with another. There is *no* other. You're not trying to get beyond the other fellow; grant him the right to use the same law to achieve his goal. His goal may be something similar to mine. But I have a goal. Then I simply apply this law toward my goal, giving him complete freedom to get his goal even though it's similar and may even be a duplicate. Well, let him have it.

So you can tell the law to anyone and it's not going to rob you. You can tell it to everyone in the world, anyone who asks for your secret tell the law, that my end is where I begin, my beginning is my end. That's where I start…I go right to the end, the thing desired, and I feel myself right into it. As I feel myself into the wish fulfilled, I drop it, and that is casting my bread upon the water when I feel satisfied. Then these two words balloon: "bread" which is "a complete, consuming, devouring thing, like a battle," and then comes the word waters which is simply "semen." Look it up in your concordance. But the word offends people if they saw the original word in scripture, so to avoid offense then they use a euphemism.

Now let us go into the Silence.

* * *

Now are there any questions?

Q: (inaudible)
A: The Holy Ghost? Personally, I don't discriminate between God the Father, God the Son and God the Holy Spirit save in function. As far as I'm concerned, they're one…although we do say three and speak of a trinity. But, if I and my Father are one, I could only differ in manifestation. So I sent myself and the being sent is one with the sender. So, he who sees me sees him who sent me. Now, I would say the Father is the everlasting abiding one, I AM; the Son is the eternally proceeding one, the one sent; and the Holy Spirit is the returning one…I return to the same being that sent me. So, the Holy Spirit is the returning one; the Son is the proceeding one from the Father; and the Father is the eternally remaining one, but yet one. For that's Israel: "Hear, O Israel, the Lord our God the Lord is one" (Deut.6:4). So we cannot get away from that foundation stone. Man should never for one moment move away from the shema—it is the Rock of it all—or you're going to make an idol. The minute you get away from more than one God and that God is I AM you're going to have an idol. Although for understanding the whole mystery they break it into a trinity…but there can't be three. It's only the function. So, the eternally abiding one or infinite love is the unthinkable origin; infinite love in eternal procession; and infinite love in eternal return. It's one…all the infinite being which is love.

Q: You say the purpose of life is to play the game?
A: Why certainly, my dear. The purpose of life is to fulfill scripture. Scripture is the Word of God, and his Word cannot return void but it must accomplish that which he sent it to do, and prosper in the thing for which he sent it. It must fulfill its purpose. So, he's given us the written Word which is the Old Testament; that is his promise, but it's done as a forecasting. The New Testament is the fulfillment of the Old. They are not two different religions. People think they're two religions and they aren't. It is only the fulfillment of the Promise. So, the New Testament is the fulfillment of the Old. But it's not a new religion; it's as old as the faith of Abraham. All the promises find their yes, their fulfillment

in Christ Jesus. But the Christ Jesus of scripture is the Christ Jesus *in you*, and that has to fulfill scripture. So the purpose or goal of life is the fulfillment of scripture…that's the goal.

But while we're waiting for the fulfillment to take place in us—because the seed has been planted, the Word has gone forth—before it erupts, learn the law by which the game of life is played. For we have to pay rent in the world of Caesar, we have to pay for shelter, we have to buy food, and we have all these things in our world. Learn how it's done so that we have not the struggle that those who will not learn the law go through. For these things…someone said here recently, I forget who he was, speaking of the eternal: "The most permanent thing in the world is a temporary tax." Well, you bear it in mind. I know in the deep of the Depression they brought in a penny tax in New York City, called it a sales tax, and we were told then that this is to help to buy food and charitable things for the unemployed…and there were millions. Well, no one resented that; but it was only temporary, temporary in this sense, instead of taking it off they added one to it and so it was no longer one cent, it was two cents. That was temporary in the sense they made it three, then they made it four. Now it's five cents…all sales tax. So the most permanent thing in the world is a temporary tax. While we're living in the world of Caesar we might just as well learn the law. You can't condemn it. If you condemn it, if you curse it, your world will mold itself in harmony with that curse and some other thing will annoy you. Simply earn enough to pay it.

Like John Kennedy our late President. The story is told that one day at one of the huge big Kennedy parties of that enormous family that the father with all of his millions said to the family, "My family is spending too much." His son John, who was not then the President and having a keen sense of humor said, "Well, there's only one solution to this problem. Father has to make more money." That's the only solution, for he wasn't going to curtail his spending and the others were not, therefore, the only solution is for father, the giver of all, to make more. So the only solution is for the Father in me to make more. But he gave me rules and he'll make it as long as I fulfill the rules. So, you know what you want? Yes, now feel that you have it…that's what he tells me. Assume the feeling of the wish fulfilled. In biblical words, "When you desire, believe you have received it, and you will" (Mark 11:24). Can I do that? Well, the Father will keep his promise. When Caesar puts more and more taxes upon me, instead of criticizing Caesar apply my Father's rules and he'll give me all that Caesar will be demanding.

Q: In this Imagination, do you have to vividly picture in your mind what you want?

A: You should certainly know what you want, but you don't have to have a vivid outline of the means employed to get it. If a friend of yours would congratulate you after he's heard of your good fortune, all you need do is to bring your friend before your mind's eye and have him congratulate you. Try to give that moment of congratulation tones of reality.

Q: Do you have to see him vividly?

A: No, no sir. Can you hear his voice? If you can hear the voice but you can't see it, the voice will do it. The voice is enough to impregnate you. Or if you know his hand, the feel of his hand, and you can't see or hear but you can feel, well then, feel his hand in yours congratulating you. Use any sense that is the easiest to use. Some people because of their profession the sense of touch is easier than the sense of sound. If you're dealing with music and you have a good pitch, it wouldn't be difficult to hear anyone's voice if you once heard it. I have friends of mine who can go to a piano, put them in another room, hit not only a single note, any note on the piano, and they'll instantly…you don't have to wait… they're on the ___(??). As though I said I'm going to speak now and you tell me what letter of the alphabet I am sounding and I say a "b." Well, they don't have to wait, they'll reply "b." I say "z"…well, it is just as keen to a good ear, the notes on a piano, as my alphabet is to one who understands the alphabet. I have done it. A friend of mine in New York City she played at the Music Hall, and I would test her. I would hit a chord, any chord, and she would instantly call it. I could hit a discord and she'd call it. Now they say that Toscanini had that pitch. I know ___(??) had that pitch. So even the slightest little off, he could stop the instrument and tell the man that whatever he was playing "You are not giving me what I want." He had perfect pitch. Not very many have that pitch. But you don't have to have *that* kind of a pitch to hear a friend's voice. If you listen carefully and listen as though you heard him and then put on his tone what you want him to say. Just put on that tone what you want to hear…and don't tell him what you did. That's casting your bread upon the waters.

Well, until Monday. Good night.

THE ONLY GOD IS I AM

3/10/69

The only God that man will never outgrow and therefore never lose is the God he knows in the first-person, present-tense experience. When he finds this God, he then tells his brothers, "As you are told in scripture, if I had not come and spoken to them, they would have no sin, but now they have no excuse for their sin." He comes to reveal God as the eternal contemporary, and man finds it difficult, almost impossible to keep the tense, for he reveals God as *I AM*. "Unless you believe that I am (is) he, you die in your sins" (Jn.8:24). No man who will think of God in the third-person knows God. When you address God in the second-person you do not know God. You will only know God in the first-person, in a present-tense experience.

Just imagine that no one sinned until he came. In the fullness of time God reveals himself and man had never sinned before, for it's not held against him until God comes and reveals himself in the first-person, in the present-tense. Everyone who believed in him who has the experience continues the tradition and tells it in the first-person, present-tense. But he will receive no greater reception than the one who first came to tell it, because they will say of him, I know this man, I know his parents. How can he say 'I came down from heaven?' We know him. When the Christ comes no one will know how he appears, for man is looking for Christ to come from without. He doesn't come from without. The revelation is whispered from *within*. It *seems* to come from without, but he's approaching from within. It is all the individual…he is awakening from within. "I have been crucified with Christ; it is not I who live, but Christ who lives in me; and the life I now live in the flesh I live by the faith in the Son of God who loved me and gave himself for me" (Gal.2:20). He actually became me.

Now, what is his name?—I am, that's his name. "Unless you believe that I am he you die in your sins" (Jn.8:24). Is that his name? Well, isn't that the name of God?—yes. You mean he is God?—yes. Tell me who is your Father? If you knew me, you would not ask, for no man can know me without knowing God, for he and I are one. So here, the revelation is "I am"...not a thing in the world, but God. What child in this world is not aware that he or she *is*; and to be aware that we are is to say I am, and that is God, and all things are possible to God. But man has great trouble in keeping the tense; he is always speaking of God in the third-person and occasionally if he's in the Silence or praying, he might speak of God in the second-person, and address him as "thou." But how many know him in the first-person, in the present-tense? For *that's* God, and there is no other God. "Against thee and thee only have I sinned" said David in his 50th Psalm. "Only thee can I sin against." I don't know you, but I must know you only in the first-person, in the present-tense.

Will it work? Well, put it to the test, just try it. Just try it. There is a lady in New York City...I'm going back now years and years ago...she had little, but very little, lived in a rooming house in Brooklyn. On Sunday morning she would go out and buy a Sunday morning paper for her next door neighbor who was an old lady, and she thought the old lady was simply on charity and relief of some kind for she lived very frugally. When she heard me, she *assumed* and she named it, $50,000 in cash. She didn't have 50,000 pennies...she didn't have 5,000 pennies...but she assumed that she had $50,000 in cash. That's what she wanted. Well, within a year the old lady died...and she who thought the old lady was on charity...she left exactly in cash $50,000 to this lady whose name was Miss Needy. Odd name, but that was her name, Needy. She also left in excess of $30,000 in jewelry...old fashioned and an old-fashioned cut, but it was valued at over $30,000. So she got an estate in excess of $80,000 by keeping God in the present-tense, I am. She started there, well, "I am wealthy. I have $50,000 in cash." She didn't go beyond it...but remember it is always pressed down, shaken together and running over. But she did get her $50,000 in cash. Then she got in excess of $30,000 in jewelry. That lady now lives in Boston, because whenever I go to New York City she comes in and spends the three weeks that I'm in New York City lecturing to attend all the lectures. I go there and spend four or five weeks and give a series of say fifteen talks in a three-week period...and she is always there. She has found him.

I want everyone who hears me to find him. When you find *this* you'll never lose him. First of all, you can't outgrow him. One can outgrow any God outside of self. One believes in astrology and the day will come you can't believe in it anymore. You will believe in teacup leaves, you'll believe in all kinds of things, like science, and you will grow and outgrow, grow and outgrow. But you can't outgrow the God you find in the first-person, present-tense experience. You just can't do it. That is the God and the only God...and one day everyone will find him. When they find him, they talk about him and they tell their brothers, because there are brothers in eternity looking down on this world of Caesar and saying to each other, "Awaken. Soon they will awake; soon they will return to us," for we are one with those who have already awakened. We can only rejoin the heavenly society and they're constantly contemplating this world and they're looking, seeing everyone...the little ___(??) where we are awakening from the dream of life.

"So if I had not come," said he, "and spoken to them, they would have no sin." They couldn't miss the mark because they didn't have any; but *now* they have no excuse for their sin. I revealed God to them in the first-person. "He who sees me sees him who sent me." Well, who sent you?—"My Father." Well, who is your Father? "My Father is he whom you call God, only I *know* my Father and ye know not your God." So this is my Father who sent me and we are one. Well, they did not believe in him. So when he comes he says, "I will convince you of sin." What sin? "Because you did not believe in me... you did not actually believe in me."

Now we are told the story has been taught and told to every creature under heaven, can you believe that? That's what you're told in Colossians, the first chapter, that every creature under heaven heard this story but has forgotten it. How did we hear it? We are told the story was preached to Abraham before that the world was, for "The scripture foreseeing that all would be saved through faith, preached the gospel beforehand to Abraham, saying, 'In you all the nations be blessed'" (Gal.3:8). Well, we all start from that state called Abraham, which is the state of faith. So we heard it and then we went astray, went sound asleep and forgot it, and made idols; and spoke of God in the third-person, and spoke to him in the second-person,. And that is not God at all. God is the eternal contemporary in the first-person: when you say "I am," that's he, that's God. There never was another God and there never will be another God. *That* is God.

So put him to the test. Without faith, we are told, it is impossible to please him, can't please him without faith. Well now, faith does work on this level, no question about it. Everything you have you brought in through faith. But the glory of faith lies in its power to link us to this heavenly realm. We heard the story...now can we keep it in spite of trouble? No matter what happens to me I can rest myself upon the vision. I know what I have experienced. I know what I'm trying to tell the world, whoever will listen to me and those who will read what I have to say: I'm trying to tell everyone of God. Here, that's the only God and the only creative power in

The Return of Glory

the world, there is no other creative power. So, my faith in God is measured by my confidence in myself. Do I really believe in myself? When I sit down and imagine a state, do I really believe it? Do I really believe that that has within itself the power to externalize itself or must I now pray to a being on the outside and ask for help there? No, I sit down and imagine a state and what I imagine I must release it in confidence that it must—for all things are possible to God—it *must* become an external fact in my world.

Have I tried it? Yes time and time again. Did it prove itself in performance? Time and time again. Then, are you sharing it with your brothers? Yes every time that I can talk to them I share it with them. To what extent I get over to them to where they can accept it, I do not know. I have no way of knowing to what extent man will accept it, because he does find trouble in keeping the tense. It's something on the outside…he's always speaking of him in the third-person. You go to church, you go to your synagogue, no matter where you go it is always "he" and he did this and he said so-and-so. And when you speak of the Lord it's not "I am," it's something on the outside; yet he comes from within. When Moses heard "I AM has sent me unto you" it seemed to come from without and yet it was whispered from *within*. So now comes the visible picture called Jesus Christ and he seems to come from without. He doesn't, he is coming from within. There is *no* evidence whatsoever in this world of any *historical* Jesus Christ. We have the evidence of Christ, but not the historical Jesus Christ.

This that is talking to you, this is only a garment, but the being within who is speaking is the Christ. This on the outside yes everyone knows his background. Those who know him know his parents, his physical garment, his limitations, all these weaknesses they know. "How do you say you came from heaven? How do you say you came out from God and you call him your Father when we know your father, Joseph and your mother, Wilhelmina, all these things? How do you know?" He said, "I do not know what you know concerning this. I am from above." How could you be from above? "You are from below. I am in the world; I am not *of* the world" (Jn.8:23); for the being that woke within me is the one that is speaking. This is not the same being that has fun in the social world, the world that will dine and drink with anyone in this world and have fun. But the being who speaks is the being of which I am totally aware who came from within, who awoke within me…who is not in any way part of this world. That's the being who is talking to you and that's the being that is in you that I'm trying to reach when I speak to you…trying to stir him awake. For it can't be too far away when that one that I'm trying to address will awake. Then all together return to those who have already awakened, and together they form the Lord, the one grand I AM.

So here, believe me when I tell you the only sin is the sin against the being that you really are. "Against thee, thee only, have I sinned." Who?—the Lord. He's still speaking of "thee," of another...he's addressing him, "Against thee." Suddenly he realizes it's all within *himself*; the whole book is all about me and I inspired the prophets to write what they did. Finding no one to play the part I came in to play it myself. I conceived the play and then came in to play it, to fulfill what I had predicted, what I'd foretold that I would do. And now here is the pattern: Christianity is based upon the affirmation that a certain series of supernatural events happened in which God revealed himself in action for the salvation of man. Did these events really happen? I know they did, for I've experienced every event recorded in that gospel...but every event.

Today I was going over my little notes as I mark it against the passages to find even a simple little thing like, "What you must do, do quickly." And here, I read it and against that I had marked the day when it happened to me, the 10th of October 1966. Where they're all seated as told you in that passage, all seated and then suddenly he who has to do it quickly, rose...and it was quick. He didn't delay, he simply jumped from that position where he was seated on the floor and departed quickly. Then just as quickly came the authority to whom he had revealed what I said concerning the Word of God, for I was preaching to this crowd of twelve men all seated on the floor. Then this one jumped up and went quickly to the door. And then came this one in glorious attire, beautiful robes, costly robes, straight as an arrow, about six feet, four inches or more. Then he circled the room in a square, and then came before me and unveiled my arm. "To whom has the arm of the Lord been revealed?" (Is.53:1). He took the entire sleeve off and then hammered the peg into my shoulder which he did first. But here, the one who revealed it moved quickly and he rose and moved quickly...that same little statement. Take a red-letter edition of the Bible and find the Word of the Lord and these are the words not yet in the Old but related, and just read the red letters and see how everything about it *you* fulfill.

The entire drama unfolded within me so I know who Christ is. It's a *pattern*, the perfect pattern that God sent into the world. So I have been crucified with Christ and so have you. You can say these words, "The crucifixion is over, because the first shall be last and the last the first." Well, in the story the last would be crucifixion...it's the first. We *have been* crucified with Christ. "It is not I who live but Christ who lives in me; and the life I now live in the flesh I live by faith in the Son of God, who loved me and gave himself for me" (Gal.2:20). He actually became me. Christ became you? Yes. You mean his name is Christ? Well, his name is I AM, that's his name. That's the Lord God Jehovah...that's Christ. He is God the

Father and he became me. He died in the sense of completely forgetting who he was to believe that he's actually this being that he's now playing. "Unless I die thou can'st not live; but *if* I die I shall arise again and thou with me" (Blake, *Jerusalem,* Plt. 96). So he rose within me. He proved that he could rise having died, but when he rose, I am he. He actually became me in the most intimate sense of the word, so I am he. And then he talks to me from within and reveals himself to me from within. In the beginning he seemed to have spoken from without, yet it is being whispered from within; and he seemed to appear from without, and yet he was coming from within. Finally, when he completely came from within, everything said of him in scripture unfolded within me.

Can we actually accept it and keep the tense? It's so important to keep the tense and never turn to the second-person or the third-person. It's all from within us…I am he. "Unless you believe that I am (*is*) he, you will die in your sins" (Jn.8:24). Put the little word "is" in between it to give meaning to it. As you read it now "Unless you believe that I am he you will die in your sins" and you think a being on the outside is speaking to you. If you put the little "is" in between it, "Unless you believe I am (is) he you'll die in your sins"…you'll keep on missing the mark. So, I want to be rich, I want to be this, I want to be that. Well, if I don't believe that I am the cause of wealth, the cause of poverty, the cause of everything in my world, then I keep on missing the mark.

The *real* mark is to know who God is. You'll never lose this God, never in eternity, when he reveals himself within you in the first-person, present-tense experience. All of a sudden he comes, all from within, and the whole thing is God unfolding. But he doesn't call himself God—his name is I AM. So who rose in that tomb?—I did. You mean "I"? Yes, I rose. Was there another? No, there's no other, I rose. And who came out?—I did. I came out of the tomb. Was there any help? No, I pushed the stone away myself. And when I came out and looked back at that out of which I came, what happened? There were witnesses as told me in the Book of Genesis, for did I not inspire the prophets to write it? Did not three appear before Abraham, the center of it all where I started? Was he not seated in the tent, the door of the tent in the heat of the day and suddenly appeared? Who appeared?—the Lord. Three men appeared, but one as he spoke he knew he was the Lord, and he's speaking concerning the child. Did you find him? Yes I found him. Did he promise a child? Yes he promised one that laughed. He called him Isaac, and Isaac simply means "he laughs," that's all that it means (Gen.17:15-19). Did the child laugh? Oh yes, he laughed. And did you take him in your arms like Simeon? Yes I did. Did you hear the storm wind that accompanied it? Yes I did.

Well then, who is Christ? Who is the Lord? Does it fulfill, does scripture fulfill itself within *you?*—yes. "I have come to fulfill scripture and scripture must be fulfilled in me" (Lk.22:37). So the whole thing was fulfilled within me. Well, did you see the temple and it was torn from top to bottom? No, *I* was torn from top to bottom. That's right—you are told in scripture that you are the temple, are you not? And so if the curtain of the temple was torn from top to bottom and you are the temple, then you would have to be torn from top to bottom. Well, that's exactly what happened. The mountain was simply torn from top to bottom, one went north, one went south, and here the entire riven being stood before me, and then I went up. So the whole thing unfolded in me.

Well now, did you find the one that he set in the beginning to reveal to you that you are the Father? Yes. Well, who is he?—David. Well, that's not what the priesthoods teach. I don't care what *they* teach, I'm telling you what I found and I'm telling you what scripture confirms. For I have found David and he cried unto me, "Thou art my Father" (Ps. 89:26). So I found him. I don't care what they say; I am telling you what *I know*. They do not believe in him so they continue in their sins. So they are worshipping a false god. All the priesthoods of the world, all the rabbis, are worshipping an idol; for you cannot worship the true God in any tense other than the present. His name is I AM. There is no other name for him.

So you go to a church and you see a picture on the wall and they say that's the Christ. Christ, nothing! And when they give a great big statue and they say that's the Lord…that's *not* the Lord! "Make no graven image unto me" (Exod.20:4). If you do not see him as yourself, you will not in eternity find him. When he comes, he reveals himself by the use of his Son and his Son reveals God the Father. Then the thrill when you look and you see *your* son that in the beginning you set up. You played all the parts, everything in the world, and you condemned none; not one part in the world did you condemn, for all contributed to the end. Well, he'll rise and you'll rise to find God, for the goal of life is to find him and you find him not on the outside, you'll find him *only* within yourself in the first-person, present-tense.

The world thinks you're insane when you talk about it, because you are still wearing a garment of flesh, and as long as you wear it you're weak and subject to all the weakness of the world as long as you wear this body. But one day he will reveal his Son *in* you…not to you…in you, and the whole drama unfolds within you. Then you know how true the whole wonderful world is and it is for a purpose.

Then…I can't explain it and I cannot describe it in words to anyone for it would make no sense…the joy that is yours when he awakens. The world into which I go night after night and to return to darkness into this world every morning; but an entirely different world that has not a thing on earth that I can use as an image to describe it, can't do it. It's an entirely different world and you leave it night after night to return here to tell it to everyone who will hear it. Some believe it and some do not believe it. Your closest most intimate friends may not believe it because they know you and they will judge you by your human weaknesses. Your relatives will judge you by the fact that you came out of the same womb, sired by the same father, and they know you. They cannot for one moment believe that your experiences are related to scripture. You can point the whole thing out, but they can't follow you…and they don't want to follow you.

Well, I'm only asking you to believe it. Believe it, that you may not be convicted of sin. *If* you believe it and accept it, he said, "What must I do to be doing the work of God? Just believe in him whom he has sent." And, when I tell you *I* have been sent, he who sent me is one with me. He's not another, yet when I stand in his presence he *seems* to be another, and we fused and became one. Where did I meet him, from without? No, he came from within. He simply came from within. You mean the recording angel also? Yes, she was from within. The book? Yes, that was from within. Everything is from within, for in the beginning he foreknew me. He?—yes, I foreknew myself. "And those whom I foreknew I predestined; and those whom I predestined I called" (Rom.8:29). That was the moment of the call from the world of Egypt, the world of death…called that night from within myself…for now this is the end of your journey, so I call you. I was called by myself within myself by the infinite being of love who was clothed in the human form divine which is infinite love, and then embraced and fused. For there was a *seeming* separation for a purpose: the separation was to come out into a world that was not mine, a world that was a strange world, among strangers, and go through hell, go through all the horrors of the world. Then in the end to be called and then having been called, he justified me. In other words, I was acquitted; no matter what I did he acquitted me, the being within myself which is myself. Then came glorification… whom he acquitted, he justified, and whom he justified, he glorified.

Now go and tell it. Tell it to everyone in the world who will listen to you and let them have their entire hope set upon this. Oh, that you can become independently secure, certainly. All these things are possible. But the *real* objective is to find him. That man can become rich I do not hesitate for one second to tell a man who is completely illiterate that you can become as rich as anyone in this world *if* you believe in God. Well, he says, "I'm an atheist." Alright, do you believe in yourself? Can you believe that "I am rich?"—not a man called Neville—speaking of yourself when you haven't one nickel in the world? Could you believe it and night after night sleep as though you were? You'll become it! And then, eventually, you'll find the one God you'll never lose. You'll find the one who made it...and that is God. For millions will speak and say I believe in God, and there are others who say I don't believe in any God, yet they may believe more in God, the true God, than those who say I believe in God. For, there are hundreds of millions who are worshipping God in the third-person, so they do not know God. To say I believe in God doesn't mean that you know God.

But when he comes and reveals who God really is, he always reveals him in the first-person. If you take the Book of John it is one "I AM" after the other, which goes back to the 3rd chapter of the Book of Exodus, the 14th verse: "Go say I AM has sent you." So when he comes, "Say I AM has sent me unto you" and that is the theme through the entire Book of John. He is revealing this, but they know the outer garment and they judge him by the outer garment. He is Joseph's son, he is Mary's son, the brother of these and his sisters, and they know everything about him and his weaknesses; but they do not know the Lord. I tell you, when he comes I can't tell you the shock and the thrill and the awe when it happens. But it *will* happen and everyone will find the whole drama unfolding within himself.

In the meanwhile, in the world of Caesar test it. There is no limit to his power, none whatsoever. So you simply take the power...and he *is* the power. So I...and you name it, you put the name on it, and night after night sleep as though it were true. It will take you no time to prove it in the testing, no time. Miss Meany within a year got her $50,000 and $30,000 in jewelry. And I can't tell you her thrill. But she knew exactly what she did. The last person in this world she would have thought could be used as the means to give her $80,000 was the little old lady. When she gave her the little paper every Sunday morning, it never occurred to her that the little old lady could afford the paper. She went out and bought the Sunday morning paper for a dime. In those days the *New York Times* (and the *Herald Tribune*) was a dime, a huge big thick issue, and she took it every Sunday morning and gave her the paper. She said, "I'm doing my good work as a Christian." Then the little old lady died in a year and because she was the one who befriended her—she had no relatives—she left her this entire estate of $80,000; but $50,000 was in cash.

Now, Miss Meany might have forgotten it. She hasn't forgotten that it works and she comes to all the meetings, but listening to her she is still inclined toward speaking of him in the third-person. Just...it's a habit of man...and Israel forgot and found it troublesome to keep the tense. So you say to any Jew today, "Have you ever read Exodus?" Well, maybe they have. It's part of the tradition that you read the five books of the Old Testament, the first five books in three years and you read passage after passage and

The Return of Glory

it takes three years to read it. Then you go back and start all over again. So every good, well-trained Jew is familiar with the five books, but he still speaks of God in the third-person. He finds it so difficult to keep the tense. And one who boldly steps out and keeps it they think is arrogant. Yet it's the only way to find him.

Well, when he comes, you don't have to go out and brag about it. You know who you are. When they call you by your name you respond, but you know that's the outer man that they are calling and yes you respond. Maybe you're going to have dinner together, have a little party together, but the being within they are totally unaware of that being, and you don't always throw the "pearls before swine." You don't try to go into a meeting and instantly begin to unload what you know within, because they are not prepared to receive it. So you don't do it. You go to a party, thoroughly enjoy the evening, and let the outer man play his part. But the inner man they do not know and *that* man is Jesus Christ. Not another Christ; there's only one Christ, so he's in every being in the world. "I have been crucified with Christ"—everyone can say that—"And it is not *I* who live but Christ who lives in me, and the life I now live in this flesh, this blood and flesh, I live by the faith of the Son of God who loved me and gave himself for me." God actually became me that *I* may become God and rise to the one being that we are.

But, on the other hand, we came down from God; we are the gods. But we had to drink the drink of complete forgetfulness to play these parts. The actor who does not know that he is a part isn't playing a good part. As long as he steps upon that stage and he knows he is an important person, that he is the great actor that the world recognizes, he can't lose himself in the character. When you leave your personality in the dressing room and you step upon the stage you *are* that character. So when God stepped upon the stage wearing this, he was Neville, one hundred percent Neville. He had to completely forget that he was God, knowing that contained within the garment that he's wearing a little while after he wears it it's going to start erupting. Then I will know who I am. But he had to completely play Neville in order for the something within me to awaken…and it was God within me.

So look upon Jesus Christ as the pattern. And then he tells of the pattern, how it erupted within him. Man ignored it; he came unto his own and his own would not receive him. He told it and they would not receive him. So what *he* told and what *we* who heard it are capable of receiving are entirely different things. Can we receive what he told as his own personal experience? I can tell you from my own experience it's true, the entire story is true from beginning to end; and to set your hope fully upon the grace that is coming to you at the unfolding or the unveiling of God within you. For God either is in you or you're not alive, and in you his name is "I AM." He has to go through a certain series of supernatural events and when they come to the end, you tell it to those who will hear it. It doesn't matter who accepts it or who does not accept it, you simply tell it.

Then in the end, when you take it off, one night you will take off the garment and you'll return to that world that you go to night after night in the interval that you can't describe to anyone on earth. To the most intimate friend on earth you can't describe it; there are no words to describe it, there are no images of earth to describe that world. So then you're told, "Eyes have not seen nor ears heard the things that are *already* prepared for those who love the Lord" (1Cor.2:9). So when you actually enter that world, you can't... they'll ask you, "Well, what does it look like?" and you can't describe it. How are you going to describe *life itself* where everything is alive, but everything is alive, and you are in control of everything in the world? How are you going to describe it? So I know of nothing here that I can use as a symbol to describe that sphere. I only know you pass beyond the world of dream into this world of reality, and you return to the world of dream into this world that is the world of death. You keep on doing it night after night after the experience until that moment in time when it pleases the depth of our own being, who is Father, to simply take it off and call it a day, the end. Everyone is going to have this experience.

So, "to sin" is not to sin against me, you can only sin against yourself, and the self of man is God. Any time I speak of God in any tense other than the first-person, present, I am entertaining an idol, entertaining a false god. No matter how you name it it's a false god. So when you walk through these doors tonight in the consciousness that I AM is God, you are walking in the knowledge of the true God. Now, all things are possible to God, so you walk tonight as though things are as you want them to be, and then complete trust in God. This is loyalty to unseen reality and that's faith. For we are told only two thing displease God: one is lack of faith in I AM he and the other is eating of the tree of knowledge of good and evil, to set up a standard using yourself as the criterion as to what is right and what is wrong. A man wants to grow a beard let him grow a beard; long hair let him grow the long hair. If he wants to wear skirts let him use the skirts. You are not the criterion of good and evil, so that eating of the tree of knowledge of good and evil displeases God and the lack of faith in I AM He displeases God. There is no other displeasure...only two things displease God. I have searched the scriptures and I can't find third. So if a man is going to put himself up—and we all seem to play that part at some time as to what is right and what is wrong using ourselves as the criterion—well then, you're displeasing the only

God in the world. Let them alone and let everyone be what they want to be, provided they don't step upon your toes or the other fella's freedom. Grant him the freedom that you insist for yourself and don't deny him his right to express himself.

Now let us go into the Silence.

* * *

Let me again remind you, I AM *is* the Lord Jesus Christ. The Lord Jesus Christ is Jehovah. When you say "I am" that's he. Now trust it implicitly, for *all* things are possible to God.

Now are there any questions, please?

Q: From your experience, Neville, how do you interpret the Beatitudes that say, "Blessed are the pure in heart, for they shall see God"?

A: Yes, "Blessed are the pure in heart, for they shall see God" (Mat. 5:8). To see and to know are the same words in Greek. You will *know* God and you will find him as yourself. No one can tell me what it means to be pure in heart. I know in my own case, if I use the human standard of purity, I could not have judged myself worthy of that experience; and yet I've had the experience of knowing God the Father as myself. So, it's an entirely different standard. In the world of flesh and blood, we are animals. As told us in the Book of Daniel we became the *animal* world, subject to all the horrors of the animal. You were given the brain of an animal, the heart of an animal, and we were made to eat grass like the animals. Times and times go over us until we discover that the Lord God rules the affairs of men and gives it to whom he will (Dan.4:16). So I could not honestly be as kind to myself as I have been kind to… by the presence within me who set me free…a complete exoneration, a complete acquittal of all the parts that I've played. So the pure in heart cannot be based upon man's concept of what the pure would stand for. At that moment in me, he completely frees me of all things and he reveals himself as myself. So I free myself because I saw not another…I am he.

At first he *seemed* to be another, and that was thirty years before the event; but when it began to erupt within me there was no other, it was myself. Thirty years before in the summer of 1929 I seemed to stand in the presence of another who was infinite love. Thirty years later, as told us in scripture, he began his ministry when he was about thirty years of age (Luke3:23). So when it began to erupt within me it was not another, it was myself in whom the entire story unfolded. So I can say that *everyone* will find himself exonerated, everyone will find himself the pure in heart, and he will know himself to be God the Father. And that is *seeing* God. Because no man has seen him, but the Son [David] who is in the bosom of the Father he has revealed him (Jn.1:18). So it takes the Son to reveal the Father…and I'm not looking into a mirror when the Son stands before me. He is revealing *me* as God the Father; it's not another. For no one has ever seen the Father. But the Son who is in the bosom of the Father he has made him known. "No one knows who the Son is except the Father, and no one knows who the Father is except the Son and anyone to whom the Son chooses to reveal him" (Mat. 11:27). So the Son suddenly appears and reveals me as God the Father. So, that's *seeing* him yet without looking into the mirror, and that is *knowing* God the Father.

Q: What does the Bible mean when it says that Moses lived 900 years?

A: That one lived 900 years or 1000 years or 100 years…in Hebrew every letter has not only a numerical value but a symbolical value. And so, you must know the alphabet, from the twenty-two letters and the five finals, and each has a numerical value. When we are told, "I send you into a land and you will be enslaved for 400 years," it doesn't mean 400 years chronologically speaking, measured by the clock. This is 400. It is the twenty-second letter of the Hebrew alphabet and the symbolical value is a cross and this [body] is the cross. It's called in Hebrew, Tau. So as long as I wear this body of flesh and blood I am on the cross, and therefore I will suffer on the cross. I hang on the cross for 400 years.

Now you are told in another scripture it was 400 and thirty years. Well, the thirty is simply right after the call—that's when the eruption starts to take place, thirty years after the call. You are called from within, you stand in the presence of love, you are embraced, made one with the being from within you, and then you are sent into the world. After thirty years you start the ministry, and the ministry is simply the eruption that takes place within you. The whole drama unfolds within you and then you tell it. So, then a man's age in scripture is not necessarily the age that we speak of here. I'm sixty-four years old; it would mean nothing in scripture. In scripture they speak of these numbers and each number has a letter in Hebrew and each letter has a symbolical value. So 900 would be the *serpent*. Nine is a Teth…and then you multiply it, expand it to 900, Tzaddi.

Q: You say the world of Caesar, what do you mean by that?

A: This world is the world of Caesar. Even though the Caesars have gone from it as far as the names are concerned every tyrant in the world is a Caesar. You could almost say that this world is B.C.…before Caesar,

The Return of Glory

before Christ. Even though it is 1969, until he is born in you, you are still living in the world of Caesar. Every child born of woman is born in the world of Caesar or born before Christ. For Christ has to be born *in* man: "Unless you are born from above you cannot enter the kingdom of heaven" (Jn.3:3). For, flesh and blood cannot enter the kingdom. So it's simply B.C. Well, the world of Caesar and yet we speak of this as 1969 A.D., after the birth of the Lord. But the birth of the Lord happens *individually*, not collectively; therefore, until it happens to the individual he still is in the world of Caesar, the world of the tyrant, the world of slavery.

Everything here is enslaved. I wear this garment and I'm a slave of this garment. If I had all the money in the world and all the power to command millions of slaves, they cannot perform the natural functions of my body for me. Oh, I can have a bathroom made of gold, I can have the bowl of solid gold, the bathtub solid gold, everything about gold and all the precious stones in the world, but I and I alone must enter there and perform the functions of the body. I can't command anyone to go in there and perform for me the elimination processes. I have not only to eat for myself, no one can do it for me, I must assimilate and what I can't assimilate I must eliminate. When I must eliminate, I must do it for myself and no one can do it for me. Well, isn't that a slave of the body?

So I take upon myself a body and become a slave of it. So the richest man in the world, the wisest man in the world must perform all the normal, natural functions of the body himself, or herself, and he can't pass it off to any slave in the world. So am I not then a slave of the body? Can you conceive of wanting to perpetuate it through eternity…to have a body similar to this where it must assimilate and eliminate? Well, I can't conceive of such a thing as desirable, I can't. And you do not, for you're *Spirit*. And so flesh and blood cannot inherit the kingdom of heaven, for God is Spirit and only the Spirit can. These bodies one day will be taken off *after* the birth from above takes place within you and the entire drama of Christ unfolds within us. But the richest, the most powerful cannot command anyone to perform for them these normal, natural functions of the body. If they're not normal and natural, they are sick.

My old friend Abdullah said, "Neville, if anyone tries to upstage you in his world, but anyone…" He was very down to earth, a brilliant, wonderful mystic, who spoke and wrote Hebrew and he understood all the great mysteries. He said to me one day, "Neville, if anyone ever tries to upstage you to make you feel little and he is big, make a mental image of him sitting on the toilet and you'll bring him right down to earth… for that cannot be any lower." So make a mental image of him, sitting just there performing the normal, natural functions and taking care of himself too. Well, that is the most marvelous thing. You meet someone who thinks he's so important or she is so important—she is the most fashionable person in the world and she's numbered among the three and a half billion in the world as one of the ten best dressed women in the world—make the mental image if she ever tries to upstage you and see how well-dressed she is!

Good night.

THE MYSTERY OF THE BIBLE

3/14/69

Tonight, I'm speaking of the greatest of all mysteries, the mystery of the Bible. One must experience the gospel for himself before he can begin to understand how perfectly wonderful it is. Think of this whole fabulous world of ours, we're all here in the world, and we go through the horrors that everyone goes through, all the violence; and then at a fullness of time, one man is called and then incorporated into the body of the author of it all, and then sent back into the world to tell what he heard, what he saw, what he felt.

Now here is the story of salvation. In our New Testament we find every author—and no one knows who they are—but each claiming that he is one who is *sent*. Each claims he is an apostle and apostle simply means "one who is sent." But we do not know the authors as they're all anonymous: Matthew, Mark, Luke and John are unknown characters. And all the others…no one mentions the others in any contemporary work of the time that these are supposed to have been written. So here, all the authors are unknown but each claiming to have the experience of being called, because to be called is also to be sent. So, they come and they bring the story that they heard and that which they saw, and that which they experienced. When Paul tells it, he makes the statement, "I will now tell of visions and revelations. I know a man in Christ, who fourteen years ago was caught up into the third heaven—now whether in the body or out of the body I do not know…but he heard that which cannot be told, which man may not utter" (2Cor.12:2). Now Paul is telling his own story, whoever Paul is, and he's simply telling his own experience.

I personally have had no restraint of that nature. I feel that the unknown author of the Book of Jeremiah, which by definition means "Jehovah will rise," for he said, "If I say 'I will not mention it, or speak any more in his name,' then there is in my heart as it were a burning fire shut up in my bones, and I am weary with holding it in, and I cannot'" (Jer. 20:9). I cannot restrain the impulse to share with my brothers that which has happened to me. So I, too, was called. You're called while you're here in this world of horror. Who knows that secret of electivity? No one knows. Who knows when anyone will be called and from what strata he'll be called? It's not based upon anything, any code, any order of arrangement known to man. There is no aristocracy of privilege, none whatsoever. You don't have to be a brilliant giant of a mind; you could be washing floors, you could be shining shoes, you could be in the eyes of the world, unlettered. There is not any, I would say, standard by which man is elected. But he is called out of this world while he's walking in this world.

Now whether in the body or out of the body...you seem to have a body because you see, you can touch, you can hear, you can observe; and the body that you see, into whose body you are incorporated, is a solid body to you. When he embraces you, you feel the embrace, you feel the complete fusion of the two, you and the one with whom you are now united. Then in the twinkle of an eye, from infinite love who embraces you, he now wears the garment of infinite power and he sends you as power. For, when you come into the world then you are the power of God and the wisdom of God. It's not the wisdom of man and it's not the power of man. You do not need the things that we call here expressions of power, like fabulous wealth or social standing or political standing. You still are the same being you were before; you come only to tell the story. But you were called, incorporated into the body of love; then, because this being is a protean being and can assume any form instantly in one twinkle of a moment he now wears the form of power. You stand before him and he sends you into the world; you're hurled back into your body. You do not now whether you were in the body when the whole thing happened or whether you were taken out of the body. You only know that you are back where you were...and the whole world is full of light. As far as you are concerned the room is simply filled with light and there's no reason for light. It doesn't subside right away, takes the longest while for it to actually subside and return to its norm, which is four in the morning and therefore dark. Filled with light! You are completely, well, I wouldn't say confused but awed. You are startled by the experience. And then you go through life playing the same little part you were playing before, when the whole thing begins to awaken within you. Then, after an interval of time, you start your work; thirty years later you begin your ministry to tell...because then something really explodes within you, suddenly erupts within you, and *that* is your beginning, which is your resurrection from within your own being.

So here, the whole vast world…we are the gods who came down and took upon ourselves these dead bodies of weighted nerves—that is all that they are—without a mind, and we animated them. Then because they are weighted nerves we began to suffer as we now wear these garments of weighted nerves. We suffer everything that they are capable of experiencing in the world, every pain, every disappointment, but everything. And it seemed that we would never depart this world of hell, for this *is* hell. Then one moment in eternity, one from this world is called and when he is sent into the world his name is changed and his name is Jesus. So everyone who is called and sent is the same being. He only brings a pattern, and the pattern then unfolds within him, and that is the pattern of redemption. It's a definite *plan* of redemption, a series of supernatural experiences unfolding in him. So when he departs at the end of his little spell here for the last time, he leaves whatever record he can leave to encourage everyone who heard him, who will abide in what he said…if his words will remain in them.

Will they? I often ask myself to what extent are we so ground into it that they really will abide in us? Well, I've told you the story as I personally have experienced it. I have not elaborated, I have not minimized it, and I do not feel for one moment any restraint in the telling of it, telling it in detail just as it happened. I have no compulsion not to tell it, such as Paul, whoever Paul is. I felt I must tell it to encourage everyone. Quite often you think they heard it to the point of accepting it. And then, today for instance in this tiny section of time, you meet friends you know well that came to the meetings. They're people my senior in years; I'm sixty-four, they must be seventy, lovely home, adequate income without labor, they don't work, trust funds, investments, no children, just the two of them. And then because they listen all through the night to the Joe Pines of the world, they are afraid at their advanced years of seventy to remain in California which is going to sink. So they take their little old garments up and rush off to Arizona to wait out the interval of time. They haven't the courage to tell me why. They make all the excuses that it's the rain, the constant floods, the constant this. They've been living here for years and years. It isn't that at all, but they haven't the courage to tell me why they're moving out for two months, looking for a place in Arizona and if they find it, they'll be back some time in the end of May or early June, then to dispose of their properties here. That's not what they're thinking at all. They've been so frightened by all this *nonsense* on radio and TV. Even today you find it the *L. A. Times* the political cartoonist making a cartoon of a man all dressed for the occasion. He has his lifebelt, he has his snorkel, everything.

You have no idea, you think you are getting over, and you think you are reaching a certain person or persons, and then their behavior belies the fact that they ever heard you… ever heard you to the point of acceptance. Because why? They know you. So he said, "So you know who I am and where I come from, but you do not know the one who sent me. Him you do not know." "But do we not know your father, your mother, your brothers, your sisters?" And he tells them of a different birth. But they can go back to his physical origin and pinpoint the day he appeared in this world from the womb of a woman, and he had brothers and they named the brothers and he had sisters. Then he tells them something else happened. Well, they can't believe it. They can't believe that that's what could have happened. That would change the entire outlook of the entire world.

It is all from here that we are called. We all came down into this world of horror for a definite purpose; not for punishment but for an experiment. For this is the world of death and we all came down to die, as told in the 82nd Psalm: "You are all sons of God, sons of the Most High, all of you; nevertheless, you will die like men and fall as one man, O princes" (82:1,6). So here we are in a world that is a fallen world for a purpose. And then in a moment in time, the first one is called, and then the second is called, and eventually all are called. Then everyone who is called is incorporated into the body of the risen Lord, everyone.

Now, we are told, "In that day"—speaking now of the very end—"the Lord will be king over all the world and his name will be one and the Lord one." And "David, his servant, will be their prince forever and forever" (Ezek.34:24). David will be their prince. Well, don't tell me that any man who was born prince say of England…if I were born as I was under the British flag, that he was any prince of mine. If I am not a prince and he's my son then I am king. So there is no one in this world who is any prince of you. Let him be the prince of his own father who is king, but not any prince of you unless you are his father. So David is the prince forever and forever. That's what we are told in Ezekiel and we're told it all through in Zechariah, all through the Bible: he is prince forever and forever. If he's prince and he's *my* prince, then I must be that one spoken of as the Lord who is king over all.

I can tell you from my own experience that is your destiny. When you will be called I do not know, but listen to the words, "As the Father has sent me, even so I send you. He who sent me is one with me. He has never left me alone." He who sent me is one with me; he has never left me alone. So if the sender and the sent are one, and then I am called, incorporated into the body of the sender and sent, I am one with the sender. So whenever I return I am the sender. When I call, as I will, I will send. And you and I will be one. I have told you his name: his name is Father. "I have made it known and I will continue to make it known, that the love with which thou hast loved me may be in them, and they in me, and I in them" (Jn.17:26). For, the sender and the sent are one.

So on my return, I am one with the one who sent me and he is God the Father. Then I will be in the capacity to embrace you into my body of love, and then clothed in the garment of almightiness to send you and you will tell the story. But you will be one with the one who sent you and you'll return having told your story. Then you too will be able to say, "I've finished the work which thou gavest me to do. Return unto me now the glory that I had with thee." For that moment when you incorporated me into your body of love, that was real joy, ecstasy beyond the wildest dream of man. So return to me that glory and then I am one with that body. And, may I tell you, no one knows the beauty of that body, the glory of that body until they see it and are incorporated into it. To describe him as love...oh, I can say love, it's the human form divine, it's infinite love. But he doesn't send you from the garment of love; he always whirls you back into this world from the garment of power.

So Paul could describe Jesus Christ as "the power of God and the wisdom of God" (1Cor.1:24). So he's telling his own story that he knows—talks about that he knows a man in Christ. To be "in Christ" is to be caught up into a cosmic purpose and you're through with this world altogether. It's a cosmic purpose now, something entirely different, and you're caught up into that garment which belongs to an entirely different sphere, a different age. So then he tells you that he knows a man in Christ, who fourteen years ago was caught up into Christ. Now whether he was in the body when it happened or out of the body, he said, "I do not know." Well, no, you really don't know. You come back to a body that's on the bed, or it can be seated on the chair, but it is in this world. You can't deny that you had a body. It never occurred to you that you should have examined the body and see what it looked like, for it's Spirit, yet it's a body. You aren't looking into a mirror to see it reflected; it's a body, a living body because you could see, and that being before you asked you a question. You could see the recording angel as the name is recorded or checked off. You could hear the voice of the one who asked you and when he embraced you after you answer him, you felt the embrace. So you felt a body, you felt a body and your body was felt. So he said, "I do not know whether I was in the body or out of the body, but this I do know that I heard things that cannot be told."

Well, I never heard that. I was told it was time to act and the only action I could think of was to tell what I had just experienced. Then thirty years later, as told in scripture, he began his ministry; and the ministry was from the moment of resurrection. Then after the resurrection within himself, and his birth, and his discovery of the eternal prince who calls him Father—well, if the prince calls me Father, I am the king spoken of in Zechariah. So he said, "In that day, the Lord will become king over all the world; and the Lord will be one and his name one" (Zech.14:9). Only one Father, one God and Father of all, and *you* are destined to be that one God and Father of all.

So, keep it in mind and let these words abide in you. No matter what sorrows you go through, hold this divine vision in time of trouble and lean against *it* and don't listen to the Joe Pines and rush off trying to hide the little garment which in the not distant future you'll take off anyway. He might tonight close his eyes in Arizona and wake to find he's not there at all. Whoever's left behind returns to find that the little house hasn't gone. He'll go blindly on selling products, for the only purpose for all these silly things on TV and radio is to sell products…it's a commercial venture. Hasn't a thing to do with the true vision of God.

So when he said, "I am now going to boast"—that's how he starts the twelfth chapter of 2nd Corinthians—"I must boast," for he'd been criticized for the claim that he was an apostle. And he knew that those who criticized him might have been more learned, they might have been, well, he claimed he had a thorn in his side and they might not have had any inhibitions or any limitations. So he thought that he must go on record and tell that he'd had what they did not have. But he should have spelled the whole thing out, just exactly what happened to him, so he claims he's not allowed to tell it. May I tell you, tell it! When it comes to you, you tell it, tell it as vividly, but don't elaborate, don't exaggerate, just tell it. It must conform to scripture. We are called to be witnesses. Well, the word witness and the word martyr are the same in scripture. To be a martyr is to be a witness. It doesn't mean that you chop off your head or you had it chopped off, or that you were stoned to death…no, you're now a witness and to be a witness, a good witness, it must conform to that one witness which is the external witness of scripture. There are two witnesses: the external letter and the internal Spirit. And the Spirit must actually conform to what is written through the prophets. So, is it in scripture? If it's not in scripture then your testimony is not acceptable, for if the testimony of two and they are different and they agree in testimony, well, then it's conclusive. If they do not agree in testimony, well, then it's not conclusive, because the testimony of one is not acceptable.

So here is the Bible, that's the testimony of one and that's external. When you in Spirit have the experience as recorded in scripture and it dovetails, well then, you have two witnesses: the external witness of scripture and the internal witness of the Spirit. Then when you've completed scripture, you return to the sender. But while you are here in this world, in this world of ours doing the work, you are still the sender. From the moment you were sent you were one with the sender...he never left you...even though no one sees it. They can't look at the mask that you wear and see him who sent you. You know who sent you and you're conscious of his being every moment of time. You know that no one sees the being that you know that you are. You know that you are the Ancient of Days and yet you're a man in your sixties or seventies or maybe fifties...but you know you are the Ancient of Days. By Ancient of Days I don't mean that you look like an old wizened person. No, it's beautifully described in the Book of Daniel, and you'll know when you see him that you're in the presence of infinite love, and he is the Ancient of Days; and when incorporated into his body, you are the body of God and you are the Spirit of God. Because, there's only "one body, one Spirit, one hope, one Lord, one faith, one baptism, one God and Father of all" (Eph.4:4). *You* are that.

So you walk still wearing your mask until that moment in time when you take it off for the last time. What was it until you ___(??) it? It was only a weighted nerve, weighted nerves without a mind. You, by taking it animated it and from then on started to suffer, because the nerves allowed you to suffer and to experience this world of death. Without wearing that garment that could be animated into suffering, into joy, joy and woe in this world, you would not have the experience. But the body without you is dead. Then at the end, you take it off, return to the sender who sent you, and you are one with the sender. Then those that you receive here—for no one comes unto me here in this world of Caesar except my Father who sent me draws them—and I will not lose one, it is said, not one. So he who comes to me and accepts what I say based upon my own experience of scripture and these words remain in him and abide in him, then I return to the one who sent me (I am the sender) and then I will call those that he gave me while I was here...everyone...not one will be cast out, not one will be lost. And they will be incorporated one by one into the body that then is mine in a conscious way; and then whirled back into the world where their body remains...with the knowledge that they have been called and sent. Then they will tell their story.

The story, tell it vividly and don't restrain the impulse...just tell it over and over. For this is such a fantastic story you can't tell it once and expect acceptance. It's too profound, it's too altogether wonderful to think you are going to tell the most incredible story in the world and have people accept it. For they are going to say, "I know you." Well, you say you know me, you know where I come from. "Oh yes, we know where you come from." And you know my father and my mother? "Yes." Well I didn't come in that way at all. The one who now speaks to you came from heaven. "Well, we know where you came from. What are you talking about coming from heaven?" "I was lifted up into the third heaven," said he. Well, three is simply a symbolic number for the *resurrected* state, for three is simply the number of resurrection: "On the third day the earth rose up out of the deep." So the third heaven is simply a nice way of saying it is the world of paradise, the resurrected world, the New Jerusalem; and there you're taken into the state, incorporated, and then sent. And you can't forget it.

Paul said fourteen years ago; I go back forty years. It was 1929 when I was called and sent. But it was not until 1959, thirty years later, that the ministry began in the true sense of the word. Prior to that I was talking only on the law: if you know what you want, believe that you have it and you'll get it (Mark11:24). If you persist in that assumption, though at the moment your reason denies it and your senses deny it, if you persist in it you will get it. So I was only talking about the law; I knew nothing of the promise. But in '59 the promise broke upon me and all the promises of God began to unfold themselves within me. So I can truly say that his promises have found their yes in me, for there's only one being in whom the promises can be fulfilled and that is the one he called and sent. He always calls and sends his pattern and the pattern man is called Jesus Christ. There is only in the end Jesus the one man; but he is housed in every man waiting to be called. He is called and, I would say, fertilized, fertilized by entrance into the body of love, and then sent into the world. Then this thing erupts within him and he is the one spoken of in scripture.

So, Father, as thou sent me even so I have sent them. And he who sees me sees him who sent me, and he who sent me has never left me alone. And, Father, I have finished the work which thou gavest me to do, now return the glory that I had with thee (Jn.17:5). I had it; now return it. So the garment comes off and you return to the *glory* that was yours when he incorporated you into his body, and you are one with the body of the Lord. You *are* the Lord, for you're one Spirit and you are the God and Father of all. Then those he gave you while you were in the world…as you are told, and the word is used that way…"As thou hast sent me into the world, so, Father, I send *them* into the world." So I was taken from the world, incorporated and sent back into the world. And when it comes my turn to call those he gave me when I was in the world, I will incorporate them into my body, which is our body, and send them back into the world where in this world that pattern will erupt and everything will unfold within them. And then they will return and we are one. So the love with which thou lovest me I have loved them that they may be one as we are one.

So let no one frighten you about the world coming to an end. It's not in scripture. The end is simply the end of your journey, that's the only "end" spoken of in scripture. The end and the buildings falling...that's all symbolical. I had that back in 1960, where all the buildings fell and I knew exactly this would fall and that would fall and the other one would fall. But it hadn't a thing to do with buildings in this world of Caesar: these were the *beliefs* by which I lived. After the incorporation and being sent into the world and then the whole thing erupting within me, all that I formerly believed because I was taught it in that manner crumbled. I could no longer believe in the little historical Jesus. I could no longer believe what my mother taught me is the Christian faith, and the churches still teach is the Christian faith, and the Jews teach in their faith. I couldn't accept it after the experience.

So all the structures of the mind by which I lived began to fall. I had the vision of all the buildings, every one, fell right down. I had to build from scratch, build a new foundation, and the *only* foundation is Christ. And Christ is not some little historical figure of 2,000 years ago; I'm speaking of the cosmic Christ who is buried in every child born of woman. In the fullness of time the individual is called, incorporated and sent right back into the world wearing that same body. He has to confront those who know him and then meet the challenge—"But don't we know you? Aren't you so and so?" Yes I would answer to that. You know my physical origin and to that I will answer, but I am not the being that you formerly knew. Something has happened and another *birth* has taken place that I cannot share with you...I cannot tell you save in words. I cannot take you and show you the actual event. I can describe it in words for you, but will you believe it? And the chances are they would say "No, that's all fantasy, that's all self-begotten fantasy." You leave it right there. That's all that they can accept.

You take them to scripture and you show them the scripture, but to them scripture is secular history, that they were not historians who wrote it, and that their one consuming desire was to transmit to man this message of salvation. That's all that they were interested in because they were saved, for they were called and sent; therefore, they were an apostle. The minute you are sent you are an apostle and the apostle, the one who is sent, is one with the one who sent him...the sender and the sent. So if one is sent by God the Father and he in turn tells those who listen to him that now I send you, well then, if he is one with God the Father and he sends you, then you are one with God the Father. The minute you are sent you are one with God the Father. You can't get away from this argument in scripture.

So I say to everyone, the day is not far off when you'll be called...if what you heard abides in you...if you aren't going to run away to save the little skin which is going to be taken from you before you can reach the plane. But when you know these people and you know them, and you love them dearly, and they seem intelligent, with an income of in excess of $800 a month without having to go to work. They get up, they need not leave the door and that comes in every month. They have no children, no obligations to society, a home that is completely free of all indebtedness, and a few acres of land, beautiful orchards, lovely flowers, everything that people would desire. Well then, they turn this silly little thing on at night and go and absorb all that nonsense, and then act upon it, proving that the words did not abide in them. So you're told, "If you abide in me and my words abide in you, just ask what you will and it will be done for you." They can remain right here if these words abide in them and ask for confirmation. But ask it for something.

Well, they would never hear what the professors at Cal Tech said about it. They wouldn't read that because that's in conflict with what they heard this ignoramus say on radio. Oh, so he makes a hundred thousand, maybe a half-million dollars a years, so what! My father used to have a saying, and it's a true saying, "Money doesn't care who owns it." It doesn't…it doesn't care who owns it. In little Barbados, we had what is known as a lazaretto for the lepers. From all over the islands they came, for we were the most healthy of all the islands, so they built it in Barbados, and then they came from all the islands. There were never too many, but I mean, it was a place for those who had leprosy. Well, the only thing that ever came out of the lazaretto that came into it, outside of the doctors and the nurses, was money. If you sent in clothing it was burned when it was no longer usable. If you sent in food, the dishes were never sent back, so you sent in on tin dishes…things of that nature. But you never got anything out in those days. The only thing that came out was money. They would allow you to send in money. If you had a friend in there or a relative, you could send them money and they could go to the top of the wall, and when the huckster came by selling candy or selling syrup or any little thing they didn't get on the inside, they were allowed to buy it and the exchange was money. But when you put the syrup beyond the gate, and they had the syrup, that little tin can never came out because that was a colony of lepers. So my father very wisely said, "Money doesn't care who owns it"…filthiest thing in the world. If you took any coin in the world and could actually tell the history of that coin, what a history, the hands through which it passed—the miser's hand, the censor's hand, the thief's hand, every hand, that one coin. If it was long enough…and what a history if you could only follow the history of a coin.

So that the man makes a quarter of a million selling a lot of nonsense and poisoning the minds of people…perfectly all right. No man can come unto me except my Father calls him and I will not lose him, not one that he's ever called to me to hear the message that he gave me to say can I ever lose, can't lose one. But the only way you can tell that they are those that

The Return of Glory

were really called is when the words that you mention to them concerning the experiences that you've had in the third heaven *abides* in them. Will it support them in the time of need? Will they lean against this vision when things are rough? If they will lean against it in the moment of distress, well then, they are abiding in the Word. And when you depart...not long, you depart it instantly...you don't go through little areas. You are instantly back to the sender and you *are* the sender. Now those that heard and abide you start calling. It doesn't take long, you start calling them one by one incorporating them into your body and sending them back into the world. For that's where you got them...he gave them to you when you were in the world of Caesar. You call them into the third heaven where you are now, and then you send them back where that body waits for them. Then they bring back the memory of the experience and then begin to tell it. That's how the Word is revealed.

So may I tell you, the greatest story ever told is the least understood; it's the story of the gospel, and the individual must experience it before he can begin to understand how perfectly marvelous it is. When the whole thing unfolds within you, you can hardly believe it. You mean the whole book was written about me?—yes. And written about him?—yes. And all?—yes. But in the end it will not be a bunch, just one...all coming back into the one body, the one Spirit, the one Lord. Just see it like a play or a beautiful poem, and the poem existing not for itself but for the author of the poem. You desire to have it exist for itself and there's no way to do it unless you come down and animate it. So you animate the entire poem, making each alive; and then you take yourself back, one by one...each now having played the part perfectly, each individualized.

So the poem...like a Shakespeare...take any play of Shakespeare...it existed only for Shakespeare, all within him. Hamlet did not exist for himself nor any character in the play. And so he comes down and plays all the parts, and now in the end he calls himself back. Then the play now exists not only for the author, it exists for itself. And that is the glory of this marvelous, marvelous play.

Now let us go into the Silence.

* * *

SIMON LIFTS THE CROSS

3/17/69

I think you will find this very practical tonight. But to me the most practical book in the world is the Bible. We are told they found one whose name was Simon and they laid on him the cross to carry it behind Jesus. Well, the word Simon in scripture means "to hear with understanding and then to consent to what you have heard." You may hear it and deny it, that's not Simon. Simon is one who hears and consents, he agrees to what he has heard.

Now, who is Jesus, for he carries the cross behind Jesus? The gospel tells what happened in the soul of Jesus…events that were seen and heard by none save by him. Through these experiences he gained the certainty that he was the Son of God and eventually God himself. The story is told and few will accept it, for his interpretation of scripture of the secret of Messiah as against the interpretations of the *priests* were poles apart. But Simon understood what he heard and could follow it, and now he carries the cross. I hope tonight that everyone in this room could call himself or herself a Simon.

Now who is the Simon? He said, "Bear ye one another's burdens and so fulfill the law of Christ" (Gal.6:2). Well, the law of Christ as described in the Sermon on the Mount is imaginal, it's wholly psychological. "You've heard it said of old 'You should not commit adultery.' But I tell you that anyone who looks lustfully upon a woman has already committed the act in his heart" (Mat.5:27). Well, the word "heart" and the word "self" are synonymous in the Bible. When we speak "And he said in his heart" he is saying to himself. When we are told, "He communed with his own heart upon his bed" he is communing with himself. He has already committed the act when he looks lustfully on another. So the whole law of Christ is *mental*, it's imaginal.

Now he carries the burden, for "In as much as you do it to one of the least among one of these, you do it unto me" (Mat.25:40). So Paul makes the statement, "From now on, we regard no one from the human point of view; even though we once regarded Christ from the *human* point of view, we regard him thus no longer" (2 Cor. 5:16). He saw the meaning of Christ: that Christ was the *pattern* buried in every child born of woman. That is the pattern. So he could not see *a* little Christ; he saw the universal Christ, the cosmic Christ, buried in everyone in the world. There's only one Christ, so when you do it to anyone, you're doing it unto me.

Now the one who heard and believed he's called Simon. So he goes out now to bear the cross and lift the burden from the back of the one being who has taken the entire cross, for every child born is the cross and collectively they form *the* cross that the cosmic Christ bears. So the one who hears the story and believes it, he goes out in his belief to lift the weight of that cross. He sees someone who is struggling—can't pay rent, can't buy food, he's embarrassed financially or he may be this, that or the other in the world, ostracized—and he lifts the cross. He knows he's doing it only to himself... it can't be another. And because he does it psychologically, he represents the other to himself as he would like to see that other were he that other, knowing that he *is* that other. To the degree that he is self-persuaded that this that he is imagining is so, it becomes so. He is the Simon who bears the cross; not moving it toward any little point in space, no, all through life he's bearing the cross, lifting the weight. And many a man today is behind the eight-ball, because no one ever believed he would be anything other than what he is.

Fortunately in my own case I had a mother who...and she would take us separately, which we did not know until I went back after twelve years in America. Having cocktails on the veranda this evening it came up for the first time. But she took me and persuaded me that I was her favorite, and that I would never let her down. "Well, no, mother, never." "You're going to make mother very proud of you, aren't you?" And naturally you say, "Yes, mother." She would curl my hair, because I had long white curls, and she would curl them up and push her finger in the curl, kiss me, and send me on my way. Then the next one came to have his hair combed or curled. She told the same story to everyone, but because it was mother's secret you couldn't violate mother's secret, and each grew into manhood believing he was the favorite. We were not going to set a little enmity among the brothers and tell the others that we were the favorite. We couldn't betray mother's trust.

Then I returned after twelve years in America and we're having cocktails on the veranda and it came out in some spontaneous way, and everyone told the same story. Mother just sat there and chuckled. She had simply accomplished her purpose. She got over to us the feeling of being important, because we were her favorite and we couldn't let her down. Everyone had to be simply right. She didn't expect us to make a fortune in the world, but to be something of which she would be proud. Well, she was a very wise mother, so that we became in our own separate spheres a success in her eyes before she departed this world. And many a man today is what he is, in the gutter, because no one ever believed he would be anything other than where he is today.

So I say, if we really hear the story and believe it, that there is only *one* being—there seems to be three-and-a-half billion—but there's only one being and there's one *real* cross made up of all the bodies in the world. So every child born of woman is that cross, and the being that animates that child is Christ Jesus. So I can't do to any child in this world— whether it be a little infant or one departing this world—that I am doing to *another*. "So bear ye one another's burdens and so *fulfill* the law of Christ. For in as much as you do it to one of the least among one of these, you have done it unto me." Well, if you believe it then you are bearing the cross, because you put it into practice. If you hear it but you don't really believe it and you're so engrossed in your own little world so that "let him take care of himself," you see him as another. You don't see him as a projection of yourself.

If you really believe the story, you'll become Simon and Simon bears the cross. He is the one who finds the child. For Simon in the Spirit comes into the temple, and as the parents bring the little child into the temple, Simon takes him up in his arms and said, "Lord, let now thy servant depart in peace, according to thy word; for my eyes have seen him, the salvation of God" (Luke2:28). Well, read now the 52nd chapter of Isaiah, where the little child symbolizes the unveiled arm of God. The unveiled arm is the symbol of his *creative power* and the child symbolizes that power (52:10). So he takes it up in his arms and now he wants the promise to be kept: "Now let me depart in peace, for I have seen the salvation of God." And in this wonderful 52nd chapter it speaks of the unveiling of "the arm of God," which is the salvation of the world. So here, as the arm is unveiled —and you'll have this experience—where the entire arm is unveiled. And it would seem to you that one betrayed you, because someone came in following the betrayal and unveiled the arm.

What did Judas betray? He betrayed the Messianic secret of Jesus and the place where he might be found; for he heard the secret and he betrayed it, and he betrayed where he *might* be found if you could still find him there. Well, they found him there: it all takes place within us. So there must be someone who must first hear the secret and tells the secret. I have betrayed it by writing my book called *Resurrection*. I have betrayed it from beginning to end, so I have played the part of Judas. I experienced it and that was the part of Jesus. Then I told it in print so that everyone coming behind, when I'm gone from this sphere, and the unborn generations coming in if the book is still available that they will see the secret. So who did he betray? He betrayed the secret, the Messianic secret, which was unlike what the priesthoods of the world believe. They believe in *a* man, a little man coming from without who is going to save them. And it isn't so at all. He comes from within because he's a *pattern*. The pattern erupts within man, unfolds within man, and as it erupts within man he knows by this experience *he is* the Son of God. Because he knows his scripture, he goes back and he searches to find that here it dovetails with all that was foretold. He continues the experience to discover that he's not only the Son of God, he is God himself; for, now the Son [David] calls him Father.

And now he tells it to everyone who will listen. The one who hears it with understanding and accepts it, consents to it, he becomes the Simon who will now pick up the cross and ease the burden from the back of the cosmic Christ. So you meet someone in the world who is unemployed, instead of passing the buck and passing by stop in your tracks and represent him to yourself as being gainfully employed. Persuade yourself that he's gainfully employed. You meet someone who is in some way limited, then represent him as being exactly what you would like him to be…to set him free from what he *seems* to be. Then you are bearing the cross. So, bear ye one another's cross and so fulfill the law of Christ. For, there is a law and the law is all imaginal. So everyone goes out to fulfill…if he hears it with understanding and having heard it with understanding he consents to it. Well, I can hear something I understand, but I may not agree with it. I may say that it's stupid, it's silly. Well, this is the most incredible story that could ever be told man, so when you hear it if you're a brilliant mind, it doesn't mean that because you're a brilliant mind that you'll accept it. You'll understand it if you have intelligence, but you may completely discount it. And the more brilliant men are today, it seems the more they discount it as a myth. They can't believe for one moment this story is true…and yet it *is* true.

Everyone who accepts it will one day experience the entire gospel unfolding within himself, for the gospel is nothing more than that which happened within the soul of Jesus. Well, Jesus means "Jehovah" and Jehovah is the Lord. Well, Jehovah is *in* man, which is I AM, so that everyone when he hears it with understanding and experiences it is Jesus. If I use the word Jesus and you think of a man 2,000 years ago and you don't see the Jesus in everyone…he's sound asleep and carrying a tremendous burden while he's asleep. If you have accepted the story and you're beginning to stir, you're beginning to awaken, you will lift the burden from the back of Jesus and you will carry it because he walks behind Jesus. So you're told, they seized Simon and having seized him they placed upon him the cross that he would carry it behind Jesus. So he carried the cross. It only means the individual in the world, any individual who hears with understanding and consents to what he has heard.

Well, if I really consent to it, I can't pass by anyone and not do something to lift the burden. So they come to the door and you might say to them, "No, I don't have what you ask me" or "I don't need your books." So they come to the door and want to sell you $100 worth of books or $100 worth of magazines. All right, that's their little game…they've got to make a living. They've got to pay rent…maybe they're married and they have an obligation to their family. So you say no physically to their appeal, but as they leave you, inwardly you see them successful, and as they leave your world, you persuade yourself that they are as you represent them to you. To the degree that you are self-persuaded they will be. But they don't know that you've done it. They need not know that you lifted the cross for them. They will go on and things will happen in their world and they will actually become what you have seen them to be. They will not have the slightest idea who did it. Well, who did it? Christ did it, because there is only Christ in the world. You take no credit because you're only doing it to yourself…the whole vast world is yourself pushed out. So representing anyone to yourself as you would like them to represent you then you are simply lifting the entire burden of the world.

So when he comes in and he picks up the little infant, which is called a *sign* in the Bible, it represents the creative power of God, the unveiled arm of God. And that arm creates everything in the world and when it's unveiled in you, you can't fail. Whatever you imagine will come to pass, I don't care what it is, for the arm has been unveiled. The entire sleeve has been severed, leaving the arm from the shoulder to the finger tips free to carry forward your sword of victory. And you see everyone as you want to see them and they become it.

So I ask you tonight to just dwell upon it and see if you fit the pattern of Simon. See if you in the course of a day if for only one person you can lift the burden. Maybe tomorrow you'll do it and you will lift the burden. Don't let it remain, because you're only letting it remain upon your shoulders… there is no other. So as you simply lift it you are lifting that burden off your own shoulders…for there is only Jesus Christ in the world. There is nothing but God. The play begins with the call of Abraham, and it comes to its climax and fulfillment in Jesus Christ. Everyone has to come to that climax. The curtain comes down on it. And when you reach that point, the curtain comes down and you depart and join the heavenly brotherhood who contemplate this world of death. "And those in eternity who contemplate on death," as Blake says, "they say thus 'What seems to be *is* to those to whom it seems to be'" (*Jer.*, Plt.36). Well now, can you assume any state for another and it seems to be? Then, it seems to be and it will become so..."Even of torment, despair, and eternal death. But divine mercy steps beyond and redeems man in the body of Jesus." For in the end there is Jesus Christ, only one body, only one Lord, and you are Jesus Christ. The one *risen* body you will wear as your own body; and the one Spirit that inhabits it you will be that Spirit; and the Lord that is the Lord of all you will be that Lord.

So today, we aren't aware of it, but Paul makes it very, very clear in his 2nd letter to the Corinthians: "If we have been united with Christ in a death like his, we shall certainly be united with him in a resurrection like his" (Rom.6:5). You see the difference in tense? That we have all died with Christ; but we *will* all *live* with Christ...that's in the future. Well, it comes when the pattern contained within man erupts, when it unfolds and the story as told in the gospel unfolds within a man; and *he* is Jesus Christ.

Now, whenever he tells this there's always a sneer, the laughter because they know him by reason of his physical origin; they do not know him by reason of this spiritual birth. They only see the outside man and the judge from appearances. They know him and they can trace his origin right back to his little beginning, so what is he doing making these bold claims, for that's blasphemy, the claim he must make for having had the experience? So he tells it and a few will believe him; and of the few who will believe him, he will get a number of them who will become Simon...to lift that burden and transform lives as he meets them in this world...no matter what it is. So you want x-number of dollars or you want so-and-so, this, that or the other...he simply hears...that's all that he does. He hears as though you told him that you *had* what you really asked him to hear, and he goes his way believing that what he has heard mentally is a physical fact to confront you in the not distant future bearing witness to that state. Or maybe he will hear it through the grape vine that it has worked. But he doesn't seek praise, no thanks. He *knows* it must come into being. So he's lifting the burden, lifting the cross.

So he carries the cross behind Jesus. He hears the pattern and he believes in the pattern and that's believing in Jesus. Not *a man*; you believe in the pattern, the pattern of salvation. *Then* you believe in Jesus. Well then, if you really believe it and everyone contains that pattern and everyone is Jesus, you can't leave anyone distressed. Yet you do not give them one nickel from your pocket, you do it all in your Imagination. Because you could give from now to the ends of time and not give yourself. No, this is giving yourself when you imagine a state and simply go your way believing in the reality of what you have imagined. So in this case, you are lifting the cross, lifting the burden. "So bear ye one another's burdens and so fulfill the law of Christ." That's told us in the 6th chapter of Galatians (6:2).

You can actually feel it, the joy of having done what you've done. You don't wait for the phone to ring, you don't *do* anything. A friend of mine, last night, told me a story. Well, he knows that quite awhile ago he told me of some work that he had done for one that he likes very much. It's an artistic work. But they never paid and it was an agreed contract, not a written contract, between two friends who trusted each other that this money was due and therefore it was paid. Well, he knows that we discussed it and that after we discussed it I certainly heard that he was paid. And we never discussed it following that. Last night he told me the money's in the bank. Out of the blue—he didn't persuade her by argument—this one came forward, she's an artist, and gave him a very large check. Now, I would say to him, that check or a similar check should be coming quarterly, and that multiplied by many. Because she is only one artist and there should be many artists needing your talent. And it would be a joy, as far as I'm concerned, to see many artists seeking his artistry, his talent that they may improve theirs. It's only one being playing it, and then a check similar to that coming from many sources quarter after quarter.

Don't say it can't be done…the minute that you say that you're going to limit someone. Don't say that someone because of his background, his financial background, social background, political background or anything, that he can't make it. You're going to limit him. Don't put the cross that heavily upon him. Lift the cross because we are in a world of horrors, really. But as Blake said and Blake understood it so perfectly: "Don't let yourself be intimidated by the horror of the world. Everything is ordered and correct and must fulfill it's destiny in order to attain perfection. Follow this path and you will receive from your own ego a deeper insight into the eternal beauties of reality. You'll also receive an even deeper release from all that now seems so sad and terrible." But if you know this story, you will lift the burden. Yes they'll carry it, because they have to carry it. But why must they carry it when you yourself are carrying it because, you're carrying all the crosses of the world. You can't meet a stranger in this world; there isn't one being that is a stranger. Regardless of the pigment of his skin, regardless of his tongue, regardless of anything, we're all one…for God is one. As we're told in the great shema of the Hebrew confession of faith, "Hear, O Israel; the Lord our God the Lord is one" (Deut.6:4). And never forget it! If he's one, there can't be a second. So in the end you and I will be the same being, the same Father, and we'll have the same Son.

Now, I have been sent into this world to convey one thought. I have conveyed it and I've recorded it. I've recorded that the *true Son* is David. It's been 2,000 years since the unveiling of the mystery of God. It has never been done before, and I have not much to convey now. I've completed the work I was sent to do, because the priests do not know the mystery. They do not know it, they're men without vision and they're arguing from a book that they do not understand. My mother used to say to me, "But after all, Neville"...a priest to her was the wisest man in the world..."and you can't contradict him." Well, I wouldn't contradict my mother and I wouldn't argue with my mother. She was simply to me something altogether wonderful, so I could not discuss it with mother. But I knew they were stupid anyway. I heard it discussed with the priests, discussed with the other ministers, and I overheard these conversations and I knew this whole thing was stupid, it wasn't so at all. Because from the time I was a boy I had visions, and I knew it wasn't what they were talking about. They didn't have the slightest concept of what they were talking about. But I couldn't tell that to mother, because mother would not have understood her little boy who was uneducated and a very limited background, how could he challenge what she considered the wise, wise priest? Because he could speak Latin or maybe he could read it too, and maybe he could read Greek...that meant he was intelligent. A lot of learned nonsense! He didn't know what I knew from vision, for mine was all vision, it wasn't from study.

Then as I matured I was called and sent. I know today the reason for the call and the reason for being sent and that was to reveal the *true* Son of God...the one Son that unifies humanity. Because if all have that one Son as his Son then we are one; the Father Jesus Christ is God the Father, and David is his Son. Jesus Christ is in you and David is his Son. The day will come he will awaken in you, he will rise in you, and you will meet David; and David will call *you* Father. Then you will have this certainty beyond anything in the world. You know what you had for dinner tonight, and maybe I could contradict you and tell you and get you to change what you believe you had. But you can't get anyone to change when you have the experience of being the Father of David. There's a certainty beyond the wildest dream of man when you meet him. There's no uncertainty in it whatsoever. Well now, if everyone has this identical experience, then are we not one? If we all have the same Son, we are the same Father.

So tonight, the practical side of this is to go out and to the best of your ability play the part of Simon. May I tell you, you aren't neglecting yourself, because the one you are helping *is* yourself. But aside from that, it comes back to the center from which it came. As the story of Job tells us, when he prayed for his friends his own captivity was lifted. So while he was locked in his own little desire to free himself of the sores and the pox and all the things that befell him, when he forgot himself completely and prayed for his friends, all these things disappeared; and then all that he lost returned to him a hundred-fold. So when I pray for my friends my own captivity is lifted, the cross becomes lighter, and finally it's just light itself. "So take my yoke upon you and learn from me," he said, "for my yoke is easy and my burden is light" (Mat.11:30). If you really put it into practice, it will become very light. You ask no praise, no thanks from anyone, no financial gain; just the joy of seeing the cross lifted, for it's being lifted from your own shoulder. So if I actually hear a man's need and instead of ignoring it I represent that man to myself as one who has had that problem solved, and become self-persuaded that it is solved, and then I find that in the not distant future that it is, I don't have to tell him what I did. I have the joy and the satisfaction of knowing that this law of Christ never fails, that it works!

So believe in the reality of your own imaginal acts. For faith is really *loyalty* to unseen reality. I must have faith, and I have faith not in things seen but things unseen. I don't see the unseen imaginal act as an external fact now, but I must remain loyal to the unseen reality, and then in time the unseen will become seen and the world will see it. So this is the practical side of this night…how you and I can lift the cross from our own shoulders. If I'm lifting it from yours, I'm lifting it from mine. And in a way I do not know blessings fall upon me to the degree that I am lifting the weight from the shoulders of myself-pushed-out. For, everyone I meet is myself made visible; there is nothing but myself and there is nothing but God.

So when you read these passages and put them together into a mosaic, it tells the most beautiful story. It's simply the most marvelous picture… if you take it that when you do it unto the least among one of these, you've done it unto me. You mean the little one that everyone ignored? Yes, if you did it to him you did it unto me. Well, who are you? "I am he the world is seeking, I am the Christ, the Lord," he said. And the little one, you mean the insignificant little one, that's Christ? Yes. "So lift his burden, because you're lifting mine…you've done it unto me."

You try it. May I tell you, it pays dividends beyond measure, just beyond measure, when you least expect it. And now you may never recognize your own harvest, because quite often our memory fades and we don't recall that maybe five years ago someone asked a favor, and you did it in your Imagination. Then five years later you encounter that person and you've forgotten completely. You only know that, well, aren't you lovely and things are going in a marvelous way for you. And you don't realize that five years before they sought you out and asked you to help them, and you did, in your own wonderful spiritual way, and it worked. Maybe even they have forgotten. What does it matter? The burden has been lifted. So we go forward to lift the cross playing the part of Simon.

The day will come, you, too, will play the part in the most tangible manner of taking that little sign called the child wrapped in swaddling clothes, lifting it up in your arms; he only symbolizes the power of God that has just been unveiled. Here is the power of God. You read it in the 52nd chapter, I think it's the 10th verse of Isaiah…the whole thing is unveiled. What is it? The arm of God has been unveiled and it's the power of salvation, symbolized as the child. When it happens I can't tell you the thrill when the entire scripture unfolds within you. You see it not as secular history at all; the whole thing is supernatural from beginning to end. From the call of Abraham to the climax in the story of Jesus Christ the whole thing is supernatural. Hasn't a thing to do with history as we understand history here. They were not telling any event that took place on earth; it was taking place in the soul of a man as he walked the earth. And no one believed him, because they knew his parents, they knew his brothers, they knew his sisters, and how could he make these claims for that was sacrilege and the priests did not believe that. They turned to the priests; they were the authorities, they were the ones who should know. So they turned to the rabbis and the rabbis said, "No, he's an imposter." So he goes and he tells it, and finally he finds a small, little circle that believes him to the point of putting it into practice. Then he came to them first and unveiled himself, and they began to be unveiled too. And the God in them that was the God in him begins to unveil in them. And the rabbis remained veiled. So even to this day when Moses is read a veil is on their mind…they don't see it. I pray for all of them, no criticism, because it's myself blinded; and they refuse to accept any change in that fixed belief of theirs.

So I have come to do one thing, and I've done it, and I've recorded it: that is to make clear to the entire world who will listen who the *true* Son of God is who will unify the entire world: Jesus Christ is God the Father and his Son is David. When David calls *you* Father, you will know you are Jesus Christ the Lord. For if I am a father, there must be a son to bear witness for that relationship. Well, he comes and he comes into one's world. So I've told it and so far there are a few thousand books in print and sold, and a few thousand more back in print and they'll be sold. So at least it will reach in the English speaking world a certain segment and they'll know. Whether they will accept it or not I do not know. But I have told what I came to tell, that the Son of God is David and David is not a physical being. It is in Spirit that he called him Father. So, "David in the spirit called me Lord" he said, "How then can I be David's son?" (Mat.22:42). So he called me Father in fulfillment of scripture; and everyone is going to be called Father by the one being that is David. When he calls you Father as he has called me Father, then you and I are the same being: we are God the Father. There's only one God the Father; without loss of identity we are one.

Now let us go into the Silence.

*   *   *

Now are there any questions, please?

Q: Does David ever become a father?
A: David? No. Out of David comes the Son who is the Father, as told us in the 7th chapter of 2nd Samuel (7: 12): "Go unto my servant David and say unto him that when your days are fulfilled and you lie down with your fathers, I will raise up your son after you, who shall come forth from your body. I will be his father and he shall be my son." For David is the culmination of the journey. When you come to the very end, though you wear the name of John or Neville or any other name, at the end of the journey David is the very last. He was all anyway, because he's played the part that you willed him to play, because all that you've done you did it, and David is the culmination. Then out of David comes one who rises within him. So you rise within your own body called John or call it what you will, but you're coming out of David. So what comes out of David is the Son of God, and the Son of God and God are one. So, "I and my Father are one" (Jn.10:30). So you awake within yourself and you come out of a body and that is David. But David is the one who does all the Father's will: "I have found in David, the son of Jesse, a man after my own heart who will do all my will" (Acts13:22). So every part that you have played was subject to your will. And it went through hell because you put it through hell as you in your dream entertained unlovely thoughts or lovely thoughts; and the David, which is the part that you played, had to go through all the horrors. Well, in itself it was dead. You, the God dreaming in these bodies, had horrible dreams; but in the end, you come out of the state into which you have placed yourself to dream. So David is the Son and he's always young, always the youth.

Q: You said that Jesus Christ was in you. And you said what David was…I didn't catch that.
A: Well, the "you" in which is Jesus Christ is David, you. In you is Jesus Christ. When Jesus Christ wakes in you it's I am…it's you waking. But he wakes in you that which you think yourself to be. That which you think yourself to be is the David. But remember, the drama is not taking

place in flesh and blood; it's taking place in the *soul* of man. The soul of man that is animating all that is David…it's something that makes the body alive. In that that dreams it, the being that is dreaming it, is God who is Jesus Christ.

Now, if I became this body and it refused to obey my will, it isn't David. It must obey my will. So "I have found in David the son of Jesse a man after my own heart, who will do all my will" (Acts.13:22). So I come into the world and I think that you are terrible, well, I've got to see in you the terror or he hasn't done my will. I come into the world and I see you are lovely, and I see you *are* lovely then he's done my will, because everything that I imagine it must do. So when I imagine that you are successful then you must become successful, he's done my will. Because no one sees me; I am Spirit, I am Spirit invisible to mortal eye. But when I actually assume that this is so-and-so and that is so-and-so, it must become so-and-so for it to do my will. But man not knowing his own imaginal acts, he denies that he is doing the things that he reaps in the world. He's totally unaware of his own harvest and denies that he had anything to do with it. You hear it from numberless lips, "Why should this happen to me?" And you say, "Well, why shouldn't it?" "Well, look here, I'm a good person." "By whose standards?" They will tell you, "I'm so good, I'm so kind and I'm so wonderful." They'll give you all this praise for themselves. That's all right…so they're making all these claims, and then something happens.

A lady wrote me from Florida the other day. She had the crust to rewrite the Book of Revelation. So she gave me a copy of it and it was just trash, nonsense beyond nonsense. Well, her husband died at the age of eighty-four and she wondered, "Why should this happen to me?" Meaning that she rewrote the Book of Revelation and she is a very wise person, a very kind person, a great teacher. Well, what can you say to a person like that? How can you answer her letter without offending? "Why should it happen to me?" Now she'll turn right around and become an atheist because he died at eighty-four. She told me in New York City only four years ago the man is eighty-four, so he was then eighty, and she was telling me of his physical and sexual power. At the age of eighty, "Just imagine Neville that he is just as though he were forty…" and I am wondering am I in an insane institution or not? She is thinking of the sexual power of a man eighty and she is my senior in years, and you wrote Revelation, that you dare to change the Word of God! And you think of a man eighty who satisfies you at eighty and you are now seventy, what on earth are you two doing? It took place in my lobby in the hotel in New York City. She came on a Sunday morning and she had to see me. I went down stairs to see her—Bill wasn't dressed for anyone to come upstairs to our room—so I went downstairs and spent an hour. I wondered, really, if I'd come into some insane institution. And she's teaching "the truth"...she has her own center in Florida. He was teaching music. As she told me all these things, I wondered what am I here for? Here is a sheer waste of one beautiful hour; I could be upstairs sitting in a robe. I had to get up early and shave and come downstairs to hear that nonsense.

If I told her that in heaven that man is above the organization of sex, she'd drop dead! What, no sex in heaven? She wouldn't want that at all. I said, no there's no sex in heaven as you understand sex, but there is a creativity that makes sex as we understand it look like nothing. There is an emotion and a thrill that takes anything here that we call sex and makes it look like a little fizz. That's the thrill of creation in heaven compared to what we think the thrill is here. But if you told her that in the resurrection men are above the organization of sex, she wouldn't want it, and she would close the book. Then she writes me that he died at eighty-four, so what? So he died...now he finds himself twenty and more virile than ever.

Any other questions, please? I knew you were going to come up with one.

Q: My grandmother's ninety-two and sick. How do I know whether I should...what should I do?

A: My dear, your grandmother is ninety-two and she's ill. I have had many of these, and what I do I simply assume they have never known such *freedom* in their lives. And quite often they close their eyes and go. My dancing partner's father was sick a week, he was sixty-six years old, and he had a suite of rooms. I went into his bedroom at the hotel and he said, "Nev, help me to the bathroom." So I raised him off the bed and I held my arms around him this way. He said, "Oh, I'm so tired!" I said, "Pop, what would you like?" He said, "Just to be free." I said, "Close your eyes...close your eyes" and I closed mine and felt he was as free as the wind. He fell in my arms and he was gone.

Another one in New York City, she was very wealthy and he is very wealthy, but for four years he was in a coma, knew nothing, with three nurses around the clock. But that meant no problem to them because they had money, oodles of money...but three around the clock to watch him. In four years they never spoke because he was always unconscious. She came to see me and her problem was her little vanity. She also had a little center and she was talking on things. She hid this thing from her people, that they wouldn't think for one second that her husband was four years in a coma. So she came to my meeting one night and sought an audience backstage and she did. I said, "Why don't you let him go? It's all vanity on your part, trying to hold him here." She said, "How would I let him go?" I said, "Assume that he's free...that he has never known such freedom." One week later she went into the room—which was not often that she did because he was always unconscious. As she went into the room he regained consciousness for fifteen minutes and dictated the terms of his will in the presence of the nurse, and he could sign it. For four years he was not conscious...and then he died, just like that.

We're holding on to things. Your grandmother's ninety-two years old? Well, if I thought I had to live until I'm ninety-two, I would say he really doesn't care for me. What, ninety-two? At that age most of them...well, Churchill lived to be ninety, but did he live? In the last few years of his life the mind was gone. When the mind isn't there, where are you? He was a dotty old man, but no one on the outside knew it. I read a story told by Mountbatten and when Mountbatten came to see his old friend Winston, Winston was completely a gone man. He rambled and rambled and took things that he never experienced and blended them with things that he had and made a story out of it. What he read in the papers and books to him became facts as *he* had experienced them. When Mountbatten left his presence he said, "I felt so sad, for here was this giant of a man who today is simply an idiot." But the world didn't know that. So you want to just simply vegetate? If your grandmother is ill and she's in pain and she's ninety-two, well, let her go back to the age of twenty, which she will when she takes off this old garment. She'll find herself radiantly happy at the age of twenty. And everyone does until they reach the end and they are resurrected. Only the resurrected transcend the return and enter the new age.

Well, until Friday.

GOD'S PLAN OF REDEMPTION

3/21/69

People understand best not bare truth but truth embodied in a tale…truths so that they can be seen in pictures. Our evangelists, who are the unknown authors of the gospels, understood this and so they took the greatest of all truths, God's plan of redemption, and they too told it in the form of a tale so that it may be seen and not forgotten. They knew the risks that they ran; that those who heard it and would see it mentally as the story was told would mistakenly take the *personifications* that conveyed the truth for persons themselves, and that the vehicle that conveyed the instructions for the instructions. So Paul said having done the same thing, "O foolish Galatians! Who has bewitched you, before whose eyes Jesus Christ was publicly *portrayed* as crucified? Let me ask you only this: Did you receive the Spirit by works of the law, or by hearing with faith? Are you so foolish? Having begun with the Spirit, are you now ending with the flesh?" (Gal.3:1).

Well, the entire Christian world and the Jewish world have ended with the flesh. They can't think of Jesus Christ as a *pattern* that is actually contained in man, a pattern of redemption; they only think of him after the flesh. They see him as a man, a unique man that differs from us, just a man, not a pattern man. So Paul discovered him to be the pattern that is contained in every child born of woman, and there it remains as the pattern until one day it is fertilized. Then after fertilization the time element enters for its development, and no one in the world can stop that coming on time after fertilization. The egg is in a woman; this egg is in everyone, but it does not unfold until fertilization. After fertilization then that built in time begins to awaken and then it comes into bloom; and that is the Christ, the savior in man. It is a pattern.

So speaking of Jesus Christ man instantly thinks of *a* man, something external to himself. It's *not* something external to himself: *he* contains within himself the pattern which is God's vision of man. Christ is God's vision of man. So, it's not going to change, that vision is forever. He said, "Write the vision; make it plain upon tables, so he may run who reads it. For the vision has its own appointed hour; it ripens, it will flower. If it be long then wait; for it is sure and it will not be late" (Hab.2:2). So the pattern is perfect and from the moment of fertilization that built in time begins to unfold and then it comes into full bloom. So, I tell you from experience how it unfolds in man.

Now don't think for one second it's unique to the thing called Neville. I am speaking of a pattern and it's in you, in every child born of woman. It has bloomed in me in its fullness, but it does not mean because it has bloomed in me that I am different from others in the world. I happen to know that Jesus Christ is simply God's eternal plan for man's redemption. It happened to me suddenly. So when I go up and I tell it, I don't make any claim to be better, to be above, simply to tell you how it happened, that's all.

Now here, when we read these stories…we're told in this month they're going to dramatize it. And he took twelve and he went up to Jerusalem, and he said to them, "All that is written of the Son of man will be accomplished" (Luke18:31). But they did not understand him. These things were hid from them and they could not grasp what was said. They were hid because they could only be told by the *risen* Christ and only the risen Christ can interpret scripture. Only his finger can trace these strange, peculiar complexes in scripture and make them give up their heavenly meanings. They're all ambiguous. You read one thing, but it has multiple meanings. If you bring reason to bear upon it to interpret it, you can get any kind of meaning. But the *real* meaning can only be traced by the risen Christ. Why?—because he has experienced it. So when you read "You must be born from above" only the one who has been born from above could actually trace it. I have heard unnumbered arguments about it, that it means a radical change in one's character, one's behavior. They were once violent and now they're kind and tender and considerate. It hasn't a thing to do with that! That they were once this, that and the other, and now they're so and so, it hasn't a thing to do with that. It's an actual *event* that you are born from above. So when you read these statements they're ambiguous yes, because you could take it in multiple ways. It is strange, it's stated "You must be born again, you must be born from above." Well, the word is *Anothin*, and it literally means "you must be born from above."

Now let us take this simple statement, "All mine are thine and thine are mine" (Jn.17:10). Now we are told in the 50th Psalm, "The world and all within it is mine. The cattle on a thousand hills is mine. If I were hungry, I would not tell you" (50:10-12). It's all mine, so I would take it. Now, if all mine are thine and I'm speaking now to God the Father, and thine are mine, must I confine it only to things, like the world and all within it? One could take it that way...that we would share the world, it's yours...and all mine are thine and thine are mine. No, it goes a way beyond that; it goes into his *nature*. What is his nature who owns the world and all within it? Well, he is a father. Now, *that's* mine. He is a father and that is mine, but I am not a father, well then, this has not yet been realized in me. Because all mine are thine and all thine are mine, well then, and you are a father, I must be a father. If you are a father there is a child bearing witness of that fatherhood and that is mine. It goes a way beyond things in this world. It goes right into the very nature of God: that God has to give himself to me 100 percent if that statement is true in the 17th chapter of John, "All mine are thine and thine are mine." Only his finger who has experienced it can trace this ambiguous statement and compel it to yield up its heavenly message, its meaning.

Well, suddenly it happens in you and you realize you are actually God the Father. Then why are you limited, why are you weak, wearing this little garment?—because of the incarnation. The incarnation is not a masquerade where God is masquerading in a human body of flesh and blood. He had to empty himself of all that is his and though he was rich he became poor that by his poverty I may become rich...a complete emptying of his entire being. So he is not playing a little part, he is not masquerading. The incarnation is a complete embodiment with all the limitations of human knowledge. So I take upon myself all in the little time slot in which I find myself. I came in in 1905 and will depart in the not distant future from that little short interval of time. Well, in that interval I, too, must take upon myself all the beliefs related to that time. I was born in this garment, born a Caucasian, born under the British flag, adopted the American flag. But here these are my restrictions and the beliefs that I inherited as a Britisher, the beliefs I then inherited as an American. All these are woven together within the time slot where I found myself in this world...and these are limited.

So man...a complete incarnation to make it real has to actually take upon himself all the beliefs of the time into which he was born. If he does not, then it is not a real incarnation and he simply masquerades...but he's a God masquerading. And there's no God here masquerading, not in this world. We actually emptied ourselves completely of the being that we were to take upon ourselves the limitations and all the restrictions of this world. While we're in it, in this time slot, then this thing unfolds within us. It's a pattern that unfolds. It's personified in scripture as a man called Jesus

Christ—but *you* are that man. You are the being who will one day have the experience of the pattern unfolding in you. And that is the story of the gospels.

Now man cannot understand it in its unvarnished, unveiled state; so he understands best not the bare truth as I will tell it to you but the truth embodied in a tale. So you tell it in a tale and then the whole vast world of Christendom and the Jewish world, numbering almost one billion in this world, now completely forget it's a great *principle* that is *personified*; and they worship the personification and completely forget the principle. So if I tell anyone tomorrow—not you, but I mean those who are not familiar with this principle, who do not know it through your eyes—that Jesus Christ is in you as a pattern, they'll come right back, "You mean he didn't live?" And you say to them, he's the only reality, the only thing worthwhile, because unless he unfolds within you, no matter what you accomplish in this world of Caesar it is as nothing.

So he is in you as a pattern. Hope that the day is not far away, if it has not occurred, that you will be fertilized. "Well, what do you mean by that?" I mean that God will call you, actually call you, and you'll be called while still walking this earth wearing these garments. But who does he call? He calls the *real* you and fertilizes the pattern, for that is his vision of you. Christ is God's vision of man. When it's fertilized by union with God, well then, the timetable begins and you can count the days up to the very end and it will come to 1,260 days from the first little appearance of the first green sprig. It will be thirty years between the embrace and the beginning of the first appearance on that tree of life, for you are the tree of life. The first appearance, God counted them, 1,260 days.

Now that is the story that we're going to reenact in the not distant future on the sixth day of April, and we're going to think that is a unique day. All right, it's a lovely thing to keep in mind I would not deny that... although Paul condemns the keeping of any day. He said, "I notice you keep and observe days and months and seasons and years. I'm afraid I've labored over you in vain." Because we keep it for a person and it is *not* a person; if we could only bear in mind that this is when the first thing erupted. Well, it wasn't on that day at all...any day it could erupt. It could erupt now, right in this audience, at any moment in time if the time is fulfilled. If you have been embraced and had union with the risen Lord, you can count it to the very day, it's going to be thirty years when you will start your mission based upon *experience* and not based upon theory. Then the first will appear within you and that first is resurrection. Resurrection is nothing more than the transformation of the cross—this is the cross—and resurrection is the cross transformed. That's transfiguration. It's a complete change of being from what people think you are and think themselves to be into an entirely new being, a being of Spirit, no more flesh. But you still remain in the flesh and you tell it to the best of your ability, and try to modify that misunderstanding. They can't all take it, but you try to modify and bring it down so that they can actually see it as *principle* rather than as a little historical event, because it is *not* an historical event. It's only history in the sense that it happens in a person at any moment in time.

Well, it started 2,000 years ago. That was when the time was fulfilled and then the tree of life began to bear. The tree of life is in every child born of woman. Now, they're searching for it throughout nature. As Blake said so beautifully: "The gods of the earth and the sea sought through nature to find this tree; but their search was all in vain: there grows one in the human brain" (*Songs of Experience*). That's where the entire thing begins and ends… it's all in the human brain. When the first little sprig appears upon it is when you can see something resurrect. If you see a dead tree in the winter and suddenly you come out one morning and you notice one little branch that has green on it, well, you know that that tree is resurrecting. It seems dead through the winter, but now it is alive, it begins to resurrect. And *you* begin to resurrect in this body that seems so dead. Suddenly you awake within yourself and suddenly you come out of this dead body. Well, it looks dead when you look at it. It's as dead as dead can be and out you come. From then on watch the leaves as they unfold. They're all blooming now one after the other and it's all scripture…only you the resurrected who is the resurrected Christ.

Well, how can you tell that to the world who believes in a little flesh and blood Christ? You're walking and you're covering that which is happening within you. You tell them what is taking place within you and it's all scripture. Only *your* finger can trace this ambiguous phrase or phrases all through scripture because you've experienced it. Then it actually yields to you its heavenly meaning. So you take it and you present it. It's not what they were looking for; it's not what they were taught when they were children, and they're not going to accept it. Go your way…you're told it was hidden from them and they could not understand it, and they could not grasp that which was said, not until the risen Christ interpreted to them the scriptures. As you're told in the 24th chapter of the Book of Luke, it was only then after the resurrection that anyone understood what he talked about; prior to that no one understood it, not even his closest, those who were called his twelve, they didn't understand it. What does he mean by rising again on the third day? What does he mean that he has to suffer first and then rise, and then bring them with him into the same kingdom that he has gone and prepared?

So here this month we'll all be celebrating these external mysteries and thinking that we're keeping alive the memory of a man. It's not so. In you this night is God's *pattern* of redemption for *you*, the same pattern that was buried in me when I was born that was my redemption. It is God's vision of you, it was God's vision of me, and his vision will not in any way change. He keeps the divine vision in time of my trouble. He first sees me as that pattern in full bloom, and the vision has its own appointed hour; and it will ripen and it will flower. If to us it seems long in coming then wait, for it is sure and it will not be late...not for itself. You can count today as I'm standing here that between the first appearance of the first little sprig, which is resurrection, and the last bringing the tree into full bloom, which is the descent of the dove; count the days, add them all together, 1,260 days.

Now, what on earth could you hear comparable to this story? For if you owned the whole vast outer world but you did not actually become God, it is nothing. For everything here is going to fade, but everything is going to fade. How many civilizations will rise and fall before the culmination of the whole, who knows? We think that today we in America are forever. Forget it! Russia thinks they are forever, forget it. England thought the same thing, ancient Rome thought the same thing, ancient Spain thought the same thing and Greece thought the same thing. And they came like a wave and then they ebbed and off they went leaving nothing behind. Everything simply vanished. So we are a power today, but don't think for one second it's a *permanent* power. It will come to its climax and it will wane and it will go. Russia will come to its climax, China will come to its, and they will wane and they will go. They will continue, yes, as nations to hatch out others. But the important thing is not that we become the biggest most powerful land in the world of Caesar, but that within us individuals are hatching out the pattern, God's plan in the beginning, which is himself. That pattern which is called Christ is the radiation of God. He "radiates and reflects the glory of God and bears the express image of his person" (Heb.1:3).

So that pattern in you is God's vision of you. And he just waits for that moment in time, after the suffering. Who knows what you have gone through? It's been hidden. In his infinite mercy he hides from us what we have suffered. And how we have suffered! But it seemed an essential part of the unfolding pattern. Then at the moment and not one second before and not one second later, he calls. At that moment you're embraced and that's the moment he fertilized you. Then from that moment that timetable was built in, and you can start counting it...it's going to be thirty years. Then thirty years latter the first little sprig will appear in the form of resurrection, followed instantly by birth from above. Then comes the great discovery of the fatherhood of God, and *you* are God the Father revealed by his Son, and no one in the world could reveal him but the Son [David]. Then you go through one after the other to the descent of the dove.

In this current issue of the *New York Times Book Review* it's devoted to religion. They make so little of religion. They speak of all these myths... they're all nothing more than simply myths not based upon any reality whatsoever. And they give all these credits, this one is doctor so-and-so, this one is doctor so-and-so, this one is the great leader of a certain theological school. They are men without vision, not at all exposed to this picture, and they cannot for one moment believe that this is true. Because you discover the non-historicity of Jesus doesn't mean the story is untrue and the evangelists realized that when they told it in the form of a story. They knew it is the best way to get it across into the mind of man. Just as the poet Tennyson said, "Truth embodied in a tale shall enter in at lowly doors." And so if you tell it in the form of a tale then men will accept it. They can't think differently. So you take thoughts and put them into pictures and then with these pictures they explain the story. But the uncovered picture, the uncovered truth they can't retain.

So I tell the average person in the world, you contain within yourself now a plan and scripture speaks of it as Jesus Christ. You're told in scripture that Jesus Christ is in you, and it is your hope of glory, and set your faith and your hope fully upon this grace that is coming to you, it's a gift. It was given to you, this pattern of redemption, so now set your hope fully upon it as it begins to unveil. So I tell you it is a pattern. Well, the average person would rather not have that. They'd rather believe that some man is responsible for me; he died for me, he's on the outside of me, and he's watching in some strange way...even though I suffer...but *he* will do it. He, on the outside rather than a pattern on the inside, is going to do it when you reach the fullness of the tribulation, after the tribulation. And you will not be delayed one second, may I tell you, it will come so suddenly.

So they ask, well, when and how will it happen? Today we're thinking of earthquakes, thinking of convulsions, and if you saw today's TV where they took our new man of defense and you don't call him man of war any more. They've changed that little title from the secretary of war to the secretary of defense. There the entire Senate questioned for hours. Well, I had not a thing else to do so I watched it and there he is speaking of billions and billions of dollars. We have enough today to destroy every person in the world a thousand times over, but we need more. All these billions to build beyond what we now have and we can destroy the population of the world multiple times over, each person. We have enough to destroy everyone so many times over, but we need more. So I sat there wondering, well, if this is not an insane institution what is it? These are so-called intelligent men, all of them; all are the senators who just gave themselves a raise of forty-three percent. You and I are now without our consent taxed ten percent. They call it by some other name, a surtax. I saw in this morning's paper that our city has granted our utility, the gas company, the right to raise us four percent to pay *their* surtax. No one is going to pay mine! I got my return today from my accountant, and here I'm paying my own surtax. Now the utility company, I must along with you, pay their surtax of $21 million. They promise to take it off when the surtax comes off. You want to bet?

So here, all this and we like sheep being led to the slaughter...when I saw this thing today these so-called intelligent men giving themselves a forty-three percent raise denying the right of individuals to ask even for a modest raise. No, hold it down while we raise ours forty-three percent. And they're talking of these billions, multiple billions and we can already kill the entire world. We don't need the help of Russia. We have enough here to wipe out everything in the world, rub it out completely, but we now must build more out of our pockets. And I wondered if this really insane...the whole thing is insane.

So I say wisely, I do not know and no one knows how many civilizations will rise and fall before the ultimate has been attained. But God is in control and he's planned everything as it has come out and as it will be consummated, so rest in that. It doesn't really matter. You will not be lost even if they go mad, go wild and push the button. I'm telling you from experience, that pattern has bloomed in me in its fullness. There's not a thing else left other than to tell it. I am like Paul, remaining in a body that is weak and telling it. And so, Jesus Christ is nothing more than that wonderful pattern of redemption that is contained in every child born of woman and that is God's vision of that child. He doesn't see the horrors that he must go through; he sees his vision of that child. And that child...one day that vision will erupt in this series of events, and when it erupts in this series of events no one can stop it. No one can delay it and no one can hasten it. When it erupts that individual is then conditioned for the new age called the kingdom of God.

So, this month and in the early part of next month when we all through habit, through tradition observe these days like Easter, it's lovely. Even though Paul says that he thinks that he's labored in vain because we still keep alive these days, doesn't really matter. You keep alive these days if you feel like it. But if you should go and your friends go, without criticism, know what you're observing. You are observing a *pattern* contained in man. That pattern...and you can't tell the day it's going to happen unless you know the visions of that individual. As some of you have taken me into your confidence and you have told me certain things that have happened to you, and so I can predict from my own experience the length of time between what you told me and when it erupts. That I do know. I know it from my own experience and I can trace it out in scripture for you if you want it. For having risen from within, my finger can trace that book and show you all these ambiguous phrases, and compel them to yield their hidden and wonderful meanings because I have experienced them.

Now a few of you have shared with me your experiences and I know that you have been, I would say, fertilized. Having been fertilized, if you knew the day that it happened and made a record of it, well then, you can count thirty years. Then from then on you can count 1,260 days for this whole tree to bloom. For the final bloom is the descent of the dove. Speaking of that, in the current issue, as I mentioned it, the Book Section of the *New York Times*, they made so light of the descent of the dove, treating that as though it were the most stupid thing in the world and that people over the years believed that, but in this modern day how could anyone believe the stupid little story? And yet it is so true! These wise men get before a camera and when they are on camera, may I tell you, they know it. You should have seen them today. They're all very well-groomed, all actors playing their parts and they knew they were on camera…everyone is trying to mug that camera because he's being exposed to a whole nation. They made it quite obvious in the paper this morning that it would come on at ten and would go through for hours. So, they had hours of exposure and all over the country they were being looked at. So now they have…their face is now registered on the minds of those who think that they're important. They go blindly on. And the only *important* thing in this world is to awaken from this dream of life, to awaken from this world of Caesar with all of its horrors. And the only thing that can awaken you is that gift which is the pattern in you called Jesus Christ. It is actually in man and there it is and it sleeps. His sleep is your waking in this world; his waking in you is your redemption when you leave this world of limitation and enter the world of eternity.

Now let us go into the Silence and then have our questions.

*   *   *

Now do me a favor and you dwell upon that statement "All mine are thine and thine are mine." Was the Lord's body split in two from top to bottom? Yes, and all mine are thine and thine are mine, well then, mine too must be split from top to bottom. Did the dove descend upon the Lord? Well then, he must descend upon me if all thine are mine. Did the Lord find David and David said unto him in the Spirit, "Thou art my Father"? Well then, I must find him in the Spirit and David must say unto me, "Thou art my Father." Is it said of the Lord that he rose from the tomb and left it empty? Well then, I must rise from that tomb and find it empty when I vacate it. Was the name of that tomb Golgotha, which means the skull? Well then, it's from that tomb, and not some cemetery in this world, from which I will rise. Did the Lord find that some sign was given proving that *he* had been born from above? Was it a little babe wrapped in swaddling clothes? Yes, well then, that sign too must be found and pronounced by those who find him that it is the sign of *my* birth from above. For if mine are thine and thine are mine, I will not stop at owning the earth, I want *your* nature. And it's God's purpose to give himself to man as though there were no others in the world, just God and you…and because you're one just you *as* God. So these are the things that happen to God, and you can say all mine are thine and thine are mine, so then you must have these experiences.

Now are there any questions?

Q: (inaudible)
A: The Passover? Well, really the Passover and Easter coincide. It's really Easter is the resurrection and without Easter there would be no Christianity. His death speaking of it as a story would be just any other death…but to rise! So the Passover is passing into the new age. The Jew does not understand it. They think it means a redemption in the world of Caesar, leaving the slavery of Egypt and coming into a promised land. No, that is an *adumbration* of the story of resurrection. It's a foreshadowing of man's freedom from these bodies of death, for all bodies die. Egypt is a land of slavery: I am enslaved by this body that I wear. I must take care of its every want. If it coughs I feel it. Every function of the body I must perform. I must eat, assimilate, eliminate, and no one can do it for me; therefore, I am enslaved by the garment that I wear. Resurrection is its transfiguration. Even though you still wear it for that little interval of time after your resurrection to tell it to encourage all your brothers to hold on and do not lose faith in the eternal vision, that vision that is the story of redemption. Do not lose faith in it. No matter what happens to you, keep the vision! So the Passover is really synonymous with Easter, only Easter is its fulfillment and the Passover was its foreshadowing.

Q: (inaudible)
A: Well, if she wanted to believe that and it serves her, satisfies her and comforts her, don't disturb her. Let her believe that he passes over her house because the little mezuza is at the door. I had many of them given to me and I've given them to friends of mine who are in the Jewish faith. They were so surprised that I, a Christian, would have one of these.

Well, I had many of them given to me and so I kept them in my jewel box. When someone felt the need of such a comfort, it was not beyond me to give them one. The little thing bears with it the Commandments. So you give them and they will tie them on their...as people tie a cross on their neck, Christians wear crosses...they will wear the mezuza or the Star of David. Nothing on the outside is going to help...but until one awakens to it.

I'm speaking now of my own intimate family. My family wouldn't listen to what I'm telling you tonight...to them they could not believe it. They're all secure in the world of Caesar, living very well, with a full complement of servants, each with a lovely home, all the comforts of this world, so what am I talking about? To them I'm a little bit off center because I will not accept their invitation to come back to Barbados and live as comfortably as they now enjoy. They see that as the height of insanity, a man would have to be a little bit touched not to accept this offer. But it's an open offer and it could be accepted tonight, tomorrow or any time at all, if I ever accept it. It's still there, the book isn't closed. But the telling of the story to me is the most important thing in this world. To tell it and to tell it...and it takes reiteration forever and forever, for man quickly forgets. The average person who thinks he's completely ground into it and he goes out and someone will say, "You know Jesus Christ is in space," a man of flesh and blood is conjured in their mind, not a pattern of redemption but a being who lived 2,000 years ago. Not one in whom that pattern erupted 2,000 years ago, but one who is different from all the others in the world, and he is the one and only God. They don't see the pattern contained in man that is Jesus Christ. So you mention the word God and instantly the mind jumps on the outside to something on the outside, when his name forever and forever is I AM.

Q: What do you mean when you say God?
A: Sir, when I say God I mean your own wonderful human Imagination, as you are seated right there that is God. When you say "I am" and you begin to imagine, that's God in action. That is actually God in action. God became you. You know why?—because he loved you. And you know why he did it?—that you may become God. That is the purpose: God became as I am that I may be as he is. And who is he in me?—my own wonderful human Imagination, that's God. By him all things are made and without him there is nothing made that is made (Jn.1:3). Well now, test it. Start imagining something that at the moment seems impossible...just start imagining something. But be faithful to that imaginal act, don't waver, believe in it, believe in the reality of that imaginal act. If it comes to pass then you have found God.

Q: (inaudible)
A: This is God's plan before the world was. Before this vast wonderful world was this is God's plan. This is a theater to express himself. You are more important than all the lands of the world. They're going to vanish; you will not vanish. Countries will come and go, fabulous nations will rise and fall, but you will not. You are *forever*. He brings in the theater, but when the play is over he strikes the theater and the theater vanishes and leaves not a rack behind. That lovely statement in the book of *The Tempest*, read it, Shakespeare's first play. What a play! That man had vision. Besides the fact he was the greatest user of the English tongue that we've ever heard of, he was a man of vision. And his play *The Tempest*: "All men and women are merely players." You are loved, loved beyond your wildest dreams by the one who brought you into being, and he will never waver in his vision of you. His vision of you is the image of himself, and his image reflects his glory and radiates his glory. So don't let anyone rob you of that belief. I tell you that it is true. The story in the gospel is the truest story ever told for that will not fade. All the others will fade, but it will not fade.

Today they think that after all we've outgrown this myth, we've outgrown this nonsense. And so let them go blindly on…they've outgrown it. They've outgrown the century in which Shakespeare lived, too, and I would like one of them to rise and duplicate one of his verses. Let one of them who are so critical of that age let them rise and attempt to write one page, any one of the pages of Shakespeare. But don't copy him just try to be as alive as he was. Just let them be…let them try to write something comparable to one of the Psalms…these who are so critical of the Bible. Just let them write it. Let them give me something comparable to the 17th chapter of the Book of John. Those who today are receiving Nobel prizes for their wonderful books and receiving all kinds of great gifts, why their use of words compared to anything in scripture is like a little kindergarten child to a great professor. Yet they are so wise and they're getting $50,000 for that nonsense. Oh, there are four-letter words in scripture, too, but not used to shock just for the sheer sense of shocking. Well, let them take any one of Shakespeare's plays and try to come near it in writing a play. Yet they can criticize him. You go see one of Shakespeare's plays today and you will see in little small type William Shakespeare, but the one who has simply re-written it for a picture, huge big block letters that he did it and little Shakespeare down below.

I love that cartoon of the Beatle John Lennon…I think it was Conrad who did it…when he said he was better known than Jesus and more people knew him than they knew Jesus. And then, of course,

Conrad came up with this cartoon "The gospel according to St. John Lennon, yea, yea." But his name is John, so St. John Lennon, yea, yea. I hope he has it enlarged and stuck up on his mirror so he can see the nonsense that he represents in the world.

Q: (inaudible)

A: My dear, I haven't the slightest idea why one at a certain moment in time has the eye opened and the ear opened, I cannot tell you. It can only come at the end of his journey, it wouldn't come before. We are *sealed in* and in the end of the journey the eye opens and then the whole thing erupts and the experiences from within parallel those that are recorded without in scripture. So he doesn't condemn anyone whose eye is not open when he's so critical, simply is amused as I am when I read this nonsense. You don't sit in judgment, you don't condemn them. They'll be all right so leave them to themselves. He believes that going to Madison Square Garden and having maybe 25,000 people scream… and there's no record that such a number ever screamed with the one in whom it first erupted called Jesus. But that is only a personification of a principle that unfolded in someone. So now he's better known in the year 1960…it was '68 when he made that statement or '67. And in the not distant future he'll go into the graveyard wherever the little body is placed eventually, if it ever gets there, and you'll see and read the name John Lennon and no one will know who he is, any more than we know today the prominent names of previous ages.

I made so many trips to the West Indies, trips to London, and it was my pleasure to go into cemeteries and read these old tombstones. Many of them are very, very humorous…but just to read them…and no one knows who they are. And these decaying pieces of marble or pieces of stone mean nothing, for they were never put there, they are immortal beings. And all this attempt to keep alive in this little world some accomplishment by a man in the world of Caesar is just all nonsense. It's within us that God is buried; within us he will rise, and then his vision for us has been accomplished. No one will fail, may I tell you, no one. He began the good work and he will bring it to completion (Phil.1:6.)

Any other questions, please?

You hold to your faith. Hold to the faith as told you in both Old and New. The Old Testament is God's promise; the New is its fulfillment. All of his promises find their *yes* in him; and the one spoken of as that "him" is the Christ *in you*; and that Christ in you is the pattern of redemption.

Good night.

WORD BECAME FLESH, DWELT IN US

3/24/69

Tonight we will take a look at the most incredible, exciting and amazing story that the world can ever hear: God's plan of redemption for us. How on earth could the Creator of the universe so love us that he became us and then slowly transforms us into himself so that we are no longer the created, we are the Creator? We are no longer that which was made, we are the Maker. How on earth is this possible? Well, this is the story of the gospels.

Let us turn now to just passages and weave them together for you. "In the beginning was the Word, and the Word was with God, and the Word was God" (Jn.1:3). Now it turns into a person: "He was in the beginning with God. All things were made through him and without *him* was not made anything that was made. In him was life and the life was the light of men." Now, here we have it established that the Word that was with God *was* God, and then it becomes personified. Here, we have now a person. We go forward, "He was in the world and the world was made by him and the world knew him not" (Jn.1:10). It has been established that he is called "The Word." Now the Word was made flesh and dwelt *within* us. The word translated "among" is the preposition "in" or "within." "He dwelt within us full of grace and truth" (Jn.1:14). Now suddenly and without warning a name is introduced into the narrative and that name is Jesus Christ. Now the secret is out that God's eternal *Word* is Jesus Christ, for we are told as we go forward, "Grace and truth came through Jesus Christ" (Jn.1:17). So the Word was full of grace and truth. Now it names who this one is that was in the beginning with God, Jesus Christ. He dwells in us, not on the outside, he dwells *in* us and he is the Word that created the whole vast world and is transforming us into himself so that we become as he is…not two, just one.

Well, where does it show this in scripture? We are told, "Your Maker is your husband; the Lord of hosts is his name" (Is.54:5). My Maker is my husband…you mean I am his emanation, I am his wife? Yes 'til the work that he started in me is over and he will bring it to completion (Phil.1:6). When he brings it to completion what is the completed state? We go back now to the seed plot in Genesis: woman came out of man, therefore man must leave father and mother and cleave to his wife and they become one flesh. Here is the man spoken of out of whom all things come. I come, you come, and we are his emanation, his wife, and he must leave everything and cleave to his emanation, his wife, and they become one, one body, one Spirit, one Lord, one God and Father of all (Eph.4:4).

How on earth can he do that? How can we the made, we the created, be so completely *transformed* that we have no beginning and we are the Creator, we are the Maker? Well, this is the story of the gospels, the most incredible and the most exciting story that man could *ever* hear. You can't top it! So when the poet said, "There is an inmost center in us all where truth abides in fullness…and to know consists rather of opening out a way whence the imprisoned splendor may escape than in effecting entry of a light *supposed* to be without" (Browning, *Paracelsus*). If grace and truth in their fullness abide in Jesus Christ and Jesus Christ is in us, then truth in its *fullness* is in us. We don't have to try to affect some entrance for this light supposed to be without, for it's all within us.

And then, he unfolds himself in us in the most miraculous manner and when he does we simply tell it. Don't think for one moment that you're going to find complete acceptance, because you are talking about the most incredible thing in the world. Here, everyone knows you are made. They see your beginning, they know your earthly parents, they know your background, they know everything about you, and you dare to tell them that the life of God unfolded itself in you? For he doesn't become you just to the point where you are two, man and wife, no, you become one. You leave everything. Who leaves it? Not the woman, it is the man. Although I am a male in this garment I am in scripture the woman, I am the emanation, the thing made. Regardless of your sex here, you are in scripture that emanation and therefore the wife. And the "he" spoken of in that 2nd chapter of Genesis represents Jesus Christ, the Creator, the Word. So he sent his Word… where? He sent his Word into me, but the one who sent it is the same one who is sent…for in the beginning was the Word and the Word was *with* God, and the Word *was* God; then the Word clothed itself in flesh full of grace and truth. So he is not pretending; he clothed himself in a garment of flesh and blood and he is within me.

Well, can I trace him? I can trace him. If he makes everything I can trace him, because I can start now to experiment. And I cannot come to any other conclusion other than he is my Imagination. I can't come to any other conclusion other than this presence that created the whole vast universe that became me, is my own wonderful human Imagination. I set a little task and all I use is Imagination. And then I've come to the conclusion that, here, his name is revealed. What was the name? The name was Jesus. Well, what does Jesus mean? It's the same identical meaning as Jehovah, and Jehovah means "I AM." Jesus means "I AM." Well, I say, "I am"…that's he. How does he differ then? He was with God and yet he is God. Where is the difference? When I say "I am," that's the eternally abiding presence. When I say "I am imagining" that is the same presence in action…God eternally abiding and God in action. So Jesus is called the one that is sent. Well, the minute I begin to imagine, I am sending *myself* to fulfill what I am imagining. The minute I begin to imagine, I am sending myself into the world to complete that, to fulfill it, to experience what I am imagining.

So, God has imagined himself into us and taken upon himself a garment of flesh and blood. But he set a purpose…there is a purpose behind the Word which is himself that he sent, and it cannot return to him empty. It must accomplish his purpose and prosper in the thing for which he sent it (Is.55:11). And for what did he send it?—to transform that which was his emanation into himself. So he cleaves to it until it becomes one with him, not two, just one. So when you awaken within yourself, who is awakening?—I am. And when you come out and push that stone away, who is pushing it?—I am. And when you hold the child in your arms and it looks into your face, who is holding it?—I am. And when the Son now stands before you and calls you "Father," who is hearing it?—I am. He means me when he's speaking to me…and I have it without any doubt whatsoever he is speaking to me— I am. And when the body is torn from top to bottom and I am experiencing that complete severance, who is experiencing it?—I am. And when the dove descends upon oneself and smothers one with affection, who is experiencing it?—I am. Well, what is Jesus' name?—I AM.

So Jesus *in us* is the Word that was sent to completely transform us into himself and he is the Creator of it all. There is nothing created that he didn't create. So although I seem so limited in the world and can't make anything, I can imagine certain things and see them made without knowing how they work. I can imagine a certain state and remaining faithful to the imagined state it happens. So I know *how* it happens or at least *why* it happened… because I imagined it. Well, if he makes everything and I know I imagined it before it appeared, then it appeared *because* I imagined it. Well then, I know who Jesus is: Jesus in me is my own wonderful human Imagination.

I do not know if you are interested in sports, I am. I do not go to the races often; occasionally I go just for the fun of watching them run. But every Saturday when they are on TV I always look at the feature race. Last Saturday, a young chap by the name of Angel Cordova, this is the first time that he ran a race at the track. He had five mounts, that is, five races, all long-shots. When you saw the tote board, the horse that he was riding no one backs it to the point where it would come in beyond the sixth or seventh place. He had four, five all together, but the first four were completely long-shots paying off forty dollars for his two dollars, or thirty-seven dollars for his two dollars. He brought each one in first. When it came to the feature race, it paid off for the owner $38,000, and he, the jockey, got ten percent of it. He brought that long-shot in first…a feature race, to bring in a long-shot. He didn't come in fourth which is out of the money, or third, or second, he came in first. And when they asked him about his riding ability, he said, "It is all feeling lucky. I came to the track feeling lucky. I have never ridden on this track before. I know nothing of the track and when I came to the track all day long…when I got up in the morning I felt lucky." So he puts on a lovely, colorful suit, I think it was a purple suit, and gay colors he wore in his outer garment, and he came to the track looking like a circus clown. But he *felt* lucky he said. Took off his outer clothes, put on the things he must wear with the horse, and brought in four long-shots, all because he said, "I felt lucky. It was no such thing as the ability to ride the horse. I could have the best horse in the world, if I don't feel lucky he doesn't come in." So he *feels*.

Well, what was it…was he not imagining? Was he not imagining that he was lucky? From the end of one day he could take home maybe eight or ten thousand dollars in earnings from the track just running the races. Well, that's what he would have been paid receiving ten percent of the winnings. And here, that whole story is so beautifully told in a simple fellow, a little jockey. He truly was an angel. His name was Angel Cordova, and he really knew how to make that horse fly. Well now, he may not know that his ability to imagine something and feel lucky was Christ in him, for if he makes *all* things he made that. If I trace it back to what the jockey did, he imagined himself a lucky being. So he could not have been lucky if he lost all the races. He could only have been lucky in his own concept of what luck is if he brought them in. So he brought them in by feeling lucky: "I just felt lucky."

Well, I'll take anyone who has succeeded in applying this principle and they will feel that same emotion, and when they feel that emotion they've set it in action. And no power's going to stop it because all things are made by Jesus Christ and Jesus Christ is our own wonderful Imagination. By him all things were made. Now he is taking our Imagination and lifting it to the level of the Creator not that we may have one little glimpse, the union is forever. When he succeeds in uniting himself with us, then a series of events unfold within us and that series ___(??), and then forever and forever you are the Lord Jesus Christ. But man has been taught to believe that Jesus Christ is some little thing on the outside of himself. No, the Word became flesh and dwelt *in us*. See it clearly, not *among* us but *in us*...not just in me, in you, but in us; therefore, it's a universal being. It's not *a* little man. It's personified as a man saying he made all things and without him was not made anything that is made. But that personification in that third person singular does not mean simply *that* little man...it's simply us. He became us and dwelt in us, full of grace and truth.

Now we go forward after that statement is made, "Yet grace and truth came through Jesus Christ"...that's the 17th verse (Jn.1). Now, going to the 18th verse, which is the prologue to the end, "No one has ever seen God." Now our three earliest manuscripts read in this manner, "No one has ever seen God. God, only begotten, in the bosom of the Father, he has made him known." Our scholars claim that that's a very odd way of translating this Greek passage, and they have come to the conclusion what they really intended because there is no article before the word "theos" which means God. So they say, "God only begotten." So this is their present translation. "No one has ever seen God; he"—no name to it—"who is in the bosom of the Father, he has made him known." It doesn't say Jesus, and it doesn't call him by any name. "He, who is in the bosom of the Father, he has made him known" (Jn.1:18).

Well, we go back to the first verse...it's already been established that the Word is Jesus Christ, one with God the Father. So the one in the bosom of the Father is *not* Jesus Christ, but he is "the only begotten." It doesn't say anything else..."the only begotten." So we start searching scripture and we can't find any other "only begotten" than we find him in the form of *David*. We find him in the 2nd Psalm and the 89th Psalm. We find him all through the Psalms as that only begotten, the only one who can reveal man to himself as God the Father. I can tell you from now 'til the ends of time that *you* are, and you won't believe me, not with that peculiar certainty, that you *are* God the Father.

You still are limited for you are still wearing the garment of flesh and you will continue to wear it until your ministry in the world is over. That ministry scholars have tried to estimate and there are a variety of estimates. They run all the way from a few months up to twelve years. No one seems to take him beyond twelve years from the time he starts with the resurrection, for this entire ministry begins with the resurrection. It does not begin with any little physical birth coming from a woman's womb; it begins with the second birth coming from the skull of a man. And then he interprets scripture based upon his own experiences and gains that certainty that *he is* the being spoken of in scripture as he traces the entire thing going from book to book.

But no scholar has taken him and his ministry beyond twelve years. A few said a few months, others said four years, others seven years, and no one has taken his ministry beyond twelve...from the time that he was born from above. So, the one who is born from above starts his ministry, and he can't stop it. Whether he has an audience as I have or whether he is head of a huge corporation and is telling it only to his intimate friends, he still cannot stop talking about it. And his ministry in the telling will not exceed twelve years so claim the scholars. I have not searched the scriptures for that aspect of it, but that is what they claim...from the moment of the resurrection to the end of his earthly days will not exceed twelve years. Be that as it may, the one who has had the second birth then must begin his ministry from the moment of the birth.

So here, we go back...in the beginning was the Word. There was a meaning behind the entire plan and that meaning, that Word, was with God and it actually *was* God. "By him all things were made and without him was not anything made that was made. He was in the world, the world was made by him, and the world knew him not." You listen to all of the wise men today, not one in maybe a hundred million will pinpoint the Creator of the things of this world as your own wonderful human Imagination. You will say John Brown did it, you will say so-and-so did it; few if any will say his Imagination did it. The Christ in him did it, for he is all Imagination. They don't think that at all. The word has been so bandied around that it has practically no meaning. "He's a man of Imagination"...you can use that flatteringly or you may use it in the most disparaging manner "that's all Imagination," the same word. So here, is it all Imagination meaning nothing? Or do you speak of it as a man of Imagination, where he really can use that power in him, but you give credit to the mask that he is wearing, this being or the being who is wearing the mask? You give it to the mask rather than the wearer which is Christ in man.

Christ in man is man's own wonderful human Imagination. That is the one that erupts within us. That is the one who comes out. That is the one who bears his name, for his name is I AM. Well, that's what the word Jesus really means. Jeshua means I AM. The word is Joshua and Joshua is simply the same form as the word Jehovah, the identical form, it is I AM. And when it happens to you, you are all alone; there's no one else because the union has been completed. He cleaves to his wife—that's you—until you become one flesh. So there's only one body, and in becoming one body, there's only been one Spirit, for his name is I AM. And when you say "I am" you don't think of a second or you'd say "we are." But you don't say "I am" and think of any other. So when you awake, you're all alone and who is awake?—I am. Who pushes it? I am pushing it. Who comes out? Well, I am coming out. The whole thing is within us; it isn't on the outside at all, the whole drama. For as Browning said, "Truth is within ourselves and it takes no rise from outward things, what ere you may believe...and instead of trying to affect some entry from without"; no, it is all coming from *within*.

So everyone here, you are blessed. The whole world is, but they don't know it. They think they must earn salvation and you don't earn it. It is grace and the grace is already within you, for Jesus Christ is within you. He died in the most literal sense of the word, completely forgetting that he is God who created the universe to actually become you that he created. And his love for you was so great he yielded himself completely and cleaved to you...and then eventually you become one. And when it is completed you awake. It's not he anymore, you the individual, I'm awakening. And I awake to find myself completely entombed. Well, that's where the Word fell, for the Word is called the seed of God, and the seed must fall into the earth and die in order to be made alive. Unless it dies it remains alone, but if it dies, it bears much fruit (Jn.12.24), and the fruit it bears is to awaken as God himself.

So, in this prologue in the gospel of John, in the first eighteen verses, if you will start with the first four and then skip, if you must, the few verses that are talking about John the Baptist which simply ties the story together. Go to the tenth verse and here you'll find "He was in the world and the world was made by him and the world knew him not." Who knows that Imagination has made the entire world? Who knows that a change in imagining tonight will change the whole vast world in which we live? Who knows that if one could now begin to imagine entirely different things concerning life instead of accepting what the so-called wise people believe it must be...but a complete radical change of imagining...his world would rearrange itself to reflect the change within him? He's in the world, the world's made by him, and the world knew him not. It doesn't know that Imagination made everything and is still sustaining it. It knew him not.

Now, the next couple of verses speak of the kind of birth of which he speaks: "Born not of blood, nor of the will of man, nor of flesh, but of God." An entirely different concept of what is going to take place in the one who actually finds him, believes in him, holds onto him, and trusts him implicitly to bring everything into the world that he wants brought in.

When you prove he does exist in you, that he does change things in your world as you change your imaginal structure then you've found him. Then you will realize that 14th verse: this one called the Word actually became flesh and now dwells in us full of grace and truth. And by this one called Jesus Christ. As the name is introduced what a shock! There is no warning to it, came suddenly, and without warning he introduces the name.

So from now on as I read the story I can't see Jesus Christ as some historical being on the outside, for he became flesh and dwelt *in me,* as he dwells in you. So from now on if anyone mentions the name, my Imagination jumps: he is calling *my* name. You speak of Jesus Christ and I don't' bend the knee like a slave before some image that one places on the screen. If you call the name Jesus Christ you are calling my name; he dwells in me. And the day came ten years ago this coming July when he *woke* in me...and he wasn't another. He so loved me his emanation, his creation, that he actually became me and took upon himself all the afflictions with which I was afflicted, every one. He was equally afflicted because he was the life of me. In him was life and that life was my light, my consciousness, my awareness. And so he is my life and it's my own wonderful human Imagination.

Now, no one could ever tell me that I am God the Father but he who was in the bosom of the Father. That 18th verse introduces a new name: "Father" comes in for the first time. And so here, a Father, and there's someone in the Father's bosom that will reveal the Father? Yes, doesn't tell you who he is. Just wait and one day he appears, and you start searching the Word of God, for his Word came out through the prophetic voice of the prophets, and here you find him. Here he is, it is *David*. Here is David who now calls you Father; you know he is your Son, he knows you are his Father, and here you are revealed as God the Father. But you have to continue telling it and perform your ministry for the allotted span whether that be a few months as some claim, four years as others claim, seven years or twelve. But you tell it for the allotted span, and then you take off the garment of flesh and you are no longer of this world. You are not of this world, you are of the world of God, for you are one with God—one body, one Spirit, one Lord, one God and Father of all.

Now, isn't that the most incredible story! Isn't that the most exciting story that man could ever hear! How could you top it? How can a man who is feeling so little, finding it difficult to pay rent, difficult to buy food, difficult to clothe himself properly, and that *he* will one day look out upon this fabulous universe not as a portion of it, a little insignificant thing called man that you couldn't see, well, just a few miles in space you couldn't recognize a man, and that he looks out on this fabulous world, where they speak of light years running into unnumbered billions of years, and he created it? Yes! That's the incredible story. Yet the Creator of it all so loved him, man, that he actually became man, and then suddenly with man transformed him. And when man reached his destination then his play that was contained within him erupts within man and man knows who he is. He is God the Creator, God the Father. And that is true of everyone in the world.

But I must warn you, although I am convinced that not one will fail, that's my deep inner conviction, there is a warning given in so many passages in scripture that one must be watchful, for there's always a possibility of turning back, sliding back. But I can't see any warning where it's ultimate failure. It could only be a turning away from it and refusing to accept this incredible story. And so our priests will accept it as something on the outside, Jesus as a savior. That's *not* it. He is the Word of God, the eternal Word of God, which actually took upon himself our garment of flesh and blood: the Word became flesh and then dwelt in us, full of grace and truth. Even though he dwells in us he is abiding forever and will continue in the affliction even when we turn back. But because he does *abide* in us, I can't conceive of the Word not fulfilling its purpose as we are told in Isaiah, that "My word shall not return unto me empty. It must accomplish that which I purposed and prosper in the thing for which I sent it" (Is.55:11). So the Word being in us and the Word is God himself, he can't fail in his purpose. But if I would be free then I must be free also to turn back, to slide back, or to turn aside. Nevertheless, ultimately with all of his sufferings and his afflictions he will bring us toward his predetermined purpose which is to make us himself. So, that no one eventually can fail, they just can't fail.

But I cannot conceive of anything that man could sit down to imagine…you take a good mystery story and they're fascinating, and you take the most marvelous play in the world, how could it compare to this concept? That warring nations, families that fight over a dead body, a little estate that is left, and that he could so love this that he actually became it, and so became it that they don't even know that he actually exists? That he is in the world, the world is made by him, and the world knew him not? That a man who walks the street and is so unaware that he is not conscious of the fact that what he is now encountering he once imagined? That he is totally unaware that he is encountering his own harvest? He can't recognize his own harvest and denies completely that he had anything to do with it?

Now, how many who saw that race on Saturday actually heard the words of that little fellow? Well, how many are interested in sports to the point of reading that page? I read it thoroughly every morning. Well, when I saw this review of the interview with the little Angel Cordova I read it from beginning to end, and he stressed over and over "You have to feel lucky." So here, I go back now to two ladies who came to my meetings, one here on the West Coast and one in New York...both were behind the eight-ball. They didn't have a nickel, both were advanced in years, no one to turn to, and all I asked them to do was to assume the feeling of the wish fulfilled. One said in her letter to me, "I simply wondered what would the feeling be like. Then I felt as I would expect to feel after these things should be." And then in the not distant future, one that she knew intimately, but twenty-odd years ago, meeting a mutual friend who inquired about her and finding that she was penniless then responded. He had made all the money in the Second World War and set up a trust fund for her to give her more than she needed. A new car every year, her rent paid, clothing, entertainment, all that she needs to live graciously, not penuriously but graciously without getting out of bed to go to work. And by her own letter she was already fifty-six years of age, and this came out of the blue on the heels of feeling what it would be like if she had all that it would take. So in her own words, "I felt as I would expect to feel after these things should be."

Now, back East I told that story. She had the book and she read it over and over, but she'd never seen it. You can read something over and over and still not see it. So she read it and I called her attention to that one story which I thought would fit her. She began to apply it and in the not distant future, in the matter of one week, she comes up with the first $600 a month, and then two years later when she discovered it was so easy doing it, "Why don't I try it again?" She tried it again with another $600 added to the first six, which means $1200 a month. She can't spend that, so the money is now invested and re-invested. Today, it must be around $1600 a month that she has coming in. She is a single lady in her seventies living modestly. I know her place. And so, it happened in her case. What did she do? She used her Imagination.

Well, if all things are created by Jesus Christ and without him there's not a thing made that is made, good, bad or indifferent..."I kill, I make alive, I wound, I heal...I do all these things" (Deut.32:39). Who?—Jesus Christ. "Oh, Jesus Christ couldn't do that, he couldn't kill, he couldn't wound," well, then there's another Creator. If he does all things *but* what you call the evil then he is not altogether the Creator. If he is absolute in his creation, he has to create *everything* in this world. So we are told in the 32nd of Deuteronomy, "I kill, I make alive; I wound, I heal; and none can deliver out of my hand" (32:39). This is the Lord speaking, his name is the Lord and he is the I AM. Who else could kill if that is a creative act but the Creator? Who could heal but the Creator? Who else could wound but the Creator?

So she began to apply it. Now today her little world is inundated with her $1600, without getting out of bed, and in her working days never earned more than seventy-five dollars a week, and as a single lady that was before taxes. Today, without working an income of $1600 a month...all by believing in the Lord Jesus Christ but not as she was trained to believe in him. You can go out and pray to him on a wall forever. He's just as dead there as any other place if he's on the outside. You pray to something on the wall that's something that is dead. Nothing on the outside, it's all within. He became flesh: the Word became flesh and dwelt in us. Well, if the Word became flesh and I'm flesh and blood and he dwells in me, I've got to find where he is. I must find who he is and how to reach him. Well then, I find him: he is my Imagination.

But I'm going to test it first before I go all out and say that he is. So I imagine a certain state. They say you can't get out of the island. Can't get out of the island? Well, all things are possible to Christ and he's in me, for he became flesh and dwells in me. Well now, I will do exactly what he told me to do: believe that you have it. Well, if I believe that I have it I'd walk up the gangplank, wouldn't I? So I walk up the gangplank. Then they called me, I didn't call them, and I sailed just as I imagined that I would sail. Well, if he makes all things then I've found him, found exactly who he is, and he is my own wonderful human Imagination.

Now go and tell it, Neville, tell it to the whole vast world. You will not get acceptance, because they still want to believe in a little Jesus Christ on the outside and pray to him. And so when this little picture is worn out tear it up and get another one just like it. I know in Vaudeville days this little girl, sweet little girl, had a nice little act, and she had this little icon, a picture which she called Jesus. Well, she used to wear very thick greasepaint, her lipstick, and she would kiss it three, four times a day as she would go onto the place for good luck. You couldn't see the face after awhile it was filled with lipstick. That was her little Jesus Christ and she really believed that *that* was Jesus Christ. Well, she's not alone; multiply her by hundreds of millions of people in the world. They have an external Christ and they can't believe the words.

You commit to memory those eighteen verses, the prologue. A prologue is a preface to a play. For the 19th verse on to the end of the 20th chapter you'll find the narrative that is the play. The 21st chapter is an epilogue. But take the prologue, the first eighteen verses, and everything is woven into that preface that you are going to find in the dialogue. It's going to take place from the 19th on. But the whole thing is there and you find out who he is, for suddenly it's slipped into the narrative, unannounced, unexpected and the name is Jesus Christ. He is the Word that was full of grace and truth, and the Word was God, and God then is in me and dwells in me full of grace and truth.

So I don't have to seek truth on the outside or seek grace on the outside. Grace comes from within: suddenly he erupts and we are one, we aren't two. And you're looking out on a whole fabulous world. You can't see it through this little garment. But you know that that which happened in you, which was unbelievable, the promise that when you finally take this off, you will realize that you are the Creator of it all, for he gave you himself. You aren't going to share it with him; he actually became you as told us in the story of the great Melchizedek. And here, he has no father, no mother, no beginning, no end…and in the end we all become members of the Order of Melchizedek who had no father, no mother, no beginning, and no ending. That's the end of everyone when he finally takes off the garment. And the whole vast theater, infinite universe, you the seeming little insignificant thing that was created is the Creator of it all.

Now, this is really incredible. I read here recently…and I've always admired and still do admire the great Einstein…but he said, "To me survival of the disintegration of the brain is unthinkable. I can't conceive of survival. I rejoice in discovering a few of the unalterable laws and the uniformity of the laws of whomever it is that we call the Lord. But that man should survive the disintegration of the brain to me is unthinkable." So, if a man as wonderful as Einstein feels the story of the gospels is incredible and unthinkable then condemn no one, because, you can't deny the greatness of the man. You couldn't deny how gentle the man is. He was tender, he was kind, he was considerate of those who knew him, because I know a few who were intimate with him, and they said the man was simply tender as a lamb, a gentle, tender, wonderful man. But in spite of that gentility he was quite satisfied to simply revel in the uniformity of the laws of nature whoever was behind it if there was one.

But I tell you there is one behind it and he so loves you he became you. And the day is coming that you will know that *you are he*. You are not the created that day; you are the Creator. You are not the made; the Maker was your husband and he left all and became you. So whether you are male or female don't be embarrassed to feel yourself the emanation of- the Lord yet his wife 'til the sleep of death is past.

Now let us go into the Silence.

* * *

THE TWO SIDES OF THIS TEACHING

3/28/69

Tonight we'll take the two sides of this teaching—that which is on this level and that which applies to the real purpose for being. On this level we see things happen like wars, revolutions, convulsions, and peace. No matter what happens in the world I say all things spring from other than the causes attributed to the real cause. War comes into being and we are told in the press, told on radio, told on TV, told all over the reason for the war, and that we do not really know, we cannot see the hidden cause. Yet the hidden cause is right here in the Imagination of man. So all things spring not from the *ostensible* causes to which they are attributed even though they seem quite adequate.

In the current issue of the *Atlantic Monthly*, which is April, the former Commandant of the Marine Corps David M. Shoup goes all out and makes this bold, bold claim. Now bear in mind his position…he was the Commandant of the Marine Corps, and he claims that there is an ambitious elite of high-ranking officers who are turning our country into a militaristic and aggressive nation. They prefer war to peace…only through war can they receive promotion and glory and all the distinctions that they want and to them serving in a peacetime Army is a dull, frustrating prospect. They plot and plan war to test their theories and their new instruments and they dream of war and it's only war to them. He claims that is taking place in this elite, high-ranking officer corps in our country. Now, this is General David M. Shoup who is making this claim. He said, "Our civilians cannot understand it and cannot even believe that such men trained in our land to protect us would conceive of this and rush us into war for their own ambitions, glory and prestige. Nevertheless, that is taking place in our land." You read it in the current issue of *Atlantic Monthly*, the April issue. There was a little summary of it in yesterday's *L. A. Times*. You might have read that.

Where is this hidden state? The hidden state is in the Imagination of man. You can use it infernally, as they are, or you can use it as you should, towards the kingdom of heaven. You can sit down here and bring before your mind's eye an individual who needs help, and represent that one to yourself as though they were all that you would like them to be and persuade yourself of the reality of that imaginal act, and then drop it, and they will conform to what you have done. Or you could take them into your mind's eye and make a mess of them and they will conform to that. So you can use this creative power which is Christ in you infernally or in the most wonderful blessing way. It's entirely up to you.

Well, when you hear these words coming from a man who was Commandant—you can't go any higher in the Marine Corps—and here he was the General of all the Marines, this able body, and he tells us that today we have an ambitious elite of high-ranking officers preferring war to peace so that they may receive glory and prestige and promotion. And they plot and plan war, only war, for to them living in a peacetime state, performing their duty in peacetime is dull and frustrating and the most horrible prospect. He claims that our involvement in Viet Nam is the result of their ambitions. He goes right out and states it. You and I are burdened with this enormous tax to continue this effort and here a small group is performing it.

Well, the poets have said this throughout the years, for the poets seem to be so far ahead, the poets and the prophets, for both seem to be inspired by the same voice. Yeats said, "I will never be certain that it was not some woman treading in the winepress who started that subtle change in men's minds, or that the passion for which so many countries have been put to the sword did not begin in the mind of some shepherd boy, lighting up his eyes for a moment before it ran upon its way." Who knows who is treading the winepress this night? What person in solitary confinement is not using this *only* power in the world, which is Imagination, infernally or in a state of blessing? I ask you to use it in a state of blessing for numberless reasons, for there is nothing in the world but yourself pushed out. And I know from my own experience that a man imagining intensely with feeling can influence myriads, and act through many men and speak through many voices. A single man unknown to the world can influence myriads and really act through unnumbered men in the world, as this little group is acting for their own little promotion and what they call glory. The day will come when all the thing is over. Those who are completely be-medaled like Stalin was and Hitler had no more room left for the medals he gave himself. You will find the costumes worn by murderers the most ludicrous costumes ever worn by

God. God wears it yes; but here was a complete misunderstanding of the power of God, the power of Imagination.

So I ask every one here who hears me to believe it, for I am speaking from a level of having awakened from the dream of life. The entire story as told in scripture I have experienced and I know it is a true story from beginning to end. Everything said in the gospels is the pattern which one day must be repeated in everyone in the world. For every child born of woman has behind it and supporting it an ancestral self, a heavenly being... the one who said in scripture, "I will never forsake you, never in eternity." For, the one born of woman is the emanation of that ancestral self who is the Son of God. And as we are told in scripture he has set bounds to the peoples of the world according to the number of the sons of God (Deut.32:8). So, behind everyone that is born there is that son of God, the immortal you, that ancestral you. He will never forsake you, not in eternity.

So remember how *precious* you are in his eyes. And he is the power of powers. Don't misuse the power; use it only in love. No matter who you meet in this world, regardless of the pigment of skin, regardless of the nation behind him, or the so-called sex, remember behind that one is a brother of yours who is immortal as you are, an ancestral being, who has really no beginning, no end. And that one is taking him through the necessary experiences to make him one with himself, and eventually all return to that one.

Now here, we are told in scripture he turned to his disciples and he said, "There are some standing here who will not taste of death before they see the kingdom of God" (Luke9:27). Scholars claim the prophecy failed for they died and they did not see the kingdom of God. That is because they do not know what the kingdom of God is. Are we not told in the 17th of Luke "The kingdom of heaven is within you" (17:21). Who would see your entry into the kingdom of heaven but you? If you told them, it is not what they expect so they would deny it and they claim that completely. So they claim that they did not enter; yet the promise is made and the words of God will not be broken. They cannot be broken: "There are some standing here who will not taste of death before they see the kingdom of God."

Well, to see the kingdom of God and to enter the kingdom of God is the same thing. You see it, you enter it, but it's all within you. Well, how do I enter it? When the curtain is split, and then looking at the base of that split curtain, which is my body, I see the blood of my ancestral being who died for me, who became as I am. And I see that blood in which there is life, I fuse with it, and then like a bolt of fire, spiral fire, I enter heaven. For, the drama began in the holy sepulchre which is my skull, and there it ends. So I go up like a fiery serpent into my skull, and when I enter, it reverberates like thunder, as we are told in the 11th of Matthew: "The violent take it by force" (11:12).

Well, the word translated violent or violence simply means "life." It means "to press oneself into, to find a place within" but it means "life," for there is life in that blood. For, "life is in the blood" and that was the blood of God himself. Contemplating it I fuse with it. Then at that moment when I became it, I had life in myself. So, "As the Father has life in himself, he has granted the son also"…at that moment I was granted the right to have life in myself and to become one with my Father who emanated me, that ancestral being that I now am. And then you weave yourself like a spiral fire into the very holy sepulchre which began the entire drama.

So here, the statement is true "There are some standing here who will not taste of death before they see the kingdom of God," and that is true. But who is going to know it?—only the one who experienced it. And it goes on and on and on forever. If you are looking for a kingdom on the outside, you will never find the kingdom, for you are told "The kingdom of God is within you" (Luke17:21). If it is within me, how could I enter it on the outside? How could I ever enter into the kingdom of heaven other than entering it from within myself? And you do. Matthew speaks of this entrance as the Son of man entering it in the 16th chapter. They speak of this in the 9th chapter of Mark and the 9th of Luke, and they speak of it as the kingdom of God.

On the heels of this he then turns and picks three, Peter, John and James, and he takes them into a high mountain and his countenance is completely altered before them. Now you think that that is on the outside. No it's not on the outside; this is also on the inside. But the evangelist took this appearance of resurrection and then went back and incorporated it into what is known. If you read the story on the outside, as Jesus' external ministry…which is not at all as this is external…so I am telling you what has happened *within* me…so this is external imagery. So they bring it back and tell it as though something took place here…where I took three people on the outside…and you don't do it that way.

Now, a lady wrote me that she found herself in a cave, and in that cave she saw three men etched in gold, and a woman holding an infant in her arms, and she is the observer of the entire thing. She is in a cave with one exit, but three men etched in gold and a woman holding an infant in her arms. She can't be far from the experience as this is an adumbration, a perfect adumbration. The first appearance of the three we find in Genesis when Abraham sat in the door of the tent in the heat of the day, and three men suddenly appeared before him. Then we find in Peter's 2nd letter, the first chapter, he remembered when three men were eye-witnesses to his

The Return of Glory

majesty. Then he goes back to remember when Peter, James and John were called to witness to the majesty of the one that is about to be born. Always the three!

So she now finds herself in a cave. Well, the cave is the holy sepulchre; it's your own skull where the entire drama began and where it comes to its climax and fulfillment. She sees now the three. She called them. She sees the woman with the child—that is only a *sign* of what is about to take place in her, her birth. But there must be these witnesses to her birth and there will be, for here comes first, she will wake within that drama and then as she wakes she will come out and the three will witness *her* birth, and the birth will be simply God. She, the emanation of her ancestral being, became awake; which is nothing more than the return now to her ancestral being which enhances that eternal Son of God. She is one with her ancestral being, but while in this world of Caesar we seem to be detached from it and lost.

So here, I say to every one of you, take this wonderful power that is yours, your own wonderful human Imagination and use it lovingly on behalf of everyone in the world. What does it matter if these officers who are dreaming tonight of war and still more war? We have enough today to kill the entire world and yet they put burdens upon our shoulders to make more…the overkill they call it…that they may get a little medal, that they may be promoted from their present state, maybe a captain to a general, and maybe a five-star general, maybe they'll become president. So what! And then be buried in some wonderful place where others will come and see where, and then two generations from now no one will know that they ever existed. Go through the cemeteries of the world and see those who thought themselves so great and no one recalls who they were. You must be an historian or be interested in such things in this world to recall these names that in their own day thought themselves so important.

So, as it is said, what does it matter if you owned the world and lost your life? For the word spoken now as violence means "life" and it means "power." You come into a power unknown by mortal man. And so all the atom bombs and the hydrogen bombs in the world will mean nothing compared to the power that you fall heir to. Can you imagine a power that can look out upon a world and still it? Of course, you will never have this power were you not guided by love. Suppose you had that power and you were not restrained by love. You could take a whole nation, still it, and face it toward the ocean, march it into the ocean and drown it. You could…but you will know power only to the extent that you have *love*. I tell you from experience. When I was taken into the divine society, it was love that first embraced me, then it was power that sent me, but love first embraced me. No power in this world could I ever exercise unless it was conditioned by love, for love first embraced me. For, just imagine such power, such almightiness not conditioned by love. So, all the power known to man on earth is as *nothing* compared to that power. Just imagine you can stop any being in the world, stop him in his tracks, and turn him around completely in a different direction, and he doesn't even know there has been a change within him. He can't complete his intension, because you've changed it having that power.

As you are told in that greatest of all dramas which we will re-enact in a week: "Do you not know that I have power to crucify you and power to set you free?" and he answered, "You have no power over me were it not given you from above" (Jn.19:10)...no power. Just imagine having that power from above! But he came to play a part and play it completely from beginning to end and re-enact the entire drama for man. Because everyone is going to re-enact the entire story of Jesus Christ and re-enact it within himself; and all you can do is tell it, because it takes place in heaven and heaven is within you (Luke17:21). Those who hear it either believe it or disbelieve it, and you have not a power to persuade them otherwise. They'll either believe it or disbelieve it.

But those who do not believe in it, they sit in judgment and here they are dreaming war as this man Shoup said. Read it...if you haven't the story it's available...it's the current issue. And you stand there as you read the six pages and you wonder what on earth is taking place? If a layman wrote it, all well and good; but this is not a layman, this is General David M. Shoup, Commandant of the Marine Corps. They can't do a thing now, because he has resigned his post and he is now retired; and the money that he is bringing in today from his position as the highest general in the Corps must keep on coming. They can't take it from him, so now he is free to tell exactly what he observed...that this *ambitious* elite of high-ranking officers in our country preferring war to peace is leading our country into a country of aggression and a militaristic state for their personal ambitions of promotion, glory and prestige. The very thought of performing their duty in peacetime to them is the most frustrating, dull and offensive thing imaginable. Now, he said, "Civilians can't understand it, because we trust these men to protect us having paid them their salaries, paid them everything, and all that's done to them. Who pays it but the civilian who works? For the country has no money...it comes out of the pockets of the workers, so everything they get comes out of those who work. And we think, well now, they're going to protect us, that's the purpose of training them...and that's not their purpose at all. Their purpose is to shine and to use us as pawns, and to become more and more glorious in their own little mind's eye.

But I tell you, you know the truth now. Your ancestral being, called the Son of God, actually shed his blood for you. I know it from my own experience. For, when this was torn in two from top to bottom and I saw that, I knew it to be the blood of God. Well, that God was my own wonderful ancestral self…an extension of that self that I am, not another. That would be a greater creative power in the world. I know from experience that the fairest body that he ever wore was the body of love; and I wore it with him when he embraced me and will return to that and wear that forever and forever, the body of love. We will not be two. I am simply an extension of himself and then brought back. And then we are more glorious yet one, more luminous, more translucent, more creative because we have a greater creative power by reason of this extension of himself where I play the part in the world. And while I am still with you, to tell you what you ought to do— to use your Imagination lovingly forever and forever on behalf of everyone in the world, and believe in the reality of your imaginal acts.

If there is one here tonight for the first time, may I tell you how it works. If you desire this night to change a friend who, say, is unemployed and you would like him to be gainfully employed, represent him to yourself in your mind's eye as one who *is* gainfully employed. Then listen carefully as though you heard his voice. Become completely concentrated on the voice you know to be his voice. You know his hand clasp, well, use that too. You know what he looks like, well, use that sense too. And then every sense that you can possibly bring to bear upon this imaginal scene you bring it to bear upon it, and re-enact a scene which would *imply* the fulfillment of your desire for him. When you feel the thrill, that imaginal thrill, that intense thrill, drop it. Just drop it completely and let that seed…as told in scripture… the kingdom of heaven is like a little seed and it grows, like a mustard seed. Don't pick it up, just leave it. It will grow and bloom and he will actually conform to what you imagined him to be. Try it! Before you judge it, just try it and you will see that it works.

And when it works you will know what this creative power in you truly is. It's called in scripture Jesus Christ. In the first chapter of Paul's first letter to the Corinthian, "Christ is the power of God and the wisdom of God" (1:24). Well now, you prove it by imagining, and you prove that you did create this change in his life, then you have proven the existence of Christ. Well, that is Christ in you, your own wonderful eternal being and he will never leave you and he will never forsake you. That's what we are told in the 13th chapter of Hebrews, "Never will I leave you, never will I forsake you" (13:5). And so, there is that in you no matter what happens to you. If someone imagines the unlovely and you are swept into that state and go through hell, there is still that in you which will not leave you and will not forsake you.

If you know this principle, you can always detach yourself from that and get out of it. I was pulled into it and I got out of it. Without shooting one bullet, without doing anything, I got out of it. Well, the same thing that he writes today in the April issue could have been written in the first day of time, for the first great frightful act is Cain slew Abel. He slew his own brother. So the same thing is taking place over and over. Well, when man knows that he need not be pulled into that whirling, or call it by any other name, he can get out of it and detach himself from it by simply ignoring the laws of the moment as I did. They said "You can't get out." Alright, I can't get out. And so I dared to assume that I was out and then I mentally acted as I would act were I out and persisted in this state for nine days. On the ninth day, the same one who denied me my freedom granted me my freedom, and I was simply sent out honorably discharged. So no matter how you are pulled into it, this Charybdis, this whirling thing that pulls all things into it, you can get out of it.

So if today you find yourself in any state...there are people planning a Depression, do you know that? For personal gain! There are those who will sell short for personal gain. All kinds of things for one simple little moment in time, a little glory, that they may be put into the papers as a billionaire. They gloat over the thought that they are now a billionaire...and their name is called tonight and they leave it behind to those who don't care whether they lived or not. Their nieces and nephews and all the others will simply spend it for them, and they will simply still be working over some other great fortune. They move into another world just like this. So when you are told that there are some standing here who will not taste of death, may I tell you, no man leaves this earth, no man—by man I mean generic man—'til he awakens, because earth does not terminate at the point where my senses cease to register it. You drop tonight and you are still on this earth, in a body just like yours but young, vital, wonderful, everything that you would want as a young body. But the environment in which you find yourself is not that same place with the billion behind you. You may drop in this world tonight only one billion, to find yourself best qualified to shine shoes tomorrow in order to earn a living. It may be your lot tomorrow based upon your lot today for your ancestral being in you knows best what it will take to weave you into the likeness of himself, for you must be perfect as he is perfect. You will not be brought to an end until you actually can be superimposed upon his image and fit it. Then you are one, the two are one.

So, if I think...not knowing there must come an end in this little journey...that I will pile it up and pile it up to find that as I pile it up and multiply it, at the very end it totals the same that it was before. And I depart to find myself in a little environment, without loss of identity, so that no one actually leaves this earth *'til* he awakens. When he awakens he departs from this age which is in earth... for this earth stretches for a length of time long beyond the threescore and ten...just like this, terrestrial, with all the struggles we have here; we marry, we die, we labor, just like we do here. We go from one little section of time to a section of time to a section of time until we are in the eyes of our ancestral self as he is. And when we are we awake.

So here, the statement is true: "There are some standing here who will not taste of death until they see the kingdom of heaven." The apostles who were called did not taste of death. Not a power in the world could have snapped them out in that section of time until they actually went up that spiral roadway into the sepulchre where they began. So every one of them actually did, but scholars don't know that so they say the prophecy failed. The prophecy did not fail, because the kingdom of heaven is not on the outside that mortal eye can see it. The kingdom of heaven is within and if it is within I enter it from within. And when you are told that they pressed their way into it violently, I know that from experience. When I went up with such force I can't tell you the pressing into this area of my head. If now the whole head represents the kingdom of heaven, that's the area where I am pressed in...a little bit left of center...right here. I tried my very best to go beyond it. But you are told in the definition given to us in the Concordance "pressing oneself into." And it's life itself. It is so crowded. You press yourself right into it as the living jewel, and when you enter it is with a force unknown to man. It has to be a force of that power to get in, so we are told, "The violent take it by force." Read it in the 11th chapter of the Book of Matthew: "The kingdom of heaven is taken by violence and the violent take it by force" (11:12).

The old age is behind us, which is the law and the prophets up until John the Baptist. They did violence to their own appetites hoping to get in. You don't get in that way. You live a normal life in this world. Whatever your normal, natural outlets live a normal life. Make no violence against this body of yours, whether it be in diet or the suppressing of the normal urges of life. That will not get you in. When you are one with your eternal self so that you can be superimposed upon him and the same image, *then* you will find yourself split in two and the life of that being that kept you alive here as something on the outside you absorb it. Like a sponge absorbing it you become one with it, and now there's life in *you*; and then you return and return with violence, and the whole thing reverberates just like thunder.

But on the side of Caesar, know that there are people in this world who dream violence and plot violence. You don't try to counter them. You plot and plan things of love, things of affection, and they'll pass by and they will not be able to draw you into their little circle. Oh, they'll draw many because living as they do, plotting all day long through their ambitions to be glorified by men and to have some great distinction in the world. They even plot their funerals where they'll be in some little caisson pulling into Arlington. To them that is a great accomplishment. See, they have nothing in their mind's eye beyond this little section of time.

I tell you, you are an eternal being, you are immortal. Before the world was, you were. You were the Son of God long, long before the very universe came into being, and it was brought in as a theater for this great experiment. Then you *radiated* yourself; you are a ray of the being that you really are one with the radiating being. And he radiates it and he does not in eternity forsake you…it's himself. He puts you through all the paces and fashions you into his own likeness. And then he receives unto himself all the experiences through which you have passed; and he is enhanced and glorified by these experiences. Oh, he is afflicted as you are afflicted, he suffers as you suffer, for then you come back and you are one. For, the being radiating is one with the ray that came out.

So here tonight, you take it seriously, and take a friend…maybe yourself for that matter…but take a friend who is in want and then represent him to yourself as one that you would like to see him express in this world. Persuade yourself that what you have imagined is true, believe in the reality of your imaginal act, and see him conform to it. He will…on this level he will.

The day will come the thought will be believed and that's when you return to your ancestral self…no time between the imaginal act and the fact. That I know from experience. There are levels: a level here, then a dream level, and then a level that is difficult to describe, and then a level where you are completely awake, which I call "Spirit waking" where really the thought is the fact.

But you come to these barriers, and this is the lowest barrier, where that ray is completely concentrated and limited into these little garments of flesh. And here we became slaves; we are slaves to this mortal body. I must serve it morning, noon and night—feed it, clothe it, shelter it. And when I feed it I must assimilate what I give it and what I can't assimilate I must eliminate. I must take care of these bodies. That is the slave. So every child born of woman is a slave, because he is a slave by reason of the *body* that he wears. And there is no slave in the world comparable to the slave in the body. So, if tonight I was a slave and someone held me as a slave and fed me and clothed me and did all these things, I would be called by the world his slave; yet he is as much the slave as I am because he, too, is slave to his body. And if he had a million like me, he cannot command us to perform the functions of his body; he has to perform them all for himself. He has to eat, assimilate and eliminate, and that is the greatest of all slavery in the world. No one can do it for him, no matter what power he has in the world. So everyone who comes into this world becomes a slave to the body that he wears. And you're told in Philippians (2:7-8), he emptied himself of all that was his and became obedient unto death, even death upon the cross. When he came in he found himself a slave and was born in the likeness of man…that was the slave. He found himself born in the likeness of man and that was his slavery.

So I can't conceive of any slavery in the world comparable to the slavery of the body. Just imagine, you have to wash it, shave it, bathe it, and do everything for it. And then it wears out and you've got to go and get a little help. You go and get glasses, you go to the dentist, and you get false teeth; and then an organ wears out and you go to a surgeon who cuts out that one and puts in another, and then you go…well, all these things…you patch it up from the beginning to the end, and still you are a slave of it up to the very end. Do you know of any greater form of slavery in the world? So luckily when we are in our teens and in our twenties we never think that it will ever get old, that it will ever wear out, and we brag and brag of our strength. Then all you have to do is to wait and watch him when he turns the little corner of time, and he may for a little while hide his weaknesses, but they become so obvious in time. Then he gets weaker and weaker, and the little body simply wears out, and he is still a slave 'til the very end. Well, I can't conceive of any grater slavery.

So, you try living this noble life, for I tell you, you are immortal. You cannot in eternity die, for he who radiated you will never in eternity forsake you. He couldn't, for you and he are one. And when you return from the journey, you are one with the one who radiated you; and you were that being before he radiated you.

Now let us go into the Silence.

*   *   *

Now, are there any questions, please? None? Well, if there aren't any… and there should be on a night like this. Nevertheless, remember what I have told you and that I am speaking from experience: you are immortal. You didn't begin in the womb of your mother and you will not end in this little state called the grave. You came out from your ancestral self and he is the Son of God, and all the sons of God together form God. We are the gods who came down (Acts14:11) and we are playing our parts, and we are the gods who will return, and all will form the one God. For, the one became many and then the many will return to the one. But while we are here, knowing that everyone can misuse this creative power, let them misuse it, but do not allow yourself to be pulled within that circle.

And just imagine that here a man who certainly should know what he is talking about comes out in public print and makes this statement. For, if I wrote it you could say I'm prejudiced, but not a man who is the highest that one could go in the Marine Corps, who after a whole career rising to the highest, the Commandant, to make that statement, and he knows whereof he speaks, that these men plot and plan, preferring war to peace for their own ambition which is to have glory and prestige and promotion in this world of ours, using unnumbered men, slaughter them if necessary, while they get the glory. And it doesn't phase them at all. That's what Gen. David M. Shoup said in the current issue of *Atlantic Monthly*. It would be a very good thing to read, but you don't have to...I've given you the highlights.

Good night.

OUR RELIGION OF EASTER

3/31/69

This is the great concentrated week of the Jewish-Christian faith. They really are one, for Christianity is simply the fulfillment of Judaism. It's not a new religion it's simply the fulfillment of all that was said in the Old Testament. So we'll take just a section tonight, because here this week we have Passover, we have the triumphal march into Jerusalem, then the trial, the condemnation, crucifixion, the burial, and resurrection…all in this one concentrated period.

Let us take it now through the eyes of one who has experienced it, but not as tradition has it. So we'll turn to the 18th chapter of the Book of John and here is a discussion between Pilate and Jesus. Pilate said to him, "What is truth?" There was no response. And then Pilate went out and said, "I find nothing in this man worthy of condemnation." But here he makes the claim, "I came only for one purpose, to bear witness to the truth. Now, he had already claimed "I am the truth" and then he claimed "Thy Word is true." It takes now the *living* Word to interpret the written Word, for no one looking at the written Word understood it. As we are told in the 1st letter of Peter, the very first chapter: "The prophets who prophesied of the grace that was to be yours searched and inquired concerning this salvation; they inquired what person or time was indicated by the Spirit of Christ *within* them when predicting the suffering of Christ and the subsequent glory. It was revealed to them that they were serving not themselves but you" (1:10-12). The time had not yet come. They were doing a work the full import of which was hidden from them. They searched and searched, but they could not understand that which they wrote. For they heard it…they were conditioned to hear and quite often to see, but more so to hear the Word of God and then to write down what they heard. As we are told in the Book of Daniel, he said, "I heard it, but I did not understand it" and then he was told to seal it until the time. "The time is not now...seal it until that time" (12:4,9).

Then comes the living Word embodied in flesh, and the Word unfolds *within* man, and that man now understands the written Word. He interpreted as it was never seen before. No one suspected this is what it meant. And he came and he interpreted to them that which they had *misinterpreted* through the centuries. And even after having interpreted it, we still today misinterpret it. There are hundreds of millions who will go to church this week—Good Friday for three hours and then Sunday for he is risen—and we'll have this pageant all over the Christian world...and they do not know the Word. When one comes who is also sent and he tells it, you will find a small, little group who will accept it, and from that group even a smaller still who will understand it to the point of complete acceptance.

I tell you it is completely misunderstood. To understand the written Word one must first be called, and then after he is called he is incorporated into the body of the risen Lord, which is love, all love. And then he is whirled back into this world of death...this is the world of death...to await that moment in time when it unfolds within him. And he is as surprised as anyone could be in this world. Then he goes out to tell what happened to him and those who have the crowds who are telling it cannot believe it... it's not what they were taught. And he *knows,* not as others do, for when he becomes the witness he cannot say "I think" or "I believe." His must be an assured "I know"...not by belief but by experience. And so we speak of the great creed, "I believe" they start off. Well, "I believe" is marvelous, but can you say "I know, I know from experience"?

I recall many years ago in New York City I came from a rehearsal—I was a dancer then—I got into a cab and headed towards my hotel. And I slammed the door...no harder than I normally do when I get into any car, and when I got to the hotel the driver asked me to pay for the broken glass. Well, I know I had not broken any glass. I suspected that maybe he had been using that little gimmick all through the day with every fare...that he had to collect from them the eight dollars for a broken glass. So I didn't pay him. I paid exactly what the meter read plus a very generous tip. Then I went to my room and in a little while the phone rang and the operator said, "There's a policeman in the lobby and he wants to see you." "I'll be right down." So I came on down and he said to me, "This cab driver tells me that you broke the glass on his door." I said, "I did not." Well, he said, "You must go with me to the night magistrate." This was now around the dinner hour, so we went over to the magistrate. He began to claim I had broken the glass and I said to the magistrate that I did not break the glass. Then he said to the cab driver, "Are you sure he broke it?" and he said, "I think he did." That was all that the judge wanted to know. "You think or you believe he did, but you don't *know*. Case dismissed." I became a very close friend of that cop for years until he departed this world.

So, one must have an assured "I know" and you can't have it unless you have experienced it. So I came here tonight saying I *know* this mystery and it's not as it will be re-enacted this coming week in all the Christian churches of the world. Christ *in us* is the hope of glory. That living Word one day will…and you cannot plan it, no one will know, it's not for us to know the day, the time, the season that the Father has already hidden within us. It will come so suddenly upon you, and then that living Word begins like a tree to put out its blossoms, its fruit, its flowers, and they're all related to the Old Testament, for, the only scriptures that the Christians had was the Old Testament. That was their only Bible. They were called "the people of the way." Who do you think wrote the New Testament? They were all Jews…even the unknown ones called Matthew, Mark, Luke and John were Jews. We know by the confession of Paul that he was a Jew, and he gave us thirteen letters forming the bulk of the New Testament. Well, maybe Luke-Acts would be a little bit longer…but here are these thirteen letters and they came first. He said, "I am a Jew, a child of Abraham of the tribe of Benjamin." And he never denied it. He laid the foundation of the Christian faith. And man forgets it. He thinks they are two religions; they aren't two, it's one. The foundation is Judaism; its fulfillment is Christianity like the flowers appearing on the tree or the fruit appearing on the tree.

I tell you this is the greatest of all stories that could ever be told. The crucifixion has *already* taken place, and I'll tell you from my own experience that it was not a painful thing, it was the most ecstatic thing that one could ever experience. The six points are the hands, the feet, the head and the side, the right side, and they are whirling vortices that nail you to your body. Nailed who? The Word of God…and the Word *is* God, don't forget that. "In the beginning was the Word and the Word was with God and the Word *was* God." There is meaning in that Word, for the word logos means "meaning." There is a plan, there is a purpose in the entire drama, and this drama took place before that the world was. It's not some little emergency thinking on the part of God; before that the world was he chose us in him before the foundation of the world. And one man carrying all—we were all crucified with Christ and Christ is in us, crucified on the only cross in this world, which is this body, your body. This is the cross that he bears. This he became a slave to, a slave to this body, and he will wear it until he awakes. For death does not stop the wearing of this cross. I can take this body tonight and cremate it, and this body cremated and therefore gone from mortal eye, hasn't gone. It is restored and the wearer continues to wear it at a point in time, much younger than he is now. But only in my own particular case I will not wear it any longer, for the Word has erupted in me and the story as told in scripture is true from beginning to end.

But everyone in whom it has not yet erupted will find himself when he is called dead, not dead but restored to life. If our late President Eisenhower has not had the Word unfold within him, no matter what eulogy you have heard, no matter what they will do and build all the things around him, he is already restored to life, a young man, twenty years of age, in a world terrestrial just like this, in an environment best qualified, best suited to continue the work that was started in him by the son of God who is his ancestral self. And when I say son of God, I mean his true being called in scripture sons of God. No child is born in this world who does not have a son of God who is his ancestral self supporting him and dreaming him into being. So tonight he is restored in a world just like this. What section of time he has moved into I do not know. It isn't my concern, I'm not interested. My only interest is to bear witness to the truth and the truth is told in the Old Testament that is the Word of God.

The Word in me has erupted and is fulfilling all the words of the Old Testament; therefore I bear witness to the truth, and "thy Word is truth...and his name shall be called the Word of God" (Rev.19:13). And his testimony, the testimony of Jesus, is the spirit of prophecy, all that is prophecy. Now, when it erupts within us, well then, *we* are the spirit of prophecy. We make it alive, because on the page it is dead, the letter is dead. And they speculate and they will say, well, I think this is what the phrase means, I believe this is what it means, and they will go on from now 'til the ends of time, but they do not *know* until it happens within them. They can say "I believe" and trust the one in whom it's happened. "I believe he's telling me the truth and now I will readjust my thinking to conform to what he tells me he has experienced." But not until the individual himself has experienced it can he say "*I know*. I know because I have experienced it." I cannot become a witness to the truth and come before the judge and say "I believe it." It will be thrown out, the case is thrown out. I must actually say "I know. I am a witness. This is what happened in me."

So this coming week, or rather we're on it now, they will only celebrate the trial, the crucifixion, the burial and the death...not the birth. Yet the birth is the other side of the coin of the resurrection. Christianity is an Easter religion. Without a resurrection it would be just a little ism like any other little ism in the world, meaning nothing. All these little ism's, oh, they're helpful. They're psychological...positive living, how to assume a certain attitude of mind and walk in that state and therefore live a freer, a healthier, and a more wonderful life, and it's all good; but that's not religion. So, all the little isms belong to a certain psychology of life.

But when it comes to this, this is the religion of Easter, the religion of being risen from the dead. And the dead is not a little cemetery, but these bodies. All these are dead and this world is the world of death, and this is the story of salvation. The story where the gods...for we are told in Deuteronomy, "He has put bounds to the people according to the number of the sons of God." Not a child could be born who has not an ancestral self who is one of the sons of God. These are the sons who as one man fell, and all of us fell with that one containing all; and all will return, but each in his own good time. No one can tell you when that hour will come, no one. You long for it and I don't blame you. One should hunger for it, but may I tell you, until the hunger comes; when he said, "I thirst," do you think he is thirsting for water? No, "I will send a famine upon the land; it will not be a hunger for bread, or a thirst for water but for the hearing of the words of God" (Amos 8:11). So the cry on the cross "I thirst" is fulfilling scripture. So they gave him vinegar...that also is scripture...you find it in the 69th Psalm...so they put that to his lips.

All this is fulfillment. "I've only come to bear witness, to testify, to the truth...and thy word is truth" (Jn.17:17). So everything that happens within that Word when it becomes alive within you and it erupts just like a seed erupting, you go back into the Old Testament and there you find word after word after word simply erupting within you, and you *know* the truth of scripture. Then you go to the world, your world, but you are told they will not receive you. Even his own brothers did not believe in him, because they knew him, they knew the physical background of the man. They did not know what is taking place *in* that man, and that man was the Word of God unfolding before the eyes of the world, but they couldn't see it. He could only tell them about it, and then point out the scripture that he is experiencing within himself. For now he comes to interpret the scripture, because the prophets who wrote it could not understand it, the scribes, the wise men, could not understand it, and they lived externally by the word, the external word, and he brings now the internal word to match the external. So we are told in scripture, unless two different persons agree in testimony that testimony cannot be held; but if two different persons agree in testimony, it is conclusive. And the two is the external word of scripture and the internal word unfolding within the individual. Do they agree? When they agree, well now, that testimony is conclusive.

So, when he said, "For this I was born," it doesn't mean this little birth. He speaks of himself only as one who was born from above...for this I was born from above. They would say, "What's born from above? How could a man be born from above?" Well, he tells you, "Unless you are born from above you cannot enter the kingdom of God" (Jn.3:3). Well, no one in the world of Caesar can understand that second birth. It doesn't make sense. One must be born biologically from the womb of a woman. And he is speaking of an entirely different birth, which is the birth of the Spirit coming from above not from below; for this I came into the world. All right, he came into the world, for the Word became flesh. It's in flesh, flesh and blood, and now it dwells among us and dwells *within* us. It is said of him he came clothed in a robe drenched in blood and his name shall be called The Word of God (Rev.9:13). Well, is not this drenched in blood? Our cardinals put on red robes on the outside and they'll think now they're wearing the robe of Christ...they're princes of the church. It hasn't a thing to do with an external red robe. Every child born of woman is wearing the red robe. Is this not a body of flesh and blood?

So he comes into the world. The Word is made flesh, that's the incarnation. *You* are the incarnated Word of God. But at a moment in time you are called and when you are called, you don't volunteer, you can't resist the call. You are called and the Word is written into the Book of Life, it's checked off. You are incorporated into the living body of love. God's most radiant and fearless form that he wears is the body of love. It is that which incorporates you and now you are one with that body, with that same Spirit, with that same Lord, with that God and Father. Then you are whirled where he wears another body, he wears now the body of power, almightiness, and then he sends you into the world. Then you wait your time, it's thirty years. And you do the same normal things that you do as a man, making all the mistakes of man, and then suddenly it all erupts within you. You tell it to anyone who will hear it, but because it's not what tradition has taught them many will ignore it. Many will turn their backs, even the closest member of the household. They will not believe, because they cannot see it with mortal eye.

So I tell you, when you see it this week and they go for their three hours. It took me just a flash, not any three hours, the night I walked in procession leading them into the house of God. So that is true...it *did* happen that way. I am walking with an enormous crowd and as I walked with them the voice rings out, "And God walks with them." Then a woman questions the voice, no one could see the form, "If God walks with us, where is he?" and the voice answered, "At your side." She turned to her side, looked into my eyes and became hysterical, because she is looking at a man that she knows. A man that is weak, a man that is frail, who could succumb to temptation to anything, and she knows it. She said, "What? Neville is God?" and the voice answered, "Yes, in the act of waking." Then the voice speaks only for my ears, and the voice is coming from the depth of my soul, and the voice said to me only, "I laid myself down within you to sleep. As I slept I dreamed ..." and I knew exactly what he was dreaming...he's dreaming that he is I.

And then, I reenacted the crucifixion. The crucifixion did reenact itself within me like the journey reenacted, for I am reenacting scripture. So the night of my journey into Jerusalem leading that enormous throng, a gay procession, as you will read it in the 42nd Psalm. Here, I am leading it right into Jerusalem when the voice is speaking and tells me that he laid himself down within me to sleep, and as he slept he dreamed a dream...and I knew exactly the dream that he was dreaming. It took a split second to feel these vortices in my hands, in the feet, in my head, and the right side of my body. That's exactly where he's pierced, all six points, the Mogen David, the Star of David, here right on my body. And may I tell you far from being painful it was ecstasy beyond the wildest dream...that was the crucifixion. But it did happen on the night of the triumphal journey into Jerusalem, so they are right in tradition in keeping it in the same time slot. But they don't tell it correctly.

We are told in the Book of Acts...quoting now from Deuteronomy, "Cursed be everyone who hangs upon a tree" (Gal.3:13). The crucifixion took place upon a tree, but the tree is *in* man, right in man, not any wooden tree. As Blake so beautifully told it, "The Gods of the earth and the sea sought through Nature to find this tree; but their search was all in vain; there grows one in the human brain" *(Songs Of Experience)*. If you will take the human brain and call it the root of the tree, and see it turned downward into generation...if you ever saw the human body with the skin off as you've seen in pictures and all the veins and arteries turned down from the brain. Now that tree has to be turned up. As told in the Book of Daniel, it was felled and stripped of its leaves and it's fruit and they were scattered, but leave the root...don't' interfere with the root. And then after seven times passes over that one who fell and he knows that the Most High rules the kingdom of men and gives it to whom he will, it will turn up (4:10). That tree will be reversed and from the fall it will now move from generation into *regeneration*. And the whole thing becomes the most glorious tree, growing still out of that root. So it fell in that crucified state and we are crucified on the Tree of Life, this living tree, and then will come the day it turns up.

Now, the resurrection follows it. On the heels of this, here comes the resurrection: that's when man *in* himself awakes. It's the most glorious... disturbing yes, I'm not denying that...but one awakes. And where does he awake?—in the holy sepulcher (skull) where the whole thing began, for it was there that God himself entered death's door and lays down in the grave of man to dream the dream of life. And it's there that he is going to awaken, and it's there that he is going to come out. He will come out of that holy sepulcher and look back on the thing that contained him, that body of a slave...and then will come all this imagery of his birth from above. So then he makes the statement, "For this I was born, for this I came into the world to bear witness to the truth...and thy word is truth." So "thy word," the written word is experiencing it. I am not a scholar...and they say, "How does this man know these things seeing that he has no learning?" You don't have to have learning, because you now have knowledge based upon experience. Learning can cause you to believe, learning can cause you to say "I think"; but experience...you can't say I think or I believe. I don't have to think about it any more, I don't have to believe it, I *know* it...I know it from experience. I do not have to believe in the Christian faith; I *know* it to be true. And I know it's the fulfillment of the Old Testament, that's all that it is.

That is man's departure from this world into a new age altogether. So when he takes off the garment after the Word has erupted within him he has taken it off for the last time. So he puts it on no more. And he knows that everyone in this world, those that he knows and those that he does not know, do not die because the Word is in them; and the Word is immortal so that no one can die. He *appears* to die, but he doesn't die. He simply finds himself restored in a world just like this...a living being without change of identity, and he continues his journey until that Word becomes now activated, becomes alive within him. And when it becomes alive, it doesn't witness to anything but the written Word of scripture. He doesn't come to change Caesar's world...whose coin is this, well, give it to Caesar. He wants taxes? Give it to him. I'll tell you how to get it: *assume* that you have it. Caesar will be satisfied because you will have it and you will simply meet Caesar's demands. Now, you want something else? Don't quarrel with it: assume that you have it.

So you don't change the world of Caesar. Caesar is just as much a slave as you are, for he is a slave to the body that he wears, and he cannot compel anyone to digest and assimilate or to eliminate for him. He has to do it all by himself. He is a slave to the body that he wears, and when he dies in the world, as we all die in this world, we aren't dead; we simply are restored into a body that is just as much a slave body and we are slaves to that body. Don't think for one moment those who have gone beyond are not now performing the normal, natural functions of the body...they are. And there they have a sex body just as they have it here. There is hate and love just as it is here... it's the same world. So my world does not terminate at the point where my senses cease to register it, it continues just like this, as though I left the stage but remain the actor. I haven't changed my identity. I simply left the stage unseen by the actors who remain on the stage, that's all.

So, here in this wonderful week the drama is so concentrated. But it is not being told. And man finds it, all right, I can't blame them, because man finds it easier to see thoughts when they are put into pictures, and so they put them into pictures. But the dramatization of the story of salvation as Paul reminds us in his first letter that he wrote which is his one to the Galatians he asks us if we have forgotten the Spirit, are we now moving into the flesh, believing in a fleshly garment (3:1)? Haven't you gone to the theater and you are so carried away with the acting of a certain actor or actress that when you came out you raved about the actor, about the actress, and you forgot the message that they were trying to portray? Many a play is not just to amuse, but to educate. Well, the story of salvation is to educate and it's not to amuse.

So that is the greatest play that was ever conceived in the world, but man goes to the play and he sees the actor and he forgets. Falling in love with the husk he doesn't know the kernel. So Paul when he made the statement, "Who has bewitched you, before whose eyes Jesus Christ was publicly *portrayed* as crucified?" That word portrayed means, literally, "a moving picture" like a movie. It moves before your eyes in individual shots, individual pictures. "Have you forgotten? Let me ask you only this…" and then he asks a simple, simple question concerning the law and concerning the Spirit, he doesn't wait for an answer, he's asking, "Did you actually receive it by the works of the law, or hearing with faith? Are you now so bewitched, are you so foolish, that you're now turning from the Spirit to the flesh?" (Gal.3:1). And then he said, "From here on I regard no one after the flesh. Even though I once regarded Christ from the human point of view," that is from the flesh, "I regard him thus no longer" (2Cor.5:16).

And so, we're going to celebrate a *physical* death and it isn't physical at all. We're going to celebrate an individual and it isn't so at all. This is a universal Christ, the cosmic Christ, who is buried in every child born of woman. And that cosmic Christ is represented by the sons of God, who altogether form the Lord God Jehovah. But there isn't a child born who doesn't have an ancestral self who is one of the sons of God already individualized. May I tell you, you are already completely individualized, and you are known more intimately than you are known here on earth behind this mask. You are completely individualized and then this mask begins to experience within itself the eruption, and your real identity is returned, and you know who you are. No one on earth knows who you are, but you know who you are. It's entirely different from anything that anyone sees here. You are returning to your ancestral self that was and still is one of the sons of God…and it takes all the sons to make God. The word Elohim is plural. We are the sons, the Elohim. Put us all together and it forms Yod He

Vav He, Jah Adonai the Lord. And not one can be absent from that body or the body would miss something...something would be missing.

So here, in this wonderful dramatic week you are fortunate you know the truth concerning this great drama. For, I can only paint it for you from this platform in words. I can't dramatize it in pictures; the world has tried that and they have misled the world by pictures. Yet man finds it easier to think in terms of pictures than to see truth unwrapped, unvarnished. He can't quite follow it. I know that in talking to my closest most intimate friends, because they have been so conditioned to believe in the historicity of this principle as an individual, a single little individual, that they can't follow the argument when you tell them it is not one little man but it is the cosmic Christ buried in the whole vast world of humanity. And in the fullness of time he simply erupts, erupts, erupts, returning to the one body, the one Spirit, the one Lord, the one God and Father of all.

I'm telling you what I know, not what I believe. It's so easy to say, "I believe this"...that's how the creeds are written. But this boy at Oxford turned to the teacher, this professor came to college to give a series of lectures, and he said to him, this was a very prominent theologian, "I'm very interested in what you believe. I think your confession of faith as to what you believe is most interesting, and thank you. But I'm not really concerned about what you believe. I would stay here all night if you'd only tell me *why* you believe as you believe. In other words, can you tell me from your own deep knowledge...have you experienced it? Or are you simply repeating some little code, some little word that was written and you call it a creed, the Nicene creed, call it what you will. Can you tell me that you *know* it?" But he couldn't...yet he was the great theologian. Day after day we find it in the papers what this one said, and when you read what they said it's what they believe, what they think. And they'll take a word and tear it apart trying to analyze it, but not one can tell you what they *know*.

I'm telling you what I know. So when I bring something that is startling to you...that you are God the Father, but you will never know that you are until you meet your one and only *begotten son* whose name is David. When David stands before you and he knows that you are his Father, and you know without any uncertainty that you are, and that he is your son, then you *know* God the Father. For this mystery is to bring us towards the Father. He said, "No one comes unto the Father except by me." I am the *pattern* and this pattern will unfold within you. I am the pattern man and as it unfolds within you, it will bring you to the Father. And no one will ever know the Father except the Son, and no one knows the Son except the Father (Mat.11:27). So he brings you by unfolding within you...for the living Word begins to unfold, you come straight to the Son...and then you know who you are. You've been searching through eternity for *yourself*, that's who you've been searching for. You aren't searching for any other being; you've been searching for yourself, the being that is God. You are God the Father. But no being can persuade you to believe it until you experience it, and when you experience it you don't have to think it and believe it any more, you *know* it.

And so, these words become your words: "For this I was born. For this I came into the world to bear witness to the truth." And so when reason personified, called Pilate, asks, "What is truth?" you, personified truth, do not answer. How could truth ever persuade reason concerning the truth? Well, what is the truth of which Jesus spoke?—the true knowledge of God. As he said in the third verse of the 17th chapter of John, "And this is eternal life to *know thee* the only true God." Let the others have all kinds of gods, like the stars, and let them bring it down into a certain ism called astrology. Let them have gods like numerology, all kinds of gods in the world; but this is eternal life to know thee the only *true* God. Then the evangelist adds the words, "…and Jesus Christ whom thou hast sent." Well, he did…he sent a pattern. He sent himself which is the Word into you: you say "I am," that's the Word. But it hasn't reached the fullness of time to burst the shell and unfold the pattern. The pattern is in you and it will lead you to the only true God, and when you find him you find *yourself*. And you will never know you are God until God's only begotten stands before you and there he is *your* Son. Then you know it! And then for the little while left before you take it off permanently you tell it. The same pattern…it can't be another pattern.

History as we understand it isn't history at all. There's nothing accurate about secular history. You take even a little section of the last World War and there aren't two accounts of any event, the same event, that resemble each other. Take what Eisenhower's son has written in his book concerning what his father experienced from all his father's papers; and his father's right-hand man, Montgomery. For, he was under Ike; Ike was over all, but Montgomery was next in charge as far as numbers. Read the two accounts of the same war. You might just as well be reading two different happenings, not the same happening, they are completely different. You take the account of Will Durant concerning Russia, and read what Khrushchev who followed Stalin, who was his successor, not immediately but soon after Stalin's death he became Premier of Russia, and he said the man was a monster, a madman, who killed twenty million people. But now read what Will Durant, a great historian, said about Stalin. You would think that here is the Lord himself wrapped in love walking the earth. Read the two accounts and all about the same man.

So there's not a thing here in secular history that is accurate, but God's history, sacred history, is forever and forever the same thing. So when you experience it, it will be right there. It will not alter one little bit. That sacred history is forever and no one will change it. So you are warned in Revelation and in the Psalms, warned in Proverbs, "Do not add to or take from the Word of God." Leave it just as it is. You don't understand it? Leave it as it is. The day will come, the Word, the living Word, will unfold in you and interpret the written Word for you. But don't try to add to it, don't try to change it. Yet scholars without vision have tried time and again to change the Word to make it conform to their beliefs and what they think, not what they know.

So this week is truly a great week. Not that we should take one week to observe it, for we are warned in Galatians, "I notice that you observe weeks and months and seasons and years. I'm afraid I have labored over you in vain" (4:10). For this could happen at any moment in time…it doesn't have to happen now. This is simply, well, to dramatize it, and we take a week, but it doesn't have to be this week. This drama unfolds at any moment in time. And it's a crowded thing, so it's good that they've taken the week to dramatize it, they'll bring it back into the mind of man. But this is not the story of scripture. The crucifixion began in the very beginning before that the world was. Easter comes at the end of the age, the age of Caesar, and the beginning of the new age called the kingdom of God. And Easter is one side of the coin; the other side is birth from above. Then the entire drama unfolds within you as the Word unfolds, for he sent his Word and his Word cannot return unto him void; it must accomplish that which he purposed and prosper in the thing for which he sent it (Is.55:11).

And so, it will go back and claim and it will be true, "I have finished the work thou gavest me to do." You gave me only one work to do: to testify to the truth. What truth?—the truth of thy Word…that's all that I came to testify to. I didn't come to make a lot of money. I didn't come to leave my name in granite or my face carved on a mountainside. I didn't come to change anything in the world of Caesar. I didn't come to judge it, or to condemn it or to praise it. Leave it just as it is, for God planned everything just as it will come out and as it will be consummated. So leave it just as it is. And you walk in the faith of this grace that is coming to you. Set your hope fully upon this grace, and day after day just hope it is today that the grace will erupt within you, for that's all that matters in the end. I have come to bear witness to the truth, nothing else, and thy Word is truth, so I've come to fulfill scripture, that's all.

Now let us go into the Silence.

*　　*　　*

Now are there any questions, please? Yes, Jack.

Q: (inaudible)
A: Jack, this section of time where you and I are now is the most concentrated of all sections of time, and God takes upon himself the limit of contraction, and that would be the infant. My experiences lead me to tell you what I tell you concerning meeting those that I know who have departed this world to find them…like last night my brother Lawrence…he was a year older than I am. He departed two years ago… he looked much older because he was in great pain for about year before he departed. But here is this young, wonderful lad in his very early twenties, the same joyful Lawrence that I've always loved and known… and he knew that he had departed. I met my father, he's a young man. He died at eighty-five, about ten years ago, died in '59, and he's a young man. Well, I met my mother who died a painful death…she was riddled with cancer and died at sixty-one, and she looked so much older than she was at sixty-one. The very day that she departed she came to me a girl of twenty.

So I can only tell you what I know. I can't explain the mystery any more than any scientist in this world can tell me how a little, tiny spermatozoa grows into a baby. As we are asked that question in the Book of Proverbs, "Who knows how the bones grow in the womb of woman?" They can give me all kinds of speculations. Let them speculate and speculate day in and day out. Tomorrow morning's paper may bring some new concept from some anthropologist, and they'll tell me I didn't really come from a monkey, but I came from a tree, or I didn't come from this…and they're changing it all the time. Or the year, that we're not really fifty billion years old, we're really fifty-one and a half, some nonsense like this…and the papers give it space.

So I can't tell you. I am just as much at sea as they are as to *how* it happens. I can only tell you that I know. I know these worlds, for I've stepped into these worlds…with my body lying on the bed. I know exactly where the body is and I know exactly what I'm doing. My eye opens from within and I'm seeing what I ought not to see. My physical eye is shut, but my spiritual eye is open, and suddenly I am seeing a world just like this. I become curious and I step into it, and then the world closes on me, and this world is shut out, and I am shut in that world into which I stepped. I meet people just like you and they're just as we are. When I came upon them in the hallway of a hotel they were scared to death of me, because I said something that would frighten anyone. I said to these two ladies as they passed by "Ladies, this is a dream. This whole vast world is a dream." Well, if you met two strangers in the hallway of a lobby and they didn't know you and suddenly you said, "This whole thing is a dream," well, they'd think he's mad, we'd better start walking rapidly...and they did. They did exactly what they would do in this world. They walked as rapidly as they could, they almost ran, and then when they got to the end they looked, took one quick little look back at me. And I'm holding this object in space and they disappeared.

But they were solidly real and they heard me and saw me. And this thing above me, which I thought was just a memory image of something that I'd seen before, wasn't...it was solid. And then I said, "You'd better wake up, Neville. You have unfinished business where you left that body behind." I did, I had unfinished business. Well, I opened my eyes and I'm still standing there. Closed them again and tried, and I'm still shut out, completely shut out and there's no way back. Then I remembered, I remembered that *feeling* would get me back, and while I'm standing erect I began to imagine that I'm feeling a pillow under my head. If a pillow is under my head chances are I'm in a horizontal position. I began to feel myself in a horizontal position; and then I'm back, but I'm cataleptic. I can't move, can't open my eyes, can't move my hands. I'm completely alive in a dead body. And then after a while I could move the wrist, move it a little bit. A little bit longer I could open the eyelid and then I could see the familiar objects on the wall and in the room. I came back from a world just like this. But night after night you pass through these worlds and you come back to this world, and these worlds are real.

But to come back to your original question...I do not know. I have not a thing that could cause me to feel in any way to accept what they call reincarnation. I don't call that reincarnation because I'm the same identity. There was no loss of identity and in all of my experiences I have never lost the sense of identity. I have known a world where I was very, very wealthy, but I did not grow spiritually. I was decadent with my wealth, because I catered just to the superficial as all of those who are fabulously wealthy do today. They like to feel themselves the very best-dressed woman, the best-dressed man. They are so proud of being one of the ten best dressed, and they'll spend a fortune to be named in *World*, or whatever it is, as one of the ten best dressed. Well, I experienced that, but I was still Neville. I was still the I that I am, and I recall that I didn't die there, I vanished. I went out of that world deliberately and never returned to it leaving my entire estate. I have a very, very vivid consciousness of that.

The Return of Glory

I also have a vivid consciousness of returning to it as everything is caught in eternity and nothing passes away, like a play. The first act of Hamlet is still the first act of Hamlet no matter where it's playing tonight or where it will play tomorrow or in the years to come. It's still the first act. And that act I recalled vividly. So I went back into that act and those who served me as my secretaries and my full complement of servants were still in the act, and they all knew me and treated me with the same deference, the same feeling of "my lord." That's how they spoke to me. Not "my Lord" in the sense of the being I have awakened to, but the lord of the earth, the world of Caesar. That's how your servants would address you in that section of time. And I recall the very ones who usurped my place. And I didn't want any part of it, for I moved from that decadence into poverty in order to become *truly* rich. As we are told in scripture: "And although he was rich he became poor that by his poverty *you* may become rich." So he became poor that he may get the *real* wealth of the world: the kingdom of heaven. But, Jack, I cannot tell you that I know from experience how it works. I only know that it does, but I can't tell you how. Here is a miracle that stuns one, because how can someone be cremated and only dust remain, and you tell me that the being before your eyes was completely cremated and gave you a little dust in your hand that's the end of that being...and he stands before you and he's a young man or a young woman, beautiful...they're all young and not one little part missing.

Now, I had an experience back in 1946 coming through the Caribbean Sea into Mobile, Alabama. Whether this is what the ascended man does, I do not know, but I know that a huge, enormous sea of human imperfection was all waiting for me. And that night, I heard a heavenly chorus and it began to sing, "Neville is risen, Neville is risen" and I actually came through my head in the form of a serpent, like a serpent. I came right through my skull and my body was simply made of fire and air, just a living vibrant being. I simply glided, I didn't have to walk, right off the surface of the earth. And this heavenly chorus is singing, "Neville is risen." When I came to this enormous sea of human imperfection, every one was made perfect. There were none left that were old or eyes missing. Their eyes were missing when I came, but as I came by eyes came into their sockets, empty sockets, arms came back, everything came back, and they were all restored to beautiful normalcy, but really beautiful.

So maybe that is what one does...takes a sea of the dead, the withered, the lame, the halt and as he, the perfect, walks by they are all restored. I couldn't tell you how those eyes did it. I only know I didn't stop for one second to do it. I didn't seem to have compassion for them, I simply walked by and being perfect myself every one was made perfect. I didn't stop to think anything or listen to one request. They were all seated on the ground waiting for me and I knew they were waiting for me. As I walked by, every one was made perfect. The blind, beautiful eyes that function; the limbs that were missing all came back, everything came back and every one was made perfect. And when I came to the very end, the chorus exulted and it sang out, "It is finished"…the very last cry on the cross.

So, is that my duty to walk by when those who are dead and lame and aged and withered who by my walking by restore them? I do not know. It may be, for I had that experience back in 1946. Is that my destiny when I take off this garment this time? It may be…the restoration of the so-called bodies that fire cremated. But I know it was an enormous sea of human imperfection, and as I glided by knowing that it was my duty to walk by…and I only did my duty. These who were completely maimed and disfigured instantly were molded into perfection because I was perfect. So you are told, "Be ye perfect as your Father in heaven is perfect" (Mat.5:48). Now if that is my task when I take off this garment, well then, let it be my task…to restore garments and make them perfect. And every one…not one was old when I went by, all became young—not babies, young—and the eyes that were missing, the arms missing, the legs missing, there were none missing, all came right back and they were perfect. And this chorus was exulting and all they are using is the same simple phrase, "Neville is risen, Neville is risen." That's all that they used, but how can you take one little phrase like "Neville is risen" and do such beauty with it? A heavenly chorus is singing it and they only change at the very end when they now exulted and said, "It is finished!"

Good night.

CRUCIFIXION: I AM THE TRUE VINE

4/4/69

Well, today as we know is Good Friday, and undoubtedly millions attended service today to hear some portion of the last seven words of Jesus Christ. But how many of them know who he is and what these words really mean?

We are told that God became man that man may become God. Accept it literally, for it is true. Now, the first word spoken, which really is a sentence, "Father, forgive them for they know not what they do" (Luke23:34) and the last word spoken is, "Father, into thy hands I commit my spirit." But that's only a portion of the verse that is quoted. That's the quote from the 5th verse of the 31st chapter of the Book of Psalms, the 31st Psalm. The completed verse is: "Father, into thy hands I commit my spirit; thou hast *redeemed* me, O Lord, faithful God." So here we find the redeemer and the redeemed are one. For here is the redeemer, "Thou hast redeemed me"...he speaks now to the Father. Then he tells us, "I and the Father are one" (Jn. 10:30). So here, the redeemer and the redeemed are really one.

Let us look at it through different eyes tonight...not through the traditional eyes of the church. He said, "I am the true vine, my Father is the vinedresser. I am the true vine" (Jn. 15:1). Let me tell you who he really is, this true vine: "The eternal body of man is the Imagination and that is God himself, the divine body, Jesus, and we are his members" (Blake, *Laocoon*). Christ became *humanity*...not *a* little man but humanity, every child born of woman. Now here we have the divine body Jesus Christ and we are the members. In what sense?—our own wonderful human Imagination is Christ in us. It is the redeemer of us and yet it is the one redeemed.

Now let us look at it through these eyes. When I first heard it or experienced it, may I tell you it was quite a shock for I was born and raised in the Christian tradition and I knew no other religion. And then suddenly to find that my little physical Christ was not the true Christ, that he actually was not something on the outside to worship, that he became me literally. In the most literal sense he actually became me, my own wonderful human Imagination, that that was the Jesus Christ. Well, there's a little poem that suits it perfectly: "Behold this vine. I found it a wild tree, whose wanton strength had swollen into irregular twigs. But I pruned the plant and it grew temperate in its vain expense of useless leaves and knotted, as you see, into these full, clean clusters to repay the hand that wisely wounded it." When I discover that my own Imagination was this eternal vine, the true vine, that everything in my world grew upon me...and they were simply irregular twigs. I never thought for one second that my misuse of my Imagination caused the deformities in my world and that when things were happening in my world relative to me that I am the sole cause of it. But what a shock and what a responsibility and what a pruning then had to take place.

So the Father and the Son are one, and I, as Father, had to start pruning this vine. I am the true vine and now I have to start pruning myself. When I allowed myself to entertain the unlovely thoughts of a seeming other, not knowing the other was a branch growing from me the true vine I didn't cut the branch off. The pruning is not in that way, the pruning is *revision* called in scripture repentance, "a radical change of attitude towards an individual or a situation in my world; a complete revision and the acceptance of this unseen imaginal act as reality." And then, to see in time it grows out of the same vine, for now I become aware of a radical change in my world relative to this person, that person, or this condition in my world. And then I have found him; I have found the eternal vine, the true vine, and I've found the Father who pruned it. And he pruned it! And if I don't keep on pruning it day after day, it simply grows into irregular twigs and will not know and form itself into these full, clean clusters to repay the hand of the vinedresser, the Father who pruned it.

So here today, it's not *a* man on a cross. Listen to the words carefully from Paul's letter to the Philippians, "Although he was in the form of God"—now he's speaking of Jesus Christ—"Christ Jesus who, though in the form of God, thought it not robbery to be equal with God, but emptied himself and took upon himself the form of a slave, being born in the likeness of men. And being found in human form he became obedient unto death, even death on the cross" (2:5-8). Well now, this is the only cross upon which Jesus Christ was ever crucified. Your body is the cross that Jesus Christ wears. And he will wear it...in the same book, it's a very short little book Philippians..."He will transform our lowly bodies to be of one form with his *glorious* body" (3:21). That's the purpose of it all: to actually take upon himself this body of humility to which I am a slave. I'm a slave to this body,

I must feed it, bathe it, clean it, assimilate what I can, and what I can't I must eliminate it, and no one can do it for me. I am a slave to this body. And I am *not* of this world any more than you are, and here we are going to completely transform this into our glorious body, for bear in mind the redeemer and the redeemed are one. I came down and took upon myself this body and then I will redeem it; and when I've redeemed it, the thing redeemed and myself the redeemer are one.

So the true vine is your own wonderful human Imagination. When you make that discovery you cannot continue to think and imagine as you formerly did. You prune that plant every day of your life. If you are in the habit of feeling remorseful or depressed or regretful or any of these states, we stop it. If my attitude toward a certain person has been unkind then I change it, because he's actually myself pushed out. He couldn't grow in my world, he couldn't appear in my world, he couldn't come to me in my world unless my Father calls him, and I and my Father are one. So no one can come unto me unless I call him, even though he brings poison. He can only bring what I myself gave him to bring.

And this is the story that is re-enacted today but not understood. He took a sop, called a morsel in some other translation, and gave it to Judas, and then Judas went out quickly for he had to do something. The sop is simply a gift of the greatest of friendship. So when you take that sop and dip it into whatever you would put it in, you pass it always to the honored guest, the one that is closest to you, the dearest friend, and that's Judas. Only Judas could betray because only Judas knew the secret. No one can betray me who doesn't know my secret. How could you betray me if I had not taken you into my confidence as a friend and told you my secrets? So Judas goes out as the friend, to tell who is the *true* Christ, the real Christ in the world. And he leaves now a sign...he tells them that this is the sign: "Whosoever I shall kiss, that same is he; hold him fast" (Mat.26:48). Don't let him go, hold him fast. You must eat that body, that *doctrine*, feed upon it, drink it. Don't let it go but let everything else go in your world. When you have found the sole cause of the phenomena of your life then let everything else go.

People tell you "this" will commend you to God. Nothing that goes into the belly can commend you to God, I don't care how well you eat. All right, eat well for your physical sake, but don't think for one second that anything you do *physically* commends you to God. As you are told in scripture not a thing in this world that you can do on the outside could ever commend you to God. What comes out of the heart of man either defiles him or glorifies him, so not a thing that you do on the outside in any way will change it. It's what you are doing on the inside and what you are doing is simply your wonderful imaginal acts. How are you imagining? For, that is the vine and

331

that true vine is your own wonderful human Imagination. So who would he kiss? He comes…and I tell you the story is true, I've experienced it. When one actually experiences the entire drama, then one comes in and he actually embraces you, and he kisses you after someone quickly leaves the room. And here you are explaining the Word of God; and one jumps up quickly and you know exactly what he's going to do. He's going to reveal your secret, tell exactly what you told concerning the cause of creation, the cause of all the phenomena of life. And then quickly one comes in… it's the same being returning.

He comes in. He now comes into the room and the one that he kisses, that is the one. Don't let him go! "Hold fast, hold him fast." The word hold as defined in the Concordance means "almighty," it means "power," for Christ Jesus is defined as "the power of God and the wisdom of God" (1Cor.1:24). The word fast is defined in the way that we have just experienced it in forty days, "to abstain from all food," to abstain from any food other than the one that you've held. You feast upon him and no one else. Where others will try to come in and say, "Well, try this, too. This will help you"…like a little numerology added to it. Now, did California go down today? It didn't, did it…unless we're all in the other world now, I don't know. So it didn't go down and they all went off to their Oregon and other homes, groups of them, and now they're praying and hoping to prove themselves right even if it took seven million of us to go down to prove their little minds right. One of the greatest weaknesses in the world is the necessity of always being right. And how they will try this night to pray until they break their skulls to simply prove themselves right, these little soothsayers.

Now, that hasn't a thing to do with scripture. Christ Jesus, who is God himself, actually became you, individually, and when you say "I am," that's Christ Jesus. When you imagine, that's God in action. Now, when you know this and you have found the true vine, that's the true vine. You know now who's going to prune it, your Father; and I and my Father are one, we're one. If I really know it, I will start pruning it. If I don't believe it and I believe Jesus Christ is other than myself, I will continue to let this wanton energy puff me up into irregular twigs and bear the most unlovely things in my world: men and women who are in need, and I do nothing about it, yet they are in my world. I draw them, I become aware of them, and yet I go blindly on doing nothing in my Imagination to lift them from that state. I am more inclined to discard them, simply ignore them. That's not what I should do. What I should do is represent them to myself as the men, as the women, I would like them to be, and persuade myself that they are what I've *imagined* that they are. Now, they will simply change, that branch will change in my world. And I will be pruning my plant morning, noon and night.

And then, suddenly when I least expect it…for this is how it happens, it comes like a thief in the night…then this tree that I have properly pruned will erupt. And then in a series of the most wonderful supernatural experiences God reveals himself *in* me, not as another, as my own very self. He unveils himself, and who is he?—I am he. So God became as I am that I may be as he is, and when he rises in me I am he. He will not rise in any place outside of you, for he is not dwelling in any place outside of you…God actually became as you are.

Now we are told in the 17th chapter of Luke, "They will not say, 'Look, here it is'" or 'There!' for I tell you the kingdom of God is within you" (17:21). It is within you. If it is within you then don't look there and do not look here, it is within you. If the kingdom of God is within me and our congregation as some translations have it—and others commonwealth, but I'd rather use commonwealth—our commonwealth is in heaven from where we expect a savior, the Lord Jesus Christ, who will refashion our lowly body to be one with his *glorious* body (Phil.3:21). This body of humiliation, he's going to completely change it to be one with his glorious body. The exalted Christ will have no body that will differ from your body. Well, it's completely transformed by Christ in you. So do not go any place when some one tells you "There he is" or "Here he is," for the kingdom of God is within you. And if it's from the kingdom of God that I expect a savior who is the Lord Jesus Christ, then he has to be within me. He can't come from any other heaven, for the only heaven is within me. So when he comes he comes from within, in a series of the most majestic, mighty, supernatural acts, and he unveils himself in me; then he rises in me and I am he.

So when Blake said so beautifully in his 96th Plate of *Jerusalem*, "I behold the visions of my deadly sleep of six thousand years dazzling around thy skirts like a serpent of precious stones and gold. I know it is *my self*, O *my* Redeemer and Creator." My own Creator, my own Redeemer and I am he. I can't tell you the thrill when you see it…when the Son of man looks upon that pool of golden, liquid light, after he has been split in two from top to bottom, and knows it is himself. And then, as told in the 3rd chapter of John, he ascends like that fiery serpent in the wilderness: he returns into the kingdom of God within him. That's where the kingdom is and I know it is myself. Here I thought I was praying to an outside Redeemer. I was taught to pray to someone on the outside. And suddenly when the whole thing was split and the being was revealed to me, I am he. It's a golden, pulsing, living light. I fuse with it and then like a serpent up I go right back into the

333

kingdom of heaven within me…a living stone in the living, living temple of the eternal God. That's what everyone is going to experience.

So here, the drama that was told this day in these seven wonderful sentences…here, the first one, "Forgive them." If I know that everything in my world I am the cause of it, well, can I not forgive it? Must I go on condemning the shadow when I am the cause of the shadow? When everyone who comes into my world…and no one comes unto me save my Father draws him…and I and my Father are one. So he comes and he insults me, he offends me, but if I know *I am* the cause of his seeming offense, I can forgive him: "Father, forgive them, they know not what they do" (Luke 23:34). They're under compulsion to play the part that they are playing, because I have imagined what I have imagined. I might have forgotten my imaginal act and even deny that I have ever in the past entertained such thoughts, but they couldn't come if I had not. Therefore, "Father, forgive them; for they know not what they do."

Now, when we come into the very end, take the one, this is the sixth word, and here, "It is finished." When it is finished, what does he ask for? He said, "I have finished the work thou gavest me to do; and now, Father, return unto me the glory that was mine, the glory that I had with thee before that the world was" (Jn.17:5). "I emptied myself of this glory and took upon myself the form of a slave and became obedient in this garment of a slave to death, even death upon this cross" (Phil.2:7). Now I've finished the work that thou gavest me to do: you sent me to redeem this slave, and I became it, we became one, we fused, and we are one. Now I will rise, but, Father, return unto me the glory that *was* mine, the glory that I had with thee before that the world was. So the whole thing is just one being returning. So God the Father and God the Son that is sent are the same. And the Son that is sent comes in and possesses me and redeems me, his own creation; so when I rise I rise as the one who was sent. I then am the Son, and the Son and the Father are one. So when he finishes the work, he only asks for the return of the glory. And by coming down and doing what he did, coming into the world of death, he overcame death; therefore, on his return his brilliance is greater, his translucence is greater, everything about him is greater by reason of the victory over death.

Everyone is going to do it. And what a joy! If you accept this, your days cannot be what they were in the past. You couldn't possibly get up in the morning and start your day…if you really accept this, don't let it go. Fast to everything *but* this and feast upon it. "Eat my body and drink my blood," said he, "but don't let me go" (Jn.6:54). You fast to everything you've ever heard before; give up everything concerning *causation* other than the one cause and that one cause is your own wonderful human Imagination. It is the cause of everything in your world, good, bad or indifferent. So when it comes, you can't deny it. I may not remember the imaginal act in my past that brings this now, but it has to be related to something in me or it couldn't come. So instead of denying it or trying to rub it out, I would accept it and *change* it in my world. So I would beautify my world. As I begin to practice this law suddenly the whole thing erupts within me, for "The kingdom of heaven is at hand. Repent and believe the gospel" (Mark1:15). Believe the doctrine, the story of God; the story of Jesus Christ, the story of redemption.

So it is not some man who died for us 2,000 years ago. *You* and *I* died with him in the beginning. "I have been crucified with Christ. It is not I who live but Christ who lives *in* me, and the life I now live in the flesh I live by the faith of the Son of God who loved me and gave himself for me" (Gal.2:20). He actually became me. Not something 2,000 years ago in space in the Near East, no, right here in this land. Wherever you were born that's when the incarnation took place. That's when God became man, that's when God took upon himself the form of a slave. And the true slave is simply man; not a person who enslaves another and that other is called a slave, which happens all over the world. In parts of the world there are still slaves of that nature, but the one who is a slave master is still a slave. He is a slave to the body that he wears and *that* is the slave. He can't command anyone to take care of the normal, natural functions of his body; he must perform them himself…that is the slave. But the day will come, he'll redeem the slave…a complete transformation will take place. And it will be like the exalted being that he *really* was before he emptied himself and came down and took upon himself the form of a slave.

Well, I can't tell you the thrill when this garment is worn by you. It's beyond…well, you can't describe it. My best description is simply a being of fire and air, but can that really describe it? All the power in the world is vested in it. There is nothing it can't do and yet it does it effortlessly. How can it form eyes and mold them perfectly into empty sockets and the eyes see perfectly? And arms into empty sockets and the move perfectly? And withered bodies completely shrunk beyond measure concerning age and then suddenly it returns to a beautiful form twenty years old? How did it do it? What magical power? Well, that's that power you possess when you wear that body. I wore it one night in 1946…just like a demonstration of that which is to be my permanent body, the body that I gave up to take upon myself this to redeem this. And in that night I still was Neville, so Neville wore that body, and I, the invisible, became a visible being. I actually nailed myself upon this cross and wore it until that night when the whole thing was revealed.

So I can't tell you the thrill that is in store for you when this body that is being transformed that you are now wearing is transformed into *that* body. And that's your body, your *immortal* body, because the being that you are cannot die...Jesus Christ cannot die. He was before that the world was and he came down into the world of death and became victorious in a world of death, raising with him every being in the world. So this one comes now, that one comes tomorrow, that one comes the next day, and everyone is going to be redeemed.

So the last cry...after he said "It's finished..." and when he said "I thirst," you think it means for water? No. The Book of Amos tells us what he's thirsting for. He prophesied the entire thing: "I will send a famine upon the world; it will not be a hunger for bread or a thirst for water, but for the hearing of the words of God" (Amos8:11). So every word has to be unfolded *in* him...that's his thirst. So after these whole marvelous supernatural things unfold within you the hunger is still on, and then one after the other unfolds within you. Every word of God proves true, and you are cast in the star role. You experience the entire book in the first-person singular, present-tense experience.

So this is this wonderful day of the crucifixion. And I wonder what percentage of our world...? And millions of us today attended service... some could not take three hours so they went for maybe a half hour... and there are only seven words that they will speak. They will simply try to explain the words. I wonder to what extent they explain them. How do the ministers today...and there were seven ministers in one church here on Wilshire, each one took a word, and a word is a sentence, and each one took a sentence and attempted to explain it. I wonder to what extent they really understood it and could explain it to those who came hungry for the Word of God? For these are only the words of God being repeated today, each with a *seeming* explanation. So how would you go about explaining if you have the traditional concept of Jesus Christ when you say, "Father, forgive them"? You would be incapable of forgiving someone if you didn't really believe he's only yourself pushed out. How could you forgive him? He has just murdered a friend or your loved one and he's yourself pushed out. Well, how on earth did I bring that about? I had to have brought it about, because no one can come unto me except my Father draws him, and I and my Father are one. Well, how will I forgive him? Only when I know who Jesus Christ really is. When I know who is the *real cause* of the phenomena of my life... and if I know I am the cause of the phenomena and by cutting it off I can't stop it, I have to rearrange it. I have to completely transform it by the story in scripture called repentance, which I prefer today to call by another name.

Here, when I *revise* a thing I have really repented in the true sense of the word.

So, the vine when I found it, I must confess I could hardly sleep for days and days. I was so disillusioned and the responsibility that would then be on *my* shoulders. I always placed it upon the shoulders of another and here all of a sudden I was told who Jesus Christ really is, that I am he and that he is the cause of everything in the world; therefore, I am the cause of all that I observe and I can't pass the buck. I have to now actually do something about it. Now the Father prunes the vine…read it in the 15th chapter of the Book of John…the whole chapter is devoted to this pruning of the vine and he starts off, "I am the true vine and my Father is the vinedresser"…and what does not bear fruit, he prunes it and gathers it for the flames. But he prunes it for a purpose: that it may bear more fruit and more luscious fruit. And so you who keep gardens know it may sometimes pain you to cut a certain branch, but you know you've got to do it if you want good fruit next year. And so, it may be all twigs now and it's such a lovely thing you don't want to cut it, but you've got to. Whether it be a rosebush, to bring forth beautiful roses or figs or anything in the world, you've got to prune it.

Well, that is life. My consciousness is this wonderful eternal vine, my own wonderful human Imagination, because, "Man is all Imagination. God is man and exists in us and we in him…this eternal body of man is the Imagination and that is God himself the divine body Jesus: we are his members" (Blake, *Ann. to Berkeley; Laocoon*). Therefore, humanity is truly the body of the Lord Jesus Christ. But every child born of woman, I don't care what that child is, what race, what nation, what sex, every child is part of the universal body of the Lord Jesus Christ. And when he knows *who* Jesus Christ is, that Jesus Christ is his own wonderful human Imagination, well, he goes out with a load for the first while until it rearranges itself within him. And then he takes himself in hand to do something about it… and I tell you from my own experience when you begin to take yourself in hand and really believe that that is Jesus Christ and turn to no other *causation*, and do something about it morning, noon and night, your whole vast world will change and mold itself in harmony with the change that takes place within you. As you change within yourself the outer world reflects it. It can't do anything other than to reflect the change within you.

So this is the great story that is told today. Not a man, *a* man, who was nailed on any wooden cross. That's not the cross. You are told in the Book of Acts he was hanged upon a tree, but the mystic knows what the tree really is. It is not on the outside: man himself is the tree, the inverted tree. The brain is like the root, and if you take a man and take off his skin and photograph him with all the veins and arteries, he looks like an inverted tree. The tree was felled, as told us in the 4th chapter of Daniel, but now the tree must not have the root disturbed. The root must remain in tact, and then the tree will reverse itself and go up and reach to heaven. The same tree that was felled now turns around and that turning around is called *regeneration*...when the force that went down into generation is turned up into regeneration. And one day you will see it and everyone will see it.

I am convinced that those who are here, who through their presence time and time again show their hunger for the Word of God, when *that* hunger is upon you the day isn't far off. But let no one deceive you and tell you that the kingdom of God will come with signs. It will not come with signs to be observed we are told. When it comes, it comes like a thief in the night, comes suddenly upon you, so let no one tell you, "Here he is or there he is, or here it is or there it is"; it's all within you. The being that you are seeking is within you. You are seeking your own cause which is God the Father, and God the Father is in you. You are seeking his kingdom and that is within you. The whole drama unfolds within the individual.

And what a joy when it unfolds! You sleep differently; you wake differently, and there isn't a moment in time that you could not close your eyes and depart willingly. There would be no restraint whatsoever if the moment happened to be now, because it has happened within you. And the Word continues to unfold within you night after night. There are experiences all based upon the promise of God, for the entire Old Testament is the blueprint which the New unfolds. Every night something happens within you and if you search the scriptures you'll find it there.

Now two ladies present wrote me a letter and both had similar dreams. They differ in a certain manner. One had a dream of two horses and one had a dream of three horses. But bear in mind, a dream is a parable and a parable has a *single* point of truth. Don't try to put into it what isn't there... just what is there, only a single jet of truth. This lady had this dream, she is driving down this highway with her husband. He's at the wheel and there's a long cliff about thirty-five feet tall. She looks back and she sees these two horses, like wild horses. They're coming pell-mell and the younger of the two leaps across the highway into a patch of green, into a pasture, perfectly. The older of the two leaps but can't quite make it and falls to the highway. She knew by the impact that he was injured and she felt sorrowful for him. And then he seemed to get to his feet and he could by his own steam come to her almost for comfort. She noticed that the feet had been taped and a little ooze of blood. But the young one had made it completely.

Well here, a horse is simply a symbol of one's understanding. She doesn't have to completely discard the old...it wasn't at the point where it had to be shot, as she said, it could recover, but it was not equal to the new one. A new understanding of the eternal truth made it beautifully across that highway. The old one...she can extract from all of her teachings of the Christian faith what can be incorporated into what she now hears, because she is riding this new understanding. And the horse could not come into her world unless this new understanding had really become alive within her. It's real within her. That's why this dream of the horses. You don't sit down and conjure the horses, they happen, and you're told in the 12th chapter of Numbers that God speaks to man through the language of dream. If God is speaking, one *should* pay attention. So here, a new understanding of the eternal story has come to her and does not mean a complete destruction of the old, but an incorporation of those portions of the old that still can be woven into the new understanding...the same story of Christ.

The other lady had it with three: the white horse and the black horse and the pale horse. She had this enormous estate, thousands of acres, and she was offered a fantastic price for the estate. She realized, when she decided to sell, that what they really wanted was her white horse and she didn't want to part with the white horse. She would part with the land but not with the white horse, which, in Revelation, is the horse that the Lord Jesus Christ rides (19:11). So the understanding comes to the point of really riding *that* horse. Now, this horse in her dream was her redeemer. Time and again they tried to kill her, tried to hurt her, and the horse always appeared and redeemed her. In the most human manner he redeemed her. So, she wasn't completely in control of it, but she has found him, and he redeems her even though he is still being sought by her, because those who are her enemies are nothing more than herself pushed out. The thoughts still come back based upon your early training.

Now in her own letter to me she did not see the red horse. Well, the red horse is the horse of war. And she wonders in her letter, "Well, maybe I already rode that horse." Don't try to put something into your dream that you did not dream. You didn't dream of the red horse...why bring him in? That red horse doesn't mean a thing. He's not in the dream. There's the white horse, the black horse, the pale horse. So forget what you didn't dream. If I start that way, I will come to no end of things I didn't dream. The dream has only *one* simple little jet of truth...and here, your redeemer who will one day reveal himself *as you*. You are not only the redeemer, you are the redeemed, and you are working with it. But you have found him or the white horse could not come. You could not have ridden him. Even if at times you were off the horse and the horse comes and saves you, using his feet as man would use his hands...to pull her out of a ditch where she was hiding from those who wanted to kill her. So, you have found your redeemer. Our redeemer is your own wonderful human Imagination...that's the white horse. But all the other horses are also found in your Imagination, and we've all played the part of the red horse, the horse of conflict, the horse of war, and every one in the world is simply riding the red horse. But after we have ridden it then he is injured. He is injured, but I can't blame him for the work he did because I was the cause of it, and so I can say, "Forgive him, Father, for *he* knew not what he did." I didn't know what I was doing…that's why he came into my being as that one of war.

So you keep up the letters and keep up the visions and share them with me. But don't try to see more in a parable than a single jet of truth. That's all that matters.

Now let us go into the Silence.

*　　*　　*

Are there any questions, please? Lots of time…

Q: What does it mean in the Bible when it says, "Go and tell no man"?
A: Not always but occasionally it is said, "Go and tell no man." Well, if you went out tonight and you told those who have no interest, who are complacent and satisfied with their present concept of religion, you would offend them. They would offend you and you would not help them at all. If they are seeking an idle word they will hear it and others will not hear it. But to go to force it down and to proselyte is not part of the teaching. No one will come until your Father calls him. So to go out and try to *make* him see as you see is futile, because he cannot at that moment and that level of consciousness could not accept it. They will give every interpretation in the world.

That goes not only for the unschooled, but that goes for those who are considered brilliant minds. They just cannot see it. And I go back now to many that I met. When I say many, well, say a few dozen that I had the pleasure of meeting and I like them as friends, but they couldn't understand one word that I was talking about. These were men whose books are read in all the great universities in the world. Many of them have been translated from our English tongue into many tongues, but they couldn't understand one word I'm talking about. They tried to pigeon-hole it into what formerly they believed. And I know that one night at a dinner party with Aldous, Aldous Huxley, and he couldn't understand one word I was talking about when I spoke of the resurrection and the birth from above and the discovery of David. It was just like talking to him in an entirely different tongue, because to him he wasn't conditioned to follow that at all. To him it was a secular story.

It was not supernatural as I told him it was; to him it was secular. And he tried to pinpoint it by saying, "Caesar did this, you know, and we do have evidence..." and he mentioned some other character like Herod. And because of these two he'll take the entire book and call it secular where there is no evidence that we can find—we haven't found it in 2,000 years—for the historicity of the characters of the New Testament outside of the two that he mentioned. Well, I can mention any two to tie a story together.

And yet, he is the one who in his book *Ends and Means* that came out in '38 said, "I had motives for not wanting the world to have a meaning; consequently, I assumed that it had none, and was able without any difficulty to find satisfying reasons for this assumption." I was in the Ebell Club the night his home burned to the ground...it had no meaning...and all of his fabulous library, unpublished manuscripts... not only his own, but he told me of one that D. H. Lawrence gave him, it was never published, and so many marvelous things he had planned to give to a university, but he hadn't yet. He was going to leave them to a university after his death. I came out of my lecture night and here the hills are in flames and one was Aldous' home. The only thing that he saved was the suit he was wearing. Everything went right down into ash, because he said he had motives for not wanting the world to have a meaning, consequently he said, "I assumed that it had none." Well, if I assume that it had none, assumption hardens into fact and he found no difficulty in finding satisfying reasons for this assumption. I witnessed the entire destruction in just a matter of moments. It didn't take an hour to bring that whole thing right down into ash that took his entire life to collect. He had things that before he was born that came from his ancestors; for he had quite a long line of physical nobility, but nobility in the sense of literature...and they were all in his library, a beautiful library. I can see it now.

But, the world had no meaning! He didn't want it to have meaning and he confessed in this book that it was all based upon sex. Because of a certain expression of sex he didn't want the world to have a meaning to condemn him. So if it had no meaning then it wouldn't make any difference to him what he did. And it was all based upon that drive. Well, he could have done anything he wanted without saying that the world had no meaning, for that also had meaning. Whatever the sexual act was, God made it so because God loved it (Gen.1:31). He never would have made anything that he had not loved. But Aldous couldn't see that. Now, he's gone from this world...and whether he now can see that this story I tried to tell him on a few occasions is true and that this pattern will unfold in him one day as it must unfold in every child in the world. Jesus Christ is the pattern man and that pattern erupts in man like a tree, and unfolds. The same pattern…it does not alter. So you try to tell it. I tried to tell it to him and he is considered a brilliant, brilliant mind. Today, if you mention the name to any circle familiar with the English tongue, they will know the works of Aldous Huxley. In every library you'll find his books, all of his books. It's almost required reading in certain schools, certain universities for the use of English. But he couldn't understand me because he wasn't trained that way. So do not caste your pearls before swine…not that they are swine…but a pig would not appreciate a beautiful pearl. They might swallow it but couldn't digest it. They wouldn't know what to do with the pearl and because it's not edible chances are it would…

Are there any more questions?

Q: What is the meaning of Jesus entered Jerusalem riding on an ass?

A: It is simply a triumphant journey into Jerusalem. Jerusalem means "from above." As we are told in Galatians, there are two Jerusalems—one from below who bears children into slavery and one from above who bears children into freedom. And our mother is from above, she bore us into freedom. So this is a triumphant journey into Jerusalem moving towards the place of birth. For if you're moving towards the resurrection, which is the goal of going to Jerusalem, you must first move towards birth. For resurrection and birth come the same night, they come together. Resurrection from above is followed instantly by birth from above. So it is simply the triumphant journey *inward*. Well, the riding on the ass is only to fulfill Zechariah for "Your Lord will come riding upon an ass."

I saw a picture of Billy Graham riding on one in Jerusalem the other day. They had him in the morning *Times*. Then he got news of Eisenhower's death and so he got off the ass and flew back for the funeral. But there he was sitting on the ass coming into Jerusalem which is part of the ___(??), and the camera was there to take a picture of him. Well, let him continue in his little folly. One day he, too, will hear who Jesus Christ *really* is and when he hears it, oh, what a shock! I tell you it is the most disillusioning thing in the world after you've been raised as I was raised to believe in an external Jesus Christ then to find that he's within you, and you better be careful because he's within you and you are held responsible for every imaginal act that you do. And you can't avoid it…you can't say, well now, this is a little light one. Plant the weed and you're going to grow the weed.

So that is simply the journey, for you are told he did everything according to a chronological map. My time has not yet come, said he.

All right, when the time comes…as the time came he moved in and as he moved in the whole thing was the unfolding of a drama. Just like going to the pictures, going to a theater, and watch the chronological unfoldment of a play, he simply unfolded the play. Man has completely mistaken the personifications for persons and the vehicle that conveyed the instruction for the instruction itself. So man is completely confused.

But this triumphant ride, I experienced that. I wasn't riding on any ass; I was walking in a crowd and leading them towards Jerusalem when the voice rang out, and that was the triumphant ride in fulfillment of the 42nd chapter of Psalms. I can see it. The whole thing goes over and over in my mind. You and I played this drama completely *before* we came down, and then we forgot it. Every one of us were rehearsed individually in the entire drama, as you are told in the 3rd chapter of the Book of Galatians…only there we are called Abraham: "And the scripture, foreseeing that God would justify the heathen through faith, preached the gospel *beforehand* to Abraham" (3:8). So then in the 8th chapter of John, Jesus could say, "Before Abraham, was I am" (8:58). Before Abraham, as my friend brought out, was I am. And "Abraham rejoiced that he was to see my day; he saw it and was glad" (8:56). So he was shown the entire drama and all of us were in Abraham, for we are all children of faith. We saw the entire drama; we were well rehearsed in it. So when we have these experiences now it is simply a reenactment of the eternal drama, and that's when we go back after we completely reenact it, having forgotten it through these unnumbered years.

But now you all know who Jesus Christ is and he's in you. Don't turn to anyone on the outside; don't turn to any place on the outside as a holy place; for the kingdom of heaven is within *you*. The kingdom of God is within you and God is in his kingdom, therefore, God is in you. And who is he?—I am. Now, if I really believe that, I will start pruning my tree and not continue in the nonsense which I did prior to the discovery of who Jesus Christ really is.

Good night.

OUTER WORLD RESPONDS TO IMAGINAL ACTS

4/7/69

"All that you behold; tho' it appears without, it is within, in your Imagination, of which this world of mortality is but a shadow" (Blake, *Jerusalem,* Plt. 71). You cannot conceive of something that is not already contained within you. If you imagine it and enter into that state as though it were true, the outer world will respond to bear witness of this imaginal activity within you.

Now you try it. And if you prove it to your own satisfaction that it does work, then you come to this conclusion—you'll read it in the 13th chapter of the Book of Acts: "I have found in David the son of Jesse a man after my own heart, who will do all my will" (13:22). Now if the entire world responds to my imaginal activity, well then, that is David who will do all my will, for, he is doing my will. Well, if the Lord said David does my will and I by a simple imaginal act command the outer world to respond to it as though I struck a chord and everything in sympathy with the chord struck must respond to bear witness to this that is active within me, well then, who is the Lord? If I notice the world responding to what I am imagining, and David is one after my own heart who will do all my will, I see who David is: David is the outer world responding to my will. Now, it's not "will" as the world will use it…I will "will" it to be so. No, I will *imagine* it to be so. I am inwardly convinced that it is so. If I imagine that it is so and persist in that imaginal state as though it were true and the world responds, I have found David. And I have found the Lord…the Lord being my own wonderful human Imagination. The imaginal act in its response is David…there is David.

The Return of Glory

Now in Hebrew thought, history consists of all the generations of men and their experiences fused into one grand whole; and this concentrated time into which all the generations are fused and from which they spring is called eternity. Now we are told in Ecclesiastes that "God has put eternity into the mind of man, but so that man cannot find out what God has done from the beginning to the end" (3:11). Only in the end will we find out what God has put into man's mind. Well, he's put eternity which would contain *all* things. If all the generations of men and all of their experiences fused into one grand whole is put into the mind of man, every conceivable variety of experience is contained within that one grand whole. The word translated eternity is also translated "the world." But it is also translated and quite often in scripture as "the youth, the *stripling*, the young man" and these are three titles used of David. He said, "I have found David the son of Jesse." Well, Jesse means "I am" and that's the name of God. "I have found in David"—the Son of God, the son of Jesse—"a man after my own heart who will do all my will." Well, now I see that he really is the entire vast world of humanity and all of their experiences, but I do not know this until the very end. In the very end of the journey I find him personified as a single youth; not as unnumbered people, one single eternal being. For, eternity is personified as youth and not as an old man as the Greeks did. It is simply one single being and he is the youth called David. I will know this only in the end.

Now here is the day after the great event that tens of millions celebrated yesterday, and I wonder what percentage of them really understood what they witnessed. Listen to these words, this is the 20th chapter of John: And Peter went into the tomb and he saw the linen clothes lying, and the *napkin*, which was on his head, lying not with the linen clothes but rolled up in a place by itself (20:6-8). Well, you would wonder, "Why on earth would you put that into a story that is so dramatic, so all-together marvelous, why would you tell it?" You see the linen clothes and you see the napkin and they are not together, they are separated, and he finds this in the tomb. Now we are told that when he was brought to the tomb the tomb was called the skull, and there he was buried. There he was first crucified and there he was buried. So Peter goes into the tomb that's the skull, but *him* they do not see. He and his partner when they went in did not see the one that was put there, but they found the linen clothes and they found the napkin, and they were not together. The napkin was rolled up in a place by itself.

If you take it as a secular story, you will think a man died, had him in linen clothes and they covered his face with a cloth called a napkin, and then when they went in the third day the tomb was empty…he wasn't there but the linen clothes…well, you will think in terms of these. But that is not the symbolism of scripture. The linen clothes represent the physical body and

345

that's what they found. They found the physical body, the garment that he wore, but they did not find him. You would say then he was dead. No, that is not the story that is being told. They found the napkin. Well, in ancient times the word napkin had a far wider range of meaning than it has today. We have a dinner napkin, a cocktail napkin…we also have today a sanitary napkin. But this was a different kind of napkin. This napkin symbolizes the *placenta*, the afterbirth. If you know the true symbolism of scripture it is telling you a birth took place and it came from this. For, the napkin symbolizes simply the afterbirth…and here is the body that you found. Well now, something was born.

Now, this is in the Book of John, it is not in the other three gospels. John insists on a birth from above. Matthew and Luke who tell the story of the birth do not tell it in this manner and you would on reading that story imply a woman called Mary gave birth to a little child, as you were born, as I was born, but it differed from us. That's not the story. When you see the story in John, who is the most profound of all the New Testament writers, you see the birth and then you see who Mary is. Mary was the skull; Mary was that *womb* in which God entered. Or as Blake said, "God himself entered death's door with those who enter and lays down in the grave with them, in visions of eternity, until they awake and see Jesus and the linen clothes lying which the females had woven for them" (*Milton*, Plt.32). Well, my mother wove this garment, this fleshy garment. My mother wove it in her womb, this is the linen cloth that mother wove and she wove it for me. When it came forward, then following it came the placenta. The uterus had to expel it…it had to be discharged. It was no part of her. Here is the napkin telling that something entirely different took place, some birth, some *unusual* birth…something that was not known to man before…and it took place in the skull. The drama begins in the skull and ends there.

So here, unnumbered millions yesterday attended this service and they heard that he is risen. Well, yes he is risen, and so will you, for he is speaking of you…the whole story is all about you. God actually became as we are that we may be as he is, and he entered death's door, which is my skull, your skull. He enters and then has visions, visions of eternity, and all these horrible visions that you and I have which come forward as physical effects in our world—wars, famines, convulsions—everything in the world you and I imagine or it couldn't happen. So when I imagine a state and I find a response coming from without, I have found who God is. But "All things are made by him and without him is not anything made that is made" (Jn.1:3). But he also has to have one who will do all of his will. Then I find that 500 different people, male and female, were responsive to my imaginal act, and they seemed to be the instrument through which it became visible in my world—then I have found David. For, if David is a man after my own heart who will do *all* my will then humanity is David. But, in the end of my journey the *whole* is fused into a single youth and that youth is then personified as David. And strangely enough, coming from within you, then you stand and you face him, and he calls you Father. As told us in scripture, he will call God, the Lord, Father—"I have found David and he has cried unto me, 'Thou art my Father'" (Ps.89:26), and when he calls you Father the journey is at an end. But it took all the generations of men and all of their experiences to bring you to the point of confronting all of it fused into a single being, and that being is David. That's in store for every one in the world. Every child born of woman will discover eventually that he is the God who created the entire vast universe. He is the God who wills everything to happen; so in the end he forgives every being because everyone did his will. But everyone summed up simply means to him David: "I have found in David the son of Jesse"—which is I AM, my own son—"a man after my own heart who will do all my will" (Acts13:22).

Now in scripture you find these words, I, Jesus, tell you I am the root and the offspring of David (Rev.22:16). I created humanity, all these bodies that were dead, and then I entered them and animated them. They became animated, they could respond to my imaginal act. And then I came out of humanity. Having played unnumbered parts I came *out* of humanity, so I am now the offspring of humanity. I am the root, therefore the Father, and yet in the end I come forward from it as I promised myself that I would. So, go say unto David, "When your days are fulfilled and you lie down with your fathers, I will raise up your son after you who will come forth from your body. *I* will be his father, and he shall be my son" (2Sam.7:12,14).

So, I created humanity, came forth, and buried myself *in* humanity. For, a seed must fall into the ground and *die* before it is made alive. Unless it dies it remains alone, but if it dies it brings forth much (Jn.12:24). So God must die, so he comes into humanity. Humanity is made of the dust, the earth, so the seed falls into the earth called man. And then *in* man because it comes from God and is God, he says "I am." That's the name of God forever and forever. So here in these bodies you say "I am," well, that's God. Then you imagine a certain state and the world responds, good, bad or indifferent. Well, if it responds it's doing your will. So whether it be a single person who did it or unnumbered persons who did it, they represent David...for I have found David who does my will. So regardless of your present name, your present race, your present anything, you are David if you respond and make visible to me that which I have imagined. I not only have found David in the response, I have found the *cause* of that response, and I have found it in myself—that my imaginal act was the cause of the response of the world relative to me. So I have found the Father and the Son.

In the end of my journey, when I come to the very end and I am setting myself free from this world of death comes this wonderful mighty act. And the whole thing is fused before me into one single youth and he stands and there he is as described in the Book of Samuel, just as he's described in Samuel. And here is eternity that was buried in me: "God has put eternity into the mind of man yet so that man cannot find out what God has done from the beginning to the end" (Ecc.3:11). So all of a sudden, I'm in the end and the journey is over, and I am enhanced by reason of the experience of creating bodies that are dead, entering the bodies that are dead, and playing a part. I play all the parts and you will play all the parts. Your presence here tells me you have played them or you wouldn't be here, because no one comes unto me save my Father calls him...and I and my Father are one. So you wouldn't be here as you are without an interest. Your presence night after night proves that interest, and therefore proves that you are at the end of playing all the parts...with the same identity, no loss of identity. But you have played the part of the well-known and the unknown, of the wealthy and the poor, of the disgraced and the honored. You have played everything in the world, for everything is contained within you, and you can't conceive of a plot in the world that is not now a reality in you. But you need not animate it. If you enter into that state and assume that you are it, well then, not one power in the world could stop that from responding. And if it takes a dozen or ten dozen or a thousand men and women to respond to bear witness to that active state within you, they must respond, for they will do your will. "I have found in David a man after my heart who will do all my will." Not once has he ever failed me in doing my will...and humanity is David.

That is the Hebrew thought concerning history. This is their real concept...when I say "their" I do not mean the person you will know who is calling himself a Jew. I'm speaking of the Sanhedrin; I'm speaking of the giants in that wonderful setup. Yet the giant did not understand the word when he said you must be "born again." His name was Nicodemus and he was a member of the Sanhedrin and he said, "How can a man who is old re-enter his mother's womb and be born again?" (Jn.3:4). He said, "You, a master of Israel and you do not know? Except you are born from above you cannot enter the kingdom of heaven." In other words, you cannot enter the new age. And this whole drama is simply one being playing all the parts... one being expanding himself by first limiting himself to his own creation.

So he creates humanity. It's part of the structure of the universe and it's dead. Now he animates it. It is said, "He breathed upon them." Well, the word breath and the word spirit are one and the same in Hebrew and in Greek. So to breathe upon is simply to possess it. I possess the body and as I possess it, spirit enters it. That is animating it. But I am now in a body that is dead. I must now go through the horrors of the journey, and when I reach the very *end* of it then I begin to awake. And I awake just where I started the dream…I awake in Golgotha, the skull, the tomb, which is the skull of man. That's were I entered, and that's where I awake, and when I awake I emerge from it. I look back at that which I occupied for 6,000 years and it is ghastly pale. It's the linen clothes that my mother wove in her womb. And then I depart, leaving, and the body expels that which is the *napkin*. And I come out, and others come to find me. They find only the discarded body and they find now the thing which symbolizes my birth. It's only a symbol of my birth from above.

Having had the experience I can tell you exactly how it happened. You start in the skull and you end in the skull…and the whole drama begins in man. The drama is all about God and there is nothing but God. It is God who created it, it is God who is playing it, and in the end it is God who extracts himself, and he rises from his own state which was a dead state. That is resurrection.

But if you think in terms of one little being called Jesus Christ, you miss it completely. That is not the mystery. Jesus Christ is your own wonderful human Imagination, and *that* is God himself. When you imagine a state wait for the response…it will come. Everything will come. It will come just like any sound that you make will bring a response, because in your world there is something that is attuned to the note that you struck. It will come. Everyone in the world will play the part they must play *if* I remain faithful to any state into which I enter.

So when Paul makes the statement, "Remember Jesus Christ descended from David according to my gospel," he's telling you now that it's *my* gospel and that he experienced it. He does not deny the descent of Jesus Christ from David, yet he knows that David was created *by* Jesus Christ. He buried himself in it and died…forgets himself completely as being the one who created it, and then extracts himself from it…now far more luminous than when he entered it, far more translucent then when he entered it, far greater in power and wisdom than when he entered it. For God is truth and truth is an ever-expanding illumination and there is no limit to the expansion. So when he comes out and he begins to expand, he is enhanced by the experience of coming into the world of death and overcoming death. So resurrection is simply the rising from the dead, and the dead is simply theses bodies in which we are now encased.

So the little napkin...don't look for it as the world sees it. It's a symbol just as I have told you. I know what I am talking about. You won't find it; I didn't find it. I knew what happened, but I knew why John placed the word napkin there and gave such importance to it, such significance, because he was the one person who stressed the necessity of being born from above. "You *must* be born from above." Well, the one sign of birth would be that. If you come and you find that, then you find a body. And that belongs to the body, but it was not with the body, because it can't be with the body after the birth. It's only with the body prior to the birth. But when the birth takes place, when the offspring comes out, that is then discharged from the uterus. And it's a *sign* that something came out of this, but this one they do not see, for he is now born from above. And no one can see Spirit with mortal eyes. So they came in and they saw the remnant of the things he wore, but him they did not see.

This is the story as told us if one understands the symbolism of scripture. And the day will come that you'll experience it. Everyone will experience it, and you and I will once more be back into the one body we occupied before the descent into these bodies. For the body of the risen Christ is not something that is finished; it is in the process of erection, made up of the redeemed, made up of everyone who has had that experience. And everyone *must* have that experience, so eventually that body will be the most glorious thing in eternity, for it will be far more luminous and more wonderful than it was prior to the descent into its own creation of death. It was done deliberately.

You didn't do one thing that was wrong to come into the bodies of death called man. You are God. You are not some little worm coming out of the slime, moving from there into some little bird, and from the bird into something else, then something else, and finally man. No, all of this is part of the structure of the universe. You descended into man and animated man...all of us. And no more can descend into humanity than the number of the sons of God and it takes all the sons of God to make God. The word is plural, the Elohim...these are the gods, the sons of God that together make up *the* I AM. And you can't have more in this world than there are sons of God. So every child born of woman could only be born and be animated because a son of God, an ancestral being is in it and animating it, controlling it, and putting it through all the paces by putting himself through; and in the end he extracts himself from that body. That body was his David, his beloved, because the whole vast world is David, because the world has to respond to his will.

Someone now sitting in a dungeon feeling abused, by some intense Imagination entering into the image conceived by her is causing disturbances in the world. She is completely unknown, buried in a dungeon, and she is treading the winepress. While completely unseen and unknown by the world she is causing a response in the whole vast world. Who knows who is actually causing the response today in this conflict, that conflict and the other? No one knows. Some unseen person can be the source of the conflict. We don't really know.

And we go forward giving what is called advice, more and more so-called good advice when scripture doesn't speak of giving any good advice; it speaks only of giving good news. Go and tell them the good news, that you created it, and you will simply extract yourself from it. And so, you are the immortal being. Don't give any good advice. Let people be just what they want to be. I don't care what they are, let them be. They want to grow beards and long…well, there was a time that everyone grew a beard. Let him grow his beard, let him grow his mustache, let him do all the things in the world as long as he doesn't interfere with you. As far as you are concerned if you don't want to grow one, don't grow one. And no one will disturb you if you in your own wonderful way imagine you are free, free as the wind, and live in that state. And the world will respond to you and treat you with all the respect you do. But if you get entangled in it, trying to work against shadows—for they're all shadows if they respond to my imaginal act then they're shadows—how can they be causative in my world? If I give them the power of causation, then I'm transferring what rightly belongs to me to them, and they're only shadows. The whole vast world bears witness of the activity taking place within us, and so the whole world only mirrors what I am doing within myself. That's all that it's doing. If I know that, I am set free!

I keep on to the very end. And when this terrific series of events begins to unfold within me and I'm at the very end of the road, tell the story. Tell it to encourage your brothers, because we're all brothers. "Go and tell my brothers I am ascending unto *our* Father. Go and tell them I am ascending unto our God" (Jn.20:17). And when we get there we *are* the Father and we are the God. It is not you and I as brothers and he as Father; we together, collectively, are the Father…we are God. So go tell my brothers I am ascending unto my Father, your Father, unto my God and your God. So in the end we are only one, one wonderful being. And the body is now being slowly erected out of the redeemed and everyone will be redeemed. I can't conceive of one being lost. One of my brothers lost in the world of death? Why, I would leave the ninety and nine and go in search of him. I could not leave one in a body that is still not yet awakened. He would have to be redeemed or the temple is missing a stone and it's not finished. So everyone in the end is going to be redeemed. Yes, Hitler, Stalin, all the so-called monsters of the world, for they only responded to the fears and the frightening, horrible things that men set in motion.

My friend, who is here tonight, gave me a letter last Friday and she said that she rarely buys a paper, but several weeks ago she bought a Sunday paper and going through it she came across a story, a short story of this woman who called herself "a great medium" and, naturally, California is going to go right into the Pacific. So she took all of the members of her family and went off to Spokane. Then she said, "Weeks went by and a friend of mine called and she brought in a paper. As I told you I do not buy papers and that was simply an occasion when I bought that Sunday paper. So she brought in a paper and I took the paper and went through the pages and here I came upon a little news item; the same woman, the same medium who took her family from California and went off to Spokane died suddenly of a fatal heart attack, age twenty-nine." All right, so California did disappear, as far as she is concerned her world vanished. She is now in a world like this, but it need not be in her little California. She's in some section of time best suited for the work yet to be done in her to bring her to the knowledge of who she is. This frightened little thing...so she died at age twenty-nine. And she is one of the great soothsayers who has frightened so many in this state. Friends of mine left it, went off to Arizona. But they don't realize you can only take yourself with you. You can go from here to the ends of the earth. If you make your bed in hell, you're still there, because God is there and you are God. You can't get away from being God, although you may not know that you are, and so if you are afraid here you're going o be afraid there.

So in her case the fear possessed her. It's like Job...he said, "My fears have come upon me" (Job3:25). He was so afraid, he was creating his own disaster and then it came upon him. Now we are told in the end that it was God who brought it. But in the end he realized who God was: God was himself. He said, "I heard of thee with the hearing of the ear, but now my eye sees thee." Now I *know*, I experienced...I was praying to a God external to myself and all of my fears came upon me while I pleaded with a God who did not exist to *do* something about it. In the end, the very last chapter, the 42nd chapter, "I have heard of thee with the hearing of the ear, but now my eye sees thee" (42:5). He now sees the symbol that reveals to him that *he is* God the Father. And all that he had lost returned to him because it had to return...but it was double. Because when God comes out of this and extracts himself from this fabulous experience, everything that he was is doubled when he comes out.

That's the story of Job. Job didn't do anything wrong; he simply imagined the wrong things. It began with a so-called devil. Well, the devil doesn't exist outside of man. The devil is *doubt,* that's all that it is. Satan is the doubter. And so, I doubt the reality of my imaginal acts...all right, so that's Satan. I can't believe in the reality of the unseen imaginal act. Well, then don't, but you still will imagine anyway. You will not believe in the reality of *this* imaginal act, but you'll turn from this, you'll turn to another, because you can't stop imagining, for imagining is God and imagining animates the world. That is the power of the world. So in the end, I have heard of thee, but I didn't see you. Now my eye sees you, and then all the things that were taken from him are now returned a hundred-fold.

So here, this wonderful birth that was celebrated yesterday is the birth from above, but they celebrated it only as resurrection. Resurrection and birth from above are two sides of the same coin; it takes place the same night. And it doesn't have to take place on any first Sunday after the full moon in Aries. That is simply a mark set up by the priesthoods of the world. It can take place at any moment in time and it is still taking place every moment of time. For, the temple is being constructed and the whole thing is being rebuilt on a more glorious scale out of living bodies. For, we are the living stones that will now form the New Jerusalem.

So believe me when I tell you your own wonderful human Imagination is Jesus Christ. That is the being that entered death's door, you skull, and that is the being who is dreaming the world in which you live and that is the being which will emerge. When he does, you are Jesus Christ and there never was another one and there's only one. So when I awake, I am he; when you awake, you are he; and we all awake, we are he. And so, together we form the one being and that one being is the Lord God, the Creator of it all.

So don't envy anyone, don't condemn anyone, for a judgment is an activity of your own Imagination and with what judgment you judge will be judged on you. You'll fulfill it. So leave them alone. You'll find people always trying to get you into a certain little circle to make you pass an opinion. What do you think of the hippies? What do you think of is one? What do you think of that one? Well, I'm quite sure if any of us had a memory long enough, we could go back and trace everything we now see in the world to some ancestor. If we go back far enough all were our ancestors: we had hippies, we had thieves, we had murderers, and we had everything. I think it was Lord George when he tried to bring in a change in the land reforms of England, and he got up in the House where he was prime minister, and he was trying to bring about some reform of the land reform. He turned to the opposition and he said that "every Englishman today in order to trace ownership of his land must go back to the ancestor who first stole it." Well, he got a lovely reaction on that, because you can't go back far enough unless you find the one who stole it. We speak of kings today...no one was originally born a king. He had to steal that position and maintain it by arms, because who ever appointed him as king? Who appointed anyone in a position of that nature? You go back far enough and they all stole it. So when he was trying to bring about land reform in England he said, "You can lay claim to this land only by going back far enough to find the ancestor who stole it."

Now, you don't have to go back and change anything. Leave it just as it is. He wants a thousand acres, let him have it, a 100,000 acres, let him have it. You are satisfied with just simply living in a lovely apartment, all right, take the apartment. But you will say, "Well, I can't afford it." If you say that you can't afford it, that's your imaginal act. I would suggest to you when you say that you can't afford it, this night to sleep in that apartment, mentally, as though you occupied it, with all the funds necessary to pay for it. And in a way you do not know the world will respond and you will get the necessary funds to pay for it. If you don't want that and you want to own your own home then sleep in a place as though you owned it and the necessary funds will come; because the world only responds, it doesn't cause. It responds to your own imaginal act, for there's only one God and that God is *in* you as your own wonderful human Imagination.

Now, before you judge it, may I ask you to try it. If you try it, you can't fail! And if you really try it and you prove it in the testing, well then, you become one who will spread the good news to your brothers, and tell everyone that you meet how things work in this world. So they will not feel, "Well, I didn't have it at birth. I didn't have the good chances as a child. I didn't have the parents who had it, the proper education." Forget all of these things and just simply take this principle and you can't fail. "For an assumption, though false, if persisted in will harden into fact" (A. Eden). That is true. So when you know what you want, just assume that you have it, and persist in that assumption as though it were true, mentally seeing the world that you would see if it were true. And as you walk, you are calling a response to it. And eventually, in the not distant future, you will find yourself occupying that state physically in this world.

Well, now don't forget it. We go to sleep after we realize our dream and try to hold onto the dream that is now solidly real in our world and try to protect it with secular means. Don't! Hold on to it only in your Imagination, for we are given a warning that this man said, "I have all that it takes, more than enough. I will now build bigger barns to house and then take my ease" and the Lord said to him, "O fool, tonight your soul is required of thee." You don't have to hold onto anything…hold on only in your own wonderful human Imagination. If something is taken from you, all right, somewhere along the way you allowed it by assuming that you had lost it, toying with the idea what would it be like if it were true that I had lost it. And then you dropped it, forgetting that you did that, and then comes the moment that you lose it. If you *want* to lose it, all well and good; if you don't, then hold onto your things only in Imagination and don't build barns to house them.

But don't forget the story of the birth as told in John. He does not describe it as Matthew does, and as Luke does, but he tells us it is essential to enter a new age. And then, in the very end he gives it to us in the most beautiful symbolism, but the symbolism is not understood. They see death. And yet it's only through death that one lives, so "The seed must fall into the ground and die before it is made alive. If it dies, it bears much; if it doesn't fall into the ground it remains alone" (Jn.12.24). So God dies: "Unless I die thou can'st not live; but if I die I shall arise again and thou with me" (Blake, *Jerusalem, Plt. 96)*. And I rise out of death.

Now let us go into the Silence.

* * *

Now are there any questions, please?

Q: If I'm imagining a thing a certain way and I'm involved with another person who's also doing imagining about the same thing, but there's a difference in opinion and they're thinking an opposite way, what's going to happen?

A: The minute you know that *he* is doing it in the opposite direction you've transferred the power that rightly belongs to you to the other. There is no *he;* he only reflects what you are imagining. But the minute you believe that another has power greater than yourself, you are now dividing the power that is rightly yours and giving it to hm. It doesn't really matter what others are thinking, what are you thinking? And so, it is entirely up to you to either believe completely in the unity of God, the oneness of God. "Hear, O Israel, the Lord our God, the Lord is one" not two. So when they say, "If the Lord is one" you say "I AM, that's his name forever." He didn't say "we are" but "I AM." So the minute that you say he is doing it, well, you've taken the one grand confession of faith, the shema, and divided it. That is not the confession of faith.

When asked to name the greatest of all Commandments, that's what he named. He did not name any of the Ten Commandments; he named the shema, "Hear, O Israel, the Lord our God is one" (Deut.6:4). So when I say, well, I'm doing this and someone tells you but he is doing the opposite, who is he? He is put into this world to bear witness to all that *I do*, not to take from me the power that is mine. So he never gave it to another. Let the whole vast world do what they feel like doing. You will find in the end that it's all been resolved.

I have heard women say to me, "You know, I want *that* man and only that man, and I don't want any other man; and don't give me any criticism about it. I want him." I said, "But he's married." "It doesn't matter, I want him"…the only man. But, I've gone to their weddings and it was not that man. What they really wanted was to be happily married and they tied it to *a* man. What they wanted was the state of blissful marriage. I've gone to their weddings and they always get a little smile on their faces, a little embarrassment, because they know the discussion that they had with me about *that* man.

I'm not speaking of only one woman, I'm speaking of quite a few that I knew back in New York City who had these problems that they had to have that man…and it wasn't that man. And as time went by, they realized that he never could have filled the bill. I know this from experience, so I'm not concerned when they tell me, "Now, don't try to dissuade from this person…it has to be this person." I'm not interested… tell me what you want and don't give me all the problems about what's going to stop it.

The minute you start that, you are taking the shema and shattering the entire confession of faith: "Hear, O Israel: The Lord our God is one Lord." And I can't even say "we are" in that confession, I have to say "I am." And "When I go to the people and I say that the Lord has sent me, and I say he is the God of our fathers, the God of Abraham, and the God of Jacob, and the God of Isaac, what shall I say? Just say, 'I AM has sent me unto you" (Exod.3:13).'" He didn't say, "Go and say we are"—like three fathers, one of Abraham, one of Jacob, and one of Isaac—the same one—and his name is I AM, and that is my name forever and forever. So the minute I go out and I say "you are" that's something that is a shadow. And "he is" that's even further away. So I must walk in the assumption that *I am* that which I want to be as though I were. And you get closer and closer to that wonderful confession, and you live by it.

Until Friday. Thank you.

CREATING ONE NEW MAN INSTEAD OF THE TWO

4/11/69

We are told in Ephesians that "He is our peace, who has made us both one that he might create in himself one new man in place of the two, so bringing peace; and that this one broke down the wall of hostility between the two" (2:14). Now, this bond of peace is not a doctrine or philosophy or any kind of abstraction; it is a person, an actual person. The being that will break down that wall of hostility between you as you are seated here and the being that you really are is a person. That person is God. It's the Son of God, and the Son of God and God are one and the same person.

Now here, a lady writes a letter and she said, "I saw myself radiantly perfect, but I mean perfect. And yet I knew that we were two, two persons. I knew at one time as I remembered I was not perfect, I knew it, and I remembered when I heard the words 'Be ye perfect." And now I know that as I looked at this perfection it was myself as I am *now*. So I woke having seen this radiant being that I am, and she was perfect. Yet as I woke I stumbled into the door and then lost my temper and bawled out my children for pouring soap on my nice clean carpet. So it must have happened in some other dimension of my being—for certainly it was not here where I lost my temper—when I saw my own perfection." She's right. While we are still wearing these garments of flesh and blood, let no one tell you that you will not lose your temper, that you will not do all the things that people do in this world. Are we not told that the perfect one, who was the pattern man, when he said, "Go tell that viper, Herod." Are we not told in scripture of all these unlovely things that the perfect one said "You whited sepulchers," and all the other words that go with it? While we are encased in a body of flesh and blood certainly we will lose our temper. We react just...maybe not as we formerly did...but then we were not ashamed of what we did...but now we pick ourselves up, as she did, instantly. She lost her temper with her children for pouring—well, who wouldn't?—soap on her nice clean carpet after this perfectly wonderful vision.

So he is our peace who broke down the wall of partition and made of the two of us, made one. Now how is this brought about? We are told the primal wish of God was "Let us make man in our image, after his likeness." We are told that "He who began a good work in you will bring it to completion at the day of Jesus Christ" (Phil.1:6). We are told that Jesus Christ is the *image* of God, the perfect image, who reflects and radiates the image of God, the *glory* of God; that he is the express *image* of God. Well now, that is the good work that is being done in us and when that image can be superimposed upon the one who is doing it and they are one, well then, *you* are God. There is only God in the world...there is nothing but God. So God actually took himself the limitations of man, just as you are, and he is working from within and working you into *his image*. And when the image is superimposed upon the one who is making it, it's not you *and* the image, you are the Maker. You are God himself. Then he rises, enhanced by reason of the experience of making an image of himself that radiates his being and reflects his glory. So her vision was perfect, perfectly marvelous, all based upon scripture.

Now, here is another beautiful one. She said, "I found myself in a beautiful forest and here I am sitting on the ground leaning against a tree. Then I heard a voice calling, 'Father, Father' and I did not answer because I did not want to be discovered. Suddenly a youth appeared dressed as a shepherd boy, and it was you. You said to me, 'Why did you not answer me? I've been searching and searching for you.' Then she said to me, "You're always searching for me, but you always seem to find me in spite of the fact that the Good Book tells us that after my labor I should rest on the seventh day. But you never let me...you're always calling and you always find me... so you never let me rest." Then she said, "I looked at you and I smiled the smile of an indulgent father, and then strangely enough, I, a woman—and I consider myself very much a female—felt that I was the Father. It didn't seem strange to me to be a father. I was not a mother, and I was not a female, I was Father."

Now here is scripture, the 4th chapter of Galatians, "When the time had fully come, he sent forth the Spirit of his son into our hearts crying, 'Father! Father!'" (4:4,6). But the Father doesn't want to respond. As we are told in the 44th Psalm, "Rouse thyself! Why sleepest thou, O Lord? Awake!" (44:23). The Father is sound asleep in man. And when one awakens who is called the son of God—and all are the sons of God—that son awake is sent into the world to call the Father. And those in whom the time has fully come still do not want to respond. They always want to postpone the day of wakening, still holding on to these little garments of flesh and blood, but he always finds them. He always finds them and does not let them rest. He keeps on crying "Father!" So we are told in the 5th of John, "Truly, truly, I say unto you, the dead will hear the voice of the Son of God, and those who hear him will live" (5:25). Well, she heard him so she is not far from the awakening. She heard him and recognized him. He was the shepherd boy, the one who was sent to do God's will, for he was the Son of God, and the Son comes only to do the Father's will, calling the Father in man to awaken: "Awake, you sleeper, and rise from the dead" (Eph.5:14).

So here in this world of ours, God became as we are for the sole purpose of making us, his image, as he is. And when the image is completed in us, so it superimposes itself upon the Maker of that image and they are one, then it's perfect. As she said, "I knew I was perfect and I recall having heard the words 'Be ye perfect.'" Well, the completed sentence is "as your Father in heaven is perfect." "So I heard the words 'Be ye perfect.'" When you are perfect the image is perfect, well then, you become one with your Maker, and you begin to awake from this dream of life, and the awakening is the resurrection. Without the resurrection this would be infinite circles, a repetition over and over and over again. Having moved around the circle unnumbered times, then comes the image and the image then turns into a spiral and moves up *as* the being who created it.

So here in this world, you can write all the documents in the world concerning peace…you'll never have peace. You can write every contract in the world between nations, between people, between everything. You will not have peace until he, in you, has so made you that you are as perfect as he is perfect and the two become one. So "He is our peace, who has made us both one, and has broken down the dividing wall of hostility." He breaks it down between the two so they aren't two any more, they're only one. And you walk without telling it to others, knowing who you really are. You tell it to the world and they only mock you, they laugh at you…because while in this world, as she is in this world, you will bump into a door and lose your temper, and someone else will ask in a way you think they should not and you'll lose your temper…just as she did even though she has seen her own perfection.

So everyone in this world is here for a definite purpose and when purpose is revealed—and it's only revealed through revelation—then it gives *meaning* to the whole of life. Without purpose, what has the world to offer? If tonight you owned everything that you could possibly buy with money and you had all that it takes, and tonight your soul is called? No, you will not die, I assure you. I'm speaking from experience, you will not die. The world will call you dead and they'll cremate you, scatter your dust, but you cannot die. But you're in a world just like this, going over the same things, over and over and over again. Oh, maybe not in the same situation, but just as solidly real as you are now; returned to a lovely beautiful form, twenty years old, to continue aging as we do here, to marry, and to lose your temper, to bump yourself into doors once more, until finally the image is perfect. When it is perfect and superimposed upon the maker of that image, then up you go into this one body, one Spirit, one Lord, one God and Father of all… and you are that one. That is the great temple, the living, growing temple, as we are told in scripture. It grows, for it's added to every moment of time as one comes up and is incorporated into the living body of the living God. You will eventually know that you are that body; you are that Spirit, you are that ultimate being that is God the Father of all.

It seems incredible as you sit here a little person, as I stand here a very weak, little person, and that is my destiny? To know myself to be the Creator of it all, the whole vast world, to share with all in a unity, that one body, that one Spirit, that one Lord, that one God and Father of all? Yes all. And I am telling you what I have experienced and having experienced it, sent back to tell it, to record it, for just a short while in the hope that those who are on the verge of moving up in the same direction into the same body, and the same Spirit, may hear it and be encouraged to know that one did do it.

So when Paul makes the statement, "I stand before you on trial for the hope in that promise that God made to our fathers. O King Agrippa, why should it seem incredible to any of you that God raises the dead?" Why? Is it not the promise to our fathers? You can search the scriptures, where is the promise made?—right in the seed plot of scripture which is Genesis. And we are told in Genesis, "And the Lord said unto Israel in visions of the night"— read it in the 46th chapter of Genesis—"in the visions of the night." And he said, "Jacob"—as you know, Israel was the name given to Jacob and Israel means "the man who shall rule *as* God," not like God, *as* God, he is God. "Jacob?" and then Jacob answers, "Here am I." Then the Lord speaks to him, "I am God, the God of your fathers. Fear not to go down into Egypt, for there I will make of you a great nation. I will go with you down into Egypt and I also will bring you up out of Egypt" (Gen.46:3,4). That was the promise. You mean he only came down into this world? Well, this world is Egypt. Egypt is not a little place in North Africa; the world is Egypt and Egypt is the world of death where everything seems to disappear. It appears, it waxes, it wanes and it vanishes. So everything in the world comes in,

The Return of Glory

grows, wanes and disappears…that's Egypt. "I will go down into Egypt with you, but I will also bring you up again."

"I stand before you on trial in these chains for believing in that hope that God promised to our fathers. And why do you think it incredible that God raises the dead?" (Acts 26:6,8). We have no answer in scripture from the king, King Agrippa, he was the last of the great ___(??). That world was coming to its end, like our present British Empire. Well, it is coming to its end. Anyone born now who calls himself a prince is almost ridiculous in this fabulous world in which we now live. So they come in to inherit what, a fading empire…not a fading, one that is gone, all its glory is gone. So he comes in still a prince, Prince of Wales now in a matter of moments. And so here he stands in chains before the prince of that day whose kingdom was fading, but he still had to hold onto it. We are in this world, the same world here. It goes over and over and over.

So I tell you, God actually, literally became you, just as you are, with all the weaknesses, all the limitations of the flesh. And there is no peace in the world for you until the image that is being formed in you by the Maker of you is perfect as he is perfect. When they are superimposed one upon the other, well then, you awake, awake from the dream of life and you ascend into your true, true being, the being that is called the kingdom of heaven. That's your true home…our commonwealth is in heaven. We are sojourners in this land that is strange to us, and we are enslaved while we are here and maltreated. All are beaten in this world. But have faith and set your hope fully upon that moment in time when the image is perfect, and it is unveiled within you, and you are the being who made it. Though you are the made, you are the Maker, for the Maker and the made become one as he breaks down the wall of partition, of hostility, between them. Then they aren't two any more, only one. So you'll return to your heavenly state *as* the God who came down and you are enhanced by reason of the descent into Egypt. So, it is as though you are speaking to another, but, really, in the end it's not another. I purposely imposed upon myself this limitation. I have no sense of another now, yet formerly there were actually feelings within me of two. Now I have no feeling whatsoever of another. It's simply the one who formed me into his own likeness and I awoke as he is. He and I are not two, we are one.

And so, this lady could see me coming in the garb of the shepherd boy doing my work, because I sent myself. The Father and the Son are one and the one that is sent is always called the Son. So he sends the Spirit of the Son into the world, into the heart of man crying, "Father, Father." Read it in the 4th chapter of Galatians (4:6). And here the man who hears it—in her case she heard it—yet in the very end of her vision it didn't seem strange to her that she was a man and the man was a father. Here in this world she is not married. She is very much a lady but she is not married, but very much a feminine person. And in her own words to me she said, "I have always shied from marriage. The very thought of marriage to me was offensive and the very thought of sex was always offensive." And here she is very much that retiring being and still it didn't seem strange to her that she was not only man but a father. The father who was hearing the word "Father" being called and he did not respond. He didn't want to be disturbed. For, as she said in her letter, "Haven't you heard? Do you not know it is said in the great book that after my labor I, on the seventh day, should rest...and you never let me rest?" No, the Son of God never lets the Father rest. He is calling forever, "Awake, you sleeper! Awake. Why sleepest thou, O Lord?" (Ps.44:23)

And so, the Father in man really cannot fully awake until he completes his work. "For he who began a good work in you will bring it to completion at the day of Jesus Christ" (Eph. 1:6). And Jesus Christ is the image that he is forming in you, for that is the image of God himself, the express image of God who radiates and reflects the glory of God. So when it is completed, well then, you will awake. So I am crying and crying through the night in the forest ...and she is seated on the ground...she's not alone, others are hearing the same voice. "For, I tell you truly," said he, "the dead will hear the voice of the Son of God and those who hear will live" (Jn.5:25). They will awake from the dream of life and awake and return to what they were, only more glorious, more wonderful than they were when they descended from that exalted state. So everyone here is destined to fulfill that state, everyone.

Now tonight, we have quite a few friends—I haven't seen a few of them in years—they haven't heard anything like this, because they haven't been with me in all the years. And so you will tolerate me for a moment to go back and pick them up where we left them off. I left them off with the law, not with the Promise. They heard nothing from me about the Promise unless they read my book that came out since I met them. They haven't been to my meetings they told me tonight not since the Ebell. Well, that's a long time and so *The Law and The Promise* was not brought out then. So for their sake, it is the same thing only raised to a higher level. But for those who only knew the law, let me now pick it up for you, just the law.

The law is very simple. There are infinite numbers of states, infinite numbers—the state of health, the state of sickness; the state of wealth, the state of poverty; the state of being known, the state of being unknown. They are only states. You're always in a state. Every moment of time you are only in a state. The state to which you most often return constitutes your dwelling place. So we all have one state that we feel more at home in that

The Return of Glory

state, and so we return to it moment after moment. That constitutes our dwelling place.

But if it is not a pleasant state in which to live, we can always get out of it. But we remain in the state and try to get out of it through external means...and that is not what we teach. You don't get out of it by trying to pull wires form the outside, manipulating things on the outside. You get out of these states simply by a mental adjustment within yourself. As you fell into the present state either deliberately or unwittingly—chances are you did it unwittingly—so you are in a state and you are the life of that state and the state becomes alive and grows like a tree and bears the fruit of that tree. But you don't like the fruit that you are bearing—it may be the fruit of poverty, may be the fruit of distress, the fruit of all kinds of unlovely things. Well now, how do I detach myself from this unlovely harvest that I'm harvesting all the time?

I do it by simply an adjustment in my own wonderful human Imagination. I ask myself what do I want instead of what I seem to have. When I name it, I ask myself, how would I see the world if things were as I desired them to be? How would I see them...what would the *feeling* be like if it *were* true? When I know exactly what the feeling would be like were it true, I try to catch that feeling. And to aid the feeling I imagine that I'm seeing people that I know well and I allow them to see me as they would see me if what I am feeling were true. I let them see me in my Imagination and when the whole thing is adjusted in my mind's eye so that they see me as I would see them and it now produces in me the feeling I desire, then I sleep. I fall asleep in that assumption. That assumption is a state, that's all that it is, it's a state. Now, let me make that state as natural as I made the former state that I did not like. If I find myself returning to this new state *constantly*, all of a sudden it becomes natural. As going home tonight, it will seem natural to me to go home and undress and sleep in my familiar bed.

If tonight I went to some other place, no matter how glorious it is, beautifully furnished and everything at my command, it wouldn't seem natural. When I leave here to go to San Francisco or New York and go into those lovely hotels, certainly, I pay much more money in these hotels than I pay in rent where I live, but it's not as comfortable and not as natural. So you go to a hotel and you pay twenty-two, twenty-three dollars a day. Well, I don't pay that sort of money in my rent, but it doesn't compare to my natural state where I am. I feel so natural when I go home tonight and just get into my bed, get into my place. Well now, you must make this state just as natural. At first it seems unnatural like buying a new suit or buying a hat... it doesn't seem natural. So you walk down the street and no one knows you, but you have a new hat, and you really believe that every one who passes by is looking at your hat, that they can see a new hat, and they don't care whether you are living or not. But you are aware of the fact that it is new and until it becomes an old hat in your mind's eye you are conscious of the fact that you are wearing a new hat. Well, you're conscious of the fact that you are wearing a new state until you make it natural. So the state to which you most constantly return constitutes your place of home. I call it your home.

Now, most of us have this great weakness. We know what we want or we think we know what we want, and we construct it in our mind's eye, but we never occupy it. We never move into it and make it natural. I call that perpetual construction, deferred occupancy. We don't occupy it. I can have a lovely place where I think one day I am going to go, but I keep on postponing the day, postponing the day, and I don't occupy it. I wish so-and-so were…and I name it. But if I wish so-and-so were as I would like them to be, that's the state from which I view them. Well, I've had the state, I've built it, I've constructed it, but I don't occupy it. Perpetual construction, all day long I have the state. If she were only and I name it, but I don't go into the state and view her *from* that state…I don't occupy the state. So she remains in my mind's eye in the unlovely state in which I see her.

Now that's the world in which we live. There are only states, an infinite number of states. You can't think of a thing that you could not reduce to a state, but the *life* of the state is the individual when he occupies it, because his Imagination gives *life* to the state. You can't give life to it from without, because God's name is I AM. God's name is not "you are" or "they are"; his eternal name is I AM…that's the light of the world, that's the life of the world. So, if I would make a state alive, I must be in it. So I can say I am here. If you are here, what are you seeing? Well, I am seeing her and she is lovely. Things are just as I've always desired them to be for her. So that's how I'm seeing her right now…I'm in the state.

Now make that state natural. Sleep in that state for her sake and then you'll make that state and incorporate it into your own lovely state so that whenever you think of her you're thinking of her *from* that state. You can take everyone, one after the other, and make it a natural thing for them until finally when you discuss them or refer to them or think of them, it is always from that state. Others may not see them in that light. It doesn't really matter what they think. I'm quite sure if I took some survey concerning what people think of me in my small world, no two would agree. Some would say, well, he's a charlatan, why, he's a deceiver; others would say I think he's the nearest thing to God that I've ever seen. You have all kinds. What a range, from the devil to God, and all about the same person based upon the state in which you are when you're called upon to define me. And so, you define me based upon your state. So, everyone in this world *could* be what he would like to be if he knows this principle and *applies* it. We are the operant power; it doesn't operate itself. I may know it from A to Z, but knowing it is one thing and *doing* it is another. Can I really do it? Well, I can do it…then *do* it. Don't say knowledge is enough. Knowing it will not do it. I am the operant power.

So, for you who are here for the first time in many years then pick it up from there, because we've had a long interval between the law and the Promise. Because I fell heir to the Promise in its completeness back in 1959 and if you haven't heard me since, then what I have been teaching since this revelation from within me would be something entirely new as far as you're concerned…like a new world, a new language. Yet I cannot deny the law, for I came not to destroy the law and the prophets who prophesied of the law and prophesied of the Promise. I came not to deny or in any way to obliterate them but to fulfill them. As I stand here before you tonight I have fulfilled them; I have fulfilled the Promise in its entirety. And all I ask is that you share with me your fulfillment of that wonderful Promise.

Now, I've told you that in the resurrection man is above the organization of sex, and in the resurrection man can change his sex at will. I've been waiting for someone to bring forward an actual vision to testify to the truth of that statement. Well, one came forward in a letter that I got today. He is here tonight. He is married and he has a lovely girl and he is every bit a man. His attitude toward sex is always the opposite, that is, the man. Yet in his experience, he said, "I found myself lying in a bed and I'm a woman and reveling in the feeling of being a woman and wanting not men but *one* man. I knew exactly the man that I wanted…he was Oriental in caste, of olive skin. And I knew exactly what I wanted, and here I assumed that I found him and he appeared. It was exactly as I had assumed: here is a man, olive skin and he was Asian. I felt so thrilled." He didn't carry it through to any act whatsoever. It was simply that at that moment he woke and said, "Does it have any significance?"

All in the world! You only verify the truth of what I've told you from experience. I've told you that in the resurrection man changes his sexual garments at will and in the resurrection he is above the organization of sex. He creates without the divided image of male-female. And so you've had it, you've had the proof of what I've told you and you now know from experience that it's true. Well, he trusts me implicitly concerning all the other things I've told him. But I will say to him, you, too, are on the verge, for this is really moving toward resurrection. So what you had is proof of what takes place only in the resurrection… and you had it. So I think your vision was perfectly marvelous, perfectly wonderful. Here he is now in this room and he came back to this world surprised that it could have happened to him because he's such a man. But in the end, you are every being in the world.

Like this one who is unmarried but so feminine and she finds herself responding to my call as the shepherd boy calling "Father, Father" and she responded, but she hid. She wouldn't answer my call, but she said, "You always seem to find me." I always will in eternity, for when you are sent you cannot return void. For the one sent is the Word of God and he is the Son of God, and he comes back bearing the fruit of his efforts. I shall not return unto my Father void. When I come back I will bring back that for which he sent me, that purpose for which he sent me. And so, I stirred in her the feelings of the fatherhood of God.

So, you who are going along with me on the Promise and those who are here for the first time in a long interval, pick it up, and still apply the law. Don't for one second fail to do it, because while we are in the world of Caesar, we must master this principle and live knowing there are only states. There is no such thing as a good man or a bad man. He's in a good state as he conceives it and the other one is in a bad state as he conceives it, but the occupant of the state is really God. And so as Blake said in his *Visions of the Last Judgment:* "From this you will perceive I do not consider anyone either good or evil, just or unjust, but simply to be those who unknowingly fell into states." They fell into states, identified themselves with the state, and then they were pronounced by others to be good or to be evil. They are only in states.

So tonight, if you are unemployed or you find it difficult to get promotion in your present employment, or you are in need, remember all the solutions of your present state are still states. I hope I have made clear how you move into a state. You move into a state by knowing how you would see the world if things were as you desire them to be, and then you begin to see them in your mind's eye as though it were true. And then you sleep in that assumption just as though it is true. That assumption, though at the moment is denied by your reason and your senses, if you persist in it and make it natural, will harden into fact.

Now let us go into the Silence.

*　　*　　*

Now are there any questions, please?

Q: Are there circumstances at times which conditions will cause reverse action to take place? I have had some circumstances work perfectly in which that which I have desired to manifest has done so. Yet there have been others that worked in the reverse fashion. An example: I wished to demonstrate an appearance of money, a certain denomination, and in so doing I convinced myself I had received it already. It did occur, but in a rather strange fashion. About three months from that time period I found myself in an auto accident which cost me exactly this amount of money that I had imagined to be mine. So literally, it was taken from me rather than presented to me. I feel that it was a result of that, but perhaps in some way I had mis-worked the principle at the time.

A: Well, I would not relate that as reversal in that sense. That is far deeper than our present state...the present one will come. But if you go back far enough, you planted that and did not recognize the harvest when it came up. You entertained the sense of loss somewhere farther back and then came the harvest which you did not recognize. Now, if you are self-persuaded of the amount of money that you lost in the accident, then do not go back on that, that will come. And I hope you will be awake to recognize the harvest equal to the time of sowing. But you do not remember the sowing that brought about that accident. So everything in the world is coming in, and this would be a world of sheer hell forever if there were no resurrection to lift us out of it...only cause and effect, cause and effect, cause and effect. It would be terrible. Nevertheless, we are living in such a world and you planted it somewhere. You cannot go back. I wouldn't even go back...you planted it and you reaped the harvest; you lost that amount of money. Now you also planted that sum of money to come in a way that you did not know, did not expect. It will come! Don't think for one moment that that was a reversal of that. That was a harvest of something you did.

Q: How, when you find yourself in a period of negative harvesting, can you work out of that state?

A: In the midst of the bad harvest plant...keep on planting lovely things in the midst of it.

As you are told in Galatians, "Be not deceived; God is not mocked, as a man soweth, so shall he reap" (Gal.6:3). So don't deceive yourself, you're going to reap it, but admit the fact I must have planted it or I could not be reaping it. It had to be planted, but now I will not condemn myself. I'll start planting in the midst of this horror the lovely things I should have planted prior to this moment and plant them now. They will come up as this present harvest that is unlovely came up. It always comes up. But man goes out after an argument with someone and feels sorry for himself...that's planting. You get into an argument with your wife or she with you and then you are sorry that these things happen in a loving relationship, and then for a moment you entertain certain unlovely thoughts…that's planting. They're going to come up, everything's going to come up. But if we are alert we'll recognize our harvest. The old, old story: I'll go into the back and eat worms getting even with mother, and so we do it whether we are children or adults.

Now, the lady who saw herself beautiful, altogether beautiful and perfect, the word she used was perfect, and she remembered when she was not, and she also remembered when she heard the words "Be ye perfect." Well, haven't you heard lovers say of each other "We were *made* for each other"? Well, these were the two lovers when they become perfect, and they can mate, and be one, only, in fulfillment of scripture. And he leaves everyone and cleaves to his wife and they become one. So, they were *made* for each other. That is a statement I think everyone in our world has heard. How often I heard it "Why, they were made for each other." If they were made for each other, it's just in the sense of perfect peace because they are one. You can't fight with yourself in that sense. You always create some mental image to fight with it and then you are two, but not when you are one. So if my image is superimposed upon me and loses itself in me as my very being then we are one.

So in the midst of an unlovely harvest, plant. Nations just like individuals…a nation has a fifteen percent loss in its harvest in the course of a year. All right, who's doing it? You find the world entertaining all these unlovely thoughts of a certain person, a certain family, a certain group, but the God in you sees only your heart. He sees your intentions, your motives. He doesn't see the external act, that doesn't mean a thing to the God in you. There are nations in this world and there are individuals who will do everything for show, for the external act, the gesture…the gesture is important. I read here recently that Peru has expropriated one of our oil companies, Standard Oil of New Jersey, and they valued that at $160 million. Peru made the grand gesture and publicized it and gave them a check for $160 million. Well, the whole of South America saw the grand gesture, but they stopped payment on the check the moment they issued it. But they aren't publicizing that. They told how they paid the $160 million, and they stopped payment. Then they brought suit against Standard Oil of New Jersey for ten times that amount, and that over forty-four years they had extracted so much more than they claimed that they had, they owed them that much more. So therefore now they are suing for a billion…having paid and pulled back the payment. But South America is totally unaware of the stopped check and to them they feel that they paid the $160 million. That's the gesture. So they live on gesture and not on intent.

The Return of Glory

But God sees the intent, not the gesture. So when the sons came before him, and the first one was tall and majestic, he said, "I have rejected him." Samuel thought, "Surely he is the one that you're going to anoint in the place of Saul." "I have rejected him." And he marched them all by, "I reject him." Then came the last one, David, and he said, "Rise and anoint him; for this is he" (1Sam.16:12). He saw the heart, for he speaks of David as "a man after my heart who will do all my will." So it is the intent that God sees, he sees the motive; doesn't see the gesture at all.

I know a friend of mine in New York City, awfully nice chap, and a mutual friend was distressed. The mutual friend turned to him and asked for a certain loan to take him over the heap. He said, "I'll tell you how to raise it. You go to say six or a dozen of us, 'Put me down for $150 a month.' Go to Neville and he'll give you $150 a month...and then Neville's other friends; and you'll raise, say, $1,500 a month. Say to all of them, 'Don't look for one penny of this money until six months goes by. In that six months, I will find a job and I'll be on my feet.'" So he made the gesture, "Put me down for $150." So on the strength of that he came to me and I said, all right, put me down for $150. Goes to my friend, who was a very wealthy man, and he said, "Put me down for $250." He got his $1,500 a month with a six-month guarantee that no one would look for a penny until six months.

He goes to the first one who suggested the idea and he says, "Oh, what a terrible time to come to me. This is the time I don't have a nickel to put out." All the others of us met our obligation, but he made the grand gesture. Had no intention from the very beginning of giving him one penny...but we fell for it. All right, eventually he paid it back, paid every penny back. But here was one who went through life that way. His whole life was one of a gesture; he owed every person in town and went right through, always this grand gesture....owning apartments, owning cars, owning country homes, owning all kinds of things...and owning nothing. But he lived that way... in the grand gesture. Well, God sees only the heart, sees the motives, the intent, and doesn't see the gesture. And the world has so much to do with gesture—to be well-dressed, to be presentable, and all these things. God doesn't see that. That something that no one sees he sees. He sees the motive behind the gift of bread. Was it given with the intent of one day demanding more or was it given without hope of return, no thought of return?

Oh, I could tell you these stories time and time again because I'm speaking from experience, I know them. One chap in New York City came on when I didn't have any money, didn't have much, and I thought it was his pleasure...I thought it was. And so, he would bring in on a week night, say, a round of sandwiches and maybe a few cartons of milk and things of that nature. No liquor, because he didn't have that much...he was an impresario. And one day came during my lectures here, I was living at the Town House, and I got a letter from him and a little note on the inside where he had itemized all the sandwiches and all the milk, everything, the pickles...where he sat down and ate everything...and not I alone but five or six of us got around and ate. He brought it in and that was his pleasure...we thought it was his pleasure. He itemized the entire thing and then sent me the whole thing, and said he wants the money immediately. So I sat down and wrote him a check and sent it off to him. Then he wrote back asking if I could let him have, now, $500. I said no thank you. So I sent him the check... he brought it up to something like $350. Well, in those days you could buy a sandwich for twenty cents. How he arrived at that figure I'll never know, but it came to $340-odd and I sent it without question. I sent him a check for $340.

So he went to his little grave about ten years ago and he's gone forward. At least that account has been closed. Like Socrates, "Give him a cock...I owe him a cock. There's one thing I must pay before I die. I'm taking the hemlock tonight, but please give him a cock, because I owe him a cock." So he went off with his slate clean. As far as he is concerned my slate is clean. I gave him the $340-odd, but I don't know how he arrived at $340-odd when he brought it in as his grand gesture. He wanted to have a feast and it was our place, so he came into my apartment, and we put on the coffee and made coffee, and then he would have milk, and he brought all these things. Then he had itemized it and kept it...even gave me the dates. How could I check it? So you see, he was doing everything with an intent and that gesture was as phony as a three dollar bill.

So in this world of ours be normal, be natural. You don't have to do anything to anyone, go within yourself and appropriate a state. Then if it takes 10,000 people to aid the birth of that state, 10,000 people will come...without their consent, without their knowledge. Then they won't have to send after many, many years a little bill, saying how good and Christ-like and generous you were, and pay it up, and pay it now.

Thank you.

MAN IS SOUL AND BODY IS EMANATION

4/14/69

Tonight, I trust will be a very practical night and all will see it clearly...I hope so. We are told in the Book of Nehemiah, the 8th chapter, the 8th verse, that "They read from the book, from the law of God, clearly; and they gave the sense, so that the people understood it clearly." As they read it, they interpreted it.

So, tonight we will take a passage and attempt to interpret it that you may apply it this very night. We go back to the 2nd chapter of the Book of Genesis, and he said, "This is the bone of my bones and the flesh of my flesh" (2:23). Here is someone making a bold, bold claim, and he's called a man. And then we are told, "And now a man leaves his father and his mother, and he cleaves to his wife, and they become one body." In this passage he makes the claim that she came out of me, completely out of me, and I will cleave to that which came out of me until we become one body. Blake makes the statement that "Man has no body distinct from his soul; that called body is a portion of soul discerned by the five senses, the chief inlets of soul in this age" (*Marr. of Heaven and Hell,* Plt. 4). He further states that "Thou art a man, God is no more. Thine own humanity learn to adore" (*Everlasting Gospel,* C, Ln. 41).

So here he identifies man as soul and that his body is but his own emanation: "My emanation, yet my wife 'til the sleep of death is past." So here is my body...it seems to be that I am wearing a body distinct from myself...and he claims that it is not, that he has no body distinct from his soul, that that called body is a portion of the soul discerned by the five senses, the chief inlets of soul in this age. So, destroy the body, well now, how will I simply bring it back? It was always a part of me and I'll bring it back by the seed of contemplative thought. I will contemplate myself as I would like to be, and reproduce that which was seemingly destroyed in the world, and the world would call it dead. No, I pass through the gate called death, and you cremate it, and here is a little dust, nothing but dust. But, I, by the seed of contemplative thought, reproduce the being that I am. It is my image. Here is a union so wedded it is connubial. I am so wedded to the image that I wear that you can destroy it a thousand times and I'll reproduce it. I'm in love with it. There is nothing *but* my wife. This is my wife—a male, yes, the father of children, a husband—and yet *this* is my emanation. Regardless of your sex, *that* is your wife, your emanation yet your wife 'til the sleep of death is past. When you completely awake from the entire dream, you and your emanation are one, and you are enhanced by reason of that experience where you emanate your own likeness.

In other words, as though you said to a beautifully cut stone "If it had dreams, I think this is what it would dream itself to be." Did you ever go into a home, a beautiful room, and you can't see anything that you would change you so love it...the library...everything about it is so perfect. And you say to yourself, if it had dreams I'm sure this is what it would dream itself to be. Whether it is inanimate stones, inanimate books, inanimate anything, this...but some human Imagination conceived it and produced it. Well now, this body that I wear and the body that you wear, no matter what you think of them, that's what you, the real you, the God in you, is dreaming itself to be. It's in love with its emanation. *You* are the emanation of God, and you *are* God, and there's nothing but God. Destroy it and you will once more reproduce it by the seed of contemplative thought, bring it back into being.

Now we are told, "Be ye imitators of God as dear children" (Eph.5:1). Well, is that what he did? He contemplated himself and out of his own being he produced this garment?—yes. And this is what he loves more than anything in the world?—yes. "Naught loves another as itself." You can't conceive of loving another as yourself. You may think you do, and you will deny what I have just said and say "Oh no, I love this one and that one and my country more, my flag more"...you're only kidding yourself. You're lying to yourself. "Naught loves another as itself, nor venerates another so, nor is it possible to thought a greater than itself to know" (Blake, *A Little Boy Lost, Songs of Experience)*. You can't conceive of something and think that it is greater, and you revere it, and you reverence it. Oh yes you may...but if God wants me, if I am his emanation and God in me is my own wonderful human Imagination, if he wants me to know him, he has to raise me to himself. It is impossible to thought a *greater* than itself to know, so how would I know my Creator if this thing is created unless he raises me to his level? He has to actually lift me to his level that I may know him as he is. If I do not know him as he is, he will never have me as one who can see him beyond what I am capable of seeing myself to be. So God becomes as I am that I may be as he is. If he doesn't actually become as I am, he can't lift me to the level that he is so that I may actually know him as he is. So everyone here is but an emanation of the God within them.

Now, I would take it from here on this level. I desire and I name it, I don't care what it is, I name it. Where did it come from? It came out of me...I desired it. Now I must actually do the same thing, I must become an imitator of God as a dear child. God became me that I may become God. I must actually...something comes out of me, it's a desire, and I must actually become *it* so that it may become as I am. I name it, health, wealth, call it by any name, it comes out of me. I desire to be and I name it. I must go into that and actually wear it as God wears this. God is wearing this garment tonight; he's wearing your garment tonight. His name is I AM forever and forever. Now, something comes out of me...I would like to be and I name it. As I name it, I must go in unto it and actually possess it and become it... as God became me that came out of him. And I must actually wear it until it seems natural, it seems normal. Reason denies it, my senses deny it. So what! Let them deny it. But in time if I go in unto the state and wear it as though it were true, and make it natural and make it normal to me, then I will externalize it in the world. It will become real in my world.

So I will take a cue from scripture, and "The man said, 'This at last is bone of my bones and flesh of my flesh; she shall be called Woman, because she was taken out of me, taken out of Man" (Gen.2:23). "And now a man leaves his father, his mother, and he cleaves to his wife, and they become one body." Now I take it from this level and I put it into my Caesar's world. It comes out of me...my emanation yet my wife. In this case, my wife now becomes a state called health, called wealth, called fame, called by any name. All right, call these names. Do I so love it? It came out of me, it's bone of my bones and flesh of my flesh. I must leave everything in my world and now *yield* to it, and assume that I am it. I dare to assume I am what at the moment of my assumption reason denies and my senses deny. As I move into it, it becomes bone of my bones and flesh of my flesh. It came out of me and it is my wife, my emanation. Yet, although it is my emanation, it is my wife until the sleep of death is past. When I reach the very end of the journey, we are no longer two, we are one. I raise it up to my own level that it may understand me and see me as I am...for it is impossible to thought a greater than itself to know.

So if God would have me, his emanation, know him as he is to be known, he has to become me and raise me up to his level, for I cannot know anything greater than myself. I may simply worship some little icon and I may think, well, he is a wonderful man, he's a richer man than I am, he's a wiser man than I am, and he is so and so. Do I want to really change my identity for him? What man in this world would give up being what he is for any man in this world? He should be completely rubbed out. A man who would so want to give up his own identity for another…that man isn't. No, you would like his wealth, like his intelligence, like this, but you don't want to change your identity and give it up for some other identity.

So God is in man. Man's own wonderful human Imagination is God. There never was another God and there never will be another God. And so he became as I am that I may be as he is, and he is raising me slowly through all the pains of the world that I may actually know him as he is. When I really know him, I've got to be him. I can't be another knowing him. So I am his wife and he leaves everything and becomes as I am, his emanation, and raises me that I may know him as he is. In that day, we are one body, one Spirit, one Lord, one God and Father of all (Eph.4:4)…can't be another.

I can take that same thought and take it on any level in this world. So you want to be…and you name it…I don't care what it is. As you name it, it came out of you, it's your emanation. Well, you've got to do the same thing as you are told in scripture. So I will read the book and read it with understanding so that the people who hear it will understand it. So you give it meaning, you give the sense to what you read. So here, "As the man said, 'At last this is bone of my bones and flesh of my flesh. She shall be called Woman, because she came out of Man. Therefore, man will leave his father and his mother and cleave to his wife and they become one body." Well, you know in the world of marriage we don't really become one body. Oh, she'll bear my name and my children will bear my name, but don't tell me that my wife is my very self. She's an independent individual with opinions of her own and she doesn't reflect mine. We are not one body. We have together born a child and that child is as independent as a hog on ice. You can't tell her anything that is in conflict with what she wants to hear. She is an independent being, so she is certainly not one with us, any more than my wife is one with me.

Then what is the wife spoken of?—this body. "Man has no body distinct from is soul. That called body is a portion of soul discerned by the five senses, the chief inlets of soul in this age." So you destroy it…tonight I drop and the body is cremated and you think, well now, he is gone. No, I restore it by the seed of contemplative thought. I'm only contemplating myself and I reproduce my image. I'm in love with it. God is in love with his image. I don't want any other image. Well, I've seen it. I saw the being in contemplation. One afternoon, sitting in the Silence, not thinking of anything in particular, and here all of a sudden I see a stone, a quartz. Suddenly the quartz fragmented itself into unnumbered little pieces, and then it quickly gathered itself together into one being and the being is seated in the lotus posture contemplating the deepest contemplation. I'm looking at it…I'm looking at myself…here I'm looking at the very being that I recognize as myself. And it began to glow like the sun, and it glowed and glowed, and it reached the intensity of the sun and then exploded. Then I awoke in the room where I was seated. I saw the being meditating me. This is his image with which he is in love, and when he awakes from his meditation, I am he…it is God. In everyone there is God, the Son of God meditating himself, and he projects himself upon the screen of space and puts himself through all the fires of the world, shaping that image into the perfection that he is. For he is perfect and you must be perfect as he is perfect. When it's perfect, you are superimposed upon him and you are one; and he is enhanced by reason of the experience in this world of death.

So here, we take it from there and come down to this level. We're still living in the world of Caesar. And if that's how he does it, then while I am here I start to try it in the world of Caesar. Now out of me comes not an expression of myself—I know what I look like when I look into the mirror, it's not *that* that I want to bring about—but in the world of Caesar you want to bring about a better way of living, a greater security, a greater this, a greater that. That's out of you, too. But in the same way we must become imitators of God as dear children as told us in the 1st verse, the 5th chapter of Ephesians, "Be ye imitators of God as dear children." So I find myself desiring. That's how it begins, "Let us make man in our image"…that's the primal wish. Well now, as man, I want now to be other than what I am as a man. So that's my wish. I must do the same thing that God did to make me himself: God became as I am that I may be as he is. As man I must become conscious of being wealthy if that is what I want, conscious of being healthy if that's what I want, conscious of being famous if that is what I want, I don't care what it is. Ask no man his permission to be anything in this world… you simply go right into the state desired. It came out of you, but you've got to *occupy* it and actually become it in the same way that God had to become you to make you God. So you have to become the state to make that state yourself. So what do you desire in this world? You name it and ask no one in this world if it's possible. All things are possible to God and God dwells in you: your own wonderful human Imagination that's God. There never was another God and there never will be another God.

So God became as I am that I may be as he is. And while I'm playing in this world of Caesar he tells me to imitate him. Imitate the same principle which he adopted in order to make me as he is. So, something comes out of me. What came out of me?—a desire, all of a sudden. But I can't do it, I have no one to help me, I have nothing in the world. I have not the educational background, the social background, any background worthy of this that I now desire. All right, you desire it. It came out of you, didn't it? Well, do the same thing;, imitate God as you are told in scripture to imitate him. How could I imitate him? He became me. If he didn't become me, he could never raise me to himself. It's impossible to thought a greater than itself to know, therefore, he has to become me, and lift me up that I may know him as he is. When I know him as he is, I have to be God, because I can't know him as he is unless I am he. So I can't know this now as it is unless I become it. So I move right into that state: what would the feeling be like if it were true? How would I feel if...and then I look at my world mentally and I see my world as I would see it if it were true. When I mentally see it as I would see it if it were true, I dwell in that state, I live in that state. Then that state in a way no one knows crystallizes and becomes a concrete reality in my world. How? I do not know. It has ways and means that my little conscious mind cannot fathom. If I dwell in it, one person or 10,000 people may be used to bring it to pass. It doesn't really matter how many are used. They'll be used either knowingly or unknowingly to bring about that which I have assumed that I am. So my assumption though at the moment seems false if I persist in it, it will harden into fact, it will become a reality.

Now, do I know that from experience?—unnumbered times. I could not enumerate and tell you how many. It's simply a law by which I live... and hope I can persuade others to live by the same law. If you accept this law then you are free and you're no longer a slave. You are as free as the wind. No matter where you are this night...you could be bound. If you actually believe this, you'll become loosed, and you'll be set free to fulfill whatever you are assuming though you be in a dungeon. If you don't believe it, then you're going to accept the facts of life and limit yourself to what your senses dictate, and there you remain, remain in prison, and remain bound in this world. But if you believe it, that all things are possible to God and God is our own wonderful human Imagination, well then, you'll go out of here believing it, and live by it, and become an imitator of God as a dear child. Because you are destined, everyone is destined to one day awaken as God himself.

It seems the height of vanity, but why did God say, "Let us make man in *our* image"? Not the image of another. He's in love with his image. Analyze it. "Let us make man in our image after our own likeness." Well, to do it he had to become me. That's the story of Christianity. He actually had to become man. So God became man...that's what we are told in the Christian faith...that man may become God. And man has been taught to believe that *one* little man called Jesus...no, that is not it. Humanity is Jesus, humanity is the Christ. He became all of us. What child in this world doesn't know that it *is*? If it knows that it is, it is saying "I am" and that's God. That is God becoming man. Now, it takes it from there and actually raises that being through all the horrors of the world to itself. One day it awakes and when it awakes it is God, and there's nothing but God. So he's in love with his image.

Now, something came out of you. It's only a desire, you say, but you fall in love with it. You may not really be interested in the ultimate at the moment; the hunger is not upon you. That thirst for God may not be upon you, but it could be a thirst for something in the world of Caesar. All right, so you take it from there, and you move right into it, and wear it just as you would wear a suit of clothes and make it natural. As it becomes natural it's going to personify itself, externalize itself on the screen of space, and you will bear witness to the fact that this is how it works. It actually works in a simple way. That man knows what he wants to be, reason tells him he can't be it, his senses deny it, he dares to use his Imagination and *assumes* that he *is* it. His reason now denies his assumption, but his assumption if persisted in hardens into fact. If it once hardens into fact and he sees it, then from there on he picks it up and continues...and eventually he falls in love with the ultimate which is to awaken as God himself! And he will...because God in man has determined to raise man to the level of himself, and when he does, he is God. There is nothing but God.

So in this fabulous, wonderful world of ours there is nothing but God. You can forgive every being in the world when you know this. It doesn't matter what he's done, whether it's good or evil. What does it matter if you know the struggle that is taking place in him? You can completely forgive him, because God in him is raising him to the level of God. And may I tell you, we are all brothers...every one of us is a brother. And we came down into this world of death and limitation and we took upon ourselves these garments. We are the sons of God, all of us, and *collectively* we form God, the only God. But in this wonderful division we are the sons of God. As we are told in the 32nd chapter of Deuteronomy, "There are no more people in the world than there are sons of God" (32:8). Limit them today as the world wants to limit production and stop the multiplication of children. All right, if you multiply them a thousand times over, or reduce it, still no one can be born who is not a son of God. By any pigment of skin, by any sex, it doesn't matter, a son of God occupies that little body...whether it be warped, whether it be shrunken, whether it is demented...it's a son of God and he'll take it from there. All things are possible to God. So he'll take it from there and raise it through unnumbered experiences to the level of himself that it may know himself. He wants to be known. As he is known by his image, he and his image fuse and they become one. Through the experience he is enhanced beyond what he was when he descended into these bodies of flesh and blood.

So you take it tonight and test it. "Know ye not that Jesus Christ is in you?" (2Cor.13:5). There is no Jesus Christ outside of the Christ in you. That's the only Christ and this is the cross that he bears; he is tied to this body of flesh and blood. He will rise not on the outside; he'll rise here, for he's buried in this garment. So you destroy it and I will by the seed of contemplative thought reproduce it and he's still buried in it. So I go through this little gate called death and once more I find myself clothed in a garment just like this, young, healthy, and Christ is buried in it because I am saying "I am"; and that's his name forever and forever. I'll continue my journey, go through another gate called death, finding myself once more restored as a physical being until that moment in time comes when I awake within this garment, and *I am he*. So this is the eternal story.

Tonight you put it to the *extreme* test; just as we are the emanation of God, his wife 'til the sleep of death is past, and he has to leave everything and cleave to his wife and they become one body, for there's only one body. Now something comes out of you in the world of Caesar. There must be only one body. It can't be you *and* your desire...you must go into your desire and occupy it as God came in unto his wish and occupied it: "Let us make man in our image." He had to come into me. He couldn't in any way make me from the outside; he had to actually become as I am that I may become as he is. So in the same way I must imitate him: "Be ye imitators of God as dear children." In the same way I will do the same thing now. I will desire, and I name it. Now I must go in unto it and wear it as he wears me. He wears this garment and he says "I am Neville." I must go in unto health and say "I am healthy." I must go in unto wealth and say "I am wealthy." I must go in unto the state called "I am known" and say "I am known." Whatever it is that I desire, I must go right in unto it and wear it in the same way that God came into me and wears this garment and he says "I am Neville"...in the same way. So we must become *imitators* of God as dear children.

So they read from the book as you're told in Nehemiah, but they read it and gave sense to the Word so that the people understood the reading. How many on a Sunday morning when they go to church take any passage and really give it meaning? No, they take the pulpit and all of a sudden they start off on all kinds of political things in the world of Caesar. No one takes the

Word of God and actually gives *meaning* to it. They'll take one little thing and call it the text of the day. Then ask anyone who comes out of the church, "What did he say?" Well, he said, "You know what? I don't think Nixon is doing such a good job." That's all that they heard. Not one word concerning the text or the Word of God, because not one gives meaning to the Word of God. But you can forgive them, you know why? They don't understand it…and that goes from the pope down. They don't understand it. If they understood it, you could not read what they say in print. It's something entirely different from the Word of God.

We have the Word of God in the Bible from beginning to the end. Well, take any passage and try to give it meaning, because without meaning what does it matter? What would life be to us if it had no meaning? If at the end of one's journey no matter what he has accomplished in the world and that was the end and there was no meaning…well, horrible…cut the child's throat when it's born. That's the best thing you could do to it if life has no meaning. But find meaning, find a purpose, then everything falls into place. There is meaning to it all and the meaning of life is that we in this world become God. We only become God because God becomes us. If he did not become as I am, he could not raise me to what he is; and it's impossible for thought a greater than itself to know. So I can't know him unless he actually becomes me and lifts me to himself. How else would I know him?

And in spite of the fact that we think, "Oh, I love him more than I love myself"…well, I would not deny for one moment that this night if you gave me no alternative and you said either you die or your daughter, I wouldn't hesitate to say I die. But it doesn't mean that I do not love myself, the image that I am. I'm confident of restoration, confident of a complete change in my world when I leave this world. I would, without hesitating for one moment, say, "Save her. She hasn't gone through my experiences, give her the chance." But that does not mean that (___??) because I say take me now, shoot me now but leave her and let her have the experiences that I've had. For, I've gone through these experiences…I have fulfilled scripture. I know exactly what the whole thing is about, because I've fulfilled it. Everything promised in scripture has happened within my soul, not on the outside for human mortal eyes to see…but it doesn't mean that there is still another that I love more. You may want to say that there's someone I certainly love *more*. You analyze it. "Nought loves another as itself, nor venerates another so, nor is it possible to thought a greater than itself to know: and Father, how can I love you or any of my brothers more? I love you like the little bird that picks up crumbs around the door."

Now, read the entire poem, very short, five or six verses. And the priest heard the little boy say this and then he picks him by his hair, and he burns him, tortures him and the poor parents heard the screams of the child but could not help him for he is the authority. That's the world over. Here is this mighty one who knows right and wrong, good and evil, not knowing that it's eating of the tree of good and evil that displeases God. If my mother, whom I love dearly, or my father, committed any crime in this world, I wouldn't care what he did; I would still want him set free. I wouldn't care what he did because I love them. But the priest couldn't see this. It's called *A Little Boy Lost* in Blake's wonderful poem of *The Songs of Experience*...*A Little Boy Lost*. He's having this fantastic experience and he knows he can't possibly love another as himself or in any way reverence another more. He knows he can't. Since, how can I love Thee or my brothers more, because he knows it's impossible to thought a greater than itself to know. He knows that.

How can you? You can admire an Einstein's mind. You can admire the great artists of the world. You can admire all these things, but don't tell me because you admire them that until you are raised to that level that you can really understand them. But even when you can't understand them—because it's impossible to thought a greater than itself to know—don't tell me because of their greatness that you love them more than self, because you don't! We're only lying to ourselves when we say I know someone I would like to change places with and lose my identity completely and become that one. I can't conceive of someone wanting to completely lose their identity in the identity of another. Can't be!

So tonight take it. As you're told in scripture, God became man that man may become God. Now, be imitators of the same principle. Is God setting a pattern? Yes. He became as I am that I may be as he is. Well, finding myself in the world of Caesar, something comes out of me, but it's something different. For I must live in the world of Caesar and Caesar demands taxes, so I want more money to pay his taxes, his demands, and Caesar demands this, so I must want that. It comes out of me. So I must do the same thing that God did in becoming me: he became me that I may become God. So I must become wealthy so that the state called wealth may become as I am, and so I become one with it. I move into it and say, what would the feeling be like if it were true? How would I feel if it were true? How would I see the world if it were true? What would I hear my friends say to me and what would I say to them if it were true? Then I carry on these mental conversations with myself from the premise that it *is* true and I walk in that state as though it *were* true. Then if it crystallizes into fact, well then, I've found the principle. Now I pick it up from there and I move into all kinds of states as I desire to make them real in my world. Knowing that he who became me is slowly raising me to his level, and eventually he will unveil himself, and I am he.

Now let us go into the Silence.

* * *

First of all, may I thank you for your letters and please keep them coming, giving me your dreams, your visions and your experiments on this principle. One wrote this past week, he found himself in an egg, a huge egg. He felt himself completely awake, like a waking vision. There was a very thick wall and he knew that he had to break through that wall. He knew that when he broke through that wall he would awake from this state in which he found himself, which was like a waking dream. And then he woke. Well, that is an adumbration. We're all like encased within an egg, and when we break that shell, we will come out. The shell is our skull. That's where we're all buried and that's the egg. So this is nothing more than a foreshadowing of that day when he will come out, and he will be the being who fell asleep in that egg, and that being is God. So thank him for his wonderful experience and sharing it with us.

A lady wrote one concerning finding herself moving into another world. "I'm going into another world, another place." But before she left for the other world she investigated the present world and it was all old buildings. Many of them had no furnishings and filled with bugs, but she knew she was going into another world…and carrying with her her child. Then she saw in this room devoid of furniture, save a rocking chair, a man in the chair rocking, and she went over to him and felt him and he was solidly real, as solid as any person she has ever known in this world. He was real, he was solid. Then she looked away and when she turned back he and the chair vanished. Then she went into the other world and someone said to her, "Let us see your baby" and she presented the child. For the child is the sign of one's birth from above: "And this shall be a sign unto you, you shall find a babe wrapped in swaddling clothes" (Luke 2:12). That is a *sign*. It is not *you*; it is a sign of *your birth*. So she's moving into a new world. Now, this is a most wonderful adumbration, a foreshadowing in the symbolism of scripture. Moving into a new world, for you have to go, and the sign of your birth from above is a child wrapped in swaddling clothes. So thank you so much for your letters and keep them coming, please.

Now, are there any questions, please? Yes sir?

Q: (inaudible)

A: No sir! There is no outside force but that which we give to the *seeming* outside force.

___(??). Well, I'll say this much about this power called Imagination: it will do nothing for us until we have assumed the *feeling* of the wish fulfilled. You can't compel it. It refuses to act under compulsion. I can't compel myself to believe anything. It will only act by persuasion...what would the feeling be like if it were true? I'm trying to persuade myself into that feeling. But to say I *will* feel it, it will simply bound back. So you cannot compel it, you can't command it. It will only act by persuasion: what would it be like? How would I see the world? What would it be like? What would I feel like if it were true? And so only by persuasion would it respond. So try to persuade yourself. It'll work that way, work like a charm. If you really believe your Imagination is Jesus Christ, if you really believe that that is God the Lord, and no other God, no other Lord, then what are you imagining? All things are possible to God; therefore, all things are possible to Imagination. You can't deny that you can imagine anything that one tells you if you understand what he is talking about. You may not *believe* that what he has said though you can imagine it is possible. That's *your* limitation, because you can imagine it. Tell me anything in this world, if I can understand the tongue in which you speak, if you speak in my tongue, the English tongue, I can follow you. You can take me into all the styles of the world...don't take me into mathematics where I can't follow you...but take me into any vivid description, word description, I'll follow you. I may not *believe* you, but it doesn't matter. If I don't believe you that's my limitation, that is not yours. If I can believe anything, I can fulfill it. It was said of I think it was Thomas Arnold who was headmaster of Rugby School in England, and the boys used to say, "It's a shame to tell him a lie, because he believes it." So the boys didn't tell him any lies, because he believed one. That was Thomas Arnold. He was so given to his boys and so loved them that he trusted them and they all agreed that it's a shame to tell him a lie because he believed one.

I'll tell you there is no lie...*all* things are possible to God. What today you and I take for granted like going around the moon, tomorrow we'll land on the moon. And turning on lights...do you know, when I was born we had none of these things in Barbados. We had a little carriage drawn by a horse, no thought of an automobile, an airplane, a missile. Yet all of these things are in our world. They were not always in our world until someone actually believed them. First they conceived them and then believed them. You can't conceive of anything that isn't true in God's world, because *all* things are possible to God. But here we're living in the world of Caesar…so make it a practical world until he who began the good work in you brings it to completion, which is to make you as he is.

But when it comes to opposition, you and you alone will give it, because really there is no opposition. The seeming opponent may be used tomorrow as an aid in fulfilling your desire. What seems today to be a disaster will prove on reflection to be the turning point in your good fortune. That I speak from experience. My father was a junior partner in a small, little grocery business, and his partners ganged up with a few others to get him out, to ease him out of that partnership, and made these false accusations. My father never looked at a book, so he knew nothing of what was going on, and when he was confronted with this false claim he came home and took to his bed for about two or three weeks. He was flat on his back he was so stunned by it all. And they thought they had him exactly where they wanted him, so they got him out giving him nothing of his equity. That was the turning point in our family's good fortune. From nothing, but I mean absolutely nothing literally, and when he died in '59 he could leave his family millions and millions of dollars. He had ten children. His wife had died ten years or more before—she died in '41, he died in '59. But in 1922 when this thing happened to my father, he simply didn't know where to turn. But that was the turning point in his life… because he trusted them all. And then he went only on his own with no partners, just himself and my second brother; and he took it from there with a small loan from a friend, and then multiplied and multiplied and multiplied. What it's worth today I haven't the slightest idea. I do not know what the businesses are worth, but I do know they run into multiple millions. And he had no formal education, no social background, no contacts in this world at all, but he did believe in this principle and he lived by it.

So what seemed to him to be the end of the world was the beginning of his world in the world of Caesar. Every year they get bigger and bigger. You can't stop it after a while. As long as they have good management you can't stop it…simply gets bigger. They're not "holding their own," they're simply moving out, moving out and moving out like a conglomerate…can't stop it. And yet in '22 no one would have given a farthing for the family. They didn't have a farthing, they had nothing. But you see, he believed and he really believed it to the point where the whole thing multiplied itself from nothing. It simply became something and then that little something became multiplied.

383

So I tell everyone, I'm speaking from experience, not only in a mystical sense but from Caesar's world. I'm telling you the story of my family. I'm also telling the story of Christ in me, because the whole thing unfolded within me. So I speak from experience and I'm not theorizing. As I stand here, I'm not in any way theorizing or speculating. The whole story has unfolded itself in me, so I speak from experience.

Well, until the next one…which is Friday. Thank you.

FORGIVENESS AND THE IMMORTAL EYES

4/18/69

Tonight we'll take two aspects of the great mystery: one is forgiveness and the other is the immortal eyes, the eyes that really see.

He said to them, "When one or two are gathered together in my name, there I am in the midst of them also. Then Peter said to him, 'Lord, how often shall my brother sin against me, and I forgive him?' He said, 'Seventy times seven'" (Mat.18:21). This is something you and I must practice and practice daily, but how many know the art of forgiveness? Repentance and faith are conditions of forgiveness. But really, forgiveness, if you look at it, there is no worldly wisdom in it, we all know that. Then what are people Christians for? The story itself makes no sense…the story of Christianity and its doctrines, none whatsoever. Well then, what are we Christians for? When you read the promises made in scripture that the dead shall rise into an entirely different world, clothed differently, it doesn't make sense when you see it all turn before you into ash as the body is cremated. Yet man is called upon to believe the story of redemption.

So here is the only way a man can forgive: learn to distinguish the eternal human that walks about and among these stones of fire, in bliss and woe alternate, from those states or worlds in which the Spirit travels. This is the only means to forgiveness. I must learn to distinguish between the state and the *occupant* of the state. If I can see the most horrible acts in the world knowing that that is an actor and the script is written for him. If he is cast in that role he has to play that part. If there's any condemnation it must be to the author who wrote the part and not the actor who is playing the part.

So here, if I can distinguish between states and the occupants of states, then I can forgive

Now, how do I forgive? By identifying the one that I would forgive with the ideal that he has failed to realize. The highest ideal would be to identify him with the divine image itself. When we are told, "Let us make man in our image," well now, that image is the image of God. It's called in scripture Christ. To take a man unknown in the world that is condemned by the world, and still identify him with the image that is Christ that radiates and reflects God…that doesn't make sense. Yet I am called upon to do it. I must actually identify him in my own mind's eye with that divine image. But I could fall a little short of that and take an ideal that he has failed to realize. The ideal, well, in his own world of Caesar it could be that he is affluent or at least he has an income equal to his responsibilities, even though he has nothing, and identify him with that. Until I am strong enough to go beyond the barriers of appearances and see him as really the divine image itself. Well, I am called upon to set this in motion and to practice it, and not only practice it but to talk about it and tell it.

So when the statement is made "Where two or three are gathered together in my name, there I am in the midst of them." In the *Mishnah*, which is a Hebraic work interpreting scripture, it is said that if two sit together and there is no word of the Torah between them, they are seated in the seat of the scoffers. As it is written in the 1st Psalm, "Blessed is the man who sits not in the seat of the scoffers, but rejoices in the law of God day and night. For that man shall prosper in all that he does" (1:1). So they associate this with the 1st Psalm…if a man who does not discuss the Torah, the law of God and his prophecies, though he is known and a brilliant mind, he is actually seated in the seat of the scoffers. Now we are told in the last book of the Old Testament, the Book of Malachi, we read it in the 3rd chapter, "If two fear the Lord"—and the word fear means "to reverence, to respect"—"if two respect and reverence the Lord, they will discuss his word and they will talk together." Those who talk together discussing the word then the Shekinah which means "the Glory of God" is between them.

Well, you can say the whole vast world certainly is not filling that bill. You think of a cocktail party and who at a cocktail party is discussing the Word of God? They look upon you as something that, well, was just dragged in. I mean, if perchance this thing happened, "What on earth did you bring him to the party for?" Go to a dinner party…I recall that about five years ago I was invited to go to the Maskers. This friend was just initiated, he's now a member, and the man who just recently died, Alan Mowbray, was the head of the party… just one joke after the other and each getting more and more into the gutter. So we sat there and we had a certainly nice dinner and they're all telling jokes and they called upon me to tell one. So I excused myself and said that I love a joke, but I'm not a good story teller, not of that nature, although I love jokes and I'll listen to you all night. But they insisted that I would say something, so I rose and I told them about the law.

Now, Mowbray played successfully in over 300 pictures. He certain didn't need any instruction from me concerning success, for he played in over 300 pictures and numberless TV appearances and a man of means in the world of Caesar. And so, when I got through telling him of the law of assumption—an assumption, though false, if persisted in will harden into fact—and I'm addressing this bunch of actors, then Mowbray had to, naturally, say something after the stranger spoke. For I was the stranger, the invited guest, and he said, "I didn't realize that we had invited one of these longhairs here tonight" and that was his attitude toward the Word of God. Well now, he just departed this little sphere. He'll find himself restored to life that I do know from experience, and he didn't know it before departure. He is restored in a body just like the one he wore only young, in a world just like this terrestrial, but without his background or the money in the bank that he left behind him. In this world of ours we leave all these things behind. We take our consciousness that we do take, the knowledge of what we have done and who we are, but we leave things.

In this world if I give you something I lose possession of it. If I sell you something, I lose possession of it. That's not so in the heavenly world. In the heavenly world I can give you my eyes and keep them, and the eyes remain yours to use as you will. And then you can give these eyes that I gave you to another and yet you keep the eyes. It's a world of sharing…not one thing is lost in heaven. I can give you everything that I know and give you every faculty that has awakened within me, and it becomes yours if I give it to you, and you will use them, and then transfer them to another or give them to another, and they will use them. It's their possession to use just as they will.

But now we come to the immortal eyes. A week ago tonight, two ladies who are here tonight were in their car driving home and then they parked the car when they got to their place…at least that's what's inferred in the letter…they undoubtedly were discussing what they had heard a week ago tonight. I couldn't tell you what I had said a week ago tonight. But suddenly, one to whom I gave my eyes two years ago, and by eyes I mean my immortal eyes, she had this vision, it was a true vision, that I took my eyes out, came forward, and put them right into hers. It was then, or soon thereafter, or just before, that in a vision she was told that she is an incurrent eyewitness. Well, an incurrent eyewitness…the word incurrent is "to give passage to a current that flows inward," like the pores on a sponge where it draws it inward.

Now Blake said "I rest not from my great task! To open the immortal eyes of man inward into the world of thought, into eternity ever expanding in the bosom of God, the human Imagination" (*Jer.*, Chap.1, Plt.5). He wasn't interested in the external eye because it doesn't see. As we are told in scripture "You have eyes and see not, ears and hear not." He wanted to give them *his* eyes and he did. While walking this earth he was resurrected. Resurrection does not come when the body is being cremated; it is while in this garment of flesh, which is the world of death, one is raised. And while he walks the earth he selects the one to whom he's going to give his eyes or his ears, his faculties., and it's a complete gift; yet he hasn't lost it in the giving, he's retained it. And she or he to whom the gift is made takes the gift and they, too, in the higher world can give it to whom they will.

So, seated in the car a series of visions possessed her. Now when I tell you these visions come, you don't have to go into any meditation for them, you don't have to go to sleep for them. They could come while you walk the street and you are seeing what is not there to be seen by mortal eye. You could be seated in a theater, and a party going on, and suddenly they are possessing you and you can't stop it. You are seeing the mystery of God. And so while seated in the car—I cannot go through all of them, there is a series of them, I'll take one—she said "At the first, I was in a long, elongated place like a church and a red carpet was right down the aisle" and then she painted a word picture concerning the altar and the things pointed out by this angelic being in that altar. Then suddenly it changed and here was a coach drawn by a team of horses and it came rushing up, stopped, and then the door was flung open, and out came a being...it could have been Hercules himself. "Never have I seen such a majestic form and the light radiating from parts of him, and he had a sword and the sword was bathed in light. He looked into my eyes and I looked into his...we simply stared at each other. Then he reentered the coach and off it drove."

Then another scene interrupted, not related really. Then the coach reappeared, this time with white horses in front of it. And then it came screeching forward and it stopped, and then the door was flung open and I stepped out. I looked at her and simply smiled, and she said "In all of my visions when you appear you have the same smile, like a cat who has just swallowed a mouse...as though you are about to now either illustrate or reveal some mystery and it amuses you as you are about to reveal it. And so there you vanished before my eyes. But the door was open implying something else is coming out...and three women came out with black bonnets. Then a miraculous thing happened, this pallet on which a corpse is placed, and it came floating out. I looked at the corpse and it is you and across your mouth is a piece of cloth that bands your mouth and then it's tied behind your head. Someone began to dig, but suddenly you are placed upon a cross, the cross is raised, and then it is set aflame. The whole thing is burning and it burns right down to the stump. I looked at the stump and in the stump is liquid, molten gold. That changed and then came the coach again. This time someone, a majestic being, is standing and he's the driver of it now. Before there seemed to be no driver, now one is driving. His feet are placed far apart…this majestic creature. And as he came up, suddenly a man like the Ancient of Days appeared—white hair, white beard, a blue robe and a white gown—and he had a large white book in his hand and a large pencil and he was writing in it. Then he pointed at me. And that was it."

But I've told you time and again concerning this golden liquid light how it works. Blake made the statement, "How they came forth from the furnaces…and how long, how severe the anguish ere they find their Father, were long to tell" (*Jer.*, Plt.73). No, it doesn't mean that I, as a man, was on any cross that was burned. It could have been, but that's not the story. Yes, man's inhumanity to man has revealed that many of us in the inquisition, say, were burned alive to satisfy some sadist who thought he was serving God. But that's not the vision. The furnace on the cross…this body is the cross and the furnace is the furnace of experience. When we have *completed* the journey, having played all, we are reduced to the stump. And you are told in the Book of Daniel "Do not touch the stump, leave it alone. Strip the tree, throw the fruit away, sever the branches, cut it down, but leave the stump" (4:15). And from that stump the new being grows. That being is golden, liquid light and that is the blood of God itself.

That rises into what? They asked Paul and Paul said in his 15th chapter of 1st Corinthians, "Someone will ask how do the dead rise, with what body do they come?" and he answered his own question and said, "It is as God has chosen." Conceive of an infinite being—not big in the sense of taking up space, but a being that is perfect that could contain all humanity. In that one body…as you're told in Ephesians "There's only one body, one Spirit, one Lord, one God and Father of all" (4:4), so in that one body is a body that is unique for every being in the world. What it will be like, who knows? But you will fill it with yourself…that is the golden liquid light. It takes the molten gold to be cast into that form, and you rise up like a serpent into that heavenly state; and you empty your being that is all molten gold which is the result of your experiences in this world.

This world is a furnace, the furnace of experiences, and it is far more burning than if tonight you were consumed in a flame, for that would take only a matter of moments. Take yourself now and douse yourself with gasoline and set yourself aflame…it wouldn't take long to depart this world. But to remain in this world, and live, and then to depart it normally, or even in violence, to find yourself restored to life in a world just like this, with problems just like these, to continue the furnaces to the very end when you are reduced right down, and there's only yourself left, and that self is that liquid molten gold. And when it rises, you will rise as it, you rise into the mold waiting for you. That is the body that God has chosen for you, and it is unique. There is no one who can fill it but you and it is waiting for you.

So everyone in the end is redeemed in the one body, the one Spirit, the one Lord, the one God and Father of all. So in the end we are not anything that is here. Paul made it so distinct: "Don't try to compare the mortal frame that you wear here with that which is your immortal self. It is planted a physical body; it is raised a spiritual body. It is planted in weakness; it's raised in power. It is planted in dishonor; it is raised in glory in a translucent state." So everyone here will go through these experiences...I don't care what they will say.

So I give my eyes to one in my spiritual world. Having been risen from this state it is my choice, my privilege, to give it to whom I will. To her I gave them and she in turn gave them to one who now sits next to her tonight...and this is hers. Having heard her relate the vision while seated in the car, this other lady who heard them as they were being told, went to bed that night (which is a week ago tonight) and in this she said, "I saw a match scratched upon the earth and then the whole earth burst into flame as far as the eye could see. That horizon was like a prairie fire in Kansas." If you've ever seen the flatness of Kansas, when the sun comes up in that vast, vast prairie flatland, that whole thing is simply like a flame. So she said, "It looked just like the flame of Kansas when the sun is rising. And then some dark object came out of what seemingly was the center of that flame and came straight towards me, an enormous object, and it was a serpent. It came straight to my nose and then turned to my left, and then what I had not seen before was a cross, and the cross rose from the earth and became erect. That serpent transformed itself into a man, and the man climbed up on the cross; but instead of being *on* the cross, he was *in* the cross." She actually saw the transformation of a serpent into a man, being transfigured on the cross from within it. And the whole thing was aflame. So here, they paralleled each other in the vision of the night.

So what I've told you is true. You have immortal bodies, a body that is imperishable. In this world of Caesar we are fighting shadows. We think the other is another...and there is no other. There is only God, there's only one being in this world. So here I am looking out upon a world that seems to be multiplied by billions of people...each seems to be separate and individual and distinct...and maybe an enemy of mine. There is only one being in the world and that being is God, God fragmented into all of these

The Return of Glory

little garments. In the end, it is gathered together, and in the end, only one being...yet without loss of identity, for you are individualized. But the body that you are going to wear is not this. Yet, may I tell you, I will know you and you will know me.

So having been raised from the dead, when I presented myself to her and to others who have been attending, they knew me. But I can vanish from them at will, appear at will. Others will see me in different characters. You become a protean being. But you can't show them *that* body until they arise to where you are. That is something that you can't display to anyone. You can display the fact that you *have* risen from the dead, but then man not understanding this, he thinks, well now, "When Neville dies and they cremate him or they put him in the grave, will he reappear to me?" That's not resurrection; resurrection takes place while you are here. This world is the world of death, everything here is dead. As the thing that he wrote, have you ever thought of it, that all of our food is dead food? We have to kill the animal; therefore it's dead before we eat it. Whether it be a bird or whether it be a fish or the vegetable or the fruit, everything is dead that we consume and the world is the world of death. So he overcomes the last enemy which is death.

So we go out fighting against *shadows*, and we think he is another or she is another. They are not others. We are all brothers and collectively we form one being and that one being is God. We are the sons of God, but it takes all the sons of God to form God. He is made up of all of his sons, and God is housed in his sons. Say "I am" that's God, that is the one and only God, there is no other God. That's his name forever and forever.

Now, if I would forgive you, I can do it only as I keep in my mind's eye the difference between what you are doing and who you are. I must learn to distinguish between you, the immortal you, and the state into which you have moved, either wittingly or unwittingly. So as Blake said, "You can see from what I teach I do not consider the just or the wicked to be in a supreme state, but to be every one of them states of the sleep into which the soul may fall in its deadly dreams of good and evil" (*Vis. of Last Judgment*). Take your mother that you love, no matter what your mother did if you really love her, what would it matter to you concerning good or evil, wouldn't you forgive her? I wouldn't care what she did.

I had my mother...she's gone from this world now...but I'm quite sure that if Mother were here in this world and she did the most horrible thing I could forgive her. I could forgive any of my brothers, I know that much...my mother, my father. Learning now to put my circle further out to encompass my friends, and then to encompass a larger circle, those that I do now know as friends, for in the end we are all one being, we're all brothers. So he said,

"Go and tell my brothers I'm ascending to my Father and your Father, and to my God and to your God." Here is a man who pushed out the circle to encompass *all*, because he realized there was only one being in the world playing all the parts. But I can't forgive unless I can discriminate between the being who occupies the part that he is playing and the part that he is playing. Then I can identify him with the part that I know he would like to be, and to the degree that I am self-persuaded that he is that, he will become that.

So it is entirely up to me to practice the art of repentance. Repentance is not what the churches teach; repentance is simply "a radical change of attitude." So I see it, it's obvious, there he is. He's committed the act and he confesses to it, but it doesn't matter, so he's confessed to it. He was in a state when he committed that act. Now I must learn to separate him, the actor, from the part that he was playing and identify him with the part I know in my heart he would like to have played. And as I am persuaded that he is *that* being, he changes from the outer world into that state, and becomes the transformed being that others may see it. So I am called upon to practice repentance...for the first word recorded in the earliest gospel—that is the earliest by actual date which is Mark—is "The kingdom of heaven is at hand; repent, and believe the gospel" (1:15). Believe the most incredible story that was ever told to man...the story of Christianity. It doesn't make sense, and so if you are going to judge it on a human level, well then, it is complete nonsense. Worldly wisdom should throw it through the window, and yet I'm called upon to believe it.

So if I believe it, I must now put it into practice. If I call myself a Christian, what are people for if they aren't going to practice it? So I either practice it or just take the word just as a name and say I'm a Christian. We go look for a job or you're inducted into the Army and they ask you that question, what's your religion? and you say, I'm a Christian. They're not even satisfied with that answer. You've got to tell them what denomination. You say, I'm a Christian, but that's not good enough. Are you a Roman Catholic? Are you a Protestant? That's not good enough...what denomination of the Protestant? And all this nonsense they ask you...when it's simply "I'm a Christian."

Well, what is a Christian?—the fulfillment of the promises of Jehovah to man, to what is called Israel, through his prophets, his servants the prophets. Christianity is only the fulfillment of Judaism. So if I said to her who asked me the question, "I'm a Jew," then she would assign me to a rabbi. But I said, No, I'm a Jew for the simple reason I'm a Christian; I could be a Jew and not be a Christian, but I can't be a Christian and not be a Jew, because Christianity is the fulfillment of Judaism." So how could I be a

Christian and not be a Jew? I would have to be a Jew first before I can be a Christian. And so, if I actually unfold the story and I experience Christianity *in* myself by reenacting within myself the entire story of Jesus Christ—without thought, it just happens—if the whole thing unfolds within me, then I am the fulfillment of God's promises to Israel, and fulfillment of that promise is Christ.

Now go and tell the story to the whole vast world...at least to those who will listen, to those who will hear you. And then when you are moving in your heavenly sphere, you select from wisdom that is from above, not from below. For on this level if I had to give my eyes to one, I would definitely give them to my wife, and next to her I would give them to my daughter. But on a higher level when there is no uncertainty as to whom you should give it to, I gave it to another. I only know this lady at a distance. I've never seen her home. I know her husband. I've never seen her children. I only know her in this place. I know her, I love her like a sister, but I certainly have never seen her socially, never met her socially, only here. And yet the one person on this level to whom I would have given my eyes, if I used this wisdom and this feeling, it would be my wife. Following my wife it would be my daughter. Yet when you are functioning from above you aren't using the wisdom of Caesar; you are seeing it entirely differently, and you select from those who come the one to whom you will give it. And then the gift is so complete she can do with it what she will. I'm quite sure she would have given hers to her husband or her mother or her children (she has two), but she didn't. She gave it to one who is not related as the world calls relationships in this world. You do it from above; you don't give the gift from here.

But fortunately, the gift that you give you retain, you do not lose it. In fact, by giving you have increased it within yourself. And your visions are all together wonderful and they come when you least expect them. When you are in the theater and you're seeing a crowd, suddenly you've dropped out, and then these things are happening within you. You are at a cocktail party, and you don't go into any meditation. Or, this nonsense of going off to some little place in India. Or, some fella coming over here with his long beard that should be washed. Have a beard but why not keep it clean? And then he goes off and takes $500 from each person. If you can't afford five, he'll take three. Then who is kidding whom in all this nonsense? And he's going to teach you how to meditate. You don't have to be taught how to meditate. When the visions come they just come and you can't stop it.

And when you have been placed upon that cross—and this [body] is the only cross Christ was ever placed upon. It is Christ *in* us that is the hope of glory and this is his cross. The prairie fires that she saw, and her friend to whom she gave the eyes saw, the fires are the fires of experience; these are the furnaces. As Blake said, "How they come forth from the furnaces, and how long, vast and severe the anguish before they found their Father were long to tell." That's the one goal in this world: man is seeking for his Father. His Father is not an earthly father; his Father is himself. The Father is the cause of his own experience in this world. He is looking for the cause of the phenomena of his life. Why are these things happening to me? He is trying to find out why. And when he finds the cause, he's going to find himself, and that cause is the Father, and *he is* the Father. So you can say "I and my Father are one" (Jn.10:30). He *must* find the Father before he finishes this search in the world.

So how long, vast and severe the anguish before they find their Father was long to tell. No one can tell you how close you are to the discovery of the Father, but it will begin with your resurrection while in this world. And soon after your resurrection, which is the same night, you are born from above. And then days later, to be exact 139 days later, you find the Father. Then 123 days later comes the splitting of the curtain of the temple, which is your own body…and there you see what the lady saw, that liquid, molten gold. And then like a serpent…as you fuse with that gold you move up like a serpent back into your own skull, which is heaven (Luke17:21). Then 998 days later the dove descends upon you, because the whole thing is over and here the Spirit of the Most High has rested upon you (Jn.1:31-34). Then *you* can say, as it is said when he begins the story in Luke, "The Spirit of the Lord God is upon me. He has anointed me now"—this is the anointment—"and he has sent me to preach glad tidings to the poor and to open the eyes of the blind" (4:18). We all think we see, and we think the blind are those without eyes or impure eyes so they can't see. No, we have eyes and see not… we do not see the mystery behind this façade.

So tonight, learn to forgive. It is essential. And you can only forgive when you can start to discriminate between the state in which a man is placed and the man who is the occupant of that state. If I can discriminate between the two, I can forgive any being in this world. For if I am cast in the role of a murderer, I've got to murder. If I'm cast in the role of the wonderful person, I must be that being. But if you like the part I'm playing, all praise belongs to the author and the author is God. So he wrote the play and then we are the actors playing the parts, and in the end when the curtain comes down we will understand the reason behind the entire play.

Now let us go into the Silence.

* * *

Now are there any questions, please? Don't be embarrassed. The purpose of this meeting is simply to find out all we can concerning the great mystery behind the phenomena of life.

Q: If we forgive, then are we forgiven?
A: In fact it's contingent. You're told that your heavenly Father will forgive you *if* you forgive. If you don't forgive, you are holding that image in your own mind's eye not knowing it is your very self. So you are bound by the thing that you haven't loosed. If you loose on earth, it's loosed in heaven; if you bind on earth, it's bound in heaven. And so it's simply a condition imposed upon man. To the degree he is willing to pardon he is pardoned; therefore, he is self-pardoned, because the Father who forgives is himself.

I know it does not make sense. In the worldly sense it's stupid. There's no worldly wisdom to this at all, but if you understand the mystery, if you can accept Christianity, which certainly doesn't make sense, and really believe it, then you must put into practice the doctrine. I ask you to think in terms of the one you love most—be it your husband, your wife, your mother, your father, a child—and see if you can't forgive her no matter what she did. I'm quite sure that if you really love her you will. You might not condone the act. It may cause you tears and great embarrassment and horrors, yet you can't condemn her. And if you go beyond it now and see the difference between the state that caused the act and the one who occupies the state, well then, you can really forgive. You must learn to discriminate between the two.

We are living in a world of infinite states and they're only states. You move into a state whether it be rich or poor, *you* are neither rich nor poor. We think we are rich in this world, we think we are this…if you want to be rich read that 3rd chapter of Revelation, "Come buy from me gold refined in the fire, that you may be rich" (3:18). That's the gold that she saw at the base of that stump. You come and buy it; it will take all the experiences of the furnaces to produce that gold. So, "Come buy from me gold refined in the fire that you may be rich…and ointment to anoint your eyes that you may see." Read it in the 3rd chapter of Revelation. That's the real gold, the gold that she saw after the flames had consumed the cross leaving only the reality; and that reality which is that molten gold is the blood of God himself. You are the blood of God, because the life is in the blood. Now you have life in yourself when you fuse with it. Before you are only animated bodies, but from then on you have life in yourself. For the first man was simply a breathing, living body, but not a life-giving Spirit. When you reach that point of fusion with the gold, you are then a life-giving Spirit, one with yourself who is God.

So it is contingent, my dear. As you pardon, you are pardoned, you are self-pardoned. So, practice forgiveness by practicing *repentance*, which is not feeling remorseful or regretful. It hasn't a thing to do with regret. It's simply a radical change of attitude toward the condition in the world…but you must put something in its place. Don't ignore it, put something in its place, and become self-persuaded that the imaginary act is real, that it's factual.

Any other questions?

Q: If we're all cast in a particular role, then it wouldn't behoove us to change that role, would it?

A: Why certainly! You are called upon to make the effort. We're not automatons.

Q: Well, if God is expressing himself in that particular individual at that time…

A: We are called upon to make every effort to get out of poverty into security rather than stand upon the feet of others. You are called upon to take this statement, "Whatever you desire, believe that you have received it, and you will" (Mark11:24). If a man is hungry and he can't afford to buy a loaf of bread, is he satisfied with that state? He is not and he doesn't want to steal it and run the risk of Caesar's law putting him behind bars. He would like to be able to buy it. Well then, assume that you have all that it takes to buy it.

You're called upon to make the effort to break through this shell. So we move from state to state to state…divine dissatisfaction. But, not to be complacent…the whole vast world of India, they are complacent. They won't eat the cow, so forty million cows roam the streets eating up all their food…they haven't enough food. And then they use the waste of the cow for their fuel, and then criticize us to whom they turn for our surplus food. We have so much it's rotting, and they have none because they have their monkeys that they worship and they have these cows, sacred animals. So they are complacent. They say reincarnation… forget it! You are an individualized being and you tend forever towards ever greater and greater individualization. There is no loss of identity. They teach loss of identity; that the reason why I am now what I am is because I was formerly that which I don't remember, I don't know and don't care about, and so I must now suffer because of this stupid theory. Hasn't a thing to do with it. That is not this teaching and it's not Christianity. You are what you are because you have assumed that you are what you are, and you are playing it in this world.

Now play the part fully. But you don't have to cast yourself forever in the same part. The actor who is satisfied because of a good check at the end of the week to play forever one part...well, there are plays on Broadway that ran five years and seven years and any actor who felt insecure and continued in that part for seven years, he is not an actor. So he gets his check every week for seven years and he comes out and they say, "What have you done?" "Well, I played in *Abbey's Irish Rose.*" "Well, what else?" "I played in *Abbey's Irish Rose*" and that's all that he can say. He played in it for seven years. But can you now play this part? No, he can't play that part, because he always played this tiny little part. He knows nothing about pouring himself into another part. The real actor will take a play even when it's at the very top, standing room only, and after six months he quits, goes into another. He doesn't want to be stymied in one part...not the real one. Suppose you have a perfect orchestra leader and you can do everything with one grand number, and the critics hail you, are you going to play that forever and forever? Aren't you going to be challenged and take something entirely different and try to bring out of that music that something that is in you? Or are you going to play the one thing because it is easy? No, that's not living. Take a challenge!

This is the most challenging religion in the world...the religion of Christianity, which is the flower of Judaism. There is no complacency in it at all.

Until next Monday...thank you.

THE LAW AND THE PLAN OF REDEMPTION

4/21/69

Our presentation of the gospel must clearly show that it has specific relevance to life *now* as well as hereafter, for secularized man is far more concerned with the present than the future. So if you would interest anyone in this work, first appeal to what they can do here and now. For the Promise is so fantastic that they may turn from you in disgust. Show them what *can* be done right here in this world now and then you'll get their interest. Then you might find them becoming more and more interested in the Promise.

Now here let me share with you a couple of stories that came to me this week. You'll see why I tell you this. He's not here tonight but he's here quite often, and he wrote these two stories. He said, "About ten days a go my wife told me of this little girl, fourteen months old. My wife is a very dear friend of the grandmother of this little girl. And the little girl had cancer. She developed certain lumps in her neck; took her to the hospital, and a little biopsy was made of the tissues and they brought back the verdict, cancer. Another doctor looked at it and he questioned it, he wasn't quite sure, not convinced, so there was a difference of opinion there. Then they brought in three specialists separately; each brought in the verdict, cancer. So here were four and one not quite convinced. But they kept the child in the hospital for further examination.

Now this night ten days ago his wife told him the story. He said, "I sat there and I listened to much of the story and then I tuned her out to the point where I couldn't even hear what she was saying. I reconstructed the entire story in my mind's eye and redid it along the lines that I wanted to hear and I actually heard my wife's voice telling me an entirely different story. As she was telling me the story, I completely revised it at a certain point. Then that night when I was completely alone and not distracted, I redid the whole thing to make myself convinced and to be sure I actually heard my wife's voice telling me the revised story." The child was kept in the hospital and then they made another test from another lump in the neck and a unanimous vote was brought in: the child does *not* have cancer, and therefore because they had no remedial treatment done in the hospital she never had cancer. They couldn't conceive of any other treatment...they did not give her any radium, gave her nothing, no injections. Therefore, they were 100 percent wrong they confessed the first time, because without treatment the child could never have overcome the condition. So, when the wife heard the new verdict of a complete change in the little fourteen-month old child, she told the mother and the grandmother what her husband had done.

Meanwhile, the neighborhood has been told this and they are agog, but they can't for one moment credit an imaginal act as causation. That imagining creates reality is the height of insanity. Nevertheless, this is his story...that as every mystic knows that every natural effect has a spiritual cause and *not* a natural one. A natural cause only seems and it is a *delusion* of this world. And man has a very, very poor memory. He can't relate what's taking place to any imaginal act in his past, because he's looking for *physical* causation. And he cannot believe that he did anything that would have produced this, not knowing that the doing was imaginal, not physical. He sat alone and he imagined, and he set in motion a cause and when the cause came into the world and he saw the effects, he did not go back into the psychic state of his being; he went back into the physical state. And he can't remember where he ever did physically anything worthy of this thing that he is now reaping. So, his Imagination is setting the whole thing in motion, but his memory is faulty, and that is the vegetating memory that simply disintegrates because it *isn't*, really. So, he looks upon the man who claims that it is all Imagination as a fool. As Blake said, "The idiot reasoner laughs at the man of Imagination." So I tell you, everything in your world is caused by an imaginal act.

Now, he said, 'I was driving home and suddenly I thought here comes April the 15th and I could use a little more cash. Uncle Sam is making demands upon my income, so I could use a little more. Then, in my Imagination I simply imagined that lovely, green, crisp currency was raining upon me, gently raining upon me. And then for about a minute I simply lost myself in this little shower of green currency. Then the traffic demanded my complete attention so I dropped it instantly and came back to this world. It only took about a minute, if a minute. And then I continued home in my normal alert state. I never thought about it again. On the morning of the 15th my boss came into the office and he said to me, "You will receive a ten percent raise in salary retroactive to April the 1st" and then gave me a check retroactive with a ten percent increase in salary." Now he said, "I simply took this green currency falling gently upon me. But let me warn you tonight… wait 'til you get home to do it if you're driving the highway. Be alert while you're driving. You can do it just as well while you're reclining in your bed preparing yourself for sleep. Or do it when you are sitting down in a chair. But it works! This actually works." Everything is an imaginal act. There is no such thing as a physical causation, it's imaginal. But the world will not accept it. We are looked upon as simply idiots and they laugh at the man of Imagination when he tells you that everything in this world is caused by some mental act.

Well, try to disprove it. You can say that man struck so-and-so, and therefore that was a physical cause, and the blow that he received that was the effect, and therefore the whole thing was simply constructed physically. It wasn't so! What preceded the impulse to strike him? You go back to an unseen cause and it was an imaginal act. The whole vast world is brought into being by Imagination, sustained in being by Imagination, and when Imagination no longer sustains it, it dissolves and leaves not a trace behind, not a trace.

So here, one must approach this gospel on this level first and you get their interest on this level so that they prove it in the testing…as my friend proved it. He received a ten percent raise retroactive to the first of the month. And then the little girl, fourteen months old, instead of having cancer as five doctors agreed and then they changed their opinion. But to justify their false judgment they had to admit it wasn't so in the beginning, because nothing was given to her. There was no treatment and unless treatment was given, it could not have ever been cancer, therefore it never was. Well, that's all right with him…it's perfectly all right. The child has not received any verdict by the doctors of cancer.

Now you'll say how can a little girl fourteen months old, why should she suffer? To you she is fourteen months old, to you. She isn't any fourteen months old. The garment she wears judged by human standards is fourteen months old, but not the little girl that is there. She's old as God himself and God has no beginning, no end. He chose us in him before the foundation of the world. Not when she came out of her mother's womb, but before the foundation of the world. Before physical creation, you and I were chosen in him for a purpose. Now without that purpose, without that meaning, what would it matter if you this night owned the entire world and there was no meaning to it, and death closed the book and that was final? Well, many a tyrant believes that. You can't blame him for being a tyrant. If he really believes it, well then, how can you blame him? Who wouldn't do just what he did if you really believe that death ends it all? Shakespeare in his *Macbeth* is perfectly right: "A tale told by an idiot full of sound and fury, signifying nothing." That's what it would have to be if there were no Promise, no purpose, no meaning behind the entire thing.

So the Promise comes in then *after* you get their interest and they can test it and prove it in performance. When you can prove it in performance, then you can give them the most incredible story in the world, and hope that they will believe you or begin to believe you. Nothing that is said of Jesus, not a thing about Jesus is proven outwardly, but nothing. Only the visionaries know him…he who this dark body, this mask…they see what a friend who walks the earth with them clothed in flesh tells them that he had experienced. So a man or a woman suddenly has this entire drama rapidly unfold within him or within her, and takes friends into his or her confidence, and tells them that these things happened to me. "Now, you know I am not dead and yet do you know I know what it is to be crucified"—and they listen attentively—"and then to be buried, and then to be resurrected? Now believe me and in time I'll prove it to you."

And then, in your heavenly wanderings you choose one to whom you give your immortal eyes that are turned inward, not outward. And then you reveal the drama and she sees you buried, on a cross burned to the ground, and the golden liquid light that is just a residue of the entire thing…just as you told her it has happened to you. Now you could not in eternity persuade her that she did not have that experience, any more than you could persuade the man who told her the story that he did not have the experience. So she knows who Jesus is…seeing behind and beyond the mask of her friend, who is fragile, who has all the weaknesses of the flesh, all the limitations of the flesh. She goes beyond the mask through vision and sees who Jesus really is.

Well then, who is Jesus? "He has made known unto us the mystery of his will, according to his purpose which he set forth in Christ as a *plan* for the fullness of time, that he may unite all things in him, things in heaven and things on earth" (Eph.1:9). Therefore, who is Jesus?—he is the *plan*. The plan is in man. That plan suddenly erupted in a man and he happened to be a friend of a few who would listen to him; and they believed him, in a way…and hoped he was telling the truth. Well, he told them of another aspect of this principle that they *could* verify on this level. They tried it and it worked. Then in the fullness of time he gave his eyes and still kept them; for in the heavenly sphere you keep what you give, therefore you only share it, you don't really lose possession of it. So she has the immortal eyes that she may see inward into the world of thought, into eternity. And then she sees her friend on a cross set aflame and reduced to molten gold, as he told her that it happened to him. Now she *knows* because she received the eyes that could look inward.

Now, only the visionaries know, actually know who Jesus is. For not in eternity no matter how you search will you have any proof externally of Jesus…for he is not of this world. He's entirely different. We are from below, we are told, and he is from above. "You are of this world, I am not of this world" (Jn.8:23). So why look for him in this world? And yet throughout the history of man they have been looking for him in the Near East, and then those who do not know, who have not the vision, say this is the spot where he was crucified and that's the spot where he was buried and this is the robe that he wore and that is a piece of wood that came from the cross on which he was nailed. They build up this fantastic tradition. As we are told in the 15th chapter of Matthew: "The traditions of our fathers have voided the word of God" (15:6). The word of God has completely gone from you because of the traditions of your fathers. You have kept these traditions alive believing in a physical Jesus and it's not a physical Jesus at all. Jesus is the *pattern* buried in *every* man, and it suddenly erupts in the fullness of time. The one in whom it erupts is just as surprised as anyone could be. And he simply tells it, still remaining in his little weak garment, the garment that is very weak, and still subject to all the temptations of the world. But he can't deny what has happened to him. So he tells it.

Then he gives to one, who in turn gives it to another, who will in turn give it to another, and they all become in scripture eye witnesses. So when Luke begins his story, he said, "In as much as many have undertaken to compile a narrative of the things which have been *accomplished* among us"—not the hope, that have been accomplished among us—"just as they were presented to us by those who were from the beginning eyewitnesses"—and then he adds the thought—"and ministers of the word, it seemed good to me also to write a narrative concerning these things of which we have been informed" (1:1-4). So he is now going to tell the one who loves God, he is called "Theophilus, O dear or blessed Theophilus." He's now going to tell him the truth of these things because of the eyewitnesses.

Now in time the eyewitnesses depart this world and then the ministers of the word multiply. They *haven't seen*…they haven't seen what the eyewitnesses saw. So they depart this world leaving only the ministers of the word and they never knew the eyewitnesses' friend when he walked in flesh whose story they witnessed because he gave them his eyes to see what had happened to him. And so they witnessed the drama as it unfolded within him. But then comes the inevitable departure from this world. So they all vanish, including the one who had the experience, leaving only

The Return of Glory

now the ministers of the word. And they build an organization...which is so completely unlike what *actually* happened. Then they make a little god out of a being who was like all the other beings in the world only it erupted in him. They speak nothing of the eruption; they speak of an external man, and there is no such thing as an external being, there never was. He is the *inner* man, the *new* man. You can look from now 'til the ends of time and you will never find any convincing evidence of the historicity of one called Jesus. Yet he is the most real, the most true being in the world, for he is *in* every being in the world. "Christ in you is the hope of glory" (Col.1:27) and "Do you not realize that Jesus Christ is in you?—unless, of course, you fail to meet the test" (2 Cor.13:5).

So you begin to test on this level with his power called the law, so that you can actually bring all things to pass. Like my friend who simply allowed crisp, crisp bills, not debt but currency to fall upon him. And having received it like a gentle shower then in a matter of days the boss comes in and tells him a ten percent raise has been voted for him and it's retroactive. So, his so-called immediate problem has been solved. But now it continues, it wasn't just for the month, this now continues as long as he is employed by this company. From what I have been told they certainly do want him in their employment.

So you start...if you're going to tell this story, you start by telling it on this level and show that it has a specific relevance to life *now*, and do not start in the hereafter. You can bring them into that afterwards, but bring them first into the working of the law. Do not allow anything in this world to confront you with something impossible. *Nothing* is impossible to Imagination and the whole thing is done in Imagination. So you are not responsible as a reasoning being to *make* it so; you simply imagine that it is so. My friend who told me the story, what did he know about cancer? If he saw the cancer under the microscope, what is called cancer, he wouldn't recognize it. He doesn't know a thing about the human body, any more than I do, but he would know what his wife would tell him if the verdict were reversed. And so now she goes out trying to convert the grandmother and the mother of the child to the belief that imagining does create reality. Well, she has a task. They are going to believe the wise doctors that she never had it anyway, that they were wrong in their diagnosis. She could not have shown it under the microscope and then in a matter of days, say within two or three weeks, to show no evidence that it was ever present. That was impossible, therefore she never had it. Not that she had it and an imaginal act dissipated it, oh no, because they can't believe in causation as mental. Causation must be under that microscope as a little physical thing. Though you can't see it with a normal eye, you can see it with the extended eye of the

403

microscope, and therefore it is still physical. So the entire structure has to be physical for them. They take it now, put the little biopsy, the little tissue, and go right down with their aid, the microscope, and they see what is called a cancer cell. Then ten days or three weeks later they don't see the cancer cell, therefore, they could not have seen accurately the first time.

They know nothing of my friend's attitude toward life, that the whole thing is imaginal. Since he started coming here he has gone up and up and up by simply imagining. He doesn't burst a blood vessel. He simply tuned out his wife's voice as it was coming through going beyond the point he wanted to hear. He heard enough, that the little child fourteen months old had cancer confirmed by all the doctors and there were five. Only one questioned; he didn't deny, only questioned. But three *experts*, all coming in singly, not together, each went out on the limb and said it was cancer. So there were four against one for cancer. But he tuned her out and simply reconstructed the entire drama in his mind's eye and listened to his wife's voice that he knows well, completely changing the entire picture and tells him what he *wanted* her to say. He heard it distinctly...that was all that he did. And that word of his could not return unto him void, it had to accomplish that which he purposed and bring it into fulfillment. He determined that. Well, then he did not a thing. He knows nothing of the human body. He *did* nothing but remain faithful to that imaginal act, and the verdict came in.

So I ask you to try it. Try it and then turn to your neighbor, in a quiet way and ask if they ever thought that their imaginal acts are causative. You might get a little wedge in that way. "Did it ever occur to you that the things that are happening to you in your world are caused not by the obvious but caused by some unseen imaginal act?" Well, you know, you may interest them that way, and then having received their interest for a moment then you can ask them to try it. You can construct a scene for them and have that scene come to pass in their world. If it is duplicated and repeated again and it works, well then, you've got them.

Now you may present them with the Promise, the most incredible thing in the world, that here this little weak garment and can be so completely transformed that it can rise from the dead. Completely rising from the dead, not restored to life as the world is always restored, but a completely transformed being...something entirely different. Yes, the face is human, the hands human, the voice human, but don't go beyond that because you don't know the form. Face human, yes, that I tell you, the hands human, the voice human, but don't try in any way to describe the form. We'll come only to the point of light...how can you have a body that's of light? Well, don't go beyond it.

I'm giving you my own experience: the head, yes, beautiful beyond measure and human, and the hands yes. The one thing that separates man from the entire creation is the hand. Look at the entire world. If it doesn't have a hand…the monkey doesn't have a hand, and it can't fashion, it can't make. Without a hand if I were the wisest being in the world, without a hand I couldn't execute my contract. Give me a hand I become a builder. So the first word is a hand: Yod He Vau He. Yod is a hand, the hand of the creator, the hand of the director, that hand that can fashion. If I couldn't fashion then I would go around nude; I couldn't fashion a suit of clothes. I couldn't fashion anything. But give me a hand and you turn me into my Father's image. I have a human face, I have hands, and I have a voice and it's human. Now the being that you're destined to be is that. But now don't go beyond it in trying to in any way conceive of what the form is like. That's the being, that's the fiery being that you really are, and you are destined to be, and you'll awaken as that being.

But you tell this to someone who would rather be the same little thing restored… something that they must carry to the bathroom several times a day and perform all the normal functions themselves, and perpetuate that forever, can you imagine such hell? No, that's not the body that you're going to wear. You're going to wear the body that is the body of God himself, for you're destined to awaken as that form. But while you're in the world of Caesar, don't neglect the law, don't treat it lightly. Use it every moment of time and there's not a thing in this world beyond your ability to imagine. It's not your responsibility in this world to *make* it so. You simply imagine that it is so and let it be so and then in a way that no one knows it is crystallizing itself into this world and becoming a fact. That is the world in which we live.

Now before you judge it, I ask you to try it. It would be stupid to pass judgment on something that you haven't tested…and so many people do that. They will say "I don't like that." "Have you ever had it?" "No, but I know I won't like it." Well, you can acquire a taste for anything. I know the first time I had an oyster…it was on the little island of St. Croix. In those days we spoke of it as Santa Cruz. It was owned by the Danes. Mother told me, when I left Barbados to go to Santa Cruz, to watch what other people did, because they were a different people and therefore they ate differently and they ate different foods that I didn't know. I was only eleven years old. She said, "You watch." In those days there were no hotels, only rooming houses, and so you sat down at the same common table. If there were twenty roomers, well then, there were twenty roomers and the man and the wife who ran the place sat with us and they conducted the whole thing. Well, in Santa Cruz where I am it's 1916, they're all speaking Danska, they're all

Danish, and I couldn't understand one word. But I could observe what they were doing.

And so, the dinner started off and they were all around the table and here before me were these six little things on shells. Never saw one before. Mother said to watch what the host did. So she took this little fork, something I never saw before either, little tiny fork. She first put all these little condiments on the thing. Then she took the fork and stuck it into the...and then that face was like heaven...what she anticipated. When she got it into her mouth it satisfied her and it was simply consummation of that glory. Well, I expected the same thing. I did the same thing and stuck it into my mouth...it wouldn't go down and I couldn't bring it up...it just couldn't...can't expectorate it. Mother said that after all you couldn't spit it out...no matter what happens, if I die I have to swallow it. And it wouldn't go down. Finally, when I swallowed then I looked down and I must have turned green...there were five more to go and I couldn't say no. I had to actually put these things together and swallow it and then down they would go. Well, today I love oysters, love them. When I go to New York, we get these lovely oysters. Every dinner I precede my meal with either oysters or the little clams, the Little Neck, not the Cherry Stone, not my favorite, but the Little Neck. They're limited in supply and that's what I order or the oysters. And here, today I thoroughly enjoy them. I can enjoy an oyster in any form. I prefer it in its raw state, but give it to me fried, give it to me Oysters Rockefeller, any way. I had my first experience at the age of eleven. So you can acquire a taste for anything in this world.

So you can acquire a taste for the Word of God. But introduce them first with the law and tell them how it works and then show them how it works. Ask them to repeat it. No matter how difficult the problem let them confront it with this principle. Then slowly get over "Do you know who Jesus really is?" Well, naturally, he's going to say yes because he's a Christian. So he believes he knows exactly who Jesus is, this unique son of Mary who had no father, but the father was God; he was physical and he came out of Mary's womb. That's what they're going to tell you—one billion Christians will tell you that story. That's what I was told. Then you will say, "You know, I know a friend of mine and he's a normal person, not formally educated, no, doesn't have any of these qualifications, completely unknown, just a normal person, married...in fact, he was once divorced, so he has a family, a son from the first and a daughter from the second." Right away they'll close the book, if you're going to tell me anything about him and associate it in any way with spirituality. But, nevertheless, you go on and you say, "You know what? Everything said of Jesus Christ in the gospels he experienced."

"And you know what? A friend of mine, just as normal as he is, she too has been married twice and she has two children from two different men; and one night in vision he gave to her his immortal eyes that she may see. And then she saw the same one, as he told her he had experienced it, hanging on a cross, and the cross set aflame, and reduced to molten, golden, liquid light. And they were digging a hole to put the body, and she saw the body on a litter, on a pallet. She has seen him on other occasions manifesting the power he tells you he now exercises when the body sleeps upon the bed. So she knows who Jesus *really* is. No, he is not that little garment. Jesus is a *pattern*, an eternal pattern of redemption which sleeps in every garment; but in that particular garment he awoke. And now *he* knows who he is, because when he awakes, the one in whom he awakes is the one who awakes. And so, he became humanity that humanity may become God. So God sleeps in everyone and in everyone he will awake; and as he awakes, the identical drama has to be experienced by the one in whom he awakes. So *that* is Jesus…and there never was another Jesus. There is no other Jesus.

Now, if they are very ardent they may turn from you even though they become enriched by the law that you taught them. Perfectly all right, it takes quite a while to break down these traditions. But you go back and you read it in the 15th chapter of the Book of Matthew, how for the sake of your traditions you have made void the word of God. So they'll keep alive all of these things, and wear all these silly little garments on the outside, with their purple robes and their red robes and all these thing and hats so heavy they can't even hold them up. Here they are, they think *that* makes them very, very important. And the unthinking millions will think themselves blessed if they can but touch the garment as he walks by, or if he will smile on them, of if they can even attend service where he, the great one, is conducting the Mass. They firmly believe this nonsense and they go blindly on doing it morning, noon and night.

But I'm telling you what I know from experience. You take it seriously, because at my age, even if I lived on for a few years, it can't be that long and I must depart. And those of you who would have seen as I have told you that you will see will depart too. And when the eyewitnesses depart they only leave behind them the ministers of the Word, and they invariably turn it into some institutional concept, and therefore void the Word of God, completely void it. But you take me seriously and start tonight—of course, you've already done it—with the law and prove it. And you'll prove it— you'll become exactly the man, the woman that you want to be. But don't forget the Promise in the proving of the law, for without the Promise what would it mater if you owned the earth? What would it matter?

I read Stalin's daughter's book. You might have read it, and you recall the passage. She was present when her father died. She said she has never seen such an expression of hate in her life. He was paralyzed on one side, and on the un-paralyzed side he raised the hand in an expression of anger. He couldn't have seen, because the brain was gone, but he saw something not with the physical eye. He saw something and the response came out in a physical manner. "Whatever he saw," she said, "I've never seen such hate in my life as expressed on my father's face, as though the devil himself stood before him and he was simply defiant." He could have seen the composite picture of the twenty million that he slaughtered personified as one face facing him...and the hand, this little hand, raised in defiance. And then he collapsed and was gone. He didn't believe in the hereafter and he didn't believe that he would ever be restored. This was it, therefore, do what you want. He looked upon the entire crowd standing on the podium with him and under his breath when hundreds of thousands were cheering him he would say 'Fools!' He looked upon them just as a cast of nothing. And yet today we find all these silly people ballooning him up as an important person in this world, and he didn't care anything about anyone...slaughtered as he felt like it. But he has to face himself now and he's not playing the part of Stalin. He's playing, yes, the same being, but a young man, healthy and strong, strong enough to shine the shoes or clean the latrines or do something that's consistent with his life that is best needed to work upon him to bring out that something that is hidden in him which he denied while he was here.

So I ask you to simply try it. Take the law...for those who are here for the first time, it's simple. This is what you do. Do you know what you want? Well, construct a scene in your Imagination which would *imply* that you have realized it. Try to enter into the spirit of the scene and participate as an actor in the scene, giving as much of the tones of reality as you possibly can to the scene, giving it all of the sensory vividness that you are capable of giving it. Enter into the spirit of it and feel the reality of it. But go to *the end*. Don't consider the means! Go to the end...the whole thing is *already* done and you are now reveling in the accomplishment...and then break it. Now faith is simply loyalty to this unseen reality. That's what faith is, to remain loyal to this unseen reality; for when you did it, that was God in action. Who did it? If I ask you, you say, "I did it." Well, that's his name...who's doing it now?—"I am," well, that's God's name forever and forever.

So you do it in your Imagination and then drop it... just as he dropped the little, gentle rain of crisp bills that fell upon him. And the boss comes in and tells him you've been voted a ten percent increase in salary retroactive to the first of the month. So his little problem was solved. And then the problem which was a serious problem for the mother and grandmother of the little girl that was solved. The doctors are still looking under their microscopes to see why they misinterpreted the first, and as they see the first, they will still come to the same conclusion. How did it happen? Well, it could not have happened, therefore it didn't. They'll be confronted with it and still it didn't happen that way. It never was cancer because it isn't cancer; for if it was cancer there should have been some treatment and there was no treatment, therefore, it could not have been cancer. And they'll go over this over and over like a squirrel in a cage, because it's only in our Imagination. That's all that he did and this man lives this way morning, noon and night. As he told me in his letter, "When I first came to you I thought you were the maddest person out of the insane asylum. I thought, really, you should be put away for the good of society...that you were stark mad. I really believed you were. But I was forced to try it and so I tried it and it worked."

It didn't make sense...not any more than the Promise makes sense. There's nothing more fantastic than the Promise and it doesn't make sense...from a worldly point of view it is completely incredible. But I tell you it's true that buried in man is a plan, a plan of redemption in every man, and in the fullness of time that plan erupts and all that is said of *that* man in the gospels *you* experience. Then you know *that* man and that he wasn't here as an individual being. He simply was the plan who awoke in one being...whose name was who knows? But the name of the plan is Jesus. Jesus is Jehovah, that's what the word means. It is I AM, and so that is the being that is in every man, and every man is going to have the experience of Jesus Christ. There is not a bunch of little Jesuses running around; there is only one. So we are all gathered together one by one into the one body, the one Spirit, the one Lord, the one God and Father of all. So that's what he said that he would take us all together into the one...gather all into one being.

Now, that expression that is used in Ephesians, the first chapter, the root of that Greek word is "head." So where do you gather it? In the head, for that's where it begins. You are buried there, you are crucified there, and you resurrect there. When you return, you return there from this external world. That's where you return. So you're gathered altogether into this one state, and this gathering is the head. As though it's what Sir James Jean said, "the more he studies this infinite universe the more he has come to the conclusion that whoever the Creator is resembles an infinite brain and we brain cells in the mind of the Dreamer." So the brain cell is expanding forever and forever within the *one* brain.

Now let us go into the Silence.

* * *

PERSONS REPRESENT STATES IN SCRIPTURE

4/25/69

When you are reading the greatest book in the world, the Bible, always bear in mind that the person Abraham, Isaac, Jacob, Jesus, Peter, Paul, any name if they're in scripture are not there meant as persons: they are *states*. The name only signifies a state that they represent. If you see them as persons, you will never really understand scripture. They are simply the personification of these eternal states which were revealed to mortal man in a series of divine revelations as they are recorded in scripture.

Now tonight, we will take just a few. Go back now to Blake and his *Vision of the Last Judgment*, he said…now when he speaks of Satan, Satan is not a person, it's a state, the state of doubt, the complete un-forgivingness. If they can't touch it or they can't see it then they cannot accept it. So Satan believed that sin was displeasing to God. He ought to know that nothing is displeasing to God but unbelief and eating of the tree of knowledge of good and evil. The combat of good and evil is eating of the tree of knowledge; the combat of truth and error is eating of the tree of life. These are not only universal but particular. Each is personified. So when he speaks of Satan, it's not a person…bear in mind he's speaking of a state. It's an eternal state into which you and I or all may fall where we completely deny a state because it is not in harmony with our senses.

Now when he speaks of truth, he calls it Jesus. And as far as Blake is concerned, and every mystic worthy of the name, a true judgment need not conform to the external fact to which it relates. If I say, "Aren't they beautiful," and you see nothing, and yet I am looking at something that I say is beautiful, well, you'll think maybe Neville had something to drink or maybe he's just having a little fun. But I am seeing what I would like to see, and so I am now looking at something that is altogether lovely. I place it where I would place it if it were true to my senses. And I persuade myself that it is true and to the degree that I am self-persuaded that it is true it becomes fact. So I discover that a true judgment need not conform to the external fact with which it relates. Satan insists that it must and truth tells us that it need not.

Well, we'll take truth on a different level tonight. We'll bring it back to this and then go back into other areas of it. Jesus is called the truth in scripture: "I am the truth. I am the spirit of truth." "I came out from the Father and I came into the world; again, I am leaving the world and going to the Father" (Jn.16:28). Well, it didn't make sense, because they knew his physical origin. Here is a man who is making a fantastic claim and there is not a thing to support the claim. In scripture...that is, you'll find it in the Talmud, not our Bible, but in the Jerusalem Talmud...Messiah is supposed to come suddenly from some concealed state. As it is said, if he is in the world, he does not know it until Elijah first comes and anoints him, and then he will suddenly appear. But he doesn't know it, even though he may be in the world, until he is first anointed by Elijah, and then he will suddenly appear. That's what we are told in the Jerusalem Talmud. For the ___(??) expected was the sudden appearance of Messiah.

Now, it is said in scripture he is the corner stone. He also is the top stone as told in Zechariah: "He shall bring forward the top stone among shouts of 'Grace, grace to it!' (4:7). Well, it was said that through Moses came the law, but grace and truth came through Jesus Christ. So here he is the top stone. He's also the foundation stone, and there is no other foundation stone. A foundation stone contains the whole stone; it contains the plan of a structure, the plan of the edifice, and its purpose, why it is being constructed. There must be a plan and there must be a reason for the edifice. So in the hollowed stone laid as a foundation stone are the documents and the purposes of the building. This structure is the temple of the living God, laid up and built out of living stones, individuals who are redeemed, all built into the living structure.

Now, here in the audience sits a couple. She said, "A week ago last Monday, as I closed my eyes in the Silence, I thanked you for once more explaining the law. I thanked you for explaining the law, and I suddenly said, 'I know that.' Then I heard your voice distinctly and you said to me, 'Do you *really* know it?' Now, in the Silence tonight I heard your voice as distinctly as I hear it when you speak outwardly to my outer ear and you said to me, 'Do you *really* know it?' Then I thought, 'With my surface mind I heard it, but in the depths of my being not really.' Then I saw a pyramid…with my physical eyes shut I saw this pyramid, but the top stone was missing. About the pyramid was a sphere and above the sphere a crown, a glorious crown. Then each was outlined in a scintillating, moving white light, and then the sphere began to spin; and all became so luminous and so brilliant I thought I would have to close my spiritual eye, for my physical eyes were already closed. It was so intense I thought I would have to close my eye. Then you said as you broke the Silence, 'Good,' and I returned to this level of my being. And I haven't been able to shake the conviction since then that had my inner eye been stronger, I would have seen a being emerging from that light."

Yes, she would have, but it's not *yet* time. The being she would have seen would be herself. "It does not yet appear what we shall be, but we know that when he appears we shall be like him" (1Jn.3:2). So when Christ appears in man, it is man himself. It is Christ who is buried in man, the only grave that he ever had. That's the hollowed out stone that is the foundation stone, and it is your own wonderful skull. That's where Christ is buried: God became man that man may become God. Now when I say man I don't mean *a* little man, I mean humanity. Every child born of woman God became or he couldn't even breathe, he would have no consciousness, nothing. But God actually became as I am that I may be as he is.

So when that top stone is ___(??), and it can't be until the fullness of time, yes she will see a being emerging from that light and it will be herself as told us in the 1st epistle of John, the 3rd chapter. You read it in the very beginning, "It does not yet appear what we shall be, but we know that when *he* appears we shall know him." Why?—because we shall be like him. You not only will be like him, you *will be* Jesus Christ…there is nothing but. Christ is the plan of salvation, so forget a man…yet it takes a man to externalize truth. There isn't a truth but it has also a man, therefore it is man; so scripture is speaking of truth *personified*. Man not knowing that thinks, "Well now, he is one little unique man and he is calling himself the truth." No, truth must take a person to express it. So here, he is the plan of salvation. He said, "I am the way, the truth, the life; no one comes unto the Father, but by me. If you knew me, you would know my Father also" (Jn.14:6)…"For I and my Father are one" (Jn.10:30). Now you know him and you see him. I have seen the Father? "Show me the Father." "Have I been so long with you, Philip, and yet you do not know me? He who has seen me has seen the Father; how then can you say, 'Show me the Father'?" (Jn.14:8). I came out from the Father and he sent me into the world, for what purpose—to bear witness to his written Word. I am now the *living* word sent into the world to experience the *written* word so that I may return to him *not* void. He said, "My word shall not return unto me empty but it shall accomplish that which I purposed and prosper in the thing to which I sent it" (Is.55:11). So he sends me into the world to bear witness to his written Word which is scripture.

So here, the Old Testament is an adumbration. It's an intimation of God's plan of salvation written in the form of history, the history of Israel. The history of Israel is now actualized in an individual and he is a normal person in the world, perfectly normal, and they all know his physical origin. It's not what they were looking for; they don't expect *that* of Messiah. Messiah will suddenly come out of nowhere and surprise them as a being external to themselves. He wasn't external at all. He is buried in that hollowed out stone, the skull of man…and he does come suddenly. When his time for awakening takes place, it's sudden, and it's all within you, and you are he. Then everything said of him in scripture unfolds within you in the first-person, singular, present-tense experience.

And you tell it…and all of your friends simply smile: "I think he's touched. I know him, I know his parents, I know his family, I know all about him. And all of a sudden he dares to tell me that what is recorded in scripture as the fulfillment of the Old has happened to him, and he is the one scripture speaks about? Why, that's impossible!" So then I turn the pages and I read now the 40th Psalm, "In the volume it was all about *me*," (40:7), but I didn't know it until it happened, and when it happened in me, then I knew the whole book was about me. Go and tell my brothers now it's all about you. I am departing this world and I am going to my Father and your Father, I am going to my God and your God because we are one. There is nothing but God. God actually became one in a diversified state, in a seeming many, but you can't speak of many gods, but it takes them all to form the one God: "Hear, O Israel: the Lord our God, the Lord is one" (Deut.6:4). The word is a plural word, one made up of others, made up of the many. So it takes us all united into *one* being to form the I AM, the Lord.

So when you read it, try to bear in mind no matter what word you see it has meaning. So you even take a word like Zechariah, as I quoted earlier the 4th chapter of Zechariah, it simply means "Jehovah remembers"…he remembers his covenant, his *promise* to Israel. Well, we are Israel. Everyone born of woman is destined "to rule *as* God" for that's what the word means. Israel is "the man who rules as God." Not like a god, like a little tyrant of the world, but *as* God.

So here, the shout "Come forward" amidst shouts, and you hear the word 'Grace, grace to it' and grace came forward and was brought forward through Jesus Christ. Well, Jesus Christ—forget him now as a little man external to yourself—Christ *in you* is the hope of glory. "Do you not realize that Jesus Christ is in you?"—asked Paul in his 13th chapter of 2nd Corinthians (13:5)—"Do you not realize that Jesus Christ is in you?—unless, of course, you fail to meet the test." You mean he is in me? And all things were made by him? Yes. And without him was not anything made that is made (Jn.1:3)...that goes for the good and the ill? Yes. You mean he can create the unlovely? Yes. Any artist can do that...he doesn't have to create only the beautiful. He can create anything if he is an artist...and he is the only creator in the world. Well, who is he? He is in me and he creates everything. You mean everything in my world? Yes. Well, I'll find him and I'll put him to the test. And then I found him...I found him as my own wonderful human Imagination. That's who he is.

Everything in my world came out of my Imagination. I may not now relate the unlovely things in my world to former imaginal acts, but I can't deny those that I can relate, and if I can remember an imaginal act and see it unfold in my world and that is a fact, well then, I'll go back. Though I can't quite remember it I will go back. Jehovah remembered and Jehovah's name is I AM. Well, I say "I am"...well, go back and see where I planted these unlovely seeds in my world, as told us in the Book of Jeremiah, the 2nd chapter: "I planted you a perfect seed, O Israel, a pure seed. How did you become degenerate?" What did you do? You went after foreign gods, Baal, and you worshipped foreign gods—the gods being astrology, numerology, or wealthy people, or important people, or all kinds of things outside of self—and God is your own wonderful human Imagination.

You sought other causes of the phenomena of your life and not the *only* cause that is God, and God is your own wonderful human Imagination. I planted you a pure seed. How, O Israel, have you become degenerate, to believe in gods outside of the only God? There is only one God and God is I AM. There is no other God. And one day you will find him. You will awaken to discover that you are the one and only God. But you're not going to rub out your brothers, because it's going to take all your brothers together to form the *one* God, and when all are formed, the top stone will be put in place. Until then, it can't be placed there upon this building which is the wonderful structure that is being erected. For the body of God, the temple of God is being erected out of the redeemed of the world...and *all must* be redeemed.

Now, a lady writes (she's here tonight) "A dream of mine wakened me at seven. I went into this exquisite jewelry store and I picked up certain items. I picked up a gem, a green one, and I walked out without paying for anything...a thing on this level I wouldn't dream of doing...and it disturbs me that I could have done that." Oh, you should be thrilled beyond measure! On this level you are eating of the tree of the knowledge of good and evil. Where you are, my dear—and you ought to know it—you are away beyond this dream of the tree of knowledge. You are eating of the tree of life, and you only fulfilled scripture, the 50th Psalm: "If I were hungry, I would not tell you, for the world is mine and all within it" (50:12)— and so I would take it—"The cattle on a thousand hills are mine." If *everything* is mine, whose permission do I need to take it? You are already an incurrent eyewitness. You're not functioning here save when you open your mortal eyes on this world. So you wouldn't go into Tiffany's tomorrow and take something out and walk out with it. No, that's the world of good and evil. We're all living in this world, eating of the truth of the tree of knowledge, this is right and that is wrong. Here we bind each other and all these are the combats. But in the tree that has only the combat of truth and error...if you are the truth, the whole world is yours, so why would you ask the permission of anyone concerning what you wanted? The hunger of a man is not only for bread, the *real* hunger of man is for the word of God. "I will send a hunger upon the world; it will not be for bread or a thirst for water, but for the hearing of the word of God," as told us in the Book of Amos (8:11).

So the hunger represented by the green jewel, the green being what grows, that which is growing, like the tree; and this is the tree of life, not the tree of good and evil. When you came down to this level you thought it wrong what you did. Yet I bless you for having done it. It was a marvelous experience that you had...something entirely different. Who knows what is right and what is wrong? No one is going to agree with another; we have different values. What is right for one is wrong for the other, and we came down eating that tree of knowledge. And the only thing that displeases God is simply eating of the tree of knowledge of good and evil...and unbelief. "Unless you believe that I am he you die in your sins" (Jn.8:24). If you think *he* is the cause of my misfortune, then you will continue in your sin, missing the mark in life. If you know that the only cause of all the phenomena of your life is God, and God's eternal name is I AM, well then, if you really believe, you will live by it. You will not deny the harvest that is coming that you unknowingly planted. It was not a pleasant harvest that you are going to reap because it was not a pleasant sowing; but you know it couldn't come unless you sowed it, so you're going to take it. But promise yourself not to replant it! You will accept it and plant something entirely different, something lovely. But don't deny there is only one cause and that one cause is your own wonderful human Imagination. That is God and there is no other God.

Scripture teaches no other God. But organized churches have made all kinds of fetishes and they build all these little things...they build their little icons. And people get down and genuflect before some little thing that is made by the human hand in violation of the 2nd Commandment: "Make no graven image unto me" (Deut.5:8). You can't go into a church but these monstrous things are all along the wall. If they only had good artists making them, but no, they turn them out as you would turn out things for Disneyland. And here they go and genuflect before some little thing that is a horrible monster of a thing. You go into a home and you see all these little things in their home. I'm speaking from experience, because half of my family are Catholic, half are Protestant, and they have all these things all over their homes. So I am not speaking from what I have heard; I'm speaking from experience. I was raised in the Christian faith as a Protestant, and when my brothers grew up they fell in love with Catholic girls and a third of them married Catholics. But they were far more productive than the Protestants, so we have just as many in the next generation of Catholic children. All had to be raised as Catholics because that was my brothers' agreement. All right to have children and whatever comes to our world will be raised in the Catholic faith. So they have all the Catholic children. And you go to their homes and here are all these things.

I don't argue with them, because as far as they are concerned this is the personification of Satan. It's not what they expected. If I would only go along with them on Sunday mornings and go and do all the silly, little nonsense that they do, wonderful. But when I tell them that suddenly he the *only one* erupted within me and then I knew who Jesus Christ was, they look at me and say, "I know your origin, your father, your mother." Certainly you do, but that's not where I came from. I came just as you are told in the Talmud. I was in concealment, but I didn't even know it…not until Elisha comes out. Well, who is Elisha that should first come? This body on the outside is John the Baptist and this comes into the world, and it makes every effort to attain salvation by some physical means, like doing violence against its appetites. It goes on a starvation diet, only vegetables, for seven years. Ask a man in the restaurant, "Does this soup have any beef stock in it or chicken stock in it or any meat stock?" and he's going to tell you no. He's a liar anyway, because what restaurant worthy of the name isn't going to have a meat stock in soup? But he satisfies your conscience and you will then order soup. So you are lying to yourself right away, because you know that it has meat stock in it and you really want the soup, so you take it. And then you don't call it anything but vegetables.

So for seven years you get thinner and thinner and weaker and weaker while you are doing violence to yourself. You are young, virile, and desirous of everything that a normal man in this world is desirous of, and you go on a diet of celibacy, and have nightmares. Go into a depression, all completely down in the depths of your own being. And you wonder why is it is happening to me, I'm such a holy man? I'm so good I'm good for nothing. After seven years of this complete violence to the body, then you awaken.

Well, that's John the Baptist. He doesn't come until John is arrested. When John is beheaded then Christ comes into the world…so that's how the man has to be beheaded. When he is completely arrested and restrained then suddenly out of nowhere he comes. And he who you are looking for suddenly comes…as you are told in scripture, he comes suddenly. No one expected it…certainly you didn't. You go to sleep normally and suddenly in the wee hours of the morning this thing erupts within you and you find yourself in the tomb. The tomb is your skull. And everything said in scripture about Jesus Christ begins to unfold within you, but you are cast in the role in the first-person singular and present-tense experience. The whole thing unfolds in 1,260 days, just as told in the Book of Daniel (7:25) and confirmed in the Book of Revelation (11:3). It will take 1,260 days.

So you go out and you tell it. You find those who will look and say now he's a little bit touched. He's not violent enough to put him away, but he is a bit touched, because here he stands alone pointing the only way to the Father because he has experienced it. When Satan, personified now as error, has the authority of the world behind him; the whole vast world has accepted because all their misinterpretations of scripture are now the traditions of the church. And they go to church every day and worship their misconceptions, their prefabricated misconceptions of scripture. And one awakes within the world and he knows exactly what has happened to him and he sets out to tell it. I've gone on TV around the clock, on radio around the clock, with ministers and priests and rabbis, and they look at me as though I am completely strange when I quote their own book for them and say "What does this mean to you?" and then I take their passages one after the other. They don't want to hear it. And I say, "Who wrote this?" Well, some prophet wrote it. Well, is it not said that David wrote these words? What words? Then I will quote the 2nd Psalm…is it not said in the 2nd Psalm, "I will tell of the decree of the Lord…he said unto me, 'Thou art my Son, today I have begotten thee" (2:7). Oh, but Neville, that belongs to Jesus Christ. I said this was 1,000 B.C., this passage is 1,000 B.C. and it is said in the Psalm of David. David tells us in this passage he will tell of the decree of the Lord, and the Lord said unto him, "Thou art my Son, today I have begotten thee." And did he not in Spirit call Jesus "my Lord"? Yes he did. Well then, if he calls him "my Lord" then who is Jesus? Because he is God's Son and now he is calling Jesus "my Lord," is he not telling you that he is God?

I said to a rabbi this night in New York City that he called me Father and is that not the fulfillment of the 89th Psalm? I have found David and "He has cried unto me, 'Thou art my Father, my God, and the Rock of my salvation'" (89:26). There he stands before me calling me Father, well, am I not then the one spoken of in the 20th of Luke when he said to Christ "Thou art my Lord"? They'll put their hands to their ears to shut out this blasphemy. The same thing goes through and through the entire scripture. They call him a blasphemer, why? Because he said he came out from God and he said he *is* God. "I and my Father are one…only I know my Father and you know not your God. My Father is he whom you call God, but I know my Father and you know not your God." But he didn't deny him, he said, "You are my God but sound asleep. I'm going now to my Father and your Father, to my God and your God." But you are sound asleep. Keep on in the dream until you wake and when you wake the dreamer is God. He is dreaming your life and putting you through all the paces; and in the end when you awake, you and he are one, not two. So he actually became you that you may become as he is.

Now, on the practical side…to prove that it works try it! Well, how do I put it into the practical side? I first must have a goal in life. I must know *what* I want…that's essential. When I know what I want, knowing there is only one cause for the phenomena of life and having discovered that cause as my own wonderful human Imagination, I then conceive a scene that if true would imply the fulfillment of my dream. I reenact it in my mind's eye, casting myself into the act. I don't allow myself to be an observer; I'm a participant in the action, in the center of all this because it's all about me. So I let my friends congratulate me on my good fortune and I accept it without any embarrassment. I accept it, and I enter into the spirit of the scene which would imply the fulfillment of my dream. Then I drop it in confidence that that imaginal act was done by God. Why?—because he did it. What's his name?—I AM. Well, *I* did it. Had you arrested my thought in the act of doing it and you would have said to me, "What're you doing?" I would have said, "I am doing so and so." That's when I called upon his name. That's who did it and that is God…"My name forever and forever" and there is no other name that I will bear, just I AM (Exod.3:14).

And so, if you caught me in my meditation enacting a scene, I would have told you. If you asked me, "What are you doing?" I would have told you what I am doing and I would have said his name…what *I am* doing. So that was God acting. My imaginal act was the act of God and all things are possible to him and there is no other Creator. So he did it, and so now if I wait patiently and wait in *confidence* for the thing to externalize itself in my world and it does, then I have found who he is. I have found the cause of creation. Having found it, tell it to your brothers who are asleep, tell it to all who are waiting patiently for some change in their world and they're not activating anything. They're waiting, hoping something is going to happen on the outside and it doesn't. Not a thing happens on the outside…you have to meet him. And if you don't, you're going to read the morning paper and get more and more afraid, and you're doing something anyway because as you react to what you read you are setting it in motion. Or you turn on TV or turn on the radio, and you react to what you hear and see, that is an imaginal act, and you simply people your world with the unlovely things in the world. When they come into view for you to reap the harvest, you can't relate what you are seeing to what you did; but you had to have done it or you couldn't now reap it. Everything in the world is man pushed out…for God and man are one.

So when you read scripture in the future, try to bear in mind if you don't have a concordance, try some way of getting the true meaning of the words. When you read the word Moses it's not just *a* man; there are millions of Moses in the world but that is not the Moses of scripture. Moses is the personification of a state, and the word Moses is simply the ancient Egyptian verb meaning "to be born." That's what it means. You can take the word and get all kinds of lovely thoughts out of it—Mem Shin He—all right, "to draw out." I can turn it around and get the word "name" out of it. I take the middle letter Shin and put that first, Shema, and get "heaven" out of it. So I'm drawing something out of self, and it's coming out of heaven, and heaven is within me. So you can put it in that form, but the word is simply the old perfective of the Egyptian verb "to be born." Something is to be born; therefore, it is an adumbration. What is to be born? That which is called the Word itself is to be born…the living Word that interprets the Old. So the New is simply the fulfillment of the Old and not the other way around. The New Testament simply fulfills the Old. There would be no New without the Old, and there couldn't be a New unless there was an Old.

So the Old presents it, but in an intimation, an intimation of God's plan. The New simply interprets, it fulfills; but man has misunderstood the interpretation and they all worship the state together…started worshipping Jesus, Peter, Paul, and all these states. They are states in the Old and states in the New, but the individual man interprets within himself the whole thing. The whole thing erupts within you and he is scripture. "He sent me into the world"…sent what? He sent his Word. Well, I am his Word and he commanded me, "Time to act!" Then I am sent into the world not knowing what it is all about, only knowing what happened, the vivid, vivid experience of what happened. I looked into the face of this infinite being of love, all love, and then he embraced me, and we fused and became one being. Now being a protean being, he now is God in infinite might, and as infinite might he commanded me, "Time to act!" And I am hurled out of that back into this little garment not knowing what it's all about.

Well, I can't rub out the experience. I could no more deny that experience than I could the simplest act of my senses. And that happened thirty-odd years ago, back in 1929. Thirty years later the work that he hurled, which is myself, erupted to interpret scripture. I began to fulfill scripture within myself. And then I tell it to those who will listen and no one comes that my Father hasn't brought him. So he draws us one by one to hear his Word as it unfolded within the one that he sent, and some believe it and some don't believe it. He has no way of knowing who believes it and who doesn't believe it...only in the visions of those who come. He can tell from the visions those who accepted it. But he departs this world to return not to a restored society like this, but into the body of the risen Lord. No more restoration as all people are when they die here. They are restored in a world just like this, terrestrial just like this, with all of the problems just as we have them. But those who are redeemed, who have fulfilled the Word, return as witnesses to his Word, and they are incorporated into the one body. For in the end, there is only one body, one Spirit, one Lord, one God and Father of all.

Now let us go into the Silence.

* * *

Q: You speak of God disseminating into the multitude of the world, and yet in the same context you speak of him as still a terrestrial being or super energy or however you would like to say it...that he is still there, yet a new person injected into the world by him.

A: Very good. The world may deny it but I'm speaking from experience, I am not speculating: God is man and man is God. But in the world of humanity the one man which is the one God is fragmented, as told us in the 82nd Psalm: "And God has taken his place in the divine council, in the midst of the *gods* (plural) he holds judgment." And now he speaks to the gods and the same word is Elohim. It's first translated in the singular, "And God has taken his place"...that word is Elohim. Although the word is plural, it is translated in the singular. Now it comes into the plural, "in the midst of the *gods*"...it's still Elohim..."he holds judgment. And I tell you, you are sons of God, sons of the Most High, all of us; nevertheless, you shall die like men and fall as one man, O princes" in the 82nd Psalm.

So, the one becomes the many for the experience. You are now individualized, you were before, and you will not in eternity lose that individuality. You will tend forever towards ever greater and greater individualization by reason of your experiences in a world of death.

The Return of Glory

For this is a world of death where everything begins and ends. But I cannot deny the presence as described in the Book of Daniel, called there the Ancient of Days. And he was brought to the Ancient of Days and presented before him, and the Ancient of Days, infinite love, asks a very simple question and you will answer as I did. "What is the greatest thing in the world?" and I answered, "Faith, hope and love, these three, but the greatest of these is love" (1Cor.13:13). At that, he embraced me and our bodies fused and we became one…one man, one body, one Spirit. Then suddenly I'm not before him or with him, I'm before infinite might…a being that if he so desired he could stop the universe or shatter it. He said to me, "Time to act" and with that I was hurled out of that presence into my hotel room in New York City. That was 1929.

Q: Well, that's what I don't understand. In the beginning he was disseminated into the multitude of people yet he still retained all of his power.

A: All right, we are told, "He who sees me sees him who sent me." He has never left me. I have no feeling that I am divorced from that body of love, though here I am clothed in mortal flesh and blood. But I have no sensation of being divorced from that body. And because he is omnipresent, although I speak of him as there he is omnipresent and therefore must be here. As told us in the Psalm, "If I take the wings of the morning and fly to the uttermost parts of the sea (world), thou art there. If I make my bed in hell, thou art there" (139:9). Where would I go that God is not when God is I AM?

So it is something that comes upon one as it unfolds within himself. So he said, "He who sees me sees him who sent me" and he has never left me. If you knew me, you would know him also; but you do not know me, because you know my secular origin and you do not know my real origin. So we came out from God and fell as one man, O princes, for a divine purpose. By this experience that we have in this world, we are greater than we were when we left on the journey. There is no limit to translucency, to expansion; there is a limit set for contraction, for opacity, and man is the limit of contraction. Doubt, called Satan, is the limit of opacity or doubt—it cannot believe what reason denies, what its senses deny.

But here, when truth begins to awake within man, there is no limit to what man can imagine. If man can believe what he has imagined, it will come to pass. Whether he believes it now or not, that he could ___(??) himself of this, that or the other, it's going to happen anyway. Everything in the world is happening because man at one time has imagined it. We're going to the moon. Go back a hundred years and

421

Jules Verne wrote a book and named it and told the entire thing about the trip, even mentioning the nation that would do it. He said it would be America; the Yankee know-how, the Yankee engineers would do it. This is 100-odd years ago, before we were really tied together as a nation.

I have a book at home called *Democracy in America* by De Tocqueville, a first edition. I love to have a friend at home, and I give him a page to read, read this one page, and they will open and read the page. You would think it was written this morning. It was written and printed in 1838. He tells of two great lands in the world—one will conquer by the sword and one by the plow, Russia by the sword and America by the plow. He doesn't give you the conclusion as to which, if either, will be victorious…but then we were not a nation. California was not a part of our states. All the western states were not part. We hadn't yet bought the Louisiana Purchase. We were a small little area on a vast land. But we hadn't yet begun to expand and Russia was not a power. England was a power in 1838, France was a power, and Spain was a power. We were not powerful. And he tells you only two powers in the world and he names them, America who will conquer by the plow and Russia who will conquer by the sword. Well, haven't they conquered by the sword? We just fought this fabulous war and Russia ended up with more land than she started with, almost as much again, and she's ballooning with land; and we haven't any land beyond what we had when we started.

We didn't go out to conquer the land…and today we still conquer by the plow. We have the know-how and we can feed the world with what *we* know how to extract from the land. With all their power, or publicized power, what do they do? They've just taken over Czechoslovakia. Before that, all of Estonia and all those areas, parts of Poland, all that has been added to their land, and they have so much land. We haven't added anything.

And this man wrote it, Alexis de Tocqueville, in 1838. I fortunately have a first edition of it. I love to just simply try…I say read this page, this very short page, and when they read it they turn back and see that it's a first edition…and the dull pages… and the publishing house is long, long out of business…but here is the first edition, 1838. Here is a man with a dream. He saw these two coming up together, unnoticed by the powers of the day…and England was a power, France was a power, all these where powers and they were not. They were rising in the midst of them all and they didn't detect them, but de Tocqueville detected them. He didn't go beyond saying these two are the only two powers on the earth, one by the plow and one by the sword.

But we have the book of books in the Bible. The most misunderstood book in the world, because it is *not* history. It is supernatural history. It is not secular history and people think it is secular. It is *not* secular. The drama unfolds in the *soul* of man. It's the eternal drama.

Time is up. Good night.

A RIDDLE

4/28/69

Tonight we will take a riddle. We are so accustomed to this strange, false, secular interpretation of scripture that we do not realize how daring it is. It is not history as the world understands it. It hasn't a thing to do with the drama on earth; it's all about the soul, the reality of man. So the question is asked in the 30th chapter of the Book of Proverbs, "Who has established all the ends of the earth? What is his name, and what is his son's name? Surely you know!" (30:4). So do we know? That's the beginning of the riddle. It's a challenge and only the indolent mind would fail to accept the challenge.

Now, in the Old—for the New is only the interpretation of the Old—the question is asked concerning a father and a son. "It is the glory of God to conceal things, but it is the glory of kings to search them out." We find that in the Book of Proverbs, the 25th chapter: "It is the glory of God to conceal things, but it is the glory of kings to search them out" (25:2). Now we go to the last book of the Old Testament, "A son is the glory of his father. If then I am a father, where is my glory? says the Lord of hosts to *you*, O priests" (Mal.1.6). Now he includes in the word "O priests" all who assumed this right, the authority to interpret the Word of God, whether you be pope or one just starting a little ism, who dares to establish some little ism. So he asks a question, "A son is the glory of his father. If then I am a father, where is my glory?"—that is, where is my son, says the Lord of hosts to you— O priest.

Now, let us from actual experience unriddle the riddle. For this *is* a riddle; it's not secular history. Hasn't a thing to do with anything that took place on earth as you and I understand it. It takes place in the soul of man. Now, who is the king, the only king made by God? We're told in the Book of 1st Samuel, he said to his servant the prophet Samuel, "Go to the house of Jesse, for I have chosen one of the sons of Jesse to be king" (16:12). He will

424

serve me. So Samuel goes to the house of Jesse and announces the purpose of his visit and Jesse brings out his sons. One after the other they are rejected... that is not him, are there any others? He finally brings out the little one who was tending the flocks, a shepherd, and his name was David. As he came into the midst, the Lord said to Samuel, "Arise, anoint him; this is he. And the Spirit of the Lord came upon him mightily from that day forward." So here we find the *king* spoken of. He is the king, no other king. Man chose the king, his name was Saul; but the Lord rejected the choice of man and the Lord chose the king.

Now let me tell you, in symbolism of scripture David represents humanity. If you took all the generations of men and all of their experiences and fused them into one grand whole, and personified that concentrated time, you would find an eternal youth, and his name is David. That's what you would see. So that is the king of kings, the result of the experiences of the entire play that God has written. Every part in the world God wrote it. We are really the story of Job, an innocent being. The word Job means "Where is my father?" Here is a blameless creature who went through such *hell* that he cursed the day wherein he was born and the night that said a man-child was conceived. He heard of a Father, he heard of God the Father, but never saw him. He is searching, "Where is my Father?" for that's his name. In the end of the drama you read the words of Job, "I have heard of thee by the hearing of the ear, but now my eye sees thee." And he sees the cause of all his conflicts. It is said in scripture, the last chapter, the 42nd chapter of Job, that when Job prayed for his friends who were going through the same horrors of the world, then his entire captivity was lifted and he received a hundred-fold more than he had prior to the conflicts that he went through (42:5). Then his brothers, his sisters, and his friends came and ate bread with him in his own house and comforted him and sympathized with him for all the evil that the Lord God had brought upon him. He found who was the cause of it all and found the one who brought all the hell upon him was himself. Here, he himself was the cause of all of the conflicts of his world.

Well, that is our world. There is nothing but God in this world. I don't care what the world will tell you, there is only God. So everyone in the world going through the hell that is this world is the cause of what he goes through, and in the very end he is going to find the reason behind it. Only one being in the world can tell him that he is that God. There is not a being in the world...I can tell you from now to the ends of time...but I can't persuade you. No, you can hear it and you'll say, "Neville said it and Neville wrote it, so I read it and I heard it, and I know others who heard him; but I am waiting to see him. So I have heard of him by the hearing of the ear. I'm waiting for that moment in time when I can say, 'But now my eye sees thee.'"

Now, how will my eye see thee? We are told...and a gentleman is here tonight. I don't even now what I said last Friday night, for when I say it's behind me, it's all under inspiration and I do not know...it just comes out and I tell you and I go home. He called me on Saturday morning and said, "Neville, what you said last night on Friday night was so inspiring to me that I went home and I read the 89th Psalm. I thought I would take my concordance"—the one I recommend which is *Strong's Concordance*, which gives the definition of every word in scripture as it was *intended* when written. Not as the words change in meaning as words do; these are the original meanings of words as used in scripture. He said, "I opened up the book and my eyes fell first upon the title. Well, I thought I wouldn't take the title for granted, I will look I up." So he looked up the title...it's a maschil... the title is *A Maschil of Ethan the Ezrahite*. Well, you'd go right over that like saying the book is written by John Doe...so who is John Doe and you skip it. But he didn't. He took his Concordance and looked it up. Well, Maschil is a *special* instruction, something that is precious...that is Maschil. Do not overlook it; it is a special instruction in the Psalms.

Ethan means "permanent" and Ezrahite means "concealed, as in the bosom, something cherished, something loved, to hide oneself." Now here, this is special instruction permanently concealed within the bosom that is cherished and loved. Then, of course, you go through the Psalms and here now is a discovery of the one that was hidden in himself. For here is like a play within one's being and he divides himself into Father and Son. When he proceeds into the world and assumes the garments of men, that is Son; he who conceived the part is God the Father. Yet the Son and the Father are one (Jn.10:30), but until the play is completely played he doesn't know it. The Son doesn't know it and the Son is asking, "Where is my Father?" That's Job. The Father has hidden his face from the Son and the Son cannot find him. The Father doesn't know who he is until the Son reveals him. So here, no one has seen God, as told us in the 1st chapter, the 18th verse of John, "No one has seen God; the only Son, who is in the bosom of the Father, he has made him known." Unless the Son reveals the Father, the Father will never know he is God the Father. He is looking for the Son and the Son is looking for the Father.

Now, how do we know that he is the Son? We search the scriptures and in the 2nd Psalm we read the words: "I will tell of the decree of the Lord: He said to me, 'You are my son, today I have begotten thee'" (2:7). These are the words of David. David is recording what he heard. He hasn't seen the Father, he heard a voice like Job, "I will tell of the decree of the Lord: He said unto me, 'Thou art my son, today I have begotten thee.'" He makes him now the king of kings, over all kings. Now comes the 89th Psalm where my friend looked up the title and in the 89th Psalm the Lord is speaking, "I have found David (:20)...he has cried unto me, 'Thou art my Father, my God, and the Rock of my salvation. And I will make him the first born" (:27). Now, that in the misinterpretation is called or implied in Revelation, Jesus Christ, but that's because we do not know the story. The first born from the dead, the ruler of all kings, well, the king of kings is the ruler of all kings and that's David. When you find him and *only* when you find him and he stands before you as this eternal youth and calls you Father will you know who you are.

I prophesy for everyone in this room and for everyone born of woman— because none can fail—you will have this experience. I am speaking from experience; I am not theorizing. Were this not revealed to me by revelation I would not know it. I can't blame anyone whether he be the pope or the simplest little minister in the world for not knowing it, for it comes only by revelation. Revelation gives purpose, gives meaning to the whole vast play. And the play is horrible, horrible beyond measure. And so when he cries out in that 22nd Psalm—he doesn't know he's a father yet—"My God, my God, why hast thou forsaken me?" Go through it and see the horrors that he goes through. Now he comes to the end, and when he comes to the last two verses in the 22nd Psalm, the glory of it all, unborn generations will tell what God has wrought. He did it, he actually did it. He buried himself in the world and died as men...actually went through the gate of death, one after the other...and in the end he wrought it. He actually redeemed himself by redeeming his Son, his creative power. He redeemed himself because the Father and the Son are one, they aren't two. There's no room in God's universe for a second, there's only one. So the sons of God form God, and yet they are companions because we are individualized. Although individualized forever and forever together we form God the Father. *We are* God the Father.

So, "Who has established all the ends of the earth? What is his name and what is his son's name? Surely you know!" (Prvb.30:04). Well, he gave me the cue in the question. What is his name? That doesn't give it to me. Who established all the ends of the earth? That doesn't give it to me. But he gave it to me in this question: what is his son's name? Well, "his son's name" then he is father. The minute you say "his son" you told me who he is...who established the ends of the earth. But you didn't tell me his son's name. You told me the son's father's name and that father is Father. So you read in the 17th of John, "Holy Father, keep them in thy name that thou hast given to me" (17:11). He gave me his name and his name is Father: "Holy Father, keep them in thy name that thou gavest to me that they may be one, even as we are one." He's praying now like Job for his friends and he wants everyone to have the experience that he has had, which is the gift of the Father's name to himself…therefore he is Father.

Well, if he is father then there must be a son and the son calls him Father. That son is David. All the generations of man, take them all together throughout eternity and fuse them into one single whole, and that concentrated time into which all the generations are fused and from which they spring, personify it, and right before you stands an eternal youth. That's eternity and he's David. There's no doubt as to who he is. I have heard of you by the hearing of the ear, but now my eye sees you; and seeing you, you tell me who the Father is. He's not another. I am the Father of you and therefore I have been the cause, for the Father is the cause of all. So in the 132nd Psalm, "O Lord, favor David and remember all the hardships he has suffered" (132:1). Favor David…well, David is humanity. Haven't we suffered? Haven't you lost a friend in death? Haven't you lost a child, a parent, a friend, a relative, someone, and you lost them untimely and didn't you suffer? The whole vast world suffers…that's humanity. So, O Lord, remember David and favor him. Remember all of the hardships he has endured. Remember them and then favor him: bring him out of the grave. For David is buried in man. He is the Son. David is the Son that is buried in man, and the Son is the creative power and the wisdom of God. That's David.

Well, then who is the Father? Scripture speaks of him as Jesus Christ. Well, Jesus Christ is the same as Jehovah, the same word; it is the Lord God Jehovah. So, "When you see me," said Jesus, "you see the Father. Why do you ask me to show you the Father? He who has seen me has seen the Father. How can you say, 'Show me the Father? Have I been so long with you yet you do not know the Father?'" (Jn.14:8). Whoever has seen me has seen the Father…for "I and my Father are one" (Jn.10:30). "Well, if I am the father, then where is my son? And if the son honors the father and I am a father, where is my honor, where is my glory?" said the Lord of hosts to you, O priest. But every priest with whom I've spoken, every rabbi, every minister, every teacher of the so-called New Thought movement, not one can name me the Son. When I tell them who the whole story is and what the Son is and who the Son is, they ignore it. Once a fellow said to me, "Why, you've robbed me of 2,000 years of Christianity." I said, if I have robbed you of 2,000 years of Christianity because of what I've told you, you never knew Christianity. Yes you have a large audience, a big, big audience and you think when you get there you're doing God's work. You do not know God. You do not know the Father or the Son. You have only empty words. But I can't blame you. It comes by revelation and you refuse to accept the voice of one to whom it has been revealed.

It was revealed not by studying scripture. I went back into scripture to find support for the revelation that came within me…and there I found it by studying scripture. But it was a sealed book, the whole thing was sealed. As we are told, he sealed the testimony. Then he said, "The children thou hast given me are signs and wonders" waiting for the breaking of the seal. And they think these jaw-breaking names that he gave to Isaiah—and the word Isaiah simply means "Jehovah is my savior," the same word as Jesus. Isaiah means "Jehovah is salvation." That's what the word Jehovah means, "Jehovah is salvation." The word Jesus is "Jesus saves" or "Jesus is salvation."

See the children thou gavest me. Well, he gave me children. There were two: one was a babe wrapped in swaddling clothes and one was the Son called David. Yet they were only *signs* because in the end there is only God. So what appeared to be the Son revealing him as the Father which is the creative power that could create, he returns to himself as simply the power, the creative power of the universe and nothing but. So he buries himself in his own creation and like an author finding no one to play the parts he plays them himself. He conceives the play and casts himself in all the parts. You have played or you are playing or you will play every part. At the end, the whole will condense itself and personify itself as a son and the son will call you Father.

You will know it without uncertainty. As you look upon him you know him more surely as your son than you know your own children. I have two from two different wives and I trust them implicitly. They look or resemble me. But I trust them when they say this is your child. I take it on faith, I believe them implicitly. But *this* Son, I don't need any witness. When I look at him, I've been his Father throughout eternity that was before that the world was. I would play all the parts and having played *all* the parts, I will simply bring out the essence of it all. He will look into my face and call me Father, his God, and the Rock of his salvation (Ps.89:26).

I will bring back and save all the power that I have buried in every character that I have ever played. I have missed no character. Not one character ever played in this world have I failed to play. The world will say, well, you're not so and so. I don't mean reincarnation. I mean the tyrant? Yes the tyrant…that's a character. It need not be a Hitler or a Stalin but a tyrant. The benevolent one?—yes the benevolent one. The wise, wise man?—yes the wise man. The fool?—yes. The one who judged and the one who was sentenced?—yes both of them…played them all. And in the very end— when the race is run and I've kept the faith, as I agreed in the beginning to dream in concert with my scattered being—at the very end here comes the coalescing of the whole thing and a projection of the whole thing in this glorious, beautiful Son. You can't describe the beauty of the Son that calls you Father. And yet you know him beyond all doubt. You know him more intimately than you know any being in this world, because every being that you know here is wearing a mask, and he's playing a part. You know him when he takes off the mask. When he takes off that mask, who do you think he is? You and he are one, playing all the parts, and yet although you are one, he is individualized as you are and remain individualized forever and forever. Yet we are one...we are the Elohim that go to form the Adonai, the Lord.

So here, it's a riddle. It is not secular history. If I take the Bible and I see it as secular history, I will never understand it. So, when I say Jesus said so and so, and you think of a man talking to people, then you don't understand Jesus. If I say the Son said so and so, you don't understand: it's a mystery. So here, who is my glory? Well, the Son glorifies the Father. I'm waiting for him, waiting for him to glorify me because he radiates and reflects my glory. I must find my Son. So if I would depart this world as a glorious being, I must first find the essence of my experiences in this life that would forever radiate and reflect my glory who is the exact image of my being. He has to be. And my being is a person, for I'm a person, and he has to actually be the embodiment and projection of my person...and that is David. Everyone will have that same beautiful being as his Son. So if my Son is your Son, are we not the same Father? Everyone will have that David and everyone will be the one Father; for there is only one God and Father of all. There aren't two fathers, only one.

So here is the most daring story ever told to man. But man did not understand it and thought it was secular history...that they were writing up the story of an ancient world, how they battled, and all these things. No, it's the story of the battle of the *soul*. The whole thing takes place within the soul of man and in the end he comes out unblemished, unscathed, as though you took off the costume at the end of a play. You stepped upon the stage and they hissed you for the part you are playing, and you went through the door and took it off. It was the costume you wore that they hissed, but you the actor who wore it were the author who wrote it, and the actor and the author are one. So you conceived the whole vast play and finding no one, because God is one, not two, there was no one else to play it, so he played it all. He is the diffused. I was a scattered being into all the parts, but the same being is playing all. And we agreed in the beginning to dream this play and to dream it in concert; not to break it, and only to awaken at the end having played all the parts. So each plays all and each comes out as the one who wrote it all. It doesn't make sense to the mind of Caesar...it's stupid. But while we are in the mind of Caesar and living in the world of Caesar, having

The Return of Glory

to pay rent, he still reveals—to comfort the blows, because there are frightful blows—he reveals a principle by which we can do it.

A friend of mine, who is here tonight, said that recently he joined a group of artists. And every weekend on Saturdays and Sundays they go to different cities in Southern California and sell their paintings. He paints in oil on canvas. He went to this city and at the end of the day not a sale. The following day, it was just about the last hour of a sixteen-hour day, and it was like the day before, no sales. He said to his wife, "Come, let us get to it and bring some customers here before my canvases." He thought because she does operate the law beautifully that she had helped him. So he said, "I didn't get the feeling at first. I must get the feeling of the end "having sold," not "going to sell." So I caught the feeling that I had sold. In the last matter of moments a man came by and bought three canvases and commissioned me to paint a fourth one. Now we are packing up when another sale takes place. On Monday night I came to your lecture and in the Silence I saw this glorious landscape." And he painted a beautiful word picture of mountains, luminous edges, forming itself into one sitting posture of a man, crossed legs, crossed arms. "I felt so completely thrilled in it. Next morning one of my agents who displayed my pictures called to say he sold one of my large canvases that day." So here, he caught the feeling of the end as taught in scripture.

If I ask you, do you know what you want, and you say yes, I know what I want. Then I tell you to believe that you *have received* it. I'm using now the past tense. Suppose I use even the present, the active, not future but the active tense, "Believe you receive it." But I say, "Believe that you have received it," that's the true translation of the text. Well then, how would you feel? You sold it. Wouldn't you actually feel as you would feel had you sold it? Well, that's what he did, he caught that and that's in scripture. It is given to man to simply cushion the blows because the blows are terrible. He has rent to pay, he has food to be bought, clothes to be bought, and the normal expenses in the world of Caesar. He's an artist and these things must be sold and enjoyed by those who appreciate such art. So he caught the end…in the end is my beginning. I always begin in the end. Tell me what you want… well, now you have it…that's the end. Go through the door as though you had it and walk in that assumption. Though at this very moment it is not accepted by your senses, denied by your senses, if you persist in it, it will crystallize and it will become a fact in your world. So in his case he sold the four canvases, or rather he sold three and was commissioned to do a fourth; and then the following day one of the big canvases was sold. I ask him to continue in that light. His work will increase in value. As he sells more and more he becomes more and more the professional, more and more in demand, and actually *feel* that.

The end is where you begin. No matter what you desire, make it the end, and dwell in the end just as though it were true...as God dwells in us in the end. He's never violated his concept of what he intends. He dwells in us, as what?—as himself. God became as I am that I may be as he is. Well, he doesn't waver, he dwells in the end. He sees me *as himself* until I see that I am he. And when I see that I am he, God has expanded himself by the experience and I *am* he. So, in the end there will not be just simply a bunch of little gods, just God. He actually is expanding himself by becoming man, which is the limit of contraction, and then going through all the experiences to break the shell to begin to expand. There's no limit to expansion or to translucency; there is a limit that he set upon contraction or opacity which is man. So he takes the limit upon himself and then goes through, wearing that limit until he breaks it. When he breaks it, he has gained power and gained in wisdom by the experience of being man.

So, "Who established all the ends of the earth? What is his name and what is his son's name? Surely you know!" (Prov.30:4). Well, the world would say the name is God, meaning what? Ask any two people in the world to define God and you will not get a similar definition. Ask any two people to define the son, they will say Jesus Christ. As the priest did to me, and the ministers did to me, and the rabbi also said believing that I was a Christian, which I am, "Well, I suppose you will say Jesus Christ." He wouldn't even give me a name, because to him Messiah hasn't come, so there was no name that he could give me. All the others would say Jesus Christ and they could not define in similar terms what they meant by Jesus Christ. I tell you, you *are* God. One day you will know it, and you will know it when God's only begotten Son calls you Father. And he who calls you Father will be David, and David in the Spirit called Jesus Christ "my lord" which means Father.

So now you know who Jesus Christ is. Jesus Christ *in you* is God the Father. And because he is Father he must have a Son bearing witness to his fatherhood, and that Son is David. There is no other Son. I wouldn't care if the whole vast world, three and a half billion, rose in opposition! It would make no difference to me if they did. I would only know, wait, that's all, wait. "The vision has its own appointed hour; it ripens, it will flower. If it seems long, then wait; for it is sure and it will not be late" (Hab.2:3). Just wait...on the appointed hour and you have played all the parts. If you haven't played all the parts, you cannot by all the efforts of the world and the wisdom of the world bring David into view. He will come only when you have played all the parts, because he is the quintessence of all the generations of humanity and their experiences fused into a single whole and personified as the eternal youth whose name is David. Not one little part can be missing, so you play all the parts.

The Return of Glory

I will depart leaving you with these words, that this is the drama that *you* wrote. You will not falter; you will not break the spell. You will go through to the end so that you may actually expand and become stronger in the creative power and wiser in your creative wisdom than you were prior to the conceiving of the play. So you conceived it, became it, you played it, you are playing it, and in the end you are the God who wrote it. There is nothing but God.

So you can really forgive every being in the world for the part that he's playing. I don't care what part he's playing. You played it, you are playing it, or you will play it. So in the end, having played all, you forgive all. "Father, forgive them; for they know not what they do" (Luke23:34). Let those who still demand an eye for an eye and a tooth for a tooth, a limb for a limb, let them do it, perfectly alright, until the end. But if you knew the one who wrote the play and that being is God the Father, would you demand what you now demand? You wouldn't. But you don't yet know that he is the Father who is playing the part, so leave him alone and let him condemn. If that is the law of Caesar, then let the law of Caesar take its full course. If you mean chop off his head, chop off his head…there is no death. There's simply a departure from the scene for a moment when he continues, re-clothed in a body just like this, in a world just like this, to continue his journey. And in the very end, you return to the being that you are. "I came out from the Father, I came into the world; I am leaving the world and I am returning to myself the Father" (Jn.16:28).

So the search of man is for the Father. It is the story of Job: "Where is my Father?" When you read those forty-two chapters—and they're not long, very short, you can read them tonight—it begins, he was a blameless man and one who feared God. The word feared means "to respect, to reverence." And he had no part of evil. Then Satan, which is the embodiment of doubt, comes upon the scene to make him doubt. And then he is filled with sores and all the horrors of the world take possession of Job: the loss of his estate, the loss of his family, the loss of everything. When his wife said to him, "Curse God and die," he didn't curse God, but he cursed the day wherein he was born and the night that said a male child or a man child is conceived.

But in the very end, when he went through everything, he could say… as he prayed for others…because now he has heard it. For these words come first, "I have heard of thee with the hearing of the ear, but now my *eye* sees thee." After that confession within himself, he could only see God if the Son revealed him: "For no one has ever seen God but the Son who is in the bosom of the Father, he has made him known" (Jn.1:18). So if the Son had not appeared and called him Father, he never would have known who the Father was. Now he prays for his friends, because they must all go through the same horrors that he has gone through. So he prays for all of his friends and all of the good that was taken from him is returned. Showing the power multiplied a hundred-fold and everything is doubled in his world a hundred-fold, for all the evil that the Lord God had brought upon him. He discovered *he was* the Lord God and he brought it upon himself by the play that he wrote.

In the end you can pray for everyone…no matter what happens to them…to cushion it, because it's yourself really. We're invited to pray—even though they haven't yet seen the end—to cushion them. To meet today's deadline, to meet the tax bill, to meet this, to meet the other, and these are problems. Don't say, "Well, alright, it serves you right." No, use your talent to lift it a little bit, because you're lifting it from your own shoulders. You're invited to do that.

So here, this is the riddle. As we're challenged in the Bible, who will accept the riddle and try to unriddle the riddle? He asks the priests if they could do it in that Book of Malachi, which is the last book of the Old Testament. So he said the of glory…"The son is the glory of his father. If then I am a father, where is my glory? says the Lord God of hosts to you, O priests" (1:6). You dare to teach my word and you dare to change my word. So when he asks the question in the 30th chapter of Proverbs, he said, "Every word of God is true. Do not change the word lest you be called a liar" (30:6). Do not add to it to give it sense…wait for the revelation.

But one who has had the revelation, listen to him. Hear his words…it has been revealed to him. He wasn't a wise man in the sense of the wisdom of this world that he could unravel it by reading scripture. He only read scripture *after* the event for confirmation of what happened in him. For, he did not foresee it by reading of scripture and no priest told him. Suddenly it happened *in* him, and knowing the word was recorded, he searched the scriptures for confirmation; and here he found the written word was witness to the witness in him. So, he was the living word that interpreted the written word.

Now he tells it to those who would listen in the hope that they will accept it. But he knows whether they accept him now or tomorrow, eventually they themselves will have the identical experience. He can only hope that what he tells them as his own experience will be some kind of a prop against which they can lean in time of trouble. So, if they remember the experience and knowing that they are destined to have the same experience, no matter what happens to them they can lean against this when the troubles come…as they will come. They all come.

Now let us go into the Silence.

* * *

ONE BEING FELL CONTAINING ALL

5/2/69

We are told in the Book of John, the 11th chapter, that "it is expedient for you that one man should die for all" (11:50). One man should die for all. Here, you and I, raised as we were, think in terms of one man, an individual man. I would have you change that now for a moment and think of a *cosmic* being containing all of us within himself—call it by any name that pleases you, call it Christ—that in all is this one being that died for all. And when he rises in one there is conferred upon that being the name Lord, for only one could rise; only one fell. So one came into all and we are called one by one according to his purpose, for he is rebuilding his temple that he deliberately destroyed to expand it into something far bigger, far greater, and far more wonderful. So one being containing all within him fell into this world of death. The same one being is rising in all, but individually. And that one being, upon that one as he rises in the individual, upon that individual is conferred the divine name Christ or Lord.

Now Paul in his wonderful letter to us tells us, "From now on I regard no one from a human point of view; even though I once regarded Christ from a *human* point of view, I regard him thus no longer" (2Cor.5:16). I do not see him any more as I formerly was led to believe that he was a man, something external to myself. And then he tells us why, and here we find events versus tradition…that Paul was led from tradition to self-discovery. For "When it pleased God to reveal himself in me, I conferred not with flesh and blood" (Gal.1:16). He went out to destroy those who believed in some external savior, as he was taught to believe someone came in that form. Then he discovers that it isn't so at all, that Christ of whom they spoke was a *pattern*, a pattern of *salvation* contained within every child born of woman. That every child born of woman contained that pattern, the pattern of salvation, and it unfolds in one way only. He tried in his way to explain how it unfolds.

I do not see the perfect pattern as he describes it. I cannot find the true, I would say, details, but he tells us to imitate God as dear children. To imitate anyone or anything in this world, I must first see it or hear it. How could I imitate something that I do not see, that I do not hear? "So be ye imitators of God as dear children" (Eph.5:1). It is my purpose to tell you how to imitate him. You can't imitate it as someone on the stage; you can only imitate it by hearing what took place and then believing it. So then I will tell you how it takes place. As he said, "How can I believe in him that I have not known, and how can I know of him unless there be a preacher, and how can there be a preacher unless he is sent?" (Rom.10:14). And so, if he is sent then it is through faith that I can believe. I can't believe otherwise, for I haven't seen him and I haven't heard him, but if you tell me that you came from him, well then, I will simply accept if you tell me the truth, and I will set my hope fully upon this that is about to be unfolded in me. For if one being became all and one being fell, and one being is going to rise, he rises in all, but each in his own good turn. He calls us according to his purpose. So he will call me...as he did in '59 of this century, 1959. He will call you, maybe tonight, but he will call us individually according to his purpose, and the same being is calling, the same being is rising in everyone in this world.

Well, I cannot conceive of anything in this world comparable to this. For unless we are called, we remain in a world of death. And the wheel of recurrence goes over and over and over, for there is no escape unless we are called out of the world of death. But I can assure you from what I know from my inner vision that everyone will escape, because he can't leave one section of himself in the world of death. But he calls us all individually according to his purpose as he now erects the temple. The temple is made of the *redeemed* being that is Jesus Christ. One being fell containing all, one being rises raising all; but he raises each according to his purpose as he builds them into the redeemed and greater structure called the temple of God, which is the house or *body* of God.

So if I would imitate him...as I'm told "Be imitators of God as dear children"... I must first have a pattern. Well, a pattern is a fully, I would say, realized form. Here is an original form that I will now accept or propose for imitation. We know that in all walks of life if I have a mold, here is a mold into which some molten metal is poured to form some casting. Well now, do I have a mold? I am told in scripture that he prepared the mold for all of us, but we must first be reduced to that molten state. Is that really true? Can I be reduced to a molten state? Burn this body and I am reduced to dust. Yet to cast me into a mold I must be reduced to a *molten* state, but not by putting it into the dust and not by putting it into the furnace. It is something that happens *in* man.

Christianity is based upon the claim that a certain series of events happened in which God revealed himself in action for the salvation of man. Is this true? Is this claim of the Christian world true? I tell you from my own personal experience it is true. We have gone astray from it, and we are worshiping something on the outside that never took place. It hasn't a thing to do with any *individual* man who ever came into this world. When Paul tells his story, it is the first story told in the New Testament. His work became the first, the original revelation—it preceded the gospels by at least twenty-five years—and it hasn't a thing to do with what happens to an individual between the cradle and the grave. If the one called Jesus was a carpenter, if he was a mason, a bricklayer, if he was anything, a pimp, it would not concern Paul. What happens to the individual between the cradle and the grave is unimportant; it is what happens *in* the individual, and what happens in him he cannot share it with another save in words. He can tell it to others, what happened, but he can't persuade them to accept it. And so Paul ends his life discussing with anyone who would come to him, as we are told in the last of the Book of Acts, and he spent his days from morning to night discussing the kingdom of God and trying to persuade them concerning that kingdom. And some believed while others disbelieved (16:2).

And so that is the world in which we live. We simply tell it, what happened to the individual. It is such an unusual thing that the average person will not accept it. It doesn't make sense. They're more concerned in the world of Caesar to make an extra dollar. The pressure is on to pay rent, to buy food, shelter, all these things, clothing, and all the pressures of a man. He is more concerned with how to do it, how to meet the obligations of Caesar than to listen to this eternal word which will lift him out of the world of Caesar into the eternal world. For, this is the temporal world...but it is continuous and it goes on and on as though it is forever. It will be forever until one hears the Word of God, responds with faith, accepting it, and then waits in hope...and sets his hope fully upon the grace that is coming to him at the revelation of Jesus Christ *within* him (1Pet.1:13), where the one being containing all of us fell for a deliberate purpose: to expand beyond what he was prior to the fall.

We did nothing that was wrong to warrant the fall. We agreed to actually come down into the world of death and struggle in the world of death; taking on ourselves these garments of death and be enslaved by them, and then overcoming them in perfect confidence that he who contained us all, which is the one Father who contained all, and we are the sons of the one. As we are told in the Book of Deuteronomy, there will be no more children born in this world than there are according to the number of the sons of God. Not one child can be born in this world that is not actually inhabited by a son of God. The words are—you read it in the 32nd chapter of Deuteronomy—"He has set bounds to the people according to the number of the sons of God," so that no one can be born who is not actually a garment worn by a son of God. So he can't leave one of the sons in this world. But the son had to empty himself of everything that was his in order to actually fall with the one being that brings all into the world. That one being is God the Father. He raises us individually as himself, because it takes us all to form the one being that is God the Father.

Now, it's a pattern. When I speak of Jesus Christ, I do not think of a man. Paul said, "I no longer regard Christ from a human point of view. I once regarded him from the human point of view, but I no longer regard him from a human point of view." Well, how did he regard him, for here is the first outpouring of the mystery? How did he regard him? He regarded him as a *pattern*, the pattern man that unfolded in him...and it began with resurrection. Paul found himself, as I found myself, awakening within the grave. I had no idea until that moment in time on the 20th day of July of 1959 that I was buried in my own skull...as you are buried in your own skull and you don't know it. But I tell you I prophesy for you. It may happen tonight and I hope it does.

But it comes suddenly, unexpectedly. It comes upon you like a storm wind and you are awakened within yourself to find yourself buried, entombed in your skull. Then you emerge from it, you come out of that skull, and that is your birth from above. Which we are told in the Book of John is essential: "Unless you are born from above, you cannot enter the kingdom of God" (Jn.3:3). The kingdom of God is simply the new age, spoken of in scripture as "that age" as against "this age." This age is the age of death, where everything begins and ends in death. "That age" is eternal life, where those who came down into the world of death became victors, they overcame death. They're victorious and they rise; and upon the one who rises, the same one who fell, is conferred the name of "Lord." Well, "the Lord" is the name of God. So he was God who came down. You are God when you break the shell and rise. And there is no other being in the world.

So, no matter what a man does, Paul is not concerned. Whether you are a thief by tradition, by your profession—there are those who are a thief by profession—he doesn't condemn them. There are those that are everything in the world that the world will condemn; he doesn't condemn them. He doesn't care what happens to the individual between the cradle and the grave. His only hope is that they will hear his story and believe it, and in

The Return of Glory

believing it then break the shell, and then rise above all this nonsense in the world of Caesar. So he doesn't really care what happens between, say, birth as we understand it and death as we understand it. He is only concerned about telling the story.

Now he said, "The story was told to us as it was to them, but it did not benefit them because it was not received with faith in the hearers. They heard it but they discounted it and they did not believe it. They believe in this world and getting better and better intellectually, and more and more financially. And so I read the story concerning Russell, Lord Russell. Bertrand Russell, you know him. He is very proud of the fact he calls himself a socialist, but don't for one moment ever discount the fact that he is very proud of being Lord Russell. He is an Earl and very proud of that fact, although he will claim that he is a grand socialist and atheist. These are his words and I quote them, "I regard religion as a disease born of fear, a source of untold misery to the human race." That is Lord Russell. He is now pushing 100 and he has not vetoed that statement or in any way modified it. He simply believes in it.

Then H. G. Wells, also receiving all the honors of the world, said, "Christianity…" and you know the famous statement but he changed it to suit his purpose. You've heard the statement "the ever present help in time of trouble." He calls it "the ever absent help in time of trouble."

Now these men receive all the honors of the world conferred upon them and they love it. They are still seeking more. One is gone from this world and one is doting at the age of…well, why shouldn't he…at the age of 100. He sees nothing wrong in killing twenty million people in Russia, but he sees everything wrong with the destruction of 100,000 in Viet Nam. He sees nothing wrong with the horrible slaughter that Stalin did in the world, but he sees everything wrong in America because we took over the British Empire. We didn't claim the part, we set them free, and now they are as much a colony of America today, little England, as America, this fabulous land, was a colony once of England. He can't see his own prejudice. He can't see his venom against this land is based upon his Lordship is no more, because we in this country look upon all these titles as so many silly little things. It's like Alice in wonderland. But he can't stand it, because he's a grand socialist…but don't you fail to recognize the fact that he is Earl, he is Lord, Lord Russell. So to him religion is a disease born of fear.

Well, I tell you, it is not a disease. Yes there are numberless false interpretations of the great mystery. Paul tells us himself, he didn't know, he thought Christ was a man, a little man who came into the world and claimed that he was the Messiah to save the world. But then it was revealed *in* him in a series of supernatural experiences. For, Christianity is based upon the claim that a certain series of supernatural events happened in which God revealed himself in action for the salvation of man. Then he realized that these series of events spelled out the pattern man and the pattern man was Christ, and it was no other Christ. Christ was not *a* little man. Christ is the pattern man buried in every child born of woman, and it takes all the blows of the world to reduce us to that liquid state. And it *is,* may I tell you, a liquid state.

The first unfolding is the awakening within the grave. The grave is not in some cemetery, the grave is your own wonderful body; but the location of that grave is your skull and that's where you are buried. And the day will come and a storm wind will awaken you. There is in the *Talmud,* the *Jerusalem Talmud,* a tradition that the Messiah was born in Bethlehem the night of the destruction of Jerusalem, and he was carried away by a storm wind. It's a tradition of the great *Talmud.* I tell you it is true, it is a storm wind that possesses you...something so fantastic that you can't quite describe it. I can't describe it save to tell you that you reverberate from head to toe, and you feel the whole thing is coming apart, the whole body is being shattered. But you aren't shattered, you simply awaken. Something happens in you and all of a sudden you are awakening. Naturally you expect to awaken where you have awakened day after day as long as you live...but it isn't so. You awake as you've never awakened before and you awaken in your skull. There you find that the skull is a tomb and you are in that tomb and it is sealed.

Then you come out. You actually force yourself out of that tomb and come out as you came out of a womb; but this is the womb from *above,* rather than the womb from below. For you must be born from above; for unless you are born from above you cannot inherit the kingdom of God and you can't enter it. So you come out from above. And then the entire imagery as told us in scripture surrounds you...witnesses to the event. You are told that the angel of the Lord said to those who are going to be witnesses, "Go and you will find it...God is born this day in Bethlehem"...and the proof of that fact that he is born you'll find a little babe wrapped in swaddling clothes, and he is lying on the floor (Luke2:11,12). They went hastily and they found exactly what they were told. But he who was born was unseen by those who witnessed the *sign* of his birth. They couldn't see him because now he is Spirit. God is Spirit, therefore, God is born...and God cannot be seen by mortal eye. So God is born. They couldn't' see *him,* but he detected every thought of theirs as though their thoughts were objective to him. He didn't have to speak it as they were all completely outside, just as though they had voiced what they had not spoken. And yet they began to speak... he heard every word they had to say, and he, the invisible one that was born, the sign of his birth was there and it was carried away by a storm wind. The wind was fantastic, an unearthly wind. Now he is God, and God is God the Father.

God the Father if he is father must have a son, and the son stands before him and calls him Father in fulfillment of the prophecy of scripture. Well, the son who is God's son is calling him Father, revealing to him that *he* really *is* God the Father, though still one to return to the limitation of his cross and share it with his brothers to tell them and encourage them what is in store for them. So here, he returns to this state having seen his only begotten son, who is God's *only* son, and that son is the consummation. If I took all the generations of men and all of their experiences and personified them, it would be *that* son proving that he has finished the race. He has completely gone through the entire *fight* of this world, and now the crown of righteousness is his. He is now ready to receive the crown of salvation because all of the generations he played them. He has played every lovely and unlovely thing in this world, and then he sees it all coalesced and projected into a single youth, beauty beyond measure, and that is his Son calling him Father.

Now the third mighty act shows you how it is reduced to molten metal. And here he finds himself, as told us in the Book of Zechariah, standing upon the Mount of Olives, and then the Mount is split from east to west, and one-half moves northward and one-half moves south. Here, this entire valley…well, he sees the entire…but the Mount of Olives is his body. He didn't know that before. He read it in scripture, but he didn't realize the Old Testament is an adumbration…it is simply a forecasting, a foreshadowing, in a not all together conclusive and immediately evident way. It's simply an adumbration: the complete shadow but not the actual substance. So here, it is told as a mountain, and the mountain, we are told, he stood upon the mountain and the mountain was split from east to west, and one side moved northward and one side moved south. Here he realizes that that whole story is about himself. His *body* is split from top to bottom, from east to west, and one side moves northward and one side moves southward. And at the base of the body split from top to bottom is a golden, liquid, molten metal. It's living. He looks at it and he knows it is himself. He fuses with it and up he goes into his skull. The kingdom of heaven, we are told, is within you (Luke17:21). He returns now from that state where he was in the world of generation into the world of *regeneration*, and the whole heaven reverberates like thunder.

So here, he returns in a molten state and is cast into that mold which was prepared for him before the foundation of the world. Here now he becomes a living jewel that radiates and reflects the glory of God, and he is the express image of God, and the express image of God is God himself. So, "Let us make man in our image" (Gen.1:26)…that's the primal wish…so he actually has made him. And the gods…one of the sons—and all together form *the* God, *the* Lord—that one has completed his journey. But because we are all brothers, he is compelled to remain in the world after the event and tell it in the hope that many of his brothers who are still asleep will believe him that Christ of scripture is a *pattern*. It is not a man separate from himself. It is a pattern, the pattern of salvation. And there are four mighty acts that form that redemption, and it begins with his awakening within himself. Then comes his discovery of his own fatherhood, who is God the Father, through the Son who calls *him* Father. Then the splitting of the temple where he is reduced to molten metal, rising up like a serpent and casts himself into the mold prepared for him. And that mold, two years and nine months later, is observed by the Holy Spirit, and he approves of the work done. He descends upon him in bodily form as a dove and smothers him with love. Now he knows that he has filled the entire mold and that it now is shining. It is a glorious living stone in the living body of the risen Christ.

So Christ is the *one* being who fell containing all within himself. "He chose us in him before the foundation of the world" (Eph.1:4). And then pre-arranged and agreed to…we agreed to fall with him, all of us because without all of us he couldn't fall. And that was simply an agreement for expansion beyond, because truth is an ever-expanding illumination. If God now reached the limit of expansion then let him die. But there is *no* limit to expansion, there is *no* limit to translucency; there is only a limit to contraction, to opacity. So he put a limit upon contraction which is man, and the limit on opacity which is called doubt and is personified by a thing called the devil. So, when one doubts what he hears, that is only the devil personified.

So if I can't believe it…any more than Bertrand Russell believed it, any more than many of the wise people. But as Paul said *after* his revelation: "The wisdom of this world is foolishness in the eyes of God…and he takes the weak and confounds the mighty. He takes the foolish and puts to nought the works of the wise" (1Cor.1:25). So we really believe that we are getting wiser and wiser, so we think, and there is no wiser and wiser, save wiser and wiser nonsense. Here, we have gone into Viet Nam with all of our power and we can't extricate ourselves. Here our present President spoke of this little thing as a fourth-rate power, but he can't get out…a fourth-rate power. He criticized the previous President for his handling of the problem, how they shot down our planes…the same thing…and what is he doing? He criticized his predecessor for not going in and acting, and he hasn't gone in and acted. We have mighty power and we can't use it, just can't use it. So the wisdom of the world is foolishness in the eyes of God, and he takes all of this nonsense and lets it go on. Let one add upon it and add upon it and give each other medals. So undoubtedly Mr. Russell has unnumbered medals upon his chest that were conferred upon him because he was a great mathematician, and he was this, that and the other. Undoubtedly, a brilliant master of the English tongue, he could match words to thoughts beautifully. Because of that he confuses the world.

And so, Paul could match them too. But he realized after the revelation that that was not what the Bible was about at all. He thought that the coming of Messiah would come from without, until he realized that it all came from within. That one man fell and his own book, the 82nd Psalm, told it: "I say that you are gods, sons of the Most High, all of you; nevertheless, you will fall like men and *die* like men, and you will fall as one man, O princes" (82:6). Can you imagine that? There it is in the 82nd Psalm, we'll fall as one man, all of us. And then he calls us princes. Well, if we are princes then our Father is king. If our Father is the King of Kings then he is he Lord of Lords, and he is the Lord God Jehovah. Now he is raising us to himself so that each becomes fully aware of being God the Father. We are sons *destined* to be fully aware that we are the Father, for the Father is comprised of all of his sons. Regardless of your present sex, you are a son of God, and in the end you are destined to awaken *as* God the Father.

So here in this wonderful story of scripture, which is completely misunderstood, you and I are called upon to hear a story from one who actually was sent. I tell you that I was sent. Now how can there be a preacher unless he is sent? Well, the preachers who are preaching today are *not* sent. They have not yet been awakened, so they are giving you all kinds of stories concerning the interpretation of scripture. I am not. Prior to 1959 I would have, but since 1959 I can't, for I was called and sent. Only one who was called and incorporated into the body of God is ever sent. And when you are called and actually incorporated into the body of God, it's like an impression made by a seal on wax or clay, so you come out bearing the *image* of God… but mortal eye can't see you. You simply disintegrate, as all bodies do, and you'll die before your friends' eyes. They see you as a mortal being, full of weaknesses and all the limitations of the flesh, and so they are mislead. They can't hear what you say because of what they see. They see a body disintegrating before their eyes. They see one in need as *they* are in need, and they can't believe what they are hearing from you because they are judging from appearances. They can't quite understand that God does not see as man sees. Man sees the outward man; God sees the inner man and the inner man has been impressed upon God like a great seal upon wax. When he returns to his little body that will continue to disintegrate, he is unseen by mortal eye. But if you could see him, he is radiating and reflecting the glory of God and he is the express image of the person that is God. But only those whose eyes are open could ever see it. They could never see it with mortal eyes. They could only see the body slowly disintegrating before their eyes.

But I promise you who hear me—and I hope you receive it—no matter how young you are in this world it isn't long before you depart this world. Don't be afraid, you'll be restored to life in a world just like this to continue your journey. But if you actually believe it and hear it, you will not see me in that world. I will *not* be in that world, but you will know *of* me. They'll be talking there where you will go of the work that I did here, because I will not be there. I have left the world of death, only waiting for the moment when this little garment is taken off. I will not be restored to this world of mortality. "I have finished the race, I have fought the good fight, I have kept the faith, and now there is laid up for me the crown of righteousness" (2Tim.4:7). Into that I go, but I'll be there waiting for everyone in this world, because we're all brothers, and all must come into that union and be the one being that came down bearing all.

Now mark my words, I am not fooling you…it isn't long to wait. No matter how young you are in this world, it isn't long to take off this garment to find yourself restored. And you'll find many of your friends who have gone before who will come after, and they'll be in a world terrestrial just like this, laboring in a world just like we do here. Possibly in a different profession, but you will labor. You will say "Where is he who taught us?" You won't see me, but *eventually* you will because you'll come where I am. I tell you I'm going to where you cannot *now* come but you *will* come, for everyone will come there. For everyone will awaken as God the Father… everyone in this world.

Now I'm not trying to persuade you to change your attitude for one moment concerning the speaker. I am telling you what I know. I am not manufacturing it. I did not receive it from a man. Just like Paul, no man taught it to me. I didn't get it from man; it came through a revelation of the *true* nature of salvation…something entirely different. Salvation: not a man saving me, but a *pattern* man buried in me that awakens in me. And when he awakens in me, he awakens in the first-person, singular, present-tense experience. *I am* having the experience and then I know who he is. I was taught to believe he was another, but when he awakens in me I realize I am he. Now, remain in the world long enough just to share it and tell it.

So the unknown author of the Book of Hebrews: "Holy brethren" he said "look to Jesus, the apostle, the high priest of our confession" (3:1). Holy brethren he calls everyone he addresses…we now are sharers in the great gift. Let me now look to Jesus the apostle. Well, the apostle is the one who is called first and then sent. Now, he speaks of him as the *only* apostle. He's right. Everyone who is called *is* Jesus, because your true name in the end is Jesus. That's who you really are. He calls the apostle and then sends him, for the apostle is one who is sent. Sent to do what? To tell the story of salvation, that's all...to tell the gospel, the good news. But not everyone who hears it responds with faith. Many hear it and discount it. They are far more interested in the honors of men, and tonight if you told it to many of the prominent people in the world, they would be completely disinterested. They are not interested. They may have fifty million dollars and their interest is not fifty million but a hundred million. They may be eighty years old when they hear the story, but they still want more of what they must leave behind. They won't take it with them as you know. They will enter a world just like this, devoid of what they have compiled and built here, and cast in a role best suited for the work yet to be done in them by the son of God who is wearing that garment.

So he may cast them in a role from a fifty million dollar surplus into shining shoes or cleaning latrines. It's the best that could be done for them for the work *yet* to be done in them. And they're right in this world and the world is just like this. May I tell you, I'm speaking from experience, I am not theorizing. But how can I take you with me when I sit on a chair and suddenly I'm unexpectedly...something is happening in me and I'm beginning to see what I should not see. I am seeing a world that is real, just like this, and then consciousness follows vision and I step into that world. Here I'm in a world just like this, then it closes upon me, and this world is shut out. Here I am exploring a world just like this. To return to this world...and when I was in that world my body was real. It was seen by others and heard by others, but it was body just like this. You ask yourself a thousand questions...well, if in that world I had a body just like this and yet those who knew I sat on a chair saw that body sound asleep, then how did I get that body? That's how you get the body when you die here. That body was just as real to me and to those who saw me and heard me as the body that you now see. So this body if destroyed would not have destroyed that body that was in that world. It was just as real. And so "you cut down the oak by the axe and the little lamb is slain by the knife, but their forms eternal remain forever and they are simply reproduced by the seed of contemplative thought."

When I stepped into that world I knew what I was. I was a man called Neville. I was so aware of being Neville I clothed myself in the body that was Neville. Yet I knew, clothed as I was in that body, that there was a body that others knew to be Neville that was sound asleep on a chair, or reclining on a bed. And here I am still Neville, clothed as Neville, fully conscious of being

Neville. How did it happen? It came by the seed of contemplative thought. So when you die here, you actually remold yourself in the likeness that you know, only reduce it in age, and you take it back not to an infant, you take it back to what pleases you. What would please the average person in this world? To be twenty with the same intelligence that he has when is eighty. So if I could only be twenty with what I know as a man who is eighty, wouldn't that be marvelous! Well, you do it. You return it by the seed of contemplative thought. Who does it? The God in you does it. So you return, not through the womb of a woman but by your own being of contemplative thought.

And so, that seems to be the ideal age that man returns to, because that to him seems to be, "If I only had more time what I could accomplish." And he returns to that age and he is exactly what he wants to be. He is not sans teeth, sans eyes, sans anything. He has *all* that he wanted which he lost when he struck the age of seventy. He was without eyes, without teeth, without all things when he struck seventy. But not when he goes back and he is clothed and he is perfect, with everything that was missing while he was here as they simply cremated the body. And then he goes on in that world just as he does here, and he matures, and he gets older and older, until that moment in time when there is that eruption in him which is the pattern man that is buried within him…which is God. Then that pattern unfolds within him. And when it does and completes it, he leaves this world permanently, and returns to the *one* that is awaiting all. That one body which is "the one body, the one Spirit, the one Lord, the one God and Father of all" (Eph. 4:4) and *all* must come into it. So he simply now looks upon the world he has left behind, with all of his brothers clothed male and female, and contemplates them, waiting for them to awaken as he awoke.

Now let us go into the Silence.

*   *   *

Now are there any questions, please? Well, if there aren't any questions, we are here every Monday and Friday, and will be until June. So thank you. Good night.

THE WISDOM, POWER, GLORY BURIED IN US

5/5/69

Blake said, "Why stand we here trembling around calling on God for help and not ourselves in whom God dwells?" Well, does he dwell in us as something other than ourselves or did he actually become us, become man? I will tell you, *you* are the being that became man, the being Blake refers to as God. God is your own wonderful human Imagination. It did not begin in your mother's womb and it will not end in the grave. This is the pre-existing being, the being that existed before the foundation of the world, and you emptied yourself completely for a purpose. Tonight, we will try to touch on that purpose.

So Paul in his letter to the Philippians speaks now of God in action as Jesus Christ. He said, "Though he was in the *form* of God, he did not consider it something to grasp, but emptied himself"—a complete emptying of himself—"and took upon himself the form of a slave, and was born in the likeness of men. And being found in human form he humbled himself and took upon himself the cross" (Phil.2:6-9). This [body] is the cross that he took.

Now, this is all behind us. The being spoken of here we are that being. Now he tells it as though there is another and he said, "Therefore God has highly exalted him and bestowed on him the name that is above every name, that at the name Jesus every knee should bow, on earth, in heaven and under the earth, and every tongue confess that Jesus Christ is Lord, to the glory of God" (Phil.2:9-11).

You read this and you think he is speaking of another. He is *not* speaking of another. It is *you* who completely emptied *yourself*. You had all the glory of God and all the power of God and all the wisdom of God, and you were not pretending when you became man and were nailed to this cross that is man. You couldn't pretend it and accomplish anything. You had to completely empty yourself of your power, your wisdom and your glory; and actually take upon yourself the humility of a garment of flesh and blood which enslaves you. For you have to cater to it from the cradle to the grave. You feed it, you bathe it, you wash it, and when it cannot assimilate what you give it, it has to eliminate, and then having eliminated then you have to clean the body again. And so, from the cradle to the grave you are enslaved by this body on which you are crucified.

Now Christ is crucified on man. He is buried in man. When he rises in man, that is the risen Christ and there is conferred upon the risen Christ in the experience of men the divine name Jesus. Through this experience a new age is ushered in. So Jesus is simply a name conferred upon the risen Christ, but the risen Christ is present in every child born of woman. The word Jesus means the same thing as the word Jehovah, "Jehovah saves." Jehovah's name is I AM. So here, this is not another being other than yourself. You are suffering from *total* amnesia. You had to completely forget your power, your wisdom, and your glory, and actually become what the world thinks to be a little man, a little woman, born a few years ago who will play a little part and then depart this world. But there is an immortal you that is in it, buried in all. So then Blake said, "Why do we stand here trembling around calling on God for help and not ourselves in whom God dwells?" He dwells in us.

Everything in this world that you can think about is *present*. You can't conceive of something that is not already worked out in detail. But they are shadowy to those who dwell not in them, mere possibilities; but for those who enter into them, they seem the only substances. When I enter into a world that is just like this, prior to my entrance into it it's a possibility, an image. But let me now actually enter into that world so that my consciousness follows my vision and I enter, it seems more real than this room when I leave it tonight. At the moment I am in this image and this room is real. When I depart here tonight, it's a memory image, just a memory picture, and wherever I am at that moment that's more real than this room that is *most* real in my life. This is more real *now* than any part of my world. I left a home which was real when I left it and it's now a memory image. But when I re-enter that room, it will seem to be the only substance in my world. When I came here, coming here it was an image. As I entered the room it took on all reality, all that was real. Now, we think this is a normal procedure. No, everything in the world exists just as this room exists and your home that you left exists, and everything exists. The job you want exists. It's only a dream, a mere image, while you're not in it; but when you

The Return of Glory

enter into it, it seems while you are in it to be the *only* reality. And you can't conceive of a state, not one state that is not already worked out and finished, waiting for occupancy, waiting for someone who desires to experience that to enter into that state.

To come into this world you emptied yourself completely of your power and your wisdom and your glory. The day will come—having gone through the gamut the God in you, which is your very self, not another, he's actually your very self—will rise in you and you are he. That rising in you is of the being that emptied itself. Then memory returns and then is conferred upon you that divine name, which we are told in that letter to the Philippians when it is heard every knee is bowed, in heaven and in earth and under the earth, and every tongue confesses that Jesus Christ is Lord, to the glory of God...because *you are* God. But in order to come here and take on this limitation, you could not pretend. No one can get anything out of this and pretend that they are a man. They had to actually become a man and take upon himself all the weaknesses and all the limitations of the flesh.

Now, does the Bible in any way suggest it? Yes, we are told in the Book of John, the very beginning, "In the beginning was the Word, and the Word was with God, and the Word was God" (1:1). Now, "The Word became flesh and dwelt within us" (1:14). If he was with God and *was* God, that certainly implies pre-existence. "Before Abraham, was I AM" (8:58). Does that not imply pre-existence? "Tell me, master, who sinned, this man or his parents that he is born blind? I tell you, neither this man nor his parents, but that the works of God be made manifest in him" (9:2). Isn't that pre-existence or did he sin in his mothers' womb? Either he sinned in his mother's womb and this is the result, or else here is implication telling us of a pre-existence. And yet he is blameless...this is a state that he *had* to experience. You don't avoid anything...you play *all* the parts of the world.

Now we find in the 17th of John, he is asking, this is a prayer, and he's asking the Father, which is himself—for he said "I and my Father are one" (Jn.10:30)—he wants everyone to be where he is. And then he tells you why he wants everyone to be where he is, "that they may see my glory that thou gavest me and the *love* with which thou loved me *before* the foundation of the world." You and I were loved. We are part of the body of love. We were loved before the foundation of the world. But we came to do a job, to expand our power, expand our wisdom, and expand our glory. And to do it we had to come down and reach the limit of contraction which is man, the limit of opacity which is doubt; and completely forget the being that we *really* are, and doubt that we ever were, or that such a being ever existed. So here we are in this world, in the limit of contraction and opacity. Then comes that moment when the risen Christ now, Christ who is in us but so asleep

449

he appears to be dead, completely dead...and then he is disturbed. The storm wind, which is Spirit itself, begins to stir him, and he wakes to find himself encased in his tomb. He comes out of his tomb...but it begins with his resurrection. He rises first before he is born from above. As he comes out of this tomb from above, there is conferred upon him this greatest of all names. It's called *the* name, the name Jesus. So in the end there is only Jesus, the cosmic Christ—we are the Cosmic Christ—buried in all. When he rises individually, that name which is the name Jehovah, that's the name of Jesus, is conferred. He is the Lord God Jehovah. Well, who is rising?—I am. What's God's name?—I AM.

What is David's Father's name?—I AM. That's what scripture teaches. So here, the essence of all that man could ever experience stands before him personified as the crown of his journey. It's a son, a son bearing witness to his victory over death. He actually died: he became man, entered the world of death, and rose out of it. And as each rises, each in that act of rising receives the name Jesus. So we can say in the end, after the transfiguration, Jesus only. All are gathered into one body and that one body is the Lord Jesus Christ.

So in this world all things appear to be, and as they appear to be, they become what they seem to be. Again, as Blake said so beautifully, "Those in great Eternity who contemplate on death"—and this is the world that they contemplate—"said thus: 'What seems to be, *is,* to those to whom it seems to be, and is productive of the most dreadful consequences to those to whom it seems to be, even of torment, despair and eternal death; but divine mercy steps beyond and redeems man in the body of Jesus" (*Jer.,* Plt.36, Ln.50). When it seems everything is lost, then you begin to awake and you awake within yourself. You don't see another, it's *you* who awakes, and it's you who goes through every stage of the entire drama. It's all in the first-person singular, it's all in the present tense, and there's not another, it's you. You are the Christ Jesus spoken of in scripture: "Christ *in you* is the hope of glory" (Col.1:27). "Do you not realize that Jesus Christ is in you?" (2Cor.13:5). Well, where is he? Say "I am"...that's he. So why call upon another? Why stand we here trembling around calling upon Christ Jesus as another and not ourselves in whom he dwells? He dwells in me as my own wonderful human Imagination...and there never was another.

I got a card today from Norway. Many of you know this lady, and she reminded me in the card that she said to me on occasions if there is one place in this world that she would like to visit it would be Norway. But she felt she couldn't afford it...she could ill-afford to live here, far less go to Norway. But if she could go to Norway it could be to make a picture, to appear in a picture. Well, she writes from Norway today stating that she is working on a picture being done in Norway, and her dream has come true, and here is this lovely picture of one of these beautiful inlets in Norway. So there she is! How she got it I don't know…it doesn't really matter. But it was a mere shadow in her world prior to this, standing here talking to me, voicing this request. And I said to her as I would say to you, "Dwell in it. If you were in Norway, how would you see the world? You would see it *from* Norway. You wouldn't see it from Los Angeles if you were in Norway. Don't ask me how you are going to get there. So you have no money, you can ill-afford to buy food, but you want to go to Norway. Well, it costs money, but you will render unto Caesar the things that are Caesar's, and you'll go *if* you apply this principle and you dwell in Norway. Tonight when you sleep, you sleep as though you were in Norway and then this state into which you go will seem the only substance. You may fall into it this night and have a dream where you are in Norway and it seems so real." Well, she doesn't confess in her card to me that she had any such experience, only that she did dwell in the state as though she were there. Then comes the casting, then comes the picture, and she's making a picture in Norway.

So you move into any state. I don't care what the state is, it's *already* done. Everything is completely worked out in detail, the most minute detail, and you simply step into it. From a shadowy substance or a shadowy state it becomes the only substance. Everything seems so on the outside and so shadowy when you only think of it. When you enter into it, it takes on reality and everything seems as completely real as this room seems real now.

So here, the being that is housed in you when you say "I am," that was in the beginning with God, and it *was* God: "In the beginning was the Word, the Word was with God, and the Word was God." You are not another. You are the creative power and wisdom and glory of God. But you as God had to completely empty yourself of this glory, this wisdom and this power, and not *pretend* you are entering the graveyard called earth. And these unnumbered bodies are all graves, that's what they are…every body is a grave. And you actually came down and took upon yourself and *entered* the grave; and because you are an immortal being your presence animates it. You made it alive because you are in it. It couldn't breathe unless you were there because you are breath. The words breath and Spirit are the same in both Hebrew and Greek. It just couldn't breathe if you had not entered these graves called men. I mean generic man, male, female. So you came right down into it, and animated it for a purpose, and you completely forgot so you don't recognize your own brothers when you see the other, and you war against them as though they were others.

You are told in this passage that I quoted tonight in the 2nd chapter of Philippians, it starts with this lovely thought: "Let each of you think not only on his own interests, but also on the interests of others. And let this mind be in you, the mind that you have with Christ Jesus" (2:4). The same mind...it's not another. You can't tell it any better. How could you tell it more beautifully than "my interest should be your interest, and then it should be our interest" because, really, basically we are one when these garments are finally taken off? They are taken off one by one and we re-enter the one body that fell. In the end, only one being, the glorious being that is the Lord God who is the Father of the entire drama.

So, I got this letter this week, in fact, I got it last Monday. All are coming close to it. He gave me a series of dreams, all on a single night. The final one is the cue to the dream, like three stages. In it he saw a being and to him it was a huge monkey, a horrible thing, and it clung to his back. He said, "I wasn't afraid of it, but it seemed unclean and strange. I wished it would go away, but it wouldn't. And then it began to make love to me and that annoyed me, but I was not afraid. I didn't want to hit it or tear it off, because I thought it could even kill me. But even then I was not afraid of it, though I felt it had the power to kill me. Then as it continued in its love match, I tore it off, and in the tearing off from my back, I awoke."

It's a perfect vision. One day he will see the complementary side. This is the "dweller on the threshold." This is man's symbol of his *misuse* of the creative power of God, that is, the misuse of his Imagination. Every man has one...let no one boast...everyone has one. Every time you have misused your Imagination by imagining something unlovely either of yourself or a seeming other you feed this monster. You brought him into being by your misused Imagination. You also brought into being one that he didn't see but he will one day, a glorious being, an angelic being, beauty beyond measure. And she is the personification of every lovely imaginal act of man. One day you will meet them together, and you will see this monstrous being, just like a huge I would call it an ape or orangutan. But it speaks...it has this guttural voice and it speaks. Then you will see this glorious being that is also your creation, but you don't know it.

They seem completely independent of your perception of them. This one, you see nothing leading to you, and here you see this beautiful creature, an angelic being, you see nothing attached to you. Suddenly as this one begins to speak it calls this one "Mother" and you are so annoyed with this monstrous thing calling this angelic being mother you pummel it, you beat it. You realize it gloats and it grows on violence. Every blow it becomes stronger and it loves it. It loves every violent act of yours even on itself. It's like a masochist appealing to you to be violent even on it. Then you realize this is my creation. And so is this one. This is all that is good in my world personified and this is everything that is evil and horrible in my world symbolized. And you make yourself a pledge, for there is no one to whom you can swear. God has no one to swear but himself. So finding no one, he swore by himself. And you will swear by yourself that if it takes you eternity you will redeem this monstrous thing that should *not* live. It never should have been brought into being...but your misuse of power brought it into being.

As you pledge yourself that you will redeem it if it takes you eternity, at that very moment it dissolves. It dissolves before your eyes and leaves no trace of ever having been present. But as it dissolves the energy isn't wasted, it comes back to you, and you feel a power that you have never experienced before. That is, you don't remember ever having such power...because the whole thing returns to you. It's only *misused* power and power cannot be wasted. It will simply coalesce into a garment like this. But it cannot be wasted, so it returns to the one who used it and misused it. And on the other hand, as it returns to you and you begin to feel the *power* that returns, this beautiful creature glows like the sun. And then you awake.

So everyone will one day be confronted with these two. They are self-creations, and man goes through in this world creating both of them. He feeds this one with every lovely, noble thought he ever entertained; and he feeds this one with every ignoble thought he ever entertained. As he goes into violence, this one gloats and it grows in it; and this one remains un-phased. But every time you entertain a lovely thought on behalf of another, this one is fed and it gets more and more glorious, more and more beautiful. So this thing that clung to him like a monkey or like a cat, the same element would take their form, as someone wrote concerning a cat. It was a vicious thing that seemed about to claw the hand. He wasn't afraid of it and yet he didn't like it. That's only the symbol of the misspent imaginal power that is God. For God in man, that divine body that is crucified upon man, is man's own wonderful human Imagination. There never was another God and there never will be another. That's the only God.

So while we are unmindful, because we gave up everything, we can still hear the voice of one who has heard it from within, the voice of one who *has* risen from the grave, and believe him to the point of testing it. Put this to the test as this lady either wittingly or unwittingly put it to the test, and then she can write from Norway. Well, she couldn't afford the passage of a ferry boat. She wouldn't know if there were a ferry between here and Catalina...she couldn't take it. She was reduced to that state and yet she can write me from Norway where she is making a picture...all because she dared to imagine she was in Norway. She reminded me of that moment with me when she simply expressed the desire of all the places of the world that she would like to see it would be Norway. But she got a job in a picture and there she is now making her picture.

So don't discount this principle. Just test it! As we are told in that 13th chapter of 2nd Corinthians: "Do you not realize that Jesus Christ is *in* you?—unless of course you fail to meet the test" (13:5). I trust you will not discover that *we* have failed in the test. And so he knew exactly what he wanted and he entered the state, and the state took on substance, and became to him real. I have gone into world after world, and when I step into these worlds it is the only reality; and this that I leave behind like my apartment tonight it's only a shadow now, just a shadow. I expect to return to it to find it wrapping itself around me and taking on substance, taking on reality. But at the moment this room is far more real to me than any place I've ever visited. It may not be as thrilling, but it's more real at this moment. And wherever I am at that moment, that place is real, it takes on substance…but it's only an image.

So I walk into an image. Whether I walk physically from here into another image or whether I do it as I do it constantly from my chair or from my bed, I see a world and into that world I step, and the world becomes real and surrounds me. People are real just like these and everything about it is real. The body that I wear is real. Where did the body come from? Isn't that also in my Imagination? Where did the clothing come from? I sleep in the nude. I've slept in the nude for the last forty-odd years regardless of winter, summer, spring or fall. If it's ten below, I get under those and in a matter of seconds I am warm if I have enough covers on me. But it gives me the freedom I enjoy…having once tasted the freedom of sleeping in the nude. Well, I was in the nude when I stepped into this world and yet I'm clothed. Where did the clothing come from? Where did the body come from? I knew the body was on the bed I knew that much, and I knew that body was in the nude, and here I am clothed and I am in a body. I know my identity; I know exactly who I am, so where did it all come from? The power begins to return and that power can clothe itself in any form in the world. It's a protean being, yet that identity remains unchallenged forever and forever; yet you will bear the name, that divine name that is above every name, and the name is Jesus.

So no one sees him here, but we will all know him because all will be Jesus. In the meanwhile, the power of God which is Christ is buried in us, the wisdom of God is buried in us, and the glory of God is buried in us. And when it is raised in us the power is enhanced and so is the wisdom and so is the glory. So you are a pre-existent being. You did not begin in your mother's womb; you cannot end in the grave. You were before the foundation of the world. That's the being of whom Paul speaks when he addresses that letter to the Philippians. He is addressing it to posterity and he is addressing it to you, to me, to everyone, for he is speaking from experience.

Now tonight, I can speak from experience, for I have had all the experiences that are recorded in scripture concerning the Lord Jesus Christ.

I mean *all* of them. And yet, I am just as weak while this garment remains, just as limited, and will continue to be until one day I'll take it off. At that moment that I take it off, I return to my former state but glorified beyond it. So I, too, can say, "Return unto me the glory that was mine, the glory I had with *thee before* that the world was. I have finished the work that thou gavest me to do" (Jn.17:5). What work? He proclaimed through his servants the prophets what would come to pass and only God could fulfill them. So God himself emptied himself of his wisdom and his power and his glory and took upon himself the opacity and the concreteness of death, and then went through the entire gamut, and then he came out victorious over death. And when he comes out as the victor over death, his power returns, his wisdom returns, and his glory, but by reason of the experience each is enhanced. And now he expands beyond what he was prior to coming into the world of death.

So let no one scare you, let no one frighten you. You are a prenatal being, a being that has preexistence. And the existence did not begin some 6,000 years ago; it was before the foundation of the world. So when our scientists tell us…and they change it every year, they jump by billions… so when they say the universe is not now so many billions, but it's so many trillions of light years, let them put any number of zeros next to that number, it doesn't make any difference. Whatever number they come up with, before that *you are*. Before the foundation of the world, I am. So it doesn't matter how many billions of light years they think it is, whatever they come up with, before that the world was, I am. So he says, "Father, return unto me the glory that was mine, the glory that I had with thee *before* that the world was" (Jn.17:5). Why?—that they may see my glory, the glory that thou gavest unto me. For I radiate that center called Father and yet as I radiate it I am the Father. I also reflect that center of the Father. And now he goes beyond that…he not only wants them there to see his glory, but he makes this statement, "And the love with which thou loved me before the foundation of the world." Here, God, infinite love, loves us all. He foreknew us all, he chose us all in him, all his one being, and all together fell. One man fell carrying with him all into the world of death.

But bear in mind, as we're told in the 32nd chapter of Deuteronomy, he has set bounds to the peoples of the world. In other words, not one child can be born unless there is a Son of God which is Christ Jesus housed within that child. He set bounds to the people according to the number of the sons of God. If he was not in us, we couldn't breathe. He is the breath of us… couldn't breathe. And when he removes his breath, you are that breath. You are he who came in. And your friends cry over the garment that you wore. They do not know the occupant of that garment was God himself. And you who had a child, that child you called it Grace, call it by some other name, that child was Christ. That child is destined to receive the name which is Jesus, and no power in the world can stop it from receiving that name eventually. Meanwhile, he's Christ...everyone in the world is Christ, the power of God and the wisdom of God (1Cor.1:24).

And then he is resurrected. When does it start? You're told in the first chapter in the Book of Romans, "He is designated Son of God in *power* through his resurrection from the dead" (1:4). He's walking the earth as a man. Maybe he's the mason, maybe the carpenter; maybe he's a musician, maybe a professor or some other thing. No one knows him, he's playing his part, and one day he is resurrected. At that moment, he is returned to his power, to his glory, to his wisdom. So he is designated now Son of God in power through his resurrection from the dead. He looks back and sees his whole vast world and knows that everyone is destined to be resurrected as he has been. Everyone is destined to form into the *one* body, as now he is, and in the end one glorious brotherhood, transcending the wildest dream of love in the world, all sharing in that divine love. For, love is the human form divine.

I can't describe it to you save in a few words, but how can I describe the mood that possesses you when *love* stands before you, when love embraces you? I can't describe it. It is an ecstasy beyond anything that the word ecstasy could describe. You speak of ecstasy, it can't describe it. It can't describe that body that embraces you, and then you are incorporated into the one body, the body of love, knowing that everyone in the world must come, but everyone must come because he loved all before the foundation of the world. And not one could be lost because God would be lost. How could one be lost? And in the end all are vindicated. Yes, the cutthroat, the murderer, the thief...I don't care what he has done...in the end everything is vindicated like the blind man in the 9th chapter of the Book of John: "No, not this man nor his parents but that the works of God be made manifest *in him.*"

One day I was confronted with this huge sea of the imperfect, and I played all those parts. They were waiting for me to redeem them, for they were the costumes that I wore; all these were the garments that I wore. And then when I was lifted up on high, I walked by and every one was made perfect because I was perfect. "Be ye perfect as your Father in heaven perfect" (Mat.5:48). And where is heaven?—"Heaven is within you" (Luke 17:21). So when he has made it perfect and you are perfect, you are lifted up and you walk by all the parts and every one is made perfect. You could not improve it, because you can't improve upon that which is perfect, or it was not perfect. There is no room for improvement in the perfect. And everyone was made perfect as I walked by. In the very end the chorus sang out, "It is finished"...the last cry on the cross..."It is finished" (Jn.19:30).

And then, you come and you tell it. Tell it to everyone who will hear you. But eventually all will hear. So you will depart the world and others will pick it up just where you left off. They will have the similar experiences and they will tell it, and then others will tell it. Don't expect to find 100 percent acceptance. There are those who will believe because you have used scripture to support your argument, and those who will disbelieve, doesn't really matter. Leave them just as they are and you go about your Father's business telling exactly what happened to you. For, when I tell you what has happened to me, I can speak more convincingly than if I am theorizing. I can speak with *conviction* when I am telling you what I actually know from experience. For, the truth man knows from his own personal experience he knows more thoroughly than he knows any other thing in this world, or than he can know that same truth in any other way. I may hear someone tell me what he has experienced and I believe him, I trust him, and I will say yes, I believe you implicitly, but I can't speak with authority; it's hearsay. I can't go into a court and be a witness unless I witnessed it myself by experience. I can't come in and say, "Well, I heard it said"…that doesn't matter. I must come in and say "I know." Here is an assured "I know," not I believe nor I think, but I know. How do you know?—because I experienced it.

And so, bring me two witnesses. I have one on the outside…that's scripture. Now I must parallel scripture. Well, have I had experiences that parallel scripture? Yes…then there are two witnesses and when two agree in their testimony then that is conclusive. Here is scripture and here is mine dovetailing scripture. Well then, I have two witnesses: one is the written word and one is the living word interpreting the written word. And so, step into the kingdom, for you brought back the truth of God's word. He sent you the living word to interpret and verify the written word which he gave to his servants the prophets. Now that you have actually interpreted scripture yourself by unfolding scripture within you, enter the kingdom. For that's the only purpose for living. There's no other purpose he said in these words of the 8th chapter of 2nd Corinthians: "You know the Lord Jesus Christ, who though he was rich, yet for your sake he became poor, that by his poverty you might become rich" (8:9). In dollars and cents, no. He was rich in power; he was the power of God. He was rich in wisdom; he was the wisdom of God. He was rich in glory; he glorified God. Gave it all up and became poor, and entered the world of death, that by his poverty, now you may become rich. So when you awake *you* are the Lord Jesus Christ…and there never was another. There is no other.

Now let us go into the Silence.

* * *

Now are there any questions, please?

Q: (inaudible)

A: My dear, from the time I was a little boy I had things I could not understand, so I can't go back to that. But I had mystical or psychic experiences that I did not understand that scared me to death. My one great one that began it all was when I was taken into the divine assembly and brought before the risen Lord. I've told you that story and I have written it. Well, that happened in 1929, in the summer of '29. Thirty yeas later began the unfolding of these mighty acts of God within me: the resurrection and the birth, the discovery of the fatherhood of God, the splitting of the curtain of the temple and the descent of the dove. All these came after the resurrection....that began the great, dramatic thing in me, but it was preceded by that union with God by thirty years. So you are told in scripture, again, that he began his ministry when he was about thirty years of age. Yet in the Book of John which is chronologically perfect, you read all the time, "My hour has not yet come." Yet, even though a few hours later he is going to go up to Jerusalem, he turns to his brothers in the 7th chapter and says, "My hour has not yet come"...can't go now. So everything is measured as though it is a play. You can't make your entrance before your cue, and you can't depart the stage before your cue. Everything is done on cue and so he says, "My hour has not yet come."

All through the Book of John it is so beautifully done chronologically...the great play. Well, in the Book of John they said, and these are the words and it struck me forcibly, "You know our father Abraham, and you are not yet fifty years of age?" Well, if you want to add, in the month of July 1959, I was not yet by six months fifty years of age. That's how he does it, it's a play. "You know Abraham and you're not yet fifty years of age?" (Jn.8:57). Well, I was forty-nine and a half, being born in 1905 in the month of February...and July 20th, add it up, not yet fifty years of age.

It's a play. The whole story is about us. You are the Christ of scripture, but as you're told in John, "I cannot go up" when he said to his brothers, "If you can do all these things, go up to Jerusalem and demonstrate it, show your wonder-working power." He said, "My hour has not yet come." So everything is done chapter after chapter on a chronological basis: you came in on cue, you depart on cue. And without the resurrection this would be the most horrible play in the world. There would be no escape. There would be a recurrence like a squirrel in a cage. And so we are told in the Book of Ecclesiastes, "There is nothing new under the sun." It's a constant recurrence, but man has no memory so he can't remember. But comes now the fullness of time when the being who came down and died, literally died, resurrects. And he knows he's not alone, he knows from now on he is speaking for the whole vast world. Because not one child born of woman, yes, even the imbecile, that which came in without any intelligence whatsoever, or that couldn't see, couldn't hear, couldn't taste, could do nothing, yet it breathes. God was present or it couldn't breathe. God is breath. You know that every being in the world is going to be redeemed, because God is going to redeem *himself.*

So no one is going to be better than the other. Forget this so-called being better than. You go to a play tonight and the king comes through and then all of sudden the other one comes through that is the servant, but at the end of the play when the curtain comes down, who was the star? It could have been the servant. When you go to see *Hamlet*, there are kings and queens in it, but who is the star? Prince, yes, but there are other plays where the star is not like *Tobacco Road*. You want to see a play where the star was really the bum of bums…but he was the star. And so, don't judge from appearances. This one is presented to you as though she or he is most important, and they will tell you, "You know, she makes a million dollars a year." I say, "Isn't that nice, can she enjoy a nice sweetbread any more than I can? Or would she know what it's all about? Can she really enjoy a lovely meal and let that palate really be exercised, or is she on a diet to keep her weight down?" And so you go through the entire gamut.

This one is important and they will tell you why: has money. It seems to be the one standard today. Tomorrow morning's obituary in the *New York Times* or the *L. A. Times* only mentions those who have money and tell you he's a millionaire. He's dead now, the richest ghost in the graveyard, but while he was here, oh, he was important because he had money. They don't tell you how he got it…no, that's hushed. I'm not saying you shouldn't have money. If that's your dream have it. It's all here, but it's all vain anyway, it's all vain. You need it to pay rent, buy clothes, food, you need it, but Caesar is going to take it all from you. In the end, you're going to pay it out in taxes or leave it to those who will waste it. It's from shirtsleeves to shirtsleeves in just a few generations, and it goes on that way. But we still give credence to these false values in the world.

Thank you.

HOLDING TO OUR FAITH?

5/9/69

We are told to examine ourselves to see whether we are holding to our faith. "Test yourselves. Do you not realize that Jesus Christ is *in* you?" (2Cor.13:5). Faith is not complete until through the testing and until through the experiment it has become experience. When I've tested it and proven by the testing in my own experience that it works, well then, I have the faith. Now, I'm testing Christ...and Christ is *in* me. I must first find what he is, where he is, who he is, and if he is in me. I'm not called upon to test anything that is the tradition of man, something on the outside, just that which is within.

You might have heard tonight's radio broadcast that the Vatican has just rubbed out forty of its saints as non-existent. Hundreds of millions of people over the years prayed to these saints. One of them was St. Christopher. When you think of the hundreds of millions who bought the little St. Christopher's medal, and the little icon, the little figurine that they carry in front of their car, because he was the saint of the road, of the traveler. If you go into battle you wear the little thing around your neck and he would save you, because you are travelling now from home. If you took the highways, you took this little thing with you and some priest blessed it. They just discovered that he never existed. Our city of Santa Barbara was named after St. Barbara; she is now deleted as one who never existed. So, now they'll tell you that that's why we're all broke...because she did not exist...a non-existing being to whom hundreds of millions over the years prayed.

If you read scripture carefully and do not go along with the herd, you will see there is *no* intermediary between yourself and God, none whatsoever. No need for a saint, a priest, a minister, a truth teacher, or any so-called healer. You need *no* intermediary between yourself and God: "Christ *in you* is the hope of glory" (Col.1:27). So examine yourselves to see

The Return of Glory

whether you are holding to *this* faith. "Test yourselves. Do you not realize that Jesus Christ is in you?" Then we start to put it to the test. I have found from my own testing and experience that this creative power called Jesus Christ is my own wonderful human Imagination. That is Christ in every being in the world. It is *this* Christ that creates everything in the world... good, bad or indifferent (Jn.1:3).

Now tonight we will turn to the 14th chapter of the Book of John. It begins, "Let not your heart be troubled," You'll find this statement repeated in a different way over and over by the master of souls, which is Christ in you. The awakened Christ in you is Christ awake and he discovers that the bane of man's existence is fear. He said, "Fear not. Be not afraid, be not troubled." If we could abolish fear from our life, there would be no need whatsoever for any psychotherapy. None whatsoever for any tyrant; tyrants could not exist. For a tyrant to come into our world he must first scare us to death and he may do that by slaughtering hundreds of thousands, even millions. When he puts that fear into us, then he has us. If man did not care if he died now this very moment, or any friend of his died, or his family died, and he remained un-scared, there could be no tyrant in the world. Tyranny can exist only as he first scared the world. The world must be scared. That goes for all the tyranny in the world whether it was Hitler's Germany, or Stalin's Russia, or it could happen here as it happens on a small scale. And so, all over the world, if you would be a tyrant you must first scare people and make them afraid of you. There's that little morning knock on the door, and they disappear never to return, and then it spreads, and you frighten people. So he said, "Be not afraid. Be not anxious. Fear not."

So this chapter begins, "Let not your heart be troubled; believe in God, believe in me also. In my Father's house are many mansions; if it were not so, would I have told you that I go to prepare a place for you? And when I go and prepare a place for you, I will come again and take you to myself, that where I am there ye may be also" (Jn.14:1-3). Now the *place* you know and the *way* you know. Thomas said to him, "Lord, we do not know where you are going; how can we know the way?" And he answered, "I am the way, and the truth, and the life; no one comes unto me, my Father, except by me... no one comes to my Father except by me" (14:6). Then Philip said to him, "Show us the Father, and we'll be satisfied." He said, "I have been so long with you and yet you do not know me, Philip? He who has seen me has seen the Father; how can you say, 'Show us the Father?'" (14:9).

Now here, let us take it on this level first and then take it into the other level. "In my Father's house are many mansions." The word translated mansions means "to stay in a certain place or state or relation or expectancy, to abide in it as thine own." We'll take it now, there are infinite states in the world, unnumbered states, and a state is your relation to the world. You enter a state and that state could become your home, a place where you abide, or it could be simply something you pass through momentarily. But it is a state, it's a relation. What would I feel like relative to my circle of friends were I now the man that I would like to be and I hope that they as my friends would like me to be? Well then, I *assume* that I am it. Then mentally I see them as I would see them if it were true. I simply see them just as I would see them if it were true. Now, can I *abide* in that state? For the word simply means "to stay in a certain place, a certain relation, a certain expectancy." But I must abide in it.

When I leave here tonight, I expect to go home to the place that I left an hour ago...I expect to go back there. At the moment, this is more real than my home that is an image, a mental image; this is real, it's solid. But I'm going to go back tonight to that home. Well, what is a man's home?—the state to which he most constantly returns. Do I return to the state as seeing you seeing me as the man I would like to be? Or do I take it as just a passing fancy and then drop it? Do I *abide* in it? For that state to which I most constantly return constitutes my abiding place, my home, my dwelling place. So I will simply imagine that I am now the man that I would like to be and see my world as I would see it *if* it were true. I'm going into that state and preparing a place.

Now there are the two: Christ in me is speaking to the outside Neville, the rational being, and Christ in me, my own wonderful human Imagination, is saying, "I'm going to prepare a place for you." You are afraid aren't you that you can't meet certain obligations. All things are done! But now I will go and prepare the place for you. And so I close my physical eyes upon the world and let not my heart be troubled, neither let it be afraid; all things are possible to Christ and Christ is in me. He will now prepare the state and the way, for he is *the way* to the fulfillment of that state. I close my eyes against the obvious, the facts of life, and then I dare to assume I am seeing and hearing what I would see and hear if it were true. But, I must tune it fine like a radio. You turn on a radio and there are four or five stations coming through, you throw the whole thing off, and you can't stand the confusion. It must be fine tuning...fine tuning not only on the radio but on a TV.

Well, there is no set in this world comparable to you who made the set. How can that which mind creates be greater than the mind that created it? So we get amazed at the perfection of a little instrument called a radio. Take it out...no wire connects it with anything in the world, a little battery, and out of the nowhere it is coming. We stand amazed at this little thing and the mind that is amazed created it. The mind is infinitely greater than what it created. Then we came upon the visual side of it. Now we can take that out without wires to connect it. When the wire connected it, we had a peculiar feeling that

The Return of Glory

some other power is coming out there. Then we take it off the ground, carry it in our hand, there's no connection and a picture comes through and it's perfect. We don't want that, we turn another one, turn another...and at this moment in this little room everything that is being broadcast and telecast in the world is right here now. We haven't tuned in...and we have an instrument infinitely greater than anything that the mind that created the instrument could ever create. The mind that created it is infinitely greater.

So, do you know a man's voice who is a friend, one who would truly rejoice with you in your good fortune? Tune him in until you get a fine tune, and that's the voice, the only voice you want to hear, and let him tell you his thrill because of your good fortune. Actively listen until you actually hear that voice. May I tell you, if you're tuning in a very fine manner you will hear it. But, imagine that you are hearing it; and to prove that you are hearing it, you can discriminate between what you think you are hearing and another voice. Even though it's not yet audible, it is in the depth of your being audible. Well, tune it in and let it become very, very fine. Listen carefully to the sentence that you put upon that voice and you are actually hearing what you would hear if it were true. Now believe in the reality of this unseen sound, unheard sound by the outer ear. Believe in this reality. If you do, you are living by this faith.

You see, it's so easy and yet so fatally easy to make the *acceptance* of the Christian faith a substitute for living by it. Tonight, after the pope's decision to cut off forty of these so-called saints, do you know the turmoil in the Catholic world? In my family half of them are Catholic. I do hope that my Protestant brothers who did not marry the Catholic girls will be big enough not to mention it. Of course, they'll read it in tomorrow morning's paper... but not to hurt them. For they all wear these medals. I'm quite sure that not one of my sister-in-law's children who are Catholics could travel without Christopher around their necks...and now he never existed. Well, it takes the Christian spirit not to mention it. Don't mention it to her...she is hurt enough. But here, it never was and she spent a goodly sum giving each their little medals and giving each one for the front of the car and to carry around in a little bag when they travel.

I recall about twenty or thirty years ago when I first came here I went to a home of this Catholic family and my wife said to me, "Now don't be concerned. They're ardent Catholics. They don't care anything about you, because you are not saved. Because you're a Protestant you're damned. Therefore, you can enjoy yourself in the pool and have fun...and they loved my father devotedly. They were mad about him...but he too wasn't saved because he was a Protestant. We'll go there and enjoy a good dinner and a lovely time at the pool." Each, as they jumped into that pool, the

463

three boys had a St. Christopher medal. One who was three years into the priesthood when he quit and went into the Army came back without the capacity to hear. One came back without a foot. And one without an arm... he was crushed by one of our own tanks on the beaches in the Pacific. The other came back with TB. But they all had their little medals. Here they're discussing at the pool that without this medal they would have died. It would have been far better if they did...to come back maimed like that. They thought their belief in St. Christopher...now tonight, what's happened to that family? He never existed.

The only Christ that ever existed is your own wonderful human Imagination, there never was another. When in one being it awakes to discover all that was foretold in scripture is taking place in itself, then it knew who the *power* really was...and told the story. Some believed him and some did not believe. Then those who heard and believed it wrote the story, wrote it in the form of a story, because truth embodied in a tale shall enter in at lowly doors. Truth is far more acceptable if told in the form of a story. So they told it in the form of a story and we have the four stories in the gospels. If they told it as it really should have been told—one day we will be big enough to hear it without the story form to support it—that it's all within man. It was foretold and recorded in the Old Testament, but not understood by those who recorded it. The prophets who actually prophesied of the coming of Messiah searched and inquired concerning this grace that was to be *ours*, and it was revealed to them that it was not for them to know. The time had not yet come. It was for us. When the time had been fulfilled, the horrors had been fulfilled, then it began to erupt in the individual. What was buried in us before that the world was begins at a moment in time to erupt. The whole thing erupts in us. Everything said of Jesus Christ you are going to know is said of you; that the whole vast book is all about you.

Now, before it actually happens you put it to the test. If Christ is your own wonderful human Imagination, as we're taught in scripture, "All things were made by him" (Jn.1:1), and it didn't say only the good. You can imagine the unlovely things of this world and the unlovely thing imagined is going to be made, and that's Christ making it...because there is no other creator. To say that Christ makes only the good and devil makes only the evil...the devil is just as phony as Christopher. He never existed save in man's *doubt*. When one doubts the power of Christ in him that is the devil. "Unless you believe that I am he, you die in your sins" (Jn. 8:24)...unless you actually believe that I AM is the *he* that you are seeking and pray only to him by *exercising* him. That's the only power in the world.

So what would it be like? What would I hear? What would I see? What would I do if what I would like to experience in this world I am hearing, seeing and experiencing? Put him to the test. If this is true, what you tell me is true concerning my Imagination, well then, I should be able to prove it in the not distant future. All right, I call upon you to try it. Costs you nothing...you pay no intermediary between yourself and God. There's no one waiting for a five dollar bill tomorrow morning that you call up tonight and ask to help you. You don't go between anyone and God. Now test it. If you test it you'll prove it in performance and then you'll know who Christ is.

Now, "No one comes unto the Father except by me." I'm going to tell you exactly how you're going to come to the Father. It's not spelled out in scripture, it's implied, and one has to search. I didn't search until it happened to me, because I was taught, as all of my brothers and my sister were, by my mother first, then Sunday school second, and then the regular grammar school, high school, third. I was taught what the world Christian world is taught and that's not the story at all. So I'll tell you exactly how you'll go to the Father. One day you're going to find a lad, as told you in the 16th chapter of the Book of 1st Samuel, a lad chosen by God to be his Son. You're told first of all he's ruddy with beautiful eyes and very handsome, a lad in his early teens. And the day you meet him—not only the day you meet him, the very moment you meet him—you know exactly who he is; and only then do you know who you are. The very moment you encounter him you're looking right into the eyes of the Son of God, and *you* are his Father. Then and only then do you *really* know that *you* are God the Father. So, "No one comes unto the Father except by me" and "I and my Father are one." As he tells us in the 10th chapter, the 30th verse of the Book of John, "I and my Father are one." In the 14th of John, the 6th verse he said, "I am the one through whom you come to the Father." Then in the next verse he makes the statement, "I have been so long with you and yet you do not know me, Philip? He who has seen me has seen the Father. How then can you say, 'Show us the Father'?" He is one with the Father.

So union with Christ is the only way to the Father. You're one with Christ: "He who is united to the Christ is one spirit with him" (1Cor.6:17). So you are united to the Lord and he takes you the only way you'll ever go to find the Father: he brings out David. You're told in the 89th Psalm, "I have found David and he has cried unto me, 'Thou art my Father, my God and the Rock of my salvation" (89:26). A simple little word like "found" you take it on its surface. I found...all right, I found something. Well, look it up and see what it means. It means "to bring forth, to actually bring forth one that has been hiding." "He put eternity, the eternal youth, into the mind of man yet so that man cannot find out what God has done from the beginning to the end" (Ecc.3:11). In the end you bring him forth and he's been hiding there all along, because you'll never know that you are God the Father until you bring him out. When you bring him forth, he stands before you and calls you Father. Who is he? The one to whom the Lord said and then he recalls and records what the Lord said to him, "I will tell of the decree of the Lord: He said unto me, 'Thou art my son, today I have begotten thee.'" Read it in the 2nd Psalm, the 7th verse. These are the words of David, he said, I will tell of the decree of the Lord: He said unto me, 'Thou art my son, today I have begotten thee.'

Then comes that moment at the end of the journey when you bring him out from hiding. Where was he?—in your own skull. For that's the area that exploded and when everything settled and you are seated, where do you think you are seated? He is standing leaning against the side of an open door looking out on a pastoral scene, but he's leaning with his left shoulder against the side of an open door. He is looking at you and you are his Father; you are to his right: "The Lord is at my right hand…I shall not fail." You are at his right hand and the story is "The Lord is at my right hand." You are the Lord, the Lord God Almighty.

So, the story is the truest story ever told. But men, for the traditions of their fathers, have voided the Word of God and built this stupid edifice called saints. This one becomes a saint…and about 100 are up for sainthood…every little neighborhood pushes someone into this place for a saint. What man on earth can make a saint? The only saints are the redeemed and no one could ever put them up. What saints? The redeemed of humanity are the saints who form the body of the risen Lord; but everyone is *destined* for that redemption, not one will be lost. So why pick this one out and that one out and call them saints and then add to it beings that never existed? Can you see the blushes on tomorrow's faces when you meet your friends? And they'll read the morning paper. It will undoubtedly be in the morning paper. You go into an office where you know this one has been praying for years to St. Christopher and Santa Barbara. Of course, they also added to it St. Nicholas…poor old Santa Claus…he is gone now. St. Nicholas is off the list, never existed. Now you can't tell that to little children. They've built the whole thing up anyway. What the other thirty are, there are thirty nonexistent and ten that didn't quite come up to the…or fifteen…didn't quite come up to the specifications. And mortal men without vision are appointing themselves to judge saints when it hasn't a thing to do with anything on earth. You could be a drunkard in the road, you could smoke and it comes through your ears, you could be a chaser of all the men and women in the world, male or female, and yet believe in him. It hasn't a thing to do with the ethical code of man, not a thing to do with it. It's entirely up to the being having gone through the entire gamut. And when you have played *all* the parts and only the God in you who is Jesus Christ knows that you've played it all, and when you've run the race, you've finished the race, you've fought the good fight and you've kept the faith, *then* the crown of righteousness is laid up for you, and then you'll awaken from the dream of life (2Tim.4:7). Having awakened from the dream of life, you are the saint, the redeemed.

But your friends know you as the bounder…and they don't believe that such a thing could be a saint. They have the strangest concept of what this creative power is. When Browning said in his *Reverie*, "From the first, power was I knew. Try but for a closer view, love was as plain to see." Power was from the very beginning and that I knew, and yet from the very beginning *prior* to power was love, and it's just as plain to see if you would strive for a closer view. Well, in my own case, striving for it could not have revealed it to me. It had to be revealed to me by the one *in* me who *unveiled* himself as love. God in me unveiled himself as love…the Ancient of Days. And yet he wore another garment who commanded me and that garment was power, Almighty God. He wore both; he wore power and he wore love.

We will exercise power in the world to come because *we* are love. To give us power here before we are incorporated into the body of love would wreck havoc in the world. But there is love, God is love, infinite love, and God is power, almighty power; and that God of whom I speak is sitting right here in everyone that is here. You are the God Almighty and you are the God of love…but the God of love in you has not completed the journey. All parts must be played, and when he completes the journey he unveils himself to *you* his emanation; and then he embraces you into his own being, and you cease to be another, and you are one with the living God. Then you tell your story in the world to all who will listen. Some will believe it and some will disbelieve it, but you keep on telling it anyway until that moment in time when he takes off the garment for the last time and you are one with the risen Lord. The risen Lord is made up of all the redeemed of humanity, and in the end when *all* are redeemed this being that was before the world was is more powerful, more wise and more glorious. It's a constant *expansion* of power, wisdom and glory. This was the being by which he could expand the power and the glory and the wisdom.

So tonight, learn how to tune it in a fine, fine manner…you'll know. Some of you are musicians and you deal in music, and you know how it grates you—others who are not so finely tuned it would not disturb them—but even they know how disturbing it is to go to a concert and have someone sit in front of us or behind us or next to us and they're singing a little ahead to prove to you they know what's coming next. Or they're doing this, tapping, with a stick or something, beating out something for you. Insensitive! I may not be tuned that fine to what others in this audience tonight are, but I do appreciate music. So leave me alone with my being to hear what's coming. Well now, I can tell a voice and tune in on that voice until I hear it. If I hear that voice then I can put upon that voice the sentence I want that voice to utter. Now, can I believe in that? Can I actually test it by believing in it? Can I actually believe in what I'm hearing? For, faith is simply belief in the unseen reality, something that is not shared with anyone other than yourself, you heard it, so you believe in that unseen reality, and look upon it as something that is real. If you can, it will come to pass.

When you will say? Every imaginal act is like an egg, and no two eggs unless they are from the same species have the same interval of time for hatching. So the little bird comes out in three weeks and the little sheep comes out in five months, the horse in twelve, and a human baby comes out in nine months. So we are told, "The vision has its own appointed hour; it ripens, it will flower. If it be long, then wait; for it is sure, it will not be late" (Hab.2:3). Not late for *itself*. Don't expect that little lamb, because it's being brought to birth in the same creative manner as a little chicken, will come out in three weeks. It's going to take its five months and the little human baby's going to take nine months. If you know the moment...well, 280 days... can you tell when it began? It's going to be 280 days unless there is some premature birth that happens. But you don't want a premature birth...you want it to come on time. So an imaginal act is a creative act and that's when the seed or the state was fertilized. Now it's going to take its interval of time.

Now today, you assume that you are the man, the woman that you would like to be and actually assume that you are it. Let people in your mind's eye reflect the truth of your assumption. Now, be faithful to it. Persist in it, as we are told, persistency is the way to bring it to pass. But you don't persist through effort and through fear, because you lose all fear if you know it's going to happen. If the pressure is on you, and the pressures come from all sides, it doesn't matter if you know what you did is a *fact*. You wait for the birth of it. It will come!

Now a friend of mine wrote me a letter which she gave me last Monday. In it, I won't go into all the details, she found herself walking down the street holding a fish and the fish was still, like a dead fish; but she could see its pulse, therefore, it still had life. She found a little cup in which she placed water and put it in the water. Then, as happens in a dream, it jumped out and it was lost again...but she found it. This time she put it in a bigger area where you would keep fish. And then two catfish attacked it from each side, bit it, wounded it, and it fell to the bottom. It seemed to be in its last stages of, well, gasping for its life. She reached down into the very bottom of that area and pulled it up. Then she had to make a long journey, so she got a glass bowl and she didn't realize there were holes in it. A man couldn't wait, he was in a hurry, so she put it on the side. When she got to the point of getting off, she went around to collect the fish, and this time it's a little minnow. Well, what to do? She took this little fish and then all of a sudden she began to feel responsible for the fish...she felt the whole thing depended upon her for its existence. And then she began to awake and a voice said to her—and it's her own voice though it was a male voice, and she's very much a girl—she heard a male voice saying to her "O my God." Then she woke.

Now, her analysis is a true analysis what she said in her letter to me. But for the benefit of you, everything contains within itself the capacity for symbolic significance, but everything. A fish has always been one of the symbols of the savior of the world. The savior of the world is your own wonderful human Imagination. The very one that throws you into the ditch will take you out of the ditch because you had to imagine yourself into it to go into it, and you imagine yourself out of it to get out. So the savior of the world is your own wonderful human Imagination. By finding this little fish that was almost dead and then she resuscitated it, and then it was attacked by the catfish and then it almost died again, she by her own confession knows that human Imagination, which is her Creator, the savior of the world, that she has neglected it.

Living in a rational world you turn to reason first and get lost in the maze of reasoning: How will it ever work? I don't know this one or that one, I'm of this age, I'm of that age, and all these things take us out of feeding Jesus Christ...Christ being your own human Imagination, and all things are possible to Christ. If we would ignore the facts of life and simply walk in the imaginal act which is the wish fulfilled then we are *feeding* Christ. So this was only to warn her...a warning by her own being, who is Christ within her, that she had been neglecting him. Here you know what to do and here you haven't done it.

So she knows the fish symbolizes the savior within her and she has neglected to exercise this power by giving all attention to reason and rationalizing everything in the outer world, when she should ignore everything and walk in the assumption of the wish fulfilled. Though at the moment her reason denies it and her senses deny it, that assumption *if* persisted in will harden into fact. So at least she recognized that she has neglected to feed this power within her. It can't die even though it was stiff and the stiff fish is the dead fish. It still had a pulse even though it got smaller to the point of a minnow; nevertheless, it came back. Then it was attacked from both sides...reason again attacking it...telling her that she's stupid to put faith in such a thing; because, it's so easy to accept the Christian faith and use it only as a substitute for *living* by it. So, one must live by it.

I had that experience in the form of another symbol of Jesus Christ which is a pig. The pig is the symbol of him. I found myself this night in a huge display of flowers and trees and everything that grows. Then as it was closing and I was alone I realized I must get out now because it's just about to close. This was one of those lovely displays for a day. As I was about to leave, I looked down and here was this little runt of a pig, small little fella. So I picked him up and I put him on a card table, not much taller than this. I took branches from the trees, flowers, all the things to cushion him. I couldn't find any food, but I figured if he got hungry in the course of the night he could eat the leaves, eat something because this was edible, and tomorrow morning, when this place was open to display the merchandise again, whoever came first to find the pig would feed him.

As happens in a dream, suddenly the scene shifted and from the interior of this huge big display of all the things that grow I'm in a huge big supermarket. My family owns the supermarket. Here at my side is a pig. He's grown in stature but he's thin, not at all well fed, tall and thin. I realize that he's my pig. I turn to my little daughter—she was then a little girl in my dream—and I said, "Vicki, go and get me some crackers to feed my pig." She said, "Daddy, I don't have any money." I said, "But you don't need money here…we own it all…all of this belongs to us. Go and take all the crackers you want for my pig. You can bring them to me." She went over to a huge big pile of crackers that were simply laid in the form of a pyramid, and she took it from the base instead of the top and dislodged the whole pyramid. Down it came, the whole thing fell.

So, she brought me a cracker, that is, a box or two. I started breaking them up. My brother Victor came by and said, "What are you doing?" I said, "I'm getting some food for my pig." Well, he took from a paper bag what looked like a white creamy gravy, and took his hands this way and said, "This will give substance to it," putting three huge handfuls of this white gravy into what I was breaking up as food. With this, a little candle where she had taken the entire pyramid began to go up in flames. Under this pyramid was a little candle. Then I said to Vicky, "Don't touch it. Now the candle is lit and it must never go out again." Then came the words from scripture: "And his candle was lit upon my forehead and by his light I walk through darkness." "And the candle of the Lord is the spirit of man, or the spirit of man is the candle of the Lord" (Prov.20:27).

So here, the candle was lit now. I recognized that I had neglected what I had discovered, for prior to this vision I had discovered that my Imagination is God. He was the only God who ever existed. And yet, in spite of my discovery I didn't feed it. I kept applying the rational approach to life where everything had to be rational…things planned on a reasonable basis. Here I found a power that didn't need reason, that it could do anything without reason, and I neglected to feed it…I neglected to exercise it. So the symbol of that power was the pig and though he had grown in the interval he was still thin and he wasn't well fed. I determined when I saw that light, from then on I would not let that light go out or get dim…I will feed this pig. The pig only symbolizes the being in me that is Jesus Christ.

For Paul said, "I want you to refer to me hereafter as a steward of the mysteries" (1Cor.4:1). Do you know what the word steward means in scripture?—"the keeper of the sty, the keeper of the pigs," that's what it means. So when we are told to follow the work of the dishonest steward who falsified the record, the word steward means "the keeper of the pigs." So I'm supposed to keep the pig. To be a steward of the mysteries I must feed this pig so that I know what I'm talking about. So I must exercise this power morning, noon and night and not neglect it. If you give a man who knows this power a million dollars and it is well invested and he doesn't have to work, he's going to neglect the feeding of the pig because he has it all. He will say, "Now I have all the money that I need so why exercise any power? I'll sit and clip my coupons." He will completely neglect the pig and he will go right down and become a very thin pig. Then one day he will see that his neglect presented itself to him for him to see what he had done to the power within him—he hadn't exercised it.

Well, you who are musicians or you are in a business where you must apply a certain talent, the day you stop practicing it is the day lost. You stop it for a week and you know whether you be a singer or a violinist or a pianist you aren't qualified to give a concert. Not until you keep this thing tuned up day after day after day are you really prepared and qualified for a concert. So this is something that is daily practiced. But if you had a fortune, you would neglect it and you would not be qualified to teach it or tell anyone anything about it. Because what would they think if Rockefeller told them tonight to imagine it when he inherited a billion dollars? You'd say…I won't tell you what you'd say. What would you say to anyone who has inherited—and didn't earn it—a billion dollars? What does he know about Imagination? What does he know? But those who haven't an enormous inheritance and have to apply the Imagination towards the production of fruit upon his tree he knows. That one is becoming more and more qualified for the last, which is the discovery of Christ within him who is God the Father, who comes only through the Son, David, who stands before him and he knows exactly who he's looking at.

Now let us go into the Silence.

*   *   *

Now are there any questions, please?
No questions? Then thank you.

ALL THINGS POSSIBLE TO HIM WHO BELIEVES

5/12/69

We are told in scripture and this is the 9th chapter of the Book of Mark, "All things are possible to him who believes" (9:23). There is no limit set upon the power of belief. Then in the 19th chapter of the Book of Matthew we are told, "With God all things are possible" (19:26). So here we see God equated with the believer. In other words, you seated here tonight, you believe you're here, don't you, and you believe you are what you think you are? Well, that is God. All things are possible to him who believes, and with God all things are possible, so God is equated with the believer. Well, I believe I'm here, I believe I'm in this room, but can I go beyond what my reason and my senses dictate? Because *all* things are possible to him who believes must I limit my power of believing to what reason dictates and what my senses dictate? That's entirely up to me. Will I really believe what scripture teaches, that all things exist in the human Imagination? For if I believe it has to be in my Imagination. If I go beyond what reason now dictates it can only be my Imagination that could take me. Well, if all things now exist in my Imagination, can I go beyond what at the moment my reason dictates and my senses dictate?

Now, here we just had this eruption in the Christian world concerning the little icons, the little nonsenses that people have made over a thousand years and worshipped. Now let me turn you to the 115th Psalm, "Your idols are silver and gold. They have eyes, but they do not see. They have mouths, but do not speak. They have ears, but they do not hear. They have hands, but they do not feel; feet, but do not walk; and no sound is heard in their throat. Those who make them are like them, and those who trust in them are like them" (115:4).

Now you may make a million dollars a year and trust in the little icon that you place—made by human hands—in the front of your car. You might have read it in today's paper this very famous actress and she in her Rolls Royce had a little accident. The car was smashed; she was injured, but not fatally. She attributes her life to the little St. Christopher. She's just like the one who made it and sold it to her, but she doesn't know it. So you have a million dollars, so what? Don't judge anyone by their little possessions in the world. They got it by belief. Well, they do not know who to believe. They do not know that their very being is the one who created everything in this world. She believes it was her little silver or gold (she could afford gold) a little gold medal that saved her from a fatal accident. Not a thing saved her but her *belief* in that stupid little thing that is man-made for profit. She bought it not knowing who really was the one in whom one should trust.

So all things are possible to him who *believes* with God all things are possible. So here we equate God with the believer. Well now, you certainly are a believer…when you go home tonight you expect to find the place that you left, and sleep in, and expect to rise in tomorrow morning. You believe you will, so you do believe. You believe you're clothed right now. And so, this capacity to believe is God and there is no other God in the world. Your own wonderful human Imagination is God. There never was another and not in eternity can there be another.

Now, can we go outside of the restriction that we ourselves placed upon us? What restriction?—the body that I wear, the body of my senses, the body of my reason. Reason tells me that I'm here and I'm not elsewhere. Reason tells me that I have so much and no more, and can't get any more unless I make a physical effort. But I could wish I had more, couldn't I? Well, let me tell you what faith is. "Without faith it is impossible to please him" (Heb.11:6). Faith is the subjective appropriation of the objective hope. "I wish" that's a hope, that's a wish. Now, faith is the subjective *appropriation* of the objective hope: what would it feel like if it were true? Just how would it feel? Can I assume that state? That assumption is faith if I really can believe it. Can I believe in the reality of my assumption? I assume that I am what at this very moment my reason and my senses deny, but can I really believe it? For all things are possible to him who *believes*. Can I persuade myself that though my reason denies it and my senses deny it that my mere assumption makes it so?

Blake in his wonderful *Marriage of Heaven and Hell* said he had an intercourse with Isaiah and Ezekiel, and he asked them if a strong persuasion made a thing so. Isaiah replied, 'The poets"—that is the prophets, they were the poets—"the prophets believed that it did, and in ages of Imagination a firm persuasion moved mountains. But many people are not capable today of a firm persuasion." They can't believe it...yet everything in this world was once only believed. What is now proved was formerly only something that one desired and believed. The building, the clothes I wear, everything here was once only believed, and then it came into being. But you will say, "Man made an effort." I'm not denying that. Let man make an effort: you believe that you are and you name it. It may take a million men to prove it. Alright, so they'll work for you without knowing they're doing it for you. You don't have to persuade them to do it. You assume that you are what you would like to be, and then let the whole vast world, which is yourself pushed out, go to work to make possible that which you've assumed that you are, and you *will* become it...for all things are possible to him who believes.

I don't have to go out and make the physical effort. I go to the *end*... that's where I start in this world. As we are told by the late Robert Frost, "Our founding fathers did not believe in the future, they believed it in." And the most creative thing in man is to believe a thing in...to believe it in. That's what scripture teaches. He said, "Our founding fathers did not believe that the mere passage of time would produce this country as they desired it to be." They wanted some wonderful democracy, not a monarchy. But sitting down and waiting for it and hoping it would come wouldn't do it. They had to appropriate it and so they believed it in. How did they do it? Well, faith is the appropriation of the hope. How do I appropriate it?—the subjective appropriation of the objective hope. I would like to be and I name it, say in San Francisco. Well, I can't afford the time, I don't have the time, but I would like to be there. I don't have the money, I don't have this, I don't have that, so I sleep where I slept last night because I can't afford it. Yet I am told to *ignore* the present moment and dare to subjectively appropriate the objective hope. Your objective hope is San Francisco. Well, if I really appropriate it, where would I sleep this night? If I really am in San Francisco and I fell asleep, though physically here, how would I see the world? Would I not see it through the eyes of one who is sleeping in San Francisco? Would I not fall asleep and see the whole vast world as I would see it if I were there? That is the subjective appropriation of the objective hope. Now I wake tomorrow morning and I'm in Los Angeles. But all of a sudden in my sleep things happen, and I'm compelled to make the journey whether I have the money or not. I will make that journey to San Francisco where I have appropriated that subjective state, which is nothing more than my objective hope.

So here, all things are possible to him who believes and with God all things are possible. We don't question that second statement, because man believes that God created the world and God does all things; but he doesn't equate God with himself the believer. And the Bible teaches man to equate God the creator of everything with himself who has the capacity to *believe*. Belief need not be determined or restricted by the evidence of our senses. It need not rest where my reason dictates, I may go beyond it. But everything in this world tells me I had to go outside of reason. This little light tells me that sometime man had to go outside of lighting a candle and lighting a little oil lamp and lighting a little gas lamp and finally came to this. Now he goes beyond that. He will go beyond it to the point where he doesn't need any light, for *he is* the light of the world. He'll go outside of everything in this world and he is God who is the light of the world, who is infinite love, who is infinite power, who is infinite wisdom. That is what he is expanding into, these states, breaking through the barriers of reason, breaking through the barriers of his senses.

So here this night, take the challenge. The Bible challenges you: "Examine yourself, to see whether you're holding to the faith. Now test yourself and see" (2Cor.13:5). Test what? Test Jesus Christ. Well, who is Jesus Christ? Jesus Christ is the power and the wisdom of God…that's who Jesus Christ is. As told us in the 1st letter of Paul to the Corinthians, "Christ the power of God and the wisdom of God" (1:24) and I am called upon to test it. Will it work? Well, doesn't cost you anything…just try it.

Now, we are told that God, who is my own wonderful human Imagination, speaks to me and speaks to you through the medium of dream, and reveals himself in vision (Num.12:6; Job33:14-16). One night it was shown me so clearly how to do it. I found myself in New York City on 5th Avenue at the turn of the century in one enormous mansion. And here in this mansion there were two generations, but they spoke of a third. The third was invisible…that was the grandfather. They spoke of grandfather or father depending upon which generation spoke. Here, this enormous mansion…everything that money could buy is in the mansion. This is what they said—I am invisible to those who are present—and they said, "I remember what grandfather would say while standing on an empty lot, he would say, 'I remember this empty lot.' Then he would go from there and he would build in his mind's eye the most fabulous building that he wanted. Then he would say, 'I remember when this was an empty lot.'" He remembered when it was and it still is, but he would build in his mind's eye what could be done with this lot. In his mind's eye he constructed the scene.

Then the scene shifted and came back and repeated itself. "I remember when" and here's this fabulous building now, an actual building is standing there, and he said, "I remember when this was an empty lot." Scripture teaches that if the dream repeats itself it means that God will shortly bring it to pass (Gen.41:32). It was teaching me the most marvelous technique. Who was the grandfather?—I was the grandfather. I was also the second generation and the third to pass it on to other generations. This is how you do it. You stand in a barren state (you have nothing) and say, "I remember when it was barren." If you say I remember when it *was* barren, you are implying it is no longer barren. You construct in your mind's eye exactly what you want for the scene, and it comes to pass in that manner.

Out of the nowhere this thing happened within me telling me exactly how this law works. Go and tell it to everyone who will listen to you. So they have nothing in the world, but nothing, what does it matter? If all things are possible to him who *believes* and the one to whom you speak is a believer, he can believe. He may believe the most stupid thing in the world but he can believe. He can believe in that silly little thing called St. Christopher's medal…but he can believe. It's a stupid little thing. Forty of them have been demoted, but it served a purpose. Now they're coming to the point where they're trying to get over to the sheep that what they formerly believed to be outside of themselves must now come into themselves and now believe in self. That's what he's trying…to bring man into the fold. It took a long time, one thousand years believing in the nonsense. I think he's very big in this day and age to bring it now to the point where the individual who comes to church doesn't have to cover your head any more. That is not necessary and yet for all these years it was necessary. Was it ever necessary? You don't have to believe in St. Christopher saving you when you go on a journey. Was it ever necessary? Maybe it was. Maybe man in his child-like state couldn't believe in himself, and he had to believe in something created by the human hand. So he created out of silver and then he made it out of gold that was more precious, so those who could afford it bought the gold and believed in it.

Well, it produced results: *belief* produces results. But did *it* produce it? No, the believer produced it. "All things are possible to him who believes, and with God all things are possible." Now we equate God with the believer. Well, what is God's name?—his name forever and forever is *I AM*. Don't you know that you are? Certainly you do. Knowing that you are, don't you say that "I am"? Before you can say John, if your name is John, you say, "I am John." I say, "I am Neville." I may not always say "I am" but if you say, "What's your name?" I may say "Neville." But before I said Neville, I was aware of being, and then I place upon this awareness of being a name called Neville. So I didn't have to repeat the words "I am," but I was actually aware that I am. That is God and that is the believer, the only God in the world. There is no other God, none whatsoever.

So, all things exist in the human Imagination, all things, not just the good things, all things. Listen to the words, "See I am he, even I, am he, and there is no God beside me; I kill and I make alive; I wound and I heal; and there is no one who can deliver out of my hand." Read it in the 32nd chapter of the Book of Deuteronomy (32:39). Who can kill but God? We say, "I did," well, *that's* God. "I killed him," well, that's God's name. You killed him because you didn't know who you were. You hurt…that's God…because you didn't know who you were. For, "*I* kill and I make alive; I wound and I heal; and there's none that can deliver out of my hand. See now that I, even I, am he; and there is no god beside me." There is no other God. As you are seated here you have the capacity to believe and you do believe. You may this very night believe the most stupid thing in the world, but you believe it. And may I tell you, it's going to work.

The one we speak of as God is our mightier self yet our slave for purposes of his own. "He waits upon us as indifferently and as swiftly when the will in us is evil as when it is good." He conjures images of good and evil just as though they're equal. The same being that is now my mightier self is my slave; and allows me to imagine anything in this world, and he projects it upon the screen of space, and I experience it. I actually come upon it and don't even realize that in my thoughtless moment I planted the seed. Here I'm confronted with my own harvest and I don't recognize it.

So here is the being that you really are: the God of scripture is your own wonderful human Imagination. There never was another God and not in eternity will there be another God. When you say "I am" that's God. Well, can we go out this night in the deep, deep conviction that we are what we would like to be by assuming that we are? That assumption is simply the appropriation subjectively of the objective fact…and that is faith…and without faith it is impossible to please him. So I walk as though it were. When I go home tonight I will ride home with my friend by sight. We will pass certain streets, certain familiar objects and go home. Well, when I walk by faith I do not walk by sight; I walk by an invisible setup. Now how would I see the world if it were true that I am what I would like to be? I set *that* up. And that's when I walk by faith, ignoring completely everything in my world, no matter what it is, that would deny that state. Then I walk by faith and not by sight. As Paul tells us in his letter to the Romans, "Let us walk by faith and no longer by sight." So we all know what it is to walk by sight, we know our way home if we go by sight, but we're called upon to break the spell and go outside of the sight and walk by faith.

So what would it be like this night if we, as we are seated here, were *now* the embodiment of the man, the woman that we would like to be? I tell you it is possible to do everything that you want to do. For the believer—and you're a believer—and God of the universe are one...they aren't two. All things are possible to God and all things are possible to him who believes... so they are equated. So don't now divorce yourself from God. Well, who is God? Say "I am," that's he. "Unless you believe that I am (is) God, then you'll remain in your sin," (Jn. 8:24). Sin is called "missing the mark." You'll miss the mark—the mark is simply a *goal* in life, that's what the mark is. You'll miss it because you do not believe that you are already the one you would like to be. It's just as simple as that. I'm not saying that it's the easiest thing in the world, no, I would not tell you that; but I tell you, you and I must practice. If I took the greatest violin in the world and put it in the hands of a great artist, he could lift me to the nth degree of joy, in the hands of the artist. Put the same violin in hands of one who cannot play, he'd drive me insane. Lock the doors, and I would really rather die than continue to listen to what he's doing with that violin, the same violin. Out of the same violin one brings the most beautiful harmony and the other brings the most horrible discord, same violin. So, I kill and I make alive out of the same instrument. That instrument is my own wonderful human Imagination. I can make all the discords in the world until I learn to play it.

Here we are in a world I call educative darkness learning to play the instrument which is God; and God is your own wonderful human Imagination. Now reason's going to deny it, I know, so what? You'll simply assume that you have it. And you may say, I don't know anyone in this world who can give me, say, $10,000. I have no relative who is alive that could ever mention me in his will; I have no one to whom I could turn, so what? Are *all* things possible to God? Yes! Oh, you'll say yes to that right away. Well, do you believe that God is your own wonderful human Imagination? "Oh, hold it a minute, no, I can't believe that, because God is all love and I can imagine the most unlovely things in this world. I have and still do, so that couldn't be God."

Then, therefore, God is not all powerful. If you can imagine something that he cannot, because of your own stupid concept of what God is, then he can't produce a discord. He is not as good as that violin...he can't produce a discord, and if you can produce a discord you transcend him. You can hit, even by accident, a chord that is beautiful, well, you did it, it's a harmony; and then you strike a discord, but he can't strike a discord, you are greater than God because he can't hit one. Well, you can't be. Therefore God: "I kill, I make alive; I wound, I heal; and none can deliver out of my hand" (Deut.32:40). *All* things come out of me, whether they be harmonious things that give me joy or the most frightful discords in the world. No matter what I do in a discord, when I really learn the instrument I can resolve it into a dissonance. I can take any discord if I know how to play, which I do

The Return of Glory

not, but if I knew I could resolve it into a beautiful dissonance to the ear that is trained to appreciate a dissonance. So everything can be resolved, even though in our learning we make the most horrible mistakes in the world. So don't condemn yourself for anything that you have ever done or that you're doing or that you may do. Learn to play this instrument. The instrument is God himself and that instrument is your own wonderful human Imagination, and there is no other God. There is no other creative power in this world.

What is now proved in the world was once only imagined. I went in to my tailor and I said, "Let me see a few suit lengths." Louie—he's been my tailor for thirty-odd years—so he brings me out these things. He knows I like conservative colors, so he brings out simple things. I picked out this that my wardrobe needed and something else, I picked out three, and then using his Imagination he took the material and executed three. But it first had to be imagined before he could cut the cloth. He didn't take his scissors and start cutting cloth hoping something would come out...he imagined it. When I go to my dentist he looks at my mouth and sees what ought to be there instead of what is there. Well, I'm not saying it's going to grow out of my mouth. He has to first conceive what ought to be there, and then he goes about his business of doing what he feels ought to be done. But it first had to be imagined. So *everything* in this world had first to be imagined before it could be executed into what is called a fact in this world.

You can imagine and that capacity to imagine is God. That is God himself. Now we do not observe imagining as we do objects, because we are the reality that is named imagining. We don't observe it; you observe the thing created. I observe this room—this was once only imagined—but I don't really observe the creative power that is conceiving it all. I only observe the things created...but not the creator. It takes one being to reveal that creator. You'll never know him until that one being, which is set up all in scripture, appears before you and calls *you* Father. Then and then only do you really know who you are...that you are God the Creator. For here stands his only begotten son before you, and when he stands before you at that very moment, not a split second past it, then for the first time in this long, long pilgrimage you know who you are. *You* are God, God the Father. Here he stands before you, this beauty beyond the wildest dream of man. As he stands, *he* knows that you are his Father, and *you* know that you are his Father, and you also know that he is your son. So you've gone through the entire gamut, coming towards *that* point, and when you arrive at that point, you know the creative power of the world is your own wonderful human Imagination.

From whom would you keep that knowledge? No one! Not everyone will accept it; they'd rather have the little icon. I'm quite sure tonight this Italian actress, if you saw it in this morning's paper, who had this accident in her wonderful Rolls Royce, maybe a $40,000 Rolls, and she attributes her recovery from the accident to the little icon that man made with his hands. Well, she's not alone. There are a hundred million tonight who will not give up the little medal. I saw where Cardinal McIntyre confessed that he had put his seal of approval on the reverse side of this little medal by the tens of thousands. Undoubtedly, they all received his blessing when he impressed on the reverse side this approval of the cardinal. On one side is a face that never existed, St. Christopher never existed, and he approved the reality of that which is not. He is a cardinal, speaking with the authority of the prince of the church. What nonsense! Stupid, ridiculous nonsense! But he can't retract it now, it's all done.

His own cathedral is no longer a ___(??), and here this saint never existed and they go blindly on in his nonsense.

But it works, why?—because they *believe*. Well now, it's time for man to stop believing in something and start believing in the *only* reality in the world which is his own wonderful human Imagination. Stop all the *outside* icons, outside gods. "You shall make no graven image unto me" (Exod.20:4)...that's the Second Commandment. Yet they go blindly on making all these graven images outside of ourselves. "Make no graven image unto me and thou shalt have no other God beside me." Beside whom?—beside me, literally. You mean my own being? Yes. But I didn't have anything when I was born. I have no education, I have no money, no social background, not a thing, so how could I believe? Believe...but go outside now of your reason, go outside of your senses, because all things are possible to him who believes and with God all things are possible. So the believer in you...well, who is believing...I am and that's God.

Now, can you go outside of your senses and believe what your senses deny? Try it! Put it to the test...put it to the extreme test. And then if it proves itself in performance, what does it matter what the world thinks? If I have something to testify to what I have done, does it matter what anyone thinks? Here I have proved by my own testing that this thing works. Well then, I have found him. Having found him I will share him now with another. So I will go to Philip and I tell Philip. Well, who is Philip?—the "lover of horses." Well, what is the horse?—the mind. He loves how the mind functions. So I will go to Philip and I will tell him. So he goes and he tells Philip, and Philip wonders, "Who did you find?" "I found him of whom Moses in the law and the prophets spoke" (Lk.24:27). They spoke of him. Who is he? He is called the Messiah. Where is he? "I will take you to him" and then they take him. But they can't find a man. I will tell you who he is. I'll take you this night to see who the Messiah is. I have found him of whom Moses in the law and the prophets wrote: Jesus Christ, the Messiah that was promised. Well, take me to him...I'll take you to him: now say "I am". "I am." That's he. "Oh, you're silly, Neville." No, I'm telling you the truth... that's he. Say "I am" again. "I am." Now say, "I am secure, I am wealthy, I am free." "But I'm not!" I'm not saying what you are now based upon your senses, I'm asking you to repeat what I said. "I am free, that I am secure, that I am known." All that you would like to be make it now a subjective appropriation of the objective hope.

Now, reason is going to try to tear from you what you have just done, but I ask you to play the little game with me. Go through the door and walk as though it were true. Sleep this night as though it were true. And if you do this night, you couldn't go to sleep seeing the world as you saw it last night; you have to see it differently. If this day, factually, someone gave you a check for $20,000 and you deposited it to your account, you would not sleep tonight as you slept last night, would you? You couldn't; you have $20,000 that you didn't have last night. Well now, tonight without waiting for it to be fact, go to bed as though it were true, just as though it were true. Put him to the extreme test: if all things are possible to God and if all things are possible to him who believes, and you can believe, can you believe that? Try to believe it! I'm not saying you'll succeed the first night, because you've been so trained to accept only what reason dictates, only what your senses dictate that you may find it difficult, almost impossible, to believe what really you could believe.

This morning coming through from the deepest, wonderful experience, here was a series like shadowy beings. The first one was blind and could see nothing in the world. And I'm the wearer of all these things. The second one could see what the first one couldn't; the third could see what the second one couldn't; the fourth one could see and hear and do what the third one couldn't. I woke actually saying to my friend, Bob Crutcher, "Why, Bob, I have just seen a series of events that with your talent to write...this is not for TV, this is for movies...you could write this story with your talent. And I'm telling you exactly what you'll get for it, you'll get $300,000." I woke actually thinking of my friend Bob with his talent to write and with my vision, put my vision—don't give me a penny of it, I don't want one nickel for it—I'm telling a series of them—as you put it on, you see what it is allowing you to see. When an actor plays a part, he must feel to some extent the part that he's playing, and try to identify himself with the character that he depicts. Well now, all these were characters...all these were simply shadows, and I, the perceiving one, took one after the other, and I was limited by the state that I perceived. As I took it on I couldn't see; the third one, I went beyond this one; the fourth, beyond that; the fifth, beyond...a series of them.

Bob has the talent. And I heard someone say, "Well, $300,000 for a movie for that" and I thought of only one person, my friend Bob. I woke screaming, "Bob Crutcher you've got to do it." Well, I mean, that is something that really is part of our world. Here is my wonderful friend a writer, he has all the ideas, I know he has them, but this is something that came to me from the depths. Here's a series, something not done by any man: that man is simply restricted by what he wears. To play a part I must feel the part, and then to the best of my ability I must actually feel myself to be the character that I'm depicting. Well now, if the thing is blind, I'm going to feel myself all over the world and feel things. Then all of a sudden I put on another garment and it isn't blind. Well, I can see so I don't need the feeling. Then I put on another garment...and all of these were a series of garments.

As I came from the depths of my being, this interrupted my depth just for a moment, because I was coming back from a tremendous depth of my being where something entirely different takes place...nothing in this world...something outside completely. But I was interrupted by this series, and here I was thinking only of my friend Bob Crutcher. I was just about to tell him when I woke that the series is for a picture. It would be a fantastic picture, never mind if they will believe it or not. There are a few in the audience who will catch it, who will see he's only playing a certain part. Now the part need not be something that was given you at birth, you could pick it up at any point in time. You could *now* play the part of a wealthy man when it was not given you twenty-four hours ago, and you never had it before, and suddenly it's a part. It's only a part and you play it. Well, what would you see if it were true? And you play that part just as though it were true.

This is scripture. All that I'm telling you tonight is from the Bible. "I kill and I make alive; I wound and I heal; and there's none that can deliver out of my hand. I, even I, am he...and there is no God beside me." Read it in the Book of Deuteronomy, the 32nd chapter. There is no other God, no other savior. "I am the Lord your God, the Holy One of Israel; and besides me there is no savior," the 43rd of Isaiah (43:11). But man will not believe it, he thinks that's crazy. But these are the words of God revealed through his prophets in the Old Testament. The New is the fulfillment of the Old, and he comes in and he fulfills it all. He tells you, "Whatever you desire, believe you *have received* it, and you will" (Mark11:24). That's the fulfillment. That's how easily you apply it...for the assumption though false and denied by your senses if persisted in will harden into fact. I am telling you, you are

God; there never was another God and the being in you is God. You and I are one because there's only one God. There aren't two Gods, there's only one. So in the end you will know that you and I are one. You will know it by this wonderful Son.

But I'll tell you the next time of another revelation: not the Son revealing the Father, but the Father revealing the Son.

Now let us go into the Silence.

*   *   *

Q: ___(??). Is that a reasonable interpretation?
A: It is a very reasonable interpretation. The word Jonah does mean "dove" in Hebrew, but Jonah in the story of Jonah—a very short book—was the one who taught *repentance*. So he came to teach repentance and men would not repent. Repentance does not mean feeling remorseful, it doesn't mean feeling regretful. It's simply "a radical change of thinking." That's all the word repentance really means. The word is "metanoia" in Greek, and the word defined in the Concordance is "a radical change of thought." So I see you and I don't like the way I see you, well, *I* must, myself, not you, I must change my thought relative to you. I must change it to the point where I'm self-persuaded that this change is fact, and not what I formerly saw. That is repentance.

So when he went to Nineveh, the Nineveh-ites believed him and they repented, and so God did not destroy Nineveh. So this generation refuses to repent...they will not change their attitude toward things. They believe what their senses dictate and that's all there is to it. But it does also mean in the ultimate sense "the dove." The *sign* that you are going to get at the very end will be the dove. So Jonah does mean "dove" in Hebrew. And so when the dove descends upon you, it's the physical symbol, the visible symbol of the Holy Spirit. So you're perfectly right... that is the ultimate. But he did teach repentance, and Nineveh repented, and saved itself from destruction, while the evil generation refused to believe what their reason would not dictate.

Thank you.

THE LORD'S ANOINTED

5/16/69

___(??) of Toynbee's latest work and he said that the Judean-Christian faith leaves him cold. Now here in the eyes of the world he is a brilliant mind. At the age of three he could read Greek and Latin, and all these tongues were to him as easy as his own mother's tongue which was English. But he was completely untouched, and is today at the age of eighty-odd, by the Jewish-Christian faith because he had no vision. He thinks he can arrive at some great pattern for man, and force them into a certain pattern based upon his rational mind and his knowledge, so he claims, of history.

Now here, you read in the Book of Revelation, "Jesus Christ the faithful witness, the first-born from the dead" (1:5). Now, you'll think that is one man, Jesus Christ, for the whole world thinks of Jesus Christ as a unique being that came into the world 2,000 years ago. The word Jesus Christ *really* means—Jesus is the same as Jehovah—and Jesus means "the Lord." Christ is the same as Messiah and the word means "the Anointed." So really, the word Jesus Christ is "The Lord's Anointed" (Jn.1:41). Not one man...the Lord *and* his Anointed. Well now, who is his Anointed? We are told, "The sum of thy word is truth"...the sum of them. "Thy word is truth," do not alter it leave it just as it is.

Now, Jesus comes to fulfill scripture and that's the Lord himself coming to fulfill scripture. This Lord is *your* own wonderful human Imagination. That's the only Jesus in scripture and that's the only God. When Crabbe Robinson said to Blake "What do you think of Jesus?" he said, "Jesus is the only God," and then he hastened to add, "And so am I and so are you." Well, man will not believe that. Man will not accept the fact that his own wonderful Imagination is God. He sees this little tiny thing here suffering and he can't conceive that the God who created the universe and sustains it is one with his own wonderful human Imagination. But Blake meant it and meant it literally, that your own wonderful human Imagination is God. So he said, "Jesus is the only God, but so am I and so are you." Then unfortunately they went in to dinner and there was no further discussion between Robinson and Blake.

Now, he tells us, "Thank you that you hid these things from the wise and the understanding and revealed them to babes" (Mat.11:25). Well, the word babes does not mean a little child, whether infant or a child; it means "the unlearned." That is the child of scripture, the unlearned. But God would choose the unlearned to confound the wise, because he would reveal himself to the unlearned. So, "You've hidden these things from the wise and the understanding and you revealed it to babes, for such was thy gracious will." Then he adds, "And no one knows who the Son is except the Father, and no one knows who the Father is except the Son" (Mat.11:27). Now, "Take my yoke upon you, and learn from me" (11:29). "Take my yoke" is an expression in Hebrew for learning the scriptures. Take my understanding of the scriptures based upon my own personal experience and not upon the traditions of men. Take it. I'll tell you who they are. Is man willing to accept that which is in conflict with the traditions of men?

Here we just saw ninety saints defrocked...not only defrocked they were non-existent. After making hundreds of millions out of the poor people selling them little medallions and selling all these little things, now they come out and say they did not exist, just one grand myth. Who started it?—the church, for monetary reasons and made fortunes. But today the pressure is on to stop this nonsense and they brought ninety down to zero. Having sold hundreds of millions of theses little medallions to protect someone from what when there is no intermediary between yourself and God? For, you are God...your own wonderful human Imagination that's God. Say "I am," that's he.

Now, let us see who this Christ is..."Jesus Christ the faithful witness, the first-born from the dead." That's *not* Jesus; that is *Christ* who is the first born. Christ means "the Anointed." Who is the Anointed? He said, "I have come only to fulfill scripture." So I go back to the Old Testament, for he can only fulfill the Old Testament, there was no New. So he turns to the Old and in the 1st Book of Samuel, the 16th chapter, "Rise and anoint him; for this is he" (16:12) and Samuel took the holy oil and anointed *David*... that was the Anointed. In the 89th Psalm, "With my holy oil I have anointed him" (89:20). He's speaking now to David: "I have found David and David has cried unto me, 'Thou art my Father, my God, and the Rock of my salvation'...I will make him the first born" (89:26). Now the words cannot be broken. He is the Christ of scripture and he is the Anointed. The Jesus of scripture is the I AM, which is God himself. It is God who comes into the world wearing these garments that you now wear...I mean your blood and flesh. This flesh and blood being that you are, that is the garment that he wears. You say "I am," that's he. But you will play all the parts.

Now, what parts does he play?—all of them. In what sense? Listen to the words carefully, "And I, when I am lifted up from the earth, I will draw *all* men unto me" (Jn.12:32). What earth? He said, "He made a garment for man and the garment was made out of the earth, out of the dust"...this garment (Gen.2:7). And when I am lifted up from this garment of flesh and blood I will draw all men unto me. What men? The word "men" has been added to give sense to the sentence; it isn't in the script. But, "I will draw *all* to me." Now, "God only acts and is in existing beings or men" (Blake). He acts in me. Well, who is he?—my Imagination, that's God. He only acts in us.

When I've played *all* the parts, but every one, then the sum of all the parts personified is his Anointed David. The *sum* of all the parts that man is going to play—because God is man and man is God—the sum of all the parts personified is the eternal youth David, the Anointed, the Christos, the Messiah. No one will stop playing these parts until he plays all... because you cannot resurrect David. The promise is I will not leave you in the pit: "Thou wouldst not leave me in the desolate pit." And then he cries, "Thou hast redeemed me, O Lord, faithful God" (Ps.31:5). Well, the God that redeems David is your own wonderful human Imagination. You are the one who wears the garment and buried in you is this mighty power, your son. When you have played all the parts, suddenly there is an eruption within you and standing before you is *David*. This is sacred history, this is not secular history. This thing goes on forever and forever.

So here, the being that you really are is God. There never was another God and there never will be another God. For God is one: "Hear, O Israel: The Lord our God the Lord is one" (Deut.6:4)...not two. So, say "I am," you can't divide it. Well, can't you say "I am"? I say, "I am." Now, how can you say "I am" and I say "I am" and we say "I am," and say it isn't divided? The one fell into division and we are now the scattered, all scattered. We are the Elohim. It's a plural word, but it takes all unified to form the one. So the one falls into division, and after playing all the parts, it then is resurrected into unity; and that unity is simply God, I AM. So at the end of the journey I don't care what part you're now playing, you have played many. This may be your last part, I do not know. But you will not leave this world of death where God became crucified. The crucifixion is over; the death is over; the burial is over; into hell is over. For *this* is hell and we rise from it. So do not say you are man going to hell, or when did he go into hell...he *is in* hell.

This world is hell. Ask the question, how does he rise form it? He rises out of it only by playing all the parts, for that was his promise to himself in the beginning. You and I were together as brothers, and together as brothers we formed the one that is called the Lord, for this is the word Elohim. Whether we translate it as God, we translate also the word "I am" as the Lord. Can't find any better way to translate it…"I am" that's the Lord.

Now, who is the Father of David? You're told in scripture it's I AM. For the Father's name is Jesse and Jesse is "any form of the verb 'to be,'" which is "I am." So, "I have found in David the son of Jesse a man after my own heart, who will do all my will" (Acts 13:22). So, when you know this you can't condemn any being in this world for what he has done and he is doing and what he may do. For when it all comes to the end you played them all anyway…you played every part. If you haven't played it you could not conjure David. David comes at the end. He was destined before the foundation of the world, but made manifest in the end of the time. Only at the very end of the play do you see David. No one will find him…and in finding him you know who the Father is because David stands before you and he calls you Father. It's not just *a* David, it's *the* David of biblical fame. Then you realize that it's not secular, it's sacred. The whole story as told in the Bible is sacred history, it is not secular history. And a David may or may not have lived as a king on earth, that means nothing; but *the* David spoken of in scripture is sacred history. When he stands before you he calls you Father, and you know without uncertainty the relationship between yourself and the one that you observe: here is your son. Before you started the drama this was part of the plot, but you will not encounter him until the end.

So the story is not that the Son reveals the Father, which he does, rather the Father reveals the Son. So, where is the Son? As you are told in the last book of the Old Testament, "A son honors his father. If then I am a father, where is my honor, where is my son?" (Mal. 1:6). And the Old Testament closed upon the question mark, "Where is my son?" For if it takes a son to honor his father and I am a father, where is my son? Then you wait for the unnumbered years to fill up the time, and then starts the New, which is only the fulfillment of the Old. It's one book. There could be no New without the Old and the New is only the fulfillment of the Old Testament. The Old is not secular history; the Old is sacred history. Then man begins to unfold within himself, and the whole drama as told us in the Old makes sense when it begins to unfold within man.

Here is a man born in this century in the year 1905. What relationship have I to any character in scripture? If you could trace it back as someone tried to trace someone back, and say you go all the way back to Solomon, what Solomon? You go all the way back to David, what David? Go back to

Abraham, what Abraham? These are *eternal states* of the mind; they are not physical flesh and blood beings. These are eternal state of the mind through which man passes. And when man passes, God passes, because God became man that man may become God. So here, the journey is from crucifixion, which is a *self*-imposed limitation. He said, "No one takes away my life, I lay I down myself" (Jn.10:18), yet we condemn a race of people for taking the life of one who didn't live any more than St. Christopher lived. That is not the Christ of scripture; that is not the Jesus of scripture. The Jesus of Scripture is your own wonderful human Imagination…that's Jesus, and there never was another Jesus.

So, *in* man Christ unfolds. Who is Christ?—David, he is the Anointed. When God plays all the parts then the sum of the parts becomes personified and it stands before him and he looks into the face of one that he knew before that the world was. He knew the end result, and David is the end result of the journey through death. This is the great mystery of the seed falling into the ground, as we are told, "Except a seed falls into the earth and *dies,* it remains alone; but if it dies, it bears much fruit" (Jn.12:24). So, God, by restricting himself to the limitations of man, which is the limit of contraction, the limit of opacity then he goes through this world of death, this world of generation. And having played *all* the parts, condemning and doing all the things that we do, in the very end when you arrive at the end of the journey then there is an explosion in him. As you are told, "He was buried in Zion." Well, Zion is your own wonderful skull, that's Zion. That is the stronghold that David took, and he took it by going up the water shaft, building it into a *spiral*. So he could only build it and take it by moving in a spiral form up into the skull. That's where he is buried.

One night there's an explosion within your skull, and when the whole thing settles, here you look out…you, the observer who is God. Well, who is observing?—I am. Well, what's God's name?—I AM (Exod.3:14). That's his name forever and forever. Well, who is observing it?—I am. What are you observing?—my son. And what's his name?—David. Here is my beloved in whom I am well pleased, here is my Anointed. Scripture then is fulfilled in me, for "I have come only to fulfill scripture," not to do anything in the world. To be rich, all right, if you want to be rich; to be poor, all right, if you want to be poor…because, you have played all the parts anyway. But you aren't *destined* to be rich or to be poor. The predestination of scripture is sacred. You aren't destined to be rich or poor, you can be either.

And now, by taking this wonderful power that you really are, which is your own wonderful human Imagination, and dare to assume that you are what at the moment your reason denies, your senses deny…if you walk in the assumption that you are what they deny—knowing who is walking in that assumption, and all things are possible to God—you will externalize it in your world. How? It doesn't really matter. The whole vast world must play the part necessary to aid the birth of that assumption. That assumption may be false and is false at the moment of the assumption, but it doesn't matter. If you persist in the assumption, it will harden into fact. Because who is assuming?—God, when *you* assume. And so, I dare to assume that I am, and I name it, then I dare to walk in that assumption as though it were true. If I am faithful to the assumption of seeing the world as I would see it were it true, it has to crystallize and become an objective fact. But, all these objective facts are only shadows and they fade anyway.

So the *real* predestination spoken of in scripture is *not* secular; it is sacred. That was before that the world was, and then God came down into the world of death and assumed these garments of flesh and blood and is playing all the parts. I speak from experience. So when I say from scripture "Take my yoke upon you and learn from me," I ask you to believe my own experiences. For, you are told, "And I, if I be lifted up from the earth, I will draw all men unto me." Well, I have been lifted up from the earth and in being lifted up from this body in a spiral form to find myself clothed in a body of fire and air—no need of the sun, the moon, the stars, for I am the light of the world. I had no need of any external light. There I was lifted, literally, off the earth. Not only out of this garment, but I didn't stand upon the earth, I glided above it. And I came upon a scene of imperfection, human imperfection—the blind, the lame, the halt, the withered. They were all waiting for me, all seated, and as I glided by, each was made perfect because I was perfect. Then scripture comes to mind, "Be ye perfect as your Father in heaven is perfect." Well, who wore that part?—the Father wore it. Well, who is the Father?—I am. And when I came to the very end and each was made perfect then this heavenly chorus sang out, "It is finished!"...the last cry on the cross.

This is the cross. There is no other cross that God ever wore. Man in his mistaken stupid concepts of scripture has nailed men to a wooden cross. But God is not nailed to a wooden cross; he is nailed to this garment of flesh. This is the cross, the only cross. When I came to the end they cried out "It is finished," and I once more congealed into this little garment, the cross, to tell the story to all who would listen. Some will believe it and some disbelieve it, but tell it anyway to encourage those who may be persuaded to modify their fixed concepts and inheritance. You are born into a certain environment and so they inherited their religion. And they think now this is the only thing and they find it difficult to modify it, because their fathers and their forefathers taught them that. But I tell you, the whole thing is within us, the whole story of the Bible is contained within man and must unfold within man. When it comes to the end of the journey, there are only two—the Father and his Son. The Father you'll discover when you come to the end to be yourself. You are God the Father and the son is David as told in scripture. "This is my son" in the 2nd Psalm: "I will tell of the decree of the Lord, 'Thou art my son, today I have begotten thee'" (2:7).

Now, take a small passage from the 4th chapter of the Book of Acts. The Book of Acts was written by the same one who wrote the gospel of Luke, the same author. Whoever he was no one knows…they're all anonymous anyway. Matthew, Mark, Luke and John no one knows who they were. These are simply titles, but we do not know who they are. We do know that the Book of Luke was written by the same author who wrote the Book of Acts. Now here, our so-called wise men, the great scholars, cannot bring themselves to believe what is in the script. Let me quote it from the 4th chapter of the Book of Acts: "Thou Lord, who by the mouth of thy servant *David* have said, 'Why do the nations rage and why do the people imagine vain things…against the Lord and his Anointed?'" (4:25-27). Now, the word translated "servant" means in Greek—and every time it appears outside of these little peculiar points where the scholars cannot bring themselves to believe it is actually what it's supposed to be—it is translated "son or child." If it is found before the word Jesus, they'll call it "son." If it is found before the word "David" they call it "servant." It *isn't* so at all. For in the same 2nd Psalm—this is now the first and second verses—in the seventh verse, "I will tell of the decree of the Lord"…the same being speaking…"He has said unto me, 'Thou art my son, today I have begotten thee'"…and the word of God cannot be broken.

So we are told, "Do not add to it; do not take from it," leave it, and one day you will fulfill it, for you have come into the world only to fulfill scripture…that's all that you came to do. So your accomplishments in the world will all vanish, vanish like smoke as told in scripture: "And the heavens will vanish like smoke, and the earth will wear out like a garment, and all within it likewise; but thy salvation will be forever and thy redemption will have no end" (Is. 51:6). But everything else will vanish. Men today making fortunes, all right, let them make fortunes, and they want to leave behind them some library. Our new President who has just gone into the White House he's now beginning to build a library as a monument to himself. He hasn't made any dent so far upon our world, but right now he's making some preparation to leave a little footprint on the sands of time, and the little tide will come in and wipe the whole thing out as though it never existed. Bless him, may he have his desire fulfilled with a lovely library and all these things.

But it's such nonsense when the only purpose to life is to fulfill scripture. He said, "I have come to fulfill scripture" and then taking the Bible he explained to those beginning with Moses and the law and the prophets and the Psalms, all the things concerning himself (Lk.24:27). For he said, "In the volume of the book it is all about me" (Ps.40:7). Well, here is a simple man telling men born as he was born that the book is all about him. But it's not the garment that he's wearing talking, it's the being *within* who experienced scripture, who understands scripture. And then he interprets it based upon his own experience, and now invites the world "to take my yoke upon you and learn form me." Don't take the traditional concept handed down year after year, for it is false. And so, what Christian this night hearing the word Jesus Christ would not think of a unique single being who was born in some unusual manner 2,000 years ago? And it isn't so at all. Yes, there is an unusual experience within the *individual*, but it's going to happen in everyone. And it is a birth. But it's not the birth from the womb of a woman called Mary or any other name; it's from the womb of one's skull. You come out of your own skull and all the imagery as described in Matthew and Luke surrounds you. Then you know it is all about you: "In the volume of the book it is all about me." You didn't realize it until it happened.

But it all begins with your resurrection. You awaken within your skull to discover yourself entombed as though…well, it's sealed. The tomb is sealed, there is no opening. Then, having awakened completely within your skull, in a way you were never awake before, you come out. As you emerge from your skull, you come out in the same manner that a little child comes out of the womb of a woman, and then surrounding you is all the imagery as told in Matthew and Luke concerning the birth of Jesus. And the word Jesus means "Jehovah". It's the birth of God. In other words, it's a *higher* expansion of himself. There's only God in the world, there's nothing but God. And so, God is ever expanding. He makes a limit of contraction, but there's no limit to expansion; a limit to opacity, but no limit to translucency. He takes upon himself the limit which is death, this world of death. This is hell! Then having gone through it, he breaks the bond, and he comes out of it. But in coming out of it having gone through it, he is expanded *beyond* what he was prior to his descent into hell.

You say, well then, God is not absolute. If God were absolute, there would be no joy, there would be no son, and you couldn't expand. How could you ever expand if you were completely beyond expansion? And that sameness would be hell beyond measure. But the joy of *constant* expansion… truth is an ever increasing illumination. You can't pigeon hole it and say this is forever, it goes on forever. Having played the parts and having brought *all* out and united all within himself once more, he is greater by reason of the experience. Well, then he conceives another play, a far greater and more difficult play, and takes upon himself the limitation of it all; then he bursts the bonds of it and comes out resurrecting once more. For the resurrection is God's mightiest act.

So here, you are God. God became you. I don't mean this little tiny thing called Neville is God, no, the being that is speaking to you is. The being that had the experience is. This is still subject to all the pains of mortality. It can this night get a headache, this night it can drink too much and go to sleep with a big head and wake tomorrow with a bigger one. All those things it can do haven't a thing to do with the being that I am. If you're going to judge me by what I do physically, you'll never know the being that I am. You'll never know the being who anyone is, for the being of every being who is playing the part is God. "God only acts and is in existing beings or men." And so he is acting in me as my wonderful human Imagination...that's God. There never was another God and there never will be another.

Now you can put this to the test in this world. But take from me what I have experienced: take my yoke upon you and learn from me. I tell you, you are here for one purpose...to fulfill scripture. And the part you are now playing is adding up towards the whole. When you have played *all* the parts, the sum of the parts will confront you as a single being, and that single being is the eternal youth David. For you are a father and if you are a father there must be a son bearing witness to your fatherhood. So there must be the result of the experience, and David is the result, the son bearing witness to the experience that you as father have had. And this whole thing unfolds within you.

Now, on this practical level you can put it to the test. You mean, my Imagination really is God and all things are possible to him? Yes. How do I go about testing it? Well, what do you want? That's the first question. What do you want...and you name it. Don't suggest to anyone what they should want, let them name it. If it comes within your code of decency, well then, do it. If you said to me I want this one to die, then go to someone else. You'll find others who will pray with you, but don't come to me. I want this one to break his neck, this one to break his foot, well, don't come to me. It doesn't come within my code of ethics. If he said I want to be rich that's all right, I want to be known that's all right. Things that I feel would *not* hurt anyone in you becoming it; but if you're going to hurt someone in order to fulfill your desire, don't come to me. But I can't deny a principle and I'll tell you the principle and leave you to your choice and its risks. So you may want to hurt someone...I can't deny that you could apply it towards that end. But in the end you will discover one day it wasn't another that you hurt, it was yourself, because ultimately there is *no* other...there's only God and one God is playing all the parts. So if you want to hurt someone, in the end you'll discover you're really hurting yourself. As we're told, "And Job prayed for his friends and his *own* captivity was lifted" (Job 42:10). When he forgot himself in his love for friends and sincerely wanted them to succeed, and then entered into a state of empathy for them, his own captivity was lifted. He became twice as rich, twice as great as he was prior to the horrors that he experienced.

So, what must I do? Well then, you name it. As you name it you give me something that I can construct. When I hear what you want and it's something that I could really want for myself then we have a goal. I will say, well now, you name it and I know what you want and I will assume that you have it. I will try to persuade myself to the best of my ability that you have told me that you have it, and I will believe in the reality of this imaginal act. This imaginal act of mine is God in action, for God is my Imagination and I am imagining. So if I imagine that you are what you would like to be, that is God in action. That's God's word and his word cannot return unto him void, it must accomplish that for which he sent it, and actually bear the fruit so that he knows his word is a fertile word. Well, if my Imagination is God, my imaginal acts are God in action. Look into the room...do you see anything in this room or in the whole vast world that wasn't first imagined? The clothes you wear, the chairs on which you are seated...everything in this world was once only imagined and then it became fact...the pictures on the wall. All of that is out of man's Imagination.

All right, so he first imagined it. My tailor took a piece of cloth that had no shape, and when he discovered what I wanted as to color, he said, "Do you want single-breasted, double-breasted? Single breasted, all right. Now leave it to me, Neville, I know more about making a suit than you do. So don't tell me how you want it pinched here or there...let me make a suit." And then he used his Imagination to execute a suit. It had to be first imagined before he even started cutting the cloth, and then he produced what was once only imagined.

This building was once only imagined and then it became fact. You can't stop a man from imagining. So let no one tell you that one man can in any way enslave the world, because he can't stop men from imagining. He may have the joy for a few years of being the tyrant of tyrants like a Hitler, like a Stalin, they were the tyrants, but he can only frighten them into accepting him as their leader. The minute they stopped being afraid of him, he was afraid. He could only be a tyrant as long as he can scare people. The minute that people are not afraid, you can't scare them and then you cannot enslave them.

Now, "Be not afraid," all through scripture, "Let not your heart be troubled" (Jn.14:1). Fear not. So the minute you become afraid they've got you. If I can sell a tooth paste tomorrow on a fear campaign, I've got you. You'll buy it even though your teeth are falling out and keep on buying it and buying it because I can scare you into buying it. Well, that's the story of the world...scare them and you've got them. Whether it be a food product or some little cosmetic or something else, just scare them to death and you've got them. Our entire economy is based upon fear, the war scare and the peace scare. Can you imagine that, having a peace scare? Well, they have a peace scare and the market goes way down because it's a peace scare. But you must scare them, you must frighten them. Well, I tell you, fear not! If you can lose all fear...that it doesn't really matter if they shoot you, it doesn't really matter if they cut your head off, what they do, if you can lose all fear.

Then in our own wonderful Imagination imagine what you would like in this world in spite of what *seems* to be, and if you persist in that state, you will rock the whole vast world to bring it to pass. If it took unnumbered tens of thousands to play the part necessary to take your imaginal act and aid in its birth, they will play it without knowing that they're playing that part. You don't have to go out and appeal to them, you simply remain faithful to your imaginal act and everyone in this world who can aid its birth will come to that assistance of that imaginal act. And they're complete strangers to you. You don't need to know who they are...it could be men who speak a different tongue. But they will bring to birth exactly what you have imagined if you *persist* in the imaginal act, because it's God in action. But if you quit then you don't know who God is. As you're told in scripture, "My word that goes forth from my mouth shall not return unto me void, but it must prosper in the thing for which I sent it" (Is.55:11). It must! It must return to me bringing the fruit of that which I intended when I sent it out. Well, *that* word is your imaginal act.

So believe me, the Jesus of scripture is the Jehovah of the Old Testament, and the Jehovah of the Old and the Jesus of the New is your own wonderful human Imagination. That's God. And the Christ of the New is the Messiah of the Old, and the word simply means the Anointed, and the Anointed is David. David stands before you...and the strangest thing about it is when you look at him *memory* returns. It's all the returning of memory. So here you are in this century and here is someone who is supposed to have lived a thousand B.C. All of a sudden, you without any change of identity are looking at your own son. It's the return of memory, as though you suffered from a long amnesia. Here he stands before you and you know he is your son and he knows you are his father. So when you see him it simply means you have finished the game. And you're like Paul now, you can say, "I have fought the good fight"—for it is a fight—"and I have finished the race and I have kept the faith. Now there's laid up for me the crown of righteousness" (2Tim.4:7). Well, what is the crown of righteousness? He said, "The son is the honor of a father." Now I've found my son and he is my crown, he is my honor. I can't return to a more exalted state than that which I left *unless* I take with me the result of my journey, and the result of this journey is David. So you take back the sum total of all the experiences of man. So take all the experiences of men and *fuse* it into one grand whole, and personify that whole, and you get David.

Then the world may not believe it. What does it matter? Leave them just as they are; bless them, knowing that each and every one must go through the identical parts. So in the end he forgives all the parts. You can't condemn a part when you yourself as the author wrote it. You wrote the play and then finding no one to play it you came down, diversified, and played all the parts. Then you resurrected into unity and return with the result of having played all the parts.

Now let us go into the Silence.

* * *

Now there is one point I would like to make tonight based upon a letter that a friend of mine wrote me. You'll find it a fascinating letter based upon a few dreams of hers. I have told you from my own experiences that there is no death, that you find yourself when men call you dead in a world that is terrestrial just like this. And you are solid just as you are now, young, not a babe, twenty years of age, but in a world just like this, making a similar struggle and afraid of death as you're afraid of death here. But as far as you are concerned you are alive, as alive as you are here and just as solid as you are here. She said in her letter to me, "I found myself in a dream talking to a friend that I knew well, his name is Jack. I said to Jack, 'Well Jack, I thought you died.' He said, 'No, it was my wife who died.'" Then in another dream soon after she found herself in the world of dream talking to one she knew in high school, one of her flames, and they were discussing in the same lovely old way, reminiscing, and it seemed—she capitalized the whole thing—SO NATURAL, SO NORMAL. And yet I knew I hadn't seen him since 1940. But many years ago my mother wrote me that he had died."

Now, when your loved ones depart this world to you they're dead and to them you're dead. You can't touch them so they're dead, can't hear them, can't see them, so you saw the body cremated, a little dust, and so as far as you're concerned they're dead. As far as they're concerned you're dead, because they know they're alive, and they can't see you, can't hear you, they can't touch you, and so you're dead. And this goes on in this world of death—this is the world of death, it's called hell in scripture—until you have the experience of which I spoke tonight, until you meet David. When you meet David you are of the resurrected, and you enter a new age, an entirely different age. Don't ask me to describe it, because there are no images on earth to describe *that*. It's a new age, an entirely new world, and you are the resurrected, one of those who go to make up the body of the Lord; for you *are* the Lord.

Now, are there any questions, please?

Q: Can this resurrection or liberation be experienced in this physical realm?
A: It *must* be experienced here. All the supernatural experiences as described in the Book of Exodus—the entire Old Testament for that matter—but take the Book of Exodus and its supernatural experiences must be experienced here in this age. Having been experienced, the age continues, but the one who experienced it disengages himself from this age and enters *that* age…but the age continues. He who experienced the experiences…and all the things of the Old are but adumbrations, they are foreshadowings in a not altogether conclusive or immediately evident way…but they are foreshadowings. When you have them then you understand them. The whole thing becomes clear as crystal *after* you've experienced them. You who experienced it in this age while you walked the earth, a simple man, normal man, subject to all the weaknesses and limitations of the earth, you are now lifted up into an entirely different sphere. When you take off this body and the world calls you dead, you died for the last time. All but the resurrected are restored, instantly restored, to continue the journey until they are resurrected. For there is only God and God is playing all the parts. He has to play *all* parts in order to bring in the sum and the sum total of all the parts is David. Not until he finds David can he escape from the world of death. So in the 89th Psalm, "I have found David," the Lord cries out, "and he has cried unto me, 'Thou art my Father, my God, and the Rock of my salvation'" (89:26). He finds his son. Until he finds his son, which is his own creative power, he can't depart this world. For, he is the creative power of God, the wisdom of God. He finds the sum total of all of his experiences gathered together and personified in the youth called David.
Q: (inaudible)
A: You will continue in this world whether you are known in this section of time or another section of time…there are only sections of time. The play has a beginning and an end, but it repeats itself. It's not linear; it's like the Book of Ecclesiastes where the whole thing is circular. Go to

a play tonight and go to the same play tomorrow night, and the play repeats itself. Life does not begin in the cradle and doesn't end in the grave. Because I cannot touch those who have departed, it doesn't mean that the world came to an end that moment when they departed. They are simply in another section of time.

Q: Is it possible for an individual to know when they have found David?

A: You cannot miss it. When you see him you could never in eternity forget it, because you know what you are intended to find before you set sail; and when it happens it's like memory returning. No one tells you he is David you know it, as no one need tell you the name of your son. If you've known your son and lived with your son and he was lost, when you found your son he doesn't ask you who you are…my son….you know that you found your son. "For this my son was dead and he's alive again. He was lost and he's found" (Luke15:24). And so, David when you meet him…the thrill of meeting David! It comes with a terrific explosion in your head *after* your resurrection. You find yourself first resurrected and born from above, and then 139 days later, based upon scripture, you encounter David. Then 123 days later your spiritual body is split from top to bottom, and then like a serpent you, the Son of man, ascend like a fiery serpent into your skull. Then 998 days later, completing a circle of 1,260 days, the Holy Spirit in bodily form of a dove descends upon you. You put your hand out to receive his descent, which is the dove, and he smothers you with love, kissing you all over your face, your head, and your neck…and while he's still smothering you with affection the vision comes to an end.

Good night.

GOD IS THE GREAT ARTIST

5/19/69

God is the great artist and there is no artistry so loving but that which perfects its work through ages in the making of its image. God has but one consuming objective: to make his image...making his image in us to reflect himself and to radiate his glory.

Now, on this level, he exists here as our own wonderful human Imagination. All things exist in the human Imagination, because the human Imagination is the divine body called the Lord Jesus. That is God. On the highest level his artistry is towards the making of his image. On this level we're asked to do something similar...and so I say to a friend, what would you like to be? And he answers, "Well, I would like to be a doctor." All right, that's an image. And you, "A business man." And you...and then he names this, that and the other. Well, we, too, are the artists lowered to this level. For we are the artist on the highest level making ourselves the image, which would radiate and reflect the glory of the being that we *really* are who is God. But while we are there on this level, we simply single out what we would *like* to be.

Now, are we willing to give all of our time to making of this image in the world of Caesar—to become a great doctor, to become a very successful businessman, and to become...and you name exactly what you would like in this world? Well, how does God do it? God is the great *dreamer* in man. And here he is bound in a deadly dream until he forms in himself the image that we name in scripture, Christ. Only when it's formed in him will he awaken from the dream. So he is bound in a deadly, deadly dream. Well, we can be bound in a dream, too. And so the dream is, well, what would it be like if it were true? What true? That I am a great doctor, that I am a most successful business man, that I am a great painter, a great musician. What would the *feeling* be like if it were true?

Now I am told in scripture that all things are possible to him who believes. Can I believe it when at the moment I assume it that my reason and my senses deny it? Can I persist in that image of myself? "When you pray, believe that you have received it, and you will" (Mark 11:24). Therefore, what is prayer but Imagination drenched in feeling? What else is it? It certainly isn't using a lot of empty words. Taking any prayer, I don't care, even the Lord's Prayer. Every Sunday in church they all repeat the Lord's Prayer and come out just as they were when they went in…no prayer is answered. Now they're going to stop praying to these demoted saints, but *all* the saints are equally mythological, all of them. There aren't any! Read the 115th Psalm and see what those things really are; and those who believe in them are just as stupid as those who make them and sell them.

So here in our world, how would I go about being the artist that could make myself into the image of the successful…and I name it…the successful minister of the word of God? Why, I have to start just as I did on the highest level: that I have finished it. I must actually go to the very end. I assume that I have done what now I am starting to do, and remain faithful to the end. For the most creative thing in us is to believe a thing in. I bring it into existence, objective existence by believing it in. So can I really believe that something is already objective in my world that at the moment no one can see and my mortal eyes can't see it, but I can walk drenched in the feeling that it is? Can I support that feeling in my world until it becomes an objective fact? Well, that's how *all* things are brought into being. For *all* things exist in the human Imagination, but everything! And the human Imagination is God himself; that is the divine body that we call in scripture Jesus the Lord. So am I willing to step out completely and ask no one if it's right, wrong or what else, and dare to walk in that assumption as though it were true? I tell you it *will* come to pass.

Let me share with you now a simple little story. I've told it before. I don't think many of you present ever heard it. This chap is a very dear friend of mine. He lives in New York City. He was born in Odessa, Russia of a very poor Jewish family. He knew what it was to be frightened when he heard that they were coming, meaning the Cossacks. They burned, they ruined, they caused pain for the sheer joy of frightening people and destroying, and they had their pogroms. Well, here was a boy, not more than nine or ten, the oldest of a family of five. His mother died soon after the last one was born. He was the head of the family. The father had no money. He worked, yes, but he had little to really maintain a family of five without the help of his wife, and so little Joseph went out to work. Naturally at the age of nine, what could you do but simply go to the bank and change the money into smaller denominations, or be a busboy or something in a store. Every day Joe would go to the bank with his large denominations and change them into smaller ones and bring them back. Well, he had never known what it was to wear shoes. He always wore his feet wrapped up in whatever they do to wrap them up, because he had no shoes. He'd never known what it was to have a pair of slacks that his father bought…they were always given to him by charity. They were simply collected by the Jewish element and then these poor families received worn-out clothes. So he had his slacks given, his shirts given, everything given. He never knew what it was to have a new pair of slacks or a pair of shoes.

So this day in question—and no one taught him this, it came from the depth of his soul, because man brings into this world with him innate knowledge. He looked at this bearded teller, this cashier, as he put the money through, and he noticed that the big copper things and the silver things when rolled into paper resembled each other; but in value they were widely separated in value. So he said to himself, not to anyone else, "Wouldn't it be wonderful if he made a mistake! Oh, wouldn't it be marvelous if he made a mistake!" And then, all in his Imagination, when he rolled the money through the window to Joseph, Joseph took the money in the same assumption that he had made the mistake, and walked in a sense of joy back to his place. Reason told him he had not made a mistake, but the thought he would have fun. "What a joy if he had made the mistake! I would buy a pair of slacks, a pair of shoes, and eat until it came through my ears"…a thing that he had never experienced before, to get up from a meal satisfied. So he walked back to his place of business and took in the rolls of money, and it was exactly what he was sent to get. But he had the satisfaction of that long walk of many, many blocks in the mood that he had what he wanted.

The next day he went back to the same bank, the same teller, put in similar denominations to get similar reduced denominations, and he saw the man make the mistake. He saw it and he knew that man made the mistake when he passed it through. He went back and he wrestled with himself on the way back, but his hunger, his poverty, his embarrassment were greater than the ethical code that his mother tried to instill within him. So he went to another bank and got it changed into the real denominations that his business expected. He would not take from the business anything…took them back exactly what it was. Then he had all this money left over, so he went and bought himself a pair of slacks, and bought himself a pair of shoes, and he went into a restaurant and ate until he could eat no more. Then he went back to the business and gave them the money.

"That night," he said, "I didn't sleep. I wrestled with my conscience all through the night, for my mother was dead and she didn't teach me this. She gave me a different ethical code...not to steal...and the Ten Commandments were woven into my brain. I couldn't justify my acts, but at least I learned a lesson: I learned that an assumption, though false, if persisted in will harden into fact." Now, these are not his words but these are his sentiments. The words I just quoted are the words of Sir Anthony Eden. He didn't need money, this need was position, but he knew a law, which undoubtedly he used through his years when he came out of Eton and came out of the highest university that Europe had to offer. But he learned a lesson.

My friend Joseph today is a multi-millionaire. I'm quite sure far, far richer in Caesar's dollars and cents than Anthony Eden. He learned it and lived by it. And today Joseph tells me, "I never dun a customer, for I feel I cannot afford to lose a customer. When he is long, long overdue in payment, I sit alone when my help has departed, and I simply mentally write a letter thanking him, not dunning him, thanking him for his check. I *never* ever post the letter. I simply write it, make it clear in my mind's eye and, Neville, within three or four days that check comes. It never fails! I simply do it. I have never had to lose one customer by suing, by taking him to court, or in any way dunning him. I learned my lesson as a boy through poverty." Well, if poverty would teach that to everyone, we all should be born equally poor.

Now he lives in an apartment in New York City where he pays $12,000 a year in rent. He doesn't own the apartment, it's not a co-op. I know the apartment well on the 33rd floor of Central Park South, the corner of 7th Avenue. Here is an apartment...$12,000 a year rent. His business in New York City, I know he pays $45,000 a year in rent for that street business. Well, it's not as big as this...well, yes, you take the space of this area here... not more than this. It's a long deep place. But certainly if you took the square footage of this place, that would not exceed this, and he pays $45,000 a year rent. Now, he has his businesses in Paris, in Puerto Rico, in Brazil. He learned it when he left Russia after the war when they collapsed in 1917, the Russian armies. He came as a young boy of sixteen or seventeen into France and got a job driving a truck, a garbage collector, and here he was, he was strong, picking up the garbage and throwing it into the truck. He simply moved from place to place.

One day he met, seemingly by accident, a Russian. And you know of her anyway—you may not be old enough to know her—I saw her in England back in 1925 when she was really tops—and that was Anna Pavlova, the great dancer. She said to him, "You know, Joseph, you're young and attractive, and I could quickly introduce you to so many women that would need your help. Your father used to make them back in Russia, but he made corsets. We don't need corsets today, but we need something to aid us. Even at my age, I've just turned thirty, and at my age I could use the help. With all of my exercise and I think I have a perfect figure, but when you hit thirty and go beyond, every woman could use a little help to look as she would like to look in the eyes of herself first and in others. So why don't you take up the making of these things?" and he called them "foundations." You're all familiar with his ad in the *New Yorker*...and the things. His name is J. Burleigh. You'll see his work here in Magnin's; you'll see the work in all the fashionable places all over the country. That's Joseph Burleigh. Here, he learned that when he was a poor, poor boy, never having been satisfied with a meal that his father could provide, and always wearing things given to him by the Jewish charities of Odessa. One day he simply experimented... he could lose nothing by it. That's why I'm asking you to experiment. I teach you a principle and leave you to your choice and its risks.

Now, when I've told this in the past, I've always had someone in the audience who criticized me for telling it...that I'm leading people astray. And I've always had a suspicion that those who are *most* vocal in their criticism— and I've met them at parties—were those who, I am quite sure...there's something in the depths of my soul tells me...that they would go into a store and lift what is not theirs. I know it as I'm standing before you, and they're simply justifying their behavior by telling me I'm leading people astray. I can see one lady now...rocks as big as, well, really rocks on both hands. Most unbecoming to have all this displayed, with everything hanging on her like Tiffany. So when I told this at a dinner party at the Ambassador one night, just among twenty-five of us who were gathered, she criticized me unmercifully for telling such a story. And something in the depths of my soul told me, don't leave your pocketbook on the side here, because with all of these she's going to take something from it...and I knew it in the depth of my soul. Because the pickpocket is not necessarily a poor person and the cleptomanic is not necessarily someone who is poor. You go into a party where they have fortunes and they can't leave your pocketbook alone. They can't leave anything...they'll pick up even one of your lovely napkins, part of a set, and put it in their purse while they're dining at your table, and break your set which you can't replace. I have witnessed these things.

So, I'm telling you, forget all these so-called codes...you're learning a principle. We ate of the tree of good and evil and from then on we've suffered. I'm not saying that anyone is going to go out and do it...you aren't going to go out and steal from anyone. So when she said to me, "Did he ever pay the money back?" I said, "To whom would he send it, Stalin?" For Stalin stole the entire place, not just a few little things that he did. Stalin took over the entire country and called it mine, and then even called the people "his," and slaughtered twenty million of them. So would he send the money back, when he could afford it, back to Stalin? For, there was no Czar when he could afford to send it back. In the meanwhile, they took his head off, and so to whom would he pay it? In the meanwhile, Joseph has given—not to justify his conscience but out of the goodness of his heart—tens and tens of thousands of dollars to help friends plus charities. I mean to friends, personal friends. How often I've said to Joseph, "You can afford it, here's a friend, he needs a little lift for the moment," and Joseph would never dun him. But he hasn't lost a penny, because he applied the same principle. If it takes a year, two years, three years, they'll pay it back, because Joseph will not dun them, but he will write that little letter and thank them for having sent it. He will not take one penny in interest from any loan that he makes. I know that from my own experience when I asked him to help a friend of mine. When the friend sent back on the $2,000 loan a six percent interest, Joseph sat right down and wrote him a check for that amount of interest and said, "We are friends, I'm not in the business of loaning money." This was simply a friend to a friend.

So here is this simple wonderful principle. And so God is the great artist and there is no greater artistry, but none. You can't conceive of any greater artist than the perfecting of a work through ages in the making of one's own image. Well, you want an image, what's your image? You want to be successful in business, well, that's an image. Are you willing to simply assume that you are it and wait? "For the vision has its own appointed hour; it ripens, it will flower. If it seems long, then wait; for it is sure and it will not be late" (Hab.2:3). So each has its own appointed hour, are you willing to wait for the happiness that you now seek or are you going to try to *make* it come to pass by bulldozing someone and arguing someone into some state? Are you actually willing to apply this principle? If you are, you'll become the successful business man, the successful doctor, the successful minister of the word of God, or whatever it is that you can actually state, that's what I would like to be. Now can you assume it, that you really are it? If you can assume that you are it, and you are willing to live in it as though it were true, no power on earth can stop it; because you are God and he has no opponent unless he creates one himself. Because there's nothing but God!

If man doesn't know that, then he creates an opposition called "the doubter," named in scripture Satan or the devil. But really they are as existent as St. Christopher...they're just as real. The devil is just as real as St. Christopher. Millions believed in him so they gave him power which he did not possess. Millions believe in the devil, so they give him power which he doesn't possess. Now we have all these little isms rising in the world concerning this thing you saw last Sunday in the paper in England…somebody of some so-called magic workers or devil worshippers or something, all such silly nonsense! Believe in nothing but God and God is your own wonderful human Imagination. That you will depart this world, certainly, this is a world of death. Why remain here forever? You only play your part here, but the purpose of it here is to form the image. When that image is formed in you, you are born from above. The first thing that happens to you after the image is formed you awaken, and when you awake, you are born, and when you are born the child appears, the signal of *your* birth. Then a little while later comes a second great promise in the Book of Isaiah, "Unto us a child is born"—all right, a child is born—"to us a son is given" and the son *is given* (Is.9:6). Here is the image. And you look right into the face of that son and he is *you,* but that's your eternal youth. You are the father and that is your son who *glorifies* you. That's exactly what you look like matured. If you could see yourself matured, you would see the being that embraced me and sent me into the world. That is the being and he is the image of the son when you meet the son, but the son is eternal youth. So, you form the image in yourself and then the image becomes objective.

So, faith is nothing more than the subjective appropriation of the objective hope. Here is my hope: I hope to make the image. So he said, "Set your hope fully upon the grace that is coming to you at the unveiling or the revelation of Jesus Christ" (1Pet.1:13). When that Christ Spirit stands before you, well then, he is the Anointed One, he is your son. Until Christ be formed in you…said Paul, "I will labor with you in travail until Christ be formed in you." This he tell us in his wonderful 4th chapter of Galatians (4:19). But then just before that he said, "I'm afraid I've labored over you in vain. I see you are worshipping days and months and seasons and years. I'm afraid I've labored in vain." For man turns back to these little things and he thought they'd outgrown them. They turn back to images. They turn back to days, to months, to seasons, to years and call them holy seasons when there is no such thing, not in God's kingdom. Every moment of time is holy and wherever *you* stand that's holy because you are standing there. No matter where you stand…you stand at a bar…that's a holy place because you're standing there. Others tell you it shouldn't be done. Who made it?—God. Well, wherever God is…where is he now? Wherever I stand that's where he is, that's holy ground. That's true of every person in the world.

But they won't believe it. They think they've got to leave where they are a lovely environment with their family at home and rush off through the rain on a Sunday morning to church, and if they don't get there on time then they have violated God's wish. He wishes you would stay home and love your family. And if one day you could ease the burden of the one who does it all the time, well, do it. If you can't do it as well as she does it through the week, all right, do it anyway. She'll understand and be very happy that you could ease her for that moment. And it's far better than rushing off toward some so-called church and praying to gods that do not exist, and all this nonsense in the world. I'm not telling you not to go to church…some people enjoy the comfort and the friendships that they have there. They enjoy the coffee clatch that follows it more than the service. They go out and say that's fun now…you can't miss it because right after service they're going to go and have a lovely brunch, and then they gossip for another hour and have the most marvelous time tearing people apart. So that's church. And they meet there, many of them in the hope of meeting a mate.

And so, that is not what I'm talking about. I'm talking about the great artist of the world and when you say "I am" that's he. But we're on this level, the level of Caesar, but we follow the same pattern. On the highest level you are the one who said, "Let us make our image"… you're the one who said that. We said it together, for we are the collective unity that said together, "Let us make man in our image." Then *we* became actually enslaved in this deadly dream. And we forever, this man that we are, this heavenly man will not break his pledge: he'll remain bound by his deadly dream until he forms his image in himself.

So all of my selections, while I come down to the very lowest, to be this, that or the other, they all add up while he remains faithful to that divine image. That image is to make his image in himself, and when it comes, it is David. That's his image…for that is the Christed-one and that is the one called the Anointed One. So, I have *found* him, my Anointed, my chosen, my firstborn, and he has called me Father, he's called me God, he's called me the Rock of his salvation (Ps. 89:26). And I am! I brought him into being. Now I can depart in peace, for I've made exactly what I've promised myself to do in the beginning of time. I promised that I would do it. And "It had been taught us from the primal state that he which is was wished until he were." And so, I wished that, and I did not deviate, I kept the vision before me constantly no matter what I did in the lower levels of my being. But I made it all add up, and so all things work for good towards him who loves the Lord. For, the Lord is your highest being remaining faithful to his image and taking all the choices on himself as he rises up the ladder and all goes into making that image. The image comes out personified as David.

So tonight you can take your wish…let no one tell you what you ought to be. Here, this, I would call her a friend of mine, well, she is a friend of mine now, and she shared with me a series of her visions. She wants to be a composer. I would tell her *now* you can be as great as you wish to be. In one of her visions which she shared with me she finds herself over a body of water and to the side land. She is in the company of Chopin. She said, "I didn't see him...I felt him...I knew it was Chopin and he's talking. I can't tell you I heard words, but he's talking and he's going to show me how to compose. Here I look down on this body of water...it's not only the subject but the inspiration of the composition. This young girl, she's just in her teens, is telling me this fantastic picture concerning what she dreamt. Well, then I tell her...she said, 'You know, having heard you quite a while ago I had a dream in which I was told in the dream to read Numbers.'"

Well, the 12th of Numbers tells you that it is God who speaks to you in dream and it is God who makes himself known to you in vision (12:6). Here is a vision. Now when the vision breaks out in to speech the presence of deity is affirmed. Well, it broke out in speech. He's telling her...even though she didn't see the face, you don't see the face right away...the real face you will not see until the Son appears. Just prior to that yes you meet the risen Lord and you fuse with him and become one with him and you are he. When the Son appears now he's only yourself made young. He's the image of the being who spoke to you only he's young...he is the eternal youth that is *your* Son that did all of your will.

But here in her vision she is with Chopin. Well, being by nature a pianist, what better one would you have as an instructor? And so she's being instructed in Spirit. But *she* is the Spirit of Chopin, for really in the depth of our soul we are one. And if that is my great inspiration, I will draw to myself that which I've assumed that I want to do. If I want to be as great as he, and he is great in my mind's eye, I'll draw him as an instructor. But if it's myself being instructed, I am instructing myself, for the whole thing takes place *within* us: all things exist in the human Imagination. "All that you behold; tho' it appears without, it is within, in your Imagination, of which this world of mortality is but a shadow" (Blake, *Jerusalem*, Plt.71). So take anything you want now as an image, assume that you are it, and then know it *must* come forward in the world of shadows. You appropriate it.

So let me repeat what to me prayer is: prayer is your own wonderful human Imagination drenched with *feeling*...just as Joseph drenched himself with the feeling that he had it. I can take story after story where you drench yourself with the feeling of having it...whether it be a wedding ring, whether it be a change of name which would imply that it happened, I don't care what it is. But if you're going to use reason as to why it can't happen, it just couldn't possibly happen not to me, well then, it can't happen may I tell you, for that's your image. You don't realize that you have two. And the one that is really deeper is the one that tells you it can't happen. But no real belief can be suppressed, not for long. It must...that inward conviction must...find some external objective habitation, it must. So which is tonight your deep conviction—that you are a failure or that you are a success? It's entirely up to you. For that deep inner conviction cannot long be suppressed, can't be done.

Now what is the inward conviction in the hearts of all of us here? What is the true image that you believe yourself to be? If you believe what the headlines tell you tonight, may I tell you, they thrive on crises. There are people in the business who only write headlines, and they'll be fired tomorrow if they don't scare you to death tonight. They've got to frighten you. I don't care what news is good today, they'll put it on the tenth page; but some little insignificant thing they'll put it on the first page if it can scare you. Now, the most exciting thing tonight, our boys are on the way to the moon…this great test. The first day they went off it was on the first page but a small, little item, and ___(??) took the whole thing. Now how can that compare to our boys going off to the moon? Today they got the front page. Well, see what happens tomorrow…I do not know, I haven't seen the paper. See what happens tomorrow. If there's a violent something in our area, that's going to get the headlines. So the headline writer only writes crisis after crisis. Ignore it all and remain faithful to your image. What do you really want in this world? Don't tell me it's going to be difficult for you, because if you tell me that right away you put whole blocks before you. Can you believe all things are possible to God?

No one in this world would have given one nickel as a bet upon the speaker if when I left the little island of Barbados at the sage of seventeen I had voiced a request to be a minister of the Word of God. Unschooled as I was and remain unschooled in a formal sense of the word, and that I could actually become a minister of the Word, not because I learned it from a man, not because I read it in any book…but because it was *revealed* to me. It was my one consuming desire to have a true vision, where if a man becomes what he beholds, I wanted my vision to be true. And I didn't want it to be false even if it was given to me by some huge, big giant of a person who had all the degrees behind his name, because all these could be just as false as anything in the world. So I wanted a *true* vision. For if it is true that a man becomes what he beholds, well then, I wanted to behold Truth so that I would become true in what I had to say. Well, I didn't get it from anyone. I simply insisted that I would have it revealed to me, and it did, it came all revealed.

So when I tell you of David you won't find it in any book. There isn't a book printed where it is actually printed, I do not know of any. When I speak to rabbis, ministers, all these priests, they shun it because it is not what they were taught. They bring their own pre-fabricated misconception of scripture to scripture, and I'm trying to show them exactly where it is.

Not because it's there that I had it; I had it first and then I read the scripture more intelligently and found the confirmation. So I am a witness to the truth of God's Word. I only wanted the truth...I didn't care where I got it. But I got it as Paul did. He said, "It did not come from a man, nor was I taught it by men, but it came through revelation, the unveiling of God *within me.*" And he unveiled himself in me when I was confronted by the risen Lord, and then the whole series began to unfold within me.

So tonight, don't neglect Caesar's world, you are in it. You have to pay rent, you have to buy food, and everything is being inflated, so don't neglect it here. Don't let anyone tell you that this is sordid. You've got to do it; you're in the world of Caesar. He said, "Whose insignia is this?—Caesar's. Well, render unto Caesar the things that are Caesar's" (Mat.22:21).

So he wants a gold coin. Fish, and when you bring the fish take from his mouth a gold coin and give it to Caesar, for that insignia is his. So in the world of Caesar he paid Caesar.

And when people tell you he got the truth out of the air, forget that concept of Jesus, forget it completely. He didn't bring anything out of any air whatsoever. The man in whom this thing awoke worked and labored as you do, as I do, and if you think I am being foolish about it, read the first two verses of the 8th chapter of the Book of Luke where he was supported by women, and they named by name three women. Now the modern translation says "they" implying disciples also. It doesn't say that in the original text: it only speaks of the singular, the one person spoken of as the Lord. He received from these three women from their own substance...they supported him.

Well, Paul said, I will not have anyone support me. So when Paul began to tell it as it unfolded in him, he said, "I earn my own bread and although it is the workman's part to receive part of what is earned by those that he teaches, I still will earn my own bread." That was what Paul set himself to do. So he didn't get any bread out of the atmosphere or do all these silly things that you're talking about. No, he went out and labored just as a man knowing what happened in him, and trying to persuade everyone who would hear him of the destiny that is theirs: that one day they will awaken and when they awaken they are God. And all that is said of God in the gospels they will experience as something that is personal, very personal.

So, I am telling you what I know from experience, I am not theorizing, I am not speculating. I hope you believe me and when I depart this world that you will not soon forget it. Because you will depart one day, and until it happens you'll be restored in a world just like this, and you'll continue to struggle until the image is formed in you. But may I tell you, you haven't wavered in the forming of that image. You may *think* you have, but not the depth of your own being. For the depth of your being and my being are one, and that depth, that brotherhood, has never once faltered. We agreed in the beginning to dream in concert and dream in concert we did and will continue to do until the image is formed in each. For each must reveal God and God is revealed in his image which is David.

Now let us go into the Silence.

*   *   *

Now are there any questions, please?

Q: (inaudible)
A: Did you hear the question? Would I comment on what happens to us when we take off this physical envelope? I find myself often in a world just like this, meeting those that the world calls dead…and they aren't dead. They're just as alive as they were here only they're young. They're not infants, they're young. The world is terrestrial and they are solid bodies of flesh and blood. They get married there, too, as they get married here. They look forward to the inevitable death there as they look forward here with the same sense of fear. They do not realize that they have even died.

I'll give you one interesting story. I have a sister-in-law, a pillar of the church in New Jersey, and she always said to me, "I don't believe one word you teach." I said, "All right, Al, it's perfectly all right with me." She said, "I love you dearly, because you love my sister. You're a good husband and a good father, and for that I love you, but I do not believe one word you teach." And so every Sunday morning regardless of weather she was in church. That was something she had to do.

Well, my secretary the first year I came out here, the year was 1945—I think it was the first year or the second year, I'm not quite sure—but soon after I came out, that is, at the end of my three-month tour, I went to San Francisco for a month, then came here for two months—and just before I closed I got a wire that my secretary was found dead. He was only fifty years old…not quite, going on his fiftieth birthday…and a hot summer's night and the maid went to his room to clean it up, and here was Jackie propping the door with his fallen body. So when they finally got to him, he'd been gone about twelve hours. I went back and attended the funeral and took care of arrangements for the funeral.

Six months after he was gone, I'm out in this world that they call the world of dream. I am there consciously as I am here now. I knew exactly where my body was that I left in this world, and I know where I am now. And here is Jack and here is my sister-in-law Al. I said to Al, "Al, how can you say that you do not believe what I teach and do not believe in survival?" For she did not believe in survival; she thought we survived only through our children. I said, "Look at Jack." She said to me, "What has Jack to do with it?" I said, "Don't you know Jack died?" and Jack said to me, "Who's dead?" I said, "You're not dead, Jack, but you died. I came back from California and attended your funeral, and I buried you in a good Catholic cemetery in Haverstraw, New York. The priest was there, you got holy water on you, you had all the stuff that your sister wanted, and so you are buried in a good Catholic grave." He looked at me bewildered. I said, "Yes, you died last August."

Al knows I'm telling the truth and Al looked at him, looked at me, and her face is completely bewildered, for she knows that I came back to attend the funeral. And she knows that Jack is now alive and standing before both of us, and Jack is talking to me. I said, "Jack, come over here." He came over to me. I took my hand and I put it on his thigh and said, "Al, look, he's solid. My hand does not go through him like some gossamer, he's solid and he's real." Jack did to me there what he would have done here—we were like brothers, he was my secretary but we were not boss and secretary, we were just like brothers. We dined together six days a week, he was home every day, and he was always my guest for dinner. He did this and he said, "Get your hand off me," just as he would have done had I done it here. For that was Jack. With that, the whole scene changed. From then on, Al was never quite as forceful about what I teach...she was never quite as denying. She hasn't completely come forward in this world of ours. It takes awhile to come through this concrete mind of ours. But she had this experience subjectively; therefore, it will gradually influence her and it will come through slowly into this conscious mind of hers.

But here was Jack and he was just as real as he was when he was here, only he was young. And she knew he was Jack, although she never saw Jack when he was that young. Jack died...white hair, he had a mass of white hair...but Jack had white hair when he was eighteen...lots of hair but it turned white as a young man. Here is Jack...and this young fella. When I first met him he looked like that. He could have been, say, twenty-three, twenty-two. And here was Al, she knows that he died and she knows I'm telling the truth. But I was the only one fully aware because Jack was not aware he had even died; because if you die, we die because he can't find us. We are living in worlds within worlds within worlds...nothing dies...not even the little flower that blooms once. If it blooms once it blooms forever. All, everything is alive, but this still is a world of death, because all things vanish and *seem* to die. We have to depart, not through the little gate of death, we have to depart from *this* age...this age is the age of death. And when we leave this age of death we enter the world of eternity and we are God awake. Here, we are God asleep.

Until the next time. Good night.

REVELATION OF THE WORD WITHIN US

5/23/69

In all the revelations that await us there is none so fundamental as the revelation of the Word within us. I can't tell anyone the ecstasy, the joy that awaits them when they discover that "In the volume of the book it is all about me" (Ps.40:7). From Genesis to Revelation the whole vast book is about the individual in whom the Word is revealed. He is the interpreter of the book. And when he discovers that *he* was the one who was sent—he is the Word of God who cannot return empty but must accomplish that which God purposed, and prosper in the thing for which it was sent (Is.55:11)—the thrill that *I am that Word!* The thrill that I am the Word that became flesh, and now I am clad in a robe dipped in blood, this flesh and blood; and the name by which I shall be called is the Word of God, and that this "Word of God was in the beginning, and the Word was with God, and the Word was God" (Jn.1:1). Then it dawns upon one that *he is* that Word sent for a divine purpose and the purpose was to fulfill the Word we call scripture! There is no other purpose for his being here; not to become rich, famous, known, strong, weak, only to fulfill the Word...the most fantastic play in the world.

Now he will fulfill it in a living way, for the Word in the written form is dead and the letter kills, but the Spirit makes alive. He is the living Word that comes to interpret the seeming dead letter. Then he makes that discovery that *he is* the Word, that the whole story of Jesus from his conception by the Holy Spirit to his ascension into heaven is a *sign* granted by God to those who will receive it. Formerly he thought of Jesus as someone external to himself; he thought of the Word of God as something completely external to himself. That the whole book was something that was dated, thousands of years ago, through men he referred to as the prophets, as the servants of a God that he did not know. And then comes the *revelation*. The revelation unfolds within him and he discovers that *he* is the Word, that the Jesus of scripture is himself, and he can say within himself, "I am Mary and birth to Christ must give, if I in blessedness now and evermore would live" (Scheffler). He brings forth himself. For he is the Word and "In the beginning was the Word, the Word was with God, and the Word *was* God" and he is that Word. He sees the entire book unfold within himself. But everything said of the "pattern man" [Jesus Christ] he experiences in the first-person, present-tense. Now it is taking place within me and he knows it. All said of him I am experiencing, so it is said of me, "In the volume of the book it is written of me."

I can't tell anyone the thrill, the ecstasy that is theirs when they make that discovery…the whole vast world changes. You don't care what anyone achieves in this world. You wish they could get all of their dreams in the world of Caesar. It doesn't matter what they want, grant it. It doesn't matter at all, it all fades into nothing. If they own the earth and enslave all, it still would be nothing. But the Word cannot return void. The Word did not come to own the earth but to fulfill scripture: "Scripture must be fulfilled in me." And then, "Beginning with Moses and the law and all the prophets and the psalms, he interpreted to them in all the scriptures the things concerning himself" (Luke24:27)…that this was written of me and this is what it means. For I tell you from experience this is how it happens. So, we are the Word spoken by God, but remember, God himself is the Word. The author of the play plays the parts, for there is no one else to play it. He had to become the actors in the drama and they cannot return empty. They play it completely and perfectly. But what they're really going to play…the final revelation…is when it unfolds within him and *he* is the Word.

Whether he has unnumbered fortunes in the world, that is not important. Today, when you see people so surprised and so shocked because of some so-called turning aside from an ethical code….and we take now one of our justices, why should we be shocked? What man walking the earth could cast a stone? What man that's ever walked this earth could say he was innocent of a similar deed? Because, we are told in scripture, to want it without having the courage to do it was to have done it anyway. "For you've heard it said, 'Thou shalt not commit adultery.' But I say to you that anyone who lusts after a woman has already committed the act in his heart with her" (Mat.5:27). So it's a psychological drama. What man is innocent of that lust? What man is innocent of the lust for personal gain? Why should we be shocked and offended when we see injustice and all these things in high places? Do we not have all of our officials…and they have very good reason for it…for by example of those above them they are encouraged to use their vocation for personal gain. Everyone this night is on the roster of a great agency to go out and earn a fortune giving lectures. They don't have to know their subject at all. All they need do is publicize themselves. If they can get publicized they can get a fortune, because everyone wants to know the one who is known in the world of Caesar. Out they come to see and to touch and to hear one.

In 1941 when I brought out my first book, Harper Brothers sent me over to a place called Peakings…and they said to me, Mr. Peakings himself—he's gone now, he was the oldest agent in the country for speakers; he had Mrs. Roosevelt on the list, he had Churchill on the list, he had them all on his list. He gave me a very nice wonderful interview because I came from Harpers Bros. They said they couldn't handle my books unless I got promotion and I was completely unknown…to that I admitted. Mr. Peakings was a sweet, lovely gentleman, mature in years. In those days I was a young man and he was a very, very elderly gentleman and very gracious. He said to me, "Neville, you're completely unknown. If you could go out and shoot someone and get off and get publicized, I could sell you night after night for hundreds and hundreds of dollars to all kinds of clubs. They love to meet the one who shot someone and who got off. I could sell Mrs. Roosevelt tomorrow…I sell her every week at $1,200 a lecture. I could sell her with any subject at all. She's the mother of many children. I could sell her if her subject was 'What it feels like never to have known a man.' If that was her subject it would make no difference…it is Mrs. Roosevelt they're coming to hear. And so, go out and do something that is ghastly and get out of jail, try to avoid being sentenced, and come back and I can sell you across the country…because I can only sell *names*."

Now today, someone gets up in Congress and they make the most outrageous statement that could be carried tonight on radio, TV and tomorrow's press. As they build up that name, then he gets more money for them, and off they go. Because they are encouraged by example by those above them to make what gain they can from their vocation. They all do it and stand aghast at one person in what he did. But that's not the play. That belongs here. It goes on over and over and over, and all are guilty…but everyone is guilty.

But the play, the real play is the sacred play. It's written in scripture. It's a sealed book. Only when the Word unveils itself within man does it become alive and then that which was a dead word begins to unfold within man in a series of experiences. He is not observing them taking place on the outside… not another is born from some so-called virgin. There was no such thing as any physical virgin birth. The birth is from *above*. You must be born from above and you are born out of your own wonderful skull; and because that hides you *that* is the Mary of scripture. That is the Jerusalem from above. That is the holy mother. I am Mary and birth to God—I cannot any longer say "must give," I gave. And now forever in blessedness I will continue, and share it with those who have not yet brought him forth.

But the Word cannot return empty, it has to fulfill this pattern...it's a pattern. Jesus is only the *pattern man* and that pattern no one is going to change. It starts with the resurrection...when the Word erupts within man and he is the Word, which is God himself. Because who awakes?—I awake. Well, who is rising?—I am; that's God. Now who is coming out?—I am; that's God. Who witnesses all these things around him, the three who witness the sign of the child?—I am witnessing them and that's God. And here, the whole Word becomes a witness to the truth of scripture, which no one prior to the awakening of the Word ever understood. So, "In the fullness of time, he sent forth his Son into the hearts of man, crying, "Father!" (Gal.4:4). Well, did that happen? Yes, in the fullness of time...and I looked and here he is calling me "Father." Well, who is his Father?—God. He's calling you "Father"? Yes. But you're a little man. In your mortal eyes yes a little man. But when this little garment which I purposely assumed for my purpose unknown to mortal man is taken off, then you would not have eyes to see me. You see me as long as I wear this robe dipped in blood, and you do not even know my name is the Word of God.

But the Word of God was sent forth from the mouth of God: he only sent himself. So "He who sees me sees him who sent me." I came to do the will of him who sent me, and my Father's will is to fulfill scripture. In the end, I will say, "Father, I have accomplished the work which thou gavest me to do. Now return unto me the glory that was mine, the glory that I had with thee before that the world was" (Jn.17:5). I ask for no other than to return what I emptied myself of when I and you were one, and there was no one to go but yourself, and you sent me. Your Word could not return to you void. It had to bring back that for which it had been purposed; and so, I have returned and I have finished the work that thou gavest me to do. Now glorify me with thyself! For the self is mine, the very self that was mine before that the world was. And so I return to my own being who is God. For, "In the beginning was the Word, and the Word was with God, and the Word was God." So you come out and you are the Word. But the Word has not yet reached the fullness of time to be erupted.

In all the revelation that you could ever experience, there is none more fundamental than the unveiling of the Word *in* you...when you know you *are* the Word. Then, because the external Word is called the Bible, and you read it in the 40th Psalm, you come upon the words, "In the volume of the book it is written of me" (40:7). The thrill that comes to man when he discovers that this whole vast book that the world calls, and rightly so, a sacred Word, the Word of God, and you were taught to believe it was all about ancient history and it's *contemporary*…it's all about me! Here, now I must unfold within myself this living Word that interprets the written Word. For the Word was dead until the living Word could give meaning to it. So he gives meaning to it by actually unfolding it within himself. He comes back awakened to the truth of God's Word. He doesn't change it, he doesn't in any way add to it or take from it he simply fulfills it. He fulfills it within himself.

Everyone who hears him either accepts it on faith or they don't. As far as he is concerned he hopes they will accept it, but he has to go on anyway. There are always those called "the remnant" who are now *near* the point that they can accept it…always the remnant. "So don't be concerned," said he, "Go back, Elijah, I have saved a remnant. There are 7,000 in that city from which you run, and you tell me there are no more waiting? You go back. I have 7,000 waiting who are ready to hear what you can tell them." So there will *always* be a circle who are at the point of breaking through with the seed within man, the Word of God, erupting.

As it erupts, the very first of the events is resurrection, and that's the cornerstone of the entire mystery. The sleeper awakes. Well, who is the sleeper?—God. "Rouse thyself! Why sleepest thou, O Lord?" (Ps.44:23). And so, the Lord awakes. Well, what is his name?—*I am*. Well, who at that moment when it happened to you, who did you feel awakening? I felt myself…I am the one who awoke to find myself completely alone, because God is one. There is no other…it was God who awoke. And then who came out? Well, the same being who awoke, and so I came out. When I came out what did I see? I saw what scripture, the Word of God, told me I would see: I will see witnesses to the event. But they could not see me for I was Spirit and they saw only the *sign*. The whole vast world has taken the sign for the event. The sign is *not* the event…it signifies something that actually took place.

What took place?—God is born. God was returning now to himself. He came into the world to fulfill his Word, and now he's departing from the world. To depart from the world he has to be born from above. If he's not born from above he has to remain in the world until he fulfills the Word. He cannot go back. Go back where? To his heavenly state which *is* the kingdom of God. Well, what constitutes the kingdom of God? The Father and the brotherhood of men…all the brothers together form the Father. So, *that* is the kingdom of God, and so he is returning now, leaving behind him his record. He asks no one on earth to judge him, for no one is capable of judging him, he knows he only has one.

The Return of Glory

So when he returns, is he truly a witness? Here is the book that is *a* witness. Well now, you the living one, can you testify to it as it states? Because when two come together and they agree in testimony then it is conclusive. So read the book. Well now, I experienced this. And I can't fool the watchers from above...for they see not the outer man and hear his words; they see the inner man, and they know if he bears the marks of Jesus or not. Does he bear the marks? Does he carry within himself *these* experiences as told in scripture? If he does, he's a witness.

So bring the witnesses. Here comes the eternal Word of God, the Bible. Now bring the one that made it alive within himself. Does he testify to that and do they agree in testimony? Do they agree? Well then, enter into the kingdom, into the joy of the Lord! So he enters in, in that manner, and there's no other way of entering, other than first to be resurrected which is God's mightiest act. Then, to be born from above. Then, to discover the Fatherhood of God by having his Son call you "Father." And then, to have the curtain of the temple, which is your own body, split in two from top to bottom and you like a serpent, in fulfillment of Exodus, rising into heaven like a fiery serpent. Then, to have the seal of approval placed upon you in the form of the descending of the dove that smothers you with love. Then, all the other passages of scripture in the interval are taking place within you night after night. Every part of the Word of God unfolds within you. And then you tell it...and having told it you depart the world. You know that those who come to you could not come unless the Father within you, who is yourself, calls them. So they will come and they will hear your story, and they will be encouraged by this story. You will tell them that you will be born from above through the resurrection of yourself called in scripture Jesus Christ. So, "I am born anew," said he, "through the resurrection of Jesus Christ" (1Pet.1:3).

Now he said, born to a hope, what is the hope? "Set your hope fully upon the grace that is coming to you at the revelation of Jesus Christ" (1Pet.1:13). For, this is the hope that makes it wisdom to accept the burden of this long dark night of time. For, here is really a night of terror...a night of terror. Who can say that this day the horrors didn't take place in the world, murders, stealing? Not only violent murders...that's bad enough...but when you take someone and you drive him through poverty into shame, into nothing, that's a living death. You can cut his throat...that's fair at least... but when you drive him into such an embarrassing state by underpaying him. And you don't realize what you're doing to yourself in the doing! For, you are sucking from him his blood.

Those who live on blood are the little, well, the termites of the world, really, in a sense. When you think of the fleas that live on dogs which never

517

produce anything themselves; they live on the blood of another. Blood in our language...money is the life blood of the world, and when you underpay a man for his services you are taking his blood. If you could only see yourself as the awakened man sees you, you would be horrified if you saw what you looked like. You'd be horrified! All the perfumes of Arabia couldn't stifle the odor that comes from you. You get before the mirror and you spend a fortune on all the things to beautify yourself, and you have all the beautiful clothes because you can afford it; but if you could only see what you really look like in the eyes of those who have eyes to see. You look like a huge, big, monstrous flea...just a flea, yet human but a flea. And you have no idea what a monstrous looking thing it is. Yet it comes out in the world and people are so proud to touch it, and because it's well-known they'll get $5,000 for speaking and telling all that it must tell. It gets everything because it's now publicized in the world. Take off the mask and those who are paying to hear it would run for their lives if they only saw what it looked like.

So I tell you, we are here in this world of educated darkness until he who sent us, watches, and then one moment in time the Word which is himself erupts, and then he fulfills scripture. So leave them all alone. If they want to live on the blood of others, let them live on the blood of others. If they want to do all these things, let them do it. Have no criticism of them; you've done it too. You've all played these horrible parts. But here in this room, you aren't playing these parts or you wouldn't be here. You are drawn here because the one who is speaking to you has fulfilled scripture, and no one comes unto me save my Father calls him, and I and my Father are one (Jn10:30). So having fulfilled the external Word of God, because I am the living Word that he sent into the world to fulfill it, I now return bearing witness to his Word and I can say, as we're told in the 17th of John, "I have accomplished the work which thou gavest me to do. Now return unto me the glory that was mine, the glory that I had with thee before that the world was." That's the only purpose for being here.

So let everyone...let him be. And if it comes within your code of decency, pray for him. He wants money, pray for him. If he wants happiness in this world, pray for it. It will be granted. If he wants to violate your code of decency like murdering someone, send him elsewhere. You would not accept his request, I know you wouldn't, so let him go elsewhere. May I tell you, if he is so bent, he will. He'll find someone who will take his money for praying for the demise of someone else, he will. But you go about your Father's business and set your hope fully upon the *grace* that is coming to you at the unveiling of the Word of God within you. For when the Word unfolds itself within you, well, I can't tell you the thrill. You jump off that bed…you can hardly believe that you actually experienced it. You mean that all that was said of Jesus Christ is taking place in me? That this thing is not of the past, it's contemporary? This is forever and forever, that he's unfolding himself within me as my very self? Then one after the other happens and you discover it is. Everything he said in scripture *you* experience, not as an observer but as the central actor in the drama.

So let the whole vast world say what they will concerning the mythology of scripture. All you can do is inwardly smile and let them go about their business. Let them go because they will eventually, after all the blows. For, the wisdom of this world is foolishness in the eyes of God. Let them become wiser and wiser in their own stupidity, perfectly all right. Let them feel themselves very prominent and very wonderful, perfectly all right. You don't dethrone them, and you don't join in their so-called self-adulation. Leave them alone, and set your hope fully upon this grace that is coming to you. Then you will see that if blows come tonight, all right, I must have at some time in my blindness planted the seed. I must have, for "As a man sows, so shall he reap" (Gal.6:7). So sometime in the past long forgotten I planted it. I do not recognize my harvest because I do not remember the sowing, but it could not come up into my world had I not sown it. All right, so I will now reap it, and rejoice in the fact that at least it's come for me to recognize, even in a little way. Then, know the words of Paul, "I consider the sufferings of the present time not worth comparing with the *glory* that is to be revealed *in us*" (Rom.8:18). When that glory is revealed, it's the Word unfolding and it all unfolds within us.

So I go through whatever is in store for me because of my misuse of the power that I am, for I am the power of God (1Cor.1:24). I am not only the Word sent into being, I am the very power, carrying the pattern of redemption, and I am the instrument of God's creation. Through me he created it all because I and God are one. And then he sends himself, which is the very being speaking to you…he sends him. So when you see me *after* the experiences, you see the one who sent me, for I am one with the one who sent me. Anyone who sees me sees him who sent me (Jn.14:9). And who is the sender?—my Father. And who is your Father?—the one you call God. Only I know my Father, he and I are one, and you know not your God.

But the joy when the book becomes your wonderful biography! Day after day you open that book to realize it was you who inspired the book when it was recorded by those who heard it or who had the vision. Many a time they speak of vision that came only through the audio state as in the opening of the Book of Obadiah, the Book of Amos, and the Book of Isaiah. They speak of having heard and speak of the vision: "I will tell of the vision of the Lord as the Lord spoke unto me." So they take an audio and speak of it as a vision. It's right in scripture. But when it happens to you, it's not audio alone…the whole thing is just like this room, it's all alive, it's all real.

Then when that moment in time comes for you to depart this world, you leave it never to return again, never. Those who have not quite reached the point of eruption will find themselves on departure here restored to life in a world just like this, terrestrial and real with solid bodies just like this, with problems just like these, with everything that you have here, the identical world, only they are younger, much younger, usually around twenty. Regardless of what mature age they leave this world, they're about twenty when they awake just beyond the veil. The veil is not out there; it's right here. It's so thin and just here…and yet to mortal eye it's not transparent, it's opaque. And because of different weights of vibration, they're not touched, not seen by those who are here…any more than we are seen and touched by those who are there. There are worlds within worlds within worlds until the Word erupts in man.

So when you are told in the 19th chapter of Revelation that his robe is dipped in blood, don't think of any red robe that the cardinal wears. Hasn't a thing to do with the outside, your little garment of flesh and blood that's the robe that you're wearing. "And he made for them skins"…now it's dipped in blood. For, you were Spirit *before* you came out and now you're clothed in a robe dipped in blood. And the name by which he's named and called is the Word of God…that's *you*. That Word that was in the beginning that was with God and that *was* God, that's you. That Word that became flesh and dwells within us, that's you. That Word that went forth from the mouth of God that cannot return unto him empty but must accomplish that which he purposed and prosper in the thing for which he sent it, that Word is you. When you say "I am" that's he, that's God.

Now in this world, you, too, can use that Word on this level. You can assume that things are as you would like them to be, and persuade yourself that they are. You'll find yourself carrying on little, tiny unheard conversations and these unheard little words within yourself persuading yourself that things are as you desire them to be, these are words too. That's why Blake said, "What have I said? What have I done? O all-powerful human words!" (*Jer.*, Plt.24). You have no idea what you are doing in the course of a day with these little internal mental conversations which you know no one outside hears. But may I tell you, they are responding to what inwardly you are saying, and you wonder why do they act as they do towards me? They have to because you inwardly are speaking words, too, and these internal conversations are carrying forward into the world, and the world responds in keeping with the word that you send out. You don't have to bellow the word and you don't have to utter it audibly at all. But you can't think without the use of words. You think anything and all of a sudden you find words clothing the thought. If you meet someone mentally and you will say, "Well, you look remarkably well," you will *think* he looks remarkably well. But if you want to express it you could say "You look remarkably well." Well now, *believe* that he does look remarkably well and you've sent your word. "I heard good news about you. I hear that things have gone up and up and up in your world. I hear that you've been making so much money that you don't know what to do with it." And, of course, he may even laugh in your mind's eye. But *feel* the reality of the word that you uttered. Don't say it will come in this manner or that manner or the other manner, you simply do it. Then you will know the power of these words…because you are God. God became man clothed in these mortal garments of flesh and blood that man may become God.

So when you see this disturbance in your world you might think, well, why did it happen to me? Because, in your idle moment you are not controlling your Imagination, and you are carrying on arguments with your children, with your parents, with your friends, from premises that are stupid because they need not be. If you know that all these things must come to pass, what are you doing? If you really believe that all these things are producing the results that they imply, well then, stop it. Stop it now and change the record…put on a new record.

But here, the day will come—I trust it isn't far off, but no one knows the hour, no one—that this fundamental revelation of the unfolding of the Word within you comes to pass. When the whole book that we call the sacred Word of God, and it is, unfolds and you are the central character, you are the actor playing the center part. Then you will know who Jesus is.

Now let us go into the Silence.

*   *   *

Now are there any questions, please?

Q: (inaudible)

A: Well, he's called Jesus in the beginning because his name shall be called Jesus as you are told in the Book of Luke (1:31). Again, in the Book of Matthew, it begins with the word alone "Jesus," then eventually they tied on the name Christ, which simply means "Messiah," which simply means the "Anointed One," which was the title given to David. One has to discriminate between these two titles. It's not like a man called John and his surname is Smith, John Smith, as some of these scholars believe. It's a mystery. Every time you open that book you're looking at a mystery and it's the mystery of God, not some little mystery written by one of our great mystery writers. This is something that is a mystery. Paul uses the word mystery no less than twenty times. He speaks of the mystery hidden for the ages but now revealed in you as "Christ in you, the hope of glory" (Col.1:27): it's his image. But Jesus is God himself. Jesus and the word Jehovah are one. David in the Old Testament the Lord God Jehovah called him "my son." In the New Testament, if one understands how to read it, David in the Spirit called him "my Father." So if he called Jesus "my Father," as told you in the 20th chapter of the Book of Luke, when he asked the question…no one asked the question, he brought it up. He said, "What think ye of the Christ? Whose son is he? They answered, 'The son of David.' Then he replied, 'Why then did David in the Spirit call him'—speaking now of another—'my Lord'? If he thus calls him my Lord, how is he his son?" (20:41,44). He is calling him "my Father" in fulfillment of scripture, which is the 89th Psalm: "I have found David," said Jehovah, "and he has cried unto me, 'Thou art my Father, my God, and the Rock of my salvation" (89:26).

So if I come to fulfill scripture and the only scripture you can fulfill is the Old Testament—for that was the only scripture when the eruption took place—he's only fulfilling the Old Testament. So if in the Old Testament David calls the Lord "my Father" and in the 2nd Psalm, the Lord said, "I shall say unto you, 'Thou art my son, today I begotten thee,'" then in the interval he finds him and calls him "Father." Well then, if I have come to fulfill scripture and the only scripture is the Old Testament, then I must find *David* and he must call *me* Father…for the New is only the pattern that interprets the Old.

I know it's a shock. It would be to you to be told that the whole of the story of Jesus from the conception of the Holy Spirit to his ascension into heaven is a *sign*…a sign vouchsafed by God to all who will receive it. Will you believe it is a sign? It's a plan, it's a pattern, the pattern man, which everyone when the Word in him erupts follows that pattern. There's no other entry into heaven save the unfolding of that pattern in man, because only Christ resurrects, only God resurrects…so the pattern unfolds in man.

Good night.

THE TRUE BATTLE OF ARMAGEDDON

5/26/69

A man's true environment is in his Imagination, so that "All that we behold, though it appears without, it is within, in our Imagination of which this world of mortality is but a shadow" (Blake, *Jer.,* Plt.71). Everything in our world contains within itself the capacity for symbolic significance, so no matter what is taking place it's a symbol telling you what is taking place within you. This whole vast world is yourself pushed out so that it is the image that is alive within our Imagination that really overwhelms us.

Now tonight let us turn to the one great book, the Bible. We are told there will be a finial battle…there will be a great and last war at the end of the world called Armageddon. The world thinks it's going to take place on the outside, where races are put against races and nations against nations and so on. You've heard it…you're old enough some of you to have heard that the First World War was that war and then came the 2nd World War. There are always wars, always conflicts, but that is *not* Armageddon. Armageddon is the battle of ideology…and it doesn't mean Communism against Democracy or Socialism against Capitalism…hasn't a thing to do with that. The battle takes place *in us.*

When we look into the world today and see the unrest, if you really understood what is taking place in a very large group in this world, you would rejoice…if you knew scripture. He said, "Do not think I have come to bring peace on earth. I have come not to bring peace but a sword. I have come to set a man against his father, and to set a daughter against her mother, and a daughter-in-law against her mother-in-law; and a man's foes are those of his *own* household" (Mat.10:35). It certainly doesn't mean our children pitted against us, hasn't a thing to do with that. But here you'll see, as it's described in scripture, it's the young against the old. It is simply the *true* understanding of the Word of God against the traditions of men. And then you hear it, after having built up all these structures by which you live, and you thought by these structures you would earn the kingdom of heaven, and so you would simply acquire merit. Then comes one who has experienced the story of God and he tells you as it actually happens and he knows that the entire story, the life of Jesus Christ, is a spiritual autobiography of everyone who is redeemed. So he tells it, knowing that everyone is going to be redeemed, and therefore *everyone* is going to have this as his own spiritual autobiography. Well, when you hear it, the conflict starts within you, and *that's* the battle of Armageddon.

Neutrality is impossible. You can't patch the little piece of new cloth to the old. It is either all or nothing. You can't possibly put the new wine that you're now receiving into the old bottles and say, well, I'll go along with him just so far, but I will not give up my belief in an external God to whom I bend my knee and cross my body when I stand before what represents him upon the wall. So the battle is on...until finally within oneself the story unfolds and then the victory is God's. It's over. You should have no other God but God, and his name is I AM. "This is my name forever. By this name I shall be known throughout all generations" (Exod.3:14). Choose this day whom you shall serve...we chose this day the Lord. All right, now prove it in your behavior and prove it in your life. To whom will you turn if you've chosen correctly and chosen the Lord? And I tell you from experience this story of Jesus Christ is the actual spiritual *autobiography* of the individual who is redeemed; for the entire story unfolds within him as though there were no other, just himself.

So here, Armageddon...don't look for it on the outside. Today we see the young—that's only a symbol—erupting not in our country alone, erupting all over the world, in Europe, in Tokyo, and were it known, in Russia. They only allow a little bit to sneak out, but they are erupting there too. That's a symbol. These kids think that they're going to change the world. No, to those who understand, they aren't changing the world. There's a tremendous eruption of the *truth* in the hearts of men. It's not just confined to this platform. There must be from this world picture of eruption simply an enormous eruption of truth against the entrenched traditions of men. Yes, even in so-called atheistic Russia...in lands where they are not considered Christian. But truth is not confined that way; it's confined to God. And within himself he realizes he is the being spoken of in scripture.

So religion really is in the true sense of the word a devotion, a tie to the most exalted reality that one has experienced. So when one has experienced scripture, who in this world can put him back into the little bottle? They can't do it. And here, you find all over our little world men who are supposed to speak the Word of God and encourage those who listen to them. They're involved in the shadow world. They're telling our government what they should do and how they should do it, not telling the individual who comes to him about God's *promise*. That here is God's promise, this fantastic promise that he's going to give himself to you in the most literal sense of he word: he's going to give his son to you. And because he and his son are one, then he gave himself to you. Now believe it and hope for the eruption now. Just now, this moment, the whole thing could erupt within us. And you realize it's not of another...that the whole vast drama on the outside is taking place within us and these things are but shadows...the whole vast world is a shadow world.

So when you see the young pitted against the old, and we think now this is a new generation, no, rejoice, for this is part of scripture. They burn down the buildings, and you and I will pay the taxes. We resent the fact that we may be taxed all the more to rebuild the buildings. But has it happened *in* us, that eruption? So that the new idea has taken over and completely displaced the old...that I no longer can bow to an external God? That I can no longer believe in an external Jesus Christ...that Christ in me all along was the hope of glory? And suddenly, that Christ in me awoke and unfolded his story...not as another where I observe him but as myself, redeeming me by becoming me to the point where everything said of him *I am* experiencing of myself. Now, that is the new as against my old concepts that I got from my mother first, then in Sunday school, then in school, and then as I went to church and heard it from the pulpit. That was an idea that I built within me and that structure I lived by it, it governed my behavior... and suddenly it is not true.

Now the battle is between truth and error...that's the *real* battle of Armageddon. It's not between nations and nations and races and races. It may *seem* to be on the outside, but it is not. So he comes into the world to bring the sword of truth. Now we are told, and when he comes the armies of heaven follow him, and from his mouth issues a flaming sword, a sharp sword. Then we are told that the sword is the sword of the Spirit, which is The Word of God" (Rev.19:13-15). So what does he bring? A sword by which we chop peoples heads off? No...that's only a symbol. Take off his head so that something new may come...but that's only a symbol. Horrible as it is, in the outer world that only symbolizes what is taking place *within* us. So here, the whole head comes off. Whose head?—John the Baptist. That was the end and then rising in its place is the Lord Jesus Christ. When he is arrested and his head comes off, I no longer go along with the external world...for he now simply is clothed in the external things of camel hair, camel and leather around his waist...everything that is external to man.

Now comes the man from within, for he is the inner man, and that inner man rises within me displacing the outer man. But I do see his rising as a disturbing influence, and everything that I believed in and bowed to on the outside—worshipped him because he was known, worshipped him because he was rich, worshipped him because he was an intelligent person in the world—then I discover that the being of beings, the God of Gods, is really within myself! And now he erupts and tells me if I conquer, conquer what? If I overcome all of these beliefs—I can't patch it up, I can't modify it—if I overcome everything external to myself, and see only myself as the cause of the phenomena of my life, nothing in the world but myself producing everything in my world—if I really accept that 100 percent then "to him who conquers I will give the morning star" [David] (Rev.2:26,28).

Now he identifies himself *as the* morning star. "I am the root *and* the offspring"...who's speaking? Jesus. And who is Jesus?—the Lord God Jehovah. So, I am the root and the offspring of David. I am the bright morning star. So he's going to give me if I conquer the old and accept, completely accept it, then I receive as the gift himself, the bright morning star—which is the symbol of the new day and immortality, a complete change in my world when finally this little garment that housed the old one is taken off for the last time. Then I am clothed in the new man, the man that rose within me, and repeated in detail the entire story of the Lord Jesus Christ.

So Armageddon is not taking place in the battlefields of the world. Interpret them all to be eruption. And then you see a new one coming in its place. Here is America...it's a new nation compared to the old nations. Now it supplanted the old powers. That's one grand eruption...the mightiest power in the world of Caesar is this land today. But in the midst of it we find people erupting and the young pitted against the old. And that's exactly how he does it in scripture, as you read it in the 10th chapter of the Book of Matthew. He doesn't tell you old against the new, he starts off with man against his father, and the daughter against her mother, and the daughter-in-law against her mother-in-law. He starts with the young trying to dislodge the old and the battle is on. Watch it in the world.

So everything must be interpreted as a *symbol* as we do in our dreams. Like a lady tonight who wrote me...I got it his past week...she felt in her dream that she was one of a twin and one had died. She felt that the love for the one who died was so great and she didn't want to hurt her mother, so she pretended she was the one who died and got the affection of her mother and the affection of all. She knew all along that the one who died was the one she had assumed.

Well, what a perfect story confirming scripture. Here, the one who took the heart of God the Father was Jacob, and he supplanted his brother Esau in the affections of his father. He came second, and he thought that because he was not first but second that the Father would love the first one first and most. Not knowing, and the world does not know that he who is called the first born from the dead in the Book of Revelation and in the Book of Colossians...and he said the first born of every creature is the same first born; but the first born from the dead must be seen in the *order* of events rather than in time.

So that every one who erupts in the story of Jesus Christ, that is the *first* born. You aren't second because 2,000 years you came later or 1,000 years or 3,000 years. No one comes before you, because Christ is the head...he is the first. Well, if Christ unfolds within you, you can't be second. You supplant what *was* the first. So you're told, the body comes into the world and that is first. The physical is first, the Spirit is second; but the second which is Spirit *supplants* the first. So the outer man is Esau, that's first, he comes in first. The second one comes in, that's Jacob, and he is the *smooth*-skinned lad...he is the Spirit man. Then we are told, "And the Lord loved Jacob but he hated Esau" (Rom.9:13). The outer man must be discarded, because flesh and blood cannot enter the kingdom of heaven. So it's the inner man that is to be born and he is the first born from the dead. But see that first born in the *order* rather than time, so that first he must rise. That's the one that is going to be born, the one who has awakened within. The minute he is awakened he comes out; as he comes out, he is born from above. That's the one the Lord loves, and he's one with the Lord because he *is* the Lord. "I will give you now the bright morning star," and he is himself the bright morning star who gives it...so God gives himself. There's no one, then, but you. You then control all. When you take off this garment, you are one with the God who is running the entire show.

Seen from above, this conflict today is not disturbing...they're rejoicing that there's an eruption of the truth in the hearts of men. But on this level as a tax payer, you read the morning paper and you resent the fact they're burning down these buildings that cost money. You resent the fact that people who go there to be educated cannot be educated because of the nonsense of a little percentage...but there's always only a small little percentage. But they don't know what they're doing...they're only symbols. They're playing their little game not knowing what they're doing at all. "Father, forgive them, they know not what they do." They *think* they're going to take over...they think they're going to take over the entire country or the world. No, they're only that little symbol, symbolizing that measure of the eruption in the hearts of men. For there's only always at any one time a remnant who erupts. But, oh, today when you see the world picture what a lovely large remnant. On the other hand, we are three and a half billion today as against only say a few hundred million 2,000 years ago. So here it is a larger section, but the larger is only relative, because, if I take three and a half billion, or even say, a few hundred million, you can see the difference. But today that thing has gone out and they are erupting…in this small room they're erupting, there's eruption here. Percentage-wise it's a very large eruption.

So here, a lady wrote, "I had this most disturbing dream. I found myself in my home cleaning out every piece of furniture that I'm going to take into my new apartment. It's going to be two miles from here." And so she's singling out all the ones she's going to take and then leaving these others for her husband…which care of the two she's going to take. Then she finds herself in the new apartment. She knows it intimately as she places all these things. Then she awakes in the bed with her husband to find that it wasn't as real as it appeared to be. It seemed so three-dimensional, everything was so real.

Well, that's the most wonderful experience. No, you aren't going to leave the man you love here. No, hasn't a thing to do with that. Take the symbolism of it. He is your husband, but your true husband is God. When you're told in the 2nd chapter of Genesis, "And a man shall leave everything and cleave to his wife 'til they become one flesh," that's what you did. You left everything of the earth, moved into an entirely different state, which is *motion*. The first creative act was motion: "And the Spirit of God *moved* upon the face of the deep." As God moved, everything erupted and the world came into visibility. So you moved from one state into another, but the state into which you moved was into your *true* husband who is the Lord God Almighty. That's your true husband. But the symbol of that husband is on earth and you will love him and continue to love him, and share your world with him and he with you. But you made the move *within* into the real union with God, for that's your husband, as told you in the Book of Isaiah: "You Maker is your husband; the Lord of hosts is his name" (54:5). So you move into a real relationship with the God within you, who will leave everything and cleave to you. And you did discover the great secret of moving from state to state.

So don't be bewildered as you said in your letter, "I am bewildered. What does it mean?" No, you'll find that the love will not be modified and the love grows stronger. If you pass a certain point in this world, then your affections get deeper and deeper for the one that when you first met her or met him you were fired by sex. That holds you. But when that fades, if the love is maintained as it was prior to the union, then you find that relationship deeper and deeper. You're more concerned for your loved one than ever before. It is not sex anymore. That is something that is faded, slowly fades from your world, but a deeper one takes over. Now, the motion takes place within you from what is now a relationship in this world to a spiritual relationship. And you'll find that you're not far then from the eruption of the story of Jesus within you. The whole thing unfolds within you.

So, *his* story is the spiritual biography, *auto*-biography, of the one who is redeemed. All shall be redeemed and therefore it's going to be the experience of every child born of woman. So don't look for the conflicts on the outside…interpret them as symbols. They're all symbols. So when today the youth is pitted against the old, see it not as the world is describing it in the papers and radio and TV. Don't go wild about it. Rejoice that in a large section of the world the Word, which is the sword of the Spirit, has erupted and the armies are on the march. For the armies of heaven *followed* him, and then from his mouth issues this flaming sword. The sword is called "the sword of the Spirit," which is the Word of God. And his name shall be called the Word of God. But he is the *living* Word that unfolds within man and interprets the external Word of the letter. So the whole outer world is a dead world like the letter in the Bible. It's dead until something alive makes it so, and only when it erupts within man does that dead letter become alive. So, he interprets it.

Well, many reject him. But today when you see the conflict many must have accepted it. Many must have experienced it and are telling it the world over. Where they are I don't know…not with this mask on me. But whoever is telling it is telling it from an experience. That's the only thing that can inflame the mind. You can't go on adding to the traditions of men for that's dead letters, all dead. Then you hear on radio and see on TV and read in the paper that our clergy instead of telling the Word of God are so involved in politics. They think they can buy off the eruption with money. They'll take all the money and ask for more. You can't stop ransom and you can't stop any blackmail…you can't stop it. But instead of stopping that whole nonsense and then in their own words tell the story of Jesus Christ… but unfortunately they don't know it. For if they sat here tonight they would think they're listening to the devil. To them this is blasphemy in the extreme. And yet, I am telling you from experience and they are telling you from theory what their fathers taught them. You're told in scripture that "You, for the sake of your traditions, the traditions of your fathers, you have

529

made *void* the Word of God" (Mat.15:6). And you can tell that from the top down, from everyone, no matter who he is.

So here, they make all their little saints…made out of nothing and they never existed. Then something has happened to force them to confess the nonexistence of their saints from whom they have made hundreds of millions of dollars in selling their little icons, all these little indulgences, and now they can't. They're still selling them. There are people who refuse to accept it. They still want their little so-called protection based upon the outside. You don't want it, that's why you're here, and you're quite willing to accept that the drama is unfolded in you, and not on the outside. So when the most horrible blow hits you and it comes home to your heart, try to see the symbolism in it all. Everything in this outer world is a symbol and contains that capacity for a symbolic significance. So why did it happen and how did it happen, and what is its meaning? What is the significance of the thing that happened? Just like a dream, for a dream has some significance. "For God speaks in a dream and makes himself known in a vision" (Num.12:6). Well, if God is speaking I should listen and listen attentively to my dream and try to understand what he is telling me through the symbolism of dream.

I got another lovely letter, about twenty or twenty-five dreams. Well, I couldn't, naturally, even summarize them because they're different. But I can tell her (and she's here tonight) they are perfectly marvelous. They're all foreshadowings or adumbrations of the story that will erupt within you when you discover you yourself are Jesus Christ, that he's not another. In your dreams he still seems to be another. He came as though he were another, well, that's an adumbration. Like the story in 2nd Kings concerning Elijah. Elisha said to him, "Give me a double portion of your spirit" and he said, "When I leave you and depart from you if you see me you shall get what you ask for; if you don't, you shall not have it" (2:9-14). And then fire separated them, and then Elijah went up in a whirlwind…well, that's an adumbration. You do go up in a whirlwind. The word fire…it's a fiery serpent…you go up *as* the fiery serpent. Well, that's not spelled out, because it's an adumbration. The Word had to erupt within one first in order to understand the story of Elijah going up in a whirlwind. So it is said a fire separated them. Well, may I tell you it *is* a fire.

Then you find in the 14th chapter of Zechariah, he stands—who?—the Lord is standing on the Mount of Olives and suddenly there is a complete splitting of the Mount from east to west; and then one half moves northward and one-half moves south (14:4). Now, that's exactly what happens…but it is not any mountain outside of you. The whole drama is in you and *you* are the Mount of Olives, and the Lord *is* standing on the Mount within you. At one moment in time it is split from east to west, and one does move north and one does move south, and your whole body stands before you as something split in two. Then you go up like the whirlwind, but the whirlwind is a fiery serpent. I don't see a whirlwind, it spins like a spiral. But he said fire separated us, and it *is* a fiery state because a bolt of lightning does cut you in two from your head to the base of your spine, and you move this way, completely parted. But who would understand it until one man experienced it? And then he dramatized it, the evangelist dramatized it, still leaving it as a closed book for those who have not fully experienced it. But to be understood by those who will be drawn by the one who has experienced it in the hope that in the not distant future they will individually experience the entire story of Jesus Christ.

So when you see unrest today, instead of ducking, rejoice that the young is now pitted against the old. Not that your child comes home and insults you. I am a father and I have two children. One is no longer the child... neither for that matter...both are adults, yet being the father they're always children to you. Although one is forty-five and one is twenty-six, they always will be to me children as far as I am concerned. But they've never gone against me. Oh, they go their own way; they are individuals as they should be and they have their own opinions. They don't completely go along with me at all. So it's not a conflict in my little physical household. The conflict is in my household which is all within my Imagination. So I leave them alone. The conflict is in me. Well, if I've overcome it, as the drama has proven, I may find myself one morning listening to the radio, seeing the TV, or reading the paper and you can so quietly and quickly get involved and *forget* and come down and see this nonsense in the world and become involved. Get back up to the Mount and see it all as symbolism. The whole thing is a symbol telling you what has happened and it's happening in the world.

Now, the eruption will not go on forever, because it only lasts for a certain length of time and the door is *closed* once more. The door does not remain open into heaven; it only opens at *intervals* of time. Blake gave it 200 years. How long it remained ajar he didn't say, but he said, "Every 200 years there's a gate into heaven." Well, you can see the symbol now is telling you that the door is ajar. How long it remains ajar I do not know. But you can see why the conflict rages...it is still ajar.

Now this will not make sense. You couldn't print this in tomorrow's paper, because they might have me investigated as a mental case. Yet I am telling you this is true. As you're told in scripture, "Why do you listen to him? The man is mad and he has a devil" (Jn.10:20). He said, "I am not mad and I do not have a devil, what I tell you is true. For I speak not of my own accord, I speak as the Father speaks to me" (Acts26:25). He's only telling you what he experienced. So he's not listening to a word and then telling you the word; he has experienced it. He actually experiences the entire drama, so he tells you *what* he has experienced. Why listen to him? The man is mad. We know his background, a very limited background. How does this man have learning seeing that he's never studied? How does he have learning? He said, "My words are not my words but the words of him who sent me…and he who sent me is God. But he is my Father and I know my Father and ye know not your God." Well, the man is mad…he that we know and know his background and he dares to claim he is the Son of God! Then he tops it, he said, "Not only the Son of God…I and my Father are one. So when you see me you see him who sent me." Well, who sent you? "My Father… and my Father is he whom you call God." He experienced it. Then having known the entire Old Testament—for that was the only thing he studied—he went back and showed them page after page where what he is telling is the interpretation, the spiritual interpretation of the dead letter. And so, he unfolded the whole thing within himself.

So Armageddon…don't let anyone tell you when you see nation against nation and race against race that *that* is Armageddon. Armageddon is the battle of ideology where they are pitted against each other *in you*. And I can't tell anyone what a shock it was to me to discover that the Christ to whom I prayed and to whom I turned in my prayers really was within me as scripture teaches. But I didn't take it literally. When I was told, "Christ in you is the hope of glory" these were words because I was taught and trained to turn on the outside for that Christ…not Christ in me. I could find no comfort in that Christ. I was seventeen when I left Barbados, seventeen and a half, and when I first began to pray by my mother putting my knees on the floor to pray, I did not have the courage to go to bed no matter how tired I was until I got down on my knees and prayed every night. That habit would not break for quite a while after I came to this country. Can you imagine the shock that comes to one who was trained to get on his knees and pray to an external God to find that he was not external at all! Then comes that awesome moment when it unfolds within you and you are he! You can hardly believe it. For memory hasn't faded…you know your past, you know how unlovely much of it has been. You know the thoughts, the emotions that were yours, the words that you've uttered. And all that could still be a house in which the perfect one, the unblemished one, the one that was never tarnished has unfolded, and you are he…still with the memory of the outer garment that you wore which clothed him while he was here.

Well, I can't tell anyone the shock that comes when all these things by which you lived tumble to earth. You can no longer turn to anyone on the *outside*. You can't turn to anything and blame it or praise it for what is taking

The Return of Glory

place in your world, not a thing. If it's unlovely you are the cause; if it's lovely you are the cause. Everything is unfolding within you. You are detached from the university, or you didn't go to one, and what is taking place, you are the cause? Yes. The word of truth erupted within you, and when it comes it sets one against the other. 'Well, they never heard you, Neville." I don't say they ever heard me, but the Word is not confined. And so when it comes into the world and he is here and he's erupted, he brings the new wine, and the old bottles cannot contain it. It will split and you cannot put the new patch upon the old garment. You see the whole erupting world around you and we wonder what on earth is taking place? Have we lost control of our children, they're not disciplined?

Well, you can say all kinds of things and justify it and make it come out just as you would like it...and I'm not going to deny that's your right. I find myself on occasion sucked into the same stream and passing an opinion not based upon the truth that has erupted in me...so I can't judge another. Who am I to say growing a beard is wrong or long hair is wrong or that anything else is wrong? I don't know. I can only say that when I see these things rejoice, for he has come. And when he comes he invariably sets the young against the old. And it's not a child against his physical parent, but it is the new idea that he brings that is going to disturb the traditions of men. You've been living by the traditions of men and so all of a sudden they are disturbed, and the disturbance is in *you,* but reflected in the disturbance of the world.

They don't know what they're doing. Not one of them knows this night why I'm doing what I'm doing. If you put him right down and asked him, he doesn't know. He is being led like sheep to the slaughter. Many of them, as some have analyzed it, may easily be set up, as someone firmly believes, as cannon fodder. And yet it caused rejoicing in the hearts of those who observe it from above, for it is only causing eruption of God's immortal plan...for Jesus Christ is the *pattern* and this immortal pattern of salvation is *in* man. When they see it erupt, nothing in this world, this shadow world, interests them. They are rejoicing at the eruption in man, which eruption causes the eruption in the outer world to set the young against the old...for this is the new that comes into the world.

In the meanwhile, you take what you know of this law, for the whole is true and use it towards your own personal *good* fortune in the world of Caesar. Just use it. It's simple: go to the end and assume the feeling of the wish fulfilled...just go to the end. Don't ask anyone to help you and ask no one if it's right. Do you like it? Well then, go to the end; assume the feeling of the wish fulfilled. For that being who is about to erupt himself in you is the being who will control *that* end *if* you will remain faithful to it. If you find yourself moving from it, go back to it and once more assume the feeling of the wish fulfilled and that assumption will harden into fact.

Now let us go into the Silence.

*   *   *

Q: (inaudible)

A: The Father in you. The only time he knows he is the Father is when his Son, which was before that the world was, stands before you and calls you "Father." Then you know that you *are* the Father and the Father knows that he is you. And the Son knows that you are his Father, and that Son is David. The Father is the Lord Jesus Christ. That truly is the Father who became man in the most literal sense: he died…for only through death can this awaken. It's the mystery of life through death. "The mystery of the grain of wheat that falls into the earth and dies in order to be made alive, for unless it dies it remains alone; but if it dies it brings forth much" (Jn.12:24). So the Father actually becomes man. He empties himself of all and "He who was rich, yet for our sake became poor, so that by his poverty we may become rich" (2Cor.8:9). Rich in power, rich in wisdom…that's the only wealth of the world. For with that wisdom you can create anything in the world. Take all my creations away from me, but leave me the *capacity* to create. Give me the power and the wisdom to create. Take everything from me and it would mean nothing.

So the Father in man is sound asleep. As told us in scripture, "Rouse thyself! Why sleepest thou, O Lord? Awake!" (Ps.44:23). So the search of every child born of woman is for the Father, and when he finds the Father he finds himself. He's really looking for himself.

Q: (inaudible)

A: When he finds it, he finds it in you. And the story of Jesus is a pattern by which he unfolds. He first rises in you, not as another; when he awoke in me, I awoke. It wasn't another and I was alone in my skull. Not a thing in that skull but myself, and I knew the skull was sealed like a tomb. I also knew that it *was* a tomb…this innate wisdom that you have. You are not only aware that you are in your skull but you're also aware of the fact your skull is a tomb. That's Golgotha and that's where you were placed. You don't remember when you were placed there, you don't remember when you entered there or if you were taken there. That knowledge is not yet yours, whether you did it deliberately as told us in scripture that "No one takes away my life, I lay it down myself. I have the power to lay it down, and the power to lift it up again" (Jn.10:18).

The Return of Glory

Now I have no memory of walking into that tomb myself, so I have no knowledge of entry. I only knew that I awoke in it and therefore I was either placed there or I walked in there deliberately and the whole thing was sealed. I knew myself to be sealed in my own skull and I knew my skull was a tomb. My one consuming desire was to get out. Then this area at the base of my skull rolled away. I pushed it from within and something rolled away like a stone and then it left a small opening. I put my head through and squeezed and squeezed and came out inch by inch like a child coming out of a womb. Only instead of being the womb of woman this is the skull of man: birth from above rather than birth from below.

Then the symbolism as told us in the Book of Luke appeared before me. This storm wind...that's all that I can describe it...it's a wind that was unearthly like a storm, a hurricane. Here, I look over to see the cause of the disturbance and when I look back (didn't take more than a few seconds) when I looked back my body out of which I had emerged is gone, but in its place sat my three older brothers. The oldest is at the head, the second at my right foot and the third at my left foot... as though the body was on its back. And it was, but the body had been moved, leaving now three witnesses. Then one is disturbed, my third brother Lawrence who was a doctor in this world, and he goes over to investigate the cause of the wind. He makes just a step or two and something on the floor attracts his attention. It is a little babe wrapped in swaddling clothes. He lifts the babe and announces to the other two, "It is Neville's baby!" They in turn said, "How can Neville have a baby?" He doesn't argue the point, he presents the infant wrapped in swaddling clothes, puts it on the bed where the body formerly was. Then I bent over...invisible to all for they don't see me, and I lift that visible child that they could see into my arms and I said, "How is my sweetheart?" The little child broke into the heavenly smile and the whole vision came to an end (Luke 2:12). Here is scripture unfolding now within me. And then every scene as told in scripture concerning Jesus Christ unfolded within me from then on.

So where is he? Is it not true, as told us in Colossians, it is "Christ in you that is the hope of glory"? (1:27). And what is the glory? He glorifies the Father and he actually *is* the Father. He said, "Return unto me now the glory that was mine, the glory that I had *with* thee before that the world was" (Jn. 17:5). I'm going back to pick up where I left off. But in that horrible experience coming through the world of death... for this is the world of death where everything dies, everything dies no matter what it is. We're told today the sun is slowly dying and all the suns are dying. If it takes unnumbered trillions of light years they all will eventually die. So this world is a world of death. So you come into the world of death and conquer it, you overcome death. You die, you don't pretend you're dying, you die, and yet there's something in you that cannot die, and it rises, and that is Christ in you who is the hope of glory.

Tell that story and it disturbs the mind of those who have heard the story as a secular story. For *this* is the spiritual auto-biography of man while the story as it is told is the secular biography...and it isn't so at all. It hasn't a thing to do with the secular world, it's all to do with the spiritual world.

Q: To what extent are individuals responsible for the crime, etc., that's going on in the world?

A: If one truly knew. Did you hear the question, "To what extent are we as individuals responsible for the eruptions in the world?" If man truly knew the hidden cause of the eruptions, he would set everyone who is erupting free. If man truly knew the hidden cause of the violence in the world, he would set not only the victim ___(??) free but he'd set the one who *seemingly* is the cause free.

There are such things even in our law as proximate causes. I'll give you a very vivid story. My daughter on her first trip out, she was only sixteen. She had to wait until she was sixteen to drive a car, and we bought her a second-hand car, a nice little Buick. She took off and she went down Doheny Road coming into Sunset and it's a very sharp curve. It was recently paved, beautifully paved...it was as black as you could make a road and beautifully marked with a double line because it was a curve like an S. She's going down slowly when a mad person comes blindly up in this curved road, across the double line, and seems to be coming straight towards her. This is her first trip out, solo trip, and she made a sharp turn to void the impact and ran right into a tree, a palm tree. Smashed the car, smashed her nose, and she came home with the car turned inside out. The tire was torn when she got home because one piece as she turned it over cut into the car. There was not a thing you could do with the car but give it away.

I said to her, "Darling, you aren't hurt too badly are you?" No, she was crying over her car. Here her nose was smashed, blood coming down. Well, at that moment if I could have put my hands on that nut I'd have killed him. I'm looking at my sweetheart, my daughter, and here is this nut the cause of her misfortune. Forget the car. So we paid $550 for it, it was a second-hand car...get another car. But this is her first trip out by herself and naturally she is careful and this fellow comes whirling around at fifty miles per hour, comes across the double line, and he wouldn't even stop. He heard the impact. Kept on going…didn't want to be near the accident. Well, that's a proximate cause. If you came upon the scene, she was the cause of that tree being injured and the car being injured. And the one who seemingly is the innocent one who *is* the cause of it went on innocently. So that is what is called in law the proximate cause. You drive down the highway and you think this fella is going to hit you, and so you to avoid the blow turn sharply and hit the other fella. Well, you're responsible because you struck him and he didn't strike you. Yet you interpreted his actions as an impending accident, and you are now the *seeming* cause of the accident when the true cause was what he, the innocent bystander, really did.

So hidden in the minds of men…for we're all creating in this world in our Imaginations: Imagination creates reality. Who knows who is treading in the winepress tonight that is the cause of the disturbances in the world? We have an arms industry, with all of the billions that we pour into it. We can't consume it ourselves, so we have to go out and force countries that can ill-afford to buy it to buy it. So we go all through South America or the Near East, all through the world, selling our battleships and discarded planes and discarded guns that we may keep the industry pouring. Well, these fellas who are selling it, they want to be successful so they can build a bigger home and get not three cars but four cars in the garage, and then live in the finest clubs, and be important people in their little community…selling arms! Then suddenly you read in the paper Peru has done so-and-so, this one does so-and-so. They have no way of making a gun for themselves and so we go out to sell them so that we may keep the wheels turning. So who is the unseen culprit? Well, that's the world over.

For instance, as a friend said to me one day, it was Emmet Fox, he said, "You know, a man came to see me and he wanted his business improved. I said, 'All right, I'll pray for you, my good man. I'll pray the only way I know how to pray, and I'll pray that your business is simply booming. I'm a little bit curious tell me, what is your business?'" He said, 'I'm a mortician.'"

Good night.

THE LAW OF LIBERTY

5/30/69

What we feel deeply is far more important than what we think. We may think for the longest time and do nothing. It is feeling that spurs us to action. And "God only acts and is, in existing beings or men" (Blake, *Mar. of Heaven/Hell,* Plt.17). So he in you, who is the cause of all, only acts *if* the thing is *felt*. So I can think of a thousand things and not be moved to act. But what we feel in the depth, that deep feeling, that conviction, is far, far more important than what we think.

Let us turn to scripture. Here in the first chapter of the epistle of James, "Ask in faith, with no doubting, for he who doubts is like a wave of the sea that is driven and tossed by the wind. Let not that person believe that the double-minded man, unstable in all his ways, shall receive anything from the Lord" (1:6) "Be ye doers of the word, and not hearers only, deceiving yourselves. For if you are a hearer only and not a doer, you are like a man who observes his natural face in the mirror; and then goes his way and at once forgets what he's like. But if you are a doer of the word and not just a forgetful hearer, then you look into the perfect law, the law of liberty, and persevere…that man shall be blessed in all his doing" (1:22). You find that in the very first chapter of the Book of James.

Now, how do I go about being a doer instead of a hearer? Well, I can tell you that scripture teaches that whatever you desire, and you believe that you have received it, you will receive it (Mark 11:24). Now there is no limit set upon the power of faith. In fact, the central character called Jesus in scripture sets no limit upon two things: one is the love of God, and the other is the power of faith. In fact, all of his great deeds were prefaced with this, "According to your faith." Entirely up to you…he sets no limit to the power of faith. But faith, if you understand it, will encompass feeling. If I *feel* it! Now, I say I believe it, well then, I will act. And if I act, it is God in me doing the acting. Well, who is God in man?—his own wonderful human Imagination, that's God. His eternal name is "I am," that's God. Therefore, will he act? He will act only if I feel it, if I actually feel it.

Now, how do we do it in a practical way? Here prayer is a very practical idea, a *most* practical idea. Let us see how it's performed if I'm not a forgetful hearer. I tell you what I would like to be and you tell me, "Go your way. You *are* it!" And for one fleeting moment I think, "Isn't that nice, I *am* it" and for that moment I see the world as I would see it if it were true. You told me to go your way and that's it...but I don't feel it. In one second I go my way and then completely forget what I looked like in that moment, didn't think for one moment beyond that. But if I'm a doer of the word and not a forgetful hearer, then I persevere. The word perseverance is used in the Revised Standard Version. In the King James it's the same thing but they translate the Greek word's meaning "and continue therein"...but to persevere in that state.

So I ask you if this is possible. You tell me all things are possible to prayer, the power of prayer. Now how would I look into the mirror? I look into the mirror and I see my face, but now I look into a different mirror if I'm a doer. I look into the mirror of my friends...all my friends form a mirror. If they heard good news of me this night, they would reflect it in their faces and in their behavior relative to me. They would all show it. So if I thought of them and they knew what I know and am feeling about myself, they would *have* to show it. Well, if I'm feeling it they would certainly know it. So I conjure them in my mind's eye and let them see me as they would have to see me if what I'm assuming of myself is true.

Now, will I not only see myself in *this* mirror, the living mirror, and persevere in it; or will I turn away and quickly forget what I am like? Will I walk through this door tonight in the assumption that I *am* the man or the woman that I want to be? It doesn't make any difference if something on the outside denies it, it makes no difference. I have heard it, but now I have heard it with faith, and I carry it into deep feeling. Now I am feeling it in my being. And so, I conjure a mirror and the mirror is a living mirror, the faces of my friends, my acquaintances, and they all know because they've heard the good news of me, and I've accepted it as permanent. So I see my face now reflected in their faces. And if they really love me, there's an empathy, there's a rejoicing with me because of my good fortune. So if they rejoice with me because of my good fortune, let me now persevere and not forget what I have just seen in this living mirror.

If I do that, I am told I will be blessed in my doing. This is only fulfillment, for the New Testament is only fulfillment of the Old. You'll read this in the very first chapter of the Book of Psalms: "Blessed is the man... who delights in the law of the Lord...for in all that he does, he prospers" (1:1-3). This is called the law. So blessed is the man who looks into the law, the perfect law of liberty. Well, isn't that liberty...wasn't I liberated from my past when I saw faces reflecting what I would like them to see? Wasn't I liberated, wasn't I set free from whatever it was that I want to free myself? I would like to leave behind me, say, poverty or sickness or weakness or being unknown or being anything. I have a goal and it's not achieved. Well now, if it is achieved, my friends would know it, and if they knew it, well then, I have been set free from that former limitation. So looking into the perfect law, the law of liberty...and then if he perseveres in that state, he is blessed in all that he is doing. That's what I am told in scripture.

Now does it work? I tell you from my own personal experience that it works. But we are the operant power, it doesn't operate itself. I may know it and knowing it I have heard it. Either I heard it or I read it, but do I know it from experience? Have I put it to the test? Can I say to a friend of mine, "Try this because it works!" How does it work? I'll tell him how it works. "Well, how do you know?" Can I answer, "Because I've done it? I have proved it." If I have proved it, now I can speak with an authority that I couldn't prior to proving it. Well now, I'll tell you how it works. It works in this way... but now try it. May I tell you, you are set free, completely set free. I have been in places where I couldn't get out, many places where it seems the law, for purposes beyond my rational mind, pulled me to force me to test this principle. So I had a commitment in the United States for the first of May. I found myself after the war came to an end in little Barbados, and there were no ships save two little small ships servicing all of the islands. There are really hundreds of islands. One ship carried sixty passengers and one carried a little over a hundred, and there were numberless little islands, each expecting service from these two ships, one sailing out of Boston and one sailing out of New York.

Well, I had this most heavenly vacation. I inquired and this shipping agent said to me, "You're silly...you came out of New York City where you could have booked a round trip, and you only booked a one-way passage." So I explained to him that I didn't know how long I would remain. I thought I might be here three months, now it's five months as I extended our visit. It's been pleasant and my first commitment in America is the first week of May in Milwaukee and I must get back by that date. I can fly in a matter of hours to Milwaukee. He said, "You can't get out of this island until sometime in September and even then it's questionable, for look at the list, and this is only the list of Barbados. Now get the list of Trinidad, get the list of all the other islands, and they're all depending on these two ships."

The Return of Glory

I sat as you are seated now only I was in my hotel room. I got into the living room of that suite and got a nice comfortable chair, and there I assumed I was aboard a ship. I knew the ship...I was going to New York City; and only one ship went there, and that was the smaller of the two. I assumed that I was walking up the gangplank. I assumed my family—not all of them, there are many of them but just say eight or ten of them were coming aboard with me, and that one of them, my brother Victor, was carrying my little girl. So he was taking her up the gangplank, and here, I could feel the motion of the plank. When I got to the top I had no stateroom committed, so I remained on deck and put my mental hands on the rail. I could feel the salt of the sea on that rail, and then I looked back nostalgically at the little island. And then I could smell the salt of the sea in the air. I could feel that this is the ship and I am sailing on this ship tonight. I did that over and over.

That was feeling...I *felt* every step I made up that gangplank, I felt that rail, I felt the salt, I could smell the salt. I did everything that feeling could be brought to bear upon it, but everything you could touch. It was all a matter of sensing and touching. Then when I completed the act and it seemed natural, I broke it. The very next day I had confirmation I was sailing on *that* ship that would land me in New York City just about a week before my commitment in Milwaukee. I flew into Milwaukee and gave my series of lectures on time, no delay. I asked the agent in Barbados, "How did I get it...you have this long, long list?" She did not give me the details but said, "We had a cancellation from New York that they couldn't make it." Then those ahead of me she didn't call. She called one person who had bothered her day after day over a period of months, but this time when she called it was inconvenient for this one person to make it. She called none of the others and she called me because she could put the three of us...my little girl was a little, tiny child, and she and my wife could sleep in one bed and I could sleep in the other...for there are only two beds to a stateroom. So if they could get three in—of course, the little child we paid nothing for—but she could accommodate three, and that's the reason she gave me. I never heard why there was a cancellation up north, why the one back in Barbados could not take it at that time I only knew that I got in. I am completely unconcerned.

Now, someone in the audience (I trust not you) but I've told this story in the past and others would say to me, "Was that a good Christian thing to do, because you might have caused someone to cancel their trip? You might have caused someone to do so and so." It was the only *Christian* thing to do, for this is the Christian principle of fulfilling God's law. I don't care if a thousand people cancelled it. That is not my concern. I am told, "Whatever you desire, believe that you have received it, and you will" (Mark 11:24). God never created in the hearts of any human being a desire that he did not also provide for its satisfaction. He has provided for the satisfaction of every desire in this world. And the greatest of all desires is the thirst for God. He has created in man the satisfaction for that greatest of all desires, and it is the deepest of all satisfactions.

You *really* want an experience of God? Let no one tell you, you should not apply this principle towards it. Well, how? I've just told you how. I wanted to get out of Barbados and come to America. I was told to look into the perfect law, the law of liberty and persevere. Well, I did and my answer came in twenty-four hours. He doesn't give me another law for *his* search, he gives me the same law. Could I tell someone tonight I have had the same experience of which Neville speaks? Could I tell anyone this night? Is that really my consuming desire or do I want something other than that *first*? I want a lovely home, secure. I want it with all the comforts, but I want it secure. I want the money in the bank so I can touch it; I want to know it's there. I want to know my stocks and bonds are really paying dividends. I want to feel liquid. And *after* that, maybe I will become thirsty for an experience of God. That's secondary, so don't try it. If that's the *consuming* desire then don't hesitate to try it. But if your desire is first, put first things first. If it's first to be known, to be recognized in the work that I'm doing, to be happy in this world, if that is really my consuming desire then apply this principle towards *it*, and let that thirst for God take its own good time to envelope you. When it envelopes you, well then, apply the principle towards it.

So feeling in depth! What a man feels deeply is far more vital than what he thinks. So I can go all through the day thinking, "wouldn't it be wonderful if"...but I never act. If I could only say what would the *feeling* be like if it were true? What would the feeling be like if it were true? When I am told in Shakespeare "Assume a virtue"...he is calling upon me to feel it. "Assume a virtue, if you have it not. Refrain tonight and it will lend a sort of easiness to the next restraint, and the next still more easy" (*Hamlet,* Act 3, Sc. 4). Well, I will assume it and then persevere in that assumption. If I assume it, I am feeling it. And then in the not distant future what I feel I will externalize as a literal fact in my world.

So this is what I am calling upon everyone who will listen to me to really put into practice. You can't conceive of a desire that does not have *already* provided satisfaction for itself. It can feed upon it. He would not send me into the world unless he had provided a complete satisfaction for every desire that *he* gave me. For *he* gives me the desire! When I am told in the Book of Amos: "I will send a famine upon the world; it will not be a hunger for bread or a thirst for water, but for the hearing of the words of God" (8:11). Well, when someone wants to really speak the Word of God, but they have no hunger for it, what they really want is glamour. Then let them go out in the theater; let them go and get a job in TV, radio, something where they are actually before the public. If that's really what they want, do that. But don't say that I want to speak the Word of God and teach it, unless you are *hungry* for it. When you're really hungry for it, well then, apply this same principle towards *that* satisfaction. But if you're kidding yourself and what you really want is a spotlight, well, get the spotlight. That, too, has been provided for. You want the spotlight? He has provided the satisfaction of *that* hunger.

And so, everything in this world is real, everything can be satisfied if you know how to look into that law of liberty, that perfect law which is the law of liberty, and persevere. If you do, then you'll be blessed in all your doings, whatever you're doing. So I will never say to anyone...a chap came to see me yesterday, came in from New York City. He wants a certain thing. I said, all right, if you really want that it's not in conflict with my asking, not in conflict with my knowing that you have it, and I'm not going to tell you how my reactions are to it. You want it...all right, I will hear that you have it! I said goodbye to him. He's an awfully nice chap. He's reached the age of retirement and so he would have a nice income from Macy's, for he had a good job at Macy's in the antiques department. But he has been teaching one of these isms back east, and he's tired of all the isms because he saw the chicanery of it all, he saw the phoniness of it all. And then he started a little correspondence course—and it's out here somewhere and they want a leader. They can't believe in a leader within themselves, so they asked him to come out and lead them.

So when he told me the nature of the so-called thing, I was sorry that's all that he could see in life. He wants a spotlight. He is tired of playing third, fourth and fifth fiddle to the leader back east who has made himself a million dollars out of those who are buying bricks into heaven. So let us buy a building ...he has nothing, so they're going to buy a building out of what?—out of the gifts of those who attend. He puts the pressure on all through the week to get that money up so he buys the land. Land in New York City is very valuable. Then he improves the land by building the building and then he has a huge, big banquet at one of the big hotels to "burn the mortgage." But they all pay fifty dollars for the privilege of attending a banquet, and he burns it before them. And they built it in whose name?—his name.

Well, that same man told me back in 1943 that he was coming to New York for one purpose. I said that New York City is wide open...come! I thought he meant to teach the truth. He said, "No, to make money, make it right in the so-called New Thought movement." I said, "You're in the wrong profession. Why don't you go into steel or oil or coal or something of that nature? If you want to do this work you can live well, but you never have the ambition for millions. But you can live well and graciously if that's what you want." "No, I want money!" Well, today he does have money. He has his homes in the country, apartment in the city, a lovely big building in New York City which *they* paid for. And they love it, being milked, for that's exactly what it is. Now he, having spent his off-hours out of Macy's in such an institution, he now sees how phony the whole thing has been, but he hasn't completely overcome it. He still wants the spotlight. He wants to jump from the fifth in order to the first, and out here seems to give him the opportunity through his correspondence.

Well, I'll pray for his success, not as a teacher because he's not a teacher. I'll pray for his success to be glamorized by those who really want nothing but the nonsense. They're going to start off, as he tells me, with no eating of meat, no smoking, no drinking, in fact, a complete loss of the palate. Might as well cut the palate out, they wouldn't need it, don't need it at all. Cut it out and save that much to be paid by whatever they are going to give themselves, and then go and have the stall, and then become the cattle that they were anyway. But it doesn't offend my moral code, so I can easily pray for his success in that nonsense.

So I say to you who come here who are sincere, try to create within yourself a longing for the deepest of all desires. For God has provided a satisfaction for that deepest, and that deepest is a thirst for God. If you can really want that above everything else, use the same law of liberty. This is the law: by looking into your friends' faces and say with deep conviction "I have had it, I have had the experiences of which he speaks, that entire series, from the resurrection right through to the descent of the dove upon me! So I know the truth of which he speaks. The entire thing has unfolded itself within me!" For, he has provided the satisfaction for that hunger. But if you have *not* that hunger and you really sincerely want a better way of living, don't think for one moment that's wrong. You're shown exactly how to get it. You use the same principle, the principle of the perfect law of liberty, and you look into it and persevere. You don't turn from it and forget what you have done. You sleep in that conviction.

Now here tonight, many of our friends are out because it's Memorial Day. In scripture we are told, Paul said to the Galatians "I notice that you observe days, and months, and seasons, and years. I am afraid I have labored over you in vain" (4:10). Not one moment in time is more wonderful, more holy than another. There is no place on earth more sacred than

The Return of Glory

another. Wherever *you* are that's sacred ground because you are there. Yet today millions went out. So far I have counted 200 who were killed in the going, and they estimate another 400 before it gets over. They're all going, undoubtedly, to some reunion of some memorial. And this is what man is thinking about, this little memorial…and they're not there at all.

I woke this morning around four, and just prior to waking here was my brother Lawrence. He died at sixty-two, he was a doctor. He was much older looking because he had suffered for the last year before his departure. Lawrence was about twenty-three and here is Lawrence, and he and I are fully awake, and he knows I am fully awake. He's telling me to tell his wife Doris that the money he gave her is all for her and don't try to save it for the children because he gave them all adequate amounts…they all have enough…in fact, more than most people in the world. They could give it to each, more than most people have in this world and he gave her quite a bit. So he told me to tell her that she doesn't have to save it for the children or for anyone else.

Well, I didn't tell him, but to myself while I'm talking to him I said, Lawrence, you don't have to tell that to Doris through me. She wouldn't give one penny to anyone anyway. She never has…and you expect a change in her right now? She gave nothing while you were with her for many, many years. She couldn't conceive of giving something to her four children. She knows they have much, and she's only concerned that you didn't give it *all* to her. I have gone shopping with her where my brother would say to me having bought a $150 suit, "Don't tell Doris that I paid $150 for the suit; tell her I got it for thirty dollars. That would make her feel happy." That same day I went out with Doris and she spent a thousand dollars buying extra sets of dishes that she doesn't need any more than I need a hole in my head. She has more silver and more dishes and more of everything you could ever think of. She can give a party for sixty and not borrow one plate form anyone in the neighborhood. Not borrow one silver spoon…and all the silver is genuine silver, it isn't plated. So he didn't have to tell me to tell her that the money he left her is all for her and not for the children. So I'll save my breath, I won't tell her.

But I was with him alive, and here is Lawrence, strong and strapping and handsome. He was a blond chap with brown eyes, and he is twenty-three years old, the same Lawrence with the same intelligence that he had when he left here at the age of sixty-two. Not one thought is less than that. But his age is different, he's not the old man, he's a young man, but with the memory of his family back here. But the veil is no clearer to him than it is to those on this side. Only those who are awake penetrate this veil consciously and so I go beyond the world of dream into the world of Spirit waking,

545

and there I meet him. Lawrence is very much alive, a healthy, handsome, wonderful lad. But he still would like me to tell her that it's all hers, and not to neglect herself as though he never had that opportunity to tell her to her face here. She never once did; she simply wanted to get and get and get, no matter what. A bigger and bigger house to house the things she got. That was Doris and still is Doris.

But here is a day of memorial, thinking of the dead. This is not the world of the dead…this world *is* dead, that world is dead. I'm speaking of the living God. So let the dead bury the dead. He said, "You have the reputation of being alive and you are dead." Now here I am risen from the dead and I'm speaking of the living God, a God that is alive, and a God that is real. That's the God of whom I speak. And so I cannot go to these cemeteries and put a flag or a candle on that which is not there anyway. Because, no one that they placed there as a body ever was there; the Spirit never was placed there. We're all placed in the skull, that's where man is buried, and that's where man remains dreaming this dream of life. It is from there that man will awake; it is from there that he will be born a second time; it's from there that he's going to find David who reveals him as God the Father; it's from there that he's going to be split in two, and into there that he shall ascend into the Holy of Holies. The whole thing is all in the same place where he began the dream. He began it in the skull and he's going to end it there. In the end, he is one with God, the living God, not any dead God.

So here, try to catch the *feeling*. It is told us in that wonderful treatise between the 25th and 27th chapters of the Book of Genesis, where Isaac had two sons. The second one was smooth all over, no hair; the first one, Esau, had hair all over. Isaac is blind and he calls his first son Esau and tells Esau to go and bring him some venison. Esau went off into the fields to bring him some venison properly prepared as his father loved it. Jacob overheard what the father requested and with the help of his mother Rebekah he clothed himself in skins like his brother Esau, to give him the feeling of hair all over, for Esau has hair all over. So he clothed himself in hair. So when he came to his blind father and spoke, he said, "Father, here it is the venison that you love." Isaac said, "Come close, my son, that I may feel you. Your voice sounds like Jacob, but come close." When he came close, he said, "But you feel like Esau and you have the smell of my son Esau" and then he gave him the blessing. So he blessed Jacob with the blessing that belonged to Esau, the first. When Esau came back from the hunt, Jacob disappeared. Isaac said, "I have given your brother the blessing. He came through deceit and took you're blessing, and I cannot take it back." You can't take it back after you've done it. You sent it on its way. You smothered yourself in feeling…for prayer is nothing more than the subjective appropriation of the objective hope.

So, that is what I hope for and now I give it objective reality. For hair is the most external thing on a man. So bring it close and let me *feel* it. Can I feel what it would be like if it were true? By true I mean it's objective, it's factual. So I will feel it, how would it feel if it were true? Now I'm clothing myself in the reality of an Esau. I open my eyes upon the world to discover that it isn't so at all. But I can't take it back...I have set it in motion and it can't be cancelled now. I have given to this subjective state the objective reality, and it has now to fulfill its blessing. So you'll be blessed in all that you are doing. But do it! If you don't do it, well then, you can't be blessed in it. So I clothe myself in the feeling of the wish fulfilled. That is Isaac receiving his son...his idea clothed in external reality which really was a subjective state. For it was Jacob dressed up as Esau, and Jacob came and deceived his father into the belief that he was Esau, the external reality, and not the smooth-skinned lad that is subjective. So it's simply the subjective appropriation of the objective hope. And he can't take it back after he's done it.

Well, who is the blind Isaac?—you are, I am. For, I can't see what I'm asking for, I can't see the beautifully prepared venison, it's a hope, so I'm blind to it. Well now, I will clothe myself in the feeling that I'm eating it, that I'm actually indulging in it, I'm devouring it. Instead of going to bed saying that I have not a thing tonight, I will actually feel I'm feasting tonight, and all the odors that come with it, all the tastes that would come with it, all the feelings that come with it, and I do it. Then in a way that I do not know, it will become an objective reality in my world.

So here, the importance of feeling! Then he said to him, "Come close and kiss me, my son." Well, the word translated kiss means "to set on fire." It means "to burn, to touch." These are the definitions given in the biblical concordance. "To set on fire," that's an emotion. Not lighting a match to something, but someone is set on fire, he's kindled, he's touched by the kiss, and so he's feeling it intensely. He knows it's real because it's a sense of touch. And so, feeling is touch, tasting is touch, and so I taste it, I feel it. So we're told in scripture, "He tasted death for all of us." How do you taste death?— you experience it because you touch it. You can't say, well now, I'll pretend it. No, you experience death.

And so you're told, Jesus Christ tasted death for all...so he experienced in me what it is to die, and then in that being now I am he.

Now I have put into practice all that he taught me, everything that he taught me. He taught me that when I want something, don't ask anyone, *assume* that I have it. Appropriate that subjective state which is really my objective hope. So I will appropriate the subjective state knowing it must now externalize itself within my world. So ask in faith, without doubt.

For those who doubt are like the wave of the sea that is tossed and driven by the wind. They are double-minded, and let not anyone think that the double-minded will receive anything from the Lord. Because if I am double-minded, it means I know what I am even though I want to be other than what I am. Well, that's two, and I can't be double-minded, I must be single-minded. So I know what I am and I know what I would like to be. I must now drop what I believe that I am and assume that I am what I desire to be. I stop desiring it, because I am *in* it now, and I am persisting in it! I am looking into the wonderful law of liberty that sets me free...and the law is made up of the faces of my friends, and they are reflecting in me what I want everyone to see. I am seeing them see me, and I persist in it, and it has to come to pass.

Now let us go into the Silence.

* * *

Now are there any questions, please?

Q: (inaudible)
A: Well, you'd better ask that of a priest, because I don't teach it. I don't teach these things at all. I teach man how *not* to miss the mark in life. The word sin in scripture simply means "missing the mark." Hasn't a thing to do with the moral violations of which the church speaks. If I have a goal in life and I fail to realize it, I am sinning. Though my goal is the most beautiful goal in the world, it's a sin to miss the mark. That is what the word sin means in scripture. And so, he comes into the world teaching "repent and believe in the gospel." Well, the word repent means "a radical change of attitude." If I radically change my attitude then I will hit the mark, but I can't continue in my present state of mind and reach my goal...it's in conflict. So I am sinning by not reaching my goal.

The churches have their own little concept of what is right and what is wrong, and we're told in scripture that one of the things that displeases God is the eating of the tree of the knowledge of good and evil; the other is lack of faith in I am he. These are the two things that displease God. Without faith it is impossible to please him, we are told. Faith in what?—faith in God. Well, who is he?—I am. Well, if I lack faith in myself I lack faith in God, because the self of man *is* God. So my only sinning is missing my objective when all things are possible to God. When the church tells me this is a mortal sin or another kind of sin. What are they saying today about St. Christopher? It used to be, all right, we'll bless this little thing for you and they made a face of the man and put him on the medal, or a cardinal here puts his insignia on the reverse side of the medal...tens of thousands. What sums of money they gave the church for that extra blessing I do not know and they were blessing that which does not exist. The thing called Christopher never existed. That's what they brought out from the pope. I didn't say it, the Vatican said it.

So they're just filled with all these nonsenses and all these are the little indulgences and they sell these indulgences from every church you see. Next door, not far away anyway, there's a little building selling all these indulgences of the non-existing saints. The cattle go in and buy them. They're all sheep led blindly by blind leaders of the blind. I can say it boldly because I have awakened from the dream of life and know exactly what they're doing. But you can forgive the cardinal because he doesn't know what he is doing. And they're naming saints! What man on earth could name a saint? What man could see with his mortal eye who is redeemed? And the body of Christ is made up *only* of the redeemed. No one can be redeemed, as you're told in scripture, "til you are born again"...no reincarnation...born from above. Anothin, that is the word, which simply means "from above, from God, out of your skull." Until that has been experienced by the individual he cannot enter "that age" spoken of as the kingdom of heaven (Luke20:35). So, all their paraphernalia will not get them into the kingdom of heaven.

Only the redeemed are the elect, and the elect enter into the power of God. They sit not idly at the right hand of God. The symbol of the right hand is the power, the creative power of God. So they enter into the creative power of God and become one with the Creator in his majesty, sharing his majesty, each who is redeemed. So you can see them if you are awake in that world of Spirit-waking, and you know them as God and yet they have not lost their identity to you...but you know them as God. Yet you knew them on earth and you know the man on the earth, and yet that depth of your own being knows he is God. Because he's now at the right hand, the creative power of God, and he's not idle, he's very, very active, active in a creative sense, performing all the creative acts of God *as* God.

I'm not here teaching sin save other than it is missing the mark. All through scripture one question is asked of anyone who wanted help, "What do you want?" He never told you what you *ought* to desire, he allows you to state it and then told you what to do. And he always prefaced it, "According to your faith." *If* you have faith, all things are possible to him who believes. He didn't put any limits whatsoever on the power of faith or the love of God. And so, what is sin? You have all these mortal sins…if you don't go to church on a certain day or so many days a year that is accounted a sin. It's not a mortal sin but it is a sin and so you must do penance. There's no penance in scripture; that's one of the little traditions of men. You're told in scripture, "For the sake of your traditions you make void the Word of God."

Q: How do we have these garments?

A: Thank you, my dear. How do we have these garments? My brother Lawrence is clothed in a garment just like the one here only younger. It is unaccountably young in a world just like this, terrestrial, and it is really something…well, I can't describe it. If tonight you had a dream, which undoubtedly you will, and you meet someone you'll be in a body that they can see and talk to, and you will see them and talk to them. Well, how were you clothed? It was clothed, wasn't it? Well, in the same way. You clothe it with your Imagination. Imagination is God. People don't believe this world here is all Imagination…that all this is vision, my dear, everything here is vision. When I step into these worlds of which I speak, I am clothed, and they see me clothed, yet I know where I left this garment that you're now looking at. I know it's on a chair or it's on my bed, I know exactly where it is, and yet here I am clothed in a world just like this and they hear me and I hear them. So how did I clothe myself there?—by imagining.

Here we are completely educated out of it, but in this world where you came through the womb of woman that is most important in this world. *This* section of time is most important, for this is the *limit* of contraction, the *limit* of opacity. And yet, when we go forward through the door called death, we are clothed as we are here but reduced in age. It's always a reduction in age to around twenty…unless you're younger when you depart. Then you remain that way and grow into it. In that world they grow as they grow here, and they do stupid things there as they do here, and they're afraid of death there as the are here, and they marry there as they marry here. Everything is just like this world as told you in the 20th chapter of the Book of Luke. For there were wise men then as there are today who deny immortality—they were called Sadducees—and they were then what we call today the scientists. Our scientists, believing that the brain is the cause and not an instrument, they cannot conceive that the brain when destroyed could survive; that is, that a being, called a conscious being, could survive. So they look upon the brain as the cause and not the instrument on which some invisible center is playing. So any scientist who believes that the brain is the cause of everything in the world, when he sees the brain turned into dust he feels that whatever occupied it is gone forever. Because he can't believe someone occupied it, it was the brain itself doing it. And it's not a brain doing anything...the brain is an instrument.

But you can't blame anyone who is *trained* that way to believe that the final end comes with its destruction. And yet I admire such men who believing that are still such decent human beings. There are men who are kind and generous and everything in the world, not expecting one moment beyond the moment of death...and yet they're generous and kind in every sense of the word. So I take my hat off to such men. But when you meet a man like Stalin who does not believe in survival, you can't blame him for doing what he did. He's going to have fun for his seventy-odd years and murder millions of people, like a Hitler, because they don't believe in survival. They both believe that what we call Jesus was simply a stupid little man...kind and sweet but stupid. They haven't the slightest concept of the mystery. But they will survive as they have survived. And they, too, because God is infinitely merciful, they were used to play a certain part. You're told in scripture he hardened the heart of Pharaoh. Well, if he hardened the heart of Pharaoh not to let his people go, then you can't blame Pharaoh for not letting his people go. If before the children were born he loved Jacob and hated Esau, well then, you can't blame Esau for anything he did when he came in hated. That means "the outer man." The outer man cannot inherit the kingdom of God, for God is Spirit. The second man, the inner man that is Spirit, that survives...that is the immortal being.

The outer man, this garment, gets older and older, and so gradually it disintegrates. From the time a child is born it is moving towards the inevitable gate called death. It doesn't know that—which is just as well that it doesn't know it...it would be horrible if it dwelt upon it. You don't begin to dwell upon those things until you hit an advanced age. Because up until the point that you are hitting a certain age you think you are going on forever, and you could lift all the barbells in the world and chin yourself a thousand times and do all the nonsenses in the world as you did when you were a child. One day, you can't not only lift the weight, you can't lift yourself off the floor. What a shock *that* is to man! All of a sudden, he thinks he could dance all night and do all the things all through the day and night, everything he once did, and suddenly he can't do them. Then he goes to doctors. By then he doesn't have the urge. The little that he's saved he gives out to the doctors and the dentists and all the other people in the world, trying to bring back what time cannot bring back...and all the doctors put together can't bring back. But you see, he doesn't know it, which is merciful. He lives in his little hope that his wonderful virility of twenty will be with him when he's ninety. So, even the wisest of them will fall for every stupid suggestion when it comes out in the papers that something new has just been discovered to bring it back. If he still has any money left, he'll go out and buy it.

Why, after the First World War all the great leaders who sat in judgment when millions of boys, millions of these lovely fellas were slaughtered. How many millions were slaughtered? A Russian came out with an idea to bring back virility by implanting in man monkey glands. Well, I knew the secretary of the man—so I'm speaking from what I heard from the secretary—who traveled all over Europe transplanting these monkey glands into these old boys. Well, the only one who benefitted from it was the doctor. He got fortunes from the old fellows. They were just as stupid then as when they were carrying on the war. And I know her (she's gone now from this world), she was his private secretary who traveled from France where he started, London, Yugoslavia, all over. All these old fellas had money. They didn't go in poor, but they came out poor. Then they made their little exit from this world just as they would anyway and since there's no transforming power in death, they will be just as stupid there as they were here. And it will start all over again…until that wonderful being housed in man called God erupts. And that wisdom is something entirely different… something *entirely* different. It's not the wisdom of this world at all.

Thank you. Good night.

LOVE: GOD BESTOWS HIMSELF

6/2/69

Blake said that "Man brings all that he has or can have into this world with him, that man is born like a garden ready planted and sown. This world is too poor to produce one seed." Now, he was called a madman, but he was telling exactly what takes place in this wonderful world of ours. For he said, "The human Imagination is the eternal body of the Lord Jesus." So Jesus is your own wonderful human Imagination and there never was another Jesus and there never will be. The word Jesus and Jehovah are one. Jesus is God and God became man that man may become God. So housed in man is *everything* because Jesus is in man. That's where he's buried and that's where he will rise.

So when we read in scripture, "I have heard of your faith in Christ Jesus" as you will read it in the 1st chapter of Colossians, you might think that a man has faith in Christ Jesus as an external object. No, the preposition "in" marks out Christ not as the *object* of our faith but as "the sphere within which faith lives," for everything is within man. Then why am I in this world of sadness, a world of death, a world of sorrow? Now the king in this world can give the highest honor to whomever he will, but he cannot *fit* the one who receives his honor for the high office that he's given. God not only bestows the honor but he fits us to receive it, and this is the world to fit us to receive it. We are all part of the corporate destiny of this fabulous play. The outcome is an entirely different world, a higher order of everything that one could think of. In fact, you couldn't conceive of the high order until you experience it.

So when we are told that he has heard of our faith in Christ Jesus, bear in mind that he is not for one moment claiming that you have some external being in whom you have faith. That is not the object of your faith, it's simply the sphere. And when you have been prepared you are drawn automatically like a magnet into that sphere, and all that is now contained within you awakens and you are he. You are drawn right into that sphere after you have been prepared to receive the high honor. The high honor is that God *gave* himself to you. God became me…just as I am…with all of my weaknesses, all of my limitations, and then with me goes through the horrors, the sufferings of the world. Then when I am prepared to receive the high honor, I am drawn into the sphere, and then it erupts within me like a garden ready planted, completely sown; and all that was sown within me simply awakens within me and I am he. This is true of every being in the world.

But we all have different parts to play in that body of God. So he goes on to say, and he uses the words, it's a little phrase, that we have received it, or that we have been prepared for it. It simply means, really, the part. It means the part that we have cast to play throughout this eternal state. You are actually cast into a part. And that casting in the part must then be prepared to receive that eternal form within you. So when you've been prepared…so why am I born blind? Well, some schools will tell you because I gouged out the eyes of others. No, not that at all. Then why was I born deaf? Why was I born limited? Why was I born weak, poor, why? Listen to scripture, "Why was this man born blind? Did his parents sin or did he sin that he was born blind? Neither this man nor his parents, but that the works of God be made manifest" (Jn.9:2). And so, I cast myself into this role to prepare myself to receive this high honor in the eternal body of God. So the eternal *body* of God is your own wonderful human Imagination and because that is eternal, "Man is all Imagination and God is man and dwells in us and we in him. The eternal body of man is the Imagination, and that is God himself" (Blake, *Annot.Berkeley; Laocoon).*

Now we are told in scripture God is love. We are also told that God is the life of man. If God is the life of man and God is love, then the life of man is love and everything in this world that loves is eternal, I don't care what it is. Well, who in this world hasn't loved? A woman brings a child into the world. She may in time be disappointed, but at that moment she is in love with her production and loves that child, and would sacrifice herself for that child. That is love. That woman by her expression of love is eternal. The man who looks upon the child and feels he had something to do with it, and holds that child and smothers it with love and affection, that man has expressed love. He is eternal because God is love and love is the *life* of man. Anything that loves is eternal. So you can say that to everything in the world. Our scientists will tell us, well, man is capable of love, but the animal world and the plant world, no, that's instinct. They don't know what they're talking about. They haven't the slightest idea of this universal love.

Walking on the beach in little Barbados...I was with these two little boys and their governess and then my daughter and my wife were walking up, and as boys will do they came to a huge rock on the beach and turned it over. It's normal for anyone to do that. As they turned it over, this tiny little crab, little beach crab and whether it was the father or the mother of the crab the big one ran away but only about say three or four feet and then looked with these piercing eyes at us. I said to the little boys, "Be quiet, just be quiet. Be perfectly still." This tiny crab was under the rock that they had turned over, and when we were perfectly still, this big crab—whether it was father or mother I do not know—but it came slowly back looking at us and then quickly grabbed the little one and held it to its breast, and ran like a devil and hid itself from us. Well, wasn't that affection, wasn't that love? And is that instinct? The little crab, that crustacean, could never express love? That *was* love! God made everything in love. "Never wouldst thou have made anything had thou not loved it." That's what we're told in scripture. The little crab was made by God and God is love, and in my experience I saw the crab express love and therefore the crab is eternal. Everything that loves is eternal.

But man has been trained, as I was trained as a child, to believe in an external God. So if I read that at the age of twenty or thirty or even forty that "I have heard of your faith in Christ Jesus." Well, I was raised a Christian. In no other faith was I raised. Went through all my schools as a Christian, always said I was a Christian, and I still say I am a Christian. But I would have said, "Yes I believe in Christ Jesus" meaning an external being that was the object of my faith, and it doesn't mean that at all! Not the *object* of my faith...the preposition "in" shows me that it is the sphere. It is not the object of my faith but that sphere within which faith lives.

And one day in 1959 having been prepared through the part that I played throughout my long, long journey, I was drawn magnetically into that sphere; and what was already planted within me waiting for that motion into that sphere suddenly erupted. The whole drama of Jesus Christ unfolded itself within me, casting me in the central role as the being who gave himself for me. But he had to prepare himself *as* the very being that you call Neville, and I speak of myself as Neville, prepare me, suffering all the way with me until it was done. When I had been prepared to receive the honor, then the honor was conferred. What honor?—God gave himself to me. So everything said of him unfolded itself within me. And I know it's true of every child born of woman in this world.

But it is difficult to convince those who are trained as I was trained *before* their time. They do not wish to stand upon their own feet...and they can't at the moment. They have to go through the mill and going through the mill they suffer. And who suffers with them?—the one who bestowed the honor upon them. For unlike the king of this world who can't suffer with them, he bestows the honor although they're not fit to fulfill the job. But God in bestowing it also qualifies us to receive it, so that we can execute that part in the corporate body that is God.

So everyone here playing the parts that they're playing, you're playing it for a purpose. If your child is mentally deficient, don't think for one second you had anything to do with it. Oh, science will tell you that you did and others will tell you that you did something wrong. You didn't do a thing that was wrong. That individual is being prepared to receive this great honor, and he has to go through everything in this world. As he plays these parts then having been perfected, the honor that was originally bestowed quickly and suddenly erupts within him, and *he* is the very one who gave the honor. He is God himself, for in the end there is nothing but God. So, when Blake made that statement and they said, "You know, he's mad!" Blake also came back and said, "There are states in which the visionary is always considered a madman. And so, I will admit to your definition of the visionary if you say I'm a madman, meaning that I am experiencing what you haven't, not as yet, but you will." Everyone in this world *will* experience this.

Now, what part you will play in the body of God, I do not know, but whatever part it is, it is perfect. And all this was done before that the world was. Now we are told he casts all this by lot. If you read the story in the Old Testament, in the Book of Joshua, from the 14th to the 19th chapter, in theses chapters when the distribution of the land is about to be given to Israel, it was all done by lot. It means simply the *part* that is allotted, not a piece of land, I am casting it into a part. Now you'll notice, as he casts us into the parts among all the twelve tribes of Israel, it also came down to the individual. To show the world which condemned a certain aspect of this world he gave to Caleb a portion of that which he gave to the tribe of Judah. Judah is mentioned in the genealogy of Jesus as the one to whom the entire being unfolds. And he gave to Caleb a portion of that which he gave to the tribe of Judah. Now, Caleb means by definition "a dog." The word dog in Hebrew is Caleb…but by actual spiritual definition it is "the homosexual." So he gave to him…right in the very heart of it, the fourth son of Jacob…he gave him eternity. He's part of the eternal play of God. Right into it. So he gave everyone—you read this in the 15th chapter of the Book of Joshua, the 13th verse—unto Caleb he gave this portion of the tribe of Judah.

So he justifies everything that he has made in this world. When people sit in judgment about this, that and the other, and one doctor tells us, well, he has so many hormones of this and he has a lack of this, all of that is nonsense. They haven't the slightest concept of scripture. They do not realize what is actually taking place in the depths of the soul of man. The whole thing is taking place in us, and not a *thing* is to be condemned, for he would not have made anything if he had not loved it. And he is love. I know from experience that God is infinite love, eternal love. I stood in his presence and he, this infinite being embraced me, incorporated me into his body, so I became one with the body of love. I *know* God is love.

Well, anyone who loves in this world or anything who loves…so they wouldn't call a crab one, they call it a thing. Well, if a thing loves it is eternal because love is God, and God is eternal, and God is infinite. So everything in this world that God made God loves, therefore it is eternal. This world in which we find ourselves, as Blake said, "It's too poor to produce one seed. We come into this world like a garden ready planted and sown." We bring everything with us that we have or will ever have, and it's all within us. Why don't I play the part of the mathematician? It's there, but I'm not cast in that role. Why does he not play the part of the mystic? He isn't cast in that role. He condemns the role of the mystic; all right, let him condemn the role of the mystic. He has it within him but it's dormant because it's not a part that he must play in this world. He is cut out for a certain part in the play and he'll play his part perfectly. But in the end, all will be in the one corporate body of the risen Lord.

Now, what part you will play or I will play, I do not know. I could only tell you from my own experience where I entered, where I re-entered the kingdom of heaven, for it's out of the kingdom of heaven that we all came. We fell from there into division, and now we are rising back into unity. I can only tell you exactly where I came when I rose like the Son of man into the kingdom of heaven. What it means no one will know until all are gathered into it. I will know it when I drop this body. You will know it when you, for the last time, drop the body and we will all then be brothers, brothers in love. "So go to my brothers and tell them I am ascending unto my Father and your Father, unto my God and your God" (Jn.20:17). So we are all brothers in the kingdom of heaven. Everyone is God, for there's only God… not a thing in this world but God.

So let no one tell you that you are some little tiny thing because you are playing a small part. Jesus is *in* you or you couldn't even breathe, for Jesus is the *life* of the world. The word Jesus and Jehovah are the same thing. The true definition of the word is "I am "…that is the name of Jesus and that is the name of God. No man could breathe were it not that he is aware of being. So, even the idiot knows that he is. He may not know even where he is and what he is and who he is, but he knows that he is, because Christ Jesus is in him. That is the Lord. Now when you read the word Christ Jesus…if I could only get it over to the whole vast world…in the 11th chapter of the

557

Book of Revelation they speak of the Lord *and* his Christ (11:15). They don't speak of the Lord which means Jesus, Jesus Christ; they speak of the Lord *and* his Christ. The word Christ simply means "the anointed," that is what the word means. In Hebrew it is "Messiah"; in our English world it is "the Christ." But Messiah and Christ are the same, and Messiah simply means "the anointed one." The anointed one in the scripture is *David*. "Rise and anoint him; for this is he" as you read it in the Book of Samuel (1Sam.16:12). As you read it in the 89th Psalm, "David, thine anointed, Thou anointed him with thy holy oil" (89:20). He is called in the 89th Psalm, "The first born from the dead" (89:27).

He is the first born. Well, what is he? I tell you David is the *resultant state*. It comes out as the result of your being prepared to receive the highest honor in the world which is God himself. He gave you himself! So David comes out as a result of having played all the parts that you have played. When you have played the last one, which has prepared you for the reception of the great honor that's bestowed upon you, then this one comes out as a resultant state. And who is he?—David. And who is David relative to you?—he's your son. And who is the Father of David?—God. Therefore, who are you?—God. "Thou art my son, today I have begotten thee" said the Lord to David (Ps.2:7). In the Bible it is said that he said it to Christ. Well, that is Christ. Christ simply means "Messiah," Messiah means "the anointed," and the anointed is David (1Sam.16:12). He is the one he calls "my king." Man made Saul the king and God rejected him and made David king. So, "I will make him the highest of the kings of the earth and he is my son." So when God in man plays all the parts, the resultant state that comes at the end of all the parts is David. David comes out as a result...that's David. So if you take all the parts you've ever played and condense them, and then project it and personify it, you'll see David. There is no uncertainty in your mind when he confronts you...here comes the resultant state...and then you know exactly who you are.

But you also know that *everyone* in this world, those that you may formerly have disliked, that he, too, is destined to come to that state where the resultant is the same son that is *your* son, and because it is the same son then you and he that you formerly disliked are one. That no one in this world is a stranger, no one is another, and everyone is coming towards the point where he is God the Father. The Father must be a father only if he has a son, and the son stands before him, and he knows it is David.

So you came into this world not some poor little boy. So you came in as a poor boy as I did. I came in a very, very poor child, one of ten. We had no money, no social background, no intellectual background, nothing, but nothing, period. Yet, here that little family moved based upon a plan. For when I was a child, there were two in Barbados, one was a colored person and his name was Prophet Jordan. They called him the prophet, and he foretold when I was just a boy of about four what I was destined to do. Well, I did it. He said, "He belongs to the Lord…do not touch him. Don't try to make him a business man, a doctor, a dentist, anything for he belongs to the Lord. He has come to do the works of God." He told my other brothers, the second and the third, exactly what they would do and they did it. One became the most successful businessman man in Barbados, and he was then only six when the Prophet Jordan told him. And then my brother Lawrence, the doctor, he told him, "You'll be a very wonderful doctor, a successful doctor." Well, he was, he became the doctor. But he said, "Don't touch the fourth one; he belongs to God. He has come now for the purpose of fulfilling God's word" and that is what I have done. I had no idea what he meant when he said it to my brother, and I didn't know that he said it until I was very, very on in years, when my brother Victor told me what the Prophet Jordan had said. Then another one, when I was about nine, also went out on a limb and prophesied what I'm doing. She said that she saw it in her vision.

So everyone has a pattern in this world. You may not have been told what it will be and sometimes it's quite right that we do not know. Well, if I knew at a certain moment in time what I was destined to do, I might have hesitated to go along that pathway. But it is hidden from us so that we may be conditioned to receive the high honor, which is to receive God himself. But man finds it difficult to believe that he is destined to become God. He thinks that's blasphemy, that's the height of blasphemy. I have heard men from the pulpit, men today who bear the highest title in the churches—they are bishops, they are cardinals, and I heard them when they were not—and they say that these people who believe that God is in them are insane. I heard them say that, and I wondered at the time how they could make this statement. They knew nothing. Then when it happened in me, when I was drawn into this sphere where the spiritual experience revealed itself in me as the *plan* unfolding, and see them still in that same state of mind and now with higher honors upon them, I wonder is it not altogether told perfectly in scripture "the blind leading the blind"? There they are, blind as you can make them, with all their little robes, and they think that's the way God dresses…when God is clothed in love. Not a thing to do with these little garments that they make for themselves with their purples and their reds and their so-called links. It's lovely if they want to wear those robes, dress up, dance like some ballet dancer, perfectly all right, but it does not endear them to God, and God doesn't see the outer man, he only sees the *heart* (1Sam.16:7).

And when that heart has been prepared, then that individual is drawn into the sphere of spiritual experience, and it is there he returns knowing the faith of which the scripture speaks, for that's where faith is alive. When I came back from that, if I stood before all the wise men of the world and they forced me to recant like Galileo. Yes, if they pained me beyond the measure of endurance, I would have said yes you are right and I am wrong, as Galileo said it too. But he knew in his heart he was right and they were stupid, he knew that. Now today we're going around the moon and we know that the earth goes around the sun, we *know* that now. Well, when Galileo lived, it was from the pope down, all the cardinals compelled him to confess publicly that he was wrong and they were right. Now we know *they* were wrong and he was right. But they still go blindly on making others confess concerning their wisdom and they haven't any wisdom at all, for they are men without vision. They haven't experienced the Word of God.

So, if I were put this night under physical pressure, I, too, would confess that you're right and these experiences are all hallucination. But in my heart I would know that if these are hallucinations, then you are, because, you are no more real before me now as you condemn me than my experiences are. So I could not deny them anymore than I could deny the simplest evidence of my senses. I see these here now…I can't deny they are here. They'll become a memory image an hour from now, but at the moment they're objective fact. I can't deny them. Well, I can't deny the experiences I have had concerning scripture. Everything said of him who is the central figure I experienced. And so I know everyone is going to have it, but he has to be prepared to receive it. It's not something that is given you that you cannot actually experience. It is something bestowed and then you are prepared to receive the thing bestowed.

We know in our own land—not so far, but it may come under his administration—but in the previous administration, I recall one person being appointed and confirmed as an ambassador and when he was asked if he knew the place, he didn't even know where it was on the map. They asked, do you know who is the head of the government of that place? and he didn't know the head of government. But he was confirmed as ambassador to this place. He has contributed generously to the campaign and he has money, and here he is now an ambassador…a very high honor. So he received an honor and he was not fit to fill the bill. Well, when God gives us the honor he then qualifies us to receive the honor, and so he actually puts us through the paces, everyone goes through the paces and then you come out and you're qualified.

So the word is used in scripture, "The Father has qualified us to share in"—and that phrase "to share in" means "for the part." That's the literal meaning of the word "to share in" is "for the part" as you will read in the 1st chapter of Colossians: "The Father has qualified us to share in"—what—"to share in the inheritance of the saints in light" (1:12). Here, there's a part but I must be prepared for that part. I must qualify, because I'm going to play that part in eternity in the body of God, as is everyone. Then "to share in" is simply "for the part." But when you read it now, "to share in," you think in terms of something waiting for you like material goods. It isn't that at all. If I actually share in for the part, I share for the part of being God, and God is all. I don't need goods. I only need the creative power that is God and I can create anything that I desire. *If* I am the creative power of God, if I am the wisdom of God, then I can create anything in this world. That's what he's preparing us all for…to receive his gift…and his gift is his power and his wisdom.

So I can't tell you how altogether glorious that you really are! If you dwell upon this alone, you will stop feeling that you are little. No matter where you were born and where you are today, if you walk this earth in the feeling that God selected me for this eternal part in the new world, the new body that he's building out of living stones, and we are the living stones, and we are all God. If you dwell upon that wonderful hope and knowing he's preparing you, and he's not going to stop it no matter what you will go through, you'll accept it. You can go through hell and you will accept it. As Paul said in his letter to the Romans: "He does not consider the sufferings of this present time worthy to be compared to the *glory* that is to be revealed *in us*" (8:18). A glory, what glory? It is God himself. So if it's suffering, all right, suffering. And who hasn't suffered? You may not have suffered so far physically, but you've suffered with the loss of a loved one. That's suffering! That's something that goes on and on and it seems to eat your heart out. But that is suffering and it is preparing you to receive the glory that God has predetermined for you.

So this may not seem to be practical, but, may I tell you, it's the most practical talk that you could get. I could tell you how to go about getting a better job and more money and all these things, but do you know the most practical thing in this world is that which is most spiritual? What is most profoundly spiritual you'll find in time to be, really, the most directly practical. For while your mind is removed from trying to become something great in this world and dwelling on something far, far greater, beyond the wildest dream of man, things are moving within you. Then, all of a sudden, you give your entire heart to that, the far *nobler* state, and then you are drawn into the area. The moment you are drawn into it, the whole thing suddenly unfolds within you without warning, because you are actually *in* the sphere where what is planted within you suddenly erupts. But it took all the time to prepare you to be drawn into that sphere. And when you're drawn into that sphere, it's nothing but the power of God in that sphere. And you feel him as the wind, the unearthly wind, and you hear it, and the whole thing is erupting within you, from the birth to the descent of the dove.

So let everyone...I wouldn't blame anyone if they're here for the first time tonight to smile and to laugh and to have fun...perfectly all right. You laugh and you have fun and you carry on. But I promise you, you will have it! If not now, beyond the state that the world calls the grave, for you don't die, nothing dies, because you're created by the living God. You have loved... if it's only for one fleeting moment you've loved...even if it was only a flower, you loved it. That moment of love made you an eternal being, for God is love and you loved. So go on, and you smile if you want to, carry on. But beyond the grave you'll find yourself restored to life just like this and still going through the paces. Then in the dim future, you will remember you once heard a mad man say things like this, a way, way back. The memory will return and you heard him say something like this. But *then* you'll be close to the sphere in which it will erupt within you.

And then, you will know that no one in the new generation differs from those of the old generation...all ages are equal. We haven't today turned out any Shakespeare. I wonder where they are...those who think they are so far removed from the present generation. Where is the modern Shakespeare? Where is the modern Raphael? The great artists, where are they? Well, they're strumming guitars today. But where are the Beethovens and Bachs? Where are they? No, they're out with their banjos. So, all ages are equal, fitted for the thing that is being done upon all of us in this world. Not one age really differs from the other. It's only preparing man. This world is a world of educative darkness where the individual is being prepared to receive the gift that God has bestowed. That gift is not a huge, big castle; the gift is himself. God *gives* himself to man, and God is all, so man receives all.

Man brings into this world all that he has and can have; he comes into the world just like a garden that is already planted and sown. The world in which we live is too poor to produce one seed; because the reality of man is Jesus, and the reality of man is his own wonderful human Imagination and that is God himself. And that body contains *everything* in eternity; the whole vast world only objectifies what is within that body that is God in man. That body that is God *in* man is his own wonderful human Imagination.

Now let us go into the Silence.

*   *   *

Are there any questions, please?

Q: (inaudible)
A: Yes, as you're told in the 9th chapter of the Book of Isaiah, "Unto us a *child* is born, unto us a *son* is given" (9:6). It's not the same one…these are two separate events. The child, the babe wrapped in swaddling clothes unto us that is born. It is found by the wise…the shepherds of the night, and they proclaim the one whose birth it signifies. It's only a *sign* that God was born that night. And the one that they name is the one that is God, born that night, and the child only signifies his birth. Then, five months later comes the one that is *given*. God gives his only begotten son to that one. And if he gives his only begotten son to him—not as a friend, not as a brother, not as a companion, but as *his* son—then he succeeded in giving him himself. For if God gave me his son as my son then I am God. I will never know that I am he unless *his* son calls *me* Father, so his son comes. There are two separate events. And then the four great titles are placed upon his shoulder.

Q: What is your purpose for speaking this?
A: What my purpose in speaking is? To tell you, who are here for the first time, that you are infinitely greater than you ever thought yourself to be; that instead of being a little man in this world who dies when you die and are forgotten in the not distant future after you're gone that you are eternal. You're here for a purpose and the purpose is to receive the gift that was given you in the beginning and that is God himself. You are being prepared to receive the gift.

Q: (inaudible)
A: Well, not everyone will receive it. Not everyone would receive what Einstein had to say and they thought he was mad, too. It is said when he first brought out his equation in 1905 only six could understand him. But the world today stands frightened to death because his equation was true. Now they're spending billions to protect each other that should be spent in schools and streets and all the lovely things we need in this world. But his equation in 1905 only six understood it and it was not proved and only partially proved in the year 1919 when Lord Rutherford could conceive of the means of testing it. But it was not really tested, only partially tested. Then came 1945 when the actual test was made and we know Nagasaki and we know these things, Hiroshima. Now today we've gone beyond that using an entirely different means…but that was the foundation. They thought him mad then.

Q: (inaudible)

A: Well, the one was energy is equal, no, it is mass is equal to energy multiplied by the square of the velocity of light.

Q: (inaudible)

A: Well, I wouldn't go into that. I'm not a mathematician. I only know that when he brought that out in 1905 our great mathematicians laughed at him. Six understood him in part, but it took fourteen years before we could devise the means to even test it. And the testing proved that the man was at least partially right. Then came the bomb based upon his equation. Now today what I am telling you may be laughed at by all the people in the world, but I tell you, you'll never disprove it because one day you will experience it. And I'll be waiting for you in the heavenly sphere.

Q: ...I've had an experience myself of Jesus Christ...

A: Good, you've experienced Jesus, wonderful. I know the story is true. I know the story of Jesus from beginning to end is simply the autobiography of man, which one day he will experience and he'll be cast in the central role.

Q: May I ask why you chose Jesus Christ as your symbol of love?

A: Because I experienced it. I'm speaking from experience...I am not theorizing, I'm not speculating.

Q: (inaudible)

A: Yes, I experienced the risen Lord. It's a man and it's a body of infinite love that is just man. Don't ask me what he looks like, what kind of a face. He has a human face, human hands and a human voice. Don't ask me how when he embraced me our bodies could fuse and yet I did not lose my identity. We became one being, one body, one Spirit, one Lord and yet I did not lose my identity. When he sent me back to tell the story of the *risen* Lord, I knew at that moment although I was sent and seemingly separated, I was representing the being who sent me. If you could see me without mortal eyes, you'd see that being, for we cannot become defused after once being fused. There's only one body being built and it is built out of the redeemed of humanity, and all will eventually be redeemed.

Q: (inaudible)

A: Well, you may say that. I'm telling you what I actually experienced. Because the question asked me...although you may say with modern science that I asked myself the question, and objectified it coming from a seeming other...but that was not the story as I experienced it. I was taken in spirit into a divine society, and here was a recording angel actually recording as you're told in the Book of Daniel (12:1). She looked at me and then turned back to this book and recorded a name. I didn't see the name, but she recoded it as she looked at me. Then I was taken into the presence of the risen Lord, and he asked me to name the greatest thing in the world. In his presence what could you name other than what you saw… and I named love, quoting the 13th chapter of 1st Corinthians, "Faith, hope and love, these three; but the greatest of these is love" (13:13). At that he embraced me, and we fused and became one body, one Spirit, one Lord. Then I was sent back into this world of tears to tell what I had experienced…that the risen Lord is a fact. I'm speaking from experience, I am not speculating.

So let the others speculate. One comes out of the university tomorrow, as they will all be graduating in the immediate present, and it's all theory. They have to go into the world of Caesar and experiment and prove it. Well, the same thing is true when you come out of the seminaries where you heard this, that and the other concerning theology. You must wait until you have experienced it, then you will speak with an authority that no one in the world can unless they have experienced it.

Q: (inaudible)

A: Well, have you had the experience of the birth from above? For you're told unless you're born from above you cannot enter the kingdom of God (Jn.3:3). Would you care to tell me what you actually experienced?

Q: (inaudible)

A: Very good experience. But that is not the birth from above. It's a very interesting experience, but you will one day have all the experiences described in scripture concerning Jesus. He was born in a supernatural manner; you will have *that* birth. You will discover that you are God the Father when God's son calls you Father. You'll have all these experiences. That's what I'm telling the whole vast world…that Jesus is *in them* (2Cor.13:5; Col.1:27). Were he not in you, you could not experience anything concerning Jesus, for he simply is the pattern man, and that pattern is in every child born of woman. And everyone will experience it in good time.

Good night.

THE NATURE OF GOD IS REVEALED IN US

6/6/69

It is in us as persons that the nature of God is revealed. A scriptural episode is not a record of an historical event but a parabolic revelation of truth. To see Jesus or David as an historical character is to see truth tempered to the weakness of our souls. The minute you see them as characters in history you are not seeing what they represent.

We'll take any episode of scripture, but any, and show you where it unfolds within you. The title of the 54th Psalm is "And David is in hiding within us." The King James Version translates it "And David is hiding with us"; the Revised Standard Version translates it "And David is in hiding among us." But the word is *within* us...that's where he's hiding. That is where every character is hiding. So when we say that "All that you behold, though it *appears* without, it is *within*, in your Imagination, of which this world of mortality is but a shadow" (Blake, *Jer.*, Plt.71), I mean that literally, the whole vast drama unfolds within us. So Jesus, David, Abraham, Moses, all are but *personifications* of these eternal states. We encounter them as we are moving towards the ultimate which is the awakening of God in us.

If the poet Browning had not experienced this, he never could have written the poem *Saul*, or the one on *Paracelus* for that matter. But in *Saul* he tells a story in the 16th chapter of the Book of 1st Samuel that David cured Saul of the evil spirit which had come upon him sent from the Lord. Well, we see right away who Saul is, if we know scripture. Saul represents humanity, the human being as described in the 4th chapter of the Book of Daniel: And the watcher said, "Hew down the tree and cut off the branches, strip its leaves, and scatter its fruit. But leave the stump" (4:14). And now

The Return of Glory

it turns from a tree into a person, "Let him be watered with the dew from heaven, and let him move with the beasts of the earth" (4:16,17). Let him now be taken from the human state: "Take from him the mind of man and give him the mind of a beast; and let seven times pass over him until he knows that the Most High rules the kingdom of men, and gives it to whom he will, even to the lowliest among men."

So here we have not the mind of man but the mind of a beast...and that was Saul. Saul went insane...did not remember who he was and was violent. David cured him of his insanity and then David tells him of the coming of Messiah. David said to Saul, "O Saul, it shall be a face like my face that receives thee, a man like unto me thou shalt love and be loved by forever. A hand like this hand shall open the gates of new life unto thee; see the *Christ* stand" (Browning, *Saul*). He's standing before him. Now, you think this is an episode in the pages of history. No this is a drama that takes place in man, this insane being looking for an external savior as man does, and one day this that never walked the face of the earth...but he knows for all revelation has the mood of certainty about it...there is no uncertainty in revelation. Then David stands before you, and you who one moment before were insane in a way...for you didn't know who you were and that's certainly a form of insanity, a man who doesn't know who he is, a form of amnesia any way. So Saul did not know. And suddenly that which had no flesh and blood stands before him as a being of flesh and blood and speaks to him and he to this being. And he now sees the real relationship and the revelation as to who he is.

But now, who is he? He is no longer Saul. Saul has been turned into Paul. For the name was changed from Saul into Paul. *Paul* now makes the statement, "Henceforth we regard no one from the human point of view; even though we once regarded Christ from a human point of view, we regard him thus no longer" (2Cor.5:16). For, he was trained in the belief of an external historical past of Israel, and to him David was the king of kings. And now, as God reveals his son *in* him...as he said, "It pleased God to reveal his son *in me* and now I do not discuss it with flesh and blood. What man believing as he formerly believed could understand what he is talking about, when he himself knew that he tormented anyone who did not accept the historicity of the revelation of the Old Testament? Now he can no longer believe in any historical character of either Old...and there was no New, the New was not yet written...but they're discussing a Messiah and now he knows who Messiah really is. Now he knows who the Lord Jesus really is. So now he sees the Lord...that is, not what the world believes to be Jesus... but he sees *himself* as that Lord and what the world believes to be Jesus. But he sees himself as that Lord...and what the world believes to be a man who was a mighty king is his son, his begotten son (Ps.2:7). And it wasn't flesh and blood at all, for this happened in the Spirit. And "When it pleased God to reveal his son *in me*, I discussed it not with flesh and blood" (Gal.1:16).

So here, to see Jesus or Abraham or Moses or Jacob or any of the characters as flesh and blood external to yourself in the pages of history is to see truth tempered to the weakness of your soul. Because most of us until the revelation takes place are unable, ordinarily we are, to stand the force of that light of revelation. There is nothing more difficult in the world than to give up a fixed idea, especially concerning religion or politics. You are born into a certain religious group and you do not know why you are born there. You are taught it as your mother taught it, and then you go to a school and they confirm what your mother said, that these are fixed characters who lived in time and space and who left behind them a record of their physical existence…and it isn't so at all. These are all revelations of an eternal drama that is *in* man and man's *real* being is his own wonderful human Imagination.

So they say, "But don't you believe, Neville, that there was a man called Jesus?" That's the one thing I get from my family in Barbados, "But you do believe that, don't you?" I said, "Are you putting words in my mouth? No I do not." I did believe it, may I tell you. I formerly believed it as you now believe it. I can no longer believe in the historicity of *any* character of scripture, for I encountered them as *states*, personified yes. But the last one which is Jesus Christ himself, he comes right out of your very being and *you* are that *state*. When you are brought to the very end of the road, you yourself are Jesus.

Well then, who is the Christ? Surely he is…no, the son is the anointed, the one who was anointed with the oil of gladness above his fellow men. Well, who is he?—that is David. David in the Spirit calls him "my Father." That is scripture and not in the flesh, for time if you take it chronologically separated these two events by 1,000 years. Yet you find the whole thing is contemporary, it is not something of the past; that God is contemporaneous with us.

Now, this very moment he is my very being, my reality, and that is Jesus, that is the Lord. But if he is a father, as we are told in scripture, "Holy Father, keep them in thy name, that thou hast give unto me; that they may be one, even as we are one" (Jn.17:11), it's interchangeable, the father-son relationship, they are one. At one moment in scripture as you read it he is speaking as the son; another moment in the same chapter he is speaking as the father. Then he jumps back without giving any warning to that of the son. And man is confused…they think it's simply one being of flesh and blood. It's an inter-relationship of father-son, they are one.

A lady who is here tonight wrote me this letter this week. She said, "In my vision I saw a table and at the table sat a man and his son, a young son, and I knew without uncertainty I was that son"—now this is a lady speaking—"that I was that son *and* I was that father. I also knew that that father and son were one, and I was that one." Now, the same lady in another vision of the same period said, "A friend of mine" (who is here tonight) "Louise Roach in the vision called to me in a very loud voice and told me that I was pregnant, bringing forth the Son of God." She said, "At the moment I was embarrassed, because a huge crowd was present and she is proclaiming my pregnancy bringing forth the Son of God." Well, she *is* bringing forth the Son of God, and who brings forth the Son of God but God. "Born not of blood nor or the will of the flesh nor of the will of man, but of God" (Jn.1:13). So she is that being who is the Jesus of scripture bringing forth God. And because God is a father as we just heard, "Holy Father, keep them in thy name, which thou hast given me" (Jn.17:11). So the *last* gift of God to man is himself; and if he's God the Father and gives himself to me then he gave me his Son. He sent his Son into me calling "Father." He sent the spirit of his Son into my heart crying "Father" (Gal.4:4,6). Well, if he calls me Father, then I am God the Father. And if God the Father is the Lord Jesus, then that Christ is simply the anointed one, and the one he anointed was *David:* "Thou art my son, today I have begotten thee" (Ps.2:7).

Now this, I tell you, is a great shock. It's a frightful shock to those of us who were raised in the Christian faith. It's also a shock to those who were raised in the Jewish faith, for there's no more historicity of the characters of the Old Testament than there is of the characters of the New. These are the *eternal states* through which man passes from darkness to light, and when he comes to the end *he* is that state personified, and that state is himself, and it's God the Father.

So David is in hiding within us. Now who told him this? We are told it is the Ziphites. Well, the Ziphite in scripture is of the tribe of Judah. If you read the genealogy, the only son of Jacob mentioned in the genealogy is Judah. So this now brings it to David. David now has been notified that Saul has been notified that he is hiding within us. Now the insane man can't follow this. If he's hiding within you, where do I look for him? Wait and he'll come out. At a moment in time there is an explosion, a real explosion; and it is that that releases David who is hiding within you. For, this is told to Saul. And we are the insane of Daniel. We are the ones…look at the world today…if we aren't insane when we murder each other. Look at what is taking place in the world. Getting the better of the seeming other and there is no other. For the prayer is that they be one as we are one, and yet we don't realize that we *are* one. Not a thing in this world can bring you to that realization but the revelation of the Son to the Father. For when you tell me, as this lady has told me in her adumbration, that she had been seen by one who is here all the time as being pregnant, bringing forth the Son of God, I know she *is*. I also know you are! You may not be as near to the actual birth, but you are bringing forth the Son of God.

Three other ladies in this audience tonight...and one wrote me this. She is sleeping on a little, I would say, couch in the home of a friend...in other words away from her own home. And there she sees a babe and the babe...there's a blanket there. At the moment that she's about to pick the babe up, this little infant and it's a boy, the door raps...someone is knocking at the door. So she answers the door, holding the new child in her arms to her chest. When the door is opened it's her daughter who is there, and she's embarrassed that this little child is in the nude, because she has a friend with her. She says, "Mother, put something on your baby"—she called it "your" baby—"because there is someone here." Well, it was a friend of the mother's, too, that she met about a year ago. So the man came in and patted the infant on its back and said, "What a beautiful, wonderful looking babe that you have there." Then she went back and began to cover the baby with a blanket, with the swaddling cloth, when she woke. That's a wonderful adumbration, a forecasting of the event. Then she will know what the real event as recorded in scripture truly is concerning the birth of God.

Then another one...it was her sister's child, and she took the child up, and the child fell for a moment. She picked it up; it wasn't injured, just a little scratched. But it was this lovely boy. And then she realized her sister said, "Give me back the child" and "the child's face turned into that of a cherub, from the little infant into the actual face of a cherub and smiled at me. Then I said, 'I cannot give this back, it is mine'" and with that she held it knowing the child was really hers. Now that is an adumbration...all these are foreshadowings.

Now, these ladies who wrote me these letters are mothers, they have their own children. The last one has five children; one has two. One speaks of a child "her daughter" was at the door. How many others? At least she is a mother...all these are people who have the physical children here. But *this* is a spiritual child. The whole Bible from beginning to end is a supernatural document where man treats it as an historical fact, and it isn't. So to see Jesus...and I don't care who you are, whether you be the highest in the Christian faith today, the head of all the bodies on earth, and you believe that Jesus is an historical character, it's because you have not yet the strength to see the brilliant light of the revelation of truth, you can't stand it.

I know when it came to me I can't tell you how the things fell within me. But we are told, all the buildings will fall in the end, and these structures are the structures of the mind by which we live. The belief in the historicity of Jesus is a structure; the belief in the historicity of the Bible is a structure. You see all these buildings, aren't they beautiful! You see them externalized as churches, cathedrals of the world. Now they will all fall... in the last days they will all fall, and you will have that experience. You will see all these buildings within you actually fall. Then from the ashes of these buildings will rise that which is permanent, for now you are not living by any external object in the world. It's all within you and everything has to be unfolded within you.

When you are told that he went into the garden and here he said, "I will give you a sign" and he gave him a sign as to which one is the secret, and he said, "I will kiss him." So he comes in and goes right up to one and kisses him, and then departs. You are told that in the 14th chapter of the Book of Mark. When you read it you think here is an episode, a record of some historical past. It isn't, it is actually something you're going to experience, and you'll see how this whole drama is *now*, it's contemporaneous with us now...for I have had that experience. I am teaching the Word of God and telling them of the experiences that I have had, therefore, I am the Word that went out. I sent it out from myself, clothed myself in flesh, so the Word became flesh and dwelt within me, and all that it implied unfolded within me. As I am telling this now one departs. No sooner had he departed than I knew he is revealing what I am teaching. Then one enters. Well, the one who enters fulfills the 14th of Mark, "This is a sign that I give you...the one I kiss" (14:44). Do not hurt him, treat him kindly, but don't let him go. If this is the truth, don't let the truth go, for this is the truth I'm going to kiss. So he comes in and kisses me, and then extends his arms in adoration like a cross. Well, the word Judah is simply "to pray with extended arm." And it was he who kissed me, who then embraced me, severed the sleeve and revealed the arm of the Lord fulfilling scripture. "And who has believed our report and to whom has the arm of the Lord been revealed?" (Jn.12:38). Well, now it was revealed. This is simply the symbol of power, the creative power of God, that's all. But it is so all-together beautiful in imagery, and the image is all perfect because you fulfill it in its perfect symbolism. So here was the man, this beautiful being about forty, gloriously dressed, and he did everything scripture tells you he would do when he comes and kisses the one who has the secret. That's the one who has the secret...hold him and treat him gently; do not let him go but let everything else go. All that you formerly believed let it go, but don't let *that* go. That is the word of truth, and these are the words of scripture.

I can't tell anyone prior to the actual experience what a blow it is to one who has to give up, or at least struggle to give up, his belief in the historicity of scripture. When I first came here back in 1945, I was invited to come out and tell my story of the Bible. The head of the organization—I won't mention his name and you know the organization, there are maybe 100 across the country now. They've grown quite rapidly and they're quite successful in their numbers. The very first night that I arrived I'm going to address all of his graduates, and there were about, I dare say, four to five hundred of them. He didn't give me one minute...I'm taking the platform right away because I'm late, the plane was late. But I was taken to a late dinner party, and so I couldn't arrive there until about five minutes before eight, and I'm supposed to be on the platform at eight. He takes me aside and in that little short interval of time he tells me I must not speak on the non-historicity of the Bible to his people, because he believes in the historicity and teaches it and I must not in any way disturb his people. I thanked him. I said, I'm your guest tonight so I will abide by your decision, but beginning tomorrow when I'm speaking, don't tell me what to say. *No one can tell me what to say!* Again, I'm quoting scripture, "Whether it is right in the sight of God to listen to you rather than to God, you must judge." For I cannot but speak of what I have seen and heard, and I know it is *not* historically true—it is truer than that, it's eternally true. And these records are forever, and one day you will experience it. Even though you call yourself the dean of this institute, not in my eyes are you any dean concerning the Word of God, because you do not know it.

Then I had to take the platform and go on, and naturally change what I had to say, and speak to them on an entirely different level. I couldn't that night as his guest speak on the truth as I had experienced it. For at least I had experienced it based upon its law, but I was getting glimpses of it, that it was *not* historically sound, that this episode recorded in scripture was not a record of some historical fact; it was something entirely different. It was simply a revelation of truth, which would stun the man if he had the strength to stand it. But, may I tell you, when it happens to you, when you actually experience it, it's perfectly all right and there is no uncertainty, none. There may be a little uncertainty up unto the moment of experiencing the truth, because you will hear it from one you trust and you would like to believe all that he tells you. Certain things seem a little bit too much and you take it under consideration. But when it *happens* to you everything goes out, because you know now it *is* the truth. So, you take all the stories, every one, and they are true...but not as they are recorded. They were not writing history as we understand history. It is not secular history; it is divine or sacred history and this is forever. So you can't speak of it as something in the past or something to come…it *is*. The climax has been reached and it is always being reached in the moment of time.

So, the Jesus of scripture is seated right here tonight *in* you. And his Son bearing witness of his fatherhood is seated right here, and hiding in you. Read the 54th Psalm, and they said unto Saul, "David is in hiding within us." Well, how would the insane man ever know that? How would he find out if he's hiding within me, where would he look? How do I go about looking for him if he's hiding within me? Wait! He'll come out. He will come out one day when some explosion takes place within you, and when he comes out he is standing. That's why I say Browning must have had the experience, because the symbolism that he uses is actually perfect: "See the Christ stand" and he's standing. And here, David is standing, so "See the Christ stand." The word Christ means "Messiah." He goes to Saul to explain the coming of Messiah and then he tells Saul, "It shall be a face like my face, a man like unto me. This is the one that you're going to love and he will love you *forever*." That relationship between you when he stands before you is one of infinite love and it is forever. A man just like me, he's telling him. He's telling you *he is* Messiah; therefore, *he* is the Christ, he is the anointed of the Lord. Then he said, "The hand just like this hand will open the door of new life to you." Now he comes to a point, he said, "See the Christ stand" and he's standing before him (Browning, *Saul*).

But that man could not take it. Those who read Browning say isn't that a lovely thing and pass right on, because it is in conflict with what they have fixed in their mind's eye concerning the historical Jesus. They think Jesus is the Christ. Jesus is God. Jesus is the Lord, the Creator of it all. But he is a father, and the final revelation of God to man is the fatherhood of God. The *final* gift of God to man is the gift of himself. So if he gives me himself, he can't take back one little bit. He gives me *all* and in giving me all, he gave me his Son. Is it in scripture? Yes, "And he has sent his Son into my heart crying Father" (Gal.4:6). He is calling me Father. Well then, when he calls me Father, I will know who I am. As he stands before me and I see him and hear him, I know who I am. Until then I do not know. I'm confused…I've heard it this way and I've heard it that way. And you have to disturb people. You never go into a place and disturb them, but from a platform like this you ask for it, perfectly all right. But to come to your home and then to volunteer this information would be silly, because you simply are out of order. You are taking your pearls and throwing it before those who are not yet qualified to receive it. So leave them alone and don't disturb them. But you who know it and you're called upon to voice what you know then voice it, tell it.

You, who are moved to really teach it, go and teach it. Don't modify it! As Paul said, "Take the words, the true words of the pattern that I have given you. Do not change them." He tells Timothy, "Hold fast the pattern of the true words which you heard form me" (2Tim.1:13) and he calls it "my gospel." Well, here was one who was very proud of the fact that he was born a Jew. He said, "I was born of the seed of Abraham of the tribe of Benjamin. I am a Pharisee of the Pharisees" (Acts23:6). And then the whole thing unfolded within him and he realized the non-historicity of his own great book, and therefore that whatever came out of it would be equally un-historical but equally true. All these are the states through which man passes.

So do not be disturbed when you read in scripture Moses said this and Abraham said that and it's beautifully painted in words. Take it, accept it. You will one day experience all these states. You'll experience the state of Abraham and know what faith really is when you see it personified. When you look into his face and see that being leaning against a tree, and wound around that tree is a serpent, the serpent with a human face, the serpent with the wisest of expression on its face. As you're told in Genesis, he was the wisest of all the creatures that God had made. You see that wisdom personified in the form of a serpent. And you see in Abraham's eyes looking not into the distance but into time. He is staring into time. As you're told in Galatians, "And the scriptures, made known unto Abraham *before*"…he was given a preview of the end of time. Before it actually began to appear in man, Abraham was shown the end. So when you look at him, he's focused not only in the distance but the distance is the distance of time. The tree under which he stands is just like the human brain, just a wonderful oak, all the knotty, gnarly oak…every little thing is like some part of the human brain. You look at it and you know where you stand in scripture: you are seeing the beginning now of the great journey.

Wisdom is present in the form of a serpent; faith is present in the form of Abraham. Then you see his name was changed from Abram, which is "exalted father" to Abraham, which is "father of the multitudes." Well, how did they change it? By putting one letter into the name and that's the fifth letter, which is "grace". That is the letter He, which is the symbol of grace. So grace is put into the name so that God will now give to his creation the work of his hand; all the gifts, all the things you could ever conceive of he gives them now to his creation; and the final gift is the gift of himself. So he puts the gift of grace into the name of the father of the multitudes and then the journey starts.

So here, when you read it, try to bear in mind, and it may be difficult at first, that you're dealing with infinite states and they are eternal states. Jesus…it doesn't take anything from you when you say that Jesus is a state. *You* are Jesus when you find the Christ. When you find the Christ, which is the anointed of the Lord, you find David; and he'll call *you* Father as he called him Father. "In the spirit he called me Lord, how then can I be his son?" (Mat.22:45). Now these are interchangeable terms, father and son. As you read it, without giving you any notice he becomes the son speaking, then he becomes the father speaking, because they are one: I and my Father are one" (Jn.10:30). "He who sees me"—he's speaking now as son—"when you see me you see the Father"; but one moment before he's speaking as the son. So keep it in mind as you read scripture.

But I'll tell you, if you'll accept what I told you this night, it will make it so much easier for you; so much easier to completely accept the responsibility that *should* go with every being who knows this truth. You don't pass the buck. You simply know exactly what as the Lord you can do and imagining *does* create reality. You can, because that is the *real* you, and that is Jesus and that is the Lord, you can imagine anything and then sustain it in faith. As you walk in the faith of what you have imagined is so, it will become so. If not this moment, it will become so. Just walk in the assumption that it is done *because* you have imagined it, and having imagined it, it will become a fact. That I do know. So take anything, take a challenge and then do it.

As I was telling a lady tonight...we were discussing one little venture that she's started...I reminded her that back in 1943 when I came out of the Army I was looking for an apartment and I found one. I told my wife before what I was going to pay for it, a rental. It was a duplex, a lovely duplex in the heart of Manhattan. When I came home that night I told her I found it, it's a lovely one, and I committed myself to it. She said, "What are you paying?" Well, I was paying more than I told her I was going to pay. She said to me, "Well that's not demonstrating this principle, is it? Because you're paying that much more, a third more than you said that you were going to pay." Well, I paid the month of September and October. Went downstairs to pay my month of November to the manager and he said to me, "Mr. Goddard, I have an apology to make. An authority from the city came in and looked over my books, and discovered that the apartment that you have I had formerly rented it for less than what you are now paying." He told me what he had rented it for...and it was to the dollar what I said I was going to pay. He was notified that it's retroactive and "now you cannot receive this money from Mr. Goddard. Not only you can't receive it, but it must go back to the first month that he came in." So he told me, "Take your check upstairs and tear it up and bring me a new check."

So it took me three months of faithfulness to what I said I was going to pay. Even though I was paying more, I didn't. I got it all back at the beginning of my third month, the whole thing came back. I committed myself in my Imagination as to what I was going to pay, and I went looking.

Because I was going to pay more in his eyes he gave me all kinds of things he would not have given me if I paid him what the former tenant did. First of all, he said, "You pick out the wallpaper"; I picked out the wallpaper. "Pick out all the colors you want." I said that I have a lot of books, so I want you to build in a lovely bookshelf for me, the whole wall for my books…"All right." He did everything I wanted because he thought on a long term lease he is going to get a third more than he got from the previous tenant. Then he discovered that he didn't get one penny more, but he put all these things in and he couldn't undo them. So had I gone in there and gotten my place for the amount of money I said I was going to pay, he would not have built the bookcase for me, he would not have given me my wallpaper, he would not have painted the entire place. Well, he painted it to specification, exactly what my wife wanted in the colors and the paper, everything just as we wanted it. The bookcase was perfect and took care of all my books. I get it and then the whole thing went back to the first day of September. And we were there almost fourteen years.

So I tell you, it doesn't fail *if* you are faithful. So, what can I say when I'm confronted with a negation of it? My wife had every right to say "but you didn't demonstrate it." She had every right to say that, because she knew that I was paying more than I told her I would pay. So I paid it willingly, and paid the second month, and went down with my check for the third month to be confronted with this wonderful gift. So I tell you, don't give up! Set your goal high, set it high. Assume the feeling of the wish fulfilled, and then sleep on it. Persist in it! And if you persist in it, not a thing in this world can rob you of that thing that you've assumed that you have.

But the most important thing is what I told you earlier in the meeting, that which is housed within you is God's plan of redemption, and he only redeems himself. He came down into the world and housed himself in man, and now he's going to discover who he is in man, for it is in us as persons that the nature of God is revealed.

Now let us go into the Silence.

*   *   *

Now are there any questions, please?

Q: Isn't there some historicity in the Bible?
A: You could take the name, say, Herod and put Herod into a certain part, but that's not the story that they're telling. I could take any of our characters that are historically true and weave it into an eternal spiritual drama, but that's not the story of the Bible. Jesus tells you, "I am from above." Therefore,

if he's from above and he said, "I'm not of this world," then where was he born? "I am from above, I am not of this world; you are from below and you're of this world." I read this in the Book of John (8:23). Then where is Jesus? If *David* is hiding himself in me, then where is the physical, historical David? I know they have places in the Near East and they call it the tomb of David, as they call it the tomb of Jesus. Well, I know that if you have read certain works…and I think of Mark Twain. He went across the world and when he came back he wrote this work, and he said he saw more pieces of wood that came from the cross and it was necessary to build a huge, huge temple…and yet one man carried it? He saw more pieces of cloth that came from the robe than you would need to clothe a whole army…and one man wore it? So they've been fooling the people since the day one with all this nonsense. Just like the saints…just dethroned ninety of them. Well, if they dethroned ninety that's only a start.

This whole thing is the most glorious story ever told and it's the truest story because it's eternally true. But when, say, this is 1969, well, ten years ago it was 1959…and that's approximately 2,000 years A.D. David is *supposed* to have lived 1,000 B.C., therefore he was separated by 3,000 years. And here stands David and he's calling me Father, without any loss of identity as to myself, and yet I know I am his Father. My name isn't Jesse, yet in scripture the father's name is Jesse, and yet that is true because Jesse is any form of the verb "to be"; in other words, it's I AM. Well, I know who's hearing it and who's seeing it, I am…so I am Jesse. So here is the story. His father in scripture was called the Lord and the Lord is Jesus.

Q: (inaudible)

A: Well, my dear, it's a foreshadowing. The child doesn't come from the womb below; it comes from the womb of God, which is the skull of man. By man I mean generic man.

It's out of the skull of man. The drama begins with the death of God, and he's buried in the skull of man. The real drama now in the fullness of it comes to its end by the resurrection of that being who is buried in the skull and it's *you*, for you *are* God. That's where when you come out, having been raised within your skull, you emerge from the skull. It's then the symbolism of the birth appears before you—the infant wrapped in swaddling clothes and three witnesses to the event as told in scripture. "Go, and this shall be a *sign* unto you, you shall find a babe wrapped in swaddling clothes, and lying on the floor"…lying on a manger, that is, on the floor (Jn.2:11.12). And they went…the shepherds or the kings.

So the shepherds—and tradition has it there are always three—so three are there to witness. They see what? They don't see you because

God is Spirit and he is invisible to mortal eyes. They see the *sign*; they see the child wrapped in swaddling clothes, because they were told, "And this shall be a sign unto you, you shall find a child wrapped in swaddling clothes." But the event that they observe only witnesses what they cannot see: the birth of God. One of them knows whose child it is and when he pronounces a man that they knew as brother, as a friend, they can't believe that such a being could be God born, because man is not looking for man as God. It stuns man to be told that God is man and that man is God.

The average person, even those who call themselves very religious, they have no concept of God as man. They speak of an over-soul or some impersonal light. God is very much a person and all will be gathered one by one, without loss of identity, into the one body which is the Lord. No loss of identity, but it's your body. You are gathered into the body—and it's your body—by the one Spirit, and you are that Spirit. For, "He who is united to the Lord becomes one spirit with him" (1Cor.6:17). So it's "One body, one Spirit, one Lord, one God and Father of all" (Eph.4:4), and is all. Everyone is drawn in, and everyone who is drawn in will be the Father of the same David. There's only one David, only one anointed, "Rise and anoint him" (1Sam.16:12), only one anointed by the Lord. Others take kings and queens and our priests anoint them. When the queen was made queen or crowned, the Archbishop of Canterbury simply took out this little holy oil and touched her on her breast. He calls that making her a holy person. Nonsense! The only holy one was David. David was the sum total, the resultant state of the long journey that God made in this world.

What you saw, my dear, is a very interesting experience. So all of these births are foreshadowings, but the real birth comes from above. He said, "You must be born from above" (Jn.3:3). The Greek word is "Anothin" translated "again." People have misconstrued it to mean "reincarnation." It doesn't mean that. For when it appears elsewhere in the Bible...for instance, it appears at the trial. He stands before a man who is now judge of mortal men, and he would not speak to him. He says, "So you will not answer me. Do you not know that I have the power to free you and the power to crucify you?" And now he answers, he said, "You have no power over me were it not given to you from above" (Jn.19:10). The word "from above" is Anothin. Yet when it appears in the 3rd chapter of John, it's translated "again." When it appears in the 1st of Peter, it's translated "anew": "We are born anew through the resurrection of Jesus from the grave, from the dead" (1:3) But the word is "Anothin" and it means "from God, from above." So he makes the statement: "I am from above, you are from below; you are of this world, I am not of this world" (Jn.8:23). He's a completely *supernatural* being, for God is and that's God speaking...but you don't know it yet. You will one day know that you are the God of scripture, that you are the Jesus of scripture. He is the *only* reality.

So, far from not believing in Jesus I want to meet the man or woman in this world who believes in Jesus more than I do. But I see no one after the flesh; I do not see him as a character in history 2,000 years ago. To me he is more than contemporary for the simple reason his Son called me Father...and there aren't two Lords and there aren't two sons. Then comes the challenge: Well, if that is so, why don't you command these stones to be made bread. Why don't you throw yourself down? Is it not written he gives his angels power to support you? Why don't you get down and worship me and I'll give you the world? And to all of these, "Get behind me, doubter" (Mat.4:3).

So everyone will put you to the test. You make a statement that imagining creates reality and one fella on radio one night...he's a professor of psychology in an eastern college...and he said to me, "Turn that yellow pencil into red." So I said to him quite innocently, "You are fulfilling scripture." He said, "In what way?" I said, "There will come in that day, in the last day, scoffers scoffing, saying 'Where is the promise of his coming?' (2Pet.3:3) and so you are the scoffer." He turned red. *He* turned red, not the pencil, because he told all of his students to listen in...he was going to take this man over. We had one of these long marathon nights, six hours on radio without breaks. We ourselves had a break at midnight or about one in the morning, with a few sandwiches and some black coffee. But we went on at midnight and came off at six in the morning. We had one little interval...there was constant talk and the phones ringing, people bringing in all kinds of questions and challenges. So he told his class to listen and he was going to take this thing over. He didn't want to go back and face them and explain why I called him a scoffer, but he will.

Q: This statement "the only son of God," is there anything else on it?
A: It appears in the 2nd Psalm, the 7th verse, and the Psalm is attributed to David. The words are, "I will tell of the decree of the Lord: He said to me, 'You are my son, today I have begotten thee.'" At the end of the journey David appears as the resultant state. So you are promised that when you come out, you will be as I am and I am a father...so you start the journey. If I really am as he is, when I reach the end, he *must* appear.

So I knew nothing of being the father of David until that moment in time on the morning of the 6th of December, 1959. I never heard it from anyone else, never read it in a book and although I read scripture, I never saw it. "You have eyes and see not, ears and hear not." I read it, but I was given a misinterpretation of it, because all of the churches believe it is of Jesus, that Jesus is the Lord who said it. Jesus is the Lord who said to him, "I have begotten you, thou art my son." Jesus is the Jehovah of the Old Testament…he is the Lord God Almighty.

But man will not believe it and our priests don't believe it, they think he is some good man. Every Sunday morning or Wednesday night…and all the time they're speaking from their pulpits they are always talking about politics, what's happening in the world. He never discussed politics. "Render unto Caesar the things that are Caesar's. Whose inscription is this?—Caesar's. Well, give it to Caesar and then unto God what is God's" (Mark12:17). But they become big business. You don't have a portfolio of $100 billion and tell me you aren't in business. That's what our estimate in this country alone is of our churches. I didn't make it up; I read it in *Life* magazine and in *Time* magazine and in the *New York Times* and the *L. A. Times*, who quoted the source which was *Life* who made the survey. The Catholic Church came in with the majority. They had forty-odd billion dollars in America, not the world. The Protestants came behind with a little over thirty billion, and the Jews came with a little over eleven billion, and then other denominations were not considered one or the other. It comes close to 100 billion dollars that is tax-exempt. That's why I pay…every dollar that I take in here I pay tax on it, as though I'm selling merchandise. I have nothing that I can call or say now this is religion. I'm not a minister, I'm not a priest, I'm not ordained. I've been offered all kinds, but I said no, I don't want to be ordained…I was *sent* of God…what on earth could you give me? You couldn't send me, God sent me. So I pay on every nickel that comes in here. My books are so I have no exemptions, and they aren't exempt, I pay taxes.

I don't care, let them keep it, but don't tell me that's religion. They're in business and what a big business! I don't care what they do with it. But when they start going into competition with people who are paying taxes—and I don't mean me, I mean these regular businesses—I think the line should be drawn somewhere. But I'm not here to go into politics. I'm here to tell you what I know from my own experience. So when God has revealed himself in me, what can I tell you but what was revealed. So his Word is there, written down by men from supernatural experiences which they did not understand; then comes the *living* Word who interprets the written Word.

Good night.

PURSUE TRUTH WITH CEASELESS QUESTIONING

6/9/69

Take nothing on external authority of a church or the Bible without pursuing it with ceaseless statements. Here we have all these statements in scripture, statements from the church and statements from individuals like the speaker. Do not accept it because it comes from the Bible, comes from a church, and comes from a speaker...not until you have found God or a *living* truth in what they say or what the speaker says. If I tell you something, I am telling you from my own experience, but still don't accept it until you with ceaseless questioning prove it *within* yourself.

To accept it because a church said it or the Bible said it or Neville said it is really silly. You must pursue it with ceaseless, ceaseless, I would say, questions. Why? Because along the pathway of the Spirit world where you and I are traveling there are many Babels, and like Babel no two speak with the same tongue. One will tell you give up all meat and you'll enter the kingdom of God; another will tell you give up so and so and you will enter, and no two will speak with the same tongue. So you will find it all the way as man travels the spiritual way, the road called the road of Babel. It's not multiple tongues as we have it today—we can overcome that with someone translating for us—but when someone tells you *this* is the way and that one tells you *this* is the way and they don't agree this is Babel. So here we find Babel along the pathway of the Spirit.

You will find it very restful if you always fall back on *first principle*. Tonight we'll fall back on first principle: "Be still and know that I am God" (Ps.46:10). No matter what happens to you, let that be your first principle: Be still and know that I am is God and with God all things are possible.

Well now, put that to the test. If you put that to the test regardless of any change in your outer world and it proves itself in the testing, then you are free. It doesn't matter what one calls on this side, what calls on that side, you know you've gone back to the first principle. And you don't have to give up this and give up that and *do* anything in this world to enter the kingdom of God. So we go back to first principle, which is "I am God." That is the first principle. Is it true? Well, just test it.

Now, let us go back to some of the "I am" statements in scripture: "I am the resurrection and the life. I am the way. I am the truth" (Jn.11:25; 14:6). Well, is this really true? Long before I proved it to be true I took it in this way...being human I wanted certain things, as undoubtedly you want certain things, and so I took it getting things. Like a trip when I could not afford it and I didn't have a nickel and the trip would cost quite a lot of money. So I took it, "Be still and know that I am God." Well, if I am is God and all things are possible to God, what I am imagining within myself should come to pass. So I tried it and it worked. I tried it again and it worked.

Having proven this in my own experience, I waited then for the other great statement that "I am the resurrection." Now, how would I go about that? I knew no way to go about that. How would I prove that "I am the light"? I couldn't do that. "I am the way, I am the truth," these I couldn't do. I could prove it in the world of Caesar that "I am" does create things in my world if I have absolute faith in it. So I am...and I named it. I began to imagine that I am on a ship when I didn't have a nickel and I'm sailing in a certain direction. Then I got a letter from the family saying that "you're the only member of the family not present at Christmas. We're enclosing a draft to buy passage. We'll take care of all expenses on the ship, use it freely; and we'll greet you on the ship when you arrive and take care of all expenses. This is simply to buy maybe a suit and some linen that you may need, and then the draft will take care of these things. We've notified the agency in New York City to issue you a ticket."

Well here, this happened out of the blue. I simply assumed that I am on a ship sailing for Barbados, when suddenly after twelve years they were moved to ask me to come, and made it possible to come. I proved it there. Then I tried it and tried it and tried it, and when I kept on trying it I realized that statement is true: that God really *is* my own wonderful consciousness, my I am-ness, that is God! So when I'm told in that 46th Psalm, "Be still and know that I am God" I proved it (46:10). Then came these fantastic claims, well, how did you prove that? I couldn't by taking the same action...I had to wait.

Then I proved that "I am the life" first of all, for I found myself moved in Spirit into an environment and suddenly I'm seeing things that seemed independent of my perception of them; and yet intuitively I knew that if I could arrest what I am feeling within me, everything that I am seeing would stand still, because I was the life of everything that I perceived in this world. I knew it! I no sooner knew it than I tested it. I arrested the activity within me and everything stood still…not only the animate, say, men and women, but the so-called inanimate. Falling leaves could not fall, the little moving grass, yes, that could move, but it didn't move after I stilled within me what I was perceiving: I was perceiving moving grass and I stilled the activity and the grass was frozen. The leaf was frozen, the bird was frozen, the people dining were frozen, the waitress walking was frozen…everything was frozen. I knew that statement is true, "I am the resurrection and the life" (Jn.11:25).

I proved first that I am the life before I proved that I am the resurrection. Then came that day in my experience when I proved that I am the resurrection; because I felt myself resurrecting within the grave of my own skull, and that was proof of that statement in scripture that I am. Well, who resurrected? I did. Well, who is resurrecting?—I am. "I am the resurrection"; I have proved that. I have proved this then that I am the resurrection before I proved that I am the Father. He said, "I am the Father"…I didn't know that. How could I prove that I am the Father? Suddenly, after having proved I am the resurrection then I prove by the Son who called me Father that I *am* the Father. He tells me that he sacrificed himself. I didn't know that to be true. I knew that I am the Father before I knew that I am the one who was sacrificed, the one whose body was split in two from top to bottom. I read that in scripture, but I didn't know that it was true until it was proven true *after* I discovered I *am* the Father. Because I am the Father it was the Father whose body was split from top to bottom. It's only the Father who made the sacrifice. So here, *I* am the Father and my body is split from top to bottom. I proved that. But I didn't know that I also was the one on whom the Holy Spirit descended in bodily form of a dove until it happened. So I proved that I am the Father before I proved that, and then *that* happened. So I tell you, from my own experience these things I now speak from experience, therefore I speak with the authority that can only come to one who has experienced them.

So I say to everyone here, if it comes from me or it comes from a church or it comes from the Bible, you simply pursue it with ceaseless questions until you have found God or the living truth in that which was said either from the page of the Bible or from the pulpit in some church or from here when the speaker speaks. Accept it, but then go back to first principle and ask these eternal questions of the one being that could answer it, and the one being is your own wonderful I am-ness. So is it true? For I am told, be still, that is be relaxed. No stillness physically and internally, I'm all tight...no, be relaxed. And just ask, are you really God? I speak now to myself, "Are you really God?" I can address myself as that as though we were two. "Be still and know that *I am* God." Well, be still and know that I am, as though it's another, is God. Are you, really? Well then, prove to me this. Now, God can do all things, so I will now ask and see if it proves itself in performance. Ask again and see if it proves itself in that...and keep on asking. When it proves itself here, well then, let these things you can't put to the test but you've done it here, and see how it comes through in performance, and it will.

Then everything opens up in scripture. Then you see the wide difference between what seems on the surface the same thing. You read in the Bible that Christ is in us. That seems straightforward, Christ is in us. Then we read in the Bible that "we are in Christ" and on the surface it seems to be the same thing. It's all the difference in the world! Christ in us is the hope of glory. That's a universal son-ship, for Christ is the anointed one, and he is in every being born of woman...that's a universal son-ship. All right, is it the same as "we in Christ"? It is *not* the same. That comes to you in the most marvelous way, I in Christ. If I am in Christ, I'm told in scripture that I'm a new creature. Christ in me does not make me a new creature. The Son is in me and through that Son I have life, for in him is life, and the life is in me. "In him is life and life is the light of men"...the *consciousness* of men...the very life of men (Jn.1:4). So he is in every child born of woman, Christ in us.

But it's not the same thing as "we in Christ." When "we are in Christ," we are the elect, we are the called; we are called and incorporated into the body of the risen Lord. It is entirely different. So Christ in us makes us the son, for we are the son in the world. Then "we in Christ" is when we are called, when we are elected, and we are drawn into the presence of the risen Lord and incorporated into his body. That makes us entirely different. It's not Christ in us any more; it's we in Christ...all the difference in the world. And we find the entire book opening up page after page after page *within* us.

If I question everything that I hear from any pulpit, from any speaker and from the Bible, I must question everything and keep on questioning, until it actually proves itself *in* me. I must find God or the living truth in what I have heard or what I have read. So you trust me, I hope you do, but even though you trust me you question and question everything that I tell you. But whom do you question? Me? Do you go to some priest, do you go to some rabbi? No, they can't tell you anything. Don't go to anyone. Fall back on first principle and the first principle is, "Be still and know that I am God." So I go to bed tonight..."I heard tonight and this is what I heard, is it

The Return of Glory

true?" Ask *yourself* is it true? I tell you we're living in this fabulous world of shadows. It's so difficult to believe that this is a world of shadows.

This past Thursday morning as I was coming through to the surface, I was arrested just for a moment, to see the race at Belmont, and here I am seeing the entire race. I'm closer to the horses than anyone could be at that track. I'm closer than anyone could be on TV. I see it in the most vivid color, colors that were not revealed on my TV set...which is a nice color set. And here I'm seeing the horses coming up and here I'm seeing Arts and Letters first, Majestic Prince second, and Dike third. Although I'm seeing it in my vision I'm disappointed, because through sentiment I wanted Majestic Prince to come in first...just through sentiment. I do not know the owner, the jockey or the trainer. I know of them, but I do not know them. It's simply a sentimental feeling I have towards that horse because he won nine, trained out west, born back east in Kentucky...but trained out west. The eastern riders made little of him because they thought he hadn't really gone against *real* horses. Then he took the Derby, then he took the Preakness, and then they changed their tune. But I saw the triple-crown, the third one, and I saw where he came second and he couldn't catch that horse.

This is Thursday morning...the race isn't run for two more days. I woke at five, then had breakfast around six, and said to my wife, "Well, the Prince came in second." She said, "Oh, no!" I said, "Yes I saw it, saw it just about an hour ago. He is second and he is second regardless of what the world will say and Arts and Letters came first. I saw it in the actual post position in which they finished." Arts and Letters on the rail, Prince is second, could be in the second or third post, but he's moving into second, and here is Dike coming up. I saw it so clearly, so vividly that if I had a billion dollars I would not have hesitated to put the whole billion on the nose of Arts and Letters. It could not be reversed; the whole thing was *fixed*.

So you ask yourself, what on earth is this world...just where is it and what is it? What part does it play in this entire world round about us? Here we find it a school of educated darkness. Man thinks he's going to change it and in some strange way he's going to improve this world, improve it and make it home. You don't turn a schoolroom into home; it remains a schoolroom. This world is a world of educative darkness, it's a school, and you aren't in eternity going to turn it from a school into a home. There's nothing in scripture that suggests that the kingdom of heaven is interested in improving this world. It's only interested in taking people *out* of this world into itself, which is an entirely different world. We are in a school here and the whole vast world is in a school.

To what extent can we change it? That's where I know *revision* comes in to make us make the effort. If you don't make the effort, the whole thing

585

is written just like a book that's already been printed, it's been finished. I have no desire whatsoever outside of a sentimental interest in revising that race, none whatsoever. When my daughter, who was out of town at the time in San Francisco, when she came back and we met on Friday, not a thing came up then. But on Saturday morning she was going off to our friends to the pool, and I said, "Are you going to see the race in color?" She said yes. "Well, this is how it finishes" and I told her. "Oh," she said, "no! You stop your dream." I said, "I can't help it…that's what I saw. So when you go to Jane and Sarge tell them, "Don't get excited the race is finished." 65,000 saw it at Belmont and 65,000 had a dollar or two dollars on the nose of this, that and the other, and 65,000 went wild rooting for this one to be a triple-crown winner. Tens of millions in our country saw it on TV and all are eager, and they didn't know the race was run before that. The whole thing was completely finished. I saw it in detail, I saw the colors of the jockey and I saw all the colors that they wore. Even that they couldn't change for everything was cut and dried. And you wonder, what is this world? Just like a schoolroom and the textbooks are all there and all these things are done.

Now you can bring about a little rebellion within yourself and revise certain things and make the effort. That is called, and rightly so, in scripture *repentance*, a radical change of attitude. But I had no emotional reason to change that, because my tie was only a little sentimental tie. There was nothing vivid about it in me, only this little sentimental tie. To what extent is this whole vast world losing itself trying to burst a brain to change something on the outside…and you can't change it on the outside anyway. If one could only remember as they come through to the surface mind in the morning the little things they pass through, which are taking place tomorrow or the next day or next week in this world of shadows. But he comes through suddenly and quickly jumps out of the bed, washes his face, and here he is locked in the world of shadows, and he doesn't know what he passed through.

So I say, everything I tell you, everything you read in the Bible, everything you hear from some pulpit you ceaselessly question. Keep on questioning and questioning until it actually proves itself so that you can find God or what is called the spirit of truth, the living truth *in* what they say. Whether it be the Bible, the pulpit or the speaker from the platform, is it true? I'm telling you what I know from experience and I know it *is* true. I know that you will one day find within yourselves that you are the light of the universe, so everything in the world that you think external and independent of your perception of it is really within you. The whole vast world is yourself pushed out and you are the life of it.

I can't tell you my thrill the first time that it happened to me that I could stop within myself an activity and stop everything moving in my world. Well, I did it. The waitress couldn't walk, the diners couldn't dine, the birds couldn't fly, the leaf couldn't fall, the grass could not wave beyond what it did at the moment it stopped. Here I'm looking at a dead world. And then I released the activity...not there but in me. As I did it, everything continued as it intended and completed its purpose: the bird to a certain branch, the leaf to the ground, the waitress to the table to serve the food, and the diners to complete eating what they were eating. But they were arrested for eternity, because I in myself I am the life of the world.

So when you read that in scripture, "In him was life and the life was the light of men...and yet men knew him not" (Jn.1:4, 10). He is *in* man and man knows it not. That being begins to stir and proves himself to be the life of the world. He stirs in a man *as* that man, and the man discovers he is that being. The next thing he discovers is that he also is the resurrection. So you're told, "I am the resurrection" (Jn.11:25). You say he's dead? "I am the resurrection. Though a man died, if he believes in me yet shall he live." And then comes that moment in time when I discovered *I am* the resurrection. I first discovered I am the life; then I rose from the dead, so I am the resurrection. But I didn't know then I was the one spoken of in scripture as the one of whom the angels spoke saying that God is born. And the *sign to prove* to you that he is born is this...and the little sign was given to the shepherds watching their flocks at night. I didn't know that and suddenly I discovered I am the one of whom they spoke. But I know that every being in my world that I address is *that* being, and one day he will discover he is that being. I knew that before I knew God the Father. I knew that I was God the Father before I knew that I was the sacrificed one, the one whose body was completely split in two from top to bottom. And I knew *that* before I knew that I was the one on whom the Holy Spirit descended in bodily form as a dove.

So here, I found these things are true. Now I know scripture *is* true, because I questioned scripture. But I started questioning scripture based upon law, for I was more interested then in things. When I had no money I wanted a trip. All right, so I wanted a trip. When I had nothing I wanted this and I got this. Then I began to tell it to others, and I wanted to see them do the same thing that I did. I couldn't keep it to myself! I wanted to see others take this same principle and test it in their lives on this level, and they did. I told it to as many as would listen to me. I asked those who proved it to tell it to others and keep on telling it. Things you can't put to the test here, because you prove other things on this level, then you have hope that things are equally true...and suddenly they become true. So, certain things you can't put to the test, but you can put the law to the test in this world. Then you can accept the promises on faith based upon what you've proven by the law.

So I say to you, do you know what you want? You really know what you want? Well now, here is a simple way to get it: what would the feeling be like if it were true? Is that all? That's all! What would the feeling be like if it were true? You feel as though you would feel, what you *would* feel, if it were true. Then what else, Neville? That's all. Now having done it you walk in that state and see the world as you would see it if it were true, and you walk in that state. And forget it, completely forget it! He knows what you did. Well, who is he? He's not outside; he is in you. He's your own wonderful human I am-ness, your Imagination, your consciousness—that is God. Well now, try that. And when it works, try it again on something else. Tell a friend, share it and share the good fortune with a friend. Tell others and tell others and have them tell others.

Then take all the other on faith because you proved this in the world of shadows. Now the other is the world of reality. For truth...he is called truth, "I am the truth" and truth is the *eternal* reality. We are living in a world of shadows. When he declares in the I-am-ness no matter what he declares he is declaring eternal truth. So, he says "I am the resurrection" and that is eternal truth. "I am the life," that is eternal truth. "I am the way," that's eternal truth. So when he makes these bold assertions with the "I am" preceding it, these are eternal truths. So anyone in the world who screams at you along the way from their towers of Babel telling you of some other way, forget it. There is no other way! You don't have to give up anything in this world... no matter what you are doing...to enter the way. And there is no other God.

Now, it is not God the Savior's pleasure that anyone should be lost as we are told; it is God the Savior's desire that every man be saved. If it's his desire, every man will be saved. I do not wish to go out on any limb and speculate as to numbers; I say *everyone* will be saved. When we are told in scripture concerning remnants and told in scripture concerning a certain elect, I leave that in abeyance. For there is a word in scripture, you'll read it in the 1st Timothy (2:4), it is his pleasure, his desire that every man be saved. If it's God's desire and God is in us, every man will be saved. So I will not go out and say that because this one proved with himself first, that is, before another one, that he is the life, that he is the resurrection, and he is God the Father, that he differs in any way from another. I will not accept that. I will simply say I know I have experienced these things and I trust that everyone here before I depart, if I depart tomorrow, it will happen to you tonight and *prove* these thing, because you have proven in the world of Caesar many things. You've taken a certain objective and you've assumed that you have

The Return of Glory

it when reason tells you that you don't, and it worked. I could tell you unnumbered stories concerning dollars and cents…of people actually taking even a definite sum of money and proving it to the penny in what they're going to earn, what they would inherit, and they do. They didn't injure anyone, didn't hurt anyone; they simply took this law at face value and they proved it.

So I ask everyone here to take all the things that I'm telling you and even though I tell you it's true, still challenge it and have ceaseless questioning within you. But who do you question? Me? No. You go to the priest and ask him if I'm telling you the truth? No, the first thing he's going to tell you is no, because he is Babel too. He's along the way screaming at you in a different voice. Go to the rabbi? No, he's another Babel screaming another voice. And so I ask you not to go to anyone, but go to first principle, and first principle is "Be still and know that I am God" (46:10). It's a fantastic chapter that 46th Psalm. I have read where certain people in their little jokes claim that Shakespeare wrote it. You can start with the first… it's the 46th Psalm…and you go through to the first word to the forty-sixth word, and the forty-sixth word is "shake." Start at the end and go back forty-six words and it's "sphere." So they say Shakespeare incorporated himself into the book. Well, I mean it's a funny thing…but nevertheless, all these things in the book.

It's said that it's called Luther's Psalm. Well, Luther lived in the 16th Century. He did claim that this inspired his majestic hymn, the hymn that, I would say, moves everyone who hears it. But although it moved him to write the hymn he certainly did not lay claim to the psalm. It is a psalm of the sons of Korah and who knows who the sons of Korah are? Korah means "bald headed" like Elijah, "the shaven head." Who knows who he is, who the sons are? But here is something that goes back a thousand B.C., and some little jokester found this Shakespeare in it in the 46th word, coming from the beginning to the 46th word, and starting from the very end back to the 46th word and it spells Shakespeare, so he said Shakespeare wrote it. But you and I know that this is one of these fantastic revelations. And in the tenth verse, be still, that's all, "Be still and *really* believe that I AM is God."

So tonight when you go to bed, don't turn to any being in the world. Ask no one for any help, don't turn any place and just within yourself say "I am"…now say anything you want, and believe it, as though you're speaking to the God that actually created the universe, your own wonderful I-am-ness. Now you imagine anything. Who's imagining?—I am. Well, that's God. Imagine it and then go to sleep. You don't burst a vessel, you simply imagine it believing that all things are possible to God and you've found him…he's your own wonderful human I-am-ness, that's God. Go to sleep and see if it works. I tell you it *will* work. You don't need to get down on your knees and pray to any being outside of yourself. You don't need to cross yourself before any little icon in the world. It's *all within* you—your own wonderful human Imagination, your own consciousness, your own I-am-ness is God.

Not a thing in this world can really cease to be, for he created it in love…that same being that is in you, your own I-am-ness. The day will come—I know it must come as it happened to me—that instead of being as you're told "Christ is in you," you will be "in Christ." So Christ is in you making you now a son of God. This is the universal son-ship, for Christ is Messiah and Messiah is the anointed one, and the anointed one is David (1Sam.16:12), and that is *in you*. That is the beloved. One day *you* will be *in*, and then you will find that instead of being the son of, that you are the father of. That's when man matures…when he becomes his own father's father. And the whole thing unfolds within us.

So do not take anything at all on face value. I know when I take the Bible and tell you that it is true that I have proven it is true. But don't you take it, question it and keep on questioning. What do you mean that I am the resurrection? Tell me. What do you mean that I am the life, that I am the truth, that I am the way? And you question it. You will see the whole thing unfolding within you. Then you ask the question when the virgin said, the prudent virgin to those who had no oil, "No, go and get your own oil" for when the bridegroom comes they wanted enough, and you wonder why? That isn't the teaching of God. Why does it not give to those who had none? One night you have the experience and you realize the bridegroom had *not yet* come. When the bridegroom comes, that union with the bridegroom reveals to the prudent virgin now they have limitless oil to give all…to give to every being in the world, no restrictions. Prior to the coming of the bridegroom they thought there was a limit to the amount of oil that they could give. But when the bridegroom comes…and who is the bridegroom? The bridegroom is the Lord.

We are told in Mark (8:38) and we speak now of an adulterous generation, well, who are these adulterers? The adulterer is one who has turned away from her spouse, and the spouse is the truth. You've turned from the truth, you've turned from the Lord, and turning from the truth you've turned into adultery. That's all that it means—this adulterous generation. Hasn't a thing to do with what the world would think. Anyone who has heard the truth or has been exposed to it and still will seek something outside, something other than what you've been exposed to, they have gone into adultery. They've turned from their spouse and their spouse is

I AM. To turn to any source other than I AM as the cause of the phenomena of life is to become an adulterer. It's just as simple as that.

If you saw the race last Saturday, you heard all these wise men after the race speculating as to what ought to have been done. Here is Arcaro who won many of these races, an outstanding jockey, and he said that it was run too slow, that the first section of it should have been run in eleven seconds instead of sixteen. They're all now having this post-mortem concerning how frightfully the race was run. They could not have helped it! Not one person on that field could have done anything other than what they did. I saw it, but who would listen to one who can't ride a horse? Who would listen to one who knows nothing of training a horse, what even to give them in order to keep them in form? I don't know. I only know I saw the race and I saw it so vividly. I've never seen a race more vividly and I saw it exactly as it came in and told it at least to two witnesses, to my wife on Thursday morning and on Saturday morning around ten I told it—which is seven hours before the race was run back east at 5:30—to my daughter. I said you go and tell Jane and Sarge who's going to win. If they know anyone who'll take a bet, fix the bet put it all on Arts and Letters. I'm not putting any money on the race, but I know who has won, and now it's like going to the same show twice. So when I sat down to see it, I couldn't get excited. All my excitement was gone because I knew exactly who was going to win. So this one starts off, the other one starts off. There were six horses in the race, and they're all moving back and forth to different positions, and I knew exactly the end, so what am I going to start screaming about? So you see, if everyone knew the end there would be no excitement.

We are living in a wonderful world, thinking we all are going to change things, but not a thing is changed on the outside. It can only be changed where I saw it, on the inside. But I had no interest, other than a sentimental interest, so I would not attempt to change it. I saw it just as it would *have* to come out……unless someone who knows the law changed it from within. So I ask you to apply it and change these seeming inevitable ends from within, for you'll never change it on the outside. But take everything that I tell you, and I tell you I'm telling the truth based upon my own experience. It's not something that I'm theorizing or speculating about; it's what I *know* that I've experienced. So when I hear someone from the pulpit and he doesn't know what he's talking about and he's quoting "I am the resurrection and the life" he thinks a being on the outside is saying it. He's telling you of some being and he calls him "my Lord" and prays to "my Lord" external to himself as the one who is the resurrection, no! "Be still and know that *I am* is God." That's the one who is the resurrection. Where is he?—in you!

One day you'll know he is the life...the life of what, this body?—yes, and everything in the world. He is the life of everything in this world. The bird that is flying, that you'll even shoot; you are the life of it. Everything in the world you animate. You are the life of everything in this world. I know that, I know it from experience. What on earth would allow any rational being to believe for a moment that a simple man as the speaker would come into a restaurant and know in the depth of his own being that if he could arrest what he is feeling within him, which is a vibration, and stop the vibration that everything that he is perceiving is going to die and yet not vanish. It will simply stand still and it wouldn't decay; it's there forever. It could not decay; it's frozen *forever*. It doesn't slowly decay...it is...and it's simply without life, because I am the life. Then I release the activity within me and everything becomes animated and continues to fulfill its purpose. Then you realize that statement is true...though I haven't yet proven the other part of it. He said, "I am the resurrection and the life." I first prove the life. When will I prove now the resurrection?

Well, it came in the same spontaneous unsought manner. I didn't sit down to do it, it happened. And then came the night when I rose in the grave to realize *I am* the resurrected being. Then I am the one of whom the angel spoke when he said to the shepherds, "Go, God is born and this is the *sign* that you will find, and the sign will tell you that God is born." This is a *sign* of his birth. I didn't realize that it was all about me. Then I knew *that* before I knew, that is, five and a half months before I knew that I was God himself, God the Father. I knew *that* before I knew I was the one who was sacrificed for it all; that *my* body was the one that was split from top to bottom, and it was my blood that was the saving blood that would save the Son of man and raise him up like a serpent into heaven. And I knew *that* before I also knew what begins the story. For in the Book of Luke, the first beginning it is the 61st of Isaiah...in the beginning, and it came at the end..."The Spirit of the Lord God is upon me." I didn't know *that* before I knew I was God the Father, and all of a sudden that happened.

So all these statements of scripture I know from experience that they are all true. And yet I ask you not to accept them because I tell you, but to question and keep on questioning, and keep on asking the one being that can give you the answer. He will give it to you when he reveals himself *in you*. And he reveals himself in you and you are placed in the character in the first-person, singular, in a present-tense experience having all these experiences. So I know that everyone in this world is going to have it. In what order he does it I do not know, I could not tell you. Let no one tell you that they can tell you. If they do, don't believe it. Don't let anyone tell you that you have so many days, weeks, months or years or lives to come.

Challenge it now. You're here to hear one who has experienced it. And you take it now and prove it to me now…that's what you ask…and then let it unfold within you. Then when it does, not a thing in this world has any value. You wonder, what are they fighting for? Why are they all trying to get more and more of shadows? So they have a billion and they want two, and then they'll become the richest guppy in the world, in the grave. You go and you read their tombstone, "He was the richest man on earth." He survived, but he took nothing with him. He had the satisfaction of having most of the shadows of the world.

So criticize no one…leave them alone. They want more shadows? Pray for them if it doesn't interfere with your ethical code. They want money? Pray for it. They want more homes and the have three or four now, pray for them. Do it simply. Ask the only being that can do it, which is your own wonderful human Imagination. You don't do it with any struggle. When they ask of you, who is listening?—*I am*. Well, that's he. Now he heard the request; you grant it. Just simply…don't struggle with it…you grant it and just let it happen. If they tell you that it's slow, make no comment. You heard it. He heard it when you heard it, because he is your own wonderful I-am-ness. So he heard it and you grant the request, for all that you ask of me in my Father's name he will grant. So you grant it and you take it. When you see it working in their lives, just ask them to share it. Not what they got, not their money, but to share the news, the good news with others and tell them how they can become free by reason of this good news. Don't ask them to give one nickel to someone else, no let them keep it. They want it, let them keep it. But you ask them to share it as you share what you found of God. You shared it with them so you share it with others.

I know when anyone calls me at home on the telephone, the minute I answer the phone if the request is within my ethical code it's granted. I don't do anything beyond that. Before I hang up that phone, I feel that they've actually told me that they have it. I get the *mood*, I possess the mood before they actually hang up that receiver; I *feel* it's been granted. I go to bed not thinking for one moment about anything beyond that it's been granted. Then they confirm it…if not tomorrow or next week or next month, some never confirm it. Well, that's perfectly all right. Scripture teaches only one in ten will do it, so I'm quite resigned to that. The one in ten will do it and that's enough for me. Nine will not come back to say thank you, but one will always come back, one in ten. You meet them months later, sometimes years later, and they will tell you, "You know, many yeas ago I wrote you or asked you so-and-so, and you know, it worked." *It* worked…something on the outside, some impersonal thing. But they never told me until we were confronting each other seemingly by accident, and then they tell me. But

I'm not surprised, because only one in ten will tell you anyway. Were there not ten of you, said he, and only one returned to say thank you (Luke 17:15). But he wasn't disappointed...that is the average that will always return to say thank you.

But you do it, regardless if one comes back or no one comes back. Just share the good news with others and set them free in the world of Caesar, for this is really a terrible world, a world of disorder. And not a thing in scripture tells me that I am going to change this world. I am not going to make this world, which a schoolroom, into a home; it will remain a school. I would not turn it into a home and I *can't* turn it into a home. It's not intended to be turned into a home. But I've been telling you and tell everyone else that he is not going to turn this into a home, but to take us out of it into the eternal home.

Now, for anyone who is here for the first time this is what I mean by applying the law. It's a very simple, simple technique. If I asked you right now to pray for me, the first thing you want to know is what do you want? You just can't pray for you; what do you want? So I must voice it, I must name it so that within your ethical code it is all right and it's acceptable by you. Well, it isn't going to hurt you any if I tell you that I want...and I name it. If it isn't going to hurt someone or hurt you, well then, I name it. All you do...for as you're listening to my request *you* are hearing it. Well, the one who is hearing it is God, for *you* are hearing it. Who is hearing it? You say, "I am," well, that's he.

Now grant it: just *feel* you have it. What would it feel like to you now to say to me and to know it's true, "Well, you *have* it." You need not tell me in words, but in your own heart you *feel* that he has it, and go about your business. He has it! That's all I would ask of anyone that they would in themselves actually have confidence in that imaginal act. For the imaginal act is really the subjective appropriation of the objective hope. I hope for this...so at that very moment you subjectively appropriated my objective hope and granted it. That's all that you do. If you are faithful to that, no matter what I am doing I will get it. I may not come back and thank you—I would be one of the nine—but don't despair, that is the average in the world. But do it for everyone in the world.

And don't think for one moment like the prudent virgins that if they gave to this one, they wouldn't have enough for themselves. They discovered that *after* they meet the bridegroom and union with him gave them a limitless flow of oil so they could give and give and give and never exhaust the flow. But they had not yet met union with the bridegroom. I have been united with him, so I can't exhaust the flow.

Now let us go into the Silence.

*   *   *

Now are there any questions, please?

Q: If you call everyone into your life then where do you draw the line at changing them to make them conform to what you want as opposed to what they want?

A: Well, personally I don't change them, because I find in scripture the eternal question which is "What wantest thou of me?" I learned that lesson with a blind man. I would have thought any man who was blind and still young and healthy in body and in mind would want to see. So I said to him one day—his name was Clyde Munroe and we called him Brother Munroe—and he said he didn't want to see. Then he gave me all the reasons why he didn't want to see. He'd rather have the adulation that came with blindness than when he had sight as a young boy in Kansas City on a farm where no one cared whether he lived or died. He could see until he was about fourteen and then he went totally blind. Friends got together and sent him off to New York City in the hope they could do something for him with operations. They discovered that the whole thing was gone, the eyes were gone, might as well take them out. But then people read to him, because he didn't read before, and they read him good books and he had a good memory so he could memorize the books. Then, because he was blind he could get permission to speak publicly in the public square. In New York City in those days it was allowed. So he had an American flag and a little box and he would get up with his long hair—he had long hair before the hippies had long hair, down to here. He looked like, well, the so-called traditional picture of a prophet. With a good memory and all these lovely poems people read to him he would simply spout. But he couldn't tell how many listened to him and he would ask and they would say, well, Clyde, you had twenty tonight or thirty tonight. Oh, he said, that's thirty people who would listen to me when not one person ever heard me before when I could see. So he had an audience and he loved it. He told me quite frankly that he didn't want to see and he meant it. So in scripture the question is "What wantest *thou* of me?" You never take it upon yourself to say another one should do so-and-so.

You go into a home and you find a little argument. There are people who will jump to conclusions and say, well, she should leave him or he should leave her when that is part of their nature to have a little argument and they love each other dearly. Some nut will come in and give you all kinds of reasons what they should do. And all these psychiatrists…you find one fellow on TV all the time, just brought out a book, and he thinks he is the biggest ever. All these silly little children, all permissiveness, and you should do this and he plays this little, tiny part of a child. You want to slap him. Here is this stupid little thing, no discipline whatsoever, everything is just "allow me." Well, you don't do that.

We have a little dog, that is, our daughter has one, and we are baby sitters for the dog four days a week when she goes off to work. Well, he better behave himself in my place…I'm not going to have a kennel. So when he wants to go out I will always take him out and he has his own way of telling me. He'll come and lick my foot and lick my hand as I'm reading the Bible. Today three times he came and licked my hand. I'm hoping he doesn't lick the Bible. I don't want to spoil it. So he licked my hand…that's perfectly all right, licks my foot. When first I didn't respond he goes and looks at me as though "Is he stupid, has he gone to sleep or something?" He comes back and does the same the same thing all over again. Well then, I know that he is right and I'm wrong, so I get up, put him on the leash and take him out and walk him until he performs whatever he's supposed to. He does, he isn't lying to me, and I always give him some little tidbit when he comes back. But he is disciplined. Well now, if he wasn't disciplined, she couldn't leave him in my home. I'm not keeping that sort of a house. So bring him yes. I love my daughter and she can leave all of her animals here. She has birds and a dog…if you'd allow it she'd bring an elephant. She loves all kinds of animals.

Well, I'll take care of as many as she wants. I've taken care of the birds and the dog many a time when she goes away, say for a weekend. But every four days a week, because her maid comes on Wednesday, so we don't get the animal on Wednesday. We get Monday, Tuesday, Thursday, Friday…we have a dog and I have to walk him. But he lets me know when he wants to go out…he has his own sweet little way of telling me. I can't delay too long, because should he perform then it is not his fault, it's mine. He's a disciplined dog. Well, *every* child should be disciplined. Imagine some man, because of this permissiveness, still performing these functions of the body at the age of manhood no matter where he goes. He's an animal and not a disciplined animal. No, I say every child should be disciplined. The Bible teaches that if you love it, you discipline it; if you don't, let it become an animal and then push it out into the wilds.

So I never say to anyone that I think you should really want so-and-so. I ask them what God in them is telling them: what do you want? Because, I know tonight there are millions of people in the world who would not want to change places with anyone in the world. In fact, everyone should be in that place where you don't want to change places with anyone in this world. If people will think because this one has a billion dollars, wouldn't you like to be in his place? So what?

Would anyone in this room tonight like to be in the actual shoes and be the person, say, Getty is? Well, he has a billion and a half, so what? From reports he's found no happiness tonight. It hasn't brought him any happiness. You're happy with your wife or your husband, with your family and you go home knowing that you're wanted. Such people will never know when they're married that they're ever wanted. Because girls can play some very interesting parts and make you think that you are the last thing in this world; in fact, that you are everything a woman could ever want…and all she really wants is your money. He will never know that he was ever wanted for himself. Well, a man must feel that he is wanted for himself. And so a woman should feel she is wanted for herself and not because she has money or social position. What percentage of the world tonight would actually believe that Jacqueline married Onassis for his looks and his physical prowess? What percentage of the world would believe that? I don't think you'll find anyone who'll believe it. But she married him and she does have a half-billion dollars. With all her money it still was not enough.

Do you know it is never enough? When I made eighteen dollars a week at Macy's, I said, O Lord, if I could only make twenty-five dollars, wouldn't that be marvelous! I made twenty-five dollars and that wasn't enough. If I could only make thirty dollars…couldn't go too far, couldn't envision more than that. Then I made thirty-five dollars and that wasn't enough because it bought a bigger room in which to live. And then you did something else and bought a better suit of clothes. Then fifty dollars was not enough. I made $100 and that was not enough; then I made $500 a week and that was not enough. I've never made enough. Less than *all* is not enough.

Good night!

GOD'S MYSTERY OF CHRIST

6/13/69

Paul in his letter to the Colossians said, "I strive for you to have all the riches of an assured understanding and the knowledge of God's mystery...of Christ" (2:1,2). Now, you wouldn't think there's any mystery to it. You ask any Christian if they know who Christ is and they instantly reply, yes, Jesus the Son of God. Paul doesn't state that. He is striving with man to change these fixed ideas of the past, that they may have this assured understanding and the knowledge of God's mystery of Christ. I find most of us are very careless when we read it, so we come to it with fabricated misconceptions, and these fixed ideas that we bring to what we read will color what we receive from the written Word.

Now here, in scripture we find the expression "Christ" used of the human race viewed *ideally*, and the one man of that race who attained to that ideal. So here, we find the human race referred to as Christ, 'Christ our life,'" we are told in the same Colossians (3:4). Then we find "the Lord Jesus Christ." But Christ is our life and that is of humanity. If you took all humanity, all the generations of men, and their experiences, and condensed them into a single being and *personified* it, you'll find *David*. David is the personification of humanity, the eternal youth. All men in whom this ideal flowers is represented by the being called Jesus. We're told that David contains within himself the Christ-seed and he was anointed by the Lord. We're told, he will bring forth a son, and the son will be the *Lord's* son; and the Lord's son and the Lord are one. Therefore, he's going to bring forth a being that instead of being his son, he's going to be his father.

Now that's a mystery, how can I give birth to my father? So in David is the Christ-seed. The Christ-seed is the Son of God that is Christ. When man brings forth the Christ-seed so that it buds and flowers and it comes into fruitage, *that* one is Jesus. Now every being in this world will flower and every being in this world because they're bringing it into fulfillment will be Jesus the Lord. "No one can say 'Jesus is Lord' except by the Holy Spirit" (1Cor.12:3). We can all say that Christ is this, that or the other, but we cannot say that Jesus is the Lord save by the Holy Spirit; and the Holy Spirit is one who brings to one's remembrance all that was told him in the beginning.

Now to understand this we go back to a parable. For the story of Jesus Christ is really an *acted* parable, that's what it is. So we go back now to a parable, the parable of the prodigal son. If you're familiar with it and I think you are, the one who was left at home complained when the one who went into the prodigal state returned and they killed the fatted calf and they brought the robe and the ring and put shoes on his feet, and made much over the one who wasted all things. He complained, and then was told, "Son, all that is mine is yours. It is right that we should make merry and be glad, for this your bother was dead and he's alive; he was lost and he's found. So now that he's returned, remember he came back from death and he was lost" (Luke 15:31). Well, we enter into this world of tribulation and death. Before we entered this world of death we *were*, but we did not know that we were. We were dead to what we had; for all that the Father has is mine, and mine is his, but I didn't know it. I had to come into this experience of tribulation and death to know it is all mine, and the only way it can be *all* mine is if I become the Father, for it is all the Father's. So I did not know it was all mine, and I could have this whole earth today and die of starvation not knowing it is mine for the taking. I may not have a dollar on me and I may think I must have a dollar to buy the loaf of bread, not knowing it *is* mine.

So before I came into the world of tribulation and death I was, but I did not know that I was. So I was dead to all that I owned. I came in here and became lost. What loss? My consciousness wandered even from that state, and that was being lost in this world. At the very end of it I'll return; and the Father will embrace me and place upon me the robe of authority which is his and the ring of authority which is his. I'll be completely covered, and the fatted calf, a symbol of abundance, will be mine. I'll be set free by the shoes, for only slaves went without shoes, so they will shod me and therefore I'll be one that is free.

Everyone is going to have this experience. At the end of the journey, that which is personified as humanity is David, just as I'm standing before you. No one is going to change it. It's not spelled out in the scriptures, but as Blake said—and he was quite the student of the scriptures—"That which can be made explicit to the idiot is not worth my care." They wanted to rouse the faculties to act so that it was not completely spelled out that man would dig and digging find it within himself, for this seed is within man. Every child born of woman contains the Christ-seed, this incorruptible seed, and you cannot lose it. It contains within itself the power of not only self-expression but self-development. The whole thing will unfold within a man, every man, and in the end man will mature. For maturity is when man becomes his own father's father. For, if I came out of humanity, humanity is my father. If the symbol of humanity is David, and I'm told in Samuel that I come out of David, as I come out of David then David is my father. But I begin to mature and discover that I did not really come out of David in the sense that he is *forever* my father. I use humanity to take this seed and bring it to fruition that it could bud and flower and attain, well, the fullness of all that was contained within it. So when it completely does its job I look back and here what I came out of—as it were who fathered me—stands before me and I am *his father*. So man matures when he becomes his own father's father...and that is the mystery of Christ.

So you're told, "When you are gathered together and you lie down with your fathers, I will raise up your son after you, who shall come forth from your body"—and this is the Lord speaking through his prophet Samuel—but "I will be his father, and he shall be my son" (7:12,14). He comes out of your body and seemingly is your son, but "I will be his father." And then this one is made to say, "I and my Father (meaning God) are one" (Jn. 10:30). So everyone here will discover one day he is God the Father and his son is humanity. But humanity brought into focus as one single being is David. So everyone is going to have the experience of being God the Father; and because he is God the Father there must be a son bearing witness of his fatherhood; and that son is David.

I can't spell it out any clearer than that, and I think it is clearer than you will find in scripture, and yet I am only giving you my experience of scripture. I am not manufacturing it, I'm not adding to it, and I'm not speculating; I am taking it right out of scripture. They were right in not spelling it out possibly, but the time has come, as far as I'm concerned, to spell it out just as clearly as I possibly can, and not leave any doubts in your mind. And then he said, "I strive for you that you may have all the riches of an assured understanding and the knowledge of God's mystery of Christ."

Well here, God's mystery of Christ...and we find that the term is used to express both the human race and that *member* of the human race who actually attained the ideal that David represented. So that, the human race certainly is not an ideal when you see it scattered, when it's always at war; but when we see it brought together into one single point at the end, it is a beautiful being. We can't see the beauty in war when the whole thing is being shattered. But in the end of the journey, all this horror that...we only see the horror...when it's brought together and *personified,* it is the most glorious youth you could ever conceive, and that youth is David the Son of God.

And what comes out of this horrible experience called humanity is God himself. It was God who buried himself in man, and in the very end he comes out of man. Because he comes out of man, you would naturally say he is the son of man. So the scripture will go along with that and say "I will bring forth from you your son." But when the son comes out he is not humanity's son, he is God who is humanity's Father. Humanity is gathered together into a single being, not multiple beings, and personified. The individual man in whom that Christ-seed blossoms and fruits looks out and sees the fruit of his labor. And now he shares that labor, that bread and that wine—which is simply the personification that stands before him—with everyone who will listen to him. He shares the fruit of his labor and tells them of the mystery of Christ.

Go back and see now in this prodigal son story it was the second one that came out. We go back now to the first second-son, and that was Abel. He was killed: "And Cain killed Abel." We go now to the second second-son and we find that it is Isaac. We are told that Ishmael, the first, tried to destroy Isaac, and he had to be sacrificed, or was offered in sacrifice to the Lord. We come now to the third second-son and we find that it is Jacob. We are told the Lord loved Jacob but he hated Esau. We come now to the fourth and we find now the twins of Tamar, whose father was Judah. We find when the first one comes out, the midwife puts a little red string around the finger to identify him as the first who came through, but he pulled the hand back. And then comes Perez and Perez comes out and says, "What a breach you have made" and so they called him Perez which means "breach" (Gen.38:29). And then he comes out. Now read the genealogy of Jesus and you'll find these second-sons all in it (Mat.1:1). So the second-son is simply the—not a second son of the womb of a woman, not a thing to do with any second son in this world—but the *choice* of God. They were chosen by him in the beginning of time; before the foundation of the world we were chosen in him, and we came out that we may know our inheritance, and that we know we are *one with* God. There's nothing but God.

But he left unnumbered for a future age. No matter how many we are in this world, billions, and there will be billions and billions, more numerous than the stars of the heaven, more numerous than the sands of the sea. And yet, there are many who did not come out. They are not going to come out at this period of time. They will come out eventually, but we will all be back as God the Father before we decide on another venture into this world. So here, you are blessed because you're out; and because you are in this world you are the second son, and the second son is beloved by God. And in the end he tells Jacob, "I am your inheritance...you inherit me, you inherit God" (Ezek.44:28). And how would I know I actually inherit God?—when his Son calls me Father. There is no other way I'll ever know that I am God the Father save through his only begotten son David who calls me Father. This is the story of the scripture.

But this is the most fantastic, incredible story that man could ever accept. How can he believe that a man becomes his own father's father? And that's exactly how the Book of Matthew begins: "The book of the genealogy of Jesus Christ, the son of David, the son of Abraham." Then he turns the entire thing around, because the whole Bible is based upon a peculiar reversal of order: the second becomes the first all through the Bible, down to the very end. So here, I find myself coming out of humanity. Humanity congeals and forms itself into a single being and stands before me and calls me Father. And yet, I came out of humanity...something came out of this body...and coming out of this garment of death, I didn't know it then. I knew I was born from above, but I didn't know, not yet, waiting. Then five months later, 139 days later, humanity stands before me, collected into one single being and calls me Father. Then I knew that I only experienced that state to join the heavenly being called Jesus the Lord. For Jesus is the personification of all those in whom the Christ-seed erupted into flower and fruitage...as David is the personification of the sum total of all of humanity and the experiences of humanity.

So when you dwell upon it, you'll see the most fantastic things waiting for you. For he is anointed, and what was the anointment? He was anointed with the destiny of Lordship... that was his anointment. And so, then you're told "Rise and anoint him for this is he" (1Sam.16:12) and Samuel took the holy oil and anointed *David* in the midst of his brothers. David never lost a battle, as recorded in scripture...not one battle did he ever lose. And yet everything that man is accused of doing David did, and the Lord said it was good and very good. Even when he took the other's man's wife the Lord did not condemn him, not really, because he did the Lord's will. He said, "I have found in David the son of Jesse a man after my own heart, who will do all my will" (Acts13:22). So everything is just the will of the Lord: "As I have willed it, so shall it be, and as I have purposed, so shall it stand" (Is.14:24). "And my will will not turn back until I have executed and accomplished the intents of my mind. In the latter days you will understand it perfectly" (Jer.23:20).

Who can understand what we read in the papers of the horrors of the world? I saw in today's paper that here back east this vast A and P store, I had no idea what an arsonist or arson had caused them last year, or in the last two or three years over fifty-odd million dollars. That a certain crowd, they call it the Mafia, whoever they are, wanted to sell A and P a certain detergent, and they made a test of it and found that it was not good, it was no earthly good. It would simply destroy rather than help any housewife, and they refused to carry it in their enormous chain. They were threatened and two managers were shot by the gang. Then they started putting on the pressure and they burned down so many warehouses and it ran over fifty-two million dollars. They just caught one young lad, twenty years old, who was just used as a front to do it, while the big ones with their ___(??) billions remained hidden, they didn't do it. This is what is known as a proximate cause. He is now judged and will be judged as the one who did it. And he did...and possibly they paid him a hundred dollars for the job and he was proud at the age of twenty to serve these mighty fellows that he thinks in his mind's eye are mighty fellows.

Now when you read that, you wonder what good could there ever be in God's world? Time will prove that it's good. Time will prove everything in this world is good, that "All things work for good for those who love the Lord" (Rom.8:28, KJV). There isn't a thing in this world he cannot resolve, because he is the master artist, and the most horrible discord in this world that you and I judge as discord he will resolve into an accord, something that the human ear can appreciate. In the end, everything is going to stand before us collected into a single being; and he is so beautiful you can't believe that he came out of humanity and that he is the sum total of all that is human. That every being in the world with all the horrors, all the things he's gone through and what he might have done, in the end it all goes to make that beauty that is called David. He is the complete personification of the human race, and you cannot describe his beauty. Well, you can't say that of man, can you? And yet I saw David. In my mind's eye the impression is so great that when I think of David I can see him as vividly as I see my mother or my father or anyone that I know intimately and that I love. His face is just as vivid in my mind's eye right now as theirs.

When you see him, you can't describe the beauty of David. And who is his father?—God. Well, *I am* his father...that experience I have had...and so in scripture, "What think ye of the Christ?" Now here comes another use of it, "What think ye of the Christ? Whose *son* is he?" and they answered, "The son of David." And then he answered, 'Why then did David in the Spirit call him Lord? If David thus calls him Lord, how can he be David's son?" (Mat.22:42). When you speak of the Lord, you speak of the Father, for the Lord is the Father; and even in ancient days a child always referred to his father as "my lord." So David stands in the presence of the one called "the Lord," called "Jesus," and he calls him "my Father," and calls him "my lord." So he's telling who he is and they still did not understand it. For in the very end he says to them, "Now I'm going to my Father and your Father, my God and your God. But I and my Father are one." Remain until it comes to you, he told them: "Remain until you are clothed with power from above" (Luke24:49). The power of what? The power of understanding; the power to really grasp the things that Paul has been trying to say. He said, "I *strive* for you that you may have all the riches of an assured understanding and the knowledge of God's mystery, of Christ."

So I have given it to you this night...that is, God's mystery of Christ. For the word Christ is used both as the human race when completely personified in the ideal form and that ideal viewed properly is David; and also of the one of that race who actually realized the ideal. So everyone in whom that ideal is realized joins Jesus as the same Jesus, not another, because there aren't two Jesuses, only one. So the minute it's realized in you, you are the Lord Jesus. You still bear your present identity, you still bear your present name among those who know you by that name, but you when you take off the garment for the last time you are the Lord Jesus. While you are here and you put the garment down in what the world would call sleep, you are then the Lord Jesus doing your work. And what is the work? The work you do...not building homes...simply stirring into a quickening state those who you've drawn unto yourself. Night after night you're trying to awaken them, trying to lighten the eyes so they would not continue in the sleep of death. Everyone that comes to you that's the work you do night after night. Come back to this world and pick up the little thing because you have chores to do in the world of Caesar. You will do it, and yet the minute you put your body down, you're off doing the work because you are *already* one with the Lord Jesus...you aren't going to be. But that wonderful inheritance cannot be actual or at least become real in the normal sense of the word, until you finally take off the garment for the last time. When you take it off for the last time, instantly you are one with the Lord Jesus and you aren't two, yet without loss of identity.

So you come into this world for the purpose of knowing what you possess. It was given to you, but you did not know it: "Son, all that is mine is yours. It was fitting that we should make merry and be glad. For, this your brother was dead and now he's alive; he was lost and is found" (Luke15:31)... only because he came out. But you didn't come out, you remained in, and you served me in your only wonderful unconscious way just like the functions of my body serve this body in its own unconscious way. Right now what I had for dinner is being digested, assimilated, built into my body as bone, tissue, blood, and what I can not assimilate the body will unconsciously expel from my system. So it's all part of me, but these are playing their unconscious roles. But you and I came out to play *conscious* roles in the body of God, and that conscious role is being *God himself.* For there is only God awakening, and the awakening will go on forever and forever and forever. For there is a limit to how many he will take at any one time to bring them into this world of tribulation and death, and they are measured by the number of the sons of God which he chose in himself before that the world was.

So everyone here is destined to have the identical experience of the discovery within himself of the fatherhood of God. How does he know it: when God's son, which is humanity, calls him Father. So every part in the world that one could ever play when summarized is David, and I came out of him. I came out of one being and he summarizes all of the parts in the world. He gave me birth, I came out of the body, so he gave me birth; and yet I matured, and as I matured I realized that *he* is *my* son and I am not his son. So how can you say he is David's son when David in the Spirit calls him "my lord?"

I hope this is becoming clearer and clearer, for it's so important that you get this distinction between the two aspects or uses of the word "Christ" as they appear in scripture. When you see the word, don't do what the whole vast world does think only in terms of the one in whom the ideal was attained. Think of humanity that *contains* that ideal in the form of that precious, incorruptible seed that is called the Christ-seed; and every child born of woman contains that Christ-seed. It cannot be corrupted. It contains within itself the power of its own self-expression, its own self-development, and it is going to unfold in every being in the world. Every being will one day stand as the Lord; and confirmation that he is a father, the son, the sum total of humanity, will stand before him in that heavenly beauty and call him Father.

So these parables are to instruct us and the whole story of Jesus is an acted parable that's to instruct us. So when Paul thought he had it, he came back to the Galatians and he said, "O foolish Galatians! Who has bewitched you, before whose eyes Jesus Christ was publicly *portrayed* as crucified?" Now are you going to leave this and start worshipping some little flesh? He asked them, how did you get it? "Did you get it by works of the law, or by hearing this story with faith?" "Are you so foolish? Having begun with the Spirit, are you now ending with the flesh?" (Gal.3:1-6). Well, the whole vast Christian world has ended with the flesh. They see a fleshly being, a body, called Jesus, a man of flesh and blood who raised up a body of flesh and blood.

When he tells us in the gospel of John "I and my Father are one and my Father is Spirit," if I and my Father are one and my Father is Spirit, what am I? Am I not Spirit? So he asks you, are you going to finish with the flesh when you began with the Spirit? Today the entire Christian community worships a man of flesh and blood. So when he said, "No longer will I regard anyone after the flesh. Even though I once regarded Christ from the human point of view, I regard him thus no longer" (2Cor.5:16). Well, who is he regarding? Now he's talking to people and if you were present he would say that you are flesh and blood. You speak to me, you're flesh and blood. Then who is he talking about? He's talking about the *characters of scripture*. These are the ones he would no longer regard as flesh and blood. He now sees that the whole thing is an *allegory*.

Then he tells the story of Abraham, and tells quite clearly "and that is an allegory." So, "I no longer regard anyone from the human point of view; even though I once regarded Christ from the human point of view, I regard him thus no longer." He's referring to the characters of scripture; because as a devout Jew he thought Abraham lived as a man and Isaac lived as a man and Jacob lived as a man. Now he sees *none* of them after the flesh. And so he cannot now see these are the background, the spiritual eternal states that culminate in the one in whom the ideal is in bloom. He cannot see the blooming ideal as flesh when he goes back in time and sees all the others are Spirit; eternal states of the Spirit through which the immortal soul passes, and comes to fruition in that one state called Jesus, which is simply the fulfillment, the fruition of that seed that was planted in the beginning in man. That's the seed called Isaac. So you'll find that the second was always sacrificed: Abel was sacrificed, Isaac sacrificed, Jacob, Perez, one after the other, and culminates in the one grand being who is God himself.

I hope it is clearer tonight, because I gave much time to it this week. I have but two weeks left, that's four lectures, and it is my real desire...I can say with Paul, "I strive for you that you may have all the riches of an assured understanding and the knowledge of God's mystery, of Christ." That you will not when you hear the word suddenly jump in your mind's eye to some being in history of 2,000 years ago, but see that great distinction between the two uses of the word Christ: one representing humanity in its *ideal* form, and one representing the *man* from that human race in whom the ideal was attained. Everyone in whom that ideal is attained is Jesus Christ. There's only one Jesus Christ and yet without loss of identity we are all Jesus Christ. That's the great mystery.

So when you read it in the future, try to keep this great important division, this dual state concerning the use of the word Christ. So he speaks at one moment in the name of the Father, the next moment he's speaking in the name of the Son, and you've got to discriminate between the two. All in the same chapter he is speaking. One moment he is the Father, one moment he is the Son, and you've got to actually discriminate it as you read it and see how he's playing the part. And so, you're playing God's part, you're doing God's will, and he planned it just as it has come out and as it will be consummated. So in spite of the horrors of the world, the end result will be so beautiful, so beautiful! You can't describe the beauty of the summary of it all when he calls you Father; and he is the sum total of all humanity and all of the experiences of humanity. How could such beauty come out of it? It does...and that was the plan before the beginning of time. So he gave us all in that state a preview of what we would experience. But we did not know that at the end of the experience that wonderful promise that we would become God himself. How could man actually believe it? For the son is still complaining that he never once received a kiss. He said, I have been with you always and you did not give me even one kiss. And here this wastrel goes and he wastes everything, finds himself at the end eating the husk that belongs to the swine, and he returns and you kill the fatted calf. I never had a kiss. You give him the robe, the best robe, you give him the ring, and you put shoes on his feet, and you make merry and you are glad. Why? (Luke 15:20-39), He tells him, but the boy cannot understand it.

Many years ago I had this vision to illustrate this point. I came upon an enormous sea of sunflowers, beautiful sunflowers, and each flower was a human face, beautiful faces, each flower rooted in the earth. When one swayed, all swayed, if one smiled, all smiled. They moved in unison. I was standing there alone, certainly not as beautiful by the wildest stretch of the Imagination as these individual beautiful flowers...for every face was beautiful, angelic...and yet I knew at that moment I was freer in my ugliness, in my limitation than all of them put together. For, they moved together, and not one could detach itself and leave that crowd. Not one could frown if the other smiled; not one could stop bending over if all bent over. So all moved in unison, they all bent together and they all smiled together, and they all did everything together. They were the sons who never came out. I came out and having gone through hell up to that vision, then I showed the marks on me of my experiences. Compared to the beauty of these, well, you couldn't compare them. Yet I knew that I enjoyed a measure of freedom that they could not dream of. All of them put together couldn't conceive of the freedom that I now enjoyed because I could walk among them. I could smile and I could laugh and I could cry, and I could do all kinds of things. They couldn't do it unless all did it.

So they did not know that they owned all that the Father owned. So he said, all that is mine is yours, but you wouldn't take it...and if you don't take it it's because you don't know you have it. You would hesitate to take it, because you'll think in terms of the consequences were it *not* yours. If you took what is not yours, you could be arrested and imprisoned. So the feeling that, well, it isn't mine then you don't take it. So you go back to the Father *as* the Father and *everything* is yours. Then you understand that 50th Psalm, "If I were hungry, I would not tell you; for the world is mine and all within it. The cattle on a thousand hills are mine, and were I hungry I would slay and eat." Why tell anyone if it's all mine. Why ask any man's permission for something if it's mine. You don't say, "May I use it?"...you use it.

So this is the whole story. But man is not aware of his inheritance until he has the experience of the birth from above. When he is born from above, then he will not be concerned with raising $5,000 towards a house or payment on a house. The minute he or she is born from above it will come. In the meanwhile, we make efforts to bring it to pass, and that's all right, it comes to pass. But apply the law towards that amount of money, and assume that you have it, and sleep as though you did, and in that manner it will be drawn to you. You keep on applying the law towards this end, and these many ends, lovely ends, until it happens. When it actually happens within you and the body comes off for the last time, you are the Lord Jesus. But no one can say that Jesus is Lord except by the Holy Spirit: "The Holy Spirit when he comes brings you into all remembrance of the things that I've told you." That is what we are told in the 14th of John (14:26), when he comes he'll bring to your remembrance all that I have told you. Now, all that he's told me he enacted in the drama and, therefore, I will have to *re-enact* that within me. Then it's the Holy Spirit in me guiding me into the action of which I was told. I saw the preview of the play, down to the end, and the end has come: I am he.

Now let us go into the Silence.

* * *

Now are there any questions, please?

Q: Several years ago, Neville, you dwelt at some length on the term "mystery" and I have sort of lost some of that. I wonder if you would briefly touch on that.
A: Well, Paul uses the word mystery no less than twenty times in his letters. He insists that it *is* a mystery and asks people to listen carefully or to read his letters carefully. A mystery is really by definition a sacred secret. That's what it really is, a sacred secret. But he will let us into the secret as he was let into it: "When it pleased God to reveal his Son in me, I then communed not with flesh and blood" (Gal.1:16).

So a mystery...my birth from above was prior to the event a mystery to me. I never heard anyone describe it. It came suddenly and it was an awful shock. My resurrection was to me a mystery...it was never described to me. Although I read the Bible, it is not described in scripture, just the empty tomb. The reason of certain things being found in the tomb, as John describes it, that was never described to me...yet I know now what they represent. No one I've ever heard even remotely mentioned David as the son of God, not remotely. This, to me, if I've given one thing that no one can say that I even saw as a glimpse in a book, it is *this* revelation that came 139 days after my resurrection and birth from above. That's the mystery. I share this great secret, this sacred secret with everyone who will listen.

Now, how that temple was torn in two from top to bottom I didn't know how. Because the world believes it was an actual temple made with hands, even though we read in scripture that "We are the temple of the living God" (2Cor.6:16) and "He dwells not in temples made with hands" (5:1) for God is Spirit, and we are the temple of the living God. I read it, but I didn't understand it until it happened. So that was a mystery. And then, the descent of the dove...I read that...I thought it happened 2,000 years ago once and for all time. I didn't realize it *is happening* and that when it is perfect just as it ought to be then the seal of approval descends in the form of a dove. He is so enamored with his work he smothers that one with love and affection, and he *remains* on him while the vision is coming to an end in keeping with what John the Baptist is made to say, "And it remained on him" (Jn.1:32). Didn't fly away...it was still on me while the vision is coming to an end.

I knew none of these...these are all mysteries. The mystery of the betrayal of Christ by a kiss...I didn't realize that that was how it was done until it happened to me. The betrayal was simply the revealing of the one who holds the secret, for that's what he said, "The one I kiss is the one." He is the one that is claiming these fantastic things for himself, that he came down from heaven to do his Father's will, and his Father is God. Well, no authority in the world of Caesar could stand that, for it would mean the end of their reign...even though he said that I did not come to bring about the end of Caesar's reign, for my kingdom is not of this world. But then comes this betrayal, which is the revealing, for the betrayer is a revealer. He reveals the *truth* that is present: this one has the truth and he comes and he kisses him. That's exactly what he did to me.

So, I am not making it up. Theses are things that I have experienced and these are all the mysteries. I'm letting you in on every mystery that happens to me. He uses the term twenty-one or twenty-two times. There are many words he will use which also has the base of mystery, but the actual word translated "mystery" he uses over twenty times. People think it's secular history. There is no mystery to secular history. If these things happen, record them; therefore it's not a mystery. If this battle cost 10,000 men on one side and 20,000 on the other, and we know the count, well then, that is not a mystery. It might be a frightful tragedy but it's not a mystery. For the mystery is simply sacred, that is, a sacred secret. No one knows the secrets of a man but the Spirit of a man that dwells in him. Likewise, no man knows the secrets of God but the Spirit of God who dwells in him as we are told in Corinthians (1Cor.2:11). Therefore, only these things as they unfold within me could be known by me.

But then I am called upon to share it. I could not be sent into this world trained as I am and feeling as I do, if I was locked in a secret. I can't keep secrets, and so, he never would have picked me and sent me into the world to tell the story if at the same time I was told to keep it as a secret...I'd burst! I can't wait to take the platform the day I have a wonderful vision. I can't wait for the next lecture to share it. That part of me was known to him who called me, for he never would have selected me to go now and tell it. It's time that this *true* story of the Christ be told, Christ being the son, the anointed, and God's son. And he is not what the world thought Jesus...Jesus is the Lord himself. Christ is his son, and Christ is David, and David is the sum total of the human race, all the generations plus all of their experiences fused together and personified is David. And he's the Son of God (Ps.2:7).

So when someone will tell you, well, humanity is God's child, you ask them what do you mean by it, explain it. You said humanity is God's child, well now, in what sense? If they haven't had the experience, they cannot tell you, unless they too heard it from one who had the experience. So the human race truly is God's child, containing within itself that wonderful Christ-seed, the incorruptible seed that cannot be corrupted. Death, as we call death, cannot destroy it. It still is in that being that seemingly died, but she or he didn't die and that seed is there. One day it's going to unfold all of its mysteries and they will complete... they start to bud, then they flower, and then fruitage. The whole thing is the marks called "the marks of Jesus." When Paul said, "I bear on my body the marks of Jesus" (Gal.6:17), these are the flowers, the great mysteries as they unfolded within him.

Q: When you were kissed in the betrayal there, were you kissed on the cheek or on the neck?

A: No, on my neck. Kissed me on the right side of my neck and I kissed him on the right side of his neck. And he stretched his arms out like a cross, and that was the ___(??).

Q: Are you speaking of the last embodiment ___(??) of the Christ-seed?

A: Yes.

Q: Do you have any revelation on how many embodiments?

A: My dear, there are so many I couldn't tell you. I only know I saw this night a sea of human imperfection and they were all waiting for me, knowing that as I came by they would be made perfect. They were blind, lame, halt, withered, shrunken, every conceivable imperfection that you could think of formed this sea of human imperfection.

That was the night that I was lifted up on high and a heavenly chorus sang...but I can't describe the beauty of the voices..."Neville is risen!" Then I felt myself standing above the earth, buoyant, in a body made of fire and air. I was self-luminous; I did not need the sun, the stars, the moon or any external light. I was light unto myself and radiated as far as I wanted to. I came upon this sea of imperfection and each man and woman and child was made perfect as I glided by. Didn't stop to speak to one, didn't have any compassion, and showed none of that, my own perfection made them perfect. They could not remain imperfect in the world where I went by.

So, I return all the parts to their primal state of beauty and perfection. I've played them and therefore I must have messed them up, just as we all do. This body is certainly not the body that I knew as a man of twenty when I was strong as a bull...unusually strong...if I say it myself. One solid piece of muscle, that's what I was until I was about thirty. Well, now I certainly wouldn't take my clothes off before anyone. Frighten myself far less the other one. So you see, I've torn this body apart, to pieces too. But I haven't...well, after all, it is sixty-five almost... can't be too long to wear it. Then I am one with the body of the risen Lord and I am he.

Good night.

THE I IN ME IS GOD HIMSELF

6/16/69

In the nature of things, it is impossible for any child born of woman to go unredeemed. When I say "I am," I am proclaiming all that is divine in my flesh. How then can God cast away that which is the "I" in me, the "I" that constitutes me? He will be casting away himself as useless, and that is impossible.

Does it teach this in scripture? Yes it does. All the little statements in scripture, all the little stories are parables. The life of Christ is a parable. We must distinguish between the story as it is told and the message that it intends to tell. So we are told in the 18th chapter of the gospel of Matthew: "And calling a child, he put him into the midst of them...See that no one despises these little ones; for I tell you that in heaven always they behold the face of my Father who is in heaven" (Mat.18:1,10).

They never deviate. They're always beholding the face of my Father who is in heaven. It is said in certain manuscripts that they're angels beholding. Well, we must see what the word angel means and what the word child means. So, he calls a child...the word translated child means "an infant"; it also means "a term of endearment." The word translated angel means "a messenger"; it also means "to bring forth." So here is a child that is always beholding the face of my Father who is in heaven and he's bringing forth a message, we become what we behold. The reality of man is symbolized in that of the Christ child, the incorruptible seed that is always beholding the face of the Father, molding this into a father's image so that he may become one with the Father.

So he casts the shadow into a certain role and we judge the role. Yet that innocent child, molding itself into the image of the Father is casting a shadow of itself into this world as a part that we are playing, and I say, "I am rich, I am poor, I am known, I am unknown." And here, the innocent little child, the Christ child, this incorruptible seed, beholding the face of the Perfect One is molding itself into the image of that which it beholds. Having seen it clearly, it is my desire constantly to see so clearly. To see what clearly? To see the truth, to see it truly, that I may become an image of truth and share it with every one in the world who will accept it. For the whole vast picture that you see in the world that frightens you, that is horrible, and men who do not understand it tell you that you are damned, that you are not saved…nonsense! It is not possible for any child born of woman not to be redeemed, it can't be done. For the being that is the reality of you has never left the face of the Father, molding himself into the image of what he beholds, and he becomes what he beholds. But he casts it into the world. It takes at this moment the part of the rich man as he molds it, the part of the poor man, the part of this; but still allowing all the freedom in this world by another precept: Whatever you desire, believe you have it, and you will (Mark 11:24). He allows that freedom which is a fantastic freedom in this world. But he's always molding and molding himself into the image of what he is beholding, and he's only beholding the face of my Father. My Father is your Father, and my God is your God. Eventually molding myself into the face of my Father, I am he.

This is the picture of the entire world in which we live. It seems fantastic but it's true. I am telling you what I know— not what I am theorizing, not what I am speculating—that no one can fail. No one being in the world can fail. Hitler can't fail, Stalin can't fail. The story is told us all through scripture that he hardened the heart of Pharaoh. Who hardened it? The Lord God Almighty hardened it and made him to *not* let his people go, and then he gave him the blow after blow after blow and then he hardened it again. Therefore, who was responsible? In the story of Job, who played that part but the child within: "I had heard of thee with the hearing of the ear, but now my eye sees thee" (42:5). I now see why I went through hell and then was given a hundred times more than he had before. He brought him out as the perfect one. Well, you're being brought out as the perfect one, so you play a certain role now and you played unnumbered roles in the past. Here in this gathering you haven't very many roles to play…many of you are playing the last. You haven't many more to play while you're here, but you've played unnumbered roles. Each role was for a perfect reason to get you into the image of that which it was beholding. And so, I am beholding the image, always hopeful that I would not deviate from that perfect image so that I may become an image of the perfect one, of the truth.

Now he tells you, "You will abide in my word…if you abide in my word, you will know the truth." But he said, "Who is the truth? I am the truth"

(Jn.14:6) and then you'll be set free. But who will set me free?—the Son. "If the son sets you free, you are free indeed" (Jn.8:36). And then you will know the truth and I am the truth. I will set you free...the minute you meet me, you'll be set free. So you're molding your own face into the image of what you're beholding. You don't see it now, you see the shadow world, the whole vast shadow world, and you're carried away with it. But believe me, and then come back time and time again and lean against this vision in your moments of distress. Just lean against it, it will support you. For, I am not theorizing, I'm not speculating; I'm telling you what I know. The little child, as we are told in the 8th chapter of Proverbs, "In the very beginning when he created the universe I was beside him as a little child. I was daily his delight, rejoicing before him always. He who finds me finds life; he who misses me injures himself; he who hates me loves death" (Prvb.8:29-39). There are those who can't stand this thought and they are in love with this world and this is the world of death.

So here in this world of ours we start with "I am"...that's God, that's consciousness. When I begin to view consciousness I must see the two relationships. First, being, pure being, unconditioned I am; then conditioned being, well, I'm a man now, Neville, a speaker, a teacher. Another one is a banker, another one is a thief, another one is something else, and these are the conditioned states of being. But there are two and I must not confuse them. A state of being is simply "I am" and then *conditioned* being...all of this is conditioned being. I do not care what part you are playing. The little child—which is only a symbol of the being that you *really* are who you never see here—is casting you into that role and you are playing that part perfectly. You do not see the little child until the end.

Now, the thing called "child" in that statement that I quoted in the beginning—"And calling to him a child he put him into the midst of them"—the word child means "a term of endearment" but also "an infant." The day will come you will hold that infant and you will express the most endearing feeling towards it, and it will come forward in speech. In my own case I said, "How is my sweetheart?" Holding the infant in my hands I had this impulse and I could not resist it and I said, "How is my sweetheart?" in keeping with the statement, "And he called a little child and placed him in the *midst* of them." Then when you find the child you find life: He who finds *me*—the little child that was beside him when he created the world—finds life; he who misses me, injures himself; and he who hates me—hates the very thought of it—loves death. He's in love with the world of death and everything here is mortality...every condition in the world is mortal. The billionaire leaves it behind him. The one with all the medals in his world pinned upon him leaves that behind him; and the tunic itself upon which they are pinned will decay; the medals will decay and they'll all vanish.

But he cannot vanish. That little child within him that was one with God, and *is* God, is changing the image as he watches it. He watches the image and he has to be as perfect as his Father in heaven is perfect. So he is building the same image, and when it reflects it and radiates it, you find him. You find him, and you hold him, and as you hold him you come forward with a statement, a term of endearment; and in my own case, "How is my sweetheart?" Then the whole thing vanished. The child was but a *sign*, a sign of my own being that was casting myself into these roles. So I cast myself into the role of a poor boy in a poor family, unknown, having no background whatsoever, no social, financial, intellectual, but no background. That was the role into which the little child within me which is my being cast me. This was the end of the entire journey. He cast me into that role. Then he brought me out in his perfect image which was the image of the Father, and then the Father unveiled himself *as* my own being. And that is the story of everyone in this world.

But he does give me a cushion and tells me that by a precept as I walk the earth, though you go through hell, take this precept and *apply* it. When you are against the eight-ball, when you are up against it, apply it. How do I apply it? Know what you want. First of all, you *must* know what you want and then assume that you have it. You must *assume* that to the same extent that I am assuming, that I am seeing and I am what I am beholding. For man becomes what he beholds! I must behold myself secure if that is what I want; I must behold myself healthy if that's what I want; I must behold myself known if that's what I want. I must see it actually as he in me is seeing the face of the Father. He never deviates from that, but he casts his shadow, allowing his shadow to apply it in this world.

So everyone here is as *free* as the wind if you know who you *really* are. No matter what you've gone through—and you've gone through hell—and what you are going through and what you may go through, you *must* be redeemed. For, he in you will not falter, and he's always watching the face of the Father. Not for one moment has he changed it. So here in the world as Blake said so beautifully that it doesn't really matter: "You will see from what I teach" said he, "that I do not consider either the just or the wicked to be in a supreme state but to be every one of them states of the sleep into which the soul may fall in its deadly dreams of good and evil when it left paradise following the serpent," the symbol that you will not really die (*Vis. Last Judgment*). "God said that you would die? I tell you, you will not really die, but you will become like God, knowing good and evil" (Gen.3:4). So we come into the world eating of the tree of good and evil…and we judge one another. This one is bad and that one is good, and we go through life this way. But now see *behind* the mask the one that really is there. It doesn't matter what he is doing and it doesn't matter what his little plan in this world is. So he wants to plot and plan to get the better of you, leave him alone. Leave him alone and let him do exactly what he is planning, but in your own mind's eye you apply this principle and assume that you are as free as the wind from all encroachments, knowing in the depths of your own soul you are seeing the face of the Father.

When you see him at first you don't know he's a father. A child knows its parents before it knows that it knows its parents. You'll meet God and know God before you know God is father. You'll know the Father before you know the Father is yourself, for this is how consciousness awakes in the world. So the Son comes into the world to save those who are lost. So what? I am lost only by wandering consciousness...I wandered from the state, that's all. I'm not lost. When I say "I am," I am in, I am of, and I'm moving towards *the* I AM. How could I move towards the I AM when I am in him and I'm of him? I could only move in awakening, moving in consciousness, moving towards the awakening *as that* I AM. So everyone is moving towards that I AM. But when he says "I am," he is in it, he is of it, and he is moving towards it. He's only moving in consciousness. So his only loss is simply a *wandering* consciousness, and everything appeals to me to wander away from *the* I AM— believe in this, this is going to help you; believe in that man, he is rich; believe in that one, he is known; believe in this; and everyone is trying to move me away from what I really am.

Doesn't really matter...I can't be lost! But the Son of man comes... who is the Son of man? The Son of man is the one in whom the ideal was realized, called in scripture Jesus. But Jesus *represents*—he's only the personification of—all in whom the incorruptible seed awoke. It budded, it flowered and then it simply came into fruitage, and the one in whom it brings in the fruit that one is Jesus. Jesus is the personification of the ideal that is housed *in man*. David is the personification of the whole of humanity reduced into a single being and projected as he is personified, that's David. And I'm coming towards fatherhood. I can't be a father unless there is a son and that is David.

Now last lecture night I had hoped that I'd told it as clearly as I could, and I think I did to the best of my ability. I got two telephone calls and they were thrilling to hear, because they got more than ever before; but they were outweighed by other numbers who never understood it at all and they told me, "I just couldn't get you at all. Either you are beyond my head or it is something that is new to me." Well, they come...not regularly... but they come. So I asked them to go home and simply dwell upon it.

The Return of Glory

In essence it was this…it's very simple…that in scripture the expression "Christ" is used of the human race viewed *ideally*. It is also used of the one member of that race who had *achieved* the ideal. The human race and all of its generations, all of its experiences, condensed into a single being and projected, personified, it would come out as the eternal youth David. That is the whole of humanity condensed into a single being and then projected is David.

Now, the being in whom the ideal is *completely* realized is projected and it's called Jesus. He is the Father, he is God the Father. You can't be a father unless there's a son: David is the son. So everyone in whom the ideal is attained is Jesus. There is *only* Jesus in the end…there is only God the Father. There's only "one body, one Spirit, one Lord, one God and Father of all" (Eph.4:4). So everyone who actually attains the ideal will be confronted with the son bearing witness to the fact he is God the Father. For *David* is the son of all the generations of men and the experiences fused into a single being and then personified. That's the eternal youth that is David.

I am telling you what I know. I am not speculating. That is a fact. It may not be the easiest thing to grasp, but you dwell upon it. Lean upon it in times of trouble. That's what Paul really meant when he said he was not unmindful of it, and he never doubted for one moment this vision, this heavenly vision, which was the promise of God to the fathers…but he didn't spell it out. I am trying my best to spell it out to everyone in the world who will listen to me. Those who will not listen to me now let them read it after I am gone in what I left behind me in the written form, that the son of the whole vast world of humanity and all that it has ever experienced, put it all together and bring it into *one* being, and then put it out and you'll see how beautiful it is. That all the horrors of today that you and I will condemn on this level, when the end comes, it took all of these horrors to produce David. So in the end you'll say, "Father, forgive them; because they know not what they do" (Luke23:34). On this level we are judging this man, that woman, and judging every being in the world in the most horrible manner, and yet it takes all these parts to produce David. And in the end, when David is brought forth and you look at him and he calls you Father, you are God the Father, and that is Jesus.

So that's what I tried to bring out the last lecture night. Tonight will help those who found it difficult the last time. There is in you…but now this is a mystery…he calls a child, he calls an infant. How would I call an infant? And then he takes the infant and he puts the infant in the midst of them. Now he tells you, "Let no one despise one of these little ones; for I tell you that in heaven their angels always behold the face of my Father who is in heaven" (Mat.18:10). And man invariably becomes what he beholds. I can take anyone in this world and if I represent him to myself as the man, the woman, I would like him to be and if I do not waver in that representation, he will conform to it. I want someone to be big in my world, then make him big in my mind first and treat him that way morning, noon and night, and see him as that being, and he cannot fail. I'll bring him into that picture regardless if I do not fail, because I must become what I behold. I'll bring him right into it. But we waver, we hear rumors that he did this or she did that, and then we change the picture. Don't change the picture!

I'll go back and show you these silly little things in our world today. Many years ago I read the story of famous theatrical mothers and their sons that had no talent to begin with. One was Milton Berle and his mother. She would go out—he wasn't the only child she had, but she singled him out—she would go out when they were playing ball and she would say to all the boys who were playing baseball, "Milton is a star and he has to be a star, and you must all play around him. Whatever Milton says goes" and she meant it! "If you don't play like this, we'll take away the ball and take away the bat. There'll be no game." I could go through a list of a dozen in this story where every mother of these fellas who became stars held that ideal of their son in their mind's eye, and did not falter for one moment. If the mother didn't, then they couldn't, because they become what she's beholding. When a mother compares me to a neighborhood child and finds me wanting, well then, she has completely broken the image. She sees me less than the neighborhood child and she thinks that's the way to get me to be spurred to make a greater effort. That's not the thing at all. If she really wanted me to be great, then do not falter in her image of me. Don't try to *make* me do it. If she really wants that for me, do it.

Well now, there's something in you that has never left the face of the Father. Not in eternity will it leave it until you are perfect. So it casts a shadow and now you must play the part of a bum, for it's *necessary* to bring this image into focus. Now you play the part of something else, and it casts all these images, and here we are in the flesh. But what is the reality in the flesh? When I say "I," I am proclaiming that which is divine in the flesh. That is my divine being and it cannot be cast off unless God is willing to lose himself…for the "I" in me is God. The "I" in you, that's God. So when I say "I am" that's he, that's his name. So it cannot, not in eternity could it, fail to achieve the predetermined goal which is to fashion itself into the image of the Father, and eventually to become the Father. What a mystery!

But here, the whole thing was done before that the world was. You are predestined to become the author of the entire world; the one who wrote the play and who is playing it; and the one who supports it and sustains it. That is the God of our scripture; that is the Lord God Jehovah; that is the Lord

Jesus. You who have done all the horrible things in the world of which you have certain memories…and you are Jesus? Yes, you are destined to be Jesus. When the image is perfect, you will awaken and you are the Lord Jesus. Well, the Lord Jesus is God the Father, and if he is God the Father, there must be a son, and the son is humanity. But humanity gathered together into a single being and projected is David. And that is the mystery. When you come to the *end*, you awaken as God the Father.

What is the next play, I do not know. I only know that until everyone is awakened it isn't complete. So we don't criticize, we don't condemn, because from *above* we will aid every being in this world to come back. So, we are the ones called "those who came to save the lost; to first seek him and then to save him." Save what? We bring him back…that wandering *consciousness*…we bring it back to the vision of the Father.

Now, my one consuming desire is to simply see truly. In seeing truly then I become an image of truth, and then I can tell it just as it happened to me. Instead of going out and trying to make you feel you must make a greater effort in some moral cause or this cause or the other cause, no. I'm not asking you not to give to charity if you have money, not to do the lovely things in this world. Do all the things you want to do, but that is *not* what will save you at all. There is something in you that is focused on the face of the eternal Father…and he's becoming what he is beholding. So as he actually sees it, he casts a shadow. It needs now this experience in poverty, this experience in wealth, this experience. But he gives to each one that *cushion*. While I am actually forming the image of my Father, which is my being, I am now allowing my shadow world to apply a certain principle: "Whatever you desire, believe you have received it, and you will" (Mark 11:24). So, though I cast myself in the role of the poor one, I'm not going to anchor myself there…he may become rich. I cast myself in the role of the rich one; need not remain there, he could become poor as he wanders from the thing into which I have cast him. I am molding my image.

So, I am telling you this wonderful story. It's a simple little story… and you read these scholars as they write it, like one I read today, "And the little child was brought" and they wonder who the little child was and what ever became of that little child. They see it as a secular story and it hasn't a thing to do with anything that took place in this world. Jesus is not a man of secular history. Jesus is the representative of every man in this world who attained *within* himself the ideal…that incorruptible seed blossomed and then bore fruit within him. The fruit I have marked out time and time again for you. I need not go over it again. You know exactly what I mean when I speak of the fruit: these are the *signs* within you, the resurrection, the birth, the discovery of the Fatherhood, and all these things take place within you. That's the fruit that you are bearing.

There's not a thing in this world that's comparable to it. If tonight you were the biggest in this world, you had all the money in the world, you have everything in the world, what would it matter if this that I am telling you were not true? And who knows who will call you this night? But if I tell you as I am and what I'm telling you is the truth, you *are* an immortal being and you cannot die. Dead though the body seems, *you* cannot die, for the reality of you is "I am" and that's God. There is no other God; there never was another God; there never will be another God. You are awakening slowly to the realization that "I am God" who did the entire thing in this world. Not one will be greater than the other. In this world we all try to be better than the other. Let me sit at your right hand, Lord…let me do so and so. All will simply awaken and all will be one, for there is only one Son and one Father. And if I am the Father of that one Son and you are the Father of *that* Son, you and I are one. Now we understand the great shema: "Hear, O Israel: The Lord our God is one Lord" (Deut.6:4). If he's one and he's the Father, then he can't be two. But if he's a father there must be a son, and there *is* a son, and the son is David. That son bears witness of my Fatherhood. But if you have the identical experience and you are the Father, and the same Son calls you Father, are we not one?

So in the end, there is only *one* God, *one* Father, *one* Son. So, the one fell into division into this completely scattered, divided state. In the end, we all awake and we are the Father…yet without loss of identity. I will love you dearly as a seeming other and yet knowing that we are one. It's a peculiar mystery, but we are one in the end. There is no other being, only God. But God is a father. That's the last revelation of God when he reveals himself as father. He first reveals himself as power, almighty power, and it's a man that describes power, real power. Then he reveals himself one after the other. In the end, he reveals himself as *infinite love* and that is Father.

So why are we here? Blake put it beautifully; "We are put on earth a little space that we may learn to bear the beams of love" (*Songs of Innoc.— Little Black Boy,* Ln.13). You could not stand the beams of love in your present state, you couldn't stand it. So we are put on earth a little space that we may learn to bear the beams of love because God is infinite love, and it's power, sheer power. We speak of power today like going to the moon and contemplating going to Mars and Venus; well, that is little firecrackers compared to the being that brought the whole vast universe into being and sustains it. And *you* are that being. It's impossible to get it over on a certain level, how could you be the being that brought the world into what we call

The Return of Glory

the universe, and you *are* that being? Here we are in this world fighting each other, and yet that is also part of the play.

So in the end, everyone but everyone, will awake. I do not care what a man has ever done in this world. Put yourself now in the part of a father and your son is now accused of the most horrible, monstrous act in the world. But you are a father and you love that son, wouldn't you want him to go free? I know I would. I wouldn't care what he did, he's my son. If he is my son and I love him, I wouldn't care what he did. I would regret that he did it, but he is my son. So in the story of David, David did every conceivable horror in the world…but he was God's son. If you read the story of David, there wasn't a thing that man could do that he didn't do. He never lost a battle; he won every battle into which he went. He sent Uriah into battle knowing he would be killed to get Bathsheba. All right, so he stole the man's wife. Although he had a thousand wives of his own, he wanted one more. Yet he was called the perfect man: "I have found in David a man after my own heart who will do all my will" (Acts13:22). And who is he? He is the Lord's son; David is the Lord's son (Ps.2:7). But David is *not* a little man born of a woman. You must take *all* the generations of men and *all* of their experiences and fuse them into a single being, and personify that being, and it comes out as an eternal youth, beautiful beyond the wildest dream of man, and it is David.

Now, the world will say no, that it's Jesus Christ who is the Son. You don't understand the mystery: Jesus is the Lord. That is the mystery, for David in the Spirit calls him Father, David calls him Lord. So humanity is the Son, humanity is the Christ viewed *ideally* and Jesus is the Father. Now I can't open up the skull and force this mystery into it; I can only give it to you in words. But I'm telling you the day is coming that you will have it as an experience. Your skull will explode and the drama begins to unfold within you. Everything said of Jesus Christ you experience in the first-person, singular, present tense. You are cast in the major role, and then you know who you are. Yet you remain while in this world a very limited being, because this is the world of mortality. There isn't a thing in this world that doesn't die. The stars are dying, the planets are dying and everything here dies, everything dies. You came into the world of death to overcome it, for the seed, that incorruptible seed, had to fall into the earth and die to be made alive. So you and I came into this world with something hidden within us which is the incorruptible seed, the seed known as the Christ-seed. It is beholding the author of it all transforming us into that image, because there's only God. When we are transformed into the image then we are God. He can't beget another; he is begetting himself.

While we're in this world take it in this wonderful precept of his: "Whatever you desire, believe that you have it, and you will" (Mark 11:24)—no restriction placed upon the power of belief, none whatsoever. And he doesn't ask you to go and consult with a so-called holy man as to whether you should have it, he asks you to be the judge of what you want. *Whatever* you desire, believe that you have it, and you will. To the degree that you become self-persuaded that you have it, you'll get it. Because we're all one and if it takes one million people in the world to aid the birth of that assumption, all right, it will take a million people. You will do it without their knowledge, without their consent. You don't have to ask anyone to aid you; they will aid you not knowing they are aiding you. All you are called upon to do is *assume* that you have it. "An assumption, though false, if persisted in will harden into fact" (A. Eden). That is the principle.

So, behind this fantastic play, where you are awakening as God, we have a secondary state in *this* world to cushion all the blows. So I am cast into the role of a poor man...but I have to meet Caesar's obligations—he demands taxes, he demands rent, he demands food, he demands this—and I need Caesar's coin. Well, "Whose coin is this?—.Caesar's. Well, render unto Caesar the things that are Caesar's." Well, how will I get it? *Assume* that you have it; just assume that you have that which Caesar demands of you. He wants taxes, well, assume that you have it. Let the world shake itself to pieces, and it will, and you will get whatever Caesar demands of you *if* you dare to assume that you have it and remain faithful to that assumption.

But in it all, something else is taking place in you which is infinitely greater than Caesar's world, for Caesar's world will come to an end; but the kingdom of heaven will not, that goes on forever. "For this is life eternal, to know thee the only true God" (Jn.17:3). So if I know the only true God, I am entering into an eternal life. To know Caesar's world is the world of death. But if I know the only *true* God, well, the only true God is my own wonderful human Imagination...that's God. That is the eternal God and he has a play to reveal it to me. Instead of saying in words "my Imagination is God" which doesn't satisfy me, I want to know that this ancient script really is revealing it. Well, it tells me when you see David he is going to call you Father...when you see him. You will never see him until you are ripe, until that picture is perfect: "Be ye perfect as your Father in heaven is perfect" (Mat.5:48).

When you see David it is because you've reached the end of the journey and he appears before you. You've played all the parts—you've been a thief, you've been a good man, you've been a known man and an unknown man—you've been everything in the world. When you come to the end of the journey and have played *all* the parts and the race is over David stands before

The Return of Glory

you. You are now the conqueror and that crown is yours waiting for you, because now you are the Father. If you are a father, where is my son? Here he comes, standing before you to prove that you are the Father. He is God's son and if he is *your* son, then who are you but God! "Thou art my son, today I have begotten thee" (Ps. 2:7). To whom did he say it?—to David. And when David calls *you* Father then who are you but the one called God in the scripture.

It seems so silly for a little man, one of billions in the world, to make these extravagant claims. But they are true! A little man went to the moon; he wasn't a big man. A little man conceived the idea of this energy today; his little name was Einstein, a little man. He's dead, but he conceived the idea and man believed to the extent of bringing billions to play upon his equation, and then they proved that he was right. So a little man walks the earth but certainly he is not the one spoken of. It happens *in* the little man, for he is only wearing a mask. He isn't the little man; he is the God who created it. But he can't come into his inheritance until he takes off the little garment for the last time.

So, bring me the little child and put him into the midst of everyone, and don't despise him, for he was the one who was with me in the beginning of time. When I laid out the foundations of the world he was beside me as a little child. He was daily my delight, delighting forever in the affairs of men (Prov.8:31). He who finds him finds life; he who misses him injures himself; he who hates him loves death (8:35). That's the little child. The little child is the *symbol* of you molding yourself into the image of the Father and casting yourself into these shadow worlds, playing certain parts as you mold yourself into the perfect image of the Father. When you are perfect so that you can radiate it and bear the very stamp of his nature, you *are* God the Father.

Now, let us go into the Silence.

* * *

Are there any questions, please?

Q: If, for example, we who come to your lectures, if we get so close to the truth and are exposed to it through your teachings in this part, I can't understand it and to my own understanding it seems almost kind of cruel…for some still to be subject to pain and limitation and frustration. And then on the other hand, you say that everyone is cast in their role. I mean it's almost like it doesn't matter anyway because it turns out all right, and if you're already cast in this role, it's almost inevitable that you're exposed to it. Still, knowing this…

A: No, my dear, as Paul said so beautifully in his 8th chapter of Romans, "I consider that the sufferings of this present time are not worth comparing with the *glory* that is to be revealed in us" (8:18). Suffering yes…this is the world of tribulation and death and every child born no matter how healthy it is moves toward the inevitable gate of death. No matter what comes into this world it dies. You buy a suit of clothes and you think now isn't it lovely, and long before it wears out it becomes horrible by the fashion of the day, and you will not be seen wearing it even though you thought it was altogether wonderful when you bought it. Then fashions change rapidly today because of our economy and you would not be seen in it. Long before it actually wears out it wore out.

And so, bodies wear out. Every body that comes into this world…a little tiny child, such a lovely healthy child…and if it lives to be a hundred it will still wear out. Many around it when it reaches 100 will wish it would die. The so-called loving grandchildren say, what's wrong with grandfather, why doesn't he die? His contribution is nil and he's eating up the little that he has where we could use it. So what was seemingly in the beginning a lovely thought, wonderful to have him, he's productive, now he becomes not productive and so he's using "theirs." That's life…it's part of this world of decay, yet it all adds up to awakening *as* God. God fragmented and God gathered together into one being, yet without loss of your individual identity. Like a brotherhood, a fabulous brotherhood, all making up *one* being, and the being is Father. So we are the sons and yet we are the Father.

Q: I heard you years ago, I've read all your books, and one thing I don't understand, why did you have to stick with Jesus? After all, he was a sick boy.

A: You see we have different concepts of what the word Jesus means. The word Jesus means "Jehovah," the same thing. Yod He Vau He is Jehovah, the Lord. Yod He Vau Shin Aiyn is Joshua in Hebrew, which is the same word as Jesus in the Anglicized form. Well, people get off into the strangest concepts because of their background. Jehovah and Jesus are the identical names. If you take the root Yod He Vau begins both. And the sacred name in the Hebrew world is Yod He Vau He, which we pronounce Jehovah. Well, the root of that word is the root of Joshua, and Joshua is the Hebraic form of the Anglicized form Jesus…same word.

Q: Well, they are two different characters Jesus and Jehovah.

A: No, not if you understand the mystery. No, if one understood this great mystery. The Bible is not secular history. It hasn't a thing to do with history in this world. It's a mystery to be understood only as it unfolds

The Return of Glory

itself within in the individual. The day will come that David, who you believe to be an historical character of 1,000 B.C., will reveal himself to you as your own son, and here you are in the 20th Century. You preceded him if he is your son. But David is not an individual born of a man called Jesse. The word Jesse is the same I AM—Jesse is any form of the verb "to be"…that's what the word Jesse means. So "I have found in David the son of Jesse a man after my own heart" (Acts 13:22). So that's what Jesse means.

Well, if he is a father and I say "I am," then I am the Father. But I must wait until I actually know it. I could tell you from now 'til the ends of time that you are the Father of David and that you are Jesus Christ. I could tell you that from now to the ends of time, but not 'til you've experienced it will you believe it. I don't have to believe it anymore; I have an assured I *know*. So the Hebrew world that is called the Old Testament and the New are the same. One of the most famous of all Jews, Disraeli, said "Christianity is only the fulfillment of Judaism." That was Benjamin Disraeli…a brilliant, brilliant mind who understood what he was talking about. He understood the Hebrew tongue. He was a Jew and never denied it, but then he understood what the outcome of it was and not Christianity as taught in our churches. That is not Christianity…it hasn't a thing to do with Christianity. Christianity is the fulfillment of Judaism, but *not* in a secular manner; in a supernatural manner because Judaism is completely supernatural in manner. It is the foundation stone.

As someone said and wisely so, "I am a Jew"…now he is born and raised in the Catholic faith. He became a priest, a very prominent priest in the Christian world, but he was born in the Catholic faith. He said, "I am a Jew because I am a Christian." Now he said, "I could be a Jew and not be a Christian, but I can't be a Christian and not be a Jew." How could I be a rose and not be the rose bush? I could be a rose bush without bearing roses, but I can't be a rose unless I came out of a rose bush. Christianity is only the flower coming out of the tree that is Judaism. But man is expecting a different kind of Messiah than that which comes—it comes within you and not from without. They are looking for some being coming from without that's going to save them, and you aren't saved from without. You are saved by fulfilling scripture. Scripture unfolds itself within you as your own wonderful biography.

I'm not speculating, I'm telling you what I know from my own experience. So everyone in this world will actually have the identical experience, everyone. And it's the Judea-Christian faith…but not as practiced by either orthodox concepts. Hasn't a thing to do with any

625

external worship, none whatsoever! To stick a little cross on the wall is nonsense! To stick a little Mogen David on the outside that's nonsense. It's all within me; that's how it unfolds. But man is taught to believe that if I abide by certain dietary rules I'm building up a certain treasure in heaven, building merit. Hasn't a thing to do with it. If I go to Mass, that's good for me. Hasn't a thing to do with it. If I buy all these little icons called saints like St. Christopher who never existed, then that's good for me. All this is nonsense. The whole thing unfolds *within* man...man is the book.

Q: Will you discuss the relationship between the Old Testament, B.C., and the New Testament, A.D. and what it means?

A: That should be obvious to you. Here we have a revelation through men conditioned to receive an inner voice and hear an inner voice. They did not understand what they heard as told us in the Old Testament. Daniel said, "I heard but I did not understand" and then the voice said to him, "Close the book; seal the book, Daniel, until the end. You don't understand it, but write it carefully and don't try to change it (12:4)." "Do not add to my words...put it down just as you heard it" (12:4,8). So he recorded what he heard. All the Old Testament begins, "And this is the *vision* of Isaiah, this is the vision of Obadiah, this is the vision of Amos." They're visions. God makes himself known to man in vision as told us in the Book of Numbers (12:6). So the Old Testament is the collection of the promises of God to man. But it takes time...it's like planting something and expecting it to grow over night. It doesn't, it takes time to grow. "The vision has its own appointed hour...it flowers but just wait for it" (Hab.2:3). Eventually the whole thing will come into blossom and you will see the fruit of it.

So, when someone who is born a Jew...as we are told in scripture, "I am born a Jew and I am telling you the truth concerning Judaism." He wasn't born outside the Jewish faith; Christianity began in the Jewish faith. All of the books of the New Testament are written by Jews. Paul said, "I am of the seed of Abraham of the tribe of Benjamin, a Pharisee of the Pharisees" (Phil.3:5). He was the one who wrote the first series of books of the Christian faith. That was Paul...his name *was* Saul, changed into the name Paul. He told his own people what the words meant, but they would not believe him. He said, "I'm telling you what the entire prophecy concerning the coming of Messiah means." He wasn't speaking of a being outside of himself called Jesus; he found him within himself and told the story.

So it was so graphic it changed B.C. into A.D., a new age altogether. But this is still B.C. to everyone who hasn't had it. No one today although we sign our letters 1969 that is 1969 A.D., but not to the one who hasn't had the experience. It is marked from the one who has first had it and all those since—it is to them A.D. But not to the billions that are living in this world. They are still living in B.C., for they have not experienced Christ. So it's a convenience to put down '69, but not to the one who hasn't had it. I had the experience in 1959. I am only ten years in A.D. Others will say, "I'm 1969 A.D." Like fun they are! They are not in the world of A.D. until they have the experience. But the one who first had it it was so graphic and unfolded the entire story that it marked the division between A.D. and B.C. Every one is living B.C. unless they have had the experience. Mine came in July 1959, so this coming month of July it's been ten years since I entered the new age. So the whole vast world is still living before Christ, before the coming of Messiah…for he hasn't come to them. He is in them, but he hasn't awakened. If he hasn't awakened, then he hasn't come.

Well, it's after the hour. Good night.

PERSONIFICATIONS, NOT PERSONS

6/20/69

In the Book of Nehemiah we are told that "They read from the book, from the law of God with interpretation, and they gave the sense so that the people understood the reading" (8:8). I wish that were true of today's preachers; but unfortunately they have mistakenly taken personifications for persons and the gross first sense for the ultimate sense intended.

Here in today's paper 325 graduate students of fifteen Catholic colleges were asked to name their ten heroes in the order that they are to them heroic. No restrictions as to time…they can go back in time as far as they feel like…and Jesus came in fifth. They see him as a person. But even if he were a person, he is fifth in the order. Now, these are graduate students of fifteen Catholic colleges. The late President Kennedy came in first and his brother, Robert, came in second and Martin Luther King came in third… here came the order, ten of them. And you wonder what are they getting? After four years in college they still see the book as secular history. If you never went to college all well and good, but if you read it as literature as many of them do in college you would discover it is not secular history.

Now here, in biblical thought a name is not a mere label of identification; it is an expression of the essential nature of its bearer. A man's name reveals his character. To know the name of God is to know God as he has revealed himself. As the Psalmist said, "Those who know thy name put their trust in thee" (Ps.9:10). But it is a progression of revelations of the name. It is first revealed as God Almighty in the name El Shaddai. Then it comes in the name of plain awareness, I AM. We are told the first was given to Abraham, Isaac and Jacob, just as Almighty Power. Then the second revelation came to Moses and that was given as awareness, I AM. The full disclosure of his name we find in Jesus Christ, and that was the name of

The Return of Glory

Father...a father-son relationship. "I have made manifest thy name to the men whom thou gavest me out of the world. They were thine and thou gavest them to me. I have made known unto them thy name and I will make it known that the love with which thou hast loved me may be in them and I in them" (Jn.17:6).

But now, who are these characters? They have names too. We speak of Abraham, Isaac, Jacob, Moses, Jesus. Are they persons? No they are not persons. They are *personifications* of the eternal states of God's play, and man has completely mistaken these as persons as you are a person and I am a person. These states are eternal. Learn to distinguish between man and his present state. In what state is the man now? It begins with Abraham. The call of Abraham as a state; the state of love, the state...he was a friend of God. The state of *faith* is really what the state is. In that state, you and I were shown the entire play in detail. Then the play comes to its climax and fulfillment in the state called Jesus Christ. It's a state and when you reach *that* state then the play is over...and you are the author of the play.

But to say he is my hero and I put him fifth as a person is to completely misunderstand the story in the Bible. It's not understood at all if you can name him among characters that are characters of history. As Blake said that it ought always to be understood when you open the Bible and you are reading anything in the Bible, "It ought always to be understood that the persons Moses and Abraham are not here meant, but the *states* signified by those names; the individuals being representatives or visions of those eternal states as they were revealed to mortal man in the series of divine revelations as they are written in the Bible." Now he said, "I have seen these states in my Imagination; when seen at a distance they appear as *one* man, but as you approach they appear multitudes of nations" (*Vis. Las Judg.,* Pp.76-77).

I say to you I have had that experience with Blake. Blake was born in 1757, died in 1827, eighty-seven years before my birth in this world of Caesar. And yet I know Blake. I met Blake this night and after discussion of the usual theme "the mystery of God"...what else to discuss...he said to me, "Fall backwards...a complete abandonment of self, no restraint at all. It doesn't matter if you smash yourself into nothingness...just fall backwards." Then as though I fell off the earth I am hurtling through space like some interstellar body. Could be a star, yet I'm hurtling through space. And when that motion ceased and I came to a stop, I looked up and here in the distance is a single man, all aglow. His heart was like a flaming ruby. But as I approached him, here that one body contained multitudinous nations and races, all the people of eternity in that one body. Just as he told me "Fall backwards" and I took him at his word and fell backwards and fell off seemingly into interstellar space. Here I am coming closer towards a being, a

629

glowing being, one being containing all the races, all the nations, everything in the universe.

Now we are being gathered back into that *one* being *after* the journey. It starts with the state called Abraham. Abraham was shown the entire thing before. As we are told in Galatians, "And the scripture, foreseeing that God would save and justify the heathen, preached the gospel beforehand to Abraham" (Gal.3:8). You wouldn't have thought Abraham if you take it as a secular story, a being of history, that he, preceding by 2,000 years, could have been shown the gospel. You would say, well, the gospel hadn't yet taken place by 2,000 years and yet he was shown the gospel, God's plan of salvation. Well now, how does it work? "God himself entered death's door, the human skull, with everyone who enters and lays down in the grave with the one who has entered that skull in visions of eternity, until they awake and see Jesus and the linen clothes lying there that the females had woven for them and the gate of their Father's house" (Blake, *Milton,* 32, ln.40). Well, who entered? Jesus is not a man. He is the Son of *redeemed* man, all gathered together after the resurrection, after the experiences of redemption, gathered together into one being, and that one being is personified as Jesus.

Well, who was it that entered? You are told it was the *seed* of God, it was the Christ seed, God's son, who entered, and God's son and God are *one*. In Galatians, the word translated seed that entered and that man must bring forward is *sperma*. It means "the sperm of man"...man is now identified with God. It's not the physical sperm, that's only a shadow producing bodies of death. It is the spiritual sperm. It's called Christ in scripture, defined here as the seed and called the seed in Galatians (3:16, KJV). It also means "to draw out," that is through the idea of extending oneself. God is ever-extending himself. So he plants himself in the human skull. Now seemingly we are two, but we aren't two any more. Through the dream and it's God dreaming; then the barrier is removed and we become one, and we are individualized and emerge *as* God in the very end. When we emerge we are God, the Lord Jesus Christ.

But the thing personified has been accepted as the thing signified when it's only a *sign*. Jesus is a sign like Abraham is a sign, Isaac a sign, these are signs. But who is talking or witnessing to the thing signified? So here, when you read it try to keep in mind that these are only personifications, and try to find out what they are personifying. What is the thing signified by the name when you read Abraham, Isaac, Jacob, Moses, Jesus or any character in scripture. Until you get the thing *signified* behind the sign, you're going to miss it as you start to read scripture.

Quite often you find a Classic telling a far greater story than the things you hear from the pulpits on Sunday morning...infinitely greater. Here is a man who is a mathematician, and you know his play. You've all seen it and you've laughed your heads off at it. I could see it every week it's so altogether wonderful—*Alice Through the Looking Glass*. "Let's go and see him. Come, go and look at him," cried the brothers and then they each took one hand of Alice and led her up to where the king was sleeping. Tweedledee said, 'Oh, he is dreaming now, I wonder what he is dreaming about?' Alice said, 'Nobody can know that.' Then Tweedledee said to Alice, 'Why, he's dreaming about you and if he stopped dreaming about you, where do you think you will be?'" The dreamer in man is God, but he has to dream it in the sequence in which it unfolds, and it comes to the climax as Jesus Christ. You can't omit any part of the dream. As our forefathers played it so will we. And the one who is playing it, who is the *only* actor in the dream, is God. God is playing every part in this world. So God is in the actual…right here dreaming and he has to dream it just as he wrote it in the beginning and showed the dream. It was essential to awaken himself and extend himself… for you *were* before that the world was. When you came down you were the son of God, an "I" of God, and he's extending that, the same son, only enhanced by reason of the dream which he predetermined. So in man is the dreamer and that dreamer is God, the only God in the world, which is I AM. He's dreaming everything.

So this mathematician known to us as Lewis Carroll…Dodgson was his name. Here we take a book, this lovely…we call it a child's Classic. Child's nothing! It tells so much. Everything was possible through the looking glass, everything. As told in scripture, "With God all things are possible"; so with the story, all things are possible…things are what I say they are. He dreams it and dreams it and brings it into its climax, into its fulfillment in Jesus Christ.

When we find today our boys and girls coming out after four years of college and they could name this personification as a character of history that is bad enough. But to put that in the fifth place is unbelievable and these are Catholic colleges. I'm not saying that it would not happen in a Protestant college, it would happen there too. They might have put him in the tenth place. Many of them have no *feeling* towards him at all, no feeling towards the story, and they don't believe it. But the dreamer is taking them through, as it is taking you through, as it took me through, and we go through everything in this world.

Now, it casts its shadow in this world. And in the shadow world we imitate God. That's what he did…he is dreaming, he's dreaming me. I heard it one night so clearly: "I laid myself down within you to sleep. As I slept I dreamed a dream" and I knew exactly what he was dreaming: he's dreaming that he's I. When he wakes, he *is* I and I am he. So he's dreaming that he's

I, but now in this shadow world, for this *is* a shadow world. I must learn to imitate him. Well, if he dreams me into being and is dreaming me through all the things that I have experienced in the world, then I can start to modify *some* of it by imitating him and start to *dream*. Well, what would the feeling be like if it were true? That's a dream…it has no fact to support it, not a thing in this world to encourage me to continue in that dream, but it's a dream, a day-dream. If he dreams me into being and then asks me to imitate him as a dear child in this world, wearing this garment of flesh and blood, I'll imitate him by singling out a *noble* dream for myself, my friends, for strangers for that matter, and then *dare* to dream it. What would the *feeling* be like if it were true? Just, what would it be like? Then get into this state just as though it were true and see if it doesn't come to pass.

I know from my own experience it does come to pass. But I want to encourage everyone who hears me to actually try it…and start tonight. What would it be like? What would the *feeling* be like if it were true? For we are encouraged to use *feeling* in the story: "Come near, my son, that I may *feel* you" (Gen.27:21). You have the voice of Jacob, but come near. You tell me that you're Esau, let me feel you to see if you really have the external reality with which I associate my son Esau. Jacob has no external reality, he's a smooth skinned lad, but Esau has the external. This world is Esau right now; my *dream* is Jacob. But I must clothe Jacob with external qualities and clothe it with all the things I can muster to make it feel to me externally real, objectively real. Now, "Come close, let me touch you, let me *feel* you." As he came close he felt like Esau, although the voice did have the sound of Jacob, but touch superseded the sound. The father was blind so he couldn't see.

So, "Come close and now let me touch you." Touch has that fantastic sense of reality. I know when you're out of the body and you are awake, completely awake as you are here, well, you can touch something and it doesn't give, it's solid, it's real. You look at something, you touch it and it's real. You meet people, you hold them and they're real. You hear them… all right you can hear them in dream too. But here, you see them, hear them, and when you touch them your hand does not go through them. You embrace them and you embrace a solid being, just as you'd embrace someone here. You know that you're out in that world, that it's not this world, but it's just as real as this world. Then you begin to shake yourself loose from what the world tells you is the *only* reality.

You can't return to this world and ever again see it as you formerly saw it. No one can tell you that anyone is dead, and therefore by dead he is gone and he has ceased to be. No matter how wise they are who tell you that you can't go along with them, because you've experienced other than what they are talking about. They are theorizing and you are speaking from experience.

The Return of Glory

You step right into a world and you meet them. No one can tell me that I haven't met them any more than tell me now I am not touching this lectern, that I am not in this room talking to you. This at this moment is more real than anything else now. But when I am in these worlds, they are more real than anything else...they are solid, solidly real.

So, go back now to the sense of touch, take anything and can you imagine that it could be touched? Well, you say, how could you touch money? You can touch money. Money even has an odor. And that's one of the senses that he used. He said, "Come close, my son, that I may touch you." When he came close and he touched him, he said, "You feel like my son Esau, and you smell like Esau...you have the odor of my son." So he took two senses that to him were like touching, because he had to come close for him to detect the aroma, and he called it his son Esau. Then he blessed him and strangely enough he could not take it back. When he discovered that he was self-deceived, he could not reverse his blessing. You can't reverse it unless you make a tremendous effort to change it. You set these things in motion and in their own good time they're coming to pass, and *every* one will come to pass. They will confront you and you will not even recognize your own harvest. You'll wonder when did I do it, but you had to have done it or it could not come to pass.

But in the *big* dream, it is God dreaming it and God is dreaming everything in the world. Well, you can't mention one thing today that we think is new, fantastic, that is not recorded in scripture openly. You mention one vice...I'll show it to you in scripture. Mention one vice, I'll show you the entire thing in scripture and we think this is something new. I'm not denying that we have new lands, new this and the other, but I'm speaking now of the realities behind the appearances. They're all recorded in scripture...everything is there.

So here, when you open the Bible and you come upon a glorious name like Jesus, still no matter how you've been trained in the past as I have been trained to see it as a person, an individual who was born of a woman in some strange manner, 2,000 years ago, *don't*. Jesus is simply the personification, the representative of all who have achieved The End. Everyone who has come to the climax of the play is gathered into the one body and that one body personified is the Lord Jesus Christ. But who's coming up? It's the seed, the Christ seed, which is the Son of God. Listen to the words in the 3rd chapter of Galatians, "And the promise was made unto Abraham, and to Abraham's seed. It does not say seeds, referring to many; but referring to one...and to your seed, which is Christ" (3:16). He identifies the man now with God...he became one with the one who made the promise. And then you are told in scripture he was told, "You are going into a land that is not

633

yours"—it's a foreign land—"and you will be enslaved and you will suffer for four hundred years; after that you will come out and inherit 100-fold more" (Gen.15:13). It's an expansion of what you were...a hundred-fold greater than what you were. That's the purpose of the entire play, to bring us who were sons of God and still are sons of God back into the kingdom but expanded beyond what we were when we started the dream.

So we entered death's door with the Seed and together we are in the grave in visions of eternity. These are the eternal visions and they're all eternal states and the states are real. So if you leave a state, don't think you've rubbed it out any more than the traveler passing through a certain city when he departs from the city. It would be stupid for him to think the city has ceased to be because he has departed. The city remains, but you the traveler move on. You, the traveler in time, you move from state to state to state...and the *final* state is Jesus Christ. When you enter *that* state, you are born from above. You are completely awakened in the grave and you come out of the one gate called "the gate of your Father." You come out and look back at the linen clothes which are the body and you see that that was what the females had woven for you. Your mother wove it for you, your earthly mother, and you come out and the whole drama surrounds you, everything that is recorded of Jesus. He's only the *sign* you are now actually experiencing in the most solid manner...not gossamer, a solid reality.

So the Bible is an allegory and like all allegories you and I must discover its fictitious character, and having discovered that then try to ferret out what it is trying to tell you, what its real meaning is, and learn its meaning. So the story of Jesus is an allegory from beginning to end. It's an acted parable, but man, unfortunately, has mistaken the personifications for persons and the very instrument itself that conveyed the instruction for the instruction. What arguments you hear from the pulpits Sunday after Sunday concerning these characters who are only personifications, and they speak of them as these graduate students spoke of him as their fifth hero.

I tell you...believe me...it is true what I am telling you. I, too, thought that these were historical characters...that they lived, as we were told, a thousand years ago, 2,000 years, 5,000 years and so on, depending upon the age of the book that you are reading, but they did not. It's a play that was conceived in the divine mind. It's not of human composition; it has a divine origin. When you experience it, you know and you can bear witness to it. Now, he calls individuals from time to time and sends them to be witnesses. They are the ones who are called in scripture apostles. But the apostle lives *now* in the world. Anyone who is sent has first to be called from this world. He is called out of this world into the heavenly world and there he is commissioned and sent, picking up the same garment that he left behind on the chair or on the bed, awed beyond measure with what he has experienced. Now he can witness to the truth of the gospel.

He can not only preach it, but he is a witness to it. He tells you the difference between the thing signified and the sign. Are we not told in scripture, "And the Lord himself will give you a sign. A young woman will conceive and bear a son, and they will call his name Emmanuel" (Mat.1:23). Well, Emmanuel means "God with us." He is with us, with every child born of woman…and that *already* is the conception. The Seed is already there awaiting a certain, well, you can call it fertilization at a certain moment in time; and from then on it quickens within; and then the individual, himself, is the one who comes out. All that you see surrounding you are only signs bearing witness to *your* expansion. Your expansion was your birth; and you came out of the grave. Then you rose, you ascended, and the Spirit himself descends upon you and smothers you with love, because he seals his approval. He approves of everything that you are now…having gone through the dream. And who did it? God did it. And who awoke? God awoke. So when he awakes, you awake and you are he, even though you must still continue in your limited state until you finally take off the little garment of flesh and blood.

So try not to forget it when you read it. And I do hope you're reading the Bible daily. As far as I am concerned I find no book comparable to it, no matter how well it's written and beautiful they are. But the Bible…but you get nothing out of it if you see it as the world sees it. Yet if you see it through the eyes of the mystic who has experienced scripture, then you will know who Jesus is, you will know who Abraham is, who Isaac is. Well, take the very names. When you hold that infant, well, who is it? "He laughs." And what is Isaac's name? "He laughs." Who was promised? Abraham was promised and he was promised what?—a son. And what did he call the son's name?—"he laughs." Yet it is only a *sign*. "This shall be a sign"—go and meet that little child wrapped in swaddling clothes, and he laughs. When you lift him up and you use an endearing term, he laughs. Then the whole thing vanishes.

Now, go to Moses. What does it mean? What does the man's name mean? It simply means "to be born." He could not yet enter the Promised Land because he wasn't yet born. The word actually means "to be born." It's the old perfective of the Egyptian verb "to be born." So Moses is to be born. The whole thing is leading up to the one being, which is yourself… for it's all contained within you. Believe me, I saw the one man and I saw him containing the entire universe. How can a man contain all? But I saw it. It seemed one man in the distance, and as I approached the one man a multitude of nations and races and people all in the one man. Then you'll

635

understand the vision of Blake: "All that you behold, tho' it appears without, it is within, in your Imagination, of which this world of mortality is but a shadow" (*Jer.*, Plt.71). The whole vast thing is yourself pushed out. In the end, you come out and you are that one man. All will be gathered together in the one being spoken of in scripture as the Lord Jesus Christ. In the end there is only the climax.

I wish I could tell everyone and convince them that there's only one true gospel of Christ and that it is this: Mankind *is* redeemed—not going to be, mankind *is* redeemed…it's done…the whole thing is done! If you're passing through towards the climax, it doesn't mean you aren't going to reach there. There's not a thing you can do in this world to prevent your reaching there and having the experience, because the drama is over. It *has been* accomplished. Christ *is* risen, so mankind *is* redeemed, and no one can be lost. There isn't a beast in this world, a man so frightful, that he is going to be lost. Are we not told in scripture, "The Lord hardened the heart of Pharaoh." Well, if the Lord hardened it, how can you condemn Pharaoh for not letting his people go? It is all part of the play. At a certain level you can't see it and you will curse God like Job…as his wife said, "Curse him and die." Curse God and die…why go through this? Yet Job is the story of every child born of woman, an innocent being put through hell by the will of God as told you in the last chapter, the 42nd chapter. Then his friends and his relatives came to Job and they feasted with him, and they loved him and comforted him for all the evil that the Lord God had brought upon him. No one else brought it upon him. The dreamer brings it upon you…*you* dream ignoble dreams and that dreamer is God. He does everything in the world.

Now, you take hold of yourself at the very end…as you are now. You're coming into the last stretch as it were, and then *alter* the play. Make it conform to your noble dreams, your lovely concepts, and dream it in the same way the Father dreamed all the way through taking you with him. In the end when he brings you to the climax, you are he, not two anymore. He leaves everyone and cleaves to *you* his emanation, his wife, for he's called in scripture "your husband." "Your Maker is your husband, the Lord of hosts is his name" (Is.54:5). So in the end the husband and wife aren't two; they have become "one being, one body, one Spirit, one Lord, one God and Father of all." No room for two; there's only one.

Now here, we're coming to the end of our session. Not only dwell upon these lovely things concerning your ultimate end, but before we meet, if we meet again, you have the world of Caesar. You have so much to do in the world of Caesar that you need. You need homes or apartments, more money, this, that and the other. Don't hesitate for one moment to dream it. Well, how do I dream it? I *assume* that I have it. My assumption is the beginning of my dream. I persist in my assumption…I am persisting in my dream. Although reason denies it and my senses deny it, my assumption though at the moment denied by my senses if I persist will harden into fact. I have watched it unnumbered times. It will harden into fact. So have a noble dream. It will not interfere with the basic dream that is taking place in you; no reason in this world why it should interfere, and it *cannot* interfere. Take your lovely wonderful dreams and persist in them…just walk as though they were true.

Try to touch them, give them reality. If they can give an odor, well then, try to detect the odor. I have tried it with just plain odor and taught others just to take the odor. One lady one night said, "I will test it now." She wasn't altogether certain it would work, but she embraced a huge, huge bunch of flowers, roses. She could detect the aroma of the rose. It's unlike any other aroma. When she was completely saturated with the feeling and the odor of roses, she simply dropped it. Not that night but the following night… she lived in the Waldorf Towers…as she was going to her room, here, she detected this aroma of roses. She wondered where they were coming from. She stopped in front of a door thinking it's coming from here. It was so potent the entire hallway was permeated with the odor of roses. She looked into her own room, the window was open and so the draft was great as she opened her door, and here came this enormous overpowering odor of roses. She looked into her room and on her bureau three dozen beauties.

It appeared that the Queen Mother, the present queen's mother, was in New York City and this huge banquet, over a thousand attended for the English-speaking banquet, and she was the honored guest. So these beautiful roses were grown for her and were named after her. The next day when they were cleaning up, they asked the maitre de what to do with the roses and the maitre de said, "Well, I know that Mrs. Niemeyer loves flowers. Give her three dozen, and give so-and-so a dozen and give so-and-so a dozen." But she was singled out because she loved flowers to be given three dozen beauties. They were simply perfect the night before, so they were just as perfect when they were brought to her room the next day. Here she was overpowered with roses. That's putting it to the test.

So I don't care who you are and I invite you to test it. I invite you to take the challenge. Are you not invited in the 13th chapter of 2nd Corinthians, "Do you not realize that Jesus Christ is *in* you?—unless of course you fail to meet the test" (13:5). So test him and see. You are invited to test him and see. Well now, that's how I would test him, for he is the power of God, the wisdom of God, the love of God…all in that seed and that seed is in you. So long before he awakens *as* you, you can test him. Can't you feel a rose now in your hand? There's no rose here, but you can feel it. Feel that velvety quality of a rose and you can detect the odor if you know the odor of a rose…and who doesn't? You can take any of these things and test it. If you say even just for the fun of it—for she did it just for the fun of it—she can well afford to buy roses. But she didn't…she was *given* three dozen beauties.

So tonight, when you leave here make a pledge to yourself that you will live by it: lean against the hope that Christ is awakening in you. Because, you can't fail anyway, so just lean against it. Then take his promise that you can assume any state and it will become a fact…for that's his promise. It's not stated in these words but stated even more beautifully: "Whatever you desire, believe that you *have received* it, and you will." You can't state it any clearer than that. These are the words of an awakened man who is God, for every man who awakes in Jesus Christ is God. He has not a thing to do but bring forth himself. If you have Strong's Concordance, look up the word that is translated "seed" in the 3rd chapter of Galatians, and you will see that it is the male sperm from the idea of extending oneself. It's called "the seed" and it's called "the Christ seed" (3:16).

So for anyone who is here for the first time…and I don't think there is one for the first time…when you know what you want, construct a scene which would imply that you have it…any scene to you that would imply that you have it. When you've constructed it, just simply without bursting a blood vessel assume that you are seeing it, and try to touch it, try to hear it if hearing would do, try to see it with your spiritual eye. Bring all of your senses to bear upon this scene implying the fulfillment of a dream. After you've done it, persist in it in the sense that you *know* you've done it, that the whole thing is behind you.

Now, it seems strange to tell you, but our present moment is *not* receding into the past; it's advancing into the future to confront us. So if I do it now, it's not receding into my past, it's really advancing into my future and I'm walking only to confront what I'm doing now. But man thinks what I have got now has receded and that's past, that's gone. It hasn't gone; it's *always* moving to confront me.

Now, let us go into the Silence.

*   *   *

Are there any questions, please?

Q: What is intuition?
A: What is intuition? Well, I can't give you the dictionary's definition of the word, they may differ; but I feel that man brings into this world *innate* knowledge. He gets nothing from this world. As Blake said, "The

world is too poor to give him anything…he brings it with him." And so then he knows intuitively in the sense he knows it; he has an innate knowledge of something. That to me is intuition.

Now, you may have a vision and that's not intuition, because that to you is so graphic that no power in the world could dislodge it. When I saw the race three days before it took place, there's no argument that anyone could give me to tell me I didn't see it, and I saw it just as it came out. Had I any amount of money I would have placed it right on the nose of the one that really came first, Arts and Letters. I saw the end and I saw Majestic Prince second, the next post position, and I saw Dike third. I saw it. How could anyone tell me I didn't see it? I saw it, saw the colors, and told my wife the next morning, and told my daughter on Saturday morning. She was going over to a friend's who wanted the Prince to win. Well, I wanted him to win, too. But I didn't know the jockey, the owner, didn't know the trainer, I knew of them. But I had no personal interest, only a sentimental interest. So there was no reason for me to start doing anything. I wanted the Prince to have the Triple Crown. But I saw the race in the wee hours of Thursday morning, about four. I was closer to that race than I've ever been to any race in my life when I'm viewing it through these eyes, or even if I'm on the finish line. I couldn't see it as closely if I had them up with glasses, for with the spiritual eye you see all the colors in detail. You see everything. I saw the horse come in on the rail and not a thing could catch him, pulling out, pulling away. I could hardly believe I saw it. And I awoke, may I tell you, I woke disappointed. I was disappointed because I wanted to see other than that. But I saw it and I had to go with my vision, for God makes himself known unto me in vision. And that was the end. It's just as well that man does not know all that God has planned. He's mad enough as it is. What would he do if he saw these fixed ends?

Any other questions?

Q: What can you say about these beings who wrote the Bible as related to time and space?

A: They are men conditioned by divine providence for the part that they played. They were completely unknown. Their names bear a certain significance. Tonight I started quoting Nehemiah, which means "Jehovah has comforted." There is a great comfort if I can read something with understanding, and so in the 8th chapter, 8th verse, I quoted tonight that they read from the book the law of God with interpretation, and they understood that which was read, for the men gave the sense to it. Well now, that's a great comfort to a man if he knows as he reads what is behind what he is hearing or seeing. The average person reading the book doesn't see it, because Jesus has become to the entire Christian world and those who oppose the Christian faith, *a* man. They don't see the mystery behind the word "Jesus." It is the *one* name because that is the climax, the fulfillment of everything that belongs to the play, and all are gathered together into the one being. The word "Jesus" means "Jehovah"...same thing...it means "savior." So everyone who has reached that state, although all *are* redeemed they have to pass through the drama as it were and arrive at the point of redemption. But he is redeemed because the one man contained all, and *all* are redeemed. I'm not distressed when I hear of this one or that one—a lovely person goes to jail, all right, so he goes to jail. I'm not distressed. I can only say, what's wrong with *that* one going to jail when others went to jail? So the papers make much of it if the man who is in jail has prominent parents...then he gets free space, an advertisement. He doesn't differ from the other inmates.

Q: In the span of a man's lifetime, how much is predestined and how much isn't?

A: The fixed things concerning the *drama* are all predestined. In the world of Caesar, you and I have a talent and we can exercise it. Your wonderful experience that you wrote me last week, I think it's perfectly marvelous. When you realized after you tried to drown this one in a cage that you yourself were in the cage. Nothing wrong with that...simply a state... trying to let go or dispose of a state. You hadn't completely let go of it, because it was still alive. But you recognized yourself in it. I think your other one concerning the child is perfectly marvelous...a wonderful adumbration of the event. You wanted that child with all your heart and you knew it was yours. The number seven is significant, for the seven means "a spiritual experience"...seven is always spiritual. So I liked your letter immensely.

Until Monday...thank you.

FORMING OF CHRIST IN US

6/23/69

I have always felt that what is most profoundly spiritual is in reality most directly practical. I will tell you a story tonight from scripture. It's so little understood. I've never read about it in any book, but I know the inner meaning of it. And I'll show you how altogether practical it is in this world of Caesar. In all the revelations which await us there is nothing so fundamental as Christ in us...the *forming* of Christ in us.

Now how is it formed and by whom is it formed and where? I say *in* us...where is the sphere of the forming? To come to it, we'll go to a story. Paul takes an old story. If we take the scholars concept of time, their chronological time as we give it in the Bible, it is placed at 1856 years B.C... the story. He ties it with another story, which our scholars give in the year 400 B.C.; and then he gives the interpretation without much explanation in the 1st Century A.D. So here is a stretch of 2,000 years. Let us see who he is talking about.

He tells us the story of the twins in the womb of Rebecca. She prayed for a child and the Lord heard her prayers and answered her. Well, then there was a conflict within her. As the children began to form within her there was a struggle and she asked the Lord why should she live? And the Lord said to her, "Two nations are in your womb, and two peoples, born of you, shall be divided; the one shall be stronger than the other; the younger shall be served by the elder...the elder shall serve the younger" (Gen.25:22). Then came the birth of the twins and the first one out was covered with hair, his name was Esau. The second one out was smooth, he had not a hair on him, and they called him Jacob. Then, afterwards, Jacob was renamed by the Lord and Jacob became Israel.

Now Paul in telling the story tells it this way to show you a certain measure of predestination…but it's not understood. He's not telling us that you the *outer* man is predestined in the way that man believes it. Listen to his words—it's taken from the 9th chapter of Romans: "Though they were not yet born and had done nothing that was either good or bad, but in order that God's purpose of election might continue, not because of works but because of his *call*" (9:11). He made one the one he loved and the other the one that he hated. He said, "Jacob I loved, but Esau I hated" (9:13). Now here is an elective love. They were not yet born and had done nothing that was either good or bad, but in order that God's purpose, his purpose was election, and that that election should continue not because of works but because of his call. He calls and he loves one and he hates the other.

Well, who are these two sons and why did he love one and not the other? Who is this Israel? Israel is *not*, as the world has been taught and still is, Jews who are descended from Abraham. Israel is not the descendants of Abraham from some *physical* state. Israel is the *inward* man…the feminine part of us. There is an inward man that is the feminine part of us. I call that inner man my own wonderful human Imagination and that's the inward man that God loves, that is Israel, "the man who will rule *as* God." That's the one that is wedded to God: "Your Maker is you husband, the Lord of hosts is his name. The Holy One of Israel is your redeemer" (Is.54:5). It is this one *in* you, your own wonderful human Imagination that is the Israel of scripture. No descendant of some man called Abraham, but in you is that being I call your Imagination. That's the inward man, the feminine part of your nature. It is that that God has wedded himself to; it is that that he cleaves to and leaves everything until the two become one flesh. It is in this sphere that Christ is formed and Christ is his son, and that son is David. You actually by this union become God, your own wonderful human Imagination and the Creator of the universe. He is in love with his emanation, yet his wife 'til the sleep of death is past. But how will he know that this union is productive? Only as his son is formed in you and that son is called "Christ *in* you the hope of glory" (Col.1:27).

So when Paul takes that passage from the 25th of Genesis and ties it in with the 1st chapter of Malachi, a separation of over fourteen centuries, and then he begins to treat *it* to show the predestined *you*, he's *not* talking about this *outer* man. This is not loved by my Father, who eventually I will find myself to be. Then what is this that he dislikes? What is it that he hates? I'm in this room and I see it and I'm very happy to be here now. But there are many places that I find myself where I am not happy to be, yet my senses tell me that I am there and anchor me there. This is the *outer man* of the senses. I find myself behind the eight-ball, maybe financially, maybe physically, in some other way, and my senses confirm that position in my world and anchor me there. He *hates* that!

But the one within me that he loves can in the midst of hell visualize harmony, visualize heaven. And because he is the Lord of the whole earth he is omnipotent to produce his purpose and he so loves me, his wife, that if I dare to assume that I am anything that the outer man Esau denies (he hates Esau) he will accept my vision and he will work it out for me in the world of Caesar. It will come to pass as surely as tomorrow morning will come...*if* I remain faithful. He, my husband—for my Maker is my husband, the Lord of hosts is his name; the Holy One of Israel is my redeemer, the God of the whole earth he is called (Is.54:5)—infinite power to realize that which his bride is claiming. He gives to his bride everything, and he loves his bride... and his bride is your own wonderful human Imagination.

That's the emanation of God. That's his wife and he cleaves to his wife until the two become one flesh. That union he wants to be productive and so he wants a son. For, "If a son honors his father, and I am a father, where then is my honor?" said the Lord to you, as you read it in the 1st chapter of Malachi (1:6). If I then be a father, and a son honors his father, then where is my honor, where is my son? That son is being formed in the feminine part of me, and when it is completed and completely formed, then there will be an explosion and our son will come out. But by then it isn't *ours*, it's *mine*... because we became one flesh. We aren't the little bride *and* the fabulous Lord of Lords. No, then *I am* that being that man worships as Lord.

You can prove it in the life of anyone who has had the experience... many of you sitting here tonight...because this "him" spoken of in scripture has several names and appears according to the sensitivity, the sympathies and the needs of the individual. He may come as the spirit of holiness, the spirit of truth, the spirit of power, or the servant of the Lord...depending upon your need when he appears. But anyone in whom the fusion took place, they are not two any longer, they are one, for "He who is united to the Lord becomes one Spirit with him" (1Cor.6:17, RSV). When he is united to the Lord and he becomes one Spirit with the Lord, then there must be a child to bear witness to that union, and the child comes out. From then on you will meet that being. You may not believe him on this level because you see his weaknesses and his limitations and you are looking at the outward man that the Lord hates. You do not see the *inward* man that is now one with the body of the risen Lord. But you will meet him according to your need, because he is sent on his errands throughout the universe doing his work and he is a protean being. He will appear, in my case, mostly as power. Whether I proclaim the Word of God or *implant* the Word of God, it is with power that it is done

But I am not confined to the appearance of power. I could appear to you…as one lady who is here tonight—I can't take all of her dreams because she gave me these visions and dreams numbering well over thirty and I can't take thirty and even condense them—but here is one. I know her nature and I know how she feels about the historical Christ, and it will take time to change it somewhat into the being of whom we speak here. But because of her need and because of her sympathies, I appeared to her in the form of what is to her the crucified Christ. There she saw me on the floor, stretched in the same form that she entertains in her mind's eye, with the head bent on the right and down on the shoulder, leaning forward, and the stigmata very obvious. She said, "Neville, it was you in the crucified form with the stigmata very obvious, wearing only a loin cloth." So she saw the entire picture, but her need was for that.

Now why was that her need? That she may be encouraged to believe all that I am talking about, for that is her picture of the one who said, "I am the truth." So she may be encouraged…if she can't follow me completely, she's encouraged to go along with what I am saying even if some night or at some moment she can't quite get it, she still will believe that I am speaking the truth, presented to her in the form of the one who gave his all for humanity. Being a protean being, in that dimension of myself, you can appear in whatever is the need for the one to whom you appear. But I was sent by power, fused with love…that's the fusion. But, when sent into the world to do what I'm doing it was power who sent me. So most of the time I am seen clothed in power, whether I am speaking the Word of God in this other dimension of my being, or whether I am implanting the Word of God by fusion, by union with those that I am sent to do it for that purpose.

So here in *this* world, that profound story that is not understood…and scholars will not even touch it because it doesn't make sense how altogether practical it is in this world. I look out on a world and everything tells me I can't have it. I haven't the background, I don't have the means, I don't have this, I don't have that. Everything is denying that I could ever realize what really I desire. I want it, and this outer man is telling me I can't have it. So my Father who is now my husband and we became one, he hates this outer one. He hates Esau that would dare deny his bride what the bride wants, for he gives her his all, and he has all. So whatever she wants he gives her. But the "he" spoken of in scripture is this Jacob who is renamed Israel, who is the inner man of every man, and I call that inner man "your own wonderful human Imagination."

So you look at anything in this world, I don't care what it is. You may not want it. I don't want buildings…I wouldn't want the responsibility today of owning a building. I don't want any of these things in the world. I don't want a home; I like living as I live in someone else's home and pay rent, so I can get up and go when I feel like it. I really don't wish the responsibility of a home and I have a wife who will go along with me. She has no feeling that to have a home is going to give her security. She either finds security in what I'm talking about or she's not going to have it. I can give her security in the world of Caesar, and who knows but tonight there could be a revolution in my little island and all that the family has could be completely wiped out over night. Where is the security? It could happen, so she can't look upon that that I can give her tonight as security.

Man thinks he has it because he has pieces of property or he has this or the other. Your own security is in the Lord, the Lord you know now to be your husband. Whose Lord is he? He's the Lord of the universe and he loves his emanation, your own wonderful human Imagination, and he can't give enough to his bride. But the bride in this world is clothed with the outer one called Esau. He hates Esau and he loves his Jacob. So his Jacob, who is his Israel who will rule as God, is your Imagination. You simply in your Imagination see what you want. You can see it. When you see it *clearly* in your mind's eye, trust you husband...he is the Lord of the universe. Accept it completely as fact and walk in that assumption that it's done and let him do it.

Now, you will discover in this picture that Christ is formed not only *in* us, he's formed *by* us, for I am one with the Lord with whom I am united. If the Lord forms his son in me, his bride, and he cleaves to me and we become one being as he is forming it, then I am forming Christ, too. Christ is formed *in* me and *by* me, for I am one with the Lord. So everyone here is forming Christ in them. He's being formed in you and by you, and when he comes out it's the most surprising thing in the world. That's why I said earlier, in all the revelations that await us, nothing is so fundamental as the revelation of Christ in us. It's such a shock when he comes out. That's not what man expected and yet here is this glorious son. It's the most difficult thing to describe, because you can't describe the beauty of this son, this eternal son who now honors he father; and then you are called "the Father."

But don't be ashamed if you are a man to speak of this being in you that is more you than anything you can see reflected in the mirror as feminine, because it is feminine. That is the bride of the Lord. And so, the inner man is the feminine part of me and that inner man is my Imagination. It can conceive to begin with...can a man conceive? So it can conceive. So it takes in its embrace the seed of her husband. And so Israel, I would say, owes her uniqueness to this covenant marriage. This is a covenant...he's going to marry Israel he so loves her. He marries Israel and then he wants a son from that union, and the son comes out, and it's Christ, and Christ is *David*.

David calls the Lord "my Father," as told us in scripture. So when David sees you, you are his Father and you are the Lord to David.

The story told in the 25th chapter of Genesis, which doesn't make sense when you read it...she struggled within her and talked to the Lord, and the Lord told her she has two nations within her womb and two peoples born of her shall be divided: one shall be stronger than the other, and the elder shall serve the younger (25:23). Well, make this younger the power that it really is, and make the outer one serve it. The outer one will say to it, "You can't do it, it's impossible," but when it's done he adjusts to it. You can't possibly own that home, it's beyond your means; and then you own that home and the outer one sleeps in it, and adjusts very nicely to it. Yet he would resist everything the inner one is desiring because he can't believe it possible. He does not know that the inner man, the feminine part of my nature, is wedded to the Lord. The Lord so loves his wife that he left everything to make the two of them one...just one flesh and not two anymore.

So this is the most practical thing you can hear. You can take anything in this world, but you must really want it, *really* want it. Now put it to the test. Do you know what you want? Well, use your same Imagination that is forming Christ in you to conceive a scene implying the fulfillment of your dream. Just use your Imagination...what would you see if it were true? What would you hear if it were true? What would you do if it were true? Well, begin to do it in your Imagination, and when you go to bed sleep in it.

I'll show you how he comes in strange ways. Always bear in mind that God is a protean being. A young girl whose father comes here every Monday and Friday, a sweet child—there are five children in the family—and she has a pet rabbit, a doe. The rabbit developed something and they took it to the vet. So she sent a message by her father to ask me to pray for her pet rabbit, her doe. The vet did what he could and said that maybe for the rest of the life of the animal you'll have to drain it, but we don't have to destroy the animal. Well, we don't have to drain it either...that too will stop. But she has her pet rabbit at home. So the father, loving his children, that night he thought of her, and she now has her wonderful rabbit and she doesn't have to lose it. Next morning this is what he saw. He said, "I swear I actually saw it with my eyes open and yet I could not have seen it with my eyes open. Was it a dream, was it a waking vision, what was it? I seemed so much awake. Standing at my bed is a man, a tall man, but his head is that of a rabbit, and he said to me, "Thank you for helping my people." And he said, "I felt this must be *Midsummer Night's Dream* only this is a rabbit and not a donkey." Thank you for helping my people. Who do you think wore the form?—God. He sends himself in everyone that he sends, and that one sent is one with the sender, and he, too, is the protean being and can assume any shape, any form. So he asked for help, and he got the help the minute I heard that he had the help. Well, this now encourages him to really believe it all the more.

Like all fathers of five children he can use some more money. It's not the easiest thing in the world to raise five children—clothes to be bought, food to be bought, all these things, schooling, and so he can always use more. Well now, he knows that happened in his world, and the one sent clothed himself as a big rabbit—but it was man because God is man—and thanked him for helping my people. Instead of putting it out of its way because, well, why keep it, a rabbit is a rabbit. No, a little operation and she has her pet, this little doe. So this is how he speaks to everyone in the world to encourage faith, for by faith all these things are made. I must have faith and faith is simply loyalty to unseen reality. So if I imagine a state that's unseen by anyone in the world…but I've imagined it, I've assumed that it's true, and he is the God of truth. And who is he? He is my husband. And where is he? He's wedded me and he so loved me, we became one. So when I imagine it, he imagined it…only we're not two anymore, we're one.

So everyone in this world will find that union one day and the fusion will take place. When the fusion takes place you are not you *and* God; God actually became you that you may become God. That is the story of scripture. But the man that he became is not this [body]. He doesn't like this one and he uses the very forceful expression "he *hated* Esau," the hairy one, the outer man; but he loved Jacob the smooth skinned lad…didn't have a hair on his body. He is the subjective you, the feminine part of your nature, and that feminine part of your nature is your own wonderful human Imagination. So don't be ashamed to admit there is in you the man which is feminine that is loved by God. But God will become that…absorb that being right into his being…and then he will awake *as* God, God the Father. For when that child calls you Father, you are a male and you are the Lord.

So Christ is being formed *in* us and it's the most fantastic revelation ever. It comes as such a shock when you see him, this glorious being that "today I have begotten you…not of blood, not of the will of the flesh, not of the will of man, but of God" (Ps.2:7; Jn.1:12-13, KJV). I formed you in me. Well, how did I form Christ in me? First of all, I received his Word, his seed, by fusion. That embrace was the reception of the seed and then it developed by my use of my talent which is to use my Imagination. Start with any little thing in the world. It doesn't have to be the biggest thing in the world. The smallest little thing when you use your Imagination pleases God; *not* to use it displeases him. So use it. How do I use it? First of all you must know what you want, either for yourself or another. When you really want it for another, believe it. You don't have to sit down and burst a blood vessel, you simply as you walk the street imagine the friend telling you that it has worked.

A friend of mine called today to thank us for the aid in selling a home. She has this enormous house in Highland Park, but no one wanted it. It's so big you'd have to have a raft of servants. There sits the house...it's empty since she's had it. She has two other homes, so she doesn't need this one. Someone came to the door...and she has a little girl in the inside just watching. And the little girl was warned not to open the door, and to ask from the inside who was there, and to give them the information concerning her telephone number...tell him to call the owner and this is the telephone number. So she got a telephone call from the man on the outside. The little girl could not describe him, because she couldn't see him, and she's simply talking from the inside. He said, "I pass this house often and I'm interested, is it for sale, because you have no sign?" She's never had a sign on the outside because it's empty, and these fellas may throw rocks and break the windows or something if they know it's for sale. Well, the deal was closed today. It's only a matter of two weeks since she told me the first story that this man came, he liked it, he thought he could raise the sums of money or finance the deal, and today it has been sealed.

What did I do? I imagined that she told me...that's all that I did. My wife imagined. We see her once a week...she comes home once a week. And all I did was to imagine that she told me that she had sold the house. This afternoon about 3:00 the phone rang and she said, "I couldn't wait until tomorrow," because she's coming to see us tomorrow. She had to call today, because she's sold the house. It's an enormous thing...in fact she calls it Fort Smith. It would take an army to protect it it's so big, so she didn't want it. And she unloaded it just because someone heard. All things are possible to God, and he so loves the one with whom he is one that he abides by any request of that one.

May I tell you, try it! Try it and you will never disprove it. The more you try it the more you please your husband, for you are wedded to God, and God is the God of the universe. He's the God of the whole earth. Therefore he is omnipotent to achieve any purpose in this world. The purpose there was to sell a house; the purpose there was the rabbit. Certainly I didn't care whether the little rabbit died or not, but I did care for the little child. So the little child wanted her little pet, she didn't want it to die, that was my only interest, not in the rabbit. If I'd been told by him the little rabbit had died, I would have been just as indifferent. But the rabbit lived. I heard her tell me—whether in person or through her father—that the little rabbit didn't have to be destroyed. That was her request and I was not going to modify it. I was not going to tell her, you can get another one because there are millions of rabbits. No, she wanted *that* rabbit, that was her pet, her little

The Return of Glory

doe. So don't modify it if it's within your ethical code; certainly that would come within one's ethical code. There is a helpful thing.

So you appear to all under different names. You could appear as the spirit of holiness, the spirit of love. I know in my own case, when my Father implanted himself within me in that union he was love. But when he sent me he wore the garment of power, for that would be the part I would play *most* of the time...so, many of you have seen me on the outside in vision, in power. Marta, who is gone from this sphere, was the first one to reveal the power as she saw it, and the whole thing surrounding the revelation of that power. But that was done for a purpose: that Marta may know the truth of what I'm talking about...for here he's described as power. On this level, certainly no power...just a normal man with all the human weaknesses of any outer man. All the money in the world doesn't give you power. I'm not speaking of that kind of power. They just buried a man who left behind him 500 million dollars. So while he was here, all right, he had 500 million; didn't take one nickel with him. He's now possibly the richest spirit in the graveyard. Nevertheless, he had 500 million. Started off with nothing practically...that's what I read in the paper.

So here, a story that makes no sense. I have at home maybe a dozen scholarly works on Genesis, and not one will even come near it. They don't understand it. They will give you the right translation of the Hebrew words, but they cannot begin to give meaning, to give it any sense. So when you read the story of Paul in the 8th chapter of the Book of Acts—because he comes into the 9th chapter, that's when he begins—he implies he was present at the stoning of Stephen, but the name does not appear until the beginning of the 9th. Well, here in the 8th the eunuch is reading the Book of Isaiah, the 53rd chapter, and Philip comes by and Philip says to him, "Do you understand what you are reading?" and he said, "How can I without a guide?" Then he asked Philip to help him, so Philip got next to him and interpreted the chapter on the suffering servant, what it really means. Because he asked Philip, "Is the prophet writing about himself or about another?" (8:30). He took it just as the world would take it; he took it on this level. He wasn't writing about any other as I would think of a man of flesh. He was telling an eternal, immortal story of this suffering servant. That God so loved me he wouldn't alter my Imagination. If I imagined the most horrible thing in the world, he would fulfill it, and he suffered with me, because I had to fulfill all that I imagined. So he allowed me to use it unwisely, and he fulfilled it with me. That's the suffering servant. But in the end, he rejoiced when he realized what he had wrought, what he had done. He went through hell with his love of the one he loved most, and then when he came out, he became as he is. So that is the story that makes no sense if you do not see it beyond the page.

So tonight, put it in this simple, simple way. As you are seated here, the outer man who looks into the mirror and sees a man, that's Esau. The man who is looking into the mirror and doesn't like what he sees, but now in his mind's eye sees what he would like to see...in that same mirror the outer man is still there, but in his *mind's* eye he is seeing the man he would like to see, *that* is Jacob. His name is "supplanter," so he supplants in his mind's eye what he is seeing with the outer eye. That is Jacob and he *loved* Jacob. Now he will grow Jacob into the likeness of what he sees.

Now, I've told you that when man dies he finds himself in a world just like this, terrestrial and solid and real. This same lady who saw me in the crucified form said, "I was lying in bed, I was awake, and I closed my eyes and I saw my mother. She was younger by many years. I blinked my eyes to see if it really is true, and there is mother again, this time younger still. I blinked several times and each time she was younger. And then she said to me, 'This is my husband.'" Now she knows the truth of what I have been telling you, that in the world into which all people go, they marry there too, and they grow there too, and they die there too. They are afraid of death there as they are afraid of death here until the union is *complete* and they are one with God. And then they resurrect and they die no more, and marry no more, for the union is complete. There's no need of any other weddings. They are married to the Lord and they're one with God...the two became one flesh. So now, forever there's no need of any more marriages.

But while it has not been completed—we haven't brought forth the Son of God to bear witness to the union of the inner you, the feminine you, with God—you go into another world, you marry, and you struggle just as you struggle here. So she saw her mother and then she blinked her eyes to see is it really true, and suddenly the mother became younger. She blinked her eyes again and her mother became younger and in ten-year jumps going backwards in time. Not just a little bit; these were ten-year jumps in time backwards. Then the mother said, "This is my husband." Now she did not tell me in her letter whether she saw the husband...anymore than my other friend who is here when he saw his mother. He did not ask her if she was married again, but he felt she was married again and not to the man he knew here as his father. But he felt that his mother was married again, and she was a young woman. She told him, "When I came here I found myself twenty years of age" and she died in her seventies and looked older because she had worked hard in her life. Then he met her ten years after her death and she was a woman of about thirty, radiantly beautiful, more so than he had ever known her before, even though he has pictures of her when she was a young girl and a young woman. He has no picture comparable to what he saw in the flesh and he felt mother is married again, and it's not to my father. So he knows the truth of what I'm saying here.

In this lady's case, with her mother going back in time and then seeing me in the crucified form, and he who was crucified declares "I am the truth," she will know now what I'm talking about from this platform is true. I am not discussing politics, for that I would go astray. When I take the Bible which is the Word of God and let my intuition play upon it, it comes to the surface...*why* it was written in the form in which it was written. It will last forever in *this* form and it would not in any other form. So it is written in this way to make you dig, because if it's made simple, you'll forget it. Man has to dig and dig, to ask why, and then it comes in revelations one after the other.

You will know one day why I'm telling you tonight concerning the forming of Christ in you. Of all the revelations—and they're all stunning, one after the other—but this is the most *fundamental*. There is no other way that man would ever know that he is God. You can be split from top to bottom; you can come out of the grave of your own skull; you can find the little child that symbolizes *your* birth from above; but not a thing in this world could ever happen to you to bring you to the consciousness of *being* God outside of seeing the Christ that was formed in you who stands before you and calls you Father. Then go back to the very book that is all about *you* and see where in the 2nd Psalm he said, "I will tell of the decree of the Lord: He said unto me, 'Thou art my son, today I have begotten thee" (2:7), and you realize who you are. No one in the world could ever tell you that you are God save the son and only *that* Son can tell you, the Son who is the Son of God...and God's Son is called Christ. Christ in you is being formed and when he's formed it's because union has been completed: you and God the Father are one and *you* are the Father. Then he stands before you and you know who you are, for, "No one has ever seen God; but the only Son, who is in the bosom of the Father, he has made him known" (Jn.1:18). He comes out and then you have found him. He has been formed *in* you and *by* you, because by now you are God...and he was "born not of blood, not or the will of the flesh, not of the will of man, but of God." And then you know who *you* are and who the Son is.

There isn't one nth part of one percent tonight who would accept it, but I will not change it one iota, because I know the day will come when they will experience it. So they will deny it today, as they have done through the centuries, but the day will come they will experience it. And when they do, their marriage states are over, because they have now *one* husband and he is *themselves*. That covenant of marriage is one's redeeming power...for, he is your redeemer, who?—your husband. Who is your husband?—the God of the whole earth. Then where is he? "I've been so long with you" said he "and yet you still ask me to show you the Father? When you see me, you've seen the Father" (Jn.14:9). Therefore, he never looks at the man of flesh and blood, for that is not the Father. The man of flesh and blood was *hated* by God the Father. The one of the Spirit was loved...and you do not see the Spirit, for the Spirit is your own wonderful human Imagination. It will take any form. But you'll meet him, and this outer form is a *faint* resemblance, but it is the outer form. They are twins, and the outer is a faint shadow that is not perfect, but it resembles the perfect inner one...the one that God loves.

So bear in mind the sphere in which the Christ is formed is the *inward* man, who is the feminine part of your nature; for it takes woman to conceive...and Imagination conceives. That is the great power and that is the bride of the Lord. So let every man be big enough and bold enough to claim that within himself there is that eternal woman that God loves. That woman is his bride and he left everything for her, and brought her into himself, and made the two one flesh. And to prove that they really are mated and they are one in love, their child must come forward bearing witness to that union. The child comes forward and it was the Christ that was formed in them. That Christ comes at the end of the journey when now he takes it off for the last time and discards the Esau forever, returning now to the heavenly sphere as God the Father.

So you who may not be here on Friday treat it seriously. Put it to the test and see if it does not prove itself in the testing. It will. For in the very attempt to test it you are pleasing God...as you are told, without faith it is impossible to please him, and faith is simply *loyalty* to the unseen reality. So, no one sees it, but you remain loyal to it. That's subjective appropriation of the objective hope...that's faith. You subjectively appropriate it. No one sees what you are doing. You could be sitting in a bar and being far more noble in mind with what you are thinking and what you are doing in your Imagination than the one who is conducting the service in the cathedral. He may be seeing if certain wealthy people are not present today. He may be looking all over the congregation to see if the wealthy ones came today because he prepared a subject that would please them. He didn't want to give it to the poor and waste it on them.

So you could be at a bar enjoying the company of a friend and in your mind's eye having the most glorious time in the most heavenly manner, and you are pleasing God by the exercise of your Imagination. And do it *lovingly*. Take any man's request and you don't have to do anything about it other than *assume* that it is done; and your Father by reason of the fact that he's the God of the whole earth has the power to make it so. He'll take everyone in the world and use them if it's needed to bring what you have assumed to pass.

Now let us go into the Silence.

*   *   *

Now tonight when you go to bed, remember what I told you. Dwell upon just imagining, and know that *this* is the bride of God. You will not waver then and play the part of the harlot and believe in people outside of self and trust them more than you trust your husband. It's not very flattering to see a woman put more interest in another man than she does in her husband. He isn't flattered I assure you. She either has faith in him or she doesn't, and when she turns from him to the belief in any power outside of the Lord, she has gone a-whoring. That's what the Bible teaches. When she played the part of the harlot, she simply wandered in consciousness from the feeling of being the bride of the Lord to the belief in some power external to herself. What a comforting feeling it is just to play that part as you snuggle into that pillow, that here is the bride of the Lord, and the Lord is with you, for we are one. He became you that you may become the Lord.

Now are there any questions, please?

Q: (inaudible)
A: Well, of course, I do not divide them male, female from the outside. The *inner* man …I speak now of the generic Man…is the Imagination of all, male and female; that is the inner of either. The outer is a male or a female, but the *inner* of everyone is female, the bride of the Lord. Now this one who spoke, he might have had a vast audience of females and he's going to play the game and appeal to all the ladies. But I could not go along and say that a woman necessarily because she is a woman is more potent in imagining than a man.

I wouldn't cut it that way, because I wouldn't offend any man in the world…because he has a female *within* him and that's the female of which I speak. I'm not speaking of the outer female; I'm speaking of the female in Man and by Man I mean generic Man. So that Man that is generic Man is God. So here we have a division, the female from the male; not man from woman. The Woman comes out of Man and the Man is capitalized in scripture if you read that 2nd chapter of Genesis (2:23). So she comes out of Man. That Man is God; it's Man's emanation, generic Man which is God. And the female which is one's Imagination is the emanation of Man who is God, and yet she is his bride until the sleep of death is past. So both male and female who separated came out of Man, as you are told, and she came out of Man and he called her "womb-man," Woman.

But here, on a whole I know, well, they say that most of the wealth of this world is left in the hands of women anyway. They outlive men, so they have the wealth...which is perfectly all right. I have a daughter and I hope that she loves the man she marries, and I hope that he will be successful and be able to do for her in this world what your heavenly Father, who became your husband, is doing for you in the heavenly world. So I have no qualms about leaving everything to my wife; I do not know anyone that I could better leave it to. So I don't think anyone, if he has a wife and he loves her, that he has any outside interest to leave it to someone else. She got older with him, and as they grew older she became less and less competent to earn a living, so to whom would he leave it when she needs it more now than when they first got married? So I am all for giving it to the women anyway...let them have it. But don't you give up the power for making it!

I can't deny that in my own case my father had that outgoing personality and he never could see failure in anything. My mother applied this law simply and quietly and got everything she wanted. She "allowed" him to give her...that's how she acted. When she wanted to take a trip to America, she assumed she was in America; then he would come home and say, "You know, Wilsey, I've been looking at you and you look tired and you know what I've done? I've booked you a passage for next week and you're going to America for three months." She would protest, "Oh no Joseph, no...you can't afford it, no." She knew exactly what she wanted, she wanted those three months. She only wished that he had given her maybe an extra week's notice so she could get some more clothes. But she could also tell him, "Joseph, you gave me no notice and so when I go north I'm going to have to buy some clothes"... so more money.

But she did everything that way. She did it with us as children. She would comb our hair, individually, kiss us on the cheek, and then as she sent us off she would always remind us, "You're going to make mother very, very proud, you know that don't you?" Well, you had to say yes. Then she would tell us all individually, "You are my favorite." We didn't know until we were all grown men and married that she told everyone the same thing. But you kept mother's secret and you felt that, well now, I'm her favorite and I must make her proud. I can't do anything that would dishonor mother or in any way reflect upon her loveliness, for she was, in our eyes, the most beautiful person and the most desirable person. So mother instilled that thought in us that we would make her proud.

But we didn't know it, because we couldn't tell the other one, they'd beat us. If I told my brothers, "I'm mother's favorite," they'd all jump on me, because we were raised to understand that we had no favorites. If I said to someone that he's wearing my pants or wearing my shoes, my father would remind me, "Whose pants? They're all mine, I bought them." So at Christmas time he gave us a cricket set or a football, something that we could share in common. If anyone complained that Neville's shoes are my shoes, he would remind them, "They aren't your shoes or Neville's shoes, they are my shoes and I'm letting you use them." So we had a little thing in our household, "The first one up and the first one dressed is the best dressed." That's a fact. The first one dressed was always the best dressed, and I'm not fooling, it's true.

Until Friday. Thank you.

WE FIND THE FATHER IN US

6/27/69

I have told you everything that I have heard from the Father and I have held nothing back. From the time the Father revealed himself to me, I have shared that revelation with you. Whether it be on this level of Caesar—how to achieve objectives—or on the true level where we're all seeking the Father. For finding the Father...little else is worth finding and it is *in us* as persons where we find the Father.

Wednesday night as I retired, it was quite early, between 9:30 and 10, I was communing with myself; and I said that I'm closing on Friday, is there any better way to explain this principle to those who are coming, any more simple way than I have told you? Naturally, I assumed that there was in some strange way a simpler way...and let it be revealed if there is a simpler way. When I woke in the morning around 5:00 I woke with this experience. I found myself in a space ship on the way to the moon. I was not alone, maybe a dozen of us, and here I am coming straight to the moon at this enormous speed, yet in control of the space ship. I came as close as I could touch it, and then the ship turned and entered the moon, this dead body, into what appeared to be a tunnel. Then I said to someone, "Well, do I get out?" and he answered, "Yes you get out." So I got out, and here is this, the end of the voyage, the moon...that everyone on earth is "reaching for the moon." You have a big business venture: I'm reaching for the moon. It seems to me beyond my ability to attain it, but I'm reaching for the moon. Everyone has said that, long before man contemplated putting his foot upon the moon. It has been simply a goal...reaching for the moon.

And so, I arrived at the moon. When I got out, here it's like a sideshow of a carnival. All the trinkets, the most horrible artifacts, little cups, little vases, little lids, made not by artists. You would simply distort the name of the artist if you thought an artist did it...the most horrible little things, all being sold to the tourists. That was the end of the journey. That everything that man has as an ambition is like these little things you buy at a carnival and it all turns into dust. They were made of clay...everything was made of clay. Here was the old money register banging out and taking money, selling these little things meaning nothing... and that is the world. All their ambitions turn to dust and even when they achieve them all turn to dust.

This was early Thursday morning when I woke at five. But it taught me a tremendous lesson to share with you. I did go there, I reached it. I'll tell you how I got there and tell you that no matter what ambition, you realize it is as nothing. The *only* thing is to find the Father, for the Father is the source, the cause of all the phenomena of life. He's not found on the moon; he's found in *you*. You will find the Father in a first-person, present-tense experience, in only *one* way. There's no other way you'll find him. And that way I've shared with you. But there was a lesson in this, for everything in this world contains within itself the capacity for symbolic significance. The moon has...the reach of man is the moon, at least today. And so here was the reach. How to tell them that no matter what ambition they have, symbolized as the moon, they *can* reach it. So then, how did you reach it? Well, I was on my bed when I communed with myself and that bed is on earth so we are on earth. You could be on a bed, you could be seated in a chair, you could be any place, but you are on earth, and you're reaching for some tremendous ambition to be realized here on earth.

Well, it's like sitting on a bank and the current from a bank may not be discernible, but give yourself to it, yield to it completely, and you will see that it is in motion and it will bear you to your objective. Many a time you have sat on the bank of a river and you didn't see the current...you couldn't see it, but you did notice some little object moving on it in a certain direction. So seated on a bench or on a chair or lying as I did in bed, and you're asking for something to give them and to feed them to make it easier. Then it was shown that you simply completely *abandon* yourself to your wish as though it were true. So my wish was the highest ambition of man, every man, for I can't tell what you individually want. Some want marriage, some want money, some want recognition, some what health. But I don't know you individually to the point of knowing what you in your heart of hearts really want, because many of us will conceal the true ambition and state. "Well, I would like so-and-so for so-and-so, meaning, that so-and-so is myself. So we come with all kinds of veils hiding our true desires. But it was shown me: yield completely. I had to completely yield to this state. And here you are moving at a velocity beyond the wildest dream and yet you feel quite safe. On the bed in this city I am moving in a space craft.

So here, you can move...move, but you steer it. My goal was the moon, but when I got there they were all trinkets. So everyone who bought anything only bought dust. Horrible little cups, little saucers, little vases, little this, and here the old money register working overtime and it was worn out. Then how do you return?—by simply awakening. I awoke to find myself...I could hardly believe that I was back here in L.A. on my bed. The thing was so completely objectively real, so solidly real it was difficult to persuade myself that I had just returned from the moon.

So everything contains within itself the capacity for symbolic significance. The moon played its part and the stupid little things played their part. So even when I go now to a sideshow at a carnival they're all playing their parts. And you use them to reveal a tremendous story, a story to tell the world that no matter what they have as an ambition in the end it's trivia compared to what man's true ambition *ought* to be: which is to find the source of the phenomena of life. The source of the phenomena of life is the Father, and you'll find him only when you find him in yourself. You won't find him as another; you'll find him only *as yourself.*

So we are told in scripture, "Hereafter, I will no longer speak to you in figures"—meaning in parables—"but I will tell you plainly of the Father." Now as you read the 16th chapter of John, there is no attempt to tell it plainly. It's there, but where is it? Read the whole of John to get what he's getting at, and you will find he's revealing himself. And the whole drama unfolds within him. But as it unfolds within him, and it's told by the evangelist, people think as the world teaches this story; and that is *not* the story at all. Listen now carefully to these words. I said, "Who is the Christ?" and they say, "The son of God." Well, with that I will agree. But who is the Lord?—the Lord is Jesus. And you say Jesus is Christ? Yes. And therefore the Lord Jesus is one and the same? Well, Christians are taught to believe that is true. The Bible *doesn't* teach that. We're coming now to the end of Revelation...in the Book of Revelation, "And the kingdom of the earth has become the kingdom of the Lord and of *his* Christ" (11:15). You wouldn't say, "the Lord and of his Christ" and bring them together, would you? The Lord is one *and* his Christ...I say, the Father and his son...so, the kingdom of the lord and of his Christ.

Well then, who is the Lord? At the end of the book, the very last verse tells you who he is: "Come, Lord Jesus!" (Rev.22:20). The word Jesus means "Jehovah" and Jehovah means "*I AM.*" So the Lord is *I AM* and his Christ is his son. Christ means "the anointed," and the only "anointed" in scripture is *David*: "This is he; arise and anoint him" (1Sam.16:12). Then David tells of the decree of the Lord: "And the Lord said unto me, 'Thou art my son, today I have begotten thee'" (Ps.2:7). Here is David, the sum total, the essence of the journey of man in this world. When he comes to the end, at the very end if you took all the generations of men and all of their experiences and fused them into a single being, and projected that being, it would be David. That is David and that is the result of your journey.

So you left the Father, "I came out from the Father and I have come into the world; again, I am leaving the world and I am going to the Father" (Jn.16:28). But when I go back, I go back *as* the Father. That was the reason for my journey into this world. I came out, and in coming out, I *seem* to be the *son* of God coming into the world as told me in the 82nd Psalm: "I say you are gods, all of you, sons of the Most High; nevertheless, you will die like men and fall as one man, O princes" (82:1,6). So we came out as sons, lower than the Father; having had the experience we return *as* the Father. For in the end, there is only God and there can be nothing but God in eternity.

So he brings out himself as sons less than himself; then when we go back, having gone through the experience, we have to go back *as* God the Father. If he is a father, he has a son, and that son is simply the personification of the entire journey that we have made as men. So in the world, we pass through all the experiences that man could ever have. Summarize the entire humanity and all of its experiences and personify it, and you're going to get the eternal youth David. He's going to call you Father. So finding the Father is the only thing in this world for man.

You might have read today's paper and tens of millions must be disgusted, because undoubtedly it was all over the country. It's not only in the *L. A. Times*; I presume every paper in the country told the story lifted from the present magazine *"Women's..."* I think it's *Home Journal* and the cover story of a former first lady. Everyone so adored her. She was this glamour girl. And then you see the greed behind that picture as written by her secretary... that she sold even the gift of her father-in-law at her wedding to what was our present president. Sold it and sold gems from gifts from foreign countries to buy what she considered a more beautiful diamond. I wonder how Joe Kennedy feels tonight when he sees it in print...not that he didn't know it before. And this whole greed...and you wonder why this union took place between that greed and a half-billion dollars? And then you wonder what is it all about? It's all trinkets. When you reach the limit of your ambition, called the moon, so you reach the moon, it's all made of clay. It' all dead...the moon is dead. I saw it as clearly as I'm seeing this here and touching it like this. The whole thing is just as dead and not one thing grows upon it. It's all dead, but we colonized it and selling trinkets as we do here on earth.

We fill our paper with ads to make you buy what you don't need and what you don't want, and take from you shadows, called money. You don't need it any more than you need a hole in your head beyond what you now have. But you will go out and reach for the moon to get it, as he did, to sell the little things that the father-in-law gave her as a wedding present to his son that he loves. And those foreign countries sent their swords with jewels on them. From one she took the big emerald, because that plus what the father-in-law gave her plus something else could be sold and then she could buy, what?—another little trinket. All tonight who saw and worshipped that creature, if they read it, and they will eventually, and then down into the mire where it should go. It all belongs there. So, all the ambitions of men come to dust.

The only thing left for man…the only thing that was for man in the beginning was to find the Father. So he said he called the twelve and said to them, "We are going up to Jerusalem, and all that is written of the Son of man by the prophets will be accomplished" (Luke18:31). But they understood none of these things, for this was hid from all of them and they did not grasp what was said. Going up to Jerusalem…the Bible tells us of two Jerusalems. The one below is the human womb, a woman's womb on earth who is in slavery with her children. She bears children into slavery, all enslaved by the body that they wear. I must take care of all the functions of this body, and I can't pay any slave in the world to perform these functions for me. Whatever they are, no matter how wealthy I am, how powerful I am—whether I be a Stalin who could kill twenty million and be exonerated or a Hitler—he has to perform his natural functions for himself. If he doesn't, they'll bury him. And so, is he not enslaved by the body that he wears? The Jerusalem from below, Paul tells us, bears children into slavery along with herself. So every woman in the world bearing a physical child is herself enslaved and enslaves the very one that she bears.

But there is a Jerusalem from above and she is *free*, and she is our mother, said Paul in his letter to the Galatians (4:26). Man must be born from *above*. And then he goes through the series of events from that moment to the very end. But within that series comes his freedom…when his son appears and he has found David. David said to him, "Thou art my Father, my God and the Rock of my salvation" (Ps.89:26). He finds the sum total of his journey: he's gone through the entire gamut of human experiences, hidden in a merciful way from his present moment in time. For if he could only remember now the horrors that he's passed through, well, he couldn't go on. But when he meets the Son, the Son's presence calling him God the Father frees him forever. And he only waits for that moment in time, which can't be long delayed, until he takes off for the last time the garment of slavery, which is the body of flesh and blood.

The Return of Glory

But while we are here…though I tell you I saw it and it is all trinkets, the whole thing is dust, made of clay, nevertheless, rent must be paid, food must be bought and clothing must be found. All of these things must be in the world of shadows, the world of Caesar. And so what it was showing me to do: conceive it. It seems far away? It isn't so far. You will move with the velocity of light, really far faster than what we now say. You said days to get there? Doesn't take days, it took me a split second to get back; therefore, it could not have taken longer. Only going was more difficult than returning. Going, I am yielding myself to my wish fulfilled, and you've got to work yourself into the mood, into the emotion, so that takes longer. So you're working yourself into the feeling of the wish fulfilled, giving it all of the sensory vividness of reality, all the tones of reality, and you're working yourself into it. It might take you a minute, might take you even an hour. You may even fail to catch hold of that trap. But the minute you catch hold of it and let yourself go completely, you will go with the current and it will bear you straight to your objective. When you get there, you'll have it, you'll realize it.

But I tell you that no matter what you realize in this world as your objective, it will turn to dust. It's made of clay. The only *real* objective that will never pass away is the discovery of yourself and the being that you really are is God the Father. All the honors of men are as nothing. Yet we read them morning after morning in the paper. The man wants another medal, he wants another honor, another something else, and he will give anything… he'll even buy it to get his name in the paper. Only those who murder or do some frightful thing are mentioned in the obituary, except if you have a million dollars. If you have a million dollars you get into the obituary. It invariably will say a millionaire, so-and-so, died last night. Have a million dollars and you'll be mentioned in the obituary. Or you kill someone or do some horrible act and you'll be mentioned in the front page. But do a normal thing in this world, do a lovely decent thing in the world, who knows and who cares? That's not news. But I'm telling you what lasts as against what doesn't last. All the other ambitions of men…so they leave a foundation, providing buildings are built with their name on it and endowed, and the thing goes on. Perfectly all right, let them do it…but it all turns into dust.

If I could only take you now with me to the moon as I saw it. Colonized by us, there were only Americans there. And was the cash register busy! It was worn out from selling the junk, and all these stupid little things, like Coney Island. I've gone to Coney Island unnumbered times when I lived back east, and I've certainly gone to sideshows at carnivals, and you know what you buy. Well, it was just as junky as that, not anything of value, on a dead body floating in space. Here it was still…that was the objective, the end of man's journey. He achieved his ambition and it was made of clay. So they got what they wanted, and that's the world in which we live.

So I tell you, I asked so seriously before I went to bed on Wednesday night, "Show me something to share with them. I have shared everything that you've given me. I have told them that you and I are one. I have told them that your son is my son, confirming the oneness of our own being. I have told them how I was born from above. I have told them how I came out of the grave, how I rose in that grave, the resurrected one. How my body was split in two from top to bottom and how like a fiery serpent I ascended into heaven. And how that dove the symbol of the Holy Spirit descended upon me and *remained* upon me as it smothered me with love. But is there something else that I can tell them? I'm closing Friday."

And these were my thoughts as I communed with self on what simpler way of telling them to assume the feeling of the wish fulfilled. Then came this most vivid…if I could only take you with me into that space craft and show you the *vividness* of that journey and the dead body in space a quarter of a million miles from earth. And I could almost reach out and touch it. Then the craft moved and then entered a tunnel, into this very wide tunnel, this dead mass. But in it I stepped off the craft with permission. I said, "May I step out?" and *then* I stepped out.

And that is what Blake meant: "If the spectator could enter into any one of these images in his Imagination, approaching them on the fiery chariot of his contemplative thought" (*Vis. of Last Jud.*). You've got to enter into, for unless I actually enter into a state, I don't know it. Unless I actually become one with what I am seeing and enter into what I see, I do not see it, not really. I see it as a spectator. But if I am not a spectator anymore and become a participant, I must step into the image to become a participant. So I'm a spectator approaching that object and then I step into it. I got permission, "May I step out from this craft?" and the man said to me yes. Then I stepped into a solid, three-dimensional world just like this, and saw all this junk for sale. All these little things they were going to bring back from their journey to show their friends what they had accomplished.

So a man accomplishes a huge fortune and the children can't wait for him to die to get it. The grandchildren why they can't wait…they would ease it quicker because they want it… don't let him live too long. But the old man doesn't realize that's what they are entertaining as thoughts. And that's the whole vast world. You think that's a cruel statement? Truth is cruel, it's a two-edged sword. Can't wait for you to depart this world, because you have what I could use. And what was it?—trinkets. It was called money. I can see the old cash register now, but everything was solidly real all around. And the return journey didn't take any craft. It was longer going by getting to the

662

The Return of Glory

moon than returning, because returning was simply waking. The minute I woke I could hardly believe I was on my bed in this city of Los Angeles. It was just as real as you are now to me. You are no more real and you are no more vividly real than all the things that I touched there.

So I share it with you. How do you do it? Unless you actually *become* and enter into the thing that you see, we do not see it, not really. We have to actually enter into it and it becomes perfectly real, and when you return you've accomplished it. Leave it alone, it will come into your world and you will have it. Share it with your friends and they'll all see it as I in the not distant future will see that as I saw it in the wee hours of Thursday morning...that is, because I went to bed on Wednesday night the wee hours would be Thursday morning. When I take this off, it's all mine. I can be here, there or elsewhere as quickly as I was here when I was standing on the moon. Open my eyes and here I am. It didn't take any four days as it takes our astronauts to do it. The time was only spent in getting into the mood, getting the mood and abandoning yourself *completely* to that state. As you abandon yourself to it, then you move toward your objective and you're doing the steering. You are steering yourself toward your objective whatever it is in your world.

So here, I have shared it with you and I do not know what else I could tell you. I have told you from my own experience that I have actually fulfilled scripture; and there is no purpose in this world for man other than the fulfillment of scripture. "I have come to fulfill scripture" he said (Luke22:37). And there is not a thing else for me to do, just to fulfill scripture. Then beginning with the psalms and the prophets and the Old Testament, that is the law of Moses, he interpreted to them all the things concerning himself (Luke24:27). He is the center of the entire Bible...but who is he? Say "I am"...that's Jesus. That's Jesus and there is no other Jesus. We are buried with him; I am crucified with him. And he rose...well then I must rise with him. So we rise individually. Well, when you say "I am," that's the Lord Jesus; and when you say Christ, that's the son bearing witness of his fatherhood or his Lordship...not until the Christ appears. So in the 11th chapter of the Book of Revelation: "And the kingdom of the earth has become the kingdom of the Lord *and* of his Christ"—the Father and the Son. The summary, the sum total of all the generations of men and their experiences fused into a single being and personified is the eternal youth David...and he is your Son. All you are called upon to do then is to tell it.

Then, like Luke in his first four verses of the gospels when he tells us: "Inasmuch as many have undertaken to compile a narrative of the things that have been accomplished among us, just as they were delivered to us by those who from the beginning were eyewitnesses and minister of the word, it seemed good to me also, having observed all things closely from the beginning, to write a very clear understanding of it for you, most honorable Theophilus, that you may know the truth whereof you've been informed" (Luke1:1). Now, Theophilus is simply...the word means "one who loves God." If you can honestly say tonight that you are seeking God more than you are wealth—but I mean seeking God the cause of wealth, the source of everything in the world—if that is truly what you are seeking, then you are Theophilus and he is writing this narrative for you. He's telling you what he has experienced. Man is only telling you what he and he alone in himself experienced; because no one saw these things happening in the soul of the one personified in scripture as Jesus. Jesus is the personification of all men in whom the seed erupted, in whom it came to flower and blossomed in fullness. So everyone in whom it blossoms is that being called Jesus. So in the end there is only God the Lord and the fruit of his journey which is called his Son. And his Son is personified as an eternal youth, David.

So take what I've given you this night concerning moving into the frame. Single out your objective. It's just like a moon, really. As far as you're concerned now it's dead, it doesn't exist. You need...and you name it. That's dead, isn't it? It doesn't live...just like the moon. But to you, if you realize it, it may be the most marvelous thing in the world. You think it will be. Well now, what would you feel like and what would you see, and how would you act, and what would you do if you realized it? Now *feel* yourself into that state...actually feel it. It's like getting off the bank and giving yourself to the current that you can't quite detect. It's not discernable from the bank. You're on the bed and you can't quite see it. You know where you are. Your friends are not there to congratulate you...and yet in your mind's eye they are congratulating you. Not a thing in this world will support what you are doing. Everything denies it; your senses deny it, your reason denies it, and yet here you are seeing it in your mind's eye. But unless we actually *give* ourselves to what we are seeing, we don't really see it at all. So you simply give yourself to what you are doing and you're on the current and it takes you off. Then with the current you go, holding your ship in position, and you get to the state where you step *into* it. As I asked permission, "May I step out?" and they said, 'Yes, you may step out." So I stepped *into* the *objective* and it became like this, three-dimensional, solidly real. Then I realized it was all trinkets anyway. No matter what the ambition was, it still was trinkets.

A man once controlled the whole vast world and he sets out...like a Hitler...and what was the end of Hitler's life but ashes. What was the end of Stalin's...they changed the streets and the rivers and the cities and all things named after him; and they will eventually take his name out of the encyclopedia in Russia as one who never lived. He'll become what is said in the Communist jargon a non-person. They'll take it out as though he was never born and that whole thing was a myth. They'll take it out because such a monster could not have existed in Russia, and they'll actually delete the entire history of the man, and it will be ash. Yet he wanted to leave forever these little stamps in the world. So they follow, one after the other, and what have they in the end?

Today, as I was coming out I turned on the radio and they gave some bulletin, some woman…and I vaguely recall the case of years ago. No one who is not my age will remember this horrible murder. Her name was Ruth Judd. They found her. They thought she had long died and suddenly they found her. Well, my son would never know—he's forty-five years old and he would never know of that. My daughter certainly would not know of it, she's twenty-seven. How would she know of that? And so, they're going to bring it up and make a monstrous thing out of it. Anyone my age will know it, but isn't that ash? The papers if they can't find something more horrible by tomorrow morning will give it a headline. So why feed our children who never even heard of the woman and what does it matter? She certainly by now must have paid her price to society if society demands something from her. To live with the conscience of having done it and the consciousness of it, hasn't she paid the price? But they'll still demand a pound of flesh.

So the whole thing turns to ash. Nevertheless, if you want it with all your heart, take what was shown to me Wednesday night as I came back from this journey. Get into your own space craft…not a craft…your space craft is simply what you construct in your mind's eye, a scene implying the fulfillment of your dream, and *feel* yourself into it. You're reaching your moon, for the moon seems to be the limit of a man's ambition to reach what is, at the moment, your present ambition. That's your moon. Feel yourself right into it until you can step into it and it becomes three-dimensional. So you can talk with them and they congratulate you on your good fortune. You are thrilled because you have achieved what you want in this world of Caesar, and you are thrilled with it. Then return to your body in the twinkle of an eye…having touched the last hand, given it a fleshly tone, and accept his congratulations, and listen to his voice and accept the sound of his voice. Make everything you are doing *real*. Having made it real, open your eyes and in the twinkle of an eye you are back. But you did it! And you can't reverse it. As you're told in scripture, you gave it the right of birth, you gave it your blessing. It was your Jacob, your subjective state. Faith is simply the subjective appropriation of the objective hope. You hope to realize so-and-so. You must first appropriate it subjectively. So the subjective appropriation of the objective hope is faith. And without faith, it is impossible to please him.

So we please who?—the Lord. Who is the Lord?—I AM. He is the creator of the world; he does everything in the world. And who else is he? He is the Father. Well, if he's a father, then he must have a child. Yes, he has a child. He has an eternal youth and his name is David the beloved: "This is my beloved Son, with whom I am well pleased" (2Pet.1:17). You will find him only at the very end; you will not find him before. But take my word for it, you will find him. Because not one child born of woman can fail: God is in him and God is playing the part. There is no such thing as a lost soul in this world. Everyone *is* redeemed. If one understood the Christian faith wisely, one would know that the Christian gospel if told as it ought to be told is "humanity *is* redeemed"...not "going to be," *is*! You're simply waiting your turn to be called...when that which is already in you is fertilized. Then it is germinated, and then moves into development, and all the story concerning Jesus Christ unfolds in you. Then you know who you are. You are the Lord Jesus and his Christ which is your son David.

Now let us go into the Silence.

*   *   *

Now are there any questions, please?

Q: I'd like to know how to overcome the feeling of time...of being rushed in time.
A: Well, if by time you mean the achieving of earthly desires, I do believe it is based upon one contingency; but if it means time concerning the discovery of the Father, I believe that is all fixed in the book as it were. That "The vision has its own appointed hour, it ripens, it will flower; if it be long then wait, for it is sure and it will not be late." That is in the 2nd chapter of the Book of Habakkuk (2:3). So that the vision of the Father when one realizes he himself is God the Father, that is predetermined and that's fixed. But our objectives in this world, I believe it's based upon our faith. A complete acceptance of the goal should bring it, well, instantaneously. It should. We can delay and dillydally—it's not important, it's not pressing. You would like it now but it's not important. So we don't really give our whole to the thing desired either for ourselves or for others. But I do believe the *intensity* of imagining has much to do with the time interval on this level. But when it comes to the real objective in life—which is to fulfill scripture and discover God the Father as oneself—that is predetermined. You're told no one knows—no not even the son, only the Father—when he will awaken himself in you *as* you.

Q: Can one take an act of Imagination after it's reached a certain point toward fulfillment and reverse it and nullify it through revision?
A: Well, I teach that all the time. To revise what we know we've set in motion, what we know in our stupid moments that we did. Because I wouldn't want to revise something if I had not started it in some unlovely way…I'd let it go to harvest. But if I'm aware of the fact that I have been using my Imagination unlovingly on behalf of myself and others, well then, I should do something about it. We're told in Ecclesiastes, "Do not curse the king, no, not even in your dream, for a bird of the air will take the word and he will bring it back," (10:20), for it can't return void. No, not even in our sleep curse anyone. But we all have done it in our sleep and waking here is sleep, really, for we're unaware of who we are. And we set in motion unnumbered unlovely things in the world. We say to ourselves, as you're told in scripture, "But no one sees me, therefore, it doesn't really matter"…as though the omnipotent one and the omniscient one isn't present to see it. So we are told, "Be not deceived; God is not mocked, as a man sows, so shall he reap" (Gal.6:7). It's automatic. I can't expect to reap something other than what I have sown. You sow corn, you're going to get corn; sesame, you get sesame. I may be disappointed that I planted corn, maybe I want something else for a harvest, but I did plant corn. Well, the same thing is true of the things we are growing in this world. And it's all to educate us; this is a world of educated darkness. People are trying to change it into a heavenly spot. There is nothing in scripture to change this world into some beauty spot. It's a schoolroom and a schoolroom was never intended to be a home.

We're closing tonight. And if you're on the mailing list and if and when we are here you'll be notified. So until whenever we meet, thank you.

Good night.

IMAGINATION'S POWER

9/15/69

___(??) with the series. May I tell you, each night is complete in itself. And I want to tell you it will take between forty and forty-five minutes, that is followed by a short silence and then that is followed by questions and answers. But each night is complete in itself. There's no commitment... come when you feel like it. I hope I will see you often, but there is no commitment. Every night I try to complete the thought.

Tonight's subject is "Imagination's Power." I hope you will listen carefully. I hope I will get a nice response; that you will agree when I tell you that when I use the word Imagination, I mean God, I mean the Lord Jesus. To me they are interchangeable terms. Well, I can't stop every night to explain this is what I mean. I take it for granted that you will know when I use the word Imagination I might just as well use the word Lord, the word God. Now we are told, "Commit your work to the Lord and it will be established" (Prvb.16:3) and that anyone who believes what he says will come to pass it will be done for him. No restriction on the power of belief. It doesn't say that if you are good or that if you're evil...this is wide open whether you're kind or unkind. It's a principle. I will share the principle with you and hope you will use it wisely and lovingly, but I can't deny you the right to simply do it as you want to do it. You may be wicked in the doing, but it's entirely up to you. But this is the principle: "The eternal body of man is the Imagination and that is God himself" (Blake, *Laocoon*)...the eternal body spoken of in scripture is the Lord Jesus. That is the being of whom I speak night after night.

Now let me share with you in the beginning before we develop it what I mean by it, so you'll be fully aware of it. When my wife and I returned from San Francisco—we were there for a few weeks—and we checked in two suitcases. When we arrived in L. A., one was missing. We asked what must we do and they said to go to the Lost Department and register your complaint, so we did. They said to describe the bag and give us the contents which I did. Well, I couldn't remember all as my wife packed the bag, and so I told what I thought was there. Then they said to me that when it comes, if it does, we will send it over. Well, it didn't come...four days...we called several times, they called us several times, and it did not appear. At the end of the fourth day they said to us that it's lost and to put in a claim; itemize the contents and the value, what it would take to replace the contents of the suitcase. So my wife having packed it, she did it. Got the entire thing settled to be sent off to headquarters in San Diego.

Early on the fifth day I said now I've done all that Caesar has asked of me—"render unto Caesar the things that are Caesar's"—that's what Caesar demands. In my Imagination I saw the bag...not more clearly than you would now see the interior of your living room if you thought about it. Think of your living room. You don't see it as clearly as you see me or see your neighbor, but you can see it. You know exactly what it looks like. It was not clearer than that. It was a black and grey bag, a very big bag that my daughter gave me two or three years ago. When you go for a long trip it's heavily packed, and so it was a heavy bag. In my Imagination I lifted the bag and felt the weight of it. I could see it clearly just like this...not as clearly as this room, but I saw it clearly. Then I held it in my hands until I got the emotion of relief. For, of all the pleasures of the world relief is the most keenly felt.

You know it from experience. You expect a loved one and they're late, and then it's an hour, then it's two hours, and you know the relief that comes when you hear a familiar voice. I know a friend of mine when they saw a flame in the distance and all that they had put into their lovely home thought, "Well, certainly that is my home" and when they came to the point where it was *not*—all the other homes were burned to the ground—he broke down in tears. That was relief! So again I repeat of all the pleasures of the world relief is the most keenly felt.

Well, I felt the relief of possession. The contents, yes, I didn't want to go out and replace them, we loved everything in it...my wife's dresses, my ____(??) to replace them, things of that sort. But why replace them if you like what you have? And it would have taken at least $1,300 to replace the contents. Long before we could settle we would have to put out that sort of money. But I went to the one being that I trust implicitly. The world will call it by any other name. I call it my Imagination and I firmly believe that my Imagination is God. I believe he is the one character in scripture spoken of as the Lord Jesus Christ. To me there is no other. So I firmly believed in the reality of what I was doing.

The fifth day went by and no calls from the airport. On the sixth day when the mail was delivered, here came a letter. As I opened it...first of all, it was written in ink but printed so that no one could guess the script. When I opened the letter it simply said, "Your suitcase is in the locker. Sonny the bandit" and then he enclosed the key, #164. My wife called the airport and read the letter to the security officer. He said they'd get in touch right away after they investigated. Within a matter of moments he called back to say that they had no box no number 164, but they would get in touch with San Francisco because it was mailed in San Francisco. They called San Francisco and within an hour they called me back that the police had found it in #164, opened the suitcase, and it was ransacked...everything was just simply ransacked. But they were sealing it and flying it off to L.A. Would I come over with my wife a little after six and in the presence of the Police Department of L.A., not their security forces, examine the contents.

So we went over. It was simply a shambles...everything was turned inside out. Even a simple little thing like your handkerchiefs all were turned inside out. We bought two little presents for our daughter and a friend of hers. We went to Gump's and we asked them to please wrap them as gifts, beautifully wrapped. They were torn apart but the presents were there. Everything was in tact, not one thing was missing—our checkbook, every check was there—but it was just simply a mess. They apologized for the condition of the bag and then said, "What may we do?" I said, "Nothing. When we go on a trip that exceeds a few weeks, we invariably have everything cleaned when we come back. It's been our custom, and we'll do it as we've always done, for we would have done it anyway." Then he said, "Mr. Goddard, I'm awfully sorry, but when you and Mrs. Goddard travel the next time on our line, you are our guests, round-trip."

And so, we brought it back. Yes it was a mess. You may say, "Why did they take your bag when you teach this?" I cannot stop you from thinking what you want to think. If I'm a victim of your wickedness, well, I have to be the victim of your wickedness. But I must not forget my principle, that in spite of your wickedness I can turn to the Lord and he will retrieve that which seemingly is lost. I went to Caesar and did all that Caesar could do and they could not find it. The Police Department couldn't find it here, the Police Department in San Francisco couldn't find it. No one could find it and they considered it lost. I did not accept that and I simply assumed that I had it. To the best of my ability I simply felt the reality of that which my senses denied and my reason denied. Although they completely denied it, I still persisted in this and I committed my work to the Lord...the Lord being my own wonderful human Imagination. The reasoning being now I could do no more than I did and I left it that way. On the sixth day it came back in tact.

I'm asking you to accept the true being that is Jesus. Man's true identity is Jesus Christ, and Jesus Christ is a man's own wonderful human Imagination. There is no other Jesus Christ: man's true identity is Jesus Christ, and Jesus Christ is a man's own wonderful human Imagination. There is no other Jesus Christ. God became man that man may become God. You can do this for everything in this world. Do not accept anything because at the moment reason denies it.

Now this concept of Imagination raises a question. I have been asked would you say then that Imagination is sufficient for all things? If he is God and with God all things are possible, is Imagination sufficient for all things, or must I add a little reason just like the chef adds a little spice to make it more palatable? I say the answer to that question is this, "According to your faith be it unto you" (Mat.9:29). I cannot really add anything, but I can say, "According to your faith be it unto you." Do *you* believe it's adequate? Do you believe it's insufficient? If to your Imagination is insufficient, well then, to you it is insufficient. I can only tell you from my own experience you will never find another law and you will never find another God. Listen to the words, "I kill and I make alive; I wound and I heal; I the Lord do *all* these things and none can deliver out of my hand" (Deut.32:39). Now choose this day whom you will serve and Joshua said, "We choose to serve the Lord."

Then, Israel responded, "We choose the Lord." But Israel forgot the Lord, couldn't keep the *tense*...it seemed too much, for the Lord had revealed his name as I AM. The fundamental sin in the world is lack of faith in "I am he." "Unless you believe I am (is) he, you die in your sins" (Jn.8:24). You must firmly believe that the only Lord is I AM. I can sever this hand from the body; I can sever vital organs from my body—take out a lung, a kidney, do all these things—but I still am. Remove them, but I can't remove I am and be. I can't remove my Imagination. Where can I go in this world and not imagine? And can any man go any place where he hasn't first gone there in Imagination? No! I can't remove it, for I am Imagination. I do not observe Imagination as I do objects. I am the reality that is named Imagination.

So here, I can't get away from it. Therefore, God that is my Imagination is never so far off as even to be near, for nearness implies separation. When the world speaks of God, it's always man *and* God...they're separated. He speaks of Jesus...Jesus is the one talking about Jesus. But you cannot separate them, not the *real* God, not the *real* Lord, not the *real* Jesus. Therefore, these things happen as they happened to me. Why? I go out on a limb and teach others what I am now telling you. But I am not left apart as something different. I must day after day examine myself to see whether I am holding to my faith. It's not enough to tell *him* that I must hold to my faith. "Test yourself and see," said Paul, "Do you not realize that Jesus Christ is *in* you?—unless indeed you fail to meet the test!" (2Cor.13:5). So I must examine myself day after day.

So the bag is missing...and it's certainly missing. I have the ticket. What good is the ticket? Where are my clothes, my wife's clothes? And I need them. So to whom would I turn? I turn first to Caesar and Caesar demands things, it's part of the law, and I render unto him that which I must. But then when they all fail, I turn to the one that I pledged myself to serve. I pledged myself to serve the Lord and the Lord is my own wonderful human Imagination. There is no other Lord. And he brought it back. Yes, disheveled...so what! This night everything has been cleaned and laundered and hanging where it formerly was. It's in perfect order. And now, not that we wanted any little thing, but he did give us roundtrip tickets next time we travel. So that was a picture.

I say to everyone, you hear a friend's need. It may be the most horrible thing in the world judged by human appearances. Don't be disturbed. The very one who told you of the need, bring him before your mind's eye and see them as clearly as you can as you now think of a friend who is not here. Think of anyone who is not here. Well, you can see them clearly enough. Do you know what their voice sounds like? Listen to their voice and have that voice tell you what you wish it could tell you...and not what it did when the voice concerned about a friend's health or whatever you call it, no matter what the condition. You do *not* listen too carefully to what they complain, you simply reverse the entire thing and then you listen. Now listen to the words, "Whoever believes that what he says will come to pass, it shall be done for him." What a promise! Read it in the 11th chapter, the 23rd verse of the Book of Mark. Whoever believes that what he says will come to pass, it will be done for him! I can sit here or stand here and believe that I'm hearing a voice, and I can actually believe that what he told me—though reason at the moment would deny that he's physically present—but I can persuade myself it's true. Then I physically do nothing. Not a thing can I do beyond what I have done. I do nothing other than what I've done. That imaginal act of mine was God's act. That's how God acts. He brings things that are not seen into the world that they may be seen, and all the things that were made were made out of things that do not appear (Heb.11:3). No one saw what I imagined.

So, my Imagination and your Imagination are forever enveloping us, surrounding us, permeating us as our very being; and ever waiting for the act of faith where we cast ourselves upon Divine Imagination and then free ourselves from the bondage of the senses, from the bondage of mortality. For the mortal man did all that he could and the senses did all that they could but they're limited. Man is shut up in the limitation of his five senses; and yet housed within him the real being that he is is God, and there is no limit now. In this little world of mortality, what limit could you put upon God?

So I ask everyone here to test it, to try it. Don't say yes hurriedly...try it. Because we're creatures of habit it might take a little while for you to undo what has been done in you when you were taught the story of Jesus. For if you were taught it as I was taught it...I was taught it as one other than myself, that a man 2,000 years ago came into the world in a miraculous way, and then he died, he was killed, and then he was buried and then rose from the dead. I was taught that story, lovely story, and I believed it implicitly. My mother taught it to me and I would never question mother. It's a true story but infinitely greater than *that* story. Do you know who he is?—your own wonderful human Imagination. That is Jesus. This is the Christ of faith: one who comes into our world completely unknown, yet one who will in some ineffable mystery let man experience who he is. He has allowed me to experience who he is. And when he allowed me to experience who he is, I discovered I am he, for in the experience it was a first-person, singular, present-tense experience. I didn't see him coming from without as the world teaches; no, he rose from within *as* my very self.

And it's all there in the Bible. But man because he has been taught as I was taught looks at it and still can't see it. Listen to these words from Ephesians, "He is our peace, who has made us both one and has broken down the dividing wall of hostility...making in himself one new man in place of two, thus making peace" (Eph.2:14). Now you read it and you're inclined to go on, because the mind has been so trained you think a man is talking outside and now he's going to make peace with the Lord Jesus...something other than himself. Come back to it. *He* is our peace...he. That pronoun is emphatic. The word follows the verb. That's an expression of a central being: *he* is our peace.

Now the body of peace, as we see it here, is not a doctrine, it's not a philosophy, it's not some abstraction, but a person. You're a person, aren't you? Well, don't think your Imagination is some intangible force. It's a person...the *ideal* you, unseen by you, the one who came unknown. Now he's going to break down that wall of hostility and make of the two one new man. And when he breaks it down and they become one new man, then he rises. Not out there, he rises *as you* and you rise as the Lord Jesus Christ. No change of identity, no change of name. Is your name Peter? Then it's Peter. Is your name Neville? It's still Neville. No change whatsoever as to identity.

You're following an eternal pattern and the pattern is described in scripture as the life of Jesus Christ.

All things are possible to him so don't turn back to anyone in this world after you hear it. After you hear it, accept every challenge in the world, I don't care what the challenge is. So someone asks you this night the most impossible thing based upon reason, don't turn away and rationalize it. And don't send them away; accept the challenge in your own mind's eye as you hear it. Don't take any challenge concerning doubt, like turn this stone into bread. We don't do that...get behind me, you doubter. But what do you want? You don't want to turn this stone into bread, you want to challenge my right to say what I say and prove and disprove it. Well now, get behind me. I have no use for that. But what do you *want*? Is your mother ill? Are you unemployed and can't find a job? Are you up against it? Name it! Well then, I will get it...I'll hear *that*. But don't you come with any challenge to cause me to doubt, because I will not doubt the Lord. I made my choice: "Choose this day whom you will serve." I have chosen the Lord to serve, and the Lord is my own wonderful human Imagination.

I will admit my limitation while I'm in this world wearing a garment of flesh and blood. Yes, I am limited, very limited, subject to all the weaknesses, all the limitations of the flesh. But I know how to reach the true being that I am, my true identity, and he's not too far away—never so far as even to be near, for that would separate us, and therefore I would confess that he hasn't yet broken down the dividing wall of hostility between us and made of the two one new man. But he *has* made of the two one new man, for he rose in me as himself. And now don't ask me any more, I will yield, completely yield to what I have heard as though I witnessed it in the flesh. I expect confirmation from you who asked it of me in the not distant future. I don't care what others will say. I don't care what they're doing, I'm not interested. I only know that I've found the one that I can trust and he's not in the sky, he's not outside. He's not anything other than where I am at every moment of time, and he's my own wonderful human Imagination. That is God. His name to you is I AM, and you can't get away from it. That fundamental being is I AM.

You're told in scripture that only two things displease the Lord: the first one is the lack of faith in I am he, and the second is eating of the tree of knowledge of good and evil. He didn't make an evil man. The man or the woman or whoever they were who stole my suitcase, whatever the motive was I don't care. I don't know and I'm not searching for him. But he didn't make an evil man. He made good and evil a tree, a tree bearing fruit of good and evil, and these are *states*. You can't conceive of a state in the world that is not now in existence. So wickedness is in existence. And I could unwittingly fall into a state of wickedness, and then I animate that state, and I have to express a wicked man, for it takes a man to express the state whether it be good or evil. But he didn't make a good man and a bad man. Man is God, because man is all Imagination and Imagination is God and dwells in us and we in him. The eternal man is all Imagination and that is God.

It's not a good man or a bad man, but passing through states. Should I fall into a wicked state at my right hand will be something or two to express wickedness. And someone who has come to my meetings—why even speculate—who could have resented my interpretation of scripture because he believes that Jesus is something other than himself, and he could resent it to the point of feeling I'm going to get even with that man and then he acts. But the being to whom I turn knows everyone. He knows every being in the world. You know why? "Because all things by a law divine in one another's being mingle" (Blake). And so, he knows the one who did it and can instantly change the man's attitude toward the act, and have him put it back, and then scribble that little thing, and send it off. He need not have done it, he could have burned it or he could have destroyed the evidence, but he was compelled to do it.

Now, if I had not acted, it never would have returned. So we are the operant power; it doesn't work itself because we know who the Lord is. I have found him to be my Imagination, but that's not enough. I must day after day examine myself to see if I am holding to the faith. So do I really believe it to the point of acting upon it? For I am the operant power; it will not operate itself. So I must every day...no matter what happens...if I should have the most horrible dream at night concerning the most intimate love of mine, I must not say, "Why did it happen to me?" How often do you hear people who consider themselves kind and generous and sweet say, "Why would this happen to me?" as though they are completely apart from the vast world when they are all individuals. It could happen to everyone in this world...but anything. Only don't forget the Lord. Let it happen. He has the right to be wicked...he fell into the state of wickedness, and if I could be the victim of his wickedness, well, let it be. Only I must not *accept* it as final. I must now turn to the Lord and the Lord is my own wonderful human Imagination; and turning to him, completely abandon myself to the act and cast myself upon Divine Imagination. Then at that moment I am freed from the bonds of mortality. I am not going to call the station any more, I'm not going to write any more letters, I just let it be, and then it must come back! It *has* to come back.

So I ask everyone before you judge it try it. And when you do it and it works, you will find who you really are. In the end, you will find you will spend your days from morning to night proclaiming the kingdom of God.

And some who hear you will be convinced by your arguments, because you will use scripture, the laws of Moses, the prophets, and the writings. Then some having believed it will turn to the other side and they will disappear. They are fixed in their belief as to who God is and how he only likes the good people and he hates the bad people; and they have their concept of what is a bad person and what is a good person and they go through life that way. But you will discover in the end *all* things work for good with those who love the Lord (Rom.8:28). So everything will work for good.

First of all, you become strengthened in your faith when someone calls you and tells you that you missed something. And when they opened the plane and saw the show and they were hurt, I asked not one penny from them, didn't need their money. Yet undoubtedly they were insured, and if I sent them a bill for sixty dollars for cleaning, they willingly would have paid it. But I wouldn't have felt right, because I would have cleaned those things anyway whether they were disheveled or not. So I have to live with Neville, so I couldn't take their sixty bucks. But I did take two tickets from them.

However, this is the power of which I speak tonight. It's not in armies, no, it's not in any implement in the world. You don't do it while they use their implements…you do it all in your Imagination. And everyone in this world will work for you. If it takes a million people to bring what you have just done in your Imagination to pass, they'll take a million people and they'll do it. They'll do it not even knowing that they are doing it. All will work toward the fulfillment of what you have done in your Imagination. So you don't have to seek the army to do it, you don't have to seek out individual brains to have them do it, *you* simply do it and completely commit yourself.

So, faith is nothing more than the subjective appropriation of the objective hope. What do you hope for, the recovery of a friend? That's your hope? Well, now appropriate it subjectively. How would I go about appropriating that subjectively? Well, bring your friend before your face and have the friend tell you, "Why I've never felt better, never!" And you respond, "But really I don't think I've ever seen you look better. I've never seen you look better and stronger. You look so altogether lovely, so altogether wonderful." Well now, *believe* that, for whoever believes, what is said will come to pass. It will be done for you. Now, whatever has to be done…I'm not saying that she, he, they may not seek the help of some doctor. Whether he does or does not, it doesn't make any difference so I'm not concerned. I'm not saying they will or will not. I will not recommend him. I would just say, "All right, I've done it" and then suddenly the change will take place in them.

The Return of Glory

I had that report only this night. A friend of mine called me in tears about a week ago, and she couldn't even get out her request she was in such tears. So I said, "All right, ___(??) called me. I didn't know it…I don't go around seeking for these things, but I am here to help and I will help. Well, at that moment I simply did what I thought I had to do, which I wanted to and I reversed the entire conversation. Tonight she saw me. Yes, she's thin. What's wrong with being thin? "I'm thin but I feel fine." She's thin and she doesn't want to put on any more weight, and she said from that very moment on she felt so much better. She knows now after a whole week of not being able to eat now she can eat and it remains down. The food is down so she is actually building strength. Before that there were six weeks where she couldn't keep anything down.

And what did I do? I'm not a doctor and I know nothing of the human body, but nothing. But I do know the law. I do know the law is not out in space, I do know it's not in time; I know he's right here…I AM. I'm not saying that Neville is the Lord. I say "I am." Neville is a mask that I am wearing…but I am he. You can say the same thing. But now test it if you really believe it. It's easy to say I am he, but do you believe it? Can you actually believe that today you have what you want in this world? That your friends have what they want in this world? And then walk as though it were true. Because these precepts are to be taken literally: "Whatever you ask in prayer believe that you have received it, and you will" (Mark11:24). If you really believe that you've received it, well then, you'll walk as though it were true and then you aren't concerned.

And any doubt, "Get thee behind me, Satan." Well, Satan is only the personification of the *doubt* in man. There's no being called Satan. Everyone in the world can play the part of Satan. The pope can play the part of Satan tonight by challenging me to say what I'm saying without being ordained. He could challenge me, and in a certain manner if I were other than what I am he could fool me into believing that he holds the authority. Like the Queen of England trying to speak with authority, isn't that nonsense? What authority? Yet there are millions who believe she has it and yet she has no authority whatsoever, but they endow her with authority. And for those who know, it's laughable.

So, everyone in the world will try to dethrone you and move you from the being that you've found. Tell them to get behind you. You have made your choice and the choice is, I will serve the Lord and the Lord is my own wonderful human Imagination. There is no other Lord. May I tell you, you will not fail. So the answer to "Is this sufficient?" well, sufficient so far as I'm concerned, but if you think it's insufficient, well then, to you it's insufficient. But may I tell you, it is *not* insufficient. It's the power of the universe, the power that created and sustains the universe. It is your own wonderful human Imagination.

It seems madness, seems insane. Well, standing on the moon seemed insane not more than half a century ago. But someone imagined it a hundred-odd years ago, a Frenchman by the name of Jules Verne. He even wrote a book and he named it *Going to the Moon*. He named the people who would do it Americans…that they would have the mechanical know-how, the engineering know-how to do it. Well, they did. The Americans went first. A Frenchman saw it, but didn't have confidence in his own country to have the know-how to do it. The Americans went, and there they put the flag out, and they actually walked on the moon. You and I saw it. I saw it in San Francisco…you saw it wherever you were. I'm quite sure many of you said nothing could interest you more than one of our boys walking on the moon. You and I saw it…and so it happened. You can't conceive something that isn't possible. You can't conceive of it because why?—you are God. God became man that man may become God, and he's slowly breaking down that wall of hostility between two and making of two one. So, when he rises, you are he.

But how can I know I'm he? I didn't change my identity and I didn't change my name. Well, how do I know? He gave you a pattern: this is how God is born. He's born in this manner; he resurrects in this manner; he comes out of the tomb in this manner; he finds David who calls him Father in this manner. He gives you the entire pattern: he is the *pattern man*. So all of a sudden that pattern erupts within you and you experience everything said of Jesus Christ. Yet you still bear the same name, you bear the name of John or Peter or whatever it is that you bear, but the entire thing recorded in scripture concerning him you have experienced. So I say, Christ of faith comes to us as one unknown, yet one who is actually by some peculiar, wonderful mysterious way lets man experience who he is. When he experiences who he is, you'll know the words, "Yes I am he." For unless I believe I am he, I die in my sins (Jn.8:24). Believing prior to that experience…I couldn't quite bring myself to believe that I am he. The experience has convinced me that I am he…and there is no other Jesus.

So if any man will ever come to you saying, "Look, here he is" or "Look, there he is," don't believe him. Why? Because whenever he comes to you, you're like him. So if you look out there, no matter how close he resembles you, like a twin, he still isn't you. It can't be another. So if any man ever comes to you telling you, "'Look, here is the Christ!' or 'Look, there is the Christ!' do not believe him" (Mark 13:21). And then John answers why: "It does not yet appear what we shall be, but we know that when he appears we shall know him"— how?—"because we shall be like him" (1Jn.3:2), the

The Return of Glory

very image of him. Because, he rises in you *as* you and you are the Christ. There's only God in the world. There's not any room in the world for anyone but God and there's only God. Regardless of race, regardless of nationality, regardless of anything in the world, there's only God, nothing but God. Plays all the parts and in the end when the curtain comes down, here one being achieving this only, and you are he. It's the most wonderful play in four acts! It begins with the law of Moses, it moves into the prophets, then it moves into the writings, and then it comes into the gospel, the most heavenly play in four acts! The gospel is the good news of salvation.

Now let us go into the Silence.

*   *   *

Are there any questions, please?

Q: Would you go through the pattern a little more slowly?

A: The pattern? Well, the New Testament begins *not* as it is said with the birth...although it is written that way...not in the Book of John, in the Book of Luke and Matthew. Mark does not begin it with the birth and neither does John. But I'll tell you the pattern: the pattern begins with the resurrection. You resurrect within your own skull; that's where you're buried. God is buried in man and the burial ground is his skull, the skull of man. It's called Golgotha in scripture which means "skull." You will awaken one day to discover that you've been a long, long time asleep. Someone who placed you there must have thought you dead, because the minute you awaken within your skull you will know it to be a sepulcher. You know it's a skull, but you also know it's a tomb, it's a grave, it's a sepulcher, and you have a consuming desire to get out. You have an innate wisdom and you will push the base of your skull, and something will give, and you will squeeze your head out. You will come out like a child being born, but still you're an adult, and you'll come out inch by inch just as a child comes out of the womb. But instead of coming out of a womb from below, you come out of the grave from above. You are born now not of blood nor of the will of the flesh nor of the will of man, but of God (Jn.1:13). God is born!

On the heels of this birth, the symbolism of scripture with the child will now engulf you. You will look back at the body out of which you emerged to find it's there. An unearthly wind envelopes you...it is so powerful you think it's a hurricane and you are diverted just for a moment. You think the origin of the wind is coming from a certain direction. As you turn away for not more than three or four seconds you turn back and the body out of which you have just emerged vanishes. You don't see it removed, it's gone. But in its place will be seated three men; one at the head and two at the feet. They're equally disturbed about the wind. They can't see you because you're invisible. You are born of Spirit now and you're not flesh and blood. So no one can see you, but yet you cannot only see them, you can discern their thoughts.

One of them is most concerned. He rises and goes over toward the direction where he thinks the storm originates. He doesn't go more than a step or two when his attention is attracted by something on the floor. He looks down and he announces whose baby it is—it's the baby of the one who came out of his skull. In my case he said, "It's Neville's baby." The other two in the most incredulous voice ask, "How can Neville have a baby?" He doesn't argue the point. He lifts the evidence from the floor and puts it on the bed. It's a little babe wrapped in swaddling clothes. I took the babe up, lifted it up to my face and said, "How is my sweetheart?" It broke into the most heavenly smile. In this world of death man begins with a cry...a child is born and they spank him to get him to breathe and cry. When you're born into heaven, it's with a smile. All the difference in the world! It's the most heavenly smile into which this little infant breaks.

Then comes an interval of time 139 days in my case, where you come upon a scene and the David of biblical fame stands before you and you know that he's *your* son, and he calls you Father. You know you're his father and you know he's your son. Then, that wonderful scene as you're feasting upon the beauty of your son, a youth of about twelve or thirteen dissolves.

123 days later your body—and it can't be this body, because this body doesn't bear the marks—but it's my body and it was split from head to the base of the spine, from the top of the skull to the base, and separates about four or six inches. At the base of the spine is a pool of golden living liquid light, and as I looked at it I knew it was myself. Here I am a pool of living liquid light. I fuse with it, and then like a serpent I ascended into my skull—up the same place that was split—as told in scripture, "As Moses lifted up the serpent in the wilderness, so must the Son of man be lifted up" (Jn.3:14). He identifies the Son of man with himself and he is called Christ. So there's only that one being having all these experiences in the world.

Then 998 says later, completing the cycle of 1,260 days, your head opens and becomes translucent...there is no circumference. In this translucent, transparent head floats a dove, a lovely dove, about twenty feet above you. It hovers just as though it's floating, doesn't use its wings, just hovers, with its eyes lovingly placed on you. Then it begins to descend and you extend the hand, in my case my index finger. It lit on my finger, I brought it to my face and it smothered me with love. While it was actually drenching me with love, kissing me all over my hair, my neck and my face, a woman at my left said, "The birds avoid man, because man gives off the most offensive odor. But he so loves you he penetrated the ring of offense to demonstrate his love for you." And here is the Holy Spirit in bodily form as a dove (Luke 3:22).

So the entire pattern as it unfolds in scripture in the written form will unfold in every man in this world in good time. Each is called in his own time. So I was called ten years ago. This last 20th of July was quite an anniversary for me, for it was the day when we landed on the moon. That was my tenth anniversary, for ten years ago last July 20th it happened to me in San Francisco…the first one. Then in Beverly Hills the next two; and where I'm living the one with the transparent eternity.

That was a long question. We don't have many more moments… one here.

Q: Suppose you have an objective and you know the principle but you have some doubt whether or not the objective would be good for you, how do you deal with that?

A: If you have any doubt concerning the objective, go beyond it and actually feel that you made the wisest decision in the world. Go beyond it in time and reflect upon it as though it has worked out beautifully and I could not have made a wiser decision than that which has now come to pass. Go beyond it. The same being to whom you cast yourself and upon whom you cast yourself will ___(??) for you in actual experience. And you will know after the experience and upon reflection that it was the wisest you could ever have done. Maybe the rational mind never could have made it.

Q: Even though at the moment you are applying the principle there may be even fears that you are doing the wrong thing?

A: No…maybe I'm not quite following you…if I had an indecision concerning what I would like to have in this world and I repeated this thing, well now, I'll come back. Suppose now I really wanted someone, wanted her terribly yet they are committed; or I thought I could not in my position do for them what I really ought to do if I want them in the capacity that I want. Well now, I'm at a crossroad. I want to do the loving thing and the right thing. So I go beyond my decision and will not say I want her in spite of all the hurts in the world, that I want her in spite of all who will be hurt. No, I forget that. I go beyond it and I take, say six months on the calendar and I bring it to mind, the

15th of September…or this is Christmas, the same year, and oh what a wonderful choice I've made! What a heavenly decision! I could not have done it rationally. I would have messed up the whole thing if I had given my full will, but now everything has unfolded like a flower and now I see it perfectly. You either will realize as you now want to realize it, or you will find you don't want it. I have had things in my life that I wanted with all my heart…I thought I did…and got it…to find within the day I got it I didn't want it and gave it away. That's a simple thing, but more complex things would be what I just said.

And now you be the judge. You can have anything in this world that you want. But if you want the one terribly, really terribly, you only think of him or her or them, and you forget self. There's a saying, a true saying, "Loving, self-forgetting service to others is the shortest, the safest and the most joyful way to God." Not the result, but loving, self-forgetting service, so that you don't feel that you earned any merit for what you've done, there's no feeling of his seeing how good I am, how generous I am. No, none of these things cross your mind. No sense of sacrifice, just simply it's a loving, self-forgetting service. And you'll find, as we are told in scripture, "Seek ye first the kingdom of heaven and all these things will be added" (Luke 12:31). You'll find that imaginative living is seeking first the kingdom of heaven.

Good night.

THE DREAMER

9/19/69

Tonight's subject is about the Dreamer: "Behold this dreamer cometh" which you will read in the 37th chapter of Genesis (37:19). It's the story of Joseph, the one that his father loved the most. He made him a long robe with sleeves. He was a dreamer, he could interpret dreams, and all of his dreams came true. So you ask the question, "Who is Joseph?" Joseph is a foreshadowing of Jesus Christ. Joseph is *your* true identity. The historical evidence for Christ the man is non-existent, yet he is the only reality. He is the true identity of very child born of woman. Just say quietly to yourself, "I am": that is Jesus Christ, that is the Lord, that is God, and that is Jehovah… just I am. And this whole vast world is a dream. One day you will discover we are the dream of God, and smoothly pass their pleasure in a long immortal dream. They brought it into being by dreaming it and they sustain it by the dream. You and I are inserted into the dream…we came down into the dream. We must dream the dream of life, and one day we will *awaken* from that dream of life. Then it will be said of us, "He hath awakened from the dream of life; 'tis we who lost in stormy visions keep with phantoms an unprofitable strife" (Shelley). We will continue the dream until we awaken, and when we awaken we are the dreamer, and the dreamer is God himself.

It's not an idle dream; it's for a divine purpose. It's to extend our power, our creative power. For if God could not extend his creative power it would be horrible. If he could not expand beyond what he is in every department of being, then there would be no living. God is *potentially* infinite, but expands and expands by coming into his dream, as you are here, as I am here. And everyone will awaken from the dream because there is only God. For, "Hear, O Israel: The Lord our God the Lord is one" (Deut.6:4)…there aren't two. You and I seem to be divided and there are billions in the world, and there will be billions; but in the end, it will be resolved and it will only be one. That one is the Lord God Jehovah who in scripture is Jesus Christ.

So in this story he could dream and dream correctly and interpret the dreams of others. Not every dream was a simple dream. There are certain dreams that are so simple it needs no interpretation, but most of our dreams are symbolic and few understand the language of symbolism. He understood it and he could take a dream like his brothers' dreams of the sheaths and tell them what it meant. Then he had a dream of the sun and the moon and eleven stars bowing down to him. When his father Jacob heard it, Jacob said, "What? Your father, your mother and your brothers will bow down to you?" He didn't criticize him, but he kept these things in his heart and he pondered them.

Now here, Joseph's name was changed...Moses called him Joshua. He took the name of Joseph and simply changed it into Joshua. For the word Joshua is the Hebraic form of the Anglicized word Jesus. It means the same thing as Jehovah: "Jehovah saves." So here, the dreamer is going to become the savior, because he's going to awaken from the dream and tell his brothers what this whole vast world is all about and that it is nothing more then a dream. Here you think this is real and tonight when I sleep, oh, maybe perchance I'll have a dream, and maybe I'll remember it. That's the dream, but surely this is reality. Well, if to dream is to dwell in unreality not *knowing* it is such, what is the life of many but an uninterrupted dream? What is it? Until you have certain experiences, you will question my sanity, but may I tell you, you're going to have these experiences and then you will know that this which seems to be so consistent and so all together real is no less a dream than the dream of the night.

You say this is consistent ...it doesn't simply jump around like the dream of the night. If you could see the mind of a man in the morning as he reads the morning's paper. Starts the first page, all violence, that gets the reader— an air crash, a war, a holdup, a murder, an embezzlement—all these on the first page. Then you go through...sometimes a beautiful wedding, and they describe a wedding and who was there, how much money he has, how much money she has. Turn the pages over and then come the deaths, all the people who died. Then come the financial pages and those who are making money and those who are losing money, then the sports...through all these things in one hour. And if you could see the mind of the one who is reading it and he's lost in what he's reading, you would see the out-picturing of all that he's thinking as he reads, isn't that disjointed? They go from the first page which is always violence to the lovely page concerning weddings and all the beautiful brides and those who attended; and then who is living with whom; the columnists depending on what paper you read; and then the ten or twelve individual opinions of single men writing columns. So they write columns and a hundred papers depending upon their success, and maybe 600 will carry their columns. And here, one man's opinion…and millions reading it and lost in all the things that he's describing. He's just as false as anyone else, but he's dreaming, too.

So how do I know it's a dream? I know from experience. I know that God laid himself down within me to sleep and as he slept he dreamed a dream…he dreamed that he's I. And when he woke he *was* I. But how do *I* know that I am he? I knew it the day that his only begotten son David called me Father (Ps.2:7). For when his only begotten son—as told us in scripture and this is simply the play, the plan—and I looked into his eyes and knew—no one told me, I *knew*—he is my son. He knew that I am his Father. When he called me Father, I knew that I was the dreamer of the entire picture, and the dreamer was God. But while I remained clothed in a garment of blood and flesh, I must abide by the restrictions and the limitations of this flesh yet remembering that it is a dream, and therefore *if* I know it is a dream, I can change the dream. If it's reality, I can't change it. But if it's a dream and *I am* the *reality* I can change it relative to myself…if I am the dreamer. Well, I know I am the dreamer and so I *can* suggest a change of the dream and produce corresponding changes in the outer world, which is the dream. For, I can change the dream *if* I know it's a dream.

This I do know as he told me in the depth of my own being, "I laid myself down within you to sleep, and as I slept I dreamed a dream…I dreamed that I am you." Yes, he dreamed that he is I. And he awoke within me…and when he woke he was I. Then a few months later he revealed that mystery to me by bringing before me his son David, and David called me Father. I knew him. He wasn't simply a boy coming into my world and calling me Father with my knowledge not corresponding to it; there was innate wisdom. I knew exactly that he *was* my son, and he knew that I was his father. So here, God awakes within man. In every child in this world born of woman he will one day awake; and when he awakes he is the same God. There aren't two Gods; therefore, you and I are really one. So in the end, although we seem now to be billions in this world, in the end we are one being, one God. This was a pre-determined plan to expand the power, the creative power of God and the wisdom of God.

Here, a dear friend of mine (in the audience tonight) and I am so thrilled for him and for myself. For anyone who comes who has an experience similar to this thrills me beyond measure. You can't give me anything in this world concerning money or things that money could buy that compares to a letter that I got from him last Monday night. How could you put it into the terms of dollars and cents? He was in his own house, sitting in the living room watching TV, and he felt drowsy and he drowsed. But he knew he was drowsy and he knew that he would actually fall asleep. He allowed himself to go to sleep, but he remembered that he was watching TV. Instantly he finds himself behind the wheel of his car, he's driving his car, and his wife is at his side. He had a sense of fear, a sense of impending disaster like an accident, and she grabbed the wheel. He knew it was a dream and he was awake in his dream…a dream just like this. You can be awake right in the dream, because *this* is a dream and you are awake in this dream. So he became awake in that dream.

He finally succeeded in getting her away from the wheel. He came toward what seemed to be a pile-up, a great accident. He remembered who he was and he proclaimed inwardly "I am." At that moment he not only remembered where he was when the whole thing began but *who* he is. And as he woke, he woke back seated in his chair and looking at the TV. Then he said, "You know, this is the first time that I fully became awake in a dream to know who I am and where I was." Then he thanked me profusely and said, "You know, I can't help feeling a little bit pleased with myself." Well, he should be. All these are simply the breaking of the little threads that bind us to the dream, which means he is on the verge of waking. He will awake from the dream.

I've done it unnumbered times…sit on a chair and suddenly find myself slipping into what I'm seeing, which reason tells me I should not see. Then I step into the thing that I'm seeing and the world closes behind me and here I am in a world as real as this, a world that is terrestrial. I'm as solid as I am now. I am talking to people and they're solid, they're real. Here I am in an entirely different world, a different section of time, and yet I knew exactly where I was when it started. But there's no way to get back by taking a road. You can't go back by a road, because what road would I take tonight if suddenly I stepped into the year 1900? Where would I come back to find myself here if I slipped into the year 2000? You see, *all* things are taking place *now*: "Eternity exists, and all things in eternity, independent of Creation which was an act of mercy" (Blake, *Vis. Last Judg.*).

So the whole thing's taking place now. You and I enter certain sections of the dream, and as we enter it we animate it, and the part becomes real to us. We only become aware of increasing portions of that which already is…everything is! I can slip back in time or forward in time, and the past has not ceased to be. It is taking place as it took place and still takes place when anyone enters that section of time. The year 3000 is, and is taking place when anyone enters it. It is all taking place, as the year 1969 finds us standing on the moon. It always has been so. The whole vast world *is* and we are in a dream, dreaming all these lovely dreams and horrible dreams. But we are placed on this little space called earth to learn to bear the beams of love. We could not where we were stand the beams of love, for God is love, infinite love. And to stand in the presence of infinite love…we came down and "we're put on earth a little space, to learn to bear the beams of love" (Blake, *Little Black Boy*). I know it from experience.

Here you enter almost like a wraith, like a specter, a shadow, and to the degree you learn to love you take on *substance*. Only as you love do you take on substance. I was given an instruction not long ago in this section of time…another section of time…and there I said to maybe a dozen men around me, "Here is this wraith, a shadow, a specter, a shadow of a man, but only a shadow. I could take it and do what I wanted with it as a little piece of cloth. Then I said to the wraith, 'Go, go and love without the help of anyone on earth, just go and love. To the degree that you love you will acquire substance, and only as you acquire substance can you really take part in the entire drama and then one day awake with life within yourself.

Now you'll only be an animated being, but not a life-giving spirit. One day you will acquire substance, which is love, and then you'll become one with life *in yourself.*" To complete that thought, which is the 3rd verse of the 1st chapter of John, "All things are made through him, and without him was not anything made." That which has been made was life to him: that is the creative act…so all things exist. But this creative act truly is an act of mercy…to bring us into these states where suddenly we take on a power and we become life-giving spirits and all return to the one being. Not *lost* in the one being, we *are* that being and still we retain our own identity. I have acquired identity and I will not in eternity lose it, but gain ever more and more individualization, as you will. Yet although we become individualized still we are one, one being. There's only God.

In San Francisco on the very last night this chap told me a story just before I took the platform, and I asked him to tell it to those who were present. This is the story. He said, "It was a hot summer's day this past summer and I stopped into a bar to get a nice cold beer." Only one seat seemed to be available, because the seat next to him that was not occupied had a lit cigarette in an ashtray and a hat on the stool, so he knew that someone had reserved it, someone had left. In a little while this one came back and took off the hat from the stool, and then as men do at a bar began to talk. He said to my friend, "You know the strangest thing and it haunts me…I was in the Korean War and I was wounded and I was shipped to Japan. I was in a hospital in Japan and here I am on a bed in the hospital. I know I'm an American soldier, I'm wounded, and I'm in Japan. Suddenly consciousness fades from the room, but I remember I am an American soldier, wounded, and recuperating in Japan.

"Suddenly I am in Europe. It's a different age. It's not this century, it's the last century, and I am dancing and the ladies are all dressed in huge hoop skirts. But I know I am a wounded American soldier in Japan and I was wounded in Korea. So I said to my dancing partner, 'You know, this is all a dream!' She became a little bit uneasy…she thought maybe I am unbalanced. And people began to get around us as I began to proclaim more and more, 'This is a dream. I am an American soldier living in the year'" and he mentioned the year 1950-something. Well, 1950-something hadn't yet arrived to these people. That certainly would put him down as an entirely mad person. That he is now alive living in the year 1950-something, how could it be? So as they began to crowd in upon him he thought, "Well now, this is time to awake" and so he awoke in Japan on the bed with the vivid memory of what had happened. He hasn't yet *completely* awakened, but it's loosening. He has awakened all right to an extent. Well, one day he will awaken from this dream that seems so consistent and every precept in scripture you are going to experience in what the world would call dream.

For instance, you've read in 1st Timothy, the 6th chapter, "The love of money is the root of all evil" (6:10). You'll find it in the epistle to the Hebrews, "Keep your life from the love of money." When I was a little boy in the island of Barbados, where I was born, we had a little jaunt every Sunday, and I'd go to my grandmother with my brothers. There were many of us… there were eight boys when I was…seven boys and one sister, and then two boys came later. So there were many in my family. But four of us would go down in a little gig and a huge big jack. That's the male donkey if you don't understand the language of the farm. That's a huge animal used to sire the horses for mules…they produce mules. But here we had this enormous jack and the four of us would go down. As we left, my grandmother would always give us a coin and she gave me a penny. A penny in those days, a British penny, was worth two cents. She gave two others a penny and she gave my oldest brother a threepence that was six cents. He had six cents; the others always had the same as I had, two pennies.

But as we got out of sight of my grandmother, this man always met us with a female donkey. So he would get on the back of this donkey and for my penny he would ride right in front of our jack and the jack would go wild chasing this female donkey. We just simply held on for our lives, for we knew that after about say three or four hundred yards in this enormous race that he's going to turn that little female off at a certain angle, almost a right angle, and our jack would follow it, and all would go over and break our necks. So at a certain point we all held the rein on this side, the four of us, to hold his mouth up so he couldn't get away. So the next morning my brother had a thruppence, the others had tuppence, and I had nothing…and

The Return of Glory

this went on for a few years. Mother found it out, and one day she said to me, "You know, Nev, you aren't going to have anything in this world; you give everything away." I knew it intuitively that the love of money was the root of all evil, I knew it.

Well here recently...to show you how these things come into scripture...I found myself in a waking dream just like this, a world just like this. But I knew where this body was, in what century it was, and the century was '69, and the body was in California. I knew exactly where I left it. Here I am with a huge pile of money. I held it together by sheer pressure. There were hundreds and hundreds of hundred dollar bills, fifty dollar bills, twenties, tens and fives, and just a small amount of ones, and I'm holding it together by sheer pressure, about that far. An awful lot of money! A woman passed by, about forty years of age, a round fat face, and she saw this money and she grabbed it. She pulled out maybe forty or fifty bills. I simply suddenly squeezed and held what was left...still an awful lot left. And in her eagerness to steal this about twenty of these pieces just simply fluttered away from her, and men and women passing by seeing the money fluttering all grabbed for it. She lost her temper and got as mad as the devil...they're stealing *her* money. She just stole mine and now it becomes hers...she's just stolen it. Well, isn't that life? So a man traces his ownership of property to the one who stole it. He inherited it after four, or five, or six generations and now he lives in great comfort, and he would be mad as a hatter if anyone took a yard of his property that was stolen by his forefather. And that is life!

So here, she took this money and as she found others taking it, she became incensed. But I kept on moving through...after all it's a dream. So where am I moving? The whole thing is objective just like this, but I am moving through a labyrinthine way of my own mind. For where else would I find it save in my own consciousness: I am objectifying what I am encountering all within me. So, the whole vast world, "Tho' it appears without it is within, in my Imagination, of which this world of mortality is but a shadow" (Blake, *Jer.*,Plt.71). So the whole thing is projected in my world on the screen of space; and it seems so real, and yet it's all within me. So finally I came to an opening, a huge big square, still holding the money and a man approached me. I knew exactly what he intended, he was just the thief of thieves. He offered me his taxi. I said, "No thank you, I don't live very far from here" but I wouldn't tell him my address. I wouldn't take his taxi because I knew exactly what he intended, to take it all from me and to kill me if necessary. Then the crowd began to come around me and they intended to take everything from me, including my life. I knew if I woke I would defeat their intention, but also mine. Because if I awoke now holding all this money they wouldn't get it, but neither would I. So at that very last

689

moment my decision was made. Here's a dilemma…I'm holding on to the money, but if I wake I'm not going to have the money…but neither will they. So I robbed them and myself, and came back to bed. And that is life.

So when a man piles it up here, he doesn't have the experience, possibly, of knowing that they're going to take it from him. But when he dies, doesn't he leave it behind? So he piles up one billion and he has all the glory while he lives. The papers tell you all about him, for he is assured of a large, large obituary because he has money. All the papers always mention those who leave a million, but if you leave a billion you're going to get three columns and your picture and all the nonsense about you. No one's going to tell how you stole it, no one—that's all hush-hush—because the others who are publicizing it for you stole theirs, too. Who wants to know about the other thief…so they all keep going. But I didn't know how I got all this money, I simply had it…an *enormous* amount of money…when you consider that much squeezed together like a vice. And here, the one who stole it from me lost her temper when others took the fluttering pieces and called it theirs because they found it in space, and she was claiming it to be hers. It was an obvious stealing from me.

Now that is life. So when that is inserted in the 13th chapter of Hebrews and the 6th chapter of 1st Timothy, you think, well now, that is some little thing that the writer to Timothy, who is Paul, and the unknown writer in what's called the epistle to the Hebrews, that they were simply summing up life itself and that the root of evil is simply the love of money. No, it's based upon vision. The whole thing is based upon vision. This vision of mine is part of the eternal structure of the universe, and you'll find yourself having a vision just like that only after you've lost all desire to pile it up. That it has no interest for you whatsoever. That you have to meet the needs of Caesar, yes pay rent, yes pay taxes, yes that's inevitable…buy food, buy clothing, all these must be met. But you don't need a billion to meet them, that's all… just don't need any billion to meet them. And those who are hungry beyond measure for more and more of the same shadows, all right, they are sound asleep. So sound asleep that if they came through the door now and heard even one minute of what I'm talking about, they'd say, "I've entered an insane institution, get me out of here!" Because I would tell them that their greed is simply a far deeper insanity, for they're sound asleep and believing their dreams to be reality.

So here is a dream. Joseph was the dreamer. And his father so loved him he made him a long, long coat with long sleeves. You wonder why add the sleeves? That's all part of scripture and one day you'll have the experience. You will be actually teaching the great mystery of God and telling those who will listen to you that *they* are God, God dreaming the dream and that one day they will awake from the dream to discover themselves the dreamer, and the dreamer is God. Someone will enter and then sever your sleeve and throw it away and expose your arm from here to the finger tips. Then you will turn back to the scriptures and you will read the Book of Isaiah, "Who has believed our report? To whom has the arm of the Lord been revealed?" (Is.53:1). For *your* arm has been revealed, and the arm means "the power of God, the wisdom of God" and Christ is defined in scripture as "The power of God and the wisdom of God" (1Cor.1:24). So you have been exposed to those who heard you. You are telling them who they are; and before their eyes it happens, who you are…that you are the power of God and the wisdom of God, and you are the dreamer of the dream. The whole vast world is but a dream. You know it and you're trying to convince others, and ask them to try it to prove it. If this is real, well then, you can't change it; but if it is a dream, you could modify it, you could change it. Well now, suppose things were…and you name it. You just simply suggest to yourself that things are as you would like them to be. Well, if it's a dream it should take objective fact and others will see it's real. But you know how it started, the origin of it was a dream, and although it seems to be objective and real don't be lost in it. You know it's still a dream, and like all dreams they will fade away.

Everything in this world comes into being, it waxes, it wanes, and then it vanishes, everything. Man comes, he waxes, he wanes, and he departs. A tree comes, even the Sequoias. So they may be 4,000, 5,000, 8,000 years old, but they will go, everything will go. The stars are melting away. So you take trillions of light years…but they are melting away. Everything is melting away. Because the whole thing is the dream of the gods: "Real are the dreams of gods and smoothly pass their pleasure in a long immortal dream" (Keats). So they brought it into being, they sustain it while this grand experiment is taking place, and we are the sons of God; collectively we form God. No child is born that is not a clothing for a son of God as told us in the 32nd chapter of the Book of Deuteronomy: "He has put bounds to the people according to the number of the sons of God" (32:8). No child is born…how could he be born…he couldn't breathe were it not for the entrance of God into him. So "God himself enters death's door, the human skull, and lays down in the grave with man in his vision of eternity, until he awakes and sees the linen clothes lying there that the females had woven for him and the gate of his Father's house" (Blake, *Milton*, Plt.32:40).

So when I entered this little thing that my mother, a female, wove for me, God himself entered with me. Well, what was his name? Mother called me Neville, but what was *his* name?—I am. And then she began to tell me that I must say that *I am* Neville. At first I was only Neville, but then *I am*

Neville, and finally it became one, they coalesced, and he made of two one new being (Eph.2:14). Then one day he awoke within me and *I am* he. Then to prove that I am he, he gave me his Word called the Bible and in the 2nd Psalm it is recorded: "The Lord said to David, 'Thou art my son, today I have begotten thee'" (2:7). Then David, the eternal youth appeared before me and called me Father, and then I knew I am he. But I'm restrained by the body that I wear, limited and weak by it, until that last moment when I take it off and the world calls me dead. So they will call me dead and that's when I really rise in the true sense of the word, back to the one being out of which I came. "I came out from the Father and I came into the world; again I am leaving the world and returning to the Father" (Jn.16:28). And in the end there is only God the Father.

So if you know this, what does it matter what the world does? They're dreaming a horrible dream, and some a noble dream, but the dreamer is unblemished, untouched by his dream. To think that a being like a Stalin, who murdered millions, and a Hitler, who murdered millions, still, as a dreamer he remains untouched by the dream. All things in the end will work towards the awakening of God. So then we are told in the 44th Psalm, "Rouse thyself! Why sleepest thou, O Lord? Awake! Do not cast us off forever!" (44:23). So the appeal to awake is directed to God: "Rouse thyself! Why sleepest thou, O Lord? Awake!" Well, he's struggling to awake. And so when my friend Bill had that experience driving down, knowing that he was seated—at the same time he was driving down—in his own home watching the TV, that is a breaking of the threads that bind you. And it can't be long after these begin to break before he awakes. And how does he awake? He will awake within his own skull, for that's where the whole drama is taking place.

As you are told, when Joseph came they said, "Let us kill him and throw him into a pit." Then Judah, his brother, pleaded for his life and said, "No, he's our flesh and blood. Do not let his blood be upon us; let us sell him into slavery. Here is a caravan coming on the way to Egypt, and they're carrying three items, gum, incense and myrrh, taking them into Egypt." So they agreed instead of killing him that they would simply take him and strip him of his long robe and his sleeves, the under ___(??) which he wore, and throw him into the pit. So they did. As the caravan came by they sold him. And they bought him and took him into Egypt. Then he rose to the power of Pharaoh and it was he who saved civilization from starvation. So they threw him in, and when the brothers complained because they felt remorseful that they had done this, he said, "You meant evil against me; but God meant it for good" (Gen.50:20). So everything works for good with those who love the Lord. His name was changed from Joseph to Joshua, which means "Jesus." And here the whole thing's unfolding within us.

So they threw him into a pit. Now in the 40th Psalm, which is so often used in the New Testament concerning Jesus, in the 2nd verse, "Thou hast raised me from the pit, thou did not leave me in the miry bog. You took me from the miry bog and placed my feet upon a rock, and made my steps secure." The miry bog…the mire is defined in the dictionary as a "wet, spongy earth." Do you know of anything that more ___(??) represents the human brain, a wet, spongy earth? For man is called "the earth"…Adam means "the red earth." You took me out of it, raised me completely out of that miry bog and took me from the pit. The word "pit" means "the dungeon." So you threw me into a prison, a dungeon, and I was locked into that dungeon: it was my skull. One day you woke, woke within me, and when you woke within me, you and I were one. Then we came out of that pit, out of that miry bog, and then we were born from above.

So man must be born twice: once physically and again spiritually. He is born spiritually through the resurrection of Jesus Christ from the dead. Well, when Jesus Christ awakes, he awakes as the one who is born…*you* are Jesus Christ. There is no other Jesus Christ. So when you are raised from the dead, it's within yourself that you awaken to find your skull a tomb, a sepulcher, a grave. And you come out…then you are born, come out in the same manner as a child is born. So you are born from above through the resurrection of Jesus Christ. Well, you look around, there is no one else, and you are all alone. As you're told in that verse, and it was empty…when they threw him into the pit, the pit was empty. You are alone. So when you awaken in the pit, there's no one else, therefore, who are you but Jesus Christ. For, the whole story is about the dreamer and the dreamer is Jesus Christ. And then you come out, and all the story as told in the New Testament concerning Jesus Christ, how he was born and the little sign of the child, all surrounds you. Everything said there is true, but not as the world understands it. The world sees it as history and it isn't secular history. It's *divine* history.

So do not look upon this earth for any evidence of an historical Christ. You'll never find it. Bishop Pike went looking. He rose to the highest position in the Episcopal world and he didn't know it…a man rising to the highest position in our established church. The pope goes on his pilgrimage every year looking for these so-called holy places and they don't know it. Hundreds of millions of people turn to them as guides: they're the blind leaders of the blind. You'll never find it, because the historical evidence of Christ the man is non-existent. And yet he is the only reality, the true identity of every child born of woman. *You* are Jesus Christ. But while he sleeps, all right, he can have horrible dreams or he could have lovely dreams or a combination. But in the end, you will awake from it all and when you wake, *you* are Jesus Christ.

You have just a little while left to tell it, but to a small minority. There will *always* be a small minority, a remnant. You will tell it to those who are willing to be disillusioned and shake that little tapestry of the past and let all the false ideas fall. Then you go on, just a little shadow that walked across the earth; but in eternity you are God. You leave no trace behind you… what does it matter…what trace? Leave that for the shadows. So you walk by leaving not a thing behind you, but just in the mind of those who heard you, and hesitated long enough to listen and to believe. As they believed it took root, and then it grew within them, and then this wonderful story erupted in them. The whole thing unfolded within them and then they knew that *they* were Jesus Christ. And because there's only one Jesus Christ and only one Son, if God's Son calls me Father and the same Son calls you Father, and there's only one Father and one Son, even though we are individualized, are we not one? That is a fantastic mystery: how we, retaining our individuality, are one.

Now let us go into the Silence.

*   *   *

Now are there any questions, please?

Q: What is the symbology of the three objects that the caravan was taking into Egypt?
A: Nan, my dear, I can't tell you. But don't discount them…there were three. In my case, there were three men…the caravan has taken three. Three is a symbol of resurrection. The actual objects like myrrh, frankincense, they are not in themselves important, but the number three is important. For on the third day the earth rose up out of the deep. On the third day he rose from the grave. Not three days as we measure time, but three is significant in the sense it is significant of resurrection. So they were taking the resurrection into Egypt. But what the actual things called myrrh and gum and frankincense, I wouldn't know. I really haven't studied it. But the three…in my own case three men were present at my birth from above, as we are told in the Book of Luke, "And three appeared." So the story is true, it's everlastingly true, and it will come with such shocking suddenness. Don't think it's going to come tonight, tomorrow night, or now, but when it comes it's with such complete unexpectedness. It's an awful shock to find that *you* are the being that you were led to believe existed in time and space 2,000 years ago, that Jesus Christ is contemporary and cannot be put into one little pocket in time.

Q: (inaudible)

A: The substance would be life is in God: "As the Father has life in himself, so he has granted the Son also to have life in *himself*" (Jn. 5:26). So the shadow would have no reality. It could be moved by your mind and made to do all kinds of things that the shadows do here. And then suddenly, by love, they take on substance, and then they become beings with life-giving power, life in themselves.

Q: You said there were two births and unless man had the birth from above he is reinserted each time in another dimension in time. Does he die in each one of those? So there are a number of deaths and two births?

A: Two births. But the death is not to the one who seemingly dies; it's only to those who observe his departure. If I drop now, to you I've died but to myself I have not. Therefore, a man who has not been born from above departs this world, or any section of time, and is *instantly* restored to life in the dream. So that he isn't born again; he's restored. All things are restored; nothing passes away, because the gods restore it all by the seed of contemplative thought. The tree we cut down and burn it and all things are cut down. The little lamb is slain by the knife, but by the seed of contemplative thought the lamb reappears in the world. And so nothing disappears *permanently*...a temporary disappearance. But the one who disappeared and is called dead, to itself it hasn't died.

So, there's a physical birth and then there's a spiritual birth. The physical birth, well, we all know that, and we are born physically by the actions of powers not our own. We are born spiritually by the action of powers beyond our own. Theologians have argued over this spiritual ...what part does God play and what part does man play? As far as I'm concerned the initiation is all God's. In my own case, I slept that night as I had the previous fifty-odd years of my life, and then this sudden vibration in my head to awaken me from a dream. For, I was dreaming all along and I didn't know I was dreaming. I was in my skull all these years, and I didn't know I was buried in my skull. Hadn't the slightest idea that was the tomb in which God was buried; that God is buried in the skull of every man in this world and that's the only Golgotha in the world. So let us stop looking for Golgotha in the Near East...you'll never find it. They think they're going to find it in the Near East and they build this holy sepulcher and they build this holy church and they build this holy thing—that is big business. They've done it through the centuries and they've made fortunes out of the gullibility of people by misrepresenting the eternal story.

Q: Neville, is there a fourth dimensional world in dream, too?

A: My dear, I'm not a mathematician so I really don't know what they mean by fourth dimension. I see three dimensions here and as far as I am concerned in the world of dream it's a three-dimensional world. Time may seem different, but the duration is the same. In a dream, what would take here centuries and centuries I experienced—but in the actual appearance and the experience of it it *seemed* centuries—in just a matter of moments. So time varies; nevertheless, the experience is the same.

Q: (inaudible)

A: My dear, that question was answered in this manner in the Bible, "Eyes have not seen, nor ears heard, nor has it entered into the heart of man, the things already prepared for those who love the Lord" (1Cor.2:9, KJV). Because, if I answered you I would have to use the images of a three-dimensional world, a world that you and I know, a world that we experience, and yet it could not possibly describe that world. It's a *new* age, a *new* world. This is one age and that is another age, and you couldn't possibly describe it. Even in this world it would be difficult for people living in a certain environment to understand a man that's trying to explain the concept of higher mathematics. If I sat in the presence of Einstein and asked him a simple question, to explain to me what he meant by energy is equal to mass multiplied by the square of the velocity of light, he would answer me and say, well, "That's exactly what I mean." But I don't understand it. He'd say, "That's exactly what I mean, Neville." Well, if he tried to tear it apart and show me all the little pieces, I still wouldn't follow him, because I am not qualified to follow him in higher mathematics. And that is true of almost anything in this world.

So if the mind has to be prepared, well, if that's an entirely new man that enters that world, then that new man has new faculties, new powers, new everything. He's a *new* man. The *fundamental* issue of scripture is metamorphosis. How are you going to explain to the caterpillar the delight of the butterfly? Can't do it! The caterpillar could not understand what it is to move in an entirely different element like air. He clings to the leaf, clings to the branch, and he couldn't understand if you told him that there is an element that is lighter than all these and you move with swiftness of the wing. He'd call you a liar. So to try to explain a new world where a new man lives, or even try to describe the new man…I can tell you the new man has a human face and it has a human voice and has human hands, but beyond that I could not go. These three I do know, but I wouldn't venture to describe the body.

Q: Here is an individual who is considered insane by the people on this plane, and is he really insane because he is living in a dream, in this wonderful Imagination, that he is what he appears to himself to be? It's been a blockage for me for quite a time.

A: Well now, sir, I'll tell you, many of them that we call insane are not at all, not at all, but they can't get through and they can't communicate their experiences. They call William Blake insane, and yet here a man who is insane…he never went to school, never saw the inside of a formal school in his entire life, and yet you ask anyone familiar with English literature, ask them to name the *six* greatest users of the tongue, no one understanding English literature could omit the name of William Blake…in six, not thousands or tens of thousands who murder the tongue every day. All day long we have all this complete misuse of words. He was very perfect in his use of words. We describe someone as disadvantaged because he's stupid…he couldn't enter college by taking the exam that is required and so he is "disadvantaged"…he must be ___(??). What a complete misuse of the word disadvantaged. Every word…you listen to the plugs on radio, plugs on TV they've taken every word in the English tongue and completely destroyed it. But here is one William Blake who never saw the inside of a school; and he thanked his father for not sending him to school to be flogged into memorizing the works of a fool.

Q: (inaudible)

A: What is the distinction between insane or not insane in this man's case? Well, he thought himself a banker on the outside; another one thinks himself and is recognized by the world as a banker. The one on the outside signs a check for a million dollars and it's honored. The one on the inside signs it for a penny and it bounces. Both go through the little gate called death, and the million dollar check will bounce after he is gone, and the penny will bounce the day before. So, both left behind them a world of shadows. But while we're living in this world of shadows, we call this section of it real, a certain section of it, and the other we call unreal. Yet so many of our great poets, all through the ages, who inflame the mind when we read them were called insane, how will you draw the line? You know that if we had…a few hundred years ago the men who gave us the things we now enjoy like electric lights and telephones and television and atom bombs, if they voiced their opinions 200 years ago in Salem they all would have been burned as witches. We used to burn people because they disagreed with our opinions. If any of them lived at that one section of time they all would have been burned.

So when I tell you I sat in a chair or I laid on my bed and suddenly I am seeing a world that I should not see, it's in conflict with what I ought to see, and consciousness follows vision, and I step into that world and I explore it, and the world is just as real as this...that's insane. But because I have so many other aspects of life, they call me sane and it over-balances and they don't put me away because I'm not violent. I haven't committed any violent acts. So if I forgive a friend for doing violence to me that also is considered an insane act, for the world is an eye for an eye, and a tooth for a tooth. But if I don't seek out the man who did violence to me and try to get even, well, that's just simply a stupid act. Therefore, when you balance them all together—I do pay my rent, I don't steal my food or steal my clothes, I pay all the things, all he bills are paid, so that makes me sane enough. But so many things I say from this platform would be accounted insane...but they balance. And they find more on what they call the sane side than the insane side, so they leave me alone.

So I can't tell you what is sane and what isn't sane, because so many things that the world calls insane I have experienced. Read the works of Blake. I have experienced all of Blake. Read the stories of the Bible, I've experienced them all. And all of sudden I know that they're not in *this* section of time or in *this* age. It doesn't belong in this age; it belongs in an entirely different age where the true drama is taking place. But we have to experience it here. People think that resurrection will come at the end of history; it doesn't come at the end of history, it comes *within* history. While I'm walking the earth, it suddenly possesses me and then I wake within myself to discover that the whole story is true...but not here. If I went out tonight and I told the whole outside world that you came here at your own risk, but if I told the outside world that there is no historical evidence for Christ the man, well, the average person, the orthodox person would slap me in the face.

They just had some luncheon for Mr. Graham down in Anaheim. 6,000 ladies attended and all thought themselves in a holy atmosphere. Now he's going to start a campaign. He needs a half-million dollars to put it on, and he has one outstanding subject to publicize...and the name of the subject is Billy Graham. He thinks he's publicizing Christ; he hasn't the slightest concept of the *mystery* of Christ. But tens of thousands and hundreds of thousands will listen to him and give him money to support the campaign of Billy Graham.

I said that in San Francisco and one lady rose and she was incensed beyond measure, oh so incensed. She said, "I think that was most unkind of you to mention that of Mr. Graham, ah, Dr. Graham." Every

The Return of Glory

time she said Dr. Graham I said, "You mean Billy?" He had one who came just before him and his name was Billy, too, but his name was Billy Sunday. He used to get down on the stage and wrestle with the devil, and beat the devil. Every Sunday he would beat him, but the next Sunday the devil was back. Take off his coat, take off his tie, and beat him and beat him and wrestle with him, and the crowds went wild… so Billy is getting the better of the devil. He did it! Well, this one is not acting that way but he's doing the same thing. Hasn't the slightest concept of this great mystery: Christ *in man* is the hope of glory. "Know ye not that Jesus Christ is *in* you" (Col.1:26, 27; 2Cor.13:5). Well, you say that to him, he will want to straighten up, "Where is he?" and start looking all over the stage for him. I tell you, Christ is your own wonderful human Imagination, believe it or not.

Good night.

WHO IS PAUL?

9/22/69

It is *in* us as persons that the nature of God is revealed. So tonight we ask a question, who is Paul? To see biblical characters as characters of history is to see truth tempered to the weakness of the human soul, which is unable ordinarily to stand the light of revelation.

So we ask now the question, who is Paul? For he is the one who said that no man taught him, that it came through a revelation of Jesus Christ. Paul's conversion was not changing religion. Paul never forsook Judaism. He interpreted through revelation the meaning of the Old Testament. He never quoted any book but the Old Testament. But was Paul a person, an individual being, say, as you are, as I am? Or is he, too, one of these eternal characters? That's the question that we're asking tonight. I will tell you *all* the characters of scripture, all of them, including Paul are these eternal states. When you reach the point where *you* are Paul, whether you be male or female you've reached the end, the very end.

A friend of mine wrote me—and she's a lady and very much a woman, she has two children and she's now expecting her third. She said, "In vision, the Bible was open to the New Testament and here we are discussing the New Testament, and the voice said to me...I can't recall the relevant things concerning the New Testament...but the voice said to me, '*You* are Paul.' I was so startled I woke repeating, 'I am Paul. I am Paul.' It seemed something that was too much for me, that I am Paul. Here I am a woman, a mother, now pregnant, and I am Paul. So I fell off asleep again and the dream continued. It seemed in the dream now that Paul had written the entire book and it was all about Paul, and he tells me I am Paul." So *who* is Paul?

When you are introduced to Christianity or Judaism, and then you discover the secret behind the words through revelation, no man tells you, it unfolds itself within you, and you discover that *you* are the Lord, *you* are Jesus Christ, and there is no other Jesus Christ. Then you are God the Father, and there is no other God the Father. As Paul said, "When it pleased God to reveal his Son in me, I conferred not with flesh and blood" (Gal.1:16). To whom would I turn to ask them what they think of my visions? They would think me insane, so I turn to no man. I simply abided with the vision and dwelt upon it. So his conversion was not changing religion; he never forsook Judaism. His one disappointment was he could not convince his own fellow religionists of the truth of what had happened to him, that it all took place within him. So Paul represents every individual in this world, male and female, who arrives at that point in time where you have your religion and suddenly you see it is not on the outside at all. That these characters do not exist as you and I exist in time and space. That these are eternal spiritual states and man the pilgrim is moving toward the climax, and the climax is Jesus Christ.

So the fundamental story of the Bible is *transformation*. It's a metamorphosis, a complete change of form like the grub worm into the butterfly, changing man as we understand man into Jesus Christ. When it happens in man, well, to whom can he turn to ask anyone to explain it to him? It happened and he can't deny it. I could no more deny that experience than I could deny that I am standing here now before you. This is a fact to me and it's a fact to you. And I could not deny the experience of Christ unfolding within me as myself. I am not unique and I am not alone. That must be the experience of every child born of woman. It will happen to everyone.

So when it happens in man, it's called Paul. First of all his name was Saul and the word Saul means "to inquire, to ask." He is seeking, seeking the answers to why am I here, what is life all about, what is its purpose, what is the plan, is there a God? That was Saul's mind and your mind if that's what you feel. Why are you here tonight? What am I seeking? What is life all about? Here, we had this wonderful day today that came to an end at sundown. Atonement! If you summed the whole thing up, in that great hymn, which is a song that they sing in all the great synagogues, it is "Awake, you sleepers, you forget eternity in the pursuit of the moment." That's what the hymn is. They call it a song and they sing it every year on Yom Kippur. Here, they're called upon to awake, awake from what— from the pursuit of the moment because we have forgotten eternity. We have forgotten that we are one with eternity…we *are* one!

So here, when Paul—we mean a state now, the eternal state—discovered the whole thing unfolding within him, he said, "From now on I regard no one from the human point of view; even though I once regarded Christ from the human point of view, I regard him thus no longer" (2:Cor.5:16). Like every Jew, Paul was looking for some *external* Messiah, one that would come who would be anointed king and save Israel from the enemy. Then he discovered it wasn't so at all...it is all within him. So now he regards none of the characters of scripture...for when Paul spoke of scripture he certainly was not speaking of the New Testament. There was no New Testament. Paul's letters are thirteen and they were written twenty years before the first gospel was written, which was the Book of Mark. So he could not have quoted Mark, Matthew, Luke or John. Whenever he quoted he quoted only the Old Testament. So there was no New Testament and there was no such thing as Christianity. So he never converted in the sense that we speak of conversion today—when a Catholic becomes a Protestant, or a Protestant a Catholic, or a Jew a Christian, or a Christian a Jew. Hasn't a thing to do with that. He takes what was revealed through the prophets, and then he understands the revelation, for the revelation took place *in* him. And the one spoken of, the Messiah that was to come was himself. "When it pleased God to reveal his Son *in* me...then I conferred not with flesh and blood" (Gal.1:16).

There's a poem by Browning, a lovely poem which he has titled *Saul*, and in this poem David is telling Saul of the coming of Messiah. David said to Saul, "O Saul, it shall be a face like my face that shall receive thee; a man like unto me thou shalt love and be loved by forever; a hand like this hand shall open the door to a *new* life for you!" Then he stands and he said, "See the Christ stand." David is standing before Saul who is demented, and he tells Saul, now see the Christ stand. When you find him he will have a face just like mine, and just like this that you see now, this man that you see, the youth, thou shalt be loved by him and you shall love him forever. The hand that is my hand shall open the gate of new life to you. Now look, this is the only Christ you will ever see...he will stand before you and you will know *who* you are! When David stands before you, you will know that you are the Lord God Jehovah. For, he said unto me, 'Thou art my Son, today I have begotten thee.'" (Ps.2:7). He said this to David, so when David stands before you and calls you Father, then you will know who you are, and you will be the Lord God Jehovah. That must be and will be the experience of every child born of woman. There is no other God, for when you say "I am," that's he.

But we are limited in this world of flesh and blood, and as long as I wear this body I am restricted, I am weak, I am limited. So when Paul spoke of sins, it wasn't as the world today calls sin, a little misdemeanor or even a great misdemeanor. To him sin was falling short of the glory of God. Now who is the glory of God? We are told in the Book of Hebrews, "He radiates the glory of God and is the express image of his person" (1:3). So if *you* are not radiating the glory of God and are not now the express image of his person, you are short of that glory. For that glory comes when you enter into the state called Paul. Well, when you enter into the state called Paul, he reveals his Son *in you* as your Son. As Paul said in his letter to the Galatians, "He has sent his Son into our hearts, crying 'Father!' (4:6). So the Son comes into my heart and calls me Father, and as it unfolds within me and I see him standing before me more vividly than I see you, more vividly than I see anyone in this world.

There he stands…and he's such a picture, this heavenly youth of about twelve or thirteen, and I know his name, and his name is David. He's not *a* David; he is *the* David of biblical fame, and I in the year 1959 and history records that he lived a thousand B.C.? No not as flesh and blood!

This is the drama, this is the unfolding picture, an eternal story in which man is involved; and the story as recorded in the Old Testament was not understood until it unfolded within one who said, "I am a child of Abraham of the tribe of Benjamin, a Pharisee of the Pharisees." He never for one moment forsook Judaism, but he tried to interpret Judaism to those who would listen, and they would not listen. They rejected his interpretation, for they were still looking—and they are still looking—for a physical external Messiah who will come and destroy their enemies and establish an ism in the world. And that is not the story at all. The story is eternally true *in* every being that walks this earth. One day you will find Christ and you aren't going to find him as another; you'll only find him within yourself. When you find him, he's not another; he is your very being. When you say "I am," that's he. All of the things said of him in the Bible you will experience, for these are only eternal spiritual states through which man moves as you are moving.

So this friend of mine, a young lady…for now she's expecting her third baby…very much a woman…and the voice said to her, "You are Paul." He told her correctly. It was the depth of her own soul speaking to herself, and she woke saying 'I am Paul?' "It seemed incredulous, it seemed impossible that I am Paul." And then, she said that "the voice said to me that he wrote the entire book and he wrote it all about himself. And that she wrote it?" She writes beautifully, but certainly she will admit she couldn't write scripture. She couldn't write these marvelous revelations we have in the Bible, and yet she is Paul who wrote it? Yes, I tell her that she is. She has been called, she has been chosen, and she has been elected. She is an incurrent eye-witness to the great truth. It will unfold forever and forever and she can't stop it. Not in eternity can she stop it, for she's been elected and she's been called.

So the Paul of the Bible is a state that everyone in this world will one day attain…you'll arrive at it. And when you arrive at it, you will know that

Browning was right, for it *was* David who stood before that state when you are in it. When you are in a state, you *are* the state. If this very moment I'm in the state of wealth, no matter what I touch it turns to gold. If I'm in a state of success, no matter what I touch it's successful. Take over a business and it's failing if I'm in the state of success it can't fail. They're only states—*I* am not successful, nor am *I* a failure. I am untouched by any state. But let me enter a state and that state has to be expressed by me in that state. Let me put myself into the state of health, wealth, being famous, being known, and no power in the world can stop me the occupant of that state from expressing it. When I enter into the state of Paul, no power can stop me from unfolding the story of Paul, and it is in that state that the Son appears to me and calls me Father. When it pleased God to reveal his Son *in* me, then the Son called me Father, and then I knew who I am (Gal.1:16). I also discovered who Messiah was.

So I tell you, "A face like my face, Saul, shall receive you. A man like unto me thou shalt love and be loved by forever, and a hand like this hand shall open the gate of new life to you. Now see the Christ stand." Look at me, said he, and you're looking right into the face of David, the anointed of the Lord, and he calls you Father, so now you know who you are. "For no one knows who the Father is except the Son and no one knows who the Son is except the Father" (Mat.11:27). So if you see the Son, he sets you free. Anyone who sees the Son is set free. So who are you…whose son are you? He said, "I am the son of Jesse" (1Sam.17:56)…and Jesse is "I am"—any form of the verb "to be"—I am. So he who says "I am" is the Father of that eternal youth who is David. He is set up forever and forever.

So when today's great song sung in the temples across the world, it is "Awake, O sleepers who forget eternity." Well, the word "eternity" is Olam, and Olam also means "the youth, the young man, and the *stripling*." Yes, it means "eternity" and it's translated "the world" in Ecclesiastes and also "eternity" (3:11). And so "Who are you? I am the son of Jesse." He's telling you that he who knows me knows eternity by revealing as the eternal one who is God the Father. He sets up the Son and the Son is David.

It's the most incredible story ever told to man. But what is religion but an incredible story? Hasn't a thing to do with this world; it's all about transformation, a metamorphosis. "Meta" means "to change" and "morph" is simply "form."—a radical change of form. For the being that you are destined to be could not function with this body of flesh and blood. Where you are going, into an entirely new age, a new world needs a new form, and that form is Spirit. Yet you have a human face, a human voice and human hands, but don't ask anyone beyond that to describe the form. It's something that's entirely different. Ezekiel tried to describe it and I wouldn't question

The Return of Glory

any word of the Bible, but you can't describe it. How can I describe a form that when it embraces me I fuse into it and become one with it without loss of identity? How can I describe such a body?

So here, when I stood in the presence of the risen Lord, what question did he ask me? My answer was based upon Paul. He asked me to name the greatest thing in the world, and when I answered I answered in the words of Paul, "Faith, hope and love, these three; but the greatest of these is love" (1Cor.13:13), and he embraced me. Why did I pick out the words of Paul to answer? But it was automatic, as though I happened to be divinely prompted what I ought to say, and I said it. At that moment he embraced me and we fused and became one. We haven't been divorced; there is no separation. But while I wear the body of flesh and blood I must be subject to all the weaknesses of the flesh. Everything subject to the flesh I have suffered, all the weaknesses, all the limitations until I take it off for the last time and become one with the body into which I have been fused. That one body is gathering all, one by one by one. In the end, not one will be lost. "There shall not be one lost in all my holy mountain" because it would be God lost. For you are God, but you don't know it yet. You will know it when you enter the state called Paul. When you enter that state, the revelations will unfold within you and you will say, as you're told it in the Bible, "I did not hear it from a man, it didn't come through men, it came through a revelation of Jesus Christ" (Gal.1:12). He unveils himself within me as my very being and there is no other.

So I say to her, your dream as you call it was true. Every word you told me in your letter is true. You have been called, you've been elected. And when men meet today to nominate saints, how stupid it is. Here you are pregnant, bringing in your third child, and the only saints in scripture are "the called, the elected, and the chosen" and not by men who go around and ask questions, did he or did she do so-and-so, and so we'll make him a saint. That's the most nonsensical thing in the world. How can any man make man a saint? When you are called, you are sainted; when you are elected, you are sainted; when you are chosen, you are sainted. No man looking at you could see you as a saint. You are still capable of losing your temper and being violent. So what! It means nothing. Be violent while you're here, be everything that you are, but you are already *redeemed* by reason of what you told me as your own personal experience.

So the characters of scripture are not historical characters. To see anyone including Jesus Christ as a character who walked this earth is to see truth tempered to the weakness of your own soul, and you cannot yet bear the strong light of revelation. So Jesus Christ is the perfect state into which all are moving. When you enter *that* state, you are God. And the whole thing

705

will unfold within you, and you will *know* that you're God. There's not a thing in this world but God. God became humanity so that humanity may become God. It is God playing all the parts, he is the actor. "God only acts and is in existing beings or men; so let us to him who only is give decision" (Blake, *Memorable Fancy,* Plt.15-17). Well, who is he?—my own wonderful human Imagination. And if all things are possible to God and he is my Imagination, then how do I act? I simply imagine that I am what I would like to be. What else do I do? Have faith…have faith in the reality of that imaginal act. I want to be…therefore that's my hope. My imaginal act is simply the subjective appropriation of that objective hope. I would like to be and I name it…that's my hope. My subjective appropriation of my hope… can I remain faithful to it? Well then, that is faith. And faith is the link between God's power and my need.

So I need this, that or the other, or I think I do. He doesn't question my right to want it. Can I believe it? All right, I believe it. Well now, wait, and let it happen. For this power has the wisdom to bring it to pass in my world. It knows everything. Christ is defined in the Bible as "the power and the wisdom of God" (1Cor.1:24). Can I do it? Well, if I do it and it works, and then I try it again and it works again, and I tell others to do it and they try it and it works, does it really matter what the world thinks? If the world thinks it's insane, it's not the first time they thought something was insane. They thought Einstein was insane, and many still thought him insane up until Hiroshima. Then the old gentleman came into his own and he wasn't insane anymore. But those who couldn't follow him thought him insane. That's always the case.

And those who cannot…like a friend of mine said to me last Saturday, "You know my wife doesn't come to you anymore, because she says when she hears you it's like this." Well, what is that? "Fuzzy," said he, "it's all fuzzy. Can't seem to put her teeth into it, can't seem to grasp anything you're talking about. It's all like this." Well, I said, all right. So I love her anyway… love her dearly. If she can't grasp it, perfectly all right. The day will come it will happen in her, and then she will understand that there is no other God and that God became man that man may become God. In becoming man he isn't pretending that he's man, he assumed all the weaknesses, all the limitations of man. He's not pretending. So when he became me he had to become all that I am, and I'm very weak and very limited. He has to take them all upon himself. And this is the only crucifixion in the world, when he became man—not nailed upon a little wooden tree or a little wooden crossbar—no, this body is the only cross that he ever wore. He became humanity and so he rises from the cross *in* me. He is buried in me; his only tomb is the human skull and there he remains dreaming. So, awake, you

The Return of Glory

sleepers! You forget eternity in the pursuit of the moment. The moment seems so real and so important in the pursuit of the moment and that is ____ (??). Then he is called, and he takes off the little garment and continues the journey.

But do no forget who you really are. You are the central being of the scripture, and the fundamental purpose of the scripture is simply metamorphosis: a complete radical transformation of man into God. God has a son for he's a father and he's God the Father. And if he's a father, he has a son. The sum total of humanity is personified in the being called David…the David of biblical fame: "A man after my own heart who will do all my will" (Acts.13:22). And David is *not* an historical character; he's an eternal state which only appears to you when you reach the last moment in the journey. He's not an historical character, yet the world thinks they have found the little tomb of David in the Near East. You will search in vain to find anything concerning these characters in the Bible. You'll never find them, because they are all within *you*. Every one is within you and you pass through these states.

When you reach the very end, you are the author of the Bible. Just imagine these letters came first and he called it "my gospel, my good news of salvation," and threatened anyone who would dare to change it. This came by revelation and it came before the gospels, came before Revelation and came before all the other books of the New Testament. So his thirteen letters came first by twenty years; all the others are based upon it. He's not quoting anything in the New Testament; they quote him. But who is he? Like the lady here tonight, her revelation, that's Paul.

Everyone here will one day enter the state known as Paul. But right now, you are a little demented…and so your name is Saul. "Inquiring, seeking, asking" that's what the word Saul means. You're looking and searching and asking "Why am I here? What is life all about?" This whole thing seems crazy, and so Saul is insane, as told us it the Book of Samuel and the Book of Kings. He was insane and tried to kill the very one who tried to reveal him to himself. But he could not be revealed until his name was changed from Saul to Paul. Then when he's turned over, he's turned into Paul. And you eventually will become the Paul of scripture, even though you are a woman. But in that day, you are above the organization of sex, as you are told in Paul's letters: "In Christ there is no bond, no free, no male, no female, no Jew, no Greek…all are one in Christ" (Gal.3:28). So you are completely above the organization of sex when man is redeemed. You're not male or female; you're man and man is God. God is man, as Blake so beautifully told it, "Thou art a man, God is no more. Thine own humanity learn to adore"

(*Everlasting Gospel.*, P.98). So man looks for something entirely different and you aren't going to find it.

So here tonight, "Set your hope fully upon this grace that is coming to you at the revelation of Jesus Christ" *within* yourself (1Pet.1:13). Others are looking for him to come on the outside. Right now they are building up a huge big campaign in Anaheim where tens, maybe hundreds of thousands in one week will hear him. All will be televised for the future, and across the nation millions will see him on television. But he will have it overflowing, these enormous crowds, and he is looking for an external Messiah. He hopes to be alive in this world when he comes…he wants to go to meet him and tell him what a wonderful work he's been doing for him…that he's been bringing all kinds of people to him, having decisions for Christ. He hasn't the foggiest idea of the *mystery* of Christ, not the foggiest idea. But don't tell that to one of the hundreds of thousands who are going to hear him, for they'll slap you and think they're serving Christ. They'll slap you and throw you out, really believing that they're serving Christ in that act. He will think it, too. But he doesn't know who Christ is: "Christ *in you* is the hope of glory" (Col.1:27) and "Do you not realize that Jesus Christ is in you?—unless of course you fail to meet the test" (1Cor.13:5).

Well, put him to the test tonight. All things are possible to him; put him to the test. How would I put him to the test? I'll name something that I would like that at the moment reason tells me I can't get it. All right, I believe you, so what would I do now? I would assume that I have it. And my assumption though false that is denied by my senses, denied by my reason if persisted in will harden into fact in a way that I do not know. I do not know the means that will be employed in bringing to pass my assumption. But I will assume that I am the man that I would like to be and knowing that *all* things are possible to him who assumed it. Who assumed it?—my Imagination. Well, who is your Imagination?—Jesus Christ. Well, I will assume it…and that's the Lord Jesus Christ and *all* things are possible to Christ. All that I have to do now is to produce the necessary link, and the link between the assumption and the fulfillment is my faith in that subjective state. So I will assume that it's *done*…and the assumption though false if persisted in will harden into fact. That is law.

So test it. If you test it and you prove it in the performance, does it really matter if it seems silly? It does seem irrational, but if it proves itself in the testing, what does it matter what others think about it? You go out and test it and walk through this door tonight in the assumption that you *are* the man, the woman that you would like to be. If your assumption hardens into reality and the world can see it, then what does it matter what others think?

The Return of Glory

We witness this thing every day where someone comes out with a fantastic dream like going to the moon, and then time goes on and man does go to the moon. Well, that would be the most impossible thing, and you know that only a few years ago as we measure time if you voiced it publicly, you could have been condemned and burned at the stake for such witchery and those who burned you would have thought they were doing God a favor.

Nothing is impossible to God, but nothing. So you name it, assume that you have it, walk in the assumption that you *have* it and see how it works. In a way that you do not know and you couldn't possibly devise it will simply unfold within your world. You'll be led across a bridge of incidence, a bridge of actual events leading up to the fulfillment of that state. And you could not consciously devise one of these little events that were necessary to bring you there. All you have to do, let the other fellow alone, and just simply go about your own wonderful business assuming the wish fulfilled. As you assume the feeling of the wish fulfilled and walk in that assumption, then it follows you; and instead of receding into the past that assumption is not going back into the past it's advancing into the future, and you go to fulfill it…you go right into it.

All these things of scripture are in the same manner: they were told but not understood. It took unnumbered centuries to come to the point where the time was fulfilled. You plant something…it doesn't grow then. You plant it and then you go through hell, for this world really is hell, and you go through all the conflicts of the world, and then comes the fullness of time, and then all that was foretold unfolds in you. It unfolds in such a way that your view of what ought to be is not what it is in retrospect. After it happens, you reflect upon what happened and realize you are the one of whom the Bible speaks. You are the Father of the one he called "my Son." And when the whole thing unfolds within *you*, you hardly believe it. Your background doesn't warrant it judged by human standards. Your intellectual background, your financial background, your social background, none of these things should warrant this thing that has happened to you. But God does not judge by appearances. She has a lovely social background—her forefathers came over on the Mayflower. Of course, if as many came as we now claim, the poor old Mayflower would have sunk before it left Europe. It couldn't possibly have set off to sea. But, nevertheless, it pleases them to feel that they're all descendants of those who came on the Mayflower. If you took them now…God doesn't see any of these things at all. He sees not as man sees: man sees the outward appearance and God sees the heart (1Sam.16:12).

So if you accept what I'm telling you tonight, *if* you can accept it, then you're on the way toward entering the state called Paul. He tried his best to persuade his own friends…for it all happened in the synagogue. Christianity is a Jewish fulfillment. It's only the fulfillment of Judaism, that's all. It's not a new religion...something as old as the state of Abraham. So it was in the synagogue that it started with Jews in whom it happened, who interpreted to Jews. And then they organized it and called it a separate religion. There could be no Christianity without Judaism, how could there? We couldn't possibly have a Christian faith without the Jewish faith, for Christianity *understood* is but the fulfillment of Judaism. Many a Christian wants to divorce the two books, and put the Old Testament aside. How stupid! There could be no New Testament unless there was first the Old Testament...and the New is only the *fulfillment* of the Old.

So here to everyone, you are destined to be told one night, as the lady was, "You are Paul." Chances are you'll be just as shocked as she was, and still remains shocked, because she looks into the mirror and sees a mother and a mother-to-be, a wife, with all the weaknesses of woman. Argues with her husband, maybe there's a shortage once in a while of a dollar, and she wonders why, in spite of the fact she knows she has been called and elected. But these weaknesses remain as long as we have these bodies to the very end. But in the end, when you take it off, you have a new body, an entirely new body. Those who have not reached the state of Paul will find themselves in a body like the one they have now, restored to life in a world that is like this, just like this. It may not be the year 1969...it could be the year 1000, could be the year 3000, because you jump into a section of time best suited for the work yet to be done in you. So don't think it's going to move chronologically from this year to that year.

When a man dies, he departs the world to find himself in a section of time best suited for the work yet to be done in him, and the work yet to be done may be best done in the year 500. But, may I tell you, it will be perfectly normal and natural. You will not feel a stranger in that, not at all. Everything is perfectly normal. If you had fallen in the year 3000, it would be perfectly normal, perfectly natural, and a body just like this one. For these bodies belong to this age. You will not find yourself because you're in the year 3000 with a different kind of body. No, just like this, where all the functions of the body you must perform yourself and you cannot command anyone no matter how powerful you are to perform them for you. Therefore, you are a slave of the body that you wear. This is slavery. To put on this body made me a slave...I have to eat and eliminate, and no one can eat for me and no one can eliminate for me. It makes me a slave, no matter how powerful I am in this world. I can have all the wealth in the world, but I can't command one person in the world to perform for me the normal, natural functions of my body. They must all be performed by me, and if they're not, then I depart this world.

The Return of Glory

And so, these are the bodies of the slave. We speak of slavery as being enslaved by some tyrant. Well, that's a form of slavery, but it's not comparable to wearing a body of flesh and blood. For the tyrant, too, has to perform the functions. And all the tyrants of the world are they not the perfect personification of Saul? Wasn't Hitler insane? Wasn't Stalin insane? Wasn't every tyrant in the world insane? The minute they have all this power they're really insane, and they think in these small, little bodies that they are something entirely different. They're all insane. They are Saul. Saul was mad, as we are told in the Bible, and he tried to destroy the very one who eventually would reveal him as God the Father. But he couldn't become the Father until he changed from Saul to Paul. Only when he became Paul would the drama unfold within him. It couldn't unfold as long as he was unbalanced as Saul. So don't think that you have to be the perfect specimen of a man judged by human standards. No, forget that. You'll be just as weak as you are, just as limited, but you will strive to know the truth concerning scripture. And one day, when you least expect it, it erupts within you and you're cast in the central role, the star role, and you are he. Everything said of Jesus Christ in the Bible unfolds within you, and you are Jesus Christ. There is no other Jesus Christ, none.

Now, that may shock you if you are here for the first time. But if there's any Christ other than he who was crucified within us and who rose and continues to rise in individuals, he is a false Christ. And false teachers talk about him. But the universal cosmic Christ became humanity...that is God...and rose and continues to rise in individuals, and that is the only Christ in the world. For, he will rise within you one day, and you will know who you are, and you will be the Lord Jesus Christ who is God the Father. If a father, there must be a child, and that child is David. David will call you Father and there will be no doubt in your mind as to who he is and who you are. The relationship was established before that the world was; only, we came down for a purpose and forgot who we are, and now we're only remembering. This is simply the returning of the memory of God, all within the individual.

Now let us go into the Silence.

*   *   *

Now are there any questions, please?

Q: If we go on to an earlier period of time, does that mean we're not developed?

A: No, my dear, no, no. If tonight one departs this world to find themselves in the year 200, it doesn't mean retrograding. We are moving towards and forever moving towards the fulfillment of scripture which culminates in the character called Jesus Christ, and you are he. So, all these sections are equally important. Because we are living in an age where man stood on the moon doesn't mean we are more advanced. Are we more advanced ethically when we can take six million innocents and burn them and people do nothing about it, but actually nothing? Put them right into furnaces alive...and that happened in our century, and we call this a wonderful century. Where is that an advance over love? 2,000 years ago Paul wrote, that is the state into which one entered, the 13th chapter of 1st Corinthians, and it's all abut love. He said love was the fulfilling of the law. 2,000 years later we not only kill millions of people willfully but take six million innocents, little children as well, and march them into furnaces and burn them up. That took 2,000 years for development? Just as violent today as we ever were!. It's all part of the play; and in the end, God comes out. Like the four boys...or the three boys and the fourth one had the image of the Son of God in the Book of Daniel (3:24-26). He put three into the furnace and the fourth one went in too. "I threw three in, but I see four," and the fourth was the redeeming one. So, the same furnaces...but in spite of these attempts to rub it out, he could not in eternity rub out the Jewish faith. It can't be done, not in eternity. It is not God's will.

Q: Where is Paul thought to have gotten his knowledge of what he was taught?

A: In scripture...he got it from no man as he said himself in the Book called Galatians. He said, "I did not receive it from a man, nor was I taught it. It came through a revelation of Jesus Christ" (1:12). In my own case, I was not taught any of these mysteries concerning Jesus Christ. I read the Bible, I was born and raised in a Christian atmosphere, but I never *knew* Christ until it happened in me. I heard it from my mother, heard it in Sunday school, heard it in school, but I certainly didn't hear the mystery until it happened in me. So I can say with that state called Paul, I never heard it from a man, I was never taught it by a man, it came through revelation. I don't know of one book I ever read, or any priest that has said that *David* is the Son of God who will stand before man one day and call him Father. That man that he calls Father will *know* he's the father of David and that David is his son; and that revelation will reveal him as God the Father. I never heard anyone say that, yet I know it's true...all by revelation. The Bible only supports it.

So Paul is the state in which these things happen and no man taught it to him, because the Bible is not taught that way. I've been on panels, hour panels, two-hour panels with many ministers and priests and rabbis…well, they all think I'm mad. One fella said to me, "If that is true, then I have 2,000 years of Christianity thrown into the ashcan." I said no, you have never *had* Christianity. You are a minister yes, but you do not *know* Christianity if you are going to lose it so quickly and throw it into the ashcan. I'm telling you what I know from experience, I wasn't taught it. You were taught yours. With you it's all theory, mine is all revelation. I am not speaking from theory, I'm not theorizing, I'm not speculating; I speak from experience. I experienced it and you have not experienced it, so you're talking what they told you in the seminary. So you went to a theological school and you were taught this…how to put the water on a little boy's head or a little girl's head and then call him by a name and you call that being united to Christ. Well, it's all nonsense.

When you are united to Christ, it's an actual event when the risen Lord embraces you, and he wears the human form divine which is love, only love, and you're embraced and you fuse with the body of love. You still don't know *how* it happened, you only know it happened. From then on you're one with the body that embraced you because you fused with it. No one on earth can see you wearing that body, but you're wearing that body. "There's only one body, only one Spirit, only one hope, only one Lord, only one faith, only one baptism, only one God and Father of us all" (Eph.4:4)…not two. Eventually…one man fell and only one man will rise. For when one man fell, it broke into multiple men. We are like the rock that became fragmented. Now all the parts will be gathered together into the one that fell. And by one came death, so by one shall come eternal life…same one, not another.

So Paul doesn't describe it. I wish he had described the experiences, but he only states them. He has not described them. I do not know of any description of it other than my chapter called *Resurrection*. I have told it as clearly as I possibly can, and in that chapter I have described the actual events as they took place in me. I didn't say, "This is the event." All these are my own, I related my own experiences; exactly how the resurrection took place, how the birth took place, how David was discovered, everything just as it happened to me. So I know of no other book that actually *describes* the events…they *state* the events. Because Paul…the central theme is crucifixion and resurrection, but he doesn't describe it. The entire thing is simply crucifixion and resurrection: "I preach Christ crucified," said he, "and risen from the dead." But he doesn't describe the process of rising from the dead. He doesn't describe the crucifixion. He calls it a tree rather than a wooden cross, but where is that tree? Blake told it beautifully: "The gods of the earth and the sea sought through Nature to find that tree, but their search was all in vain, there grows one in the human brain" (*Songs of Innocence*: The Human Abstract). That's the only tree upon which the cosmic Christ is crucified; and it is *there* that he rises, for it is *there* that he is crucified… right in the skull of man.

Well the time is up…thank you.

ALL ARE MEN IN ETERNITY

9/26/69

Blake said, "All are men in Eternity, rivers, mountains, cities, villages, all are human, and when you enter into their bosoms you enter into and walk in heavens and earths, as in your own bosom you walk in heavens and earths. And all that you behold, though it appears without, it is within, in your Imagination, of which this world of mortality is but a shadow" (*Jerusalem*, Plt.71). When you read it you may ask yourself, "What is he talking about?" Yet this is the language of the Bible. Biblical language evokes rather than describes. The Bible is talking of another world, of another man, of Jesus Christ, and unless you know something of the experience it tries to express, its language can hardly come alive.

So all the places in the Bible are human! Jerusalem becomes a woman descending out of the heaven adorned like a bride for her husband. Bethlehem becomes that woman out of which God comes. We read in the Book of Micah, the 5th chapter, "You, O Bethlehem, who are so little to be among the thousands of Judah, from you will come forth for me one who is to rule in Israel, from of old, from ancient times this one was. Therefore he will be given up until that time when she who is in travail will bring forth" (5:2). Then we read in the 63rd chapter of Isaiah: "O Lord, thou art our Father, our Redeemer, from of old is thy name" (63:16). From of old is one buried in man and that one is called "the Father." Here is the Ancient of Days buried in man. You and I are members of a body which shares in this eternal purposed end. There is an end to everything recorded in scripture and it's only man. It's all about you. But it's the *heavenly* man, the man in you that is called the Ancient of Days, the one that you and I speak of as the Lord Jesus Christ. He's buried in you. And you, like Bethlehem, are in labor, you are in travail, and you're bringing forth the Father. But you bring him forth *as yourself*, because everything has to be redeemed, and there's only one being, and it is God the Father. So, you're bringing forth out of your own being God the Father, for there's nothing but God the Father.

And the day will come you will know how true these words are concerning the mountains, the rivers, the cities and the villages. You will live in an imaginative world and everything is possible to you, but everything. When you awake, you are the Father. And to imagine is to have it objectively real, I don't care what it is...just to imagine. Your imaginal act becomes an objective fact. You create your entire world and it is forever and forever, as we are told verse after verse, chapter after chapter, throughout the Old Testament. But it is in a language that man finds difficult to understand for it *evokes*. So when you read these words, how do you really understand them? "Thou, Lord, art in the midst of us. Do not let us cease." You read it in the 14th chapter of Jeremiah (:9).

Well, what is the Lord in the midst of us? He tells us in that chapter not only that "Thou, Lord, are in the midst of us, but that thou hast given us thy name." Well, the name is I AM. Do not let us cease...do not take the name from me. How could anyone exist and the name I AM be taken from him? If you couldn't say "I am" then you would cease to be. You may not know who you are and what you are and where you are, but you still exist. You could suffer from total amnesia and not know where you are, who you are, what you are, but you can't stop knowing that you are...not as long as the faithfulness of God remains.

So he remains faithful to his pledge, and as long as he is faithful you can't cease to be, you simply are, and that is God. That, buried in the depth of your own soul has to come forward and when it comes forward you are God. There are plans by which you will know it. You don't boldly claim "I am God" without any assurance that you are...that would be silly. To walk the streets claiming "I am God" not having the plan unfold within you would be the height of insanity, and they'd put you away. But when you know it, you don't proclaim it to anyone; you simply know it and you live by it. You know it because he reveals himself in you. And the only way he could reveal himself in you *as you* is to have what scripture claims to be his Son...and when his Son stands before you and calls you Father, and there is no uncertainty within you as to the relationship between yourself and the one calling you Father, and then you know who you are. "I have found him" said the Lord, "and he said unto me, 'Thou art my Father, my God, and the Rock of my salvation!' (Ps.89:26). And when this lad stands before you, you know exactly who he is, and you know who you are, and you know the relationship between the two of you. Then and only then do you know that he the eternal God who is Father rose within you and you are he.

The Return of Glory

Now you tell it...not expecting a hundred percent acceptance, but you tell it, allowing everyone to respond to what you have said. They see your weaknesses, your limitations, and they know that you are weak, that you are limited, but you tell it anyway, and allow them to respond. Some will believe it and some will disbelieve it, but it doesn't really matter. You go your way telling it until the end of your allotted time now, and then you awake—not to continue the journey—you awake as God the Father. For the weaknesses are taken off with the discarding of this garment for the last time, this body of flesh and blood. You've told it to those who have accepted it, and they will prove it in the not distant future. Acceptance on their part will simply begin to stir within them he who is buried in all or they could not exist, for he is the I-am-ness of every child born of woman. And when he wakes he is the Ancient of Days.

Strangely enough, the story is so true. When you read, "What you, you know our father Abraham?" he said, "Before Abraham, was I am" and "Unless you believe I am (is) he, you die in your sins" (Jn.8:58; Jn.8:24). "But you are not yet fifty years old, and you know our father Abraham?" "Before Abraham, was I am." They can't see with mortal eyes the being that you really are. You know that you're the Ancient of Days whose origin is from of old. It has no beginning and it has no end. You *seem* to have begun in time but you didn't really, because he who buried himself in his creation has no beginning. He is the Melchizedek of scripture—no father, no mother, no genealogy, no beginning of days, no ending of days. And so here is eternity buried in his creation and waking in his creation. When he wakes in the creation, then you are he and *you* have no father, no mother, no beginning, and no end. But because he is a father you must have a son bearing witness of your fatherhood. And the son stands before you. That son is nothing more than the personification of the whole generations of humanity fused into one single lad. If you took all the generations of men and all of their experiences and fused it into one grand whole, that one grand whole then personified would be the lad David.

When you read the scripture, you'll find that his father was called Jesse. The word Jesse means "I am," that's all it means "I am." Then you are told that Jesse was advanced in age when David was a lad, as told you in the 17th chapter of 1st Samuel. Then the Lord said...and he quotes the words, "And the Lord said unto me," said David, 'Thou art my Son, today I have begotten thee'" (Ps.2:7). So here, the Lord's begotten, which is nothing more than the sum total of all the generations of humanity and all of their experiences fused into this one grand single whole; and that personified one grand single whole is the lad called David. David one day is going to call you Father, but not until you have gone through the furnaces. I have tried

717

them in the furnaces of experience—furnaces, mind you, all these furnaces of affliction—for my sake, for my own sake I do it, for how shall my name be profaned and my glory be given to another? (Is.48:10). He can't give his glory to another; there is only God. So then he buries himself in his creation and when he rises he's still God but enhanced beyond measure by reason of the experiment of becoming his own creation and rising in his creation as himself. And so, you and I are brought out individualized and yet the one being called God. You and I are members of a body which shares in this wonderful grand play the purposed end of all things...of the rivers, the mountains, the cities, the hills, everything...for it is all humanity. All are *men* in eternity.

So, have you ever sat in a chair or reclined on your bed with your eyes shut as in sleep and then see a scene of water? It's unlike the scene of water that you now see in your Imagination. Think of a scene of water, well, you see it in your mind's eye, but I mean to go beyond that and to see it as you would with your mortal eye, and it's just as real and you can put your mental hand into it, which is a hand that is real, and it's wet, you can drink it, you can feel it, and all of this is real. If you enter into that state, you will see it does become very personal. It's very personal, and all related to that state will come into being and you'll be living in a world as real as this. That is in store for you. This is your power tomorrow when everything is at your disposal, everything in this world, all based upon your own wonderful human Imagination, for *that* is God. God became as I am, taking upon himself all the weaknesses, all the limitations of the flesh so that I may become as he is. When he awakens within me I am he, and, therefore, I will live in my own wonderful imaginative world, and everything will be under my control, but everything. Everyone in my world will be within me, to be contacted at will. And no one can escape me when I rise within myself as the one who first became me.

So this is the story of scripture. We begin to test it while we are here, and we test it based upon our needs in this world. So we are up against it and I can't afford it, I don't have the time, I haven't the means, I haven't the know-how, I haven't...well, I could call a thousand reasons why I can't get it. Then suddenly I heard the story that my Imagination creates reality. It does? Yes! Well then, let me imagine. Is that enough, to imagine it? It should be enough, but it takes one element and that element is *faith*. Can I have faith enough to believe in the reality of my imaginal act? So my imaginal act is that I am the man that I want to be. I *firmly* believe it if I've had this experience. And then, all I did is to wait for it to appear within my world; for that imaginal act has its own appointed hour, and it will ripen, and it will flower. All I have to do is to wait, for it is sure and it will not be late (Hab.2:3).

The link between my imaginal act and its fulfillment is my faith. My faith is nothing more than the subjective appropriation of my objective hope. I hope that it is true. Well now, the link between my subjective imaginal act and the objective hope is faith, and so I walk as though it were true. That's all that I do. I make no effort to make it so; I *let* it be so, for I'm now acting as God, and God said, "*Let* there be light, let the sun appear, *let* the moon appear, let this appear." He lets it appear after the imaginal act sustained by faith, for without faith it is impossible to bring it to pass. Faith is "the assurance of things hoped for, the evidence of things not yet seen." So if I have the faith in the reality of my imaginal act then it *must* objectify itself within my world.

So to really understand scripture I must have some knowledge of the experiences that it tries to express, because they're not of this world. Hasn't a thing to do with this world. It's speaking of a *new* man and that new man is the one in you that I'm trying to appeal to that can believe in the reality of an imaginal act. To the outer you reality is what it can touch, what it can see, what it can hear…all these things based upon the evidence of its five senses and based upon reason. But I'm appealing to another man, a new man that is called in scripture Jesus Christ. Jesus Christ in you is your own wonderful human Imagination…that is Jesus Christ and he's one with the Lord. So he rises *in* man, he's buried in man…man is the grave in which he's buried. He will rise in man not as someone other than man but *as* man because he breaks down that wall of partition between the two. If I speak of "he," instantly I'm implying the existence of two; if I speak of "them," at least more than two. I can only speak of one when I say "I am." I can't speak of another and still say one. So Christ becomes one and becomes my very self.

And how do I know that I am he? Well, all that is recorded in scripture concerning him I have experienced. Having experienced it and I'm told in scripture it has only happened to Jesus Christ—that my rebirth is a result of the resurrection of Jesus Christ from the dead. Well, if I rose as it is said he rose from the same grave in which he was buried, and I didn't see another when I rose, and I didn't see another grave, just the one grave which was my own skull; and if I awoke within my skull and I didn't see another; and who was saying it?— I am. And what's his name?—I AM. Well, "I am" is not two; "I am" is one. *I* experienced it and it wasn't another. It was my own skull, and that's Golgotha, and I came out in the manner recorded that I would come out. It is said that Bethlehem must bring forth someone for me, one who is to be the ruler in Israel. And, the word Israel means "a man who rules *as* God." So here comes a man (I'm a man), and he comes out. Must I now be the one to rule *as God*? Well, try it! All things are possible to him… and it's an imaginative act. Well, imagine something that at the moment reason denies and your senses deny and see if it works. If it works, then did you not rule *as God*? For that's how God commands a thing to appear. That's all that you do.

Well then, who is he? His origin is from of old, from Ancient of Days. Well, who is this Ancient of Days? You're told in the Book of Daniel and there was one, the son of man…the son of man was brought and presented to the Ancient of Days. And they became one…the ancient of Days and the son of man (7:13). Well, the word translated "son of man" is the Aramaic for the term "I" or "one," that's all that it means. So when in scripture Jesus employs the words "son of man" to designate his function as the mediator between the world of man and the kingdom of God, it is only the Aramaic for the word "I" or the word "one." So the one called the son of man is one… an individual is brought into the presence of this Ancient of Days. Now when we read in the Book of John, "O Holy Father, I have made known unto them thy name, the name that thou gavest me. Now may we be kept in thy name, the very name that thou gavest me." Well, that name he tells you now is the name of the Father, "O Holy Father." But he now wants something else, "May the love with which thou hast loved me be in them and I in them" (17:26). Well, he wears the body of love, the Holy Father. So when you step into the presence of the Ancient of Days, he is God in the human form divine, and the human form divine is nothing but love, infinite love. When he incorporates you into himself by embracing you and you fuse with the one body, this *one* body, then *you* are the Ancient of Days.

You feel it…though no one with mortal eyes can see it. So when you tell the story, they will say to you, "You? Why you're not yet fifty." In the speaker's case they would say, "Why you're not yet seventy and you say you know Abraham?" If I answered "Before Abraham, was I am" (Jn.8:58), they would do the same thing and throw at me the facts of life which are called in scripture "stones." So they throw at you the facts: they have your birth certificate, your place of birth, your social, intellectual, and financial background. They have all these things catalogued, so they throw them at you…these are the stones. For you dare to claim that you are known by one who is our forefather who lived unnumbered centuries ago, and you tell us that he rejoiced that he was to see your day; and he saw it and was glad (Jn.8:56). But not only that, that you knew him? That you came before him? That doesn't make sense. But here is that which has no origin burying itself in that which has; and raising that which began in time to its own level which has no origin.

So here we find the story of Nebuchadnezzar, Melchizedek, all woven into one. Here is an insane king, Nebuchadnezzar, like man in this world, buried *within* him is that which is now Melchizedek, who has no father, who has no mother, no origin, no beginning in time, no ending in time. And it rises in that which begins in time, but it rises *as* that, and transforms time into eternity. So he brings into the world that which transforms the world that began in time and transforms it into eternity that has no beginning and no end…and this is the coming of the Father. So the finding of the Father is all that is worthwhile finding. What else is worth finding? So you'll find a million dollars. You find all the things in the world that you think so wonderful. All right, maybe they're wonderful for the moment, maybe you think you need them, but they will come and like everything in the world it wears out. Money wears out, everything wears out…even the very heavens are dissolving. But this cannot dissolve, and that is the Father who was before that the world was.

So when he rises in us, then we are God…even though for a little while you are still wearing the garment that is wearing out. It wears out and the world will call you dead. But after he rises in you, you depart this world forever and return to the Father. Then you'll understand the words: "I came out from the Father and I've come into the world; again I am leaving the world and I'm going to the Father" (Jn.16:28). And now the same one is saying, "Go to my brothers," therefore, we do not differ from this one in whom the whole thing took place. These stories took place in the soul of one and was seen and heard only by that one in whom they took place… recorded as told either as they heard it or in themselves it took place, and they're recording their own experience. So the gospel is only the record of experiences seen and heard in the soul of the one and by no one else. So he said, "Go and tell my brothers I am ascending unto my Father and to their Father, unto my God and to their God" (Jn.20:17). There is no other Father but the one Father, and no other God but the one God, and he is in us as our own wonderful Imagination. When you say "I am," that's he. There is no other God.

But you do not know it until scripture becomes alive and you fulfill scripture in yourself. "Scripture must be fulfilled in me" as you are told in scripture. When I come into the world that's when I begin to awaken in the world…that's coming into the world. I have come only for one purpose. Not to change the world.…I didn't come to put things right as the priesthoods would say. I didn't come to make this schoolroom into a home, to transform it into some ideal state; no, I leave it as a schoolroom where man is searching for his Father. They think they will never find their Father and "How long, vast and severe the anguish before they find their Father was long to tell"

(Blake, *Jer.*, Plt.73). Who knows when he will awaken in them? But he *will* awaken, and when he awakens they will see the reason behind it all, and they will leave it just as it is with no attempt to change it.

Let the world think they're going to change it. Every day politicians think they are going to change it, others tear it down, and it goes on, over and over. Every day some new one…tonight in Bolivia a new one rises and the crowds will get behind the new junta, and they will think, "Now here comes our savior." There are only nine such governments in South America tonight. But more and more are getting into the world, all as saviors. Each one turns out to have clay feet like Hitler and Stalin and all these people, but still people will fall for it morning, noon and night. You can't stop them, because you can't stop man dreaming, and man is all Imagination. Because you can't stop him from imagining—and imagining creates reality—he will simply turn everything upside down by his imagining.

You can put a stop tonight…as we are trying now to stop cigarettes. They tried to stop alcohol back in 1919 and they did until 1933. In their doing they brought into our social world billionaires who came right out of the gutter, and made billions that they could not declare for taxes. So then after fourteen years of the experiment they were left with cash, with unnumbered hundreds of millions of dollars that you couldn't touch. The few that they got and sent up for avoiding taxes were on some little pittance like Al Capone who made $125-130 million net a year through that period. So they got him on some small little infraction for a few thousand dollars. But what happened to the $130 million a year? It was all there… then funneled, with the same mentality, into legitimate businesses. And we found in our wonderful cabbage patch, or call it by any other name, all these worms. So the good-doers will do it over and over again, and they're going to start now with cigarettes. You'll find instead of receiving six million in taxes from the industry, we'll get *no* taxes and it will still be sold. The taxes that should come into the government, for they need it, will go into the hands of those who will still see that you who want a cigarette will get it. Man never learns a lesson. It goes over and over and over.

I lived in New York City in those days. I came in 1922 when it was three years old, and I remained there until '52 when I came out here. So I know New York City backwards, and I recall all these places. You can't stop it! Prohibition is stupid. You can educate a man out of a thing, but you can't prohibit. If I tell you now that I will give you the earth, providing you will not think of a monkey in the next twenty-four hours, I'll keep my prize. You can't earn the earth, you couldn't possibly do it. So, "thou shalt not" will always be broken. Every Commandment that is negative will be broken. So you are told in the 11th chapter of the Book of Romans, "And God has consigned all men to *disobedience* that he may have mercy upon all" (11:32 RSV). Now read it. What, the Lord God who is all love consigned men to disobedience? The very moment I gave you a Commandment that was negatively worded, I consigned you to disobedience. And so they are all… there's only one that is not and that is "Love thy father and mother." That's the only one of the Commandments that is not stated negatively; all the others are stated negatively "Thou shalt not." But every one has to be broken. Man thinks he is so holy and all these people who are now against this, that and the other. So you find someone tomorrow (who will die) and they'll say to what do you attribute your longevity?—"Smoking every day since I was eight." Of course, they won't read that, they'll turn it right over. And then, to what do you attribute yours, and she died at thirty—"I didn't smoke."

My mother never smoked in her life, died at sixty-one, a painful death. Never drank in her life. My father drank like a fish and died at eighty-five. He broke every law in the world concerning health. Didn't have any health code, never read anything concerning what he should eat in order to live. He just lived and ate what he wanted when he wanted it, and drank what he wanted when he wanted it, and at eighty-five, every faculty alive, he died from sheer exhaustion. So I have two examples before me. When they give me all this nonsense about you should eat this and do this and all, I don't go for it. I'll wear out this body as I wear out the suit of clothes, and one day I will wear it out, and I can't find another one to put on, and they'll call me dead.

But this time, I will not be restored to life as the world will be. I have departed life as the world knows it. I am one with the awakened Lord, for I've experienced all the things recorded in scripture concerning Jesus Christ. He said, "Did not David in the Spirit call Christ my lord?"—which simply means "my father," or, "O Lord, thou art my Father" (Mat.22:41)…and that is my name. So he called him Lord and he is giving you a secret. But the Bible evokes, it doesn't describe. So man tries to find it written like the columnists. Well, there are three kinds of writing: journalism, literature and scripture, and they differ. So if you want to study journalism, study it, it's marvelous. Study literature? All right, take the more difficult course and study literature. But you can't study scripture, not in that sense, for its *all* revelation and it's all vision. It's written differently and so everything in scripture becomes man—the rivers, the mountains, the cities, the villages, all, everything is man.

Take the 4th chapter of Daniel, and the watchers from above, and the watcher came down, and I heard the watcher say…I saw this in my vision, said Daniel…and the watcher said, "Cut down the tree, cut off its branches, strip its leaves, and scatter its fruit. But leave the stump…and bind it in iron and bronze." And now the tree becomes a person, "Water *him* with the dew of heaven, and take from him the mind of man and give him the mind of a beast, and let his habitation be among the beasts; until seven times pass over him and he learns that the Most High rules the kingdom of men, and gives it to whom he will; even the lowliest among men" (Dan.4:10-17). So let the tree be completely cut down.

Well, the tree grows in the human brain, that's the tree. In the human brain grows the tree of life, but it's been cut down to the root, and now out of that tree of life will come a shoot, comes right out of Jesse, and Jesse is I AM. That shoot that comes out will now come forth and is what the Father is waiting for: he's waiting for himself to come out of man. When he comes out of man he brings man with him; so that man is individualized forever and forever, but now he is God. He no longer is something that began in time and space; *that* has ceased to be with the arrival of the awakening of God in him. So God who created it all became it all, and rising in all rubs away time as we know it and rubs away space as we know it…for now he is the *only* reality.

Now let us go into the Silence.

*   *   *

JUDAS BETRAYS MESSIANIC SECRET

9/29/59

Tonight we will play the part of Judas. What was it that Judas betrayed? Judas betrayed the Messianic secret and the place where Jesus might be found…a most important role in the great *mystery* of God. "I have found in David the son of Jesse a man after my heart, who will do all my will. Of this man's posterity God has brought to Israel a Savior, Jesus, as he promised" (Acts13:22). If God brought to Israel a Savior as he promised, who do you think he brought? Now listen to these words from the 43rd chapter of Isaiah: "I, I am the Lord… and besides me there is no Savior" (43:11). So if God brought a Savior to humanity, he brought himself. Now he names himself as Jesus. The word Jesus simply means "I am." In all the great I AM statements—"I am the vine, I am the door, I am the shepherd, I am the bread"—he's declaring, "Unless you believe that I am (is) he, you die in your sins" (Jn.8:24). Man must believe that "I am" is the Lord. So he's brought to Israel—"the man who will rule *as* God"—a Savior, Jesus, as he promised.

Now, when you say "I am" you don't think that is Jesus, do you? You hear the word "Jesus" and you think of someone *outside* of yourself. But no, when your say "I am" that is Jesus, but sound asleep and buried in you. One day he will awaken, and when he awakens *within* you instead of being the son of God you will be God the Father. That is the transformation that is for you, for you ventured into this world of death. You and I came down into the world of death and took upon ourselves these garments that die. They get old and they wither and they die, and continue dying, and everything dies. Yet God is the conqueror. But he sends his sons into the world and when the sons conquer by the power of the Father, they return *as* the Father. So, "Beloved, we are now the sons of God; it does not yet appear what we shall be, but we know that when *he* appears we shall be like him, and see him as he is" (1Jn.3:2). It does not yet appear, for I'm a son of God. But how when *God* appears I will know him? I will know him because I will be just *like him*.

And now he reveals the great secret to the entire world, the great Messianic secret: when we use the word Jesus Christ, begin to separate it. As you're told in the very end of the Bible, "Come, Lord Jesus...and *his* Christ" (Rev.22:20; 11:15). Christ is the Messiah. Christ is the great Son who reveals *you* as God the Father...and that Son is *David*...whether you ever heard it before or not. I cannot resist the power that tells me to tell it and tell it and tell it, for man has completely forgotten the mystery, and they're telling all kinds of things that are not related to this mystery. They speak of Jesus as a little man who was born and who lived 2,000 years ago, when Jesus became humanity, which is God himself. You say "I am," well, that's God and that's Jesus. But he's God the Father and that's the great secret of the Christian faith: to reveal the fatherhood of God and the brotherhood of man. Well, the fatherhood of God is Jesus *in* man: "Do you not realize that Jesus"—yes *and* his Christ—"is in you?" (2Cor.13:5). And did not the Christ call *him* Father? Did not David call him the Lord?

This is a mystery. If David were not in me then I would never know that I am God the *Father*. One day he comes out of me and stands before me, and I know exactly who he is even before he calls me Father. I know the relationship: and only then do I know that I am God the Father. But I also know that everyone in the world will one day have the identical experience, and there is only one God, one Father; therefore, we all are the one Father. We are members of a body which shares in this wonderful *promised* end of all things—everything resolves itself into the one, and that one is God the Father.

So he reveals the Messianic secret and tells you where you might find him. Who? Find the Lord, the Lord Jesus. Well, where will you find him? You'll find him in heaven and "heaven is within you" (Luke17:21). "If anyone should say, 'Come, look, here he is or there he is, don't believe it" (Mat.24:23) for "the kingdom of heaven is within you" (Luke17:21). When you find it, the journey is over! And then your heart goes out to every being in the world that is your brother, we're all brothers. We aren't going to *become* the sons of God; we are *now* the sons of God. We are going to become, by God's wonderful gift, God himself. God is able to give himself to all of us, to each of us, as though there were no others in the world, just God and you...just God and I. Believe that and the most incredible story ever told man becomes possible. Then not only possible...by reason of the unfolding of the "pattern man" in us, who is God, who is Jesus, we *know*

The Return of Glory

that it is true. The whole thing unfolds within us and we know we are God the Father. And that is the story of the Bible.

The Old Testament is an adumbration, a foreshadowing; but the New does not spell it out completely…it still is a rough draft. When Paul writes us of his letters, the books are the thirteen letters of Paul, preceding by at least twenty years the first gospel chronologically speaking which is Mark. And yet no book spells it out…they don't spell it out completely. It's a rough draft…the whole thing is a rough draft. It is not a *complete* exposition of the great mystery. I have tried my best to tell it more clearly than I think it has ever been told before…just how it unfolds within us. How we actually come to the full realization of ourselves as God the Father, that there is no other God and there is no other being. That God actually sent his sons into this world. He chose us in himself before the foundation of the world, and we came to perform a certain job. Then we will say at the very end "And now Father, I have finished the work thou gavest me to do…now return unto me the glory that was mine, the glory that I had with thee before that the world was" (Jn.17:4,5). It was a glory, radiating the glory of God as sons; but when I return I return as God the Father. He actually *transforms* his sons into himself and gives *us* his own Son, whose son is God's Son, and he calls *us* Father. So we are God the Father. That is what we return to by reason of the adventure in the world of death, for this is a mystery of *life through death*.

So here, when I take the Bible in my hand and I read it, the thirty-nine books of the Old is a foreshadowing. Paul makes the statement, "Follow the pattern of the true words which you heard from me"…a *pattern* of the *true* words (2Tim.1:13). I take the thirty-nine books and there is a pattern in it. Not every word has significance, not every verse, not every chapter. It is all a wonderful story, but there's a pattern in it. I will follow the pattern of the true words, but Paul does not spell it out. He makes a statement, "When it pleased God to reveal his son *in me*, then I conferred not with flesh and blood" (Gal.1:16); but he does not spell out *how* God revealed his Son in him.

The first to use the word "Christ" was Paul…by twenty years if you take it chronologically. You first find the word in the Book of Matthew, but Matthew came twenty-odd years after Paul wrote his letters. So the word Christ is the word Messiah, which really means "contact," which really means "God has touched him." He's touched this son, and this son has now become God the Father. He touches one son after the other in his own good time.

He descends upon his son in bodily form as a *dove*, and when it remains upon that one on whom it descends that one has been touched, there is contact. That contact is now the gift of the Holy Spirit. God now gives himself to his son. And then the Son stands before him—not this one, but God's Son who he decreed as his Son, the one that represents the whole vast world of humanity, called David. David is the personification of all the generations of men and all of their experiences, fused into a single whole, and personified as an eternal youth. That is David. So when he stands before you and calls you Father, and God called him "my son," and he calls *you* Father, then you know who you are. Everyone is going to have that experience.

So *that* is the great secret that Judas betrayed. He betrayed the Messianic secret, and told *where* you might find Jesus...Jesus being God the Father. You'll find this in yourself, for he is there now and your breath is his life. You couldn't breathe were it not that Jesus was within you. He is within you and his being within you caused you to live. One day he will awake within you and his rising within you is the most glorious experience in the world. As he rises within you, you have been saved from this world and have been transformed into God the Father. That is the story of Christianity.

Don't look for Christ to come on the outside. I know hundreds of millions are waiting for him to come and change the world. This world is not going to be changed; it's the world of educative darkness. It's a schoolroom and you do not change a schoolroom into a home. *Heaven* is your home; this is a schoolroom and here we are. One day we remove ourselves by reason of this gift of the Father to us, and as he gives himself to me I awaken from the dream, awaken in the grave and come out. Everything said...now the pattern of true words...he said, "Follow the pattern"—what kind of pattern?—"the pattern I laid down for you. These are the true words that you heard from me"...and then he tries to spell it out. He spells it out in the thirty-nine books, quoting the books one after the other, but he doesn't quite completely expound it. He doesn't and no one does in scripture.

But as Blake said, "That which can be made explicit to the idiot isn't worth my care." So maybe they, too, felt the same way as Blake did. Why spell it out so that everyone by reading it could read an a-b-c. No, that which causes a man to struggle within himself will force him to make an effort, and maybe that is what is necessary, to search the scriptures and ask, Why? What? Where? When? Ask all these questions and then find out he is all within you; that God, actually, literally became humanity that humanity may become God. And, in becoming God the Father, you do not lose your individuality. You are not only a member of this wonderful body that shares in the purposed end of all things, you *are* the body. You are the Spirit animating the body. Yes, a member...and yet you are the *whole*. For in God there is no division; God is one and we are one. So all of us together... and not one will be lost. No matter what our fellows are telling us tonight about how you're sinning and you're going to be lost, it is *not* God's will that one be lost. If it is not God's will that one be lost then one cannot be lost. Why?—because God is *in* him. He couldn't say "I am." If he's a moron, he still knows that he *is*. He may not know who he is, where he is, what he is, but he cannot stop knowing that he is. That's God when he says "I am." That is he.

So here, in this wonderful unfolding picture, what courage one should take from the message of scripture! It's good news; it's not good advice. They're all giving good advice—try to be this, try to be that—all good advice. Let the world give good advice. The gospel means "good news," the good news of *salvation*. That God actually became his sons in the world and transforms his sons into himself, so they all rise as God the Father. Not all the sons came out as told us in the prodigal son story (Luke15:11-32). One remained at home and complained that he didn't have anything. He didn't know that he had *all*. You may have all in the world and if you don't know it you could die of starvation for the want of a dollar. Pass the bank that holds a billion dollars of yours and not knowing it you couldn't cash a check. You would simply die of starvation not knowing it. And the whole is yours when you become aware that you are God the Father. You too will say, "I and my Father are one" (Jn.10:30). I and my Father are one, and all mine are thine, and thine are mine." In the meanwhile, while you remain in the garment after the great resurrection, you teach it and help everyone that comes into your world.

And I can't tell you my thrill when I get letters from you quoting scripture. If you don't actually quote scripture, your letter is simply one hundred percent scripture. Now here is a letter from a young lady…she's still in school, she's majoring in music, and she wants to be a composer, that's her ambition. In her letter to me, which she gave me last Friday night, she said, "I have a very dear friend of mine, he's much older than I am and I'm very fond of hm. I wanted to give him something very, very special for his birthday, which was last September"…which was really this month but a couple of weeks ago. "I didn't know what to give him. I didn't think it had to be something material; it could be something that I said, something that I did of which he would be proud…or it could be material. I was dwelling upon what I could give him when I fell asleep. At two AM in the morning I woke with this vivid memory of what I had dreamt. I dreamed that I was sitting on my bed and in my room were my mother and father. Mother was in front of me and father to the left. My father spoke and said, 'Well, here are three records. You may keep two and give him the third, and he will so love it he will play it over and over. He will never tire of playing this record.' Then a sheet of music was given to me and the sheet of music was the sheet of music from which the record was made. I noticed that the composer's name was Elam.'" She spells it E-l-a-m. Then she said, "I noticed that the title of the composition was 'Christ.'" You could not in eternity grow tired of the mystery of Christ.

Now, the composer was Elam; it really was O-l-a-m. If you look it up, it is Ion Lamed Mem which means "something that is hidden, something kept out of sight" and it means "the lad, the youth, the *stripling*." It is translated "eternity": "I have put eternity into the minds of men yet so that man cannot find out what God has done until the very end" (Eccles.3:11). He put eternity…well, he put that eternal youth into the mind of man, which youth is his Son. It's the sum total of all the experiences of humanity fused into a single lad and personified as *David*. And so here, David was the author, the composer of the music. What was he composing? It was all about himself. It was Christ, for he is the Christ of scripture. The Lord is Jehovah; Jesus is the Lord, and that is God himself. Come, Lord Jesus and his Christ (and his Son). They are all *in* man. Separate the two: Christ is not a title as the world thinks; that is the Son. Jesus is the savior and there is only one savior. "I am the Lord your God, the Holy One of Israel, your savior, and besides me there is no savior" (Is.43:11). I, I am the Lord, and besides me there is no savior (Is.45:5). Read it in the 43rd and 45th chapters of Isaiah.

So here, this young lady, still in school studying music, desirous of being one day a great composer, and she found who *really* composed. She found his title of the composition and it was simply "Christ." You can't exhaust the subject of Christ, it is forever and forever. Man is forever misunderstanding it. Crowds and crowds will go to different ones in this world and they will tell you all about some little man who was crucified on a cross by Jews. Now let me quote you one simple statement in the Book of John, "You know not whom you worship; we know who we worship, for salvation is from the Jews" (Jn.4:22). Now, if you think a physical Jew no! An Israelite is not a descendant of Abraham after the flesh, but the *elect* of God of *any* race, any nation, of anyone in the world. That's the true Israelite. It's from the Jews… well, the Jews' real book is the Old Testament. You came into this world as the son of God for one purpose: to fulfill the *Old* Testament. "I have come to fulfill scripture," he said (Luke22:37). Only as scripture is fulfilled *in me* have I accomplished his work. And "This is life eternal, to know thee the only true God and Jesus Christ"—put a little "and" between it, Jesus and his Christ—"whom thou hast sent" (Jn.17:3). I'm only here to fulfill scripture.

Now, all the actions and they're all mystical actions, every event that I experience in my mystical experiences is foreshadowed, or seems to be foreshadowed by a word in the Old Testament, it is *predestined*. It's all there, all written through his servants the prophets. Now, it's not page after page. In fact, the chronological order of both Old and New is not truly the chronological order. Here, in the New we begin with Matthew...and Mark came before Matthew. The letters of Paul came before the four gospels. So it is not chronologically exact, but canonically, as our early fathers of the church arranged it...they placed it in that order. But that is not the true order of the unfolding of the picture anymore than in the Old Testament. So, as you read it, there is a certain *pattern*: "So follow the pattern of the true words which you heard from me." I have given you from my own experience what he is telling you. He's writing this letter to Timothy...the 2nd letter that he wrote to Timothy...and he's telling Timothy *not* to deviate from what he heard from him: *this* is the gospel, this is the good news of redemption, the good news of salvation, and don't deviate. But he doesn't spell it out.

Now, I've spelled it out to you. I've told you in the best way I can just as it happened to me, and I've given it to you actually chronologically. The resurrection comes first. The crucifixion comes in the very *beginning* of time. When I came out from the Father and came into the world I was crucified on this body...and so were you. We've been crucified on these bodies all through the journey. The crucifixion *begins* the journey. So Paul said, "I know only Christ and him crucified" (1Cor.2:2)...so it begins with the crucifixion. But the real drama of redemption begins with the resurrection. After the resurrection comes the birth. After the birth, comes the discovery of the fatherhood of God and the Son David who is the Christ. The words of David, "I will tell of the decree of the Lord, he said unto me, 'Thou art my son, today I have begotten thee'" (Ps.2:7).

Now comes the fulfillment of it: the Father is now trying to find him and he is lost in a maze. "I have found David and he has cried unto me, 'Thou art my Father, my God and the Rock of my salvation'" (Ps.89:20, 26). Who found him? The Lord found him. The Lord found his own Son, and then the Son revealed him as the Lord. At that moment he thought he was a little tiny man, a man walking in a world of death and he knew that death was inevitable. As he approached the inevitable end, he prepared for the inevitable and made his will to those he loved. If he had anything to leave, he left it to those he loved. And so, he knew he had to go and the whole vast world even those that he now loved would follow him and leave what he left them, if they still have it, to those not yet born. And he thought that was life. Then, all of a sudden he finds he is God the eternal Father. What a gift! That God actually gave himself to his son. God actually became man that man may become God!

One day you will know it by this betrayal of the great secret, the secret of Messiah. He not only tells you the secret but he tells you where you might find him. Where would you find him?—where the tree grows. You find him in the garden. "And the gods of the earth and sea sought through Nature to find this tree, but there search was all in vain, there grows one in the human brain" (Blake, *Songs of Experience, Human Abstract*). That's where the tree grows…there you are going to find him, right in the garden, and he is the Tree of Life itself. One day the whole drama unfolds within *you* the individual, and as it unfolds within you, you awake, and you are God the Father. You and I who were sons of God before we came down, as told so beautifully in the 82nd Psalm (:6), when we return we are God the Father, and yet we have not lost our individuality. We have *added* to God the Father and yet remain individualized. I can't tell you the joy, the ecstasy in store for all of us on our return to God the Father *as* God the Father. "I came out from the Father and I came into the world; again I am leaving the world and I'm going to the Father" (Jn.6:28). This time I'm going to the Father *as* the Father.

So God's *gift* to us is Christ, who is his Son that is David. Christ's gift is the Spirit of Truth…and the truth unfolds within us. As it unfolds within us, we know who he *really* is: "I have found in him a man after my own heart, who will do all my will" (Acts13:22). Now, listen to these words, "I have come to do the will of him who sent me." Here, God in man is not yet awake, so he's speaking, "I've come to do the will of him who sent me." He knows he has to do that will, for that's David's will, and that is God's will through *David*. He said, "My food is to do the will of him who sent me. I have come only to do the will of him who sent me" (Jn.4:34). Well, what words are these but the one who said, "I have found in David the son of Jesse"—and Jesse means "I am"—"one after my own heart who will do all my will." He does all the will and that is Messiah who does all the will. But when I am through as the son called man, I awaken having done it all; and then humanity put together, personified as a single eternal youth stands before me, and now I am no longer of the world of death. I've been redeemed as God the Father!

So he redeems us. He doesn't bring us back as his sons; he brings us back as himself. So we came out into the world in the grand experiment, the grand adventure. Was it proven before or was it something that could have failed? Just imagine that it could have failed…what would it be if we knew in advance that it had to succeed? But when the time had fully come, the cheers went up, hosannas went up that it had happened, and if it happened in *one* it will happen in *all*, for the grand adventure proved itself. But if I knew in advance it had to succeed, what would it matter? I tell you, he didn't know in advance that it *would* have happened. But he chose us in him for the experiment and gave us in victory himself.

The Return of Glory

So we return as God the Father and that's who we *really* are. I'm speaking from experience; I'm not theorizing, I am not speculating. Jesus is in you as your own wonderful Imagination. When you say "I am," that's Jesus, that's the Lord. But he's buried there. One day he will awaken, one day he will rise; and then all that is said of the Lord in the Old Testament, that he is the Father of David and chose him to be his Son, will now stand before you and you are his father and he is your son. So when the adventure is over and it's victorious, you are God the Father. What a *glorious* concept... that God actually gave himself to me, to you, to all of us! And I know from experience that because it has proven itself in performance it cannot fail in anyone. It can't fail! Not one can fail. Not a Hitler, not a Stalin, not any monster in the world can fail, because it has been proved the resurrection is a fact. All will come out; everyone returns not as the son of God—which is glorious enough—but as God himself.

That is my message to you. And this sweet young lady, who in her desire to express herself in a loving manner towards one she admires and respects, she said, "He is many years my senior, but I respect him and I love him, and I wanted so much to give him something that was really precious to him and to me. It could only be really something that I said that he would think precious, something that I did...it could be that intangible or it could be something material. Then came my parents"—symbols of the creative power. They were not physically there...this is all in Spirit...they only represented her own creative power. Your parents are simply symbols of that creative power, and here the father spoke of "three records." Well, they are symbolic or symbols. There were three who stood before Abraham, who pronounced the coming event of the child (Gen.17:15-19) only they were not called records they were called men...the same symbolism. For everything contains within itself the capacity for symbolic expression and significance. Then "Keep two for yourself, but one you give him, and he will so love it he will play it over and over and over. He will never tire of hearing it." Then a sheet of music and she notices the name: it is Olam...Ion Lamed Mem...the eternal youth composed it, and the title of the composition is *"Christ."* He's talking about himself.

No man in this world writes anything but about himself. You read anything written by a man, what is he writing about other than himself, his own thoughts, his own feelings, his own beliefs. You think he's detached from it? Read the tripe of some of these books that sell one million copies and they're all publicized. Read the nonsense in it, he's only writing about himself. He has acquired the ability to write. Anyone can do that if they apply themselves. Go to school and simply master the technique of writing. But when you start writing, what else can you write about other than the thoughts permeating your mind? You think you are detached from your own thoughts, but you aren't detached from your own thoughts, you're writing all about yourself. So Olam, the eternal youth, was the composer and the composition was titled *Christ*. It's all about himself. And you could never in eternity tire of listening to this incredible story of Christ.

Now let us go into the Silence.

* * *

You take comfort from it...God has prepared the way for his sons to return. I've told you the way. If I said "I am the way" that does not reveal anything. If I say "I am the truth, I am the life" they are true, all these statements are true, but it does not explain. In telling you exactly what I experienced, I have told you "the way." That is the way of the son returning to the Father. He has prepared the way for his sons to return and to return as God the Father.

Now are there any questions, please?

Q: God' s name is given as "I am that I am"?
A: Yes.
Q: It's never been particularly meaningful to me. In the *Anacolipsis,* Higgins gives the grammatical translation of that as "I shall be what I am then." Do you consider that accurate?
A: I would accept that...in Higgins. I would accept that in the translation of the Revised Standard Version, they say, "I will be what I will be." They use all the verb of "to be": "I am that I am, I will be what I will be, I will be what I was." Yes, they use them all. They give them in the footnote in the Revised Standard Version. But Higgins, his *Anacolipsis* is perfectly marvelous. I recommend it to anyone. I loaned it to a friend of mine twelve years ago and she never gave it back to me. There were two volumes, these two lovely volumes that I had. But I wouldn't...if she's getting anything out of it, she can keep them. But you can't do better than Higgins' *Anacolipsis.*

But when I say "I am," you get to the point you no longer look on the outside. There is no other savior, there's only God, and God is our own wonderful I AM, and that is Jesus. That is Jesus! But he's buried in us and he *rises* in us. He rose and he continues to rise in individual men and women. But he *rose* and that is the important thing. Therefore the whole experiment has *proven* itself successful; and the cry has gone up and none can fail now because it has been proved that he rose from the grave. He rises in everyone and no one can fail. I can't conceive of one failing.

I am not close to a Stalin or a Hitler…it's not my cup of tea, that concept of life. But can I conceive for one moment of those I love dearly being left behind and I depart? I couldn't. I'd remain here forever if my remaining would in any way awaken them. But I don't have to…it's been *proven*. And I can watch from on high and see it struggle and see it move, and know the awakening isn't far away. I'll watch it…and *all* are coming in… and what a joy when one comes, one after the other, into one body. That one body is God. There's only one God, only one Lord, only one Father…and so all awaken as the Father.

What a thrill that we were chosen in him before the foundation of the world! And came into this world and put upon ourselves the restrictions, the limitations of blood and flesh; and are lost in the act of creation, but lost in it…everything is simply geared to the creative act. I mean on a sexual plane, all of our advertising, everything is based upon that; and then all of sudden to be redeemed and to be awakened out of it all into a creative power undreamt of by anyone in this world. We have flashes while we still wear this garment *after* we've had the experience, and that is "the way." The early Christians were known as the "People of The Way." And that was The Way, but it's not spelled out. For reasons that the writers…well, they either believed that was the way to tell it because no one else would have believed it if they told it in its true, real form. So they implied and implied and implied, but, by all these implications we get so many misinterpretations…and tonight we have these prefabricated misconceptions of Christ.

I read in this morning's paper, if it's a true summary of what the man said last night, he spoke to almost 50,000 people, and I wondered if this really is the age in which we live, what on earth is he talking about when he's talking about such dribble? Not what I read in the morning's *Times*. A few months ago I read it in the *New York Times* when he was speaking at the Madison Square Garden, and he feels the second coming is imminent, and he hopes he will live long enough to be here when he comes. He wants to greet him. Of all the nonsense in the world! Can you imagine! Listen to the words, "Beloved, *now* are we the sons of God. It does not yet appear what we shall be, but we know that when *he* appears we shall be like him, and see him as he is" (1Jn.3:2). I'm quite sure in spite of all of his feelings tonight he doesn't really believe he looks like him.

You will look actually like that one being who embraces you, into whose body you are incorporated. That is the one body. So man sees the outward appearance; but God does not see the outward appearance, he sees the *heart* (1Sam.16:12). It's like that lovely book which you might have read, *Precious Bane* by Mary Webb. There are two characters who dominate the entire thing one, a girl, is called Prue, and then Hector is the man. She said of him, "He goes into the cabbage patch and they're filled to overflowing with caterpillars. Hector will never say caterpillars, he will always say, 'Look at the beautiful painted butterflies-as-is-to-be." That's how God sees you. He doesn't see the horrors on the outside, the rags you wear, and these things that men judge you by; he sees that painted butterfly-as-is-to-be. He sees his image…that's what he sees.

Q: Jesus' disciples asked him why he spoke to the multitudes in parables and he said, "Unto you it is given to know, but unto them it is not. They may see but they see not; they hear and they hear not." Is that part of the program in their journey?

A: My dear, yes. If tonight I asked some great physicist to explain to me how this thing works the unfolding of the atom, he could talk all through the night and I wouldn't follow him. I am not qualified to follow what he knows concerning the atom. I would be completely incapable of following Einstein's reasoning concerning mass and light. I couldn't do it. Well, the same thing is true of this great mystery. When man has been trained to see things as they are—men and women appear in the world, they wax, they wane and they vanish—and then you introduce an entirely different being into the world, a new being, a being that is called Jesus, and when you begin to explain this, he can't follow you. Our great scientists could not follow it and our great neurologists couldn't follow it. To them the brain is dead, it's dead, and the thing who occupied it, that is dead. He doesn't look upon an occupant. He looks upon the man as the man himself. The physical organ that he's curing, or hopes to cure, is the man. It's not a garment that man wears; it is the man. So you begin to speak of the occupant and he wouldn't know what you're talking about.

So we speak in different languages. And he spoke in parable, but in his smaller circle he explained the parables. A parable is a story told as if it were true leaving the one who hears it to discover its fictitious character and learn its lesson. So the story of Jesus is an acted parable. Learn to discover the *nature* of the parable, the *fictitious* character of the parable, and extract the meaning, and apply it.

Good night.

J, E, AND P MANUSCRIPTS

10/3/6

I think you'll find tonight very interesting. In the Book of Genesis which begins one of the manuscripts…there are three that we have, the J, the E and the P manuscripts. That's all the authors that we know of, and no one knows who they are. Scholars claim all kinds of things for these initials, but regardless of that, tonight we will begin with the E, which begins with the 15th chapter of Genesis. It doesn't mention the first fourteen. And here is the story, "As the sun was going down, *Abram* fell into a deep sleep; and a dread and great darkness fell upon him. The Lord said to him, 'Know for a surety that your descendants will be sojourners in a land that is not theirs, and they will be slaves there, and they will be oppressed for four hundred years… and after that they will come out with great possessions'" (Gen.15:12). Abram believed and it was accounted unto him as righteousness.

Here, we see that it is not what man is but what man trusts God to do that saves him. Here, he believes that God the Father has prepared the way for his banished ones to return. He firmly believed that there was a way. He accepted the verdict that they would be enslaved for four hundred years. Now when you read it you might think in terms of time as you and I think of time, but that is not part of the mystery. In the Hebrew alphabet each letter has a numerical value and a symbolic value. The last letter of the Hebrew alphabet, Toph, has the numerical value of 400, and the symbolic value of a cross. The cross is the *body* that you wear. It doesn't mean 400 years, or 4000 years, or four of anything. It's simply the numerical value of the cross which is the last letter. When you reach the end of the journey then there is a way prepared to bring you out of this experience in the world of death. For here is a world of death: everything begins, it waxes, it wanes and it dies, but everything. The very stars are melting…everything is dying…but it must first reach its fullness and then it disappears.

But he has prepared a way for his sons who were banished into the world of death to return to him, and when they return, they return with great possessions. Certainly not anything on earth, like homes, since everything here dissolves and disintegrates. And so, we must find what the possession is that comes out of this experience in the world of death. Here, no matter what you have you are enslaved by it. You buy a home and you start paying insurance on it right away to protect it against all kinds of things. Here in the Western world, earthquakes; all over the world, fires; certain sections, hurricanes. But no matter what it is it's against loss. You get a huge big diamond and you're so proud of it, and you insure it against loss, and you pay on it for the rest of your days. Many a person owning a fortune in diamonds puts them in a vault and they never sees them and pays on them year after year…but they have the feeling of possession. All they do is pay the insurance on them, because they wouldn't run the risk of wearing them in public. So they get duplicates made out of inferior material and wear that, while they know they actually own the original in the vault. Now that's an actual fact and that's all over the world.

So here, it is *not* anything that you own in this world that you will take out and call it great possessions. Tonight we will see what this great possession is that we actually take out after the journey of 400 years. The 400 years will be determined in a certain manner. The Old Testament is a prophetic blueprint which is fulfilled in the New. It is not cut and dried so that you can actually see exactly what it is talking about. It's a foreshadowing in a not altogether conclusive or immediately evident way. Then it happens and is recorded in the New, but even then it is not, I would say, conclusive and vivid so that man can see it. So we must search the scriptures to see just what you and I must experience in order to depart from this world of death and take with us this fantastic gift that we actually acquire by coming into the world of death. You and I *pre-existed*. When we speak of God, there is only one God so he could send no one but himself…for the son and the Father are one. He sends his sons into the world, and it takes all the sons to make the Father.

Here in this world there is only God the Father wearing these garments that are the crosses, these garments of flesh and blood. This is our cross and we bear it to the very end. When we come to the end then we are awakened, and when we awaken we discover who we are…that *we* are God the Father. In this world we do not know it. Here we don't recognize each other, and yet we were loving brothers before we came down—intimate, loving, wonderful brothers, all loving each other in the most intimate wonderful manner.

The Return of Glory

And then we put on the mask, the cross of flesh and blood, and we are so completely hidden from view we do not recognize each other and we fight each other, and we do everything in this world of horror. Then we are gathered one by one and brought back into that original state, but this time "with great possessions," and the possession is something entirely different from anything that man has dreamt of. The possession is to have *life in ourselves*. Not simply to be an animated body as I am now and you are, but to actually have life in ourselves.

Now the Book of Zechariah...and the word Zechariah means "Jehovah remembers." The awakening man remembers and that's what the whole book is about: the awakening man remembers. When you begin to awaken, this whole thing will come back, the whole vast memory of what you were told *before* the venture will begin to return. Now let me share with you an experience. It happens the very night that you are awakened from this world of dream. When the voice calls you from the tomb and you awaken within the holy sepulcher, which is your skull, to discover that you have actually been there for unnumbered centuries dreaming this dream of life. And the dream comes to an end on a certain note, and this is the very night you begin to remember who you really are, and the whole drama unfolds before you and within you. Then you know who you are.

Now, we're told in Zechariah, the 8th chapter, "Thus, says the Lord, 'I will return to Zion and I will dwell in the midst of Jerusalem: and Jerusalem will be called the faithful city, the mountain of the Lord of hosts, the holy mountain. And in the streets of the city shall be numberless boys and girls playing in its streets'" (8:3,5). Now you read that and you wonder what on earth does that mean in a book called a book towards the revelation of God and his plan for the salvation of humanity? What on earth would that be? Yet, may I tell you, the symbolism and the imagery is perfect.

One night, and I hope it's not too far from now, but I do not know, no one knows when it comes to the individual, for we are gathered one by one. You're so unique in the building of the restored temple that you aren't drawn with another, you're drawn singly. You are a unique being. Here, the prophet Zechariah, which simply means "Jehovah remembers," here he describes in the most vivid imagery Jerusalem as it will be when city and temple are restored and the exiles have returned. The image of this night that begins your awakening...I fell asleep in the normal, normal manner that I have done over the years, not expecting anything, and then came a dream. Here I am in the most glorious city. No building was higher than three or four stories...certainly not more than four...a walk-up, no need of any contraption to take me up. The sidewalks were wider than any streets we have in the city. There is no street, no boulevard as wide as the

739

sidewalks. Just imagine how wide the streets! And they were filled with boys and girls...I mean young boys, young girls, not even quite teenagers, just lovely, laughing healthy boys and girls. There were concert grand pianos on the sidewalk at stated intervals so that one could not interfere with the other. Artists would come and play, and it was all just for the joy of those who were present. There was no charge, just they played. And they all had their following made up of boys and girls and they were their heroes. I sat at one grand piano. There came this enormous crowd following their hero, a great artist. He came over and it was an unwritten code that no one could ask anyone seated to rise. He could be there always; no one would ask him to get up. But as he came over, I rose and gave him the bench. He thanked me and sat down to play, and as he played, his music formed geometrical patterns. The most glorious patterns came out, seemingly out of that instrument, all in color. But what beauty, what artistry, as it came out of what he played!

As I stood next to him I knew that if I could arrest within me a certain imaginal activity that what I saw, this beautiful thing coming out of the piano in all these forms, that I could arrest it. Then I arrested within me this activity and here the music was frozen. I looked at it and as I looked at it the tone that I arrested increased in volume within me like a sustained note, and that sustained note within me began to build up and it began to awaken me. I felt myself awakening from this dream. But instead of awakening as I would awake say this morning, I awoke in the holy sepulcher, my skull, to find I had been there in this strange, strange, wonderful, fantastic dream, a horrible dream, throughout the centuries. Then I knew innately what I must do to get out. And so knowing it I got out, and all the imagery of scripture concerning the birth of God surrounded me, and I knew at that moment who I was.

Months later came another unfolding, and then I knew beyond all doubt who I am. That the whole thing is only God playing all the parts in the world. That every being in the world though he thinks himself a little being, unknown, unwanted, and shunned by the world, he really is God wearing his cross, as he swore to himself that he would wear it for the 400 years...the 400 meaning only wearing a body of flesh and blood.

So the tone...as we are told in scripture, "Marvel not at this; those who are in the tombs will hear my voice and come forth" (Jn.5:28). Those who are in the tombs will hear his voice...and you think of a cemetery, you think of a graveyard, no, the tomb is your skull. You are actually buried in your skull, and the *you* that is buried are God and his name is I AM. That is God's name forever and forever (Exod.3:13-15) and there is no other name for him. Your own wonderful human Imagination is God, buried in your own wonderful skull, and that is the holy sepulcher. Don't go to Egypt to find I; don't go into the Near East in what is called the Holy Land. It is not there. You'll not in eternity find it outside of yourself; you are buried in your own wonderful skull, and the being buried is God, and that is the Lord Jesus Christ.

Now, when do we awaken? That dream precedes it only by the night, and you can't really know when it's going to come. But I'll tell you, the power in you is the gift that you bring back. You have then the power to stop the entire world, but the *entire* world, and have it stand still and examine it, and then start it at will. No matter how long you arrest it, it will have no knowledge of being arrested. It will continue from the moment of arrestment as though not a thing had happened, and that interval between arrestment and the release within you could be unnumbered centuries. But it would have no knowledge, for there could be no change without time. Space is a facility for experience, but time is a facility for *changes* in experience. When you arrest time, then there could be no change. If you arrested it now, at this moment, and then kept it so for a thousand years, nothing could age because nothing could change without time, and time is simply the facility for changes in experience.

So you simply have time within you, and you arrest it, as I did that night, and saw this most glorious thing coming out seemingly from what this artist produced on the keyboard of this concert grand. As I held it and looked at it, I was holding a tone, for the tone sustained it. As I held the tone, that sustained tone…and the word translated "voice" in scripture if you look it up in your biblical concordance, it means "noise, sound, the sustained noise, the sustained sound." It is really what is also called in scripture "the blowing of the trumpet." The trumpet is simply a reverberation and that thing reverberates like a noise, a storm wind within you. As it continues in that sustained note, you awaken. You waken not like you're ever awakened before; you waken from the *dream* of life. Morning after morning you awaken from the little dream of the night; this time you awaken from the dream of life. Because you see the whole vast world as it really is and not as you believe it to be through the senses as you read.

So he said, "Believe me, I and the Father are one" (Jn.10:30). I and the Father are one. Can I be one with my Father? If I am really one with him and if he's a father then he has a son. And therefore I can't then be his son if I am one with the Father. So then who is the son? I and my Father are one; I have *become* the Father. But he still is a father and therefore show me the son…and that comes five months after this experience. But I am one with the Father. Now how on earth can a man be his father? How on earth can he be not only his father, but his earthly father's father? Doesn't make sense, does it? But I tell you it's true and all these things you are going to experience. Everything in scripture you will experience. All of these are adumbrations, foreshadowings, and you are going to experience them.

Now, in the world here you go through the oppressions as promised in the book, the 15th chapter of Genesis: "And they will be oppressed for four hundred years...they will be slaves." What man in this world is not a slave of the body that he wears? No matter how rich you are, how powerful you are, can you command any servant of yours to eat your food for you, and assimilate it, and what he can't assimilate eliminate? Is there any man on earth so powerful that he can command one of his slaves to eliminate what he can't assimilate? Must not he perform all the normal functions of this cross of flesh and blood? Isn't he a slave of it? He has to eat and drink, and he has to assimilate and eliminate. You need not be a wealthy man and live in a home. You can sleep on the outside, you can go in the nude, you don't have to have shelter and raiment, but you do have to have food. Having food, you've got to eat it yourself. Eating it you have to assimilate it yourself, and assimilating it you've got to eliminate what you can't assimilate. And that makes you a slave of the cross that you wear. No one in this world has ever been so wise or so powerful that he can forego these functions. The day he forgoes the functions they bury him, cremate him or put him in the grave.

But the real grave is your skull. That's where the *real* you, your own wonderful human Imagination, is buried. There it remains until the end of the journey when you are awakened from the dream, and you come out *as* the dreamer, and the dreamer is God. He was always God. So you come out from the dream. He has prepared a way for his banished sons to return. And all the sons together, collectively, form the Father. But we are gathered one by one. You're so unique you cannot be called in pairs or in groups; you are called one by one. I'll tell you, the night you are called it begins with the dream that I've just mentioned in the 8th chapter of Zechariah... Jehovah remembers. So, "I will send the Holy Spirit and he will bring to your remembrance all that I have said to you" (Jn.14:26).

So here we are told the story and the visible presence who tells it disappears. Well, where does he go? He sends the Holy Spirit who is the Spirit of Truth. But he proclaimed, "I am the truth" so who can he send but himself. So "God himself enters death's door with those who enter, and he lays down in the grave with man in visions of eternity until they awake and see the linen clothes lying there that the females had woven for them" (Blake, *Milton*, Plt.32, line40). Yes, my mother wove this garment of flesh and blood, and I will come out of it one day (as I have) and I saw it. There was what my mother wove me. It's called in scripture the linen garments. And I, the invisible being, no one could see me, and I am feeling and hearing this power within me. It sounded like a storm wind, the noise spoken of when I heard the voice. But the voice was simply *my* own voice, because *I* arrested what I saw just through contemplating the beauty that came out of that music. As I arrested that one tone, the tone continued to support what I'm seeing. For the whole thing was supported and it was supported, it was conjured, by the tone and supported by the tone. If the tone stopped, it would vanish; but if I sustained the tone, the tone would continue. And the tone continued and in continuing it awoke me.

So there is a tone in man, it's a unique tone, that one day you will arrest. When you arrest it, it will continue as a tone, and that sustained tone, as we are told, a sustained tone could break, if related to the tone, a glass. I am told that Caruso could take a glass and get its pitch, and then hit that note and sustain it and break the glass. Well, there's a tone in man, and one day you will intuitively know that tone. It will come in the form of a pattern, a beautiful pattern, and you will arrest it…it's a frozen tone. You will sustain it, and as you sustain the tone, it will crack the shell in which *you* have been completely sealed for unnumbered centuries. Thousands of years you have been dreaming this dream. You didn't begin in the womb and you do not end in the grave. You are an *immortal* being that came down into the world of death.

Here you are in the world of death dreaming it, and one day you will see exactly what I saw in that 8th chapter. I fulfilled the 8th when I saw the boys and girls. They filled the streets. And they were so happy…nothing sad about them…just a happy wonderful crowd, each with their own individual hero who played these grand pianos. As he played and I saw the beauty that came out of the piano, within me I had the desire to arrest what I'm seeing, it's so beautiful. I did, not by holding it with my hand, I arrested what I saw by stopping an activity within my own Imagination. That's where the power was. As I arrested it, the note continued and it was a sustained note, and it woke me. I felt myself waking from a dream, only to discover I was not on my bed where I fell asleep; I was in the holy sepulcher, my own sealed skull. Then I knew intuitively how to get out, and that shell was cracked and out I came to be surrounded by all the imagery of the birth of God, as told us in the story of the birth of Jesus. For, Jesus simply means "Jehovah saves," and the only savior is Jehovah. So when he is born, Jehovah is born; therefore, you come out from the shell into which you placed yourself.

How did you get into that shell? How on earth? We know of no way even today with all of our knowledge—we can go to the moon, we can do all kinds of things—and no biologist has discovered how an egg is fertilized. How on earth can the sperm penetrate that which is sealed? It is an egg and there is no hole into that egg. Yet unless it is fertilized it cannot bear the chicken, it cannot bear the child, it cannot bear the animal. Here is an egg completely sealed…but it must be fertilized. The sperm must penetrate the surface of that egg or it cannot become alive. So how on earth was this thing penetrated so that it was made alive, and then to come forward in the likeness of the one who penetrated it? For, all things bring forth after their kind. Well, if God is bringing forth after his kind, it has to be God that is born. So the egg penetrated was the skull. It's not simply with the eyes open and the nostrils and the mouth and the ears…it's a sealed dome. You and I entered these domes, and God entered with us and actually became us. God became as I am that I may be as he is. And you awake to find that *you* are God the Father because his only begotten son calls you Father; and you have no doubt in your mind as to who he is when he calls you Father, and who you are. So only until this relationship of father-son is revealed to man is the journey over.

Last night as I retired I was thinking on this theme which I am trying to express tonight. Then I woke this morning about, I would say, 2:30…but I did retire quite early so I had a good solid sleep, seemingly dreamless sleep until the very end. At the very end, here I find myself in New York City in the Plaza Hotel. It was much bigger than the Plaza as I know it, much more roomy, but the same old-world harmony and graciousness that you find in the Plaza of today. I had just checked out and I looked up to see one checking in, and he's my brother Fred, my sixth brother. I went over and I greeted him, and then I turned to my left and here is my nephew Philip who is his son. I didn't know my brother was in New York City and I didn't know that Philip was, so I brought Philip over and then the strangest thing happened. I turned to my brother Fred, who is the father of Philip, and I said to Fred, "Oh, I want you to meet my nephew." They acted as though they didn't know each other, that the father-son relationship was completely unknown. I said to my brother Fred, "This is my nephew Philip. You've met his father and his mother, haven't you? Haven't you met Flo and Fred?" I spoke to him as though he were another. He answered as though he knew the ones of whom I spoke…because he had no knowledge of being the father of Philip and Philip had no knowledge of being the son of the one that I'm introducing him to.

Then you turn to scripture, "And Philip said unto him, 'Show us the Father, and we will be satisfied'" and he said to him, 'Have I been so long with you and yet you do not know me, Philip? He who has seen me has seen the Father" (Jn.14:8). You see, everything in this world contains within itself the capacity for symbolic significance. Now here, my brother in the world of flesh and blood, my nephew in the world of flesh and blood, and yet in my dream they are only symbols; symbols that father and son do not know each other. So I tell you that you are the father of God's only begotten son

The Return of Glory

who is named David, but you don't know it. I tell you that David is your son and you do not know it. But I can assure you the day will come that you will stand in the presence of David and David will call you Father; and you will know you *are* his Father and you will know he is your son. This mutual understanding between father and son will be accomplished. Then the journey is over.

So here, in my dream my own brother and my nephew...and his name is Philip. I played the part of David bringing them together. Who is David? The word David is defined in the biblical concordance as "beloved" but also "the uncle, the father's brother." Read it in *Strong's Biblical Concordance*, "the father's brother is called David. So I am David and yet I am the Father of David, so "I and my Father are one" (Jn.10:30). So, as David I make the announcement. These are mysteries, and the mysteries of scripture are not things to be kept secret, but they are mysterious in nature. They confuse the rational mind because the mind wants to continue thinking on this level, the secular world, where you are a man and you have a child, therefore that's a father and that's a son, and that's all there is to it. They can't get beyond into the great mystery of scripture, and the Bible is *not* secular history, it is *divine* history. It's something entirely different. They're not writing history, those who wrote. All the names are significant, and they tell an entirely different story that unfolds in the soul of man, and that soul of man is God. *You* are God...when you say "I am" that's he. There is no other God.

But you're down in this world for the allotted time. You will bear the fardel for the allotted time. Then will come that moment in time that this tree that you are will be split from top to bottom, and the Spirit trapped set free. It will be set free and you will awaken to know who you really are... that you are God the Father. There is no other one. In the meanwhile, dwell upon it, just dwell upon it. If you owned the earth tonight and death ended it all, what would it matter? Stalin thought he controlled the world and his little world, big as it was, it was little. So he could kill twenty million people and then vanish. But he hasn't gone; he's restored to life in an environment best suited for the work yet to be done in him. He knows he's Stalin, which was an adopted name, he knows it, but he is not ruling Russia. Hitler isn't ruling Germany. They are all restored to life in an environment best suited for the work that *must* be done in them, for in the end they too will be redeemed. *Everyone* will be redeemed, because everyone is aware that he is, and to be aware that he is, is saying "I am," and that is the name of God.

But while they played their parts here they were used, and although they didn't know it, they were playing the part of God; and it was all moving towards an ultimate good, but they didn't know it. They thought differently. But forget the individual and come back to scripture, for here, I'm only here to fulfill scripture. Every night and night after night even though I have completed the entire story as told in the New Testament, I find myself re-enacting the play, the Old Testament. For in the days when the story was written, there was only the Old Testament, and it must all be fulfilled in me.

Even to this morning…by simply dwelling the night before on the subject of tonight, wondering what could I add to it to make it more vivid to help everyone who is here. Then to come through the surface like coming from the depth of one's sea, and as the waves begin to break in your own consciousness, you have this little drama unfold before you—your brother Fred, your nephew Philip, and they don't know each other yet they're father and son. It's a perfect representation of the absence of consciousness or the lack of *memory* of the father-son relationship. My brother Fred has said to me so often in the past, "Of my four children, the one I do not understand is Philip. He is the first and I never understood how he thinks I've never understood what he does. He is completely strange to me, and all the time I do not know exactly what is going through his mind." They are entirely opposite, yet they look like each other. Physically they are the spitting-image of each other, only my brother is 6'3" and Philip is about 5'8". Philip is a captain in the Marines and for the last ten years he's been in the Orient. He's flown everything that we have manufactured from the super-sonic bombers to the super-sonic fighters, down to the helicopters. He's flown every kind of mission in the Orient. My brother Fred, who is a business man, can't quite understand that desire. They have not a thing in common on this level, but on the spiritual level father and son…but they do not know they are father and son. So when I introduced my brother Fred to my nephew, I had to tell him, "Why, he is the son of Flo and Fred. You know my brother Fred and Flo." He said yes, but never identified himself with it. And then I came through to this level. So here, everything in the world contains within itself the capacity for symbolic significance, but everything. There isn't a dream that is insignificant, but we are past masters of misinterpreting the dream. We can't quite put our teeth into it and see the story behind the story.

But here, you're here for one grand purpose: to awaken from the dream! When you awaken, you will have power in yourself. "As the Father has power in himself, so he has granted the Son also to have power in himself. Do not marvel at this; for the hour is coming when those who are in the tombs will hear his voice and come forth" (Jn.5:26). And they come forth when the power is exercised. There's only one note that can awaken you. That note will come to you when the boys and girls are playing in the streets of Jerusalem, and Jerusalem is within you. Zion is within you; the Lord is within you. The whole drama unfolds within the Imagination of man.

Don't look for it in any part of the outer world. The whole thing takes place *in* man.

One day you'll be so completely carried away with the beauty of something produced by a note that you will arrest the thing by arresting the activity in you. To arrest it, you'll have to sustain that note. That note being sustained will awaken you, and you will awaken from the dream of life to discover that *you* are the Christ of scripture and that *you* are the Jehovah of the Bible. There is no other God, no other God. When you say "I am" that's he, but you don't know it until these things happen within you. There is a doubt, there is a question mark. I could tell you from now to the ends of time that you are, but not convincingly. You would remain unconvinced because you cannot be convinced until the father-son relationship becomes a reality. Not because you reasoned the whole thing out, but because you've experienced it. You must *experience* scripture to know how wonderful it is.

So I can talk about it. I can be the greatest scholar in the world. I could know Hebrew, Greek, English, all the tongues of earth and still not know anything about it. I could translate the words literally, do all these things. In this morning's paper the usual press agent for Billy Graham, and they said that he took to the platform last night a Hebrew Bible given to him by the present prime minister of Israel. So what? He can't read Hebrew. So it's a gift, a gift of a book that is completely sealed to him. And from what I've heard him say, although he speaks English, the English Bible is sealed to him...doesn't understand it at all. It's completely sealed. Now he goes beyond that into the Hebrew translation. And here he took to the platform. If that is sacred...no, *you* are the sacred one. That is an external record of a drama that must unfold within *you*. That is the witness, the external witness. When it happens in you that is the internal witness and now you have the two witnesses. But don't bring me one and say scripture said so-and-so, because you don't know what it's talking about. Have you *experienced* it? Have you experienced that chapter and that verse? Well then, come, did it parallel it? Then you are now a *witness* to the truth of God's word.

But if it has not happened in you, you cannot be called as a witness... it's only hearsay. That's what you heard. That's what you either read or that's what someone said, but you don't know it from experience. When you know something from experience then you know it. Well now, is there another witness other than your own experience?—scripture. So you bring the written word and the internal experience, and the two stand together. You need no one in the outer world to verify it. First of all, they couldn't, but you have in the depth of your own being a being who knows it, the being who experiences it. And you go blindly on, regardless of what the world thinks or does.

So here, you are the ones and into this world we came. We were told exactly what to expect, that we would be slaves, oppressed for 400 years, but then we would come out with *great* possessions and that possession is power. It's not power with money in the bank; it's power, *creative* power, that you can at will conjure anything and it stands as an objective fact before you. What do you need with anything in the world when you can at will create it because you have power in yourself as the Father has power in himself, and I and my Father are one! So I don't need anything…take it all from me and I can re-create it. But if you can't create it and now it's taken from you, then you'll have to have it insured in the event they take it from you. So if they take it from you, you've got to go and collect and try to find something similar to what was taken from you, but you can't recreate it. But to have the power of creativity within you to create anything in this world, that is what you come out with when you come out of Egypt.

But you will come out, may I tell you, one by one. You are too wonderful, you're unique, and you can't be duplicated, so you can't be called in pairs. You're called one by one as you're told in the 27th chapter of Isaiah, "And I will gather you one by one, O people of Israel" (27:12). Everyone comes out one by one. And the time, when will it come? I'll tell you the night that it will come when this dream of which I spoke tonight takes place is the night you begin to dream of the city where the streets are full of boys and girls, and they're so happy playing in the streets. Then you hear music, and some part of that structure interests you to the point of wanting to arrest it for contemplation. You do arrest it by arresting in *you* an activity that seems to animate it, and as you arrest it the note is now frozen but sustained. The tone continues and increases in volume, and that volume awakens you. That's the voice that you hear. He said, "They will hear my voice"…the noise, the storm wind…and when they hear it they will come out from the tombs, even though the world calls them dead.

Now let us go into the Silence.

*   *   *

Now are there any questions, please?

Q: In the Song of *Jerusalem*, they say Blake composed the words and the words of that, do you think he had that identical where the children were singing in the streets? Do you think he had that identical vision?
A: I'm convinced of it. You read Blake's *Songs of Innocence* all about the children. Who could have written that but one who had the experience? *Songs of Innocence, Songs of Experience*… what beautiful poems! Oh,

The Return of Glory

Blake was fully awake! But he had the capacity to tell it so beautifully in the written form, and so now we have after 200 years a work that grows and grows and grows. He was unknown in his day and 200 years later this unknown man is now a giant in the world of literature. Anyone who understands English literature, as I am told by others who are considered great scholars in the use of the tongue, if they were asked to name the six greatest users of the English tongue in all time—going back to Chaucer and coming through Spencer, all the way up to the modern time—ask them to name the six greatest users of the English tongue, no one understanding the English tongue could omit the name of Blake in the six. And he never went to school, never saw the inside of a school. Yet you could not omit the name of William Blake in the list of six of the greatest users of the English tongue. You may put Shakespeare there first, and I presume most people would, but you could not omit Blake. You might change the others from time to time, you may change his position in the six, but you would not eliminate him from the six. Here is the great William Blake...I say Blake was completely awake. You go back and you read his beautiful poems, read *Jerusalem*, why, if you understood it, why you'd stand on your head it's so beautiful. Everything about him is beautiful as far as I am concerned.

Q: (inaudible)

A: Neither am I. I know you quoted it correctly. Yes you have, you've quoted it correctly. I don't think it's Job, I don't think so, nevertheless it could be. You quoted it correctly...I'm familiar with the verse. But we are told in the 12th chapter of the Book of Numbers that "God speaks to man through the medium of dreams and makes himself known through vision" (12:6). So I would not discriminate between the old and the young as to the vision and the dream. We all dream. There are some people who tell me, and they're advanced in years, that they've never dreamt in their lives. Well, they haven't recalled the dreams, but they have dreamt. They haven't brought it back to the surface and for reasons that I do not know they just have not remembered.

Very few people have had a true vision. A vision is this...this is a vision. When you have a vision, you are awake in the dream, and it ceases to be a dream because you are awake in it. Now, this is a dream, but it ceases to be a dream the moment I awake in the morning. I awake in a vision and this is a vision. When you are in a vision you can't change it. It seems so difficult to change like this seems difficult to change. For in a vision everything seems to be independent of your perception of it. In a dream if you know you're dreaming you can change it. If man knows that this is, although it is a vision, it still is a dream, he can change it. He can change it by assuming that things are other than what they appear to be. To the degree that he persuades himself that it is so, it will change to conform to his persuasion.

Q: Are dreams a form of astral projection?

A: No, no it's not an astral projection. That's a term that I don't really use here. I have had out of the body experiences time and time again, both voluntary and involuntary, but they are not vision. That's not what I call a vision. A vision is an automatic thing that just happens. You go to sleep and suddenly you're awake within the dream. But the true vision is fulfilling scripture, for these are the visions of Jehovah and you fulfill them. You experience the visions of Jehovah to be Jehovah. So all that he did you'll do…to be what he is. But an astral projection, no. I've had it voluntary from the time I was, well, just turned twenty, and involuntary.

Q: (inaudible)

A: Dreams are very significant. But some dreams can be interpreted simply and others need the dream interpreter. As we're told in the story of Joseph he could interpret Pharaoh's dreams; Pharaoh and the astrologers and magicians could not, they all failed. And he could interpret them and they all came true as he interpreted the dream. If you take all dreams literally, then you're simply confusing yourself. Some dreams are literal, but most of them come in *symbolic* form. Now this morning, with my brother, it's a normal thing to meet your brother. I met him at a hotel where he would stop…perfectly normal for him to check in at the Plaza. It would be normal for me to go in the Plaza and register and check in, and then meet my nephew. It would not feel to us that something was different about it. We are accustomed to living that way when we travel, we travel as we live at home which is in a good manner, so I don't think it would be considered extravagant by any of us to check in the Plaza and take whatever they quote, a normal room. We live that way at home and we live that way when we travel. So to meet him it's normal; to meet Philip it's normal. But then to have Philip not know his own father and to have his father not know his own son—and I'm fully aware of what I'm doing and then I come back with the full consciousness of what has happened—I must now interpret it symbolically. Because, certainly my brother Fred is not unaware of the fact that he is the father of Philip, and Philip is not unaware of the fact that he is the son of my brother Fred, yet in the dream they were strangers. I spoke of my brother Fred as another to my brother Fred and he understood he met him as though it were something different.

Q: (inaudible)

A: No, I wouldn't give it that interpretation. I would give it the interpretation of scripture, and scripture only gives one true death and two births. I know we have many schools of thought concerning reincarnation. They'll go back forever and forever, and I'm not questioning their right to entertain these thoughts, but I go along with scripture. When you die unless you are born from above, you will find yourself *restored* in a body just like yours, but young...not a child, a young man about twenty, placed in an environment not necessarily the year after your death. But as far as you are concerned you haven't died... only those who saw you go beyond and they couldn't reach you. But you could be placed in the environment 3,000 or the environment 1,000, for all these things are taking place now. It's a closed circle.

This whole world is based upon the principle of a circular form; and redemption is *spiral* and *vertical*. Redemption from this world is a spiral motion, while this world is on a circular principal as told in the Book of Ecclesiastes. But man has little memory, he can't remember...even in this world he can't remember, he forgets. As he gets older and older his memory gets shorter and shorter...can't remember. And so, we speak of things today that this has happened for the first time. Well, Ecclesiastes asked the question "Is there a thing of which it is said, 'See, this is new'? I tell you it has been of old in ages past. There is no remembrance of former things, nor will there remembrance of things to come among those who will come after" (1:10). So we think it is all new—we're living in a new age, a new this, a new that, because we are on a very vast wheel, and our memory does not go back that far. So it's like a wonderful play repeating itself over and over until that moment of redemption when you move vertically and horizontally, in a spiral manner...vertical to this horizontal motion.

I'm after the time now. Good night.

BELIEVE IT IN

10/6/69

Tonight's subject is "Believe It In." *All* things exist in the human Imagination. The world in which we live is the world of Imagination. Objective reality is solely produced by imagining. So tonight, we hope we can show you how to take that which *already* exists within you and bring it into an objective fact...for it already exists. Our lives are nothing more than our own imaginal activities. Imagination fulfills itself in what our lives become.

The last year that Robert Frost was with us he was interviewed by someone from *Life* magazine, and they said as they quoted him, "Our founding fathers did not believe in the future. They believed it in." Now, they could have believed in royalty. They could have broken with England and then established their own royalty...maybe one of those who were the Founding Fathers...and then perpetuate the same thing. They could have taken some form of dictatorship. But they agreed in concert to imagine a new form of government, something not tried since the days of the Greeks. It's the most difficult form of government in the world, that which you and I have: democracy. But they agreed in concert to believe it in—it didn't have to take place—and that's what they agreed upon. They knew it wouldn't just take place because they named it; they were the operant power.

You are the operant power. You don't say, "I'm going to be rich" and expect because you say it that it's going to happen. If you tell it *believing* it, yes. But you can't say "It *will* be," it must be in the present tense, because the active power is God and God is I AM. "God alone acts and is in existing beings or men" (Blake)...and because his name forever and forever is I AM, you can't say "I will be," just "I am" and you name it. Although at the moment reason denies it and your senses deny it, you must actually assume it, and that inward activity that you're now establishing and perpetuating will objectify in the world.

For the whole vast objective world is nothing more than man's imaginal activity. To attempt to change the circumstances of life before we change our own imaginal activity is to struggle against the very nature of things. You can't do it. If my imaginal activity is producing the things in my world but I don't like what I'm believing but I indulge myself with my own imaginings, and I so like hating people, or hating this or hating that, and I want that little thing for myself and I expect the world to change in spite of my imaginal activity, well then, I will labor in vain. That I know from experience. I have friends who said to me, 'Oh, I so like hating him"…but they want him to change. He can't change while you who dislike him as he is persist in your imaginal concepts concerning him. If I want the world to change, I must change my own imaginal activity, for that is the only *cause* of the phenomena of life. So we can believe a thing in. Anyone can do it. But if we accept the facts as our senses dictate it and then try to reason it and try to change it in that manner, well then, we're going to labor in vain.

So here, all things are in the *human* Imagination. You say, "But in God they do," well, human Imagination is God. "Man is all Imagination. God is man and exists in us and we in him. The eternal body of man is the Imagination and that is God himself" (Blake, *Annotations Berkeley; Laocoon*). And God alone acts…your own Imagination. May I tell you, it is an actual body. You are actually tearing down yourself when you imagine, because all is contained within you. It comes out of an actual body. That body, your Imagination, is the divine body of the Lord. All right, we call it in scripture Jesus Christ; well, Jesus Christ is Jehovah…same thing. It's a story, it's a mystery, and the most wonderful mystery ever told man. But man doesn't know that the Jesus of scripture is his own Imagination and that is an actual body, it's the divine body of the Lord. He tears everything out of himself and he projects it on the screen of space. He projects it only through imagining.

Now, how do we go about it? In a very simple way. A few years ago, I can't recall how many now, not too many years, maybe six, seven, eight years ago, I was taken in Spirit and shown a certain technique by which man can change his entire world. We are told in scripture that God speaks to man through the medium of dream and unveils himself through the medium of vision. We'll take, say, a dream. This borders between dream and vision, for really vision is nothing more than a waking dream like this world…this is vision, this is a waking dream. But take the dream of the night, where you're not fully awake within it. Well, this night in question I was taken in Spirit into one of the early mansions of the turn of the century on 5th Avenue in New York City, these palatial mansions. When I arrived in New York in

1922 many of them were still standing. They were forty and sixty room homes, three and four story buildings, all with their full complements of servants. Their carriages they kept on the west side, not too far away, a block away between Sixth and Seventh. They also were palatial areas where the coachman and his staff lived, and the horses.

But I was taken into this place, and as I entered there were three generations present. One was invisible, he was grandfather; he was spoken of but he was not seen. He was the one who had made the fortune that they now enjoyed, that his children and their children now enjoyed…this enormous fortune. So the father of the present third generation is telling them of the *secret* of grandfather. I stood there, invisible to those who were present and I heard every word that he said to his children. He said, "Grandfather"—speaking to them now—"Grandfather used to say, as he stood on an empty lot, 'I *remember when* this was an empty lot' and then he would paint the most wonderful word-picture of what he wanted to establish and to erect on that lot. So he actually in his mind's eye created what he wanted on that empty lot. He went through life in that manner: he realized it objectively by first realizing it subjectively." So faith is the subjective appropriation of the objective hope. Grandfather used to say, while standing on the empty lot, "I remember when"—he's still standing on the empty lot—but he would say, "I remember when it *was* an empty lot."

Well, if I say, "I remember when this was a club where I lectured, then it's no longer a club where I lecture. I remember when it *was*…I rub it out of my mind when it was, and now in its place I put what I want it to be. I remember when you were poor, so I rub you out of poverty and put you into comfort. I remember when you were sick, and therefore I rub you out of sickness and put you into health. I remember when you were unknown, well then, that *implies* you are now known. I remember *when*, and then I change that memory by saying that I remember *when* you *were*. Then I'm implying that what I'm *now* seeing differs from what I remembered formerly. And that was the secret of Grandfather's success…and he made the fortunes.

Well, I was told that quite vividly in my vision and so I share it with you. Don't turn it aside because it came in vision. In the 12th chapter of the Book of Numbers, if you believe scripture, it is said that God speaks to man through the medium of dream and makes himself known through vision (12:6). If he makes himself known to man through vision and speaks in dream, what is more important than to remember what you have dreamt and what you have experienced in the form of a vision? There is nothing in tomorrow morning's paper comparable. You can't compare tomorrow morning's paper or any book on earth comparable to what you tonight could read if you remember your vision, for that is an instruction from the depths of yourself. God *in* you is revealing to you certain instructions. Well, that night he revealed to me by taking me into this enormous mansion, beautifully staffed, and they were all, as I said, at the turn of the century. I could tell by their clothes, tell by everything about it that I'm going now into a different section of time. Here, I am invisible to them, for I'm in Spirit, but I hear more distinctly than they're hearing and I take it in more graphically than they are, because they have it. When you have millions, who is going to tell you how to make millions? They didn't make it, they inherited it, and therefore they aren't concerned about it. They are simply going to spend it and enjoy it.

But, I was taken into this environment. And I heard the story to share with those who will believe it; and then to apply it myself. Having heard it, it doesn't mean because I heard it that I would enjoy such comfort. It means *if* I apply what I heard I would enjoy that comfort. If I will now say, "I remember when I couldn't afford to spend $300 or $400 a month rent, I remember when, that would imply I can well afford it now. If I said I remember when it was a struggle to live on x-number of dollars, and then I mention quite a sum, that would *imply* that I must have transcended that. Well now, if you put yourself into these states...I remember when she or he was single in this world and I always thought what a waste of a beautiful person in this world that they are single. They should be happily married, and the man or the woman to whom they're married should be so proud of having them as a mate. Well then, I remember when, and I then by saying I remember when, I persuade myself they are no longer in that state. I'm only moving them from a state. All these are infinite states all contained within man.

So when I say all things exist in the human Imagination, I mean that infinite states, every conceivable thing possible for man to experience *now exists in* him. But it exists in him as a state. He is the operant power of all states, and only as he enters that state does it become alive, does it become animated. As it animates itself by reason of his entry into the state it out-pictures itself. Now, he may go back to sleep and think the objective fact is more real than its subjective state into which he entered. But may I tell you, all these states exist forever. When they become objective, they are in the world of generation called vegetation. They will vanish because a state as it appears, it waxes, it wanes and it vanishes. But the *eternal* form of that state remains forever, and you can re-animate it through the seed of contemplative thought, so you bring it back into being. But it can't stop you from growing old. Everything in this world, it appears, it waxes, and it wanes and disappears. But the seed from which it sprang remains forever and you can re-animate it by once more re-entering that state.

755

So here, the most creative thing in man is to believe a thing in. Tell me what it is and I'll show you how to believe it. Now how do I believe it? Causation is the assemblage of mental states which occurring creates that which the assemblage *implies*. Causation is the assemblage of states. Now, I bring before my mind's eye a couple of friends, friends that truly would *empathize* with me. Not sympathize, they would empathize, rejoice with me if they heard good news about me. So I bring before my mind's eye a couple of friends that I trust implicitly— because I would rejoice with them if they told me good news about themselves—and I hear them discuss my good news. They are true friends and they are ecstatically happy because of my good fortune. I see them discussing it, I hear them discuss it, and then I become aware not only of what I hear but I now allow myself to become visible to them. Then I imagine— it's all in my Imagination—that I am being congratulated by them. I accept the congratulations as a fact. This is now realized eschatology in a way, for the *end* is with me and I have realized it. And so I hear them congratulating me on my good fortune, and I accept the congratulations. Then when I break that little contemplation, I firmly *believe* in the reality of what I have done, that that imaginal act is a fact!

Well, who did it? I did it. Then God didn't do it. Yes he did, because God and I are one. His name is I AM (Exod. 3:14). Must I go on believing that there's another on the outside? The great confession of faith, which I would have everyone in the world accept, is the Shema, "Hear, O Israel: The Lord our God is one Lord" (Deut.6:4). If the Lord is one, there can't be two. Therefore, if his name is I AM and I say "I am," well then, that must be the Lord. And he brought the whole vast world into being. As I am told, "By faith we understand that the world was created by the word of God, so that things that are seen were made out of things which do not appear" (Heb.11:3). We find "the word" in this case is simply an imaginal activity. It was created by an imaginal activity. So through faith we find now that the activity must be joined to faith. Faith is nothing more than the subjective appropriation of the objective hope: man firmly believing in the reality of what he has done in his Imagination. He sees the imaginal act as much a fact as though he observed it with his senses, and he firmly believes in that reality. So we understand that through faith the world was created by the word of God and so what is seen was made out of things which do not appear.

You don't see my imaginal act. They don't appear to you, but then all of a sudden there's a change in your world. And then you tell me in the not distant future, "You know, Neville, what we discussed has happened." But you discussed it and I heard what you implied when you discussed it. For if you said to me, "You know, I need so and so," that was something that you told me. If I accepted that, well then, remembered always, that's what you were. But I remember *when* she needed it, but I no longer remember when you needed it. I remember now something entirely different where you have what you said you wanted. When I meet you in the not distant future and you tell me that you have it, well then, you are only bringing confirmation of this imaginal creative act.

Well, if it works this way and it proves itself in the testing time and time again, what does it matter what the world thinks? If there is evidence for anything in this world, does it matter what others think? It costs you nothing to try it, and what a change in life it will produce in you if you try it and prove it in performance! Now, it may be in conflict with your own concept of what you believe God to be. Maybe you still want God to be something on the outside, and have two of you, and not the great Shema: "Hear, O Israel: The Lord our God the Lord is one"…not two. All right, God became man that they may not be two. He became man that man may become God. If he became man, then his name must be within me. Well, his name *is* within me. For to ask for anything I must first say that I exist, that I am. I may not know who I am, where I am, what I am, but I do know that I am. I could suffer this moment from total amnesia and not know anything other than I am, but I can't stop knowing that I am. Therefore, God became me. Well now, I may by using my senses, using reason and believe that I'm a limited little being unwanted, ignored, maltreated, and believe that. So I'll produce it, and you will maltreat me, and the world speak ill of me, and everything in the world will confirm my imaginal activity. But if I don't know what is causing this peculiar mistreatment, then I'll blame everything in the world *but* myself. And the *only* cause of the phenomena of life is man's imaginal activity…there is no other cause.

If I really believe in the horrors of the world as morning after morning it's given to me in the papers. They feed us on it and so I'm frightened every morning by the paper. They say everything is getting scarce and then I read the next morning's paper we have so much of the same item we have no storage room for it. It happens moment after moment. There was a shortage in wheat, and now we have no place to store the crop, a shortage in beef and then no place to store it. Because of the shortage, you go and you buy what you don't need and then put it in places where it will spoil anyway. We go blindly on using all the strange peculiar pressure to perpetuate the imaginal activity that keeps us fighting in the world. Yet all through scripture we hear the words, "Let not your hearts be troubled…be not afraid… fear not" (Jn.14:1). If you could rub out fear from man, you could take the entire profession of the psychologists and psychiatrists and then bring it to an end. It's a bunch of nonsense anyway…bring it all to an end. Every day they change their concepts and they are always in conflict as to what the man's attitude towards life is...no two will agree.

So I say to everyone here, the whole vast world is *now* within your own wonderful human Imagination. You can bring out of that wonderful Imagination of yours whatever you desire. But you will do it by first knowing what you want and then creating imagery *implying* the fulfillment of what you want. Now, what would it be like if it were...and you name it. Take any simple thing. Would my friends know it? Yes they would know it. Would they say something about it? Yes they would. Well then, imagine that they are now in your presence and it's being discussed. It could be even a little party given for it...maybe a little cocktail party, maybe a dinner party, maybe a little get-together over tea to discuss the good fortune of one. Well then, you create that in your mind's eye, and having created it, believe in the reality of that creation. For that's the invisible state that will produce the objective state and all objective reality is solely produced by Imagination. There isn't a thing in this world...right here in this room...take the dresses that you wear, were they not first imagined? The chairs on which you are seated, the room that surrounds you...there isn't a thing in this world that wasn't first imagined. So what is now such an objective fact was once only imagined. So imagining creates reality.

If you don't believe it, well then, you are completely lost in a world of confusion. There is no fiction in this world. What is today's fiction will prove itself tomorrow as tomorrow's fact. The whole vast world...if I write a book, a book of fiction, and I write it and I say all in my Imagination, the whole thing came out of my Imagination, therefore, it is not to offend anyone. Anyone mentioned in this book that might resemble one that you know, that is not my responsibility. So I write a book and tomorrow the whole thing becomes a fact. If we have a good memory or a good research, we could go through any library and find these things...not all, because not everything is written. Who can tell the one who has never written one word in this world, but you can't stop her or stop him from imagining. And one now feeling himself or herself wrongly imprisoned, and losing himself or losing herself in an imaginal state to get even is disturbing the entire world, because "all things by a law divine in one another's being mingle." And you can't stop but react to that force coming from one who is imagining, because behind the mask that we're wearing, we're all one, and so I can't stop it. Someone this very moment in a dungeon being lost completely in hate... and I may be an innocent victim being used to express what she or they are imagining in their hearts.

So to disengage ourselves from that, always be aware of what you are imagining. Only as you are completely aware of what you are imagining can you steer a good course towards a destined end. If you lose sight of that destined end, you can be ruled by any being in the world. But if you keep your mind on the end, dwell on the end…the end is where we begin; "In my end is my beginning." So tell me what you want and don't tell me the means, for I don't know the means and you don't know the means. Just tell me what you want that I may hear that you have it. But don't tell me what you are so I have to rub that out first to know what you want to be. Man insists on telling me all the complex things about the problem, "Listen to me first…give me one hour." If you give him five minutes, he'll take five hours, because he wants to talk about his problems and he just simply wallows in the problems. They will not believe you for one moment that when you say, "Tell me what you want and that is all you need do." So, if they only believed for one moment that imagining creates reality, they couldn't go over that old, old record and play it all over again as to what they are as against what they want to be. But they'll play it over and over…that's the whole vast world.

So I tell you, the greatest thing in our lives here in this world, the most creative act is to believe a thing in. To believe it into existence as our forefathers did, the Founding Fathers. They had no example unless they went back 2,000 years and they wanted to re-try democracy. It failed in Greece and it was rubbed out, because man changed the imaginal activity. That's the only reason for it…the dream of men within the system. We can change this…don't think for one second we have to go on as a democracy. There is nothing written in scripture that man has to go on. This thing could become in twenty-four hours a dictatorial setup…it could. Everything is possible. If the people in our midst who are tired of democracy and want to entrench themselves in a totalitarian setup, they could do it. Everything is possible. You have to be constantly watchful. If you like the system, and I love the system, then we have to be watchful and actually keep this wonderful form of government alive. It's the most difficult form in the world…where a man can really voice an opinion, voice a protest and he can dissent. You can't dissent in other forms of government. So here, if you really want to enjoy that ability to dissent, well then, keep this alive!

But if you know this law you don't have to broadcast what you want; just assume that you have it. For the assumption though at the moment you have assumed it, although it is false—that is, if you say that reason denies it and your senses deny it—although they deny it if you persist in the assumption, it will harden into fact. The whole thing will actually become real, and there's no limit to the power of believing, none. The Bible doesn't set any limit on the power of believing, none whatsoever. You read it in the 11th of Mark and the 9th of Mark…*no* limit is set to it. "All things are possible to him who believes." I think you'll find that in the 9th chapter, the 23rd verse of the Book of Mark...no limit, just *imagine*! What an enormous promise made to man! It doesn't say he must be a nice person or a good person or a wise person. If you could only persuade *yourself* that what you have imagined is true. So you walk as though it were true, and if you could only walk as though it *were* true, it would become a reality in your world. So believing something as if it were is the way to success. I don't imagine there is one successful man in the world, unless he inherited it, who would deny that he actually lived as if it were true, just lived as if it were true and then things happened. This one aided him and that one aided him. He might deny these things, but it wasn't the one who aided; *he* compelled the aid. He compelled all this assistance as he moved toward the fulfillment of his dream.

So to believe it in is the most wonderful thing in the world of Caesar. This belongs right here. As you're told in the very first Psalm, "Blessed is the man who delights in the law of the Lord...in all that he does he prospers." (Ps.1:2,3). This is the law of the Lord. The law of the Lord has been explained to us in the Sermon on the Mount as purely psychological: "You've heard it said of old, 'You shall not commit adultery.' But I say unto you, anyone who lusts after a woman has already committed the act of adultery with her in his heart" (Mat.5:27). So we see that the restraint is not enough. That would be on the outside and one must not even want to in order *not* to commit adultery. So that entire story is psychological. What I want, let me steer myself toward it, because I've already done the act in the wanting. But now I must add faith to it. I want to be successful...now I must add faith. Because without faith it is impossible to please him...so I must add faith to the imaginal act. Can I imagine the state and then *feel* that the imaginal act is a fact.

Now, in *its* own good time it will come into my world and confront me as a fact, if I will take it. Well, try it...it costs you nothing...just try it. May I tell you, the funny part about it is when we get it, it seems such a natural thing that we deny that we had anything to do with it. We will say to ourselves, "You know, it would have happened anyway" and man goes sound asleep after the event. First of all, most of us don't even realize our own harvest. We are confronted with the harvest and we don't realize that we planted it. If we do remember that we once did it imaginatively and then we are confronted with the actual fact to confirm it, as we go back reason tells us, "You know, that would have happened anyway, because look how it happened. You met this one seemingly by accident at a cocktail party, he was interested in making money, and he heard your ideas and then he did so and so, and then they did so and so, and see what happened. So, really, it would have happened anyway." And then, of course, you ignore the law.

Well, "Blessed is the man who delights in the law of the Lord…in all that he does he will prosper" (Ps.1:1-3). Don't forget the law…yet you're not justified before God by the law. But while we are living in a world of Caesar and law is necessary…learn the law of God and apply it wisely.

But you aren't justified before God by law; you are justified before God only through *faith*. You heard the most fantastic, incredible story in the world: that he would bring out of you himself, and when he brings himself out of you, *you* are the one that came out of yourself. That is God's promise to man…if man could believe it! That's *all* that he's asked to do. For it is not what man *is* in this world but what man trusts *God* to do that saves man. That's something entirely different. So you will be saved to the degree that you actually *trust* God to do what he promised he would do. But in the world he's given us a law, a law to cushion the blows, the inevitable blows, and the law is purely psychological. What would the *feeling* be like *if* it were true and I assume the feeling that would be mine if it were true. Then I live and sleep as though it *were* true, and in a way that I do not know and couldn't devise it becomes a fact.

So Grandfather used to say, "I remember when this was an empty lot" and then he would paint the most heavenly word picture of the structure he desired for that lot. And that's how he made his fortune. It was shown me so clearly that that is really the most wonderful technique. I remember when he was unknown, I remember when he was so and so, and then as you remember when he *was* you are implying he is no longer that. The power is in the *implication*. So if I remember now when he was, I'm implying now he is no longer, and that power that creates it is in the implication of my statement. You take this law and you work it, and may I tell you, you'll go from success to success as you conceive success to be.

As far as I'm concerned, the only success is the fulfillment of the Promise, and man does not do that by the law. That has been a promise: he does it only by *faith*. Is he really holding to the faith? "Examine yourselves, to see whether you are holding to the faith" (2Cor.13:5). For I've told you a story, said he, and this is the eternal story, do not change it, "God became as you are that you may become God." Now take the law and cushion the blows, but God will keep his Promise. Now commit yourself to the Lord, as you're told I think it's the 31st Psalm, "Into thy hand I commit my spirit; thou hast redeemed me, O Lord, faithful God" (Ps.31:5). It's the cry on the cross and this is the cross. As I wear the cross night after night, commit myself to the Lord: "Thou hast redeemed me." Well then, he'll prove to me he has redeemed me in the most beautiful imagery in the world, in the most beautiful experience of being born from above not of blood nor of the will of the flesh but of God (Jn.1:13).

Now, before we go into the Silence, I want to thank you who wrote me this past week. I got eight perfectly wonderful letters. I can't answer all tonight, but I'll say in a quick way, the lady with the elephant, the story of the elephant, the elephant is a symbol of the creative power of God, the same as the word Christ; Christ is the power and wisdom of God (1Cor.1:24). The new born elephant, so new it was wet, and when you dried it off and fed it, and the little elephant thought you were its mother...marvelous imagery! It's the most marvelous adumbration or forecasting of the birth of this creative power in you.

Now a lady writes that she was taken into the presence of the Ancient of Days and he asked the question and she answered. "I cannot recall the answers or the questions," she said, I only know he said to me that "I will not be late." In other words, what was promised, he will not be late in the delivery. I can say to her that is right on the verge of the fulfillment of the Promise...when you're taken into the presence of this one.

And then two ladies—one is here tonight—and both had a similar dream. Both dreamt in their own significant way concerning Mary. One was raised in the Catholic faith—she's completely accepted *this* story—and she said, "It seemed so strange that Neville is talking about Mary and it seemed so Catholic" meaning Roman Catholic. But the way she unfolded the story...it unfolded and she realized at the end that I'm talking about *her*. Another lady who was in the vision with her at the same time had a different kind of a dream which was also about Mary. She said that she saw this book about ten inches long and six inches deep, and the title of the book was *Peter* and subtitled *Or the Story of Mary*, and she was reading this story. I tell both of them that "You are Mary and birth to God must give if in blessedness you now and evermore would live" (Scheffler in Bayley, *Lost Language of Symbolism*, Vol.1). There is no other Mary. You have now been called to the point of playing the part of bringing forth the child. So you are pregnant. Pregnant...in one case, one really is physically; in the other case, she is not, but both are pregnant with the Holy Spirit. For, I am a male, yet I am Mary. I brought forth the blessed child which is only a symbol of *my own* birth from above. So you are already conceived and there is no miscarriage in the divine conception, none. You can miscarriage in this world but not in the divine conception.

So I would say to all of you, thank you beyond measure for all that you told me in your letters. They were perfectly wonderful...all leading towards the fulfillment of the covenant which is to be born from above. Please keep it up! I can't tell you my thrill when I went home last Friday night and read these eight, and re-read them several times in that weekend. Though my weekend was very, very much taken up with the ballgame, in between shots

The Return of Glory

I was reading these wonderful letters. Nothing could divert me from reading them several times, and now I have them on file. So thank you and please keep it coming.

Now let us go into the Silence.

* * *

Now are there any questions, please?

Q: When Jesus said, "Ye believe in God, believe also in me," what is the meaning of that?

A: That's the 14th chapter of John, and in that 14th chapter he tells Philip who asks him to show him the Father, he said, "If you've seen me, you've seen the Father. I am the Father" (14:9). So he's telling you that if you say you believe in God, well then, believe in me, for that's God. "Unless you believe that I am (is) he, you die in your sins" (Jn.8:24). So this is one of the great I AM sayings. Before Abraham, I am. "Before Abraham, was I am" (Jn. 8:58). So that's God…the "I am" in man is God…man's own wonderful human Imagination. He's not pretending that he's man; he took upon himself all the weaknesses and all the limitations of man. Emptied himself of everything (Php.2:7) and became man, an animal. Man is an animal as told us in the 4th chapter of the Book of Daniel. He took the heart away from him and gave him the heart of a beast, took the mind away from him and gave him the mind of a beast, until seven times went over him that he would know that it is the great Lord himself that does all these things (4:16).

So he actually is an animal. Just look what we are doing all over the world. Not only in the actual fighting, where it's obvious people are killing each other, but you don't have to kill a person to kill him, you can steal him to death. That picture of Blake *The Ghost of a Flea* with a human head and this monstrous body, no neck, a head stuck upon the body and it's the ghost of a flea. Well, it's human…but what is a flea? It's a blood sucking insect that does not produce its own blood and it lives off the blood of others. Well, if I employ you and I don't really pay you an adequate sum and I bleed you to death, that's a slow killing… far better if I killed you. When men are not paid adequately for their services, the man who doesn't pay them, if he only saw himself as the mystic sees him, he would see himself as a flea, the ghost of a flea. In the eyes of the world he's a well-dressed man, living lusciously. Goes to all the fine restaurants, orders everything in sight, goes home to a house where all the servants are there and they kowtow to him; and yet seen mystically you're looking at the most monstrous thing in the world. You're looking at the ghost of a flea, for he lives off the blood of others and in this world of ours money is the life's blood.

Now, people laugh at that and say that's stupid. Well, stupid to those who have no eyes, and the average person in this world has no eyes. He has eyes but he doesn't see and he has ears but he doesn't hear. No two people see the same tree. Some people see a tree as an obstruction and chop it down; and others see this glorious thing. "You see what I see but you do not see what I see." We both see a man, but you don't see the man that I see. So people will say, "Isn't he wonderful!" What's wonderful? "Well, he has twenty million dollars," and if you saw him as I saw him you'd see a wonderful big flea. But who sees the man? And you're told that God sees not as man sees, for man sees the outward appearance and God sees the heart (1Sam.16:12). We have eyes but we see not and we have ears but we ear not. So let them go, perfectly all right, playing their parts.

If you want to be mentioned tomorrow in the obituary column of any paper in our country either kill someone or die a millionaire. But don't die a gracious, gentle person who has been kind and unknown or you would hardly be mentioned in this section. But do leave behind you some violent end or oodles of money. They rarely ever tell you in the obituary how he got it. I think of that Lloyd George when he tried to propose a law in parliament to bring about a change in the ___(??) so that others could have a little land in England. He said to those most… he was addressing the House of Lords plus parliament…and he said, "In England all that a man has to do to prove ownership is to trace his ancestors back to the one who stole it." And that's part of the world and they live in that manner. Perfectly all right, leave them just as they are. But I would say to you, Set your hope fully upon this *glory* that is coming to you at the unveiling in you of God's secret which is Jesus Christ (1Pet.1:13). He unveils him in you *as you, not another*: "Christ in you is the hope of glory" (Col.1:27).

Q: Is there any way one can train himself to remember his dreams?
A: Oh yes. People will say that I do not dream. Everyone dreams! When you wake in the morning even if it seems not a dream the first thought that occupies your mind is consequent upon a dream. So instead of jumping out of bed and running to the bathroom to brush your teeth or put the kettle on for water, remain just for a few moments and ask yourself, "Why am I thinking what I am thinking?" It's consequent upon a dream. And your mind will go back to the ladder of events that led up to the thought that occupies your mind. Even though the thought seems

a natural thing because it's part of the day—you have an appointment and you woke because you remembered the appointment, and it would seem that. But go back, that was only the last rung in the ladder that led you from *deep* self to outer self. So every last section of a dream is consequent upon the dream, even though it's seems only an idle thought occupying the mind. You can train yourself to remember dreams.

Thank you.

NO OTHER FOUNDATION

10/10/69

Tonight's subject is "No Other Foundation." We are told in the letters of Paul and you'll read it in the 1st Corinthians, the 3rd chapter, "No other foundation can any one lay than that which is laid, which is Jesus Christ" (3:11). Then he states in his 2nd letter to the Corinthians, the 13th chapter, he said, "Do you not realize that Jesus Christ is in you?" (13:5). Well, the average person does not realize that Jesus Christ is in him. So they ask, "Who is this Jesus Christ that is in man?" For there is no other reality!

Now let me tell you, a man dreaming—and that goes for every man in the world—is creating his own world. The entire dream of a man is his own creation and that is the foundation of the world. Everything in the world is his dream and that is the only foundation the dreamer. The dreamer *in* man is his own wonderful human Imagination, and that is called Jesus Christ. Man doesn't know it. He thinks of Jesus Christ as something other than himself on the outside, and yet Jesus Christ is within him. "Do you not realize that Jesus Christ is *within* you?" (2Cor.13:5). If he's within you, then where within and what is he or who is he? I'll tell you, he is your own wonderful human Imagination. The whole vast world is your dream. It's not only the dream of the night which anyone can discover to be himself, the most fantastic dream still is your own being pushed out. Maybe you can't write a letter, or you're incapable of painting a picture, or doing anything, and yet you dream it, and the dreamer is within you, and that dreamer is your own wonderful human Imagination.

Now let me take you with me into the greatest story ever told man. It's in the Bible, but it's not understood; because when you hear the word Jesus Christ you think of another, when you hear the word Lord you think of another. I want to show you tonight who the Lord Jehovah is, who God is, who Jesus Christ is, and to show you that *you* are the being spoken of in scripture. The entire Bible is your own wonderful *auto*-biography. You dictated it, it's recorded, and then you came into the world to fulfill it. You fulfill it in the most marvelous way in the world by a series of events *within* you. You don't fulfill it on the outside. People today are looking for the coming of Christ but Christ is *already* within you. The coming of Christ is the *awakening* in you of the dreamer. So the dream comes to an end and he awakens in a series of events which was predetermined in the beginning of time. That series simply was before the world was. Let man in his dream speculate as to the ends of the earth and the moon and all the things round about him, perfectly all right. That's part of the dream, too. But when you come to the end of the dream, you begin to awaken, and you awaken in a series of mystical events.

The events are in a very simple way not seen on the surface, but I'll tell you what they are. You will find yourself awakening *within* yourself, awakening within your skull. That's where you are buried...man is buried within his skull...and the man buried within his skull is the Lord God Jehovah, and that is Jesus Christ. He awakens within his skull and then he comes out of his skull. As he comes out of his skull it is recorded in scripture that "We are born again through the resurrection of Jesus Christ from the dead" (1Pet.1:13). And no one here thinks he is dead...he thinks he's very much alive. We think of those who depart the scene as the dead and they're no more dead than the actor who leaves the stage. They are restored to life in a world just like this to continue the dream, and they continue it just like you and I continue it here. They are restored in a body just like the body they left only it is not as old if they die as an old person; and they are restored at a normal age of, say, twenty to continue the dream in a section of time best suited for the work yet to be done in them...until this series takes place in man.

The series begins with a man awakening. It's a peculiar awakening, and he begins to awaken within himself, and he finds himself in his skull. The skull is a sepulcher where he was entombed. Then he comes out, and the symbolism as described in scripture surrounds him—the birth of a child. No, he doesn't bring forward a child; a child symbolizes *his* birth. He is born "not of blood nor of the will of the flesh nor of the will of man, but of God" (Jn.1:13). It is God the dreamer who is awakening, and he simply foretold exactly what would happen in symbolism when he awoke from the dream of life.

Those who are not awake from the dream of life will continue fighting shadows, for the whole vast world is simply the world of shadows. Everything in the world is simply himself pushed out, and he's fighting only himself. So as Shelley said of the one who awoke, "He has awakened from the dream of life. 'Tis we who are lost in these stormy visions and keep with phantoms an unprofitable strife." So man who is fighting today against the establishment, fighting against this, that and the other, doesn't realize he is only fighting against the objectified images of his own mind. He is the dreamer dreaming the entire world...and he's simply carrying on the dream.

The day will come that he will suddenly awake within himself. And then it is said of the one who awoke and who tried to tell it to others, they call him in the Bible, they call him Jesus. Well, the word Jesus and the word Joshua are the same, and they both mean the same thing as Jehovah, which means "the Lord saves, Jehovah is salvation, or Jehovah saves." A man is saved from the dream and he is simply returned to his *normal* state before he began the dream.

Now, they said of him, is this not Jesus when he told the story. He said, "I came down from heaven." "Is this not Jesus, the son of Joseph, and do we not know his father and mother and his brothers and sisters? How then can he say that he came down from heaven? Why, he has a demon and he is mad. Why listen to him?" (Jn.6:41). Why listen to a man with such nonsense? Because man is looking for the coming of savior on the outside to change the establishment, to change society, to change the world and think it is here on earth when it hasn't a thing to do with this world of dream. When he comes he comes from within you, for he *is* within you, and he awakens within you in this wonderful series of events. Everything said in scripture is said of him, and it's all about *you,* for you are the dreamer and the whole vast world is your dream pushed out. So fight with it if you will. Do what you want. You will not awaken until you have experienced the dream of life. Everyone must dream this dream of life, and in the end he will awaken from the dream of life to find himself God. There is only God in the world, there is nothing but God, and God is your own wonderful *human* Imagination. There is no other God, no other Jesus Christ, and no other Lord. *This* is the God of scripture.

I'll tell you the series of events that will take place. It begins with your resurrection. You don't resurrect in the cemetery...there is no cemetery... all that is big business. All the cemeteries of the world were conceived by a greedy man to make money. There is no holy ground outside of where you are. *You* are the holy ground, and the holy sepulcher is your skull, and that is where God is buried. God became you, man, so that man may become God. So he's buried in man in his own wonderful human skull. And one day, after the dream has been completely dreamed to the very end, you will find yourself waking. Instead of waking as you've done day after day to find the same world confronting you, a world that you either like or dislike, you find a world, but it's not this one. You awake within your skull and you're completely sealed, may I tell you. It's not just a skull, it's sealed like an egg, and you have to break it from within, and you come out. You come out in the form of the same being that you are...there is no change of identity.

But the symbolism of scripture...when you are told a little child signifies the birth of God, you will find that symbol, a little infant wrapped in swaddling clothes. You'll find witnesses to your birth and it will be three. Two will deny that you could bring forth a child because they take it literally. But one will find the evidence, find the infant wrapped in swaddling clothes and present it to *you,* the one who came out awakened from the dream of life. Here, you'll take that little infant in your own hands and speak to it with the most endearing terms. In my case, I simply said, "How is my sweetheart?" and as I held it in my hands, the whole scene dissolved.

Then you go from there into another section of scripture, for you were the Spirit of Jehovah who inspired the prophets to write the Bible. You are not other than Jehovah...you are the Spirit of Jehovah who inspired the prophets to write what we call the Old Testament. What is called in the New Testament Jesus Christ is nothing more than the same Spirit of Jehovah who controlled the lives of those who wrote the stories of the New Testament... the same being and *you* are that being. Then following this, birth from above...for you are only born from above through the resurrection of Jesus Christ from the dead (1Pet.1:3)...and you are Jesus Christ. So you simply awake and you are resurrected and then the whole thing takes place within you.

The second great event is this. You inspired the psalmist to say these words, "I will tell of the decree of the Lord: he said unto me, 'Thou art my son, today I have begotten thee'" as you read it in the 2nd Psalm (2:7). So you must now fulfill it, for you've come into the world to fulfill your own prediction. So you come in to fulfill this: "I have found David and he has cried unto me, 'Thou art my Father, my God, and the Rock of my salvation" (Ps.89:20, 26). So the second grand event will come when suddenly standing before you will be this eternal youth, *the* David, not *a* David, of biblical fame. There will be no uncertainty as to the relationship between you and the David that you're seeing, and you'll know the relationship is son to father, and father to son. He will know it, you will know it and yet you're living in this century, the 20th Century. Here you see this wonderful being who stands before you and who is the result of all that you've experienced. For all the generations of man and their experiences if you would fuse them into a single being and personify that being, it would come out as David. David is the result of all the experiences and all the generations of man.

Here is the eternal youth. So you brought forth from your experiences of humanity this being who is your son. He stands before you, this beautiful lad just as described in the 16th chapter of the Book of 1st Samuel, this lovely lad (16:56). You can't describe the beauty of David. He's not just a boy, he's not just a David; he is *the* David of biblical fame. Here you are living in this century and he is supposed to have lived, if you take it chronologically, 3,000 years ago.

But the Bible is not secular history, the Bible is salvation history. The Bible is written not concerning anything taking place here. This is the hell into which man, which is God, descended, and we dream the dream of life in a world of hell. But before we descended into this...so then he says, I came down from heaven..."I came out from the Father and I came into the world; again I am leaving the world and I'm going to the Father" (Jn.16:28), it is only the Father. *You* are God the Father and there is no one else in the world but God the Father. So he comes into this wonderful adventure for the purpose of *expansion*, for if the limit of expansion were already reached, it would be hell. Just imagine if you could never go beyond what you are. So, we speak of omnipotence that is not part of scripture. When we speak of any of these omni-so-and-so...there must always be the opportunity for expansion. So God is ever expanding in wisdom, expanding in power, expanding in everything. And so, he limits himself to a contraction called man, to this opacity called man, and then he breaks through this contraction, this opacity, into this wonderful *expansion* beyond what he was prior to his descent from his exalted state into this limited state. So man goes through these events.

Now, we are told in scripture, "As Moses lifted up the serpent in the wilderness, even so must the Son of man be lifted up" (Jn.3:14). Now, this Christ comes not as the world expects him to come; for you're told, "When Christ comes, no one will know where he came from; yet we know this man, we know where he came from" (Jn.7:27). Well, when he comes no one will know...certainly no one will know. They know where the speaker came from, they know his baptism certificate, born in the year 1905, February the 19th, on the little island called Barbados, and here is his little appearance in the world, so all who know my appearance in the world can follow the record. They know that this little thing called Neville appeared at that moment in time in this century. Then I tell my brothers, my sister, and my family and friends that I am *not* of this world. I came down from heaven and I've only just remembered. All along I have been suffering from amnesia, total amnesia, and I thought that I was Neville Goddard, a member of a certain family, a member of a certain race, and all these things. Suddenly my memory returned and now I remember who I am. I came down from

The Return of Glory

heaven. I came from my own being, who is God the Father, and I came in for a purpose into the world and wore a garment that is called your brother, that is called your son, called your friend…and here I am wearing a garment called Neville Goddard…and yet I am not. I am a being who came out from himself and came into the world, and now I'm leaving the world and returning to myself having accomplished the purpose for which I came.

And they say, "Are you sure you're feeling all right? Are you really? Because this man has a devil and he is mad. Because he does not believe in an external God; he believes that he *is* God, and what can he do in the world?" Then they challenge you, all right, if you are God, turn this stone into bread, fall off the cliff, and see if he does not give you support to move without the aid of something else (Mat.4:3). And you say to such a doubting Thomas, "Get thee behind me." I cannot share with you what I have experienced. I can tell you what I have experienced and tell you that you will in time have a similar experience. You will simply duplicate what I have experienced: you will know one day that you are God the Father. For just as *you* inspired, because God is one, there aren't two Gods, only one: "Hear, O Israel: The Lord our God, the Lord is one" (Deut.6:4). And so the God who inspired the psalmist to say, "I will tell of the decree of the Lord," *you* are that Lord who inspired them to write the words, "Thou art my son, today I have begotten you" (Ps.2:7).

So you come in to fulfill your own words, and then he has to stand before you; and he is but the result of all the experiences of humanity. You've gone through *all* the experiences; you've played every conceivable part before you come to the end. You were the rebel, and you were the conservative, you were this, you were that, you were the other. You play every part in the world, and having played all the parts then you can bring forth that which is the *result* of all the parts. So don't think for one second that someone today who is now the rebel hasn't played or will play the conservative, or who is now the conservative has not played or will play the rebel. You have played *every* part in the world, and having played all you will forgive all, because it takes *all* to bring forth the result. The result is a son, "Thou art my son, today I have begotten thee" and it's David, the eternal David that stands before you.

Then you will find another event as told us, "As Moses lifted up the serpent in the wilderness, so must the Son of man be lifted up" (Jn.3:14). The Son of man is the Christ in you, your own wonderful dreaming being. And you'll find the event so beautiful—when you experience it you can hardly believe this could have happened to you—but you will find yourself split from top to bottom, from the top of your skull to the base of your spine, and the two parts will simply separate, maybe six inches. At the base of your spine you'll find a golden, liquid light, and that light will be a pulsing living light. As you look at it you will know it is yourself, and you will fuse with it, and then like a fiery serpent you will move up that spinal cord into your skull. You'll simply move right up and your whole skull will reverberate like thunder. I can't describe it other than to tell you that is what is going to happen to you. You will try your best to get out. You won't get out, for your skull contains all; the whole vast drama is all within you.

Then will come the final one and in the final one, suddenly your skull will become translucent, transparent, infinite, and there is no circumference. Then you from within looking up will see a *dove* circling over your head about twenty feet above, as though floating. It's not using its wings, just floating. Its eyes are lovingly fixed upon you and your eyes upon it. Then you will raise your hand automatically. In my own case, my left hand went out and the index finger came out, and the dove descended and lit upon my finger. I brought it to my face and it smothered me with kisses, all over my face, my head, my neck, smothering me with affection. Then a woman at my side said, "They avoid humanity because man gives off such an obnoxious odor, an offensive odor. But he loves you, and because of his love for you he penetrated this ring of offense and descended to demonstrate his love for you." And while he was smothering me with love then the whole scene dissolved. And "He upon whom you see the Spirit descend in bodily form as a dove and *remains*" (Jn.1.32, 33) that is he.

But I am not alone; I am only a sample. I'm telling you what has happened to me and what will happen to every being in this world. So let it go on, let them riot, let them carry on, let them do all the things in the world. It's been going on forever and forever and there's nothing new under the sun. Man *thinks* it's new. I saw in today's paper that Professor Urey has just brought in his verdict concerning the moon dust and the rocks as the same age as that of the earth. He claims four and a half billion years old. And the whole thing simply started together, the whole thing, just together. No evolution. Evolution is only in the affairs of man, but not in the Creation of God. Yes, I move from using a hoe to a tractor, and from walking the distance between here and the east to now a jet plane; and crossing the ocean I go by plane today; but before that I went by ship…not a sailing vessel, or by rowing, or by simply moving with the current…but I used power.

Here I find an evolution in the affairs of man but not in the Creation of God. The whole thing was one grand explosion like an orgasm and all at one time. The only place that could cradle this biological experiment is earth. They found nothing on the moon but that which could not cradle life. They will find nothing on Mars or Venus or Mercury or any of the planets where they seek. In this fabulous explosion it is only here, this little spot called the earth. As Blake said, "We are put on earth a little space to learn to bear the beams of love." So here we are. You don't see any evidence of learning to bear the beams of love. You see nothing but hate and violence, man against man. He's going to tear down everything and set himself up as the criterion of what you should follow. He doesn't know that time moves on, and he, too, will be old like the speaker, and he, too, will be called old. No one will trust him because he's my age; today they don't trust anyone over thirty. But after all, they won't be thirty very long. They'll be soon forty and then the boys who are fifty won't trust them, and then they'll be sixty and they're old, old people. And it goes on and on, the same thing over and over. There's nothing new under the sun. They think they're going to arrest time and maintain that twenty-five or twenty-eight forever and forever. Well, if they ___(??) it, let them be it.

I'm telling you what I know from experience, and what a man knows from experience he knows more thoroughly than he knows anything in this world. Oh, you can know something by hearsay, but you don't really know it until you have experienced it. When the dreamer in you dreaming this world begins to awake, then you realize how, really, the whole thing is a dream. And you can prove it right here in this world. If this world is a dream, this waking world of mine is as much a dream as my dream of last night, and then I should be able to control it. In the dream of last night I might have been startled, I might have been frightened, I might have thought for one moment that it was a reality outside of myself and beyond my control. I woke to discover it was a dream and had I known in the dream I could have controlled it, and I could have changed it. But I didn't wake within the dream, therefore, I was scared, I was frightened by it. Now I wake into what the world calls a waking state, I'm awake now so this is all right…these are facts, these are realities outside of myself and so it's not a dream. Last night was a dream and I didn't know it or I could have controlled it. Now I know this is not a dream…isn't it?

This *is* a dream, my dears, this is as much a dream as the dream of last night, only it's more difficult for man to control, because he sees it's so real and so objective and so independent of has own perception of it. But to prove to you that you can control it *assume* that it is a dream. Then assume that things are as you would like them to be and persuade yourself of the *reality* of your assumption. Don't make any effort to make it so, just trust the power within you to make it so. For the power who assumed it is the Lord Jesus Christ, and all things are possible to the Lord. So simply assume that it is and you'll prove to your own satisfaction that an assumption though false at the moment that it is made—that is, it's denied by your senses, denied by your reason—if *persisted* in it will harden into fact. When it hardens into fact, it will happen in such a normal, natural manner that you might say to yourself, it would have happened anyway. That is the dream. When it happens through normal channels you'll find yourself saying, well, that would have happened anyway. On reflection it happened so beautifully...this one met that one and that one met others, and then together they formed a certain chain of events, and the events culminated in this which I had assumed. But certainly my assumption was not the cause of this chain of events. And so, we see it happen before us and we can't quite believe that we are the cause of the phenomena of life.

But I tell you, try it. Try it once, try it twice, and after you try it a few times and see it does work you'll stop all the fighting in the world. You'll stop all this conflict in the world as far as *you* are concerned. Leave it to the dreamers who are still sound asleep and let them dream their violence, perfectly alright, let them dream it. In the midst of their violence you walk through just as though you are protected...and you *are* because the dreamer has awakened. It is your dream too, and no dreamer can be destroyed by his dream. You've stopped dreaming the dream of violence, and now you start an entirely different dream while you are here. And you tell it to the best of your ability to those who will listen...not everyone will listen. They will call you mad and that's the eternal picture. The man has a devil and he's mad, why do you listen to him? Why listen to him? The man is mad. He tells me he came down from heaven, yet here we know his father, his father is Joseph, his mother is Mary, and he tells me he came from heaven. Now he tells me that before Abraham was that he is, but how on earth could he know my father Abraham? How could he living in this century know Abraham who preceded him by 2,000 years? He must be mad! How could this one today in the 19th Century, 20th Century, know David and know him as his son? Why, that man is completely mad. And he doesn't believe in reincarnation. If he doesn't believe in reincarnation then how on earth can he be David's father?

He only believes in two births—one physical birth that never comes to an end until the second takes place—and only one death. The death is not when he departs this world and the world calls him dead, but death took place in the beginning of time when he completely emptied himself for this purpose; and took upon himself the form of a slave, and became actually embodied in a body of flesh and blood, and became a slave to it (Phil.2:6-8). So he had to eat and assimilate his own food. No matter how powerful he was he could not command another to do it for him. What he couldn't assimilate he had to eliminate, and he couldn't command anyone to do that for him. So he was a slave of the body that he took upon himself. That was in the beginning of time when he took upon himself a form called man. In the end he is re-born, and the rebirth is only the awakening from the dream that he self-imposed upon himself for this divine purpose: to expand his power and his wisdom beyond what it was when he made the decision.

So here, we are living in this *fabulous* world that *we ourselves* created. We agreed in the beginning to dream in concert, and we're dreaming in concert, allowing everyone to dream the dream he wants to dream. One dreams he wants to change the entire world like a Hitler, like a Stalin, and they seemingly kill millions of people. But not one that they seemingly kill truly dies. They just depart it and they move into another section of time clothed as they were. Others will come behind them with similar dreams to change the world and set it all up in their image. They know exactly what it's all about…and they don't know the whole thing was done *before* that the world was. That the whole vast world as we see it now is simply the unfolding of a purpose, and that purpose is the purpose that you and I as God agreed upon before we began the adventure.

So here, no other foundation! Oh, you'll find all kinds of foundations. Our scientists are constantly devising new hypotheses upon which to experiment, and they'll do it forever and forever. Don't stop them, leave them alone. They are dreaming too. Tomorrow, Professor Urey will find that some other professor, equally prominent and equally respected, will think that it's not four and a half billion but maybe six billion years. Oh, they chuck these little numbers around as though they were nothing, and they call these light-years, unnumbered light years, and all that is wonderful. Now we must study evolution in school. No one tells the students it's a *theory*, it's a hypothesis…it's not a fact. It must be taught as fact, and there's no evidence in the world to support it, none whatsoever. Yet we must come out and actually say that it is a fact. It's *not* a fact! This whole vast world was the orgasm of God…and only one little spot, a tiny little spot, called earth was the cradle where the great experiment could take place. And then the dream began and *you* are dreaming this dream.

If you don't think it's a dream, well then, you take some section of your life that seems beyond repair, beyond redemption, and rearrange it in your own mind's eye as you would like it to be, and persuade yourself of the reality of that assumption. And do nothing! Just wait…because "The vision has its own appointed hour; it ripens, it will flower. If it be long, then wait; it is sure and it will not be late" (Hab.2:3). It will come in the objective world and bear witness to the reality of your assumption. Then you will know the whole world is a dream, the whole vast world is a dream; and you are the dreamer, and you are the Jesus Christ of scripture. Jesus Christ of the New Testament is the Lord God Jehovah of the Old. The Old is an adumbration, a foreshadowing in a not altogether conclusive or immediately evident way. The New is the interpretation and the fulfillment of the Old. So when you hear the word Jesus and you think that it's a man other than yourself, you don't know Jesus. So when priests and ministers and rabbis are looking for the coming of the Messiah, they are looking in vain. He has *already* come or they couldn't even breathe. He is the life of every being born of woman… and he awakens in them. He doesn't come from without; he awakens from within *as* the being in whom he awakens.

Now you try it. What I've told you tonight concerning the coming of Christ as the *only* foundation you will not in eternity disprove, not in eternity. For I am not speaking from speculation, I am not theorizing, I'm telling you what I have experienced. So when this little garment is taken away in the not distant future, I will no longer be part of this age. There are two ages: this age that goes on beyond the grave. You find yourself in a world restored to life just as you are with no change of identity, only young, not an infant, about twenty years of age, in an environment best suited for the work yet to be done in you until the dream of life is over. When the dream of life is over, the series of events that I have just mapped for you will unfold within you, and you too will awaken from the dream of life. Then we all return as *one* being, for all together will form one being who is God the Father.

Now let us go into the Silence.

*　　*　　*

Now are there any questions, please?

Q: Why haven't I heard about this philosophy until now if it's true?
A: Well, sir, as Tennyson said, "Truth embodied in a tale will enter in at lowly doors." Man finds it difficult to accept bare truth, but thoughts put into pictures are acceptable. And so, the story is told in a way that you would think that a man called Jesus Christ lived 2,000 years ago, born of a woman who did not know man. So it is told in that form because man at a certain level can accept that in some strange way. But the Christ of *faith*, and we have to accept that story on faith, only comes to us as one unknown. One who in some ineffable mystery lets himself be experienced by man. When man experiences Christ, he knows *he is* Christ. So it's told in a strange wonderful way in the form of a story. My mother told me the story as every person born and raised in the environment in which I was raised in the same manner. I was born and raised in what is known as the Episcopal faith. Where I was born it's called the Anglican Church of England. But it's the same story, and I heard the story, and I cried as I was told certain aspects of it…how he

The Return of Glory

suffered. Well, I suffer…no one suffers more than you and I. This is Christ suffering, because Christ is your own wonderful I-am-ness, your own wonderful Imagination. But if Mother told me that story as a child, and she wouldn't know the other story, I would not have understood it. I could not have understood how some God could suffer when I am suffering, because I didn't know that I and he are one. Not until it happened in me…and then I realized that the suffering of Christ is my suffering.

But it happened to me suddenly…ten years ago this past July in the city of San Francisco. I was teaching the law all through the years since 1938, how to get what you want. That's all that I knew, the law of assumption…that consciousness creates reality. If I could create within myself the right state of consciousness, then I would out-picture it in my world. But I had no idea that behind it all was this great reality until suddenly one morning on the 20th day of July, 1959 it suddenly unfolded within me, and I was cast in the central role in the first-person, singular, present-tense experience, and all that was said of him in the New Testament I experienced. But I must continue in my same limited weak manner until I take off this garment, which is like a great musician trying to play the violin with a mitt on his hand. Take the greatest violinist in the world and put a mitt on his hand and say, "Go on and play." Oh, he might get a few notes out better than the amateur, but can he play? Put it on him and say, "Here's the grandest piano in the world, perfectly tuned, go on and play." He can't play it. So I'm still restricted until that moment in time when I'm taking off for the last time this garment of flesh.

And so, I will tell it as long as I am here to tell it and also in the hope that those who hear it and who believe me will continue to tell it after I'm gone. I've told it and recorded it in my book *Resurrection*, in the last chapter. The first four books are all based upon law—how to get what you want, which is good in the world of Caesar—but my last chapter is my own personal experience. I could not have told it before because I didn't experience it. It comes so shockingly sudden. And I would not criticize our leaders in the religious world because they don't know. They are appointed by men as our government leaders are appointed by men—they are *not* divinely appointed. When they make a claim that they are direct descendants of any Peter…there is no Peter… they're all states of consciousness. *All* the characters of the scriptures are eternal states of consciousness through which man passes. So it's not secular history; it's salvation history. So don't talk to me about he said so-and-so, quoting some character from scripture, any more than you say in Shakespeare, "You know what? That's what the king said." No that's what Shakespeare said. And "that's what so-and-so said"…no that's what Shakespeare said. Go back and read it. The author is Shakespeare and the king didn't say that. The chances are he was incapable of writing it. But Shakespeare, the grand poet, who understood human nature, and he wrote it and put these words into the mouths of characters. But they didn't say one word that he said.

So here, the Bible is simply the most glorious vision in the world. It's an eternal vision. These characters are reality but they're states. When you, the immortal you enters a state, it becomes personified because you are a person and you see the state as a person…but it's not a person. You enter the state of Abraham and you see this faith-beyond-measure as Abraham, but Abraham is only a state. *You* animate it and personify it when you enter the state of faith.

Thanks. Good night.

THE STATE OF PAUL: THE FREE MAN

10/13/69

Tonight's subject is on "The Free Man," the man who is set free. Paul, if we take him as a person, and I do not, but we'll take him as a person that you may understand the mystery. He was the first man in history to be set free, but Paul really represents *all* who are set free.

The first book in the New Testament chronologically speaking is Paul's letter to the Galatians. When you read it in scripture it is not the first, but that is only the canon of the fathers; they arranged all these in *their* own order. But all scholars are agreed that Galatians came first, and his thirteen letters form a quarter of the New Testament. He begins it in this manner: "Paul an apostle—not from men nor through man, but through Jesus Christ and God the Father, who raised him from the dead." If you understood that verse, it really tells the entire story…just that simple verse, the first verse of the first chapter of Galatians. An apostle is one who is sent on a mission. The mission in this case is to tell what he has experienced…to tell the story of salvation. So he tells you that he's an apostle and he never saw any Jesus Christ after the flesh, never. But the mystery was revealed *in* him, and then he came out to tell it. He didn't get it from a man or from any man in the world, any of them. He got it from Jesus Christ, having *experienced* who Jesus Christ really is and from God the Father who raised him from the dead.

Then he makes the statement in the same first chapter, "For I would have you know, brethren, that I did not receive this from man, but it came through a revelation of Jesus Christ" (1:11, 12). He doesn't deny that he heard the story from others, as you have heard it, as I have heard it. My mother taught me the story and she told it to me as secular history. She died believing that it took place in one little individual 2,000 years ago. That's how she taught it to me, that's how she was taught it by her mother, and throughout the ages men have been taught it in that manner. So, she heard it from others. He couldn't quite believe that that was what the prophets intended, because the only scripture was the Old Testament. So when he was told the story of Jesus Christ, of a peculiar, remarkable, miraculous birth, and a resurrection and an ascension, and a being who was man dared to claim that he was God, that he actually *was* God, God the Father, well, he rebelled against that until one day in this shocking suddenness it unfolded itself in him, and he realized the story of the mystery of Jesus Christ. So he did not deny he had heard it from others; what he insisted was defending *his interpretation* of that story having experienced it,

Now he said, "It pleased God to reveal his Son in me" (Gal.1:16), but "No one knows who the Son is except the Father." He's telling you right away who he is. "It pleased God to reveal his Son *in me*"...the preposition is "in"; it's not "to" as some translations have it. It revealed itself in me. And "No one knows who the Son is except the Father, and no one knows who the Father is except the Son, and anyone to whom the Son chooses to reveal him" (Mat.11:27). So right in this revelation of his, when it pleases God to reveal his Son, he's telling you exactly who he is...for only God the Father knows his Son. No one knows the Son but the Father, and no one knows the Father but the Son. "No one has ever seen God; but the only begotten Son who is in the bosom of the Father, he has made him known" (Jn.1:18). So Paul is revealing exactly who he is in that first statement, that "Paul an apostle, not from men nor through man, but through Jesus Christ and God the Father, who raised him from the dead." And we go on to read what Paul is saying to all of us...he tells you, "I am free." He said, "Am I not free? Am I not an apostle? Have I not seen Jesus our Lord?" (1Cor.9:1).

Now, you can take that in two ways. He actually saw the risen Lord and became what he saw. He realized *he* was God the Father in seeing the risen Lord. The union took place. You can also take it, not only he became it in that way, but he understood the mystery. He said, "I will tell you a mystery which has been hidden for ages and generations, and the mystery is the mystery of Christ *in you* that is the hope of glory" (Col.1:26, 27). He tells you, "Christ is the image of the invisible God" (1:15)...and yet Christ is *in* you.

Now, as I said, there was only one scripture and that was the Old Testament. There was no New when these words were written. We turn to the Old and we read the words, "Keep me as the apple of the eye. When I awake, I will be satisfied in beholding thy form" (Ps.17:8, 15). He's speaking now to the Lord and this is David speaking, the 17th Psalm: "Keep me as the apple of the eye. When I awake I will be satisfied in beholding thy form."

The Return of Glory

The phrase translated "the apple of the eye" literally means "the little man of the eye." Look into any man's eye whether he be an evil man or a good man, and what do you see if you look right into the eye? For the apple of the eye is that which is hollowed out, that dark spot that is like a gate, and it is called "the gate." Well, it's called "the little man of the eye." You look into anyone's eye, you look right into the pupil, and you do not see the man, you see yourself. So, "Keep me, O Lord, as the apple of the eye." So the Lord looks into my eye and sees his own reflection, and his reflection is Jesus Christ who is God himself. He's not seeing another, he is seeing himself as he looks into my eye having hollowed it out and forming a pupil that could reflect. In the darkness of the pupil God sees only himself.

Now, be faithful, O Lord...and be faithful to the image, faithful to the vision that you've seen. He only saw himself. "Let us make man in our image" (Gen.1:26). He looks into my eye, into your eye, and he only sees himself; and he keeps the vision in time of trouble. As Paul said, "I was not disobedient to the heavenly vision. I kept it in time of trouble" (Acts26:19). So God keeps his vision of himself no matter what you do, no matter what furnaces he puts you through. He'll take you through all the fires of the world in order to bring out himself as a living being, *as* himself. So, "Keep me as the apple of the eye," said David. And Paul realized after the experience what scripture really meant: that God beholds himself, but not when he looks at you outwardly, for he sees *not* the outward man, he sees only the inner man. So he looks at you and he sees the same image that he saw when he looked at me, and he looked at the whole vast world whether you be black, yellow, pink, white, and looking into the eye he sees only himself. That's all that he's going to bring out; he is going to resurrect himself. He sees himself *buried* in man, and he will bring out of man the being that he is, endowed with all that he is, power, wisdom, and clothed in the body that God wears, which is infinite love. So you may be a violent, horrible creature, but when that one is awakened within you and it comes out, it will be *God* wearing the form of God, and that form is infinite love. I know that from experience.

He doesn't tell you that having had the experience that the remaining years will be pleasant. No, his story is one of horror. He was imprisoned, he was beaten, he was left for dead, and he was ship-wrecked. All the horrors that could take place in man took place. So that represents man. Don't think because a man has experienced scripture that he is in any way set free from the horrors of the world, which is this world. He still goes through it until the very end, but knowing that at the very end when he takes off the garment that he's been wearing, which is his cross, that he is set free and he is now radiating the glory of God and reflecting the glory of God and he is the express image of his person. So when you see him, you see God... can't see another. You will see God—everyone individualized, no loss of individuality, and yet wearing the form of God and with the power of God, which is a protean being, able to assume any form, any shape in the world that suits your purpose when you are sent on a mission. You are sent on a mission, for you are now the apostle, the one who was called and sent.

So here, the story of Paul is the story of the free man in the world. Who is Paul? Who knows? His first name is Saul and Saul means "Ask Paul." He is seeking. Paul means "the little one." As we are told in scripture, "How can Jacob stand? He is so small!" (Amos7:2). You look into the pupil of the eye of anyone and the little reflection of yourself is so little. But Jacob's name is changed to Israel and the word Israel means "the man who rules *as* God." Not *like* a God, *as* God. He only sees himself. And he changes the name Jacob, which means "the supplanter," into Israel, "the man who rules as God." So nothing in this world can really fail in God's purpose. As Paul made the statement, "He has made known unto me the mystery of his will, according to his purpose, which he set forth in Christ as a *plan* for the fullness of time" (Eph.1:9). So Paul discovered what man has yet to discover, that Jesus Christ is a *plan*, a plan set forth in man. It is called in scripture, Jesus Christ. But that is not a man *outside* of you; that is the plan *in* you. And when it unfolds, it is man, for you are man, and it unfolds in you in the most marvelous manner.

He described it the best he could and he told it to the best of his ability. If we have discovered all of Paul's letters, no one knows. We only have thirteen. There might have been others...or he might have taken into his confidence those who did not record it...and maybe he didn't write it. But I'm quite sure he would have written the identical story as I've told you concerning that plan as it unfolded itself in me. It's the same story. Two cannot have different plans; there's only one plan. "He has made known unto me the mystery of his will, according to his purpose which he set forth in Christ as *a plan* for the fullness of time" (Eph.1:9). When the time is fulfilled, it erupts within *man* and man discovers he *is* God, and he *is* the Lord Jehovah; for the plan simply unfolds in him as a seed would unfold if it is dropped into the earth.

So whoever Paul was...and he certainly is not named in any non-biblical source in the 1st Century. How could a man go through all those experiences as recorded in the Book of Acts and recorded in his letters, where he was imprisoned, he was charged, brought before the governor, brought before King Agrippa, and he said, "I was not disobedient to the heavenly vision" (Acts26:19)...and "why should any of you think it incredible that God should raise the dead" (11:19)? "Why do you think it incredible when God promised our fathers that is what he would do? And now for the hope that is the hope of our fathers, which God revealed to them through prophets, I stand before you a slave, enchained."

So here, that is not recorded in anything outside of the Bible, and yet there were works of the 1st Century where if the man lived as an individual then certainly his imprisonment, his arrest, his ship-wreck, all these trials certainly would be recorded, for we have all the others recorded. So he is no more a person than Jesus Christ, or Abraham, or Isaac, or Jacob. These are eternal states. When you reach the state of Paul then you are set free, for the mystery of Jesus Christ unfolds within you and you know who you are. Then you are that little one who *was* Jacob…and how can Jacob stand seeing that he is so small? But God will take his image as reflected in the pupil of your eye as he beholds himself. He is not beholding the thing beheld like your form—he sees not the outer man—he only sees the inner man, and the inner man is God himself.

He is bringing forth from you himself and it is God that is born. But you're told in the story that Jesus Christ was born. "He was born not of blood nor of the will of the flesh nor of the will of man, but of God" (Jn.1:13). And who was born? A Savior was born. Well, who is the Savior? The Lord God Jehovah: "I am the Lord your God…and besides me there is no Savior" (Is.43:3). So if a Savior is born, it has to be the Lord God Jehovah, and what is his name? His name forever and forever is I AM (Exod.3:14). Well, who is having the experience?—I am. Well, that's God. And what was the experience? I felt myself waking from a sleep. You mean you were waking from a *sleep?* Yes, something unlike any other sleep I've ever had. I began to wake from a sleep, and to find myself in a holy sepulcher, and it was my skull. That was the place where I was born but buried, and that's the place where I was born. I came out of it as I formerly came out of my mother's womb, but this time it was different. I came out without loss of identity, knowing exactly who I am. Then the symbol of my birth presented itself before me, and then everything as recorded in scripture I have experienced.

Well now, go and tell it. Go and tell it to the world and encourage them to believe in the eternal story and to repudiate all authorities, all institutions, all customs, and all laws that interfere with the individual's *direct* access to his God. No one in this world has the authority to aid you towards that. That image is *already in* you, for God beheld himself in you. So you don't need any authority, whether it be called by the name of a pope or some archbishop or some rabbi or priest or some institution. You need *none*! Therefore completely reject and repudiate all authorities, all institutions, all customs, all laws that would in any way interfere with the individual's direct access to his God. He one day will awaken *as* God and not something other than God. There is only God in the world. Everyone in the world is going to have that experience, but everyone.

So I tell you from my own experience the story is the only true story in the world, for all the stories you read in the papers today about who made what and what they did and what they're going to do and what they're planning, all that will fade as though it never existed. But this eternal story which is planted in you will erupt, and when it erupts it interprets the Old Testament. The Old Testament contained it, but as an adumbration, as a foreshadowing, which could not be understood until it happened. When it happened in the individual then he understood the Old. Until it happened *in* one called Paul, he never understood the Old. He thought that you must abide by the laws, the external laws like the dietary laws, and all the ceremonies. We have kept these things through the centuries and none of these thing really matter. It doesn't really matter if you never saw the inside of a church...never saw any so-called holy man. That doesn't matter. Nothing must come between you and your God. When you find your God, you'll find him in yourself *as* yourself.

And he does have a Son. His Son is called David, and David is simply the result of your journey through fire. You are the one who came through the fires of experience in the world of death. The result of all the experiences that man could ever pass through stands personified before the man who has passed through the fires; and that personification is an eternal youth, and his name is David. He's not *a* David; he is *the* David of biblical fame. You'll know how true the words were when he said, "I will tell of the decree of the Lord: he said unto me, 'Thou art my son, today I have begotten thee'" (Ps.2:7). Well, here he stands before you and there's no uncertainty as to the relationship and the identity of who he is, and who you are. Then you will know the words, "When it pleased God to reveal his Son *in* me, I conferred not with flesh and blood" (Gal.1:16). To whom would I go in the world who has not had the experience and ask them for an interpretation of the experiences when there is *no* uncertainty in me as to what happened? How could I go? So he went into Arabia...no contact with anyone in the world... just went into himself to commune and ponder this fantastic thing that was so true and he didn't know it.

Here was the one who said, "I am of the seed of Abraham. I am of the tribe of Benjamin. I am a Pharisee of the Pharisees...keeping all the laws, and I did not know it until it pleased God to reveal his Son in me." And because no one knows the Son but the Father, when he revealed the Son then the one *beholding* the Son *is* his Father. And he knows it. It isn't something that this must be so because...you just simply know it. You know it more surely than you know any physical child of yours as your own child. A father is told in this world that he sired this child and he believes his wife. He trusts his wife or the woman whether she's his wife or not...and maybe it resembles him. It's not a duplicate, but it resembles him, and so he'll say "All right, it is my child." But he has no certainty that it is really his child. The woman if she's in some sleep when she delivers, she doesn't know whether it's her child that they give her when she leaves the hospital or another woman's child. What assurance has she? But there is *no* uncertainty as to this relationship between you the Father who is God the Father, and the Son who bears witness to your Fatherhood

So, it pleased God to reveal his Son in me and then I knew at that moment who I really am; prior to that I didn't know. I thought I was a little man born of a certain woman, of a certain father in this world and that was it. I was taught to believe and taught first by my mother and then by my school and then by the traditions of the world as I went to church, that all this happened 2,000 years ago, and that it's not related to this age. But the whole thing is contemporary, it is *taking* place. God came and comes into human history in the person of Jesus Christ...but Jesus Christ is the *pattern* of salvation. It is the pattern man that is buried in man. The moment God beheld himself in the eye and he called it the apple of his eye. So we are told in Zechariah, which means "God remembers," "He who touches you touches the apple of God's eye" (2:8). To touch him, you're touching the apple of God's eye. Now, don't interfere with him, leave him alone. He may be kind, he may be unkind...he's going through the furnaces. And "How long, vast and severe the furnaces before they find their Father were long to tell" (Blake, *Jerusalem*, Plt.73). How long will it take? Who knows? No one knows but the Father.

In that moment when suddenly it appears, it's the Son who appears to reveal the Father to himself and it is the Father who awoke. The Father's memory returned and he awoke from a long wonderful dream, but a frightening dream, and the dream is this world. This is the dream where God is dreaming everything in the world. "Rouse thyself! Why sleepest thou, O Lord? Wake! Do not cast us off forever" (Ps.44:23). These words are addressed to the dreamer and the dreamer is God. A man dreaming is caught up in a reality that is his own and entirely his own creation. Even though it's his own creation and he is the sole author of everything that is happening, he may be frightened by what is happening, he may be startled, just as though these events that he is now observing and experiencing are outside himself and beyond his control, just as in waking hours. And that is the dreamer in us. We are the dreamer and the dreamer is God. Everything in my world I am conjuring; and everything has some symbolic significance for me *if* I could interpret it. The story of the Bible it all begins "And this is the *vision* of Isaiah, the vision of Obadiah, the vision of Ezekiel"…and these are all the visions. And here, all the visions are spelling out one thing: how God became man that man may become God.

So everything in the world is the unfolding of God and he's unfolding in you *as you*. You are not some little thing on the outside cast away; you *are* God himself…but dreaming. You are dreaming undoubtedly horrible dreams and some lovely dreams. But mostly…you read the morning's paper and the daily press and listen to the radio and TV and they are horrible dreams. Yet in the end you will awaken from it all to find that you are God, clothed in an immortal form, and that form is love, "the human form divine." Yes you're human and God is man…let no one tell you he is not man. Oh, they can tell you but don't listen, don't be persuaded. I tell you God is man. "Thou art a man, God is no more; thine own humanity learn to adore" (Blake, *Everlasting Gospel*). For, he actually became humanity and this is the cross that God wears. He never wore another cross. There was no cross of wood, no cross of a tree. The tree is *in* man. Let our scientists search through Nature to find the tree. May I tell you, they will search in vain, for there grows one in the human brain (Blake, *Human Abstract*). That is where God is crucified, right in the skull of man. That's where he's buried and that's where he will rise; and when he rises he rises in you, and you are God.

His only begotten Son will stand before you, and he doesn't even have to speak, although he will, but he'll stand before you and you'll be so in love with your Son, this heavenly eternal youth that is David. He has no mother and you are his Father, regardless of your sex here. May I tell you, forget your sex here, for in the resurrection there is no Greek, no Jew, no bond, no free, no male, no female (Gal.3:28). You are above the organization of sex. You are not a male, you are Man. Capitalize it. It is Man, not a little male which is a divided image of male-female. And you will find yourself completely fulfilling scripture.

So the basis of Paul's authority was *experiencing* scripture. Not a dead written code as you read a Bible. You take up the Bible and start to read it and you'll say, "What does this mean? Isn't this horrible! What on earth could this be?" You can't understand it. But *after* the experience, it's an open book and all the seals are broken and you see it clearly. Everything in the book Man is capable of doing; he has done, is doing, and will continue to do until he has awakened from the dream of life. One day he will awaken from it all and just as he awakens he awakens as God the Father. Yet he continues in his little garment of flesh and blood, in prison, in bondage. And he too will cry out, "O King Agrippa, why should it be thought for one moment incredible that God raises the dead? Is this not the promise that God made

The Return of Glory

to our fathers through the prophets? And now why am I standing before you chained as I am? Would that you are all as I am—minus the chains" (Acts 26:22, 29). That's what he said.

So he did not get rid of the limitations of the flesh, the weaknesses of the flesh, while he wore the body on which he was still crucified. But he knew what he had experienced, and he knew that at the very moment that it was taken off it would be taken off for the last time, and he would come into his *glory*. The glory was simply the radiation of the glory of God. He would not only radiate it but reflect the glory of God, and he would be the express image of his person. He was a person: God was Man. So when you met him in the future, you met God. You didn't meet a little being; you met God, clothed in his immortal garment which was infinite love.

So the Paul of scripture is like all the other characters of scripture, all are eternal states through which Man passes. He passes and the states remain…but the pilgrim passes on. You started in the beginning with faith in the story that was told you…as Paul makes the statement that the story was revealed to Abraham. Can you imagine the gospel being told to Abraham when if you take it chronologically they are separated by thousands of years? It is said, "The scripture, foreseeing that God would save the Gentiles"—call the word heathen—"through faith, preached the gospel beforehand to Abraham" (Gal. 3:8).

Now he tells you that the story of Abraham is an *allegory* (Gal. 4:24). Do you know what an allegory is? It's a story told as if it were true leaving the one who hears it to discover the fictitious character and learn its lesson. One should apply the lesson after having learned it. So he tells you in Galatians that Abraham—speaking now of the character which he tells you is an allegory—had two sons, one born into slavery and one born into freedom. Then he makes the statement, a bold statement, "This is an allegory." Well now, if that is an allegory and the New Testament begins in the canonical order of the books with these words, "This is the genealogy of Jesus Christ, the son of David, the son of Abraham"…if Abraham and his story is an allegory, then what is his offspring? So what is the genealogy? These are the states of consciousness through which the *immortal you* must pass.

So I can't begin with an allegory and arrive at something that is called reality. All ends run true to origins, and if the origin is an allegory, then what is the end? "You see yonder fields? The sesamum was sesamum and the corn was corn; the silence and the darkness knew, and so is a man's fate born" (Sir Edwin Arnold, *The Light of Asia*). So if this story is an allegory, then let me now sift it and separate the wheat from the chaff, and find out what it really means. Find out just what that story which is an allegory is trying to tell me. There are two births. This one is born of a slave, it enslaves me as long as I wear it, and it was born from the womb of a woman, "my mother" I call her…a very wonderful lovely mother, my mother. But there's another birth and that is born not from the womb, not of blood, not of the will of the flesh, nor of the will of man but of God. And that is God himself—he begets himself. As these beget themselves, so God begets himself: one is born into slavery and one is born into freedom.

So the first man in history to be really set free is represented in scripture as Paul, and everyone who is set free by the identical experience is Paul. He is the free man, freed from this world of bondage and made in such a way as the son of God. And he tells us in the 8th chapter of Romans (8:19) that the whole creation is actually in turmoil and in slavery and in pain waiting for the liberation and the setting free of what?—of the sons of God. For, we're all sons of God and it takes us all collectively to form *one* being, and that being is God the Father. No child is born in this world who is not a son of God. As told us, "He has set the bounds to the peoples of the earth according to the number of the sons of God." Read it in the 32nd chapter of Deuteronomy. No child could be born who is not actually a garment worn by the son of God and it takes all the sons to form the Father. The same word, may I tell you, the word is Elohim. It's sometimes used in the singular and sometimes in the plural, but it's the same word. Elohim is really a plural word as told us in that 82nd Psalm, "And God has taken his place in the divine circle, the divine assembly, and in the midst of the gods"—the same word now translated plural gods is the word translated God in the singular. And then he turns to the gods and he said, "I say you are gods, sons of the Most High, all of you; nevertheless, you will die like men, and fall as one man, O princes" (Ps.82:1,6).

So we are the gods who came down into the world in this fabulous biological experiment, the only spot in eternity that could really cradle this experiment. And the gods took upon themselves the limitations and the weaknesses of the flesh, and they were formed in this manner. Now he's redeeming himself, for he and his sons are one. "I and my Father are one" we are told (Jn.10:30). So he is redeeming all of his sons, and when all are redeemed they form the Father. And there's only one Father and there's only then one Son. For you are the Father and the result of the experiment is personified as David the Son.

So, having had the experience I do not deny that the story was first told me by my mother and then I heard it when I went to school. I was beaten unmercifully for misquoting—which I did not misquote—but he was a sadist that I had as a master, and corporeal punishment was allowed where I was born, and he beat me until blood poured, for simply saying "Take up thy *bed* and walk." When I could not produce my Bible, because his translation said, "Take up thy couch and walk." To satisfy his own sexual pleasure, for he was a sadist, he simply went in and got a long cane that he could bend into a circle, made me lean over a chair, and beat me unmercifully. That was allowed. And when my father that night saw what he had done, for my brother Victor told him what I looked like, when my father came in and saw the condition of my body, he started dressing. It took all the family to restrain him and the neighbors to restrain him, which was good because his intention was to kill him, and he would have. He could have...he was a big strapping strong man, my father, and in those days he was a very young man. But luckily they restrained him. One year later this man blew his brains out. Of course I was taken out of school that very day. So, driven into my mind was the book of God...beaten unmercifully for quoting correctly, but it wasn't quite what his Bible said. And maybe it didn't say that, but he was looking for an opportunity, some excuse, to beat me.

So here, I tell you the book is the only true book in the world. All the others are theories. Today's great theory of the moon, oh, they'll change it...give them a few months and they'll modify the age of the moon, raise it from four billion to maybe six billion or drop it down to two billion. Oh, they'll throw it around and they will have all these theories. We're always modifying our theories, for our men of science are constantly devising new hypotheses upon which to test and to experiment with their little concepts of life. You and I have *one* and we need not change it. I call it God...and God is your own wonderful human Imagination that is God. Can you imagine? Well, that's God, the only reality in the world. That's the dreamer in man and the dreamer in man is God. That is called in scripture Jesus Christ. It contains a plan, a plan that was devised before that the world was to awaken all of his sons and bring them back from this world of death.

For we came into this experiment—and what a glorious experiment—but we were warned that we would die, we the immortal ones would experience death, and all of our friends would die, our loved ones would die. Yet we were told, "You will not surely die." You will die but not surely die. And while it lasts, we have no assurance that that statement is true...we only see them die. We can't touch the hand that we love, we can't hear the voice that we love, and they disappear from our world. And we have to go along believing...is it really true? Is it really true that they didn't die, the woman who bore me that I nursed, who loved me and protected me? My father who when he was about to depart this world that he would take all of his earthly goods and divide them among his children, and give them to his children, so that I came into an inheritance from him, and that he is no more...that I would never see him again?

Well, I *know* that's a lie, but my senses would go along with that and reason would confirm it. For how can you take a man and cremate it and turn it into dust before you and tell me something survived? And yet I know that something survived in a world just like this and he continues in a world just like this, in a body that I recognize, only much, much younger, not an infant, a young man. And he continues in a world, learning and experiencing all that he must until that moment in time when it is ripe. Then the pattern that was in him from the beginning of time, when God beheld in him his image and knew him as the apple of the eye, then in a moment when it is fully ripe it erupts, just like fruit coming out of a tree. What comes out? That pattern as described in the story of Jesus Christ: that miraculous birth, following on the heels of his resurrection. It comes first as a resurrection from the grave, coming out of the grave like a little sprig coming out of the earth. That coming out of the earth is his birth. He's surrounded by the symbolism, as told us in the Book of Luke and Matthew: the little infant wrapped in swaddling clothes. Then he knows that this is the *sign* of his *own* birth and it's the birth of God. And yet there's no change of identity and no loss of identity. Then comes the discovery of the Fatherhood of God and he is the Father. So in the end, he is not my father…he and I are brothers and *we* are the Father. We have the same Son and the Son is David.

So here, my earthly father ceases to be my father…he becomes my brother. Then we understand the words, "Now go unto my brothers and tell them I am ascending unto my Father and your Father, unto my God and to your God" (Jn.20:17). Here is the one who had the experience who is telling, "Here is the pattern and all are brothers regardless of the pigment of skin, regardless of your race, your nation, anything." In the end we are all brothers and together, collectively, we form one Father, and *we are* the Father. The result of our pilgrimage in this world of horror and death is a Son called David, that eternal youth.

Now let us go into the Silence.

* * *

Now are there any questions, please?

Q: If I understand correctly, in meditation we keep still to listen to the still, small voice within us, and reduce ourselves. But if we use our Imagination, aren't we doing the opposite here, exerting it to a greater degree to bring something to it that we want? Are they compatible?
A: Well sir, you can do either. In the Silence you can be still as you're told in the 46th Psalm: "Be still and know I am God." You could do that. Or if

the pressure is on you and you are in need of something in the world of Caesar, you can use the power that you are, which is God's power—your own wonderful human Imagination—and construct a scene implying the fulfillment of your dream, and persuade yourself of the reality of this imaginal act. And if you are persuaded that that imaginal act was God's act, and you believe that all things are possible to God, you could walk through the door in confidence that in a way you do not know it will take place.

So you can do it either way. You can use it for the world of Caesar. He does not deny that in scripture...when they said taxes are due, he said, "Now bring me a ___(??). Now let me see the coin, and whose face is this, whose inscription?" He said, "Caesar's." "Render unto Caesar the things that are Caesar's" (Mat.22:21). In this world of Caesar I have to pay taxes, I have to pay rent, I have to buy food and clothing, and I have obligations to a family. These things must be met. I assume that responsibility. Well, I can use my talent—he gave me a talent and that talent is my own wonderful human Imagination—to simply imagine certain states and *trust* the power within me implicitly to take that imaginal act of mine and externalize it for me. I don't have to devise the means and work out the means. "I have ways and means that you know not of." So I just simply *let* it happen.

But you can do both. I find simply dwelling...because you're told in scripture that your Father knows your need...you have need of these things he knows. On the other hand, man may not be quite confident so that he's sure that my Father knows my rent is due in three, four weeks...maybe better remind him...so we then start applying this principle. But you are told the Father knows what you have need of: "Seek first the kingdom of God and all these things will be added unto you" (Mat.6:33). Well, seeking first the kingdom of God, we simply "Be still and know that I am he" (Ps.46:10). If I am he, then he would know the garment's need that he is wearing while I am in this world. But man is not quite that confident, and so he better prompt him. We feel more secure if three weeks in advance there was a certain deposit in the bank. Why wait until the last day to be startled? And so, it's entirely up to us. But I'm hoping that everyone will begin to live more and more by faith. We are told in scripture, without faith it is impossible to please him.

Q: What is the open eye that you see in the forehead just above the bridge of the nose?

A: Well, Ina my dear, I wouldn't speak of that eye. Tonight when I spoke of the eye, I spoke of the iris of the eye, which is the apple. It's called "that which is hollowed out, the little dark spot, called the pupil"; and in that when God looks he sees himself. But the other eye that mystics speak about and occultists and all those who teach otherwise it isn't mentioned in scripture. They speak of the all-seeing eye and then draw some big eye on the forehead of a man, and all of this is an attempt at *self*-salvation. Salvation is by faith: it's all grace, grace, grace and only grace.

Q: But I have it.

A: Well, my dear, if you have that eye that you speak of, I do not know of it. I do not know of that eye of which you speak. I know of visions. I know of the story of scripture. It is not mentioned in the Bible. But there are certain schools of thought that will teach self-salvation, and how they're simply going to conjure from the base of their spine a certain force, and all of this is self-deception, complete self-deception. It is faith, faith in whom?—faith in God.

I walk limited in this world…I'm so bound to this garment. When I heard this story, I didn't understand it. Because mother told it to me I believed it, but I couldn't quite understand it. And then came the eruption of the story *in me* and then I understood it. If she were here tonight and I told her what happened in me, that darling would not quite accept it, I know. Mother would be too disturbed and she would not want to believe in this power within herself. She would rather believe in what she believed before she departed this world, an external savior, something that is on the *outside*. And though she loved me dearly, because I am her child and she nursed me and raised me, she knows all the weaknesses and limitations of her son, she couldn't quite go along with me.

So I wouldn't blame anyone else if my own mother would not go along with me. I know my brothers don't…they think I'm completely mad. That's what they said of Paul. They said, "That is to say, O Paul, your great learning is driving you mad. He answered, Festus, I am not mad. Were that everyone in the world were as I am…minus these chains" (Acts 256:25, 29). But he thought him mad. Here was the Pharisee of the Pharisee making a claim and defending what formerly he tried to rub out because it hadn't yet happened in him. When it happens in a man, what can you do? You can't deny the evidence of the senses. It's more real than anything that happens in this world, it's forever. So he was not disobedient to the heavenly vision. It's the body that I wear when I am not in this body. It's not anything that you can describe. It's a human face, human voice and human hands…don't go beyond it. It is human…don't try. He said, "I will be satisfied when I awake with thy likeness" (Ps.17:15, KJV). Until then keep me as the apple of the eye. So I will be satisfied…when it happens I will be satisfied. *That* body will be the human form divine, which is all love, infinite love. That's what it is, nothing but love. You can hardly believe this world as we see it is really guided by a being of love, and it is.

Now, just a couple of minutes left, any questions?

Q: What part of the Bible is it where you say that Paul was accused of being mad?

A: The 26th chapter of the Book of Acts.

We're here every Monday and Friday through into the early part of December. You're all welcome. Every night is complete in itself. You don't have to come night after night. Any night you feel like coming remember it is simply a complete evening in itself. We don't try to tie into next time by leaving you in midair. That is not our purpose. I try to get everything together in the one evening. And if you feel so moved the next time, come every Monday, every Friday at eight.

Thank you. Good night.

SCRIPTURE MUST BE FULFILLED IN ME

10/17/69

According to a rabbinical principle what is not written in scripture is non-existent. The story of Jesus Christ follows this principle. "Scripture must be fulfilled in me" he said. "All that is written about me must be fulfilled. And beginning with Moses and the prophets, he interpreted to them in all the scripture the things concerning himself. And they said to each other, 'Did not our hearts burn…while he opened to us the scriptures?' And then he said to them, 'Everything written about me in the law of Moses and the prophets and the psalms must be fulfilled.' Then he opened their minds to understand the scriptures" (Luke 24:27,32, 44).

The one who wrote these words, the unknown one called Luke—for they're all anonymous—they were only telling their *own* experiences. It is the Christ in you of whom he speaks; he is not speaking of any Christ outside of you. That is the false Christ and false teachers talk about him as coming from without. So when they read in the scriptures, "Scoffers will come in the last days scoffing, saying, 'Where is the promise of his coming?' For ever since the fathers fell asleep, all things have continued as they were from the beginning of creation" (2Pet.3:3). Why certainly they do and they will continue—graft, war, dirty politics, poverty, you name it—it will continue forever and forever in this age. So do not look for any sign in the outer world for his coming, because this age will continue. In the midst of poverty, in the midst of graft, in the midst of war, in the midst of everything that is unlovely he comes. He comes like a thief in the night suddenly, when you least expect him, *within* you. And then he awakes. He awakes within you.

"In many and various ways God spoke of old to our fathers by the prophets, but in these last days he has spoken unto us by his Son" (Heb.1:1). When the Son comes, he reveals God the Father. Until then man is searching and searching on the outside. He will find all kinds of things as to how things are made, but he can't find the Maker. As you're told in the 19th Psalm "The heavens declare the glory of God; and the firmament shows forth his handiwork" (19:1). There is the handiwork, and our chemists and our great scientists are tearing it apart...going off into the heavens now. We've gone to the moon to bring back dead earth...never once anything lived upon it. Bring it back, analyze it to find it's just dead; it's been dead since the beginning of time. They'll find it is *all* dead no matter where they go. It is *here* that is his handiwork, but you won't find him no matter how you analyze his handiwork. You'll tear it apart and think I'm finding the secret of life. Today someone, three fellow citizens, received the Nobel Prize for their great work in trying to analyze this wonderful land of ours. They'll find many wonderful things about it, but they won't find the Maker. They will find the made, and they will find all kinds of things in this world that are made, but we will not find the Maker. He comes only when you find the Son, and only as you find the Son is the Maker who is God the Father revealed.

So the Bible is all about *you*: it is your own personal spiritual *biography*. Every child born of woman is written up in the Bible. No, your name is not written there as John or Neville or Brown; it is Jesus Christ. That's your name, that's the true being that you really are. So then you're told in scripture concerning the things to come, for the Old Testament is nothing more than a prophetic blueprint of the life of Jesus Christ. So then you are told in the 9th chapter of the Book of Isaiah, "To us a child is born, to us a son is given; and the government shall be upon his shoulder, and his name will be called 'Wonderful Counselor, Mighty God, Everlasting Father, Prince of Peace'" (9:6). So you read it and you wonder "What is it all about?" May I tell you, nothing could be truer.

It is not in the order in which the prophet recorded it, or some scribe recorded it… it is not in that order…but these names are true and it comes in a perfect order. A child is born and then the name given is Mighty God. The first name revealed to man was El Shaddai, God Almighty. That is Mighty God. Well, suddenly you—individually now, I'm speaking to you individually—you will feel something you've never felt before, a vibration that seems to you the very end and you think it's death. Far from death, it's waking you from death, waking you from a long, long sleep. You awake within yourself to find that you had been entombed for *unnumbered* centuries. You do not know how you got there and why. I'll tell you, you went there voluntarily. No one took away your life, you laid it down yourself. For you have the power to lay it down and the power to lift it up again (Jn.10:18). You went deliberately into that grave, the human skull, and you laid down in that grave to dream the dream of life.

Here for unnumbered years...some mystics claim 6,000 years. I have no vision to support a time interval, none. I'll go along with Blake if he says 6,000 years, but I have no vision to support it. I only know you feel as though you've been there for unnumbered ages when you wake. And for a moment you wonder 'how did I get here and why am I here and who placed me here?' Then you read scripture, "He is not dead, he but sleepeth. I go to awaken him" (Jn.11:11). And one day he shall hear the voice of the Son of God, and hearing it he shall awaken from death. For they hear the voice of the Son of God and those who are dead awaken from *sleep*, for it really was a sleep. "He sends his Son into our hearts crying, 'Father'" (Gal.4:4), and we hear it and awaken from this long, long *self*-imposed sleep.

So the first name is Mighty God. When man awakens within himself it takes this *enormous* power that is God to stir himself, to awaken himself from this sleep. That is the child that is born, for the child surrounds you. You see it and you know the child is the symbol of the *birth* of God. It is not the same as the Son is given. When you read it in the 9th chapter of Isaiah you think the child and the son are one and the same. No they are not. The Son comes 139 days later. When the Son comes it is *then* that you know who the Maker of it is and who is God the Creator. For the Son comes and when he comes you know exactly who *you* are. Prior to that you did not know; you were like the scientists trying to find the Maker of it all and looking *outside* yourself and it's *not* outside yourself. He comes from within and stands before you and calls you "Father." As he calls you Father you know this relationship is eternal, and you *are* the Father and he *is* your Son. That is the name then given to you, Eternal Father, Father forever.

There are four titles given to you. The first is Mighty God and the second is Everlasting Father. The third...and this is a strange one because it is given first when you read scripture, but it is not first, it comes third. And the third is based upon a peculiar wisdom; it is called Wonderful Counselor (Is.9:6). Well, the Wonderful Counselor in scripture is associated with a serpent. In the beginning it said, "The wisest of all God's creation was the serpent" (Gen.3:1). It was the serpent who suggested that you eat of the tree of knowledge. And then when you're told "God said you would die," it was the serpent who said "No you will not really die, not surely," he did not lie. We experience death, we tasted of death, but we did not *really* die. Even though we *seem* to die and all vanish one after the other, we don't really die. We depart from this world to be restored to life in a world just like

The Return of Glory

this to continue the journey for unnumbered centuries, but we don't really die. And the serpent was very wise as told in the same chapter. Then God said to the gods, "The man has become like one of us, knowing good and evil" (Gen.3:22), just as the serpent said he would. If you ate it, you would know good and evil, and you would become as the gods. And so, only as coming *down* into this world of experience...and now that third title is called Wonderful Counselor...it has much to do with the serpent.

Now we are told in scripture, "No one ascends into heaven but he who descended from heaven, the Son of man" and "As Moses lifted up the serpent in the wilderness, so must the Son of man be lifted up" (Jn.3:13,14). When you read it, it doesn't make sense until someone experiences it and then tells you about it. What you will one day experience and therefore to expect it... it's going to come. Then that third title is conferred upon you and his title is called the wisdom of God, this Wonderful Counselor. You can give all the advice in this world...it means nothing...for when this title is conferred you speak from experience, you *know*. You can say that you will not die, not surely die; for in the day that you eat it you will become as the gods and your eyes will be opened and you'll know from experience good and evil. And yet you will not die, you will return. You'll return by an ascent back into that heavenly state from which you descended. Just as the Son of man descended so the Son of man ascends...but he ascends like a serpent.

Now the serpent in scripture is described as the seraphim. Beyond that 6th chapter of the Book of Isaiah nothing is said about him, not a full description (6:1). He simply surrounded the throne of God. It is by definition a fiery serpent, a *fiery* being with human face, human voice, and human hands. He does give him six wings: two to cover his face, two to cover his feet which is a euphemism for his creative organ—he covers his nakedness with two—and then he flies with two. But beyond that he's not described, this heavenly being, the wisest of all God's creation and that is *you*! You are the gods that came down (Jn.10:34; Ps.82:6). You're not some little thing here that our scientists are trying to find out coming out of the mud and starting as some little amoeba. No, you're not that. You came down from heaven and you emptied yourself of all that you were in order to come here and assume the limitations and the weaknesses of the human flesh, this thing called flesh and blood. You aren't pretending that you are man; you became man with all of man's weaknesses. Assumed the poverty though you were rich; you assumed the weaknesses though you were strong; you assumed all these things though you were an infinite being so that you may have the experience that only *this* could give you. The whole vast world declares his glory, but *only* here on this little earth is his wonderful work revealed. Here on this little earth you and I came. We were brothers before we came. We have forgotten we are brothers and we fight each other here. We will one day awaken and return to our brotherhood, for when we return we are God the Father. It takes *all* the brothers to form God the Father. So that is the third title that is conferred upon you. The first was Mighty God, the second Everlasting Father, the third Wonderful Counselor, and the fourth Prince of Peace.

That latter one will descend in the form of a dove *on you* (Luke 22:37). Don't read it as something 2,000 years ago. It won't happen physically. No, it will happen and only you will know it…no one else will know it. As you're told in the earliest gospel, which is Mark (1:10), and if you read it carefully, no one but the one in whom it descended was aware of it. He's recording the event. But it is not seen by another, no one saw it but you. You had the experience and you alone, and that is the fourth title conferred upon you which is Prince of Peace.

So you bear the four titles and therefore you and you alone experience scripture. You foretold it and you came down to fulfill it. "Scripture must be fulfilled in me…for what's written about me must have its fulfillment" (Luke22:37). And so, "The testimony of Jesus is the spirit of prophecy" (Rev.19:10). And the name by which he is called is the Word of God and "the Word of God cannot return unto God empty, but it *must* accomplish that which he purposes and prosper in the thing for which he sent it" (Is.55:11). You are the Word of God. And the Word was in the beginning, and the Word was with God, and the Word *was* God (Jn.1:1). You were not only with God…you *were* God. And here comes a fragmented God, fragmented into all of his sons, for it takes all the sons to form the Father.

And so here, you came down into this world to *experience* the horrors of this world, so don't think for one moment you're going to change it. When our politicians promise you they're going to change it, they're going to stop poverty, stop wars, stop this…in today's paper we're going to stop war. In the last six years we have sold to other nations close to fourteen billion dollars in conventional arms. The Communist world, they've sold to the same poverty ridden nations close to $16 billion in conventional arms. They can't afford to feed themselves and we force upon them to buy what we're manufacturing. And then we go out with this pious look and ask people to sign a little paper to stop war when we are feeding that nation that can't feed themselves not food but armaments. $13 billion in six years…a little over $13 billion, and our factories are pouring it out and forcing these nations who can't afford anything…they need tractors. But you can't stop this world from being what it is. It was never intended to be anything other than what it is—a world of poverty, a world of war, a world of dirty politics, a world of graft. Read the papers and see what is taking place in high places.

You aren't going to change it; it will go on and on and on, because the story of Christ is *redemption*. He redeems himself in this world. He lifts us out of the world in that *spiral* motion; for this world is a circular principle and it goes over and over and over. Redemption is based upon a spiral principle where one moves up from this world into the world from which he came, and he moves like a serpent, like the seraphim, this burning one.

So when he comes, what must I see? Well, he said, "As the lightening shines from the east unto the west, so will be the coming of the Son of man" (Mat.24:27), and people are looking for some lightening on the outside. No, it's an actual fact...it splits you in two from top to bottom. It's a bolt of lightening. As told you in scripture, he stood on the holy mount, the Mount of Olives, and then it was split from east to west. One half moved north and one half moved south, and there was a valley, a great valley (Zech.14:4). You think of some little place in the Near East called the Mount of Olives...*you* are the Mount of Olives. On this mount, your own wonderful head, that's the Mount of Olives. Then the whole body is split from top to bottom. Your body is parted about, oh, four to six inches, that entire valley, and at the base of your spine is a pool of golden, liquid, pulsing light. It's the blood of God...your own blood. And you will see it and you will fuse with it, and then like a spiral fire you will ascend into your skull, and it will reverberate like thunder. This is the thunder that you will hear.

I tell you what you are going to experience. Whether you can grasp it or accept it tonight, I do not know. I know you will not disprove it. You may fall back into the sleep and dream the dream that you are dreaming now... for this is a dream. A man dreaming is the sole author of all that occurs when he dreams. He's caught up in a reality that he himself is making. Even though what he sees may frighten him and he would have horrors in his dream and really believe for a moment that what he's seeing is part of a reality outside himself and beyond his control. You've done it and I have done it. Haven't you had a dream where you're scared to death...not knowing that you're the cause of all the difficulties? Well, the same thing is happening in the waking dream, but man doesn't know that this, too, is the dream until he awakes from it.

He will awaken in the manner in which I've told you. You will one night be sound asleep and the sleep will seem to be the kind of a sleep you've endured through the years when suddenly something arouses you, something that is different, something that is not felt before. And you will think you're waking as you have awakened day after day over the years, but it is not. You wake to find yourself in your skull, and your skull is a sepulcher and you know it. It's a grave and you know it; and only the dead are placed in the grave and you know it. But you are not dead, you're alive. You weren't dead; you were sound asleep. But someone must have thought you dead to place you there; or when you went into that place voluntarily and fell asleep the sleep was so deep that others thought you dead.

Then in the course of time, in the fullness of time, you heard the cry of the Son of God and that voice woke you. You awoke within the grave and then you came out, born from above this time. Not from below for these bodies were made for you by woman, by your mother, and they're made from below. But you must be born from above if you would re-enter the kingdom of heaven, for unless you are born from above, you cannot enter the kingdom of God (Jn.3:3). So everyone in this world is in this world because they're born from below from the womb of woman. But man, while here, must be re-born and born the second time from above...and that "from above" is his skull. He comes out and he has no mother. Eventually, he's going to find that he has no father, and that *he* is the Maker of it all. He finds it out only as the Son appears before him and reveals him to himself as the being who did it all.

Here we are in this tiny little planet, so small you couldn't see it possibly beyond, say, the moon. I dare say if you got far enough away it wouldn't be seen...this insignificant little thing. Yet it is the *most* important thing in the whole vast universe. No one little speck in the whole vast universe could cradle this biological experiment that expands the power of God, expands the wisdom of God. For without this, God could not expand, God could not grow in wisdom; and therefore no matter how wise he appears to be it would be stagnant if he could not expand beyond what he is. So, God is an ever-increasing illumination, an ever-increasing creative power, and ever-increasing wisdom. By reason of this one little speck called the earth, where these little garments are being worn by God, he could now fulfill his promise to himself and awaken *within* himself. And the whole play is told us in the Bible.

So the story of Christ is not what the world is talking about: he isn't going to change anything in the world. Tomorrow's generations will think it's going to be different; they'll find poverty as you find it now, and they will find all the things that you find now. Oh, changes yes. Changes in fashion...if you live long enough the fashions will go back to what they were. It's like a wheel, it's a circular principle, and so not one thing is really going to change. The only change is going to be when man comes out of it *spirally* and that is when man is redeemed. He goes back to the world from which he came, but this time *enhanced* by reason of the experience of death in this world called earth.

So this principle of which they speak is a true principle. So let me repeat this principle of the rabbis that what is not written in scripture is non-existent. So, are the presidents and the kings and the dictators names of the world are they written in scripture? No, therefore they are non-existent… all the little characters, all the little parts. They can't help but play the part that they play. They have to play it, because they are in a state. All of this is infinite states. When you enter a state you animate the state and the state *seems* real to you and to others who observe the state, but it's only a state. In this world you can play any part. You can play the part of a rich man or a poor man, the beggar man or the thief, he known or the unknown. You play any part in the world if you know they're states. But if you don't know they're states, you're unwilling to give up what you are to become what you would like to be. You could become what you would like to be in the twinkle of an eye by simply assuming that you are. The day that you dare to assume that you are what at the moment reason denies that you are, and remain faithful to that assumption, it will begin to externalize itself in the world.

But you may go sound asleep when it becomes a reality like a dream. The minute the dream starts and you are possessed by the thing you have created, you forget that *you* are the creator, and go sound asleep observing your own creation, and then become all puffed up depending upon what you did create. You can create something noble and become so puffed up in your own concept you forget that you created it. Or you could create poverty and become so embarrassed with your poverty, not knowing that you created it. You can create everything in this world by a mere assumption. So I dare to assume that I am the man that I would like to be. Having assumed it even though others would deny it, I don't discuss it with them. If I would like to experience that in the outer world I will continue in my assumption, and my assumption if I persist in it will harden into fact. That should teach me it really is a dream.

Well, I know a boy, eighteen years old, no money, one of a large family, but intuitively he knew that if he could look at a certain building and see on that building's marquee a name which would imply that it was owned by his father and his brothers that in a way that he did not know it would happen. So he did, he tried it. He only took one person into his confidence and that was his mother. He told his mother what he was doing, that every day twice a day on his way to work and his way back from work he would stop opposite the building, which occupied a whole block at the widest area of the main street, and there he would see his father's name and the words "and sons"…including all of his sons. Then his mother told him not to do it because he could only get hurt…that we had no money and therefore what he was doing could never come to pass.

Well, he did it anyway. He told no one else and his mother told no one else. Then two years later a total stranger on the day of the sale bought that building *for* the family which had no money, no collateral, but he trusted them implicitly to pay it back over a period of ten years plus the interest on it. Then when it was completely paid off he came back to the family and asked them to take the money back and this time give him not six percent but four. In those days you could get four percent. Six percent was an enormous interest and this goes back to 1922. That building became the foundation of the family's growth, and they started only with my brother's Imagination, that's all that he used. Today, from that small little beginning, I don't think you could buy them out for millions and millions, because their gross business today exceeds thirty million a year.

That's from the little early beginnings of a man who had the guts to imagine and believe his Imagination creates reality. He discovered that that was God in man and man's own wonderful human Imagination was God, and there was no other God. If this is God and God creates all things, and then over the years he has tangible proof to prove the reality of what he did, then who in this world could persuade him that it was all a fluke, just a mere strange coincidence, when he's lived by that principle and built his fortune by simply using his own Imagination? Of course there are intervals in the interval having created so big and vast an enterprise. He may go sound asleep and believe that those he employs...now he has many employees, a thousand people he employs today...and he might think that *they* are in his way, or this one...because you may forget how it started. We're all inclined to forget that we are the makers of all that's happening in our world, and then blame our own dream. This is our dream...the whole vast world is yourself pushed out. But man doesn't know it and it's so easy to place the blame on an aspect of self rather than on the maker of the dream. But once in a while he jacks himself up and gets back to the original thought that started it all, back when he was only a boy in 1922.

So here, I ask you to try it. Try it and don't give up. It won't fail you! But the other aspect of it is far greater: to depart from this world. But you can't do it by taking thought. It happens in the fullness of time when the Father in you who fell asleep begins to stir. He wakes and as he wakes, you and the Father are one...not two, just one. And these names are conferred upon you and each name carries a special power. Mighty God is your first name as you awake from the dream. Everlasting Father, that's the second title. Then the third Wonderful Counselor. And then comes the fourth, Prince of Peace... and of his reign there shall be no end, not in eternity. You are the being spoken of in scripture that men worship outwardly. You hear the ministers and the priests of the world talking about his coming, waiting for him to come, and trying to interpret signs on the outside, that when things get horrible then he is coming. He doesn't come at the end of history, he comes *within* history. It's not at the end of human history; it is at the end of the individual's history. It only comes individually. So tonight, in this audience one of you could have his coming. No one knows but the Father in you.

But "Ever since the fathers fell asleep, all things have continued as they were from the beginning of creation" (2Pet.3:4) so don't look for any change. When they promise you all kinds of changes—they're going to give you this, that and the other, —all right, don't argue, smile, as you have done through the centuries—for they aren't going to change anything. These are infinite states and you and I fall into the states unwittingly or we can deliberately go into a state as my brother did into that state. That was a state. He was a poor boy. The family had no relatives that had any money and no one to whom they could turn. So he deliberately went into the state of wealth. He simply actually went right into it not knowing how it would work. When he told my mother she said, "You're only going to hurt yourself. Were I you, Vic, I would stop it and I wouldn't do it any more. You know we could never own that building." We not only owned that building, we owned the bigger one right opposite and others on the same main street and all through the islands…all started from the dream of a boy who *persisted* in his assumption.

So, this is simply, persistent assumption will do it. What have you assumed? That you are what the mirror reflects and what the background tells you? Don't unless you like it. If that is not what you would like to live with in this world, don't accept it. Now, look into the mirror of your mind and then don't look away, persist in that assumption. What would you like to be? Then declare that you are it and persist in that assumption. Morning, noon and night you live in that assumption as though it were true, and no power in this world will stop it from becoming true in the world of effects. But you can't go from side to side in the doing of it. As you're told in the Book of James, if you look into the mirror and see yourself and turn away and forget what manner of man you look like, well then, it's simply this inconstant being and not a thing will happen to you but the perpetuation of your former unlovely state (1:22-25). Look into the mirror of your mind and continue in that state as the man that you would like to be. See it, sleep in it, wake in it, live in it, and it will become.

But in the end you're going to depart from the world which is this world, and you will go up back into the world from which you descended. For, you came down from heaven. You are the gods spoken of in the scriptures, you are the Elohim. When people tell you that you are some insignificant little thing, forget it. They will say, "Neville, you are blaspheming. You are taking the name of God in vain." Let them say what they will. They are always

803

afraid to claim their birthright, they all do. So they're turning to a God on the outside who never existed, and they make little images of him and stick them on the wall, and then get down before their own creation and bow before it. Is there any cross in the world that wasn't made by a man? Is there any image of Jesus Christ? And there's no description of Jesus Christ in the scripture…not the faintest description of what a person looked like, and yet we have unnumbered *pictures* of him hanging all over the Christian world and people bowing before that which is made with human hands. Read the 115th Psalm, and if you have one of them, feel ashamed when you read what the Psalmist said in the 115th Psalm concerning making any image and then bowing to it as some power that could help or hinder you. "If anyone should say, 'Look, here he is!' or 'Look, there he is!' believe it not" (Mark 13:21). Why? Because when he appears you shall know him. Why shall I know him? "Because I will be like him" (1Jn.3:2). Can't be other than myself when he appears: I am he. For, "Unless I believe that I am he, I die in my sins" (Jn.8:24).

So here, the Bible is all about you. And you're only here in the final picture to fulfill the book that *you* dictated before you came down. You inspired the prophets who were only ___(??) of revelation. The Son is by his very nature and being the *revelation* of God. So when the Son comes, God is revealed; and he reveals *you* as the Father of the Son who stands before you. So the Son is God's Son, and he reveals you as his Father…therefore, who are you? And this I know from experience. I am not speculating, I am not theorizing. I am telling you what I know from my own personal experience. I did not hear it from a man nor was I taught it. Like Paul it came through a revelation of the true meaning of Jesus Christ. And it's all in scripture and every one of you will experience it. When we take off these garments, and all rise, you and I will be in a state of ecstasy…the brothers who have returned and all together form the one eternal Father. For, we all have the same Son. So if his son is my Son, are we not one Father? And there aren't multiple sons, no, one Son. We're all individualized and we will never in eternity lose our individuality, and yet in spite of our individuality we are *one* in Spirit by reason of the fact we have the one Son. That Son is our Son, therefore we are brothers, and *collectively* we are God the Father.

So the principle upon which the whole thing is based is that man, true man, has come here only to fulfill scripture. And, "All that is said about me in the law of Moses and the prophets and the psalms must be fulfilled" (Luke 24:44). That's all that I'm here to tell you, how to simply understand the book. But you'll understand it best and only really understand it when what I have experienced *you* experience. You *will* experience it …there is no aristocracy of privilege in this story…we're all one. One is not better than the other. One awakes; he can only wait for the other to awake. Nothing does he want more than for the awakening of all, because without all awakening the Father is not complete. So tell it over and over and over until everyone hears it and everyone sets their hope fully upon this wonderful story that one day must erupt within them.

Now let us go into the Silence.

*   *   *

Now are there any questions, please? Lot's of time…any questions? Well, I hope it was as clear as your silence implies. But if it wasn't clear, this is the time to make me clarify it. Well, if there aren't any questions, it must have been clear. Now we're here every Monday and Friday until into December. You're all welcome. Come when you feel like it. We try to make it a meeting that is complete in itself, so you don't have to feel that you must continue the next one and the next one in order to understand it. We hope that we can make it as clear as possible all within the one night. And so come when you feel like it and bring a friend.

Thank you. Good night.

SORROW PRODUCES GLORIOUS END

10/20/69

We're told in Paul's letter to the Romans that this world in which we live is a world of sorrow, and he gives us the reasons for it...and what a glorious end it produces. He said, "I consider that the sufferings of present time are not worth comparing to the glory that is to be revealed *in* us. The creation waits with eager longing for the revealing of the sons of God; for the creation was made subject unto futility, not of its own will but by the will of him who subjected him in hope; for the creation will be set free from its bondage to decay, and obtain the glorious liberty of the children of God" (Rom.8:18-21).

So here, the redemption of the entire universe depends upon the revealing of the sons of God. And here we are buried in this world...we are the sons and we do not know it. It is our revealing of ourselves when we unveil who we are, and to the degree that we are all unveiled is the entire world redeemed. It did not subject itself; *we* subjected ourselves. No one took away our lives we laid it down ourselves, for we have the power to lay it down and the power to take it up again. So we came in for a purpose, and the whole vast world was subjected not by its own will but by the will of him who subjected it in hope that we who deliberately became what we are would one day rise from it, and then redeem the whole vast world, and set it free from this bondage to decay.

Now, your connection with the "plan of redemption" which is called in scripture Jesus Christ can be told in this manner. It is like a visible history compressed within a few years *and* a history that is continuously unfolding throughout the ages, a history that we call the history of salvation. At a moment in time they come together and unite into one person, and that is the Son of God...that is the unveiling of the being that *you really* are. They come together condensed into a few years. What is 6,000 years against

The Return of Glory

a background of eternity? So there is a history, *divine* history completely finished. You and I departed from that world of eternity and came here for a divine purpose and we go through human history. And here the real humanity, your real humanity, and the true divinity of Jesus Christ *unite* and become one person.

Now, I'll show you how it happens. Think for a moment of Jesus Christ as divine history. Read it in the gospel that is divine history. It is *not* secular history; it's divine history. When this history begins to be experienced by you who are in the world of human history, you will know the time has come. You will know that you are at the end. You will have it. I'll show you how they tell it in scripture, and then link it with the most wonderful experience that I will share with you tonight that a friend of ours, I would say, gave me this past week. She's not here tonight, but I will tell it. Well here, we'll turn to the story of the raising of Lazarus. This is divine history. You'll see how the evangelist by the name of John…no one knows who John is, for he's an anonymous person. Matthew, Mark, Luke and John are unknown; they're not historical characters. Who they were, who wrote it, no one knows, but they took the source material and then they wrote it in their own way. So they took events that were separated in time and rolled them into one dramatic scene that seemingly took place at one grand moment as an experience when they were really separated in time. But that's their privilege, that's their right as evangelists to take these widely separated events and fuse them into one grand dramatic scene.

So we'll see now what is told in the 11th chapter of John. It starts off by saying that the one that you love…so he's stated right away to be one loved and he's loved by the Lord Jesus Christ. He is made aware of the fact that the one that you loved is dead, so he delays his journey even though he heard that he was dead. When he comes in, the sister of the dead man meets him and tells him, "If you had not left us my brother would not have died." He inquires, "Where is he buried?" and they brought him to the tomb where there was a stone over the tomb where he was buried. He was buried in a cave. Then he gave the command to remove the stone and Martha said to him, Martha the sister, "Lord, by this time there will be an odor, for he has been dead for four days." Prior to that, he said, "I am the resurrection. Do you believe this?" She answered indirectly in this manner, "Yes, Lord; I believe that you are Jesus Christ, the Son of God, who is *coming* into the world" (11:25-27). Now you listen carefully, "He who is coming" therefore, where are you addressing the being? If I said to you, yes I believe that you are and I tell you what I think you are, will I continue in this world to say you are coming into it? So where is the conversation taking place?

"Yes, Lord; I believe that you are the Christ, the Son of God, he who is coming into the world." He doesn't respond. He gives the command to remove the stone. Then she tells that he has been dead for four days and by this time—the King James Version uses the stronger expression "by this time he stinketh." In the Revised Standard Version, they say, "By this time there would be an odor." It should be stronger than that...but nevertheless, there would be an odor. He commanded them to remove the stone and the man who was dead hearing the voice, for he said, "Lazarus, come out!" came out, bound hands and feet and his head covered with a napkin. Then he commanded them to loose him and let him go...unbind him and let him go. Now, you read that and you will think it is secular history. No, John took events separated in time in *divine* history and wove them into this one grand experience. I will give you *my* experience. He took the first event, which is resurrection, and then he took that last event, which is the descent of the Holy Spirit in bodily form as a dove, and he wove it into one grand complex picture as taking place at one moment...yet they are separated in time by three and a half years.

Now let me give you my experience. After my resurrection and birth from above—for they are inseparable, you cannot separate these two aspects of this wonderful experience. They happen the same moment like two sides of a coin. So, we are born from above through the resurrection of Jesus Christ *within* us...that comes first. Now, John takes the resurrection and he's going to raise someone, and then he ties it in with the last event. Unless you've had the experience or you know someone who has had the experience, you could not see it. No scholar that I've ever read—I have so many books at home on the Bible, exegesis after exegesis, and no one touches it—no one touches it. They can't get it because you cannot in any way discover truth through some logical process. Truth is *revealed*; it is not logically proved, it proves itself.

So here, the very last event in my own case was the descent of the Holy Spirit resting upon me in bodily form as a dove and remaining upon me, smothering me with love, kissing me all over my head and my face and my neck. Here it descends and remains. But prior to the descent, or as it is descending, a woman on my left—that's Martha—and she said to me, "They avoid man because man gives off such an offensive odor. But he loves you and to demonstrate his love for you he penetrated the ring of offense so that he may show his love for you." So here, the identical thing: an offensive odor. Not just an odor...there are pleasant odors...but "by this time there will an odor." That doesn't quite reveal the intensity of the disgust that they feel towards the world into which the sons of God have descended. Everything here decays, but everything decays. There isn't a thing in the world, no matter how long it *seems* to live, it decays. Whether it be an animate or inanimate object it vanishes from the world…it decays. And death has a peculiar odor; it is the generative organs in a state of decay. I have on many occasions turned in the morning to my wife and I would say, "You know, this morning at four, so-and-so died" because of the odor, and I associated it instantly with that individual. The phone would ring during the day to tell me that my friend or my mother, my father, my so-and-so died…and give me the hour of departure. It's associated with the decay of the creative power of God. This whole vast world is built upon it.

And so, in my case when the dove descended upon me it was a woman, not a man, who said to me, "He loves you." That's all that I told when I told the story in *Resurrection*, but she went beyond that, she said, "They avoid man, because man gives off such an offensive odor." He stinks in this world of decay, and to avoid it they don't come. But at that moment in time there will be contact between the two histories: the human history that is compressed within a few years, what, 6,000 years, and the eternal history of salvation. Then when they touch they create within that touch one *new* person instead of two…yet you do not lose your identity. I am myself and yet I am the being that touched me, and that being is Jesus Christ. It is the Pattern Man, the Eternal Man, the Heavenly Man. So therefore you leave this world eventually. Soon after that moment you'll take off this garment and take it off for the last time. Then you will come into your heavenly inheritance which you cannot now fully appreciate while you are still wearing the garment. But when you take it off, you will see it in its entirety. What is you inheritance? The heavenly garment that is the body of the Lord Jesus Christ that *creates* anything at will. Its wish becomes an objective reality. That is the power that you are inheriting, with a body to fully appreciate it. Now here the creation waits for such contacts for the unveiling of these sons, for the creation has been subjected to futility. It was not subjected by its own will but by the will of him who subjected it in the hope of the revealing of his sons…and all of us are the sons. Whether you be a woman or a man, you are the son of God.

Now let me share with you what came to me this past week. About three years ago in a vision I gave her my eyes. In the vision she was told she was the incurrent witness. An incurrent witness is one who gives passage to a current moving within—and the kingdom of heaven is within— when you see reality. When you give something in Spirit, the one to whom you give it receives it in its fullness; but you retain the gift and the gift is enlarged by reason of the gift. I give you anything…I not only give it and you really receive it, but I retain the gift and it grows beyond what it was at the moment that I gave it. That is the peculiar thing that takes place within man. So she has the capacity to see reality coming from within.

She said, "I found myself in a group of people"—and it's a vision—"I felt unlike anything I ever felt before, and coming out of the blue were bolts of light coming directly at me. I must confess I felt a little bit afraid. I was a bit startled and a bit frightened. Then suddenly I began to feel what I had never felt before a power, a strange, strange power. In this power I felt I could have stilled the universe. I could have made everything stand still I felt so powerful. Before me stood a man dressed in black, and he was the personification of something that humanity, including myself, but humanity has feared through the ages. He was the embodiment of everything that would be something to fear. And then my memory began to return and I knew that he came into being when I lost my memory. He was there, but as my memory returned he was now on the very verge of demise, and he knew it. My memory had not completely returned but enough to bring him to an end, and that he knew. He didn't want to lose his power which was a power usurped from me when I lost my memory."

Here, he was dressed in black. There is a rabbinical legend that Satan, who was the personification of human frailty, man's doubts, all of man's weaknesses, is always dressed in black silk. Here is a personification of a being that man called Satan, who is only the personification of man's doubt, man's unbelief, man's frailty. Now, as memory returns and this is the memory that came back to her, she knew without any uncertainty that "I am"—speaking of herself now—"I am Paul and I am Jesus Christ. It didn't seem strange," she said to me, "that I am a man, totally a man." To those who are not familiar with this lady, she's a young lady, a mother of two and now pregnant expecting her third in the not distant future...very much a woman. She said, "I was totally man and I am Paul—not *a* Paul but *the* Paul—*and* I am Jesus Christ, and I have all the power that I formerly had minus that much memory that is not yet returned. My power seemed to have struck him and he fell back on his elbows. He looked at me as though he was boring holes through me with these peculiar piercing, fiery eyes, trying to find some weak spot where he could once more recapture a bit of the power that he knew that he took from me when I fell asleep and forgot who I am. As he actually tried—I could feel him almost burning through me—I knew and he knew it was hopeless, for my memory was returning.

"Then he said to me, 'You don't remember when you met me, do you?' and for that moment I said, 'No I don't.' That would be technically true, I don't, but something flashed through my mind like an ancient dream that I had forgotten to record. What flashed through my mind was a tree and a man standing beneath the tree; and *he* was that man beneath the tree who

The Return of Glory

told me to *eat* of it. And I knew, the whole thing then began to come back, it was *that* that put me into my forgetfulness and I dreamed the dream of life. He became the most real thing in my world, causing all the things that have ever happened to me and yet it was *myself*...for he was the power. And now I am going to redeem that power, for it has to return to me. It can't be lost and it can't be simply dissipated in space, for *I am* the only power. I am Paul and I am Jesus Christ."

So here is Paul. Who is Paul? His name was Saul and Saul means "to ask for." Paul is "the little one." Paul was blinded by the truth when, as Saul, destroying everything and being moved by this personified hate in his world, he touched the eternal story; and the union of the two transformed him from Saul into Paul. Paul is simply the *redeemed* man who knows he is man and yet he knows he is the Lord Jesus Christ. So everyone is destined to become aware of being Paul and still at the same time Jesus Christ. That is the story of scripture.

So, we take the events in the history, the divine history of the Lord Jesus Christ, and then we tell it in the form of a gospel. We take liberties as poets do and they take events widely separated in time, fuse them into a complex picture as though they're all taking place now at this moment. They don't tell you that is what they did...they leave you to discover it. Because you can't take something as great as this and spell it out so that a child in kindergarten can understand it. As Blake said, "That which can be told to the idiot's understanding isn't worth my care." The ancients discovered that what was not too explicit was best fitted for instruction, and so they wrote the story of the gospel, the story of the Bible. They took events which could only be revealed; they cannot be discovered by logic. You can sit down from now 'til the ends of time and you're not going to discover it. I haven't found one book written by a brilliant mind—who has not had the experience, mind you—who knows what it's all about. He's going to change the entire world and set it up on a new foundation and make everything just right. He hasn't any idea what he is talking about. For truth is *revealed*; it is not logically discovered. It proves itself...so you don't have to go out to prove it.

I am telling you what I have experienced based upon divine history. You will experience it, and you will experience it in the manner that I have told you. I really need not take the time to give you the chronological order, for the evangelists did not do it. None of them followed the chronological order. They took, for their own reasons, these events that are all true in themselves, completely true, and they wove them into a new story, and told it just as it should have been told, possibly, because "truth embodied in a tale shall enter in at lowly doors." Man finds it difficult to accept bare truths. He finds it easier to take thoughts put into pictures. So you take these individual experiences and put them into pictures and the individual now picks up his book and reads it and he thinks, "Now isn't that a mighty act, a man was raised from the dead." He wasn't resuscitated...we have that every day in our world. In the summer days there isn't a beach where crowds go that we do not have a dozen or more where someone's looked upon as dead, but there are trained men to bring them back to life, revive them by mouth to mouth resuscitation and they come back. They weren't dead, but they would have died if they were not revived.

Well, this is not resuscitation. They use the word "four days" because it was common practice in those days, and still today there are certain groups who will keep the body three days and then cremate it on the fourth day. Right here in our state in Oceanside there is an ism known as the Rosicrucians and they have an international setup. Not the one in San Jose, the one in Oceanside, called the Hymer group, and they keep their dead three days in a cool room. If he doesn't revive, they cremate him on the fourth day. Well, that's not new. This is something as old as civilization. They firmly believed that the soul hovered over the body in the hope of reviving it for three days, and if it didn't revive then they departed permanently. That was their concept. And so, in keeping with that concept when it was written 2,000 years ago, she said to him that he has been dead four days—meaning there is no hope of resuscitation. Then by this time decay has set in and decay will produce a stench. Then he commands him to come forth.

No one was in any little tomb on the earth; this was an adumbration. This is a foreshadowing in a not altogether conclusive and immediately evident way of what you one day will experience. You will experience not here, but you will experience it in divine history. You will come back and you will ponder the experience. You've touched the garment, you've touched the robe. For this history unfolds forever and forever. It's not like the human history that begins and ends; this is eternal history, the history of salvation. And the minute you touch it and these things begin to unfold within you, you know you are one with the body of the Lord Jesus Christ and this union will produce one person, a new man. You will be not Saul batting your head up against all things in the world; you will be Paul and you will be at the same time Jesus Christ. You will actually know "I am Paul" and you'll know at the same time "I am Jesus Christ." And all the things that happened in this world that we frowned upon with our little moral codes are so natural and so right in the heavenly world. It didn't seem strange to her that she was a man, and yet in this world she is so much a woman, so *much* a woman, yet there she is man and she knew she was man.

Now listen to the words as told us in the end of John. John has two endings. The real ending is the 20th chapter, while the 21st is an epilogue. So in the 20th chapter the unknown author makes this statement, "Jesus did many other signs"—they're all *signs* in John, never calls them a miracle—"Jesus did many other signs, that are not written in this book; but these are written that you may believe that Jesus is Christ, the Son of God, and believing have life in his name" (Jn.20:30). There are numberless things that you're going to experience related to that eternal history that are not written, but these that he wrote down seem to be what everyone experiences within a given period of time. Those that I have given you came within that definite period of time, yet before and after I still have these experiences all related to divine history because I can find their parallel in the Old Testament. So after the descent of the Holy Spirit in the form of a dove I had other experiences concerning the Old Testament, where it all came back like a memory returning…that the whole drama was played out completely before we descended and lost our memory. We are only remembering. Within our memory as it comes back a certain section of time in this little area of the world it happens. But it happens outside of the region that you can take any friend and share that experience with him. You can tell it, but you can't share it, because it doesn't take place in anything known to man.

So here, her experience is perfectly marvelous. It's true. She *is*, by actual experience tonight, Paul and she *is* Jesus Christ. Here, every moment of her time she is very much a woman. Yes, she can be jealous of her husband, she can be envious…just like any woman in this world who is in love with her family. Not that I think for one moment that he has ever given her reason for doubt, but, nevertheless, she is so given that she can do it. Very much a woman…and yet tonight she knows she is Paul and she is Jesus Christ.

But this is not reincarnation. Paul is only the personification of everyone who has been transformed from what was Saul into what is Paul. And it was Paul, under the name of Saul, who was persecuting this divine history. It was called "The Way." When he heard the words, "Saul, Saul, why persecutest thou me?" He said, "Who art thou, Lord?" He said, "Jesus, whom thou persecutest" (Acts9:4). Where was it? It wasn't here. Here I hear the story and I turn away from it completely, turn my back on it, and refuse to accept it. That's persecution: I deny him. Well, that's what everyone in this world does at some time, some moment in time he does it. Then comes the fullness of time when it suddenly erupts within him and he *is* the Lord Jesus Christ. Now he goes through the entire divine history and it all unfolds within him.

So who would have thought that simple little statement in the 11th chapter of John, "By this time he stinketh"…you will think, well, after all, that's some little comment made by a woman in this world about a dead brother who had died four days before. But it hasn't a thing to do with that. When the woman turns to *you* and tells you that the Holy Spirit avoids man because man stinketh, you will know what section of the gospel you are now re-enacting. For he speaks of the Holy Spirit who descends upon you and now he comes in the form of a dove and here he *remains* upon you. So now you know this is he: the one on whom you see the Spirit descend and remain that is he. That's the chosen one, that's the elect, and so one more son of God has been unveiled. And to that degree the groans of the world…for creation is groaning and waiting eagerly for the revealing of the sons of God. All the revealed sons in the end form *one* and that *one* is God the Father. It takes all the sons to form the Father.

So, there's no book in the world comparable to it. Everything else is commentary. I don't care what it is, it's all commentary. *This* is truth, not discovered by any logical process but revealed. Who on earth would have thought that that simple little statement made that he stinketh, or there would be an odor, had any significance to it? Here, everyone is going to hear that same word coming from a woman. A man didn't tell it to me, it was a woman…that was the Martha of scripture. Here she stood on my left and said in a very commanding voice…she knew exactly what she was talking about…"They avoid man because man gives off the most *offensive* odor." If you could only put that qualifying state to it…not just say an odor, but the most offensive odor, then you would know exactly what the King James translators meant when they said, "He stinketh." Because every man stinks and the whole vast world gives off the most horrible odor to those watchers in eternity who watch eagerly waiting for the "stir" so that they may come down to redeem the one that is but the externalization of themselves. For these are the sons in eternity waiting for this to simply stir. The minute we in this world touch the eternal garment, then virtue goes out and then we are healed. And then we begin to move from this world into the world of eternity.

Then we tell it. You come back and you tell it, just as it happened to you, and try to show through scripture that the story is true. Some will believe what you say from what you've done and others will disbelieve it, and it doesn't really matter. They will never disprove it. Let them remain because their time has not yet come. Everyone eventually will be redeemed and everyone will have the same experience.

But the story is told…there is no reason to retell it. I can tell you as I've done over the years in the chronological manner in which it happened to me. But whether it is a chronologically true story or simply the individual's experiences woven beautifully by the poet, for these were poets who wrote the gospels. As someone once said to me, I think it was Huxley, "There are three kinds of writing: there is journalism, there is literature and there is scripture." The greatest writers of the world considered the giants in literature can't write scripture. He himself admitted "No I couldn't write scripture." It's something entirely different. The journalists, you wouldn't call them men of letters, but they write beautifully and excitingly in our papers and magazines. But they certainly would not be considered the mental giants in the use of words as to real literature. On the other hand, those who write literature, great literature, couldn't write scripture. If you really understood scripture as it is written, I'm quite sure the whole thing was poetry. But our translators couldn't quite get the measure of it and bring it into its poetical form. For it is poetry...it is truly inspired. Even if it is not measured as you would measure a poem, when you read it no one can tell me he isn't moved by it, because it is speaking to something in the depths of one's soul. So don't treat it as literature...it is not literature.

I saw in today's paper some ex-nun, was a nun for ten years, and now she's teaching at, I think, UCLA, some class in religion. Or it's a branch of UCLA...I think it's Irvine or some other college, but it's part of UCLA. She said what an enormous class that she has, but she treats it as literature. Well, if you want to, but that's not religion. It certainly is not history for there was no place on the face of this earth where a man was buried for four days having been proven dead who rose from the grave. Yet *you* have been buried for thousands of years and you don't know you are, and yet the watchers in eternity receive from you, multiplied the by billions of us, a stench beyond the wildest dream of man. If you've ever gone to Chicago and gone near the stockyards, you know what a horrible odor that is. Well, multiply that by the whole vast world. Not one small area in Chicago but the whole world, and the stench is beyond the wildest dream of man. That is the stench of humanity. But the love is so great he penetrates the ring of offense to demonstrate his love for that chosen one on whom he will now descend and remain. They will ascend together. He is now a transformed person, and he is Paul, the transformed being, and he is Jesus Christ. Then they go back together...two that are really one.

So when you read it in the future, don't discount the simplest little thing about it. I tell you that you will experience it...just what I told you tonight...and you will know that Lazarus is not something on the outside. The word simply means "God has helped." No man can redeem himself, God has helped. Yet there are numberless schools teaching self-realization, self-development. If you don't do so-and-so then so-and-so will happen, and they give you all these little things for you to do and promise you self-salvation. Well, if you want to believe that, you'll believe it only through the help of those who teach you. The only help that they get from it is to take from you the money that you've paid for having heard it...for they can't deliver the goods. This comes through *grace*, grace and still more grace: "Grace and truth came through Jesus Christ." So let no one fool you that by doing certain things you are going to be saved. You will be saved not by anything that you did other than to "Set your hope fully upon the grace that is coming to you at the revelation of Jesus Christ" (1Pet.1:13).

Hear the story. Don't reject it, believe it. And then really set your hope that it will come in the not distant future. That hope that you have set firmly believing in the story without doing anything on the outside will materialize in your world. You will share it with others. Not every one will believe you. And even if others believe that you did have the experience they will discount it as a nice, sweet, wonderful dream. Not having had any similar experience they will call it just a dream or hallucination. It's so easy to simply shake it off if you don't know what is being said. That goes from the highest to the lowest, so don't expect because a man is intelligent that he really understands what you're talking about when you get off into these depths. I know that from my own personal experience from trying to share it with men who consider themselves very able. They have their Ph.Ds and they're so brilliant in their own mind's eye, and they write tomes about each other. All must be Ph.Ds and so anything below that isn't worth their consideration. They shake off their ignorance by telling you, well, it's an hallucination. They'll go home, possibly, and burst their little brains trying to find out something about it, but they couldn't confess to you that they didn't know.

So they're very proud of the fact that they are agnostics. I read here recently that someone in a very humorous vein said, "The man who proves himself on agnosticism is only confessing that he's an ignoramus as stated in the Latin. For ignoramus is "we do not know." So the agnostic is "we do not know," so he proves himself on agnosticism which is only a confession in Greek for the Latin "ignoramus." Well now, you tell that to someone and he will slap you in the face because he is a Ph.D. But having once heard what it means, I reserve my feeling about it. It's a very humorous...and yet people spend seven years to get it and therefore let them have it, and let them indulge themselves in the belief that they differ because they spent seven years to get the Ph.D. What they have to commit to memory... volumes and volumes that tomorrow will be disproved. In fact, when they start to do it they must commit to memory volumes that have *already* been disproved. But unless they have a good memory for such nonsense they won't get their Ph.D., and unless they get their Ph.D. they can't get a better job in our universities. It goes over and over...all this nonsense.

But the truth of which I speak is not acquired in universities; it is revealed. You cannot bring any logic to it, it doesn't make sense yet it is the eternally *true* story. So it's the wedding between a visible history compressed into a few years and the eternal history of salvation. When they meet, they then create a new being, a new being in one person. So you are Paul *and* you are Jesus Christ. So her story is perfect just as she experienced it.

Now let us go into the Silence.

*   *   *

Now are there any questions, please?

Q: (inaudible)
A: Yes, Ina, but I don't want to go beyond that…because I asked the question. Well, as I brought out tonight and I think I've answered you in tonight's lecture, the two histories touch each other. One is a visible history condensed in a few years and the eternal history of salvation. When they touch, the ones still wearing the garment of the visible history will have the eternal history unfold *within* themselves. Then they're not male or female when it completes itself, they are man. Man is *above* the organization of sex; he's not female neither is he male. Man is not a divided being. So as you brought out earlier, well, the regeneration of one and the regeneration of the other…and it's not based upon a sexual manner.

Q: (inaudible)
A: Ina, if you try to bring it into *this* world and try to explain it here, you're going to confuse yourself. If you identify that eternal history within any man in this world, you're leading yourself astray. It is not here. He is coming into the world: I believe, "Yes, Lord, I believe that you are the Christ, the Son of God, he who is *coming* into the world" (Jn.11:27). Well, he comes from *within* man in a series of events…that's how he comes. That's how I will know that he did come, because I experience all that it is said of his history. He was present at the resurrection of a friend that he loved. He was present at this…and what did he say? For I heard the woman, the same woman repeat that "it stinketh"…it's a most offensive odor…this identical thing that took place as recorded in the 11th of John. So when I know these things are taking place in me then I know that he came. So he becomes as I am, and in that moment I am no longer Saul batting my head against the wall, I am Paul, fully aware at the same time that I am Jesus Christ.

And you can share it with those who will understand, but the majority of the world knowing your weaknesses and your limitations will turn their back upon you and think that you are in need of a little psychiatric treatment. So I would not tell anyone. They do not understand…they just don't. Why throw it before someone who could not digest this food? They can't digest it. If you served this tonight or took that tape and played it back for those who are now cardinals and heads of the great dioceses of the world, they would think whoever took it down is blaspheming, and the one who spoke it is the embodiment of the devil, because they have the strangest concept of who Jesus Christ is. They do not see Jesus Christ as the "pattern man." They see Jesus Christ as a little man who lived 2,000 years ago and he was brutally murdered, the innocent being that he was, and then he rose. One little being that's what they see and they teach that, and really believe that they're doing God a service in teaching that nonsense.

The whole thing is the most glorious story ever told. You and I are the gods who came down (Acts 14:11; Jn.10:34; Ps.82:6) and assumed the weaknesses of the flesh, the limitations of the flesh. And while here, that which was before that the world was, the pattern man, in the fullness of time of our horrors and our sufferings we touch it. As we touch that history, our little visible history compressed as it is into a few thousand years is now completely transformed into eternity, and we are one with that which was before that the world was.

Good night.

WE ARE GOD HIMSELF

10/24/69

To tell you who you are would really shock you. Here we sit in this world of ours frightened, scared to death, and here we are God himself, the very God who created the whole vast universe and sustains it. And to tell you that, well, the first thing you do you resist it, because it seems impossible and the one who utters it must be insane.

It tells you, "God was in Christ reconciling the world to himself...and entrusting to us the message of reconciliation" (2Cor.5:19). Has he really entrusted to us the message of reconciliation? Yes. As he awakes within us he entrusts to us that message and we tell it to our brothers who are equal with ourselves. We are no better off, we're no greater, and you can't be greater than God. You tell it to those who are still waiting and are confused by reason of the dream and of the sleep into which they have placed themselves. When it happens to a man he is called in the mysteries, Paul. He resisted everything in the world. Then it happens *in* him...a plan awakens within him...and then he said, "From now on we regard no one from the human point of view; even though we once regarded Christ from the *human* point of view, we regard him thus no longer" (2Cor.5:16). No longer? Then what did he believe Christ to be? What the whole vast world still thinks that he is...they think he was *a* man, something divorced from them, something distinct, and something on the outside that came in some unique manner. They do not see Christ as God's *plan* of salvation. God prepared the way for his sons to return to himself and Christ is the *way*.

Why should we be disturbed and be surprised when we read in scripture that a serpent spoke? We take that for granted. We read that the serpent said unto the woman so-and-so; then Balaam's ass spoke; then in Daniel a tree became a man...and we read all these things. But then you hear that Christ is a *plan* that also has a voice and that everything is personified in scripture. So when you read, "I am the way, and the truth, and the life; no one cometh unto the Father except by me" here is a *plan* (Jn.14:6), the only road to God, with a voice, a plan is speaking, and the plan is in man. Why should I be surprised if a plan takes a voice and not be surprised if a serpent speaks? This is scripture and this is something entirely different from anything that you would sit down to write.

So, God was in his plan reconciling his sons to himself. He banished his sons for a purpose. You and I are the sons, all of us are the sons. "He has set a bound to the people of the earth according to the number of the sons of God" (Deut.32:8). Not one child can be born that is not simply a mask that a son of God wears. No one can be born who is not the mask that God's son wears. So he has set a bound to the peoples according to the number of the sons of God. Now, he is *in* his plan. Christ is called "the plan of God." He prepared a plan for his sons to return to himself. Returning to himself he has given them what he really wanted always to give: he wanted to give his sons himself. God's plan is to give us himself.

He couldn't give us himself until he first banished us, and we were sent out into this world, a world of death, a world of horror, a world of despair. But he had prepared the plan before that the world was, that when he brought us back by this plan that we would be God himself. Because, really, there is *only* God. "Hear, O Israel: the Lord our God, the Lord is one" (Deut.6:4). There's "only one body, ultimately, only one Spirit, only one hope, only one Lord, only one faith, only one baptism, only one God and Father of all" (Eph.4:4); that in the end, all constituted the one body, the one Spirit, the one hope, the one Lord, the one faith, the one baptism, and the one God and Father. So in the end there is only one.

So, "From now on," said he, "I regard no one"…it happened *in him*. He went to take all the people who were called the people of The Way and to bind them and bring them into Jerusalem. While he was on the road—and the word road is simply "a progress," the same word as "the way"—he was blinded by the Truth. It happened in him. And then he had to defend what happened in him against those who were still blind. Standing before those who were blind he said, "You cannot prove anything against me, for all that you will now try to prove against me is only what our fathers believed: that God would raise the dead. Not a thing you can prove against me that is not what you now believe…only in me it has happened and in you it *will* happen." That's what he is telling those to whom he spoke. So here, every being in this world, I don't care what he is, what he has done, what he's planning to do, it is all God. The whole thing is God and there's nothing but God.

The Return of Glory

Now let me share with you. I've told you in the past what has happened to me. I know from my own personal experience that God is love. When I say love, you can't describe it. You use the word love…and we do know what it is to love a child. We who have had a child, we know what it is to love a child. We know what it is to love our wives. We know that's a feeling that you can't describe…you *know* what it is. But when it comes to a child you know what it is to love that child. To stand in the presence of infinite love and have love embrace you—having first been asked a very simple question, to name the greatest thing in the world—and then you answer in the presence of love that the greatest thing is love because you can't think of anything but…there's nothing but love. At that moment of incorporation you *are* love, that's all that you are. From then on, though others may not see it, you are wearing the body of love. So you tell others what happened to you. They may or may not believe it, but you can go right out on the extreme limb and tell them, "There are some standing here who shall not taste of death before they know the truth of what I say." (Luke9:27). They shall not taste it, they shall not depart this world—but really nothing dies, not in God's world, nothing really dies—but you shall not depart the world until you know the truth of what I say, that this pathway to God is a series of mystical experiences in which God reveals himself in action for the salvation of his sons. He brings them all back into himself *as* himself. They are God himself. So I've told you that I was incorporated into the body of love, and from that moment on, though not seen by mortal eye, it's the body that I wear. Whether I am awake or asleep, judged by human standards that's the body that I wear.

It's her privilege to give the eyes to anyone in this world; but when you give in the Spirit, you keep what you give and the thing that you give increases in its potency. Love increases if you can increase it. I thought it was infinite and how can you increase infinity? But, nevertheless, there it was. It still increases, wisdom increases, power increases if you give it. And so you give your immortal eyes so that they may see the truth of what you say, and she or he to whom you give it, they can give it and still retain it. You never lose your gift if you give it spiritually, it augments itself.

So here comes this experience of one who's here tonight and she tells me that "I awoke within this dream. It was a complete waking state, because I heard the most heavenly music, and it was coming from this huge house in which I lived alone with my father. He and I shared this house. So I got out of bed and I went into the foyer, and I heard heavenly music surrounding me. I looked into a room and there this brilliant light, a ball of light, seated at a little pulled out chair playing the piano like a concerto. The most heavenly music was coming from it. But within the light was the skeleton of a child, a skeleton of a child in radiant light. I said to myself, I must find someone who is a witness to what I am seeing, I must. I don't believe that Neville himself would believe it. I must tell him, but I can't see how he could even believe this incredible thing that I am now witnessing…and I must find a witness. For if two agree in testimony and the two are different and yet they agree in testimony then it's conclusive." That is scripture. But there must be two; one cannot witness to himself.

But she lived in the house with her father. Scripture tells us that when he confessed, they said to him, "But your testimony is of yourself, therefore it is not true." He said, "Yes, you have a law that only when two agree in testimony is it conclusive, but my testimony is true for I am not alone. The one who sent me, who is my Father, he witnesses with me" (Jn.8:13-19). So here, the father, the earthly father, is but a symbol of the heavenly Father in her vision. She actually lived in the household with her father (who is really herself), for the whole vast world is seeking the Father. The Father is the cause of the phenomena of life, but man does not realize that it's not another than himself until he finds the Father. Finding the Father he finds the Father is himself and he is the sole cause of everything that is happening in his world. There is no other cause in the world.

So she lives in the home with her father. She wanted to find the father. Seeing this now she hears a noise coming from the room. It's her father and her father is on his way to work. It's quite early…and as he comes out she says to him, "Do you hear what I'm hearing?" and he said quite simply, "Yes, I do." She was astonished that he heard because she knew this was a vision; yet he knew it, he heard it. As she held him by the hand as he was about to go through the door to work and she dragged him and opened the door to look in, and the scene she saw before is still there. Here is this brilliant ball of light with a child's skeleton in the light playing this heavenly concerto. And he said, "Yes, I see."

Then she had a witness now. She wants to come and tell me the story with her witness which is her father. So she started towards my home. As she arrived at the home, it is not the father, it's her friend Natalie. And here, Natalie is with her, but Natalie knows nothing of what the experience was; her father knew it. So they came into my house. As they entered the place they knew that here was his living room, my living room. They knew, that is, she knew and Natalie with her, that my wife Bill was asleep upstairs. But here my living room was not what you'd call a living room but it was a garden, a heavenly garden with the most beautiful flowers and there I was surrounded in a body of love. She's looking at you…"I knew I could not disturb you. You seemed to me to the prince of light, completely enveloped in a body that is only love. I can't describe it other than it was simply love.

I looked at you, you looked at me as though you didn't even see me, and I knew that what I'd tell you would be silly to you for you knew it all. You knew it completely so why even disturb what you were doing. You were watering these flowers and gathering these beautiful white flowers for the one that you loved. She was sound asleep upstairs, but you would take these flowers to her that you had watered and you had given life…for you were life itself; and then you gave it love and brought these flowers in a bouquet to her while she slept as morning after morning you did it in this wonderful place that was your garden, which was your living room." Whole vast world is simply a shadow. Everything here is but a shadow. Your earthly parents are simply *symbols* of your heavenly Father. The one who now tells you the story is now sent.

I have told you I have been enveloped in the body of love. And the one to whom I gave the eyes would have to, before I depart the world, see the truth of what I'm telling you. This was a messenger. God was in Christ, which is simply use the word instead of Christ, God was in his *plan* of redemption, his path of redemption, reconciling his sons to himself. He banished his sons for a purpose and then *we* become the messengers of reconciliation. He's entrusted to us the message of reconciliation *after* we experienced it. And you can tell it to the whole vast world confidently that you will not depart the world until someone testifies of the truth of what you've said. You are now enveloped in love, when she saw the child, a skeleton that has all through the centuries been the symbol of Christ. Christ is always the child. Then you clothe it in love: the pathway you experience. He said, "I am the way, I am the truth, I am the life" (Jn.14:6). This is a pathway speaking, it's a path speaking, the way of redemption that is speaking, as the serpent spoke, as the tree became man and spoke. So a way of redemption takes on the human form and speaks to man. We enter the pathway. It takes man to externalize and awaken the path, because only man could do it because God and man are one.

It takes man who is the *living* way. Here is a way…it seems not to be alive…and then you come upon the way. And there's only one way to the Father. As you enter the way you are really the one resurrecting the way. It begins with the resurrection and you resurrect the entire way within yourself. You are the one truly living way to God the Father. When you arrive there *you are* God the Father. Then you are now entrusted with the message of reconciliation and you tell it. Some will deny it as they're more interested in things of the world. They want…like today's paper shows a diamond that was sold for one million and a few hundred thousand dollars on a lady's finger. Well, there are certain ladies in this world who would want that more than what I'm talking about. They would love to have that beyond anything in the world. But to tell them to have *this* which is a living way awakening within yourselves where it takes them back from the outer world of death into the living world of being God the Father, they wouldn't be interested. Oh no! They'd rather have that and show it and brag about it all and love it. She would not be alone. There are millions tonight who would love that piece of dead stone…but valued by man in the outer world at a million plus…and that would be to them the most marvelous thing in the world. But to tell them this story, he said they were stubborn and they would not believe it. They were not interested. They'd rather have the acclaim of man and the honors of man, but certainly not this.

So I tell you what I know from experience. I have gone "the way," and the way is not a man. *You* are the man who animates and activates "the way" when you enter it. And there is only one way back from where we are to where we were; and where we were was the Father. "We came out from the Father and came into this world; again we're leaving this world and returning to the Father" (Jn.16:28). The return to the Father has been fixed for us and before we came out that pathway was done. He prepared the way for his loved ones to return. But we went berserk all over this world having all the experiences of death. Then comes that moment in time when there's only one way back. It's a very narrow way, for you can't go through it in any other way than simply by this series of events. Diets will not take you back. Your position in the world will not take you back. Whether you are socially prominent, financially sound, intellectually a giant…no matter what you are in the outer world that will *not* take you back. There's only one way back and that way is a series, and only *one* series of mystical experiences in which God reveals himself in action for the salvation of his son. He brings his son back, and when the son comes back he *is* God the Father. And that is the destiny of everyone in this world.

So now that I have heard one tell it I am completely satisfied. Yes, one saw me clothed in power. Yes, I am at moments clothed in power, clothed in wisdom, but now one has seen me clothed as I really am. For in the story when he embraced me he was love. That's the one in whom I am incorporated. I am forever in that body as you will be forever in that body when you go through the series. You're right back into the one body and that body is love. You can't describe it. As she said, "I could not describe it. I only knew standing in your presence you were the prince of light." Well, listen to the words of the 82nd Psalm, and God is speaking in the presence of his sons, he said, "I say that you are sons of the Most High, all of you; nevertheless, you will die like men and fall as one man, O ye princes" (82:6). You fall as princes because you *were* princes, but you're going to go back as the *king*. You are princes, but you will return into the body who is king of all, Lord of all. For in the end, there is only one God containing all of his sons. But he now shares his being with his sons and they're all the same being: they are the Lord God.

So I tell you, you can give anything away in this world and you'll keep it…if it's a spiritual gift you'll keep it. You do not lose your gift; the gift becomes augmented and becomes an expansion of what it was. If it was love, love increases. No matter what it is…although it seems how on earth could this be increased? You can't conceive of this love that embraced you ever growing beyond what it was…it seemed infinite. Yet in some strange way by the return of all of his sons maybe that love *can* be increased. Maybe that wisdom and that power can be increased and it's not really infinite. It is simply an ever-expanding illumination. So I thank her for sharing it with me, and she in turn has given her eyes to others. The others who received it will give it and yet all will retain the gift, and by giving the gift is increased.

So here, when you use the word Christ, think of Christ as the *plan of redemption*. When you read, "I am the way, I am the truth, I am the life" do not see it as just a single man 2,000 years ago making this bold claim; and then 2,000 years after you're thinking *of* that being and turning to him and worshipping him. You see, the prophets' vision was really foreshortened and they saw as present what was future. Now, the present moment is not really receding into the past; it's advancing into the future. What I have told you now if you hear it and believe it, it is advancing into your future, so that really the bygone is not gone, it's oncoming. We read of these things as something that took place 2,000 years ago and we think now 2,000 years ago and we've progressed since then, so it must have receded, for they told the story that happened 2,000 years before they were telling it. They told the story of Abraham that was 2,000 years B.C., that is before it happened. Well then, 2,000 years later…that's 4,000. And you think it is always receding into the past; no, it's advancing into the future. All these things that are happening are not happening now once and for all, it's continually happening.

So everyone who is here this night, it's my hope before you depart this little sphere that it will happen in you. I can't tell you…looking at you with my mortal eye I couldn't tell you. I could not give anyone the gift that I gave her from this level; I could only give it in another level. So when I gave it I would have given it to my wife or my daughter. That would have been my feeling that I must give it to the one who bears my name here, but I was not in control from this level. When the gift was given, I gave it from a different level of my own being. Of all the people in the world…here is one I do not know socially, and yet it's to her in the Spirit world I gave it, because it happens that way. She was just the one to whom it should be given. I retained the gift and she received the gift and now her eyes are opened inwardly into the world of thought. As Blake said, "I will not rest from my great task! To open the eternal worlds, to open the immortal eyes of man *inward* into the worlds of thought, into eternity ever expanding in the bosom of God, the human Imagination" (*Jer.,* Plate 5).

So you give it and she shares it. She cannot give it to anyone who asks for it, because she can only give it in Spirit. If she gave it in Spirit as she did this night in seeing the story of one clothed in love…and you can't describe it…how can one be clothed in love? Well, when you see it you see it clothed in love, incapable of doing anything save in love, and therefore everything in his presence is harmless. That perfect love casteth out all fear. In the presence of love not a thing could harm it.

Isn't that strange that here we go into the jungle and we're afraid of the wild beasts. And when you're clothed in love everything in this world is as harmless as a little kitten that is completely domesticated. Not a thing could harm you when you're clothed in love and you are destined to be clothed in love…that little skeleton of a child. And every mystic knows exactly what that symbol means. Here he will clothe it now. In the 37th chapter of Ezekiel, all the dead bones…he will lift them out and when he clothes them, well, he has only love so he clothes them in love. And the harmony of the spheres comes into being, and she heard the most heavenly music coming out of a piano played by a ball of light. The skeleton itself was radiant light and it was a skeleton of a child. So when you see the child you see the plan and not one bone shall be broken. Don't break one bone…that's the plan. On that little bone structure will be built the body and the body will be the body of love.

And so you see, you do not lose your identity. She knew me to be the Neville that she knows, even though I'm clothed now in a body of flesh. But she knew Neville and yet she knew that he was the prince of light and she knew he was the embodiment of love. She couldn't disturb the work he was doing which was simply raising flowers, beautiful flowers. The flowers of scripture…read the flowers of scripture. And her name, by the way, is Sharon. In the Song of Solomon we speak of the rose of Sharon, and he who spoke of her as "my sister" and yet "my love" and then "a lily of the valleys" (2:1). And all these flowers come into being and they mean so much in scripture: the things that are blossoming in the world of man. They are symbolic of what is taking place *in* man. They are only the fruit that love bears.

So, in the end, may I tell you, you are really God who is *infinite love.* So when you read in the epistle of John "God is love" don't think for one moment these are idle words. These are based upon experience, God is love. It's not an attribute of God. Wisdom and power, all these things are attributes of God but not love. God *is* love and that is God himself. Then he incorporates you into his body as you go along the way and then the son has returned as the Father. And when you see that one thereafter you see nothing but love and yet you see your friend. Eventually you will know him as your brother and you'll be clothed as he is clothed, and everyone will be clothed in love. Can you imagine the end of this drama when the curtain comes down upon it having brought back every one that he sent out? Can you consider for one moment, for one moment conceive of the thrill, the joy beyond measure, when all the sons return, all clothed as God the Father who is nothing but love? And the harmony she heard in her house, why, that beautiful as it was to her it is nothing compared to what you're going to hear. I heard it, I heard it just for a moment back in 1946, and you can't describe the beauty of the heavenly chorus that sings your redemption. When the whole chorus comes in, in one little theme, calling you by name by the way, because you're so unique no one can take your place. Although we are one as the Father, we are distinct as sons, and no one can take the place of another. You are forever individualized, forever and forever, and yet together we are one Father. I can't describe it in words, it can only be experienced.

And so, you bear witness to yourself, he said. *One* cannot bear witness, it's a false witness; it would not be acceptable. And so he quoted scripture, "If two persons agree in testimony, then it is conclusive." If these two differ and yet their testimony is one, then it is conclusive. Well, I have one who testifies to me and that is my Father. So she began the story with "I live in the home alone with my father" and he heard what she heard and he saw what she saw, so he testified to the truth of what she witnessed. Now she wants to tell the man who told her of the path to God. She found when she got there that it was not her father but a friend—"I call you friends... I no longer call you slaves" (Jn.15:15)—the most perfect fulfillment of scripture in this vision. Then she comes in and instead of seeing what mortal man would see in the living room, beautiful this, that and the other, man-made, she sees God-made, a garden of flowers and a lovely greenery. She said, "A jungle that was not a jungle because everything was so beautifully done, but flowers coming up," and I am watering and giving light, for I was the prince of light giving light to the flowers and giving love to the flowers. Then taking these flowers day after day to the one that I loved who was asleep above...waiting for the waking of that one.

So everyone must wake in this world and when they wake they go the same pathway. There's only *one* way; there aren't two ways to God. Today they have numberless ways that people teach, but they're false ways. You can go on a vegetable diet from now 'til the ends of time. You can go on any pathway other than this and that pathway will be false. There is only one way and that one way is made up of a definite series of mystical experiences. It begins with the resurrection and the same night like the other side of the same coin is your birth from above. Then a few months later, five months later comes the third experience. The first is a dual experience. Then what would be the second—but still if you take these two and separate them, which you shouldn't, call then that second one the second experience—and that is the discovery of the Son who reveals you as the Father. Then the third experience is the splitting of the curtain of the temple which is your own wonderful body; *and* your ascent into heaven, which causes the whole heaven to reverberate with your return. Your return! It's a joy! Then the fourth is the descent upon you of the Holy Spirit with the stamp of approval of the work that is perfect. You are now as perfect as your Father in heaven is perfect; and you are one with your Father, and now he is holy and you are holy. And that is the end. Now you are assigned a little, I would say, purpose in life for the remaining years to tell the message. So God was in Christ reconciling the world to himself and has assigned us the ministry of reconciliation. So we are now ministers of the Word. We are simply telling the message of this pathway from this world, which is the outer world of sin and death, to that wonderful inner world of God and heaven which is perfect.

So I tell you, don't despair. You are *destined* to awaken one day as God who created the whole vast universe. Yes, not a little being but God who created the universe and who sustains it. When all the sons have returned and all are back as God the Father, in the twinkle of an eye it will come to an end. It will not take time to *dissolve* the universe; it will come to an end. It was brought into being just for this purpose. Let our scientists speculate about the age of the universe, billions and billions of years and so many light-years. Let them do it, perfectly all right. The end will come suddenly. The beginning came suddenly in spite of what they tell us. It was one grand explosion. Now we've just discovered that the moon that they thought came before or after is the same age as the earth. They'll find that the sun is the same age as the earth. They'll find the whole vast thing came into being as one grand scenic beauty for a purpose, and the *only* little place that could house it, which is a stage, is earth. Earth…and you're on it. This is where all the sons are. Sons will go back to the very being out of whom they came and they go back to the Father. So you are infinitely greater than you could ever conceive yourself to be…but I mean infinitely greater.

So here, tonight you may envy someone, dislike someone, well, that's because you're wearing a mask. And because of the mask you can't recognize behind the one that you envy the one that you loved before you came out, really loved. He was a brother and there was nothing but love. You're going to go back with that same love only increased by reason of the experience of coming into this world. There will be no envy, no tears, no darkness, nothing of that world. All of this will come to an end when we go back. So I am so glad that I can tell you tonight there is one to whom I gave the eyes and then I remained long enough for her to have the experience of seeing me clothed in the body of love. For, I have told you time and again, and you have the tapes to record what I told you concerning the experience of love. Though mortal eye cannot see it, I feel it all the time. I sleep in it, wake in it, and it is always the clothing that I wear. Yet I must take this body up morning after morning and put it on, and have dim eyes, and not see quite what I ought to see. But the day will come when this is taken off and I am clothed as she saw me, clothed in a body of love, which is protection beyond measure; not a thing can harm you clothed in the body of love. For all fear is cast out…for love casteth out *all* fear. What you do not fear cannot hurt you. You walk in a world that is created by you. And everyone is destined to be clothed in that body.

So here, you are *infinitely* great and you are moving towards the discovery of it. Everyone in the world is really seeking one thing: seeking the Father. So in the household she lived with her father; and he said, "Yes" quite innocently "I hear it." She was stunned. "I see it, just what you see." And then he seemed to vanish as she traveled the road towards my home, and now she's in the presence of a friend. Then comes the unfolding picture of a garden. We came out of a garden and return to a garden, but this time we are fully conscious of who we are and we're God the Father…in that beautiful living garden.

Now let us go into the Silence.

* * *

Now on Monday we'll give you a very practical one, it will not be like tonight. So if you're interested in the practical side while we are still living in the world of Caesar, it will be on Monday night. We have to mix them up and give you one like tonight and then one on the most practical side… how to really realize any dream in this world while you're here. Again, there's only one way to do it. You either do it knowingly or you do it unknowingly, but you do it, and there's only one way. So Monday night it will be on that theme.

Now are there any questions, please? We have lots of time…Ina, a question?

Q: A question did arise though when you were speaking of the destruction of the earth or the world. What about the land of Atlantis and Lemuria that they are speaking of so much, do you believe that they were lost continents?

A: Ina, my dear, I do not know, really. In my visions I have not seen that. I only see earth and I see the heavenly world. Now whether these things were once parts of this land of ours and sank as some people teach, as Plato taught…Atlantis went down and then Lemuria went down in the Pacific…so they teach that. Well, it's an exciting story, but I do not know from experience. I do not know anything concerning what they're talking about. My visions are all of the heavenly vision. But if these things really happened, it still would not mean that those who went down cease to be any more than when I depart tonight that I have gone…only from one who can't touch me. But I haven't really gone.

Yes, my dear?

Q: Well, I know a lady that used to come here and when she first came she had the most marvelous visions and seemed to open up centers. And then suddenly she had terrible visions and she really is quite disturbed now. She seems to have opened centers that take possession of her instead of her taking possession of…I don't know how she explains it, but…

A: Well, my dear, I have people that will make that statement…you open up centers and this, that and the other. You still have her as a friend, don't you? Well, tell her that it's not anyone opening up any centers, none whatsoever. There are certain schools of thought that teach these many centers in a person. A friend of mine who saw me last Wednesday, no, it wasn't Wednesday, was it Thursday? Jan, when were you home, Thursday? Yesterday…well, only yesterday. And she told me she went to this place and they were asking certain questions and the spoke of seven centers. "And now when you get to seventh center what do you think you're going to find?" And Jan very boldly and I'm so proud of her for having said it, she said "Nothing!" Well, the lady was so distraught because she was setting herself up as a teacher having gone to a little maharishi or something who talks of all these centers. She said, "Don't you understand that you aren't going to find anything? You're only going to find *yourself* at the very end of the road! So what are all these so-called centers?" The lady began to cry, because she thought that she was now a teacher and all should obey her and listen to her as one endowed with this power.

Q: I'm not putting over what I mean about centers. But it seems that what she said was at night she would have these terrifying experiences. I don't know whether people would come, but…well, I'm sorry, I just can't explain it.

A: Well, you know, my dear, few people will confess what they do in their silence, so they do not recognize their harvest when it appears in their world. I was in the company last night of a very wonderful, dear couple, friends of ours who have gone through a great tragic thing in the last few years, and she told me for the first time last night at dinner that she gave her mother a great deal of trouble when she was a little girl. Then the mother in her advanced years developed cancer and lingered for quite a few years in frightful pain. In the meanwhile, she, the daughter, had two little girls; one gave her more trouble than the other. And she said to her God—long before she came here to discover that God was within her as her own wonderful human Imagination—and she talked to God as millions of people do, and thought she could appease God for the things she had done to her mother. She said to God, "I wish, God, you would take the one I love most and save my mother." She's going to sacrifice the one she loved the most, her own child, like the story of Abraham and Isaac. She took it into her own heart and made that bargain with God. Well, the mother eventually died, she was an old lady.

Then came a third child who did all the things that this mother wanted her to do. She was a great dancer, she was in the public eye, and she did all these things. And then this girl for no apparent reason, no apparent reason—she had everything in the world to live for, a good job paying her $500 a week, everything, a young girl…then she committed suicide. Now the mother told me this last night…and of course she still can't get over this blow of two years ago. Here was a girl making this fabulous fortune, no obligations to anyone, a single girl, young girl, and then commits suicide. She made a bargain and it's not forgotten. This is a play, the most wonderful play in the world. "Be not disturbed; God is not mocked, as a man soweth so shall he reap" (Gal.6:7). And so, many people …and there are today people who sacrifice children, sacrifice people on the altar to appease God. That was common practice centuries ago. And that little thought has still come through the minds of men, and you don't actually sacrifice them but you ask God to make his choice of one. You're willing to give up the one you love the most to appease your own heart for what you think you did to your mother… and now she's suffering with cancer. And so you feel you're contributing towards what she's now suffering because of your attitude towards her when you were young; and you're willing to give up the one you love the most. The one she really loved the most was the last one that did all the things that she herself wanted to do. But I did not tell her there are moments when silence is golden. Why add to her hurt. It just simply came up at dinner, just the four of us, the two of them and the two of us, this wonderful confession out of the nowhere. But it had to come out, as she was asking for some reason for the death. She had just preceded the reason by the story she told me.

This is the most marvelous play in the world...there's *only* this play. And it's *not* as Shakespeare said, full of sound and fury signifying nothing. It's full of meaning. Every little thing is full of meaning, but man has so little memory, it's so short. So man sits down with himself and he thinks now he's not going to be seen by anyone, and the only one who is worthwhile looking at him is within him. It's himself who is called the Father, and he sees everything that he is doing on the outside...and he will give it to him. When he gives it to him, he wonders, why should this have happened to me, for I am so good, I am so clean, I am so holy, I give to the poor, I do all these things. But they don't know what they did in the Silence. The 8th chapter of Ezekiel will tell you that they say no one sees us and there they are engraving on the interior of the mind these horrible, horrible monsters and they say, "No one sees us" (8:7-13).

Well, the time is up now. We're here, as you know, every Monday and Friday into December, then we close for a very short while. Come and bring a friend.

Thank you.

THE INVISIBLE GOD BEHIND THE MADE

10/27/69

I think you will find this hour a very practical hour and yet a very spiritual hour. We are told in the Book of Romans, Paul's letter to the Romans, the very first chapter that all the invisible things of God are clearly seen being understood by the things that are made (1:20). So man is called upon to look at the made and then to discover the invisible God. All of the invisible things of him are clearly seen, and how do I know? Well, I look at the things that are made...and I begin to reflect upon what I did. For here I find myself in a world and am I really responsible? I try to find out why. I look at all the things round about me and finally I come upon a certain thought. You know, when there was not a thing in the world to support my belief, I began to believe that one day I would experience this...and then I experienced it. So I relate the things seen to the unseen.

Could that be God? Well now, Paul tells us in the very next verse, "Although they *knew* God they did not honor him *as* God." Oh, I found the relationship between the things seen and the unseen reality, the imaginal act, but I did not honor him as God. And then I turned to images resembling man and I thought man on the outside was the cause, because he seemed to aid me in bringing this to pass. I turn and I exchange the immortal God for images resembling man. Or I might have turned to other images, that of a man, not only a man but that of a reptile, that of an animal, that of a bird, and I turn to these and think that *they* are the cause of my good fortune or misfortune. And I gave up the truth about God for a lie, and began to worship and serve the thing created instead of the Creator; for I could relate the outer world in which I live to an imaginal activity within myself. Then

I knew that that was the cause of it; for if God is the cause of everything in the world and I discover how it happened and then I will not accept the fact, I do not honor him as God.

Read it in the 1st chapter of Romans, from the 20th to the 25th verses, this wonderful revelation to all of us, for he's addressing *us*. This is not just for those to whom he sent the letter 2,000 years ago; it's to everyone who reads the letter. Stop for a moment and see if you can't relate the things around about you to something *in* you that caused them, *and* if you're perfectly honest you'll see a cause in yourself. The cause was an imaginal activity. But then you will not...or I hope you will...but I mean he said, "But then they did not honor God as God." They did not honor him as God. They saw it, but did not in some way accept it...it was too great. And then they turned to man, an image, and turned to the created rather than to the Creator.

Tonight let us see how we bring about these things in our world. The Bible begins on this note, "In the beginning God created the heavens and the earth" (Gen.1:1). He created the within and the without, and God dwells *within*. You're told that he created the heavens, well, heaven is within you we are told (Luke17:21). He created the heavens which is within, and then he created the without. Now how did he bring anything on the outside? We are told that "the Spirit of God moved upon the face of the waters." We find that *motion* was causative, that without motion it is impossible to bring forth anything, so God moved. Well, how does God move? We've discovered that he is our own wonderful human Imagination, for I can relate what happens to me to my own imaginal act, so I know where he is. But now how does he move? It's impossible to detect motion unless you have some fixed frame of reference against which motion moves; because motion can only be detected by a change relative to some other state.

Well, what would I do now to move from not only *where* I am but *what* I am to that which I would like to be? Eyes can be open or shut, it doesn't matter...I'm doing it all in my Imagination. So I imagine now that I am... and I name it...and it differs in what a moment before I thought myself to be. How do I know that I have moved? Well, I look at my world mentally and I must see a change. I must see that which implies that I have moved. I'll take it spatially first. If you are familiar with San Francisco, and here we are in Los Angeles, I put myself in Union Square in San Francisco. How do I know? Well, my eyes are open and I'm seeing the St. Francis Hotel. If I turn around, my back is to the St. Francis Hotel and I'm looking towards the other side of the Square. I go beyond it in my mind's eye and I go down to Market Street. I *feel* that I'm there. Well, how do I know?—now think of Los Angeles. I think of Los Angeles and I see it 500 miles to the south of me. If Los Angeles is 500 miles to the south of me, I must be at least 500

The Return of Glory

miles north. But now I will locate myself in San Francisco by these familiar objects, and then think of Los Angeles and see it 500 miles to the south. Well, that's where I am.

But I am told I can't be double minded. Let not the man think that he will receive anything from the Lord if he's a double-minded person, for he's nothing more than simply a wave of the sea that is driven and tossed by the wind (James1:8). So when I sleep this night I must sleep as though I were in San Francisco, and as I'm falling off to sleep I must think of the place that I formerly knew which is Los Angeles and see it to the south of me 500 miles away, and fall asleep *in* that assumption that I actually am in San Francisco. That is a motion and without motion it is impossible to bring forth anything. This is true of everything in the world. In the beginning God created the inner and the outer, and then the Spirit of God moved, and then Creation began. So everything is within us…*everything* is within us.

But now how do I bring these things forward? Well, by the same simple, simple technique. I found that I did it and it worked. I don't want to fall into that category spoken of in that first chapter of Romans that although he *knew* God he did not honor him as God. I found how it worked. I found that if I slept while in New York City as though I were in Barbados…and to prove I was in Barbados I thought of New York City and saw it 2,000 miles to the north of me. Then came a letter from my brother giving reasons justifying why I should come to Barbados, and then making it possible by enclosing a draft. In the letter he stated that if I would go to a certain steamship company that he had already written them and they would give me a ticket for Barbados; that I needed no money, the draft would take care of my normal needs aboard the ship and that I could sign for anything that I wanted. If I used the bar, sign everything that I wanted, and he would meet me on arrival and pay all expenses that I incurred on the trip. I did not write him to ask anything of him. He, at the same time that I was doing what I'm telling you that I did, he had the impulse to write me and give me reasons why I should come to Barbados—that I hadn't been there in twelve years and the family gathering at Christmas needed me to complete the link of the family. I was the only missing one of all the members. So his letter justified the draft, justified the expense that he would incur. And all that I did, I simply imagined that I was in Barbados. I didn't have a nickel, literally.

Now, I know exactly what I did and therefore I found God. For all things are made by God and without him not a thing is made that is made (Jn.1:3). So if I've found God, am I going to fall into the trap now? That although I knew God, I did not honor him *as* God, and then turn to an image resembling a human being and say he was the cause of my trip? And give all credit and all praise to my brother who sent me the draft and

835

notified the steamship company to issue me a ticket so that I could come in and present myself and give proof of my identity and then get the ticket? So, did I fall into the trap that he was the cause or did I remember the God that I discovered? That's what Paul is asking everyone who reads that letter. They found God and then they did not honor him as God. They found him and then they exchanged the truth about God for a lie. For, to turn to see my brother as the cause of it…though he wrote the letter I had set it in motion long before he wrote the letter. The one who set it in motion he was causative…that was causation.

So here, nothing is happening to us that we have not set in motion in our own wonderful human Imagination. I tell you that you can be anything you want to be in this world. But when you voice your request and you say verbally I want to be so and so, it must be a *genuine* desire and not something that you just flippantly say that I would like so and so. You must so want it that you're going to remain faithful to that change in position relative to a fixed frame. If you want to be other than what you are, well then, you can't just assume for one little moment that I am it and then go back to your former state. Let not the double-minded man think for one moment he'll receive anything from the Lord as we're told in the Book of James. Don't for one moment think that I can be double minded and get anything from the Lord. I want to be successful in business? I don't care what the register told me today that I have and what I sold. I must sleep tonight as though it were all that I expected it to be, even though reason tells me it isn't and my senses deny it. But I've got to actually assume that things are as I would *like* them to be, and then regardless of all the things round about me denying it, persist in that assumption. If I do it in this way, I cannot fail. This is the law by which we live in this world. So take it to heart.

The God spoken of in scripture is seated right here in everyone who is here and he is your own wonderful human Imagination. When you say "I am" that's God. Now what are you imagining? If I could be so sensitive and I could feel your motion…that now you dare to assume that you're other than what reason tells you that you are; and if I said, "Who has moved?" and you answered, I would say, "Tell me who is now moving because I can feel it?" and you would say, "I am." Well now, you've called his name. That's his only name. I am moving from where I thought I was to where I would like to be. I thought I was behind the eight-ball and now I'm completely clear. Things are rolling just as I want them. I moved from where I was to where I would like to be, and I detected the motion and wondered who is moving and then you replied "I am." That's God, and all thing are possible to God. So without the consent of anyone in this world you simply move from where you are to where you would like to be by a change of attitude, a simple change of attitude. But it has to be fixed. You move and then you fix it so that when you walk or when you sleep that attitude is yours. For that state to which you most *constantly* return constitutes your dwelling place. So that I constantly dwell upon this state and in this state, that's where I live. And that's where I will return to no matter where I go in the course of a day. I go back to *that* state. Then that will externalize itself in your world.

So, all the invisible things of him from the creation of the world are clearly seen. How?—by the things that are made. So when they come into the world you recognize your own harvest. You're bringing them in anyway, but man is unaware of it, and he exchanges the truth about God for the lie. He exchanges the *immortal* God for an image of a mortal man. And because a man was instrumental in aiding you to bring it to pass, you think he was the one who did it, that he was the cause. He's not the cause at all. If tonight you inherited a fortune, don't think for a second the one from whom it seemed to have come was the cause of it. No, preceding that you assumed it and he was only the *instrument*, the actor playing his part in giving it to you. A total stranger could be the one. You don't need a wealthy uncle, a wealthy aunt, a wealthy grandfather.

I had it in my own family…a brother who…yes he did befriend a friend, but certainly there was no reason for him at the end of his life to leave him the sum of money that he did, a considerable sum of money. He had a wife and he had two sons and a daughter, and in his will he left it so that no one could break it. He said, "I gave them all that I thought was due them" and then he left everything that he had to my brother Victor, and it was a considerable sum of money with all other things attached to it. My brother certainly was in his own mind's eye assuming that he's a wealthy man…he kept assuming that "I'm a wealthy man." That was his consuming desire and there was no divided mindedness in my brother. He wanted that more than anything in the world. He actually wanted it. To this very day money to him is power and he wanted power. He was tired of poverty and he was tired of being shunted around. Then dreaming power, just dreaming wealth, then out of the nowhere people came and opportunities came.

Well now, if he forgets the cause, he turns from the immortal God to an image resembling a man. That's what you'll read in that first chapter. And here he turns to a man and thinks that he was the cause of my good fortune, he gave me x-number of hundreds of thousands of dollars…and it wasn't that at all. He had to or whoever it was. He's only one of numberless who would have to do it at the very spur of the moment, because someone is dreaming that he is wealthy. Though he has not a thing to support his dream, he is dreaming that he is.

So I say to everyone, you can be what you want to be, but you can't be double minded. You are told, "Let no one believe that looking into the mirror and turning away forgetting what he is that he will receive anything from the Lord; for the double-minded man is unstable in all his ways." So I say, well, I want it…and many a person will say to me I want so-and-so, and you meet them a week later and they forgot they even told you. How could you forget that was your request and then ask me, "Where is it?" This is not some little magical thing; this is based upon principle. You want it? You can have it! Are you willing to give up what you *are* to be what you want to be? That's the only price you pay for it. You don't make any sacrifice outside of giving up the state in which you find yourself to move into the state in which you want to be. They're only states.

So here, without motion it is impossible to bring anything forth, for everything *is* in the invisible world, but everything. Now, how do I do it? I think of you who would actually congratulate me if you heard good news about me and I bring you into my mind's eye and allow you to congratulate me. I know what this implies. The power is in the *implication.* What are you doing? You are congratulating me on my good fortune. I accept that congratulations and I don't duck it, I accept it as fact. That is my subjective appropriation of my objective hope…because I am hoping that one day you will know of it and therefore you will congratulate me. So I go ahead in time and I go into that state and I allow you to congratulate me now. When you do it in the not distant future then it is only confirmation of my imaginal act. But I will remember what I did, and having done it I will not forget what I did. Then I'll go about my business. When I think of you, I will let you know in my mind's eye that you know of my good fortune. The day *must* come, it must externalize itself. So it externalizes itself, you will know of it, and you will congratulate me on my good fortune.

So he brings things that are not seen into the world that is seen. As you're told in the same Book of Romans, "And God calls things that are not seen as though they were seen, and the unseen becomes seen." You'll read that in the 4th chapter, the 17th verse of Romans (Catholic Bible; KJV). He calls a thing that is not seen just as though it *were* seen and the unseen becomes seen. So how would I call it? In this simple movement…I move from where I couldn't see it to where I could get a good look at it. Well, I can't see on your face any expression other than what I would now see if you knew my present condition. If I don't like that present condition, I want to see the same face but I see it differently. Now, if I move from what I am into what I would like to be, I would still know you, you would still be my friend. So I bring you into my mind's eye and I let you see me as you would *have* to see me if things were as I want them to be. Then I don't move from that. I mustn't be double minded and go back and let you see me in my *former* state. I must *persist* in this one state where you are seeing me.

Now this is true of everything that you do in this world, I don't care what it is. If you want to be known, I don't care what the world will tell you, you may have not a thing in this world to show to the world that would cause anyone to look back at you and point you out as someone that is known. Forget that. You want to be known, you want to be rich, you want to be this, you want to be the other, well then, *dare* to assume that you *are*! For these assumptions, though at the moment you assume them, are denied by your senses, if you *persist* in them they will actually become externalized… they'll become facts in your life.

A friend of mine who is here tonight, and he's promised to write it out for me, but here he said to me, "I started with $180 and I had so many debts that's all that I had not so long ago in a small little restaurant in a small place, Ojai." Now he's contemplating an expansion into San Francisco. He said, "Tonight, Neville, the estimated value of my business is over a hundred thousand dollars." I know him well. I first met him in San Francisco and he heard this. He was born and raised an ardent Catholic. In his mind's eye he is still a deep, deep Christian, but he does not call it Catholicism or Protestantism or any other ism, but he was raised in the Catholic faith. He heard this from me in San Francisco and he believed it. He began to apply it and things worked. But we forget as he forgot, and then he remembered again, and then he forgot again. But now he has remembered and I hope this time that the memory is permanent.

So he started in this manner and everything fell into line. Yes, men came in to help, all these things happened, but they were not the cause. The cause of everything that happened to him was all in his own wonderful Imagination. He would turn to his wife and say, "What have we forgotten to do? We aren't applying this principle." So when things did not go as they *should* go, he remembered there was a law behind it all: things are not just happening and they're happening only because he is creating them. Then he got back on the ball. Now here is this wonderful opportunity for expansion in the city of San Francisco, and it all just happened. Today, they're all about to incorporate and the value is in excess of a hundred thousand dollars…and he started with $180. Now this is not too many years ago.

So I say, everything in this world is possible to everyone if he knows *who* he is. If I asked the average person in this world, do you know God, and they were brutally honest, they would say, no I don't. They speak of God, but Paul is not speaking *of* God. Paul said, "And they *knew* God, yet they did not honor him *as* God." They knew God, for they found that one day they imagined a certain state and something happened that was related to that state. Now, you might have read in yesterday's paper or the day before yesterday's paper, that this young lady, twenty-five years old, she read all these papers and read the magazines, she saw the TV, heard the radio, of all these murders of the young girls, and she became frightened. She read of these many nurses in Chicago who were killed, one after the other, because they didn't cry out. She swore to herself she would cry out if it ever came to her life, and she took a knife and slept with a knife under her pillow for about two months. It was a knife and she toyed with the idea of getting a gun, but she said, no, I wouldn't want a gun in the house…but she did have a knife. Then she put the knife back where it was in the sink area.

Here, the girl is working undoubtedly in a very nice job, because she pays $160 a month rent, so she must have a nice job. Then she heard a sound coming from the kitchen and she saw a shadow. Next thing she knew a knife was at her throat. This tall blond man with long hair to his shoulders, about 6'2" and estimated weight about 190, and he said to her, "How old are you?" She said, "Twenty-five." He said, "Take off your pajamas." And she thought, "This is it, he's going to kill me." All these things she had done and imagined in the past, and what she would do if it ever happened to her. So she had a knife, mind you; but she didn't have the knife this night, he had the knife. Then in some way she got out of the bed by his order to take off her pajamas, she got the knife and began to stab him all over his back. Then he ran leaving a trail of blood for at least a block. So she must really have done quite a job on his back. I don't see how he can avoid being detected. He has to go to some hospital or some doctor to be repaired. But everything she had imagined having been exposed to TV, exposed to radio, exposed to all the things in the paper, came to pass. She may not relate it, but she did state that as she read it in the paper that all these things she did imagine and put herself as the victim and what she would do even to the point of getting a knife to protect her. And it was a knife; it was not a gun.

So, not a thing happens in this world by accident: this is a world of law. The most horrible things had first to be imagined and the most beautiful things had first to be imagined. So everything is being imagined, good, bad and indifferent, and these things are happening to us from morning to night. We have found God, as Paul said. The average person will say, "No, I haven't found God. I never saw him. What does he look like?" Well, didn't you see the phenomena? He tells you *how* you find him: "All the invisible things of him are clearly seen from the beginning of time." How? By the things that are made! Well, that was made, that scene was made. Well, how could that be God? "I kill and I make alive; I wound and I heal; I do all these things, and none can deliver out of my hands" (Deut.32:39). That's God speaking…not just some outside being. I kill, I make alive; I heal. I

The Return of Glory

am the Lord and beside me there is no God. Well, do you say "I am"? That's he. You mean I did all these things? Yes, I did all these things, good, bad or indifferent. But I found him.

So they have found God. Although they knew God, they did not honor him *as* God. "Oh, I know that I imagined the thing and then it happened, but don't tell me that is God, because that's not my concept of God. I have a different concept of God...something up in the sky...but certainly not here in my own Imagination. Because I am capable of all the unlovely acts in the world and that could not be God." But they don't read their scripture. If they read the scripture they would hear the same God saying, "I kill, although I make alive; I wound and I heal." Well, who is stabbing a person? She said, "I am." Well, that's God, that's his name; his name is I AM. Who held the knife? I am! That was a person. And he was imagining all things, too, for he had imagined that "Suppose I'm not successful, what are the consequences of my act?" He had imagined that, too. So the whole vast drama is the unfolding of God within man, and there's only one God that's God.

If you really have a desire...but it must be a genuine desire so when you voice the wish it is not just an idle wish. It must be something that is so genuine that you mean it. Then I'll tell you how to get it: you simply move from where you are mentally, not physically. People do all things on the outside. You don't do it that way; you do it on the inside. What would the world look like if you were now the person that you want to be? What would it look like? Well, see it that way. If you see it that way, you have moved from where you were to where you would see it as you would see it if it were true. Well now, what would you see? Then move...the motion is all mental, all in your Imagination. But it must be genuine. If it's genuine, you remain in that state. Don't go from place to place, just remain there. "Into whatever house you go remain" he said. Just remain in it. So I'll go into a state and I remain in that state regardless of what the world will do. If I remain in it, I will bring it into visibility. But it is impossible without motion to bring anything from the invisible state into the outer visible state. You can do it...everyone can do it...because you have an Imagination and that is God. That is God *in you,* and without him not a thing is created. Whatever is created is created by God whether it be good, whether it be indifferent, whether it be an evil thing (Amos 3:6).

So take me at my word. My friend is here tonight and I've asked him to write the story up for me in detail which he promised to do. But to start with $180...and that is not $180 clear, as he had debts, all kinds of debts in trying to make a little restaurant go. Then from there to suddenly find it growing and growing, and out of the *nowhere* someone comes down from San Francisco and said, "You know, this is my third visit here, all the way from San Francisco, because this is what old San Francisco used to be, and now it's all tourists, all sophisticated. This is the real old San Francisco way of dining." Then he proposed that he come to San Francisco, he'll find him the place, and he'll incorporate, and do all these things. Then the present value of this today is a hundred-odd thousand dollars from an investment of $180…which is not really $180, because he didn't have any money and he had so many debts. Now he said, "Tonight I have the pink slip of everything in my restaurant. There is not one penny owed on anything in the restaurant, and I have the best material, the finest most modern equipment and everything. I hold the pink slip by simply applying this."

So, I don't ask him how you were born? He was born in a very devout Irish-Catholic family in Boston. His father is gone from this world but he went as a devout Catholic. His mother is still here and undoubtedly she's a devout Catholic. They love him as a son, but undoubtedly before the father left he wondered, and the mother wonders, "What happened to my son?" But he found God. And they're not yet…they found him, but they don't believe that he's God. Because no one can live a full ripe life and not at some time find a thing happening in their world and cannot see the relationship between what they imagined and what has happened. They refuse to believe that they are causative; they can't believe that this is the cause of the phenomena of life, and so they will ignore it and brush it aside, but they found God. As he said in his own words, "Although they knew God, they did not honor him *as* God; and exchanged the immortal God for an image resembling man, and exchanged the true knowledge of God, all that they knew about God, for a lie." Then they worship and serve the creature rather than the Creator. The Creator is your own wonderful human Imagination. That is God.

If you are in control of what you are imagining, not a thing in this world is impossible to you. But you will find that when you find God your values will change: you will not worship things; you will worship God the Creator. You'll be so thrilled when you can imagine something for a friend and see it work and then give thanks to the one that did it…all within you. So you thank God and you worship God and you serve God. When your friends give you the good news and it confirms what you imagined for them, you are thrilled and you honor God. You thank the friend for bringing the good news, for you knew it had to come some day, for you had *imagined* it. Therefore, thank him, but the *real* thanks goes to God for you've found him. And now you *honor* God because he never lets you down. You don't have to burst a blood vessel to make it so…you *let* it be so. You knew the request was a genuine request. The man wanted this, the lady wanted that, and these wanted so-and-so, and you simply imagined it and trust him implicitly to do it. It was not based upon your moral code, your ethical code, no just your trust in God that he would do it. So you knew that what you had imagined was God in action and that God is faithful; therefore, it would come to pass in a way you could never devise, so you couldn't tell them what to do to aid the birth of it. You only knew that you did it and therefore it *had* to work.

So I ask you who are in business, who have…if you're not in your own business and you want to transcend what you are, imagine that you have. Don't ask yourself if you are qualified…you'll be qualified. All that it takes you will get. All that it takes to fill the better job will come to you; the know-how will come to you. You simply assume that you *are* the man, the woman that you would like to be. Then in a way that no one knows it is going to take place. Your businesses will grow, your family will grow, and all these things will grow just as you have imagined it.

So when you read that the Spirit of God moved upon the face of the deep, you know who he is. He is your own Imagination, and it moves. You can stand perfectly still and move. And may I tell you, you can so move that you can be seen spatially at the point in space where you've imagined that you are. I've done it; I'm speaking from experience. Two thousand miles away I appeared to my sister, for I wanted her to see me, and yet physically I was in New York City in my own home. I wanted her to see me, and she came in and she saw me. She could not see what she ought to have seen with her physical eyes. She should have seen her son, but she couldn't see her son, she could only see her brother Neville, for that's what I wanted her to see when she looked at her son. Here I am physically in New York City, and yet to my sister in Barbados across water…and how did I move? I simply moved in my Imagination and yet in Barbados she saw me.

Then she sat down and wrote me and said, "Neville, the strangest thing has happened to me. I went into the room to look at Billy and I couldn't see Billy, I only saw you. I rubbed my eyes, I did everything, and no matter how I looked I couldn't see Billy. My son was not there, it was you. Will you please explain it to me if you can?" At that very moment I was doing what she said that she saw and witnessed. And when I came out I told my wife and told a friend who was waiting for me to come out of my bedroom exactly what I had done. Eight days later came a letter from my sister asking if I could throw some light on this strange thing that had happened to her. Had I told it eight days before, then they might have believed me afterwards, yes, but there would have been a question. But they could not deny that I told them eight days before what I had done. It came not by air, because in those days you couldn't get a letter by air, so it came by boat. It took eight days to bring that letter.

I tell you that all things are possible to man because God and man are one. So you'll find this night a very practical night, and yet you'll find it a very spiritual night. You take it, but you must be sincere in your wish, so that you're not moving from place to place. Do you really want…and you name it. You want a glorious home? Don't say, "Well, I can't afford it." Do you really want it? Then sleep in it as you will conceive it. Do you want this, that or the other? Well then, sleep in it as though it were true…and that's your motion. You move from where you were into where you want to be. But *remain* there! When you rise in the morning and the world tells you that you're not there, you simply walk through the door just as though you were. You're leaving *that* place. And in that state you remain and then everything happens. If it takes the entire world to aid it, the entire world will aid it.

It took a man to come from San Francisco three times to enjoy a meal, a wonderful meal, but it's not an extravagant meal, but a *tasty* meal. The kind of environment that he said old San Francisco used to have. He lived there for thirty years, and he said, "This is the kind of place we always had in old San Francisco, the décor, the atmosphere, the food, everything about it. Now today, all the restaurants have gone into catering to tourists and that old atmosphere has gone, and I would like to rebuild it, at least in one place. I tell you that when we open we'll turn away everyone outside, because we'll have so many of the local people coming, and they'll come only by reservation. You'll have no extra room for outsiders." So I asked him to save me a spot anyway, coming from L.A. I know he will.

So take me at my word, it is impossible without motion to bring anything into this world, and the motion is all within you. The motion is a simple motion…all you do …you know exactly what you want. Well, if you had it, how would you see the world? If you see it as you now see it, you haven't moved. If you see it as you *would* see it after the result, then you've moved. Now continue seeing that, for motion can be detected only by a change of position relative to another object. If I say I am moving now and I see everything as it is now, then I haven't moved. But if as I move I look at the same frame of reference and I see it from a different angle, then I've moved. So I use as a frame of reference my friends, your face, and on your face I let you see me as you would *have* to see me if you knew of something that you do not *now* know. You have to see me differently. If you heard news of me that is not now known, when you meet me the next time you would see me differently. If that's what I want you to know, then let me see on your face the expression that would *imply* that you know of that news. If you would be one who would congratulate me on that news, then let me accept the reality of your hand and the reality of your voice and the words coming congratulating me. Having done that, let me know that was *true* and let me

The Return of Glory

have faith in this unseen reality. If I do, no power in the world can stop it, they can't stop it. If man only knew this, he'd be free, really free. But today he doesn't know the source of the cause of all the things that happen in this world. He doesn't know causation, he doesn't know the cause of phenomena, and he thinks the president is doing it or the army's doing it or the Pentagon or something on the outside...his competitor is doing it. Not a thing is doing anything but what is taking place within him in his own wonderful human Imagination.

In the deep Depression of 1929 we only hear of the hundreds of thousands who lost everything on paper in the stock market. For in those days you put up ten percent and even then you didn't have to the way they manipulated it. So if you were wiped out and you say you're wiped out of a half-million all on paper, you didn't have it at all. But there were others who made fortunes. So, we read only of those who lost, but we do not read of the tens of thousands of men who became multi-millionaires. Because all stocks...I read in this morning's paper that RCA dropped from this fantastic height down to eleven dollars and found no buyers, and the boy on the floor just as a joke bid one dollar for a block of stock at one dollar and got it. There were no takers and he got it at one dollar a share. Whether he could raise a few dollars to buy them I don't know. But it kept on tumbling all the way down and they thought at eleven dollars it couldn't possibly go lower. Then he put in a bid at one dollar a share and it fell to him because there were no takers. If he held on to it...and it has been split and split several times...what would that little boy who ran errands on the floor be worth today? But he was only one of that kind. There were those who had cash and they took advantage of it all and they simply bought. It tumbled and all stock lost seventy percent of their value. So, there were those who could buy.

But I'm not going into that side of it. I'm just saying, if you remember God...and God is not on the outside; God is on the inside and he's your own wonderful human Imagination. He brings everything into being by moving. So he moves from one state to another state. He remains faithful to the state into which he goes, and then whatever is there must project itself on the screen of space and bear witness to his creative power. So, all the invisible things of him are clearly seen from the very creation of the world through the things that do appear. So they appear and you know exactly what motion he made. When this appears, that's the motion that he made or it could not appear. If Depression appears, that's the motion he made. If the papers begin to suggest to you that things are going to be on the way down, and you *accept* it, then you'll move, suggested by a paper, a magazine, or some so-called expert, and then it will appear. It appears because you moved based upon some suggestion by what you thought to be an authority. And

845

it isn't that at all; it's all within you. If you ignore the suggestions and do not accept them at all and keep on moving where you want to be, well then, you'll move, and if you remain in it, it will externalize itself in your world.

Now, you'll find this the practical night and yet you can't divorce it from a very spiritual night because you've found God! What is more than finding God? And God is your own wonderful human Imagination. The day will come you'll find him in a more wonderful way by the series that I've spoken about night after night, which we'll pick up again, because that is to me far more important. But nevertheless, one should know who they are while they are here, that you're *not* a victim of circumstances, you are not a victim of people on the outside; *you* are God! And there is no other Creator but God, there is no other Savior but God; and God is one, he's not another, and he's you.

Now let us to into the Silence.

* * *

Now are there any questions, please? Well, above all things apply what you heard, and then share the results with me. Don't give me anything, but tell me the story…that's gift enough. I don't mean that you apply it toward a fortune and then share your fortune with me, no, I'm not asking for that. But to tell me the story is enough. That's a gift! For I love to hear the story, love to hear your dreams and your visions. So, until the next time… thank you.

FUNDAMENTAL REVELATION: JESUS CHRIST IN US

10/31/69

In all the revelations that await us, there is none so fundamental as the revelation of Jesus Christ *in* us. Nothing about Jesus Christ can be known outwardly. It is only the incurrent eyewitnesses who know him—those whose immortal eyes are opened inward into the world of thought, into eternity, who are dazzled seeing through the mask of the body some flashing of the light he said he was. When one begins to awake, the being who awakes *is* the Lord Jesus Christ. But no mortal eye can see him and the mortal mind knows him from the record—where he was born, his parents, his brothers, and his friends. They know all about him and the weaknesses and the limitations of that individual. They do *not* know the being who has awakened within him.

So tonight, we will take the being who will one day awake within every child born of woman and try to show you who you really are. For Jesus Christ is the true identity of every child born of woman. He said, "I am the light of the world" (Jn.8:12), but he also said that you are the light of the world. This claim which is the most fantastic claim in the world was not claimed for *one* little individual; for Christ is the *universal* being that is the life of every child born of woman. So when one awakes, he claims it not only for himself, he claims it for every one in the world: *you* are the light of the world. But mortal mind cannot understand it and they said to him, "Tell me, who are you?" He said, "Even what I have told you from the beginning"—the beginning of what, the year one A.D.?—no, before that the world was. Before that the world was you and I heard the story that you and I would descend into this world of death and experience death, and trust the story, the *plan*. For it was a collective plan that we would come out of it and return enhanced by reason of the experience of death.

So, even what I have told you from the beginning...well, they didn't understand that...because they knew him. Beginning of what, just a few years ago? That's not what ...because he's not a physical being but one who actually experiences something entirely different from this world, and yet living in this world until the silver cord is snapped he cannot but tell it. When the silver cord is snapped, he returns, *if* he has had the experience, to the world that was his before that the world was...with all the glory that was promised by the experience of coming into this world.

So, who then is this being that I tell you that you really are, the being called Jesus Christ? We are told that we must be "born again" and then we are told, "We are born anew through the resurrection of Jesus Christ from the dead" (1Pet.1:3). That's how we are born. Our birth is conditioned upon the resurrection of Jesus Christ. And you might think that it was 2,000 years ago if you are thinking of it today. That's not it at all. Here is another statement concerning the same mystery as we read it now in Revelation: "Jesus Christ the faithful witness, the true witness...the first born of the dead" (1:5). Well, you'll think in terms of time, wouldn't you? If I now said concerning children, well, who is this one? He was the first born. And this one?—he is the second born. Well now, that is in time. But this hasn't a thing to do with time. We must now regard this in the *order of events* rather than in time. We're dealing with a mystery—"Jesus Christ the faithful witness, the first born of the dead."

There is only one Jesus Christ and he is buried in every child born of woman. If I am the beginning and the end, then I cannot be better at the beginning than I am at the end. I can be foremost, because of the first or the last. Here I am...I encompass the all. So if today at this moment you awaken and the whole story of Christ awakens within you, you are no better than one who will awaken tomorrow. And you do not precede him for this is not in time...they're speaking of the order of events. Now listen to it carefully, "Jesus Christ the faithful witness, the first born of the dead." There are two events that take place simultaneously—you cannot be born from above unless you are first resurrected. So we are resurrected first and then we are born. As we are told, "We are born anew through the *resurrection* of Jesus Christ form the dead." So, only as one is first awakened from the dream of life can he be born from above. So don't think in terms that you are preceding the other and you are better than the other. It's simply, this is an event not measured in time, but this is *how* the events take place: I am born from above through the resurrection of Jesus Christ from the dead.

Well, Jesus Christ is *in me*; not some being who 2,000 years ago rose from the dead and that was my salvation. No, in the fullness of time it began to erupt. What?—the Christ buried in *all* of us. This is now the age of the awakening. This is entirely the awakening. Everyone is going to awaken no matter what he has done in this world, for whatever he has done it was God who played the part. If he was the most horrible being in the world, he's forgiven because he played a part. I don't care what he did, it was simply a part and all things are moving towards the fulfillment of a predetermined end.

Now there are a series of events. The first event is resurrection. And as you are told in the 15th chapter of 1st Corinthians, I think it is the 51st verse, "We shall *all* be changed." Changed in what sense? He said, "In a moment, in the twinkling of an eye we shall all be changed; for the trumpet shall sound, and we shall rise from the dead, and all will be changed." At the end of what, at the end of a long, long journey? Yes…but individually. Not, say tonight, that the whole vast world will hear any trumpet. It is so unique. You are so completely unique you can't be replaced. No one in eternity can take your place. When you are awakened and you are now brought back into this infinite being that you really are—sharing the whole body, for you *are* the whole body. You play a unique, distinct part, and no one can take your place. "We shall all"—not a few—"be changed in a moment, in the twinkle of an eye; for the trumpet will sound." And when the trumpet sounds, then they shall awaken from the dead and *all* will be changed.

What is a trumpet? The word trumpet in scripture, you look it up, it simply means "a vibration." But may I tell you, it is the most unusual vibration that you have ever felt. Why, I've heard numberless vibrations in the world as you have. You go to a concert and everything you hear is a vibration, all synchronized into a harmony. But they're all vibrations, the piano, the violin, the cello, everything is a vibration. But this is a *peculiar* vibration. It is something that is centered in your head and you can't arrest it, you can't stop it, and it goes on until finally you awake. And you awake where?—in the sepulcher, in your skull, for the first time since you entered that state. How long you've started no one knows. They all speculate. I'll go along with Blake, but I do not know from actual experience…no one from within me told me the numberless centuries that I slept. I only know that I awoke within that sepulcher and that it was a peculiar vibration. And on the heels of the vibration came my birth from above just as it is symbolized in scripture.

So it took only a moment. "In a moment, in the twinkle of an eye, the trumpet will sound." As the trumpet sounds then they will awake. But it's not a collective state, it's the individual awakening. And as he awakens within, all right, so he awakens within…that's the beginning of the series of events. So when we are told, he was the first born, don't look upon it as a time; see it now as of the order of the events. So that this begins the series of events and then they continue for forty-two months. And then, you're still tied to this body because the silver cord has not yet been snapped. You must tell it to encourage everyone in this world to continue…he has to anyway. But you tell it and tell it and tell it and everyone who is hearing it will be encouraged. For not a thing in this world concerning the wisdom of man is really important; in the end it will all be proven nonsense. All that he thinks the world is made of isn't so at all. They will get all their Nobel prizes and their wonderful prizes and all the money for it and the honors that go with it; and it isn't so at all. You're not going to find life in any test tube; you're going to find it within yourself. The day is coming when *you* will see the entire world as something external to yourself, and then you will arrest within yourself an activity that you feel, and then the world will stand still. And you can do with it what you will…you can actually do with it as you will. You can change it and turn it, and make it come out as you want it. That is *life* in yourself and you're not going to find it in any test tube.

So here, the story of Christ is not to be seen, not to be understood externally. Jesus cannot be known or proven. You cannot prove the existence of any Jesus Christ externally. Only the incurrent eyewitnesses know him, those whose immortal eyes are open inward into the world of thought, into eternity. And then they are startled, for they see the truth of what one who awoke from the dream actually claimed for himself: he claimed, "I am the light of the world" (Jn. 8:12) and that is the most fantastic claim in the world. But everything claimed in scripture you're going to experience; you will know that *you* are the light of the world. May I tell you from my own experience, you will have this experience, you will feel and actually see and know that you are the center of infinite light, pulsing living light. There is no circumference, none whatsoever. You are the center and there's only light. Not a thing within it, no worlds, and no suns, no planets, but nothing. Just you and you are infinite light. You will know that from an actual experience. When the eye is open in those that you told the story to, they will see you as light, and yet know you as the being that they knew and loved. They know you and yet they will see you as that being of light, the prince of light.

Now, it is said of him, God is love. They will see you and know you as love, clothed in the form of love. It is said of him that he is power and he is wisdom, and they will see you clothed in the body of power, in the body of wisdom. Everything said of Jesus Christ in the scripture you are going to experience. And others will see you when the eye is opened inward into the world of thought. They will see you clothed in these garments of love, of power, of wisdom, of light. And eventually all will return and only one being will be there...and yet all of us individualized. There is no absorption into this being, just *union* in the one being. All are completely individualized and each the being of love, the being of power, the being of wisdom, the being of light. All of this is ours and this is the Christ of the scripture.

So of all the great revelations that await us, there is none so fundamental as the revelation of the unveiling of Christ *in us*. So let the world do what it will. So they simply murder each other. But no one dies. So they murder, they steal, they do all the unlovely things of the world, but in the end, behind that mask that being that is buried there will awaken and he will come out. When he comes out, all is forgiven, because he did all the unlovely things, too. It isn't one person today doing it; everyone who ever came out did it all, because he was the cause of it all. In last Sunday's *New York Times* magazine there is a story told by this being called Speer. He was Hitler's right hand...many thought he would really succeed Hitler. He spoke of this man, he said, "I can't describe it...the man had the capacity to make everyone obey his will. He seemed to have no center. He had a mind that so completely controlled by himself that we were like puppets in his world. That every one of us who stood before him, regardless of what we were—they could be intellectual giants or simple people—they were simply *puppets* in the presence of Hitler. But he seemed not to have a heart; he had no center. And in the end, he blamed his own people for failing. Having slaughtered millions, having burned millions, when they did not succeed, he said, 'All right, the stronger power has succeeded and they will rule, and it serves my people right." The voice of hell is always self-justification. He had failed to completely control it up to the very end, but he did for years. Yet in the end he lost the control he thought he had forever, because all things are planned by God.

God planned everything as it has come out and as it will be consummated. And so, he was used for a purpose...what you and I consider a horrible purpose. Bur as we are told in Genesis, you intended it for evil but God intended good...and raised me to the level of the Pharaoh to save civilization from starvation (50:20). But God knew he could use me and not you for his end, for his purpose. So you intended evil against me but God intended good and raised me to the level of the Pharaoh to save civilization from starvation. So here, he was used. It doesn't seem right judged by our normal moral standards in this world, but read the story of Job, the innocent man who was used. He did nothing that was wrong, and in the end he realized why. He is the story of every child born of woman; every one in the world is Job. In the end he will bring out what was buried within him, which is a plan, the plan of redemption. So he said, "I have heard of thee by the hearing of the ear, but now my eye sees thee" (Job 42:5).

So here, in the very end, after all that you've gone through he who is buried within you, which is the reality of your own being, your true identity, will erupt just like a tree coming into blossom and bear its fruit. The first fruit is to awaken. And after that the very night, happens the same moment, in a moment, in the very twinkling of an eye, then comes the birth. Both come together, one after the other. But awakening comes first and then comes the birth. Then comes the discovery of the fatherhood of God and *you* are God the Father. Then comes your ascent back into the heavenly sphere, and you go back to where you were before you came down. For, "No one returns into heaven but he who first came down from heaven, even the Son of man" (Jn.3:13).

So if you ever rise into heaven, it's because you first came down. And you came *down* from heaven, that's why you're going to go back, but enhanced by the experience of this world of hell. For this is hell. This is the only hell you'll ever know. This is the horror into which man, which is God, descended. And then comes that glorious peaceful state when the whole thing is consummated and the seal of approval is placed upon your return. And then you're redeemed. You leave this sphere, leaving it completely to your brothers, because they're all brothers, and you'll become one of the watchers from above. You will watch faithfully and lovingly, waiting for the return of everyone from this sphere. But no one is going to be lost, not one. Listen to it carefully, "*All* shall be changed in a moment"...not one, all. "Lo, I tell you a mystery"—that's how he begins the story—and the mystery is "All shall be changed." In a moment; doesn't take a long time. They go through as though not a thing is going to happen, and then one moment, in the twinkling of an eye, there's a change.

The change comes at that moment when you begin to awaken, and you're fully awake, and then you're born from above. Others with mortal eyes don't see you; they see the *sign* of your birth. But they cannot see you, for you're now born of God and you *are* God. He only brings back his son, expanded beyond what the son was prior to the descent into this world. So they see the child which is only a *sign*, the child is only a symbol of what took place. They do not see you, but you see them, and you read their thoughts, everything they think is objective and that's what the one born of God sees. He sees everything that you're thinking, everything that you've planned; everything is just as objective and more so than this room. So they see him not, but he sees them and all that they are plotting and planning. The whole thing completely unfolds within us.

The Return of Glory

So the story of Jesus Christ actually takes place in a series of events *in* the individual. Dwell upon it, take it to heart, as you're told, and pray. Try to remember...for it's only a matter of remembering. As you're told in the last chapter of the Book of Ecclesiastes, "Remember your Creator" (12:1), try to remember what he told you before that the world was. And then he tells you of the breaking, the snapping of the silver cord, and the breaking of the golden bowl and the pitcher before the dust returns to the earth (12:6). Then he calls upon us to dwell upon these words that are gathered together by one shepherd; and they are like pegs driven in, in a secure manner, like one man driving them into the lives of many. So one who has had the experience tells you his experiences, and they become many pegs driven into the minds of many. Beyond these, he warns us not to think of anything, for of the writing and the making of many books there is no end. Take *these* sayings, said he, the sayings of the shepherd; and one shepherd gathered them all together and they're like pegs driven into the being. So when one person awakens, he finds many to whom he can speak, and then he becomes the one man driving these pegs into many, many minds, and asks them to dwell upon them.

You're carried away tomorrow with news of today...what happened to the plane that flew from here to the east and then to Ireland and then to Cairo. And all that is exciting, but that's not important. Some little insane boy did it or someone did it, and the motive behind it, what does it matter? I do not know and it should not interest us. What should interest us are the collected sayings of the *wise* given to us by one shepherd, and you'll find them all in scripture. There they are. You dwell upon them and try to find out what it is all about. Well, who are you? They said "Even what I have told you from the beginning." I am the same being that spoke to you when we all gathered together in eternity before we came down; and you and I are one. You are sons of the Most High, all of you. But now we're going to have an experience, we're going to fall as one man and have the experience of dying like men, and fall as one man, O you princes (Ps.82:1,6). Every one is the prince, of what? Of light, of love, of power, of everything named in scripture concerning God...for you *are that* being. Then we simply return...that's all.

May I tell you, you'll all have the experience of which I speak. I hope it will be my pleasure to pass those eyes on. But I can't do it from this level...do it from a higher level. It's done with the consent of the watchers in eternity. All those who are already redeemed from this world decide, this one, give the eyes to this one. Then they will see the truth of what you say. So when you make the statement, "I am the light of the world" (Jn.8:12), infinite living pulsing light, it seems stupid for a little man so weak, so limited, to make that claim; and yet the one to whom you give the eyes will see you as that prince of light, that prince of love, that prince of power and wisdom. Yet you continue until the silver cord is snapped. When the silver cord is snapped and the golden bowl is broken and the pitcher is broken, all this, well then, you enter and return to those that you've always known. They are eagerly waiting for your return, return from the world of death. So it is from death to life, from darkness to light, from bondage to freedom. So we came down voluntarily and assumed the limitations of the flesh, this bondage; came down into darkness and took upon ourselves the world of darkness, and forgot that we were the light of the world. We came down into death, and yet were eternally alive. Gave it all up and took this in confidence that we had the power and the wisdom to return.

So everyone here will go back, go back regardless of what you've done or what you may still do or what you're now planning to do. I can only tell you, everyone, yes, including Hitler, including Stalin, including every monster that ever lived on the face of the earth, and they were all used. They were so constituted that they could be used for a certain purpose. No, you don't love the individual who played the part, but beyond the mask...through that mask of the body, one day he will serve and you will see the same being that is described in scripture as the Lord Jesus Christ. So the Lord Jesus Christ cannot really be proven, cannot be known by any outward means, no matter how you search it. You can search it from now to the ends of time to find where he was born, but you can't find any birth place on earth. You can't find any genealogy no matter what the priests will tell you. You can't find anything concerning Jesus Christ *outwardly*. Only those who have their immortal eyes opened and turned, as they must be when they're open, inward into the worlds of thought. They are the incurrent eyewitnesses and they know the truth of all the claims concerning Jesus Christ.

In the world a man will come or a woman will come and tell you that they have experienced the story of Jesus Christ. And then you either believe it or you don't. For when it's told like John telling the story, he said, "I'm a witness to what I have heard and seen, but I've actually seen with my own eyes, which I have handled with my own hands, concerning the word of life." Now John is not some professor who gives to society a convincing set of arguments; he is simply telling what he actually heard outside of this region. He's telling the world what he actually saw and heard that cannot be explained with the rational mind, and invites everyone who hears the story of redemption to believe it. But he leads the individual up to the point where he himself must decide whether he will accept it or reject it. It's entirely up to the individual. And so, the individual says no, it doesn't make sense and rejects it, or he will believe it and completely accept it on faith.

Now, the Christ that you accept on faith comes to you as one unknown, yet one who will in some mysterious manner let you *experience* who he is.

The Return of Glory

You first must believe the story...it comes to you through a story, and it's told as one unknown. As Paul told us in his letter to the Galatians, he said, "Did you receive the Spirit by works of the law or by hearing with faith? Are you so foolish, having received the Spirit by faith are you now ending with the flesh?" (Gal.3:2,3). Are you thinking of Jesus as a being of flesh and blood, when "flesh and blood cannot inherit the kingdom of heaven?" (1Cor.15:50). So are you really thinking of it as a being who walked as a physical being? Didn't you receive the Spirit by the hearing of the story and accepting it with faith? And that was the Spirit? If you heard it in that manner and believed this incredible story, well then, go your way, and it will unfold within you. If you reject the story, you're only delaying that moment in time when you will experience redemption. So the wise men of the world who think they are so wise by their rejection of it are simply delaying their wonderful redemption. When they now turn to dust, as they will, they will find themselves restored in an environment best suited for the work yet to be done in them to the point of acceptance of the incredible story.

Don't think for one second that you drop here at the age of seventy with all the medals of the world conferred upon you, with the wisdom of the world, and you'll continue in that state. No, God is merciful, and that may be a completely wrong direction to awaken one who is all-wise. Because all the things that man is discovering concerning the secret of life isn't so at all. To tell you that you'll come upon a scene just like this...and you don't have to receive a Nobel Prize in physics or in chemistry to understand life... suddenly you look upon everything and it's all active, moving in its own direction, each moving as it intended to move; and then you arrest it and stop all intentions, and everything is dead, completely dead, and you and you alone are alive. Everything about you stands perfectly still and you go over and you look at it...dead as dead can be. But everything is dead, everything is so still, and you've never known such stillness. If you saw a still day, a very still day, there's still some little thing moving. Not this! Everything is as still as you would see it in a museum...as if you walked into a museum and saw only the dead stuffed animals. And then you release the activity in you and they all become alive once more.

Then where was life? Life was in you. And so "As the Father has life in himself, so he has granted the Son also to have life in himself" (Jn.5:26). But only as he awakes does he have life in himself. And you will see it's not in a test tube. It's not where people *think* it is...where people are receiving fortunes for their so-called discoveries of the mystery of life. That life is an activity of Imagination: *imagining* is life. As you begin to imagine you are bringing things into being. The whole vast world is coming into being because we unwittingly are imagining what we are imagining. Don't tell

855

me that you can write papers and magazines, radios and TV's and all these things and not influence an unthinking, uncritical mind. They see all these things and entertain these thoughts, and then they execute the thought. Then behind the scene those who are making fortunes out of it hide behind it and say, oh, no, we didn't influence at all. And there isn't one thing you see in the world that wasn't in some way influenced in that manner...unless one is completely isolated and then conjures the whole thing through hate within himself.

So I tell you, the whole vast world is the Imaginations of men pushed out into the world of effects. But behind it all a merciful God steps beyond and redeems us, awakens us, and brings us out in a series of events. The series begins with your resurrection and at the same moment your birth from above. So in a moment, in the twinkling of an eye, all will rise because the trumpet, the vibration, will sound and the dead will rise and *all* shall be changed. Changed from these bodies of darkness into immortal bodies, imperishable bodies that are bodies of light, bodies of love, bodies of power, and bodies of wisdom. I can't describe it to anyone, not until you see it. Fortunately for me there was one to whom I gave my immortal eyes—yet still retained them—who saw it only recently. I've been waiting for someone to bear witness to it all. For one must witness the truth of what one, who has actually experienced it, claims that he has. So I claimed that I have... fantastic claims: I am the light of the world, I am all that is said of Jesus Christ in the scripture, all that is said of God. Yet until the silver cord is snapped, I am as weak as any man that walks the face of the earth. I am as limited as anyone who walks the face of this earth, making all the mistakes while I'm tied to a body that is made for mistakes, it's weak. But the moment when that thing is snapped I will return instantly to that which I have experienced unnumbered times, time and time again, a body of light, a body of wisdom, a body of power, and above all things, a body of love.

Now let us go into the Silence.

*   *   *

Now are there any questions, please?

Q: Neville, when you take off this body, you said there are worlds within worlds, do you have to return in this dimension to have the experience?
A: My dear, death that we call death is not death...any more than departure from one scene on a stage is the death of the actor who left the scene. You're restored, not resurrected— restored to life instantly, there's no delay—in a glorious body like this, young, attractive, altogether

wonderful like all young bodies are and approximately twenty years of age. You may be in an entirely different pigment. May I tell you, all these pigments...this is not evolution as the world calls evolution. Evolution is...there's not a thing in scripture concerning evolution. It's a *theory* with no facts to support it, none whatsoever. The jump between the fish and the mammal, they can't find the link. Between the little mammal and man, they can't find the link. Or the bird and the animal, they can't find the link. Evolution belongs only to the *affairs* of man: instead of always digging with a hoe we now use a tractor, and between the hoe and the tractor there are numberless stages. Instead of floating across a body of water on a raft I now use an ocean liner, atomic energy...but between that there was a sail boat, a steamboat, and all kinds of things. Now instead of walking a distance I can take a jet and maybe a missile. And so, there's evolution in the affairs of man, but not in the creation of God. And so, the pigment of the skin that you now wear hasn't a thing to do with any so-called evolution. Let no one tell you that that is behind the times as some people will say. You could tomorrow find yourself a blue-eyed blonde lady and one who is now a blue-eyed blonde lady in the pigment that you wear if that is what is necessary for the unfoldment of Christ within you. The whole thing unfolds within and Christ is playing all the parts, but *all* the parts. So let no one tell you that we came out of any monkey and from monkey into this and that. Don't believe it, my dear.

But at death, unless this thing happens before the silver cord is snapped, you will find yourself in a garment knowing who you are, no loss of identity, in a world terrestrial just like this, in an environment best suited for the work yet to be done in you by the being that you *really* are who is God. "He who began a good work in you will bring it to completion at the day of Jesus Christ" (Phil.1:6). So let no one in any way tell you that they know from what is taking place now what you're going to be tomorrow...and reading auras and all this nonsense, and reading horoscopes and reading numbers. Forget it!

When you hear people who are supposed to be teachers, as I heard today, someone called long distance from New York City, and then they told me about some kind of wedding that some astrologer saw, and I wondered, "What have I been doing all these years?" I've been talking and talking and talking and I wondered, "Who is hearing me? Just what am I saying that is ever heard...to what extent is it ever heard? What degree am I getting over?" Here is one...she called twice in the course of four hours. The first call was for some distress about a nephew, and four hours later she called to say she got him out of jail...that it happened. I only heard what she asked me to hear. And so what he did? I didn't ask what he did, I don't know what he did, but she got him out. And then all this nonsense concerning marriage all based upon astrology.

People read this nonsense. In the morning's paper, men who are really in big business and you wonder, my Lord, you better take your money out of that stock. They won't leave the house until they find out what their little sign is going to do today. Don't think for one moment it isn't so, they do it. And the only one who makes any money out if it is the one who writes it. Oh, he fattens himself out of writing this drivel. But you can't break these little superstitions over night; it takes time to dislodge it, and tell you that your true identity is Jesus Christ. If Jesus Christ is my true identity, then I'm suffering from amnesia and then the whole story is *remembered*! So the last chapter of Ecclesiastes begins, "Remember, remember your Creator in the days of your youth" (12:1)… the whole thing is appealing to man to try to remember.

In the Book of John, "He will bring to your remembrance all that I have told you" (14:26). The whole thing…the 42nd Psalm, "These things I remember: how I went with the throng, and led them in gay procession to the house of God" (42:4). It's a constant remembrance, calling upon man to remember, for man is suffering from total amnesia. He has forgotten his true identity, and his true identity is Jesus Christ. That's what man really is. And here he fights with each other, he does all unlovely things to each other, and he doesn't know who he is. So you are playing whatever part you are playing because the God in you thinks it best and *knows* it's best, for the work that he's doing in you and still to be done in you.

So let no one tell you that we're moving in some little direction towards a climax in a certain pigment. No, you are outside of this altogether. You are a being of light yet human, may I tell you, a human face, a human voice, human hands…and I will not go beyond that. I will not go beyond that much concerning the form that you will wear when you're resurrected. But it is a human face, a human voice and there are human hands…beyond that let no one try to describe it. How would the butterfly explain to the chrysalis what it is to be a butterfly? When you awaken how could you ever describe to the being in whom you awoke what you were wearing? I tell you it's the body of love that I wear and a body of light and power and wisdom, yet tied to this until I break that silver cord. But I can't describe it to anyone's satisfaction what I look like unless you have incurrent eyes…and then you are an incurrent eyewitness.

Any other questions, please? Yes, Ina?

Q: Well, don't you think there has to be a code or something in the world in which men live? And then this idea of God playing all the parts and one goes ahead and does something ugly when maybe he might have a touch of conscience about him, but yet he thinks he's justified because it is God playing all the parts?

A: Well, Ina my dear, you have always been in the theater, so you're very familiar with Shakespeare. You go tonight to see a Shakespearean play and the great artists step upon the stage, and we're all ready to receive their interpretation of the great Shakespeare. They step on by different names...one is called by this name, one is Burton, this one is Taylor, this one is so-and-so, and they're all playing to the audience. Yet they are only witnessing the dramatization of the mind of Shakespeare. Every word that you hear was uttered by Shakespeare. It's difficult for man watching it, not to think because he heard it coming from the lips of an actor who wore the mask of Hamlet, that it isn't really Hamlet who is saying it, it was Shakespeare who wrote it. And then, that one who stabbed the uncle and he was killed, it was Shakespeare who did it... everything that you saw as you saw the whole thing unfold before you.

And I have seen the uncut version of Hamlet; it ran about five hours. We went out to dinner after two and a half hours and came back an hour later. It played on 44th St. right off Broadway. We went to Sardi's for dinner and my wife and I came back after dinner and continued for the next two and a half hours...five hours of the uncut version of Hamlet. Everything you saw—and you were moved to tears, moved to passion, moved to all those things—and you only saw the mind of the author projected, that's all that you saw. There isn't a thing that you saw there that was not out of the mind of the one who wrote it and it wasn't there at all. The actors were paid for what they did; they played their part well. But in the end it was only one being who wrote it all and because there was no one else to play it, he played it all.

Good night.

THE RIDDLE

11/3/69

The Rev. Dr. Trusler criticized Blake for his abstruseness and said to him that he needed someone to really elucidate his ideas. Blake said to him, "You ought to know that that which is grand is necessarily obscure to the weak." Then he went on to say that "You also ought to know that what can be made explicit to the idiot isn't worth my care, and that the wisest of the ancients considered that what was not *too* explicit fittest for instruction, for it rouses the faculties to act." Then he asked the Rev. Dr. Trusler this question, "Why is it that the Bible is more entertaining and instructive than any book? Is it not because it is addressed to the Imagination, which is spiritual sensation, and only but immediately to the understanding or reason?"

Now tonight, we will ask a question based upon scripture. It's a riddle and the riddle is this, "What is it that becomes his own grandson and vice versa?" How is it that that which is called the Divine Creator, who created me, is my child? How can the Divine Creator, my father, be my child? Now we'll take the riddle and show you how these parts are put together. It's not addressed to those to whom you must take it apart and show it in little detail; it's addressed to the human Imagination. I doubt that any logical, reasoning mind could unravel it; it has to be revealed. When it's revealed you stand *amazed* at the statements as told in scripture. Now here, we go back to three passages from the Book of Isaiah. The 7th chapter is the first. It is translated in some translations "a virgin" and in others simply "a young woman, a maiden." "A maiden will conceive and bring forth a son" (7:14). Now this will be a *sign* you are told, and it is that the Lord will give you a sign, and the sign is this: a maiden will conceive and bring forth a son and will call his name Immanuel. Immanuel is translated as "God with us"; it is better rendered, "God *in* us" as confirmed in the New Testament, "The

The Return of Glory

kingdom of God is within you" (Luke17:21). So it is not "God with us" as something on the outside, but is "God *in* us" that is the true interpretation of the word Immanuel. "And she'll call his name Immanuel."

Now we pass on to the 9th chapter and here we read "Unto us a child is born…and his name shall be called the "Everlasting Father" (Is.9:6). Here, to *us*—to us the human personalities—and yet what we bring forth as a child his name is Everlasting Father. I am bringing forth that which created myself. The Everlasting Father and the child are now told to be one. His name is Everlasting Father, and the Everlasting Father is the self-existent, the ever-creating being that created the entire universe and sustains it. Yet I am told *I* bring him forth…I bring him forth as *my child*. My child is my Father. That is what is implied in the statement.

Now we go another two chapters into the 11th, and here we find in the 11th chapter "And there shall come forth out of Jesse a stem…and out of the stem will come a branch…and this branch will be the ruler of all" (Is.11:1). Out of Jesse will come a stem and out of the stem will come a branch, and this branch is ruler of all. (11:10). The solution of the riddle you will find in the names. The word Jesse means "I AM," the eternal everlasting name of God. Now we are told, out of Jesse comes the stem…well, Jesse's son is David as told us in scripture (1Sam.17:58). So here we now find David. And now out of David comes a branch, and the branch is one with his grandfather.

Now in the New Testament the same riddle is proposed, but not answered: how can they say that the Christ is the son of David when David in the Spirit calls him Lord? No one answered…it's simply stated to describe in the 20th chapter of the Book of Luke, you read it in the 41st and the 44th verses. "How is it that they say"—meaning the scribes say, the wise men say that David—"the Christ is the son of David when David in the Spirit calls him Lord"…calls him "my Father?"

Now here, we will take these passages and put them together. Here we find first the name of the son is Immanuel, which is "God is in us." That's the name of the son. The name of the Father is David…and David is "the beloved." The name of the grandfather is Jesse and Jesse is "I AM," the everlasting God, the everlasting Father. Here we find these three separate generations as it were. And then we find that the son is one with the grandfather and the grandfather and the grandson are one. That is what you find in scripture. Now who will un-riddle the riddle?

Then we come back now to David. Well then, what is David? Who is David? He's called "the beloved." I tell you now not from any logical reasoning, because Truth is *revealed*. It is not logically unraveled, not logically proven at all. It is revealed and were it not revealed to me I wouldn't know, any more than anyone in the world would know unless it was revealed to them. So I'm sharing with you the revelation: David is all of the generations of humanity, but all of them, fused together into a single being, and that single being is personified as one youth, an eternal being, and the *beloved* of the eternal Father. Out of him he begets himself. The whole drama is nothing more than the reproducing of the Divine Imagination in the human Imagination, that's all that it is. A constant reproducing of itself, for there's not a thing in the world but God. He's reproducing himself in every being in the world. But it takes something in which he reproduces himself and that is humanity. Humanity is the *mask* that he wears. The sum total of all the experiences of men fused into one single whole and that whole personified comes out as a youth and the youth is David. So humanity in that sense is his son. But out of humanity comes God, which would be the grandson and the grandson is one with the grandfather. *You* are the grandfather.

This is a riddle, and only the indolent mind would fail to respond to the challenge: what is it that actually becomes its own grandson, and the grandson becomes the grandfather, and they are one? So here we find the three stages. God is begetting himself on humanity and humanity does his will. "I have found in David a man after my own heart, who will do all my will" (Acts13:22). So man is completely under the control of this Supreme Being and man does all his will, and he begets on man his grandson. Man becomes the son, and man's child is his grandson; but the grandson and the grandfather are one, and you are both. You are what you begot and you are the begetter. So you come out and you are God the Father, and you look now on humanity, personified as David, and David calls you Father; because what David brought forth is only himself, the begetter. The grandfather and the grandson are one. You, humanity, are that on which it's begotten. But when you can see humanity gathered together into one single being and personified, it's David; and David calls *you* Father, then you are the grandfather and the grandson who really are one.

I do not say that this is the easiest thing in the world for man to grasp, but I'm telling you it is true. It is a fantastic miracle that takes place. It is the riddle of riddles. So then he asks the question, "Why do they say that Christ is the son of David when David in the Spirit calls him Lord?" (Mat.22:42).

So here, I am bringing forth, and brought forth, the child. I am told that "I will give you a sign and this shall be a sign, a maiden will bring forth a son, and she'll call his name Immanuel (God is in us)." What came out as a child that is a sign is "God is in us." Now we move over to the 9th chapter and we find "Unto us a *child* is born" (9:6). Here is this wonderful child and his name is "Everlasting Father." You mean the child is Everlasting Father?

Yes. So he begot through me his own grandchild. I am his son, but now he's going to raise me...I begot his grandchild. And then his grandchild stands before me...it is my son and he is his grandfather, and I am looking at him, and I see *David*, and David which is the being out of which it came, therefore, who am I? I am the grandfather. And the grandfather and the grandson are one.

I am not telling you this is the easiest thing in the world to grasp, but I thought this is time for you to hear it. We have reached the point in time for you to hear it...that the grandfather and the grandson are one. These are the three as named. First, out of Jesse—Jesse means I AM, the eternal name of God the Father, the Everlasting Father—will come a stem. Well, Jesse's stem is called David. All right, we'll call David humanity. And then out of David will come a branch and that is called Christ. Now Jesus asked the question, "What do you think of the Christ?" (Mat.22:42). How can scribes say that he is the *son* of David when David in the Spirit calls him Lord? By then he is the grandfather, and as the grandfather he is the father of David, so the grandson and the grandfather are one. David is that on which he molds himself and brings out himself; and then raises you, the individualized you out of which it came, to himself. So you are the grandfather *and* the grandson. And then humanity remains on which to mold himself throughout eternity.

Humanity is simply David. If all the experiences of man could be gathered together and fused into one single whole and that concentrated time projected into a single being, it would appear before you as an eternal youth. And you don't have to ask anyone his name, his name is David. But he represents all the experiences of humanity, but *all* of them, fused into a single whole, and that single whole projected and personified is David. So you've gone through, or you will go through, all the experiences of humanity. And when you've gone through it, you'll bring forth the son, your son. And your son is but the grandson of God the Father, and he and his grandfather are *one*. You then become the grandfather and you are God himself! The eternal divine imagining is reproducing itself in human imagining, so that the "I am" of man is one with the universal I AM. There can't be any other...there is no other...there is *nothing* but God.

So all the horrors that you see in the world and all the frightfulness that you experience, and have experienced, or may experience, it all adds up to the birth of the wonder child. "Unto us"—to us—"a child is born." So here, we find three generations. Here we find Jesse, the universal I AM; and here we find the "us," a human personality—to us is born...*we* have the experience of what?—of this wonder child. But his name bear in mind is Everlasting Father. You mean, how can I, begotten of the Eternal Father, produce the Father? That's what I have to do, I bring forth, because he can't beget anything but himself. So *I beget* the Eternal Father. And then, having begotten the Eternal Father, I have the experience of this glorious son David who made it possible. So I became humanity that I may beget myself. Humanity remains…no matter what horrors you have heard of humanity, no matter what things you have read about it, and the history of humanity is horrible, but it took all these things to produce a son which was the grandson of the Eternal Father…and the grandson and the grandfather are one. The son remains humanity and humanity condensed into a single being is David.

I hope you will dwell upon it. I'm not telling you it is the easiest thing in the world for you to grasp, but I thought this is full time to tell the riddle. For there are many things to be said and time is short. But here, this is the riddle: the Eternal Being, who is God the Father, entered into the eternal structure of the world…for that's humanity. Man as you see him is part of the eternal structure of the world and on it he is reproducing himself in this part of the eternal structure of the world. When he brings out his likeness, it's his grandson. Then the grandson said, "David called me Lord" and the Lord is David's Father. Therefore the grandson, the Christ, was called the Lord by David and therefore he's one with his grandfather, the identical image of his grandfather, and one with it. Then he looks out and David calls him Lord, so he is one with the eternal Everlasting Father. So it's only the search for the Father that is taking place in this world and there is nothing but God the Father.

So I am not saying that it is the easiest thing for you to hear tonight. I am quite sure that most of us here tonight are not here for the first time and you're fully aware of what I've been trying to say over the years. So it should not be difficult for you to simply dwell upon it and sense it until it actually is revealed to you by a wonderful mystical experience. It will be revealed to you and you will be the eternal God, God the Father. For the universal I AM and your I am are not two I AM's; it's the same I AM. So he's bringing forward himself by molding himself upon that part of eternity which is the human family. And it's a very painful process to bring out his likeness, to reproduce himself the Divine Imagination in the human Imagination.

There's no better way to do it than to put it in this manner. So these three passages in the 7th, 9th and 11th chapters of Isaiah and then the 20th chapter of Luke all propound the identical riddle. The riddle put into our language would be: what is it that becomes its own grandson and how is it that the grandson is one with the grandfather? How can that which begot me actually become my child and in becoming my child, raise me to my begetter who is God the Father? And then to look back on humanity and

The Return of Glory

all the experiences of humanity fused into a single being standing before me and calling *me* Father?

So you dwell upon it. It's not the easiest thing to grasp, but we're going to give you lots of time to challenge me tonight or to ask questions. You'll find this most stimulating, and far from being not practical you will find it the most practical thing that you've ever heard. Far more exciting than anything you heard or read about today on TV, radio or in papers, for not a thing said this day by any person in the world would compare to it. All the plots and plans of men concerning bringing this war to an end and all these things is all part of a divine plan. The plan is not the wars and the peace as the world sees it but to bring out himself—he's only begetting himself. Divine Imagination is reproducing himself in the human Imagination; and they are not two, they are one. They differ only in the degree of *intensity*.

But the purpose of it all is that you will be able to wish anything and realize it. "I have come that you may have life and have it more abundantly" (Jn.10:10). That, you'll ask for anything and realize it, that's the purpose of the entire scheme. That you will not be a slave of anything in this world, not be afraid of anything., for you'll know you are one with the Creator of the universe and that you can ask and expect instantaneous return as far as the answer goes. That comes with the complete revelation of what I have told you tonight. Now, you will not find it spelled out as I have this night to you, but you can read scripture and having heard my story over and over again you will follow my argument.

So the problem is and the riddle is, what is it that becomes its own grandfather and vice versa...the grandson becomes its own grandfather? And then, if this is so, where is that father of the grandson and where does he fit in? His name is David. And you'll find out when you bring forth the wonder child, whose name is Everlasting Father. You wake a few months later to find that you instead of being his son you are the father of David. So instead of coming out of humanity as humanity's son, which you did, for it took humanity and all the horrors that God the *real* Father experienced to produce his being, his likeness...and his likeness is himself. So then you awake as God the Eternal Father. Humanity remains; but this time not a multitude of faces, only one face. All the faces put together and fused into one body stands before you and David calls you "my Lord." So how then can he be David's son when David in the Spirit calls him "my Lord"? You follow? I hope so.

If you haven't followed it, I do hope that many of you have taken it down on the tape and you'll play it over and over. For it is a profound truth and I think nothing deeper in scripture will come to you. For this is the story of scripture. So Blake was perfectly right, "Why is the Bible more entertaining and more instructive than any book? Is it not because it is addressed to the Imagination, which is spiritual sensation, and only immediately to the understanding or reason? Therefore, what can be made explicit to the idiot is not worth my care. And the ancients, the wisest of the ancients, consider what was not too explicit fittest for instruction because it rouses the faculties to act." So here comes a riddle and you've got to respond to that challenge. Where on earth could it be and how could such a thing happen? How can a grandson become his own grandfather? For that is what he's telling us in these three passages of Isaiah and in that passage of Luke. You say that the Christ is the son of David, but I ask you now, how then can he be the son when in the spirit David calls him "my Lord"? If he's the son of David and David's father is "my Lord" and David in the Spirit calls him not "my son" but "my Lord," then he is his own grandfather. Do you get it?

You dwell upon it! And maybe this night because it's been given to you this night something may happen. Something may explode within you to lead you to an understanding of it. But the full understanding comes when you *experience* it, when the whole thing unfolds within you like a wonderful unfolding flower; and there is only the Eternal God unfolding in humanity. And you'll find these three generations constantly throughout scripture. The Book of Matthew, which begins our New Testament, begins with three generations: "This is the book of the genealogy of Jesus Christ, son of David, son of Abraham." Three generations…doesn't state any more. Then it begins to project into the genealogy, the generations. But the names now, Abraham is "the father of multitudes"…that's all that it states. That's what the word means, "father of multitudes," nothing but. Here we find David in the middle again; he is the father of Jesus Christ, he is the Beloved, that human being that brought forth the image of God. The image of God is called Jesus Christ, but the image of God and God are one, so it goes back now to the grandfather.

So tonight, although it may seem profoundly spiritual, I must repeat what I've said time and time again, whatever is most profoundly spiritual will prove in time to be the most directly practical. Instead of wrestling with a problem, you dwell upon these wonderful revealed truths and the problem solves itself. Instead of going to bed and bursting a blood vessel to find out how you're going to meet this, that and the other commitment, you go to bed dwelling upon these, and the commitments are met. Your Father knows what you have need of: "Seek first the kingdom of heaven and *all* these will be added unto you" (Mat.6:33). They will all be added. While you sleep, things will happen in your world. While you dwell upon these profound thoughts of revealed Truth everything will come! You sit down to work out one problem and you simply involve yourself with another and another. But

The Return of Glory

dwell upon revealed Truth and then all these things that you need in this world—your Father knows you need shelter, that you need food, that you need clothing, that you need all these things. But you dwell upon his Word and try to wrestle with his conundrums, these wonderful, well, riddles.

You may not unravel them. But dwell upon what I've told you tonight because I'm telling you what I know from experience. I did not arrive at these by any logic in the world. I am not trained in logic, I'm not a philosopher. I simply am one in whom the Word unfolded, completely unfolded. There isn't a thing else that I can think of in scripture that hasn't unfolded within me. But you're told, in time you'll be urged to tell it, in good time. So you tell it at a certain moment in time and you who hear it this night, you dwell upon it...that *you* are giving birth to Christ. And Jesus Christ—who will be your son because he came out of you, that is, the wonderful child—is one with your Father, who would have to be his grandfather. He is one with *your* Father and as he came out of you, and he's one with *his* grandfather, which is your Father; finally you awaken to find you are the Everlasting Father. Because now you look down upon yourself called man, which is now personified as David, and David calls *you* Father.

Now that we may have a full evening of questions, let us go into the Silence.

*   *   *

Q: In regard to what you said about the grandfather and grandson, does this equate with Mary conceiving of the invisible Father and bringing forth a son, and is man then Mary?
A: Yes. "I am Mary and birth to God must give if I in blessedness for now and evermore would live" (Scheffler). Think of humanity as feminine... the soul of man...think upon it as the bride of the Lord: "My Maker is my husband" as told us in Isaiah (54:5). Then he will cleave to me, leaving all, and become one with me. He leaves all and cleaves to his wife and they become one flesh. So I am Mary.

I said that one night here, oh, about two years ago, and one took issue with me and he's never returned. Perfectly all right. He will wake one day and he will know that he *is* Mary and he has to bring forth the Christ child. But you're told in the 7th chapter of Isaiah, "And the Lord will give you a *sign*" (7:14). A woman—translated a maiden, a virgin—but the word simply means a young woman, whether she is a virgin or not. Who in the world is a virgin if they've ever had a mental affair with the opposite? Who in the world is a virgin when you are told in scripture it's all *psychological*? You are told that you should never lust after another, but anyone who lusts after another has already committed the act in his heart with her (Mat.5:27). Therefore, it is a psychological motion. If I want but restrain the impulse, impulse was the act.

So you can call it a virgin or a young woman, but "I am Mary and birth to God must give if I in blessedness for now and evermore would live." And so I brought forth the child…and only Mary brings forth the child, so I am Mary. Mary is the bride of the Holy Spirit who brought forth the child, and the child and the Holy Spirit are one. The child, my son, and his grandfather are one. But by then when I bring forth the son, he has finished his work in me, and the cleavage with me, on me, has been complete and we aren't two now, we are one. So, the three become one. And yet humanity remains that upon which I can continue to mold myself. It's the Divine Imagination reproducing itself upon humanity, and in the end you will actually come out as God the Everlasting Father.

Q: Is there in scripture passages that bear witness to your experience of seeing David that spells out he is the symbol of humanity?

A: Not in the sense that I have explained it. But it is, "I have found David and he has cried unto me, 'Thou art my Father'" in the 89th Psalm (89:26). There are certain words in scripture that are not translated. If you translate them, go to the Concordance and look them up. You'll find one word used only once in the 16th chapter of 1st Corinthians and it is left just as it is. Some take the word before it, which is anathema, which translated means "a curse" and join it to that word. But then you think that the original manuscripts had no punctuation marks. In fact they had no vowels; they were all consonants and not punctuated, no sentences, no paragraphs, no chapters. That was done centuries later.

So the King James Version takes the word and puts a period after these two and leaves the word anathema and the word maranatha which simply means in the Revised Standard Version "our Lord has come" (16:22). It *has* come, it actually *has* happened, this whole thing has happened. That's how he ends his first letter to the Corinthians. Just about the verse before the benediction comes this word un-translated in the King James Version but translated in the Revised Standard Version. You shouldn't join it to anathema, for if you do not believe in the Lord Jesus Christ anathema means "be ye cursed," because you *will* be by not believing in this eternal story of salvation. But then the next word should be something entirely different beginning the sentence which means "Our Lord has come." It has actually happened! That which was promised or foreseen throughout the centuries has finally happened.

Now some will translate it instead of saying "our Lord has come," they will translate it like the one in the end of Revelation, "Come

Lord Jesus." Meaning it has not yet, but please, we're hopeful. It's the great hope of man. But I know from my own experience it *has* come and it's continuing to come in the lives of humanity, because it can't fail. Everyone is simply being worked on where God the Father, the Everlasting Father is begetting himself in man. When he begets himself he's completed the work. When it comes out it is the Christ child. And what is begotten is one with the begetter; and that out of which it was begotten was his bride. Then she awakes without any change of identity, and she is God the Father. Then humanity stands before her...fused together into a single being, and that single being is a youth, the eternal youth called David.

It's all there but not spelled out. As Blake said, "If it could be made explicit to the idiot then it isn't worth my care." Then he said, "The wisest of the ancients consider what was not too explicit fittest for instruction, because it rouses the faculties to act." But if you take it just as a little story, a story that is a secular story, well then, anyone can write scripture. But it isn't that. The whole thing is a hidden book that is completely contained *in man*, and then suddenly it comes to the surface. Man having gone through hell...luckily our Infinite Father, who we are destined to awaken *as*, is merciful, and has hidden from us the memory of the horrors through which we have passed. You have only glimpses of the horrors. Sometimes someone threatens a certain thing and then a faint memory returns. It wasn't a threat in the past, it was a fact...it actually happened to you.

I know when I was a boy in Barbados...and he said it quite without taking thought...he was a fisherman, a black fisherman, and little boys in Barbados...there's no reason for bathing suits or thing of that sort, and I came out of the water in the nude, running toward the other part of the beach where I left my little clothes with a rock on them. He didn't mean it...he never would for one moment have intended what he said... but suddenly a flash returned that that same event happened to me in the dim past. He said to me, "Come here, I'm going to castrate you!" But memory fades. I recalled it vividly at that moment and I was scared to death at what he said. But that was an experience of the past that my Father, in whom I have awakened *as*, in his infinite mercy he hid that memory picture from me until that one little incident revived it.

So everything in the world has significance. *Everything* has significance! And he was perfectly innocent of what he said, he was simply kidding in his own way with a little white boy. I came out of the water and here was this Negro taking care of his nets, he was a fisherman, and getting all the knots out, getting it ready to dry before he would go off to sea the next day to catch fish. Undoubtedly if I asked him at any time for a fish he would throw me a half dozen of them. They were all lovely, wonderful men, so he didn't intend to hurt me, but he revived a memory. So the whole thing comes back. And in the end, the whole thing comes back and you are God the Father who began the whole thing. For in the end, there can be nothing but God the Father.

Q: This is my first visit…how do you view the devil symbolically? I've never heard your views.

A: Well, the devil is everything that God is not and God is the *only* reality, so the devil is not.

Q: But in your line of thinking, if we are evolving towards, being awakened to the realization that we are in fact God?

A: Well, put it this way, God is affirmative. We're told all the promises of God find their *yes* in him…that's affirmation. Then negation would be in the devil. When something seems impossible, that is the devil. If I say all things are possible to God but something may not be, well then, that is a devil. So here comes now negation in my world.

Q: So anything that negates yourself?

A: Yes, that is the devil, that's Satan..

Well, my dears, it's almost the time and I do hope that you listened attentively tonight, because really you will find it something so altogether wonderful when you dwell upon it: what you are destined to awaken to. You are destined to awaken to the fact that you are the Everlasting God who created the whole vast universe, brought it into being, and you sustain it! Good night.

THOU ART OUR FATHER, OUR POTTER

11/7/69

In the 64th chapter of the Book of Isaiah we read, "O Lord, thou art our Father; we are the clay. Thou art our potter; we are all the work of thy hand" (64:8). Well, when you read it you might think, "All right, O Lord" and you think of another. Then you say, "Thou art our Father"...that's the same other. We are but clay and thou art our potter. Well, it's identified with the Lord and with the Father, so you think also of another, and we're all the work of thy hand.

The word "potter" by definition simply means "Imagination." The word "Lord" is Yod He Vau He, which is defined for us as I AM. You mean that my own wonderful I-am-ness is the Lord, is my Father, and is my potter? That I am actually shaping myself and shaping my world? Yes, that is exactly what it means, that the Father is the Lord and the Lord is the potter shaping my entire world. But *I am* the shaper shaping it into a form, molding it into a form. Now, can I prove it? Am I really *all* Imagination as everyone who has experienced it knows? That "Man is all Imagination and God is man, and exists in us and we in him...that the eternal body of man is the Imagination, and that really is God himself" (Blake, *Annotations to Berkeley*).

Now let me share with you a story I read two weeks ago in the *New York Times*, the magazine section. It was written by one who was imprisoned on the island of Amorgos in the Aegean Sea. He was a Greek imprisoned by the present regime that has taken over Greece, the generals. He was under house arrest and he was watched twenty-four hours a day. He was allowed to leave the house for a restaurant and by doctor's orders to go for a certain walk after he had signed in at 6 PM with the police. Every morning at nine he had to sign in at the police and at 6 PM to return and sign in. Then he could go for a walk. These are his words, he said, "I began to imagine the scene in the village of horror the day *after* I escaped." Then he imagined, "the elderly would be drinking coffee at nine in the morning, and then the cobbler would have opened up his doors for business, and then the scent of fresh bread would come straining through the windows of the bakery. By 9:30, because I had not registered, they would inquire of the one who had always sat in the public square dressed as a civilian looking at my apartment, and he would tell them that he had not seen me…I had not come upon my balcony. By 10:00 they would come to investigate themselves and then they would knock down the door. Then by 10:30 it would be, well, the news would scattered abroad and all would know that I was not there. Throughout the day the villagers would pass in their silent way, secretly but in a knowing way look one to the other that he isn't here. That night they would gather in secret around their little shortwave radios listening for news from abroad of my escape. And so, I began to imagine that scene. The scene that gave me the greatest happiness was the scene when they all would know that I had escaped."

Well, it came to pass, and he wrote his letter. His name is George Mylonos. It was on the 26th day of October, this last month that that letter appeared in the *New York Times* magazine, the Sunday issue. It all began in his Imagination. He was there for 409 days. At first it was only a dream, only a daydream. Then in the end he began to really do something about it. Now he told a story—which I will question because he wants to save the other prisoners on the other islands, also on the mainland—concerning exactly how he did it. Oh yes, there were physical means, but the means came into being as a result of his imaginal activity. To attempt to change circumstances *before* you change your imaginal activity is to struggle against the very nature of things. For this world in which we live is a world of Imagination. *You* are all Imagination and God, your reality, is all Imagination. Divine Imagination has reproduced himself in the human Imagination; therefore, all things exist in the human Imagination for all things exist in Divine Imagination.

Is it really true? Well, test it! He did. I wonder how many people who read it only two weeks ago would relate his escape to his imaginal act? They would read the letter, but what percentage of them would read the letter anyway? Because the *New York Times* weighs pounds…it's about that thick…and so you would spend the whole day and not cover it, depending upon your interest. Well, how many would even see it? But here, this simple letter occupying not more than a page—it's on three pages, but only one column to a page, so put together it would only take up one page. How many would read it? And of those who read it, what percentage would relate his imaginal act to his escape? And that's exactly how he escaped.

Now you don't have to be a prisoner on Amorgos. You could be a prisoner financially or socially. You could be a prisoner in a thousand ways, physically in health. Now, will you do the same thing that he did and imagine the scene that would take place the day *after* your escape. The day *after* it is heard that you do *not* have what you thought you had and others heard that you had; the day after you are not financially embarrassed and that you have all that it takes to live graciously. The day after…and you just mention anything in this world. Always go to the end; the end is where we begin. In my end is my beginning. So I go to the end…the day *after* my escape. Then I imagine the scene that would take place. He thought, "Well now, the elders would be having coffee at nine, the cobbler would be opening up his doors at nine. Then the odor of the bread, the fresh-baked bread would be coming through the windows of the bakery. By 9:30 they would notice I had not signed in. By ten o'clock the police would call to ask that plainclothes man who always sat in the square looking up at my apartment, and he would say "I didn't see him and he did not come on his balcony today." By ten they would investigate and getting no response they would break down the door. Then the villagers would know it…and that was my greatest thrill!" That's where he started, letting the villagers know it in his mind's eye. This is all in his Imagination.

Now, you have friends…or if you don't have friends, which would be a horrible thing if you didn't…but you do have friends, and your friends know your present position in this world, the conditions that surround you. Maybe they're pleasant and you'd like to perpetuate them. But maybe they are not pleasant, maybe they are not exactly as you would like them to be. You start with letting your friends know—not verbally, not outwardly—all in your Imagination. You see them seeing you as they would have to see you if things were as you desire them to be. You start there, the day *after* they know that things are just as you want them to be and then you let them see it. In your mind's eye they are seeing it and you start there. Then ways will open that you do not devise. No one knows how it's going to happen, but in a way that no one knows it will unfold and you *will* fulfill it. You'll walk across a series of events, some bridge of incidents that you did not consciously devise which will take you from where you are in prison to your freedom whatever that end is…whether it be health, wealth, or in his case, an actual physical escape from a life imprisonment. Because, as long as the present regime reigns in Greece these political prisoners would be under house arrest.

So here, you can verify it. I read it and I now share it with you. It's the 26th day of October in the Magazine section of the *N. Y. Times*. I think, if my memory serves me correctly, it begins on the 16th page. So it's not long. It's a very thick magazine because all these issues especially now coming into the fall when all things are being sold for Christmas, and the magazine is now three times its size and the paper is three times its size. But I get it every week and it comes on Wednesday. And here, a man, a simple man, political prisoner of the current regime, wondered what it would be like *if* these things were true.

So I tell you, "Man is all Imagination and God is man, and exists in us and we in him. The eternal body of man is the Imagination, and that is God himself." When this God awakes within man, that man in whom he awakes is clothed with everything said of God in the scripture. It is said of God that he is the light of the world; it is said of God that he is love; it is said of him that he is the power of the universe and the wisdom of the universe. May I tell you, when you awake (and you will) you'll be clothed with power and wisdom and light and love. And those who have eyes that are open into the inner worlds, open into the eternal worlds of thought, into eternity, will see you clothed as God. There is only God in this world. So God is begetting himself: Divine Imagination is reproducing himself in human Imagination. And when he reproduces himself in the human Imagination, that being in whom he is reproduced awakens and he is clothed as God himself is clothed. When you see him, you'll see him clothed in light, in love, in power, in wisdom. Everything said of God in the Bible will be said of you by the one who sees you.

But if the eye is not open, they do not see you and they only see the little garment that you wear with all the weaknesses of that garment, all the limitations of that garment. You will wear it in a world that is limited not quite fully inheriting what you really are while you're still tied to this. For your heavenly inheritance is not completely actualized, not fully realized by you while you're still in the world of flesh and blood and tied to a garment of flesh and blood. But at night when you sleep and you are detached, you are in the world of eternity. And those who have eyes will see you functioning in that world. You are fully conscious of what you are doing. But when you return you come back through a quick series of events, strange little things that pull you back to this waking surface of the mind. And then you continue to tell your story. Tell it over and over in the hope that all that hear it will believe it. But one day they will believe it, because one day they will all experience it. Everyone will experience it and not one in eternity will fail. Let no one tell you that anyone is going to fail. They *can't* fail for the whole thing is reproduced in us. There's no abracadabra about it. You don't *earn* it, it simply awakens within you in good time.

The Return of Glory

So here, he started by simply imagining what the villages would do. And can you put yourself into that place? Here, under house arrest because you're for the king, the legitimate ruler of the island of the place of Greece. And then came the junta; the generals who had their own ambitions, their own desires, and so they ousted the king, sent him off to Italy, him and his family. Then they took over and imprisoned all opposition. They're all intelligent, brilliant minds, and they were all under house arrest as they are today. If they only would see the secret of the story, not the means by which he escaped. Because God is infinite in his creative power and he doesn't have to duplicate the means: "I have ways and means ye know not of; my ways are past finding out" (Rom.8:33 KJV). So don't try to duplicate the means; the means are not your concern.

But the *technique* is our concern, so listen only to his technique. Because what he said happened I question...because he is saving others who are going to read his letter and they are all tuned into the fact that he has escaped from the island of Amorgos. He is now in Europe, a free man, who undoubtedly will be given asylum in this country and tell his story to the world maybe in a book form. But forget the story of the means...that does not interest us. Give me principle! What did he do? The means follows the principle, and what he did, he simply imagined a scene which would imply the fulfillment of his dream.

I create a scene in my mind's eye, but the scene must imply *the end*, not the means. "So I see faces and they're all my friends and they're all gathered around the little shortwave radios, and they do it in secret because these are outlawed. They must not listen to outside areas, only what they pump into their controlled press and controlled radio, but not the shortwave that would bring in the outside world to tell me what happened. So they're all gathered together quietly, secretly, and they're listening and here comes the news from France, from Italy, from America, saying that George so-and-so has escaped the island of Amorgos. That's all that he wants. And the thing that thrilled him the most was when that news came through. Not the elderly people drinking coffee...that happens every day; not the odor that comes from the bakery, that happens every day; not the cobbler opening up his shop at nine in the morning, that happens every day. But this: "they all know that I have escaped...that doesn't happen every day, for I have been there for 409 days." But this day is different and that gave him the *thrill* of his life!

So I tell you, start now...don't delay it. Start now to create the scene which if true would *imply* the fulfillment of your dream. And there is no power in the world that can stop it! Because our Lord is Father, and our Father is our potter, and we are all the clay in his hand. So, "'Arise, and go down to the potter's house' said the Lord to the prophet Jeremiah 'and there

875

I will let you hear my words.' So I went down to the potter's house, and there he was working at his wheel. And the thing in his hand he was making of clay was spoiled in the potter's hand. But he didn't discard it, he *reworked* it into another vessel as it seemed good to the potter to do" (18:1).

So someone comes into our world and you don't turn your back because you can't spend the time. They're down and out, they're up against it, they're unwell, they're physically limited or they're financially limited, call it by any name. You don't discard them. It's in *your* hand, *your* Imagination. You take that same vessel and you rework it into another vessel as it seems good to you to do. That's *all* that you do. You reshape the individual in your mind's eye. He's unemployed and yet he does need a job. He has obligations to life, he has a family to support, he has rent to pay, food to buy, all these things, and these are musts. Well then, in your mind's eye you rework him into a man that is gainfully employed and he was never happier in his life, never. And you see this in your mind's eye…that's *all* that you do.

Now, the means that will be employed to bring him into that state where he is gainfully employed is not your concern. Your only concern is to be the perfect potter. So when it came into your world it was spoiled. That thing is a spoiled vessel and I don't like it. All right, so you don't like it. Don't discard it! Rework the vessel into another vessel as it seems good to you to do. Read that in the 18th chapter, 2nd through 4th verses of Jeremiah. So I was told, "Arise and go down to the potter's house and there I will let you hear my words." So I went down to the potter's house and there he was working at his wheel. But the vessel in his hand he was making of clay was spoiled, so he reworked it into another vessel, as it seemed good to the potter to do." And when you know that the potter is your own wonderful human Imagination…so you encounter someone and they casually say, "Oh, I wish things were better"…it need not be for themselves it could be for someone that they love. Like tonight someone asked me concerning someone they love dearly. It need not be what you call a blood relationship. But, in the end, may I tell you, we are all related, we're all intermingled, we're all really *one*. We're not really as separate as you or the world thinks that we are.

I couldn't see you this very moment if you did not penetrate my brain. So, really, literally you are within me, even though at the same time you exist seemingly independent of my perception in the surrounding world. But I can't deny that you do literally exist within me. Now if you should change on the outside and I become aware of the change, the corresponding change would take place within me relative to you. If you change in any form whatsoever, either socially, intellectually, financially or even in appearance, if I encounter this change then that penetrates me and I will rectify, modify the image of you that I held to conform to what I now see, what I now hear.

But now, must I wait for that thing to change on the outside to produce in me a corresponding change? Or can I produce in me the change and then produce outwardly a corresponding change? If the change is made on the outside and that change penetrates my brain and compels me to modify my image of it to conform to what I'm seeing or hearing, well then, need I wait for that to take place first on the outside before I produce the change on the inside? No, not if I know who the potter is. The potter is my own wonderful human Imagination who is making everything take place in this world. "O Lord, thou art our Father; we are the clay, and thou art our potter; we are the work of thy hand" (Is.64:8). And, the potter, the Lord, and the Father are the same being, and it is my own wonderful Imagination. When I say "I am," that is God the Father, that is the Lord and that is the potter. If I know that and believe it and trust it, well then, I don't have to wait for things to change on the outside. If I desire changes, I can, because they do penetrate me now, they exist in me. Because, having reproduced himself in me all things now exist in my Imagination. So I don't have to wait for changes on the outside if I desire changes. I can produce them on the inside, and then compel the outside to conform to the changes that took place within me as I the potter brought them to pass.

Well, the only way to prove it is to try it. And we try it by simply imagining what the scene would be *after* the thing is done. No means... don't consider means...do not consider anything concerning *how* it's going to happen. You go to the "end." The end is where I begin. The *most* creative thing in man is to imagine a thing into existence. As we are told in the Book of Hebrews, "The things that are seen were made out of things that do not appear." You will read that in the 3rd verse of the 11th chapter of Hebrews. All of the things that you see were made out of things that are not seen and they do not appear. No one can see what you are doing when you sit in the Silence. So, you do it in the Silence and they're unseen by the outer world. But you do it and remain faithful to what you have done, because without faith in what you have done it will not appear in the world. "Without faith it is impossible to please him," because it is through Imagination and faith that man creates and sustains his world.

So I tell you, all that I've told you is based upon experience. I am not theorizing, I am not speculating...all these I have put to the test. And having awakened from the dream of life, I have told you that I have experienced all the things concerning the one spoken of in scripture as the Lord Jesus Christ. When he said, "I am the light of the world," I know from my own experience I am the light of the world. A friend of mine gave me a letter last Monday night, she said, "I was with my friend Sharon"—they're both here tonight—and she said, "I saw you sitting on the outside of the stage in a blue suit, and you were so thin, so pale, so weak, and the blue suit seemed as weak and worn as you. Sharon and I knew you needed some kind of strength, and so we got you a chocolate pudding and then we got you a chocolate ice cream, and then a chocolate bar to give you some substance, some energy to go onto the platform. So we led you to the platform. You suddenly disappeared and re-appeared as nothing but light, only your head was there. You were a giant of a man, towering over all, and the stage seemed to be enormous. There was no light but you, and only your head which shown like the sun. The light was so intense that it woke me. And may I tell you" she said as an afterthought, "what Sharon and I bought you, the ice cream, the chocolate bar, and the chocolate pudding cost twenty-eight cents." So I owe you twenty-eight cents.

They gave me twenty-eight cents worth of food to get me onto the stage, and then suddenly that little garment disappeared and I became the light that filled all. I'm telling you, I know it. See, her eyes were given to her by the one to whom I gave my eyes, and so she too can see the truth of what I'm talking about. For Sharon gave her the eyes I gave Sharon. Yet in the giving you do not lose the gift; you retain the gift, and the gift becomes stronger and stronger by reason of the fact that you gave it. Every gift that you give spiritually you retain and it increases in its power, in its wisdom, in it is everything that is that gift. So she saw what only a few weeks before Sharon saw, the prince of light. But no one who has not the incurrent eyes to be an eye-witness could see it. I am telling you the truth. I have experienced it and I live in that world. And the day this little thing drops, which she saw as a little thing clothed in a dark blue suit, frail, fragile, and could hardly make the stage until she could give it some substance based upon this world. For the body that it wore was of this world and chocolate would be a quick producing energy in this world.

But as I stepped upon the stage the whole thing enlarged, and suddenly it disappeared and I was nothing but light. All she could see towering above her was a giant and the head was my head. It was all that she could see. The whole thing was radiant light and the head began to be as intense in light as the sun, and then it was so intense she woke. Then she wrote me the letter. So I must now give her twenty-eight cents…repay my debt like Socrates. He owed a rooster, owed a cock, and he asked that please before he dies after he's taken the hemlock, please give the cock for he must not be left owing anyone in this world.

But here, may I tell you, you are all *Imagination* and you are not a prisoner save you are a prisoner by yourself, because you brought it all to pass and you can change it *if* you know who you are. So when you read the words "O Lord," don't think of something on the outside. The word "O

The Return of Glory

Lord" is Yod He Vau He, which means by translation "I AM." "Go to the people of Israel and say unto them I AM has sent you" (Ex.3:14). That is the word "Lord" as translated in scripture. Now, "O Lord, thou art our Father," so the Father is the same as I AM. "Thou art our potter" is the same as I AM. And he molds everything in the world, so to him and to him alone is all responsibility for what is done in your world. But he's not other than yourself...so it's your own wonderful human Imagination that is the cause of the restriction or the freedom that you are enjoying in this world. There is no other cause but the Lord who is the Father who is the potter. And if he's your own wonderful human Imagination to whom will you turn to blame for anything that is happening in your world?

So the blind leaders are leading the blind, blaming society, blaming the government, blaming one party, blaming this or that, and they're all so blind. They are, well ninety-nine and ninety-nine percent. If you could measure beyond that that's how many are blind, blaming everything outside of themselves for the causes of the phenomena of their lives. There is no one outside of yourself! The whole vast world is yourself pushed out, for there is not a thing in the world that does not now exist in you because divine imagining has reproduced himself in you. Divine imagining is the Lord God Almighty, who contains all things within himself, and he's reproduced in you, therefore all things are contained within you. So do not turn to the left or the right for the cause of misfortunes in your world...it's all within you. Everything is now penetrating your brain if you are going to perceive it; therefore, it actually exists in you and yet, seemingly, it exists independent of your perception of it in the surrounding world. But don't wait for it to change to produce the change corresponding to that change in you. *You* produce the change in yourself if you desire a change and then ask no one to help you. Just simply produce that change in you and then let that change reproduce itself in the outside world, for it's only an out-picturing of the world within you.

You try it...and change your world as this prisoner from the isle of Amorgos did it. It was a most exciting story. I could hardly wait to share it with my wife Bill, and then my friend who drives me. I couldn't wait to give him the paper the following lecture night and have him read it. But as you read it, I wonder to what extent those who bought the paper read it and then those who read it saw what was there to be seen, for the cue was all based upon the day *after* his escape. And what thrilled him most in his Imagination was when the villagers knew it. Well, if they knew it then it's a fact. Not the other things...they take place day after day...they took place every day for 409 days. But they didn't know as they drank their coffee for 409 days and could smell the bread coming from the bakery, and the cobbler's shop is open that the prisoner had escaped. But when they knew he had escaped, that's what thrilled him most of all. He's trying to tell those who are in prison, who will hear the story, the cue is in the entire story…for the cue is the day *after*. It's in my end where I begin; I always go to the end and that's where I start. What would it be like if it were true? What would you tell me if it were true? What would I see if it were true?

Before I came out tonight I got a telephone call from my friend Natalie and she's flying tonight. She hardly misses a meeting here…not in years has she missed it…but I'm so thrilled tonight that she isn't here for this is the answer to a prayer. She met someone that she loves and they're flying off tonight to Mexico to be married tomorrow. So she said, "I cannot see you tonight or Monday, but I will see you a week from now." I hope not! I hope she goes off to a nice long, wonderful honeymoon. She doesn't have to rush back here. She has accomplished what she wants, to be married. And I do hope it's a blissful union, I hope so, because she's certainly altogether lovely. That's what she wanted. She loved the man that she met and that is it, so they're flying off tonight, wedding tomorrow, so she can't be here tonight. So she, too, lived in the end. But it took an awful lot of jacking up, may I tell you. She'd always forget the end and come back to the moment where it isn't. Night after night I would remind her, because I have been going along the Promise…more and more on the Promise rather than the law. Every once and awhile I felt impelled to talk about the law because people were forgetting that we are still in the world of Caesar and the law is important! As you're told in the Book of Psalms, "I delight and rejoice in thy law day and night. It is my constant meditation, thy law. And those who rejoice in the law, in all that they do they prosper" (1:2) as we are told in the very first Psalm. Rejoice in the law! Don't forget you're living in the world of Caesar. Although to me the Promise is the one grand objective and the true reality of all being, we are still here and rent must be paid, clothes bought, food bought, and multiple things must be bought with the coin of Caesar. And so she would forget and every time I would jack her up from the platform. She was very sweet about it and she would always say thank you, then the next day she would go back. But by tomorrow it will be consummated. I hope she's so busy she hasn't time to send us a card.

So here, may I tell you, this thing cannot fail you. It will not fail you! But we are the operant power; it doesn't operate itself. So when I know what I want, don't turn to any outside God. He is not on the outside. In fact, he isn't even near, for nearness implies separation. He is my I AM and where could I go where I am not aware that I am? I've seen this body detached from myself and I could point to a body, but I could never see myself detached from myself. I know from experience that I am not this garment that I wear, for I have seen it on the bed when I am not in it. But I can never be anywhere where I am not aware that I am...so that "I am" is the Lord. And I could never be so far away as even to be near, because nearness implies separation and I can't be separated from the Lord. "O Lord, thou art our Father; we are the clay"...this is the clay...but, "thou art our potter; we are the work of thy hand." So when I entered death's door I found a garment. But who entered death's door?—man. "When weary man enters the cave he meets his Savior in the grave. Some find a female garment and some a male woven with care" (Blake, *Gates of Paradise*). So I find a male garment, others find a female. But I the finder am man, not male; I the finder am man, not female. Man that finds it is one with God. He and the Savior are one, he and the Lord are one, he and God are one, and he and the potter are one.

But we find garments when we enter the cave and the cave is the human *skull*, and we find a garment woven with care, woven by the female. "But alas, one is slain and one is fled." The garment has to be slain, but the immortal man who occupied it as it walked from the cradle to the grave is immortal and cannot be slain. But he still walks asleep. The day must come when he will awake, and when he awakes he knows who he is: he is the Lord God Jehovah, the being spoken of in scripture. He is the Lord Jesus Christ.

Now let us go into the Silence.

*   *   *

Are there any questions, please?

Q: If you say everything is within you, well, what about the people who wouldn't accept this type of teaching that you are encountering?
A: Well, my dear, it really doesn't matter, ninety-nine percent of the people of the world would not accept it. Read the morning's paper, everything is happening on the outside and they're not the cause of it. Everything is happening by others. The government will notify you that you're a little number. For instance, I'll be sixty-five in February. Today, unsolicited came a letter from HEW. You know, they call it HEW, notifying me that I will be sixty-five in February and therefore go to a certain place in this city and notify them of my...take the letter down...that I'm now eligible for...what do you call it...Medicare. So I didn't even know that they knew I existed. And here I'm notified that they do know and they have me computerized, I'm a number. That's all that I am to the government, I'm just a number. And so they knew in advance I would be sixty-five the 19th day of February next year, so they notify me now

to go down to a certain place in this city with my letter that I got from them and then I would be on Medicare.

Here we think that we are not numbers? We're all numbers... that's all that we are to them. But they're not independent of us...we made it so. The whole vast world wants to depend upon something outside of itself. And so, it is we who brought it into being, brought the entire thing into being. And so, I am a number. Undoubtedly they have a dossier this high on me; all the things that I have said or my little throwaways that you get in the mail, they have those there too. Any claim that I make concerning that you can do it for yourself, they have that there too.

Nevertheless, I tell you, you are all Imagination and Imagination is God. There's nothing but God. The day will come that you will awaken from the dream of life—this whole thing is a dream—and it will fade leaving not a trace behind it. You brought it into being for a purpose and when that purpose is fulfilled, it will vanish, but not until *all* have awakened because not one must fail. My body would be incomplete if one was missing, so I will leave the ninety and nine and go in search of the one. I cannot be missing from the risen Lord's body. For *we* are the *one* body, the one Spirit, the one Lord, the one God, the one Father, and you can't have one that is missing. *All* will be redeemed...everyone will be redeemed.

Good night.

KINGDOM OF GOD: THE ONE BODY

11/10/69

When one is called into the divine assembly and incorporated into the body of the risen Lord, he then is sent; and the purpose is to re-interpret the Christian mystery in terms of his own experience and its true and abiding *meaning*. For over the years traditions and the false concepts of men bring barnacles upon it as it were. So he is sent to re-interpret the great mystery as he will experience it, and then to give it its everlasting meaning…refresh it as it were.

Tonight we will take the statement that you've all heard, "the kingdom of God," and you think, naturally, of a sphere, of a realm. But here now we turn to scripture, "Unless you are born from above you cannot see the kingdom of God." You'll find that in the 3rd chapter of the Book of John (3:3). Then you read it in the 9th chapter of the Book of Mark, and he's speaking now of *seeing* God, that you *cannot* see God, see the kingdom of God. And yet he said, "Truly I say unto you, there are some standing here who will not taste death before they *see* the kingdom of God has come with power." And then he adds, "After six days he took Peter, James and John into a high mountain; and was transfigured before them" (9:1,2).

Now, you read it and you think of a man taking three friends into a high mountain on this earth of ours. It doesn't mean that at all. I tell you what I have experienced, and then I must share with you that which I have… not only my experience but share with you my body. I must give you my eyes and give you my ears and give you my tongue, and give you my body. But in the giving I still keep it and it grows in the giving. In the Spirit I must share it, so I tell you exactly what's happened to me, and then tell you that there are some standing here who will not taste death until they *see* what I have told you…until they see the kingdom of God come with power. The kingdom of God is the transformed man, the transfigured man.

What follows on the heels of the statement reveals what is meant in that first verse of the 9th chapter of Mark, "There are some standing here who will not taste death until they see the kingdom of God come with power." Then he takes them into the high mountain and becomes transfigured before them and they see a transfigured being. This is a metamorphosis, this is a complete change of form that he shows them, and *that* is the kingdom of God, that is the power. It is not a realm; it's a power of a transformed body. For wherever it is, that is the kingdom of God, it is power. And he promises that there are some standing here who will not taste death until they see that transformed being who tells you that he was sent, sent by one, and when you see him you see the one who sent him. That's what he is telling you. Well, who sent you? The one you call God, but I call him Father, and he and I are one. When you see me you will know I am he. And so, the first one to see will be the one who will see me clothed in power; thereafter, you'll see me clothed just as you saw me clothed in light. You'll see the regal light…call me a prince or call me the king. Or you will see me clothed in love. But you will see me, just as I told you he is when he sent me. So the kingdom of God is not a realm, it's the *transformed* being. It's a metamorphosis of a being, therefore, a change of form.

Now, what else did he tell me? He said, "All that I told you, you will experience." Now he asks the question, "Can a strong man's house be plundered unless he is first bound and then his goods may be plundered" (Mat.12:29). You wonder what it is all about. These are the words of the risen Lord, "Can a strong man's house be plundered?" Well, who is the strong man whose house can only be plundered if he is first bound? You must bind him and then you may plunder his goods. The strong man in this statement stands for Satan, the doubter in man, and then the risen Lord will plunder his house because he will now exorcise everything that he holds in bondage. And this is answered in the statement when John the Baptist sent his disciple and said to him, "Tell me, are you he who is to come, or should we look for another?" "He said, 'Go and tell John all that you have seen and heard: that the blind receive their sight, that the lame walk, that the lepers are cured, they're made clean, that the deaf hear, that the dead are raised up, and that the poor have good news preached to them" (Mat.11:2-5). You go and tell them all these things are taking place and let him judge whether this is he who is to come.

Well, I tell you this takes place in me. In the speaker back in 1946 sailing through the Caribbean when suddenly, unexpectedly, certainly I did not expect it, I was lifted up on high into that body that performs all these things. As you are told, "Come, O blessed of my Father, enter into the inheritance prepared for *you* from the foundation of the world" (Mat.25:34). Then we're told, "I, if I be lifted up, I will draw all men unto me" (Jn.12:32). Well, that night I was lifted up into that inheritance which is only a body, the *transformed* body. I can only describe it as a body of light, a body of power. It was self-luminous and it didn't need any external light, no sun, no moon, no stars…simply light…it was radiant light. And a heavenly chorus sang as I was lifted up, "Neville is risen. Neville is risen." As I was lifted up into this state, I simply floated, just floated over the earth, and a sea of human imperfection—there were the blind, the lame, the lepers, the deaf, the dead, everything mentioned in this statement—and as I walked by every one was transformed into the perfection that they sought, every one. And I did nothing but simply be. I was only a being of power. I didn't stop to ask this one what you want or that one. I felt no compassion. My very being was all that was necessary to transform every one as I walked by…and I simply floated by. Everyone was made perfect as I floated by. And when this chorus came to its end, it sang out in exultation, "It is finished!" Then I felt myself condensed and returned to this little world in this little garment once more. So the question that John asked "Are you he who is to come or must we look for another?" Well, go and tell John what you have seen and what you have heard. And then you tell him all these exorcisms that you have witnessed, and tell him if that is not the one that should come, well then, tell me of another one.

So the kingdom of heaven is not a realm. The kingdom of heaven is the transformed body. I can say it safely this night that if I drop now, this very moment, I have witnesses to the fact that that body has been seen by those who have been present in this audience. One departed two years ago when I was in San Francisco, and she saw it before she departed; she saw it clothed in power. She stood amazed. She was an eyewitness to the power in which it was clothed. Peter is made to say that we saw his majesty, clothed in power. He said, "When I told you these things, we were not deceived by some myth, but we were eyewitnesses to his majesty" clothed in power in Peter's 2nd letter (1:16). She saw it and then soon after, maybe a month or two months she departed. But she fulfilled the statement, "There are some standing here who will not taste death 'til they have seen the kingdom of God come with power." He knew that much would come with power.

I'll go beyond and say it will also be seen come with love, and come with light, and clothed in these things. For I'm telling you what I have experienced, and what I have experienced everyone in the world will experience, but everyone. It's only God who reproduced himself in us and now must *unfold* himself in us. So all that is God is man and man is everything that God is. For having reproduced himself in me, he has to unfold himself in me and I be cast in the central character in a first-person, singular, present-tense experience. So when I read scripture, I see myself unfolding within it. And so, "Unless you are born from above, you cannot see the kingdom of heaven" (Jn.3:3). That is, you will not see the *form* of God—not the realm in which it operates—it's the form. For whatever he is, that's the kingdom, that's the body. Everything is possible to such a transformed body.

So here, when you read "the kingdom of heaven," do not think of some sphere where you're going to go in collectively. Think of the body that was yours, prepared for you before that the world was…from the foundation of the world this body was prepared for you. It's a transformed being…and you enter that body. I can't tell you the glory that it is when you enter that body. When you walk by, anything that was unlovely ceases to be unlovely. You walk by and anything and everything is transformed into beauty. Everything is made perfect because you are perfect. You are the perfect one in that body for the body is perfect…even though you return to this level. And you tell it in the hope that many will hear it and many will believe it. But you cannot swear that they *all* will believe it. But they will hear it—some reject it and some believe it. But you can say boldly, "I tell you there are some standing here who will not taste death until they see the kingdom of God come in power," knowing in your heart the kingdom of God is the transformed body that you are wearing and fully conscious of it, though they cannot see it. And you know in the world of Spirit you must now share not only what you know—which is called "the good news" so that the poor will have good news preached to them—but you will share your eyes and your ears.

Now, the word translated "eyewitness" in scripture—"we are eyewitnesses of his majesty"—by definition means "to gaze with *amazement* as at something remarkable." It's not a passive sight. It's not the mechanical sight that I'm now using when I look at you; it's something that I'm seeing and it's remarkable. Can you see a being before your eyes suddenly transformed, and you know the being, you recognize the face, but the face is a heavenly face now. It's not marred, it isn't scarred, it isn't aged, it isn't anything that you know here. It's completely perfect and yet it shines like the sun. You don't see a weak body, you don't see a little body; you see a being that is completely transformed. The face is human and if it speaks to you the voice is human. Should it gesture, the hands are human. But don't go beyond that, for you aren't going to see anything beyond that. You're going to see a glorious being of light if he's clothed that moment in light, and you will know him to be the prince of light. If he is clothed in love, you will know him to be one wearing the human form divine which is love. If he's clothed in power, you'll know it is power, it's infinite power. Nothing is impossible to him clothed in power, clothed in wisdom. Because everything said of God is now going to be said and discovered by some still standing who will not taste of death until they verify the truth of what he has said.

Then one day he will depart the world and others will tell the story, for the four gospels were written by the eyewitnesses…those who told it. No one knows who Matthew, Mark, Luke and John are. They were the compilers, the recorders of the eyewitnesses. No one knows who they really are. A friend of mine who is here tonight wrote me this letter in which she said, "I saw in vision John; it was the John who wrote the gospel of John. He was dressed in a toga-like gown, white hair, white beard, seated with a Bible on his lap, and next to him were two dressed in the same manner. I didn't have to ask him if he was John, I knew he was John. On the lap was this black book, it was the Bible, and it was the story of Christ, Jesus Christ." But she knew that *this* was the *true* gospel. It was not the other gospels, the other Bibles recorded in the world…that this was the true, true gospel, the true message of Christ. She said, "I couldn't tell you how I knew it, I simply knew it." Because wisdom from above is without uncertainty and she knew it.

Well, may I tell her, the *Interpreter's Bible*, which is called by the modern scholarly critics of the Bible the grandfather of all criticism of the Bible; and that the scholars who worked upon it and worked upon it for years are considered the outstanding scholars of biblical criticism. And in this volume they say concerning John, that the gospel of John before it was printed was dislocated either by accident or by design. Today, they believe it was not by accident, but the early fathers in the 2nd or 3rd Century deliberately dislocated it. It was *not* the intention of the author and they have tried to rearrange it in what they believe to be the true arrangement of that gospel. So I can say to her, your vision is true. You saw the book as it should be: it wasn't open. You saw it as it should have been printed instead of the printing as of today. Today's printing *is* dislocated. I can take that book and rearrange it and make—I wouldn't change one word of it—but when you rearrange it, it reads more simply. It flows when it's rearranged. Take the 5th chapter and the 6th and completely reverse them. I can take the 3rd that I quoted tonight and go on to the 21st and jump to the 36th; and then go back to the 22nd and finish with it, and rearrange the entire book, and it comes out more beautifully.

So you saw correctly when you saw the one true book upon his lap and the John who wrote it. But today we do not know who Matthew, Mark, Luke and John really are. They are the anonymous writers of the eyewitnesses. As Peter says, "It was not cleverly devised myths that I told you, for we are eyewitnesses of his majesty." He said, "I am the light of the world. I am the wisdom. I am the power. I and my Father are one. And there are some standing here who will not taste death until they see the kingdom"...'til they see the body of which I speak. And so when they saw it, they saw the majesty of God clothed in mortal form here. But after that form is taken off, that being of light, the being of love, the being of wisdom is clothed forever. You will meet him. But he will inspire you until the very end because he's your brother, he is one with you, and he is the Father as *you* are the Father, too.

So you are not a little pygmy here suffering as you do, ignored as you are, shunted as you are. You are not that! You're clothed with this garment of flesh and yet you are the God of the universe! You are the being spoken of in scripture as God the Father, you are the Christ of scripture, and you are this pattern man. And unfolding within you is this being. You can't rush it, it is all on time. As she said in her letter to me, "It seemed as though you were the captain of the ship, waiting, and you could not leave until everyone was called and incorporated into this state. You could not leave and would not leave until they *all* were called. And strangely enough, they were all called in order, not one before its time. It was called in order. And there you stood like the captain of the ship waiting for everyone to be called, patiently waiting... for it's all yourself anyway calling." And she wrote this voluminous letter of the vision.

So I tell you, she is the incurrent eyewitness. An eyewitness is one who sees with his own eyes and can report what he saw and become a witness to that occurrence or that fact whatever it is. But the eyewitnesses of scripture are the incurrent eyewitnesses—those whose eyes had opened inward into the world of thought, into eternity. It is to her that I gave these eyes of mine. In giving, I shared. She in turn gave, and therefore, she shared. And it comes on sharing and sharing these immortal eyes that we may see the kingdom of God, which is nothing more than the transformed form of man. And don't let anyone tell you of any realm. It's not a realm. You create *at will*. You don't go into a realm. It's not the sphere in which it operates; it is the kingly ruler that you are. It takes the power of the body that you wear that commands everything in the world. No matter where you are, that is it, that is the kingdom of God, that's the kingdom of heaven.

So when you enter this body which was before that the world was, "Come, O blessed of my Father, inherit the kingdom prepared for you from the foundation of the world" (Mat.25:34), that is the body that is waiting for you to enter. Strangely enough, like a child growing you enter it, and you are amazed. You stand amazed at its power. You do nothing to transform people...and as you walk by they are transformed—the blind see and the deaf hear and the lame walk and the leper is cured and the dead rise.

The Return of Glory

Everything in the world returns to perfection. And you did nothing...I mean not consciously...you simply...because your *body* did it. That is the kingdom of heaven and heaven means harmony...everything must be in harmony, must be perfect because you are perfect. When you come to the very end you simply glide, that's all that you do. As you glide through everyone is made perfect and a heavenly chorus sings out, "It is finished" the last cry on the cross. And it does come from the Book of John, "It is finished" (19:30). Then you return to tell it and some believe it and some will not believe it. It doesn't really matter to you who believes and who does not believe. You'll do no more than tell it. Those who believe it, you can say to them boldly, I tell you there are some standing here who will not taste death before they see the kingdom of heaven, the kingdom of God come with power. You can state that boldly.

For power will be revealed first as it was in the book of the law. He came clothed first as power, and then he comes after that clothed in his name. But he first appears as El Shaddai, "God Almighty" (Exod.6:3). So when Marta saw it, she saw only power and the expression of power, yet she knew the face that expressed that power was the one she knew as a friend on earth. And she knew him as such a friend. But she had to *witness* power and before she departed this world she had witnessed the truth of what I said. Since that, others have seen me clothed in light. You must see me clothed in love. You must see me clothed in all the garments. She saw it in power, my friend Sharon saw it in light, my friend Marge saw it in that glistening light, but you *will* see it clothed in love. For, you stand in the presence of love, and you will answer correctly, and he who wears the garment of love will embrace you. For, all the others are but expressions of love. Power is an attribute, wisdom an attribute. All of these are attributes of love, and the fundamental state is love. When you see him clothed in love, he will embrace you, incorporate you into his body, and then you'll be sent. Then you'll have all the experiences as told you in scripture concerning the Lord Jesus.

It's the only true story in the world. There is nothing but the Lord Jesus Christ. Were he not within us, we could not breathe. Were he not within us we are only clay, but because he is within us you are immortal. And one day you will wear the body of which he spoke and that body is the body of *God*. There is nothing but the Lord Jesus Christ, nothing. Everything else fades into nothingness. So "Christ *in you* is the hope of glory" (Col.1:27). And when he wakes within you, there's only one Christ. You are the same being as the being in whom he awoke who seemed to be another. You'll find that we really aren't others, just one...one body, one Spirit, one Lord, one God, one Father of all (Eph.4:4).

So here, when you are called and sent, you are never sent save by the one who is love. Power yes, you will see him, but not until you are first incorporated into love. If you have power without love, you could destroy the earth. You'll never have that power until you're first clothed with love, because love is *everything*. There is nothing but love, and power is but its attribute, as wisdom is its attribute, light is its attribute…everything *but* love. Love is its reality: God is love. And whenever you meet a being clothed in love, it is because you have been called. Your name then has come up and it's in the book, all in order. Not one before the other…it comes in order. You will see her look into that book and she will check it off. You're right and then you go before the risen Lord clothed in love and he will embrace you, and then you are sent and all said of him you experience.

Then you say exactly what is said in scripture that he said, "There are those standing here who will not taste of death 'til they see the kingdom of God come with power." You need not go beyond that. They'll see it clothed in power and you're the one who voiced it. They'll see you. It's your face, only transformed…a face that you never saw on earth…there's no blemish to it…there's nothing but perfection in it. And the body of power is power that could destroy the earth if it so desired, but it wouldn't because it was first clothed in love. They hadn't yet seen you clothed in love, but they saw you clothed power. And then others will see you clothed in light and know you to be the prince of light.

But the day will come they will see you. And she describes John quite as you will see the wearer of the garment of love. For, when you meet him he is snow of hair…that lovely face. It is the most heavenly face. You could describe it…how could I describe it? It is blond, yes. The eyes are heavenly eyes and they're blue. The hair is snow white yet he's not old, and yet he's the Ancient of Days. Nothing seemed to come before him…nothing preceded him. He's all love…and he stands before you. And how it happens I couldn't tell you, but when he embraces you, you mingle and you aren't two. At that moment you are one, you are the being who embraced you. You are now the being of love who is God himself. Then he'll send you into the world to experience all that is recorded in scripture that *he* experienced only *you* experience it now. Then you say exactly what is said in scripture and now they are your words. You tell anyone in the world exactly what happened and it happened to you. Every child born of woman, regardless of their race, regardless of their nation, regardless of the pigment of their skin will have this experience. And when the curtain comes down on the whole drama we will know and understand what it's all about.

So when you are sent you are sent to re-interpret the great mystery of Jesus Christ in terms of its abiding meanings, for all the meanings have been lost. They speak of a Christ that never existed. They do not know the *true* Christ, the true *Lord* Jesus Christ...and there is no other, no other being. So in the end, you will awaken as the Lord Jesus Christ, and yet, may I tell you, without loss of identity. That is the mystery: I will know you in eternity. Your form transformed yes into a body of love, a body of light, a body of power, a body of wisdom, and yet the face I know it in eternity. And the face is so beautiful! You can't describe the beauty of your face when you enter into that which is called in scripture "the kingdom prepared for you from the foundation of the world." This is not some emergency thinking on the part of God; this was *before* that the world was. The whole thing was plotted, the whole thing was planned.

You dwell upon it. And I can't tell you when you go to bed at night and dwell upon *this* rather than the problems of the day, what it means to your night, what it means to our tomorrows. All these things will be taken care of, because your heavenly Father and you are one and he knows your earthly needs. He knows everything you need in this world. You need money, certainly you do, you need clothing, you need shelter; you need everything that man needs in this world. But you dwell upon *this* rather than the needs and the needs will come fulfilled. Everything will come into your world—the money that is necessary, the clothing, the shelter, everything will come. I am telling you from experience that out of nowhere it comes.

So here, the kingdom of God is within you and that kingdom is your transformed, transfigured body. So he took them into the mount. It doesn't say what mount and scholars speculate as to which mount, Mount Taber, Mount this, and it hasn't a thing to do with any mount on earth. He took them into a high place, it's all within himself, and there before them he became transfigured. And one appeared representing the law, Moses appeared, and then Elijah appeared representing the prophets. And then when the eyes were completely opened and became incurrent eyes, when they saw clearly, it was *Jesus only* (Mat.17:12). The law was fulfilled, the prophecies fulfilled, all fulfilled in Jesus. There's nothing but Jesus. Everything was completely gone but Jesus himself...and *that's you*. You are the Lord Jesus Christ. There is no other reality in the world, and the Lord Jesus Christ is the God who created it all. So the Lord God Jesus Christ reproduced himself in us and must *unfold* himself in us. As he unfolds himself in us it's the identical being. One being fell and became fragmented. All are gathered together one by one into the one being, one body, one Spirit, one Lord, one God, one Father...and you are that.

You dwell upon it. I can't tell you the hour and I can't tell you the day. I wish I could say to everyone here tonight, may it be tonight. Because what else in the world is worthwhile? If it could only be tonight! No, you're not going to lose your love of people…in fact it increases. Your love of people, your love of things will increase. You don't become disinterested. No, you become more in love. I don't care what it is you just love people all the more. It's something peculiar that happens to you…you simply love. You don't lose interest in the lovely things of the world such as a good dinner. No you enjoy it. Your capacity to love and to enjoy is increased a hundredfold.

You're not ashamed to shed a tear if you're moved. The shortest verse in scripture, "Jesus wept." So you aren't ashamed to shed a tear if you're moved emotionally by something that you're seeing. I went to see a picture last night *Goodbye Mr. Chips* and there was only one little moment that called for a little tear. I knew I was watching a picture, I knew it's all acting before me… and the news came that she was killed. They changed the plot, because I saw the original with Robert Donat, where she died in childbirth. But this time she doesn't die in childbirth; she is killed by some German bomb as it fell on London. The news is brought to him that she has been killed, and then one boy in his class comes in and tells them all that Mrs. Chips is dead, killed. Of course, he knows it…no tears drop upon his face, but they must have put something in his eyes to show you the welling of the tears in the eye, a bloodshot eye. It's all in color. Well, it would be impossible to watch it and not drop a tear, yet I know I'm watching a picture. But you are comforted, because the part you are destined to play is the part of Jesus Christ and he dropped a tear when his friend Lazarus was dead. So he came…and the shortest verse recorded in scripture is "Jesus wept." So don't be ashamed to drop a tear.

So your destiny is to *completely* fulfill the story of Jesus Christ. That is your true Spiritual biography. You wrote it and you've come now to play it. It's all within you and it will unfold within you.

Now let us go into the Silence.

*　　*　　*

Now are there any questions, please?

Q: I don't understand when you said that when you're born from above because you're still bound to this body you're subject to anger, and yet tonight you said that your love and understanding increases.
A: It does. The love and understanding does increase. But while you're tied to this body, an animal body, you'll play the part of this animal but not to the extent that you did prior to the birth from above. As Peter said, the time for his departure he knows is close, he knows close, he knows it's near, and so he said I must tell you while I'm still wearing this

The Return of Glory

body. So he confesses that the body was his limitation…in his 2nd epistle (1:13), "While I'm still wearing this body" and then he goes on to tell his story of being an eyewitness, but he confesses the limitation of the body. This body is a limit. As far as I'm concerned it limits me. Well, I enjoy eating, I enjoy a drink, I enjoy all the things I do, but it's still a weak body. Got to put it to bed and take it up in the morning, dress it, shave it, bathe it, perform all the normal, natural functions. I can't command another to eliminate for me or to assimilate for me, all that I must do.

But there is a body that I wear that does not have any of these limitations. But while I'm still tied here to tell the story, I must abide by the body to which I am tied. Paul said in his final letter to Timothy, "The time for my departure has come. I have fought the good fight, I have finished the race, I have kept the faith…now comes the crown of glory that has been laid up for me" (2Tim.4:7). But while he still wears that body, it's a thorn within his side…all the weaknesses of the body are still his. No matter how strong you are, you're only kidding yourself if you tell me that at the age of eighty, ninety, if you've survived that long, that you feel as though you felt when you were twenty. I've heard men tell me that when nature has long outlawed their capacity… but nevertheless they think that. Well, they're kidding no one but themselves. They are slaves of the body that they wear. Shakespeare was right: at the very end, sans teeth, sans eyes, sans everything…in the very end. Well, that's part of the play.

Don't be afraid to keep on growing, but be willing any moment in time to let go, because you are going to let go anyway. If tonight I'm called, perfectly all right with me. I know the body into which I move, and I know there's no return, for you *can't* return *after* you've been resurrected. You can influence from above and watch longingly and lovingly all those who are still in the world of death, waiting eagerly for the awakening of your brothers who are buried in the world of death. For we gave up, we abdicated these bodies before we came down. We're not growing into them; they *were* our bodies. And we gave them up, willingly gave them up: "I came out from the Father and I came into the world; again I'm leaving the world and going to my Father" (Jn.16:28) and "I and my Father are one" (Jn.10:30). So I'm not some little thing that came out of the swamp as evolutionists teach. I abdicated my *divine power* and came here for a purpose. Then at the end of that purpose I return to my position that I held before that the world was.

Q: You said the face, the hands and the voice were human. Well, when the face comes to you there's no body with it…the face shone, the hair was white and the beard was white. The face itself shone, but the eyes were

893

dark and piercing. But it had a message for me and I had never seen the face before. About ten years afterwards I saw the picture of the face that came to me, but it had a message for me. Is it usual for a face to come to you like that without a body?

A: Quite usual, my dear.

Q: It was a beautiful face, really. Everything was just white.

A: Well, if the message given you by this face could be tested…always test the spirit, whether it be of the Lord. If it could be tested and proven in performance, well then, it was true. The perfect test is to turn to scripture and if there are parallel passages in scripture to equal what you experience, it is true. For these are the two witnesses that are necessary: one, your experience which is internal, and then the external written word. These two if they agree in testimony it's conclusive.

Well, if there are no more questions, until the next time which happens to be Friday. Thank you. Good night.

EXPERIENCE THE MYSTERY OF CHRIST

11/14/69

The hostile attitude of the world to this great mystery of Jesus Christ is their ignorance of who the Father is. You will know who you really are, the heavenly being that came down into this world, to the degree that you *experience* the mystery of Jesus Christ. And when you experience it, you will discover *you* are Jesus Christ. There never was another and never will be another.

Just follow me closely in a little drama that is told us in the Book of John. The word Pilate means "closely pressed" like a contracted form, the limit, really, of contraction and of opacity. But like all these characters they are *personified* and these are attributes, these are qualities. To see the characters of scripture as characters of history is to see truth tempered to the weakness of the human soul. They are all states, eternal states. So Pilate is not really a person as you are a person, as I am a person; it's the contracted state. The story is taking place within you. So Pilate said to him, "Are you the King of the Jews? And he answered, 'Do you say this of your own accord, or did others tell you about it?'" (Jn.18:33-38). Do you know this from experience or is it hearsay? You ask me the question, "Am I King of the Jews?" Now he doesn't deny that he is…he simply is asked the question. But he wonders if this contracted state has reached the point of being broken now. It must reach the point where the shell is going to break and then it will know of its *own* accord.

And then he said, "So you are a king?" He said, "You say that I am." For he had said, "For this I was born, and for this I came into the world, to bear witness to the truth." And then the contracted form asked the question,

"What is truth?" Based upon this level, it is true that the pitcher is here, that the glass is here, that you are here, that I am here, but he is not speaking of *this* truth. The truth of which the true being that you are speaks is the true knowledge of God. He's not speaking of anything known to the world of science. Today we're on the way to the moon for the second time, but that is not the story of the Bible. He is speaking of the being that *created* the moon, that created the heavens, and that sustains the heavens. And he's trying to tell every being in the world that the being that did it *you are* but you have forgotten. You came down into this limit of contraction, this limit of opacity. And so, do you know it now when you ask the question of your own accord or were you told it by another? Did one tell you about me? Well then, you really do not know it...you've got to know it by having *experienced* it. So to the degree that man experiences the mystery of Christ he understands Christ. Whether you call yourself the pope or an ordinary minister or a layman, it means nothing. You could be someone washing floors tonight who will know by experience who they *really* are. They'll know that they are Jesus Christ by having experienced Jesus Christ.

Now let us turn to the poet Browning. He said, "Truth is within ourselves; it takes no rise from outward things, what'er you may believe. There is an inmost center in us all, where truth abides in fullness...and to know rather consists in opening out a way whence the imprisoned splendor may escape, than in effecting entry of a light *supposed* to be without" (*Paracelsus*). He took three of the mighty I AM statements in the Book of John, "I am the truth, I am the way...I am the light of the world" and incorporated them into this very short statement: there is an inmost center in us all where truth abides in fullness...not just a little bit but in fullness. He likens this to an imprisoned splendor. And then he speaks of the way and the way is from within. To think that some Christ is coming from without is to misunderstand completely the great mystery. It's entirely *within* us. As you sit here now in this little room and you seem to be so small in this enormous universe, and yet you seated here in this contracted state and this contracted state is Pilate who questions your sanity when you begin to stir within you—and asks these questions. It's all between you...the whole contest is within the individual. And then that effulgence within comes out. It arouses itself, it awakes within this little garment and the Creator of the *universe* comes out of the individual.

I tell you, I know it from experience. You are not some little tiny being at all, no matter what the world will tell you. You've gone through hell and maybe you'll go through more, but the search is to find self, and the self you're seeking for is your Father who *is yourself.* It's told in scripture but told in such a strange and wonderful manner: "And Jesus said, 'Go and say unto

The Return of Glory

him, 'I am the root *and* the offspring of David, the bright morning star" (Rev.22:16). I am the root, the origin, the Father, and yet I am the offspring of David. I am the father of David; I am the offspring of David. Now read scripture…I will bring up out of you, O David, "I will raise up a son that will come forth from your body. I will be his father and he shall be my son" (2Sam.7:12). He shall say, "I and my Father are one" (Jn.10:30). He's coming out of David; therefore, he's David's son. And David is the son of that which created the whole vast universe. Yet he who created the whole vast universe brings out of the universe that which is himself that was buried within the universe. So here, the grandfather and the grandson are one and the same being…coming out of that which God created which is the universe. Humanity is David, and he draws out of humanity that which is himself. The grandfather and the grandson are one and the same being. So go and say, "I am the root *and* the offspring of David."

But if you see David as the world sees David you will never see the mystery. I am telling you who he is: he is humanity reduced to a single being. And when you look at that wonderful boy and you see him, he is your son. But he brought forth you…for you buried yourself in humanity and played all the parts, every part. At the very end, you extricate yourself from your own creation and you redeem your creation. For your creation became condensed into one single being, standing before you as your son, and he's the David of biblical fame.

Now he said, "I am from above; you are from below" (Jn.8:23). He's speaking within himself. "Above" and "within" are one and the same; "below" and "without" are one and the same. "He who comes from above is above all; he who is from below expresses that which is of the earth earthy" (Jn.3:31). Here we find in the Book of John that the outstanding, in fact, the one thing that they cannot take in this revelation is his revelation of the *fatherhood* of God. They have an entirely different concept of who the Father is. I tell you, *you* are the Father. Maybe you can't even this night pay rent, maybe the cupboard is bare, maybe you are in debt…and *you* created the universe and you sustain the universe! The being that you're going to discover that you *really* are is the Creator of the universe…and there is no other God! There's no room in the universe for two Gods: "Hear, O Israel: The Lord our God the Lord is one" (Deut.6:4). So when asked to name the greatest of all the commandments, he didn't mention any of the ten; he mentioned the confession of faith of Israel: "Hear, O Israel: The Lord our God the Lord is one" (Mark12:29).

Now he gives a second commandment, which is not new. You'll read it in Matthew… "Love thy neighbor as thy self" (22:39) because it *is* yourself. The whole vast world is yourself pushed out. The day will come that you'll

897

discover that the whole thing is yourself pushed out, and only as you change your attitude towards what is pushed out can *it* change. It cannot change of itself. Only as I change within me my attitude towards you can you change towards me. It all begins that I love him. Why? Because *he* first loved me (1Jn.4:19). Well, the "he" spoken of is the I AM of you. So you want someone to love you or to see you differently? You start by changing *your* attitude toward the aspect of yourself that is projected. The whole vast world is yourself projected. So you want something different to come from that projection? Well then, because I first loved him…then if it's all in me, well, I change it within me, and then the whole vast world if I change it within me must conform to the changes within me.

So he comes to speak of the truth which is a different truth altogether: it is the knowledge of God. So he said, "I am the truth." Well, if there is an inmost center in us all wherein truth abides in fullness and here is one called Jesus Christ saying "I am the truth," and that is the center in me, then where is he? The only one that can resurrect is Jesus Christ and he's in me. He resurrects *in* me and breaks the shell, and then he comes out. As he comes out, I am set free, free as the wind, and I gradually discover who I really am. Night after night I become more aware that *I am* the Creator of it all.

So when someone dies in this world, where do you think they go, to the cemetery to impoverish the relative who put them there? In the world of Caesar that appears to be true. No, he goes within me; there is no place for him to go other than to return to me. Everyone in this world who dies returns to me, for I am the center. But you can say the *same* thing because there is only one center: they all come back within me. This morning as I was waking I met a friend of mine who dropped suddenly at the age of sixty-four. He had just retired and had a lovely retirement fund all built up. He worked for Standard Oil of California and he was the head of the personnel department. He said to his wife on the day he died…they went shopping in the morning, they went off and did many things…and then he said to her, "Have you any time to give me, just for a moment?" She said, "Certainly," so she came in and they sat at his desk and he had seventeen items to go over. He took them one by one and said, "Do you understand this?" and Muriel said, "Yes, I do, I think I do." Now he told the second one, explained it in detail, went all the way down the list and she said to each one, "Yes, I think I understand." Then he came to the last item, Now you're sure you understand this one?" and she said, "Yes I'm quite sure I understand that." She had no sooner said "I think I understand it" then he went right over and he was gone.

Well, this morning he was with me…a delightful soul. I've known him for the last, well, I would say since 1947 I think I met him…no, the first year, '46, when I first came out. I've seen him every year in my visits here and my visits to San Francisco. But this morning he came and told me what a delightful passage it was, it was so easy. It was just a normal, normal conversation with my friend Al. He was a Swede, Al Olstrom. And here, he told me of this perfectly lovely departure, but Al is the same Al. He would not listen to me here. No, he loved my company socially…to get together for a few drinks and a lovely Bar-B-Q. And when I entertained him in San Francisco I had no Bar-B-Q so I would take him to the club or to a restaurant. But every year we interchanged these visits, I would go to his home one year and he would come to my hotel next year…it was always on that level. He never came to my meetings after the first three or four. It didn't interest hm. He liked to sit down on Sunday morning and play the old hymns and cry…just simply cry playing all the lovely old hymns, and that satisfied him. But to listen to this revelation no, it just didn't make any sense at all to him. So I met the Al that I knew here and he hadn't changed one iota. He's the same Al…and he's in me. Where else would I have met him this morning? I was coming back from the depth of my soul. Having told the story to those on higher levels of my being who could hear it with understanding, and coming through here is Al. Just long enough to greet him in this lovely manner.

And strangely enough where do you think I found him? In a railroad station sitting at the counter having just a little snack, there he was. Just long enough to see him in the same manner in which I left him here. That was all that he wanted of me, to join me in a little snack or a big snack, but simply a physical meal. That was the Al that I knew and he's the same Al, hasn't changed at all. He denied the fatherhood of God as I *experienced* the fatherhood of God. He had his own fatherhood of God and he would sit down and cry his eyes out while he played his lovely old hymns—"Nearer My God to Thee" and God was away out in space…and all these things he played. When I told him of the *only* God, the God that is housed within us and only to the extent that we experience Jesus Christ do we *understand* Jesus Christ…oh, no…he had his own little Jesus Christ and no one's going to rob him of that…same Al.

So I tell you, the denial of Jesus Christ was simply his revelation of the Fatherhood. They could not accept for one moment what he was telling them of the Father. So when he said, "I go unto *my* Father and *your* Father, to *my* God and *your* God…and I and my Father are one" (Jn.17:20; Jn.10:30); therefore, I and your Father are one, and therefore you and I are one, they could not believe that. That was too much, so they rejected him. And those who call themselves Christians today still reject him because they have these little icons out in space, and worship some stupid little concept of the mind. They will not believe in the revelation coming from within them. I tell you, you are God and you are God the Father, the Father of *humanity*, the whole of humanity. It's a play. This is the most wonderful theatrical play ever conceived, and God is playing all the parts. When he's played all the parts, the same God that is now in you breathing, when he's played them all in you, he breaks the shell. He breaks that Pilate, and then you the God are *self-born* and you come out. You return to yourself the being that you really are, for there is only God. There nothing but God.

So, everyone in the world is playing the eternal play, and that play is so beautifully told in scripture. When one thinks for a moment, the only scripture known when the *revelation* was made was the Old Testament. Every quotation in the New has to be from the Old for there was no New. Now he interprets the Old by telling you exactly what it meant. I could give you passage after passage in the Book of John to show you what he's talking about concerning the *discovery* of the Father. Starting off even with the very beginning…take the 18th verse of the first chapter, "No one has ever seen God; he who is in the bosom of the Father, God only begotten, he has made him known." I am quoting now from the oldest manuscripts, the three oldest manuscripts quote it in that manner. In the 4th Century the word "son" was substituted for the word "God," which I will not quarrel with at all, so it now reads "the son, the only begotten Son." It read originally, "God only begotten"—he's begetting himself. Yet I can't deny that when you do see that out of which he comes that the sum total of all humanity, the whole world of men and women, fused into a single whole becomes a single youth, and it is his Son. He calls you Father, and you know he is your son, and you know you are his father…you know it. So I do not blame the one in the 4th Century who changed the word from "God" to "Son" and rearranged the sentence from "God only begotten" to "the only begotten Son." But that's how it reads in the earliest manuscripts. "No one has seen God; he who is in the bosom of the Father"—he tells you exactly now God is Father—"God only begotten, he has made him known."

Well, I'm telling you that my mission is to let you know who that Son is. You will not find it in any work that I know of save the Bible, but the Bible is something that is so strange that people do not even see it. Priests do not see it, rabbis do not see it, and ministers do not see it. But I am telling you what I know from my own experience: it is *David* who is that *only* begotten Son. There is no other Son. The Bible tells it to you, but they do not see it because they rearrange scripture to suit the traditions of the churches. And you never hear any bold affirmation in scripture concerning "I am the traditions, I am the conventions"; but "I am the truth, I am the way, I am the life, I am the resurrection" (Jn.14:6), you hear these. These are the bold mighty I AM sayings, but never I am the conventions, I am the traditions. So we are hiding from ourselves if we keep alive the conventions. And it's now part of the conventions to say that Jesus Christ is his Son. But our Bible has been changed over and over and over again by men who had no vision, who could not see it.

Now here is a vision that I'll share with you tonight. My friend is not here, but she gave me the letter last lecture. She found herself in a casino. You see everything has within itself the capacity for symbolic significance. So she is now in a gambling casino and the owner is coming towards her with a stick to count off her winnings. Instead of counting off what you would in any casino, say, the little chips that you have, it is a long French loaf, sliced but still held together because it hadn't gone right through. It's been sliced right down, but not completely through the entire loaf. So it's a long French loaf. So he comes with his stick and he simply touches…as he taps a slice she calls off "fifty dollars" and he repeats "fifty dollars." She repeats it again and then she said "$100." "$100"…everything she said he had to repeat and he was getting more and more purply and explosive and annoyed because she would call the number and he had to repeat what she said…and it was one more slice of the loaf. She enjoyed…there was some peculiar thrill in her bones that he was so annoyed with her and disliked her heartily, but she was just simply winning all the money. It came down to the end, the very last was the last end of the loaf and she wondered in her mind's eye, "What number will I call now?" The number came to her, "$1,150" and he called it. That was the entire loaf. The whole thing bled…the loaf of bread bled. It oozed out like a rare piece of roast beef when it's sliced and the whole loaf turned into blood, and yet it was bread. And the number tone is seven, spiritual perfection…1,150.

You're told in scripture, the 6th chapter of John, speaking of the bread, "It is my body." "Unless you eat my body and drink my blood you have no life in you, for the life is in the blood" (6:51-56). Well, here is the most perfect vision and she certainly has the perfect vision of the symbolism of scripture. She said, "I don't understand it, Neville, but it was fun as I watched his face getting more and more purply as he was actually ticking off these slices as I called them by number. The very end I wondered, what number and I said, all right, one thousand, one hundred, fifty. I don't understand it." But it is perfect, perfect symbolism of scripture. Number seven…the perfect number spiritually. She had completed the loaf and the whole thing is now alive and oozing blood. That is the blood. She has accepted completely the body of Jesus Christ as her own wonderful human Imagination: that is the body of God! She has completely accepted it and she blames no one now. If anyone is to blame, it's only herself and she *knows*

901

it's only herself. When you get to that point that you can't blame another, you have to eat it all by yourself because you've accepted completely that your own wonderful Imagination is the cause of the phenomena of life, then you've eaten the loaf of bread. And then it turns into blood...the whole thing was oozing blood, the whole loaf became a bleeding piece of flesh: "Eat my body and drink my blood."

I tell you, your letters of last Monday were thrilling beyond measure. One gentleman said, he found himself in a place like the Bowl and here someone received the baton, a long-haired maestro. Innately he knew that that same performance would take place again for those who did not witness it. So he drove up to the knoll where he knew it would once more be presented to the same long-haired maestro. While he was there...and it was, it was presented...a lady next to him said, "What is that in the sky?" He took binoculars and he looked up, wondering whether it was an airplane or what, and it was a multi-colored bird resembling a parrot because it could speak. The bird said to him, "Get out of here. We don't want any part of you people!" and then it came down and whacked him on the face with its wings.

Now you will think that is an idle dream. It's not an idle dream at all. That's a wonderful adumbration of what will take place the next time, but this time it will not be the multi-colored parrot it will be the dove. They avoid man...I know that from experience...because man gives off on this level the most outrageous odor. And it was a woman in his vision; it was not a man who asked him to see what the object was in space. It is a woman when it comes to who will turn to you and say, "They avoid man...but he so loves you that he penetrated the ring of offense to demonstrate his love for you." So it's a marvelous foreshadowing of what is in store for him.

Another lady saw me dying. So many of you have been seeing me dead recently. May I tell you it's healthy, it's a very healthy state, very healthy. She was with the very one whose eyes are now incurrent witnesses. And here, as she looked and I was dying, no possibility of reviving me, and she knew that my friend with the incurrent eyes so loved me she didn't want me to die. She, on the other hand, who is having the vision, didn't want me to be touched by anyone and hold me back...because if you touch him you're going to hold him back and then he will not be set free. Then I collapsed to the floor and then I was gone. It's a wonderful vision for her to have: "For unless I die, thou canst not live; but if I die I shall arise again and thou with me. Wouldest thou love one who had never died for thee, or ever die for one who had not died for thee? And if God dieth not for man and giveth not himself eternally for man, man could not exist" (Blake, *Jerusalem*, Plt.96). So God dies. I am telling you I have awakened from the dream of life. I have been born from above and the only one who is born from above is God. And so God dies...it's a perpetual dying...that all may live. So she saw it beautifully. I can't congratulate her enough. Her vision was perfect in this that she shared with me.

I can't give the whole evening to all the visions, but they were perfectly wonderful...what you gave to me last Monday...one after the other, and every one as lovely as the other. So, I'm not here to flatter you; I'm here to tell you the truth as I have experienced it. Browning was right based on a vision, there is an inmost center in us all where truth abides in fullness. And to know...know what...the true knowledge of God. He's not trying to break through from without but from *within* and to release this imprisoned splendor. It comes from within. Listen to the story, believe it implicitly, and the crust will break and he will come out. And it's an effulgence...you are radiant light. Whatever it touches it transforms into beauty, into perfection for you are perfect. You can't go any place where you are not perfect.

For, when you inherit the kingdom, as we told you last Monday night, as told us in the 25th of Matthew, "Come, blessed of my Father, *inherit* the kingdom prepared for you from the foundation of the world." That kingdom is a *body*, the body is perfect, and it was from the foundation of the world. So you awaken into that body and wherever that body is heaven is...that's the realm. You don't inherit a realm; you inherit a body. So wherever that body is the whole vast world that is now reflecting it is perfect. You can't come upon anything that is imperfect; and if it was before you got there, instantly, automatically, it is transformed into perfection because *you* are perfect. That is what is in store for you. "Come, blessed of my Father, enter into and inherit the kingdom prepared for you from the foundation of the world."

So when this body awakens, I can't tell you the beauty, I can't describe it to you. As he said in that 5th chapter of John, "No one"—speaking now to the one below—"No one has heard his voice, no one has ever seen his form, but *I* know thee, O Lord" (5:37). He is telling those around about him, "You have not heard the voice, you have not seen his form, but I know thee, O Lord. The world has not known thee, O Father, but I know thee." And now he turns to a few, a *remnant*...he's speaking now to his disciples... he said, "And they know that thou hast sent me." He has found a few who really believe his story and they will spread it and they'll keep on spreading it. They will hear it first by hearsay; eventually they will know it from experience.

So this is the truth of which he spoke: it's the *true* knowledge of God. Anyone who talks about any God outside of you, turn your ears away, turn your attention away from him. There is no external God. You see this fabulous external world, but there is no external God. He who supports the whole thing is within you and it was he who created it. It's almost, well, the world calls it blasphemy to say this. Let them call it by any name that they wish. I tell you that it is true. The day will come you'll crack the shell and he who is now the imprisoned splendor within you will come out and *memory* will return and you will know all that you knew before that the world was. By coming down into this world and taking on the limitations of the flesh, you will now expand yourself beyond what it was prior to the coming down into the world. He said, "No one takes my life from me, I lay it down myself. I have the power to lay it down and the power to take it up again" (Jn.10:18). So he came down of his own accord because there is no one else. And he came down *as* us, because it takes all of us to form the One.

We are the Elohim! The name is a plural name, Elohim is plural. It first appears in the Bible in the very first verse, "In the beginning God"... that's Elohim (Gen.1:1). And the Elohim said, "Let us make man in our image"...that's Elohim (Gen.1:26). Then "The Lord took his place in the divine council"—that word translated "Lord" is Elohim (Ps.82:1). And he said to us, "I say ye are gods, sons of the Most High" (Ps.82:6). That word "gods" is Elohim. So it takes all of us, it takes humanity together to form the one God that created the whole vast universe and sustains it. So he's not speaking of anything on the outside. Let man on the outside find new planets, new ways to get to them, new energies in the world, new everything, and we're all for it. Why not enjoy the world while we're in it, so I'm all for it. But that is not the truth of which the scripture speaks. He speaks of the true *knowledge of God*; that's all the truth that he's talking about. You'll find in scripture that no effort is made to change society. He doesn't change anything in the world: he says, "Render unto Caesar the things that are Caesar's" (Luke20:25). He doesn't try to make the one who is in prison as a slave a free person...leave him just as he is.

And today all of our energies are going into changing everything in the world. I received a notice here recently, as I think I told you, from Health, Education and Welfare. Well, I thought it was only concerning my health. And instead of carrying my Blue Cross, as I have for years for my family, well, if the government will take it over...because I've paid in all this money since I began to pay, which was the very first month it came into being back in 1936 I think it was when I became eligible to pay my Social Security. So I went down today and she's asking me all kinds of questions that were not related to my health...all related to my retirement fund. Well, I said that I'm not retiring and I came here because this was all about what I thought was health insurance...if I had to go to the hospital or to get a doctor. She said, "That's part of it here too." She didn't ask me any of these questions; she's asking me all kinds of things about my insurance. The she said to me, "You don't have to answer any other questions because we have it all anyway." She only confirmed my suspicion that we're all numbers. We're all computerized. She has all the material in the world and she need not have asked me one question. Not one question. I gave her my passport, my only identity. I don't have a driver's license because I don't drive...I have no car. Well, "What proof do you have that you really are sixty-five this coming February?" I said, "My passport, and here it is." "Well, that is not the proof. Do you have a birth certificate?" I said, "They didn't have them where I was born...not in the year I was born...that was too expensive. Why have birth certificates? But I was baptized and somewhere I know I had the certificate, but I can't find it now." She said, "Try and find it for me or write for it, because we must have some proof that you really are going to be sixty-five this coming February."

But do you know, all these things were already known. I didn't have to go there at all. They knew exactly what I paid in taxes, what I declared, what I didn't declare, everything they know about me. So no one is really doing anything but what the government has the whole little thing all right before him. But you are not that. You created the whole vast world so don't let anyone scare you. If you go down...this was a very sweet lady, a delightful lady, and she could not have been kinder, could not have been sweeter. You would have thought she was my sister she was so kind. Nevertheless, they know everything about you. But if you don't find one as I found one, don't let them scare you. Because in you, as in the one who is going to question you, is the only God, there is no other God. The God that created the whole vast universe is within you.

And you can prove it on this level even though the body has not yet been broken... where the birth has taken place. You can prove it by simply imagining certain states. And do not raise one finger to make it so. *Believe* it to be so, go about your business as though it were true, and may I tell you it *will happen*, because that is the way everything came into being as you brought it into being. While you're here you have forgotten, but I am trying to remind you of the way that you brought it into being. You brought it into being by *imagining* and now you can simply bring things into your world by imagining. There isn't a thing in this world that wasn't first imagined. So you imagine what it would be like if you were the man, the woman, that you would like to be; and then you sustain that imaginal act as though it were true. No power in the world can stop it from becoming true, because there is no other power. *If* you believe it, there is no other power in the world that can stop it. Now try it, beginning tonight. Take a glorious concept...nothing less than the best, the very best, and simply imagine it to be true about you and those that you love. Start with your immediate circle. And although at the moment our circle may deny it by reason of what they're doing, you persist. You persist in that assumption as though it *were* true, and may I tell you it will harden into fact because there is no other creative power. Name it by any other name, there is no other creative power.

Grant all of your brothers who are still asleep to pursue God in some other direction. They'll never find him in any other way than by *experiencing* the story of Jesus Christ. They will not find him in all the laboratories in the world. They can take the little pieces apart and find out how they are put together, but they'll not find the Father. The Father is the one who is looking, the one who is seeking. And they're looking for something on the outside and the Father is within them. He will never reveal himself save through *David*. You'll never find the Father save through David. Do you wonder why the Jewish faith denied the story when no one said he was the Father of David? And it's been done so long now for 2,000 years and no priest dares say it because they have been brain-washed into believing that it's not. They think God is another, and Jesus Christ is something less, and he is the son. They don't know that Jesus Christ is God the Father. It is a *pattern*...it's the pattern in man, buried in man, and it *erupts* in man, awakens in man. When it awakens in man he is a father, therefore, who is the son?—David. Now go back to the end of the Bible, the 22nd chapter of Revelation and Jesus is speaking, "I am the root *and* the offspring of David" (22:16). The root is the origin that is the Father; the offspring is the child. But if I am both—I am the root *and* the offspring—they are one being. Therefore, what is David now? He didn't say that he was David. He said, "I am the root and the offspring of David." Well now, he used David. So if the root and the offspring are one and the same, then who is David? He tells you the "offspring" of David so David is a father. But the root is the Father of David, and he is the root, so he is the Father of David. Yet, the Father of David is one with the son of David...so here, the grandfather and the grandson are one being. Therefore, who is David? Well, David is his son. He is one with his grandson. The Son is David which is humanity altogether fused into one being and *personified* as a single youth, the eternal youth.

Well, that is what I have come to give to the world. I have never read it in a book, I have never heard it from the lips of any other person, but I have *experienced* it. And so I tell you what I know from experience; I am not theorizing. The whole vast world could rise in opposition it would make no difference to me. I would say to them, as Peter and John said to the Sanhedrin on the day when they told them not to speak any more in the name of Jesus and they answered, "If it be right in the eyes of God to listen to you rather than to God you be the judge, but we cannot but speak of what we have seen and heard" (Acts 4:19). So I cannot but speak of what

I have experienced, and I have experienced being the Father of David. And in searching through the only scripture, which is the Old Testament, I have found confirmation there: "I have found David and he has cried unto me, 'Thou art my Father!'" (Ps.89:26). And, "Thou art my son, today I have begotten thee" (Ps. 2:7).

So I found it all in scripture, and I did not know it until it happened to me on that 6th day of December back in 1959. So I'm telling you this and I know that here in this audience there are those who believe me. They say, "O righteous Father, the world has not known thee, but *I* have known thee; and these believe that thou has sent me" (Jn.17:25).

Now let us go into the Silence.

*   *   *

THY WORDS WERE FOUND

11/17/69

We read in the 15th chapter of the Book of Jeremiah, "Thy words were found, and I ate them, and they became a joy to me and a delight to my heart"—then he gives the reasons, and the reasons are as he gives them—"I am called by *thy* name, O Lord, God of hosts" (15:16). He found the words of God and he ate them, and as he ate them they became a joy and a delight to his heart. Then he gives the reason why...because "I am called by thy name." Thy name is "O Lord, God of hosts." The Word is what every man in the world—by man I mean generic man, male, female made he them, every child born of woman—must experience. He assimilates the Word: he hears it, he understands it, he accepts it, he fully believes it; and then suddenly it erupts within him, and he has an experience of the Word, and *he himself* is God. There is no other Creator, no other God.

So in the New Testament we find the story of the Word: "In the beginning was the Word and the Word was with God and the Word was God. He was in the beginning with God. All things were made through him and without him was not anything made that was made. He was in the world, the world was made by him, and the world knew him not" (Jn.1:3,11). He came to his own home and his own people received him not. And you ask, "What was it that Jeremiah actually ate?" Well, it's the Word. What is the Word? What did he discover to be the truth concerning God by whose name he was called? He discovered that your own wonderful human *Imagination* is God...that's what Jeremiah discovered.

Blake tells it in a simple way. It's so simply told that people think, well now, this is told for little children, for he calls it *The Songs of Innocence*. He calls it *The Lamb*. He said, "Little Lamb, who made thee? Dost thou know who made thee? I'll tell thee who made thee...for he calls himself a lamb. He is meek, and he is mild; he became a little child. I a child, and thou a lamb, we are called by his name. Little Lamb, God bless thee!" And we think that's a nursery rhyme. Blake is telling you the most profound thing that one could tell. Here, he calls himself a lamb and yet he is the little child, the Christ child. Well, "I am a child" said Blake, "and thou art a lamb, and we are called by his name." He's repeating the same story as told in the 15th chapter, the 16th verse, of Jeremiah.

Here, your own wonderful human Imagination is the God of scripture. Listen to another statement of Blake's: "Babel mocks"—well, that's the world, Babel is the world with its multiple tongues—"Babel mocks, saying there is no God nor Son of God, that thou, O Human Imagination, O Divine Body, art all a delusion; but I *know* thee, O Lord, when thou arisest upon my weary eyes, even in this dungeon and this iron mill. For thou sufferest with me tho' I behold thee not." And then the divine voice replies "Fear not! I am with you always…only believe in me, that I have power to raise from death thy brother who sleepeth in Albion; fear not, trembling shade" (*Jerusalem,* Plt.60).

Here, your own wonderful human Imagination is the God of scripture. It is the Jesus Christ spoken of, for John identifies Jesus Christ with the Creator, and here the Creator's name is called "the Lord." He is called "the Lord" and he is called "the Lord, God of hosts." And Jeremiah, which means "God or Jehovah will rise," is telling you that he is called by the name of the Lord: "I am called by thy name" and then he names it, "O Lord, God of hosts." Then man discovers that he is actually the Lord, the God of hosts. But while he wears the garment of flesh he is restrained, he is restricted to all the weaknesses and all the limitations of the flesh. And he decays as all bodies decay…everything decays in this world. But in spite of the decay of the thing that he wears like a mask, he, the wearer of the mask, is the Lord, the God of hosts.

One day he will experience that he *is*. No matter what the world will say, he knows there is no such thing as "I believe" anymore; there is an assured "I know" for I have experienced it. Even though I must continue in the world wearing a garment that slowly wears out, and eventually it must be so worn out it has to be discarded. But after the experience, you're no longer restored into another garment similar to the one that you've worn out. You depart from this altogether into the body that *was yours* before that the world was. And wherever that body is there is heaven. For heaven is only the body that is alive, this infinite body, and wherever you are, the realm in which you dwell is harmonious, it is heaven. For heaven is a body, the body that you will wear in eternity; and no matter where you go everything is transformed into the perfection that your *body* is.

So you don't go into a realm called heaven; you *are* heaven by reason of the fact that you wear the body that now you have awakened within you, which is the imaginative body. Wherever that body goes it is heaven. Not a thing can remain imperfect in the presence of one who wears the risen body. If you went into hell, instantly—not over a period of time but instantly it's transformed into heaven. No matter where you go it is heaven. And if you are not wearing that body, wherever you go it is really hell...as this world is hell, all decay, all conflict...everything in the world is really in a conflict.

So when he said, "Thy words were found and I ate them," how would I eat words? Do you know many a person has taken the Bible and eaten the Bible? I went to the mental institution in Barbados with my brother Lawrence, who is now gone from this world, who was the doctor there. Here, all these mental patients, many of them with their Bibles tearing them up and eating them. Eating the pages...I actually saw it and I could hardly believe my eyes...they were eating the Bible...they took it literally. And we aren't helped by the early church fathers who changed the Word of God. For here, the prophets inspired as they were wrote what they heard and what they saw, and the early church fathers added to the Word of God to make it conform to their traditions, their conventions, and changed the entire picture.

I'll give you just a couple of examples. In the 3rd chapter of the Book of John there's a conversation between one called Nicodemus, who was a master of Israel, a member of the Sanhedrin. He would be like any Cardinal today, the master of what is considered the right thing concerning God. He encounters now one who stands in the presence *as* God, for he has *experienced* God, and he said, "When you see me you see the Father. I am the Father." Then he makes the statement, "Unless you be born from above, you cannot enter the kingdom of Heaven" (3:3). Nicodemus replied, "How can one who is old once more enter into his mother's womb and be born?" He said, "You a master of Israel and you do not understand?" Now take the 5th verse, "Truly, truly, I say unto you, unless one is born" and now they have added "water and." It isn't so. The verse now reads "Unless you are born of water and the Spirit, you cannot enter the kingdom of God." The words "water and" are added; they are not in the original script. These are added by the editor, the early fathers of a church, to give support to *their* tradition of baptizing a child with water.

Now the 8th verse—I've just quoted you the 5th verse— let me read you the 8th verse: "The wind blows where it wills, and you hear the sound of it, but you do not know whence it comes or whither it goes; so is everyone who is born of the Spirit." Now the word "water" is not used in the 8th. Here in the 5th he has added "water and"; here in the 8th water is not...that is gone from the script. You must be born of the *Spirit*. And now he likens the Spirit to the wind...and the word in Hebrew and Greek for Spirit and for wind is the same word. So, as the Spirit blows or moves, you may say...but he uses the word, the translator calls it now "wind"..."as the wind blows where it wills, and you hear the sound of it, but you cannot tell whence it comes nor whither it goes; so is everyone who is born of the Spirit."

Well now, when my mother came to this country when my little boy was two and a half years old, one of the first questions she asked of me was, "Where was Junior baptized?"...that's my little son, two and a half years old. I said, "He wasn't baptized." "Oh," she said, "Neville, how could you? Suppose he dies?" I said, "What has that to do with anything?" She said, "He couldn't go to heaven. If he isn't baptized, he couldn't go to heaven." Mother was stuck with that one little word which her minister taught her, "You must be born of water and the Spirit" and "the water" he explained to her—and to millions in the world who call themselves Christians—is baptism by water. It hasn't a thing to do...that's been added by the early church fathers just to support and sustain *their concepts* which they practiced. It's quite an income. You're not charged for baptism, but it is expected that you *give* something. It amounts to a considerable sum of money. This is one of the little things, one of the little indulgences of our churches and you can multiply that all over the world.

I know from my own experience having been born from above that the wind is correct and the water is false. You hear a wind and the wind is in your head, but it also comes from without, seemingly from without. You do not know whence it comes...you think it's from this direction and you look over here. At the same time you're looking there, you also feel it in your head. Then when the whole drama is over and the infant appears, then the wind disappears...so you cannot tell "whence it comes or whither it goes; so is every one who is born of the Spirit," and not a thing to do with water. When the side is pierced and out comes water and blood *that* has been added. It's a symbol of birth, yes, but that has been added. If you take the 6th chapter, which is one of the most difficult chapters in John, all based upon a peculiar thing concerning "eating my body." Well, the "body" of scripture is the Word and the *Word* is God—you understand it and you assimilate it and you're eating it. You actually eat it by *assimilation*. What you cannot assimilate, like the physical world, then you will reject and therefore you eliminate. I can't quite understand this and so I will simply eliminate it; I can't quite take it in and assimilate it.

So we'll start with the 51st verse of the 6th chapter. You can eliminate from the second half of the 51st verse right through to the 58th verse and go into the 59th...and it's all about "eating my body." He said, "I am the

911

bread that came down from heaven. He who eats my body will live forever." This he said in the synagogue. In between these nine verses you find all the things that support the Eucharist, support the Holy Communion. And just to support the traditions of the church the early fathers added those nine verses, from the second half of the 51st verse through the 58th verse of the 6th of John. We could take you through the entire book and all the other gospels, the ___(??), and show you where the redactor made it conform to the traditions of the church. And today, well, as my mother said to me concerning my little boy's baptism…so I went down to please my mother and arranged with some Episcopal minister to baptize him. Well, the only thing that happens to a little child in baptism, or to an adult when they're old, could be catching a cold. Not a thing happens *spiritually* may I tell you.

My first wife who got religion at the advanced years and joined some…I don't know…Baptist? No, she joined the…oh, what was this…well, it will come to me eventually. But she joined it and took my little boy over to an indoor pool at the St. George Hotel in Brooklyn. She was going to be completely immersed. She couldn't swim anymore than my little boy could swim, and they almost got drowned. She was going to be just completely immersed and so she's going to get religion. All she got was just on the verge of death. And my little boy who couldn't swim, she did the same thing to him, not knowing that when he was two and a half, because of my mother's fear that he would go to hell if he, an innocent little boy, wasn't baptized, I allowed this performance.

So I tell you, throughout the book when you read it there are so many things that the early fathers incorporated in spite of the warning which they would not heed. You read it at the end of Proverbs, "Let no one add to or take from the words of the prophecy of this book" (30:6). In the very end of the Bible, in the very last chapter of Revelation, we are warned against adding to or taking from the words of the book (22:18). But they would not heed the warning. They are going to make it conform to their traditions and their conventions. And you never heard the statement in scripture coming from the mighty I AM states, when all through John he said, "I am the light of the world, I am the bread, I am the door, I am the way"—all these mighty I AM statements—it never said, "I am the conventions, I am the traditions." But to support their traditions the early fathers inserted and added to the Word of God.

So here, I tell you behind the mask that you are wearing is the *only* God. There is nothing but God. Divine Imagination reproduced himself in you in your own wonderful *human* Imagination. And because he contains all, all is contained in the human Imagination. Man one day will awaken to this fact to discover the whole vast world is himself pushed out as the whole vast world is God pushed out. This, as he awakens in you, begins to expand within the bosom of Divine Imagination. You are the human Imagination, but it is one with Divine Imagination. So reproduced in us is the Divine Imagination. And who is the "us"?—human Imagination. Certainly not in this little body…this is only the mask that I wear.

So here, we eat the body of God by hearing the Word and then assimilating it. I hear it. I may not at the moment be able to understand it. As we're told in the Book of Nehemiah, "They read from the Word of God, and they read it with interpretation; and they gave the meaning, so that the people understood that which was read" (8:8). So it all came from *within* and they understood it. Well, when you hear it, do you understand it? If you don't understand it, go over it and over and over again. But the New is only the fulfillment of the Old. So when you're told, "I am the bread," he's only quoting from Jeremiah. He said, "I found your Words" and he is called the Word of God. Now he identifies the Word with that statement in Jeremiah: "Your words have been found and I ate them, and they became to me a joy and the delight of my heart; for I am called by thy name, O *Lord*, God of hosts" (15:16, KJV). Well, man is embarrassed to be told he is the Lord, the God of hosts when he can't pay rent, when he can't buy clothes, when he can't eat as he would like to eat…and he is the Lord, the God of hosts? Yes, limited by the body that he is wearing. And no one imposed it upon him; he did it all by himself: "No one takes away my life, I lay it down myself. I have the power to lay it down and the power to lift it up again" (Jn.10:18).

So I did it for a purpose: I did it that I may *expand*. For the joy is constant expansion. I could not expand unless I first contracted. So I reach the limit of contraction called "man" and this contraction is the limit of opacity. Then at a certain moment I break the shell, and what is contained within is the God who created it all, and it begins to expand. And everyone in this world will succeed…not one can fail. So I may be satisfied today with my little earnings in the world, my little place in which I live, but all of this is a *contraction*. The day will come I will actually eat the Word of God: I will experience the Word of God, and when I experience the Word of God then I will know that *I am he*.

But not until I am that hungry will I do it. As we are told in the Book of Amos, "I will send a famine upon the land; it will not be a hunger for bread, nor a thirst for water, but for the *hearing* of the words of God" (8:11). The average person is not interested in hearing the word of God. When they go to church what do they hear? I read in this morning's paper some sermon given yesterday in Santa Monica, and the minister is telling the congregation that religion should be rooted in *reason*. Of all the asinine things in the world! Religion is revealed truth which cannot be logically proven. It's *revealed* truth. How could you explain to anyone logically the story of the birth from above? How could Nicodemus ever grasp until he experienced the birth from above how it could be done? I am born from below as the whole vast world is born from below, from the womb of woman. How could I, a grown man, approaching the grave, be born from above? And where is "above"? The world thinks the above is out there, and the above is within; for in scripture "above" and "within" are the same, and "below" and "without" are the same. So I came into the world by being born from below; I enter into my eternal state by being born from within. That "within-ness" is from above, and that "above-ness" is the skull of man. That's where I was born from above, and not any water was present in the birth, so, no baptism of that nature whatsoever.

So here, we find the words "water and" and we delete them in that 5th verse of the 3rd chapter of John...just delete them. You're not born of the water and the Spirit; you are born of the Spirit...so forget the water. And so, if it pleases the family when a little child is born to have the child baptized, then please the family...that's all. I pleased my mother when I took my little boy down and had him baptized for *her* satisfaction, that she would feel that if he should die at least he would have a chance to enter heaven. And you only enter heaven from here when you are born from above. When I say here, here does not end with death. The world does not terminate at the point where my senses cease to register it; therefore, when someone departs this life they are still here in a world terrestrial just like this. So they go on, and they will be born from within, which is from above, from their skull. They will be restored to life. All are restored except those who have experienced the birth from above, and they now can die no more. They can't pass through any more departures from one state to another. They are now sons of God, and the son of God is *one with* God: I and my Father are one (Jn.10:30).

So here in this statement of Jeremiah, he discovered that Jehovah rose within him. When he rises within me, well then, when I wear that garment in which he rises—which is my garment that I took off to come into *this* garment—then all impossibilities will dissolve at that touch of exaltation which his rising in me imparts to my nature. So wherever I go then clothed in that form is heaven. So heaven is not a location; heaven is the body that I wear and wherever I go wearing that body is the realm called heaven. For everything is transformed in harmony with the perfection that is now springing and rising within me.

So I know from experience that these things are really inserted and they have violated scripture by adding to the words of God. So that statement in Blake when he identifies the human Imagination with the divine body of the Lord Jesus Christ. And then the world denies that there is a God. The mocking world says, "There is no God nor Son of God, that thou O human Imagination art all a delusion. That thou, the human Imagination which is the divine body of God really does not exist. But I know thee, O Lord"—he knew exactly the one who returns morning after morning upon his weary eyes, because he could bring through the vision right down to the moment when he once more awoke within the garment of flesh. So he came through remembering exactly what he had done and how he came back through this bridge of incident that led him into the so-called waking world of this mundane state. So then, he returned upon his weary eyes... he opened his eyes to know how it came back. For in that state whatever he imagined happened and he knew the power of the Creator, that all things were made through him, and without him was not anything made that was made (Jn.1:3). If you awake in a dream, you can control the dream, and you know exactly who is doing it: your Imagination. If you ever catch yourself dreaming, you either quickly awake, as you undoubtedly will, or in that state you control everything that you do and you know exactly the controller and the begetter, and he is your Imagination. If you awake and not awake here, then you will control everything that you are doing and make it come out.

So when you return upon the weary eyes in this dungeon and this iron mill, you still remember the Lord and the Lord was your own wonderful human Imagination. One day, you will completely awake in that body and *that* is the Lord Jesus Christ. There is no other Jesus Christ. *Everything* in the world is but your own wonderful Imagination pushed out. Here in this world you did this for a purpose, a heavenly purpose. The restriction you imposed upon yourself was for the purpose of expansion and you could not expand until you first reached the limit of contraction, the limit of opacity.

I can't tell you the thrill that is mine when I'm getting your letters and reading how you are awakening, one after the other, as the visions are coming through. But *everyone will.* Those who tonight would deny it completely, condemning it then forgive them. It makes no difference. Let them condemn it forever. I am not speaking any longer as one who will say, "I believe it...I was told it by my mother whom I trusted and I believe her implicitly." I don't have to say that any more. Mine is an assured *I know*! Mine is not rooted in reason; mine is revealed truth. Truth is *revealed*: it is God's unveiling himself in the individual, for God became man that man may become God...so in man he unveils himself. It's revealed. You cannot in any way logically come to any of these conclusions. You cannot prove truth by any logic in the world; it simply unveils itself. And then you tell it...some believe it and some deny it.

So when you read Blake bear in mind he wasn't writing for any little child as you understand a child. He was telling the most profound truth in the language of the child that it may be kept alive. Because it is so beautifully told it will it will live forever and forever. "Little lamb, dost thou know who made thee? Little lamb I'll tell thee. He is called by thy name, for he calls himself a lamb. He is meek and he is mild; he became a little child. I a child, and thou a lamb, we are called by his name." So he's telling you in the most beautiful manner exactly the experience of Jeremiah in the 15th chapter, the 16th verse of Jeremiah. So when we speak of the lamb being slain, all right, not a little lamb...that's a symbol. I took my own life when I came down here, you took your own life when you came here, and we are the one being who did it. He calls the one being Albion, the universal *humanity* in which all are contained.

So in this one man all men fell, and we individually rise back into the one man. So the one man is gathering himself together, one by one, into the same one man who is God, who came down into universal humanity. And not one will be missing; every one will be gathered. He will leave the ninety and nine who are saved and go in search of the one because the body is not complete until *all* are redeemed. So all are brought back into the one body that fell, and that one body is God. You and I are contained in him and we are called "the gods in the one." So the word translated "the Lord" would be singular and the word translated "God" is plural, it's Elohim. So when we speak of the great confession of faith of the Hebrew, "Hear, O Israel: the Lord," that's singular..."our God," that's plural..."the Lord," singular, "is one" (Deut.6:4). So the one became fragmented into the many, and all are gathered one by one into the same one Lord. So you hear this wonderful confession, "Shema, Israel, jah adonai elohenu adonai achad." One Lord... the numberless gods gathered together in the one Lord. Every one is going to have this identical experience.

And so, if I could take from you the few little things that have been added into scripture because they confuse the mind, forget the word "water." You are not born of water and the Spirit; you are born of the Spirit. No physical baptism has anything to do with your second birth. Completely forget it...whether you were completely immersed in the river or a little water thrown on your head. Most of the little children cry anyway...if you've gone to these baptismals...they scare the little things to death. But that is not important. If it pleases, as it did my mother, then do it to please the one rather than offend her. But don't think for one second you have to be baptized by any person in this world. Who by the laying on of hands in this world can do anything for you? Who by taking a little water and putting it on your head can do anything to you spiritually? But you will find a real baptism when you stand in the presence of the risen Lord whose body is gathering together one after one after one, and then he embraces you. That is baptism by the Holy Spirit. And then you are sent to have the experiences of the Word of God: "For my word cannot return unto me void; it must accomplish that which I purpose, and prosper in the thing for which I sent it" (Is.55:11). So the Word is God himself and he's *in* you. He sent himself and then you go through all these afflictions of the world, and then one day it suddenly erupts within you, and *you* are called by his name and you are the Lord, God of hosts.

You are looking upon the whole vast world and you realize it is yourself pushed out…everything in the world is yourself pushed out. So if you don't like what's going on, you can only change it by changing your attitude towards it and change it within yourself. It cannot change unless you first change your attitude towards it, because the whole thing is within you. And when you see it changed to conform to the change in you, then you really have confirmation of what is taught in scripture. Then one day you awake, and you know when the final day comes after you're awake…it can't be delayed too long…well then, you enter into that garment that was yours before that the world was. Then you become one of the watchers from above who contemplate the world of death, waiting eagerly for the return of all your brothers, for we are all brothers. We were before the world was, we still are though we don't recognize each other, and we will be when this world ceases to be. But all will be enhanced by reason of the experience of coming into the world of death and conquering death.

What I'm telling you tonight I tell from experience; I am not speculating, I am not theorizing. Weak as I am in the world of Caesar, limited as I am, I still know the experience and I cannot deny the experience. I could no more deny this experience than I could deny the simplest evidence of my senses. I had dinner tonight, I drove here with a friend, I know exactly what happened and I couldn't deny that. Well, I couldn't deny my experience. If I deny that, it's like saying I didn't come here tonight with my friend and my wife. I can't deny it, it is so real to me. And I know that everyone here is going to have it, but when I cannot tell you. The day, the hour remains the secret of the Father in you, for he will not awaken within you until he has accomplished his purpose. He sent himself into the world clothed as you. When he awakens, you are the Lord God Almighty, but still restricted until that moment in time when you take off the garment as you would as an actor…take it off and hang it up in the costume department. Then you depart from the stage, depart from the theater.

Now while we are here there is a technique given to us where we can make it easier…knowing who God is, and God is our own wonderful human Imagination. We can imagine that we are the man, the woman that we would like to be and *persuade* ourselves that we are; and to the degree that we are faithful to that assumption that assumption will harden into fact. If I could now persuade myself that I am...but I must first of all *want* it. The world will say to you, well, why don't you want to be rich? Well, maybe you don't want wealth. It's the most difficult thing in the world to convince someone that you really don't want to be rich. They think you're insane, you must be insane. Don't you want to be well-known like, say, Richard Burton, who could spend a million dollars for a diamond for his girl? And you say, no, I have no desire to have a million dollars to spend on a diamond for my wife, none whatsoever. The little that I gave her she doesn't wear, and so she has no desire for that, and I have no money to that extent, none whatsoever. Well, they think something's wrong with you. Well, that's perfectly all right. Leave that individual just as he is. If he wants a million to spend on a diamond, let him have it, and pray for him that he may have it. But personally I have no such desire, none whatsoever. I'm not alone, I'm quite sure I am part of the majority. Because I had no desire to be known when *everything* in this world is fading and will vanish and only the *immortal you* will remain and he doesn't function in this world. So everything you ever accomplished in this world will pass and really pass forever and leave not a trace behind.

But the you of whom I speak and to whom I am speaking are immortal...that's the eternal being. And when you awake, you awake in an immortal body. It is perfect, it cannot be improved, and wherever you are that realm is perfect. There can be no blind, no deaf, no halt, no weakness, no limitation wherever you are. Everything in your world as you walk by is transformed into the perfection that is *you*...and that is heaven. So, really, heaven is not a locality, it really is a body, it's a character, and that character as it moves in the world, the universe, transforms every place where it is into heaven. That becomes then the realm for the time that you dwell in it and leave it for anyone else, for when you go on wherever you go is perfect, for it is heaven.

So when you read this, don't think a man is going to eat a piece of paper as I saw them in Barbados doing it. And that's not alone they do it all over the world. When you eat the Word of God, you first hear it with understanding, with interpretation, and you say yes to it. When you can say yes to it then you accept it and you're eating it, you're assimilating it. You can't take it all at the same time. Certain portions of it you can't digest, and so you simply reject it for awhile. Eventually you'll eat the entire loaf...as my friend saw the entire loaf alive and blood pouring from it. It was all bread, beautiful symbolism, beautiful imagery and so true. She has completely accepted the fact that all things spring out of her own wonderful human Imagination. And he could not for one moment alter the fact as she called the number one after the other and it all added up to the whole loaf. "Eat my body and drink my blood." She doesn't have to go to any church to have a little piece of wafer and a little sip of wine. She saw the entire thing because she has eaten the body of God: she has completely accepted the fact that imagining creates reality. Whether she proves it in performance or not she still accepts it one hundred percent. So she may falter in proving it in the testing, but she has completely accepted it and *that's* why the symbol came to her in a vision.

And so, she may tomorrow because she's married, she has two children and third is coming, she may find moments of difficulty in her life, but having seen that symbol she will always fall back upon it and know she can't pass the buck. She can't blame her husband, John, or her three children, as the one is to be. She has to turn and say, "No man takes it from me I lay it down myself. That, no man cometh unto me save my Father calls him, and I and my Father are one." So you are a rascal and you couldn't come into my world unless my Father called you, and I and my Father are one. So you came to take from me what is mine, and if you succeed in taking it, I still say you could not have come unless I called you. You could not have taken it unless I by my attitude toward life allowed it. So the whole vast world is myself pushed out. I either control it or I don't control it.

And that's the story of scripture. There is no other God than your own wonderful human Imagination. So when you speak of Jesus Christ and you bow you head mentally if not physically, do the same thing when you think in terms of your wonderful Imagination. For *that* is Jesus Christ, that is the Word of God who is God himself, and by your own wonderful human Imagination the world was created and that world is supported and sustained. It changes only as you change your Imagination. Believe that and you will live in a wonderful, beautiful world.

Now let us go into the Silence.

*   *   *

Q: (inaudible)
A: Well, my dear, I gave you tonight the words of God. I could give you no deeper than I gave you tonight: you are God. When you look into the mirror you see a lady and you say here is ___(??), and that's the name you'll answer to if I call you by it. But your name as told tonight is the Lord, God of hosts. Yet without loss of identity and though you are the Lord, God of hosts, you will respond to that name. You love the name.

I respond to the name Neville. When I heard the heavenly chorus sing my praises when I was risen they called me by my name Neville. They said, "Neville is risen." They didn't say the Lord, God of hosts or God of hosts; they said Neville. So they'll call you by name. You're completely individualized and not in eternity will you cease to be. In fact, forever and forever you'll be more and more individualized, so that you're distinct and you're not going to be absorbed into one body. You *are* that body, but you have your individual being. That's the joy of brotherhood. I will know you in eternity and know you as one that I knew before that the world was. And like a great masquerade, it's always hilarious when the mask comes off and we see who we love behind the mask that we did not recognize when they wore the mask.

But when you have these experiences, ___(??), write them for me… write them out. Let me just dwell upon them for awhile, will you?

Q: When you talk about identity, do you mean when you are aware of being? If when you awaken you don't lose your identity then your identity is like exactly where I am today?

A: Your true identity is the Lord Jesus Christ and that's your *true* identity forever and forever. But the Lord Jesus Christ comes to us as one unknown yet in a mysterious manner he lets us experience who he is, and when we experience who he is we discover who we are. So without loss of identity you are the Lord Jesus Christ. I am still Neville and yet I have experienced everything said in scripture concerning the Lord Jesus Christ, including crucifixion. And it was not as painted in scripture, a sad event; it was ecstasy. It's a joy beyond the wildest dream…no blood and water came out. There were six points in my body, but they were ecstatically done, whirling vortices, six not five…two feet, two hands, my head and my right side were vortices and the ecstasy that you enter into when you feel it! And this is only a remembrance. You can remember the event and relive it, but not to the extent that you do when you first lived it. This is only a remembrance, mind you, and yet the ecstasy was so great.

So I tell you, we have been crucified with Christ. It is not I who live but he who lives in me and the life I now live in the flesh I live by faith in the Son of God who loved me and became me (Gal.2:20)… and that was God himself. So I could not lose my identity. I recall it vividly…it was the fulfillment of the 42nd chapter of the Book of Psalms. That was my triumphal journey into the holy city, when I heard the voice, and the crowd that I led in procession to the house of God. What the voice said to me and it was heard only by me from the depths of my own soul. Then came the crucifixion and it was ecstatic, it was *beautiful*...whirling vortices in my hands, my head, my right side, and the soles of my feet. So, far from being a sad event, it was a heavenly event! And the churches do not teach it that way. They have completely misrepresented the mystery, because the men who ran the churches are men without vision. You aren't elected as a cardinal because you've had a mystical experience; you're elected cardinal because of your capacity to raise enormous sums of money. If you can prove you're a good business administrator and raise enormous sums of money, you are right in line for the next little cap. Don't tell me any pope was elected in any other way than we now elect our presidents. This does not mean that he has any spiritual vision whatsoever...any more than Mr. Nixon has. I don't think he would claim that he has. He was elected as a politician by pressure groups who have been promised that they would get certain things *if* he was successful in getting the election, and he has to keep his promise or not run the second time. Well, the pope is running for office in the same manner. It's never unanimous. They go in there and spend hours, sometimes days, before the smoke comes through the chimney. If it was a unanimous decision from on high it would be *automatic*. It's never a unanimous decision. How can God, who is one, not bring in a unanimous decision?

Q: When you awake you find out your true identity, which is the Lord; then when I awake, my identity will be the Lord, which is the same as your identity—the true identity is the same for everyone—then how can you all raise up in a body with your own identity if it's all the same?

A: Here, if you are the Father of my Son, are we not one being, though seemingly two? See, there's only one Son and the one Father, so if all of us have the experience of being the Father of that one Son, we are one (2Sam.7:12-14). Now read carefully, and may I tell you, try to commit it to memory, the 17th chapter of the gospel of John: "I in them and they in me...that they may be one as we are one. And Father, I have made known to them thy name and will make it known" (17:23-25). The name he made known was "Father." So I tell you, I dwell in you and I am the Father and I have a Son. If I dwell in you and I awake in you without changing your identity, I awaken you as Father. Then the same Son that called *me* "Father" when God awoke in me is the Son who's going to call you "Father." Well, if you are the Father of my son David, then he doesn't have two fathers...there's only *one* Father. Then you will realize the *unity* of humanity. And today, no matter what skin he wears, when he awakens and he is God the Father because of the Son calling him Father, and the same Son called me Father and I *know* I am his Father, you will have the same innate knowledge that you *are* the Father.

This wisdom from above is without uncertainty, so you will know it. Well, knowing that you are the Father of that one Son who calls me Father, you will know when you look at me that you and I are one.

And if you will ever forgive yourself for an act that you did wittingly or unwittingly and you heard that I had done it, you would know that you did it, and therefore you'll forgive me. So, "Father, forgive them; they know not what they do" (Luke 23:34). If you would like to be forgiven for an act which you heard that I had done and you would have the experience I have had, you would willingly forgive me, because you would know that you and I are one. There's no other way that we would ever know the unity of being save through the Son revealing us as God the Father. And I'm telling you, and I've never read it before save in scripture—but I didn't know it in scripture until I experienced it—that the true Son who reveals man as God the Father is David. It's in scripture. You will realize that he called Jesus Christ "Father"…also in scripture. And so, when he calls you "Father," though to the world you are a little person that is ignored, not worthy of a second glance…they pass by not knowing that they just passed one who knows he is the Lord Jesus Christ.

Should they be told you are, they would not be impressed, because they're judging from appearances and they do not know (1Sam.16:12). But go into a restaurant and say "Look who's over there" and you say, "Well, who?" "Well, look at that person, know who he is?" And you don't know. "Well, he has a billion dollars!" And of course, they're so impressed because he has a billion dollars. They never tell you how he got it…that is hush-hush. The third generation from that inheritance will enter the social register and they will be in all the great books of the world because they have money. You will walk by having had the experience of being the Lord Jesus Christ and no one will know or care, because that's not the Lord Jesus Christ that they are expecting. They're expecting some being to come from without. He can never come from without: he comes from *within* and he allows the individual to experience who he is, and when you experience who he is, it's who you are. That's how he allows you to experience who he is. So you never see him as another; you can only experience him as yourself.

When I hear Billy Graham getting up and saying that he hopes that he'll live long enough to meet the second coming of Jesus Christ, and he'll go forward and shake his hand. Well, millions hear his voice and he's highly publicized and they go all for it…the second coming of the Lord Jesus Christ. When I read that in the *New York Times*, well, I could hardly believe that I'm seeing correctly. I reread it and reread it…

yes, unless they misquoted him, which they could...but he's waiting eagerly and hoping that he will live long enough, because he thinks that signs that are about now are the signs of the coming of the Lord for the second time.

He hasn't the slightest concept of the mystery of Jesus Christ. But I say that and they say, "Now what are you talking about, were you ordained?" Of course, knowing that they're orthodox in mind, I say, "To the degree that Jesus Christ was ordained. Who ordained him?" What man had the power to put his hand upon his head and add anything to him...if you think of a personal Jesus Christ? Did he go to college? What college did he attend? Is it not said in the 7th chapter of John, "How can this man have such learning seeing that he is not schooled?" (7:15), so did he? Name the college. Was it Harvard? I don't recall they said it was Harvard or Yale or Princeton or USC. I have no knowledge that he said these things. Well then...but his background...he tells you is not what the world thought it was...his background is God. He said, "I came out ...the one you call God...but I know my Father and you know not your God." Well, how can this be? We know his father and his mother and his brothers and his sisters, how can he make this claim? Well, I do the same thing. You know my father and my mother, two delightful people, gone from this world, but you know them...or you can investigate their backgrounds. You know my brothers, most of them are still here, and my sister. Well, how can he make these claims? So everything said of him I can claim, for I have experienced the identical story which is my personal spiritual *auto*-biography.

Good night.

GOD ONLY ACTS AND IS

11/21/69

Blake said, "God only acts and is in existing beings or men." That is, God is the only actor in the universe. It is God who embraced the fire of experience, and was consumed and rose from its ashes, and continues to rise as Jesus Christ or Divine Imagination. Good and evil are not conditions imposed by some malevolent deity, but states of experience through which the soul of man must pass in order that having experienced good and evil he will surpass them and awaken as God himself.

Tonight I'll share with you certain experiences of mine, of others, and one lady, who is not here but I'll tell it. I'm quite sure she never heard or never read the letter written by Aldous Huxley, which is printed in Walter de la Mare's anthology on dreams. For she said, "I had a dream and this was my dream. I was someone who could be anything that I desired to be. I looked at anything that intrigued me and I could instantly put myself right into it and feel its emotions and share with it its thoughts, its environment. I actually became the being or the thing." She didn't name the thing…she just said "the thing." "And throughout the night I seemed to go from one to the other, actually putting myself right into that individual or that thing. Then I woke, reluctantly, slowly, and hated waking as I was so enjoying the experience of being anything that intrigued me."

Now here, I will quote it. It may not be an accurate quote, but close to it. He is telling of his experience with D. H. Lawrence, and he and Lawrence were close, intimate friends. In fact, when his home burned a few years ago here in the Hollywood Hills, he had unpublished manuscripts of Lawrence that Lawrence gave to him. They were close, most intimate friends. And this is what he said, "To be with Lawrence was like an adventure. It was simply a discovery, because he himself was really not of the order of this world. He belonged to a universe that was not of this world. When you were with him as he told his experiences, you felt that he knew from actual personal experience what it was to be a tree, to be a daisy, to be a breaking wave, to be the mysterious moon itself. You felt in him that he saw things that no mortal eye ought to see. Here was the most sensitive man that I have known; an intelligent man, a man who could cook, he could sew, he could embroider, he could do woodwork, you name it and that's what he could do all to perfection. And yet he could sit perfectly alone doing nothing and be completely happy. He could put himself into the skin of an animal and tell you what it was like to be that animal. He could describe in the most convincing detail that dim inhuman thoughts of the animal. I never tired of listening to him. He was not of the order of these things."

Well, I'm quite sure that my friend never read that. But to her I gave my eyes. And may I tell you, without boring you with my own experience I've tried to tell it time and again. But why tell mine? I'm waiting for others to tell it. Well, she told it, "I went from state to state." She did not itemize them, she did not name them, but she said, "Things or persons, I knew exactly how they felt, I knew exactly what they did, all their emotions I shared." Because, God is the only actor...there is not a thing in this world but what it is God, not a thing in this world. She is the actor, you are the actor, but when the eye is not open you think it is another.

Now, Blake made the statement: "Eternity exists, and all things in Eternity, independent of Creation which was an act of mercy. You will see by this that I do not consider either the just or the wicked to be in a supreme state, but to be every one of them states of sleep into which the soul may fall in its deadly dreams of good and evil" (*Vis. Last Judgmt.*, Pp.91). Here, everything in the world *is*. And I'm telling you from my own experience the day will come—I hope it's now with all of us here, that you too will see that everything in this world is yourself pushed out; that you can actually enter into the skin of any animal in the world and experience its emotion, experience everything about that animal...it's only yourself. The day will come and you will see it. It will stand perfectly still, perfectly dead. And then you will know who you are, that you are the animating power of the universe.

So then we are told in scripture that "All things were made by him and without him was not anything made that was made" (Jn.1:3). Now we are told what he made. What is it that he made? He made life and that you become the animating power of the entire universe. You will see it one day, and when you see it you will feel within yourself that something that is alive. The thing is dead as you look at it and then, within you, you will allow it to become alive. It is not alive outside of you; it's alive *in* you. You will animate it and you will stop it and let it go, and you will stop it and let it go, and prove to your own satisfaction that *you* are the life of the universe. So when he said, "God only acts and is in existing beings or men" he meant it in this sense, God is the *only* actor in the entire universe (*Mar. Heaven and Hell,* Plt.15-17).

Well, how does he act? He acts imaginally...all in one's own wonderful human Imagination. The day will come that you will think say of your home tonight as you are seated here. You see it in your mind's eye, but you don't really see it as you see me now or as I see you. But the day will come you will think anything and you will see it more vividly than you now see the speaker. You will enter it and it will not be a shadow; it will be three-dimensional just like this. You will sit in a chair or you'll lie on a bed, and with your eyes shut as in sleep but you're not asleep, you know exactly what you're doing, you know exactly where you are. You will see through closed lids what you should *not* see if the lids were open. You will know exactly where you are and know exactly what you're doing. Consciousness will follow vision and you will step into the image. The image will not be simply a flat shadow; it will be three-dimensional. It will close around you and then you will explore. Then you will know these words of Blake, "If the Spectator could enter into these images"—now follow it closely—"*enter into* these images in his Imagination, approaching them on the fiery chariot of his Contemplative Thought...if he could make a friend and companion of any one of these images, which always invites him, intrigues him to leave mortal things (as you must know), then would he rise from the dead, then would he meet the Lord in the air and then he would be happy" (*Vis. of Last Jud.*,Pp.82-84)

Sitting in my chair, how often have I done it or lying in my bed, knowing exactly where I am and knowing what I ought to see were I to open my eyes. But I didn't open my eyes; I left the eyelids closed. And my eye, my inner eye is open, and I am seeing what no mortal eye could see were they sitting where I am sitting or lying where I am lying. And then I allowed my consciousness to move. Then you discover who you really are! They call it by your name...all right, Bill, Jan, Neville, call it by any name...that's what you are to them. Then you move out of it, a conscious being in the world that you are seeing, and that world closes itself around you and you explore. You ask yourself, "Who am I?" If anyone entered the room and saw that thing on the bed or on the chair, they would call you by name and say he or she is asleep. Yet you are fully awake and you, too, are looking at it as something external to yourself. Everyone thinks when they see a person in this world they are looking at that being, and they're only looking at the mask. They do not see the *immortal* you that cannot die. When this thing happens to you, you know you cannot die, that no one in the world can ever die. He is not the thing that they put into the furnace and consume. He is not that which they can put into the grave and bury. He is that which is I AM. And how can you describe it? It is simply *consciousness*...it's simply your own wonderful human Imagination.

You explore a world just as real as this. The world is three-dimensional just like this. No one knows this wonderful mystery until they really experience it. So he said, "God only acts." Well, I acted. I sat in the chair and saw what I should not see, and then my consciousness followed what I am looking at; and I stepped into the image and the image was not a flat surface, it was three-dimensional, and clothed me with it...completely clothed me. Well then, I walked into that state and then I explored.

So when she tells me in her letter, "I was one in my dream that could become anything that intrigued me. No matter what it was, if it intrigued me, I became it, one after the other, and I woke from it all reluctantly. I didn't want to wake, I hated waking, but I had to wake from this fantastic experience of the night." And I know she did not read this which is said by Huxley of his friend D.H. Lawrence that he was not an ordinary person, he was not of this world, and he didn't live in this universe. Yet, in this universe he had more talents than anyone that he knew. He could sew as no one could sew that he knew, he could embroider, he could do work, carve all kinds of beautiful things in wood, he could cook. He could do everything... you name it and he could do it. He gave his entire time to the thing that he was doing. And yet, he could do nothing and be perfectly happy in doing absolutely nothing. He said he saw more than the human being ought to see.

Yet the same Huxley when I tried to tell him of mine, he showed no interest, none whatsoever. When I tried to tell him of the birth and tried to tell him of David and all the things that I have told you, Aldous showed absolutely no interest. He liked me as a friend, but he had his own limitations, as everyone has. You open your mouth and the minute you pronounce a certain word you're catalogued in a certain social world. You pronounce it differently and instantly you are simply catalogued as one who is not of the "in" as it were. He would not listen...he liked me as a friend... but I didn't speak as he spoke and as he thought anyone should speak. So I could have told him things beyond the wildest dream of his friend D. H. Lawrence, but he had his little stumbling blocks and he couldn't listen. So we walked in to dinner together, breaking a thought that I wanted to complete, but he showed no interest. When Blake said to his friend who asked him "What do you think of Jesus Christ?" he said, "Jesus Christ is the only God" and then he hastened to add, "But so am I and so are you."

Then came dinner so he didn't complete the thought or he didn't develop the thought...and what a loss because there was dinner.

So I tell you, you as you're seated here tonight, *you* are the only God. There is no other God. The day is coming, and I hope it is not too far away, when as you think of anything in this world, instead of seeing it in your mind's eye you will see it as you're now seeing the speaker. Because that eye when it opens allows you to see it just as though it is here. Whether it is something ten thousand years ago or a billion years ago or what you might think to be future, it is here. When the eye is open there is nothing that is not here, and you enter right into the state and the thing is completely real just like this room here is now.

So when he makes the statement that he does not consider the just or the wicked to be to be supreme states, he means it. You can forgive every being in this world for what he has done. It seems stupid, horrible based upon this level, but may I tell you, they are only states and they can't help it. Man has to pass through all of these states. Good and evil are simply states of experience through which the soul of man *must* pass in order that having experienced good and evil that he will then awaken to the being that he really is: the one who actually embraced the fire of such experiences, was consumed, and then from the ashes rose...and continues to rise in every being in the world. For he is the only one being playing all the parts. So he rose in one, he rose in others and he is rising in all. The only one being is the being when you sit here and you say "I am"...that's he. One thinks, "How could it be?" Well, I'm telling you from my own experience and I cannot deny it. I could no more deny what I have experienced than I could now deny that I am standing here.

And when the eye opens, I can't tell you the thrill that is in store for you. The eye to all appearances is shut, and it isn't shut...you're actually seeing for the first time. The ears are open for the first time, and you hear what no mortal ear can hear, and you see. A few days ago, last Thursday, really a week ago last Thursday, I went down to this area where I was called concerning my Medicare and they asked me to prove that I would be sixty-five. Well, I couldn't prove that I would be sixty-five. I had my passport, and they said, "No that's not good enough. We want either a birth certificate or a baptismal certificate. I must have that in order to register that you actually are sixty-five this coming February." Well, I didn't know where to find such things. They may not be in existence in Barbados. But I knew once upon a time many years ago I did have to have it when I went off to London, and I wrote for it and got it. But where it was I didn't know.

Well, two nights ago, about 1:30 in the morning, my brothers said to me—not my earthly brothers but my divine brothers—"Go and look in your wallet; it is there." And I awoke, went to the bathroom, it was too early to disturb my wife, because she sleeps in one room and I sleep in the other, and so I didn't think I should go in and open up the drawer to look at a wallet. It's a wallet that my wife gave me back in 1938. I don't carry wallets. I carried it for about a year or two after she gave it to me. It's still as new as when she gave it to me back in 1938. And they told me to look there and there it was.

So the next morning when I woke about five, I completely forgot it. Went downstairs and got my paper, made myself a cup of tea, and here I am reading my paper, and about 8:30 it all came to me. Well, they told me this morning at 1:30 to go to the wallet and there I would find what I'm looking for, my baptismal certificate. So I went right in, opened up a thing I hadn't seen in years, and there was my baptismal certificate. They told it to me. I was coming through from the depth of my being when they're talking to me and said, "Go, and you'll find it. There it is." So then I picked it up and brought it out to my wife and showed it to her. It's all falling apart it's so old. It was 1924 that I got it. When I got my passport to go off to England on some dancing career I had to have it to prove that I really came into this world in some strange way. There it was, this peculiar falling-apart thing, and they told it to me.

So I can tell you that when the eye is open and when the ear is open, you can hear and see anything in this world that you want to. That's your destiny. And when you are completely awake, you are God. There is nothing but God. God is the only actor in the world. So when you imagine anything in this world, I don't care what it is, and if you will now couple it with faith by really believing in the reality of that imaginal act, it will come to pass. It *surely* will come to pass.

And so, eternity exists. What does it mean, "Eternity exists and all things in Eternity independent of Creation which was an act of mercy" (Blake, *Vis. of Last Judgmt.*, Pp.91-92). It means that this little garment that I've seen sitting on a chair, lying on a bed, when I am not occupying it, others would come in and say that Neville is asleep…and I am hearing them and seeing them and I am *not* asleep, I am very much awake. But they're looking at the garment and they only know me by reason of the garment. And that is a garment that anyone can wear and, may I tell you, many will wear it. It is the garment in which one *awakes*. But I am not the garment anymore than I am any part I ever played in the few plays that I have played. Oh, I have played…six plays on Broadway…but I am not the characters that I played, I was the actor. Well, God is the actor in *all* these parts and God is your own wonderful human Imagination. That is God and there is no other

God and there is no other actor. He plotted the entire thing before he came down.

Now, we are told in scripture, the serpent spoke and told man…in this case it is said he told woman…"that you will not die, for God knows that in the day that you eat of the tree of knowledge of good and evil, your eye will be opened and you'll become like God knowing good and evil" (Gen.3:5). You'll actually know good and evil. It's something you *must* know, and knowing it you surpass it, and then rise beyond it as Divine Imagination. But you must know it. So the serpent said, "You will not die." In the day that you eat of it you will embrace the fire of experience. You will be consumed as its victim, and then you will rise from the ashes, and rising you are God himself! That's the story as told in scripture.

So then Blake added to this wonderful thought that we left paradise following the serpent. We left—that implies that we did not begin here on earth. If I left paradise following the serpent that told that I must embrace the great experience of good and evil, I *must* embrace it and be *consumed* in this fire…and yet I will not die 'tho I turn to ash, and I will rise from it. In John we are told "I came out from the Father"—it's a more lovely way of telling it—"I came out from the Father and I came into the world; again I am leaving the world and I'm returning to the Father" (Jn.16:28). So I did not begin here, you did not begin here. When we came down here and we found these garments, the little garment *seems* to begin, but it didn't *really* begin. It is an eternal part of the structure of the universe. You pick it up and it seems to be a new garment. In my own case, 1905 it *seemed* to begin; that little garment was *always* so. It was always growing into manhood and always departing at the age in its sixties. Always appearing, occupied by God, moving towards a certain point, and then disappearing. And all these are but garments. You pick them up and you wear them and they seem to grow. People think you are the garment. They do not know you who are God who wears the garment. You are the Lord Jesus Christ. There never was another, there never will be another, *you* are God. So God only acts and is in existing being or men. There is no other God. He is the only actor in the entire universe.

If you want to test it, test it tonight. Dare to assume now that you are the one that you want to be. Though the eye is not open and the ears are not open, it doesn't matter. I tell you from my own experience, for in me they are open. I tell you from my own experience they need not be open to test it. You could now dare to assume that I am…and then you name it. You remain loyal, remain faithful to this assumption, and though everything in the world denies it, if you remain faithful to it you will become it. It doesn't matter who you are today. If doesn't matter what the world thinks of you.

The Return of Glory

As I told you earlier, in my own case if he had only listened to my message rather than to my English. I'm a colonial in his eyes and like all Englishmen, the colonials are looked down upon...they're colonials. If you don't speak with an Etonian accent, with the Oxford accent, or the Cambridge accent, you are simply a colonial. So, in their eyes you are simply not quite one of the boys. Had he only listened I could have told him things beyond the wildest dreams of D. H. Lawrence.

I know what it is to be not only the wave but the ocean. I told it in my little book called *The Search*. When I was but a boy, years before puberty—in fact, it stopped at puberty—but it lasted for years before that. And I knew the night it was going to happen. I didn't want to go to sleep, because I knew exactly what was going to happen. It scared me unto death. I was the ocean...that was marvelous, to be the ocean. Oh, but to be the wave, the breaking wave, that frightened me. I, the ocean, would toss myself, the wave, into the sky and then catch myself upon my own bosom as I fell. I went up thrown by myself, the ocean. The ocean was marvelous. But to be the wave, that small portion of my being, the ocean, I threw myself up and then caught myself coming down. I would go to bed frightened to death, because I knew exactly what was going to happen. It happened once a month over a period of years. I could have told him that. He said that his friend Lawrence knew what it was to be the breaking wave and I could have told him what it was to be the ocean.

I could have told him what it was to be infinite light—but I mean *infinite* because there was no circumference...but my accent was colonial. And that's the barrier the world over. They see someone and they judge by appearances. They judge by his voice, they judge by his looks, they judge by the clothes that he wears. They judge by everything that is external, and that is *not* the being at all, because the being you do not see. He is unseen. He comes to us unknown, unseen. But in his own wonderful mysterious manner he lets us experience who he is; and when we experience who he is, we experience it in a first-person, singular, present-tense experience. We experience him *as* ourselves. There is no other.

So I tell you—I'm not flattering you—you are God. Everyone is God! The one who stabs you, the one who murdered, is the being with the one who is murdered. We all experience all of these experiences of good and evil in order that having experienced good and evil we will *surpass* good and evil, and then rise as Divine Imagination, who is God himself. So I came down, as you came own, and we embraced this fire of experience, and we have been consumed by it. Many a time the little garment that we wore turned to ash, only to find us restored in a body that is similar. From that ash we restored it and found a new body just like the old one, only new and healthy and wonderful, and not a thing missing in it. Then we were consumed in that. And we keep on being consumed one after the other until that moment in time when we rise from it all. We aren't consumed and restored any more; we rise as the Lord Jesus Christ, *God* himself. So there's not a thing in this world but God...nothing but God.

So when he said, "God only acts," he really meant that he is the only actor. He not only acts, he is the *only* actor. And when you sit tonight at home or sit here, and when you begin to imagine anything, may I tell you, it will happen. I was late tonight. I had a friend at home for brunch yesterday. She knows my friend who brings me here all the time, and she said to me, "Isn't he unreliable?" I said, "No! Never! Always right!" She didn't want to hear that; she wanted to hear that he was unreliable. She's a very intense lady, very intense. She *wanted* to hear that. This is the first time in the months that he has been bringing me that he called from the Valley to say he couldn't make it. An *intense* imaginal act produced what she wanted to hear. But she will not get the satisfaction from me. She'll never hear from me that he was ever even late far less not coming. But she's a very intense lady, intensely intense, and she said it quite openly in the presence of my wife and myself. She came to brunch and asked all about him. I said, "He's perfectly wonderful." "Well, have him call me." He's in the audience so I will tell him what she said, but I'm not going to ask him to call her at all. She knows exactly how to reach him. Then she said, "Isn't he unreliable?" I said, "No. Not at all! He's all together wonderful" which did not please her.

Well, do you realize that people in this world who on the surface are altogether wonderful, perfectly marvelous, and it's a veneer? Below the surface is that intensity. They do not realize what they're doing. They haven't the slightest idea what they're doing. Because they're doing it only to themselves; they're not doing it to another. She can't do it to me, although undoubtedly she has tried. It will boomerang in a way that she will never know, because I would never resist it. And I love her dearly, just love her dearly, but she's intense. Also, of the same school that if you are not of that physical background, well then, you are not "in." I have told her unnumbered times that I have no, not the slightest little feeling toward any aristocracy in the world. When I speak of being a descendant of Abraham, it is not after the flesh; it is after the Spirit, where I actually believe 100 percent in the story that was told me *before* that the world was. That is what Abraham represents. There is no *physical* aristocracy, none whatsoever. The only aristocracy are the called, the elected—those who are called and embodied into the body that is the risen Lord.

But I could tell that to her forever and forever and she will not understand it. She still believes in physical aristocracy, and there is none.

May I tell you, let no one in this world ever try to impress you with his own greatness relative to you. As I stand before you now, I have never been able to feel anyone my superior. Physically yes, they can knock me down with one blow; intellectually yes, no question about it; financially certainly. You name it, they're all superiors. But I cannot meet anyone…I've never been able to meet one person in this world…that I felt my superior. Oh, he could be a giant intellectually, a mathematical giant, a musical giant, giant in a thousand ways, but that does not mean for one moment I feel inferior to him. I have never felt it and I cannot feel it…I just cannot feel it.

I was surprised today when I looked at my baptismal certificate. It amused me. Back in 1905 this huge, big, enormous thing…and the parent's profession. My father's profession in 1905 was a meat vender. He had a butcher shop, so he was a meat vender. Well, right away that would have disqualified me completely from this lady's picture of being socially acceptable. But, may I tell you, let no one in this world ever make you feel less than anyone in the world, because you are infinitely greater than all the characters put together in this world. You are the *God* who is playing the parts. You've played all the parts. You've played the phony parts, the decent parts, the rich man, the poor man, the known, the unknown. You've played them all or you would not be here. And the reason why you're here is because you're on the verge of waking. You will awaken from the entire dream to find that you created the play, and finding no one in the world that could play the part you're playing the part yourself. You've played all the parts and in the end you awaken. You awaken by a certain definite series of events that take place *within* you.

When they take place within you, all these inner things open. The eye is opened and the ears are opened as mine were this morning when they said, "Go and look, look into the wallet." Well, I haven't used that wallet. It was given to me in '38 and after all this is now '69, so that's thirty-one years ago. I don't think I used it more than a year before I simply put it away. As I told my wife today, "What use have I for a wallet when you give me a dollar when I go out? I have no use for one." I get a dollar and change, and so what do I need with a wallet? It's perfectly new, it's a lovely one…she brought it back from Paris back in 1938. And here, the certificate was there…this crumpled little yellow page. They told me so vividly and I woke. It was too early to disturb her, so I went in, and then completely forgot it when I woke at five. Had my tea, had all these things, and then at 8:30 I remembered that they told me to go and look in my wallet. Went to the wallet and there it was.

So I tell you, there isn't a thing in this world that isn't *now*…absolutely here! They speak of the age of the moon as billions of years, but you cannot measure your age because there never was a time when you were not. Nor will there ever come a time when you will cease to be. There *never* was a time when you were not. You didn't begin in time. You came down into time which you yourself created to experience good and evil, to expand the being that you always were. For, that is a constant, constant expansion of the being that you are. So you did not begin, even though your little birth certificate will say you began. No, you didn't begin. You are the wearer of the garment and the wearer of the garment is the actor, and the only actor in the world is God. There is nothing but God and you *are* God. You can't even say that he's near to you, because nearness would imply separation. He's not even near: you *are* God. When you say "I am" that's he. Begin to believe in your own being who is God and whatever you imagine to be so, firmly believing that it is so, may I tell you that it *will* be so.

Now let us go into the Silence.

*　　*　　*

Now are there any questions, please?

Q: ___(??) In Job, is Satan representing the nature of the individual that is doubtful?
A: Satan is only doubt. God is the affirmative. As we are told in scripture, "All the promises of God find their Yes in him" (2Cor.1:20). Well, all the promises of God find their No in Satan. "If you are the Son of God then command that this be turned into that." He doubts that it could be done. So every doubt in your mind is simply Satan speaking, for there is *nothing* impossible to God (Luke 1:37). When anyone will challenge you, don't accept the challenge, not for one second. You'll have to repeat it every day from now to eternity. They will say that was an accident, and tomorrow they'll challenge again…that's an accident. If you did it a million times, it's still an accident, because to them it isn't that which can be done. The devil is only or the anti-Christ is only any idea or person who denies the Christian revelation, that's all that it is. Anti-Christ is not something coming out of space. Alright, he could come as a person who completely denies the Christian revelation, like a Hitler, like a Stalin. He personifies the anti-Christ to the degree that he completely denies the Christian revelation. But that's only a part that he plays and God played the part. God will, one day having played the parts, play the part where he awakens as Jesus Christ. All must awaken as Jesus Christ. And there is nothing but Jesus Christ.

You decided to play the part you're now playing. We decided to embrace the fire of experience and play these parts. And how close you are to the awakening no one knows. Let no one tell you. Only the Father knows, and the Father is within you, and you are the Father. You and he are one. But you must be one in the sense that you must be just as perfect as he is perfect, and when the perfection is done then you awaken. Let no one tell you that they know when…no one knows. It comes with startling suddenness, comes so suddenly, so unexpectedly.

Q: The garment that we wear, you said they are eternal parts of the universe. For instance, the family…have they been in that family before to continue experiences or are they just there…wandered into that family for the sake of experience in` that particular thing?

A: Well, Ina, in this sense. You take the play of Shakespeare, *Hamlet*. All the characters exist, all, since the year, what, 1580 or 90, back into the early 17th Century when he wrote them. They all exist and through the centuries men have been playing them. The relationships between Hamlet and his mother and his father who was murdered, and his uncle who murdered him, and all these characters remain the same, and different actors play the part.

Q: You think that's similar to what happened in this world?

A: Well, this is God's play. This whole thing is God's play. It's God's play and these parts are forever, because they are part of the eternal structure of the universe.

Q: Do we go back into the play?

A: Well, my dear, you were *before* Ina. You are God who has no beginning. You came down and play a part which is part of the structure of the universe, but you are *not* that which began a few yeas ago in this world. You are the immortal God, the immortal being playing the part. And this part has a definite…like a play…you will play it differently but still the same part.

I have seen so many Hamlets and no two were alike…and yet all used the same words. Their faces differed because they were different beings. But they wore similar costumes, spoke the same words, but they played it differently. And their relationship to the mother in the play was the same although they played it differently. I saw Burton in the modern Hamlet and he used certain impressions, certain I would say, inflections that would differ. In fact, it was completely different from anything I ever heard before. When he said to his mother, "Assume a virtue if you have it not" he didn't treat it seriously, he treated it lightly. It's not the way I heard it before or I would read it. I do not read that in a light vein, "Assume a virtue if you have it not." But he did it as though it was a lark, not believing that she could ever assume one. Well, that's the way he interpreted it, but he did not change the words.

Q: Is that what you meant when you said of members of your family that when your family assembled again, you won't be one of them?
A: I must leave this little costume. I'm leaving it forever when I take it off, but the costume remains as part of the eternal structure of the universe. These things are forever, all these are forever. And when I take it off now in the not distant future I have played my final role. To play the final role you must have these experiences that I have mentioned over and over and over again: such as the resurrection, and then the birth, and then the discovery of the Fatherhood of God. When these things happen in man, well then, he has played his role for the last time. So in this present play I am playing it as one called Neville, but I have played the last role. And until this that I have mentioned takes place *in* man, he has not played the last role.
Q: Someone else might pick up the role?
A: Why certainly. This is going to be played over and over and over.
Q: Thank you very much. You clarified it.
    Good night.

ALL DREAMS PROCEED FROM GOD

11/24/69

The Bible recognizes one source of dreams: all dreams proceed from God. In the 33rd chapter of the Book of Job we are told that God speaks to man in two ways, but man does not perceive it. Then it states the two ways: "In a dream and a vision of the night, when deep sleep falls upon men, while they slumber on their beds; then he opens the ears of men and seals their instruction" (33:14). Now, you tell that to a psychiatrist, he will think you are insane. He will tell you that all dreams are from the individual dreamer, because he separates the dreamer from God. He does not understand what you are talking about. God's eternal name is I AM, so who is dreaming? Well, I am…well, that's God…that's his name forever and forever. So I'm not separating the dreamer from God.

All dreams proceed from God. Some are simple and you need no interpreter; others are revealed in a symbolic language which is not understood and then you need the interpreter. As told us in the story of Joseph, who could take the story of the butler and the baker, and even Pharaoh himself, and interpret their dreams for them and it came to pass just as he interpreted it (Gen.40:8). The cue is given as to who he *really* is when they said, "We have had a dream that's why we are disturbed," because he looked upon their faces and they seemed so disturbed. Then he said to them, "Only *God* can interpret the dream. Tell it to me, I pray you." If only God could interpret the dream, then why tell it to *him*? But you see he is a personification of God. His name was changed from Joseph, which really is Hosea—which means "salvation"—to Joshua; and Joshua is the Hebraic from of the Anglicized Jesus, which means "Jehovah is salvation." So he's telling you "Tell it to me, I will interpret it for you." So he tells you who *he* is.

Now here, the year is 1954, the month is November, November the 28th, and waking from a dream I heard the words, "You do not move in waking any more than you move on your bed in sleep. It is all a *movement of mind*. And the intensity is determined by the strength of the vortex you create. This is just like a whirlwind with a center of perfect stillness. You only believe that you are moving when you are awake as you *think* you believe in sleep." Well, I'm a rational being as you are and so reason could not accept that, but I wrote it down and placed it where I place all these visions in my Bible waiting for a future revelation that would in some way illuminate it, explain it. But I wrote it down...it came from God. Yes, psychiatrists will say it came from yourself and I'm not denying that. It came from a level, a depth of *my* own being that my rational mind could not reach; but I wrote it down just as it came, waiting for some future revelation that would explain it. How on earth could that be explained to the reasonable mind?

Today our three boys returned from the moon, a trip of a half-million miles. We have the record. You and I came here tonight in our cars...a friend of mine brought me here, I can't deny that. I travel all over the world. I travel so much on earth. I have travelled in my dreams. Like Blake said, "I have traveled through a land of men, a land of men and women, too, and heard and seen such dreadful things as cold earth wanderers never knew" (*The Mental Traveler*) and then he describes this travel. Well, I travel, you travel, and here I can't go back on what I heard, I wrote it down. You mean that I've never really traveled save in a dream...that this is no more than a dream? For when I woke in the morning I must confess I was still on the bed on which I fell asleep. I know I did not physically leave my room. I did not physically leave my bed, yet I heard these words. And night after night I sleep on a bed. I do not *leave* the bed 'til I wake in the morning, and yet I travel. You mean this waking state is no more than a dream and there is a dreamer dreaming in the depths of my being that looks upon this as a dream, just as I at night on a little lower level of the dream wake to find I didn't really leave the bed?

Well, when I was born from above, which came after my resurrection from the dead, for as we are told, we are born anew through the resurrection of Jesus Christ from the dead to discover that the Jesus Christ is the Jesus Christ *in us* who is God himself. There was no one else who woke...but I woke...I felt myself waking from a dream, waking from a deep, deep sleep, and a waking that I've never experienced before. Suddenly I began to feel myself waking. It was a vibration, it was a storm, a terrific wind, all centered in my head and still coming seemingly from without. I found myself waking within the sepulcher and the sepulcher was my own skull, where it was in my own skull that I fell asleep. And here, I awoke within my own skull. And then out of my skull I came to find the symbolism of the Christian mystery surrounding me, like the infant wrapped in swaddling clothes, and the witnesses to the event, and I unseen by the witnesses for I was Spirit and they could not see me. They spoke of me as the father of the child, which was only a sign. "For this shall be a *sign* unto you; you shall find a babe wrapped in swaddling clothes and lying on the floor, on the manger" (Luke 2:12). They found it as told in scripture, but calling *me* the father of it, "It is Neville's baby."

Now, I woke from a dream. It seemed to me that I had traveled. But I know that when I woke I woke in the same little room in the same little hotel in San Francisco in which I slept and I hadn't really gone anywhere. But I woke this night from a far deeper level of my being to find the symbolism of my waking from the dream of life…as night after night I wake from the dream of the day. Could it really be that that revelation is literally true? Reason denies it. Reason questions it and reason doubts it and reason rejects it. Well, if it is true then reason is rejecting Jesus Christ, for Jesus Christ defines himself as "the truth." He said, "I am the truth" (Jn.14:6). Well, if the revelation is true and reason rejects it then is not reason the doubting one, the devil Satan who denies the revelation of truth?

But how can you logically prove that this is true? And yet I have it written down. I had completely forgotten it. But I put it in the *Interpreter's Bible*…there are twelve volumes and four of the dictionary. Picking up a dictionary today…I took up one of the four volumes and there was my record back in November the 28th of 1954…that "you do not move in waking any more than you do on your bed in sleep; it is *all* a movement of mind and the intensity is determined by the strength of the vortex you create. It is just like a whirlwind with a center of perfect stillness. You only *believe* that you are moving when you are awake as you do and think that you move in sleep." I had completely forgotten that…and there it was written recorded on the 28th of November 1954.

July 1959 in the city of San Francisco I had the experience of waking from a profound sleep all within my skull. That sleep was not twenty-four hours, that was an eon, an age. There are two ages: this age where men appear in this world not knowing that they are dreaming. They have no idea that God within them is dreaming the dream of life, and they're actually experiencing motion and all these things in the world, violence, everything. They are totally unaware that the dreamer in them is sound asleep and the dreamer is God, as told us in the 44th Psalm, "Rouse thyself! Why sleepest thou, O Lord? Awake! Do not cast us off forever!" (44:23). He is *dreaming* and he is *occupying* his dream, and in this dream he has the *sensation* of travel and motion and all the violence in the world. He will continue until he awakes from the dream of life. When he awakes from the dream of life, he really hasn't gone anywhere. He simply deliberately fell asleep in the sepulcher and the sepulcher is the skull of man. That is where Jesus Christ is buried and it is there that he was crucified on man...no other place in the world was he crucified. He became man that man may become God. So he's buried in man, sound asleep, and dreaming this dream of life.

Now, I want to clarify a few points tonight. We are told in the Book of John, "You do not and you have not heard his voice and you have not seen his form; neither does his word abide in you" (5:37). Then he gives us reasons why: "Because you do not believe him whom he has *sent*." Now, many of you have had this experience...those who have completely accepted the fact that I have been sent. I have been sent as vividly and as clearly and as definitely as any apostle in the world has ever been sent. Call him by any name, I stood in the presence of the risen Lord and was embraced by him. I became one with the risen Lord— union with God, one body, one Spirit—and then I was sent. That body was infinite love that embraced me. When he sent me, he wore a different form. In the twinkle of an eye he wore the form of power; Almighty God sent me. It was not love. Love embraced me. But God is a protean being and plays all the parts. You can see him as wisdom and power, but his true being is love. That was the being that embraced me. But he wore the garment of power when he sent me to tell the story...to tell my experience.

And so, I have come to tell the experience. You who have actually accepted what I've told you, who believe it implicitly, one hundred percent, you have had an experience, and you interpreted it on this level as a physical, sexual experience. Many of you have. This is a shadow world. It is a creative act, no question about it. But complete acceptance of what I've told you concerning the birth of God in man will result in such a union on this level; yet I, the speaker, am totally unaware of such an act. I am totally unaware of such a creative, sexual act on this level with any of you. But your complete *acceptance* of the story will reveal itself to you on this level in such an ecstatic creative act...far greater than any sexual act on the physical plane. As you know from your own experience, it transcends anything that you've ever experienced on this level...you who have had such experiences sexually on this level. But I, the individual with whom you had it, am totally unaware of it. It only means that you have completely accepted the Word. Having accepted the Word that I bring to you, the story of Christ, then it *abides* in you. And now that it abides in you it will erupt within you and everything that I have experienced *you* are going to experience.

The males who have completely accepted it will find union with me not in a sexual act but in an embrace where I'm wearing the body with which I am now one. I am one with the body of the risen Lord...and he's all love, infinite love. You, too, will be asked the same question. Because I wear that body and I wear that face, you'll be asked to name the greatest thing in the world. You'll name it as though you were divinely inspired and you'll name it quoting the words of Paul from the 13th chapter of 1st Corinthians, "Faith, hope and love, these three; but the greatest of these is love" (13:13). And I will embrace you and you will fuse with me, for I am one with the body of the risen Lord. "He who is united with the Lord becomes one spirit with him" (1Cor.6:17). So I am one body with him, one spirit with him, and that will be *our* union. The female garment will see it in a different manner; they will see it as a creative sexual act. But let me tell you, I have no knowledge whatsoever of the event which is only a *symbol*. Everything in this world contains within itself the capacity for symbolic significance. So union with the risen Lord in the female takes that form, which means that you've completely accepted what I have told you as the messenger who was sent from the risen Lord..

It's a break with the past, a complete break with the past, as told us in the terms of the very first words uttered in the Book of Mark, "Repent and believe in the gospel" (1:14). The gospel is the "good news," the good news of *redemption*...that man is not lost. Repent and believe in the gospel. So I've brought you the true gospel; it's not secular history, it is divine history. It's a story that was before that the world was. The whole thing was plotted and planned before that the world was, and then God entered his own creative play, and God is playing *all* the parts. It is God in man who awakes. We are the sons of God, all of us, as told us in the 82nd Psalm: "I say that you are gods, sons of the Most High, all of you; nevertheless, you will die like men and fall as *one* man, O princes" (82:1, 6). I have quoted the Revised Standard Version in the marginal setup, which is the true translation of the Hebrew. You will fall as one man, one man containing all, and then you became diversified, fragmented. These are the sons of God. It takes all the sons of God to make God. So we're all gathered together one by one into the same one body that fell, and that one body fell into humanity. *Humanity* is the son of God. But buried in humanity is God and he extracts himself from humanity, individually, one by one, because we are unique. You cannot be duplicated, neither can you be lost. Not one in eternity can be lost or God would cease to be what he is. He would have to leave the ninety and nine and go in search of the one. So everyone is to be redeemed, but everyone, because in everyone God is buried.

The story of Jesus Christ is the truest story ever told to man. All of these things that are happening...oh, they happen, certainly they happen. Today I watched the splashdown. It was exciting! Watched every little bit of it and it was most exciting, a trip of half-million miles. And then I had to go back and reread what I wrote back in 1954, November the 28th that you do not move in waking any more than you do on your bed in sleep. Now, reason can't accept that. I saw them come back and we have a record of the journey. It was a half-million miles round trip, and yet we do not move? Well, I must confess that I do have experiences in my dreams where I travel as you do, and we travel and travel. Yet we have to admit when we wake on our bed in the morning, we have to confess we never left the bed, did we. We didn't leave the bed. Well, could there now be a dreamer far deeper than *that* dreamer who is dreaming this seeming waking state? And when he awakes from the dream of life, would he not look upon the dream of life as you look upon the dream of the night and know you didn't leave the bed?

Well, I'll tell you from my own experience when I woke within my skull to realize I had been there for unnumbered centuries, that I was buried in my skull dreaming the dream of life, dreaming violence, dreaming love, dreaming all kinds of things and thinking everything to be real as I do any dream. Then to awaken from it to discover I must have been in that skull all through the centuries; that I had been dreaming that I am a man walking this earth, dying, as told in scripture, being restored to life to die again, and keep on being restored and dying until that moment in time when I awake in the sepulcher where in the beginning I was buried. I was buried in the beginning in a skull, Golgotha, that's my Calvary and yours. There we are buried, dreaming this dream. I see myself here, I get up and shave in the morning, bathe, eat, make an effort to make a dollar to pay the rent and all these things…and it's all a dream!

There's a purpose behind it all. God limited himself to this little thing called man: he became man, the limit of contraction, the limit of opacity, so that he may *expand*. For there is no limit to expansion or to translucence; there was only a limit to contraction, to opacity. He took upon himself the limit of opacity and contraction and began to dream, and he dreamed the dream of life. This whole vast world is a dream. Dream *noble* dreams because all dreams can come to pass if you know that you are the dreamer. You can make it come to pass. It is a dream. If you believe it to be a dream, you can change anything tonight. The minute you know it's a dream you can change anything. Course, the chances are you'll awaken. If you find yourself dreaming, you usually wake, but do you know there are ways to prolong the dream and change it? Well, you can change it in the waking dream, really change it, and make it conform to what you want in this world. But look upon it as a dream…as a very fluid state.

Now, how would I change it? I bring before my mind's eye those who know me, my inner circle of friends, and I let them see me as they would have to see me were I the man that I want to be. I *let* them see me, and when

I am self-persuaded that this is a fact, they do see me. It hasn't yet appeared in the world so that they see that, because it hasn't yet become a fact. But I believe in gestation…there's a interval of time between impregnation and birth. And so I allow them to see me as they would have to see me in that day when I become the man that I'm assuming that I am. So I dare to assume that I am. I let them now reflect by the expressions on their faces and the sound of their voices and what they say that they see in me what I want the whole vast world to see. When I am convinced that they *do* see me, I break the spell, having assumed the feeling of the wish fulfilled. Then I abide and wait for that impregnation to take place in the world of dream. For, while I live in the world of Caesar, I must abide by the laws of Caesar. "Whose inscription is this, Caesar's? Well, render unto Caesar the things that are Caesar's." Give to him…he has to have them—rent must be paid, food bought, raiment bought, all these things, taxes paid. So render unto Caesar the things that are Caesar's and this is the way that you render it, waiting for that moment in time when you awake from the dream of life.

And so, I'll tell you, you who have had this experience with the speaker, don't be ashamed of it. You are married and blissfully happy and you love your husbands, and you would not be unfaithful to your pledge to your husband. You were not! You simply believed implicitly in the story that I've told. I have told you my own personal experience. I am not speculating, I am not theorizing. I have told you that the whole story of Jesus Christ has unfolded itself within me, but every little part of it. What I told you tonight which is not recorded in scripture is in this way the very last verse of the 21st chapter of John: "And many other things that Jesus did which are not recorded in this book, but *these* are recorded that you may believe." For if all were recorded, perhaps the world itself would not be big enough to hold all revealed to me. It so does fit in with the statement of the very last verse of the epilogue of the books (21:25). And so that is not recorded, no need for it to be recorded, but it was John. Well, John ends on the 20th and the 21st is the epilogue. And all these things happen and many more, but only these are recorded that you may believe.

And so, what has happened to you is the most marvelous thing, for it simply means to me, when you told me the stories as you've written them, that you have completely accepted the story as I have told it. Therefore, union with me is only confirmation of the complete acceptance of that story, the true story of Jesus Christ. For over the years barnacles have gathered around the ship. Men in the interest of their own doctrines have added to the script in the Bible. They are redactors, and in spite of the warning in scripture not to add to or take from the words of the prophecy of this book, they have added to in order to support their own traditions and their own conventions. I could go through the Bible and show you where these things have been added. It was not in the original text and it was not the intention of the author who had the vision and recorded the vision. He could not understand it, but he recorded it, waiting for that time when a greater revelation would come and he would then understand it.

For, in '54 I could not understand what I heard, but in '59 I knew that I awoke from a profound dream. And here, I'm awaking not on my bed, I'm awaking in my skull. I am alone. I come out of my skull to find the babe wrapped in swaddling clothes and the witnesses to the event are seeing a babe wrapped in swaddling clothes. They know it is my child, but they can't see me because I am born of the Spirit. They are of the flesh; they are not yet born of the Spirit. What is born of the flesh is flesh and what is born of the Spirit is Spirit. And so, I was born of the Spirit, so how could they see me? But they knew the *sign* of my birth: "For this shall be a sign unto you." No, I didn't bring forth a little baby; the child is but a sign. "And this shall be a sign unto you, you shall find a babe wrapped in swaddling clothes" (Luke2:11). What was the sign?—that God is born. God is begetting himself, bringing forth himself that he buried in humanity. He is redeeming himself. And there's only God in the universe...nothing but God.

It's not a moral book...hasn't a thing to do with morals as you hear from all the pulpits of the world. They get up and tell you all kinds of things about how to change the world. There is no attempt to change the world in scripture. The world is a school house and you don't turn a schoolroom into a home. It is nothing more than a school of educative darkness, and we're moving from darkness to light. There's no attempt in scripture to change it: "Render unto Caesar the things that are Caesar's." And we're going all out today to make this world a nice, sweet little place in which all will be happy, have enough to eat, enough to drink, enough to do this. That hasn't a thing to do with the mystery of Jesus Christ! There would be no struggle and there would be no effort in the world to awaken from the dream of life. You'd go into a deeper, deeper sleep. So let them be. They're all going to march along and then tell the world how to become good people, and how to become kind, and all this nonsense. You aren't going to be, may I tell you, not while you wear these garments of the animal. He took from *himself* the heart of God, the mind of God, and then took upon himself the body, the heart, the mind of an *animal*. Read the 4th chapter of Daniel...the whole thing is an animal world. And while in this world of violence God awakes from the depth of his own being to discover he hadn't gone any place: he only dreamed the dream of life. Then he awakes and he is the Lord Jesus Christ, and there is nothing but the Lord Jesus Christ.

Were it not that Jesus Christ is in you, you couldn't breathe. Your breath, your very breath, is his life. For the word breath or wind and the word Spirit are one and the same in both Greek and Hebrew. Your very breathing is the Lord Jesus Christ. The day will come and you will awake, and when you awake you *are* the Lord Jesus Christ. And David, the sum total of all of humanity, all of the experiences you've had in your dream as man, will stand before you completely solidified as one being, a youth, and he's David. Not *a* David, *the* David…only the one David. And he calls you Father, he calls you "my lord." And then you fulfill scripture, the 89th Psalm: "I have found David and he's cried unto me, 'Thou art my Father, my God, and the Rock of my salvation" (89:26). Then you find him and you find who the son really is. The son is humanity fused into a single youth, personified before you, for you've played all the parts of man and *that* is your son who did all your will. "I have found in David, the son of Jesse"—and Jesse means I AM; it is any form of the verb "to be," or I am—"the son of Jesse, who will do all my will" (Acts 13:22). And so, you find him…he did all your will, for you dreamed it and you played all the parts.

And when you awake in your skull, which is Golgotha, you come out of that skull and you are born from above. "We are born from above" as told in Peter, "we are born anew through the resurrection of Jesus Christ from the dead" (1Pet.1:3). Well, you see no one in the skull but yourself, and you know that you are waking from a dream, a profound dream. You are waking in a tomb, your skull, and you come out of that skull to find the symbolism of your birth surrounding you. And then you know who Jesus Christ is. While the world worships him as something coming from without, you've found him *within*…not as another but as yourself. There is only God in this world; there is nothing but Jesus Christ. So you come out of yourself and here you are the dreamer, the dreamer of life. So the great poet saw it so clearly when Shelley said, "He has awakened from the dream of life. 'Tis we who lost in stormy visions keep with phantoms an unprofitable strife." That's what the whole vast world is doing, fighting phantoms that are self-created. The whole vast world is himself pushed out and he's in conflict with himself, until that day when suddenly in the most dramatic manner an unearthly wind possesses him, which is the Spirit, the Holy Spirit, and then he wakes. He finds himself waking and waking, and he wakes as he's never been awake before in his skull. He has one consuming desire to get out. He has an innate knowledge and he knows that if he pushes the base of his skull there will be an opening. He does and something moves and it opens. He comes out just like a child would come from the womb of woman, but from above, from the skull of himself. The word is Anothin, "from above."

Everything that is taking place here in the world is from above. When brought before Pilate and Pilate said, "Do you not know I have the power to crucify you or the power to set you free?" He said, "You have no power over me *unless* it were given to you from above" (Jn.19:10). The same word Anothin. The whole thing is from within a man; he's in a profound sleep and he is the Lord Jesus Christ dreaming the dream of life. And when he wakes, he *is* the Lord Jesus Christ. So because there's only one being, one Jesus, all will awake and they are Jesus. Everything vanishes and Jesus only. No one can say that Jesus is Lord except by the Holy Spirit, by the holy wind. When the wind possesses you and you wake within yourself, only then do you really know you are the Lord Jesus Christ.

Now let us go into the Silence.

*   *   *

Now are there any questions, please? Plenty of time…well, if there aren't any, class dismissed. Good night.

THE CHRISTIAN MYSTERY EXPERIENCED

11/28/69

Those who experienced the Christian mystery are charged with the responsibility of telling others. The aim of their preaching is the awakening of faith in God. That is their purpose, for they have experienced God. But as Paul said, "How can men call upon him in whom they have not believed? And how can they *believe* in him of whom they have never heard? And how can they hear unless there is a preacher? And how can men preach unless they are sent? As it is written, 'How beautiful are the feet of those who preach good news!' But not all have heeded the gospel" (Rom.10:14,16). As Isaiah says, "Who, O Lord, has believed what we have heard? Who has believed what we have told them?" (Is.53:1). So faith comes from what is heard...and what is heard comes from the preaching of Christ.

Now Christ is the most misunderstood term in the world. When you hear the word Christ you think of a person outside of yourself, some being 2,000 years ago. That is not Christ. I speak of the cosmic Christ who became humanity. He is buried in every child born of woman. God became man that man may become God. So when we hear the words, "How can men call upon him in whom they have not believed?" Well, you say to the average person in the world, which may be almost 100 percent, "Tell me, do you believe in God?" Maybe many of them would say yes to that question. And you ask them who is God and they will paint all kinds of word pictures of something other than themselves. So how can man call upon one in whom he has not believed? If I tell you the only God in the universe is your own wonderful human *Imagination* and when you say "I am" that is God. He's encased in the limitation of your little garment. But that being when you say "I am" that's God. How can I call upon him in whom I have not believed? I don't believe that I am he...I don't believe in him. Well, how can I call upon him then? Then how can I actually believe in him of whom I have never heard? What preacher ever told you that your own wonderful human Imagination is God? They paint a word picture of a God outside of you and so you've never heard of the true God.

And when someone comes and tells you of the true God, to you that is blasphemy, because you can't believe for one moment that you are creating the conditions of your life. For God is the only causative power in the world and there is nothing but God. So everything in the world is caused by God. God is the only reality, the only causative power in the world. So how on earth can I actually believe in him of whom I have never heard? Well now, how can I hear of him unless there is a preacher and then how can there be a preacher unless he is sent?

You read in this morning's paper that Peter's throne is *not* his throne. That nonsense has been perpetuated for the last thousand years upon the gullible, the blind leaders of the blind. Here is man actually being told a thousand years ago this is the little throne upon which Peter sat. Now it's a holy thing encased in something to protect it from decay, and now science comes and proves by their own knowledge of time that it's only a thousand years old or 900 years old and here we are told that Peter lived 2,000 years ago. Now they have to take it out of its little cabinet and put it where it belongs. They should burn it! It was all nonsense to begin with, and it is still nonsense. And here, they perpetuate it. They'll take it out and keep it as some holy relic when it was never any more than a piece of thing upon which some self-appointed nut sat. They call him by the name and they gave him some holy name of a pope-this and a pope-that, and a holy this, or of some emperor. Here now the whole thing has been completely revealed after one thousand years of nonsense. What are we going to do when this whole thing is perpetuated and man does *not want* to hear the truth? He doesn't want to assume the responsibility that he himself is responsible for everything that happens to him. The only God in the world is your own wonderful human Imagination. That is God.

But you look out upon a world and you think if God is my Imagination, I had not a thing to do with the creation of the world. You don't know it yet. Because for a purpose not yet revealed to you by yourself, not by another God, God assumed the restriction and the limitation of his own creation. He became his created world so that he may expand beyond it, and expand a still greater world for even further expansion of himself. For God is an *ever-expanding illumination*. And he takes upon himself the limit of contraction called man, the limit of opacity called man that he may break the limit and expand. That's the glory of it all.

So anyone who has experienced it cannot conceal from anyone what he has experienced. He is under an obligation to tell it. As Jeremiah said in the 20th chapter, "If I say, 'I will not mention him, or speak any more in this name,' there is in my heart as it were a burning fire shut up in my bones, and I am weary with holding it in, and I cannot" (20:9). If tonight you paid me not to talk about it, well then, keep your money. I cannot stop talking about it. I must share my experience with others to encourage them to believe in God, but it is my responsibility to tell them who God *is*. Not to believe in God...for a billion people have different concepts of God...the little icons that someone...the little chair called Peter's chair. And when men take the characters of scripture and believe them to be characters of history, they are simply taking truth modified to the limitation of the weakness of the human soul. The characters of scripture are not characters of history; they are personifications of the aspects of the human mind, every one from Jesus down.

Jesus is a personification of the fulfillment of the plan that you yourself set up in the very beginning of time. You planned it before the world was. The world came into being, and you and I came down into our *own* creation. And Jesus is the fulfillment of our plan. So when we have fulfilled it and the whole story of Jesus unfolds within us, we've got to tell our brothers who are still sound asleep and wean them from this nonsense where year after year they are told of some external God to whom they must turn and pray...some external God to whom they must bow and pay homage to this being. And there is *no* external God. It is Christ *in you* that is the hope of glory. There is no other Christ. Christ is the plan of redemption and it is Christ in man. It is really a *pattern*, the pattern that was before that the world was, and that you and I actually agreed upon, and simply became what we created, knowing that there's a pattern that we in the depth of our own being would one day fulfill.

Now, "Unless you believe," said the pattern man, "that I am he, you die in your sins" (Jn.8:24). Put the little word "is" in this manner, "Unless you believe that I am (is) he, you die in your sins." And they did not believe that he was speaking of the Father. Well, the Father is the cause. The Father is the cause of you and without a Father you couldn't be. He was speaking of the Father and they did not understand that he was speaking of the Father when he said, "Unless you believe that I am is he." So I tell you when you say "I am" that is the Lord Jesus Christ, there is no other Jesus Christ.

Well, how do I know that he is Jesus Christ? Read his story as told in the gospel, just read it. He was born from above and he said, "I am from above and you are from below; where I am going you cannot come, not now" (Jn.8:23). And they said, "What is he going to do...is he going to kill himself, for he said that where I am going you cannot come?" No, he is returning to his own being, for he has fulfilled scripture. He's telling every being in the world, he's only returning to the source of it all, and he is the source. There is no other source. It isn't that you will not come, but you cannot come *now*. Not until here you have fulfilled what you and I agreed upon before that the world was, for you and I agreed to dream in concert and we will not break our pledge to each other. You and I came down from heaven; we are the ones who descended. We came down right into our own creation; and this is our creation, and we're playing the parts. Everything in the world you and I created.

Well, if I think of another God, I am sound asleep. So he who comes comes for one purpose, the one who is sent. By whom is he sent? He's sent by himself: "He who sees me sees him who sent me." Well, who is the one who sent you? The one you call God, but I call him Father. For I found him, and he and I are one. So now we're told the one who really broke through, his name is called Paul in scripture, and Paul spent his days from morning 'til evening expounding the kingdom of heaven and trying to convince all with whom he spoke about Jesus. He turned to the Old Testament, for there was no gospel, he turned to the Old Testament and from the law of Moses and the prophets he tried to convince them about Jesus. Some were convinced by what he said while others disbelieved. But he welcomed everyone who came, and teaching Jesus Christ, and some believed and some disbelieved. Well, that's all that I can do. Having experienced exactly what he is talking about, all that I can tell you is what I have experienced...that Jesus Christ is the only reality...it is God the Father.

Where is he? He is in you, in me. In what sense? Well, say "I am"... that's Jesus Christ... there is no other Jesus Christ. Well, how do I *know* that that is Jesus Christ? I'll tell you how you will know. You will know in this manner. The day will come when some peculiar vibration will possess you. It's called in scripture the wind: "The wind blows where it wills and you hear the sound of it, but you cannot tell whence it comes nor whither it goes; so it is with every one who is born of the Spirit" (Jn.3:8). Well, the wind will possess you. Your whole body will vibrate and you will awake. You will awake in the tomb where you buried yourself; because "No man took away my life, I laid it down myself. I have the power to lay I down, and the power to lift it up again" (Jn.10:18). And I laid it down within my own creation which is man: "For eternity exists and all things in eternity, independent of creation which was an act of mercy" (Blake, *Vis. of Last Judg.*). So man is

The Return of Glory

part of the eternal structure of the creation of the universe, and I laid myself down within man, part of the eternal structure of the universe.

Now, what is this act of mercy? I would like to change the word "creation" to "re-creation." It's a transcending of my *own* creation. I come down into my own creation and by re-creating it I transcend it, and awaken myself from this body of death. So one day you will actually awaken within your skull, and the symbolism of scripture concerning the birth of Jesus Christ will surround you. But it's all about *you*, not another; *you* are Jesus Christ coming out of Golgotha, your own skull. And the little babe wrapped in swaddling clothes is right there. Those who witness *your* birth are there, but they can't see you. Why? Because you're Spirit, you're God, for God is Spirit. They can't see you who are God-begotten. You are self-begotten and you come out. All the things told in scripture concerning Jesus Christ *you* are going to experience and then you will know who Jesus Christ is. It's a *pattern* buried *in* man which one day will unfold *in* man, and man is the entire story of the Bible. It's not about another, it's all about you. The Bible is your own personal spiritual biography. That's the story of Jesus Christ. So let them talk about all these holy relics and all these little things. Let them do it. Forgive them for they don't know what they're doing. They are the blind leaders of the blind.

Now, someone said to me, "Is that all that you talk about?" I said, yes, I talk about Christ, always Christ. "But isn't that limited? Doesn't that become monotonous? Isn't there some point where you exhaust it?" I said no, there is no end to the mystery, but no end to the mystery. I preach Christ always. I preach him crucified on humanity; not on some little piece of wood in the Near East 2,000 years ago. There was *never* any man who was crucified in *that* manner. Yes, we have insane men like our Hitlers, our Stalins, and these people who will do it man to man. In our own land we have had men who will take innocent fellows and string them up on a tree and think they're doing God's business. Yes, we have these *insane* people. But that's not the story of Christ. Christ became humanity that humanity may become God. And the one who came down and who became this was *God*. See, "No one ascends into heaven but he who first descended from heaven, the Son of man" (Jn.3:13). The Son of man descended from heaven? Yes. Buried in you is that one who is going to come out of you, and coming out of you then he is the son of man. He is the one who descended from heaven and he's the one who is God.

Listen to it carefully: "I am the root *and* the offspring of David, the bright morning star" (Rev.22:16). Yes, I am the root, I am the father of David; and yet I am the *offspring* of David. So the father of David and the offspring of David are one and the same being. So here comes the

951

grandfather and the grandson as one being, and as one being they are the father of David. David is the *symbol* of humanity, for humanity does the Father's will. Everything in this world is doing the Father's will. Say "I am," that's the Father. And whatever you are assuming that you are that you are going to do.

Now listen to these words in the Book of Samuel, "And the Lord said:—and he's speaking now to the boy Samuel, and the word Samuel in Hebrew means "his name is God." Sam-u-el, "his name is God." So here, the boy Samuel is saying...and now he's speaking because the Lord is speaking to him and these are the words, "Those who honor me I will honor and those who despise me they shall be lightly esteemed." Now you think of a being on the outside? No, your concept of yourself is either your honor or dishonor. You feel little when you meet someone, well then, you are dishonoring God. Have you ever met anyone in this world you thought more important than yourself? Oh, he's richer, he's bigger, he's stronger, and he's more handsome. He's everything that you think you are not. But did you feel little in his presence because he had more money, that he was wiser, that he was stronger, or that he was better dressed? Then you are not honoring God because God's name is I AM. And when you felt *less*-than you were not honoring God. So, he who honors me I will honor him and he who despises me then he shall be little esteemed. Read it in 1st Samuel, the 2nd chapter, and I think it's the 30th verse.

You read it carefully. It's the little boy Samuel who heard the voice coming *seemingly* from without. For he went to the old man, the prophet Eli, which means "my God," and he thought "my God" was another. He went to another and he said, "Go back and dream again, my boy." So he went back and he dreamed again...dreamed the same thing. Goes back to Eli: "Go back and dream again." He's still dreaming the same thing and when the dream is repeated it means that the Lord has spoken and it will shortly come to pass...and it did. He became the great prophet.

So here, the Samuel in us...I heard a voice say...the voice is speaking from within *me*. What did he say? "Those who honor me I will honor them, and those who despise me then they will be lightly esteemed." You talk to anyone and they say I do so-and-so and they're embarrassed of what they do? Well, if they are embarrassed because of the job that they have then they are despising the name of God which is I AM. So someone asks you in some social gathering, "What do you do?" and because they have a Ph.D. they are so proud that they have a Ph.D.; and you have to confess, well, maybe you're a busboy and you feel embarrassed. You say "I'm a busboy." They are so proud that they're a Ph.D. and so you feel little, then you're despising the name of God by feeling that way. Don't let anyone in this world make you feel little. Oh, they'll try it, but they'll only try it when *you* feel little. When you don't feel little, it doesn't matter what they are and who they are and where they are, when you don't feel little no matter what you have—you have not a nickel in your pocket but you don't feel little—you know who God is and God is *your* own wonderful human Imagination…that's God. Well, you can't be more than God!

All right, so you're God. So you walk the earth…not in an arrogant way…no, you aren't arrogant. But you don't let anyone put you down. See, I was born in a little island called Barbados. The island is just like a farm, a huge big farm. Everything is planted in order to produce a dollar. So we planted in sugar cane; and the products of sugar cane will be molasses, rum, and so on. So this is an interesting setup. From the time that I was a child we had no chemical fertilizers, none whatsoever; we only had the animal products to fertilize the fields and you and I know it is called manure. We gathered it all together, and then after about two years of gathering it, then we would simply scatter it to fertilize the fields. Do you know what we called it long before telephones were invented and radio and TVs? We called that broadcasting. Now is the time of broadcasting…which meant we took all the manure, the droppings of the animal and we broadcasted it. Well, isn't that appropriate today of the broadcasting? It's broadcasting. Long before there was such a thing as the telephone, we broadcasted. So, today you will drop your teeth, drop your hair, drop everything if you don't buy this product. Well, isn't that b.s.? Then from b.s. you go to M.S. and that's more of the same thing, then Ph.D.…it's piled high and deep. So that is the story.

Let no one in this world make you feel little. You are God. God is buried within you as your own wonderful human Imagination. That is God! There never was another God. Now you're invited to test it. Well, how do I test God? You're told in the 13th chapter of 2nd Corinthians, "Come prove him and see. Test me and see. Do you not realize that Jesus Christ is *in* you?" (13:5). Well now, that's quite a challenge. Well, if he's in me, how do I test him? You tell me he is my Imagination and I tell you Imagination creates reality, because Jesus Christ is the creator of the world and therefore he creates reality. Well now, let me imagine that I am what at the moment reason tells me that I'm not, and my senses tell me that I am not. Can I *believe* that I am what they deny? For, the purpose of this preaching is to awaken faith in God and God is your own wonderful human Imagination. So it's to awaken faith in *your* Imagination.

How on earth can I believe what at the moment everything is denying? Well, try it, just try it. Walk as though you *are* the man that you desire to be…asking no favors, asking no one anything. What would it *feel* like if it were true? For that *feeling* is brought into scripture: "Come close, my son, that I may *feel* you" (Gen.27:21). Come close that I may feel you, for I am blind and I cannot see what I am *assuming*. So the father said, "Come close, my son." His name was called Isaac. So Isaac said, "Come close" and Jacob came close. You find all through scripture the father is the blind one and the son is called, and as he is called he said, "Come that I may feel and touch you." So when Jacob was calling his grandsons he said, "I'm blind, I can't see." He called and Joseph placed his sons before him, and he crossed his hands and put one hand on the head of one boy, one hand on the head of the other and reversed it, and then he justified his act. When Isaac did it to Jacob, he did the same thing, "Come close that I may feel you."

Well, in this what would the feeling be like if it were true? How would I feel now if I were the man that I want to be? Just what would it feel like? Well now, feel *that* and believe in Jesus Christ. Well, who is Jesus Christ? Just what I did…he's my *Imagination*. When I say "I am" that's the Lord Jesus Christ. There is no other Lord; there is no other Jesus Christ. Well now, is that really true, are all things possible to him? Yes, *all* things are possible…but it takes *faith*. Listen to what I quoted earlier, "And it comes through faith, so hear it." You must hear it, and then hearing with acceptance comes through faith. "How can men call upon him in whom they have not believed?" The average person does not believe in himself. So when I wrote my book *Your Faith is Your Fortune* before I wrote the very first chapter I wrote one little line and I said, "Man's faith in God is measured by his confidence in himself." I can't tell you what criticism I've had because of that statement, but it's still there, I haven't taken it out. For, my *faith* in God *is* measured by my confidence in myself because the self of man *is* God. And so I put it there and it's still there.

So, how can I call upon one in whom I do not believe…because, the average man does not believe in himself. He has faith in everyone *but* himself. He says, oh, I'm working for a wonderful person. "You are, for whom?" "Mr. So-and-so. And you know what, today I had lunch in a certain restaurant and what do you think? I saw Mr. So-and-so dining." And you ask him quite simply, "Did he pick up your check?" "No." Then what on earth does it matter? So he dined there, and he paid for his dinner and you paid for yours and you're impressed because he came to the same restaurant? No, that is the man's mentality the world over. And so, how can I call upon one in whom I do not believe? I don't believe in myself, so how can I call upon him? And how can I believe in one of whom I have never heard? No one told you? No. And how can I hear unless there's a preacher, and how can there be a preacher unless he's sent? So the one who is sent is one who has *experienced* the mystery, and he doesn't ask favors of anyone in this world. What on earth should I ask the pope or the Cardinal of England or all these so-called leaders what to say? What on earth could they tell me after they've dethroned the little chair of Peter? They took out all the medals last year... you can't pray anymore to St. Christopher because he doesn't exist. He is no longer a saint, he doesn't exist, but he did for hundreds of years and brought in millions of dollars to the church.

So I tell you, you don't owe anything to anyone, because God himself became you. And as you're seated here and you say "I am"—even though tonight you can't pay rent and you haven't eaten well today—the being who owns the whole vast universe, who created it and sustains it is within you. When you say "I am" that is his name. So when you say call upon his name, his name is I AM. You call *with* the name by saying "I am..." and then you put a title on it "I am free, I am wealthy, I am healthy"... you put something on it, because the name is I AM and he is the creative power of the universe...and there is no other God. None! The story of Jesus Christ I personally, as I stand before you, I have experienced it in detail from beginning to end. So I know what I'm talking about; I am not theorizing. Christ *in us* is God's plan of salvation and God in us is I AM. So when you have the experience, who's having it, the other one? No, *I am* having it. So you experience the story of Jesus Christ in the first-person singular, present-tense experience. You don't see another being born; *you* are the one who first resurrects and then who is born. The whole thing unfolds itself within you.

I stand before you as a witness to it all. And I spend my last days like Paul testifying from morning to night. The phone rings, letters come, and I have to answer the letters, have to answer the phone. All that I'm talking about is testifying to the kingdom of God, and trying to convince every one who will listen to me about Jesus Christ. All that I use to persuade them is simply the Bible, the law of Moses and the prophets, and my own experience which is simply the interpretation of the law of Moses and the prophets. The *fulfillment* of the law and the prophets is Jesus Christ. He came only to fulfill scripture...that's all that he came to do. He comes *in us* to fulfill scripture.

So let no one make you feel little for one moment. You don't feel arrogant, no. I meet no one in this world that I do not respect. I can't meet anyone...he shines my shoes in the barber shop, I respect him. He will come on, he'll do all kinds of things, and he will sing and talk...to the annoyance of the boss-barber who thinks he should not be so intimate with the customer. But I'm talking to him all the time, enjoying his company, for he's shining my shoes, so what? That's God...I'm shining my own shoes in the being who's shining my shoes. I respect him. So he has a wife to go home to; he has to take money home to pay the rent, to buy the food and to buy clothing. But because he plays that part, it doesn't mean that he is less than.

Others come in because they're going to give him a quarter after he shines their shoes, and the boss-barber hopes you'll come back...so what! That's all the little business things. But we're all brothers. Behind all these masks we are brothers. I knew you before that the world was; and before that the world was we were one being and that one being is God. But we were made up of a brotherhood, infinite brothers. And in spite of the infinite number we all know each other individually, distinctly, in spite of the numbers. And we formed one being. We came down and became fragmented into our own creations. We're going back and going back to the one being that we really are. That one being is God the Father...and you are God the Father. One day you're going to know it.

Now let us go into the Silence.

* * *

Before we take the questions, we're closing two weeks from tonight on the 12th, Friday night, two weeks from tonight. We re-open on the 5th of January, Monday the 5th. I do not know whether I will send out notices or not, but make a note of it in the event I do not. I'll definitely take an ad in the paper, but you may not read the paper. I'm reopening on the 5th of January and I'm only closed for three weeks. So I'm closing two weeks from tonight which is the 12th.

Now are there any questions, please? No questions? The night is young...yes sir?

Q: I suppose by this method you can change arthritis or anything with this concept, can you?

A: Sir, I firmly believe that everything is possible to God and I do believe that your own wonderful human Imagination is God. To the degree that you can be self-persuaded that what you imagine is true to that degree it will become true. If man could only be self-persuaded. As we are told in the Book of Mark, the 23rd and 24th verses of the 11th chapter, "Whatever one says believing that it will come to pass, it will be done *for* him." Followed by the statement, "Therefore, whatever you ask in prayer, believe that you *have received* it, and you will." So all things are possible to God, but to what degree can I believe it? The only condition imposed upon man is his belief. I can imagine a state, but if reason denies it, my senses deny it, can I be self-persuaded in spite of their denial? Can I really believe in God?

That's what I tried to bring out tonight. How can man call upon him in whom they do not believe? Well, the one that you call upon is your own wonderful human Imagination. Man does not believe in him. You hear it said day after day, "It's only his imagination." And so we went to the moon and that was only once an imagined act. What is now proven was once "only" imagined. And so, we went to the moon and we came back, and yet it was all done in one's Imagination first. So, can one believe? As told us in that 10th chapter of the Book of Romans, "How can I call upon him in whom I do not believe? And how can I believe in him of whom I have not heard? Well now, that's quite obvious, because the average person is not told that the God of whom they speak is their Imagination. What priest or minister or rabbi in the world when they take their lecterns on their Sabbath ever tells the audience who God is? They paint a word picture of an external being to whom they must turn and then they point to the wall and show these God-awful pictures of a being, in violation of the 2nd Commandment, "Make no graven image unto me." And yet we turn and we see this bleeding heart and all these things all over the place...and that's called God. You're told, "It does not yet appear what we shall be, but we know that when he appears we shall be like him" (1Jn.3:2). Well, go into any of these churches and see if you look like these things. Usually they're all painted by the strangest artists...if they can call themselves artists. What monstrosities! No one resembles what they have painted to be the Lord. No, he's just like you! When you see him, he's just like you raised to the nth degree of beauty, but the nth degree. And I haven't seen any of these strange things on the walls of the churches that come near the beauty of the being that I am.

So everything is possible *if* you can persuade yourself that what you have imagined as a desirable state is true. So test yourselves and see, as you're told in Corinthians (2Cor.13:5). Test it. This is something that we are called upon to test.

Any other questions, please?

Q: Yes, Neville, what does it mean to be chained and imprisoned in your dream and yet in the end of the dream to have the truth slightly awaken in you?

A: Oh, that's a marvelous dream. Have you had that dream?

Q: Yes.

A: Well, my dear, we're all chained right now. I'm a slave of the body that I wear. I have to bathe it, shave it, clean it, feed it, dress it. After having fed it, I can't command anyone in the world to assimilate the food for me. I must assimilate it and what I can't assimilate, I must eliminate, and I can't compel anyone to eliminate it for me. Well, isn't that a slave? The chain is a symbol of slavery. You are enslaved by the body that you wear, but in the end you'll be free of it, and you'll wear your *immortal* body. The being who is within you is clothed in an immortal body. But for purposes of his own he took upon himself the form of a slave, and became subject unto death, for all these bodies die. There is something in you that *cannot* die. So the imagery is perfect, my dear, if you had that, perfectly marvelous.

Q: One time you mentioned about in a dream you had a vision of falling backward... something with Blake.

A: Yes.

Q: Well, what does it mean if you actually let yourself fall backwards?

A: Well, I can tell you, try it.

Q: I experienced it in dream.

A: And did you see what I saw?

Q: I believe you said to fall back into whatever you desire to be...

A: No, no. This night when Blake said to me, "Let yourself go, fall backwards" he emphasized *backwards*, and so like diving off a very high platform. Well, this was not just a high platform, this was diving off into infinity. I dived like a meteor falling through space, and I came hurtling through space backwards. And then all of a sudden it came to a stillness. When I looked up, here was a man, a single man in the distance, one man, his heart was aflame, just a fiery ruby. But as he approached he contained the whole of humanity—all the races, all the nations, everything you can think of—one man containing all. In the distance it was one man, this glorious being with a heart that was simply a ruby that flamed. And all of a sudden, I am approaching him or he's approaching me and the one man contains humanity.

So that's what Blake told me to see..."Let yourself go" and I did, took him at his word and hurled back, as I've done many a time as a boy...couldn't do it today...diving backwards, diving forward, diving all over the area where I was born. So the sensation of diving backward I'm familiar with that. But this time instead of diving into, say, twenty or thirty feet from a height, this is into eternity...just jumping off into eternity and hurtling through space. Then all of a sudden it comes to a stillness and here is a man approaching me when it came to a stillness. His heart was just one blaze like a ruby. It was simply this red, wonderful living being, all in here. As I approached him or he approached me he contained humanity, all the races, all the nations, all everything, one man containing all. He was telling me that one man fell, and *I* was that one man, for where did it take place but within me. As told us in the 82nd Psalm, "I say ye are gods, sons of he Most High, all of you; nevertheless, you will die like men and fall as one man, O ye princes" (82:1,6). So I was the one man falling and I saw the one man containing all. It was Blake who told me to fall and how to fall.

Man has no idea how great he is! That he who walks the earth though unable to buy a loaf of bread created the universe. And here he created the whole vast universe and sustains it. But he's going through experiences that *he* pre-determined for his own purpose. But let no one ever put you below them. In our mind's eye do not allow it. Grant them to be what they want to be, but let no one make you feel little, no one. I had that from the time that I was about this big. I recall I was in a show and the show was owned by the Shuberts. Well, they were the biggest thing on Broadway; they owned all the theaters, and they had so many millions and they were everything. This was a rehearsal and we were in Cleveland I think it was, when J. J. Shubert, one of the two boys sat in the audience, and he told me to get off the stage. Well, I didn't know him. I knew he was J. J. Shubert, but I didn't meet him personally. Told me to get off the stage and I wouldn't get off the stage. He said, "Get off the stage." I said, "I'm not leaving the stage until the director orders me off the stage. You are not the director." I knew exactly who he was and he had to turn to the director and said, "Tell that man to get off the stage." Then the director said, "Neville, get off the stage, please." I got off the stage. And Shubert went through the ceiling, because he thought everyone should get down and bow to him.

So when we opened on Broadway four weeks later, it was always his habit to send back Mr. Simmons who was his outside man to ask the entire cast to take a cut. He did it every time we opened the show. So he came on back and said, "Now, we do not know what the reporters are going to say by tomorrow morning's press, but Mr. Shubert feels he can carry the show if the whole cast will take a twenty percent cut." They came to me and I said, "I wouldn't take one cent cut. You can go back and tell it to Shubert." So all took a twenty percent cut and I got paid for the next seventeen weeks, it ran seventeen weeks, at my full price…they cut nothing. It was his habit and that's why he made millions. So, he couldn't make me feel little. Just let him have his millions. One thing, he didn't take it with him. They both died since. Tried his best to find some way to take it with him and he couldn't find it, so he left it.

No, you don't have to have it…you own the world…the 50th Psalm. If you don't believe it, read the 50th Psalm: "The world is mine and all within it. If I were hungry, I would not tell you; for the cattle on a thousand hills are mine…so were I hungry I would slay and eat" (50:10-12). You don't have to beg anyone in this world, just know who you are. "Those who honor me I will honor and those who despise me they will be little esteemed." Well, who is speaking? Your own wonderful I-am-ness is speaking. You feel that I am little because I scrub floors? Well then, you are ignoring the name of God…you despise God because you feel that you are little and that you're unwanted.

No, I never make anyone feel that way. I have a maid who comes home once a week and cleans for me, a colored maid, well, she's like my sister in the household. I don't treat her as something that is a maid. Doris to me is simply like my sister coming in, but she has to make a living and I need a house cleaning so she cleans it for me. When the boys were coming down, I said, "Doris, stop all that you are doing and come in here and watch it." She said, "But I've got to do this." I said, "Don't do anything. You come sit right here on this couch and watch these boys come down." So I had her sit there for fifteen or twenty minutes, and she and I sat on the couch together and watched the boys come down in the Pacific. For they left the moon, they were coming, splashing down. Well, Doris is like my sister. We're different pigments. She is dark and I am olive skinned, call it what you will. At least it's skin.

Any other questions, please? No? If not, let no Ph.D. get you down. Good night.

THE SEASON OF ADVENT

12/1/69

This is called the season of Advent, the coming of a great event or person… the coming of the Lord Jesus Christ. That's how the Christian world observes the season. Of course, Paul in his letter to the Galatians doesn't condemn it but he wonders if they really got the message when he said to them, "I notice you observe days and months and season and years! I am afraid I have labored over you in vain" (4:10). Nevertheless, it is not wrong in spite of that statement in Galatians that men do observe this season of the year. If they only understood it…this coming of the great event, this coming of the person called Jesus Christ.

Now tonight, I will tell you what I know from my own experience. My conviction is born of experience; it's not theory, I'm not speculating, not repeating what others said. I'm telling you what I know. Well, I have to use certain imagery in order to explain it, and ask you to follow me in your Imagination. For your wonderful human Imagination is simply a reproduction of the Divine Imagination, and, look upon all of us as brain cells in the mind of the dreamer. And just see us all going out—it's a purpose, a divine purpose—going out to infinity and curving back like a boomerang right into the very center of the Imagination of the Dreamer. But when we return we *are* the Dreamer, we *are* God the Father. We go out as sons and return as God the Father. The going out is not easy; it was never intended to be easy. It took all the horrors of the world to awaken us and to expand us to become God the Father. The day will come when the divine breath will breathe over you and you will awaken in the immortal tomb, and you will come out, and you will hold in your arms the infant Christ as a *symbol* of your return. The end of the horror is over and you are then God the Father, which you will discover in the not distant future, only a matter of 139 days later.

But you go out, as you and I have gone out, all of us have gone out. Now this is revealed in the most wonderful manner. This morning I was wondering, before I went to bed, just what I would say tomorrow? And this morning at 1:30 I am giving just a small little super for three friends. I took care of the funeral of two of them many years ago in New York City...close, dear wonderful friends of mine. The third may be gone, I haven't heard, but I did take care of the parents, father and mother. I took from a cauldron what we call in Barbados the yam. It's unlike the yam in America. We call the yam here a sweet potato, but the yam in Barbados is a root and it comes from two, three pounds up to twenty or thirty pounds, and it's snow white. The covering is dark brown, but when you cut it there's nothing whiter than the interior of the yam. And there it was in the cauldron and I took out a good big piece and placed it just ready to be served when in came a father and a mother jackal, or you could call it a big silver fox. They jumped right up where I was about to serve my guests, and the father in the most vicious manner tore out of the back of his son a huge hunk. There was a board... about that long...and the center of the board had been gouged out just enough to fit that back, so that when he put the hollow into it it would just fit. And believe it or not, here this animal began to nail his son upon that cross. The cross that extended was the wood, but he the son was simply the upright part. And then I woke.

This morning I went to the *Lost Language of Symbolism* by Bayley, and here they said that the jackal or the fox is "the path finder in the desert." He leaves the track perfectly leading to the gods. And the Egyptian god Osiris was represented as having the head of a jackal. Not only that, he was the one who brought three to the mountain. You read that and you wonder what is it all about? Well, here in the audience tonight there is a lady...two ladies. One gave me a letter this past week, that is, both gave me letters. One said, "Here is a dream which I do not understand. I was in a crowd, a very large crowd, and then I saw a woman and the crowd disappeared. Three men were around the woman; then they disappeared. She came over to me and asked me if I knew their names. I thought of faith, hope and charity...that's all I could think of. She said to me, 'You know the names.' And when she departed, I thought she really meant Peter, Paul and James, but all I could think of was faith, hope and charity."

She was right. But the word charity is translated today in the Revised Standard Version as love...and love is right, that I know from my own experience. So he brings three to the mountain top. What a wonderful vision for her. She saw the three and she knows their names. And then the woman

The Return of Glory

said to her, "You will soon remember the names." Well, she does, she knows the names, but the last one is love. Charity is a wonderful name as translated in the King James Version and maybe you're familiar with that. But it's perfectly all right; you knew the names even if you said one was charity. But it is faith, hope and love.

The Father took us, the brain cells of his own being, and we are nailed upon the cross. We go out to infinity in the most horrible nightmare. It takes that…and then, like a boomerang we curve around and return right back into the center of the dreamer of the dream, who is God the Father. But on our return *we* are God the Father. This is the great mystery that confronts us now in the mystery of Christmas, where God the Father is born. That's the story of Christmas. His name is Jesus and the word Jesus means "savior." In the 43rd and 45th chapters of the Book of Isaiah we are told, "I am the Lord your God, the Holy One of Israel, your Savior…and beside me there is no Savior" (43:3,11). So the Savior is the Lord God himself. So the word "Jesus" simply means "the Lord God, the Savior who is the Father." So if this happens, that is simply a vision of what must happen and will happen to every cell in his brain. Everyone will return into the very heart of the dreamer as the dreamer himself.

So you were nailed down and then sent out to infinity to experience all the horrors of the world, for it took that and takes that, and then you return to the being who conceived it all and played it all. This is the mystery of Christmas. So everyone eventually will know that he is the very being called Jesus in the scriptures. The word Christ is the Greek for Messiah, which simply means "the anointed to rule all the people of God." That's what the word means. So "Jesus" is the Lord God himself and "Christ" is simply "the anointed" who will rule all the people, who will save all the people from their sins and deliver them from their conquerors. Who was that in scripture? That was David. He delivered Israel from the Philistines, who conquered and brought down the giant and took his head. So Jesus Christ is really God the Father *and* his Son. But you when you return are God the Father, and his Son is our son…and that Son is David. You will see him standing before you and calling you Father. Then and *only* then will you really know who you are…that you are God the Father.

Well, it takes the horrors of the world to reveal this to you. It all comes back, and suddenly you awaken as God the Father. But in the beginning you were but a brain cell in the mind of the dreamer. The dreamer nailed you down upon the cross and this body is the cross. What I saw was simply a beautiful imagery of that which finds the path in the wilderness. But this is the cross on which you are nailed and you go out to play the part of man. You've played every horrible thing in the world, *every* horrible thing. Then comes the return and you return. When you return you come right back into the very center of the dreamer *as* the dreamer! Not a little one coming back as you went out, for you expanded in the going; and then you encompass it all. And you come back to encompass all and you are the dreamer himself. This is the mystery of Christmas…not some little being who was born in some strange way 2,000 years ago…and it is taking place every moment in time in the universe.

Another lady, who is present, in her letter that she gave me last Friday, said, "You were with me all through the night, and here you told me of the mystery of Imagination which I thought I knew. And then you said to me, 'I'll show you how it works.' At that point to my left appeared a man and then to my right appeared another man. The one on the right came in with a ledger and he had it opened, and he came over to the one on my left who you called "a brother." You introduced him to me as a brother. He came to the brother and said to the brother with the open ledger, 'My funds are exhausted.' The brother simply looked at him intensely for just a moment, and turned away and went on his way. Then you said to me, 'You see, it is just as easy as that. You simply do what is to be done and you simply go about your way doing other things. You drop it completely.' The one with the ledger, now with a face of, well, joy, ecstasy on his face, he is looking at the ledger and some miraculous thing has happened. It is not funds exhausted…undoubtedly he is seeing what he desired and wished he could see…the funds *are* there in the ledger when one second before they were not. And then my brother, the one I introduced to her as a brother, just simply looked and saw what was desired, and then went his way ignoring it all, just dropping it completely, in complete confidence in the reality of the invisible state.

Then I showed her how Imagination works. You don't labor over it; you really believe in the reality of unseen states. And so, looking at him and he desired money…he wanted his ledger to show a lovely balance, and my brother saw it perfectly. Now, I introduced him as a brother. In Paul's letter to the Galatians, he said in the first verse, "Paul an apostle of the Jesus Christ—not by men nor through man, but through the Lord Jesus Christ and God the Father who raised him from the dead"—then he goes on and quotes from whom the letter is coming and it's signed Paul but it's a corporate letter, for he said, "…and from the brethren who are with me." To him the brethren were those who enter into this union to live by faith, hope and love, the three. All the brethren, those who were awakened from the dream of life who had returned are brothers. And so I introduced a brother who will show my friend how easily this law of Imagination works. You don't labor, you are God! And now show it's an empty ledger, it's now in the red, and he looks intently, only a moment, and then ignores it and goes on his way. He sees what ought to be there instead of what seems to be there. He doesn't concern himself, he goes about his way. And he with amazement on his face is looking at this complete change in the ledger.

This is what I'm trying to convey to everyone who will listen. This you can prove. You can't prove the story of Christ until you've experienced it, but you can prove what I've told you about the ledger. If you will imagine that you are the man that you want to be, the woman that you want to be, and do nothing to make it so…just *imagine* that you are that, and just actually walk as though you were, convinced that you are, do you know that in the twinkle of an eye things will happen. Things will change in the outer world. And then the ledger will change and you will see that it's there. How? Let no one tell you that they know how. Your imagining created it…that created the change in the ledger. But it will come about in a very normal, natural way and when it happens in a natural way you may be inclined to credit the means employed rather than the imaginal act that did it. We always will say, "Oh, well, it would have happened anyway." No, it would *not* have happened anyway for imagining creates reality. Without the imaginal act it could not have changed, it could not have happened. But when it happens, it always employs a normal, natural means. It's not miraculous save to the individual who sees this radical change. But even he being normal in this world will then give all credit to the means employed rather than to the imaginal act that created the means and produced the end result.

So what we're seeing now is the birth of *that* in man, in the individual. Don't look upon some individual 2,000 years ago, for *everyone* is destined to play that part. He has gone out in the horrors of the world, and he's coming back right into the mind of the Dreamer, and when he arrives there he *is* the Dreamer. The Dreamer set up a path for his beloved sons to return. He created the path before he began the dream so that they would return. The return is told in the story of the gospels…beginning with resurrection. That's how the whole thing begins. Without the resurrection there is no birth, no expansion from above to encompass God the Father. And so, the breath divine breathes over the sleeper, that little cell in which you're nailed, and breathing over it you awake. Waking, you have a built-in innate wisdom and you know exactly where to push in this immortal tomb. For we're all in the same immortal tomb, as told us in the 87th Psalm, "And this one was born here and that one was born there, and that one was born here…" and he points out the different places, all within the same immortal tomb. So, you awake within the immortal tomb and you know intuitively where you should push from within that tomb [skull] and you come out to hold the infant Christ in your arms.

Then you can say, "Now let me depart in peace according to thy word." For you are the one who heard it, believed it, and simply continued the journey. May I tell you, no one will falter, no one will turn back. The most horrible being in the world will not turn back: he's only playing the part. He *has* to play it. Everyone will play it and in the end you will say, "Forgive them all, Father; for they know not what they do" (Luke23:34). They played it, I played it, and the memory slowly returns and the horror of the thing that I have done. So, forgive everyone for whatever he's doing or will do, because he is moving towards the End. And that end...he moves out to infinity and curves like a boomerang. Have you ever seen one thrown in space? It's an interesting thing. You can hardly believe it would ever come back. You can throw it with all your might and it goes beyond what you think you can even throw it, but it turns around and comes right back to where you're standing. You only reach and catch it. That's the boomerang.

And so, it all comes right back into the very mind of the dreamer. As he threw it out he cast us all out. I can see it now. Last night it was not a pleasant sight to see when this huge big father tore this hunk off the back of his son; and then as though he were human, having hands he took him and placed him on his back, and began to nail him upon this wood, leaving upright the son's body and hands extended to be nailed upon the extended cross. That was the jackal, the fox, the Osiris of the Egyptian, the pathfinder in the desert: the one who not only finds the path, he *is* the path; and the one who brings three to the mountain top.

So here, one lady saw the three. And we do bring the three and they are faith, hope and love, those are their names. It's not Peter, Paul and James; it's faith, hope and love. You knew it beautifully in your vision. And the other concerning how simply this law works, you saw it perfectly too. So don't strain to make it work, don't! It's all *faith*. You don't have to make any effort if you believe. If I go into the bank and I have a deposit equal to my check, I'm not concerned. I put my check in expecting that the bank will honor my check. It's a simple transaction. Well, do the same thing, treat it just as simply as that. But she saw it beautifully. There was a ledger and the funds were exhausted. That's the test. Can you treat that as simply as you would going into the bank when you know they're not exhausted and expect the teller to give you exactly what you're asking for, because the balance is there? Now, can you approach this thing in the same simple manner?

Well, you try it. Just try it. I have lived by it, really, all of my life...even to this day. Yes, I have funds, but you may have all the funds in the world and you can't reach them because they are tied up in investments and you can't reach them. Yet you need cash and you need it now, and you cannot liquidate the funds. It would take time and quite a bit of time beyond the time allotted to meet the current needs. All you do is simply apply the principle, and in a way that no one knows, may I tell you, it works!

So this is what we are about to celebrate on the 25th day of December. See, they begin it on what is called St. Andrew's Day…of course, this is all tradition. Andrew's Day is the first Sunday nearest the 30th day of November. Well, it so happens that November 30th was a Sunday, which was yesterday, the end of November. And that's called Andrew's birthday. He was the first to find the Lord Jesus Christ in the gospel story, and then he went and found his brother Peter and brought Peter. But the first disciple in the list of twelve is Andrew. He found him and then he went and found his brother Peter and then Peter came. So that is now the first or the beginning of the four Sunday's known as Advent, or the coming of the great event or person…the coming the Lord Jesus Christ. When he comes, he comes in you, and he awakens *in you* as you. You are the Lord Jesus Christ, but you will not know it until you come right back into the very center of the one who sent you out, and sent you into hell, for this world really is hell. Read the papers…read all the things that happen in the world. I need not repeat it you've read the papers today. What horrors that people do in the world and they do it not knowing, just not knowing. But it seems to take all the blows of the world to awaken and expand that little cell, that brain cell in the mind of the Dreamer. The Dreamer is God. And when you begin to expand, you go out to the very *limit* of infinity and then you curve back like the boomerang and return into the very center of the mind of the Dreamer. But this time, not as a brain cell; you come back as the Dreamer himself. You are God the Father.

He prepared the way for your return before that the world was, and he prepared it by setting up a Son, the anointed one. The anointed in the Bible as you read it I can't find where there is any other than David. "Arise, anoint him; for this is he" said he to the prophets. He called all the people before him, "No, I reject this one, I reject that one, I reject the other. Are there any others?" "Yes, there is one. His name is David and he's tending the sheep." "Go and call him; for we will not sit until he comes." David comes into the area and he said, "This is he; rise and anoint him. And from that day forward the Spirit of God came upon David mightily and never departed" (1Sam.16:12,13). Then comes all the Psalms: "This is my son, today I have begotten thee" (2:7) "I have found David; with my holy oil I have anointed him" (89:20). "I have found David and he has cried unto me, 'Thou art my Father, my God and the Rock of my salvation" (89:26). Where else are you going to find him? It is David.

So I am telling you what I *know* from experience. They have not spelled it out in scripture; they have implied it. Paul said, "It pleased God to reveal his Son in me" but he doesn't tell you who the Son is. The priesthoods of the world have actually changed the scripture to make it conform to their misconceptions of the story. Jesus is truly *the awakened God*. He is God the Father and as God the Father he has to have a Son. The Son is the sum total of the journeys of humanity personified as a single youth and that youth is David. So David stands before you and calls you Father...and that is the Christ, that is the anointed, the one who conquered. "For I have found in David a man after my own heart who did all my will" (Acts13:22). You were doing all the will of the Father, may I tell you. You've done it, you are doing it, and you will continue to do it. And it's all done, believe it or not, in love.

When you come back to the Dreamer just imagine it was all a dream, the whole vast world was a dream. This universe we study with such care is a dream and we are the dreamers of the dream, eternal dreamers dreaming non-eternal dreams. One day we will awaken from the dream to find that we have never really left our eternal home; we were never really born and never died save in our dream. But in the dream we have the illusion of a fabulous journey where Space interlocked with Time goes out to infinity and then returns into eternity. Then Time has come to its end, Time is finished, and the breath of the divine being is breathing upon you. As he breathes upon you, you awake within the immortal tomb, and then you come out. As you come out, the symbolism prepared before the world was awaits you and you take the infant child wrapped in swaddling clothes and hold him in your arms. This heavenly smile appears upon his face and then the whole thing dissolves. You have finished the journey.

Now you remain for just awhile and tell it to you brothers, for they're all coming back. You're going to tell it to all your brothers. There are those who are going out and those who are returning. Those who are here are those who are returning. No one is here who is going out; they're all returning or you would not be here. "For no man cometh unto me save my Father calls him (Jn.6:44)...and I and my Father are one" (Jn.10:30). Having returned to my Father *as* the Father then I am only drawing those who are returning to encourage them to continue for the little while that is left.

So the story of Christmas which is now about to take place in our world is not the anniversary of a little boy born 2,000 years ago. "For when the fullness of time came then he sent the Spirit of his Son into our hearts crying, "Father" (Gal.4:4, 6). Well, it takes the fullness...we had to go out to infinity before the Spirit of his Son could enter the heart and start calling us by name...calling us "Father." For, if he calls me Father, I am the one dreaming the entire dream. And so when the time has fully come then he sends the Spirit of his Son into the hearts of men and calls them Father. So the time has come for everyone here or you would not be here.

Now *when* that moment comes I cannot tell you. No one knows but the Father. There's a peculiar innate fear in man that he will never find the Father. He doesn't now what he is looking for. He thinks it's for wealth, for security, for this, that and the other. He really is looking for the Father…but "How long, vast and severe the anguish ere he finds and knows his Father were long to tell." But he will find the Father and he'll find the Father only through the Son. You will never know that you are the Father until the Son calls you Father. I could tell you from now 'til the ends of time, but I cannot convince you as you will be convinced when it is born of experience. It *must* be born of experience, for truth which has been experienced differs from any truth that you may repeat even though it is true, because it is only hearsay until you experience it. So I am telling you exactly what you're going to experience. You're going to experience that you are God the Father, and you will do it only through his Son David calling you Father. You will know it and strangely enough you'll know it more surely than you know anything in this world.

Now, there' a statement in the 4th chapter of Ecclesiastes…and remember that the New Testament is the fulfillment of the Old, not the other way around. The statement is this, "I saw all the living who move about under the sun, also the second youth who shall stand in his place; there was no end of all the people; he was over all of them. Yet those who come later will not rejoice in him. Surely this also is vanity and a striving after wind" (4:15). Now, Paul in his 15th chapter of 1st Corinthians speaks of the second, but instead of calling it a youth he calls it man: "The first man is of the earth, a man of dust; the second man is from heaven. As we have borne the image of the man of dust, we shall bear the image of the man of heaven." He calls the man of heaven the second man. I wish he had called him, in keeping with Ecclesiastes, the second youth. But, nevertheless, it doesn't really matter. It is the second being called "the new man" that when one reaches the limit, then he returns to the center out of which he came to find the whole thing when he awakes from it all was a dream. For I know that I awoke. The sensation of resurrection is one of waking. You actually wake and you wonder, "How long have I been here? Who put me here? How did I get here?"

Well, the Father put you there. You were nailed upon the rock. As Blake told you in his wonderful *Mental Traveller*: "And if the child is born a boy, he's given to a woman old. She nails him down upon a rock and catches his shrieks in cups of gold" (*Pick. MS*). Everything is that little boy that was nailed upon the rock. I saw it upon a board in the symbolism of the god of Egypt with the jackal face, and yet he had hands…he could nail him down. He had no compassion in tearing that back, a huge hunk right out of the back equal to the area that was gouged out on the board. So he placed him in and it fit it. And I gasped at the horror that I saw…the blood spattering. And here was only symbolism of how the whole thing is done. Just as I began to serve those who are dead and I am serving them a meal which I took from the cauldron, and just began to serve it when these two, the father and son in the guise of the animal. Are we not told in the 4th chapter of the Book of Daniel (:16) that he took from beings the heart of man and gave them the heart and the mind of an animal and they became animals.

Are we not animals in the world? Today's paper certainly would convince anyone that even though they are our boys, and they had all the opportunities to go to school and learn the things that we teach our children, the lovely things of life, and when they can coldbloodedly, regardless of excuses given, slaughter hundreds and hundreds, even though they might be guilty of being spies, children, men and women. It's not yet proven, but the evidence seems to be mountainous that we did it. So there are not only the Nazis who did it, or the Russians who did it, but we who always set ourselves up as an example, we did it. And if it could be done to say 500, it could be done with 5,000,000. You simply multiply the figure. But it's part of an unfolding horror, because the heart and mind of God was taken when the tree was felled, and then the heart and mind of an animal was substituted. Then *many* times rolled over until they learned who it was who did it all.

Do not ask now why? I can only tell you it happens this way. You're grateful that you finished it, that you've finished the course. That why you're here. But don't brag. The others will come back and they will be the same God the Father. When they come back they are brothers. I, too, or you will say or others who will come afterwards will say, "This is a brother." Then one will come in with his ledger and show you the funds are exhausted, and the brother, knowing the power that resides within him, will simply look intently at you, and then turn to do something else, completely forgetful of what he's just done, confident it must be done, for imagining creates reality. You in amazement look at the ledger to see what a second before was *not* there—it's now in the black and to a degree way beyond your expectancy… because one simply was a brother…and the brother is simply the awakened humanity. Members…and the only qualifications for membership are simply faith, hope and love. That's the only qualification to enter that world. Having been "born from above" in the sense that you awoke having gone through the journey to discover you really never left your immortal home. That, really, in the true sense of the word, you were never really born and you have never died save in your Imagination.

The Return of Glory

Now let us go into the Silence.

* * *

Now before we take the questions, let me tell you we are closing on the 12th. That's a week from Friday and then we re-open on the 5th of January. So we're only closed for three weeks. So I'm not sending out any notices. Try to remember the dates: I close on the 12th and re-open the 5th of January. Now are there any questions, please?

Q: In your book *Resurrection,* you mentioned the angels appeared to Abraham to announce the coming of the child.

A: Yes.

Q: Is there any definite period of time between the announcement and the actual experience so far as you know?

A: The Old Testament is the prophetic blueprint of the life of Jesus. It is an adumbration, a forecasting. Prophets always see everything foreshortened; they see as present what is future. So an adumbration is simply a foreshadowing in a not altogether conclusive or immediately evident way of that which must come to pass. So it's recorded. If you take it chronologically, it was a 2,000 year vision…but we mustn't take scripture that way. The three are mentioned. There are three, and strangely enough there are three witnesses just like my friend who saw the three. She knew it was simply faith, hope and charity…and correcting the word charity, it is love. He did not recognize them at first as being messengers of the Lord. In the next chapter, after they first appear he realizes one *is* the Lord. Not only a spokesman for the Lord, but the Lord himself. That's how the story is told.

So the interval between the three, the coming, I can say to this lady who saw them…well, she gave me the letter last Friday…I can't conceive that it's far away. And yet it's only now that she saw the three…and yet the lady said, "Yes, I'll be back and you will remember." She didn't say when she will be back, but that's only a vision, that's only, well, an image in the entire story. I will say to her it isn't far away. I don't think it's far away for any here, really. Many have seen the truth of what I've told you. Some departed this world, but they saw the truth before they departed; others have seen it while they're still here. Still others will see it. Right in this audience tonight there is a lady sitting here who's had the identical experience that I've had. She hasn't yet told me of the dove. She has told me of the birth and of David. Others have told me of the splitting. So I say, we're all upon it. God the Dreamer waits eagerly for the return of his sons. He's prepared a way for his sons to return. It is God the Father's purpose to give himself to his sons, so when they come back they *are* God the Father. That is the purpose of the entire story. We come back. We go out as sons, "Sons of the Most High, all of you; nevertheless you will die like men and fall as one man, O princes" (Ps.82:6). Oh, but when you return, having tasted death you'll return *as* God the Father.

This is the mystery that confronts us this coming 25th of December. The reason why Paul did not want days stated is because it could happen any day of the year, not just on the 25th of December. It could happen any moment of time. If we think only in terms of seasons…now we've separated the two events that really come the same night. We take Christmas on the 25th and then we take Easter as the first Sunday after the full moon in Aries. It's a movable date and it could go anywhere from late March to early April…all the way in. Because once the full moon is in the constellation of Aries takes place it could move thirty-odd days. It's a movable date. We cross the equator on the 21st of March, so anywhere from the 22nd on it could take place. But these two dates really come the same night. It begins with the resurrection and the same night is the birth. For, the divine breath breathes upon the sleeper, who is to all appearances dead. He's been nailed upon that cross and he's been sent out in his dream to dream the dream of life, which is the dream of death. He has to experience death. Then he awakens in the immortal tomb and he comes out confronted with that which was prepared before the world was to prove his return: the infant wrapped in swaddling clothes, which he now embraces. Now he has seen the salvation of Israel as promised by the prophets (Job 42:5).

So everyone is going to return. But these two events come the same night; they're not separated by months as we do it on earth…all the same night. But for reasons that the early fathers wanted, which are not explained, they separate them and call one the birth or Christmas, and one Easter or resurrection. But they are not! The ascension comes after, granted, for that is when you ascend like a serpent. They do take the ascension fifty days later, but it's *not* fifty days later, it's 123 days after the discovery of the Fatherhood of God. Resurrection and birth come the same night; discovery of the Fatherhood comes 139 days later; and then the ascension comes 123 days later; and then 998 days later comes the descent of the Holy Spirit in bodily form as a dove…completing 1,260 days. It's a *pattern*. He prepared the way for his banished sons to return, and when they return they are God the Father.

Well, the time is up. Thanks. Good night.

THE SECRET OF CAUSATION

12/5/69

When man solves the mystery of imagining he will have solved the secret of causation, that is, that imagining creates reality. So, "The secret of imagining is the greatest of all problems to the solution of which every man should aspire, for supreme power, supreme wisdom, supreme delight, lie in the solution of this great mystery" (D. Fawcett, *Zermatt Dialogues).*We speak of Jesus Christ; well, Jesus Christ is your own human Imagination. When you solve the great mystery of imagining, you have found him and then you will know who Jesus Christ is and who is the *cause* of all the phenomena of the world. Jesus Christ and the one spoken of in the Old Testament as Jehovah are one and the same being: that is your own wonderful human Imagination. Divine Imagination reproduced itself in the *human* Imagination, and because Divine Imagination contains *all* within itself and having reproduced itself in our Imaginations, well then, *we* contain within ourselves *all*. All things exist within the human Imagination. So when you solve the problem of imagining, you have found the secret of causation and you have found Jesus Christ.

Now let me share with you two experiences that came to me this past week. Here is the first one, the lady wrote me dated December the 1st…that's the date of her letter. She said, "I returned from a wonderful cruise through the Caribbean and the Mediterranean, returned to New York City. I checked my baggage at La Guardia Airport for Chicago where I expected to spend a few days with some friends. When I arrived in Chicago, one of my bags was missing. It really was my most valuable bag. Not only did it have most of my clothes, but it had all of my presents that I bought for my friends and my relatives, all my family. Plus the fact, in it I had left the most precious of all things, I left a wedding band and an engagement diamond that my husband gave me...he's now gone from this world. I had them made into a locket. So I reported the loss when I got to Chicago and it wasn't there. They said they would call me when they found it. Well, I arrived in California and there was no trace of the bag. A week later I got a letter from the airport saying that they were sorry but there was no trace of the bag. My first reaction was to curse them for their treatment of baggage, but I remembered the teaching, that which you teach us, that imagining creates reality. So I tried to reconstruct the letter that I received from them and revise it, but it didn't seem natural. I tried it over and over, but it didn't seem natural to me.

"So then, I tried to make it a natural scene. For if imagining creates reality, then what scene could I really construct that would be natural to me that I could feel in order to recover my bag? Well, I imagined that I had it. If I had it, what would I do? Well, I would put it on the bed. I would open the bag and I would put away all of my clothes and the gifts that I bought for my family and my friends. All these things I would do. So in my Imagination I took my bag, placed it on my bed, and I opened the bag and put all my clothes away plus the presents. I did it every night and sometimes during the day. If I thought of it I did it again. But every night I did it, not allowing for one moment any doubt to enter my mind that I was not doing that which causes reality. I firmly believe that imagining creates reality. Believing it as I did, I did it. And when my little grandchildren asked me, "Where are the presents?"—I always brought them presents; when my husband and I travelled together we never came back empty handed, we always brought presents, and so they asked for the presents—I said, 'Well, it takes a long time for baggage to come by freight.' I never allowed them to know for one moment that it was considered lost. I never told anyone." I assure you she didn't tell me. And under the circumstances, she would have called me and asked for help as she has on other occasions for different problems, but this time I knew nothing of it. So I'm not part of it at all. It's all what *she* did.

Then on the 26th of November...that is only a little while ago...she received a letter form the airport saying, "If you don't not pick up your bag within five days, you'll be charged storage." So she called her friend and asked if she was free to go and get the bag. The friend said yes, so the friend went over with her and she got the bag. The friend said to her, "Why did it take so long? It's been six weeks since you've been back." You see, she did not tell her friend that she had lost the bag. She told no one, didn't tell her daughter, her grand-children or the speaker. She kept it all to herself, because in her mind's eye it was *not* lost...delayed but not lost. In her letter she said, "I do believe that love's labor is never lost. Everything in it was loved. I bought every present with love. I intended to give it to those that I bought it for with love. There were no strings attached to it, it was all done in love. I knew that if this principle is true, and I firmly believe it, it would have to prove itself in the testing." And so, she has her bag, all the things in it, everything in it.

Well, I can't thank her enough for sharing that news with me so that I in turn may share it with you that everything in this world is created by your own wonderful human Imagination. *That* is God! There is no other God. You can use it wisely or stupidly. Most of us use it stupidly, use it foolishly, and we create havoc in the world. But it's the same power. There's only one power...there's only one God. That one God you and I call Jesus Christ. In the Old Testament, we speak of that same power as Jehovah the Lord; but there is only one power, there is no other power. And you can use it as the most frightful power in the world or the most heavenly power. So in her case, her first impulse was to curse the station that so stupidly mislaid or lost her bag. Then she remembered what she heard here and figured, no, I can't do that, I must actually apply it. Well, she tried revision of the letter which said they could not find it and they were sorry about it. At first she couldn't make it natural to revise that letter, so she struck upon something that would seem natural: if I had the bag, what would I do? Well, I'd take the bag and put it on the bed and open the bag, take my clothes out, put the clothes away, take the presents out and put them away until the moment when I would give them to those for whom I bought them. And this she did every night. It took six weeks to get a revised statement. Instead of a new letter here is a threat that if you don't pick up the bag in five days, you'll be charged storage. Then she goes and gets the bag.

That's what I mean by imagining creating reality. That is real faith. An assumption is faith and without faith it is impossible to please him. Please who? God! But who is God? Your own wonderful human Imagination that's God and there is no other God. Divine imagining reproduced itself in human imagining, therefore, divine Imagination containing all, the human Imagination contains all.

Now I'm going to show you what I mean by containing all. The whole vast world is yourself pushed out, everything in the world is yourself pushed out, but man doesn't know it and so he mistreats *himself*. He tries to murder himself as you see in today's paper with this strange horrible little thing that is taking place in our midst. But do not let yourself be intimidated by the horror of the world, don't. Leave it alone. It *is* a horrible thing, but that is simply a *misuse* of the power. One stumbled upon a power without awakening...and if you don't awake, Lord, what horror you can wreak in this world.

Now here is another lady. She's here tonight, too, both are here. Her letter is dated December the 2nd, only a few days ago, she said, "I found myself in my neighbor's living room and in her living room all are dressed as Mennonites." You know what the Mennonites look like…you've all seen pictures of them. They came to this country in the 17th Century and they've been here over 300 years. They originated in Zurich, Switzerland in the year 1525, and then they moved into Germany, into France, into parts of the north, and then into Belgium and Holland. Finally in the middle of the 17th Century they came here. They are supposed to number around 150,000 to 200,000 today. You've heard of the Amish…that's a branch of them. Like all these groups they splinter and they become other groups. Just as Catholicism split into the east and the west, and then the western splintered into all the Protestant world and they splintered…they all splinter. So the Mennonites splintered…but they dress today as they dressed when they came here 300 years ago; there's no change in their outward appearance. All the men dress in the same manner, all the women in the same manner, and the children in the same manner. Here is a *fixed* idea. So she saw all the people in the household in a fixed, fixed state over a period of 300 years…no change in one's attitude towards life. It perpetuates itself year after year.

Now this is the scene. It appears that the woman in the living room that the Mennonites, all brothers, had killed her second husband. It appears that she had been mistreated by her second husband, and so because they all belonged to each other, and he belonged to them, they killed him. That is the beginning of the dream—they killed him because she was mistreated by him. Now she comes upon the scene and she tries to explain to them that that was all wrong. But as far as they're concerned that is right, that was the thing to do. He belonged to us, he mistreated her, and so we killed him. No matter what argument she used it could not persuade them in any way that they had done wrong. Well, that's part of scripture and you'll find that in the 16th chapter of the Book of Proverbs, and there you will read these words, "All the ways of man are pure in his own eyes, but God weighs the heart" (16:2). In the eyes of a man what he does is pure, is right, he should do just what he did, but God weighs the heart. You go on to the next verse, "And God made everything for its purpose, even the wicked for the day of trouble." So here, you find the whole thing was perfect. They thought themselves pure and good in the doing…an eye for an eye and a tooth for a tooth.

Then she said, "At this moment a car drove up, a huge big limousine and a group of men came out, all dressed in black and carrying machine guns." They all came into the place and they were standing then on the veranda. She ran into the house and pleaded with this woman to come, but she didn't. She came quietly and reluctantly quite slowly into the house, but not before the men entered. One man held a gun to her, he was going to kill her, and the others ran all through the house. So, looking at this scene, the man with the gun right next to this neighbor of hers, this Mennonite, she said, "Suddenly I woke, but I woke in the dream. I didn't wake here, I woke in the dream and I realized that the whole thing is taking place within me." As Blake said, "All that you behold, though it *appears* without, it is within, in your own wonderful human Imagination, of which this world of mortality is but a shadow."

So, "I awoke and here I know the whole thing is taking place within me…but now they seem more real than ever. I am looking at them. Then I felt within me a certain activity which I stopped. As I stopped it, he froze. I looked at her, I stopped the activity which allowed me to see her as something apart and alive outside of me, and she froze. Then I went into the kitchen and I froze them all by stopping in *me* an activity which allowed them to appear to be alive independent of my perception of them…and they all froze. Then I came back into the living room and there they are frozen… two of them are frozen. And I turned to him and I said, 'You don't want to kill her, you love her, and she loves you.' At that, the man simply put down the gun that he held in his hand at the woman, and then with open arms he moved towards her to embrace her in great affection. At that moment, as I was about to go into the kitchen to do the same thing, my alarm went off and I woke to *this* dream." That was a dream and then she woke to this dream.

May I tell you, this is just as much a dream as *that* was a dream. But man is not awake. Man is sound asleep in this world and he doesn't know what he is doing. So he can perform the most horrible things in the world and he is innocent in his dream. When you wake in the morning and you tell of a dream, the most horrible dream that you've ever had, no one is going to sentence you for it. They'll try to analyze it for you and they all make such horrible mistakes in their analysis. They haven't the slightest concept of what a dream is all about. I mean our psychiatrists and all the so-called experts on dreams are past masters of misinterpretation. They don't realize the great mystery that is surrounding us in this world. The whole vast world is the *individual* dreamer pushed out and the conflict is within himself and not on the outside at all.

So here, she saw this whole thing taking place on the outside and seemingly independent of her perception of it. Then she realized as she became awake that she woke in the dream. But she felt within herself an energy, an activity that was animating and making real all that she perceived, and she arrested it. As she arrested that activity, the thing seen froze like a statue. She arrested one here and it froze. She goes into the kitchen, arrests the activity and they freeze. She comes back and before she releases it, now she changed their attitude, she changed their intention. Having changed with love, when she released them they were bewildered because there had been a radical change in them, and they knew nothing about it. It all took place within her. That is taught in scripture as *repentance*. Repentance is not confessing some sin in this world as the churches teach it...hasn't a thing to do with remorse. Repentance is "metanoia," a *radical* change of mind. When something radically changes in me, all of my intentions change, all of my attitudes toward life change. So she changed it.

That's told us at the trial in scripture: "You have no power over me were it not given to you from above" (Jn.10:18). What is taking place here is a drama that has been set in motion based upon attitudes from above. She was functioning from above. She tasted of the power of the age to come. That is told us in the 10th chapter of Luke, they sent seventy into the world, seventy more disciples, and they came back, and they were simply thrilled beyond measure. They said, "Lord, even the very demons were subject unto us through thy name!" (10:17-20). He said to them, "I saw Satan fall from heaven; nevertheless, rejoice not that the very spirits were subject unto you, but rejoice that *your* names are written in *heaven*." I will tell her, rejoice not that these things happened—you have a power, you tasted of the power—but rejoice because your name is written in heaven; that's infinitely greater than to demonstrate a power in this world. For, you can demonstrate it in the most horrible way in the world...but you had to demonstrate it in love.

Now, seventy doesn't mean seventy individuals were to be sent out. Seventy is the numerical value of the Hebrew letter Ion; the symbolic value is an eye. You are an incurrent eyewitness. I gave my eyes to Sharon and she shared them with you. You will share them with others, and they will keep on sharing with the incurrent eyewitnesses. It doesn't matter what number... seventy is only a *symbolic* number, the numerical value of the letter Ion, which symbolically is an eye. And the eye is the incurrent eye, the eye that sees inward into the world of thought, into eternity. Not an outside eye, no mortal eye could see it, and you have the incurrent eye. Now I tell you, rejoice not because the spirits were subject unto you, but rejoice because your name is written in heaven. And that is a true story. You will see one day when you're called into that assemblage that there is such a ledger and there is such a record of the name being written in heaven.

All this so-called imagery seems so stupid to the intelligent mind of the world, but they don't know how sound asleep they are. They haven't the slightest concept how sound, sound asleep they are. They'll try this boy who is now on trial for this murderous thing. He fell into a power of which he is totally unaware. They all became his slaves so said the papers. They didn't know what they were doing, simple people, many of them cultured, one boy three years in college, and all became slaves of one who fell into a power of which he's totally unaware. This power exercised without love is horror. But *she* exercised it in love. She said, "You don't want to kill her, you love her... and she loves you." Then having released him with a bewildered expression on his face she turned to her and said, "You love him and he loves you." Then he takes the gun in his hand and puts it down, and with out stretched arms goes to embrace her and she to receive the embrace in love. Then before she can reach the kitchen to release them from some violent state she's awakened to this dream. This is still a dream. This world pushed out is the world of the dreamer and you are the dreamer and the dreamer in you is God. God is your own wonderful human Imagination. That is God...there is no other God. The whole vast world is yourself pushed out.

So you can take it on either level. Take it on the level of my friend who came back from this heavenly cruise to find that one lovely piece is missing. Well, if imagining does create reality, then I will simply not accept the fact. That is the fact, well, why must I accept the fact? Are we not taught in scripture that whoever believes that what he says will come to pass, it will be done for him? All right, so she takes in her Imagination the so-called lost suitcase, puts it on her bed, opens the suitcase, then takes out every piece and hangs it up. Then takes all the presents that she bought for her family and her friends and puts them all away for the appropriate moment when she will give them to those for whom she bought them. She did it every night for almost, say, five weeks. She started doing it after she came back and sometimes during the day when she thought of it she did it again. She never shared that with anyone because to her it was not gone, and therefore she could not concede that it was lost. It wasn't lost, just delayed. She did it every night before she retired and sometimes through the day. Then she receives a letter, "If you don't pick it up within five days, you're going to be charged for storage."

I think that's thrilling! I can't thank her enough for sharing it with me that I in turn may share it with you to encourage you to simply control your own wonderful human Imagination. For if I would steer a decent course towards a certain port, a certain goal in life, I must ever be aware of my imaginal activity, or at least I must be aware of the *end* that I am shaping. I may have other activities, but the end I am shaping I must not allow doubt to enter for one moment. If I know what I want, then I must shape *that* morning, noon and night...and then no power in the world can stop it. They can't stop it, because I am the dreamer of my dream and I am pushing myself out into the world, shaping my world based upon my own imaginal activity. For the Jesus of scripture is your Imagination, the Jehovah of scripture is your own wonderful Imagination, and the Jesus and Jehovah are one and the same being. The same root...Yod He Vau begins both words. And Shin Ion simply means "salvation." And the word Jehovah means "Jehovah is salvation or Jehovah saves." That's what the word Jesus means. It's Jehosua in Hebrew; we call it Joshua. Well, Joshua and Jesus are the same thing.

So, Jehovah saves. Well, who is Jehovah? His name is I AM as revealed in the 3rd chapter of Exodus. I AM? Yes! You mean I am not John, Mary, Neville? No, just I AM...stop right there. Then you go back in the very first book, in the Book of Genesis, and go to the 4th chapter, the 26th verse, and the one who took the place of the first one killed, for the second one was killed...and she said the second husband was killed. Now, Abel was the second and then Seth took his place...for she bore another son to take the place of the one who was killed. Then Seth had a child and Seth called his name Enis, and then this lovely little statement, "And from that day on, men began to call upon the name of God." Literally the word "call upon" means "call with." I don't say, "In the name of Jesus or in the name of God or in the name of Jehovah." That's nonsense. All the priesthoods of the world do that: "In the name of Jesus Christ, so and so" and no one feels anything. When you call upon the name you call *with* the name and the name is I AM. Well, who is unpacking the grip? I am—that's calling with the name of God. Who's putting the clothes away? I am—that's calling with the name of God. Who's putting all the presents away? I am—that's calling with the name of God. Who's arresting the activity within them and silencing the being who stands before them? I am—that's calling with the name of God. Who is saying, "You love her and she loves you?" Well, I am—that's calling with the name of God. And from the very moment men began to call upon the name, you can change that "upon" to "with," for that's the true and literal meaning of that Hebraic phrase, calling *with* the name of God.

If you really believe it, you can prove it in the testing as these two ladies here tonight have proved it. One, on the first of December she wrote it; the other on the second of December. I can't tell you my thrill, my two dears, that you heard it to the point of *application*. That one who is the incurrent eyewitness took it into the deep...for you have my eyes now and you are seeing into eternity...for you have the incurrent eyewitness as yours. And the other hasn't yet received the eyes, she will, but she knows it and believes it and she proves it on *this* level of the dream. From this level she brings a bag back and all the contents in place.

The other one goes into the deeper level of her being to discover there is nothing on the outside but herself and that, these Mennonites are only what…expressions of fixations, for they haven't changed their outer dress in 300 years. In this land alone they haven't changed it. You see pictures of them and you wonder, "Is this back in 1969?" Yet they make lovely things, the Amish. They have one of the most wonderful refrigerators that man could buy. It runs almost a thousand dollars, and some models run higher than that, but it's a beautiful thing. So they're not against making money. They won't charge, so they claim, any interest on a loan, for that's against their ethical code. But they'll buy land and have it increase in value, and they can't see that that increase is also is interest on investment. How we kid ourselves…morning, noon and night we do it. You'll buy stock and the stock grows. You loan a dollar and will not accept six percent interest on a loan, they just want the loan back. That satisfies their conscience. But they have not a thing against going out and buying what they think is a good deal and holding it until it rises in value…that's something entirely different.

See, man has a peculiar innate something that justifies everything that he does so that all the ways of man are pure in his own eyes. So there they go across the world, maybe today 200,000 of them. For what I quoted tonight is taken from the *Encyclopedia Britannica*, which I bought for my daughter maybe fifteen years ago. Maybe the new edition will give them a larger number in our land today, because they certainly are increasing. But they still dress today as they dressed 300 years ago.

So I tell you, man's Imagination manifests itself in the Imaginations of men. The whole vast world is playing their part because you are doing what you are doing. And who knows who is treading in the winepress tonight who is causing the subtle change in the minds of men? Someone who feels himself wrongfully accused and is sitting in some jail, and there he goes over it in his mind's eye and is getting even with society. He's treading out the winepress. If he lifts that to the point of vision…as Blake said, "All that man need do in this world is to raise Imagination to the point of vision and it is done." If you ever lift it to the point of vision where you become awake… vision is simply becoming awake in the dream. This is vision because we are awake in this dream. When you dream at night, you seem to be the victim of vision, a slave of vision. Then you wake and you can choose whether you're going to look at this picture or that picture, and you become now discriminating. So you are awake in the dream here and that is vision. So she awoke in her dream and that was then vision. Then realizing it started as a dream, therefore it still must be a dream, so these things are simply myself made visible, I will now change them. You don't want to kill him…she doesn't want to be hurt…you don't want to kill her…she loves you and you love her. And then he takes the gun and puts it down and with outstretched arms goes to embrace her. A radical change within him and produced by one that he was totally unaware of who was the cause of the radical change in him.

Well, who knows who is actually producing the changes in the minds of men—to go to war or to have peace, to have this or to have the other? Someone…it could be some woman treading in the winepress, or as Yeats said, "It could be simply in the mind of some shepherd boy lighting up his eyes for a moment before it ran upon its way"; and that little boy dreaming of heroism, dreaming of noble battle where he is the hero, and he causes the blood to flow. Who knows? If you know who you are and how the whole thing operates, well then, you will start as of now to control your imaginal activity. For if you don't, it will be controlled for you by another and you will become a slave, the victim of the other even though the other is some woman treading in the winepress, living in a dungeon and going wild in her own strange Imagination. But if she ever takes it to the point that the imaginal act becomes vision, it's done, may I tell you.

But any time you exercise your Imagination lovingly on behalf of another, you've done the right thing. No doubts whatsoever if it's ever done in love. But there's always a question mark if it is not done in love. For I tell you that I know from experience that God is love. This is not the result of some philosophic reasoning; this is the result of God's self-revelation. When God unveils himself within you he is infinite love. Yes, he's infinite power as described in scripture: "Christ is the power of God and the wisdom of God" (1Cor.1:24), no question about it. But power without love could raise the most horrible ___(??).

So I say to everyone believe me the Jesus of scripture, the Jehovah of scripture, is your own wonderful human Imagination…there is no other God. And I tell you from my own experience that God is love and you will know it one day from your own experience that God is love. But in the meanwhile, believe me as the lady believed me that imagining creates reality. When I told her that, as I've told you time and time again, she believed me. So a natural human impulse is to curse the airport for their stupid handling of bags. Then she remembered the teaching and began, "No, I won't curse them. I will get my bag back; it's delayed but not lost. And so I'll perform in my Imagination exactly what I would do here in the flesh if I had it." And so she does it and the bag comes back with all the things within it.

Now, that lady was not here when I opened in September to tell a similar story of my own, because she left this city for her cruise before I opened in September when I told a similar story. So she did not hear that story. Not having shared her story with others, she knew nothing of what I did to get my bag back when it was lost. So she was not in any way influenced by my own story of getting my bag back which was lost when I came down from San Francisco. How I simply took it in my hand and held it, and then I got a notice from San Francisco an air mail letter and it said, "Your bag is in box so-and-so. Sorry" and signed "The Phantom." So I went over and I got my bag. I called up the airport, told them what I'd received in the letter, and they said, "We'll investigate." There was no such box in L.A. They called San Francisco where the letter originated, they investigated, and it was there. They opened it up and the whole thing was a mess, but not one thing was missing. Whoever took it hoped to find something that they did not find…but the whole thing was a mess. So I went over when it came down to L.A. and got my bag. Everything was in it, everything in tact, save it was all a mess.

Now, I told that story when I opened in the middle of September, but she was not here. She was already on her way to New York City to take this cruise, a month at sea through the Mediterranean and the Caribbean and return to New York City. Not having mentioned it to her daughter or her grandchildren or her friend or to me, she simply applied the principle. So she was not influenced by what I had done under a similar circumstance. I can't thank her enough for sharing it with me that I in turn may share it with you. And thank my other friend for this wonderful depth, taking with you the eyes that I gave to you via Sharon, that you may taste of the power that is to be, for that is the power. This whole vast world is a play and all these are the costumes, and you are the actor, you're writing the play and you change it as you go…as you did in your vision. Here, you set that in motion and now you're going to prove to yourself that you can take the most fixed idea in the world. Well, you try to think in terms of a more fixed idea than the Mennonites when after 300 years they're still dressing as the did 300 years ago, when men's fashion today is changing almost every six months and ladies' change every month. They change and change and change. And here are people who haven't changed in 300 years that *we* know of. They really haven't changed in 500 years, for they started way back in 1525.

So believe me, imagining really *does* create reality, believe it sincerely. If you say you believe in Jesus, well then, you'll know him to the extent you know the mystery of imagining. You will never know Jesus unless you know the secret of imagining, for *man's* Imagination is Jesus Christ. There is no other Jesus Christ. Man's Imagination is God and there is no other God. So if you really believe in God, believe in your own Imagination. Believe that Jesus Christ is the power of God and the wisdom of God. So when you do what the lady did to bring the grip back, what wisdom is in that! To influence the entire outer world to produce that so-called lost bag and bring it back.

So I tell you, there is no other power. There's only one power in the universe and that power we call by the name of God, we call by he name of Jesus. But if you think of Jesus as someone on the outside who lived 2,000 years ago, you'll never know him that way. You think of God as some impersonal force, you'll never know him that way. He's a person because you are a person. You are a person...well, your Imagination is God...God is a person. God became as we are that we may be as God is.

So you take it to heart and apply it from now on. The man that you would like to be you *can* be. But don't start dreaming about it, do something about it. And you don't do something about it by trying to meet the so-called right people. Leave the so-called right people, they're all dead. The whole vast world is yourself pushed out and they're dead. They're only *reflecting* the activity taking place within you; change the activity and you change the behavior of those who surround you. So if it needs the so-called aid of those, it's only because a change took place within you. As you change it within you, you change it within the seeming others which is nothing more than yourself made visible, all pushed out. Just as she saw so beautifully when the man is about to kill the woman, "You don't want to kill her, you love her and she loves you." Then she releases the activity having given the order that is a command...she turns to the woman, "You love him and he loves you." Then she releases in her an activity which allowed her to seem real and alive independent of herself, and then they embraced each other. Then she returns to *this* dream.

The day will come you will awake in this dream and you will see just what she saw in another aspect of the dream, that the whole vast world is as dead as dead can be and it's only reflecting the activity of your own wonderful human Imagination. Then you will awake from it all and depart from the world, and leave it just as it is for others to play upon it. And we return to the being that we really are...the Creator of it all.

Now let us go into the Silence.

* * *

Are there any questions, please?

Q: Last week in the lecture you mentioned the war with the Philistines, what is the meaning of the Philistines?

A: The Philistines? Well, the Philistine is simply the whole vast world pushed out...man is just in conflict with himself, but he doesn't know it and he thinks its another. David brought down the great giant. What giant? Whatever is your problem in the world and you bring it down by applying this principle. We speak of all these races and nations in the Bible, but they aren't really. They're simply the whole vast world pushed out. Out of what?—out of the mind of the Dreamer. The Dreamer is God and *you* dream...that's God. There's not a thing in this world but you. You are the only being in the world, pushed out.

But may I tell you from my own experience, do it in love, because really in the depth of your own being you are love. If you don't know it, you can do the darndest things in the world. Let us not judge this little boy who is now up for trial or will be. The chances are he didn't do the murder of all that they will find out, and they may find many bodies that have not yet been revealed. So far we know of seven. He could have been just simply the controlling mind and others were the slaves who performed the acts. If he didn't actually perform the act, we have no law that I know of that could accuse him, because we do not believe that such things exist. So how can you try a man for something that the courts will not accept as fact?

We have what is known in law as approximate cause. I'm driving down the highway and I think I'm about to meet with an accident...I think. And so this man is coming close and it forces me off and I in turn hit the one in front of me. Well, the actual fact is my car struck his car therefore I am the guilty party, but the one who caused me to do it goes free...that's the approximate cause. Because no one can prove that what I said I thought was about to take place really would have taken place. So I could have misinterpreted his action, but he caused me to do what I did and I am the guilty party. That's called an approximate cause.

So who today could go into court and say that a man had me under hypnosis and I performed an act when we do no accept such things to begin with? It's not part of our law. So if this little boy stumbled upon this and could control his Imagination to the point of making it vision...all that man has to do is raise Imagination to the point of vision and it's done. Those who do it do it unwittingly and do it blindly, but do it wittingly too. And they wouldn't eat meat...they're all strict vegetarians. Take the serpents out of their place or take the little snakes out of their place to the desert because they couldn't kill a snake. Couldn't eat any part of flesh, only vegetables, but they could kill men and women...slaughter them as though they were nothing...but not a snake. You see the strange mind...that is when we stumble upon this force and you have not awakened to the power that is love. So whenever you exercise this power, exercise it with love and you always do the right thing.

Thank you. Good night.

CHRISTMAS: GOSPEL PROCLAIMS EVENT

12/8/69

Here we are within a matter of days of the great event called Christmas. The gospel is the proclamation of a great event and we call it Christmas. It is an event which puts an entirely different light upon human life. It proclaims that man *has been* saved...that's the proclamation. This is the one great divine event to which the entire world is moving. Everything is moving towards this one great event and we call it Christmas. But I question seriously that an nth part of one percent of those who call themselves Christians knows what this event is about.

Tonight we'll take it...take it from my own personal experience. We're told, "No one can say 'Jesus is Lord' except by the Holy Spirit," no one (1Cor.12:3). The Holy Spirit is nothing more than one's own personal experience of the event. As we are told in scripture, "I will send the Comforter, the Holy spirit, who will lead you into all things and bring to your remembrance all that I have told you" (Jn.14:26, KJV). *Everything* was told in the beginning. The Holy Spirit is only your own wonderful experience of the event that seems incredible. Then as you experience it, you will know from your own experience that Jesus is Lord. Well now, who is Jesus? We are told to call upon his name...call upon the name of Jesus and say, "In the name of Jesus"...and nothing happens. There are millions calling upon the name of Jesus and nothing happens. So who is Jesus? We're told in scripture, "Say unto the people of Israel, I AM has sent you. This is my name forever. Thus am I to be remembered throughout all generations" (Exod.3:14-17).

There is no other Lord. Jesus is the Lord. But the word Jesus really means I AM. If you spell it in Hebrew which is Joshua it means "Jehovah is Savior." That's what the word actually means. Joshua is the Hebraic form of our word Jesus, and it means "Jehovah is savior." "Our God is a God of salvation; and to God, the Lord, belongs escape from death" (Ps.68:20). There is no other Lord than I AM. God actually became as we are that we may be as he is. God is buried in humanity. The God that buried himself in humanity to make man a living being is I AM. That same God will rise in man, individually, and that God is I AM. No other…just I AM. This is this one far off divine event to which the whole creation moves: the discovery of the God *within himself* and that God is his own wonderful human Imagination. That is God.

When he rises in us that's the only resurrection spoken of in scripture. When he rises in us in our wonderful skull he comes out and that is the only Christmas, the only birth spoken of in scripture. I come out, I escape from the tomb, the sepulcher in which I was buried, and that sepulcher was my own skull. This is the immortal tomb in which man is buried. In the fullness of time he rises. So the event called Christmas is really although it seems to be a single event these are parts of this complex…or call it a single complex, because there are many events within the one event. So we call it Christmas. But we shouldn't separate it…although we do; we separate Christmas from Easter by a few months. Then we separate these from ascension by a few months. Then we separate these many events…but they are really all part of a single complex.

So now we're approaching one part and we call it Christmas, which is the birth of God, the God of whom the scriptures speak. And there is no other God "for this is his name forever and thus shall I be remembered throughout all generations." Well, what is the name? I AM. Where could you go where you are not aware that you are? Where could man go and not find God? If I lived in hell, real hell, *there* is God. Am I not aware that I am? There is God in hell. If I live in ecstasy, *there* is God. I am *aware* of my ecstatic mood…that is God. For I AM is the only name of God and that is Jesus. There is salvation in no one else said Luke in his book called The Acts…there is salvation in no one else: "For there is no other name under heaven given among men by which we must be saved" (4:12). There is no other name. What name? To call Jesus? No, if you know what Jesus really means. When you are without using a word…when you are *aware,* you are saying I AM. That is Jesus and there is no other Jesus. He is buried in us, and he rises in us and he comes out. His escape from the tomb of our skull is the birth of Christ and that is the *only* birth. We think it happened 2,000 years ago among people who are long gone from the world. For find when it happens in us it's strangely *contemporary*. Yes, it happens and it is fact; and it is active for it continues morning, noon and night in humanity. It is not over, because it is still taking place. It's taking place in the individuals the world over. This is that one far-off great divine event to which the whole vast world is moving. That is Christmas; there is no other Christmas.

But if tonight you said to someone who calls himself a Christian, "Who is Jesus Christ?" chances are he would say, "Well, Jesus Christ is the son of God." If you said to him, "Well then, you must be God," if he were one given to anger and to expressing that anger, he would slap you. If he thinks he could get a way with it, he would say that you're blasphemous by calling him God. But if you turn back to the proclamation of the great event and you said to him, "Well, no one knows who the Son is except the Father" (Mat.11:27) and you tell me you know the Son, that the Son is Jesus Christ, you will have to be God the Father. And so you declare that you know who Jesus Christ is, so you tell me he is the Son of God. If he is the Son of God, then you are God the Father, for we are told in scripture, "No one knows who the Son is except the Father, and no one knows who the Father is except the Son" (Mat.11:27). So if you know that Jesus Christ is the Son of God, you must be the Father. You must be!

Well now, he cannot rationalize because he has not had the experience. For no one knows that Jesus is Lord, which is God the Father, except by the Holy Spirit, and the Holy Spirit is to have *experienced* the great mystery. When Paul said, "He rolled up into the third heaven…and there he heard unutterable words…words that could not be uttered by man" (2Cor.12:2,4). Some translations have it that they must not be uttered by man. It isn't that. What Paul heard, what Paul saw was simply ineffable, incapable of expression in words. How could you express it? For we are speaking here of a body, a body that man wears when he rises within himself that is not this body. This is flesh and blood, and flesh and blood cannot inherit the kingdom of God. Paul tells us in the 15th chapter of 1st Corinthians, "What you sow unless it dies it is not alive" (15:36). It cannot be made alive unless it dies. And what you sow is not the body which *is to be*, for God gives it a body as he has chosen" (:38).

I will know you in eternity, I will know everyone in eternity. But for all the identity of persons there will be a radical discontinuity of form. I'll know you, but you aren't wearing a body of flesh and blood, for it cannot inherit eternity (1Cor.15:50). It cannot inherit the kingdom of God. I will know you, your wonderful identity, but the form you wear is *divine*. And let no one tell you they can describe it…you *can't* describe it. Yesterday morning as I returned to this level of my being, I arrested the body that I was wearing just for a moment. There maybe I spent, oh, say ten or fifteen minutes in the most glorious way, right on the surface of my being. For I was wearing that form, the form…you may call it all *energy*. It's power, for "Christ is the power of God and the wisdom of God" (1Cor.1:24). You're wearing that form. It is all love…but it's power and it's wisdom. It's the power of God and the wisdom of God. And here, as though someone took…and yet I am in control of it. Mind you, I am wearing it as I would this suit that I wear now, only it is my very self. It's not something that you put on, you wear it but it is your body. You are in control of it; you can intensify the energy or you can modify it. Here, as though someone within me, and yet I am the one doing it, and here I am looking out at the most glorious scenes you have ever seen. You can't paint them. No artist on earth could paint what I saw. We wouldn't have the pigments and we wouldn't have the ability. They were all three-dimensional visions in such vivid colors that you cannot describe one after the other. But I controlled how long I would observe one and then I let it go and observed another.

All that heavenly treasure is in me? Yes. When one's eyes begin to open inwardly into the world of thought, into eternity, he sees what no mortal eye turned out could ever see. You cannot use any images of this outer world to describe what you see in this eternal world, the world that is imperishable. Can't do it! Here you are actually wearing Christ. Well, Christ is simply "the new man." You by birth are the "new man." You are the new man and that new man is the power of God and the wisdom of God. You wear it. Well, how can you describe it, because it is an ineffable mystery? Yet, in a way, although you cannot describe it, he comes to us as one who will allow the individual to experience who he is. When you experience who he is, you are experiencing who *you* are, for you are the Jesus of scripture. There is no other Jesus, there is no other Jehovah. You are the Lord God Jehovah, you are Jesus, but buried in you. And the event towards which you are moving is simply the awakening of the Lord in *you*. When he awakes *in* you, then and only then you will know who you are.

So Christmas is simply the proclamation of this far-off divine event to which the whole vast creation moves. It is not about another, it's not about one who lived a long time ago, and it's all about you. The Bible is very personal: it is your own spiritual biography, it's not about another. The Bible is salvation history. There is no secular history in the Bible. To see the characters of scripture as characters of history is to see Truth tempered to the weakness of the human soul. They're not characters of scripture; they're all within man…the whole thing takes place within man. The whole drama is unfolding within the Imagination of man, and when man reaches the fullness of time man awakes. He awakes where?—within himself. For, he is buried in himself, but he doesn't know it.

When a friend of mine told the story last lecture night, or rather told it to me and then I told it to you, *there* is what I'm talking about when I say you have a moment where you taste of the power of "the age to come." She found herself in a dream in a neighbor's house. They were all dressed in this strange garb of the Mennonites…almost a changeless group of people, who haven't changed their outer garments in 300 years, that is, the fashion of the garment. Oh, they've worn them out but bought another one just like the one worn out, no change in pattern, no change in fashion. They've been in this country for 300 years. They started in Europe in the year 1525…yet the same form, the outer form, same ___(??). She saw them all dressed in these garments of the Mennonites. One was accused of killing a man…they all killed a certain man, which was the second husband of this one woman. So here, she tried to tell them that they did a wrong thing and they would not believe it. She tried to persuade them what they did was wrong. They could not believe it be because "he was one of us, therefore, we owned him; and what he did we call wrong and so in our eyes it was the right thing that we did." She couldn't persuade them. Then came a group of men all dressed in black with guns in their hands to kill the woman whose second husband was killed, because the leader of the gang claimed that this man killed was *his* brother. He tried to persuade him that it would be wrong if he killed her. He could not understand that. Then she began to awake and she woke within the dream and she knew she was dreaming. So she awoke *within* the dream and knew that all that she saw though they seemed to be independent of her perception of them were only aspects of her dream. It was herself pushed out.

So, at that moment when she realized it was only herself pushed out, she felt an energy within her, a power within her which she felt she could arrest…and she arrested it. As she arrested the power they all froze and stood still. She went into the room where all the others were and she froze them. She returned to the living room where these two were and they're still frozen as though made of clay, and she said to the man, "You do not want to kill her, you love her and she loves you." Then she released the activity in her which allowed him to become reanimated. Then she released the woman after telling her, "You love him and he loves you." She released that activity and she became animated. Then he put down the gun and with outstretched arms went over to embrace the woman.

That is the power of which I speak, a power unknown to mortal mind, a power completely unknown to the rational mind. We think power is in the atom bomb, hydrogen energy, or money in the bank or securities, and that's power. We think that's power. Tonight, undoubtedly a dozen or more very, very wealthy men have died…they die all the time… didn't take one penny with them. They simply dropped off and left behind them what they thought was power. The power of which I speak you never lose, it is forever. These bodies die, certainly they die, and all they possess dies with them, for they can't take it with them. But the power of which I speak is imperishable. It is the power of God in man, which is called Christ. "Christ is the power of God and the wisdom of God" (1Cor.1:24). Man is slowly wakening into this power that is within him. When he feels it and he hears it and senses it, that is the power that he exercises.

Now, in her case she woke within a dream. She was dreaming and everything seemed to be taking place independent of her perception of it like in a dream. She woke within the dream to discover that the dream was her own self pushed out and that she could control the dream and change it, change the motivation of the things in the dream. So instead of murdering the one, she could command him to love and command her to respond in love. Then she released the activity which allowed them to become reanimated, and they obeyed the command.

This is your future. You come into an inheritance where everything is under your control, but everything in the universe, for the whole vast universe remains. These are only garments that God wears and the garments remain just as they are now. They are restored even though they are consumed in a furnace and we call it cremated. The bodies are restored and *others* occupy them. But the whole vast world is restored and you the occupant, the actor in the drama, you move up until finally you awake. When you awake, it is called in scripture…well, *we* call it…rather, it isn't in scripture…*we* call it Christmas. Christmas is the awakening of God *in man*. That's all that it is. It is not an event that took place 2,000 years ago; it is taking place all over the world in those who have reached the *fullness of time*. When the fullness of time has come, well then, it erupts within you. What erupts? You begin to stir, you begin to awaken, and you awaken from the dream of life, from this dream of death. You come out of your own skull, which is a tomb, and that coming out, departing from the tomb, is the birth.

Well now, these are two events that take place the same night. We separate them by three and a half months. Then we add another few months to the discovery of the Fatherhood of God. Then we add another few months to the ascension of the Spirit. But they are all parts of a single complex…all parts of one grand event. So the first aspect of the complex event is resurrection; the second is birth; the third is the discovery of the Fatherhood through the Son; and then the fourth that completes this single event is simply the ascension or the rising of the Son of man—you are the Son of man—into heaven in a serpentine form. These form the grand single event.

Tonight, those who are preparing for the great event and will sing their heads off on Christmas morning—and I'm all for it, let them have fun—but they're talking about someone that they do not know. They will sing their hearts out with all the hallelujahs thinking some being in time and space is responding to their adulation. That's not Christmas! In the world, moving among them walk those who have experienced the event, and they know that Jesus is Lord. But they know that Jesus is their own wonderful I-am-ness and there is no other Jesus. That Jesus is the Lord God Jehovah, and the Lord God Jehovah is your own wonderful I AM and there is no other Jehovah. "Say unto the people of Israel, I AM has sent you. This is my name forever, and thus shall I be remembered throughout all generations." There is no other Jehovah.

You are aware…well now, you are a living being because Jehovah is buried within you and that is Jesus. You are destined to become not only a living being but a *life-giving* Spirit. As my friend had the experience, she was a life-giving Spirit: she stopped the activity in herself which allowed them to breathe and to be alive. She changed their motivation by giving a command that was in conflict with their intentions. Then she released the activity in her which allowed them to once more become reanimated. But at that moment there was a bewildered expression on the faces of both, for now they're not going to carry out what formerly they intended. There's a radical change of attitude towards each other, and now they embrace each other. They had to execute her command. She has tasted of the power of the "age to come."

On this level, we make all the arguments of the world trying to persuade the other one that he's wrong and he tries to persuade you that you're wrong. And we end up nowhere…just where we started. But this is life on this level and this is a world of death where everything dies. There isn't a thing that comes into this world but what it waxes, it wanes and it vanishes… everything dies. But the world of which I speak is *eternal*. You are destined to enter that world, but you cannot enter that world with a body of flesh and blood. It's a new body that is required. So that what you sow unless it dies it cannot be made alive, and what you sow is not the body which is to be. But God and God is yourself gives it a body as *he* has chosen. You have chosen the body that you're going to wear. It's a glorious body, but it's a body of power, it's a body of wisdom. It is called "putting on Christ" in scripture. "Put on the Lord Jesus Christ" that's what you're told (Rom.13:14). It's putting it on and you wear it as you would a garment only you are in control of it. It is all power, for Christ is defined in scripture as "the power of God and the wisdom of God." So you put on the power of God and the wisdom of God, and you are in control of it. It's an innate wisdom…something that

The Return of Glory

you don't have to get from books. It's innate and you know from the depths of your soul and you know there's no doubt within you as to what you know.

This Truth, this proclamation is not discovered by some rational argument. The gospel is not discovered *by* us; it is *disclosed to* us. It's not something that you can prove logically; it is a self-revelation of God. God unveils himself *in* the one who now he has chosen to reveal himself. All the scholars of the world can study from now 'til the ends of time and they will never in the study of the life and teachings of Jesus find in their studies who the Father or the Son is. If they did, they wouldn't tamper with the Bible. Take the earliest of all the gospels, the Book of Mark. It's not the first in the gospels. It's the first chronologically written, but it's not in the canon: Matthew is given first place and then Mark comes second. But it begins this way, and it's the earliest gospel by all records, "The beginning of the gospel of Jesus Christ, the Son of God." Now that phrase "the Son of God" is an *addition* by a scribe; it is not an original. The earliest and best manuscripts that we have omit the phrase "The Son of God." It's, "The beginning of the gospel of Jesus Christ." "The gospel" means "the good news" of this mystery that is Jesus Christ.

Jesus *is* the Lord Jehovah; Christ is his power and his wisdom. He is buried in us and he will rise in us. You will know of his rising because the very imagery of scripture will surround you the day he rises within you, and you'll know that you are the one spoken of in scripture as the Lord Jesus Christ. Then you'll discover who the Son is. It's not written in any book outside of scripture, but you don't see it there until you experience it. For, no one will know that Jesus is Lord except by the Holy Spirit. The Holy Spirit is simply *to experience* scripture, that's all. When you experience scripture, you will know who the Son is and you will know that the Son is David. David is the *personification* of humanity. Take all the generations of men and all of their experiences and fuse them into a single being and personify that being, it will come out as the lad David of scripture. That is the Son of the Lord, and you are the Lord and he is your Son.

As you're told in the very end, "A son honors his father. If then I am a father, where is my honor?" (Mal.1:6). In other words, where is my son? That's how the Bible ends in the Old Testament. The New Testament begins it and reveals the son, but man doesn't see it and he cannot accept it until he experiences it. For he does not know that Jesus is Lord who is God the Father until he experiences in himself that he rose in his skull. It was he himself who awoke within himself. It was he who came out of the skull. It was he who held the Christ child in his own hands as his *own* sign of *his* resurrection. It was he who stood before the Son of God, David, and David called him, "Father." He knew it…there was no doubt in his mind as to who the Son was and who he was relative to that boy. He knew he was his father and he knew that he was his son.

Then he goes back and he searches the scriptures to find some reference to it, and it's all over the scriptures. "I will tell of the decree of the Lord," said David, "He said unto me, 'Thou art my son, today I have begotten thee.'" There it is in the 2nd Psalm: "I will tell of the decree of the Lord: He said unto me, 'Thou art my son, today I have begotten thee.'" Now we turn the pages over and go into the 89th Psalm: "I have found David and he has cried unto me, 'Thou art my Father, my God, and the Rock of my salvation'" (89:26). Then we go back into the Book of Samuel and there we read in the 2nd Book of Samuel: "When you lie down with your fathers, I will raise up after you your son, who will come forth from your body. I will be his father and he shall be my son" (2Sam.7:12, 14).

Now we jump to the very last book of the Bible, the Book of Revelation, and the Lord is speaking: "I am the root and the offspring of David" (22:16). Yes, I am the root, the cause, the father, *and* the offspring. So I am one with my grandson. The grandfather and the grandson are one and the same being. So that comes out of man, man being humanity. All of the members of the human race all put together, all of their experiences and you fuse them together into a single being and it's David. Now what comes out of that would be David's offspring. What is the root of David?—the Lord. What comes out of David is one with his root: "I am the root *and* the offspring of David." So here, the two become one. The grandfather and the grandson are one and the same being, leaving David as the son. So, man matures when he becomes his own father's father; when he becomes his grandfather. The grandfather *is* the Lord.

We're dealing with a mystery. If you think you're going to reach through some rational argument the story of Christianity or the story of the Old Testament, then you are searching in vain. The wisest of the wise cannot see it, and so because they can't see it and it isn't rational, they call it a myth. They all call it a myth. In fact, the wisest of the wise speak of the Bible as a grand myth…they do not know it. But I tell you, he gives it to whom he will, even the lowliest of men. And you walk the earth completely unknown, while others have all the degrees and the honors, and money, and reputation, and they are so dead and they do not know it. You do not condemn them, you do not argue, you simply walk by. Only to the willing ear do you tell the story; you tell it to those who are receptive to hearing it. Usually it is those who are not the scholars of the day. They hear it, they can't quite understand it, but you spoke convincingly because you spoke from experience and you were not theorizing. Then they heard it and they carried it and locked it in their hearts and pondered it. One day, believing it, as you hoped they would, it erupts within them and they experience it. So they know that the Lord Jesus *is* the Lord that the world calls the God of the universe, because they know it by the Holy Spirit…which is their own *personal* experience of it.

So let the world go blindly on…if it will. Eternity waits and it doesn't matter how long it takes, everyone eventually will come into it. But no one will come into it until he hungers, until he thirsts after God, a thirst that only an experience of God can satisfy. He said, "I will send a hunger upon the world. It will not be a hunger for bread, nor a thirst for water, but for the hearing of the word of God" (Amos 8:11). So he will send a famine upon the world, and the world not understanding scripture thinks a famine is coming upon us that is a physical famine. Oh, it could come…happens all over the world anyway. There are hungry people in our fabulous land. All over China, all over India they are hungry. It's not because we cannot supply the food, that's not our problem. That is simply an economic problem. We have to curtail production…we can't find bins big enough to house our surplus, and we put that enormous weight on the taxpayer to let it rot, because we do not know how to give it away. So we have to pay people not to grow what they could grow on their land.

And we talk about not being able to supply? We could from the Southern states alone in this country grow enough to feed the world and clothe the world. We don't need any more than the Southern states of our land to clothe the whole vast world and feed the whole world, but how to do it under the present economy? It' can't be done. I am not an economist, so I have no way to tell you how it can be done; but I know it is not a lack of production and it's an economic problem. I am not an economist. I know nothing of how to even start to take this enormous capacity that we have and do with it what were we really in love with each other we would do…I do not know. But let no one tell you that we are bursting at the seams and cannot feed this bursting population. It is not a problem of production; it's a problem of economy and I do not know how it could be done. But we are paying people millions and millions every year not to use their lands, and we are now curtailing the use of the land and growing more on the smaller areas, because we have found a better way to fertilize, we have found better crops, we have found better everything. We can grow more in an acre than we did in the past out of twenty acres, so we curtail it to one acre, and still we cannot sell it we grow so much.

And with the new what is known as the synthetic industry where from peanuts and the Southern Pine we make clothes, we make peanut oil, we make butter, we make everything you can think of…a thousand by-products from two items that formerly you gave away, because what to do with them—the Southern Pine and the Ground Nut. Then we discovered through this new, I would say, concept of life, the synthetic world, and here we cannot possibly give it away we produce so much. How to give it away? You can't give it away. And then they pay us...go out a thousand acres and tell the country that you're going to plant it, and they'll pay you not to. Sit back and get your check every year for not planting. Threaten them...that if you're going to plant wheat and they have no place to put it, it can only stay there and rot. And yet, India could use it, China could use it, South America could use it, and we in the land could use it. But it is not a problem that I could solve...I do not know.

I can only tell you that Christ in you is your own wonderful human Imagination. That the God of scripture, the Lord Jesus Christ is that in you when you say, "I am." There is no other Lord Jesus Christ...there is no other God. Let the world scoff at it. They will come year after year as told us in scripture, "Scoffers will come scoffing, saying, 'Where is the promise of his coming? For ever since the fathers fell asleep, all things have continued as they were from the foundation of the world" (2Pet.3:3). So let them scoff, perfectly alright. You accept it and put your hope fully upon the *grace* that is coming to you, and hope that it will erupt within you now in the not distant future. When you drop off this garment, as you must, you'll be clothed in the garment that puts you into a *new* kingdom, a new world, clothed in power, clothed in wisdom. Those who have not experienced it before they depart this world are restored to life in a world just like this, faced with all the problems that they detected here. So you do not drop off as a billionaire and find yourself with the billion you left behind you. You might find yourself a nice, wonderful shoeblack or cleaning latrines if that is what must be done to rouse you to believe the incredible story. So don't think for one moment that your present position here is any indictor of what you will be when you drop off this garment. No, you will find yourself in a world terrestrial just like this, in a body just like these but new and young. Not a baby, young. In a world where you'll be working, you'll be doing something best suited to the work yet to be done in you, and you will continue until Christ *in* you awakes. Until that power in you awakes you will continue using your rational mind in a world that is quite logical just like this.

So the Christmas that we now look forward to celebrate is one aspect of the great event. There are four definite events in the single event. The first is resurrection...it's not told that in scripture, but that's the first. Then comes the birth; then comes the discovery of the Son who reveals you as the Father. You *are* the Father; David reveals you as the Father. Then comes your ascent into heaven, as told in scripture, in a serpentine form, and you enter it violently, clothed in power.

Now let us go into the Silence.

* * *

Are there any questions, please?

Q: You don't put on the new body until you have a hunger for it and…

A: No, no, I say until one is hungry for an experience of God. He hears about it, but what does it mean? He may go to church because it pleases his family, or she may go because it pleases her family, and they go there through habit. It becomes a habit. People get up in the morning and they have a cup of coffee. One day they'll stop drinking a cup of coffee and they'll not miss it; and after awhile they don't even want coffee, you couldn't give it to them. Yet, through habit we take coffee or we take a cigarette or we take a drink, and we're creatures of habit. So the day will come that you will really *deliberately* seek God, not because someone told you about it, but you'll become hungry for an experience of God. And then you'll be fulfilling scripture. "I will send a famine upon the world. It will not be a hunger for bread or a thirst for water, but for hearing—with understanding—the word

Q: Even so, you don't experience that until…like the way I understand you…until the appointed time?

A: The appointed time…like pregnancy. In other words, we are pregnant with Christ, pregnant with the *power*, but there is a certain moment of delivery. When the time comes, you will have the experience of Jesus Christ. All that is said of him in scripture you will experience in the first-person, singular, and you will know the story was all about you, it wasn't really about another. The whole thing is about the individual in this world. So you stop worshipping anything on the outside. The Bible is your own spiritual biography, *auto*-biography. As told you in the 40th Psalm, "In the volume of the book it was written of me," all about me.

Q: You said you have to live again, you mean in another world or in this world?

A: In this world, but not the world that you now see. It's this world, but this world does not end at that moment when one cannot touch you. In other words, the world does not cease to be at the point where you seem to vanish from it. You are restored to life in a world just like this, in a body like this, only it's much younger. I would say about twenty…if you're 100, you find yourself…how? It's a miraculous discovery, but you find it. And you're solid; you'll bleed if you're cut; and there you do all the things you do here. You labor just as you labor here. And the hunger one day will so possess you to get away from this world of death...for this is a world of death, everything dies. The strongest youth today will depart tomorrow, but they never think that they ever will. When you are in your twenties, well, the world is yours. You never think for one moment that you'll ever be the one that you're criticizing who is so old, he's forty. Forty years old, my! He's the old, old person and why shouldn't he get off the earth. When you tell him, look at me, take a good look. If you survive my age, you will look as old as I do now, *if* you survive. He can't believe it; that frightens him, because he can't conceive he ever will look that old.

I only recall my mother as a grown lady, and yet I was the fourth of a very large family. When mother bore me she could not have been more than twenty-one or twenty-two. I recall many things vividly at the age of three and four, and yet I can't recall my mother save as matured lady. And yet she was a young girl when I was a little boy. I must have been, say, seven before she turned thirty and yet she was always a matured lady, and to me, naturally, I would call it old. Now today they trust no one over thirty. Take off their beards and you will see they themselves are well over thirty, many of them. But they can't believe that they will ever reach a matured age...they are forever the adolescent.

Q: When you go back into this world where you say you're young again, will you have any memory of all of this life?

A: Yes, my dear. Memory is one thing you carry with you. You do carry it with you, believe me. But when you are awakened here and experience what is the great mystery of Christmas, you depart "this age" altogether. You are in an entirely different world, a world that cannot be described in words or painted with the brush or sculpted. It cannot be described because there are no images on earth that you could use to describe it. But everything here you will find where you are going and we are all going there save those who are resurrected. As told us in the 20th chapter of the Book of Luke, the resurrected do not die any more, because they are no longer subject to death. They are now sons of God, being sons of the resurrection (20:35). Those who have not, continue and they are restored to life. But there is a difference between restoration and resurrection. All are restored, for nothing dies in *God's* world. But individual's one after the other are resurrected.

Well, the time is up. So until Friday, which is our last for three weeks; then reopening on the 5th of January. Thank you. Good night.

THE MYSTERY OF CHRISTMAS

12/12/69

Here we are on the verge of the great mystery, the mystery of Christmas. These words are put into his mouth, that is, simply a man just as we are, one in whom the great story unfolded. His words were enigmatic. And the evangelists in writing the gospels kept that great mystery as it was told.

So tonight, we will take a few of his words and try to explain them. We go now to the 17th chapter of the Book of John, the 11th and 12th verses. Here is one speaking now and he is communing with himself; and the depth of himself which has been revealed to himself is God the Father. He has discovered the Father...which everyone is destined to discover. He's addressing the Father and he makes the statement which John records: "And now I am no more in the world, but they are in the world, and I am coming to thee. Holy Father, keep them in thy name, which thou hast given to me, that they may be one, even as *we* are one" (17:11). The *only* name in the world that can truly bind us together and make us one is Father. When you and I discover that we really are the Father, then we know what this whole great mystery of life really is.

Now he goes on and makes this statement, he said, "I have guarded them and none is lost but the son of perdition, that the scripture might be fulfilled" (17:12). I haven't read in any book that I have, or in any lecture that I have heard or any discussion with anyone that comes near this great mystery. They see it as secular history and it is not. "None is lost but the son of perdition." Well, who is he? All the scholars claim it is one called Judas. Hasn't a thing to do with that. If you want to get close to it, read the 18th Psalm, which is repeated in the 22nd chapter of 2nd Samuel. Read it tonight when you go home. Well, that 22nd chapter of 2nd Samuel is a complete repeat of the 18th Psalm. It's a hymn in praise of the one who saved him from death and destruction. Perdition simply means "death and destruction." David sings out the praise to the *Lord* who saved him from death and destruction. Hasn't a thing to do with any Judas the son of perdition.

Now, let us take these enigmatic words and show you. A story is told that is the strangest story ever told which is in the gospel. Who then is the son of perdition? The one who hears it and *rejects* it. Any man who refuses to accept the Christian revelation is the antichrist, the son of perdition. Now, what are we told in the New Testament concerning it? Read it in 2nd Thessalonians, the 2nd chapter: "And the lawless one, the son of perdition, will be revealed and the Lord Jesus will slay him with the breath of his mouth, and he will be destroyed by his appearing and his coming" (2:3). So I tell you the story as I personally have experienced it. Some will say no to that, and others will say yes. Those who say no to it are the antichrist, the son of perdition. *They* will *not* be destroyed. It's the state of consciousness in which they *dwell* that will be destroyed...for it will *happen in* them. For "None have I lost but the son of perdition."

So no individual will be destroyed. How could he be when he is a Son of God? But he falls into these states. So he falls into the state known as the son of perdition, who completely denies that this incredible story is true. But, when it awakens within *him* and becomes true, then he has no leg to stand upon but to admit the experience. So, if I tell you the most incredible story in the world and you say, "Oh, that's silly, that's stupid," it's alright. I am confident that it's going to happen and you will have the experience of it. When you experience it, then what does it matter what you've said before? What does it matter what others coming after you who experience it have said or will say? When you are confronted with the experience, what does it matter?

So everyone in the world will be saved and the only thing that is lost is the son of perdition...that state of consciousness in which the individual lived at that moment when he heard the story and could not accept it. To him it was stupid, it was silly, and he completely rejected it. That is the son of perdition. It hasn't a thing to do with any Judas. Judas was the one who betrayed the Lord. Well, no one in the world could ever betray me but myself, for no one knows my secrets but myself, but no one. Judas is Judah. Judah is the one named in the genealogy of Jesus...the lion's whelp. None of the others were mentioned, just simply, "And Jacob was the father of Judah and his brothers." They are not mentioned. It's simply Judah, the one who *knew* the secret. He told the secret. So it hasn't a thing to do with any individual man. No man can be destroyed, because every child born of woman is a son of God, and it takes all the sons of God to make God, as told us in the 32nd chapter of the Book of Deuteronomy, "And he has put bounds to the people according to the number of the *sons* of God" (32:8).

So no child in this world could be born who is not an emanation of a son of God, and it takes all the sons to form God. For the word translated God, which is Elohim, is a plural word. "In the beginning God created the heavens and the earth" that's Elohim. And God, Elohim, said "Let *us* make man in our image." And the *gods* came down and buried themselves in humanity. But not one could be born of woman who is not occupied by a son of God, and not one son of God can be lost. "I have lost no one but the son of perdition" and perdition is only that state of consciousness that rejects and denies this Christian revelation. So you say, "Can't be! How can a man be consumed before your eyes, turned into dust, and yet survive?" No that is simple, may I tell you, that's easy. It's not *that* of which he speaks…for all things are restored to life. Everything is restored to life, even the little flower that I discard cannot really cease to be. All things are restored by the seed of contemplative thought…that's only restoration. But I'm not speaking of restoration; I'm speaking of resurrection where the Son is resurrected. Not the body that he wears in the world…that's always restored. But he who occupies it, who goes through the world of death, he is awakened from the great dream of death. And when he is awakened, then come the signs.

Now, Jesus calls himself "The Son of man." He speaks of himself as a Son of man. He also speaks of himself of that which is to come. When the Son of man comes, will he find faith upon earth? So he speaks of himself in the future: "when he comes." He's *always* coming and awakening in man, for God is awakening in man. So here, this great mystery called Christmas is simply the beginning of the signs: "And now this shall be a *sign* unto you" (Luke 2:34). We are told that many will reject it. Read the 2nd chapter of Luke…it's a sign that many will reject. It is for the fall and the rising of many in Israel. When Simeon took the little child into his arms and then he said, "It's a sign for the fall and the rising of many in Israel"…that out of many hearts will come these thoughts, some will reject it and some will accept it. So I'll tell the story and some hearing it will say no to that, and some will say yes to it. But even those who say no, who throw themselves into the state of the son of perdition, will find that Jesus will rise in *them* as their very being, and rising in them he will slay by the breath of his mouth, breath of what mouth? By the Word of God, for the sword of the Spirit is the Word of God. And, the Word cannot return void, it must accomplish itself and fulfill itself in that for which it was sent. So the Word goes out and the whole gospel is the Word of God.

Now, this is the Word of God: God actually became you that you may become God. He sent himself as sons into the world; then he raises his sons as himself the Father. When all return they are not sons, they are God the Father. "When you see me, you have seen the Father," said he. Don't look beyond that. When you *see* me is to *know* me. You will not see him outside of yourself...not in eternity. If anyone should say, "Come, look there he is or here he is do not believe it. If anyone ever tells you, "Come, let us go, I know where he is," go no place. You'll never find him outside of yourself and he will rise *within you*. There's only one way you'll ever now him: when God's Son—which is the sum total of all the experiences of humanity, all of their experiences, fused together into a single being personified before you—stands before you and calls you Father. When he stands before you, you know exactly who he is...he is David. "I have found in David a man after my own heart, who will do all my will" (Acts 13:22). He is the son of Jesse and Jesse means "I AM."

So man is in search of himself who is God the Father. And there is no other God, no other Father. And the whole comes in this wonderful experience that everyone will have. So though you have said in the past and maybe tonight you say, "It's an incredible story and I can't believe it," you are in that state of consciousness which is only called the son of perdition. It's the state that is destroyed by the breath of his mouth by his Word unfolding *in you*. So when his Word unfolds in you, you have not a leg to stand upon; you cannot deny what has happened. So although you denied it prior to the eruption of the Word in you, after it erupts within you and all that is said of Jesus Christ in scripture you have experienced, and you know you are he, then you can't deny it. So the son of perdition is the only one that is slain, the only one that is lost. It's part of the play.

Everyone in the world, call him by any name, is *already* saved, for the simple reason it has *already* happened. It *has* happened. And when it happened once, it would happen for all, for he is one. "That I in them and they in me...Holy Father, keep them in thy name which thou hast given me" (Jn.17:11). What is the name?—Father. And I have kept them in the name that thou gavest me. I told them that they are the Father and they're moving toward the discovery of it. Well, some didn't believe it. But, "Father, I guarded them, and none of them is lost but the son of perdition, that the scripture might be fulfilled." The scripture is thy Word. I told them thy Word as I experienced it. I interpreted to them thy Word. And Father, they heard it, and some rejected it and some believed it. In spite of those who rejected it, may I say, they cannot themselves die for they are my brothers. We came down together and all of us became fragmented.

In this morning's *L. A. Times*...I do not know if you read it, maybe you still have the paper at home...but the Book Review, it was one of the many poems of Robert Graves...and it was the first one. He printed about

The Return of Glory

five or six of them, but this one little verse…and my heart leapt within me. These are the words if I recall it correctly, "Hold fast with both hands to that royal love which alone as we know certainly restores fragmentation into true unity." What a revelation! The great poets are the ones who see so clearly and those who have the capacity to use words as Robert Graves has to say it so beautifully. "Hold fast with both hands to that royal love which alone as we know certainly restores fragmentation into true unity." Here is the fragmented one. The whole vast world is one fragmented. Regardless of the pigment of the skin, the race, the nation, whatever it is, this is the fragmented rock

That I saw in my experience back in 1934 when sitting alone in my little room…for that was the deep of the Depression, 1934, and I was a dancer, and people could not afford to buy anything, far less pay to be entertained by a dancer. So I lived in a basement apartment on 75th Street in New York City. I, too, did not know where the next was coming from. I didn't despair; I sat in the Silence, not thinking of anything in particular…just simply with my eyes shut as in sleep, but I was certainly not asleep. I was very wide awake, but my eyes were closed. Then these golden lovely clouds—they always come if I close my eyes and for just one little moment meditate; my whole head, all the dark convolutions of the brain grow luminous. And it's all gold…golden liquid light comes out of the head and surrounds me. Then it just pulses and pulses and goes off. But the whole head is enveloped in golden liquid light.

So, as I contemplated this, suddenly before my eyes, my inner eyes, for the eyes were shut, came a quartz. It could have been, what, sixteen, twenty inches in diameter, but just a quartz, this rock. As I looked at it, it fragmented. In some strange way the whole thing broke and fragmented itself into numberless parts. Then the whole thing gathered itself together into a human form, seated in the lotus posture. As I looked at it, I'm looking at myself…but a self that in my wildest dreams I could never believe I could ever attain to that perfection. What majesty of face! What beauty of features! You couldn't conceive of this face that you now see ever attaining to that beauty. That was perfect. Here it is in deep meditation and I'm looking at myself. As I looked, the whole thing is alive. It wasn't a piece of clay; it was alive. A living, living statue right before me and it's myself. As I looked, it began to glow and it increased in luminosity and reached the intensity of the sun. Then it exploded. And then I awoke seated in my chair in my little basement apartment.

Then I turned to scripture: "Of the Rock that begot you, you are unmindful and of the God who gave you birth you are unaware." Read it in the 32nd chapter of Deuteronomy (32:18). Then we read in the 10th chapter of 1st Corinthians, "And they drank from the Rock that followed them: and the Rock was Christ" (10:4). So then you're told Christ is within you, that Rock that never fails. So the imagery was perfect. Here, I sat perfectly still not contemplating anything in particular.

Because the market broke in 1929 and everything went to pieces, and there were seventeen million of us unemployed. We then only had a population of maybe 130 million. Today we have 204 million…but then we only had 130 million maximum. There were seventeen million by the confession of the government. The chances are there were many more and these were the bread winners. They were completely unemployed. They couldn't turn any place to find a loaf of bread. Our bins were filled to overflowing. We couldn't pay the taxes on these bursting bins, but how to give it away, how to distribute it? And so, in 1934 I had already gone through five years of this Depression. So I certainly wasn't thinking of anything in particular…this almost became a state of mind.

So I sat perfectly still, as I did daily, and simply turned my attention within my brain and contemplated within. And as always happens the clouds begin to appear and all the dark convolutions grow luminous, and the whole thing is moving in ___(??) golden liquid light. Then comes this rock… the perfect imagery of scripture: "And the Rock was Christ." He formed himself into me…me as the perfect being. I looked at myself and could hardly believe that I could ever in eternity attain that perfection…and yet I'm looking at myself.

So I tell you, everyone is destined to have these experiences. The words are enigmatic. Luckily for us those who wrote the story and told it so beautifully in the gospels kept the mystery in the words and didn't try to explain it in detail to anyone. Let those who deny it, alright, let them deny it, but even though they deny it they're not lost. For, not a thing is lost but the son of perdition and the son of perdition is simply the belief in destruction, the belief in death. As everyone seeing their friends depart this world have to admit to themselves that things do die. We came down into the world and everything dies here…and yet I tell you *nothing* dies. Everything in the outer world returns by the seed of contemplative thought.

But that is not the mystery of Christmas. The mystery of Christmas is that which is housed within us is that which *appears* to die. And that which is housed within us is God himself, and he's dreaming this dream of death which we call the dream of life. One day he will awaken; he awakens within us. Then there is a definite series of events that he goes through. This is the series…we call it beginning with Christmas…but it doesn't begin with Christmas it takes place the same night. It begins with the resurrection: he awakens within his own skull, which is the tomb where God is buried. Man awakens within his skull from a long, long dream. No one knows how long. Certain poets like Blake say 6,000 years, but I do not know. I have not had that experience to tell you that I can confirm it as he said 6,000 years. But it was an awful long dream.

Then I awoke within my skull. I had no idea that I was asleep within my skull. I always thought I slept on my bed, and that I was fully awake, and I was wearing a body. That night I discovered I had been asleep these unnumbered years in my skull. When I awoke, the skull was completely sealed. Yet I had an innate knowledge what to do and I pushed the base of my skull and something gave…a hole opened. I squeezed myself out. Just as a child comes out of its mother's womb I came out of that tomb. The tomb was the womb of God where God himself had entered. I saw no one, there was no companion. I alone came out. Then the imagery of scripture, as told you in the 2nd chapter of the Book of Luke, surrounded me. That is, a little child wrapped in swaddling clothes which is a sign. And I held this little child in my arms and with the most endearing manner I asked him, "How is my sweetheart?" He smiled a heavenly smile, and the scene dissolved.

There were three witnesses to the event. For they were told, "Go hurriedly into Bethlehem and you will find a sign, which is a sign that a savior was born on this day" (Luke2:12). For God is the savior of the world and there is no other savior. As told us in the 43rd and 45th chapters of Isaiah: "I am the Lord your God, the Holy One of Israel, your savior; and beside me there is no savior" (43:11). And that savior, his name is I AM. So when I awoke if anyone had asked me anything I would have said, "Well, I am the one who just awoke." That is the only being who just awoke. It is God. As told us in the psalms, "Rouse thyself! Why sleepest thou, O Lord?" (44:23). It is God who sleeps and dreams the dream of life in the world of death, who animates the whole thing, until one day *he awakes* within the tomb where he first entered; and that tomb is the skull of man. So that is called the birth, which we now celebrate on the 25th day of this month.

Then comes that great revelation where God *knows* who he is. He has no way of ever knowing who he is unless his Son stands before him and calls him "Father." The Son is David; and David is the sum total of all the generations of men and all of their experiences fused into a single being and personified before the one he's about to reveal as God the Father. So I am the father of David and you are the father of David. If you have not yet encountered him, may I tell you, you will. *Then* you will know what Graves said today in his poem which I quoted. Because, only in this dream manner will you know true unity. For if I am the father of your son, and if one you know other than the speaker is the father of our son, are we not *one* father? So in the end, are we not told there's "only one body, one Lord, one Spirit,

1005

one God and Father of all" (Eph.4:5). So *all* are coming towards the one body that fell and was fragmented and the fragmentation is humanity. So all these are the sons of God all being collected and brought back into that unity, that true unity that is God the Father.

So you are God the Father. And having played all the parts—the good, the bad and the indifferent—then you are gathered together. And that moment in time when you confront him, these are the signs of the end; for Christianity is based upon the affirmation that a series of events happened in which God revealed himself in action for the salvation of his sons. He brought all the sons back, and in the bringing them back he gave all the sons *himself.* In the end there is *only* God the Father. It takes all the sons to form God the Father.

So, all these things when you read them it takes one who has experienced it to explain the Old Testament. Who on earth would ever have believed that when we are told in the 3rd chapter of John—for he calls himself the Son of man: "And as Moses lifted up the serpent in the wilderness, so must the Son of man be lifted up" (3:14). He likens himself to a serpent, and who would have thought for one moment that the Son of man is just like that fiery serpent? And that you go up, just as he described it, in spiral form right into heaven, where heaven is within you as you're told in the Book of Luke, "The kingdom of heaven is within you" (Luke 17:21). So you go up into yourself, having split the entire body from top to bottom. "For the curtain of the temple"—and "We are the temple of the living God"—"was split from top to bottom" (2Cor.6:16). Then the Son of man, like a serpent, rose into that heavenly state, and when he rose into it, it reverberated like thunder. Exactly that...the imagery is perfect!

Who would have thought for one moment that when the Holy Spirit descends, it descends always in bodily form as a dove? It does...right upon you. It so loves you, the Holy Spirit, because you have finished the work that you yourself planned to do. For you and I agreed to dream in concert before we descended and became fragmented. We were a unity, a brotherhood of one; and then came that fragmentation in this world, and each became a seeming separate being at war with one another...and there is no other. Because eventually he is God the Father and his son is your son...so, really, he cannot be another.

So, "Hold fast with both hands to that royal love which alone as we know certainly restores fragmentation into *true unity.*" Well, I can't tell you how my heart jumped this morning when I read it. If you haven't discarded your paper, you'll find it in the *Book Review* in today's *L. A. Times.* They are all lovely...there are about five or six that he quoted...but this one... and Graves has been such a difficult poet to read because his words, too, are enigmatic, no question about it. Well, this seemed so clearly stated for those who have had the experience. Maybe others will pass it off and think, "Oh, what stupid things to have said." So beautifully said, but oh so *deeply* said.

So, one stands before you and he speaks of being here *and* he tells you he *is* to come. He is the Son of man; then he tells you the Son of man *will* come. "And when the Son of man comes, will he find faith upon the earth?" (Luke 18:8). So he's *always* coming. And one in whom he comes, when he awakens, he turns to his immediate circle and he wonders if anyone will trust him, anyone will have faith in him. Because the story of Christ is that he is a wine bibber and a glutton, a man of the world who loves harlots and tax collectors, and all the sinners of the world. He's a friend of sinners. So someone meets you and they know that you, too, like a good dinner, and you do like a good bottle of wine and you do like a few good Martinis. Well, that is not in their popular concept of what Jesus ought to be, what the Son of God is, so right away you're scratched out. You're no earthly good and you're an imposter.

So he tells them exactly not to go any other place than where they are. Don't go here, don't go there. If anyone tell you, "Come, I have found him," go no place, because he can't come from any place but within you, because he is buried within *you*. Every year you find these coming out, the false prophets claiming that they are it…and let us go and see him. When *you* see him he is just like you. "It does not yet appear what we shall be, but we know that when he appears we shall be like him" (1Jn.3:2). Why? We shall see him just as he is, and we shall be like him. So, have you seen his face? If it's not just like you, raised to the nth degree of perfection, you haven't seen him. "He is the Rock…and the Rock was Christ. We have forgotten the Rock that begot us and we are unmindful of the God that gave us birth" (1Cor.10:4; Deut.32:18). That Rock was fragmented and all the world round about you is yourself pushed out. You fought against the shadows believing it came from a seeming other and there is no other. It's only yourself; there is no other in the world. Housed within the seeming other which is yourself pushed out and you being the only God, housed in *that* is the only God. In that will awake all that awoke within you.

In the end, we all will know each other…no loss of identity. Even though I am God the Father and I tell you you are God the Father, there is no loss of identity. For all the identity of persons—and certainly not in eternity will you be other than the individualized being that you are—there is this strange, peculiar discontinuity of earthly form. You do not wear the earthly form, but you wear the earthly face raised to the degree of perfection…but not the earthly form. So let no one try to describe to you what that heavenly form is like. Face yes. Human voice yes. Human hands yes. But do not go beyond that, because they cannot describe it. It is power, it is wisdom, but above all things it is love. You can't describe the human form divine which is love. It is all love…the whole thing is love.

So everyone in the universe will arrive at the mystery that we are now about to celebrate called Christmas. You will see that it is not some little day that took place once and for all 2,000 years ago; it is always taking place. For, this is simply the coming of God, awakening *within* man, for he is *in* man. Were he not now in man, man could not dream. So he actually slays the son of perdition by the breath of his mouth and destroys him by his appearing and his coming. What could anyone tonight who stood before me—take the arch atheist of the world, by whatever name he calls himself— and I tell him the story that I've told you, and he thinks I should be put away, that I am insane. But I know that love conquers all; and the day will come that every word that I have said to you tonight is true, and therefore because it is true he will experience it. There will be no crowing. No, no crowing "I told you so" but a welcome that my lost brother has returned. No crowing whatsoever that he who today will say, "You're stupid, you should be put away, you're insane, and therefore some menace to society"…let him go on. Love…that royal love as spoken by Robert Graves, "Hold fast to that royal love which alone…" there is no other.

So, he within you has emanated the garment that you're wearing. He has emanated it and he cleaves to it. You in turn cleave to him. And you will one day begin to love only one being. And this is one being, but he's pushed out in every being. You'll see him reflected in all beings. So hold to him! What's his name? I AM. But some other name? Yes, he is the *Father*. But before they know him as Father, tell them his name: his name is I AM. One day they will love him, why? Because "He first loved them" (1Jn.4:19). He loved his emanation and he will cleave to the emanation, and they will become one. When they become actually one, he awakes, wearing that individualized face that is perfect.

And so I tell you I know it! I will meet you in eternity and I will know you. But for all the identity of persons, there will be a discontinuity of form, a form that is glorious beyond the wildest dream of man. The form is all power, it's all wisdom, but above all things, it is all love. We purposely descended into this world to accomplish this end.

Now I hope that when you get together on Christmas Day to celebrate the day with your family, which we will, that you will remember what it *really* means. Everyone present, though they laugh at the idea, nevertheless, know that everyone present and the whole vast world will one day have this experience, and they will awaken to being God the Father. Know that everyone *will* awaken, and because there's only one Father he is one with the whole vast world. And the brothers will return and the brothers in returning will be God the Father. For it was the one being's pleasure and will be to give all his sons himself. So when all return they are God himself.

Now let us go into the Silence.

*   *   *

Are there any questions, please? Well, if there aren't any questions, may this great event take place in you before we meet again.

Good night.

GLOSSARY

Affliction - Experienced for the purpose of fashioning man into the image of God which when completed the individual is inwardly awakened and shown to be God (one's own I-am-ness).

Awakening - The soul of man awakens from a profound sleep of "6,000" years to his true divine identity (the return of long memory). Man experiences a series of six visions: resurrection/birth from above; David and the father- hood of God; splitting of the temple of the body/ascension into Zion; the descent of the dove, over a period of three and a half years—all are signs of your transformation from limited man back into God.

Bible - All parable. Not secular history but salvation history. Man's spiritual autobiography. The Old Testament is adumbration and prophecy, while the New Testament is fulfillment of the prophecies: the events depicted in the story of Jesus Christ which man experiences.

Bible Characters - Personifications of eternal states of consciousness (not historical beings). Two lines of personifications run through scripture: the inner man and outer man; e.g. Eve (inner) culminating in Jesus; Adam (outer) culminating in John the Baptist.

David - The symbol of humanity—all of its generations, experiences, and the concentrated time in which they spring, fused into a grand whole, and personified as a glorious youth who (in vision) calls you "Father." God's only son (Ps.2:7); the anointed, the first born from the dead, the Christ. Also, eternity, a lad, a stripling; personification of the resultant state; symbol of man's creative power that overcomes all challenges. Only David reveals the Father.

Egypt - This age of illusion; the state of ignorance that I AM is he, as opposed to "that" age, the awakened state.

Enemy of Israel - All false gods and beliefs in causation other than the only God which is I AM (your I-am-ness or awareness of being).

Faith - Response to revelation rather than discovery of new knowledge. An assumption persisted in; an experiment that ends in experience. Loyalty to unseen reality. Opposite of faith is worry. To determine a thing.

Glory - God's gift of himself to each individual soul, ultimately. Achieved by an internal transformation of man into God by God (man's inner being) (2 Cor. 3:18). The state of awareness man enjoyed prior to the descent into man (John 17:5). Man's true identity returned, greatly expanded having experienced and overcome death.

Imagination - The eternal body of man; God himself. Man's awareness of being; the inner five senses; God's/man's creative power; the I AM (called God, Lord, Jehovah, Jesse, Jesus, the Dreamer, the Father). Man's creative power keyed low is human Imagination, the son—but the same in essence.

Imagining - Picturing a scene that implies the wish fulfilled, feeling the present reality of it, drenching self with that feeling, believing it is done, and remaining faithful to the imaginal act until it manifests.

Israel - "He who shall rule as God" (all of humanity at the end of his/her journey as man); a man in whom there is no guile.

Jesse - Any form of the verb "to be" (hence I AM; God the father of David, Ps.2:7).

Jesus - The I AM (Exod.3:14); the Father. Also called Jehovah, Lord, Jesse. Means "Jehovah is salvation." Anglicized Hebrew word Joshua. God individualized is when you say "I am." Universal humanity.

Christ - (See David above) The power and wisdom of God personified (1Cor.1:24)

Jesus Christ - Personification of awakened Imagination and man's creative power. God awake in man (two having been transformed into one, Ehp.2:14). Personification of man's soul; the animating principle of a being. Bifurcated term: "Jesus and his Christ" (Rev.11:15; 12:10). Father/Son. The pattern of salvation (six visions) buried in man's soul or buried in man's I-am-ness.

Man - God (Imagination) is man, the son, the creative power keyed low. Destined to be awakened as God. Man's power is greatly expanded by overcoming this world of the senses, of extreme limitation, opacity and contraction.

Old Testament - Series of permanent states of consciousness through which man must pass, personified as characters; New Testament is Old Testament's fulfillment.

Parable - A story told as if it were true, leaving the hearer to discover its fictitious surface character and learn its hidden meaning. (See Mat.13:3 and 13:18 for instruction on how to solve the riddle of parable.)

Paul - To find the I AM; to desist in seeking (as opposed to Saul, one who seeks; also humanity still suffering from amnesia). Paul is the symbol of anyone who awakens; one in whom the six visions has occurred.

Potter - The Imagination personified (Jeremiah 18:1). Also teaches revision of facts in order to get new results. Lord (Imagination) and Potter linked (Is. 64:8).

Power - One's ability to create by use of Imagination. The inner five senses used to to assume the wish fulfilled, which contains the way to bring it into being.

Pray/Prayer - To imagine. Defined as: motion toward, accession to, in the vicinity of, nearness at. A mental-emotional movement into a new state of consciousness by assuming the feeling of the wish already fulfilled, along with gratitude therefore. Not supplication.

Primal Form - A being of fire in a body of air.—not flesh and blood.

Purpose of Life - To learn to create imaginatively and to exercise the power of love to overcome this limitation called man. Eventually, to regain the exalted state of God, without loss of identity…a gift to man (Luke 12:32).

Repentance - A deliberate radical change of attitude towards life, called revision by Neville (called repentance in scripture). Not contrition or remorse.

Time - Two times exist simultaneously: Eternity or big time; and sidereal time or man's view of a past, present and future (temporary and part of this dream's illusion).

Transformation - The inner process conducted entirely by the Inner Being (God) on the individual to change man into himself. Man cannot earn it, nor do anything to shortcut the process or the time required to accomplish it. A loving result of the journey of the soul through fires of experience as man.

Vision - Revelation. Contains three elements: the supernatural, parallels stories in scripture and quite vivid. Issues from the only source, God (Num.12:6; Job33:14).

Visions of The End (Six) - Signs to man that the internal transformation into God (by God, your "I am") has been completed and the promises to man have been fulfilled. (For a list see above "Awakening")

World - A dream dreamed in concert for the purpose of sentient experience and expanding our creative power. The world is dead if not animated by Imagination (as is man). Also, the individual (aka, nations, cities, rivers, mountains, etc., all man).

A few sources of the quotes used by Neville:
> James *Strong's Exhaustive Concordance of the Bible* (with Hebrew and Greek dictionaries, containing the original meanings of words); Bayley's *Lost Language of Symbolism; The Complete Writings of William Blake; The Bible— Revised Standard Version* (most used).

PRODUCTION NOTES

1. The word Imagination is capitalized because it is synonymous with Lord, God, I AM, Jehovah.

2. The set of figures ___(??) is used to indicate a missing word, words, even a phrase, inaudible on the tape from which it is typed.

3. Parentheses are used at the end of a sentence to indicate book, chapter or verse of a biblical quote or other source used in the lecture but not identified by the speaker.

4. Italicizing of a word usually indicates voice emphasis made by Neville. Also used to indicate a book, magazine, newspaper and sometimes reference to a chapter within them.

Ingram Content Group UK Ltd.
Milton Keynes UK
UKHW011930300623
424349UK00001B/76